THE OMNIBUS ESSENTIAL GUIDE TO CLASSICAL CDs

EDITED BY GARAUD MACTAGGART

Schirmer Trade Books
A Part of **The Music Sales Group**
New York/London/Paris/Sydney/Copenhagen/Berlin/Tokyo/Madrid

Schirmer Trade Books
A Division of Music Sales Corporation, New York

Exclusive Distributors:
Music Sales Corporation
257 Park Avenue South, New York, NY 10010 USA
Music Sales Limited
8/9 Frith Street, London W1D 3JB England
Music Sales Pty. Limited
120 Rothschild Street, Rosebery, Sydney, NSW 2018, Australia

Order No. SCH 10147
International Standard Book Number: 0.8256.7307.0

Printed in the United States of America
By Vicks Lithography and Printing Corporation

Library of Congress Cataloging-in-Publication Data

Omnibus essential guide to classical CDs / edited by Garaud MacTaggart and Dave Wagner.
    p. cm.
  ISBN 0-8256-7307-0 (pbk.)
  1. Compact discs—Reviews. 2. Music—Discography. 3. Composers—Biography. I. Title: Book of essential classical CDs. II. MacTaggart, Garaud. III. Wagner, David, 1949-
ML156.9.S34 2004
016.7816'8'0266—dc22
                    2004008055

the omnibus essential guide to classical CDs

contents

I would like to dedicate this book to the memory of my parents, Gerard and Matilta "Tillie" MacTaggart, and my mother-in-law, Bernice Marschall. I also feel compelled to express wonder at the continued depth of support I've received from my wife, the incredible Claudia Marschall, my in-laws, the "Gettysburg Marschalls," and my "siblings" Shirley Mahut, Thom Telfer, and Ron Williams. I love you all. Without the aid and encouragement of Marty Connors, Dean Dauphinais, and Judy Galens, it is unlikely that this project would ever have gotten off the ground, and if Larry Birnbaum and the folks at Music Sales Corporation had not stepped in to help, this book would probably never have even seen the light of day. Thanks also go out to Nancy Nuzzo and the staff of the Baird Music Library of SUNY Buffalo, and to Barbara Sawka and the staff of the Stanford University Music Library for their aid.

Garaud MacTaggart

I wish to thank my family—my wife, Penny, and Katie, Nathan, and Allison—who have seen me disappear for hours on end in front of the computer and have lived with my mania for books and compact discs covering all available surfaces. And also to Brahms, the Golden Retriever and lover of classical music, who listened to all of these recordings with me and yet was kind enough not to critique my choices.

Dave Wagner

"Classical music" is a broad term that includes the work of centuries within a multitude of cultures and idioms. For the most part, this book focuses on the centuries of art music drawn from European or Western traditions, without seeking to deny the inspirational role played by the classical legacies of Asia and the Middle East on twentieth-century composers as diverse as Claude Debussy, Philip Glass, and John Cage.

Too many people feel inhibited by this kind of music, associating it with stuffiness and the ivory-tower rigors of academia. It doesn't have to be that way, however, especially since the depth and variety of musical colors within the genre are such that there is conceivably something to please and/or infuriate every listener. It is also true that boundaries between musical idioms are becoming more and more permeable. Film soundtracks and Broadway show scores have been written by some of the twentieth century's finest composers. Jazz, rock, and country music have helped shape the sensibilities of an ever-increasing number of modern, conservatory-trained composers in much the same way that folk music influenced works by Franz Liszt, Ralph Vaughan Williams, and Béla Bartók.

Many of the three hundred composers considered in this book are familiar names, but there are other personalities represented whose lives and works have helped shape the music of various eras while remaining outside the confines of current cultural literacy. Most of the articles are meant to inform the beginner or intermediate listener who wants to get an idea of what the classical music has to offer, but there is plenty of substance here for aficionados as well. Biographical entries (and many of the sidebars distributed throughout the book) are meant as snapshots of their subjects' lives and works. Included are recommendations of specific pieces and performances that each article's author(s) believe will serve as a good introduction to the composer or artist covered.

Since the writers all have their own opinions, their advice in matters of what is and is not worth covering tends to be a tad idiosyncratic. Some of the authors in this book lean towards classic performances from the monaural era, while others favor recent recordings. In many cases more than one writer has contributed to an article, and that has brought a broader perspective to the articles and their recommendations.

At this point, it would probably be helpful to explain what all the various headings within the articles mean. When the composer is assigned to a particular period in history, the timeline is roughly divided up this way:

1. Composers classified as Medieval lived between A.D. 500 and the early fourteenth century.
2. Renaissance composers generally lived from about 1400 to 1600.
3. The Baroque era runs from 1600 to 1750.
4. Classical composers belong approximately to the period 1720 to 1820.

5. Romantic works were generally created from 1820 until 1900.
6. Twentieth-century music is just that.

While classical-music scholars have come up with a variety of style headings, this book simplifies things by creating only three divisions: Orchestral, Chamber, and Vocal.

1. The Orchestral designation is reserved for instrumental music featuring more than ten musicians. This includes works like Beethoven's Ninth Symphony and the various Mahler symphonies with vocal soloists.

2. Chamber music is generally an instrumental work performed by one to ten musicians. Organ symphonies by Charles-Marie Widor and Louis Vierne are lumped into this category by virtue of the number of musicians necessary to execute the score. I realize that this may infuriate some organ aficionados (a few of whom wrote for this book),

but it is a distinction made purely for the sake of simplicity and ease of use by the novice listener.

3. Vocal scores feature the human voice and include such otherwise independent categories as Song, Choral, and Opera.

Recordings cited in each entry are generally items that were available as the text went to press. If they weren't in print then, chances are good that they will eventually turn up later on collections devoted to specific artists, as budget releases, or in used CD stores and bins. The Internet has also proved to be a boon for fans unable to find what they are looking for in local outlets. Keep in mind, however, that recordings of classical music, no matter how good they may sound, are only a reference point for concert performances and should not be the only way one experiences this art. The reward of hearing music you love performed by live musicians can be a transcendent, once-in-a-lifetime encounter that will only enhance your time on this earth.

So how do you use the *Omnibus Essential Guide to Classical CDs*? Here's what you'll find in the entries, and what we intend to accomplish with each point:

An introductory paragraph, which will give you not only biographical information but also a sense of the composer's sound and its stature in the classical—and overall music—pantheon.

what to buy: The album or albums that we feel are essential purchases for appreciating this composer or artist. It may be a "greatest-hits" set, or it may be a particular album that captures the essence of the composer in question. In any event, this is where you should start—and don't think it wasn't hard to make these choices when eyeballing the catalogs of Beethoven, Tchaikovsky, Mahler and some of the other Titans.

what to buy next: In other words, once you're hooked, these will be the most rewarding next purchases.

what to avoid: Seems clear enough.

the rest: Most everything else that's available for this composer, rated with our musical note system (see below for more on this). Note that for some artists with sizeable catalogs, we've condensed this section down to **best of the rest.**

worth searching for: An out-of-print gem. A bootleg. An import. Something that may require some investigating but will reward you for the effort.

influences: The crucial predecessors who helped inspire this composer's music.

Now, you ask, what's with those notes? It's not hard to figure out: ♪♪♪♪♪ is a masterpiece; a ♪ is a dud. Keep in mind that the note ratings don't pertain just to the composer's own catalog but to its worth in the whole music realm. Therefore a lesser composer's **what to buy** choice might rate no more than ♪♪♪; some even rate ♪♪⅙, a not-so-subtle sign that you might want to think twice about that composer.

All of what you're about to read is subjective and personal. Ultimately, however we think this guide will point you in the right direction, and if you buy the ♪♪♪♪♪ and ♪♪♪♪ choices, you'll have an album collection that will give you great joy.

A

John Adams

Born John Coolidge Adams on February 15, 1947, in Worcester, MA.

period: Twentieth century

Adams's energetic and engrossing music often features an eclectic mix of media, including electronics and video. Like other examples of so-called minimalism, his compositions, especially the earlier ones, are frequently based on repetitive tonal patterns, and much of what Adams has done builds upon the work of Philip Glass, Steve Reich, Terry Riley, and LaMonte Young. Yet he has his own, unique compositional vision, creating music that is both pleasing to the ear and challenging to the mind. For Adams, minimalism has been (as music critic Mark Swed writes) "not a restrictive art but an inclusive one."

John Adams studied clarinet with his father before attending Harvard University, where Leon Kirchner, Roger Sessions, and Earl Kim were among his teachers. Upon graduating in 1971 with two degrees in hand—a B.A. in music and an M.A. in composition (he was the first Harvard undergraduate allowed to submit a piece of music as his senior thesis)—Adams moved to California where he taught at the San Francisco Conservatory and directed its new music ensemble. It was in the mid-1970s that he began employing some minimalist techniques in his writing. *Shaker Loops,* his first significant piece in this style, was originally written for string septet. Steve Reich's ensemble was entrusted with the premiere in 1978. Later, in 1982-83, Adams revised it for orchestral performance.

1978 also marked the beginning of a productive association with conductor Edo de Waart and the San Francisco Symphony Orchestra, when Adams became its advisor for new music, and the alliance was solidified in 1982 when he was named composer-in-residence. The most important symphonic works created during this period were his *Common Tones in Simple Time,* (1979), *Harmonium* (1981) and *Harmonielehre (1985).* The first of these is perhaps his most strictly minimalist score, while *Harmonium*—for choir and orchestra, based on poetry by John Donne and Emily Dickinson—expands upon his previous work to become one of his first "mature" compositions, coupling minimalist devices to a lush, traditional musical language. In 1984 Adams began a collaboration with producer Peter Sellars and librettist Alice Goodman which resulted in his largest work to date, the boldly imaginative *Nixon In China.* The first opera to base its characters on living personages, treating them with sensitivity and ironic humor, it showed Adams's ability to adapt his style to the demands of the stage. *The Chairman Dances,* composed before the finishing touches were applied to *Nixon in China,* presents themes from the last act. It is one of Adams's most beguiling scores.

Since that time, Adams's reputation has become firmly established, and he is now one of the most frequently performed of all modern American composers. His success with *Nixon In China* has been followed up with two other semi-realistic operas: *The Death of Klinghoffer*

from 1991, about the murder of a wheelchair-bound passenger during the hijacking of an Italian cruise liner, and *I Was Looking at the Ceiling and Then I Saw the Sky* from 1995, taking its name from a survivor's response to the 1994 Los Angeles earthquake.

Orchestral
The Chairman Dances for Orchestra
what to buy: [Edo de Waart, cond.; San Francisco Symphony Orchestra] (Nonesuch 79144) ♪ ♪ ♪ ♪♪

Written before the completion of *Nixon In China,* this wonderfully evocative "foxtrot for orchestra," its melody line flexing over a steady pulse, may be the best introduction to Adams for the uninitiated. De Waart's long association with the composer has made him the leading Adams interpreter, and this is one of his best efforts. Also included are the surprisingly graceful *Christian Zeal and Activity,* a boisterous pair of orchestral fanfares (*Tromba lontana* and *Short Ride in a Fast Machine*), and the most conventionally minimalist of the composer's scores, *Common Tones in Simple Time.* A fine primer of Adams's work.

worth looking for: [*Dance Mix*; David Zinman, cond.; Baltimore Symphony Orchestra] (Argo 444454) ♪ ♪ ♪♪

The only Adams music here is *The Chairman Dances.* Zinman's performance is good and well recorded, but what makes the disc especially valuable is not just this piece or the orchestra's rendering of the mambo from Bernstein's *West Side Story*—it's the sheer number of short dance-oriented compositions by some of the late twentieth century's most interesting young American composers, among them Aaron Jay Kernis, Libby Larsen, Michael Torke, Christopher Rouse and Michael Daugherty.

Shaker Loops for Seven Strings
what to buy: [John Adams, cond., Orchestra of St. Luke's] (Nonesuch 79360) ♪ ♪ ♪♪
Solid playing by the Orchestra of St. Luke's in the orchestral arrangement of one Adams's earliest "hits" with the composer guiding them through a wonderful performance. It's coupled with the Violin Concerto, one of his most important recent works (1993), featuring soloist Gidon Kremer and Kent Nagano conducting the London Symphony Orchestra.

John Adams

Marian Anderson:
Born February 17, 1899, in Philadelphia, Pennsylvania, Marian Anderson grew up in poverty, displaying her striking vocal abilities in church choirs. She was finally able to pay for vocal instruction when her congregation raised enough money to assist her. After taking lessons with Giuseppe Boghetti, she sang in various concert venues before winning a competition to sing with the New York Philharmonic Orchestra in 1925. She won with her rendition of the Gaetano Donizetti aria *O Mio Fernando* from *La Favorita,* and was impressive enough to also secure a booking as soloist with the Philadelphia Orchestra. Most of Anderson's concert appearances from that point onward were as a featured soloist—singing at Carnegie Hall (1929 and 1936) and, from the early 1930s, doing star turns on European stages.

Anderson's most memorable and moving concert occurred at the Lincoln Memorial on Easter Sunday in 1939 as she sang before 75,000 people. This was shortly after the Daughters of the American Revolution denied her an appearance at Washington, D.C.'s Constitution Hall, a venue that they controlled and which had a segregationist policy. In 1955, toward the end of her career, Anderson broke yet another color barrier by becoming the first African-American to appear in a solo role at New York City's Metropolitan Opera, taking the part of Ulrica in Giuseppe Verdi's *Un ballo in maschera.* Without her steadfast personality, beautifully controlled contralto voice, and (to be frank) the active advocacy of Sol Hurok's management, overcoming racial prejudice in America's major operatic venue could very well have taken longer than it did. Chances are that if Anderson hadn't succeeded, Jessye Norman, Leontyne Price, and Kathleen Battle might have encountered even more obstacles to being taken seriously as classical singers.

While her repertoire included lieder by Franz Schubert and Robert Schumann (RCA Victor Red Seal 63575), along with sacred arias by Johann Sebastian Bach and George Frideric Handel (*Prima Voce: Marian Anderson,* Nimbus 7882), her most effective recital material was rooted in the gospel songs she sang when growing up. *Spiritual* (RCA Victor Red Seal 63306) features thirty sides recorded between 1936 and 1952, with her longtime accompanist Franz Rupp playing piano on twenty-seven of the songs and Kosti Vehanen acting as pianist on the trio of performances from 1936.

Mathilde August

Vocal
Nixon in China
what to buy: [Trudy Ellen Craney, soprano; Carolann Page, soprano; Marion Dry, mezzo-soprano; Stephanie Friedman, mezzo-soprano; Mari Opatz, mezzo-soprano; John Duykers, tenor; Thomas Hammons, baritone; James Maddalena, baritone; Sanford Sylvan, baritone; Edo de Waart, cond.; Orchestra of St. Luke's] (Nonesuch 79177) ♪ ♪ ♪ ♪

This is the original cast of Adams's classic opera in an obviously authoritative performance, wonderfully conducted by de Waart and well recorded. It won the Grammy for Best Contemporary Composition in 1989.

***Harmonium* for Orchestra and Chorus**
what to buy: [Edo de Waart, cond., San Francisco Symphony Orchestra; San Francisco Symphony Chorus] (ECM 821465) ♪ ♪ ♪ ♪₄

The first movement, based on John Donne's poem *Negative Love*, shows many minimalist trademarks while the second section, setting two poems by Emily Dickinson (*Because I Could Not Stop For Death* and *Wild Nights*), features some of the composer's most gorgeous choral writing—lush and enthralling.

influences: Morton Feldman, Philip Glass, Steve Reich, Terry Riley, LaMonte Young, Michael Nyman

Frank Retzel and Garaud MacTaggart

Richard Addinsell

Born Richard Stewart Addinsell, January 13, 1904, in Oxford, London, England. Died November 14, 1977, in Chelsea, London, England.

period: Twentieth century

Addinsell was a gifted tunesmith who outgrew his music hall roots and became, in spite of his relative lack of formal training, one of Britain's best known film composers. His most famous work, the *Warsaw Concerto*, originally appeared in the 1941 movie *Dangerous Moonlight.*

The son of a wealthy London businessman, Richard Addinsell received his early education at home. As a young man, he briefly studied law at Oxford before enrolling at the Royal College of Music. He never got around to graduating, however, since his studies were not nearly as interesting to him as his first love, the musical theater. After traveling through Europe and studying music in Berlin and Vienna, Addinsell returned home, where he wrote songs and sketches for a few Andre Charlot musical revues. He eventually became a protégé of the British writer and theatrical personality Clemence Dane. In 1933, at Dane's request, he wrote the well-received score for a stage presentation of Lewis Carroll's *Alice in Wonderland*. Addinsell was soon writing other shows, and from there it was a short step to writing music for motion pictures.

The British film industry in those days was very different from the Hollywood studio system, where music was turned out on an assembly line basis. In England, cinema composition was by no means a full-time career; people who engaged in it knew they would have to move back and forth between movies and other kinds of musical activities in order to make a living. In addition to his film work, Addinsell continued composing for the theater (collaborating with Dane and later with singer Joyce Grenfell) and radio (scoring BBC dramas and comedies). His gift for melody and an instinctive sense of drama served him well in motion pictures; whatever deficiencies he had on the technical side were compensated for by a series of able and talented assistants (among them Roy Douglas, Leonard Isaacs, Leighton Lucas, and Douglas Gamley), who helped him with the complexities of scoring, orchestrating, and conducting.

Addinsell's most popular composition is the *Warsaw Concerto*, from the 1941 British motion picture *Dangerous Moonlight,* which was released in America with the more warlike title *Suicide Squadron*. The picture told the melodramatic tale of a Polish pianist/composer who, after being forced to flee his homeland by the Nazis, joins an airborne unit of fellow exiles continuing the struggle from England. The screenplay called for a concert hall sequence in which the pianist plays one of his compositions; rather than use an existing work, Addinsell was assigned the task of writing a nine-minute piano concerto movement in the floridly romantic style of Sergei Rachmaninoff. It became a huge, almost instantaneous hit. No one was prepared for the enormous popularity of the piece, but in spite of wartime rationing, a recording hastily dubbed from the soundtrack sessions was rushed into distribution, cementing the work's immortality and inspiring a host of imitators on both sides of the Atlantic. During the next 50 years there would be more than 100 separate recordings of the work, with sales in the millions. The *Warsaw Concerto* would become a staple of pop-classical concerts the world over, becoming much better known than the movie for which it had been written. Incidentally, legend has it that the big romantic tune in *Warsaw Concerto* was actually a slowed down version of a rumba that Addinsell had composed in his Oxford days.

Some of Addinsell's other film scores include *Fire Over England* (1937), *Goodbye Mr. Chips* (1939), the original (and some say far superior) British version of *Gaslight* (1940), *Blithe Spirit* (1945), Alfred Hitchcock's *Under Capricorn* (1949), *Tom Brown's Schooldays* and the classic Alastair Sim version of Charles Dickens's *A Christmas Carol* (both 1951), *The Prince and the Showgirl* (1957), *The Roman Spring of Mrs. Stone* and

Greengage Summer (both 1961), and *Waltz of the Toreadors* (1962).

Addinsell retired in 1965 and spent most of the next decade taking care of his friend, the couturier Victor Steibal, who fought a long battle with multiple sclerosis. Steibal died in 1976, and Addinsell followed him to the grave about a year later.

Orchestral
Warsaw Concerto
what to buy: [*Music of Richard Addinsell*; Martin Jones, piano; Kenneth Alwyn, cond.; Royal Ballet Sinfonia, orch.] (ASV White Line 2108) ♪ ♪ ♪↓

There are many perfectly good performances of the *Warsaw Concerto*, but this one has the advantage of being part of an all-Addinsell disc, along with rare recordings of some little-known gems, well played by Alwyn and his orchestra.

various film scores
what to buy: [*Richard Addinsell: British Light Music Series*; Philip Martin, piano; Roderick Elms, piano; Kenneth Alwyn, cond.; BBC Concert Orchestra] (Marco Polo 8.223732) ♪ ♪ ♪

If you like Addinsell's music, this is the next disc to buy. The film pieces are wonderful, especially the themes from *Goodbye Mr. Chips* and *Fire Over England*. The *Smokey Mountains Concerto* is a real hoot!

influences: Morton Gould

Jack Goggin

Isaac Albéniz
Born Isaac Manuel Francisco Albéniz May 29, 1860, in Camprodón, Lérida, Spain. Died May 18, 1909, in Cambó-les-Bains, France.

period: Romantic

A supremely talented pianist, Isaac Albéniz helped play a major role in creating a national identity for Spanish art music through *Iberia,* an evocative piano suite that made extensive use of the country's folk music, specifically the rhythms of Andalusia. He was also a friend to and an important influence on his French impressionist contemporaries Claude Debussy and Maurice Ravel—

major composers whose own respective pieces *Ibéria* and *Rapsodie Espagnole* might not have come into existence were it not for this native son of Catalonia.

Born the son of a customs official, Albéniz was a child prodigy on the piano, receiving his first lessons from his sister Clementina and developing his talents so quickly that he appeared on stage at the Teatro Romea in Madrid by the age of five. The young Isaac was also a bit of a hell-raiser, rebelling against a father who saw his talented young son as an artistic meal ticket. In 1868, the family moved from Camprodón to Madrid, where Albéniz was enrolled at the Real Conservatorio, He proved to be a lackadaisical student, displaying little interest in solfège or any of the other classes he was put in.

Driven by wanderlust or perhaps just a desire to leave his strife-torn surroundings (Spain was then in the middle of a revolution), Albéniz kept running away from home. His first jaunt took him around northern Spain, but he returned to Madrid in 1874 upon learning that his sister Blanca had committed suicide after failing an audition for the Teatro de la Zarzuela. Then it was off to southern Spain, where he stowed away aboard a ship bound for Puerto Rico but was tossed off in Buenos Aires, the ship's first stop. He played in various dives all over South America, and by the time he was fifteen, he had scraped together more than enough money to book passage for Havana, where (surprise!) his father had been transferred as a customs inspector. The reunion was not a terribly happy one, and the younger Albéniz soon skipped off to New York, where he embarked on another series of concert tours that took him all over the United States. After earning enough money to finance his return to Europe, he boarded a ship for England and eventually wound up in Germany, where he studied music at the Leipzig Hochschule für Musik Felix Mendelssohn-Bartholdy.

Around 1876, Albéniz finally returned to Spain, where he succeeded in impressing a courtier to the Prince of Asturias (later King Alfonso XII), who saw to it that the young pianist was given a scholarship to study in Brussels. After winning an award for performance in 1878, Albéniz left Brussels to seek out Franz Liszt, the dynamic pianist and composer with whom he hoped to study. Two years later, wanderlust overcame him once more, and he launched yet another concert tour of the Western Hemisphere. By this time, Albéniz had started to write short pieces that he would use in his programs, foreshadowing the turn his career was to take. He finally returned to Spain in 1883, married, and briefly settled in Barcelona, making the acquaintance of the folklorist, composer, and pedagogue Felipe Pedrell, whose work inspired Albéniz to incorporate the rhythmic elements of Spanish folk music into his own scores. Gradually, Albéniz eased back on touring, and the 1890s found him splitting time between Great Britain, where he wrote operatic settings for execrable librettos by a wealthy businessman, and France, where he formed friendships with Paul Dukas, Vincent d'Indy, and Claude Debussy while teaching piano at the Schola Cantorum. Aspects of Albéniz's post-Pedrellian approach to harmony influenced many of his French contemporaries.

For years, Albéniz had suffered from Bright's Disease, an illness affecting the kidney. This led to uremia, which caused the composer's death just shy of his forty-ninth birthday. Although he died in France, Albéniz's body was taken to Barcelona for burial.

While his oeuvre includes a small number of vocal works (mainly zarzuelas and operas), his catalog is dominated by piano scores, including his masterpiece, the four books of *Iberia*. It was into these last works, written between 1906 and 1909, that Albéniz poured all he had learned of the Spanish landscape, its people, and their songs, filtering his impressions through a lively understanding of classical piano technique and a vivid use of harmony. The results have endured as a valued part of the standard piano repertoire and a defining statement of Spanish musical identity. *Iberia* has also been arranged for orchestra, with Albéniz's friend Enrique Fernandez Arbos orchestrating five of the pieces and Carlos Surinach taking responsibility for the other seven.

Orchestral
Iberian Suite, arr. Arbos and Surinach
what to buy: [Antal Dorati, cond.; Minneapolis Symphony Orchestra] (Mercury Living Presence 434388) ♪ ♪ ♪

Despite the age of these recordings, the sound is very good, dating from the days when Mercury albums were known for their excellent engineering. The re-mastering on this set is wonderful, and Dorati's vision of the arrangements is exciting, but only the five Arbos treatments (*Evocación, El Corpus Christi en Sevilla, Triana, El Puerto,* and *El Albaicín*) are included. The balance of the disc consists of excerpts from de Falla's *La Vida Breve,*

Mussorgsky's *Khovanshchina,* and Smetana's *Bartered Bride.*

what to buy next: [Jesus Lopez-Cobos, cond.; Cincinnati Symphony Orchestra] (Telarc 80490) ♪ ♪ ♪ ♪

Lopez-Cobos meshes the Arbos and Surinach arrangements into one seamless whole, making this an interesting companion to the full-length piano version, but it's not as exciting as Dorati's rendering, despite the latter's exclusion of Surinach's work. The overall performance is well recorded and competently played—finely crafted, to say the least. Those qualities may be enough for many listeners.

Chamber
Iberian Suite
what to buy: [Alicia de Larrocha, piano] (EMI Classics 64504) ♪ ♪ ♪ ♪

Alicia de Larrocha is perhaps the best known contemporary exponent of Spanish piano music, and this recording of the *Iberian Suite,* one of several she has issued, shows the skill and passion with which she illuminates the work of her countryman. Also included in this package are fine performances of the composer's unfinished *Navarra* along with five other Albéniz piano pieces.

worth looking for: [Rafael Orozco, piano] (Auvidis/Valois 4663) ♪ ♪ ♪ ♪

A pianist of sensibility and nuance, Orozco offers a more leisurely and meditative approach to the suite than de Larrocha does.

Mallorca for piano (transcribed by Andrés Segovia,) op. 202.
what to buy: [*Road to the Sun: Latin Romances for Guitar,* Sharon Isbin, guitar] (Virgin Classics 91128) ♪ ♪ ♪ ♪

As the guitar is a more portable instrument than the piano, many of Albéniz's works have achieved wider notice through their guitar transcriptions. Here Sharon Isbin explores the passion and drama of Albéniz's Spain via Segovia's arrangements for guitar. Other pieces on the disc include music from Francisco Tárrega (who transcribed many Albéniz works while the composer was still alive), Joaquin Rodrigo, Agustín Barrios, Leo Brouwer, Heitor Villa-Lobos, and Antonio Carlos Jobim.

influences: Enrique Granados, Manuel de Falla, Joaquín Turina, Claude Debussy, Maurice Ravel

Kerry Dexter and Garaud MacTaggart

Tomaso Albinoni

Born Tomaso Giovanni Albinoni, June 14, 1671, in Venice, Italy. Died January 17, 1751, in Venice, Italy.

period: Baroque

During his lifetime, Tomaso Albinoni created music that was as popular as that of Corelli and Vivaldi. However, the most familiar work ascribed to this baroque Italian—the Adagio in G Minor for Strings and Organ—is a piece constructed by Remo Giazotto (an early twentieth-century Italian musicologist) from a fragment he allegedly discovered. Later scholars, through a rigorous analysis of the composer's style (based on works that Albinoni was known to have written) have deduced that Giazotto probably erred in attributing the work to Albinoni.

The eldest son of a wealthy stationer who made playing cards, Albinoni seemed destined to take over his father's business, even though he was allowed to study violin, singing, and composition. While he initially managed to live off of the family's business receipts, Albinoni's finances took a hit when his father died in 1709 and left the bulk of his business to the two youngest sons. When the firm went bankrupt, the composer had to support his wife and children by teaching and composing. Even though he didn't actively seek professional music positions from either the Venetian court or the church (with one exception), Albinoni's talents and ability to get along with the upper economic strata of Venice secured singing students and subscribers for the publication of his works.

Albinoni was best known in his own time for the volume and quality of his operas. A prolific composer, he once claimed to have written over 200 operas, although some scholars believe that he only completed 80, of which just a few have survived. His *Zenobia, regina de' Palmireni* (Zenobia, queen of Palmyra)—initially staged in 1694 at the Teatro Santi Giovanni e Paolo in Venice—was one of his first great successes as a composer. Most of Albinoni's operas were first performed in and around Venice, but the demand for these productions was strong enough in other municipalities that many works were written for non-Venetian venues. Overseeing the

Maurice André:

Although his father played trumpet, gave him an old cornet when he was fourteen years old, and made sure that the youngster took music lessons, they both worked in the mines in the Cévennes, a rugged area in the south of France. Their joint goal was to have Maurice eventually exit from the hardscrabble life of a miner and join a military band where things would presumably be easier. Maurice shared this wish but one of the perks of his military musician job also caught his attention: a waiver of tuition at the Conservatoire National Supérieure de Musique de Paris if he displayed enough talent and passed the competitive entry exam. He did so in 1951 and within a year also won a number of prizes and competitions as a cornet player, including the *prix d'honneur*. He then switched over to taking trumpet lessons, winning first prize on that instrument in 1953.

While in school André worked occasional gigs in recording studios, where he played on a number of film soundtracks and with Michel Legrand's jazz orchestra. His first consistent job upon leaving school was with the Paris Radio Orchestra, but he later became principal trumpeter for the Lamoureux Orchestra. In 1955 he won the Geneva International Competition and began to think of a career as a soloist. It took him eight years to become known as one of Europe's finest trumpeters. André did this by winning the International Music Competition in Munich and attracting the attention of Germany's finest conductors, including Herbert von Karajan, Karl Böhm, and Karl Richter. In 1967 André also took a position teaching trumpet at the Conservatoire National Supérieure de Musique de Paris, staying on staff there until 1979. When he retired from the school he established the first *Maurice André Trumpet Competition* (now a triennial tradition), where young trumpet players from around the world could come to measure their skills.

A good sampler of André's repertoire can be found on *Trumpet Masterpieces* (Deutsche Grammophon 413853), a two-disc set of concertos and adaptations of concertos by Franz Joseph Haydn, Georg Philipp Telemann, George Frideric Handel, Antonio Vivaldi, and others. *Trumpet Voluntary* (Erato 92123) is another good option, containing selections from Bach, Telemann, Handel, Henry Purcell, and Jeremiah Clarke, with André soloing in front of either the Academy of St. Martin-in-the-Fields with Neville Marriner conducting or the Württemberg Chamber Orchestra under the direction of Jörg Faerber. While much of André's reputation rests on his work as a soloist with orchestras, some of his most affecting playing has been done in tandem with an organist, including *Maurice André Plays Baroque Trumpet* (EMI Classics Special Imports 54330), a superlative recital with André accompanied by organist Hedwig Bilgram in arrangements of music by Bach, Handel, Purcell, and others.

Ian Palmer

production of these operas meant that Albinoni traveled to Naples, where he supervised *L'Inganno innocente* (later revived as *Rodrigo in Algeri*) in 1701, to Florence for his operas *Griselda* and *Aminta* (both in 1703), to Genoa, where he presided over *La Prosperità di Elio Sejano (The Prosperity of Elio Sejano)* (1707), and to Bologna, where he supervised *Il Giustino* (1711).

Although operatic works dominate Albinoni's catalog,

his instrumental pieces are the ones that have survived over time and that were most influential among his contemporaries. He was the first to use three movements consistently in his concerto scores, and he was the first to popularize the fugal finale. While his fugal and canonic movements are more outstanding for their rhythmic buoyancy than for contrapuntal originality, J.S. Bach and Johann Gottfried Walther still found much of value in his music and used and/or arranged his works as teaching tools and concert items. Even though Bach set a pair of fugues drawn from Albinoni's opus-one trio sonatas, the twelve concertos from opus nine are the finest examples of this style within Albinoni's oeuvre.

Orchestral
Adagio in G Minor for Organ and Strings (spuriously attributed to Albinoni)
what to buy: [Orpheus Chamber Orchestra] (Deutsche Grammophon 429390) ♪ ♪ ♪ ♪♪

Most of the public's favorite baroque hits for string orchestra are here. You've got your (pseudo-) Albinoni, your Pachelbel *Canon*, a little J.S. Bach, some Purcell, a few works by Handel, a bit of Vivaldi, and Corelli's "Christmas" Concerto to tie it all together. The performances by this conductorless group are quite fine.

what to buy next: [Neville Marriner, cond.; Academy of St. Martin-in-the-Fields, orch.] (EMI Seraphim 73289) ♪ ♪ ♪ ♪

The sonics are a little older here than on the Orpheus Chamber Orchestra set (and the price is a lot less), but the selections are quite similar. In addition to the Adagio and Pachelbel's *Canon,* however, you also get Mozart's wonderful *Eine Kleine Nachtmusik* and a batch of other pleasant pieces.

Concertos à cinque, Op. 9
what to buy: [Christopher Hogwood, cond.; Academy of Ancient Music, orch.] (Decca 458129) ♪ ♪ ♪ ♪♪

If you are seeking well-recorded authentic-instrument renditions of these beguiling works, it is hard to imagine a more felicitous place to start than here. Andrew Manze, the reigning virtuoso violinist of choice for period performances, is the soloist in the four concerti featuring his instrument, while oboists Frank de Bruine and Alfredo Bernardini are more than adequate for the balance of the works.

what to buy next: [Claudio Scimone, cond.; I Solisti Veneti, orch.] (Erato Ultima 25593) ♪ ♪ ♪♪

These recordings display the great virtuosity of the performers as well as Albinoni's genius as a melodist. The most impressive playing heard here comes in the seventh concerto, where the last *Allegro* movement resembles *Spring* from Antonio Vivaldi's *Four Seasons.* For listeners seeking fine yet economical versions of these works, Scimone and his forces fit the bill.

various *Concertoa à cinque*
what to buy: [*Double Oboe Concertos and String Concertos, Vol. II*; Anthony Robson, oboe; Catherine Latham, oboe; Simon Standage, cond.; Collegium Musicum 90, orch.] (Chandos Chaconne 0610) ♪ ♪ ♪ ♪♪

This fine recording of Albinoni's concerti features performances filled with grace, charm, and lilting motion. The intonation of the string ensemble is excellent, and both oboists play their lyrical interpretations with great control and drama. Included on this disc are four concertos from Albinoni's op. 7 and four from op. 9.

influences: Arcangelo Corelli, Giuseppi Torelli, Pietro Locatelli, Antonio Vivaldi

Marijim Thoene and Garaud MacTaggart

Valentin Alkan
Born Charles-Valentin Morhange on November 30, 1813, in Paris. Died March 29, 1888, in Paris.

period: Romantic

Even though such heavyweight pianist-composers as Frédéric Chopin, Franz Liszt, and Ferruccio Busoni admired his compositions, Alkan was better known during his lifetime as a pianist of wondrous skills. It wasn't until the mid-1960s that his music found persuasive (and scholarly) advocates such as Raymond Lewenthal and Ronald Smith, who avidly displayed his musical genius to concert audiences and record listeners.

Alkan entered the Paris Conservatoire as a child prodigy, won his first *premier prix* (for solfège) when he was only seven, and by the age of eleven had garnered a *premier prix* for performance and seemed well on the way to becoming a famous touring virtuoso. A few years later the still youthful pianist was teaching part-time at his old school and found himself swept up in much the same Parisian social whirl as Chopin. But before long, Alkan began withdrawing from the circuit of salons that could have furthered his career, becoming more and more reclusive and not playing publicly for long stretches. By 1838 he had begun the first of his extended retreats from public life.

Alkan next appeared in concert in 1844, but he limited his performances to two that year and two the next and then abandoned public venues altogether once again. In 1848, though he hadn't taught at the Conservatoire for over ten years, Alkan lobbied to become a full-time staff member. Daniel Auber, the director, was put off by the pianist's often misanthropic attitudes, and the position was awarded to Antoine-François Marmontel, a young pianist and composer for whom Alkan had no respect. (Marmontel went on to become a well-respected teacher who counted Georges Bizet, Vincent d'Indy, and Claude Debussy among his students.) That year also marked the publishing of Alkan's first great piano works, the frighteningly virtuosic *Grande sonate* for piano, op. 33—*Les quatre âges* and the dozen etudes making up his op. 35.

After giving a pair of recitals in 1853, Alkan again withdrew, this time for twenty years. He spent his days teaching, writing music, demonstrating pianos for a leading French manufacturer (Erard), studying the Talmud, and undertaking a translation of the New Testament. In 1857 his most important publication appeared, the twelve etudes op. 39, a tour-de-force of keyboard writing. Innovative not only by virtue of the superhuman technique demanded in bringing the music into focus, they also represent something even rarer: a monumental sonic edifice conceived specifically for solo piano, containing an entire "symphony" (etudes four to seven), a "concerto" (etudes eight to ten), and an "overture." The only Alkan pieces published during the 1860s—the *Sonatine*, (op. 61) and the *Esquisses*, (op. 63)—draw on material written as far back as 1851. After briefly returning to the concert stage in 1873, he continued doling out a few performances a year until he died in 1888.

A final note: There is an apocryphal story about his death stating that Alkan had reached up to the top shelf of a bookcase in search of a copy of the Talmud when the bookcase tipped over and he was crushed beneath the weight of knowledge previously resting on the shelves. A more likely explanation—that he "was found stretched out, lifeless in his kitchen in front of his stove which he was probably about to light to cook his evening meal..."—came from Alexandre de Bertha (1909), quoted here from the *Musical Times* (1972) and also cited in Ronald Smith's book, *Alkan: The Enigma*.

Chamber
Symphonie, op. 39, nos. 4–7
what to buy: [*Piano Music of Alkan*; Raymond Lewenthal, piano] (BMG High Performance Classics 63310) ♪ ♪ ♪ ♪⅛

This recording dates from the mid-1960s, but the BMG re-mastering is amazing, preserving a hallmark performance of exceptional virtuosity, faithful to the letter of this finger-breaking score while it unveils the poetry at its heart. Lewenthal was an incredibly deft pianist, and his performances of the composer's Le Festin d'Esope *(op. 39, no. 12),* Barcarolle *(op. 65, no. 6), and the second movement ("Quasi-Faust") of Alkan's* Grande sonate, *op. 33 are all top notch. So too is his rendition of Franz Liszt's* Hexameron, *which closes the disc.*

Grande sonate for piano, op. 33—*Les quatre âges*
what to buy: [Marc-André Hamelin, piano] (Hyperion 20794) ♪ ♪ ♪ ♪ ♪

The superbly recorded Hamelin duplicates three of the pieces heard in the Lewenthal set mentioned above, (*Le Festin d'Esope,* the second movement of the *Grande sonate,* and the op. 65 Barcarolle). Hamelin's Sonata is a consistent revelation, matching Lewenthal's technical fireworks but presenting the entire piece instead of just a single movement. His rendition of Alkan's *Sonatine* (op. 61) is equally arresting.

Esquisses, op. 63
what to buy: [Laurent Martin, piano] (Marco Polo 8.223352) ♪ ♪ ♪ ♪

The product of fifteen years, these forty-nine little keyboard gems explore a wide range of technical problems, offering wonderful solutions that simmer and/or explode. Martin's playing, while not as virtuosic as that of Hamelin or Lewenthal, is consistently fine interpretively. From the gentle ecstasy of *La Vision* to the harmonically adventurous *Laus Deo,* there are plenty of discoveries here for piano fans.

various piano works

what to buy: [*The Railway and Other Piano Works*; Laurent Martin, piano; Bernard Ringeissen, piano] (Naxos 8.553434) ♪ ♪ ♪ ♪

This is a good budget sampler for those wishing to explore the Alkan repertoire, drawing performances from Marco Polo's series dedicated to the composer. A nice feature of this disc is its inclusion of two classic works from the op. 39 etudes—the *Scherzo diabolico* and the *Marche funèbre: Andantino*—not found in either the Lewenthal or Hamelin sets (see above).

influences: Franz Liszt, Frédéric Chopin, Sigismond Thalberg, Anton Rubinstein

Garaud MacTaggart

Leroy Anderson

Born July 29, 1908, in Cambridge, MA. Died May 18, 1975, in Woodbury, CT.

period: Twentieth century

Anderson's specialty was light semi-classical music for orchestra; he displayed a penchant for appealing melodies and popular dance rhythms while often enhancing his works with striking orchestral effects. Most of his pieces are no longer than five minutes, so thematic and musical elaboration was not the main point; instead, Anderson sought to create a mood by capturing an image stated in the title and then interpreting the concept in musical terms. In doing so, he wrote such enduring, "pops" classics as *Blue Tango, The Typewriter,* and *Sleigh Ride.*

Leroy Anderson enrolled at Harvard University in 1925 after taking courses at the New England Conservatory, where he had gained a reputation as a multi-talented musician capable of playing the double bass and tuba in addition to the piano. At Harvard he studied orchestration with Walter Piston, graduating magna cum laude with a B.A. in music. Anderson stayed at Harvard, enrolling in composition classes taught by Piston and Georges Enesco, before finally receiving his M.A. in music in 1930. From 1931 to 1934 he served as director of the Harvard University Band, leaving that position to become a freelance musician.

He was contracted to write his first set of arrangements for the Boston Pops Orchestra in 1936, striking up a rela-

tionship with conductor Arthur Fiedler that would serve Anderson in good stead when he became the orchestra's arranger (1946–1950). By the time Anderson left the BPO to strike out on his own, he had already written "Sleigh Ride," a holiday gem from 1948. Recorded by many (Johnny Mathis comes quickly to mind), it is still a Christmas favorite in the original scoring by Anderson—complete with sleigh bells, whip, and horse's whinny.

After signing a recording contract with Decca Records in 1950, Anderson began churning out such best-selling pop fare as "The Typewriter" and "Blue Tango," which received a gold record in 1952 for selling one million copies. Other beloved Anderson miniatures include "Bugler's Holiday," "Trumpeter's Lullaby," and "The Syncopated Clock." Anderson also composed the score for the 1958 Broadway musical *Goldilocks,* for which Walter and Jean Kerr wrote the book and Agnes de Mille did the choreography.

Orchestral
various works

what to buy: [*The Typewriter*; Leonard Slatkin, cond.; Saint Louis Symphony Orchestra] (RCA Red Seal 68048) ♪ ♪ ♪ ♪

Many of the composer's standards can be found on this well-recorded set, including the title tune, "Sleigh Ride," and "Fiddle Faddle." Featuring a fine orchestra and conductor and a well-chosen selection of material, this recording is a delight.

what to buy next: [*Leroy Anderson's Greatest Hits*; Arthur Fiedler, cond.; Boston Pops Orchestra] (RCA Victor 61237) ♪ ♪ ♪ ♪

Fiedler always had a knack for this type of music, and this recording will not let you down. Most of the big hits have made their way into this collection, including "The Typewriter," "Fiddle Faddle," and "Syncopated Clock."

influences: George Gershwin, John Williams, Richard Addinsell, Morton Gould

Frank Retzel and Garaud MacTaggart

George Antheil

Born Georg Carl Johann Antheil on July 8, 1900, in Trenton, NJ. Died February 12, 1959, in New York, NY.

period: Twentieth century

History is filled with musical "stars" who seem destined to blaze in the artistic firmament but, save for one brief, shining moment of glory, fade away into seeming irrelevance. Such was the case of George Antheil, who was embraced as a trendsetter by critics and musicians upon the initial production of his *Ballet mécanique* in 1926. Forty years later the noted American critic and composer Virgil Thomson wrote: "My estimate of him [in 1926] as 'the first composer of our generation' might have been justified had it not turned out eventually that for all his facility and ambition there was in him no power of growth."

Antheil began taking piano lessons when he was six years old. Later he had theory and composition lessons with a teacher in Philadelphia and at nineteen went to New York to study composition with Ernest Bloch. In 1922 he moved to Europe and attempted to establish a career as a concert pianist. He met Igor Stravinsky while living in Berlin and was impressed by the Russian composer's innovative approach to rhythm, feeling that it epitomized modern industrial society. Antheil brought together the academic grounding he had received from Bloch and the exciting rhythmic ideas in Stravinsky's music to create his own compositions. He gave them quirky titles (*Airplane Sonata* and *Sonata Sauvage*) which, along with their catchy, jazz-inflected rhythms, conjured up mental images of mechanized twentieth-century life. By 1923 he was living in Paris and found himself on the cutting edge of artistic expression, hob-nobbing with Ezra Pound (who became his most vociferous advocate), James Joyce, Erik Satie, and Pablo Picasso.

In 1926, after creating more works that played with meter and dissonance, Antheil unveiled a scaled-down version of his *Ballet mécanique*. Originally scored for sixteen pianolas, xylophones, drums, and miscellaneous percussion, he reduced the forces for this first production to one pianola (with amplifier), two pianos, three xylophones, electric bells, three propellers, a tam-tam, four bass drums, and a siren. Parisian audiences and critics reacted favorably to this percussion extravaganza, unlike the American concertgoers who were introduced to the piece at Carnegie Hall in April 1927. The New York promoter emphasized the visible over the audible, increasing the number of pianists called for in the score to eight (one of them was Aaron Copland) and placing a huge set of propellers on-stage. Instead of

hailing Antheil's triumphant return to his native shores, American critics held him up to ridicule, and audience members reportedly laughed out loud during the performance.

Disappointed and dejected by this turn of events and by the lukewarm reception in Paris of his neo-classical Piano Concerto a month before the Carnegie Hall fiasco, Antheil moved to Vienna in 1928 and began concentrat-

ing on opera. His first effort, the satirical, jazz-inspired *Transatlantic,* whose wild plot involves organized crime, big business, and an American presidential election, was fairly well received at its premiere in Frankfurt in 1930. By 1932, he had won a Guggenheim Fellowship, which paid his living expenses while he worked on a follow-up opera, *Helen Retires.* During this time Antheil also wrote *La femme 100 têtes,* a set of forty-four preludes that seemed to revert to the mechanistic style of his earlier piano works. When *Helen Retires* was finally produced in 1934, it was roundly criticized.

By that time Antheil had moved to Hollywood, having evolved from a daring young artist creating provocative music into a craftsman with more modest goals. While he still composed symphonies, concertos, chamber pieces, and operas, the need to support his family motivated him to write the music for such varied movies as *The Plainsman* (1936), *Angels Over Broadway* (1940), *Tokyo Joe* (1949), and *The Young Don't Cry* (1957). His autobiography, *Bad Boy of Music,* was published in 1945 and gave a glossy, almost cinematic, spin to his life up to that point, with fascinating snapshots of Stravinsky, James Joyce, Leopold Stokowski and other musical figures. He also engaged in more eccentric pursuits, writing a syndicated column for the lovelorn, patenting a radio control device for torpedoes (in collaboration with movie star Hedy Lamarr), authoring a mystery novel (under the alias of Stacey Bishop), and volunteering his services as an amateur endocrine criminologist to any willing police department.

Orchestral
Ballet mécanique for Large Percussion Ensemble
what to buy: [University of Massachusetts Percussion Ensemble, orch.] (Electronic Music Foundation 120) ♪ ♪ ♪ ♪

Antheil revised this score five times, but his second arrangement, from 1924, was not performed until 1999. This recording documents that concert and is quite impressive, though the album is geared more to fans of electronic music than enthusiasts of Antheil's works. Pieces by John Cage and Lou Harrison (*Double Music*), Richard Grayson (whose player-piano works follow Conlon Nancarrow's path), and Amadeo Roldán make up the bulk of the set.

George Antheil

Vladimir Ashkenazy:
In 1954, when Vladimir Ashkenazy was seventeen years old, he won second prize at the Chopin Competition in Warsaw. He then attended the Moscow Conservatory, where he studied piano with Lev Oborin, a frequent accompanist for master violinist David Oistrakh. In 1956 Ashkenazy won first prize at the Queen Elizabeth Competition in Brussels, and two years later made his first tour of the United States. 1962 found him sharing first-prize honors in the Tchaikovsky Competition with the English pianist John Ogdon. Ashkenazy finally left his native U.S.S.R. in 1963 and with his family moved first to London, then to Iceland (where his wife grew up and where he became a citizen in 1972), and finally to Lucerne, Switzerland.

While his initial reputation was as a soloist with or without an orchestra, he has also worked closely and well with a few favored musicians to create chamber music of uncommon worth. Perhaps the most justly famous of these pairings is the one Ashkenazy had with violinist Itzhak Perlman. These two artists combined for a beautifully recorded, technically assured set of Ludwig van Beethoven's ten Sonatas for Violin and Piano (Jubilee 421453) that ranks as one of the most moving recordings in either's oeuvre. Arguably their finest performances were reserved for the most famous sonatas in the group, the *Spring* (no. 5 in F Major) and the *Kreutzer* (no. 9 in A Major), both of which are available as a mid-priced CD (Decca Legends 458618).

Russian music, especially the works of Sergei Rachmaninoff, was of particular importance in the early years of Ashkenazy's career. His powerful 1970s recordings of that composer's four piano concertos with André Previn conducting the London Symphony Orchestra (London 444839) and his performance of the twenty-four *Preludes* for Solo Piano (London 443841) are also part of a six-disc set of Rachmaninoff's complete works for piano solo and with orchestra (London 455234). Ashkenazy's 1999 rendering of Dmitri Shostakovich's twenty-four formidable *Preludes and Fugues* (Decca 466066) is another high point in the pianist's recorded repertoire, the work of a more mature artist whose well-conceived interpretations are close in tempo to that of the composer.

In 1969, after having established himself as one of the finest pianists on the international touring circuit, Ashkenazy took up the baton and led the Iceland Symphony Orchestra in a few concerts as a way of familiarizing himself with the task. As a conductor Ashkenazy has developed a marked affinity for the orchestral works of Alexander Scriabin and Jean Sibelius, in addition to Rachmaninoff's symphonic fare and the piano concertos of Wolfgang Amadeus Mozart. But his most adventurous and rewarding release as a conductor is an album he recorded with the German Symphony Orchestra (Berlin) that was devoted to the orchestral music of Boris Blacher, an important but relatively under-recorded twentieth century German composer and pedagogue (Ondine 912).

William Gerard

worth looking for: [*Fighting the Waves: Music of Antheil*; Heinz Karl Gruber, cond.; Ensemble Modern, orch.] (RCA Victor Red Seal 68066) ♪ ♪ ♪ ♪

For those wondering what all the fuss was about, the

Ensemble Modern's rendition of this rhythmic potboiler should provide a few answers. Gruber leads the ensemble through Antheil's sonic morass with considerable élan, imparting an almost civilized veneer to the composer's techno-barbaric score. The balance of the disc displays a variety of his shorter compositions, with chamber works and orchestral pieces adding up to a well-rounded picture of Antheil's early oeuvre.

Chamber
various piano works
what to buy: [*Bad Boy of Music*; Marthanne Verbit, piano] (Albany TROY 146) ♪ ♪ ♪

Antheil's pianistic exuberance is given full rein here in performances that highlight his flashy, if often derivative, keyboard ideas. The earlier works (*Airplane Sonata, Sonata Sauvage,* and *Little Shimmy*) exhibit the composer's fascination with jazz, while some of the later pieces (the eleven *Valentine Waltzes* from 1949 in particular) demonstrate that Antheil was capable of creating charming works utilizing mature, fully conceived musical ideas instead of relying on attractively chaotic riffs.

influences: Igor Stravinsky, Edgard Varèse

Garaud MacTaggart

Thomas Arne
Born Thomas Augustine Arne, March12, 1710, in London, England. Died March 5, 1778, in London, England.

period: Baroque

Thomas Arne was one of the most eminent English composers of his time; for twenty-five years his theatrical works played to packed houses in London and Dublin. His opera *Artaxerxes* is a good example of Arne's synthesis of Mozartian charm, Italian lyricism, and Handelian, grandeur, but modern audiences are more likely to be familiar with his short anthem "Rule Britannia."

As a teenager, Arne became friends with Michael Festig, a member of the orchestra of the Italian opera who taught Arne to play the violin. Festig also took his young friend to Oxford, where they heard George Frideric Handel's *Athalia* performed and listened as Handel played one of his remarkable organ improvisations.

Arne, in turn, gave his younger siblings, Richard and Susanna Maria, singing lessons and joined them in an April 1732 performance of Handel's *Acis and Galatea* at the Haymarket Theatre. This event marked Arne's entry into the world of the English stage.

Two years later, his masque *Dido and Aeneas* was also performed at the Haymarket Theatre; his success at that venue led to an engagement at Drury Lane, where Arne's masque *Love and Glory* began a profitable association between the composer and the theater. By the end of 1741 he had gained a measure of popular recognition with a series of songs composed for the Drury Lane productions of four Shakespeare plays—*The Tempest, As You Like It, Twelfth Night,* and *The Merchant of Venice.* During this time Arne also crafted *Alfred,* the masque in which "Rule Britannia" made its first appearance.

In 1742 Arne went to Dublin and met Handel, who was there overseeing the production of the *Messiah* and some of his other oratorios. Arne spent the next two seasons in Dublin, planning a series of concerts that revolved around his own and Handel's music. When he returned to London in 1744, Arne was welcomed as an established composer, and he soon became extremely fashionable with audiences of the day.

Arne's greatest theatrical success came in 1762, when *Artaxerxes,* his opera based upon a text by Metastasio, was premiered. Heavily indebted to the Italian model, this score featured a bevy of virtuoso arias that propelled its popularity into the nineteenth century before it finally faded from view. In addition to publishing the theatrical pieces for which he is best known, Arne also wrote music for the harpsichord as well as various chamber works, songs, and orchestral compositions.

Vocal
Artaxerxes
what to buy: [Catherine Bott, soprano; Patricia Spence, mezzo-soprano; Christopher Robson, countertenor; Richard Edgar-Wilson, tenor; Ian Partridge, tenor; Ray Goodman, cond.; Parley of Instruments, orch.] (Hyperion 67051/2) ♪ ♪ ♪

Goodman and the members of the Parley of Instruments do an outstanding job playing a version of the score that was reconstructed and edited by Peter Holman. To hear the harpsichord played with such clarity is a delight, and the voices suit the parts, with royalty sounding like royalty and the peasants sounding like peasants.

"Rule Britannia"
what to buy: [*English National Songs: From "Greensleeves" to "Home Sweet Home";* Lucie Skeaping, mezzo-soprano; John Potter, tenor; Jeremy Barlow, cond.; Broadside Band, orch.] (Saydisc 400) ♪ ♪ ♪ ♪

Barlow and company have put together a collection of historical songs illuminating the evolution of the British character from the glory days of Elizabeth I to the twilight of the empire under Victoria. Folk melodies like "Greensleeves" and "Sally in Our Alley" mesh well with the more nationalistic "God Save the King" and Arne's "Rule Britannia" in this delightfully tuneful anthology.

influences: George Frideric Handel, Charles Avison

Marijim Thoene and Garaud MacTaggart

Malcolm Arnold

Born Malcolm Henry Arnold, October 21, 1921, in Northampton, England.

period: Twentieth century

Generally known for his film scores, Arnold is a prolific composer who has written orchestral, chamber, opera, and solo music in addition to music for the cinema. His work is better known and more frequently performed in England and Europe than in the United States, where he is best known as the composer of the film score to *The Bridge on the River Kwai.*

Malcolm Arnold has had a career not only as a composer but as an orchestral musician. His formal training in composition and trumpet took place at the Royal College of Music; he joined the London Philharmonic Orchestra in 1941, becoming the principal trumpet player just one year later. World War II interrupted his musical career, but after two years in the British military he jumped back into the orchestral fray, initially with the BBC Symphony Orchestra and a year later with the London Philharmonic.

Even though he was employed as a trumpet player, Arnold's real interest lay in composing, and in 1948 he left the security of his orchestral position for good. He had won a Mendelssohn Scholarship, which enabled him to spend a year in Italy pursuing his chosen profession. By 1950 Arnold had embarked upon a career as a composer and arranger whose livelihood was determined by the number of commissions received.

His years as an orchestral player helped him develop exceptional skills as an orchestrator. By the early 1950s his musical gifts were being recognized, and in 1952 he was commissioned to write a ballet for the coronation of Queen Elizabeth II. He was knighted by the Queen in 1993 in recognition of his years of musical work and the impact that he made, particularly in the film industry.

The casual listener may link Arnold's name with the 1957 movie *The Bridge on the River Kwai*, which won an Academy Award for best film score. Ironically, the most famous tune from this score was not actually by Arnold at all. The whistling melody known as the "Colonel Bogey March" was actually written 40 years prior to the film's production by an English composer name Kenneth Alford. Due to the success of Arnold's score however, Alford's catchy tune is often attributed to the wrong person.

Arnold has written prolifically for both amateur and professional ensembles; his catalog includes nine symphonies, a variety of overtures and orchestral dances, chamber music, two operas, and almost two dozen concertos for various instruments. Despite the serious works on his résumé, however, Arnold does not lack a sense of humor. One of his most delightful pieces, written in 1956 for the irreverent Hoffnung Festival, inspires almost as much amusement today as it did when it was first written. Even the title brings a chuckle—*A Grand Overture for 3 Vacuum Cleaners, 1 Floor Polisher, 4 Rifles, and Orchestra,* op. 57.

Humor aside, Arnold believes strongly in the power of music as a social act of communication that binds people together. To that end, his music is generally tuneful, straightforward, well constructed, and not overly chromatic. Strong melodies predominate in each minor and major work.

Orchestral
The Bridge on the River Kwai Suite
what to buy: [*Film Music*; Richard Hickox, cond; London Symphony Orchestra] (Chandos 9100) ♪ ♪ ♪

Here is the suite from the movie, along with some other great Arnold scores, including *Hobson's Choice, The Inn of the Sixth Happiness, Whistle Down the Wind,* and *The Sound Barrier.* Good, clean sound and warm acoustics mark this disc.

Scottish Dances for Orchestra, op. 59
what to buy: [*Dances;* Andrew Penny, cond.; Queensland Symphony Orchestra] (Naxos 8.553526) <4 b

Penny's budget-priced version of these four charming movements is clear and detailed, with accomplished, surprisingly idiomatic playing from this Australian orchestra. Included along with Arnold's other symphonic dances from English, Cornish, Irish, and Welsh sources, this Scottish set is an almost ideal introduction to the brighter, more appealing aspects of the composer's oeuvre.

[*Arnold for Band;* Jerry Junkin, cond; Dallas Wind Symphony, orch.] (Reference 66) ♪ ♪ ♪ ♪

This is an exceptionally fine disc recorded in Dallas's new Meyerson Symphony Hall, with great interpretations and great sonics. Here is a virtual feast of Arnold's music (ten pieces worth) at its tuneful best. It's all Arnold, and it's worth enjoying over and over again.

Symphony No. 9, op. 128
what to buy: [Andrew Penny, cond.; National Symphony Orchestra of Ireland] (Naxos 8.553540) ♪ ♪ ♪ ♪

As befitting the mystique surrounding a ninth symphony, Arnold approached this work after a particularly trying time in his life, which may be reflected in the generally meditative character of this piece. There are upbeat moments because, after all, it's Arnold we're talking about here, but the final Lento movement may contain the most impressive writing the composer had done in years. The interview between Penny and Arnold that ends the disc sheds some light on the score's distinctive use of repetition as well as other thought processes involved in the work's construction.

Chamber
Trio for Violin, Cello, and Piano, op. 54
what to buy: [*Chamber Music;* English Piano Trio] (Naxos 8.554237) ♪ ♪ ♪ ♪

There is a palpable energy to the group's performance here that can make the hair on the nape of your neck stand up. Arnold's violin sonatas (opp. 15 and 43) and the

Malcolm Arnold

five violin and piano duets from op. 84 fill out the disc, making this recital an attractive sampler of the composer's more intimate music.

influences: William Walton, Gordon Jacob, Bernard Herrmann, Erich Wolfgang Korngold

Dave Wagner

B

Milton Babbitt
Born Milton Byron Babbitt, May 10, 1916, in Philadelphia, PA.

period: Twentieth century

Beginning with his initial classical scores in the mid-1940s, Babbitt was one of the earliest American composers to use and extend Arnold Schoenberg's twelve-tone compositional method, applying it to pitch, rhythm, and other musical aspects. Some of Babbitt's most original work was produced during the 1950s and 1960s, when he became a consultant for RCA and helped develop the Mark II Electronic Music Synthesizer. He has also written relatively attractive works for voice (frequently performed by soprano Bethany Beardslee) and composed a variety of pieces for chamber groups and instrumentalist soloists.

Born in Philadelphia but raised in Jackson, Mississippi, Babbitt was interested in math and popular music as a youth. By the time he graduated from high school, he had shown considerable skills as a jazz ensemble player on clarinet and saxophone and as a composer of pop songs. He had originally intended to follow in his father's footsteps as an actuary when he entered the University of Pennsylvania in 1931 but ended up switching to music when he transferred to New York University. After graduating with a B.A. in music in 1935, Babbitt studied composition privately with Roger Sessions, then pursued graduate work at Princeton University.

Before twelve-tone music was widely accepted, Babbitt studied the music of Arnold Schoenberg (whom he first met in New York in 1933), Alban Berg, and Anton Webern, although his earlier influences had been Edgard Varèse and Igor Stravinsky. He joined the Princeton faculty in 1938, received his M.F.A. in music in 1942, and joined the mathematics faculty from 1943 to

1945, dividing his time between teaching at Princeton and doing mathematical research in Washington, D.C. He rejoined Princeton's music faculty in 1948, fresh from another kind of research.

In 1946, during a period of study and discovery, he wrote a paper, "The Function of Set Structure in the Twelve-tone System," which summarized his analyses of Schoenberg's compositional methods. Throughout his career, Babbitt has exhibited a fascination with the formal characteristics of twelve-tone (or dodecaphonic) music, initially seeking to apply the pitch operations of that system to rhythm, dynamics, and timbre. His first real attempts at building upon Schoenberg's ideas were his *Three Compositions for Piano* (1947) and *Composition for Four Instruments* (1948), the latter also showing the influence of Webern in the sparsely textured passages.

Babbitt's work with electronic sound synthesis was also a major concern. By the 1950s he had become a consultant for RCA, where he became the first composer to work with the company's Mark II Electronic Music Synthesizer, built by engineers Harry Olson and Herbert Belar in 1957. In its earliest incarnation, the Mark II was an analog synthesizer controlled by punched paper tape, which allowed Babbitt great precision and control with regard to timing and the rate of timbral, textural, and volume changes in live performances. In 1959, the Mark II was acquired by the Columbia-Princeton Electronic Music Center in New York City, with Babbitt as its primary user. The composer's first totally synthesized work was his 1961 *Composition for Synthesizer.* The same year, he also wrote *Vision and Prayer* for soprano and synthesizer, a work inspired by a Dylan Thomas poem and originally recorded at the Columbia-Princeton center with a tape produced completely on the Mark II synthesizer. Babbitt used the structure of the poem's two groups of irregular-length stanzas to furnish details and tonalities.

From 1962 to 1964, Babbitt composed *Ensembles for Synthesizer* and *Philomel,* a work for synthesizer and voice. His 1965 piece *Relata I* was his first fully acknowledged orchestral score, using synthesized polyphonic sounds in six parallel sections based on a rarely appearing but pervasively influential twelve-pitch class series. Within each of the sections, the first part features the full orchestra, while the second uses small groups within the orchestra. In 1966, the complex work was premiered by the Cleveland Orchestra with guest conductor Gunther Schuller. While Babbitt favored Schuller, he complained about the Cleveland players, saying, "The orchestra was mechanically and mentally largely unprepared and massively uninterested." Babbitt said that only 80 percent of the notes were played at all; only 60 percent were accurate rhythmically; and only about 40 percent reflected his expressive and dynamic markings. By this time, he felt that the only way to further contemporary music was to establish dedicated ensembles sympathetic to new scores and to give them adequate rehearsal time.

Today, Babbitt may be most admired for his chamber and vocal music. His 1951 song cycle *Du* is a lyrically expressive composition for piano and female voice that proves Babbitt was not just concerned about structure. Another of his more famous (and frequently performed) pieces is *Philomel* (1964), an imaginative melodic work that combines live performance with taped sound. Commissioned through a Ford Foundation grant that enabled solo performers to request works from chosen composers, it was originally written in conjunction with poet John Hollander for soprano Bethany Beardslee. The piece is based on Ovid's version of the Greek legend of Philomela, the speechless maiden who is transformed into a nightingale, and it reflects a shift in perspective that can be heard in Babbitt's synthesized speech-song similitudes, conveyed with a mellowness that would affect the character of his future live music.

In recent years, the availability of Babbitt's recorded music for multiple combinations of instruments has improved, aided in no small measure by his 1982 Pulitzer citation for a "life's work as a distinguished and seminal American composer" and a 1986 MacArthur fellowship. Despite all his honors and awards, though, Babbitt's atonal work has yet to be embraced by the public. In fact, two major American orchestras found his 1986 work *Transfigured Notes,* with its nine individual lines all jockeying for equal contrapuntal attention, particularly difficult to perform. The piece wasn't premiered until 1991, when conductor Gunther Schuller led a group of Boston musicians through twelve rehearsals and combined two live recordings for the CD. Schuller claims he lost $42,000 on the project while only managing to achieve a "less-than-perfect" performance.

Milton Babbitt

Babbitt has said he wants "a piece of music to be literally as much as possible," an attitude that, according to some critics, leads to a body of inaccessible work. However, his defenders claim that Babbitt's highly ordered works make greater demands on the listener. In any event, accessibility was a lesser priority for him than the evolution of the form. He wrote a provocative article that appeared in the February 1958 issue of *High Fidelity* magazine ("Who Cares If You Listen"), stating "that 'tradition' has it that the lay listener, by virtue of some undefined, transcendental faculty, always is able to arrive at a musical judgment absolute in its wisdom if not always permanent in its validity. I regret my inability to accord this declaration of faith the respect due its advanced age."

Orchestral
Transfigured Notes for String Orchestra
what to buy: [Gunther Schuller, cond.; Boston Symphony Orchestra Strings] (GM Recordings 2060) ♪ ♪ ♪ ♪♪

One of Babbitt's more lyrically appealing works, *Transfigured Notes* is framed on this disc by string masterpieces from Arnold Schoenberg (*Verklärte Nacht*) and Igor Stravinsky (the Concerto in D Major for String Orchestra), two of the composer's early influences. Schuller recorded two 1991 performances of the piece and combined them to yield this lustrous performance of Babbitt's slow, sinewy work. Nine smoothly blended, dissonant parallel lines from string sections within the orchestra leave little to stick in your memory, but repeated play heightens listener appeal.

Chamber
The Joy of More Sextets for Violin and Piano
what to buy: [Rolf Schulte, violin; Alan Feinberg, piano] (New World Records 364) ♪ ♪ ♪ ♪♪

Misleading in that the piece is performed by a duo, the title signifies the structure of sixes that run through it. It was written twenty years after Babbitt's 1966 work *Sextets,* also featured on this disc. Changing dynamics of the shaped phrasing and repeated lines with altered rhythmic values contribute to the exhilaration and power of the music, and these talented, seasoned players brilliantly provide an engrossing listening experience.

Vocal
Philomel for Soprano and Four-Track Tape

what to buy: [Bethany Beardslee, soprano] (New World Records 80466) ♪ ♪ ♪ ♪♪

Sparsely accompanied by sprinklings of synthesized sound and electronically enhanced vocal choruses, Beardslee soars, swoops, and quivers with masterly precision and flexibility. Her New York premiere received rave reviews, and it's obvious that she's staked her claim to this piece. Her magnificent performance of one of Babbitt's more popular works is the highlight of this disc, which also contains two performances of *Phonemena*—one for soprano (Lynne Webber) and piano (Jerry Kuderna) and the other for soprano (Webber) and tape. There are also two works spotlighting pianist Robert Miller—*Post-Partitions,* and *Reflections*—the latter composed for piano and synthesizer.

Vision and Prayer for Soprano and Synthesized Accompaniment
what to buy: [*Milton Babbitt*; Bethany Beardslee, soprano] (CRI 521) ♪ ♪ ♪ ♪♪

Soprano Beardslee sings on this historic recording (she was the original interpreter of the piece), accompanied by an intriguing and appealing assortment of synthesized sounds. Other pieces on the disc include *An Elizabethan Sextette,* performed by the Group for Contemporary Music, and five solo piano works played by Alan Feinberg. But nothing else here is quite as arresting as the performance by Beardslee and the Mark II.

influences: Roger Sessions, Arnold Schoenberg, Alban Berg, Anton Webern, George Perle

Nancy Ann Lee

Carl Philipp Emanuel Bach
Born March 8, 1714, in Weimar, Germany. Died December 14, 1788, in Hamburg, Germany.

period: Baroque/Classical

While modern audiences recognize C.P.E. Bach as the most famous son of his father Johann Sebastian, in his time he was the best-known of the Bachs, due in large part to his treatise, *Essay on the True Art of Playing Keyboard Instruments.* His compositions elicit much present-day interest, particularly his many keyboard and orchestral works, though he wrote a large body of sacred vocal music as well.

Born while his father was at Weimar, young Carl Philipp Emanuel Bach was the second surviving son of Johann Sebastian's first wife, and had every advantage of musical training and education. He began his musical studies at home with his father and later said the senior Bach was his only teacher. He soon proved to be quite talented at the keyboard, and the large volume of works he wrote for it show his continued enjoyment of the instrument. But Sebastian had more in mind for his sons than their musical training—they received a good general education at the Thomasschule, and were encouraged to attend a university as well. Emanuel studied law at the universities in Leipzig and Frankfurt-an-den-Oder, though he never actually practiced as a lawyer. For the next few years he continued to combine his academic studies with his first steps as a composer, until finally deciding upon a musical career and traveling to Berlin in 1738.

From then on the major changes in his life were few. In 1740, he was called into service at the court of Crown Prince Frederick, who in two years would ascend the throne and become known to history as Frederick the Great of Prussia. While it is not certain why Emanuel was given the appointment, it does not seem to be because of his father's influence, though other Bach relatives may have done some networking with their friends at court. Possibly the ten works he had already written for flute impressed Frederick, an avid flautist. In any case, he was called upon to play harpsichord in Frederick's chamber orchestra, an opportunity not to be missed. He remained at the post almost thirty years, until 1768, and it was within this period that he supposedly arranged for his father's visit to the court at Potsdam, during which the senior Bach met the King and composed the *Musical Offering*. During his Berlin years Emanuel also wrote his *Essay on the True Art of Playing Keyboard Instruments,* a treatise on ornamentation and figured-bass realization that goes beyond the basics of keyboard technique to more advanced subjects such as theory, composition, and style. It remains both a classic firsthand reference on correct period ornamentation, and a compendium of the performance practices associated with the "empfindsamer stile" ("sensitive style") in Germany at that time. As such it retains both historical and practical significance.

In 1768, Emanuel succeeded his godfather Georg Philipp Telemann as cantor at the Johanneum (Lateinschule) in Hamburg, where he stayed until his death twenty years

Cecilia Bartoli:
Italian mezzo-soprano Cecilia Bartoli has been hailed as possessing one of the finest vocal instruments in recent times. Noted for her rich, vibrant tone and technical agility, Bartoli has excelled in both the "pants" (young boy) and ingénue roles of Mozart and Rossini. Her open, earthy interpretations are marked by an innocent sensuality and generosity of spirit. She is equally at home in the grandeur of the opera house, the intimacy of the recital stage, and the rigorous scrutiny of the recording studio.

Born June 4, 1966 in Rome, Bartoli studied at the St. Cecilia Conservatory, but she received most of her training from her opera-singing parents, Silvanna Bazzoni and Angelo Bartoli. Her mother in particular has been instrumental in shaping Bartoli's career. At the age of nine Bartoli made her professional debut as the shepherd in *Tosca*. Television appearances with seasoned veterans Katia Ricciarelli and Leo Nucci and a tribute program to Maria Callas brought increased attention to her at age nineteen. Impressed by the youngster's potential, conductors Herbert von Karajan and Daniel Barenboim became early advocates and mentors. She made her Metropolitan Opera debut as Despina in Mozart's *Cosi fan tutte* in 1996.

Although closely associated with the signature roles of Mozart and Rossini, Bartoli has shown a keen interest in authentic performance practice, having recorded Handel's *Rinaldo* (Decca 467087) and Haydn's *Orfeo ed Euridice* (L'Oiseau-Lyre 452668) with Christopher Hogwood; Haydn's *Armida* (Teldec 81108) and Mozart's *Lucio Silla* (Teldec 44928) with Nikolaus Harnoncourt; Mozart's *Mitridate* (Decca 460772) with Christophe Rousset; and the *Vivaldi Album* with Giovanni Antonini (Decca 466569). Other highlights of Bartoli's extensive recording career include Rossini's *La Cenerentola* (London 436902), a duets album with Welsh baritone Bryn Terfel (Decca 458928), and *The Impatient Lover* (Decca 440297), for which she received a Grammy Award in 1993. Bartoli's first solo recital album, *If You Love Me—18th Century Italian Songs* (Decca 436267), is a must for any serious student of the voice.

Mona DeQuis

later. Whereas Emanuel had plenty of time at Frederick's court to pursue his interest in keyboard technique, as cantor he had to not only teach musical subjects at the Johanneum, but also was called upon to serve as musical director for the five main churches in Hamburg. With a workload similar to his father's before him, he was responsible for over 200 performances during the church year, not to mention special music for funerals, school functions, birthdays, and royal visits. After twenty years of that kind of schedule, it is little wonder that his output includes so much vocal and sacred music—the twenty-two Passions and two oratorios are just the beginning!

Emanuel's two disparate positions during his musical career are responsible for the wide variety of his compositions. While in Berlin, he composed chamber music for strings, and also several pieces for oboe and flute, in Frederick's honor. His church position at Hamburg required that he write huge volumes of vocal music, as well as larger sacred dramatic works. In addition he wrote several string symphonies that were among the first to break from the old Italian *sinfonia* style (in which the work is simply a single movement of a suite or a prelude to an opera which is played alone). Emanuel's symphonies are rather more representative of the early freestanding symphony of the Rococo period, the forerunner of the large-scale form we know today.

Orchestral
Sinfonias for Orchestra, nos. 1–4 (Wq. 183)
what to buy: [Gustav Leonhardt, cond.; Orchestra of the Age of Enlightenment] (Virgin Veritas 61794) ♪ ♪ ♪ ♪♪

These works from Emanuel's Hamburg years are great examples of just how forward-thinking his symphonies were—if you close your eyes, you might think you're listening to a Mozart or Haydn symphony at times. Leonhardt's orchestra is well recorded and, though the conductor gets his musicians to play at a brisk pace, never is there the feeling that his timing is incongruous with the composer's wishes. The second half of this two-disc set features Anner Byslma as the excellent soloist in three cello concertos (Wq. 170, 171, and 172), works which, in different arrangements, can be flute concertos (Wq. 166, 167, and 168) or harpsichord concertos (Wq. 26, 27, and 28).

what to buy next: [Yoon K. Lee, cond.; Salzburg Chamber Philharmonic Orchestra] (Naxos 8.553289) ♪ ♪ ♪♪

The Salzburg Orchestra doesn't have quite the beguiling blend of flash and substance that Leonhardt's musicians display in these scores, but the infectiousness of the music and the adequacy of the performances make this budget-priced set worthwhile. The Sinfonia in F Major by Wilhelm Friedemann Bach closes out the album in fine style.

various flute concertos
what to buy: [*C.P.E. Bach: Die Flötenkonzerte, vol. 1*; Eckart Haupt, flute; Hartmut Haenchen, cond.; Kammerorchester "Carl Philipp Emanuel Bach," orch.] (Capriccio 10104) ♪ ♪ ♪ ♪♪

Haupt, Haenchen, and the orchestra provide stately,

eloquent performances of these three lovely works which quite aptly charmed Frederick the Great. He probably didn't concern himself with the fact that they were originally written for the keyboard rather than his own favorite instrument. The pacing in the D Minor and A Minor Concertos (Wq. 22 and 166, respectively) is superb, and Haupt's cadenzas in the A Major Concerto (Wq. 169) are totally in character with this Bach's oeuvre.

what to buy next: [Martin Feinstein, flute; Martin Feinstein, cond.; The Feinstein Ensemble, orch.] (Black Box 1019) ♪ ♪ ♪ ♪

Feinstein draws some marvelous playing from himself and all concerned. He does take the tempos noticeably faster than Haenchen in the two concertos their programs duplicate (Wq. 22 and 169), but Feinstein's orchestra is able to keep up without sounding hard-pressed or unnatural. The version of Wq. 169 heard here is in G Major, however. Feinstein also includes another of Bach's flute concertos, the A Major, Wq. 168.

Chamber
various keyboard works
what to buy: [*For Connoisseurs and Amateurs: Six Collections of Sonatas, Free Fantasies, and Rondos*; Gabor Antalffy, harpsichord] (CPO 999100) ♪ ♪ ♪ ♪

A capacious collection of all sorts of keyboard works, written from 1758 to 1786. It's a good recording, but for some may be too much of a good thing, containing seventy-one pieces spread over four compact discs. Still, each of these miniatures has a charming character of its own, and it is wonderful to trace the development of Emanuel's mature compositional style over almost thirty years. Antalffy's easy performance style seems just right for these pieces—even the serious ones aren't overdone.

influences: Georg Philipp Telemann, Jean-Philippe Rameau

Melissa M. Stewart

Johann Christian Bach
Born Johann Christian Bach, September 5, 1735, in Leipzig, Germany. Died January 1, 1782, in London, England.

period: Classical

Although music historians generally regard him as a minor composer, the youngest son of the great Johann Sebastian Bach—Johann Christian, also known as John, "the London Bach"—was more famous in his own day than his father. While he was best known in his lifetime as an opera composer, it is his instrumental music (particularly his sinfonias from the opus 6 set) that is generally performed today.

The name "Bach" was synonymous with "musician" in eighteenth-century Germany, and no wonder. Johann Sebastian fathered four famous composers, the last of whom was Johannn Christian Bach. This junior Bach was instructed in music by his father and, upon the death of the senior Bach in 1750, went to live with his older brother Carl Philipp Emanuel in Berlin. Johann Christian's musical education continued under his sibling's tutelage until 1754, when he left his brother's household to live in Italy, first as a court musician and later as the organist of the cathedral in Milan. While in Italy, Johann Christian converted to Catholicism and became enamored of opera (not necessarily in that order). After writing his first three operas he immigrated to England, where he continued producing operas in the Italian manner that was so popular during this period. He also ventured into the area of public concerts with his partner and fellow composer Carl Frederich Abel. By this time Johann Christian's fame and fortune had become much greater than his father's, and his musical language was considered more modern and cutting-edge.

Johann Christian Bach moved in the highest levels of society and was a friend and confidante to many composers. He knew and admired the young Wolfgang Amadeus Mozart, who returned the favor not only by praising the older composer's music but by employing many of his compositional techniques in his own early works. Johann Christian wrote in the rococo style, which was all the rage by the 1740s, even while his father was still composing in the more learned and severe baroque manner. Light and pleasant, with clear-cut phrases and tuneful melodies but without the demands of too much counterpoint, rococo compositions were geared to be pleasing because there was a new audience for art music. No longer restricted to the aristocratic courts and drawing rooms, music could increasingly be heard and enjoyed by a much wider audience in the public concert hall. New middle-class consumers wanted music that was a delight to their ears and a treat for their memories. To this end, the younger Bach was thought by his

Kathleen Battle:
Noted as an artist of extraordinary versatility, American soprano Kathleen Battle has been celebrated for her stunning interpretations of repertoire ranging from George Frideric Handel to Duke Ellington. The natural lyricism and purity of her voice paved the way for a career that included collaborations with the world's finest performers, conductors, and orchestras.

Born on August 8, 1948, in Portsmouth, Ohio, the youngest of a steelworker's seven children Battle earned both a B.A. and a M.A. in music education from the University of Cincinnati College Conservatory. While teaching music in an inner-city school, Battle continued to audition in hopes of building a singing career, eventually making her professional debut at the Spoleto Festival in 1972 with conductor Thomas Schippers. Many engagements with leading American orchestras and a series of other momentous debuts followed, including the New York City Opera in 1976 and, in 1977, both the San Francisco Opera and New York City's Metropolitan Opera. In 1985, Battle won the prestigious Laurence Olivier Award for her Covent Garden debut in Richard Strauss's *Ariadne auf Naxos*. Fellow Ohio native James Levine became an early champion and frequent collaborator, serving as conductor for many of her opera performances and as accompanist in recital. Other noted conductors with whom Battle has worked include Herbert von Karajan, Neville Marriner, Seiji Ozawa, and Leonard Slatkin. Battle's impressive discography includes Gioachino Rossini's *The Barber of Seville* with Placido Domingo (Deutsche Grammophon 435763), *Angels' Glory* with Christopher Parkening (Sony Classics 62723), *Baroque Duet* with Wynton Marsalis (Sony Classics 46672), and *The Bach Album* with Itzhak Perlman (Deutsche Grammophon 429737). Battle, an inductee in the NAACP Hall of Fame, has been the recipient of numerous awards and honors including five Grammys, six honorary doctorates, and an Emmy. An otherwise brilliant career was tarnished by her unfortunate release from the Met production of Donizetti's *The Daughter of the Regiment* in 1994 on grounds of "unprofessional actions." However, Battle's career has carried on, primarily in the concert hall and recording studio.

Mona DeQuis

contemporaries to be a far superior composer to his old-fashioned father. Not until fifty years after Johann Christian's death in 1782 did the full importance of his father begin to be realized. The son has been demoted in importance, and few of Johann Christian's thirteen operas are performed in their entirety today, although their overtures are sometimes presented as concert works.

Orchestral
Sinfonias for Orchestra, op. 6
what to buy: [David Zinman, cond; Netherlands Chamber Orchestra] (Philips Duo 442275) ♪ ♪ ♪ ♪

Although early recordings on period instruments are all the rage now, one cannot argue with the clear intonation, fluid playing, and good musical judgments set forth by Zinman and the Netherlands Ensemble. This complete set of the six Sinfonias from op. 6 also includes the Sinfonias from opp. 9 and 18, with first rate performances in all respects.

various opera overtures

what to buy: [Opera Overtures: Vol. 1; Anthony Halstead, cond; Hanover Band, orch.] (CPO 999129) ♪♪♪♪

The overture to Bach's most famous opera, Adriano in Siria, is included here, along with those to Artaserse, Gli Uccellatori, Alessandro nell'Indie, and many more. From these kinds of overtures grew the early classical symphony. They are heard here in performances by Halstead and the Hanover Band, with brisk tempos, spirited playing, and wonderfully recorded sound.

Sinfonia Concertante in A Major for Violin, Cello, and Orchestra

what to buy: [Pinchas Zukerman, violin; Yo-Yo Ma, cello; Pinchas Zukerman, cond; St. Paul Chamber Orchestra] (Sony 39964) ♪♪♪♪

Here, modern instruments are played with the sensibility and lightness that this music demands. This sinfonia concertante, a cross between the baroque concerto and the classical symphony, comes alive in the hands of Zukerman and Ma. The recording also includes the first of the Sinfonias for Double Orchestra, op. 18, and the famous cello concerto by Luigi Boccherini, in a stunning performance by Ma that is worth the price of admission all by itself.

influences: Carl Philipp Emanuel Bach, Carl Frederich Abel, Wolfgang Amadeus Mozart

Dave Wagner

Johann Sebastian Bach

Born March 21, 1685, in Eisenach, Germany. Died July 28, 1750, in Leipzig, Germany.

period: Baroque

Johann Sebastian Bach is the composer of the Baroque period, and his achievements are breathtaking. Accounts tell us that he was an organist and harpsichordist without peer, and his compositions continue to astound us centuries later. His influence was vast

(Wolfgang Amadeus Mozart and Ludwig van Beethoven were just two revered later composers who held him in awe), and endures into modern times.

We know very little of Johann Sebastian Bach's first musical experiences, but from his son, Carl Philipp Emanuel, we hear that his earliest keyboard studies were with his older brother Johann Christoph. The elder sibling had studied with Johann Pachelbel during the 1680s and was organist at St. Michael's in Ohrdruf, where it is possible that Johann Sebastian developed his knowledge of organ construction by helping Johann Christoph maintain the church instrument. The younger Bach also met Georg Erdmann (a lifelong friend) at this time and, in 1700, the two of them moved to Lüneberg, where they became members of the Matins chorus of the Michaeliskirche. Bach continued his general education at the church's school, and probably took part in the performance of chamber music. The school also had a large library of scores, which he may have taken advantage of to further his compositional education.

In 1703, Bach became organist at the Neu Kirche in Arnstadt. In the fall of 1705 he was granted a leave of absence to travel to Lübeck to hear Dietrich Buxtehude's famous concert series, but when he did not return until February of 1706 his relations with the town and church administrators, already bad due to Bach's headstrong manners, grew worse. His reputation as a talented musician was well under way, however, and a year later Bach took a position as organist at St. Blasiuskirche in Mühlhausen, and married his second cousin Maria Barbara Bach. Organ and clavier music made up the bulk of his compositions while living there, though a number of cantatas (BWV 4, 71, 106, 131, and 196) probably date from this time as well. Bach left his post in Mühlhausen and accepted the position of court organist at the palace of Duke Wilhelm Ernst of Weimar in 1708—-a marked advance in both salary and social standing. In 1714, he received the additional appointment of Konzertmeister and was required to compose a new cantata every month. There are about seventeen extant cantatas from this time, the most important being Ich hatte viel Bekümmernis (BWV 21). Six of Bach's children were also born during the years at Weimar, including Wilhelm Friedemann (b. 1710) and Carl Philipp Emanuel (b. 1714). Despite the increase in funding that went along with his position in Weimar, Bach remained discontent. There was a growing resentment between patron and composer, culminating in 1716 when Kapellmeister Samuel Drese died and Bach's expectations of being offered the position were unfulfilled. He decided to seek a post elsewhere, finally accepting a position at the court of Prince Leopold in Cöthen. This displeased Duke Wilhelm, and the ensuing dispute resulted in the composer being imprisoned (for one month). He was released on December 2 and left town immediately.

The work situation in Cöthen was happier; Bach was handsomely paid and highly esteemed. During this time he composed a large amount of chamber music, several solo concertos, and more keyboard music, but only secular cantatas since the court chapel was Calvinist. Among the more prominent of his compositions from this time was the first book of *Das wohltemperirte Clavier (The Well-Tempered Clavier)*. In 1719 he made a trip to Berlin, where he met the Margrave of Brandenburg, to whom, two years later, he would present the six *Brandenburg Concertos*. In 1720 both Maria Barbara and Johann Christoph died, and the year after that Bach married Anna Magdalena. She was a Cöthen court singer who became Bach's copyist and assistant and bore him thirteen more children, including Johann Christian (b. 1735). Over time Bach's relationship with Prince Leopold cooled, and so the composer once again went looking for a new position.

The Kantor at Leipzig, Joseph Kuhnau, died in 1722 and Johann Sebastian was one of many prominent composers who applied. Bach was actually the council's third choice (after Georg Philipp Telemann, who couldn't get released from a post at Hamburg, and Johann Christoph Graupner, who turned down the invitation), but he accepted the position when it was finally offered to him in 1723. This marked the beginning of his most productive period as a composer. As Kantor, Johann Sebastian was to be Director of Music for the town of Leipzig, and much of his duties revolved around the Thomaskirche and the Nikolaikirche. He had academic responsibilities as well (for which he hired an assistant), and derived a large part of his income from weddings, funerals, and town celebrations. His compositions in these years include more cantatas, the *St. Matthew Passion,* the *St. John Passion,* a variety of motets, and various instrumental works. On the death of Friedrich August I, Elector of Saxony, in 1733, he composed the Kyrie and Gloria that would later be part of his monumental Mass in B Minor.

In the latter part of the 1730s, Bach tried to delegate even more of his duties in order to make more time for composition. He composed works such as the *Christmas Oratorio* (not really an oratorio, but a set of six cantatas), the harpsichord concertos, and the *Clavier-Übung* for organ. Wishing to upgrade his social standing, he sought another court appointment, and in 1736 was appointed *Hofcompositeur* for the Dresden court; his 1733 homage to the Elector of Saxony had finally paid off. Bach's final years as a composer were spent working on such pieces as the *Canonic Variations on Von Himmel hoch* for organ (BWV 769), the *Musical Offering* (composed after a 1747 visit to Potsdam, where his son, Carl Philipp Emanuel, was a court musician to Frederick II), and the unfinished *Art of the Fugue.* In 1749 Bach became quite ill, and by early 1750 he was nearly blind. He died on July 28 of that year, after two unsuccessful operations to remove cataracts.

About 200 of Bach's sacred cantatas survive (some three-fifths of what he wrote), and there are numerous secular cantatas, nearly 200 chorale settings, and almost one hundred sacred songs. Of the sacred cantatas, some of the most noteworthy include: Cantata no. 4 (*Christ lag in Todes Banden*), Cantata no. 56 (*Ich will den Kreuzstab gerne tragen*), Cantata no. 78 (*Jesu, der du meine Seele*), Cantata no. 80 (*Ein feste Burg*), Cantata no. 82 (*Ich habe genug*), and Cantata no. 140 (*Wachet auf, ruft uns die Stimme*). For secular cantatas, Cantata no. 202 (the *Wedding Cantata*), the witty Cantata no. 211 (the *Coffee Cantata*), and Cantata no. 212 (the *Peasant Cantata*) are particularly noteworthy. There are also a number of large-scale sacred works, including three passions (the *St. Matthew Passion* and the *St. John Passion* constitute two of the greatest dramatic works ever composed), oratorios for Christmas and Easter, the Mass in B Minor (In 1817, the Swiss critic Hans-Georg Nageli acclaimed this piece as the "greatest work of music of all ages and of all peoples"), magnificats in D Major and E-flat Major, four *Kyrie-Gloria* masses, and eight motets.

Bach's suites and partitas, inventions and sinfonias, the *Italian Concerto* and the two books of *Das wohltemperierte Clavier,* are all musts for any keyboard artist. And there's so much more: fantasias, preludes, sonatas; and, of course, the sublime *Goldberg Variations.* Bach wrote nearly 250 works for organ, essentially creating the lion's share of the repertory with his preludes and fugues, fantasias, toccatas, trio sonatas, numerous chorale preludes (including *Das Orgel-Buchlein*), the six chorales after Schübler cantatas, and the *Clavier-Übung* 3 (1739). Other important instrumental works include numerous concertos for various instruments and orchestra, the six *Brandenburg Concertos,* the wondrous *Musical Offering,* the sonatas and partitas for solo violin, and the suites for solo cello. *The Art of the Fugue,* Bach's last work, is unfinished, and in the absence of a specific instrumental direction from the composer, it has been performed by both ensemble and solo keyboard artists. The only genre not represented in Bach's oeuvre is opera, and that is no doubt because he didn't get the opportunity. Certainly his secular cantatas are virtually chamber operas, and we can only assume that he would have set singular standards in this area too had he been given the chance.

Orchestral
Brandenburg Concertos (BWV 1046–1051)
what to buy: [Herbert von Karajan, cond.; Berlin Philharmonic Orchestra] (Deutsche Grammophon 453001) ♪ ♪ ♪ ♪ ♪

A fine and classic recording, full of fire and quite wonderfully performed. This complete set of the six *Brandenburgs* also includes the second and third of Bach's four Suites for Orchestra (BWV 1067 and 1068).

[Trevor Pinnock, cond.; English Concert, orch.] (Deutsche Grammophon Archiv 423492) ♪ ♪ ♪ ♪ ♪

Another gem of a recording, this three-disc set contains all of the *Brandenburg Concertos* in addition to all four Suites for Orchestra (BWV 1066–1069). The budget price (relatively speaking) and original-instrument slant of the performance make this a viable alternative to Karajan's modern, full-sized orchestra version.

Concertos for Harpsichord and Orchestra (BWV 1052—1058)
what to buy: [*The Glenn Gould Edition;* Glenn Gould, piano; Vladimir Golschmann, cond.; Columbia Symphony Orchestra; Leonard Bernstein, cond.; New York Philharmonic Orchestra] (Sony Classical 38524) ♪ ♪ ♪ ♪

Gould is a master when it comes to Bach. He does not disappoint in these recordings from 1957–1959, and although the orchestral playing is not quite sublime you should get the set for Gould alone. This disc features only three of the concertos, with BWV 1052 documenting Gould playing while Bernstein conducts the New York Philharmonic Orchestra and the balance of the set (BWV 1055 and 1056) showcasing Gould with Golschmann and an orchestra of studio musicians.

[*Bach: Concertos;* Trevor Pinnock, harpsichord; Trevor Pinnock, cond.; The English Concert, orch.] (Deutsche Grammophon 463725) ♪ ♪ ♪ ♪

All of the keyboard concertos, including the ones with two, three, and four keyboards, are here in this moderately priced five-CD box. They are all performed on harpsichord, with an original-instrument bias evident in the orchestra. This is not a drawback when you consider how well sprung these performances are and how fine the recording is in general. Pinnock and company also toss in the two violin concertos (BWV 1041 and 1042) and a batch of alternative arrangements by Bach (i.e., the Oboe d'Amore version of BWV 1055, etc.). If you want it all in one fell swoop, this is the set to get.

Concerto no. 1 in A Minor for Violin and Orchestra (BWV 1041)
what to buy: [*Solo and Double Violin Concertos;* Andrew Manze, violin; Andrew Manze, cond.; Academy of Ancient Music, orch.] (Harmonia Mundi 907155) ♪ ♪ ♪ ♪♪

These are exciting yet astoundingly nuanced performances from one of the finest violinists in the original-instrument camp. Manze does double duty, playing and conducting with equal aplomb through the main piece and the other three works on this disc: the Violin Concerto in E Major (BWV 1042) and a pair of D Minor concerti for two violins, with Rachel Podger joining him in the spotlight (BWV 1043 and 1060).

what to buy next: [*Isaac Stern: A Life In Music;* Isaac Stern, violin; Alexander Schneider, cond.; English Chamber Orchestra] (Sony Classical 66471) ♪ ♪ ♪ ♪

For those listeners not wishing to jump on the original-instrument bandwagon, this disc offers a satisfying experience of the wonderful A Minor Concerto. Stern also plays the Concerto no. 2 for Violin and Orchestra (BWV 1042), the Concerto in D Minor for Two Violins and Orchestra (with Itzhak Perlman playing the second part and Zubin Mehta conducting the New York Philharmonic Orchestra), and the Concerto for Violin and Oboe (with Harold Gomberg on oboe and Leonard Bernstein leading the NYPO). The performances throughout this set are quite marvelous.

Johann Sebastian Bach

Musikalisches Opfer (Musical Offering) for Chamber Ensemble (BWV 1079)
what to buy: [Barthold Kuijken, flute; Sigiswald Kuijken, violin; Marie Leonhardt, violin; Wieland Kuijken, bass viola da gamba; Robert Kohnen, harpsichord; Gustav Leonhardt, harpsichord] (Sony Classics Seon 63189) ♪ ♪ ♪ ♪

A thrilling work, with a group delivering quality results in a way befitting this late gem.

Die Kunst der Fuge (The Art of the Fugue) (BWV 1080)
what to buy: [Christopher Hogwood, harpsichord; Neville Marriner, cond., Academy of St. Martin-in-the-Fields, orch.] (Philips 442556) ♪ ♪ ♪ ♪ ♪

Bach didn't specify the instrumentation for this final work, but Marriner and the Academy are fabulous in their interpretation. Also included on this two-disc set is the ensemble's version of the *Musical Offering*.

what to buy next: [Bernard Lagace, organ] (Analekta-Fleur de Lys 23066/67) ♪ ♪ ♪ ♪ ♪

Considering Bach's reputation as an organist, Lagace's rendition makes much sense, especially when the playing is so consistently rewarding. The work doesn't span the entire two-disc program, however, and Lagace also gives the listener solid performances of the *Canonic Variations* (BWV 769), the chorale *Für deinen Thron tret' ich hiermit* (BWV 327), and excerpts from the *Musical Offering*.

[Canadian Brass, ensemble] (Sony Classics 44501) ♪ ♪ ♪ ♪

Many different arrangements are possible with this piece, but not all are as easily assimilable as the Canadian Brass's. The engineers have done a good, if not great, job with the overall sound picture, and the results are quite pleasing.

Jesu, bleibet meine Freude (Jesu, Joy of Man's Desiring)
what to buy: [*A Bach Celebration*; Christopher Parkening, guitar; Paul Shure, cond.; Los Angeles Chamber Orchestra] (EMI Classics 47195) ♪ ♪ ♪ ♪

Parkening's playing is superb in this lovely little transcription for guitar and orchestra. It is part of an album devoted to arrangements drawn from various Bach chorales, and which have been specifically crafted to feature the guitarist's undeniable talents. Other adaptations include *Sheep May Safely Graze* (lifted from BWV 208) and *Sleepers Awake!* (taken from BWV 140).

what to buy next: [*The Stokowski Collection, vol. 1*; Leopold Stokowski, cond.; Leopold Stokowski Orchestra] (Vanguard Classics 8009) ♪ ♪ ♪ ♪

Never one to shy away from shaping old masterpieces to his own idiosyncratic needs, Stokowski was, nonetheless, a talented conductor and popularizer. The orchestral arrangement heard here, however, was created by Peter Schickele, best known to most classical fans for his comedic capers with material supposedly generated by P.D.Q. Bach. *Jesu, Joy of Man's Desiring* finds itself keeping company with works by Antonio Vivaldi, Wolfgang Amadeus Mozart, and Arcangelo Corelli.

Chamber
Sonatas and Partitas for Solo Violin (BWV 1001—1006)
what to buy: [Itzhak Perlman, violin] (EMI Classics 49483) ♪ ♪ ♪ ♪ ♪

The sheer technique required for playing these pieces is prodigious, but so too is the poetry at the heart of these wonderful works. They are a must for top-tier violinists, and Perlman is second to none in his ability to develop the subtle blend of skill and artistry necessary to convince and enchant listeners.

[Henryk Szeryng, violin] (Deutsche Grammophon 453004) ♪ ♪ ♪ ♪ ♪

Since it came out in the 1960s, this has been one of the definitive recordings, and it is still a worthwhile addition to any collection no matter how many versions of these works one already owns.

what to buy next: [Arthur Grumiaux, violin] (Philips 438736) ♪ ♪ ♪ ♪ ♪

Grumiaux upholds the fine Belgian tradition of violin artistry with a recording which makes one more aware of the music than the masterly technique that goes into presenting it. The mid-line pricing for this release makes it a very attractive option.

[Paul Galbraith, guitar] (Delos 3232) ♪ ♪ ♪ ♪

There have been other guitar-oriented arrangements of Bach's premier works for solo violin, but none quite like this. Galbraith had an eight-string guitar specially built for him and modified his already formidable technique to accommodate the demands of the music. The results, while they won't supplant the original works, are definitely worth investigating, especially when they are as well recorded as these.

Suites for Solo Cello (BWV 1007—1012)
what to buy: [Yo-Yo Ma, cello] (Sony Classics 37867)
♪ ♪ ♪ ♪ ♪

This is not just a master set by a master cellist, it is the premier set of these seminal works by the finest cellist of the past twenty years. It is also an earlier recording of the complete suites, *not* the batch he recorded later in conjunction with a PBS special called *Inspired by Bach.*

[Pablo Casals, cello] (EMI Classics 66215) ♪ ♪ ♪ ♪ ♪

These are wonderful recordings from 1936–1939 by the legendary cellist. The sonics are a bit boxy, but the performances are groundbreaking and worth a slot on your shelves.

[Pierre Fournier, cello] (Deutsche Grammophon 449711)
♪ ♪ ♪ ♪ ♪

In a sea of big-name cellists like Ma, Casals, Starker, and Rostropovich, there is still room for this set of lovely, well-recorded cello suites. Not as many people may be familiar with Fournier's name now but he was one of the finest, most subtle performers on the instrument in his day, and these recordings will surprise many listeners with the depth of feeling his aristocratic renditions can convey.

what to buy next: [Jaap Ter Linden, baroque cellos] (Harmonia Mundi 2957216/17) ♪ ♪ ♪ ♪ ♪

The reason for this set, other than some exquisite playing from Ter Linden, is that it presents the works as they might have been heard in Bach's time. The other thing that separates this set from the other four mentioned here is that the sixth suite is played on a five-string cello (an Amati instrument from c. 1600) because the work was originally meant to be played on a five-stringed instrument—perhaps a piccolo cello. In this respect Ter Linden follows the same trail blazed by Anner Bylsma in 1981, but with slightly better engineering.

[Mstislav Rostropovich, cello] (EMI Classics 55363)
♪ ♪ ♪ ♪

Rostropovich's performance of the popular Suite no. 3 in C Major (BWV 1009) reveals the strengths and weaknesses of this powerful cellist. There is no lack of emotion or technique, but there is an idiosyncratic approach to the work that leans more toward the muscular than the cerebral. Subtlety is not a strong point, but the playing is magnificent nonetheless.

Sonatas for Flute and Continuo (BWV 1030—1035)
what to buy: [Jean-Pierre Rampal, flute; Trevor Pinnock, harpsichord; Roland Pidoux, cello] (Sony Classics 39746)
♪ ♪ ♪ ♪ ♪

The great flautist Rampal teams with Pinnock throughout this wonderful set, and the result is magic. Cellist Pidoux is added to the continuo for the E Minor sonata (BWV 1034) while Rampal is the sole performer in the Partita for Solo Flute in A Minor (BWV 1013). The flautist's transcription of Bach's G Minor Sonata for Violin and Harpsichord (BWV 1020) closes out the set.

Chromatic Fantasy and Fugue in **D Minor** for **Harpsichord (BWV 903)**
what to buy: [Wanda Landowska, harpsichord] (EMI Classics 67200) ♪ ♪ ♪ ♪ ♪

This is the legendary harpsichordist as recorded in 1934, playing the *Fantasy* along with the *Italian Concerto* and the *Goldberg Variations*. Despite the age of the actual recordings, the performances come through with surprising clarity. Anybody interested in these works won't want to miss this!

what to buy next: [*Rosalyn Tureck Collection, vol. IV*; Rosalyn Tureck, harpsichord] (VAI Audio 1139)
♪ ♪ ♪ ♪ ♪

Recorded live in 1981 at the Metropolitan Museum in New York City, Rosalyn lives up to her reputation as one of the finest Bach interpreters. Here, she can also be heard playing the *Italian Concerto*, the *Goldberg Variations,* and selections from *The Well-Tempered Clavier.*

Partitas for Harpsichord
what to buy: [*Glenn Gould Edition*; Glenn Gould, piano] (Sony Classical 52597) ♪ ♪ ♪ ♪ ♪

Gould was at his best with Bach, and these classic recordings of six of the composer's partitas should be counted among his finest performances. The two-disc set also includes the pianist's idiosyncratic take on a fine selection of preludes and fugues. This is a must-have for any Bach lover.

what to buy next: *[J.S. Bach: Three Partitas, vol. 2*, Ralph Kirkpatrick, harpsichord] (Boston Skyline 132) ♪♪♪♪

When his recordings originally came out in 1959, many critics didn't quite know what to make of Kirkpatrick's groundbreaking approach to these fine works. Totally different in conception than the earlier, equally valid versions laid down by Wanda Landowska, they have since taken their place amongst the most acclaimed recordings of their era. Kirkpatrick's renditions of the B Major (BWV 825), C Minor (BWV 826), and E Minor (BWV 830) partitas still sound good today.

Das wohltemperirte Clavier (The Well-Tempered Clavier), (BWV 846—893)
what to buy: [*Book 1*; Andras Schiff, piano] (London 414388) ♪♪♪♪♪ and [*Book 2*; Andras Schiff, piano] (London 417236) ♪♪♪♪♪

Here we have the finest of playing on a modern piano by a superb artist.

what to buy next: [*Book 1*; Wanda Landowska, harpsichord] (RCA Red Seal 6217) ♪♪♪♪♪ and [*Book 2*; Wanda Landowska, harpsichord] (RCA Red Seal 7825) ♪♪♪♪♪

The great lady, a pioneer in the Bach recording arena, can be heard here in a set of fine, well-mastered performances with fairly good sound for their age. This is for connoisseurs!

various organ works
what to buy: [*The Biggs Bach Book*; E. Power Biggs, organ] (Sony Classics 30539) ♪♪♪♪♪

This has been a favorite recording over the years and is still one of the best samplers of popular Bach organ works. It contains various minuets, marches, polonaises, and excerpts from the *Anna Magdalena Bach Notebook*. Biggs is another legend, and this collection shows why.

[*Bach: Great Organ Works*; Helmut Walcha, organ]

(Deutsche Grammophon 453064) ♪♪♪♪♪

This is a two-disc set ranging across the wide variety of styles in which Bach wrote. Found here are many of the large-scale organ works, including the famous Toccata and Fugue in D Minor (BWV 565)—once associated in the minds of many listeners with the pre-Lloyd Webber *Phantom of the Opera*—one of the Trio Sonatas, the Schübler Chorales, and the sublime *Canonic Variations on Von Himmel hoch* (BWV 769). Walcha is one of the great Bach interpreters, and this set is a particularly good value.

what to buy next: [*Bach: Organ Works, vol. 1*; Anton Heiller, organ] (Vanguard Classics 2005) ♪♪♪♪

Naturally, you will find the famous Toccata and Fugue in D Minor here—since just about every Bach organ collection aimed at the general marker features it—and some of the other large works, including the late masterpiece Prelude and Fugue in E Minor (a.k.a. *The Wedge*). Heiller is marvelous throughout, and the budget price makes this a fine value.

Vocal
Mass in B Minor for Orchestra and Chorus (BWV 232)
what to buy: [John Eliot Gardiner, cond., English Baroque Soloists, orch; Monteverdi Choir] (Deutsche Grammophon 415514) ♪♪♪♪♪

This stupendous work is presented in one of the best of performances. Certainly the finest recording of this piece done by anyone working with forces approximating those utilized during Bach's lifetime.

what to buy next: [Lois Marshall, soprano; Hertha Töpper, mezzo-soprano; Peter Pears, tenor; Kim Borg, bass; Hans Braun, bass; Eugen Jochum, cond.; Bavarian Radio Orchestra; Bavarian Radio Chorus] (Philips 438739) ♪♪♪♪♪

For those unaccustomed or unwilling to experiment with the original-instrument bias of Gardiner and his forces (see above), Jochum's two-disc recording may be the perfect alternative. The recording is clean, the sound borders on lush, and the soloists are accomplished. Jochum's take on Bach's Missa Brevis in F Major (BWV 233) is included as a bonus.

St. Matthew Passion (Matthäus Passion) (BWV 244)

what to buy: [Elisabeth Schwarzkopf, soprano; Christa Ludwig, mezzo-soprano; Peter Pears, tenor; Nicolai Gedda, tenor; Dietrich Fischer-Dieskau, baritone; Walter Berry, bass-baritone; Otto Klemperer, cond.; Philharmonia Orchestra; Philharmonia Choir; Hampstead Parish Church Boy's Choir] (EMI Classics 63058) ♪ ♪ ♪ ♪ ♪

Featuring great soloists, conductor, and orchestra, this thrilling performance has been a top choice for years. In many ways the collaboration is as much a wonder as the work itself. Fischer-Dieskau as Jesus and Pears as the Evangelist are stunning.

what to buy next: [Sibylla Rubens, soprano; Andreas Scholl, countertenor; Ian Bostridge, tenor; Werner Güra, tenor; Franz-Josef Selig, bass; Dietrich Henschel, bass; Philippe Herreweghe, cond.; Orchestre du Collegium Vocale, Choir du Collegium Vocale] (Harmonia Mundi 901676.78) ♪ ♪ ♪ ♪ ♪

The engineering for this performance was very good, and the singing is absolutely wonderful throughout. Using the amazing Scholl instead of the usual soprano or mezzo-soprano is a marvelous idea, and seems perfectly in keeping with the era from which this magnificent piece comes. Herreweghe does a fine job of keeping the multi-layered score from becoming mush, and the orchestra follows his lead quite well. One hesitates to note that this is a period-instrument performance because this might discourage some listeners from trying it. That would be their loss. Those possessing a computer with the Windows 95 (or higher) operating system and a CD-ROM drive can get this same performance on a CD-ROM (Harmonia Mundi 901676.78) that includes a composer biography, a history of the Passion, the text of the Passion, a copy of the score, and an interview with Herreweghe.

Herz und Mund und Tat und Leben, (BWV 147) (Jesu, Joy of Man's Desiring)

what to buy: [*Six Favourite Cantatas*; Jane Bryden, soprano; Drew Minter, countertenor; Jeffrey Thomas, tenor; Jan Opalach, bass; Joshua Rifkin, cond.; Bach Ensemble, orch.] (L'Oiseau Lyre 455706) ♪ ♪ ♪ ♪♪

If you are only used to the instrumental version of the chorale *Jesu, Joy of Man's Desiring,* then the full-length, twenty-two-minute-long cantata from which this little

gem was lifted will be a revelation. Rifkin's group of singers and instrumentalists gives an inspiring performance on this and five other famous Bach cantatas including *Ein feste Burg ist unser Gott* (BWV 80), which builds on the Martin Luther-penned hymn *A Mighty Fortress is our God.*

what to buy next: [Ruth Holton, soprano; Michael Chance, countertenor; Anthony Rolfe Johnson, tenor; Stephen Varcoe, bass; John Eliot Gardiner, cond.; The English Baroque Soloists, orch.; The Monteverdi Choir] (Deutsche Grammophon Archiv 463587) ♪ ♪ ♪ ♪

All the singers are quite good, with Holton being especially pleasing. If there is any misgiving about this disc at all, it is only that Chance is, uncharacteristically, a bit inconsistent. However, the performances in the album's other work, *Wachet auf, ruft uns die Stimme* (BWV 140), are totally recommendable.

Schweigt stille, plaudert nicht (BWV 211) (Coffee Cantata)

what to buy: [Emma Kirkby, soprano; David Thomas, bass; Christopher Hogwood, cond.; Academy of Ancient Music, orch.] (L'Oiseau-Lyre 417621) ♪ ♪ ♪ ♪ ♪

This secular cantata shows Bach's wit and charm in a completely different way. This fine recording also offers the famous *Peasant Cantata (Ner hahn en neue Oberkeet)* (BWV 212).

Weichet nur, betrübte Schatten (BWV 202) (Wedding Cantata)

what to buy: [Emma Kirkby, soprano; David Thomas, bass; Andrew Parrott, cond.; Taverner Players, orch.] (Hyperion 66036) ♪ ♪ ♪ ♪ ♪

This is another great secular cantata, presented in a fine performance. You also get an equally well-rendered version of the sacred cantata *Ich habe genug* (BWV 82).

what to buy next: [*Wedding Cantatas*; Christine Schäfer, soprano; Reinhard Goebel, cond.; Musica Antiqua Köln, orch.] (Deutsche Grammonphon 459621) ♪ ♪ ♪♪

While BWV 202 is the better known of Bach's two *Wedding Cantatas,* and Schäfer sings it beautifully, the composer's *O holder Tag, erwünschte Zeit* (BWV 210) is another marvel that deserves to be better known. As a bonus, this disc also includes Schäfer and company in a sterling rendition of Bach's cantata *Jauchzet Gott in allen Landen* (BWV 51) in its arrangement by his son, Wilhelm Friedemann Bach.

various cantatas

what to buy: [*The Bach Cantatas, vol. 16*; Helmut Rilling, cond.; Stuttgart Bach Collegium, orch.; Gächinger Kantorei, choir] (Hanssler Classics 98867) ♪ ♪ ♪ ♪ ♪

Bach's cantatas can be quite intimidating in their variety and number. A set such as this, done by a group that is uniform in both performance and interpretation, gives the best exposure to them. Rilling has put together a fine collection of three wonderfully performed cantatas selected from the more than 200 works Bach wrote in this format, including a rendition of Bach's first cantata, *Wie schön leuchtet der Morgenstern*.

influences: George Frideric Handel, Wolfgang Amadeus Mozart, Ludwig van Beethoven, Antonio Vivaldi, Wilhelm Friedemann Bach, Carl Philipp Emanuel Bach, Johann Christian Bach

Frank Retzel and Garaud MacTaggart

Wilhelm Friedemann Bach

Born November 22, 1710, in Weimar, Germany. Died July 1, 1784, in Berlin, Germany.

period: Baroque

The oldest son of Johann Sebastian Bach was arguably the most talented of the great one's offspring, both as a composer and an organist, but he was also the most inclined toward wasting his talents. Wilhelm Friedemann Bach was an acclaimed musician whose predilection for pigheadedness, drunkenness, and a generally dissolute lifestyle interfered with his ability to obtain the consistent patronage that his younger siblings Carl Philipp Emanuel and Johann Christian would later acquire. Despite his personal shortcomings, this Bach wrote some intriguing music (especially for the keyboard) that deserves a wider audience.

A measure of the father's hopes and dreams for his eldest son can be found in the first book of the senior Bach's magnificent *Das Wohltemperirte Clavier* (The Well-Tempered Clavier), a tome that was meant in some ways as a primer for Wilhelm Friedemann. The youngster had

developed into a keyboard prodigy under the tutelage of his father, but Johann Sebastian also took care that his son would develop into a better-rounded musician by sending him (at the age of 15) to study violin with the famed virtuoso/composer Johann Gottlieb Graun. By 1729 Wilhelm Friedemann had entered the University of Leipzig, where he studied mathematics, philosophy, and law for four years. Upon graduation he went to work assisting his father prior to securing a position as organist at the Dresden Sophienkirche in 1733.

Life in Dresden was filled with cultural opportunities lacking in the more provincial Leipzig, and Wilhelm Friedemann indulged himself wholeheartedly. He observed the various musical entertainments held at court and made friendships with influential musician/composers such as Sylvius Weiss and Johann Adolph Hasse. In an attempt to move up the ladder of success, he applied for and was denied the director/organist post at the Dresden Liebfrauenkirche in 1742. Four years later he got a similar position at the Halle Marienkirche, due to the intercession of his father as well as his own skills as an organist. But Wilhelm Friedemann's stay there was a difficult one, filled with much head-butting over philosophical differences between him and the church authorities.

After the death of his father in 1750, Wilhelm Friedemann put his hand on the tiller of his life and steered it towards the shoals of profligacy with an almost single-minded stubbornness. His youngest brother, Johann Christian, had been entrusted to his care, but he shunted the youngster off to the next oldest brother, Carl Phillip Emanuel, for instruction. In 1751, just six months after his father's funeral, Wilhelm Friedemann married Dorothea Elisabeth Georgi. For the next decade or so, this Bach requested ever-more-frequent leaves of absence and overstaying the periods allotted to him by his employers. He also sent out a stream of applications for various openings, which didn't endear him to the church elders. Despite his reputation as a gifted musician and improviser, his efforts met with repeated failure, and he earned a reputation as a difficult artist to work with. Things finally reached a crisis point in 1764, and he quit his job, embarking upon the insecure life of a freelance musician and teacher.

His wife's modest inheritance was disposed of in order to support the family, as were some of the manuscripts he had acquired from his father. Wilhelm Friedemann's arrogance led him to lose some good opportunities, and his attempts to find stable employment were fruitless. The most frequently cited example of his unscrupulousness dates from 1774, when he orchestrated a smear campaign against his erstwhile friend, the Berlin court composer J. P. Kirnberger, with the intention of taking Kirnberger's job. When this unsavory son of a great man finally died in 1784, he left his family in abject poverty.

Despite Wilhelm Friedemann's obvious character deficiencies, his compositional skills were, on occasion, quite formidable. While his vocal music, most of which was written during his tenure in Halle, fulfills the basic needs of his texts, none of it is particularly noteworthy. Instead, Wilhelm Friedemann shines brightest in the instrumental scores where a keyboard (usually the harpsichord) is prominent. This is where he could best indulge his gift for melody and harmonic adventurousness, blended with the contrapuntal underpinnings he learned from his father.

Orchestral
Concerto for Harpsichord in D Major
what to buy: [Charlotte Nediger, harpsichord; Jeanne Lamon, cond.; Tafelmusik, orch.] (Sony Vivarte 62720) ♪ ♪ ♪ ♪

This work was probably the composer's most popular orchestral piece during his lifetime, and Nediger's performance is sparkling enough to make a case for the score still being relevant today. The rest of the disc contains three more of his delightful orchestral compositions plus one that was attributed to him but not positively confirmed. These performances by the Toronto-based original-instrument ensemble Tafelmusik are subtle, well-recorded gems.

worth looking for: [*Harpsichord Concertos*; Richard Egarr, harpsichord; Charles Medlam, cond.; London Baroque, orch.] (Harmonia Mundi 901558) ♪ ♪ ♪⅛

The acoustics here are not as felicitous as on the Nediger recording, tending towards the harsh and bright, but Egarr's playing is not at fault, and the accompanying works include two more of the five surviving harpsichord concertos Wilhelm Friedemann wrote. For some, these factors may tip the balance towards this disc rather than the Tafelmusik album.

Chamber
Sonata in A Minor

what to buy: [*Oeuvres pour clavecin*; Christophe Rousset, harpsichord] (Harmonia Mundi 1901305) ♪ ♪ ♪ ♪⅛

The writing in this piece verges on the music of the classical era, with a pulse-pounding third movement and a steadily progressing set of changes in the opening movement that begs to be appropriated for a contemporary pop tune. There are seven other works by the composer on this set, and Rousset has the measure of them all, especially the concluding Sonata in G Minor, which lifts a quote from the senior Bach's *Goldberg Variations*.

influences: Carl Philipp Emanuel Bach, Wolfgang Amadeus Mozart, Jan Dismas Zelenka

Garaud MacTaggart

Mily Balakirev
Born Mily Alexeievich Balakirev in Nizhny Novgorod, Russia, on January 2, 1837. Died in St. Petersburg on May 29, 1910.

period: Romantic

A major figure in the nationalist movement in Russian music, Balakirev was one of the "Five" or "Mighty Handful," along with Alexander Borodin, César Cui, Modest Mussorgsky, and Nikolai Rimsky-Korsakov. A lamentable tendency to leave major works incomplete diminished his legacy, but his exotic, virtuoso piano piece *Islamey* has kept his memory alive, and his two symphonies have long had an audience among Russophiles, with conductors Sir Thomas Beecham in particular (and later Herbert von Karajan) championing the first.

Balakirev was the oldest child of a minor government office worker barely able to support his family on his low salary. Balakirev's mother was his first piano instructor, though her knowledge was quite limited. When he was ten years old, she brought him to Moscow to play for Alexander Dubuque, a pupil of John Field. Later in life, Balakirev credited his ten lessons with Dubuque for his formidable skills at the piano, but he was unable to continue them at the time, even after Dubuque offered to teach him for free, because the Balakirevs could not afford to live in Moscow.

Back home in Nizhny Novgorod, Balakirev was fortunate enough to come into contact with an eccentric landowner named Alexander Ulïbïshev, who was working on a biography of Mozart. To this end, he had accumulated a music library and formed his own orchestra, conducted by the Viennese (or German) musician Karl Eisrich. Balakirev studied music with Eisrich for three years and, at the age of fourteen, replaced him as conductor when Eisrich left Russia. In this position, Balakirev acquired a fair amount of practical musical experience and knowledge.

As there were still no music schools in Russia, Balakirev studied mathematics and physics at the University of Kazan from 1853 to 1854, but Ulïbïshev talked him into applying himself to music again. In St. Petersburg he made a splash in 1856 playing the first (and only) movement of his Piano Concerto no. 1. The great Russian composer Mikhail Glinka recognized Balakirev's talent and convinced the young man of the importance of nationalism to the development of a Russian musical style.

Filled with missionary zeal, Balakirev acquired a circle of students, including Borodin, Cui, Mussorgsky, and Rimsky-Korsakov. Guided by the example of his own musical path, Balakirev proved to be an unorthodox teacher, however, and by Western standards all his pupils were lacking in technical knowledge and weak in their grasp of musical form. Nonetheless, their Russian style proved viable.

In 1859, famed Russian pianist Anton Rubinstein founded the Russian Musical Society, and in 1862 the St. Petersburg Conservatory was formed as an offshoot, with Rubinstein in charge. Western musical values were the cornerstone of Rubinstein's enterprises, and the Russian Musical Society largely featured works by German and Austrian composers. Balakirev, fired by his opposing vision, founded the Free Music School in 1863 and presented concerts of new Russian music. It was after one such concert in 1867 that critic Vladimir Stasov dubbed Balakirev and the circle of composers surrounding him the "Mighty Handful."

Balakirev's ambition to create a truly Russian idiom was fostered by his interest in folk music. During the 1860s he made three trips into the Caucasus, which provided him with an invaluable source of musical material. In 1866 he completed the collection *40 Russian Folk Songs*, and folk tunes inspired the themes of many of his own works. With the piano piece *Islamey*, premiered in 1869 by Nikolai Rubinstein (Anton's brother), Balakirev achieved his greatest triumph as a composer.

Considered one of the most technically challenging works in the repertoire, *Islamey* is basically a Caucasian dance, but one of its themes is based on a Tartar love song.

When Rubinstein resigned his posts in 1867, Balakirev was named director of the Russian Musical Society. It was a great victory for the nationalist camp, but Balakirev's dictatorial ways upset the orchestra players, and his utter lack of diplomacy with the board of directors—and more significantly with the Society's patron, Grand Duchess Elena Pavlovna—led to his forced resignation after only two years.

This setback shook Balakirev to the core. Within the next few years he had given up the Free Music School concerts and was working as a railroad clerk; when he returned to music, it was in minor administrative positions. Eventually he submerged himself in the Russian Orthodox Church after a life of indifference to religion. Through faith he found his way back to music, and in the early 1880s he was named director of music at the Imperial Chapel.

In 1882 Balakirev returned to conducting at the Free Music School and began to rework some of his unfinished compositions. In 1882 he completed his most famous symphonic poem, *Tamara*, begun in 1867; in 1884 he turned the *Second Overture on Russian Themes*, originally dating from 1864 and also known as *One Thousand Years*, into the symphonic poem *Russia*; and in 1897 he finally finished his First Symphony, started in 1864. Its premiere in 1898 at the Free Music School marked his final appearance as a conductor.

Balakirev's last years were marked by depression and withdrawal (after a quarrel, he refused to speak to Rimsky-Korsakov), and although he devoted his last decade to composing, he was not prolific. He worked on his Second Symphony from 1900 until 1908. It proved to be his last major completed work.

Orchestral
Symphony no. 1 in C Major
what to buy: [Igor Golovschin, cond.; Russian State Symphony Orchestra] (Naxos 8.550792) ♪ ♪ ♪₄

Conductor Golovschin makes the best possible case for the symphony, with a taut reading that avoids extremes and carefully holds together its episodic structure. Balakirev's First Symphony is typically nationalist in tone, quoting traditional themes and primarily relying on the Glinka-inspired method of continually varying their accompaniments rather than breaking the themes into motivic fragments. Thus, the first movement is not really in sonata form; it lacks a recapitulation, and its development consists largely of varying the orchestration and counter-themes. The orchestral version of *Islamey* heard on this disc was made after Balakirev's death by his friend Sergei Lyapunov.

Concerto no. 1 in F-sharp Minor, op. 1
what to buy: [*The Romantic Piano Concerto, vol. 5*; Malcolm Binns, piano; David Lloyd-Jones, cond.; English Northern Philharmonia, orch.] (Hyperion 66640) ♪ ♪ ♪♪

This set contains both of Balakirev's piano concertos as well as Rimsky-Korsakov's works in that genre. Balakirev's tendency to procrastinate about finishing his longer works is starkly evident in these two pieces. His first concerto, which helped establish his reputation, consists of a single movement because he apparently lost interest. He started his second concerto in 1861 and by 1862 had completed the first movement and played the other two for his friends, but he never bothered writing them down or orchestrating them. In his last years he finally put the second movement on paper, but the third had to be completed after Balakirev's death by his disciple Sergei Lyapunov. Had he finished them, they undoubtedly would have had a better chance of entering the standard concerto repertoire, as their mix of Russian-flavored lyricism, imaginative modulations, and spectacular keyboard virtuosity is immediately appealing.

Chamber
various piano works
what to buy: [Michael Kollontaï, piano] (Russian Season 788110) ♪ ♪ ♪

This program offers a nice cross-section of Balakirev's piano works. Michael Kollontaï is a Russian pianist whose powerful touch does not exclude a certain delicacy. Thus, though fully qualified to deliver the famed *Islamey*, which opens this disc, he also renders convincingly such sonic pastels as the *Valse mélancolique* and the lengthy, dark-hued *Gondellied*.

influences: Mikhail Glinka, Alexander Borodin, Nicolai Rimsky-Korsakov

Steve Holtje

Samuel Barber
Born March 9, 1910, in West Chester, PA. Died January 23, 1981, in New York, NY.

period: Twentieth century

One of the most important twentieth-century American composers, Barber also ranks with George Gershwin and Aaron Copland as one of the most frequently performed. The *Adagio for Strings* (his orchestration of a movement from his only string quartet) is a concert favorite that was played at John F. Kennedy's funeral and featured on the soundtracks of several movies (*Platoon, The Elephant Man, El Norte, Lorenzo's Oil*), but his Violin Concerto and a host of beautifully crafted songs have also helped ensure his place in history.

Samuel Barber's parents never encouraged him to become a musician, but there was always music in his house, and the youngster drew inspiration from his aunt and uncle, the famous contralto Louise Homer and the art-song composer Sidney Homer. Barber studied piano from the age of six and began composing a year later (a short piano piece entitled *Sadness* was one of his first attempts). He tried his hand at songwriting, and his aunt would sometimes sing his compositions. "Writing songs just seemed a natural thing to do," Barber once said. At the age of ten he even wrote one act of an opera (*The Rose Tree*) to a libretto by the family's Irish cook.

While still in high school he conducted the school orchestra and worked as a church organist, and he entered the Curtis Institute in Philadelphia when it opened in 1924, studying composition with Rosario Scalero, piano with Isabelle Vengerova, conducting with Fritz Reiner, and voice with Emilio de Gogorza. Barber's student years saw the composition of a violin sonata (1928, now lost), the Serenade for String Quartet, *Dover Beach* (1931), and the Sonata for Cello and Piano (1932). By the time he left Curtis, his scores had been performed in New York and Philadelphia. One work, the overture to *The School for Scandal,* was awarded the Bearns Prize in 1933 and premiered by the Philadelphia Orchestra.

Barber's early works (through 1938) are written in a harmonically conservative, late-romantic idiom. After 1939, his music makes greater use of dissonance (the Violin Concerto of that year marks a turning point) but through it all remains firmly tonal. Counterpoint and contrapuntal devices such as canon and fugue are always important, and Barber is masterly in their use; listen, for instance, to the wonderful fugal finale of the 1949 Piano Sonata. His orchestration glows with rich color, and his rhythms are varied and interesting; his musical materials are always deeply felt, his writing always supremely polished.

Barber was a romantic, and the emotional accessibility of his music brought him early and lasting success. In the late 1930s, he became the first American composer to be performed by Arturo Toscanini (the *Adagio for Strings* and the *First Essay for Orchestra*). Others who championed his music included Bruno Walter (the *Symphony no. 1 in one movement* and the *Second Essay for Orchestra*), Eugene Ormandy (Concerto for Violin and Orchestra), Serge Koussevitzky (Symphony no. 2), Martha Graham (the ballet *Medea: Cave of the Heart*), and Vladimir Horowitz (*Excursions* and the Sonata for Piano). Leontyne Price introduced the *Hermit Songs* in 1952, and two years later Charles Munch and the Boston Symphony gave the first performance of *Prayers of Kierkegaard.* The Metropolitan Opera staged the 1958 premiere of *Vanessa,* the Pulitzer Prize-winning opera for which Barber created the music and Gian Carlo Menotti wrote the libretto. Barber won a second Pulitzer in 1962 for the Concerto for Piano and Orchestra, which John Browning premiered with Erich Leinsdorf and the Boston Symphony.

Virgil Thomson once described Barber's style as "elegant neo-romanticism." He rarely experimented with modern technical procedures and seemed content to write in a time-honored language. Simply put, Barber's work is in the musical mainstream—melodic, listener-friendly, and formally traditional. All his compositions, from songs and operas to chamber and orchestral works, display a deep vein of lyricism, ranging from the charming, light, and airy to the intense, passionate, and even tragic. The songs and operas contain some gorgeous melodies (*Knoxville: Summer of 1915,* with its text by James Agee, and "Under the Willow Tree," from *Vanessa,* come instantly to mind), as do such instrumental works as the *Adagio,* with its tragic passion (and, one might add, its many similarities to the Adagietto movement from Gustav Mahler's Fifth Symphony), and the slow movements of his Violin Concerto and Piano Concerto. What Barber was not was an innovator. Copland already called him outmoded in 1939. By the 1960s his conservative music was dismissed by serialist and avant-garde composers, but it remained popular with audiences and concert presenters.

Given his feeling for vocal writing, his dramatic sense, and the accessibility of his style, an opera by Barber was the logical choice to inaugurate the new Metropolitan Opera House in 1966. The libretto for *Antony and Cleopatra* was adapted from Shakespeare by Franco Zeffirelli, who was also responsible for the staging. On opening night, there was much applause throughout the performance and fourteen curtain calls at the conclusion. The press, however, instantly branded the opera and production a failure, though seemingly ignoring much of what they had heard and seen. Barber was devastated, and in the fourteen remaining years of his life, he would finish only a small number of pieces. Much of his time was devoted to revising *Antony and Cleopatra,* condensing it and toning down the spectacle with the help of his friend Menotti. Adding some thematic cross-references and revising the orchestration, Barber managed to improve the work, though without solving all its problems. Menotti's Spoleto Festival first presented the new version in Italy in June 1983.

Orchestral music
Adagio for Strings
what to buy: [Neville Marriner, cond.; Academy of St. Martin-in-the-Fields] (Argo 417818) ♪ ♪ ♪ ♪ ♪

Barber's most popular piece has arguably never received a performance so right *and* so well recorded, finer even than the Schippers version (mentioned below) by dint of its superior sonics. This superb mini-survey of American composers slips in little-known works by Paul Creston (*A Rumor*) and Henry Cowell (*Hymn and Fuguing Tune no. 10*) among the Barber and other classics such as Aaron Copland's *Quiet City,* and Charles Ives's Symphony no. 3.

what to buy next: [Thomas Schippers, cond.; New York Philharmonic Orchestra] (Sony Classical 62837) ♪ ♪ ♪ ♪

Are there more recordings of Barber's *Adagio* than stars in the sky? This is still among the best of the many versions, and the disc also offers Barber's *Medea's Meditation and Dance of Vengeance, The School for Scandal, Essay no. 2* for Orchestra, *Andromache's Farewell,* and selections from *Vanessa,* as well as works by Berg and Menotti. With its wealth of well-performed material, it makes an excellent introduction to Barber's music.

Samuel Barber

[*Music of Samuel Barber*, Leonard Slatkin, cond.; St. Louis Symphony Orchestra] (EMI Angel 49463) ♪♪♪♪

Slatkin and his forces give a fine performance of the *Adagio* as well as of Barber's *Essays for Orchestra, Medea's Meditation and Dance of Vengeance,* and the overture to *The School for Scandal.*

Essay no. 3 for Orchestra, op. 47
what to buy: [Zubin Mehta, cond.; New York Philharmonic Orchestra] (New World 80309) ♪♪♪♪

This premiere recording of the third *Essay* was released just before the composer's death. The stunning Barber performance is coupled with John Corigliano's Clarinet Concerto, featuring soloist Stanley Drucker.

Concerto for Piano and Orchestra, op. 38
what to buy: [John Browning, piano; Leonard Slatkin, cond.; St. Louis Symphony Orchestra] (RCA Red Seal 60732) ♪♪♪♪♪

Barber wrote this concerto for Browning, and no one has played it better. This fabulous album presents a recent interpretation, combining it with the composer's First Symphony and his four-hand piano arrangement of *Souvenirs,* with Slatkin joining Browning at the keyboard.

worth looking for: [John Browning, piano; George Szell, cond., Cleveland Orchestra] (Sony Classics 61621) ♪♪♪♪♪

The 1964 premiere recording of the Piano Concerto, with John Browning as the featured soloist and George Szell conducting the Cleveland Orchestra, has still not been reissued. When it is, don't miss it!

Concerto for Violin, op. 14
what to buy: [Gil Shaham, violin; André Previn, cond.; London Symphony Orchestra] (Deutsche Grammophon 439886) ♪♪♪♪

Shaham's virtuoso fireworks in the Korngold concerto on this disc may make it more immediately appealing, but repeated listenings will reveal the Barber to be the more sophisticated and trenchant work. It's not that the Barber lacks passion, but his writing is less showy and more substantial than Korngold's. In any event, Shaham plays superbly, and it's hard to imagine a more impressive version of either work.

what to buy next: [Joshua Bell, violin; David Zinman, cond.; Baltimore Symphony Orchestra] (London 452851) ♪♪♪♪

The pairing of violin concertos by Barber and William Walton is interesting enough, but the addition of Ernest Bloch's heart-tugging *Baal Shem* raises this set to another level. Bell's playing is wonderfully gutsy throughout, though Zinman and his Baltimore orchestra can't quite match André Previn and the London Symphony for Shaham (above). This album won the 1998 *Gramophone* award for Best Concerto Recording.

Chamber
various piano works
worth looking for: [*The Complete Solo Piano Music*, John Browning, piano] (Music Masters 67122) ♪♪♪♪

Browning is a master when it comes to Barber, especially in his playing of the composer's powerful Sonata op. 26. The recording quality is sterling.

Vocal
Knoxville: Summer of 1915
what to buy: [*Leontyne Price Sings Barber*, Leontyne Price, soprano; Thomas Schippers, cond.; New Philharmonia Orchestra] (RCA Gold Seal 61983) ♪♪♪♪♪

Here, one of the finest of all sopranos gives a fabulous performance of this, one of the composer's masterpieces as well as selections from *Antony and Cleopatra.*. Barber himself accompanies her in the *Hermit Songs*

[Dawn Upshaw, soprano; David Zinman, cond.; Orchestra of St. Luke's] (Nonesuch 79187) ♪♪♪♪♪

Upshaw is a dream in Barber's orchestral song and also presents works by Gian Carlo Menotti, John Harbison, and Igor Stravinsky. This gem of a disc won the 1990 Grammy Award for Best Classical Vocal Album.

various songs
what to buy: [*Secrets of the Old: Complete Songs of Samuel Barber*, Cheryl Studer, soprano; Thomas Hampson, baritone; John Browning, piano; Emerson String Quartet, ensemble] (Deutsche Grammophon 435867) ♪♪♪♪

This two-disc set has (almost) everything, including fine performances of *Dover Beach* and the *Hermit Songs,* op. 29.

what to buy next: [Eleanor Steber, soprano; Leontyne Price, soprano; Martina Arroyo, soprano; Dietrich Fischer-Dieskau, baritone; Samuel Barber, piano; Juilliard Quartet, ensemble; various conductors; various orchestras] (Sony 46727) ♪ ♪ ♪ ♪

The sound on this collection varies from the 1950 monaural recording of Steber in *Knoxville: Summer of 1915* (with William Strickland conducting the Dumbarton Oaks Orchestra) to the 1967 stereo rendering of *Dover Beach* with Fischer-Dieskau and the Juilliard Quartet. In between there are marvelous performances of the *Hermit Songs* (with Price accompanied by Barber) and a hair-raising version of *Andromache's Farewell* from Arroyo and the New York Philharmonic Orchestra conducted by Thomas Schippers. These are all classic performances, and the budget price makes this album a steal.

Vanessa, op. 32
what to buy: [Eleanor Steber, soprano; Regina Resnik, mezzo-soprano; Rosalind Elias, mezzo-soprano; Nicolai Gedda, tenor; Robert Nagy, tenor; George Cehanovsky, baritone; Giorgio Tozzi, bass; Dimitri Mitropoulos, cond.; Metropolitan Opera Orchestra; Metropolitan Opera Chorus] (RCA Gold Seal 7899) ♪ ♪ ♪ ♪ ♪

Great cast, great orchestra and conductor, great music! It all adds up to a recording that will continue to delight.

Antony and Cleopatra, op. 40
what to buy: [Esther Hinds, soprano; Jane Bunnell, mezzo-soprano; Kathryn Cowdrick, contralto; Robert Grayson, tenor; Jeffrey Wells, bass-baritone; Eric Halfvarson, bass-baritone; Christian Bedea, cond.; Spoleto Festival Orchestra; Westminster Choir] (New World 80322/80324) ♪ ♪ ♪ ♪₆

This is a good live recording of the revised version of the opera that caused Barber such grief. When you hear it, you may wonder what planet the critics were on when they wrote their scathing reviews.

influences: Aaron Copland, Gian Carlo Menotti, Ned Rorem

Frank Retzel and Garaud MacTaggart

Béla Bartók
Born March 25, 1881, in Nagyszentmiklós, Hungary. Died September 26, 1945, in New York City, NY, USA.

period: Twentieth century

Composer, pianist, and (along with his friend and compatriot Zoltán Kodály) one of the first Twentieth century ethnomusicologists, Bartók is a major influence on many modern composers. He is best known by contemporary audiences for his *Music for Strings, Percussion, and Celesta* and the Concerto for Orchestra, but he also wrote one of the finest string quartet cycles of the Twentieth century.

Béla Bartók received his first piano lessons from his mother, and soon showed an aptitude for composition as well as performance, writing his first pieces when he was only nine years old. He later studied piano with Ferenc Kersch and László Erkel, and theory with Anton Hyrtl, preparing himself for entrance into the Vienna Conservatory. Though the young pianist auditioned for the school (and was offered a scholarship) in 1898, he took the advice of the pianist/composer Ernö Dohnányi, who was then the star of the Hungarian musical firmament, and chose instead to enter the Budapest Academy of Music. Bartók started at the school in 1899 and studied with Istvan Thomán (piano) and Hans Koessler (composition) before graduating in 1903. Compositions from this time (e.g., the Scherzo in B-flat Major for Orchestra and the symphonic poem Kossuth) reflect his interest in the music of Richard Strauss and Richard Wagner, although we can see glimmers of the nationalist flavor to come.

Apropos of this, of primary importance in his development was a study of Hungarian folk music that he began around 1906 with Zoltán Kodály. Both young men traveled through Romania, Slovakia, Bulgaria, Serbia, and Croatia, listening to the peasants sing and play while the composers transcribed the music—notating what they heard and recording the music on wax cylinders for later study. The duo's activities would help establish the study of folk traditions and ethnomusicology as rigorous sciences, paving the way for later scholars to utilize similar methods in other areas of the world. (Alan and John Lomax, for instance, would do invaluable field research in music of the southern United States, while Cecil Sharp in England and Felipe Pedrell in Spain were carrying on much the same work within their own cultures.) Bartók began using the materials he collected as the

basis for his own creative work, assimilating the music and filtering it through the prism of his own vision. This gave Bartók's music a totally unique flavor, completely contemporary yet rooted in the tradition and spirit of his homeland. An appointment to the academic staff at his alma mater in 1907 brought him more financial security in his dual role of composer/researcher. He was at the same time becoming an international touring artist, playing concerts in Paris and Great Britain in addition to his work within Hungarian borders.

The first all-Bartók concert occurred on March 19, 1909, and included a revised version of the work which would later be acknowledged as his first string quartet (not counting juvenilia of 1896) and an early form of his one surviving piano quintet. His 1917 ballet, *The Wooden Prince,* was unveiled in Budapest and became an immediate success, while the first version of his opera, *Bluebeard's Castle,* was started in 1911 and finished in 1912 but would wait until 1918 for the premiere of its final revision. Universal Editions began publishing his compositions in that same year, increasing Bartók's recognition amongst his international peers. By this time, his works included a number of orchestral and chamber works, among the most notable of which where the *Allegro Barbaro* for piano, and the pantomime *The Miraculous Mandarin.* In 1926, the composer also wrote a number of large piano works for his tours including the Concerto no. 1 for Piano and Orchestra, the Sonata for Piano, and the suite of piano pieces known as *Out of Doors.* The years from 1930 to 1940 were another fertile time for Bartók. He wrote his second piano concerto, four more string quartets, the *Cantata Profana, Music for Strings, Percussion, and Celesta,* his Divertimento for String Orchestra, and the six-volume *Mikrokosmos*—progressive piano exercises which built from the beginning student level throughout the virtuoso. A grant given in 1934 had also allowed Bartók to publish his research on Hungarian folksong and relieved him of the necessity of teaching at the Budapest Academy of Music.

Bartók and his second wife Ditta left Budapest in the fall of 1940, driven out of Europe by the burgeoning fascist movement in Europe, and settled in New York City. Needing to re-establish a steady income, he began working with the Ditson Foundation of Columbia University, which hired him to transcribe and catalog a

Béla Bartók

collection of Yugoslav folksong recordings which were, oddly enough, housed at Harvard. The composer had always been of frail health, but now he was slipping even further into a physical decline. In spite of this, he continued his work, composed, and gave concerts and lectures. On January 21, 1943, Bartók gave his last public performance, the premiere of his Concerto for Two Pianos, Percussion, and Orchestra, with Ditta playing the other piano. Shortly after this concert, the composer's health became conspicuously worse and he suffered a complete breakdown.

The Bartóks spent the summer of 1943 in upstate New York at Saranac Lake. Before they left, the conductor Serge Koussevitsky (at the instigation of violinist Joseph Szigeti and Bartók's former student, the conductor Fritz Reiner) came to Bartók's hospital room offering him a commission for an orchestra piece. At first he was reluctant to accept the commission, but eventually did, producing one of his most enduring successes, the Concerto for Orchestra. He was present for the work's first performances, given December 1 and 2, 1944, with Koussevitsky conducting the Boston Symphony Orchestra. The Concerto for Orchestra is the largest of Bartók's mature orchestral compositions, and would play a major role in establishing him for posterity as a great composer. Though very ill, Bartók still worked on his last two compositions: a third piano concerto and a viola concerto (for violist William Primrose). At the time of his death, Bartók had virtually finished the newest piano concerto but the viola concerto was still unorchestrated. Nonetheless, his legacy of individualistic greatness was secured.

Orchestral
Concerto for Orchestra
what to buy: [Fritz Reiner, cond.; Chicago Symphony Orchestra] (RCA Victor Living Stereo 61504) ♪ ♪ ♪ ♪ ♪

Here is an early recording, but a classic one, complete with a great conductor (and former Bartók student) and orchestra combined with a great program: the Concerto for Orchestra, the *Music for Strings, Percussion, and Celesta,* and the five *Hungarian Sketches.*

what to buy next: [Antál Dorati, cond.; London Symphony Orchestra] (Mercury Living Presence 432017) ♪ ♪ ♪ ♪

Dorati was not only a fine conductor in his own right, he was yet another persuasive advocate for his former teacher Bartók. The recording is quite fine and the accompanying orchestral pieces offer a different view of the composer from that offered by Levine (see below) and Reiner. The balance of the disc is filled out by the composer's *Dance Suite,* his early *Two Portraits,* and a pair of excerpts from *Mikrokosmos* that were arranged for orchestra.

worth looking for: [James Levine, cond.; Chicago Symphony Orchestra] (Deutsche Grammophon 429747) ♪ ♪ ♪ ♪ ♪

Levine leads the orchestra through stunning performances of both the *Music for Strings, Percussion, and Celesta* and the Concerto for Orchestra.

Music for Strings, Percussion, and Celesta
what to buy: [Pierre Boulez, cond.; Chicago Symphony Orchestra] (Deutsche Grammophon 447747) ♪ ♪ ♪ ♪ ♪

A 1994 recording with interpretations which are always unique and refreshing. The companion work, *The Miraculous Mandarin,* gets top billing on the album cover.

The Wooden Prince
what to buy: [Pierre Boulez, cond.; Chicago Symphony Orchestra] (Deutsche Grammophon 435863) ♪ ♪ ♪ ♪ ♪

Boulez conducts the best interpretation of this work and includes Bartók's wonderful if infrequently heard *Cantata Profana* as part of the package. The engineering is up to the usual high standards one expects from Deutsche Grammophon.

Concerto no. 2 for Violin and Orchestra
what to buy: [Gil Shaham, violin; Pierre Boulez, cond.; Chicago Symphony Orchestra] (Deutsche Grammophon 459639) ♪ ♪ ♪ ♪

Shaham's performance of this Twentieth century violin showpiece is nothing short of historic, rendering the composer's score with an insight and intensity that is matched by Boulez and the CSO. Bartók's two rhapsodies for violin and orchestra are agreeable fare, acting as counterbalances to the drama of the concerto.

Chamber
Quartets for Strings (nos. 1–6, complete)
what to buy: [Emerson String Quartet, ensemble] (Deutsche Grammophon 423657) ♪ ♪ ♪ ♪ ♪

It is best to savor these wonderful works as a whole, and the Emerson performances are both stunning and well recorded.

what to buy next: [Vegh String Quartet, ensemble] (Valois 4809) ♪ ♪ ♪ ♪

All of the ensembles listed here do wonderful work with Bartók's quartets, and all are decently recorded. The Vegh String Quartet, however, is just a bit rougher in its attack, exciting the senses just a bit more, taking a few more chances with the material. This set of performances may not be to everyone's taste, but for those who are willing to go along with the group, the roller coaster ride doesn't have too many dips and offers plenty of highs.

worth looking for: [Tokyo String Quartet, ensemble] (RCA Red Seal 68286) ♪ ♪ ♪ ♪ ♪

The Tokyo String Quartet performances are just as worthy as those of the Emerson. A point in favor of the Tokyo ensemble, however, is their inclusion of Leos Janácek's two string quartets in this three-disc package.

Contrasts for Clarinet, Violin, and Piano
what to buy: [*Benny Goodman: Collector's Edition*, Benny Goodman, clarinet, Joseph Szigeti, violin, Béla Bartók, piano] (Sony Classics 42227) ♪ ♪ ♪ ♪ ♪

This recording dates from 1940 and the sonics hold up quite well. The album includes works created specifically for Benny Goodman by Bartók, Leonard Bernstein, Aaron Copland, Morton Gould, and Igor Stravinsky.

Mikrokosmos (complete)
what to buy: [Dezsö Ránki, piano] (Teldec 76139) ♪ ♪ ♪ ♪

A collection that makes it easy to appreciate the artful pedagogy involved. Note the composer's transition from the (relatively) simpler pieces of Book One to the progressively difficult works in Book Six. Ránki is a gifted Hungarian technician who can invest these notes and phrases with a mixture of power and subtlety that makes light of difficulties while infusing the tiny fragments with their own kind of poetry. He also includes his countryman's complete *Für Kinder (For Children)* cycle on this moderately priced three-disc set.

Sonata for Solo Violin
what to buy: [André Gertler, violin] (Hungaroton White Label 31635) ♪ ♪ ♪ ♪

This was Bartók's last completed chamber work, a major composition for solo violin that is in the same league as J.S. Bach's famous suites. Gertler handles the astounding technical demands of the composer with all the ferocity this material needs. The other works on the budget-priced disc (Bach's Concerto no. 1 for Violin and Orchestra in A Minor and Alban Berg's Concerto for Violin and Orchestra) bracket the Bartók, creating an unusual program.

Vocal
Bluebeard's Castle, op. 11
what to buy: [Jessye Norman, soprano; Laszlo Polgár, baritone; Pierre Boulez, cond.; Chicago Symphony Orchestra] (Deutsche Grammophon 447040) ♪ ♪ ♪ ♪ ♪

An anxiously-awaited recording of a one-act powerhouse. Norman is sublime.

influences: Richard Strauss, Richard Wagner, Igor Stravinsky, Zoltán Kodály, Franz Liszt, Claude Debussy

Frank Retzel and Ian Palmer

Arnold Bax
Born Arnold Edward Trevor Bax, November 8, 1883, in London, England. Died October 3, 1953, in Cork, Ireland.

period: Romantic/Twentieth century

Although he is not well known outside of Great Britain—and probably never will be—Sir Arnold Bax was a powerfully individual composer who made a major contribution to the revival of English music between the two World Wars. He is best known for his atmospheric tone poems *The Garden of Fand* (1916) and *Tintagel* (1917).

Bax came from a wealthy family, enabling him to travel extensively, pursue many interests, and remain free of financial pressures. As a result he became something of a wanderer, rarely staying more than a few months in one place. In 1902 Bax read W.B. Yeats's *The Wanderings of Usheen,* which awakened in him a passionate interest in things Celtic. He visited Ireland regularly after that and strongly identified with the Irish and their culture. This later had a major impact on his music, inspiring some of Bax's finest work. Following a visit to Russia in 1910, Bax fell under the spell of the Russian romantics. Among his other influences were Franz Liszt, Richard Strauss, and the early compositions of Maurice Ravel. Bax's strongly individualistic personality assimilated all of these influences to forge a unique idiom.

He studied at the Royal College of Music in London, graduating in 1905 with a Gold Medal in piano. Besides being a fine composer, Bax was also an exceptional pianist, with the ability to reproduce complex orchestral scores on the piano. His own piano compositions show a great understanding of the instrument's technical and musical effects; in this sense, Bax can be considered a worthy successor to Chopin. All the more curious, then, that this fine pianist remained reluctant to perform in public for the rest of his life.

During the first years of the century, Bax's mastery of orchestral technique was virtually unequaled. He wrote seven symphonies, and even though they are uneven in quality, they nevertheless confirm his reputation as a composer of powerful and original means. Interestingly, three of those symphonies had their first performances in the United States.

Bax's music is a compelling combination of post-romantic and impressionistic elements, with an almost mystical overtone that is particularly evident in his masterly, lushly orchestrated symphonic works. Bax utilized elaborate harmonic structures filled with rich chromaticism and broad, sweeping melodies, and his best works are highly picturesque. His chamber music is just as important as his symphonic works and is beautifully and sensitively written for the instruments involved. Bax was also an outstanding composer of vocal music, although many of his lovely songs have never been recorded. Songs were among his first important compositions, and he showed great taste and discrimination in his choice of poets and texts. The outbreak of World War II all but ended his major creative output, and although he did start writing again in the mid-1940s, Bax produced nothing of great significance except for a couple of outstanding film scores.

Even in Britain, Bax's music never established itself solidly with the public, and in the years since his death, he has become almost a cult figure. He was a very fine writer, and his autobiography, *Farewell, My Youth,* is an outstanding literary work. Bax also collected many honors during his life, having received the Gold Medal of the Royal Philharmonic Society, two honorary Doctor of Music degrees, a knighthood, and an appointment as Master of the King's Music.

Orchestral
The Garden of Fand
what to buy: [*Bax: Tone Poems, Vol. 1;* Bryden Thomson, cond.; Ulster Orchestra] (Chandos 8307) ♪♪♪♪

The late Bryden Thomson and the Ulster Orchestra recorded all of Bax's major orchestral works. This compilation from that series also includes *November Woods, Summer Music,* and *The Happy Forest,* some of his most attractive and atmospheric symphonic poems. This is perfect way to get into his music, with fine performances and outstanding sound.

Symphony No. 3
what to buy: [Bryden Thomson, cond.; London Philharmonic Orchestra] (Chandos 8454) ♪♪♪♪

The third is arguably the best and most coherent of Bax's seven symphonies, and this disc presents a fine, superbly recorded performance of the work. Two tone poems, *Dance of Wild Irravel* and *Paean,* fill out the disc.

worth looking for: [Sir John Barbirolli, cond.; The Halle Orchestra] (EMI 63910) ♪♪♪♪

This legendary 1944 recording was not only the first recording ever of a Bax symphony, it is also arguably the finest recording of his finest symphony. Even though the mono sound is dated, the power of the performance comes through vividly.

Chamber Music
Elegiac Trio for Flute, Viola, and Harp
what to buy: [The Nash Ensemble] (Hyperion 66807) ♪♪♪

Some of Bax's finest chamber works are assembled here, including the Nonet for Flute, Oboe, Clarinet, Harp, and Strings (1931), the Quintet for Oboe and Strings

(1924), and the Sonata in B-flat Major for Clarinet and Piano (1934). The sound quality is excellent, and the music is played with total dedication and artistry.

Vocal
various choral works
what to buy: [*Howells & Bax Choral Works;* Paul Spicer, cond.; Finzi Singers, choir] (Chandos 9139) ♪♪♪♪

Spicer delivers an outstanding sampler of Bax's marvelous choral writing and presents four of his finest works in the genre, including *Five Greek Folk Songs* and *I Sing of a Maiden That Is Makeless.* Featuring superlative singing and very attractive sonics, the disc also includes five choral works by Herbert Howells.

influences: Frederick Delius, Herbert Howells, Gerald Finzi

Charles Greenwell and Dave Wagner

Amy Beach
(Mrs. H. H. A. Beach)
Born Amy March Cheney, September 5, 1867, in Henniker, New Hampshire. Died December 27, 1944, in New York City, New York.

period: Romantic/Twentieth century

Amy Beach was a prominent member of the New England romantic school of composers and a formidable pianist.

Born Amy Marcy Cheney, she very early proved herself a staggeringly prodigious talent. Refused piano lessons at age two, she spent two years simply watching her mother play, then sat down and played the hymns and music of Strauss, Chopin, and Beethoven she had been hearing. "I knew how to play instinctively," she said, "as a cat knows how to jump."

Amy also began composing at an early age, though without formal instruction, and can be considered largely self-taught. Her genius was immediately recognized by Boston musicians when her family moved to that area in 1875, and she promptly received the attention of the best piano teachers, debuting as a recitalist at age sixteen. Two years later, Amy made her solo bow with the Boston Symphony Orchestra in a performance of Chopin's Piano Concerto no. 2 in F Minor.

Amy Cheney's career then markedly changed direction. At the age of eighteen, she married a prominent Boston surgeon, Dr. Henry Harris Aubrey Beach, happily adopting the name Mrs. H. H. A. Beach both personally and professionally. She also went along with her husband's insistence that she be a stay-at-home wife, concentrating on composition and limiting her touring as a pianist. She was allowed to give a few local concerts but only if the proceeds were donated to charity.

Over the next twenty-five years, her major works appeared, including the *Gaelic* Symphony, the Violin Sonata, the Piano Concerto in C-sharp Minor, the Mass in E-flat Major, and the Piano Quintet in F-sharp Minor. There were also many songs, one of which, "The Year's at the Spring," has been an enduring hit. In the early years of the Twentieth century, it was found in virtually every American parlor where there was a piano. During this period, Amy became recognized as one of the leading American composers. Royalties from her compositions, which her conservative husband "graciously" let her keep, made Amy financially independent.

On Dr. Beach's death in 1910, Amy resumed her career as a pianist with a highly successful tour of Europe, where she stayed for four years. Returning to the United States, she settled into a regular routine, wintering and touring from New York City while summering in various New England locations, notably the MacDowell Colony in New Hampshire. The MacDowell Colony, a famous artists' retreat, became the beneficiary in her will of all posthumous royalties from her music.

When she died in New York in 1944 at age seventy-seven, Amy Beach was still recognized as a major figure in American music, although the revolutionary changes spearheaded by such composers as Arnold Schoenberg and Igor Stravinsky had already begun eroding the popularity of music considered primarily romantic in expression. This last category included most of Beach's work, and she remained out of vogue until the middle 1970s, when recordings began to awaken the world to the beauty of this remarkable woman's music.

Orchestral
Symphony in E Minor, op. 32—*Gaelic* Symphony
what to buy: [Neeme Järvi, cond.; Detroit Symphony Orchestra] (Chandos 8958) ♪ ♪ ♪♪

The *Gaelic* Symphony is the first—and perhaps still the best—symphony ever composed by an American woman. The Detroit/Järvi CD provides a wonderfully

---

Cathy Berberian:

The daring originality and versatility of American mezzo-soprano Cathy Berberian inspired a generation of twentieth century composers. Her impressive three-octave range and courageous curiosity led to the composition of several original works by Luciano Berio, John Cage, Hans Werner Henze, and Igor Stravinsky. Berberian was willing to push the potential of the human voice to the absolute limit, often incorporating unusual sounds and movements in order to achieve the desired effect. In this way, she is considered a forerunner of performance artists such as Joan La Barbara and Meredith Monk.

Berberian was born in Attleboro, Massachusetts on July 4, 1925. Her early training included voice, mime, and dance as well as classes at New York University and Columbia University. She moved to Italy and married composer Luciano Berio in 1950; the couple separated in 1966 and finally divorced in 1968. Berio wrote a number of works specifically for her including *Chamber Music* (a setting of poetry by James Joyce), *Air*, and *Recital*. A 1958 performance of John Cage's *Fontana Mix*, a very demanding work, served to establish Berberian as a formidable advocate for the avant-garde. The piece showcased the type of unconventional vocal techniques for which Berberian became so famous. Besides being a champion of twentieth century repertoire, she was a devotee of the music of Claudio Monteverdi. Her recordings of this seventeenth century Venetian master include his opera *L'Incoronazione di Poppea* (Teldec Das Alte Werk 42547) with Nikolaus Harnoncourt. Other significant recordings are Berio's *Folksongs* (Aura Classics 171), *Visage* (BMG Ricordi 1017), *Circles*, and *Sequenza III* (the last two each Wergo 6021); Bruno Maderna's *Dimensioni No. 2* (Stradivarius 33349); and vocal works by Igor Stravinsky including *Elegy for JFK* (Sony Classics 64136), which was written for her. She even recorded a number of Beatles songs (Aura Classics 146) on the same album as her own 1966 composition, a work for solo voice using newspaper comics entitled *Stripsody*. She also wrote, in 1971, a piece for piano one-hand called *Morsicat(h)y*. Berberian died in Rome on March 6, 1983, but her contributions to twentieth century vocal practice, performance, and repertoire are unquestioned and her pioneering influence is enduring.

Mona DeQuis

---

clean recording and performance of this work, pairing it with Samuel Barber's First Symphony and his *School for Scandal* Overture.

worth looking for: [Karl Krueger, cond.; Royal Philharmonic Orchestra] (Our Musical Past 105) ♪ ♪ ♪ ♪

Krueger's performance, more emotionally involved than Järvi's, can only be ordered by mail, directly from the Library of Congress in Washington, D.C.

Chamber
Sonata in A Minor for Violin and Piano, op. 34
what to buy: [Curtis Macomber, violin; Diane Walsh, piano] (Koch International 7223) ♪ ♪ ♪ ♪

This is strong, lyrical music that caused some critics of her day to say that Amy Beach composed like a man. Although that would be considered politically incorrect today, the writers of a century ago intended it as a high compliment. John Corigliano's sonata for the same instruments fills out the album.

various piano works
what to buy: [*Under the Stars*; Joanne Polk, piano] (Arabesque 6704) ♪ ♪ ♪ ♪

An excellent introduction to Beach's art, this volume contains the traditionally minded Prelude and Fugue, op. 81, the graciously descriptive five movement suite *Les Reves de Columbine,* and ten other works. The most immediately appealing of the remaining pieces are *A Hermit Thrush at Eve,* op. 92, no. 1, and *A Hermit Thrush at Morn,* op. 92, no. 2. Here Beach, an amateur ornithologist, quotes actual bird songs (years before Olivier Messiaen's acclaimed similar activities) in the most effortless, beguiling, and impressionistic way.

influences: Arthur Foote, George W. Chadwick

Herman Trotter

Ludwig van Beethoven
Born December 16, 1770 in Bonn, Germany. Died March 26, 1827 in Vienna, Austria.

period: Classical/Romantic

Beyond the sheer quality and inventiveness of his music, Ludwig van Beethoven is important as the first great composer to support himself as a freelance throughout his career, independent of any permanent court, church or aristocratic post, and for inspiring the Romantic period with his vision of concert music as a form of uplifting, public self-expression. Furthermore, his harmonic daring and his vast expansion of the lengths and resources of the various musical forms set the pace for the 19th century.

Beethoven was fond of pretending he was descended from nobility, but in fact he was born a commoner—the Dutch "van," unlike the German "von," merely indicates where a family was from. His father gave him his first musical training; after that, he studied with various local musicians. An adept pianist and violinist, he could also

play organ and horn, and began composing early; his first published piece was written when he was twelve years old. He found work as a violinist in theater orchestras and was an organist in the court of the Elector Maximilian Franz. In 1787, the Elector sent Beethoven to Vienna, but he was forced to return to Bonn prematurely by his mother's illness and death. With his father having become an alcoholic, Beethoven now had to support the family.

Giving piano lessons provided him with some income beyond what he could earn from playing the viola in the Bonn chapel and theater orchestras, but at that time musicians rarely managed more than subsistence without backing from the rich and (usually) noble. Beethoven's first major patron was Count Ferdinand von Waldstein (later immortalized as the dedicatee of one of the composer's most famous piano sonatas). But more important to young Ludwig's development was his introduction in 1790 to Franz Joseph Haydn, who invited him to come to Vienna for lessons. A combination of Haydn's travels and Beethoven's inadvisable step of having another musician edit his assigned exercises led to the termination of these studies, but once in Vienna, Beethoven was able to continue his training with less prestigious but equally learned composers, including Johann Georg Albrechtsberger and Antonio Salieri. Around 1793 he was invited to live with the family of Prince Karl Lichnowsky, to whom he dedicated the *Pathétique* piano sonata and who, starting in 1800, would also provide him with a generous annuity. He made his Vienna debut as a performer in 1795 with one of his early piano concertos, and his growing reputation soon enabled him to play in many of the major Austrian and German cities. His real arrival as a composer, however, came in 1800 when he put on a whole concert of his own works, including the First Symphony and Septet in E flat major.

Around the turn of the century, Beethoven was still best known as a pianist, and he made his name not only with the concertos but also with his piano sonatas. At first strongly influenced by Haydn's, these works became larger and more complex. To some extent, his piano writing was restricted by the relatively fragile fortepiano of the time, but the instrument was continually being improved, and Beethoven tested the limits of each successively heftier model. By the time his fourth piano

Ludwig van Beethoven

sonata (in E flat major, op. 7) was completed in 1797, he had vastly expanded the form's structure. Also significant are the piano sonatas no. 8 in C minor, op. 13 (the *Sonate pathétique*) of 1798, with its dramatic slow introduction, and the famous "Moonlight" sonata (no. 14 in C sharp minor, op. 27, no. 2) from 1801. The fiery "Tempest" (no. 17 in D minor, op. 31, no. 2) from 1802, supposedly inspired by Shakespeare's play of that name, is even more romantic in flavor, anticipating symphonic developments to come.

The Symphony no. 2 in D major (op. 36)—mostly written in 1802—came during a period of emotional turmoil in Beethoven's life: He had noticed that he was losing his hearing. He was advised by a doctor to get away from the noisy city, and moved temporarily to the village of Heiligenstadt, just outside Vienna. But his condition did not improve, and he became nearly suicidal, as movingly described in a letter he wrote to his brothers. Beethoven soon rebounded from his depression through hard work, and his music grew increasingly daring, even revolutionary. His hearing loss was gradual enough that he was still able to continue performing in public for several years, appearing as soloist at the premiere of his Third Piano Concerto (op. 37, in C minor)—an intensely stormy, emotional work—in 1803. The final step into a new musical era came with Beethoven's Symphony no. 3 in E flat major (op. 55), originally given the name *Eroica (Heroic)* by the composer. When he wrote it in 1803-04, Beethoven was still inspired by Napoleon, who had liberated France from its royal rulers and made it a republic, but when Napoleon made himself emperor, Beethoven scratched out the dedication. More important than its source of inspiration was the work itself, a landmark in Western music. It was the longest symphony yet written, which occasioned much comment, by no means all favorable—nor were all observers ready for a symphony containing a funeral march as its second movement. Beethoven's expansion of the symphonic structure also confused some early listeners, as did the unremitting tension caused by the way his first theme repeatedly ends on an unresolved note and the trend-setting amount of dissonance. The work's controversial aspects hardly meant that it went unappreciated; on the contrary, it was much praised in some quarters on its premiere in 1805.

In November of that year, the French army occupied Vienna, considerably disrupting life in the city. Beethoven also entered another turbulent but not unproductive period. The Concerto in D major for Violin and Orchestra (op. 61) was written for the violin virtuoso Franz Clement in 1806 and came to be regarded later in the century as the supreme violin concerto. Some of his most famous piano sonatas—no. 23 in F minor (op. 57, the "Appassionata" (and no. 26 in E flat major (op. 81a, "Les Adieux")—date from this time as does Beethoven's sole opera, *Fidelio,* which he originally called *Leonore.* The story of a woman's quest to free her unjustly imprisoned husband, it again reveals Beethoven's idealism and his passionate dedication to the concept of liberty. It would be revised considerably a number of times before assuming its final form and title in 1814; the three *Leonore* Overtures are a result of this process.

Dedications of many of the masterpieces from this period show the continuing support of Beethoven by the aristocracy: the op. 59 string quartets were written for Count Razumovsky, the Russian ambassador in Vienna; Symphony no. 4 in B flat major (op. 60) for Count Franz Oppersdorff; and the immortal symphonies nos. 5 in C minor (op. 67) and 6 in F major (op. 68, the "Pastoral") were dedicated to Razumovsky and Prince Franz Joseph Lobkowitz. The latter two symphonies, along with the Concerto no. 4 in G major for Piano and Orchestra (op. 58—dedicated to Archduke Rudolph of Austria, one of Beethoven's piano students) and the *Fantasia* in C major for Piano, Chorus, and Orchestra (op. 80) were all premiered in an extremely long Vienna concert on December 22, 1808. Beethoven himself was the pianist in both the concerto and the *Fantasia,* but his hearing loss soon put an end to both that role and his conducting.

In 1809 he wrote his last piano concerto (no. 5, in E flat major, op. 73), nicknamed the "Emperor," though' not by Beethoven, but by an English publisher looking to make an inappropriate Napoleonic connection. The concert of December 8, 1813, at which he premiered his Symphony no. 7 in A major (op. 92) and the trivial piece of program music depicting Napoleon's defeat, *Wellington's Victory,* was his last public appearance as conductor. The severity of Beethoven's deafness led to his increasing isolation and obstreperousness: when informed that his Symphony no. 8 in F major (op. 93) received less applause at its 1814 premiere than did his Seventh Symphony (included on the same concert), he responded angrily, though earnestly, "That's because it's so much better!"

Beethoven began working on the monumental *Missa Solemnis* in 1818, aiming to have it ready for the enthronement of Archduke Rudolph (his student and the youngest son of Emperor Leopold II) as Archbishop of Olmütz in 1820, but its scope became ever more ambitious, and he did not complete it until well into 1823. It was so massive—as well as difficult for the singers (Beethoven seemed unconcerned with the practicability of his choral writing and treated voices like instruments)—that it was unrealistic to present it in a liturgical context. As the public performance of sacred works was not allowed, special permission had to be obtained to include three movements in a concert. The world premiere of the complete *Mass* took place in St. Petersburg, Russia, without the composer in attendance. Similarly, Beethoven already began sketching his *Ninth Symphony* before 1817 but didn't begin actively composing it until 1823–24, Whereas previously his symphonies had appeared with some regularity, a long gap thus separated the premieres of his *Eighth* and *Ninth.* Though his groundbreaking inclusion of vocal soloists and chorus in the final movement was (and, to an extent, remained) highly controversial, the work was an immediate success.

After his deafness became virtually total, Beethoven largely turned to more intimate forms. Following a gap of four years he resumed the composition of piano sonatas, and he returned to the string quartet after a gap of fifteen years. What have become known as his *Late Piano Sonatas* (nos.27-32) and the *Late String Quartets* (nos. 12–16 and the *Great Fugue*) were composed between 1814–22 and 1825–1826, respectively. Distinguished from his earlier efforts in those genres not only by time but in style—more ruminative, more inward, unconcerned with any display of virtuosity for its own sake—these are arguably the subtlest and most searching pieces of music in all of musical literature. Beethoven had begun sketching a tenth symphony by 1825, but his final illness, beginning in December 1826, prevented him from further composition.

Orchestral
Symphonies (complete)
what to buy: [Riccardo Muti, cond.; Philadelphia Orchestra] (EMI Classics 72923) ♪ ♪ ♪ ♪⅛

There are versions with more vividly defined character, but for a well-played, digitally recorded set (on six CDs at a budget price) in which every performance is commendable and lacking in controversial points, Muti's 1985-88 cycle can't be beat. The above description should not, however, be taken as an indication that

Muti's direction leads to bland, generic music making. These are lively and joyous performances. Besides the symphonies, this set includes three overtures: *Leonore* no. 3, *Fidelio,* and *Consecration of the House.*

[John Eliot Gardiner, cond.; Orchestre Révolutionnaire et Romantique] (Deutsche Grammophon Archiv 439900) ♪ ♪ ♪ ♪⅛

This is the original-instrument version of the symphonies for people who usually find original-instrument recordings too lightweight for Beethoven. Balances are not tilted too strongly away from the strings, though certainly the winds come through nicely with pungent but never raw tone. Tempos are often quick but never degenerate into a scramble. All but radical period-performance advocates will probably find Gardiner's speed in the slow movement of the Ninth Symphony closer to an Andante (and a quick one, at that) than an Adagio. However, this is an effective interpretation, and the vocal soloists are stronger than in many other period performances.

what to buy next: [Leonard Bernstein, cond.; Vienna Philharmonic Orchestra] (Deutsche Grammophon 423481) ♪ ♪ ♪ ♪

Though some of Bernstein's earlier Beethoven recordings with the New York Philharmonic on Sony are also excellent, this set is more consistent. Lenny lived for the emotional peaks; even at tragic moments, he makes the music sound cathartic rather than beaten-down. The orchestra provides a wonderful sound, creamy in tone yet with sufficient bite where required, and the engineers have captured it well. The flaws come at the end of the cycle. The Ninth Symphony starts well but bogs down in a very slow third movement. Bernstein's whiplash tempo changes slip into mere melodrama in the finale, also disfigured by occasionally grating male solo voices (René Kollo, Kurt Moll), a shrieking, swooping soprano (Gwyneth Jones), and lots of vibrato from the sopranos of the Vienna State Opera Chorus. There are six overtures as filler in this six-CD set (*Coriolan, Leonore* no. 3, *Fidelio, Egmont, Prometheus,* and *King Stephen*), all imbued with great character and drama..

[Arturo Toscanini, cond.; NBC Symphony Orchestra] (RCA Victor 603324) ♪ ♪ ♪ ♪

Toscanini was not the first conductor to take generally quick and—by the standards of the high Romantics—

relatively unvaried tempos in the Beethoven symphonies; Felix Weingartner's admirable 1920s/30s recordings set the standard in that regard. However, through sheer force of personality and unrelenting discipline, Toscanini popularized that approach at a time when conductors were still prone to broader speeds and frequent tempo fluctuations. Though some will say that too much of Toscanini's style and personality are imposed on these pieces, they all work on their own terms, even the always tricky Ninth Symphony. Supplement these late 1940s/early '50s recordings with a few choice earlier Toscanini recordings of individual works (see below).

[Wilhelm Furtwängler, cond.; Vienna Philharmonic Orchestra (nos. 1–7; Stockholm Philharmonic Orchestra (no.8); Bayreuth Festival Orchestra (no. 9); Bayreuth Festival Chorus (no. 9)] (EMI Classics 67496) ♪ ♪ ♪ ♪

Not necessarily the best Furtwängler performances of each symphony (supplement it with the incomplete Music & Arts set below), but the most consistent complete set, now with improved sound. Symphonies nos. 1-7 are played by the VPO while the Ninth Symphony (recorded in 1951 at the postwar re-opening of Bayreuth) includes Elisabeth Schwarzkopf as soprano soloist. Furtwängler, the antithesis of Toscanini, is the ultimate master of the broad, heavily inflected approach, treating the music more organically than others of that school so that his interpretations never seem merely willful.

[Claudio Abbado, cond.; Berlin Philharmonic Orchestra] (Deutsche Grammophon 469000) ♪ ♪ ♪ ♪

This 1999-2000 five-CD traversal of the cycle, mostly recorded in concert, is a surprise from Abbado. Not only does he show a keen awareness of period practices (though obviously the Berlin Philharmonic doesn't play on original instruments) and use the new critically revised Bärenreiter Edition to ensure accuracy of the musical text, there's also a degree of emotional expressiveness that he has not always mustered in symphonic repertoire in the past. With an effervescently Italian flavor to the proceedings, the swift tempos convey rejoicing without seeming hard-driven, the *Eroica* being especially sprightly. Though this approach will not be to all listeners' tastes, especially those who favor a serious, Germanic-sounding Beethoven, the only real flaw in the cycle comes in the Ninth Symphony, when baritone Thomas Quasthoff sounds strained by his first solo, so much a focal point in this piece. However, on the whole

this set is a fine achievement.

[Otto Klemperer, cond.; Philharmonia Orchestra] (EMI Classics 68057) ♪ ♪ ♪ ♪

Klemperer's stereo 1955-59 recordings of the symphonies are for listeners who prefer monumental Beethoven. If one listens through some imperfections, these are powerful interpretations, though again not to all tastes. This budget-priced nine-CD box also includes the piano concertos and the *Choral Fantasia* with Daniel Barenboim (a surprisingly good cycle, with Klemperer thoroughly curbing the pianist's eccentric tendencies), an orchestration of the *Great Fugue*, three of the finest readings of the *Leonore* Overtures nos. 1-3, and the *Coriolan* and *Prometheus* overtures. Despite possible quibbles about some of the performances (Symphonies nos. 1, 2, and 6), this is excellent value.

worth looking for: [Roger Norrington, cond.; London Classical Players, orch.] (EMI Classics 49852) ♪ ♪ ♪ ♪♪

Norrington's adherence to Beethoven's metronome markings makes this set controversial. When these recordings were first released in the last three years of the 1980s, "authentic performance" ensembles playing Beethoven was a new and far from accepted notion. Norrington is hardly the unromantic, insensitive conductor that his detractors called him. Rather, he returns practically to the Toscanini approach, but with period instruments and a period-sized orchestra, and finds the excitement that had been missing from so many recordings searching for profundity in these scores.

Symphony no. 3 in E-flat Major, op. 55 *Eroica*
what to buy: [Otto Klemperer, cond.; Philharmonia Orchestra] (EMI Classics 66793) ♪ ♪ ♪ ♪♪

This is the high point in Klemperer's Beethoven cycle. (Note that it's the 1959 stereo version; a much-praised 1955 monaural recording offers a quicker reading but less polished playing.) Klemperer's pace gives us a hero who's poised and deliberate, with real pathos and drama in the Funeral March. Filling out the disc is a string orchestra version of the *Great Fugue* for string quartet, played nobly. A fine acquisition for those who don't want to invest in the box set.

what to buy next: [Arturo Toscanini, cond.; NBC Symphony Orchestra] (Dante Lys 079) ♪ ♪ ♪ ♪♪

Toscanini's 1939 recording finds the orchestra playing with more portamento and deeper feeling than in his 1949 version (above set). This reading has more breadth, especially in the emotional Funeral March, but not at the expense of a rousing finale.

worth looking for: [Franz Konwitschny, cond.; Staatskapelle Dresden, orch.] (Berlin Classics 9039) ♪♪♪♪

This 1954 monaural recording (with very clean sonics) is urgent but not pressed too hard, with good contrast even within movements. Broad enough to provide the requisite weightiness, yet never dragging, it's heavily accented yet well balanced dynamically, with some bold brass and wind playing. A distinctive interpretation, yet well within the mainstream.

Symphony no. 5 in C Minor, op. 67
what to buy: [Carlos Kleiber, cond.; Vienna Philharmonic Orchestra] (Deutsche Grammophon 447400) ♪♪♪♪♪

When this recording appeared in 1975, many hailed it as the best yet, and arguably no subsequent version of Beethoven's Fifth Symphony has surpassed it (with the possible exception of Bernstein's with the same orchestra). It's now coupled with Kleiber's equally praised Seventh Symphony, which, after the slow introduction, is rather quick, even aggressive, but perfectly proportioned, never sounding rushed or breathless.

worth looking for: [Arturo Toscanini, cond.; NBC Symphony Orchestra] (RCA Gold Seal 60270) ♪♪♪♪

Alas, this 1939 performance, even more thrilling than Toscanini's 1952 version, was recorded at NBC's infamous Studio 8-H and suffers from incredibly dry, overly close, one-dimensional sound. It needs to be heard anyway. The beginning is even more dramatic than in 1952 and Toscanini opens up the finale more to excellent effect. It all sounds positively operatic! The remainder of the disc is a lovely orchestral version of the Septet (op. 20) and a sub-par 1953 reading of the *Egmont* overture.

Symphony no. 6 in F Major, op. 68 *Pastoral*
what to buy: [Karl Böhm, cond.; Vienna Philharmonic Orchestra] (Deutsche Grammophon 447433) ♪♪♪♪♪

This amiable work is surprisingly hard to bring off. The

warmth and rustic geniality most of it calls for must be balanced with a sufficiently dramatic depiction of the storm movement. Many conductors manage one or the other, but not both. Actually, all of Böhm's Beethoven cycle is good, but DG has allowed the cycle by Karajan—their meal-ticket conductor—to eclipse it rather unfairly (this writer does not find Karajan persuasive in this repertoire). This disc also includes Schubert's Fifth Symphony performed by the same forces.

what to buy next: [Bruno Walter, cond.; Columbia Symphony Orchestra] (Sony Classics 64462) ♪♪♪♪₄

This 1958 recording is, as one would expect from Walter, amiable and warm-toned, but with sufficient drama and never slack. It is paired with a version of Beethoven's Fourth Symphony from the same year and with the same merits.

Symphony no. 7 in A Major, op. 92
what to buy: [*Toscanini—The Great Recordings:1926-36*; Arturo Toscanini, cond.; New York Philharmonic Orchestra] (Pearl 9373) ♪♪♪♪₄

Nobody has ever conveyed the structure of Beethoven's Seventh Symphony more effectively than Toscanini, made its rhythms flow so naturally. In this 1936 recording, it has a natural plasticity that eluded him in his later remake with the NBC Symphony, and the sound is acceptable. Available as part of a three-CD set.

Symphony no. 9 in D Minor, op. 125 *Choral*
what to buy: [Carol Vaness, soprano; Janice Taylor, mezzo-soprano; Siegfried Jerusalem, tenor; Robert Lloyd, bass; Christoph von Dohnányi, cond.; Cleveland Orchestra; Cleveland Orchestra Chorus] (Telarc 80120) ♪♪♪♪♪

For a wonderfully played Ninth in excellent sound, it's hard to beat this performance. In a sense, there's nothing distinctive about it: Dohnanyi's interpretation is middle-of-the-road with no eccentricities. He holds the piece together well, is never grotesque or bland, and, most of all, draws excellent playing from the orchestra. He makes the piece flow naturally, with clear proportions—a lot harder than it sounds, and actually quite rare.

what to buy next: [Helen Donath, soprano; Brigitte Fassbaender, mezzo-soprano; Horst Laubenthal, tenor; Hans Sotin, bass; Rafael Kubelik, cond.; Bavarian Radio

Symphony Orchestra and Chorus] (Orfeo 207891) ♪♪♪♪♪

It's so difficult to bring all the elements of this monumental work together that whenever a truly great performance results, peripheral flaws should be ignored. So the fact that this is a true live performance (no studio "fixes" afterwards) from 1982, with some audience noise (but fine sonics), should deter nobody from acquiring it. Not only does Kubelik mold the problematic structure well and bring out the music's natural drama, he has an excellent solo quartet.

[*Furtwängler Conducts Beethoven*; Tilla Briem, soprano; Elisabeth Höngen, contralto; Peter Anders, tenor; Rudolf Watzke, bass; Wilhelm Furtwängler, cond.; Vienna Philharmonic Orchestra; Berlin Philharmonic Orchestra] (Music & Arts 4049) ♪♪♪♪♪

This four-CD set focuses on Furtwängler's wartime Beethoven recordings, generally his most fiery and impassioned—not only in the Ninth Symphony but also in nos. 3-7. All the symphonies except the Third (Vienna) are with the BPO, the orchestra he led for so many years and which responds ardently to his direction. The set is filled out with a *Coriolan* Overture from Berlin and a *Leonore* no. 3 Overture with the VPO. Considering the era and the fact that these are concert performances, the sound is surprisingly listenable.

[Luise Helletsgruber, soprano; Rosette Anday, contralto; Georg Maikl, tenor; Richard Mayr, bass; Felix Weingartner, cond.; Vienna Philharmonic Orchestra; Vienna State Opera Chorus] (Pearl 9407) ♪♪♪♪

Though the sonics of this 1935 recording, and slight flaws in orchestral execution, will incline some collectors to pass it by, it's both an invaluable historical document and a superbly sculpted performance. Weingartner believed firmly in moving things along, yet he's never rigid in his tempi—in fact, he's wonderfully flexible in subtle, unexaggerated ways. The solo quartet is quite distinctive, although the men are lacking in tonal splendor. Weingartner leads the this work with such alacrity, that there's room for a bonus: a 1938 recording with the London Philharmonic Orchestra of the eleven "Mödlinger" dances, which are now thought not to be by Beethoven.

Concertos for Piano and Orchestra (complete)
what to buy: [Wilhelm Kempff, piano; Paul van

Kempen, cond.; Berlin Philharmonic Orchestra] (Deutsche Grammophon 435744) ♪♪♪♪♪

Yes, these 1953 recordings are monaural, but it's good clean studio mono, and this set is better than Kempff's stereo remake the following decade. At all times there is a delightful freshness and spontaneity, enhanced by Kempff playing his own cadenzas in the first four concertos (he was a legitimate composer whose First Symphony was conducted by Furtwängler). His technique in these recordings is still largely solid, and for all his lightness of touch where appropriate, he plays the mighty *Emperor* with sufficient weight. The orchestra is led spiritedly, and the whole set sparkles with joy. The third disc, with the *Emperor*, is filled out the solo Rondos, op. 51, nos. 1-2.

[Vladimir Ashkenazy, piano; Georg Solti, cond.; Chicago Symphony Orchestra] (London 443723) ♪♪♪♪♪

This classic set presents the traditional view of the Beethoven piano concertos in spectacular fashion. Ashkenazy's impeccable virtuosity and dramatic flair meet Solti's boldness and bigger-than-life musical gestures to create a perfect portrait of Beethoven the heroic pianist. Some may call it bombast, but it's more like an unstoppable force of nature. Ashkenazy's later cycles (with Zubin Mehta and with the pianist himself conducting from the piano) can't touch this one. At its new low price, a must-have. The pianist's performances of the six Bagatelles, op. 126, and *Für Elise* are an attractive filler.

what to buy next: [*Glenn Gould Edition—Beethoven: The 5 Piano Concertos*; Glenn Gould, piano; Vladimir Golschmann, cond.; Columbia Symphony Orchestra (no. 1); Leonard Bernstein, cond.; New York Philharmonic Orchestra (no. 2); Leonard Bernstein, cond.; Columbia Symphony Orchestra (nos. 3 and 4); Leopold Stokowski, cond.; American Symphony Orchestra (no. 5)] (Sony Classical 52632) ♪♪♪♪♪

Glenn Gould's expressed distaste for most of the traditional piano repertoire (especially concertos) notwithstanding, his eccentricities in Beethoven's concertos are not disruptive as they are in the piano sonatas (or the Mozart piano sonatas). Rather, they are thought-provoking and refreshing. The "Emperor," Gould's only collaboration with his hero Leopold Stokowski and a much more collaborative view of the work than usual, is quite special. The fourth concerto, with Bernstein, is also spectacular, and the first, with Golschmann, is noteworthy for Gould's own cadenzas, far from authentic yet quite effective.

[Alfred Brendel, piano; Simon Rattle, cond.; Vienna Philharmonic Orchestra] (Philips 462781) ♪ ♪ ♪ ♪

Brendel, long hailed as a great Beethovenian, has often seemed merely persnickety and detail-obsessed. Here, however, on his fourth (!) complete cycle of the piano concertos, everything finally comes together. Partly inspired no doubt both by the plushness of the VPO sound and Rattle's avoidance of routine, Brendel seems to come alive, to actually enjoy the music rather than see it as a pedantic chore. Compared to earlier cycles, his playing on these 1997-98 recordings is a touch more relaxed. His intelligence is not compromised, just placed in a more fertile context in which momentum is not allowed to slacken for point-making, though (in general) the tempos are marginally slower than before.

[Leon Fleisher, piano; George Szell, cond.; Cleveland Orchestra] (Sony Classical 48397) ♪ ♪ ♪ ♪

Though this is rather dry and stern compared to some cycles, Fleisher's virtuosity and the quick speeds are compelling. Szell allows more theatricality to shine through than in his desiccated recordings of the composer's symphonies. Disc 3 also includes the "Triple Concerto" performed by pianist Eugene Istomin, violinist Isaac Stern, cellist Leonard Rose, and the Philadelphia Orchestra led by Eugene Ormandy.

Concertos for Piano and Orchestra (nos. 1-4)
what to buy: [Emil Gilels, piano; George Szell, cond.; Cleveland Orchestra] (EMI Classics 69506) ♪ ♪ ♪ ♪ ♪

This budget two-disc set contains positively scintillating performances. The stern Szell smiles more than usual, metaphorically speaking, in these sunny readings, and Gilels's playing sparkles with life. Tender slow movements flow with liquid grace; fast movements with a laughing lilt—and, in the C minor concerto, there is drama, neither overdone nor too restrained, along with a spectacularly emotive cadenza. These 1968 recordings at Severance Hall also show that Szell's orchestra didn't really sound as thin as it often seemed on their original Columbia releases.

Concerto no. 3 in C Minor for Piano and Orchestra, op. 37

what to buy: [Arturo Benedetti Michelangeli, piano; Carlo Maria Giulini, cond.; Vienna Philharmonic Orchestra] (Deutsche Grammophon 449757) ♪ ♪ ♪ ♪⁴

These live 1979 performances contain monumental views of Beethoven's first and third piano concertos seemingly chiseled in fine marble by the stunning technical assurance of Michelangeli and the expansiveness of Giulini. Hardly captured on the fly, the sound is of studio quality.

worth looking for: [Artur Rubinstein, piano; Arturo Toscanini, cond.; NBC Symphony Orchestra] (RCA Gold Seal 60261) ♪ ♪ ♪ ♪

Rubinstein's later performances of Beethoven's piano concertos are a bit inconsistent and often more lightweight (though some collectors will undoubtedly respond to that approach and the beauty of his tone). This radio broadcast performance from 1944, when Rubinstein was still at his technical peak, contains more verve and power in the outer movements without sacrificing that effervescent Rubinstein sparkle; the *Largo* is deliciously expressive. Toscanini is wonderfully responsive and supportive throughout. The orchestra is recorded somewhat distantly and quite one-dimensionally in the justly maligned NBC Studio 8-H, and there's surface noise from the old transcription discs, but the piano comes through clearly.

Concerto no. 4 in G Major for Piano and Orchestra, op. 58
what to buy: [Maurizio Pollini, piano; Böhm, cond.; Vienna Philharmonic Orchestra] (Deutsche Grammophon 469112) Pollini's reading is the perfect combination of brilliance and emphasis, utterly assured, flowing easily and naturally. Böhm's velvety accompaniment is perfectly complementary. The sound is crystalline and the piano/orchestra balance is more equal than in many concerto readings, although Pollini's playing is definitely the focus of attention. The performance is back in print as part of a two disc set with Pollini performing the "Waldstein" and "Tempest" sonatas, Claudio Abbado directing the Vienna Philharmonic Orchestra in the *Leonore* no. 3 Overture, the Emerson String Quartet playing the op. 59, no. 3 Quartet, and Carlos Kleiber's rendition of the Fifth Symphony with the Vienna Philharmonic Orchestra.

Concerto no. 5 in E-flat Major for Piano and Orchestra, op. 73 "Emperor"

what to buy: [Walter Gieseking, piano; Artur Rother, cond.; Greater Berlin Radio Orchestra] (Music & Arts 815) ♪ ♪ ♪ ♪ ♪

This recording is historically remarkable, a live recording from September 1944 in stereo! Its stereo character shows up not in spread, but rather in depth of sound and brilliance of tone. Beyond these sonic qualities, which make it much easier to enjoy than most contemporaneous recordings, it is notable for its combination of light-fingered grace and exuberant joy. Though it isn't note-perfect, occasional gabbles don't affect its wonderfully organic flow. The companion performance on this disc features Gieseking playing Robert Schumann's piano concerto with Wilhelm Furtwängler conducting.

[*Great Pianists of the 20th Century—Edwin Fischer II*; Edwin Fischer; Wilhelm Furtwängler, cond.; Philharmonia Orchestra] (Philips 456769) ♪ ♪ ♪ ♪ ♪

Made in 1951 at Abbey Road Studios in London, Fischer's performance is in good monaural sound. The rapport between pianist and conductor is excellent, and though Fischer has a few finger slips in the finale, the overall conception of the work is noble and majestic. This two-disc set also features the pianist playing two Beethoven sonatas (the "Appassionata" and no. 31 in A flat major), Schubert's Impromptus, op. 90, and a pair of works by Mozart—the Fantasy in C minor (K. 475) and the Concerto no. 20 in D minor for Piano and Orchestra.

Concerto in D Major for Violin and Orchestra, op. 61
what to buy: [Jascha Heifetz, violin; Charles Munch, cond.; Boston Symphony Orchestra] (RCA Living Stereo 68980) ♪ ♪ ♪ ♪ ♪

Heifetz dispatches this violinistic challenge with great aplomb (and speed: 37 minutes and 44 seconds)—nobody has ever recorded a more dazzling version, and it's hard to imagine that this recording can be improved upon at all from the soloist's standpoint. Those who say Heifetz is not profound enough must equate profundity with slow tempos. His tonal splendor is unchallenged, his intonation supernaturally accurate in even the most fiendish passages, absolutely even in the quietest moments. The cadenzas are his own elaborations of the cadenzas by Leopold Auer (his famous teacher) and Joseph Joachim (the violinist credited with making the work popular after Beethoven's death). This 1955 recording is in early but magnificent stereo. It's coupled with a

slightly less successful reading of the Mendelssohn E minor violin concerto.

[Jascha Heifetz, violin; Arturo Toscanini, cond.; NBC Symphony Orchestra] (Naxos 8.110936) ♪ ♪ ♪ ♪ ♪

Only the 1940 sound holds this back from the top recommendation. If anything, Heifetz is even sweeter and more subtle than in his later version, and Toscanini provides sensitive support.

what to buy next: [*The Art of Nathan Milstein*; Nathan Milstein, violin; Erich Leinsdorf, cond.; Philharmonia Orchestra] (EMI Classics 64830) ♪ ♪ ♪ ♪⁴

Milstein's 1961 recording is currently available only as part of this six-CD box set. It's worth seeking out, as everything on that set is up to this artist's high standards—in fact, it's a way of acquiring all at once a sizeable chunk of the important violin repertoire.

[Yehudi Menuhin, violin; Wilhelm Furtwängler, cond.; Philharmonia Orchestra] (EMI Classics 66990) ♪ ♪ ♪ ♪⁴

This 1953 recording offers much better monaural studio sound than its current discmate, the Mendelssohn E Minor Violin Concerto which they recorded a year earlier. Unsurprisingly, they offer a broad view of the piece (coming in at just over 44 minutes), yet its weight does not at all preclude grace and elegance. It's a supple and noble reading, pulsing with life and a multitude of small spontaneities. Menuhin's rich, vibrant tone is just about at its peak here, although sticklers will note occasional intonation problems. He uses Fritz Kreisler's cadenzas.

[Aaron Rosand, violin; Derrick Inouye, cond.; Monte Carlo Philharmonic Orchestra] (Vox 7902) ♪ ♪ ♪ ♪⁴

Here is a gentler and plusher version of the Heifetz view of this work, with a more natural balance between the soloist and the orchestra. Rosand has a fabulous tone, warmer than Heifetz's if less penetrating. If he's an iota short of matching Heifetz's technique, well, welcome to the club. He plays Heifetz's cadenzas, and nearly at his tempos, though he's hardly a clone and has ideas of his own, taking a little more time in the last two movements and thus making the Larghetto a bit more endearing. His finely honed Romantic sense of phrasing makes even straightforward passagework speak emotionally. Considering that this 1998 recording is on a budget label and is paired with the Brahms Violin Concerto, there's no excuse for not owning it.

[Georg Kulenkampff, violin; Hans Schmidt-Isserstedt, cond.; Berlin Philharmonic Orchestra] (Dutton Laboratories 5018) ♪♪♪♪

Kulenkampff lived only 50 years, and his career was disrupted by two World Wars. But he was a very special player, combining North German earnestness with Romantic flexibility. This 1936 recording is rather hissy, but the sound of the orchestra and the violinist himself come through. This is a big, solemn, yet enjoyably capricious reading, full of expressive touches (including juicy slides) and fine playing from both the soloist and the orchestra. This disc includes the Robert Schumann Violin Concerto and Mozart's Adagio in E major (K. 261) with the same forces.

Concerto in C Major for Violin, Cello, Piano, and Orchestra, op. 56—"Triple Concerto"
what to buy: [David Oistrakh, violin; Mstislav Rostropovich, cello; Sviatoslav Richter, piano; Herbert von Karajan, cond.; Berlin Philharmonic Orchestra] (EMI Classics 66954) ♪♪♪♪♪

This all-star session from 1969 has claimed primacy in this work for three decades now. A confluence of big talents such as this could have easily resulted in conflicting interpretations, but the Russian soloists were friends and share the spotlight equally while still playing with great expressiveness; Karajan accompanies sensitively and the Berlin Phil is supportive without being obtrusive. The result is a big bear-hug of a performance, the full and vibrant tones of cellist Rostropovich and violinist Oistrakh matched by the big sound of pianist Richter and the smooth richness of the orchestra. The coupling is the Brahms Concerto for Violin, Cello, and Orchestra, op. 102 "Double Concerto."

Chamber
Quartets for Strings (complete)
what to buy: [Talich String Quartet, ensemble] (Calliope 3633/39) ♪♪♪♪♪

For a more intimate, profound, middle-European view of the cycle, these 1977-81 recordings (on seven CDs now priced for the cost of three) are most recommendable. The Talich isn't as lively in the six op. 18 quartets as it could be, but their warm and realistically scaled performances are most apt in the middle and especially the late works. Their playing lacks the glossy finish of the

Alban Berg Quartet, (see **worth looking for:** below), but some may prefer that. The more emotional and profound the music, the higher the yield of the Talich's approach. The autobiographical slow movement of no. 15 (op. 132), *Heilige Dankgesang (Convalescent's Holy Song of Thanksgiving to the Deity),* is especially memorable, moving yet not at all melodramatic.

what to buy next: [Alexander String Quartet, ensemble] (Nova Arte 63637) ♪♪♪♪

The Alexanders present a surprisingly attractive choice for the economy-minded. Though spread across nine CDs (in close to chronological order), it's at a budget price. Nonetheless, sonic and performance standards have not been compromised. The group's style is dramatic, even muscular, yet lyrical rather than aggressive. The players are sensitive to details and provide rhythmically lively, tonally polished and structurally assured readings. Certainly these are not the most profound interpretations the quartets have received, but they're certainly visceral enough to be an exhilarating introduction for neophytes looking for a cheap but high-quality integral set.

worth looking for: [Alban Berg Quartet, ensemble] (EMI Classics 54587) ♪♪♪♪♪

[Alban Berg Quartet, ensemble] (EMI Classics 54592) ♪♪♪♪♪

Recording the complete string quartets in concert at the Vienna Konzerthaus in 1989 bore excellent fruit for the ABQ. This pair of four-CD sets finds the group responding to Beethoven's masterful works with freshness, spontaneity, and a winning mixture of relaxed ease and dramatic intensity. There is a degree of suspense rare in such familiar repertoire, the group's strong concentration holding together some daring conceptions and keeping some slow tempos effectively tensile. None of this in-the-moment inspiration comes at the expense of the ABQ's seductive tonal sheen or telepathic precision. The quartets are presented out of chronological sequence, not ideal from a scholarly view but allowing a more varied listening experience. Their concert origin doesn't diminish the recording quality in the slightest.

Quartets for Strings, opps. 127 and 135
what to buy: [*Beethoven: The Late String Quartets;* Budapest String Quartet, ensemble] (Bridge 9072) ♪♪♪♪

This is not drawn from any of the Budapest's three studio Beethoven cycles, but rather from a vast collection of live performances at the Library of Congress, where they were able to use the Library's matched set of Stradivarius instruments. The concert readings preserved here have a special aura about them. The earliest of them—opp. 135 and 131 (1943) and op. 127 (1941)—include second violinist Alexander Schneider in his first period with the group, generally considered its peak. Op. 132 from 1945, with Edgar Ortenberg, is hardly less inspired. Schneider was back for the 1960 recordings of opp. 130 and 133 (the *Great Fugue*), with the decline in technical facility offset by an incredible intensity and excitement.

Trios for Piano, Violin, and Cello (complete)
what to buy: [Beaux Arts Trio, ensemble] (Philips 432381) ♪ ♪ ♪ ♪ ♪

The Beaux Arts Trio presents suave, finely textured readings. Their lyricism in these works is unsurpassed; their teamwork, uncanny blend, and depth of interpretation are unattainable by all-star trios that don't work together steadily. This five-disc, mid-priced set also contains trio arrangements of larger works, including Beethoven's Second Symphony.

Sonatas for Piano (complete)
what to buy: [*The Complete Piano Sonatas*; Richard Goode, piano] (Nonesuch 79328) ♪ ♪ ♪ ♪ ♪

The Beethoven piano sonatas remain, as Artur Schnabel so memorably said, "better than they can be played." No performance can reveal all the facets of a given sonata, and no complete set will ever be ideal, but this cycle certainly comes close. Goode's reasonable, uneccentric interpretations make his set easy to listen to repeatedly, yet his playing reveals many felicities; he presents the music in such an ego-less way that we are never overtly conscious of particular interpretive stances. There is "Horowitz's Beethoven" and "Rubinstein's Beethoven" and even "Richter's Beethoven," but the transparency of Goode's approach seemingly reveals only "Beethoven's Beethoven." His playing has great tonal allure, his dynamic range and control are precise and well judged, his overall spans evince great structural integrity, and the sound is natural and well captured. He sometimes takes relaxed, even spacious tempos, but without exaggeration or extremes. In many pieces there are greater—or at least more striking—individual performances available, but no other complete set surpasses his

consistency at such a high level of skill and intelligence.

[Vladimir Ashkenazy, piano] (London 443706) ♪ ♪ ♪ ♪ ♪

Ashkenazy's 10-CD set, recorded over the years 1971-81, is nearly as recommendable as Goode's, with only one flawed performance (plus a few sonic problems) but some higher peaks. Ashkenazy plays with a very attractive poise in the early sonatas, rhythmically flexible and ruminative enough to keep them from seeming shallow, yet without inflating them to the proportions of Beethoven's later styles. In the "Pathétique," his refusal to milk the Adagio cantabile with a mournfully slow tempo is refreshing. The "Waldstein" is impressively poetic, the *Appassionata* is overflowing with powerful, finely balanced feeling, and the finale of "Les Adieux" features some dazzlingly quicksilver runs. The only serious misstep is his "Hammerklavier," where he pulls the tempo around erratically in the first movement and doesn't achieve real coherence until the final movement. Otherwise, in the late works, Ashkenazy's mix of power and poetry, grace and dignity, serves him well. These are profound interpretations yet pulsing with rhythmic life. Alas, nos. 30 (jangly piano) and 32 (muddy, boomy bass) are sonically flawed.

what to buy next: [Alfred Brendel, piano] (Philips 446909) ♪ ♪ ♪ ♪

Brendel is the digital-era Schnabel, a bit more cautious (or, one could say, considerably more precise and note-accurate) and less soulful, but every bit as cerebral, offering readings that are the sonic equivalents of dissections. In this 10-CD 1992-96 cycle, he lays bare Beethoven's structures and materials, yet also plays with beautiful tone, including creamy legato in slow movements. This cycle is not without its flaws, though most are more a matter of taste than of miscues. While there is often intensity in Brendel's interpretations, it seems rather generalized. More specifically, the opening movement of his "Hammerklavier" is rather less headlong than some might prefer, not so much in its tempo as in its many rhythmic hesitations; his "Appassionata," though powerful, is inaptly dispassionate. However, Brendel finds great tenderness in the slow movements of the early sonatas, his "Pastoral" ambles nicely, he delineates the variation movements in the late sonatas with ample character, and his readings of sonatas nos. 30 and 31 rank among the finest ever. Quibbles aside, this set contains relatively consistent Beethoven playing on a very high level.

[*Beethoven: The 32 Piano Sonatas*; Artur Schnabel, piano] (EMI Classics 63765) ♪ ♪ ♪ ♪

Schnabel, a Mozart/Beethoven/Schubert specialist, was the first pianist to record all of the 32. Despite some fumbles, to be expected in 1930s recordings (furthermore, he was past his technical prime by then), he set the interpretive standard, always capturing a seemingly ideal mood. His playing is often severe, but always intelligent, and exudes great integrity—he never "plays it safe" when that would compromise his vision of Beethoven's intent. This set influenced several generations of pianists. Although it can't be a primary recommendation because of the wrong notes and the sound, no dedicated Beethovenian should be without this set.

[*Beethoven: The Piano Sonatas, volume 1*; Robert Taub, piano] (Vox Classics 7514) ♪ ♪ ♪ ♪
[*Beethoven: The Piano Sonatas, volume 2*; Robert Taub, piano] (Vox Classics 7529) ♪ ♪ ♪ ♪
[*Beethoven: The Piano Sonatas, volume 3*; Robert Taub, piano] (Vox Classics 7532) ♪ ♪ ♪ ♪
[*Beethoven: The Piano Sonatas, volume 4*; Robert Taub, piano] (Vox Classics 7544) ♪ ♪ ♪ ♪
[*Beethoven: The Piano Sonatas, volume 5*; Robert Taub, piano] (Vox Classics 7549) ♪ ♪ ♪ ♪

This budget-priced series of five two-CD sets would be recommendable at two or three times the cost, for Robert Taub is an excellent pianist who has many insights into this cycle. His readings are consistently thoughtful and also have great tonal allure (well captured by the recording quality). There are a few missteps (the "Hammerklavier" is a bit untidy, and the rhythms in no. 32 are sometimes oddly jerky), but many more moments of great felicity, with "name" highlights including the "Moonlight," "Tempest," and "Waldstein." Nos. 30 and 31 are also excellent.

Sonata no. 21 in C Major for Piano, op. 53— "Waldstein"
what to buy: [Maurizio Pollini, piano] (Deutsche Grammophon 435472) ♪ ♪ ♪ ♪

This disc of 1997 live performances (also including Piano Sonatas nos. 11 and 12) finds Pollini playing with more warmth and emotion than he is known for. Imbuing the two earlier works with wit and lightness at times and with passionate intensity at others, he then plays the

"Waldstein" with tightrope bravura in a reading that takes risks successfully and carries the extra frisson of the concert hall. This release includes Deutsche Grammophon's CD-ROM feature "CD-pluscore," with musical scores of the sonatas that can be synchronized with Pollini's performances, along with analysis and other articles.

Sonata no. 23 in F Minor for Piano, op. 57— *Appassionata*
what to buy: [Stephen Kovacevich] (EMI Classics 56965) ♪ ♪ ♪ ♪

Kovacevich's gradually accumulating cycle of the Beethoven Sonatas has been uneven, but this 2001 release (also including sonatas nos. 4, 22, and 25) is an absolute winner. Even though it's a studio recording, it has the spontaneous, on-the-edge feeling of a concert performance, nowhere more so than in the outer movements of the "Appassionata," seemingly about to explode as the torrents of notes unfurl at a furious pace, yet held together (without a dampening aura of safeness) by Kovacevich's brilliant technique. The middle movement proceeds at a faster pace than the norm, lending its relative repose an element of suspenseful tension.

[*Broadcast Recordings from the Hessian Radio (Frankfurt)*; Walter Gieseking, piano] (Music & Arts 1074) ♪ ♪ ♪ ♪

Found on a double-CD, Gieseking's 1947 reading of the "Appassionata" fully explains his reputation in a way that his later studio recordings for EMI do not. He has the lightest touch even in technically demanding passages, producing a glistening tone. Yet this is a passionate performance, balanced on a knife's edge. Amazing.

Sonata no. 29 in B-flat Major for Piano, op. 106— "Hammerklavier"
what to buy: [Sviatoslav Richter, piano] (BBC Legends 4052) ♪ ♪ ♪ ♪ ♪

In Richter's hands at the 1975 Aldeburgh Festival, the mighty "Hammerklavier" is given a reading that fully lives up to Beethoven's designation of it as a "Grand Sonata." It is not note-perfect, but as a historical recording not released until after Richter's death, this has none of the studio fixes so common on "live" recordings nowadays. Anyone knowing how taxing a work this is to perform will admire the combination of technical skill and endurance on display in the final movement, in which Richter goes for broke and succeeds brilliantly. In the slow movement, he takes a somewhat broad tempo (though others have brought it in as much as four minutes slower), yet there is not the least slackening of tension—the normal passage of time seems suspended as the lines are spun out inexorably, with nearly overwhelming emotion. Beethoven's third sonata is played in a later, heavier style, yet Richter, unlike most pianists, manages to bring off the transformation. Also included is a charming reading of three of the six Bagatelles, op. 126 (nos. 1, 4, 6). It remains only to be said that, drawn from the BBC archives, the sound quality of this concert recording is wonderful.

Sonatas for Piano, nos. 28–32 (selections)—*The Late Piano Sonatas*
what to buy: [*Richter in Leipzig—The 28 November 1963 Recital at the Leipzig Gewandhaus*; Sviatoslav Richter, piano] (Music & Arts 1025) ♪ ♪ ♪ ♪ ♪

Beethoven's final three piano sonatas form the bulk of this album. In all of Richter's playing on this CD, there's keen focus and a constant awareness of the long line. His articulation is impeccably clear without being mannered; his tone has a legendary fullness and liquid legato. In 1963 he was still at his formidable technical peak, and while the sound is monaural (with some audience noise), that's no barrier to enjoyment. There's some tape noticeable flutter in the third movement of no. 30, but this Olympian performance deserves to be heard. Richter's program also contains a trio of works by Brahms (op. 118, nos. 3 and 8 and op. 119, no. 3) and one of Chopin's Nocturnes (op. 15, no. 1).

what to buy next: [*Beethoven: The Late Piano Sonatas*; Maurizio Pollini, piano] (Deutsche Grammophon 449740) ♪ ♪ ♪ ♪₄

Pollini can lack the unbridled passion necessary for the middle-period sonatas, but in these late sonatas that's less of a concern. Here his superb structural understanding and objectivity are apt, while his brilliant tone keeps this still-challenging music from seeming dry. Pollini's recording of the A major Sonata (op. 101) is especially effective.

various "name" sonata collections
what to buy: [*Beethoven: Favourite Piano Sonatas*; Vladimir Ashkenazy, piano] (Decca 452952) ♪ ♪ ♪ ♪ ♪

The "named" sonatas are the most popular ones with the public, and this two-disc set with the "Pathétique," "Moonlight," "Pastoral," "Tempest," "Waldstein," "Appassionata," and "Les Adieux" sonatas will appeal to those who don't want to invest in Ashkenazy's complete set. He delivers impeccable readings of great power but also, where needed, lyricism.

what to buy next: [Rudolf Serkin, piano] (Sony Classics 37219) ♪ ♪ ♪ ♪

Serious, sober, but more note-accurate than Schnabel (and in stereo), Serkin leaves no doubt as to the greatness and depth of this music, yet there is also a welcome plasticity in his phrasing which transcends mere pedantry. This CD contains his renditions of the "Pathétique," "Moonlight," and "Appassionata" sonatas. It's unfortunate that Sony has not kept more of his work in print; one can only hope that the centenary of his birth in 2003 will bring a comprehensive edition.

various piano sonatas
what to buy: [Sviatoslav Richter, piano] (Praga 354022/25) ♪ ♪ ♪ ♪ ♪

This four-CD set obviously doesn't include all of the piano sonatas, (it only has nos. 3, 7, 12, 17, 18, 23, 27, 28, 29, and 31 plus the Diabelli Variations) but it does contain possibly the best Beethoven playing any pianist has ever committed to record. It consists entirely of performances taped at concerts in Prague, and like Schnabel, Richter willingly risks all in the service of his vision—but unlike Schnabel, his astounding technique is such that even in unedited live recordings, mistakes are mostly insignificant (except for a momentary lapse in the "Hammerklavier." Richter's "Appassionata"—long a specialty—is particularly spectacular here, arguably his best. It bears out the work's "name" as much as any performance ever has. The old argument that this is how Beethoven would have wanted the sonatas to sound, if he'd had at his disposal a modern grand piano, all of a sudden seems entirely plausible. More than any other pianist, Richter nearly refutes Schnabel's conviction that the sonatas are "better than they can be played." There are other fine Richter performances, but on this set Richter reaches the highest peaks. Unlike some of the Richter material Praga has issued, the sound quality is fine on all selections.

Sonatas for Violin and Piano (complete)
what to buy: [*Beethoven: Complete Violin Sonatas*;

Aaron Rosand, violin; Eileen Flissler, piano] (Vox 3503) ♪ ♪ ♪ ♪ ♪

Rosand studied with Efrem Zimbalist and carries on that great Romantic tradition. His tone is gorgeously rich and colorful, his phrasing expressive but never exaggerated. In these 1995 recordings, he is naturally and appropriately balanced with the pianist. These warm, nobly affectionate readings are unsurpassed in the stereo era for both discernment and style.

what to buy next: [Wolfgang Schneiderhan, violin; Wilhelm Kempff, piano] (Deutsche Grammophon 463605) ♪ ♪ ♪ ♪

For the German view of these works, this 1952 cycle is most recommendable, its monaural sound no hindrance—in fact, it's marvelously focused. Schneiderhan is in the tradition of Joachim and Busch, but with sweeter tone and excellent technical precision (even in pizzicato passages often merely approximated); his playing is serious, even intellectual, yet flows with organic ease. Kempff is a marvelous partner (only slightly subordinated in the recording balance), his lightness of touch combining with Schneiderhan's keen focus to keep the proceedings from becoming too weighty.

worth looking for: [Jascha Heifetz, violin; Emmanuel Bay, piano; Brooks Smith, piano] (RCA Gold Seal 61747) ♪ ♪ ♪ ♪⅛

Not all of Beethoven's sonatas for violin and piano are really meant to showcase the violin, and in none is the piano less than an equal partner. But in these performances by Heifetz, that all goes by the board. He's the star, he's the focus, and frankly many listeners have been conditioned to accept it—with playing this preternaturally perfect, it's understandable. The sound is fine studio monaural.

various sonatas for violin and piano
what to buy: [*Artur Rubinstein Collection, vol. 40: Beethoven Violin Sonatas*; Henryk Szeryng, violin; Artur Rubinstein, piano] (RCA Red Seal 63040) ♪ ♪ ♪ ♪ ♪

This set stars not the pianist (whose solo Beethoven playing could sometimes sound freakishly Chopin-like) but the underrated violin virtuoso Henryk Szeryng. Long known for his magnificent and subtly colored tonal production, he was at his peak in these 1958 and 1961 recordings of Beethoven's three most popular violin

sonatas, nos. 5 ("Spring"), 8, and 9 ("Kreutzer"). Szeryng's playing is so supernal that one deeply regrets that this collaboration did not extend to the other seven sonatas; it could have been the finest set ever recorded. There are many small but telling inflections in these lovingly tender yet rhythmically lively readings, but never anything that interferes with the organic unfolding of the composer's conceptions or calls attention unduly to the players—beyond the rapturous beauty of their tone.

Vocal
Missa Solemnis in D Major, op. 123
what to buy: [Charlotte Margiono, soprano; Catherine Robbin, mezzo-soprano; William Kendall, tenor; Alistair Miles, bass; John Eliot Gardiner, cond.; English Baroque Soloists, orch.; Monteverdi Choir] (Deutsche Grammophon Archiv 429779) ♪ ♪ ♪ ♪⅛

There have been very few totally successful performances of this immensely ambitious yet structurally troubled work; it's practically a rule of thumb that readings that require two CDs can hold attention only intermittently (not to mention taxing the endurance of the choir). Gardiner, in a period performance, brings the piece in at a mere 71 minutes and 39 seconds. It's tremendously thrilling, although a bit of a slowdown right at the end could have mitigated the abrupt ending. The sound is also excellent.

[Julia Varady, soprano; Iris Vermillion, mezzo-soprano; Vinson Cole, tenor; René Pape, bass; Georg Solti, cond.; Berlin Philharmonic Orchestra; Berlin Radio Choir] (London 444337) ♪ ♪ ♪ ♪⅛

For an equally thrilling ride through this work (also in excellent sound), with even better soloists (Varady is spectacular) and one of the best orchestral readings on modern instruments, Solti's Berlin version can't be beat. At 77:16, he takes longer than Gardiner, but just about everybody does. This is a performance of high drama. Stay away from Solti's Chicago version, which can't touch this one.

[Elisabeth Söderström, soprano; Marga Höffgen, contralto; Waldemar Kmentt, tenor; Martti Talvela, bass; Otto Klemperer, cond.; New Philharmonia Orchestra; New Philharmonia Chorus] (EMI Classics 67547) ♪ ♪ ♪ ♪⅛

This comes on two CDs coupled with the same Choral Fantasia found in the EMI Klemperer box of the symphonies and piano concertos, but it didn't have to:

Klemperer, belying his reputation as a plodder, takes 79 minutes in this 1965 recording. The soloists are uniformly good if not great, the recording perspective is odd at times (not only up-front soloists, but also some surprising spotlighting of instruments), the choir is excellent but not always favored by the miking. But the attraction here is the conductor. Klemperer shows that it's possible to deliver a truly monumental and weighty (yet also visceral and stirring) reading in less than 80 minutes.

what to buy next: [Rosa Mannion, soprano; Birgit Remmert, contralto; James Taylor, tenor; Cornelius Hauptmann, bass; Philippe Herreweghe, cond.; Orchestre des Champs-Elysées; La Chapelle Royale Chorus, Paris; Collegium Vocale, choir] (Harmonia Mundi 901557) ♪ ♪ ♪ ♪

Herreweghe favors a lean (but hardly scrawny) orchestral sonority using period instruments, but with more weight at moments of dramatic emphasis. The choir is recorded moderately closely, providing clarity and preventing the singers from being buried behind the orchestra (which is miked more naturally). The solo quartet is fine (though recorded unevenly, it seems, and less forwardly than usual) and generally avoids sounding overly operatic, though Mannion's vibrato is perhaps too intense. Herreweghe excels at bringing out the intimate, introverted nature of the work. This is recommended for those who don't want slow tempos (he brings it in a bit over 77 minutes on a single disc) yet prefer religious music to sound more devotional than dramatic.

[*Immortal Toscanini, Vol. 3*; Lois Marshall, soprano; Nan Merriman, mezzo-soprano; Eugene Conley, tenor; Jerome Hines, bass; Arturo Toscanini, cond.; NBC Symphony Orchestra; Robert Shaw Chorale] (RCA Victor Red Seal 55837) ♪ ♪ ♪ ♪

This 1953 recording is worrisome in a few moments of the Kyrie when the dynamics overpower the microphones, making the singers sound deadened and distorted. Aside from that, the sound (at Carnegie Hall) is fairly good, if perhaps too closely recorded. Toscanini's brisk pace gets him through this massive work in under 75 minutes and greatly increases its dramatic impact. The brass are so strongly weighted, whether by playing or miking, that Toscanini seems to anticipate one of the primary effects of "original instrument" interpretations. The chorus, prepared by Robert Shaw, is magnificent, singing with precision and intensity. The soloists are not well matched—in particular, Marshall and Merriman

have wildly different vibratos, and the men, particularly Conley, are overwhelmed by the women—but are more than adequate. The orchestra plays at the peak of its considerable powers. Most of all, though, it is Toscanini's taut and detailed shaping of the structure and dynamics which makes this a classic recording (now coupled with the composer's Ninth Symphony on a two-CD set with improved sound compared to previous issues).

[Martina Arroyo, soprano; Maureen Forrester, mezzo-soprano; Richard Lewis, tenor; Cesare Siepi, bass-baritone; Eugene Ormandy, cond.; Philadelphia Orchestra; Singing City Choirs] (Sony Classics 53517) ♪ ♪ ♪ ♪

Ormandy also generally gets the proportions and tempos right, and his single CD is even a budget-priced offering. At a bit over 76 minutes, he never seems rushed. The solo quartet is excellent, dramatic but without exaggeration, and the orchestra offers possibly the best playing these instrumental parts have ever had. The chorus, however, is not much more than adequate, though the distant, mushy recording may account for some of the lack of detail.

[Heather Harper, soprano; Janet Baker, mezzo-soprano; Robert Tear, tenor; Hans Sotin, bass; Carlo Maria Giulini, cond.; London Philharmonic Orchestra; New Philharmonia Chorus] (EMI Classics Special Import 69440) ♪ ♪ ♪ ♪

Collectors who prefer a slow reading of the *Missa Solemnis* will appreciate this two-CD set. Giulini's performance lasts nearly 88 minutes but has a certain inner glow, and Harper and Baker are wonderful. It is coupled with a similarly devotional reading of the earlier Mass in C major, op. 86 (also with Baker, but with Elly Ameling, Theo Altmeyer and Marius Rintzler as the other soloists).

Fidelio
what to buy: [Christa Ludwig, mezzo-soprano; Ingeborg Hallstein, soprano; Jon Vickers, tenor; Gerhard Unger, tenor; Gottlob Frick, bass; Walter Berry, bass; Franz Crass, bass; Kurt Wehofschitz, tenor; Raymond Wolansky, baritone; Otto Klemperer, cond; Philharmonia Orchestra and Chorus] (EMI Classics 67361) ♪ ♪ ♪ ♪ ♪

Ludwig is a wonderfully believable Leonore. Vickers as Florestan is perhaps a bit over-the-top in interpretation but in fine voice. Frick is effective as Rocco, and Berry is a less evil and perhaps more realistic (if less dramatic) Pizarro. Hallstein is an aptly girlish Marzelline. The other soloists are also fine. Klemperer is hardly a fiery conductor in this music, but at this stage (1962) he had not yet settled into the turgid tempos of his last years, and his long history with this music—early in his career, he was primarily known as an opera conductor—and with drama in general, informs his knowing interpretation. The studio recording is in fine, detailed sound.

what to buy next: [Kirsten Flagstad, soprano; Elisabeth Schwarzkopf, soprano; Julius Patzak, tenor; Paul Schöffler, tenor; Anton Dermota, tenor; Hermann Gallos, tenor; Hans Braun, bass; Josef Greindl, bass; Ljubomir Pantscheff, bass; Wilhelm Furtwängler, cond.; Vienna Philharmonic Orchestra; Vienna State Opera Choir] (Opera d'Oro 1281) ♪ ♪ ♪ ♪

Recorded at the 1950 Salzburg Festival, this is a strongly, lovingly molded performance featuring superb singers in the main roles: Flagstad as Leonore, Patzak as a stunning Florestan, Schöffler as a malevolent Pizarro, and Greindl as a convincingly rough-hewn Rocco. Despite rather dim sound on this radio recording of the concert, this is greatly to be preferred to the studio version without dialog Furtwängler made three years later. Here, events flow more logically, shaped organically with Furtwängler's usual skillful plasticity.

[Birgit Nilsson, soprano; Graziella Sciutti, soprano; James McCracken, tenor; Donald Grobe, tenor; Kurt Equiluz, tenor; Tom Krause, baritone; Hermann Prey, baritone; Kurt Böhme, bass; Günther Adam, singer; Lorin Maazel, cond.; Vienna Philharmonic Orchestra; Vienna State Opera Choir] (Decca 448104) ♪ ♪ ♪ ♪

Though a studio recording, this 1964 effort has the sonic effects of a stage production, but with natural, well-balanced sound and no extraneous noises. Maazel has a taut, forward-moving view of the drama. The cast, if not starry throughout, is quite consistent. Nilsson is a most heroic and noble Leonore/Fidelio, McCracken a powerful Florestan, Krause a darkly threatening yet believable rather than cartoonish Pizarro. Böhme is a bit guttural as Rocco, but then, that character need not always make beautiful sounds. Sciutti is a bit weak as Marzelline, but acts well; Grobe is an adequate Jaquino, while Prey as Don Fernando and Equiluz as the First Prisoner are much more than that. At the two-for-one price, this set offers a clearly defined alternative to Klemperer's set of similar vintage among stereo versions. Alas, no libretto, especially missed since Maazel includes most, though not all, of the dialog.

influences: Franz Joseph Haydn, Luigi Cherubini, Muzio Clementi

Steve Holtje

Vincenzo Bellini

Born November 3, 1801, in Catania, Sicily. Died September 23, 1835, in Puteaux, France.

period: Classical/Romantic

Although he began his career as a serious composer at the same time that Gioachino Rossini and Gaetano Donizetti were producing their own masterpieces, Bellini created operas (most notably *Norma* and *I Puritani*) that anticipated the Romantic movement, imbuing his works with sensuous melodies while infusing emotion and drama into the vocal line. In many ways he also serves as the pivot upon which Italian opera spins away from the relatively frivolous plotlines used by Rossini and toward the dramatically consistent character portrayals of Giuseppe Verdi.

Bellini's father was an organist and maestro d'cappella who dabbled in writing small works for use in church services. His son displayed musical talent at a fairly early age, having written his first score when he was six years old, and composed a number of technically competent pieces for the church. All of this artistic activity helps to explain why, in 1819, Bellini was sent to the Real Collegio di Musica in Naples, where he immersed himself in musical studies for six years, courtesy of a financial grant from the city council of Catania, his home town. Despite his natural talents, Bellini took a relatively long time to develop into a finished composer, especially when compared to the preternaturally gifted (and prolific) Rossini, who had already written more than a dozen operas before reaching his mid-twenties. In contrast, Bellini's first opera (*Adelson e Salvini*) was a graduation exercise and wasn't performed until just before the composer turned twenty-four years old.

Il Pirata, the first of Bellini's operas to receive a modicum of international approval, had its initial performance at Milan's La Scala in the fall of 1827. Its success opened the door to a credible career as a composer, but Bellini's almost painfully slow method of working meant that he charged impresarios progressively more for his projects. This fact probably troubled some of his employers at first but, upon counting their receipts from each succeeding production, it was not enough to stop them from funding his operations. His escalating pricing structure and the success of such operas as *La Straniera, Zaira,* and *I Capuleti e i Montecchi* paved the way for *La Sonnambula* and what many critics acclaim as the preeminent bel canto vehicle, *Norma*.

A genuine masterpiece of the nineteenth century, *Norma,* the story of a Druid priestess who bears two children by an enemy's general, is both a lament and a paean to womanhood with the *Casta diva* aria proving itself to be one of the finest vocal moments in opera. Unveiled at La Scala on December 26, 1831, *Norma* started off inauspiciously but picked up more and more admirers as the performances continued and improved. By now, Bellini's fame was quite substantial and a minirevival of his operas was taking place all over Italy. This was to spread to Paris and London when, in 1833, the composer took a trip to these European capitals for the purpose of securing more performances of his works. London audiences proved especially hospitable, with the staging of *Il Pirata, Norma, La Sonnambula,* and *I Capuleti* shortly after his arrival in late April, drawing large crowds despite a generally lukewarm reception by the critics.

Bellini's last completed opera, *I Puritani,* was intended for Paris, where it garnered much acclaim at its opening on January 24, 1835. By this time Bellini was a bankable property, and contract talks with assorted venues in France, where he had been living for two years, and various Neapolitan impresarios, were fast and furious. It seemed as though his career was on an upward spiral. Sadly, all of this activity was cut short in September of that year, when Bellini died. There is an apocryphal story that ties his death to three weeks of dysentery, but an autopsy found that his liver was abscessed and his large intestine was ulcerous.

As a composer Bellini subtly and carefully crafted the music to more purposefully follow the singer's words and emotions. He also capitalized on a relatively new singing technique: bel canto. This was an ideal that called for an enormous vocal range (especially in the high end) and florid, emotional embellishments that would show off the singer's ability to navigate a thicket of notes with conviction and control.

Vocal
Norma
what to buy: [Maria Callas, soprano; Christa Ludwig, mezzo-soprano; Franco Corelli, tenor; Nicola Zaccharia,

bass; Tullio Serafin, cond.; La Scala Orchestra; La Scala Chorus] (EMI Classics 66428) ♪♪♪♪♪

In the 1950s, most bel canto music was under-represented on opera stages. Maria Callas, however, with formidable technique and the dramatic accomplishment of a Sarah Bernhardt, turned her attention to these types of works. Of her several recordings in it, this is the most rewarding; first, because the voice was still at its peak, and second, because of the presence of Franco Corelli, an inspired Pollione.

what to buy next: [Joan Sutherland, soprano; Marilyn Horne, mezzo-soprano; Yvonne Minton, mezzo-soprano; John Alexander, tenor; Joseph Ward, tenor; Richard Cross, bass; Richard Bonynge, cond.; London Symphony Orchestra; London Symphony Orchestra Chorus] (London 425488) ♪♪♪♪♪

Recorded in 1964 when Sutherland's vocal prowess was at a technical peak, this performance has a lot going for it, though not enough in the acting department to take anything away from Callas's achievement cited above. While Sutherland is the star of the production, the rest of the cast also sings at a high level. Especially notable are Horne in her role as Adalgisa and Alexander's portrayal of Pollione.

[Joan Sutherland, soprano; Montserrat Caballé, soprano; Diana Montague, mezzo-soprano; Luciano Pavarotti, tenor; Kim Begley, tenor; Samuel Ramey, bass; Richard Bonynge, cond.; Welsh National Opera Orchestra; Welsh National Opera Chorus] (London 414476) ♪♪♪♪♪

Six years can make a difference in the human voice, and Sutherland's performance here is a perfect example. While she could still summon up a great sonic presence when needed, the consistent ability to hit the upper end of the range had diminished, a fact acknowledged by the *Casta diva* and *Mira, o Norma* duets, which were transposed to a more forgiving key. Pavarotti was a fine Pollione but the best-performed role in the set belongs to Caballé, whose secure intonation and characterization of Adalgisa is nothing short of superb.

I Puritani
worth looking for: [Joan Sutherland, soprano; Luciano Pavarotti, tenor; Piero Cappuccilli, baritone; Nicolai Ghiaurov, bass; Richard Bonynge, cond.; London Symphony Orchestra; London Symphony Orchestra Chorus] (London 417588) ♪♪♪♪♪

The blending of Joan Sutherland and Luciano Pavarotti makes this set a must-have for opera fans. During the 1970s when this performance was recorded, Pavarotti was a masterful vocalist whose singing masked his weak acting skills, and Sutherland was in top form. The pairing found the two of them flinging glorious notes about on great, youthful gusts of air.

influences: Gioachino Rossini, Gaetano Donizetti, Giuseppe Verdi

Michael H. Margolin and Garaud MacTaggart

Robert Russell Bennett

Born June 15, 1894, in Kansas City, MO. Died August 18, 1981, in New York City, NY.

period: Twentieth century

Bennett was one of the most successful Broadway and Hollywood orchestrators, writing arrangements for Jerome Kern, George Gershwin, Cole Porter, and Richard Rodgers. He also composed his own concert music, including a fine Violin Concerto that dates from 1941, but he remains best known to modern audiences for *A Symphonic Picture of Porgy and Bess,* where he rearranged elements of Gershwin's score, and for his work on the 1952 television series *Victory at Sea.*

Robert Russell Bennett began his musical studies with piano lessons from his mother, a prominent local pianist and teacher, and trumpet and violin lessons from his father, a professional musician who worked with the Kansas City Symphony. At the age of twenty-two, Bennett moved to New York City, finding employment as a dance-band musician and music copyist at G. Schirmer prior to working as an arranger for the T.B. Harms publishing firm. The latter experience proved valuable when he began working on Broadway shows, and he eventually orchestrated over 200 musicals. His Broadway arranging credits include Irving Berlin's *Annie Get Your Gun* (1946), George Gershwin's *Of Thee I Sing* (1931), Jerome Kern's *Show Boat* (1927), Frederick Loewe's *My Fair Lady* (1956) and *Camelot* (1960), Cole Porter's *Anything Goes* (1934) and *Kiss Me, Kate* (1948), and Richard Rodgers's *Oklahoma!* (1943), *South Pacific* (1949), *The King and I* (1951), and *The Sound of Music* (1959).

From 1936 to 1940, Bennett lived in Hollywood, where he arranged music for more than thirty films, including

Alfred Newman's score for *The Hunchback of Notre Dame* and Franz Waxman's score for *Rebecca.* Bennett received an Oscar in 1955 for his work on the film adaptation of *Oklahoma!* A testament to Bennett's preeminence as an arranger was a commission from conductor Fritz Reiner. After the successful revival of Gershwin's *Porgy and Bess* in 1942, Reiner asked Bennett to prepare a concert suite. This work, *A Symphonic Picture of Porgy and Bess,* was given its premiere by Reiner and the Pittsburgh Symphony in 1943 and quickly became the standard suite from the opera, even though Gershwin had prepared his own symphonic suite, *Catfish Row.*

The differences between these two versions are many and reflect the differing perspectives of composer and arranger. Bennett tended to ignore the purely orchestral passages in favor of the popular songs. While he included the hurricane music, its performance was optional, and the unity and flow of Gershwin's opera was lacking. Where Gershwin himself thought in terms of an orchestral suite drawn from his opera, Bennett put together a popular medley. It is a lighter suite, eminently listenable and quite popular in concert performances.

What of Bennett's own music? From 1926 to 1931, he lived in Europe, where he held two Guggenheim Fellowships and studied with Nadia Boulanger, the great French pedagogue who taught such American composers as Aaron Copland and Virgil Thomson. Bennett completed his first symphony and the *Charleston Rhapsody* while working with her. Over time he composed six more symphonies, two operas, a ballet-operetta, scores for band or wind ensemble, and a host of chamber works. Bennett's concert music shows a love of Americana, using a language that encompasses both classical and popular idioms. The harmonies can be adventuresome, but they never stray too far from the conventional, while the popular idioms anchor the pieces in a way that makes them buoyant, lyrical, and at times, dramatic.

Orchestral
Symphonic Songs for Band
what to buy: [*Winds of Change: American Music for Wind Ensemble from the 1950s to the 1970s*; John P. Paynter, cond.; Northwestern University Symphonic Wind Ensemble, orch.] (New World 80211) ♪ ♪ ♪ ♪₄

Bennett's three-movement suite for wind band is both charming and substantial, and this performance by Paynter's collegiate ensemble is wonderful. Also included in this anthology are works by Vincent Persichetti, Hale Smith, Ross Lee Finney, and Henry Brant.

various orchestral arrangements

what to buy: [Robert Russell Bennett, cond.; RCA Victor Symphony Orchestra] (RCA Victor 68334) ♪ ♪ ♪

Overall, this is a fairly good recording of works by Leonard Bernstein and George Gershwin, some of which received Bennett's touch as an arranger or conductor. The album is one of those compilations with snippets from various sources, which is why some works are conducted by Arthur Fiedler. One of Bennett's Gershwin treatments, the *Symphonic Picture of Porgy and Bess,* is reason enough to pick up this budget-priced disc.

what to buy next: [*Richard Rodgers: Victory at Sea*; Robert Russell Bennett, cond.; RCA Victor Symphony Orchestra] (RCA Victor 60963) ♪ ♪

This is the best-selling soundtrack to the 1952 television series for which Richard Rodgers wrote the music. Bennett's arrangements are quite good, even if the material isn't the best of Rodgers's work.

influences: Richard Addinsell, Max Steiner

Frank Retzel

Alban Berg

Born Alban Maria Johannes Berg on February 9, 1885, in Vienna, Austria. Died December 24, 1935, in Vienna, Austria.

period: Twentieth century

To say that Alban Berg was merely one of Schoenberg's prize pupils would be to miss the importance of their unique interaction: their relationship was lifelong, if somewhat prickly at times, and the mutual effect was enormous. Along with Anton Webern, Berg was one of the most prominent of Arnold Schoenberg's students. While these three composers are collectively referred to as the *Second Viennese School,* Berg was the only one who was eventually able to live on his royalties as a composer. He remains the most popular member of the trio, and his best known works include a violin concerto and the operas *Wozzeck* and *Lulu.*

As a teenager Berg composed some songs to romantic texts, and on the basis of this work Schoenberg accepted him for study without fee in 1904. That same year,

Anton Webern also began taking lessons with the master. The pioneering achievements of Schoenberg, Berg, and Webern can almost be seen as a three-way collaboration, since they seem to have shared an artistic vision, although Schoenberg would always be the dominant force. He was, after all, older than Berg or Webern and had already established himself as a composer. While Schoenberg's revolutionary ideas and concepts provided a path for the future, Berg developed his own mastery of technique, and his scores reflect his unique creativity. As Schoenberg's student, Berg composed the *Seven Early Songs,* the Piano Sonata, op. 1, the *Four Songs,* op. 2, and the String Quartet, op. 3. Berg's financial situation greatly improved in 1906 when his mother inherited a substantial real estate holding in Vienna. Since the management duties fell to him, however, he did not have as much free time for composing as he would have liked.

In 1911 Berg married Helene Nahowski and began working at the music publisher Universal Editions, where his tasks included preparing piano reductions (Schoenberg's *Gurrelieder* was one) and writing analytical guides. Between 1912 and the onset of World War I, he composed the *Altenburg Lieder* (a set of orchestral songs whose partial performance in 1913 was disrupted by the audience), the *Four Pieces* for clarinet and piano, and the *Three Orchestral Pieces.* With the *Altenberg Lieder* and the *Four Pieces* for clarinet and piano, Berg worked in miniature, although his pieces were never as brief as Webern's. It wasn't until the *Orchestral Pieces* of 1914–1915 that he began dealing with larger forms where tonal structure is absent and thematic transformations hold the pieces together. Berg's creative work slowed to a trickle in 1915 when he was drafted into the Austrian army, but weak health led him away from the frontlines and into a job as a bureaucrat with the war ministry.

After seeing a production of Georg Buchner's play *Wozzeck* in 1914, Berg was so moved that he began thinking about setting it as an opera. He worked on this powerful drama from 1917 to 1922, using a libretto that he revised from the play. Its premiere at the Berlin Opera in 1925, along with subsequent productions elsewhere in Europe, made Berg famous and allowed him to devote himself exclusively to composition. In the ensuing years, *Wozzeck* would become a repertory staple at opera

Alban Berg

houses around the world. The story of *Wozzeck* is decidedly expressionistic, relating the tale of a pathetic soldier driven to madness and murder by his wife's infidelity. While the work does stay within certain operatic traditions, Berg's innovation was the combination of arias and recitatives with themes for specific characters or events in the style of Richard Wagner's leitmotifs. Each scene is cast as a self-contained musical piece (prelude, march, etc.) in a clearly defined form.

Schoenberg formulated his idea of employing twelve-note series to add unity to music during these same years, and Berg began utilizing this method in 1925, although his usage was uniquely his own. Most often, Berg combined the twelve-tone method with freely composed sections and didn't shy away from implications of tonality. He often used quotation, referring to Wagner's *Tristan* Prelude in the *Lyric Suite* and Bach's chorale *Es ist genug* in the Violin Concerto, and even quoting from his own scores. Berg was not any less systematic than Schoenberg or Webern, but he never lost his affection for nineteenth-century romanticism, and his music consequently sounds much less radical. There is also a personal element in many of Berg's works. The *Altenberg Lieder* uses texts from picture postcards of his friend, the poet Peter Altenberg, and the *Lyric Suite* has a coded subtext written for (and about) Hanna Fuchs-Robettin, Berg's secret love. The Violin Concerto, finished in 1935, is more personal than any work that preceded it, presenting a musical portrait of Manon Gropius, Alma Mahler's daughter, who died in 1935 at the age of eighteen.

Berg began working on his second opera, *Lulu,* based on a drama by Frank Wedekind about the murder of a prostitute by Jack the Ripper, but he never finished it. He had originally planned for this work to be in three acts, but Berg was bitten by an insect, the bite became infected, and he died on Christmas Eve, 1935. The only completed portions of the work were a fully orchestrated score for acts one and two and a short score for act three with indications for orchestration. Berg had also extracted a suite, which contained some music from the third act. After his death, Helene Berg asked Schoenberg, Webern and Anton Zemlinsky if they would complete the opera from Berg's sketches. Each declined, and Helene refused to allow anyone else to finish the project. *Lulu* would be performed until 1979 in a shortened version comprising the completed acts one and two plus a spoken act three with music drawn from the *Lulu Suite*. After Helene's death, the opera was finally completed by composer

Friedrich Cerha, and the first performance of the revised work was given at the Paris Opera in 1979 under the direction of Pierre Boulez.

Orchestral
Concerto for Violin and Orchestra—*To the Memory of an Angel*
what to buy: [Itzhak Perlman, violin, Seiji Ozawa, cond., Boston Symphony Orchestra] (Deutsche Grammophon 447445) ♪ ♪ ♪ ♪ ♪

This is a superb recording of Berg's instrumental masterpiece, with one of the best available performers in the solo role. Igor Stravinsky's Concerto in D Major for Violin and Orchestra (with Ozawa conducting the BSO) and Maurice Ravel's *Tzigane* (with Zubin Mehta conducting the New York Philharmonic Orchestra) round out the offering.

what to buy next: [Pinchas Zukerman, violin, Pierre Boulez, cond., London Symphony Orchestra] (Sony Classical 68331) ♪ ♪ ♪ ♪♪

Here is another fine recording, although the sonics aren't quite up to those of the Perlman set. Also on this all-Berg album are renditions of the three *Pieces for Orchestra,* op. 6, conducted by Boulez, and the Chamber Concerto for Piano, Violin, and 13 Wind Instruments, with Zukerman, Boulez, and members of the LSO teaming up with pianist Daniel Barenboim.

Chamber
Sonata for Piano, op. 1
what to buy: [Glenn Gould, piano] (CBC 2008) ♪ ♪ ♪ ♪ ♪

This is the classic 1952 recording of the legendary pianist playing Berg's Sonata along with Webern's Variations for Piano, op. 27, and three works by Schoenberg (including the Concerto for Piano and Orchestra, op. 42). Don't let the monaural sound dissuade you.

what to buy next: [Maurizio Pollini, piano] (Deutsche Grammophon 423678) ♪ ♪ ♪ ♪♪

This recent rendering of the Sonata is a masterly performance by one of the late Twentieth century's pianistic grandmasters. Claude Debussy's dozen *Études* for piano fill out the package and provide a delightful contrast.

Vocal
Altenberg Lieder, op. 4
[*Jessye Norman Sings Alban Berg*; Jessye Norman, soprano; Pierre Boulez, cond.; London Symphony Orchestra] (Sony Classical 66826) ♪ ♪ ♪ ♪

Norman, Boulez, and the London Symphony combine in an electrifying performance. In addition to the stunning *Altenberg Lieder,* there are fine versions of Berg's *Jugenlieder* (Youthfuls Songs) and the seven *Early Songs.*

what to buy next: [Brigitte Balleys, soprano, Vladimir Ashkenazy, cond., Deutsches Symphonie-Orchester, Berlin] (London 436567) ♪ ♪ ♪ ♪ ♪

A fine overview of Berg's vocal and orchestral compositions, this superb recording (like the Norman disc) contains the seven *Early Songs* along with the *Altenberg Lieder,* but it also includes the *Lyric Suite* (in its orchestral version) and the three *Orchestral Pieces.*

Wozzeck, op. 7
what to buy: [Hildegard Behrens, soprano; Philip Langridge, tenor; Walter Raffeiner, tenor: Heinz Zednik, tenor; Franz Grundheber, baritone; Aage Haugland, bass; Alfred Zramek, bass; Claudio Abbado, cond.; Vienna Philharmonic Orchestra, Vienna State Opera Chorus; Vienna Boys Choir] (Deutsche Grammophon 423587) ♪ ♪ ♪ ♪ ♪

The concert performance recorded in June 1988 under the baton of Claudio Abbado is the best current representation of this classic modern opera, displaying its impressive writing to full effect.

worth looking for: [Evelyn Lear, soprano; Gerhard Stolze, tenor; Helmut Melchert, tenor; Dietrich Fischer-Dieskau, baritone; Karl Böhm, cond.; German Opera Orchestra, Berlin; German Opera Chorus] (Deutsche Grammophon 138991/92) ♪ ♪ ♪ ♪ ♪

Fischer-Dieskau was a very effective Wozzeck, and this is a masterly performance in every way.

Lulu
what to buy: [Teresa Stratas, soprano; Hanna Schwarz, mezzo-soprano; Yvonne Minton, mezzo-soprano; Robert Tear, tenor; Kenneth Riegel, tenor; Franz Mazura, baritone; Gerd Nienstedt, bass; Pierre Boulez, cond., Paris Opera Orchestra] (Deutsche Grammophon 415489) ♪ ♪ ♪ ♪

This was the first recording of *Lulu* to utilize the third-act completion by Friedrich Cerha, and it's still the best. Stratas is marvelous in the title role, and the sonics are spectacular.

worth looking for: [Evelyn Lear, soprano; Patricia Johnson, mezzo-soprano; Donald Grobe, tenor; Dietrich Fischer-Dieskau, baritone; Karl Böhm, cond.; German Opera Orchestra, Berlin; German Opera Chorus] (Deutsche Grammophon 435705) ♪ ♪ ♪ ♪

Here *Lulu* is done the old way, with the incomplete third act. This isn't really a problem, since the stunning performances more than make up for what's missing.

influences: Arnold Schoenberg, Anton Webern, Gustav Mahler

Frank Retzel

Hector Berlioz
Born Louis-Hector Berlioz, December 11, 1803, in La Côte-St-André, Isère, France. Died March 8, 1869, in Paris, France.

period: Romantic

A master orchestrator, enlightened critic, and gifted conductor, Hector Berlioz was also one of the supreme musical visionaries of the 19th century. Although modern audiences connect his name most often with the superbly crafted *Symphonie fantastique,* his most impressive work perhaps lies in the scoring of the massive *Requiem (Grand Messe des morts)* and, above all, in his great opera *Les Troyens,* now widely regarded as his finest achievement.

Born near Grenoble, in the shadows of the French Alps, Berlioz was the son of a well-to-do doctor who forced medical training on his son in the face of overwhelming evidence of musical precocity. At age 21, with a degree in science in hand, he bargained with his father who reluctantly agreed to continue Hector's medical school allowance while he attended the Paris Conservatoire, providing he made reasonable musical progress, reasonably soon. The success of his son's *Messe solennelle* in 1825 gave Berlioz *père* some hope, but Hector's mounting debts and failure in two attempts to win the prestigious Prix de Rome were the death knell, and all support was summarily cut off. He persisted in his musical pursuits, however, supporting himself by giving guitar lessons and writing brilliant, incisive musical criticism.

The visit to Paris in 1827 of a touring British Shakespearean troupe became a watershed event in Berlioz's life. He fell madly in love, with Shakespeare and also with the actress Harriet Smithson. He vowed to marry Harriet, but it would be five years before he was even able to meet her. Berlioz's creative juices reached maturity in 1830 by finally winning the coveted Prix de Rome with a cantata (*La Mort de Sardanapale*) and securing the premiere of the work which remains one of his greatest, the *Symphonie fantastique*. This visionary, autobiographical work details his hopeless love for Harriet through five movements of ecstatic fantasies as varied as a swirling scene at a ball, a serene and reflective pastoral interlude, and a diabolic, shrieking *Dream of a Witches' Sabbath*. Coming only six years after Beethoven's "Choral" symphony, there is no way that such a great leap forward in style and brilliance of orchestral coloration could have been anticipated. Berlioz organized another concert in 1832 with a newly revised *Symphonie fantastique* as its centerpiece, and Harriet attended. The two met, and Berlioz finally convinced her to marry him, but not without a suicide attempt as his trump card. They married in 1833, but without a common language, and with Smithson's theatrical career on the downward slope, she became dissolute and shrewish. In 1842, when Berlioz left for his first international concert tour it was with the singer Marie Recio on his arm. He finally married Marie in 1854, following Harriet's death.

In 1833 the violin virtuoso Nicolò Paganini came backstage after a concert and introduced himself, begging Berlioz to write a work with which he could display his newly acquired Stradivarius viola. The result was the symphony with viola obbligato, *Harold in Italy*, based on Byron's epic *Childe Harold*. Again, there was much travail, including Paganini's refusal to play the work, protesting that the viola part was neither difficult nor prominent enough; when he finally did hear *Harold in Italy* Paganini knelt before the composer, kissed his hand, and said that never in his life had he been so powerfully impressed at a concert, the following day sending the composer a note for 20,000 francs. Berlioz used this windfall to closet himself and compose his ultimate tribute to Shakespeare, the dramatic symphony, *Roméo et Juliette* for chorus, soloists, and orchestra, completed in 1839. This magnificent music's hour-and-a-half duration sadly inhibits many full performances, but the exquisite

Hector Berlioz

Love Scene and the eerie *Queen Mab scherzo*, with its extraordinary use of antique cymbals and perilous string harmonics, are often excerpted for concert programs.

As for the *Requiem (Grand Messe des Morts)* of 1837, there may be easier, quicker ways to gain an appreciation of the dizzyingly dynamic, brilliantly colorful, and heart-wrenchingly expressive music of Berlioz, but if you want to understand the staggering reach of his artistic vision and sonic imagination, you must know the *Requiem*. In addition to being a composer, Berlioz was also a very perceptive and articulate critic who earned his livelihood during the first half of the 1830s to a large extent by writing for various journals. So, when in the twilight of his life he said, "If I were threatened with the destruction of all my works save one, I would crave mercy for the *Requiem*," that statement could be taken as the definitive self-appraisal by the man deemed by many to be the ultimate musical incarnation of the entire Romantic movement.

Scored for huge orchestra, four brass bands, large chorus, and tenor soloist, the *Requiem* is arguably visionary beyond anything else Berlioz composed. The antiphonal effect of the four brass bands at the corners of the performance space evokes what Berlioz called a "terrible grandeur" in the *Tuba mirum*. The emotional effect can be overpowering enough to bring tears to the eyes and a knot in the stomach, while similar reactions are often wrought by the bizarre "pulling rhythms" (Berlioz's words) and shrieks of the brass bands in the *Lacrymosa*. On the other hand, equally compelling and absolutely unique are the haunting quiet opposition of massed high flutes answered by growling low trombones in the *Hostias* and in the ethereal chromatic modulations of the concluding *Agnus Dei*.

It's hard to draw the line in recommending a "Basic Berlioz" library. Even before the works mentioned above, the adventurous listener should perhaps start with the 1844 overture *Roman Carnival*, drawn from his first opera, *Benvenuto Cellini*. Its rumbustious pulse and blazing brass succinctly and excitingly establish the Berlioz vocabulary and sonority in the listener's ear. In addition, an oddity that should be explored is the devastatingly dramatic, short 1848 *Funeral March for the Last Scene of "Hamlet"* for orchestra, wordless chorus, and offstage musket shots. Other indispensable works include the beautiful song cycle of 1834, *Les Nuits d'été, La Damnation de Faust*, from 1846 (labeled a "dramatic legend" but really uncategorizable), *L'Enfance du Christ,*

(The Infant Christ) (an uncharacteristically straightforward, ravishingly lyrical oratorio), and the monumental opera *Les Troyens* (1859), regarded by many as his greatest achievement, whose epic two-part, five-act, four-hour length is yet another of the composer's works presenting production challenges.

Some of Liszt's symphonic poems owe a certain debt to Berlioz in orchestration, but the fact is that Berlioz established no "school" of composition and had no coterie of followers. There was, however, one of his contemporaries who quite independently arrived at a swashbuckling, dynamically driven style with an arching, lyrical sweep reminiscent of the great Frenchman. That is the Swedish composer Franz Berwald; parts of his wonderful 1845 Symphony no. 3 in C major—*Symphonie singulière*—are eerily suggestive of Berlioz's style.

Orchestral
Symphonie fantastique, op. 14
what to buy: [Charles Munch, cond.; Boston Symphony Orchestra] (RCA Victor 61721) ♪ ♪ ♪ ♪ ♪

If somewhat dated sound is no objection, the choice would be Munch's performance with the Boston Symphony Orchestra. The same forces also respond well to Berlioz's *Roman Carnival* and the overture to his last opera, *Béatrice et Bénédict.*

what to buy next: [Leonard Bernstein, cond.; New York Philharmonic Orchestra] (Sony Classics 47525) ♪ ♪ ♪ ♪

Bernstein's blazing energy carries this performance, and he transfers that power to the other Berlioz scores on this disc: the *Roman Carnival,* the overture to *Benvenuto Cellini,* and the "Rákoczy March" from *The Damnation of Faust.*

[Charles Mackerras, cond.; Royal Philharmonic Orchestra] (Intersound/Platinum Entertainment 2381) ♪ ♪ ♪ ♪

Mackerras's pacing in the *Symphonie fantastique* is less frenzied than that of Bernstein and his overall performance is beautifully proportioned. The budget pricing is another attraction as is Mackerras's rendition of, once again, the overture *Roman Carnival.*

Harold in Italy, op. 16
what to buy: [William Primrose, viola; Serge

Koussevitzky, cond.; Boston Symphony Orchestra] (Dutton Laboratories 5013) ♪ ♪ ♪ ♪ ♪

By all odds the finest performance on the market is the 1944 monaural recording by Primrose and Koussevitzky that still leaps thrillingly out of the speakers courtesy of this splendidly re-mastered disc. The same performers (minus Primrose) also tackle the accompanying score, *Till Eulenspiegels lustige Streiche (Till Eulenspiegel's Merry Pranks)* by Richard Strauss.

what to buy next: [*Berlioz: Great Orchestral Works*; Nobuko Imai, viola; Colin Davis, cond.; London Symphony Orchestra] (Philips 442290) ♪ ♪ ♪ ♪

Of the stereo versions available, Imai and Davis have captured the music's essence particularly well. Their performance is also part of a highly recommendable mid-priced, two-disc set of Berlioz's music with Davis conducting the *Symphonie fantastique,* the *Roman Carnival,* the overture to *Le Corsaire,* and the *Symphonie funèbre et triomphale.*

Roman Carnival Overture, op. 9
what to buy: [Zinman, cond.; Baltimore Symphony Orchestra] (Telarc 80271) ♪ ♪ ♪ ♪ ♪

There are no great interpretive problems in this brilliantly scored overture, so an energetic, straightforward approach works well, leaving the quality of sound as the major criterion. On this basis the Zinman recording offers a fine account of the music's bombast and glistening sheen. It shares a program with yet another recording of the *Symphonie fantastique* and the early, rarely heard, overture to *Les Francs-Juges.*

Vocal
Requiem
what to buy: [*Munch Conducts Berlioz,* Léopold Simoneau, tenor; Charles Munch, cond.; Boston Symphony Orchestra; New England Conservatory Chorus] (RCA Victor Gold Seal 68444) ♪ ♪ ♪ ♪ ♪

Now only available as part of an eight disc monaural retrospective of Munch's years leading the Boston Symphony Orchestra through performances of Berlioz, this is still the top recommendation. In addition to the *Requiem,* this package also includes many of the Munch recordings recommended elsewhere in this entry plus the concerto overture *Le Corsaire,* the overtures to the operas *Benvenuto Cellini* and *Béatrice et Bénédict,* as well as *L'Enfance du Christ, Les Nuits d'été, La Damnation de Faust,* the *Grande Messe des morts,* and the Royal Hunt and Storm from *Les Troyens.*

what to buy next: [John Aler, tenor; Robert Shaw, cond.; Atlanta Symphony Orchestra; Atlanta Symphony Chorus] (Telarc 80109) ♪ ♪ ♪ ♪

Aler, Shaw, and company are, occasionally, a bit on the reserved side but project the work's huge scope very well. This two-disc set also includes Shaw conducting the *Prologue in Heaven* from Arrigo Boito's Faust opera *Mefistofele* and the fourth of Giuseppe Verdi's *Quattro pezzi sacri (Four Sacred Pieces),* the Te Deum.

[Michael Schade, tenor; Noel Edison, cond.; Elora Festival Orchestra; Toronto Mendelssohn Choir; Toronto Mendelssohn Youth Choir] (Naxos 8.554494) ♪ ♪ ♪ ♪

This performance is a marvel of transparent clarity but loses something in bite and massive grandeur along the way. At the budget price, however, it is an amazing bargain.

Roméo et Juliette
what to buy: [Margaret Roggero, contralto; Leslie Chabay, tenor; Yi-Kwei Sze, bass; Charles Munch, cond.; Boston Symphony Orchestra; Harvard Glee Club, choir; Radcliffe Choral Society, choir] (RCA 60681) ♪ ♪ ♪ ♪ ♪

The best of the currently available recordings is arguably still Munch's 1953 monaural version.

influences: Franz Berwald, Franz Liszt, Richard Wagner, Ludwig van Beethoven

Herman Trotter

Leonard Bernstein
Born on August 25, 1918, in Lawrence, MA. Died October 14, 1990, in New York, NY.

period: Twentieth century

Bernstein was one of the most famous conductors of all time, a teacher by inclination rather than any official position, and a composer of path-breaking theater and concert works.

Leonard Bernstein was one of the most talented and successful musicians in American history. Driven by seemingly boundless energy, he was a star, accorded the attention and privilege that come with fame. His influence reached to the highest levels of society and government, as Bernstein often expressed concerns outside the realm of music. Whether his message had to do with politics, aesthetics, linguistics—perhaps warning about the evils in society—Bernstein's words counted because he was what he was: vivacious, charismatic, and so gifted that he could have pursued a multitude of careers.

Leonard Bernstein was a musical prodigy, educated at the Boston Latin School and a graduate cum laude from Harvard, where he studied with Walter Piston and Edward Burlingame Hill. During his last semester, he organized and directed a performance of Marc Blitzstein's agitprop musical *The Cradle Will Rock,.* In 1937, at a summer-camp production in the Berkshires he befriended songwriter Adolph Green, and that year he became acquainted with Aaron Copland, Roy Harris, and William Schuman, who urged him to become a conductor. Dimitri Mitropoulos, another famous maestro and Bernstein mentor, concurred, and in 1938 he enrolled in Fritz Reiner's conducting class at the Curtis Institute, where he also studied piano with Isabelle Vengerova. In 1940 he went to Tanglewood to study at the Berkshire Music Center with Serge Koussevitzky.

Bernstein moved to New York two years later, suffering through some lean times until Arthur Rodzinski hired him as assistant conductor of the New York Philharmonic for the 1943–44 season. His big break came on the afternoon of November 14, 1943, when Bernstein was called in on short notice to replace the indisposed Bruno Walter. The concert was broadcast nationally, and the next morning a glowing review appeared on the front page of the *New York Times.* The twenty-five-year-old conductor had become famous overnight. He made many appearances as a guest conductor and became a virtual pop idol, as much for his handsome figure, flamboyant conducting style, and undeniable flair for publicity as for his musical talent. By the age of forty he had been appointed music director of the New York Philharmonic, the first American to hold that post, remaining for over ten years. By the time of his death at the age of seventy-two, he was considered one of the world's greatest conductors and had close associations with numerous orchestras, especially the New York Philharmonic (where he was named laureate conductor for life), the Israel Philharmonic, and the Vienna Philharmonic.

Bernstein, however, never regarded himself as solely or even primarily a conductor. In the 1940s he composed two ballets, *Fancy Free* and *Facsimile,* in collaboration with choreographer Jerome Robbins. His first work for large orchestra was the symphony subtitled *Jeremiah,* which was written in 1942 and won the New York Critics' Circle Award in 1944. During his first few years in New York City, he renewed his friendship with Adolph Green and Green's songwriting partner Betty Comden and began working in what many consider his greatest creative arena—musical theater. *On the Town,* written with Comden and Green in 1944, played off the scenario of Bernstein's ballet *Fancy Free*—three sailors on leave in New York for twenty-four hours. Whereas the ballet was somewhat existential in nature, the musical is playful, witty, even bawdy, with jazzy rhythms and a remarkable zest. Bernstein proved that he could write show tunes with the best of them, and many of his songs are now considered standards.

In the 1950s Bernstein composed the score for Elia Kazan's famous movie *On the Waterfront,* as well as the Broadway musicals *Wonderful Town, Candide,* and, most famously, *West Side Story,* which updates the story of *Romeo and Juliet* by setting it in the context of a rivalry between New York City street gangs. Stephen Sondheim wrote the lyrics, Bernstein composed the music, and Jerome Robbins directed and choreographed the show. From the tryouts through the movie version up to the revivals and the recording Bernstein himself eventually made with opera singers, *West Side Story* has endured to become a classic, continuing to delight and move new listeners today. After the 1950s, Bernstein stayed away from Broadway until 1976, when a long-awaited musical collaboration with Alan Jay Lerner, *1600 Pennsylvania Avenue,* closed after seven performances.

Bernstein composed the work for piano and orchestra that he called his Symphony no. 2 (*The Age of Anxiety,* after the poem by W.H. Auden) in 1949, a third symphony (*Kaddish*) in 1963, and the tuneful, exuberant *Chichester Psalms* in 1965. He also drew concert suites from his musicals, as well as writing songs, incidental music, and two operas—*Trouble in Tahiti* and its sequel, *A Quiet Place.* Bernstein's *Mass—A Theatre Piece for Singers, Players, and Dancers,* commissioned for the 1971 opening of the Kennedy Center in Washington, D.C., aroused hostility from its shocked audience and from critics for mixing rock, serial music and characteristic Bernstein mannerisms with religious ritual. While

some of its numbers have since joined the repertory, the whole work is only just beginning to receive its due. Other compositions from Bernstein's late period include the ballet *Dybbuk, Songfest,* the *Divertimento* for Orchestra, *Halil* for flute and strings, and his Concerto for Orchestra.

In addition to being a powerhouse of creative energy, Bernstein was also a fine teacher, though not in the usual sense. He was not associated with one of the conventional educational institutions (although Tanglewood would always have a special place in his heart), but by virtue of his position as a musical standard-bearer and his personal rapport with audiences, he began to use television as his rostrum. In the 1950s, he appeared regularly on the *Omnibus* program and later hosted a series of successful *Young Peoples' Concerts.* In the 1970s he gave the Norton Lectures at Harvard, and he was always in demand to coach students at Tanglewood and other festivals. He wrote several books (*The Joy of Music* is a classic) and numerous articles. The list of accomplishments goes on and on; fortunately, a great deal of his work is documented in print, on recordings, and on video. One beautiful video package is *The Gift of Music* (Deutsche Grammophon video 440 073 200-3), a tape that offers an "intimate portrait of Leonard Bernstein as composer, conductor, performer and teacher." A more recent project is *Leonard Bernstein: Reaching for the Note,* a wonderful documentary made for the American Masters series on PBS (Video Winstar WHE71125).

Orchestral
West Side Story: Symphonic Dances
what to buy: [Leonard Bernstein, cond.; New York Philharmonic] (Sony Classics 63085) ♪ ♪ ♪ ♪ ♪

This marvelous anthology features highlights from *West Side Story* and some of his other theatrical scores. Not only do you get Bernstein's suite of dances from *West Side Story* but similar riches excerpted from *Fancy Free* and *On the Waterfront,* plus the delightful overture to *Candide.*

Symphonies
what to buy: [Leonard Bernstein, cond., Israel Philharmonic Orchestra; Vienna Jeunesse Chorus; Vienna Boys Choir] (Deutsche Grammophon 445245) ♪ ♪ ♪ ♪

Leonard Bernstein

Everyone here is superb, especially Lukas Foss, the pianist in Bernstein's Second Symphony (*Age of Anxiety*). Mezzo-soprano Christa Ludwig is the soloist in Symphony no. 1 (*Jeremiah*), while Michael Wager narrates and Montserrat Caballé sings the soprano part in the Third Symphony (*Kaddish*). Also included on this two-CD set is the Serenade for Violin and Orchestra, featuring Gidon Kremer as soloist.

Vocal
West Side Story
what to buy: [Carol Lawrence (Maria); Larry Kert (Tony); Chita Rivera (Anita); Mickey Calin (Riff); Ken LeRoy (Bernardo); Max Goberman, cond.; Original Broadway Cast recording] (Columbia Broadway 60724) ♪ ♪ ♪ ♪ ♪

The sound of the orchestra and singers is typically Broadway, a little rough around the edges but dynamically exciting. There is a magic and immediacy about this original cast recording that later performances seem to miss. The suite of *Symphonic Dances*, with Bernstein conducting the New York Philharmonic, gives further heft to an already outstanding album.

what to buy next: [Kiri Te Kanawa, soprano; José Carreras, tenor; Tatiana Troyanos, mezzo-soprano; Kurt Ollmann, baritone; Leonard Bernstein, cond.; anonymous orchestra; anonymous chorus] (Deutsche Grammophon 457199) ♪ ♪ ♪ ♪

Even though this is a fine recording, and the only time Bernstein ever conducted *West Side Story*, some of the singing may strike listeners as overly operatic. Marilyn Horne, ballyhooed on the packaging, sings "Somewhere," while Bernstein's son Alexander and daughter Nina read the dialog between Tony (Romeo) and Maria (Juliet).

Candide
what to buy: [Jerry Hadley, tenor; June Anderson, soprano; Della Jones, mezzo-soprano; Christa Ludwig, mezzo-soprano; Nicolai Gedda, tenor; Kurt Ollmann, baritone; Adolph Green; Leonard Bernstein, cond.; London Symphony Orchestra and Chorus] (Deutsche Grammophon 449656) ♪ ♪ ♪ ♪ ♪

Bernstein's last studio recording contains material deleted from the original Broadway production of *Candide* and restored by the composer in his 1989 final revision of the score. Bernstein was reportedly very proud of the results, as well he should have been.

what to buy next: [David Eisler, tenor; Erie Mills, soprano; Joyce Castle, mezzo-soprano; Maris Clement, mezzo-soprano; John Lankston, tenor; James Billings, baritone; Jack Harrold; John Mauceri, cond.; New York City Opera Orchestra and Chorus] (New World Records 80340) ♪ ♪ ♪ ♪ ♪

Even though this recording documents one of the earlier versions of the work, the performance is simply fabulous. Mills's rendering of *Glitter and Be Gay* is unequaled by any other singer's, and the recorded sound is quite respectable.

Chichester Psalms for Orchestra and Chorus
what to buy: [Leonard Bernstein, cond.; Israel Philharmonic Orchestra; Vienna Jeunesse Chorus] (Deutsche Grammophon 447954) ♪ ♪ ♪ ♪ ♪

In addition to Bernstein's stunning recording of *Chichester Psalms,* this disc includes a beautiful version of *Songfest*, with the composer leading a strong quintet of vocal soloists and the National Symphony Orchestra. The album would be worth buying for the *Psalms* alone, but the whole package is irresistible.

A White House Cantata
what to buy: [June Anderson, soprano; Barbara Hendricks, soprano; Kenneth Tarver, tenor; Neil Jenkins, tenor; Thomas Hampson, baritone; Keel Watson, bass-baritone; Victor Acquah, boy soprano; Kent Nagano, cond.; London Symphony Orchestra; London Voices, choir] (Deutsche Grammophon 463448) ♪ ♪ ♪ ♪

This 2000 release features the musical numbers from a work few have ever heard—the 1976 Broadway musical about US Presidents and the White House entitled *1600 Pennsylvania Avenue*. No cast album was ever made, and except for a couple of songs, the show has remained shrouded in mystery. This superb recording should rectify the situation and restore this score to its rightful place in the Bernstein catalog.

Mass
what to buy: [*Bernstein Century—Bernstein: Mass*; Alan Titus, celebrant; Leonard Bernstein, cond.; anonymous orchestra; Norman Scribner Choir; Berkshire Boys Choir] (Sony Classical 63089) ♪ ♪ ♪ ♪

The only recording of this marvelous, if controversial work was out of print for too long. It is good to have it available again.

influences: Aaron Copland, George Gershwin, Stephen Sondheim

Frank Retzel

Franz Berwald

Born Franz Adolf Berwald, July 23, 1796, in Stockholm, Sweden. Died April 3, 1868, in Stockholm, Sweden.

period: Romantic

Berwald's four symphonies, all composed between 1842 and 1845, mark him as Sweden's earliest important symphonist and arguably the most visionary and important composer Sweden has produced. The work most likely to snare a first-time listener is the Symphony no. 3 in C Major, subtitled the *Sinfonie Singulière*.

Franz Berwald was born and died in Stockholm. If this suggests that he led an insular, sheltered life, forget it. Despite his solid musical education, Berwald's independent temperament and uncompromising musical integrity managed to create enough friction in provincial Stockholm that his music never got a fair hearing. Swedes in the early 1800s, it seems, were enamored of symphonies by Franz Joseph Haydn and the Mannheim school of composers.

So in 1829, without recognition, Berwald went to Berlin. Needing income, he went to work for a company manufacturing orthopedic devices, finally rising to an executive position within the firm and contributing many inventions to that field. Then Berwald tested the waters in Vienna and Paris (without much luck), worked for a glass factory in Sweden, was a promising violin virtuoso (only to give it up abruptly), conducted the Royal Copenhagen Orchestra, and became the editor of a Swedish music journal.

Finally, four years before his death, Berwald was elected a member of the Stockholm Academy of Music and, with just one year to live, was appointed a teacher of composition at the Stockholm Conservatory.

Oddly, his continued lack of success came despite enthusiastic backing in high places. The legendary conductor Hans von Bülow called Berwald's 1851 Trio no. 3 in D Minor for Piano, Violin, and Cello "truly a work of utter beauty" and, marveling at the fact Berwald was born in 1796 but was so advanced in expression, called him "that ancient musician of the future." Even Franz

Liszt was an admirer, finding Berwald's advanced ideas very acceptable and always playing his music with great pleasure.

What will you hear in Berwald's music? Well, it could be described as nervous, taut, filled with short, explosive ideas and dynamic rhythms. There is also a love of repeated phrases, modulations to unexpected keys, and tense harmonic sequences coiled like springs. But above all, Berwald's music is memorable for its inexhaustible melodiousness. His Symphony no. 2 in D Major, known as the *Sinfonie Capricieuse*, contains a cosmically lilting waltz theme which looks forward to Carl Nielsen's great *Sinfonia Espansiva*, while Berwald's Symphony no. 1 in G Minor, known as the *Sinfonie Sérieuse*, concludes with one of the most arresting and original codas in the entire symphonic repertoire.

All four of Berwald's symphonies are worthy to be ranked right up there with Robert Schumann's four or Felix Mendelssohn's five. But the composer's most winning characteristics are perhaps best summarized in the remarkable Symphony no. 3 in C Major. Its brilliant scoring for brass, adventurous key modulations, and bombastic, soaring melodic lines will remind you of no one so much as Hector Berlioz, who was Berwald's ideal.

Orchestral
Symphony no. 3—*Sinfonie Singulière*
what to buy: [Igor Markevitch, cond.; Berlin Philharmonic Orchestra] (Deutsche Grammophon 457705) ♪ ♪ ♪ ♪₈

Berwald's last two symphonies are combined with Franz Schubert's Symphony no. 4 on this disc. These pioneering 1958 monaural recordings, recently reissued, are still the benchmarks.

what to buy next: [Okko Kamu, cond.; Helsingborg Symphony Orchestra] (Naxos 8.553052) ♪ ♪ ♪ ♪

If you insist on the latest high-tech reproduction, this CD will please you for both performance and sound quality. The composer's fourth symphony is included in this budget package, as is his Concerto in D Major for Piano and Orchestra.

Chamber
Septet in B-flat Major for Violin, Viola, Cello, Double Bass, Clarinet, Horn, and Bassoon— *Grand Septet*

what to buy: [Gaudier Ensemble] (Hyperion 66834) ♪ ♪ ♪

This is one of the most delightful undiscovered gems of the chamber repertoire. Two other pieces by Berwald, the Piano Quintet in C Minor and the Piano Trio no. 4 in C Major, help make this a nice sampler of the composer's works for small groups.

influences: Felix Mendelssohn, Hector Berlioz

Herman Trotter

Georges Bizet

Born Georges Alexandre-César-Léopold Bizet on October 25, 1838, in Paris, France. Died June 3, 1875, in Bougival, France.

period: Romantic

In his short life, Bizet wrote a variety of works, yet he's often regarded as a one-hit wonder, famous mainly for *Carmen,* the opera he completed a year before his death. Anyone who has ever heard the first suite from *L'Arlésienne* and his Symphony in C—both now standard orchestral fare—or Bizet's other major opera, *Les Pêcheurs de perles* (The Pearl Fishers), knows differently.

Georges Bizet was the only child of Adolphe-Armand Bizet, a singing teacher, and Aimée Delsarte, a pianist considered more gifted than her husband. At the age of four, he began music lessons from his mother, showing so much talent that he entered the Paris Conservatoire before he was ten years old. There he won a major prize for piano performance in 1851, took composition classes with Fromental Halévy in 1853, and won the admiration of Charles Gounod, who allowed the young boy to earn money by arranging some of his works. Bizet composed his Symphony in C at the age of seventeen, but the score remained hidden until its discovery in 1933 among a batch of manuscripts at the Conservatoire. It received its debut performance two years later and has since become a standard on orchestral programs, recognized as one of Bizet's finest works.

In 1857, after winning the Prix de Rome (and the stipend that went with it), Bizet was able to spend three years in Rome, residing at the French Academy's headquarters there, the Villa Medici. These were to be his happiest years, during which he developed a love of Mediterranean culture; but he also contracted the chronic throat infection that would eventually lead to his death. He wrote an Italian-style comic opera (*Don Procopio*) and worked on other compositions in Rome, few of which survive. Returning to Paris in 1860, he considered but rejected careers as a teacher or concert pianist and abandoned many musical projects during periods of self-doubt and acute depression. At the age of twenty-five, after working on a number of operas and operettas, none of them staged and many of them destroyed or never completed, he wrote his first important work—*Les Pêcheurs de perles* (The Pearl Fishers). This work—set in Ceylon and based on the eternal triangle, murder, and more—was produced on September 30, 1863, at the Théâtre-Lyrique, where it ran for a respectable eighteen performances, in spite of being torn to shreds by the press.

Bizet now suffered hard times, as his pension from the Prix de Rome had run out. Dividing his time among composing, doing drudging work for publishers, teaching a few piano students, and playing through scores submitted for performances at two theaters, he earned very little money. Many of his subsequent works were left unfinished, had only short runs, or suffered from uneven quality. He experienced further illness and a spiritual crisis in 1868, factors that led him to change his thinking about music. Still, although opportunities presented themselves, he was unable to achieve focus and abandoned some promising projects. In 1869, Bizet married Geneviève Halévy, the daughter of his old composition teacher. Their union was to be a difficult one, made worse by his wife's own frequent depressions.

In the summer of 1871, Bizet began composing incidental music for Alphonse Daudet's play *L'Arlésienne.* He reworked excerpts from that score into a suite for the concert hall a year later, and the resulting music recaptured the spontaneity of his youth in four marvelously inventive, highly expressive, profoundly evocative, and totally natural movements. (His close friend Ernest Guiraud took some of the remaining material from the incidental music and created a second suite four years after Bizet's death.) Also in 1872, Bizet began working on *Carmen*; after some setbacks and delays, the opera was premiered on March 3, 1875, at the Opéra-Comique. Based on a novella by Prosper Mérimée, the plot about thieves, gypsies, and cigar makers was not well-received by the audience or critics, who described it as erudite, obscure, colorless, melodically conventional, insignificant, and undramatic. Bizet was depressed over the reception of his opera, and his health went steadily downhill. He took his family to the country near Paris and died there on June 3, 1875, after suffering two heart attacks. Time has since completely effaced those initial unsympathetic responses, and *Carmen* is now perhaps the best-known and most popular work in the entire operatic repertoire.

Orchestral
L'Arlésienne: Suite no. 1
what to buy: [Sir Thomas Beecham, cond.; Royal Philharmonic Orchestra] (EMI Classics 47794) ♪ ♪ ♪ ♪

In this splendid performance of the wildly popular Suite no. 1, Beecham elicits the best from his orchestra through all four movements, and the sweetly appealing string playing helps make this an exemplary recording. Beecham's passion for French ballet and the music of Bizet is evident throughout. The darker second suite (also included here) is equally melodious, with greater emphasis on woodwinds and brass. This CD, which also contains Bizet's *Symphony in C,* is a must for any classical music lover.

what to buy next: [Jesús López-Cobos, cond.; Cincinnati Symphony Orchestra] (Telarc 80224) ♪ ♪ ♪ ♪

López-Cobos leads the Cincinnati orchestra through a wonderfully robust and dynamic reading of the first *L'Arlésienne* suite, as well as orchestral *Carmen* excerpts and the Symphony in C. Spanning Bizet's creative life, this gorgeous 1989 recording is a worthy introduction to the composer, especially for those not yet devoted to opera.

Symphony in C
what to buy: [Jesús López-Cobos, cond.; Cincinnati Symphony Orchestra] (Telarc 80224) ♪ ♪ ♪ ♪ ♪

A fine performance of this ever-fresh, spontaneously inventive, and now familiar work, written by Bizet when he was seventeen years old but not performed until 1935.

Vocal
Carmen
what to buy: [Tatiana Troyanos, mezzo-soprano; Plácido Domingo, tenor; Kiri Te Kanawa, soprano; José Van Dam, bass-baritone; Georg Solti, cond; London Philharmonic Orchestra] (London 414489) ♪ ♪ ♪ ♪

E. Power Biggs:
Very few organists in the twentieth century have been able to make a living just by playing their instrument. Such was not the case for E. Power Biggs, who for more than forty years championed the cause of the classical organ and its literature throughout the world. Biggs's ideas about what constituted the proper organ were highly influential. No single player had more of an impact on how major contemporary pipe organ builders constructed their instruments. Unlike his equally famous counterpart, Virgil Fox, Biggs refused to play electronic instruments, considering them crass, vulgar, and not able to produce proper organ tone.

In 1929, after studying at the Royal Academy of Music in London, Biggs moved to the United States, where he became a citizen in 1938. He quickly became a highly respected scholar and advocate for organ literature and performance. Biggs achieved a broad-based popularity with American audiences through his Sunday-morning programs broadcast on the fledgling CBS radio network from 1942 through 1958. Even though he made a number of recordings of nineteenth and twentieth century music, including Walter Piston's Prelude and Allegro for Organ and Strings and a fine version of Aaron Copland's Symphony for Organ and Orchestra (with Copland conducting), Biggs's finest work can be found in his Bach recordings. One particular standout is *E. Power Biggs Plays Bach* (CBS 42643). Originally recorded in 1973 on the four organs at the Munster of Freiburg in Southern Germany, this disc includes Biggs's take on the famous Toccata and Fugue in D Minor, BWV 565 (remember *The Phantom of the Opera*?) and a fine recording of the Toccata, Adagio, and Fugue in C Major, BWV 564.

Dave Wagner

Domingo has recorded "Don José" more ofen than any other singer. His exceptional performance on this 1975 recording of *Carmen* is further enhanced by the fine acoustics of London's Henry Wood Hall. Kiri Te Kanawa sings Micaëla, displaying the pure beauty of her voice in her scenes with Domingo as well as her arias, but it is Troyanos as Carmen, with her gorgeously rich, throaty timbre and astounding dramatic range, who steals the show. Solti draws an appropriate mixture of lightness and richness from the orchestra and chorus. Without disturbing essential elements of the plot, the dialogue in this performance has been heavily cut, but you can follow along in the 278-page libretto.

what to buy next: [Leontyne Price, soprano; Franco Corelli, tenor; Mirella Freni, soprano; Robert Merrill, baritone; Herbert Von Karajan, cond.; Vienna Philharmonic Orchestra; Vienna State Opera Chorus; Vienna Boys Choir] (RCA Gold Seal 6199) ♪ ♪ ♪ ♪

Karajan creates a real orchestral drama on this digitally remastered 1963 recording, which features an all-star cast. Although Price's voice seems a bit heavy for the flirtatious Carmen, she's still sensuously magnificent in the lead role. Soprano Mirella Freni (Micaëla) shows

appropriate girlish naiveté in her solos and partners Corelli strongly in their duets. Individually, Corelli and Merrill are also powerfully convincing, but it's the resplendent choral singing and Karajan's deft hand at blending the whole ensemble that makes his rendition such a favorite.

[Regina Resnik, mezzo-soprano; Mario del Monaco, tenor; Joan Sutherland, soprano; Tom Krause, baritone; Thomas Schippers, cond.; Orchestre de la Suisse Romande; Choir of the Grand Theater of Geneva] (London 443871) ♪ ♪ ♪

Schippers injects plenty of drama into this performance, but with a lighter hand than other conductors. Recorded in 1963 at the Grand Theatre in Geneva, this worthy performance is considerably enhanced by Sutherland's presence, but Del Monaco doesn't hold a candle to Domingo. No libretto is included with this two-disc set.

Les Pêcheurs de perles (The Pearl Fishers)
[Nicolai Gedda, tenor; Janine Micheau, soprano; Ernest Blanc, baritone; Jacques Mars, bass; Pierre Dervaux, cond.; Paris Opéra-Comique Orchestra; Paris Opéra-Comique Chorus] (EMI Classics 69704) ♪ ♪ ♪ ♪

Although this opera broke no new ground in French opera tradition, its lyrical beauty and memorable moments have earned it a place in the standard repertoire. In this 1960 recording, the fiery tenor Gedda (Nadir) grabs your attention in sparkling scenes shared with pearl fishers Zurga (Blanc) and Nourbad (Mars). Even though Micheau excels as Leila, taking the highest notes with astonishing finesse and precision, and collaborating in lovely duets with the gentlemen, it is the "guy thing" that makes this opera so appealing, as the gents prevail in scenes full of brawny fervor. The two-disc set also includes excerpts from Bizet's unfinished opera *Ivan IV*, featuring the same company under conductor Georges Tzipine.

L'Arlésienne
worth looking for: [Daniel Mesguich, narrator; Jean-Claude Malgoire, cond; Orchestre de Chambre National de Toulouse, Jean Sourisse Vocal Ensemble, choir] (Auvidis 4839) ♪ ♪ ♪

Ernest Bloch

Since both of the *L'Arlésienne Suites* are more often recorded without the narration, hearing this melodramatic, intimate blend of words and music for the first time can be a rare treat. But rather than present Bizet's original version, with text by Daudet, Malgoire has bizarrely added excerpts from *Carmen* ("The Toreador Song") and other Bizet works, as well as a song by Jules Massenet ("Chant provençal"). Unless you're a Bizet completist or a devotee of drama or spoken word recordings, you may find the narration distracting.

influences: Charles Gounod, Giacomo Meyerbeer, Piotr Tchaikovsky

Nancy Ann Lee

Ernest Bloch
Born 24 July, 1880, in Geneva, Switzerland. Died July 15, 1959, in Portland, OR.

period: Twentieth century

"It is the Jewish soul that interests me, the complex, glowing, agitated soul that I feel vibrating throughout the Bible." These are the words of composer Ernest Bloch, explaining the source of his inspiration. His best-known work is the rhapsody *Schelomo* for cello and orchestra.

Swiss by birth, Bloch was American by adoption, having first come to the United States in 1916. Although many of his students would become famous in their own right, he fostered no compositional "school." He taught that one must develop one's unique voice, writing from inspiration and inclination rather than adhering to any technical or structural device. This maxim could at times lead to music that was undisciplined, both from him and his students, but it could also be an inspiration to create something truly unique.

His earliest formal music studies took place during his teens with Louis Rey (violin) and Emile Jaques-Dalcroze (composition). Between 1897 and 1899 he studied in Brussels under Eugène Ysaÿe (violin) and François Rasse, a pupil of César Franck (composition), who gave him a firm musical footing: after all, inspiration and inclination require knowledge and discipline to function properly. In Ernest Bloch, all these combine wonderfully to create some stunning music—deeply felt and showing his sure sense of expressive means. Some of his early scores are in the German-Romantic vein (such as his Symphony in C sharp major), while others are in French Impressionist style (the symphonic poems comprising *Hiver—Printemps*). Certain aspects of these works, especially the use of modes and cyclic formal construction, would become typical of Bloch's style. Several pieces from the period 1911–16, including the Psalm settings and his most famous composition, *Schelomo* for cello and orchestra, constitute his "Jewish Cycle," all works in large-scale forms, with rhythmic features paralleling the intonation of the Hebrew language and a use of repeated notes and intervals recalling the sounding of the shofar (ceremonial ram's horn) in the synagogue on High Holy Days.

After moving to the United States in 1916, Bloch taught at the Mannes School in New York for two years before moving to the Cleveland Institute, where he served as its first director from 1920 to 1925. He abolished exams and textbooks in favor of a looser study process focused on the masterworks, an innovation that met with the disapproval of the Cleveland board of directors and ultimately resulted in his resignation. He moved to San Francisco to become director of the Conservatory from 1925 to 1930. Bloch's creative work after 1920 includes the Concerto Grosso no. 1 for Strings, the Quintet no. 1 for Piano and Strings, and *America: An Epic Rhapsody*. This last composition, scored for chorus and orchestra, was his entry in a competition sponsored by *Musical America* and garnered first prize. Dedicated to the memory of Abraham Lincoln and Walt Whitman, it features such "American" elements as Native American motifs, sea shanties, patriotic tunes, and car horns as part of its orchestral fabric.

Bloch spent the 1930s in Europe where he returned to writing in large-scale forms. The works from this period include a violin concerto and *Avodath Hakodesh*, his music for the Jewish sacred service. As European Jewry faced increasingly hostile governments, he returned to the United States in 1940 and took up a professorship at the University of California, Berkeley, which he held until 1952. During these last years Bloch added to his increasingly hefty oeuvre with compositions ranging from the neo-romantic (*Concerto symphonique* for piano and orchestra) to the neo-classical (Concerto Grosso no. 2 for Strings), even going so far as to employ the 12-tone system (*Sinfonia breve* for orchestra) advocated by Arnold Schoenberg. The writer Eric Mason summed up the composer's legacy by saying: "One does not have to be a Jew . . . to appreciate Bloch's individual artistry and the eloquent intensity of his creative vision; his best

enduring compositions owe their success to their potent musical appeal."

Orchestra
Schelomo for Cello and Orchestra
what to buy: [Leonard Rose, cello, Eugene Ormandy, cond., Philadelphia Orchestra] (Sony Classical 48278) ♪♪♪♪♪

Bloch's initially conceived this, his best-known work, for voice and orchestra. First performed at Carnegie Hall in New York in May of 1917, it has since become a classic. Rose and Ormandy bring a real sense of passion to this "Hebrew Rhapsody," and the effect is quite stunning. The album also includes cello masterworks by Gabriel Fauré, Édouard Lalo, and Pyotr Ilyich Tchaikovsky.

what to buy next: [*New York Album*; Yo-Yo Ma, cello; David Zinman, cond.; Baltimore Symphony Orchestra] (Sony Classical 57961) ♪♪♪♪

Any performance by Yo-Yo Ma is worth the price of admission, and this recording is further testament to that fact. Added treats here include Béla Bartók's Concerto for Viola and Orchestra (in an arrangement featuring Yo-Yo Ma on the rarely played alto violin) and Stephen Albert's Concerto for Cello and Orchestra.

Vocal
Avodath Hakodesh (Sacred Service) for baritone, orchestra, and chorus
what to buy: [*Bernstein: The Royal Edition*; Robert Merrill, baritone; Rabbi Judah Cahn, speaker; Leonard Bernstein, cond.; New York Philharmonic Orchestra; Metropolitan Synagogue Choir; New York Community Church Choir] (Sony Classical 47533) ♪♪♪♪

Quintessential Bloch, performed by the legendary Merrill and Bernstein. It is a shame that there aren't more recordings of this major work, but it is good to have this one. The companion pieces on the two-disc set are by Paul Ben-Haim (*Sweet Psalmist of Israel*) and Lukas Foss (the gorgeous *Song of Songs*).

influences: Paul Ben-Haim, Lukas Foss, Leonard Bernstein, Ralph Shapey

Frank Retzel

Luigi Boccherini

Born Ridolfo Luigi Boccherini, February 19, 1743 in Lucca, Italy. Died May 28, 1805 in Madrid, Spain.

period: Baroque

Luigi Boccherini was a brilliant cellist and remains best known as a composer for his numerous chamber works and the Cello Concerto in B-flat Major. Although he greatly admired Franz Joseph Haydn's music, Boccherini's own scores lack the strength and vigor of the wizard of Esterházy. Instead, his music tends to be filled with charm, delicacy, grace, and an exuberance which dazzles but never overpowers.

Boccherini made his first public appearance as an impressively talented cellist at the age of thirteen in his home town of Lucca. From there he traveled around Italy and Austria, gathering experience and a reputation as a virtuoso, before finally being granted an appointment (in 1764) as cellist back in Lucca. While ensconced in this position, Boccherini composed two oratorios (*Gioas* and *Il Giuseppe riconosciuto*), the first of his multitudinous chamber works, and an early concerto, but none of them were published until he left Lucca in 1767. That was the year when Boccherini, along with his friend, violinist Filippo Manfredi, began a concert tour which eventually took them to Paris. There they played many private concerts and were eventually invited to perform in the French capital's most prestigious concert series, the Concerts Spirituels. By this time Boccherini had also found himself a patron (Baron de Bagge), which enabled him to publish some of the compositions he had written back in Lucca: a set of six string quartets and a set of six string trios.

In 1768 the duo turned up in Spain as musicians in an opera company subsidized by Crown Prince Carlos, Prince of Asturias. It was as part of this troupe that Boccherini traveled with the royal court, playing at various locations around the country. He was seeking to expand his reputation by composing more works that would expose his talents as a virtuoso cellist, including more string quartets and trios as well as some of his very first mature orchestral works: a sinfonia concertante and an overture that he cobbled out of material he had written for an earlier, abandoned symphony. In 1770 he left the opera company to take a position as performer and composer for the Infante, Don Luis Antonio Jaime of Bourbon, the younger brother of his former employer.

Many of the works in Boccherini's catalog, including the bulk of his symphonies and a substantial number of the string quintets, stem from this year until the death of the Infante in 1785. Most of these compositions were published first in Paris, though Boccherini had also worked out an arrangement with the Vienna-based publishing house Artaria in 1780. Boccherini's wife also died in 1785; the composer was awarded an annual pension from the royal treasury but he still needed sources of consistent revenue to help support his family. Prince Friedrich Wilhelm of Prussia stepped in the next year as Boccherini's new patron, but the composer was now free to accept commissions from other supporters, including the Benavente-Osuna family and Lucien Bonaparte, the French ambassador to Madrid. While Boccherini still maintained an admirable reputation as a virtuoso and a composer, he continued having fiscal difficulties, which intensified in 1796 soon after one of his daughters died. That same year he contacted the Paris-based publishing house of Pleyel about selling the rights to much of his music, offering them up at a desperate discount. While Boccherini continued to sell his compositions during this time, including his last string quartets, all of his piano quintets, and the balance of his string quintets, his commissions were slowly dwindling. Then, within the span of two years (1802–1804), his second wife and three more of his daughters died. Added to his own increasingly frail health, these traumas may have helped further his demise. By the time he died, Boccherini's only survivors were two sons from his first marriage.

Orchestral
Concerto in B-flat Major for Cello and Orchestra
what to buy: [Erling Blondal Bengtsson, cello; Ilya Stupel, cond.; Artur Rubinstein State Philharmonic Orchestra] (Danacord 416) ♪♪♪♪♪

The Danish cellist Erling Blondal Bengtsson plays brilliantly, deftly handling the tremendous technical demands of this concerto. The dramatic and intense shifting of moods from pensiveness to irrepressible joy is remarkable as the cello hovers in the stratosphere, often sounding like a violin. The orchestra is a perfect partner for this great soloist. Haydn's two cello concertos are included, so you can compare the settings and determine for yourself the musical kinship of these two composers.

what to buy next: [Jacqueline DuPré, cello; Daniel Barenboim, cond.; English Chamber Orchestra] (EMI Classics 66948) ♪♪♪♪

DuPré's rendition of the concerto has reached classic status, and the playing still has the kind of character worth saluting. The pairing with Haydn's two cello concertos (the first conducted by Barenboim and the second featuring John Barbirolli leading the London Symphony Orchestra) is felicitous.

Symphony no. 13 in C Major, op. 37, no. 1
what to buy: [*Four Boccherini Symphonies*; Ross Pople, cond.; London Festival Orchestra] (Hyperion 66904) ♪ ♪ ♪

Pople's disc is more expensive than the one by the New Berlin Chamber Orchestra (cited below), but it makes up for the price difference by duplicating their program and expanding it by one work: the Symphony in D Major, op. 42. The sonics are less harsh as well.

what to buy next: [*Boccherini Edition, Vol. 3: Symphonies (1)*; Michael Erxleben, cond.; New Berlin Chamber Orchestra] (Capriccio 10457) ♪ ♪ ♪

The second movement of Boccherini's Symphony no. 13 is a perfect example of his technique for weaving a gossamer sound. In such moments the composer displays a marked fondness for pairing the flute with the bassoon. Other works on the disc include two more examples from his opus 37: Symphony no. 15 in D Minor (op. 37, no. 3) and Symphony no. 16 in A Major (op. 37, no. 4).

Chamber
Quintets for Guitar and Strings
what to buy: [Pepe Romero, guitar; Academy of St. Martin-in-the-Fields Chamber Ensemble] (Philips 438769) ♪ ♪ ♪ ♪

These arrangements by Boccherini of previously composed works are light, easy-to-digest works that never fail to entertain. Romero, as befits his reputation for consistent, high-order musicianship, is sterling throughout, able to blend with the ensemble or solo effectively. The sound on this budget-priced two-disc set of nine quintets is quite good.

Quartets for Strings, op. 32
what to buy: [Quartetto Esterházy, ensemble] (Teldec Das Alte Werk 95988) ♪ ♪ ♪ ♪

Boccherini developed his own model for the string quartet independently of the Viennese masters, but since he was isolated in Spain at this time and away from the

musical centers of Europe, he is seen as more of a transitional, Rococo figure, stuck on the cusp of the Baroque and Classical periods. These works were created in 1780, just prior to Haydn's opus 33 quartets, and on this two-disc set the Quartetto Esterházy does a splendid job of putting them within that context without forsaking their essentially sweet qualities.

Sonatas for Cellos and Continuo
what to buy: [Michal Kanka, cello; Petr Hejny, cello; Jaroslav Tuma, harpsichord] (Praga Digitals 250127) ♪ ♪ ♪ ♪

You would expect a cello virtuoso like Boccherini to come up with pieces testing the mettle of other players and showing off his own formidable technical prowess. The seven sonatas heard here fit the bill perfectly, using one cello as the focus and combining the second cello with the harpsichord to provide the continuo. The beguiling performances are quite good.

influences: Franz Joseph Haydn

Marijim Thoene and Garaud MacTaggart

William Bolcom
Born William Elden Bolcom, May 26, 1938, in Seattle, WA.

period: Twentieth century

Bolcom is a contemporary American composer and teacher whose stylistic range spans classical music, early American pop tunes, and various aspects of jazz. As a scholar, Bolcom has contributed articles on jazz to *The New Grove Dictionary of Music and Musicians,* edited a book of essays by George Rochberg (*The Aesthetics of Survival: a Composer's View of 20th Century Music*), co-written a book on the black vaudevillian pianist and songwriter Eubie Blake (*Reminiscing with Sissle and Blake,* with Robert Kimball), and published a number of pieces about ragtime in general. In 1988 he received the Pulitzer Prize for Music for his *Twelve New Études* for Piano.

Bolcom was a child prodigy who went to the University of Washington and studied composition there when he was only eleven years old. After receiving his B.A. from that institution in 1958, he continued his studies at Mills College with Darius Milhaud, the French neo-classicist who embraced jazz and polytonality. Bolcom followed his teacher to France where, from 1959 to 1961, he continued his classwork at the Conservatoire National Supérieiur de Musique in Paris under Milhaud and Olivier Messiaen. In 1964 he received his doctorate in composition from Stanford University, and next began a year of piano study with George Rochberg. He then went back to France and the Conservatoire, where he won Second Prize in Composition before returning to the United States, where he began working in a number of academic postings. The positions included stints at the University of Washington (1965–1966), Queens College (1966–1968), and the New York University School of the Arts, where he was composer-in-residence (1969–1970). He finally joined the faculty at the University of Michigan in 1973 and has remained there, currently serving as chairman of the composition department since 1998.

Lest it sound as if Bolcom's post-doctoral life has been spent as a dry academic, it should be noted that his recordings of classic vaudeville and parlor Americana from the early days of the Twentieth century and the complete piano works of George Gershwin, as well as a number of albums dedicated to the songs of Irving Berlin, Jerome Kern, and Cole Porter (with his wife, mezzo-soprano Joan Morris), have all proven to be top sellers. In an interview he did with Ann McCutchan (for the book *The Muse That Sings,* Oxford University Press, 1999), Bolcom said that one reason he was "involved with American popular song is that it exists close to the real choices that make us [Americans] who we are."

His own compositions generally display an acerbic, dry, witty style. While jazz elements such as syncopation can be heard as themes or quotes in many of his scores, Bolcom also produces music with atonal components in addition to huge sweeps of melodic invention. One work which encompasses all of these characteristics is his Concerto for Piano and Orchestra from 1976, a work that whipsaws back and forth between serial passages and portions inspired by the improvisatory nature of post-bop jazz riffing. The most accessible of his pieces, however, are the series of piano rags inspired, in part, by Bolcom's love of early American jazz.

Vocal works are also a prominent part of his oeuvre. Among his most important recent works in that idiom are his song cycles, *The Mask* (1990), *I Will Breathe a Mountain* (1990), and the four volumes of *Cabaret Songs* (1963–1996). Thanks to commissions from the Chicago Lyric Opera, Bolcom has also written his first operas during the last decade, completing *McTeague* (based on the

Nadia Boulanger:
Nadia Boulanger's father had won the Prix de Rome during his student days in 1863 and taught singing at the Paris Conservatoire while Lili, her younger sister, was a promising composer in her own right who became the first woman to win the Prix de Rome in 1913. Most of Nadia's early training came, logically enough, under her father's guidance but she also took classes at the Paris Conservatoire. While competing for the 1908 Prix de Rome, Nadia set the fugue subject (which had been formulated by the composer Camille Saint-Saëns) for string quartet rather than for voices as was required. This upset Saint-Saëns, who then lobbied his fellow judges to exclude her from consideration for the prize. While Boulanger was eventually allowed to continue in the competition, it is quite possible that Saint-Saëns's wrath affected the outcome of the contest even though she did end up with second prize for her cantata, *La Sirène (The Siren).*

After Lili's death in 1918, Nadia, who had begun a career as a pianist/organist, concentrated more on teaching. Her ability to goad young, unformed musicians into seeking their true musical characters proved attractive to whole generations of American composers, but most particularly those ensconced in Paris during the 1920s and 1930s, including Aaron Copland, Virgil Thomson, Walter Piston, Roy Harris, and Leonard Bernstein. Other Americans who studied with Boulanger, especially such striking individualists as Elliott Carter, Roger Sessions, and later Philip Glass, took relatively little from her classes except the reinforced desire to be true to themselves. It wasn't only Americans who sought her out for guidance, however, since Yehudi Menuhin (British), Jean Françaix (French), and Astor Piazzolla (Argentina) were also among the many students benefiting from her tutelage.

While she is best known as a teacher, Boulanger was also one of the first women to direct orchestras. Her first opportunity to do so occurred in 1933 and she went on to become the first woman conductor of not only the Royal Philharmonic Society, but the Boston Symphony Orchestra and the Philadelphia Orchestra. In this capacity Boulanger was known for her assured advocacy of Gabriel Fauré's *Requiem* (EMI Classics Special Import 61025, with Maurice Duruflé playing the organ) and her groundbreaking 1937 recordings of Claudio Monteverdi's works (Pearl Pavilion 9994, with her student Dinu Lipatti playing piano). An article that appeared in *The New York Sun* of February 15, 1938, quoted her response to questions about her gender and the experience of being a conductor, saying, "I've been a woman for a little over fifty years, and have gotten over my initial astonishment. As for conducting, that's a job. I don't think sex plays much part."

Ellen Kokko

Frank Norris novel *Greed*) in 1992 and *A View from the Bridge* (based on the play by Arthur Miller) in 1999. However, the most important of his works overall, vocal or instrumental, may be his setting of William Blake's fervid *Songs of Innocence and of Experience*. The score includes roughly two and a half hours' worth of music crossing a multitude of stylistic boundaries—from pop to rock, and from country to works evoking the spectre of late Twentieth century classical music. The *Boston Globe* hailed it as "The greatest achievement of synthesis in American music since *Porgy and Bess,*" but there has (as of press time) been no recording made of it.

Orchestral

Symphony no. 4 for Mezzo-Soprano and Orchestra

what to buy: [Joan Morris, mezzo-soprano, Leonard Slatkin, cond., St. Louis Symphony Orchestra] (New World 80356) ♪ ♪ ♪ ♪ ♪

Bolcom conceived of this work in two sections, complementary to one another: The first half features energetic waves of aural texture meshing with spurts of melody while the conclusion spotlights a text by Theodore Roethke as Joan Morris's pliant soprano sails through a sea of emotion. The second piece on the disc *Session I,* is a surprisingly effective blend of jazz and classical idioms. Riffs, utilizing parameters established by the composer, allow for some improvisation, but this is basically a twelve-tone composition written in 1965 for conductor/composer Luciano Berio and his Domaine Musical Ensemble.

Concerto for Piano and Orchestra

what to buy: [William Bolcom, piano; Sydney Hodkinson, cond.; Rochester Philharmonic Orchestra] (Vox Classics 7509) ♪ ♪ ♪ ♪ ♪₄

Bolcom treads a difficult line between jazz pastiche and serialism with amazing aplomb, delivering a fine performance of his own work that brings out both the humor and the majesty of the score. The recording is a bit soft-focused, but not enough to affect enjoyment of the concerto, and the budget pricing makes this a good first choice for anyone wishing to explore the composer's repertoire affordably. Bolcom's *Three Dance Portraits* for piano is one of the accompanying pieces, and is performed quite capably by Barry Snyder. The balance of the album is devoted to a pair of works for flute by Samuel Adler: the Concerto for Flute and Orchestra and the Sonata for Unaccompanied Flute, with Bonita Boyd as the soloist in each.

[Marc-André Hamelin, piano; Dmitry Sitkovetsky, cond.; The Ulster Orchestra] (Hyperion 67170) ♪ ♪ ♪ ♪₄

Hamelin's technique is formidable, and he makes short work of the difficulties Bolcom poses for any pianist tackling this piece. He doesn't quite have the jazz-tinged feel which the composer imparts to the score, but in the first movement, where the ragtime episodes dissolve into seeming chaos before exploding in a big, brass-filled mass of sound, Hyperion's engineers have made sure that maximum sonic value is extracted from the performance. Leonard Bernstein's piano concerto-cum-symphony, *The Age of Anxiety,* is the actual top-billed piece in this package, and Hamelin, Sitkovetsky, and the orchestra do a bang-up job of trying to convince the listener that the work has substance beyond its posturing.

Chamber

Twelve New Études for Piano

what to buy: [Marc-André Hamelin, piano] (New World 80345) ♪ ♪ ♪ ♪ ♪

Bolcom's humor and eccentricity shine here. Hamelin, familiar with Bolcom's oeuvre, never overdoes the humor, or the intricate interplay of rhythms and textures that populate this score. The études, which exploit an amazing array of piano dynamics, display aural links to some of Bolcom's American idols: George Gershwin, Charles Ives, and Scott Joplin. Hamelin is as graceful as a ghost, whispering on the keys or, like a bull in Bolcom's china shop, crashing into chords. Stefan Wolpe's *Battle Piece* is the accompanying work.

Rags for Piano (complete)

what to buy: [*Knight Hubert*, John Murphy, piano] (Albany TROY 325/26) ♪ ♪ ♪ ♪ ♪

Bolcom's charming rags have a surprising number of harmonic tricks and turns, paying homage to the past while acknowledging the present. Many of these works have shown up on other albums and in a number of piano recitals, especially the *Graceful Ghost Rag* and *The Serpent's Kiss,* but Murphy has lived with the pieces for quite some time and it is hard to imagine a better, more insightful performance of these gems.

Vocal

The Mask for Piano and Chorus

what to buy: [Margaret Kampmeier, piano; Judith Clurman, cond.; New York Concert Singers, choir] (New World 80547) ♪ ♪ ♪ ♪₄

Five pieces for chorus and piano and one for solo piano reveal an adroit juxtaposition of syncopation and atonality. The text of the choral works blends African-American poetry with Bolcom's surprisingly sympathetic musicality for an exemplary match-up of words and music, while the solo piano section sounds a bit like postmodern Gershwin. The disc shares space with songs by Mario Castelnuovo-Tedesco and sets of hymns and songs by Virgil Thompson. The sound is dynamic and the various scores work together well, providing a mini-history lesson in the art of Twentieth century American writing for chorus.

various songs by other composers
what to buy: [*After the Ball: A Treasury of Turn-of-the-Century Popular Songs*; Joan Morris, mezzo-soprano; William Bolcom, piano] (Nonesuch 79148) ♪ ♪ ♪ ♪

The composer plays the piano while his wife (Morris) sings these tunes in a most beguiling manner. The result is a wonderful introduction to American popular songs from the cusp of the nineteenth and twentieth centuries.

influences: Eubie Blake, William Albright, André Previn, George Gershwin, Darius Milhaud

Michael H. Margolin and Ian Palmer

Alexander Borodin
Born Alexander Porfir'yevitch Borodin, November 12, 1833, in St. Petersburg, Russia. Died February 27, 1887, in St. Petersburg, Russia.

period: Romantic

From 1876 until his death slightly over a decade later, Borodin worked on two genuine masterpieces (his String Quartet no. 2 in D Major and the unfinished opera *Prince Igor*) and two near masterpieces (the atmospheric tone poem *In the Steppes of Central Asia* and his Symphony no. 2 in B Minor.) The second string quartet begat the *Nocturne for String Orchestra* as well as the 1954 "hit" "And This Is My Beloved," while the *Polovtsian Dances* from *Prince Igor* later served as inspiration for the pop standard "Stranger In Paradise" (also from 1954).

Borodin had aristocratic bloodlines courtesy of his father, Prince Luka Stepanovich Gedianov, but since he was an illegitimate child, the young Alexander lived with his mother and drew his surname from one of his father's serfs (Porfiry Ionovich Borodin). When his mother married a retired army doctor (Christian Ivanovich Kleineke) in 1839, Gedianov gifted the couple with housing and remained friends with his former mistress until his death in 1843. Alexander demonstrated musical abil-

ities at an early age, playing the piano, flute, and cello, and composing little bits of juvenilia before he was ten years old. He also developed an intense interest in chemistry, creating his own watercolors for painting and (no doubt to the dismay of his mother) experimenting with homemade fireworks.

This scientific fascination would ultimately lead to his enrollment at the St. Petersburg Medical-Surgical Academy in 1850, where he demonstrated a profound aptitude not just for chemistry but botany, zoology, and other natural sciences. While he didn't abandon music totally (he still composed a variety of short pieces), Borodin used it as little more than a way of relaxing with friends. Upon graduation in 1856, he served his internship at a military hospital, but a year later left the medical profession to engage in chemical research and teaching. The next few years saw Borodin traveling all over Europe, spending most of his time engaged in examining state-of-the-art facilities in Germany and France, and attending conferences devoted to the sciences in general and chemistry in particular. He also became acquainted with a number of musicians, seeking like-minded souls with whom to make music. One of these, Yekaterina Sergeyevna Protopopova, an accomplished pianist, married him in 1862.

This was also the year that Borodin returned to Russia, began teaching chemistry at his alma mater, and met up with Mily Balakirev, the composer and teacher who would become the putative leader of the "Mighty Handful." Through Balakirev, Borodin became acquainted with Nicolai Rimsky-Korsakov and César Cui, but at this time was also delighted to run into Modest Mussorgsky, whom he had first met and befriended in 1856 when both men were assigned to the same military hospital. Urged by his new compatriots to further hone his compositional skills, Borodin began working on his first symphony, which took three years to complete. Neither this piece nor the following satirical stage work *Bogatïri* won much approval from St. Petersburg critics when they were premiered in 1868 and 1867, respectively, though according to contemporary sources the symphony appears to have been a hit with audiences.

From the standpoint of posterity Borodin's first major scores were begun almost simultaneously; his second symphony was sketched out in 1869 and the initial material for his opera, *Prince Igor*, was started when he postponed work on the symphony. Switching back and forth in his labors over the two scores (and maintaining a full schedule as a teacher and researcher), the composer finally finished the first version of the symphony in 1875. Intermittent work on the *Prince Igor* project bracketed the completion of his first string quartet in 1879, while the loss of the full score for his second symphony (a fact discovered just as he was assured of a performance) resulted in his re-orchestrating much of the piece prior to its eventual premiere in 1877. *In the Steppes of Central Asia,* his short, vibrant orchestral work, was composed rather quickly in comparison, with Borodin starting and finishing the piece during the first weeks of 1880. The next year saw the completion of his second string quartet, which he dedicated to his wife. By the time of his death from a heart attack in 1887, Borodin had not yet completed what was to have been his magnum opus, the opera *Prince Igor.* Rimsky-Korsakov (as he had done for Mussorgsky) and Alexander Glazunov took it upon themselves to prepare a performing edition of *Prince Igor,* while Glazunov orchestrated some of Borodin's piano pieces (to form the *Petite Suite*) and both men orchestrated a few of his songs.

Orchestral
In the Steppes of Central Asia for Orchestra
what to buy: [*Russian Orchestral Music*; Leonard Bernstein, cond.; New York Philharmonic Orchestra] (Sony Classics 47607) ♪ ♪ ♪ ♪

Most of the programming for this disc places the album on the cusp of the nineteenth and twentieth centuries, when Russian nationalism was coloring the music being produced. That said, Borodin's mini-tone poem sits well as part of a collection of Russian bonbons including standards by Mikhail Glinka, Reinhold Gliere, Mikhail Ippolitov-Ivanov, Modest Mussorgsky, Sergei Prokofiev, and Dmitri Shostakovich.

Prince Igor: Polovtsian Dances
what to buy: [Herbert von Karajan, cond.; Berlin Philharmonic Orchestra] (Deutsche Grammophon 419063) ♪ ♪ ♪ ♪♪

Karajan's disciplined forces combine with Deutsche Grammophon's long-heralded engineering staff to create a lively (albeit well-groomed) rendition of Borodin's oft-times unruly dances which perfectly complements the ensemble's version of Nicolai Rimsky-Korsakov's *Scheherazade,* with which it is paired.

what to buy next: [Leonard Bernstein, cond.; New York Philharmonic Orchestra] (Sony Classics 47600) ♪ ♪ ♪ ♪

While not as darkly hued as some Russian orchestras would make this piece sound, Bernstein's interpretation has a certain kick to it that, combined with a fairly clear recording, makes this piece jump out at you even more than normal. The rest of the album is a well-programmed crazy quilt of familiar ballet excerpts from Charles Gounod, Nicolai Rimsky-Korsakov, Giuseppe Verdi, and others.

Nocturne for String Orchestra (arrangement of movement from Borodin's second string quartet)
what to buy: [Leonard Slatkin, cond.; St. Louis Symphony Orchestra] (Telarc 80080) ♪ ♪ ♪ ♪

Lush string playing in this arrangement skirts the edge of kitsch but Slatkin still manages to maintain a sense of integrity. The rest of the program is packed with more proven hits for string orchestra, including the almost ubiquitous Pachelbel *Canon,* a cleanly played Ralph Vaughan Williams *Fantasia on Greensleeves,* and Tchaikovsky's hedonistic *Serenade* for Strings.

Symphony no. 2 in B Minor
what to buy: [Loris Tjeknavorian, cond.; National Philharmonic Orchestra] (RCA Victor 60535) ♪ ♪ ♪ ♪♪

Tjeknavorian has a flair for this material and communicates it to his colleagues in the orchestra, all of which results in a performance that, from an interpretive standpoint, is probably the best of those currently available. This is also a one-stop shopping package for those seeking Borodin's orchestral "hits." The other works include *In the Steppes of Central Asia* and four instrumental excerpts from *Prince Igor* (the overture and the *Polovtsian Dances* among them).

what to buy next: [Rafael Kubelik, cond.; Vienna Philharmonic Orchestra] (Seraphim 69021) ♪ ♪ ♪♪

This is part of a rewarding set of Borodin's most popular orchestral works—the second symphony, *In the Steppes of Central Asia,* and the *Polovtsian Dances* and overture from *Prince Igor*—combined with two fan favorites by Modest Mussorgsky. Kubelik, who conducts the first and third compositions, is a steady performer who can often generate inspired playing from his orchestra. André Cluytens also directs the Philharmonia Orchestra in *Steppes* while Constantin Silvestri conducts the same forces in Glazunov's arrangement of Borodin's *Igor* overture. William Steinberg's Pittsburgh Symphony Orchestra runs through Mussorgsky's *Night on the Bare*

Mountain and Herbert von Karajan leads the Philharmonia Orchestra in that composer's *Dance of the Persian Slaves* from *Khovanshchina*.

Chamber
Quartet no. 2 in D Major for Strings
what to buy: [Emerson String Quartet, ensemble] (Deutsche Grammophon 445551) ♪ ♪ ♪ ♪

If you are only familiar with the *Nocturne* in its orchestral arrangement, the original string quartet version is even more haunting in its intensity. The smooth yet taut playing of the Emerson String Quartet is a very good match for this material. Their version is packaged with a delightful take on Antonín Dvořák's *American* String Quartet and the pleasantly innocuous first effort into the medium by Piotr Tchaikovsky.

worth looking for: [Takács Quartet, ensemble] (London 452239) ♪ ♪ ♪ ♪

The Takács Quartet was entering a marvelous "middle age" stretch in their career when this performance was recorded, emphasizing the melodic content of Borodin's quartet without neglecting the rhythms that make it all work. The group's rendition of Borodin's small-force masterpiece stands up quite well to other versions currently available and has a strong disc-mate in the ensemble's playing of Bedrich Smetana's first string quartet.

influences: Modest Mussorgsky, Alexander Glazunov, Nicolai Rimsky-Korsakov, Mikhail Glinka

Mathilde August

William Boyce
Born c. September 1711, in London, England. Died February 7, 1779, in Kensington, London, England.

period: Baroque

William Boyce's lively, inventive works deserve a hearing from modern audiences to better understand why music lovers of his day considered him a worthy contemporary of George Frideric Handel and Henry Purcell. Boyce was also an important pedagogue and compiler/historian of sacred music.

Boyce's reputation after his death was based more on his sacred music than anything else, and there is no doubt that his connection to the church was longstanding and important. His first real exposure to music as a profession came when he was admitted to the choir of St. Paul's Cathedral. As a chorister, Boyce learned how to play various keyboard instruments, which prepared him for a post-choral career. His first job outside the choir loft came in 1734, when he was appointed organist to the Earl of Oxford's chapel, a position that allowed Boyce to teach harpsichord playing to a variety of students. He started writing short songs for popular consumption, in addition to weightier pieces. By 1736 Boyce's reputation had grown to the point that he was able to take a higher paying position as organist at St. Michael's Cornhill. That same year, Boyce was appointed composer to the Chapel Royal.

Boyce's choral music shows him to be a master craftsman in the art of text painting. An example of Boyce's brilliance at giving life to words can be heard in his setting of Psalm 25, *Turn Thee unto Me*. The passage "for I am desolate" is a heart-rending plea, expressed with a descending melodic line in a minor mode and in imitative counterpoint between a bass singer and boy trebles. This particular anthem features the juxtaposition of chordal writing with contrapuntal texture to convey the text's dramatic nature. His delightful serenata *Solomon* was performed by the Society of Apollo in 1742 and enjoyed frequent performances until the turn of the century, when the text (based on passages from the biblical *Song of Solomon*) was deemed too erotic. Boyce's next theatrical work, *The Secular Masque*, with a libretto by John Dryden, was first performed at Cambridge in 1749 as part of a Boyce festival. Various songs from this work were published in *Lyra Britannica*, the first volume of Boyce's song collection.

Boyce's only chamber music compositions (*Twelve Sonatas for Two Violins, with a Bass for the Violoncello or Harpsicord*) were published in 1747 and enjoyed great popularity during his lifetime. Charles Burney described the impact of these works in glowing terms: "...they were longer and more generally purchased, performed and admired, than any productions of the kind in this kingdom, except those of Corelli. They were not only in constant use, as chamber Music, in private concerts, for which they were originally designed, but in our theatres, as act-tunes, and public gardens, as favourite pieces, during many years." Boyce took his next steps towards lifetime security when he was appointed Master of the

King's Musick in 1755 and when he was named as one of the three organists at the Chapel Royal in 1758. Some of the works that Boyce composed as part of his duties appeared in the set of eight symphonies he published in 1760 and in the twelve overtures of 1770.

Boyce's fascination with the music of earlier English composers may have been facilitated by his inheriting a collection of church music put together by Maurice Greene and John Alcock. This compilation helped form the core of Boyce's music library, the largest such collection in Britain. His three volumes of *Cathedral Music* (published in 1760, 1768, and 1773) combined a host of resources, bringing together works of English composers spanning 200 years in a massive set that played a great role in preserving the outstanding tradition of English church music. Containing music by John Blow, Henry Purcell, Pelham Humfrey, and Orlando Gibbons, Boyce's *Cathedral Music* also served as source material for and played a major part in the development of nineteenth-century British church music.

Orchestral
Symphonies, op. 2
what to buy: [*William Boyce: 8 Symphonies*; Trevor Pinnock, cond.; English Concert, orch.] (Deutsche Grammophon Archiv 419631) ♪ ♪ ♪ ♪

Boyce's op. 2 contains the eight symphonies that were published in 1760. These delightful works are filled with invention and easily stand out from the bulk of the baroque material available on disc. Pinnock leads his merry band through the intriguing twists and turns of the composer's scores with plenty of elan, marking these performances as an easy place for the novice to begin appreciating Boyce's art.

Chamber
Voluntary in A Minor
worth looking for: [*Early English Organ Music*; Simon Preston, organ] (Deutsche Grammophon Archiv 415675) ♪ ♪ ♪

Be transported to the Chapel Royal with this performance by Preston. Organists should note that he plays on an organ built for Lichfield Cathedral in 1789 that was moved to the parish church of St. John the Baptist in Armitage in 1861. The rest of this recital covers works by a wide variety of composers, including such well-known names as John Bull, William Byrd, Orlando Gibbons, and Henry Purcell.

influences: George Frideric Handel, Thomas Arne, Johann Christian Bach, Charles Wesley

Marijim Thoene and Garaud MacTaggart

Johannes Brahms
Born May 7, 1833, in Hamburg, Germany. Died April 3, 1897, in Vienna, Austria.

period: Romantic

During his lifetime considered a musical reactionary or held up admiringly in opposition to the modernism of Wagner, hailed as an innovative visionary in the next century by Arnold Schoenberg (in a 1947 essay entitled *Brahms the Progressive,* he praised Brahms's bold modulations—as daring as Wagner's most tonally ambiguous chords—asymmetrical forms, and mastery of "developing variation"), Johannes Brahms is now viewed as a central figure in Western music, immortalized as one of the "three B's" along with Johann Sebastian Bach and Ludwig van Beethoven. His combination of Classical structural rigor and autumnally nostalgic Romanticism has shown its appeal to be timeless.

Brahms was born into a family of modest means and grew up in working-class neighborhoods. His father, a music teacher, gave him his first lessons on piano, cello, and horn, and by the time he was ten his exceptional talent had earned him free instruction in piano and music theory from one of Hamburg's leading teachers. He was soon performing in public, and while still in his mid-teens had already made a name for himself as a fine pianist. His first two published works were piano sonatas: in C major (1853) and F sharp minor (1854). In 1853 he became friends with the famous violinist Joseph Joachim, who put the budding composer in touch with Franz Liszt and Robert Schumann. The latter recognized Brahms as a rising star early in his career, when he was 20 and still best known as a pianist. A critic as well as composer, Schumann dubbed him the great hope of German music in the now-famous article *New Paths,* writing that Brahms was "called to give the highest and most ideal expression to his time," and thus setting him up as potentially the first symphonist to meas-

Johannes Brahms

ure up to Beethoven's standard. This may have helped spread Brahms's name, but he was distinctly conscious of being in the master's shadow, commenting to the conductor Hermann Levi, "I shall never compose a symphony! You have no idea what it is like to hear that giant tramping behind us."

In 1854 he began composing a two-piano sonata that nearly became his first symphony but was eventually turned into a piano concerto, which he premiered in 1859 with Joachim conducting. He also wrote two serenades for orchestra, practice in dealing with the challenges of composing for symphonic forces. Even a chamber work like the Sextet no. 1 in B flat major for Strings approaches symphonic dimensions—an unusually grand work for just six string instruments. One of Brahms's great friends was Clara Schumann (Robert's widow). A letter he wrote to her in 1862—the year he was appointed conductor of the Philharmonic concerts and Singakademie choir in Hamburg—includes the theme of the first movement of what he declared would be his first symphony but, a decade later, it was still unfinished.

In the interim he had written *Ein Deutsches Requiem (A German Requiem)* in the aftermath of his mother's death. The success of its performance in Bremen in 1868 and throughout Europe in the following years brought him widespread fame at last. The work is not a setting of the standard Requiem text of the Latin liturgy, but rather a carefully selected assortment of excerpts from Luther's German translation of the Bible. Brahms said it could be called *A Human Requiem*. Brahms still continued to write in smaller forms, and his next major successes included the 18 *Liebeslieder* Waltzes for vocal quartet and piano four hands, and two volumes of *Hungarian Dances* for piano four hands.

A turning point in Brahms's life came in 1872 when he moved to Vienna to take up an appointment as director of the prestigious Gesellschaft der Musikfreunde. Another important orchestral work, the "Haydn" Variations, was composed in 1873 and performed by the Vienna Philharmonic. Finally, in the summer of 1876, he completed his First Symphony, which was premiered under Otto Dessoff at Karlsruhe, Germany, a few months later. Comparisons to Beethoven were immediate—famed pianist/conductor Hans von Bülow, the source of the "three B's" remark, referred (favorably) to it as Beethoven's "Tenth," to which Brahms, typically irascible, replied, "Any ass can hear that." The success—or,

perhaps, merely the completion—of his Symphony no. 1 in C minor may have freed Brahms of his inhibitions. Certainly the next one (in D major) appeared quickly. It was completed in 1877, and premiered by the Vienna Philharmonic under the famous conductor Hans Richter (though Brahms was not fond of Richter's style, finding it too rigid).

His Violin Concerto—a worthy successor to Beethoven's, in the same key (D major) and of comparably large dimensions—appeared in 1878, dedicated to Joachim, who had provided much technical advice in its creation. The mighty Concerto no. 2 in B flat major for Piano and Orchestra—on a larger scale than any of Beethoven's, even containing an unprecedented fourth movement—was premiered by Brahms in 1881; the Symphony no. 3 in F major, again premiered by the Vienna Philharmonic and Richter, came out in 1883, and the Symphony no. 4 in E minor was first performed in 1885 by the Meiningen Orchestra, perhaps Brahms's favorite, with Bülow conducting. The "Double Concerto" for Violin, Cello, and Orchestra of 1887 was his last major work for the concert hall.

Aside from this procession of mighty orchestral works, Brahms kept up a steady stream of smaller pieces for more intimate forces, most notably for singers (lieder and folksong settings especially, but also many fine choral pieces harking back to the tradition of Bach and Mendelssohn, yet still distinctively Brahmsian in their musical language) and many superb piano pieces. The songs and piano works are often more immediately appealing than his famous large-scale works. Only by appreciating them as well can one grasp the full splendor and breadth of his achievement; balancing his abstract symphonies and concertos are the folklike melodies of some of his songs and the glorious effulgence of his *Ballades, Intermezzi, Rhapsodies*, etc. for solo piano. A more restrained, intimate, even transcendental tone entered some of them in his last, less prolific years, most notably in the piano collections opp. 116-119, the two Sonatas for Clarinet and Piano (op. 120) (of which there is also an edition for viola), the *Four Serious Songs* (op. 121), and the 11 *Chorale Preludes* for Organ (op. 122).

In his later years, the life-long bachelor became overweight from a diet of cheap food and large quantities of beer. He died of liver cancer supposedly aggravated by a cold he caught attending the funeral of Clara Schumann in Bonn in May 1896. Less than a month before his death, Brahms attended a Vienna Philharmonic concert under Richter which included the Fourth Symphony. His adopted home city had not always appreciated this demanding work, which ends with a complex movement of variations, but this time it was applauded vociferously after every movement and, deeply moved, the composer had to take multiple bows.

Much was made, especially during his lifetime, of Brahms's supposedly conservative musical tendencies (which were real to some extent, especially later in his life when, for instance, he expressed a dislike of the daring new harmonies in Richard Strauss's tone poems). Those out of sympathy with Wagner and Liszt and other avant-garde musical personalities of the time rallied around Brahms, and the resulting polarization often drove other progressives into opposing him. Hugo Wolf, for instance, is responsible for this vitriolic (and utterly wrong-headed) statement: "The art of composing without ideas has certainly found its worthiest champion in Johannes Brahms…these nauseating and vapid symphonies…are essentially a mess of hypocritical chaos and confusion with their dearth of melody, their crippled rhythms, and arid harmonies." Brahms, though he certainly had his strong opinions, largely kept himself out of this fray. And some composers identified with the Wagner camp respected Brahms greatly—-Anton Bruckner being a prime example.

Brahms was by no means immune to self-criticism, on the contrary. He destroyed a number of works that he later decided were not up to his standards, even asking for the return of pieces he had written as presents! A few such works slipped through his net; among them are the first version of the First Symphony's second movement (reconstructed from orchestral parts) and a preliminary version of the Piano Trio, op. 8 (though it's rarely heard). There were also entire compositions lost to future generations when Brahms consigned them to the flames.

Orchestral
Symphonies (complete)
what to buy: [*Furtwängler Conducts Brahms*; Wilhelm Furtwängler, cond.; North German Radio Orchestra; Berlin Philharmonic Orchestra; Vienna Philharmonic Orchestra] (Music & Arts 4941) ♪ ♪ ♪ ♪ ♪

Furtwängler was arguably the greatest Brahms conductor of the 20th century. He left a multitude of recordings of the symphonies, mostly concert performances, and

this set unerringly chooses the best one for each work. While tending to take slower speeds than the norm, Furtwängler shapes phrases and the larger structure with extreme flexibility—too much for certain strict modern tastes, but Brahms himself avowed that when he was conducting these works, he could never make too many tempo adjustments. Furtwängler conducts the orchestra he helmed for many years, the Berlin Philharmonic, in symphonies nos. 3 (from April 27, 1954) and 4 (December 12-15, 1943), the Vienna Philharmonic (with which he also had a long-standing relationship) in no. 2 (January 28, 1945), and the North German Radio Orchestra in a monumental no. 1 (October 27, 1951) from a legendary concert as guest conductor. The latter performance, in particular, is intensely profound and perfectly judged in all matters. This must-own set also features the Second Piano Concerto, with Edwin Fischer as the supremely sensitive soloist (November 8, 1942), and two readings of the *Variations on a Theme by Haydn*, one from the same Hamburg concert as the First Symphony, the other from the same Berlin concert as the Fourth. Never mind the less-than-hi-fi sonics, this music can hardly have ever sounded more emotionally transcendent than on these four CDs.

what to buy next: [Wolfgang Sawallisch, cond.; Vienna Symphony Orchestra] (Philips 438757) ♪ ♪ ♪ ♪₄

These 1959-63 recordings team up an orchestra and a conductor who are eminently comfortable in these works, but the young Sawallisch played up their drama (but not melodrama!), making this one of the great stereo cycles. The woodwinds and brass have great character without slipping into eccentricity (though there are slight touches of untidiness), and the strings, if lacking the final degree of polish, play with endearing emphasis and passion. Most of all, though, it is the conductor's vigorous, sweeping readings which make this such a compelling set. Fitting the four symphonies onto two discs for the price of one merely makes the decision to acquire this highly flavorful view of the cycle even easier.

[Kurt Sanderling, cond.; Staatskapelle Dresden, orch.] (Eurodisc 69220) ♪ ♪ ♪ ♪₄

This is definitely the biggest bargain in Brahms, a three-CD set that features irreproachable performances in the German tradition and includes equally recommendable readings of the *Haydn Variations* and the *Tragic Overture*. Sanderling shapes the music subtly yet vividly, with great rhythmic incisiveness yet no sense of nervous fidgeting—in fact, with sensitively applied and very effective agogic hesitations in performances whose considerable flexibility seems entirely organic and unfussy. The sound of these 1971-72 recordings is very forward but realistic on those terms, and the orchestra was and is one of Germany's finest.

[Charles Mackerras, cond.; Scottish Chamber Orchestra] (Telarc 80450) ♪ ♪ ♪ ♪₄

The "authentic performance" movement has even reached the late 19th century, and this is the best rethinking of Brahms to come out of it. A new critical edition is used, correcting some minor printing errors; more significantly, the cover says, "The Four Symphonies in the style of the original Meiningen performances," and that means reversion to the old orchestral seating of first and second violins on opposite sides of the platform (which reveals some antiphonal passages usually not audible), period instruments, generally quick yet flexibly inflected speeds, tasteful string portamento, and an ensemble of only 47 players, with woodwinds and brass more prominent than in larger orchestras. Of course, many collectors will not want their Brahms leaner, and those who insist on plush string sections should steer clear. Also of interest is an early version of the second movement of the First Symphony. Fillers for this three-CD set are the *Academic Festival Overture* and the *Haydn Variations*.

worth looking for: [Leopold Stokowski, cond.; Philadelphia Orchestra] (Biddulph 017/18) ♪ ♪ ♪ ♪₄

Throughout his more than six-decade career, Stokowski devoted considerable attention to the Brahms symphonies. In fact, these recordings from, respectively, 1927, 1928, 1929, and 1933 (originally on Victor) were the first complete recorded Brahms symphony cycle. It's worth listening through the unsurprisingly primitive sound quality to hear one of the world's greatest orchestras being led by the man who created its famously beautiful string tone. Stokowski could take odd liberties with music, but these are relatively unmannered readings, though imbued with considerably more red-blooded drama and measure-to-measure tempo fluctuations than most modern conductors would dare. The First in this two-CD set is one of the great readings of all time, as viscerally thrilling as any captured on record and surpassed only by Furtwängler's mighty 1951 Hamburg concert performance, which has the edge in profundity.

Symphonies nos. 2-4
what to buy: [Willem Mengelberg, cond.; Concertgebouw Orchestra of Amsterdam] (Tahra 274/275) ♪ ♪ ♪ ♪₄

Here is evidence for the assertion that Brahms used to be played faster. But though Mengelberg's tempos are quick—the Second (in surprisingly clear sound for 1940, though with some distortion at the highest dynamic peaks) seems like a sprint compared to most modern maestros—he's not at all unyielding. The 1932 Third (for English Columbia, the only recording here not made for Telefunken), the 1938 Fourth, and the 1942 *Tragic Overture* are equally fresh and lively, and also quite expressive and nuanced, with some luscious string portamento (especially in the Third). The Fourth features some delightful and quite distinctive rhythmic articulation in the first movement.

Symphony no. 3 in F Major, op. 90
what to buy: [Erich Leinsdorf, cond.; Philharmonia Orchestra] (EMI Classics 67021) ♪ ♪ ♪ ♪₄

Recorded in 1958 and originally released in the US on Capitol, Leinsdorf's is a beautiful, unusual reading. The orchestra's execution is faultless, and the *full dimensional stereo* sound was captured with a single dual-capsule microphone (nothing here was "fixed in the mix"). It's smooth but finely detailed, and not without drama where called for. Many will prefer a more boisterous conception of this work (for them, there are Furtwängler, Sawallisch, and Mackerras in the sets recommended above), but for a warm alternative approach, Leinsdorf is hard to beat. The coupling is Milstein's stereo rendition of the Brahms Violin Concerto (see below).

Symphony no. 4 in E Major, op. 98
what to buy: [Carlos Kleiber, cond.; Vienna Philharmonic Orchestra] (Deutsche Grammophon 457706) ♪ ♪ ♪ ♪ ♪

There is no finer digital recording of this great work. Kleiber keeps the VPO from slackening and drowning the work in sentiment, while the warmth of their playing, with unostentatious little touches of string portamento, keeps his relatively taut reading from seeming heartless. Although he is more emotional in the slow movement than one might have expected, the main characteristic of this performance is drama.

Piano Concertos (complete)
what to buy: [Rudolf Serkin, piano; George Szell, cond.; Cleveland Orchestra] (Sony Classics 48166 and 42262) ♪♪♪♪₄

These 1968 recordings are classics that would be just as recommendable if they weren't budget-priced. Serkin's playing is simply bursting with passion throughout. On a very few occasions his finger-work may not be perfectly clean, but his technique is nonetheless impressive: he's going for broke in the service of his and Szell's incisive, energetic vision of these pieces—with, however, ample lyricism in the slow movements. The blend of intelligence and emotion here is entirely convincing. On the disc containing the first concerto (Sony Classics 48166) the remainder of the program finds Serkin in Schumann's *Introduction and Allegro appassionato (Konzertstück)* and Felix Mendelssohn's *Capriccio brillant.* However, coupled with the second concerto are the pianist's noble 1979 readings of Brahms's op. 119, nos. 1–3 (*Intermezzi*) and 4 (*Rhapsody*).

what to buy next: [Emil Gilels, piano; Eugen Jochum, cond.; Berlin Philharmonic Orchestra] (Deutsche Grammophon 44/446) ♪♪♪♪

This is a set for collectors who prefer ruminative, broad readings of these works—for those favoring songfulness over power. Gilels is poetic throughout, even where other pianists are muscular. Of its type this set has long reigned supreme, though some listeners may not find it to their taste. This two-CD set includes Gilels's readings of the seven *Fantasias* (op. 116) as filler on the second CD, and though the first disc remains short measure, the mid-price compensates.

[Stephen Hough, piano; Andrew Davis, cond.; BBC Symphony Orchestra] (Virgin Classics Veritas 61412) ♪♪♪♪

Though these recordings date from 1989, only the second concerto was issued at the time. This is much less monumental Brahms than the norm, entirely avoiding bombast. The interpretation highlights the contrast between the urgent orchestra and the more lyrical piano. The soundstage is far more integrated than in many solo recordings, with Hough's crystal-clear articulation and deep musicality making up for the lack of "spotlighting." Not a first choice, but a most interesting and well-executed alternative.

Concerto no. 1 in D Minor for Piano and Orchestra, op. 15
what to buy: [Clifford Curzon, piano; George Szell, cond.; London Symphony Orchestra] (Decca 466376) ♪♪♪♪₄

The emphatic orchestral introduction here has Szell's fingerprints all over it. The contrast with Curzon's seraphic entrance is stark, but Curzon soon builds to a level of intensity that matches the orchestra's. This is a most dramatic reading. Although the pianist seemingly does nothing out of the ordinary—barely seems to interpret at all except for wide dynamic contrasts—there is an unutterable rightness about this classic account. Part of his secret is a liquid legato which is no longer a dependable part of young pianists' arsenals, and an ability to project without letting the tone become harsh. Fluctuations in tempo are sometimes significant yet never seem exaggerated or calculated for overt effect. This reading combines grace and fist-in-velvet-glove power. The remainder of the CD consists of Curzon and the LPO under Boult in César Franck's *Symphonic Variations* and the *Scherzo* from Henry Charles Litolff's *Concerto symphonique* no. 4.

[Leon Fleisher, piano; George Szell, cond.; Cleveland Orchestra] (Sony Masterworks Heritage 63225) ♪♪♪♪₄

This classic 1958 recording is a fiery, sinewy take on a youthful work. Fleisher—a student of Schnabel—and Szell are on the same wavelength throughout, and certainly there has never been another version that so insistently gets the blood pumping. It's not that Fleisher pounds (actually, he's quite lyrical at times), it's just that when he plays forcefully, one can sense his reserves of strength being held back, if only by a hair. It's not inferior to the Curzon and many will even prefer it, but the Second Concerto (on a second CD) is not quite at this exalted level, making this a bit of an investment. There is a fine selection of Fleisher's 1956 monaural recordings of Brahms solo works to fill out each disc: the *Variations and Fugue on a Theme by Handel* (op. 24) and the *Waltzes* (op. 39). The *Handel Variations* are especially fine, nearly Beethovenian in their strength.

what to buy next: [*Artur Rubinstein Collection, vol. 34*; Artur Rubinstein, piano; Fritz Reiner, cond.; Chicago Symphony Orchestra] (RCA Victor Red Seal 63034) ♪♪♪♪

Not quite as good as some of its advocates claim, but still superb. There's plenty of forward impetus throughout, with Rubinstein's liquid tone keeping it from sounding jagged. The recording may be from 1954, but this is gorgeous-sounding stereo. The orchestra sounds as richly toned as the pianist, and although the performance is fairly fast (46:03), Reiner's direction makes allowances to stop and smell the roses in the slow movement—just not as languidly as many other performances. The finale is thrilling in a quicksilver way, but as exciting as it gets. This recording is never about raw power, as Fleisher/Szell or Serkin/Szell can be, because Rubinstein is always lyrical above all else. The fillers are a small selection of solo works he recorded in 1970: the *Capriccio* (op. 76, no. 2), the *Intermezzo* (op. 118, no. 6), and the *Rhapsody* (op. 79, no. 1), all played somewhat dryly but not unattractively.

Concerto no. 2 in B-flat Major for Piano and Orchestra, op. 83
what to buy: [Sviatoslav Richter, piano; Erich Leinsdorf, cond.; Chicago Symphony Orchestra] (RCA Victor Gold Seal 56518) ♪ ♪ ♪ ♪ ♪

Brahms's Second Piano Concerto stands apart from the normal concerto fare, both for its four movements and relative length (ranging from 40 minutes to around 52, depending on the interpreters) and for its epic, symphonic, rather unvirtuosic character (even though it is one of the greatest technical challenges in the concerto repertoire). This 1960 recording (made under nearly ad-hoc conditions two days after Richter's first American concert) is a legendary success. It gets off to a slow start, both literally and figuratively (there's an audible edit in the piano's first solo passage) but quickly builds up momentum. Richter's sheer abundance of tone is awe-inspiring yet produced without the slightest inclination to bang—in fact, some of the most magical moments come in quiet passages, where the suspense is tangible. The only complaint is that the solo cello in the third movement could have been a bit more strongly projected. Richter's famous unease in studio recordings is not in evidence here; this is superior to his other six recordings (one studio, five live) and offers unmatched (yet never ill-judged) spontaneity. The quite substantial "filler" is Beethoven's "Appassionata" Sonata, recorded later that year.

[*Artur Rubinstein Collection, vol. 1* Artur Rubinstein, piano; Albert Coates, cond.; London Symphony Orchestra] (RCA Red Seal 63001) ♪ ♪ ♪ ♪ ♪

This 1929 reading is startling in its alacrity, coming in two seconds under the 40-minute mark! Yet the élan with which Rubinstein plays is so great that it never seems rushed in execution, only in comparison to conditioned expectations. The piece has an utterly different character here than in any other recording, obviously, but not because of untoward eccentricities. Anyone who wants to hear the Brahms Second sparkle should acquire this disc. The sound is quite good for its vintage. (The filler is Tchaikovsky's First Piano Concerto with Rubinstein accompanied by Barbirolli in 1932.)

[*Artur Rubinstein Collection, vol. 71*; Artur Rubinstein, piano; Eugene Ormandy, orch.; Philadelphia Orchestra] (RCA Red Seal 63071) ♪ ♪ ♪ ♪ ♪

And here, 42 years later in 1971, with vastly better sound from both the orchestra and the engineers (it's possible here to revel in Rubinstein's glorious tone), is another fine Brahms Second from Rubinstein. This time he takes 48:46, but while the feeling is more autumnal than in 1929, it's not more somber. The pianist sounds happy, contented but vitally alive, although he was losing his sight at the time and would soon be forced to retire. "Miraculous" is not too strong a word. (The filler is Schumann's *Fantasiestücke*, op. 12.)

what to buy next: [Emanuel Ax, piano; Bernard Haitink, cond.; Boston Symphony Orchestra] (Sony Classics 63229) ♪ ♪ ♪ ♪ ♪

Ax is a thoughtful interpreter who delves deeply into whatever he plays, and he had performed this work over 150 times before this 1997 recording, including four concerts with Haitink in preparation for their studio reading. Its tempos are a bit broader than the norm, though not extravagantly so. Above all, it is warm and tender, both in Ax's beautifully lyrical playing and in the BSO strings. The filler is surprising: Yo-Yo Ma and Ax perform an anonymous transcription for cello and piano (from Brahms's lifetime) of the Sonata no. 1 in G major for Violin and Piano—hardly essential, but enjoyable.

Concerto in D Major for Violin and Orchestra Concerto, op. 77
what to buy: [Jascha Heifetz, violin; Fritz Reiner, cond.; Chicago Symphony Orchestra] (RCA Living Stereo 61495) ♪ ♪ ♪ ♪ ♪

Heifetz's playing was unfairly called cold and shallow.

This fiery sprint (34:31) through the second most important violin concerto (Beethoven's, of course, being the first) has been the object of envy by lesser violinists for 45 years, and criticism of the finale as too fast seems unconvincing in the face of its utter success as a taut, invigorating interpretation (not to mention Heifetz's perfect tone production and intonation). There are any number of recordings of Heifetz in this work, but this one (in glorious 1955 stereo) offers the best sound and finds his technique absolutely undimmed.

[Nathan Milstein, violin; Anatole Fistoulari, cond.; Philharmonia Orchestra] (EMI Classics 67021) ♪♪♪♪♪

This 1960 rendition is also faster than the norm but also, crucially, a bit slower (36:09) than Heifetz's, and Milstein's tone is somewhat mellower, less aggressive, so those who find Heifetz "cold" but shun the over-dramatization and exaggeratedly slow tempos of many modern players may find Milstein to be their ideal. His technique is exceptionally secure but never draws attention to itself; rather, what one notices is the charm and patrician elegance of his interpretation. This reading is also included in the magnificent six-CD box *The Art of Nathan Milstein* (EMI Classics 64830).

what to buy next: [Henryk Szeryng, violin; Antal Dorati, cond.; London Symphony Orchestra] (Mercury 434318) ♪♪♪♪₅

Neither Dorati's matter-of-fact conducting nor Mercury's somewhat cold recorded sound really suits Szeryng in this 1962 recording, but as his version with Monteux is currently available only in an expensive box set, this is the great violinist's most practically recommendable reading. And make no mistake, the extra warmth of his playing in this piece must be heard. It's not that, at 39:51, tempos are relaxed, because there is no lack of tension (maybe Dorati was useful here, after all), but Szeryng at this time had the knack of connecting the notes more completely than other players—his legato is amazing—which makes the lines sound fuller and more rhapsodic than usual. The coupling is Aram Khachaturian's Violin Concerto.

[Aaron Rosand, violin; Derrick Inouye, cond.; Monte Carlo Philharmonic Orchestra] (Vox 7902) ♪♪♪♪₅

Rosand whips through the Brahms with vigorous but not exaggerated alacrity (37:50). Like Heifetz and Milstein,

Julian Bream:
Born in 1933, Julian Bream received his first guitar lessons from his father but, with the exception of a few private lessons he received from Andrés Segovia while the latter was touring Great Britain in 1947, Bream was essentially a self-taught guitarist. His talent, however, was so apparent to Segovia and members of the Philharmonic Society of Guitarists that, in 1948, they sponsored a benefit concert for the young guitarist that eventually (with the additional aid of a separate scholarship) enabled him to attend the Royal College of Music despite the school's lack of a guitar program. There Bream studied cello and piano while honing his guitar skills in his free time. By this time he had also established a performing career on the side, playing in a series of radio programs for the BBC.

Bream began delving into Baroque and Renaissance lute music in 1950, an interest that would lead to his working with the noted countertenor Alfred Deller and, from there, to the eventual formation of the Julian Bream Consort ten years later. This ensemble was one of the earliest groups of the modern era (along with the Deller Consort) devoted to the study and performance of early music, generally concentrating on compositions (and arrangements of works) from the Elizabethan era but especially favoring pieces by John Dowland, William Byrd, Thomas Morley, and Orlando Gibbons. Among the albums celebrating this period in Bream's career are his selections of Johann Sebastian Bach's *Lute Suites and Trio Sonatas* (RCA Victor Gold Seal 61603), wherein he is aided by harpsichordist George Malcolm, and the delightfully programmed *The Baroque Guitar* (RCA Silver Seal 60494), containing his performances of works by Bach, Gaspar Sanz, Fernando Sor, Robert de Visee, and Silvius Leopold Weiss. The latter album won a Grammy Award in 1966.

Although his earliest years as a professional focused on material from the English Renaissance in addition to the Spanish repertoire and Baroque transcriptions favored by Segovia, Bream also sought opportunities to work with contemporary composers and broaden the catalog of guitar works available to modern musicians. In that regard he secured the contributions of Benjamin Britten (*Songs from the Chinese* and *Nocturnal* for Guitar), William Walton (the five *Bagatelles* for Guitar), Hans Werner Henze (*Royal Winter Music I* for Guitar and *Drei Tentos*), Lennox Berkeley (Sonatina for Guitar), Michael Tippett (*The Blue Guitar*), Peter Maxwell Davies (*Hill Runes*), and a number of other twentieth century composers. For listeners desiring to hear Bream's playing of more modern scores, a good place to start would be with *Nocturnal* (EMI Classics Special Import 54901), an album he recorded in 1993 (after ending his remarkable thirty-one year association with RCA) featuring works by Britten, Toru Takemitsu, Leo Brouwer, Witold Lutoslawski, and Frank Martin, some of which were commissioned by and/or dedicated to Bream.

Ian Palmer

he comes from the Leopold Auer tradition (in his case, by way of their contemporary Efrem Zimbalist), though leavened by the Eugène Ysaÿe School. His beautiful yet biting tone, a sonically attractive recording (for a budget and mid-price label), and depth and passion expressed nobly make this a top-notch reading—the finest of the digital era in this work. The disc also includes Rosand's performance of the Beethoven violin concerto.

[*Fritz Kreisler: Early Recordings*; Fritz Kreisler, violin; Leo Blech, cond.; Berlin State Opera Orchestra] (Music & Arts 4290) ♪ ♪ ♪ ♪₎

This is a 1927 recording, and requires tolerant ears as far as sound is concerned. But Kreisler's inimitable playing is certainly reward enough for the effort—and his cadenzas are imaginative. To say this is a style of playing that has died out is, in a way, misleading, because there have been very, very few violinists who combined his silken tone, gliding phrasing, and complete bow control, even at the softest dynamics, with unabashedly Romantic yet never distorted interpretations. This is part of a mid-price two-CD collection with concertos by Mendelssohn, Beethoven, and Mozart.

Concerto in A Minor for Violin, Cello, and Orchestra, op. 102—"Double Concerto"
what to buy: [Zino Francescatti, violin; Pierre Fournier, cello; Bruno Walter, cond.; Columbia Symphony Orchestra] (Sony Classics 64479) ♪ ♪ ♪ ♪₎

This is perfect teamwork. The under-rated Francescatti and the justly legendary Fournier deliver a sweet-toned, ardent reading, exquisitely balanced sonically and with excellent support by the orchestra and conductor; that the soloists are quite spotlit (though not as extremely as on some recordings) is forgivable here. Phrasing is emphatic but not labored, tempos are moderate and well judged, and the whole performance glows eloquently. The Beethoven "Triple Concerto" on the second half of this CD comes from 10 years earlier, in poor monaural sound (Walter is the only participant in both). No matter; at mid-price the Brahms alone makes this disc worth owning.

what to buy next: [David Oistrakh, violin; Mstislav Rostropovich, cello; George Szell, cond.; Cleveland Orchestra] (EMI Classics 66954) ♪ ♪ ♪ ♪₎

This 1969 recording is an entirely different creature from the Walter set, with two stars (Oistrakh and Rostropovich) delivering ebullient, larger-than-life performances. More hot-blooded than warm, the soloists are mightily impressive if not, perhaps, operating on a scale designed to reveal all the music's charms. For those who revel in bold, even brash playing that fills up the sonic and mental picture, this has been the reading

of choice for three decades. It's paired with a compelling reading of Beethoven's "Triple Concerto" by Oistrakh, Rostropovich, pianist Sviatoslav Richter, and the Berlin Philharmonic conducted by Herbert von Karajan.

Serenades for Orchestra, opp. 11 (D Major) and 16 (A Major)
what to buy: [Jiří Bělohlávek, cond.; Czech Philharmonic Orchestra] (Supraphon 1992) ♪ ♪ ♪ ♪

Though on one level Brahms wrote these works in preparation for tackling the large form of the symphony, they don't necessarily call for interpretations of symphonic weight, density, and seriousness—quite the opposite, in fact. A general rule of thumb could be that if both Serenades don't fit onto a single CD, the conductor is overloading them with meaning. Bělohlávek emphasizes their joyous spontaneity. While fully capable of bringing out the lyrical qualities of the slow movements, he acknowledges the latter part of their tempo markings: Adagio non troppo. The Czech Philharmonic sounds glorious, rich but not overly polished, and Supraphon's sonics are clear and natural.

Variations on a Theme by Haydn, op. 56a
what to buy: [Michael Tilson Thomas, cond.; London Symphony Orchestra] (Sony Classics 47195) ♪ ♪ ♪ ♪₎

Thomas shapes this work skillfully, avoiding an overly episodic feeling and never pumping up the excitement prematurely. The orchestra plays with contained but palpable verve (the winds are especially good), in exceptional sound, on this 1989 recording; for a digital version of the work, this is hard to beat. It's also nice that the variations are separately banded. His version of the second *Serenade*, the first piece on this disc, is a bit more subdued than is ideal, but the *Hungarian Dances* (nos. 1, 3, and 10 arranged by Brahms and nos. 17–21 arranged by Dvořák) are pulsing with life.

Chamber
Sextets and Quintets (complete)
what to buy: [Cecil Aronowitz, viola; William Pleeth, cello; Christoph Eschenbach, piano; Karl Leister, clarinet; Amadeus Quartet, ensemble] (Deutsche Grammophon 419875) ♪ ♪ ♪ ♪₎

This three-CD set of 1967-68 recordings is a most useful (and economical) compendium of the two String Sextets, the Piano Quintet, the two String Quintets, and the

Clarinet Quintet. The core group is the Amadeus Quartet, augmented, as needed, by Aronowitz, Pleeth, Eschenbach, and Leister. The strings display vibrantly fulsome tone, with enough muscle to add emphasis where needed but not so much as to disrupt the musical line. Tempos tend to be on the fast side of moderate, sometimes driving but never rushed. Eschenbach blends well in the Piano Quintet while still projecting his instrument's tone. Leister's dulcet tone and the phrasing of the group as a whole find the right degree of nostalgia in the wonderfully autumnal Clarinet Quintet; their dynamic gradations are breathtakingly precise and apt. The sound is a bit closer than ideal throughout the set, as often in recordings of chamber music, but clearly defined as a result. This is a most recommendable blend of beauty and brains.

Sextets (complete)
what to buy: [Isaac Stern, violin; Cho-Liang Lin, violin; Jaime Laredo, viola; Michael Tree, viola; Yo-Yo Ma, cello; Sharon Robinson, cello] (Sony Classics 45820) ♪♪♪♪♪

While all the players here have major solo careers, they have worked together often and their teamwork and blend are impeccable. These readings of opp. 18 (B flat major) and 36 (G major) exude love. Emanuel Ax is also heard on the Theme and Variations in D minor for Piano, an arrangement by Brahms (presented to Clara Schumann for her 60th birthday) of op. 18's second movement. While certainly an interesting and offbeat tidbit, one wonders whether its inclusion justifies a second CD: the two sextets alone play for less than 79 minutes. But for collectors willing to spend the extra money, this set is easily recommendable.

Piano Quartets (complete)
op. 25, op. 26, op. 60; Piano Trios, op. 8, op. 87, op. 101

what to buy: [*Isaac Stern: A Life in Music—Brahms Trios and Quartets*; Emanuel Ax, piano; Isaac Stern, violin; Jaime Laredo, viola; Yo-Yo Ma, cello] (Sony Classics 64520) ♪♪♪♪

Brahms's three Piano Quartets, all Romantic masterpieces, are mainstays of that under-appreciated format and among his most distinctive compositions (in general, his chamber music including piano—his own instrument—seems more inspired than his works for strings alone). Ax, Stern, Laredo, and Ma offer a great emotional and dynamic range. Stern's playing (in 1986) was still

incisive as well as sweetly emotive—not that he's the focus of attention here, just the elder member. This is definitely a performance of equals, four people breathing as one. The musical gestures can get big, but they're never out of proportion. The miking is close, without any attempt at simulating an audience perspective, but that is entirely appropriate to music-making of this kind, drawing us into its ebb and flow. For the Piano Trios Stern is joined by cellist Leonard Rose (Ma's teacher) and pianist Eugene Istomin in readings of equally strong projection and brimming over with conviction. (The Piano Quartets are also available separately on Sony Classics 45846, but the three-CD set is a better value.)

Piano Quartets (complete), op. 25, op. 26, op. 60
what to buy: [*Brahms: Complete Piano Quartets*; Walter Trampler, viola; Beaux Arts Trio, ensemble] (Philips 454017) ♪♪♪♪

In Brahms, and in chamber music in general, these players subtly scale their performances to a small room, never over-projecting. Though there are some dynamic peaks, in general this is the musical equivalent of conversation rather than oration. The Beaux Arts Trio is a long-standing group (the personnel heard in the quartets are one of its later configurations: pianist Menahem Pressler, violinist Isidore Cohen, and cellist Bernard Greenhouse), and the level of cooperation and interplay between them and Trampler is considerable. The filler is the controversial Piano Trio in A major (op. posthumous), recorded earlier when Daniel Guilet was the Beaux Arts violinist. This is excellent value at a two-for-one price.

[Ruth Laredo, piano; members of the Shanghai Quartet] (Arabesque 6740) ♪♪♪♪

The playing here is emphatic, though not aggressive (the slow movements are nicely lyrical, and the strings employ portamento, though discreetly), but rhythmic alertness, strong accents, and wide dynamic contrasts—all wonderfully coordinated by the veteran Laredo and the young string players—give these pieces strong definition without any resort to extreme tempos. Laredo is prominent without being spotlit; the balance is close but natural on these 1999 recordings. Unfortunately, op. 26 occupies the entire second disc of this set, with no filler.

[Stephanie Brown, piano; Alexander Schneider, violin; Walter Trampler, viola; Leslie Parnas, cello] (Vanguard Classics 97/98) ♪♪♪

Avuncular violinist Schneider was the reason for reissuing this set, in a series dedicated to his chamber music recordings. Aside from Trampler, the other performers in these 1977 recordings (Parnas and Brown) are largely known only to chamber music aficionados, but the affectionate Romanticism of these readings gives them currency nearly a quarter century after their first appearance, in spite of competition from more finely polished groups. Alas, there is no filler.

String Quartets (complete)
what to buy: [Quartetto Italiano, ensemble] (Philips 456320) ♪ ♪ ♪ ♪

Though not as sharply defined as the Berg performances (see below), this set contains unpretentious readings of grace and beauty that may appeal to collectors who find the other group a bit nerve-wracking at times. The recorded sound is more than adequate, and this inexpensive two-CD set is made an even more irresistible value by the generous filler of both of the op. 120 Sonatas for Clarinet and Piano recorded by George Pieterson and Hephzibah Menuhin in 1980.

worth looking for: [Alban Berg Quartet, ensemble] (EMI Classics 54829) ♪ ♪ ♪ ♪♪

The great technical polish of the Bergs is not achieved at the expense of excitement or passion. It's as though the vitality and multi-hued timbral variety of an old-fashioned Middle-European quartet had been combined with the perfect intonation and control of a modern international group. The op. 67 quartet (recorded at a 1991 concert) is just as impressive as the studio efforts on the op. 51 pair. When they go for hushed expectancy, as in the lovely *Romanze* of op. 51 no. 1, tension never slackens; when they shoot for high-voltage thrills, precision never slips. A knee-jerk reaction would be to equate such perfection with coldness, yet in neither tone nor heart is that the case here.

Piano Trios (complete)
what to buy: [*Brahms: Complete Trios*; Beaux Arts Trio, ensemble] (Philips 438365) ♪ ♪ ♪ ♪

The earliest lineup of the Beaux Arts Trio (Pressler, piano; Guilet, violin; Greenhouse, cello) provides sweetly amiable but amply incisive readings of the three Piano Trios, joined by clarinetist George Pieterson for the wonderful Trio for Piano, Clarinet and Cello—one of the glories of Brahms's compositional Indian summer. Also

included is the Trio in E flat major for Piano, Violin & Horn, op. 40, with pianist György Sebok, violinist Arthur Grumiaux, and horn player Francis Orval, in a fairly low-key reading most notable for Grumiaux's beautiful tone. This is another excellent two-CD value from Philips.

Sonatas for Violin and Piano (complete)
what to buy: [*Artur Rubinstein Collection, vol. 41: Brahms Violin Sonatas*; Henryk Szeryng, violin; Artur Rubinstein, piano] (RCA Red Seal 63041) ♪ ♪ ♪ ♪ ♪

Recorded in December 1960 and January 1961, these performances of Brahms's three sonatas for violin and piano (among his most lovely and melodic music in any form) continue the success of Szeryng and Rubinstein's 1959 collaboration on Beethoven's "Spring" and "Kreutzer" sonatas. Szeryng exhibits some of the most gorgeous violin tone ever heard on record and Rubinstein's piano tone is even more fabled, of course; these pieces have never sounded more beautiful. And consider that in his youth, Rubinstein was an assistant in Joseph Joachim's violin classes! As much of a star as the pianist was, he had great respect and love for chamber music, and there's no ego on display here. Throw in superb sonics, and frankly, it's hard to imagine anyone dislodging this disc from the top spot in this repertoire.

what to buy next: [Aaron Rosand, violin; Hugh Sung, piano] (Vox Classics 7535) ♪ ♪ ♪ ♪♪

Certainly the best performance in the digital era, although not in terms of sound due to the somewhat recessed piano (in loud passages Sung holds his own, but in soft passages he loses presence). Rosand is the supreme living violinist in Romantic repertoire now that Perlman's technique is in decline, and his perfectly even tone production and subtle, entirely unselfconscious Romantic inflections (rubato, portamento, etc.) are a constant joy. Compared to Szeryng, in nos. 1 and 2 Rosand's fast movements are faster and his slow movements slower, in no. 3 the reverse is true in the first two movements, while the timings of the last two are just seconds apart. Rosand's generally greater urgency in outer movements and the greater contrast in his characterization of the music make this reading a most valid alternative.

[Itzhak Perlman, violin; Vladimir Ashkenazy, piano] (EMI Classics 66945) ♪ ♪ ♪ ♪

This 1983 recording is preferable to Perlman's later version with Barenboim, both for the extra grace of Perlman's playing and because Ashkenazy lets the piano part breathe instead of torturously dissecting it as Barenboim does. Perlman's tone, while beautiful, is slightly less evenly produced than Rosand's or Szeryng's, but his more relaxed readings will be preferred by some.

Sonata no. 3 in F Minor for Piano, op. 5
what to buy: [Emanuel Ax, piano] (Sony Classics 45933) ♪♪♪♪♪

Ax is more often pegged as an ideal "team player" in chamber-music ensembles than a piano heavyweight, but it's surprising that this decade-old recording hasn't changed that impression. This is a deeply probing account of the monumental five-movement work, glinting with emotion yet supremely aware of structure. Nicely full-bodied readings of the three *Intermezzi* from op. 117 fill out this disc.

what to buy next: [*Artur Rubinstein Collection, vol. 63*; Artur Rubinstein, piano] (RCA Victor Gold Seal 63063) ♪♪♪♪

Rubinstein's 1959 recording treats this work as more of a virtuoso piece. Whether one responds to his often lighter, fleeter, bravura reading is a matter of taste, of course, but of its type this is admirable, with a dazzling variety of tone color. Even more enticing are his 1970 recordings of the four *Ballades,* op. 10 (in Rubinstein's hands, they bear an attractive resemblance to Chopin); between those works are an *Intermezzo* (op. 116, no. 6) and a *Romance* (op. 118 no. 5).

works for solo piano (complete)
what to buy: [*Brahms: Works for Solo Piano*; Julius Katchen, piano] (London 455247) ♪♪♪♪♪

This set includes all the works with opus numbers, and of the various surveys of Brahms's piano music, it's both the most consistent and the most inspired. Katchen, whose career was cut short by cancer at the age of 42, plays with great élan throughout this concisely packaged, budget-priced six-CD box, the contents of which were recorded in the years 1962-65 (except for the *Ballades,* op. 10, which date from the previous decade—though the booklet fails to mention this—and are in monaural). His tempos in the fearsomely difficult *Paganini Variations* are spectacular. He has a brilliant tone, perhaps a bit too bright in some of the more lyrical works, though he is generally sensitive in modulating it.

In the second set of *Hungarian Dances,* using the piano duet version, Katchen is joined by Jean-Pierre Marty.

various works for solo piano
what to buy: [*The Glenn Gould Edition: Brahms*; Glenn Gould, piano] (Sony Classics 52651) ♪♪♪♪♪

Who would have guessed that this notorious iconoclast, who drained all the passion from Beethoven's *Appassionata,* would sound so utterly at home in this quietly emotional repertoire? The *Ballades* and *Rhapsodies* heard here come from 1982 sessions, while the selection of *Intermezzi* date from 1960. All are played with an intoxicating inward expressiveness and a lovely legato that's the opposite of his famously detached sound in Bach. This two-CD set is revelatory.

[Yaara Tal, piano; Andreas Groethuysen, piano] (Sony Classics 53285) ♪♪♪♪♪

For the piano duet version of all 21 of the *Hungarian Dances,* there is no better recording than this scintillating and joyous disc. The dance-like character and gypsy origins are always foremost, embodied in frequent but always appropriate (and perfectly coordinated—this is a long-standing collaboration) rubato and a beguilingly light touch, allied to splashes of brilliance. The duo's rhythmic flexibility is equally enlivening in the op. 39 Waltzes which are less famous but just as delightful.

Vocal
Ein Deutsches Requiem (A German Requiem), op. 45
what to buy: [Elisabeth Schwarzkopf, soprano; Dietrich Fischer-Dieskau, baritone; Otto Klemperer, cond.; Philharmonia Orchestra and Chorus] (EMI Classics 66955) ♪♪♪♪♪

Klemperer's version has been a classic since the day it was released. At generally moderate tempos that were actually considered a bit fast by the standards of the time, he makes the entire work cohere magnificently. This 1961 recording (with the excellent sonics of London's Kingsway Hall) comes from a period when he was stable and still in complete command of his conducting abilities. Everything is held together with his trademark granitic control, building inexorably to thrilling (but never exaggerated) climaxes. The chorus is most impressively drilled, and the choral-orchestral balance is superb. Fischer-Dieskau, in prime voice, sings with his usual interpretive intensity without sounding fussy. The purity of Schwarzkopf's voice is a joy, with a palpable (and textually apt) sense of reverent longing. Texts and translations are included. If there's a better performance of this work, it's not on this earth.

what to buy next: [Charlotte Margiono, soprano; Rodney Gilfry, baritone; John Eliot Gardiner, cond.; Orchestre Révolutionnaire et Romantique; Monteverdi Choir] (Philips 432140) ♪ ♪ ♪ ♪₅

This was the first (1990) *German Requiem* recording on period instruments, and still the best, because Gardiner invests it with considerable emotional expressiveness and stirring drama, with a wide range of dynamic and timbral shadings. His choir is one of the most perfectly disciplined groups around, and while the two soloists may not be household names, they are both excellent. Tempos are faster than average but not at all out of line. Full texts and translations are included in the packaging.

[*The Bruno Walter Edition: Brahms*; Irmgard Seefried, soprano; George London, bass; Bruno Walter, cond.; New York Philharmonic Orchestra; Westminster Choir] (Sony Classics 64469) ♪ ♪ ♪ ♪₅

This is a loveable, relaxed interpretation. One could wish for greater clarity in the 1954 monaural sound, but the performance is fine in all aspects, with Seefried especially magical thanks to the lightness of her upper range. This is probably the only one-CD version available with a significant filler, the *Alto Rhapsody*. Walter (leading the Columbia Symphony Orchestra and the Occidental College Choir) gives that work—a Goethe setting— nearly Mahlerian intensity, yet with redeeming sweetness at the end. The soloist, Mildred Miller, displays exemplary diction and modulates her timbre nicely, though her vibrato may be a bit too prominent for some tastes. Alas, there are no texts or translations for either work.

[*Brahms: Choral Works and Overtures*; Wilma Lipp, soprano; Franz Crass, baritone; Wolfgang Sawallisch, cond.; Vienna Symphony Orchestra; Vienna Singverein, choir] (Philips 438760) ♪ ♪ ♪ ♪

This 1962 recording is a fine mainstream version of the *German Requiem,* vastly better than many glitzier productions. As far as the soloists are concerned, Lipp's vibrato is a bit operatic—as is her phrasing—but Crass is excellent. Occasional moments when the choir's consonants aren't together will only bother those listening

with headphones. Sawallisch molds the phrases lovingly but not stiflingly, at generally moderate tempos. When one takes into account that this two-CD set also includes versions of the beautiful *Schicksalslied (Song of Destiny),* and the *Alto Rhapsody* plus the *Academic Festival Overture, Tragic Overture,* and *Haydn Variations,* it becomes an irresistible bargain.

[Janice Chandler, soprano; Nathan Gunn, baritone; Craig Jessop, cond.; Utah Symphony Orchestra; Mormon Tabernacle Choir] (Telarc 80501) ♪ ♪ ♪ ♪

The main attraction of this 1999 recording is that it's in English. Of course, the point of Brahms calling it a *German Requiem* was his use of texts in the vernacular, so the use of another language can also be justified. Robert Shaw's tweaking of existing translations of these Biblical texts helps adapt them to Brahms's rhythms and melodies, and the performance is, if not thrilling, far more than adequate. In spite of its size, the chorus (352 singers!) proves surprisingly agile, even in the large recording space of the Mormon Tabernacle in Salt Lake City. Speeds are moderate, and the soloists, especially Gunn, are also fine.

Alto Rhapsody, op. 53
what to buy: [Christa Ludwig, mezzo-soprano; Otto Klemperer, cond.; Philharmonia Orchestra and Chorus] (EMI Classics 67029) ♪ ♪ ♪ ♪

Ludwig is in magnificent voice in this 1962 recording, the sound is a bit clearer than on Walter's disc (see *German Requiem* above), and the male chorus is also slightly superior in tone and discipline. This is the filler on a CD featuring a fine reading of Brahms's First Symphony.

[Dagmar Pecková, mezzo-soprano; Jiří Bělohlávek, cond.; Prague Philharmonic Orchestra; Prague Philharmonic Choir] (Supraphon 3417) ♪ ♪ ♪ ♪

Bělohlávek's tempos are a bit slow, but he moves proceedings along just enough to maintain tension, giving the opening two stanzas a brooding darkness that's most effective. When the sun comes out (so to speak) in the third stanza, the effect is magical. Pecková has a rich, vibrant, but well-controlled voice and sings with great feeling, the only flaw being that she switches to an unnatural timbre to reach the very lowest passage (which lies better for true contraltos). With realistic sound, this makes a fine choice for collectors looking for a digital version of this work. The bulk of the disc contains orchestral songs by Wagner, Schoenberg, and Zemlinsky.

various sacred choral works

what to buy: [*Brahms: Motets*; Philippe Herreweghe, cond.; La Chapelle Royale de Paris, choir; Collegium Vocale, choir] (Harmonia Mundi 901122) ♪ ♪ ♪ ♪ ♪

These sacred a cappella choral works (opp. 29, 74, 109, and 110) are arguably the most purely beautiful pieces in Brahms's vast oeuvre. Many of the texts are Biblical, the rest are poetry either devotional or concerned with God as a refuge for world-weary souls. Herreweghe, just as in his numerous Bach recordings, presents the music in devotional fashion, both acoustically and in terms of its moods and meanings. Thus, these are not overly weighty performances, yet they are still reverent and largely shun overt drama. For these works looking back to Bach—full of contrapuntal passages, but with Romantic harmonies—such a presentation is most apt, and this is a very attractive program. Full texts and translations are included, but there are no notes regarding the music.

what to buy next: [*Geistliche Chormusik*; Marcus Creed, cond.; RIAS Chamber Choir, Berlin] (Harmonia Mundi 901591) ♪ ♪ ♪ ♪₆

Though slightly less atmospheric (but, on the other hand, with slightly clearer and better defined sound—so some might prefer it), Creed's program includes the bonus of the Sanctus, Benedictus, and Agnus Dei of the *Missa Canonica* that the young Brahms worked on in 1856. These are, apparently, the only movements that survived.

Liebeslieder Waltzes, opp. 52 and 65

what to buy: [Edith Mathis, soprano; Brigitte Fassbaender, mezzo-soprano; Peter Schreier, tenor; Dietrich Fischer-Dieskau, baritone; Karl Engel, piano; Wolfgang Sawallisch, piano] (Deutsche Grammophon 423133) ♪ ♪ ♪ ♪₆

The delectable *Liebeslieder* Waltzes, sets of 18 and 15 songs for vocal ensembles varying from one to four parts, accompanied by piano four hands, show Brahms having fun (not that the poems are entirely without pathos). This all-star quartet has delved deeply into them, finding more musical complexity and, especially,

shades of meaning in the lyrics, than usual. Some may feel they even go too far, making them into full-fledged art songs. Certainly there's no casual feeling here, no sense of the salon. For concert-hall intensity and full interpretive power in these works, this is the team to opt for, and their interplay is finely nuanced and unselfish. The pianists are rather in the background, but superb nonetheless. The op. 64 vocal quartets are a well-chosen

Liebeslieder Waltzes, op. 52

what to buy: [Benita Valente, soprano; Marlena Kleinman, contralto; Wayne Conner, tenor; Martial Singher, bass; Rudolf Serkin, piano; Leon Fleisher, piano] (Sony Classics 48176) ♪ ♪ ♪ ♪

For a less tightly wound—though often boisterous—account of the first and more familiar set of *Liebeslieder* Waltzes, this budget-priced disc makes a nice introduction which non-completists may find entirely satisfactory. These readings are more affectionate, more relaxed—but that's not to imply they're slipshod. The pianists fare well in the mix, emphasizing how delightfully Brahms has elaborated these little dances. The only complaint is that the men's voices are not of the same high quality as the women's. Also on the CD are bass-baritone George London and pianist Leo Taubman in the *Four Serious Songs* (op. 121), while the opening tracks find Valente and Serkin joined by French horn player Myron Bloom and clarinetist Harold Wright in two Schubert songs, respectively *Auf dem Strom* and *Der Hirt auf dem Felsen*.

[Heather Harper, soprano; Janet Baker, mezzo-soprano; Peter Pears, tenor; Thomas Hemsley, baritone; Benjamin Britten, piano; Claudio Arrau, piano] (BBC Music 8001) ♪ ♪ ♪ ♪

Another informal take on the first set, captured in concert in 1968 at Britten and Pears's Aldeburgh Festival. The mood is most informal, with some amusing exaggerations of certain melodic figures. Hemsley sounds a bit throaty and ordinary in such stellar company, but suffices. The live concert sound is not always perfectly captured, but the recording is more than adequate. The pianists accompany with considerable grace. The rest of the program consists of Tchaikovsky and Rossini songs.

various lieder

what to buy: [Jessye Norman, soprano; Daniel

Barenboim, piano] (Deutsche Grammophon 459469) ♪ ♪ ♪ ♪♪

This two-CD set is drawn from Norman's contribution to DG's Brahms Edition volume of the complete Lieder, but stands alone nicely. Her multi-hued voice, which she can present as girlish or maturely burnished depending on the context, is a magnificent instrument when used so intelligently in conveying the meaning of the text. Barenboim is less willful than usual here, aside from a few sudden shifts in dynamics when Norman isn't singing.

[*Brahms—Liszt—Lieder*, Thomas Quasthoff, bass-baritone; Justus Zeyen, piano] (Deutsche Grammophon 463183) ♪ ♪ ♪ ♪♪

Quasthoff is possibly the finest young lieder singer currently active. Here he probes the complex emotional profundities of this deeply affecting music with keenly pointed elegance, his darkly rich voice always beautiful and firmly but smoothly controlled, with a strong low range for a baritone and an easily accessed head voice. This 2000 release is especially welcome for presenting complete opuses rather than the usual assortments; heard this way, op. 32 in particular seems a most coherent cycle built on lovelorn poems. The vast bulk of the program is the listed Brahms; a few Liszt songs conclude.

influences: Franz Berwald, Robert Schumann, Antonín Dvořák, Edward McDowell, Max Bruch

Steve Holtje

Benjamin Britten
Born Edward Benjamin Britten, November 22, 1913, in Lowestoft, Suffolk, England. Died December 4, 1976, in Aldeburgh, Suffolk, England.

period: Twentieth century

Britten was a major 20th-century contributor to virtually every genre. He poured out a torrent of music for every conceivable occasion, always passionate, usually traditional sounding, and tuneful, but with a decidedly modern feeling. Best known for *The Young Person's Guide to the Orchestra*, the operas *Peter Grimes* and *Billy Budd*, and the intensely personal *War Requiem*, Britten ranks as the greatest English composer since Henry Purcell. His work has found a permanent place in the repertory

of opera companies, symphony orchestras, choirs, string quartets, and soloists the world over.

Britten was a modest man plagued by self doubt, at times painfully unsure of his talents, who never lost his boyish sense of wonder. As a composer of rare talent, he channeled all of these attributes into music that can be powerful, dramatic, lyric, memorable, religious, childish, witty, even terrifying.

He began studies in harmony, counterpoint, and composition with the composer Frank Bridge in 1924 and six years later, after winning a scholarship to the Royal College of Music, found himself studying piano with Harold Samuel and Arthur Benjamin, and composition with John Ireland. In 1933, his *Sinfonietta* was performed, but Britten achieved his first real success in 1937 with a performance by the Boyd Neel Orchestra of his *Variations on a Theme of Frank Bridge*. The 1930s saw the first of his collaborations with W.H. Auden (the song cycle, *Our Hunting Fathers*) and, in 1939, Britten (and his life-long companion Peter Pears) followed Auden's lead, emigrating to the United States where they lived first on Long Island and later in Brooklyn Heights. In America, Britten composed the *Sinfonia da Requiem* and the String Quartet no. 1 in D. Armed with a libretto by Auden, he also made his first foray into writing for the theater with the opera *Paul Bunyan*.

Physical illness and homesickness caused him to return to England in the spring of 1942. The trip across the Atlantic was both hazardous (it was the third year of World War II) and uncomfortable. Britten had trouble with customs officials on both sides who thought his manuscripts might be encoded messages. In spite of these difficulties, the composer completed the *Hymn to St. Cecilia* (to a text by Auden) and settings of English and Scottish poems for treble voice and harp on the journey home. To this last work he gave an unusual title, *A Ceremony of Carols*, although the use of plainsong at the beginning and end of the work give it the feeling of a religious service. Britten and Pears also sketched a synopsis for the opera *Peter Grimes*. With Pears singing the title role, the newly rejuvenated Sadler's Wells Opera Company gave its premiere on June 7, 1945, instantly establishing Britten as one of England's great musical dramatists. The next few years also saw a number of other important works, including his score for the film *Instruments of the Orchestra*—which would soon evolve into the classic *Young Persons' Guide to the Orchestra*—two chamber operas (*The Rape of Lucretia* and the witty *Albert Herring*), and the *Spring Symphony*. The first Aldeburgh Festival was held in 1948 in the Suffolk fishing village of that name, which would become the center of Britten's activities for the next three decades. His first work for the festival was the cantata *Saint Nicolas*. Other major works of his to receive premieres in this venue include *Lachrymae*, for viola and piano, the miracle play set to music *Noye's Fludde*, with important children's parts, the "church parable" *Curlew River*, and the opera *A Midsummer Night's Dream*. His other major operas from the 1950s include *Billy Budd* (adapted from Melville), *Gloriana* (written to honor the coronation of Elizabeth II), and *The Turn of the Screw*, a chilling version of the novel by Henry James.

One of Britten's most stunning compositions is the *War Requiem* of 1961, a work inspired by the texts of Wilfred Owen, an outstanding anti-war poet of the First World War whose work was revived during the Second, when Britten got to know it. Britten's requiem responded to Owen's profoundly disturbing poems that focused not on the heroism of soldiers but rather their transgressions against others and their own suffering. A prominent feature in many of Britten's works by the time he wrote this piece was the recurring theme of innocence desecrated and ruined, so it was fitting that the composer—a lifelong pacifist and conscientious objector—should create a piece about the violence of war, death, grief, and guilt set against the concepts of mercy, forgiveness, and peace. Written for soloists, multiple choirs, orchestra, chamber orchestra, and organ, it received its first performance in May of 1962 in the newly dedicated Coventry Cathedral (the old one having been destroyed by German bombs), and achieved a worldwide success comparable to *Peter Grimes* more than 20 years earlier.

Early in the 1960s Britten visited the Soviet Union where he was warmly received by both the government and Dmitri Shostakovich. The two dramatic works that followed his visit, *Owen Wingrave,* composed for the BBC in 1971, and *Death in Venice* from 1973, after Thomas Mann's novella, would be the last of his theater pieces. In 1973, Britten underwent surgery to replace a heart valve, and afterward his strength waned. The last three years of his life saw none of the touring and large productions in which he had taken part before but instead the composition of his subdued String Quartet no. 3 and several vocal works including *The Death of Saint Narcissus* (a "canticle" for tenor and harp on an early poem by T.S. Eliot).

Orchestral
The Young Person's Guide to the Orchestra, op. 34
what to buy: [Neeme Järvi, cond.; Bergen Philharmonic Orchestra] (BIS 420) ♪ ♪ ♪ ♪ ♪

Here is an engaging overview of the composer's style, containing not only the *Young Person's Guide,* but the four instrumental *Sea Interludes* from *Peter Grimes* and the intense yet seldom performed, *Cello Symphony.* Arvo Pärt's *Cantus in memory of Benjamin Britten,* written very much in Britten's powerful style, is also included, making this a satisfying set from start to finish.

what to buy next: [Benjamin Britten, cond.; London Symphony Orchestra] (London 417509) ♪ ♪ ♪ ♪

Any of the recordings that Britten made of his own music are fine since he was a very good conductor and worked with the best musicians. This disc also contains two earlier works by the composer: the *Simple Symphony* and *Variations on a Theme by Frank Bridge.*

[Andre Previn, cond.; Royal Philharmonic Orchestra] (Telarc 80126) ♪ ♪ ♪ ♪

This is a personal favorite of Retzel's. The *Courtly Dances* from Britten's *Gloriana* and Serge Prokofiev's delightful *Peter and the Wolf* (with Previn providing the narration) round out this charming, well-recorded, album.

worth looking for: [*Instruments of the Orchestra*; Malcolm Sargent, narrator and cond.; London Symphony Orchestra] (Beulah Video RT 152) ♪ ♪ ♪ ♪ ♪

This is a video of the original film which used *The Young Person's Guide to the Orchestra* as a soundtrack. The sound heard throughout is not of the fidelity one expects nowadays but the performances are excellent and the whole film is intriguing.

Chamber
Suites for Solo Cello, opp. 72, 80, and 87
what to buy: [*Britten: The Three Cello Suites*; Torleif Thedéen, cello] (BIS 446) ♪ ♪ ♪ ♪ ♪

These splendid, engaging, performances of Britten's beautiful, rich-toned works for unaccompanied cello display Thedéen's awesome, multifaceted technique. The cellist manages to capture the dark, churning intensity and graceful serenity found in these magnificent scores while BIS has given him an admirable acoustic within which to show off the virtues of both the composer and the performer.

worth looking for: [*Britten: Cello Suites 1 and 2*; Mstislav Rostropovich, cello] (London 421859) ♪♪♪♪♪

Along with the suites by J.S. Bach and the Zoltán Kodály sonata, these are the premier works for solo cello. Originally written by Britten for Rostropovich, the cellist delivers emotional yet technically secure, performances that deserve "hall of fame" status. Only the first two cello suites can be found here but the third work on this disc, the Sonata in C major for Cello and Piano, is a more than acceptable substitute and features the composer on piano accompanying Rostropovich.

Vocal
Peter Grimes, op. 33
what to buy: [Peter Pears, tenor; Claire Watson, soprano; James Pease, baritone; Geraint Evans, baritone; Benjamin Britten, cond.; Orchestra and Chorus of the Royal Opera House, Covent Garden] (London 414577) ♪♪♪♪♪

This opera is a classic and one listening to this classic performance will tell you why. Pears, in the role written for him, has never been surpassed as Grimes, the supporting cast is marvelous, and the overall production values (even though they date back to the early days of stereo recording) are excellent. The *Sea Interludes* and *Passacaglia* lifted from this opera to form one of Britten's more popular concert works only gives an idea of the power of the whole opera.

Billy Budd, op. 50
what to buy: [Peter Glossop, baritone; Peter Pears, tenor; Michael Langdon, bass; John Shirley-Quirk, baritone; Owen Brannigan, bass; Benjamin Britten, cond., London Symphony Orchestra; Ambrosian Opera Chorus] (London 417428) ♪♪♪♪♪

Melville's tragedy loses none of its drama in this opera, and the Pears/Britten recording is still the one to own. As a bonus, the set also includes two of the composer's song cycles (*The Holy Sonnets of John Donne* and *Songs and Proverbs of William Blake*) with Pears and Dietrich Fischer-Dieskau and Britten accompanying them at the piano.

War Requiem for soprano, tenor, baritone, orchestra, chamber orchestra, chorus, boy's choir, and organ, op. 66
what to buy: [Galina Vishnevskaya, soprano; Peter Pears, tenor; Dietrich Fischer-Dieskau, baritone; Simon Preston, organ; Benjamin Britten, cond.; Melos Ensemble; London Symphony Orchestra; Bach Choir; Highgate School Choir] (London 414383) ♪♪♪♪♪

This stunning choral work combining the Latin text of the Requiem with Owen's poetry is one of Britten's most widely acclaimed masterpieces. It is an 81-minute work of vast scope in which the composer drew on all the technical resources available along with abundant emotional power. There may be other recordings with more polish but certainly none more heartfelt.

A Ceremony of Carols for Treble Voices, Harp, and Chorus, op. 28
what to buy: [Sioned Williams, harp; David Hill, cond.; Choir of Westminster Cathedral, London] (Hyperion 66220) ♪♪♪♪♪

Hearing this work performed by a talented group of boy singers gives it the ethereal, otherworldly quality that Britten undoubtedly sought. Certainly Hill's lads give one of the finest renditions of this piece currently in the catalog. Williams is very good in her solo interlude, surely the single most sublime moment in 20th-century music for harp. Hill and his forces also work their magic on Britten's *Missa Brevis, Jubilate Deo,* and the gorgeous setting for double choir, *A Hymn to the Virgin.* Two other works from the composer, the *Hymn of St. Columba* and *Deus in adjutorium meum*, fill out the program.

worth looking for: [*Britten: The Choral Works, vol. III*; Harry Christophers, cond.; The Sixteen, choir] (Collins Classics 1370) ♪♪♪♪♪

This is one of the finest vocal ensembles around, and what a lineup of high-powered choral works is included here! In addition to the *Ceremony of Carols,* Christophers includes the *Missa Brevis,* the *Festival Te Deum, Jubilate Deo* and six more examples of Britten's skill with massed voices.

influences: Michael Tippett, Peter Maxwell Davies, Paul Hindemith, Igor Stravinsky, Dmitri Shostakovich

Frank Retzel and Nancy Ann Lee

Leo Brouwer

Born Juan Leovigildo Brouwer on March 1, 1939, in Havana, Cuba.

period: Twentieth century

Leo Brouwer's compositions include a cantata for two percussionists and piano, a ballet, choral pieces, and a series of challenging orchestral scores, but he is best known for works featuring his own instrument, the guitar. He also has over sixty film scores to his credit, including the incidental music for Mexican director Alfonso Arau's award-winning 1993 movie *Como agua para chocolate* (Like Water for Chocolate).

As a child, Brouwer was fascinated by the sounds he heard coming from his father's guitar and began a love affair with the instrument. He studied with Isaac Nicola, placing him in a performance lineage dating back to the first great Spanish guitar teacher, Francesco Tárrega, and his pupil, Emilio Pujol, Nicola's own mentor. Brouwer also began writing music, drawing inspiration from African-rooted aspects of popular Cuban culture even as he was absorbing the traditional repertoire of classical and romantic pieces associated with the guitar. He wrote his first works in 1954 and gave his first public performance the following year. After studying composition at the Peyrellade Conservatory in Havana, Brouwer obtained a grant enabling him to study at the Juilliard School of Music in New York City and the Hartt College of Music in West Hartford, Connecticut. He returned to Cuba in 1960 and was appointed director of the Music Department at the Instituto Cubano del Arte e Industria Cinematográficos, a position that enabled him to work with talented students in a program teaching the basics of composing for the cinema.

Brouwer's own scores from this time were clearly influenced by Béla Bartók and Igor Stravinsky, even though his music at its core still reflected Cuban folk traditions. He then embarked upon a new, decade-long phase, which Brouwer has since referred to as his middle period. He was the first Cuban composer to use aleatory and open forms, where elements of chance are involved in the composing or performing of a piece; he has described this period as a "big eruption, a kind of cathartic avant-garde aleatorealism." Inspired by the avant-garde music of the early 1960s, he began writing more experimental pieces, beginning with *Variantes de Percusión* and followed up by *Sonograma I,* for prepared piano *Canticum,* and *Le Espiral eterna.* Dating from this period, the *Elogio de la danza,* one of his most important

solo guitar works, illustrates how Brouwer was able to look back to his Afro-Cuban roots even as he included elements of Stravinskian aesthetics in a second movement he entitled *Ballets Russes.*

While his experimentation was valuable for what it taught him about instrumental and vocal capabilities, Brouwer became dissatisfied with that kind of writing fairly quickly and by the mid-1970s began taking a different approach to composition, one he called the "new simplicity" but that others have compared to neo-romanticism. It was during this period that he started listening to and adapting elements of pop music to the serial and traditional classical music styles in which he had been trained. By 1981 he seemed even more committed to the idea of meshing advanced compositional techniques with concepts derived from African and Hispanic historical sources. So it was with *El Decamerón negro,* one of his most celebrated works, for which Brouwer drew his inspiration from a collection of earthy, epic African tales compiled at the beginning of the Twentieth century by the renowned German anthropologist Leo Frobenius.

While Brouwer's solo guitar pieces consistently tax the abilities of performers even as they reward the ears of listeners, his works for guitar and orchestra are also valuable additions to the repertoire. In that category are the passionate, melodious *Concierto Elegíaco* (dedicated to Julian Bream and premiered in 1986) and the darkly textured *Concierto de Toronto* from 1987 (created for and premiered by guitarist John Williams). Alongside these works are the adaptations of pop and jazz standards (including Scott Joplin's "Elite Syncopations" and the seven-movement Beatles-inspired suite *From Yesterday to Penny Lane*) that also form an important part of his overall catalog. Brouwer's *Variations sur un thème de Django Reinhardt* could easily be considered in that vein as well.

In recent years Brouwer has focused more on composition, conducting, and teaching, due in part to a hand injury that has kept him from playing the guitar to his satisfaction. While there are still a fair number of recordings available that display his conducting prowess, the only disc currently in print featuring Brouwer as a guitarist is an Italian release, *Leo Brouwer Collection 4: Live Recordings of the Seventies* (Frame 9721). It showcases him performing works by Manuel Ponce, Hans Werner Henze, and Heitor Villa-Lobos, as well as his own arrangements of Scott Joplin's "The Entertainer" and "Elite Syncopations."

Orchestra
Concerto no. 3 for Guitar and Orchestra—*Elegíaco*
what to buy: [*The Guitar Concertos of Leo Brouwer*, Ricardo Cobo, guitar; Richard Kapp, cond.; Pro Musica Kiev, orch.] (ESS.A.Y. 1040) ♪ ♪ ♪ ♪ ♪

The Colombian-born Cobo, an accomplished classical guitar virtuoso, and Kapp, a sensitive conductor, manage their recording of this magnificently lyrical work with abundant flair. Cobo shines in the middle movement, a soothing oasis of sound, before a bit of interplay between guitar and marimba launches the fiery Afro-Cuban themes of the finale. Kapp also leads Pro Musica Kiev through a flawless recording of Brouwer's challenging fourth guitar concerto, the *Concierto de Toronto.*

Concerto no. 4 for Guitar and Orchestra— Concierto de Toronto
what to buy: [*The Black Decameron*; John Williams, guitar; Steven Mercurio, cond.; London Sinfonietta, orch.] (Sony Classics 63173) ♪ ♪ ♪ ♪ ♪

In the liner notes to this disc, Brouwer calls the *Concierto de Toronto* "one of my favorite pieces." It is easy to understand why in this masterly performance by John Williams, the guitarist to whom it was dedicated. The soloist is a bit forward in the mix but not so obtrusively to spoil the otherwise well-balanced orchestration. Especially intriguing is the way Brouwer meshes percussive effects (marimbas, etc.) with the string and woodwind sections. The balance of the album features one of the composer's most popular works for solo guitar, *El Decamerón negro*, along with the difficult *Elogio de la danza* and *Hika: In memoriam Toru Takemitsu.*

Chamber
From Yesterday to Penny Lane: Seven Songs after the Beatles
what to buy: [*Leo Brouwer Collection 2: Folk Songs*; Victor Pellegrini, guitar; Elisa String Quartet] (Frame 9623) ♪ ♪ ♪ ♪ ♪

Pellegrini is featured in the guitar and string quartet arrangement of Brouwer's seven-movement suite, a setting that shows off the basic architecture of the Beatles' songs ("She's Leaving Home," "Ticket to Ride," "Here, There, and Everywhere," "Yesterday," "Got to Get You

into My Life," "Eleanor Rigby," and "Penny Lane") with intimate clarity. While he presents much of the same material found in other Brouwer recitals (*Elogio de la danza, Un día de Noviembre,* and *Danza característica*), Pellegrini also offers some of the composer's short but brilliant arrangements of Cuban folk tunes, including "Zapateo," "Guajira Criolla," and the lovely "Drume Negrita."

what to buy next: [*From Yesterday to Penny Lane: Contemporary Works for Solo Guitar and Guitar & Orchestra*; Carlos Barbosa-Lima, guitar; Plamen Djurov, cond.; The Sofia Soloists, orch.] (Concord Concerto 42041) ♪ ♪ ♪ ♪

Differing from the chamber version in the order of songs presented, the orchestral setting of this work is suitably lush. But Djurov never lets the other musicians overpower the soloist, and Barbosa-Lima goes about his business with admirable efficiency instead of wallowing in the kind of sentimentality that could bury a lesser guitarist. The other major piece on the program, an arrangement of George Gershwin's *Rhapsody In Blue*, is quite nicely done, as are short works by Bobby Scott, Francisco Tárrega, Julio Sagreras, Agustín Barrios, and John Griggs.

El Decamerón negro
what to buy: [*Tales for Guitar*, Ricardo Cobo, guitar] (ESS.A.Y 1034) ♪ ♪ ♪ ♪ ♪

Cobo's impeccable technique and heartfelt passion as a Brouwer devotee make his version of the composer's intricate and melodic work sizzle with excitement and beauty. Cobo also performs works by Astor Piazzolla, Salvador Brotons, Roland Dyens, and Nikita Koshkin on this highly recommended album.

worth looking for: [*Guitar*, Jason Vieaux, guitar] (Mark Custom Recording Service 1334) ♪ ♪ ♪ ♪

Vieaux's lovely version of this solo guitar piece is coupled with more works by Brouwer and other composers. A skillful technician and tenderly expressive (especially in Brouwer's *La Huída de los Amantes por el Valle de los Ecos*), Vieaux triumphs throughout.

various works for guitar
what to buy: [*Leo Brouwer: The Complete Guitar Works, vol. 1*; Costas Cotsiolis, guitar] (GHA 126.040) ♪ ♪ ♪ ♪

Leo Brouwer

Cotsiolis premiered the sixth guitar concerto (the *Concierto de Volos*) in 1996 and has proven to be a persuasive advocate for Brouwer in his ongoing series dedicated to the composer's guitar oeuvre. This first volume includes near-definitive performances of the Sonata for Guitar (originally dedicated to Julian Bream) and the seventeen-note series at the heart of the *Preludios epigramáticos,* but Cotsiolis's playing in the *Elogio de la danza* and the first book of Brouwer's *Estudios sencillos* is also noteworthy.

what to buy next: [*Guitar Music, vol. 1*; Ricardo Cobo, guitar] (Naxos 8.553630) ♪ ♪ ♪ ♪

Cobo skillfully and passionately performs this soothing collection of Brouwer's solo guitar works. Getting inside each tune, he maintains the Afro-Cuban flavor of the various pieces, including the four books of *Estudios sencillos,* designed for young guitarists as an alternative to traditional guitar exercises.

influences: Heitor Villa-Lobos, Egberto Gismonti, Emilio Pujol, Francesco Tárrega, Manuel Ponce, Hans Werner Henze, Agustín Pío Barrios Mangoré, Tulio Peramo

Nancy Ann Lee and Ian Palmer

Max Bruch

Born Max Karl August Bruch, January 6, 1838, in Cologne, Germany. Died, October 2, 1920, in Friedenau, Germany.

period: Romantic

A real globetrotting musical celebrity, Bruch was well known in his own lifetime as a composer of secular oratorios. He had a great gift for melody, was a wonderful orchestrator, and demonstrated a mastery of form in all of his music. Today his fame rests mostly on three works—his first violin concerto, the *Scottish Fantasy* for Violin and Orchestra, and the *Kol Nidrei,* arranged for cello and orchestra.

Bruch's father was originally a lawyer but later became the chief of police in Cologne. His mother was a professional singer during the 1820s but, according to Bruch, "lost her voice early on and devoted herself to giving singing lessons." She gave him his first musical instruction, and the precocious child ended up writing a song for her birthday when he was only nine years old. His

juvenilia also included motets, short piano pieces, and the rudiments of a string quartet, all manifesting such talent that his parents sent him to Bonn to study music theory with his father's friend Heinrich Breidenstein. The bulk of Bruch's non-musical education came through home schooling and occasional visits from teachers associated with the Friedrich Wilhelm School in Cologne.

At the same time he was taking theory lessons from Breidenstein, Bruch began studying composition and theory with Ferdinand Hiller—a former child prodigy who had moved to Cologne in 1850 to take up the position of Kapellmeister—and piano with Carl Reinecke, who taught at Hiller's conservatory. Both of these musicians had impressive backgrounds: Hiller was a close friend of Felix Mendelssohn-Bartholdy, Hector Berlioz, and Franz Liszt, while Reinecke, also well acquainted with Mendelssohn and Liszt, was a friend of Robert and Clara Schumann. Bruch's sessions with Hiller and Reinecke came about as a result of his winning the Frankfurt Mozart Foundation Prize for a string quartet he wrote when he was fourteen years old. By the time he was twenty, Bruch's first opera (*Scherz, List, und Rache,* a setting of Johann Wolfgang von Goethe's singspiel) had been published; his formal musical training had ended; and he had begun teaching music.

Bruch is an example of the energetic traveling musician in the late nineteenth century. His appointments took him all over Germany and Austria, to France and Belgium, to England and the United States; he toured all the major European cities, performing his own music to great acclaim. By 1891, though, he had finally settled in Berlin, where he became a professor at the Berlin Academy and taught a master class in composition. When he died at the age of eighty-two, Bruch was a world-famous composer whose well-crafted music was filled with gorgeous melodies. But he was also a relic of the past whose last years saw him eclipsed in the public's perception by the "New Germans"—Richard Strauss, Max Reger, and Hans Pfitzner—composers whom Bruch railed against, calling them "musical social democrats."

Bruch's three most famous works were written between 1868 and 1881, when he was an orchestra conductor. The Violin Concerto no. 1 in G minor was written for the violin virtuoso Pablo de Sarasate, who made the work—and Bruch's name—famous when he played it all over Europe. In a poll conducted in 1998 by Classic FM (the

British commercial music service now competing with the BBC), the most popular work among listeners was Bruch's First Violin Concerto, which received more votes than even Beethoven's Fifth Symphony. However, during Bruch's lifetime, praise for his concerto was not universal. After Bruch played it for Johannes Brahms and asked for his fellow composer's opinion, Brahms commented on the quality of the music paper on which it was written!

Bruch's setting of the *Kol Nidre* for cello and orchestra evolved out of his work with the "children of Israel in the [Berlin] Choral Society" and takes the Jewish prayer of atonement as its source. While the solo portion of the work was originally written for the cello, the composer also arranged versions of the piece for viola and piano, piano and harmonium, solo piano, cello and organ, and solo organ. The melody line also appears in the first of the *Three Hebrew Melodies,* a choral score that Bruch was working on at about the same time. On the other hand, the core of the *Scottish Fantasy* grew out of the *Twelve Scottish Folk Songs* that Bruch wrote in 1863 and includes some of the developments used by Mendelssohn in his Scottish-themed works, specifically the rhythm known as the "Scottish snap." When the score was finally completed, it was premiered in Liverpool at a concert that also featured the English debut of Bruch's *Kol Nidre.*

Orchestral
Concerto no. 1 in G Minor for Violin and Orchestra, op. 26
what to buy: [*The Fritz Kreisler Edition, Vol. 2*; Fritz Kreisler, violin; Eugene Goosens, cond; Royal Albert Hall Orchestra] (Grammofono 2000 GRM 78579) ♪ ♪ ♪ ♪₄

Even though Isaac Stern's recording made it famous for many late-twentieth-century listeners, the top prize for a recorded performance of this work should go to Kreisler. His perfect technique is coupled with a mature interpretation and flawless musicianship. Also included in this set is Kreisler's version of the Brahms violin concerto with the Berlin State Opera Orchestra conducted by Leo Blech.

what to buy next: [Gil Shaham, violin; Giuseppe Sinopoli, cond; Philharmonia Orchestra] (Deutsche Grammophon 427656) ♪ ♪ ♪ ♪

The competition is pretty strong when it comes to this piece, but Gil Shaham wins the silver medal. His recording also includes the Mendelssohn Violin Concerto in E Minor and features more up-to-date engineering and sound than that found in the older Kreisler recording.

Kol Nidrei for Cello and Orchestra, op. 47
what to buy: [Janos Starker, cello; Antal Dorati, cond; London Symphony Orchestra] (Mercury 432001) ♪ ♪ ♪ ♪

Starker's playing is refined, elegant, and full of restrained emotion. His beautiful reading is combined on this disc with the famous Dvořák cello concerto and Tchaikovsky's *Variations on a Rococo Theme.* These recordings were originally made on 35-mm film for optimal sound.

what to buy next: [Pierre Fournier, cello; Jean Martinon, cond.; Lamoureux Concerts Association Orchestra] (Deutsche Grammophon 429155) ♪ ♪ ♪₄

Here is yet another older recording that still holds it own against the brightest and the best from the last twenty years. On this album, Fournier's performance of the Bruch masterwork is teamed with Ernest Bloch's *Schelomo* and the Dvořák cello concerto, both works featuring the cellist with Alfred Wallenstein conducting the Berlin Philharmonic Orchestra. The same performances of the *Kol Nidre* and *Schelomo* can also be found on another disc (Deutsche Grammophon 457761), grouping them with concertos by Edouard Lalo and Camille Saint-Säens in superb performances by Fournier, Martinon, and his orchestral compatriots.

Scottish Fantasy for Violin and Orchestra, op. 46
what to buy: [Kyung Wha Chung, violin; Rudolf Kempe, cond.; Royal Philharmonic Orchestra] (London 448597) ♪ ♪ ♪ ♪

The advantage to this set, other than the uniformly fine performances by the violinist, is that it combines both of Bruch's masterworks for violin and orchestra—his first violin concerto and the *Scottish Fantasia*—in renditions loaded with power, grace, and finesse. Of course, these same performances are also available at roughly the same price on Penguin Classics (460620) and Decca (460976), with the last one tossing in Kyung Wha Chung's stylishly fluid performance (with Charles Dutoit and the Montreal Symphony Orchestra) of the E Minor violin concerto by Felix Mendelssohn.

what to buy next: [Itzhak Perlman, violin; Zubin Mehta, cond.; Israel Philharmonic Orchestra] (EMI 49071) ♪ ♪ ♪ ♪

Perlman really makes this work his own, and the famous finale leaps out of the speakers with joy. Mehta's conducting on this and Bruch's lesser-known (and some say far inferior) Concerto no. 2 in D Minor for Violin and Orchestra, op. 44 is solid but unspectacular, offering support but little in the way of orchestral sheen.

influences: Felix Mendelssohn, Pablo de Sarasate, Joseph Joachim, Johannes Brahms

Dave Wagner and Garaud MacTaggart

Anton Bruckner

Born Joseph Anton Bruckner, September 4, 1824, in Ansfelden, Austria. Died October 11, 1896, in Vienna, Austria.

period: Romantic

Even though his music often seems to inhabit the same sonic territory as that of Richard Wagner and Gustav Mahler, Anton Bruckner's massive symphonic scores illustrate the monumental dreams of a humble, religious, at times overly deferential man rather than duplicating the egocentric vigor of the other two masters. While Bruckner's most performed symphonic scores during his lifetime were the Symphonies no. 4 (in E-flat Major) and no. 7 (in E Major), his unfinished ninth symphony (in D Minor) is even more compelling. His other major area of concentration, choral music, yielded two masterpieces: his *Te Deum* and the uniquely constructed Mass no. 2 in E Minor for Woodwinds, Brass, and Chorus.

Bruckner's early life centered around the rural church where his mother sang in the choir and his father, a schoolteacher, also played organ. It was there that his lifelong belief in the spiritual tenets of Catholicism had its roots, reinforcing the basic intellectual naïveté of his character in an age when other musicians and artists were often questioning the religious constructs which ostensibly governed their society. In 1841, after he qualified as an assistant teacher for elementary schools, Bruckner started on a career path which would lead from the less sophisticated countryside of Austria and into its cultural heartland, Vienna.

Although he had written several choral works by 1846

(including several settings of the Mass), Bruckner still didn't feel fully confident as a composer. He pored over works by Franz Joseph Haydn, Johann Sebastian Bach, and Ludwig van Beethoven and continued a study of music theory, using texts by Daniel Gottlob Türk and Friedrich Wilhelm Marpurg suggested by various teachers. The most significant point in his musical education came in 1855 when Bruckner was accepted as a student by Simon Sechter, a historically important Viennese composition teacher and theoretician whose roster of pupils had included Franz Schubert, Henri Vieuxtemps, and Sigismund Thalberg.

Within the next three years Bruckner accomplished and was exposed to much, if often only at the urging of friends; he became cathedral organist in Linz, was appointed conductor of a choral society (with whom he could perform some of his own works), and was granted a diploma from the Vienna Conservatory, which enabled him to teach harmony and counterpoint in music schools. In 1862 he was also introduced to the music of Richard Wagner through performances of *Die fliegende Holländer (The Flying Dutchman)* and *Lohengrin.* This would have a profound affect on Bruckner's life, not only in his handling of orchestral forces but in his unsought (and unwarranted) role as a whipping boy for conservative Viennese critics (especially Eduard Hanslick) seeking to link him with Wagner as an example of all that was wrong with contemporary music.

In 1863 Bruckner wrote a "study symphony" (now known in his canon as Symphony "00") which was essentially a student exercise; the first in his great trilogy of masses (Mass no. 1 in D Minor) was completed a year later, while the first of what would be designated as his official symphonies and the second of his major mass settings (Mass no. 2 in E Minor) were finished in 1866. Two years after that, he finished the Mass no. 3 in F Minor and accepted a post at the Vienna Conservatory as professor of organ-playing and counterpoint. Bruckner's next work was another symphony, but after its completion in 1869 the composer withdrew it from performance, in part because of a rehearsal at which the conductor questioned him about a theme. Now known as Symphony no. 0 in D Minor (*Die Nulte*), this work actually seems more indicative of the direction Bruckner was heading than the designated Symphony no. 2 in C Minor, which he finished in 1872.

All of his symphonic scores underwent repeated revisions, but his Symphony no. 3 in D Minor (often called his "Wagner symphony" because of its initial use of orchestral quotations drawn from that composer's *Tristan und Isolde* and *Der Ring des Nibelungen*) received the most alterations of any large-scale orchestral work by Bruckner, in an attempt to get it performed more often. The score for what would become his most popular orchestral piece, the Symphony no. 4 in E-flat Major (a.k.a. the *Romantic* symphony), was also tinkered with during the next few years, despite its relative acceptance by audiences of its day. Although Bruckner completed the first draft of his fifth symphony in 1876, it too underwent the revision process, but, unlike his other completed symphonies, he never heard even one movement of it performed.

The Symphony no. 6 in A Major was completed in 1881, the same year that Bruckner's fourth symphony received its initial performance. 1884 saw the final version of his *Te Deum* and the successful premiere of his seventh symphony, a work which caused Johann Strauss, Jr. to send congratulations to the composer saying, "I am deeply moved. It was one of the strongest impressions in my life." During the next dozen years, Bruckner received a number of honors from universities and other cultural organizations but also suffered more crises of confidence, causing him to embark on a further series of revisions to his symphonic oeuvre under the influence of well-meaning if misguided friends and, in the case of his Symphony no. 8 in C Minor (initially finished in 1887), an underqualified conductor.

Mental and physical ailments bedeviled Bruckner toward the end of his life, but from 1891 until the day of his death he worked on finishing his Symphony no. 9 in D Minor, which utilized episodes of dissonance and quotations drawn from his *Te Deum*.

[Note: In 1932 the International Bruckner Society sought to compile the definitive edition of the composer's works, searching through their archives to determine what Bruckner's intentions were for each composition prior to input from his various associates. Robert Haas, who oversaw the first "corrected" editions of the symphonies that came out between 1934 and 1944, was replaced shortly after World War II by Leopold Nowak, who had joined the project in 1937. Nowak went back into the archives and brought a whole new edition of the composer's works to market in 1951. While there are few variations between the two editions for most of the symphonies, significant differences exist for nos. 2, 3, 4, 7, and 8. For instance, Haas included the new scherzo

movement as well as the newer finale for the *Romantic* symphony, while Nowak ended up choosing the first revision, the newest scherzo, the newest finale, and a bit of even newer material which was discovered after World War II. The basic rule of thumb (though as with all rules, there are exceptions) is that the Nowak editions don't vary all that often from the Haas editions but when they do, the Nowak sets are generally leaner and less expansive than their counterparts. Another notable point is that the Haas and Nowak editions are not the only revised versions of Bruckner's symphonies that have been recorded. For example, Gustav Mahler completely re-orchestrated an edition of the fourth symphony which had already been hacked up by Ferdinand Loewe, and that particular version was recorded in 1984 by Gennadi Rozhdestvensky and the USSR Ministry of Culture Symphony Orchestra.]

Orchestral
Symphonies (complete)
what to buy: [Eugen Jochum, cond.; Dresden Staatskapelle, orch.] (EMI Classics 73905) ♪ ♪ ♪ ♪₄

As in complete sets of anything, it is hard to maintain excellence in every performance. That said, Jochum's cycle with the Dresdeners is impressive, probably as a result of the conductor's long, loving association with the Nowak editions he has used (in the later symphonies) for years. His version of the fourth symphony, though lovingly shaped, isn't quite as inspired as an earlier recording for Deutsche Grammophon (see below), but the first three symphonies, usually glossed over by many conductors, are revealed to be quite inventive, and the sixth and seventh are truly monumental.

worth looking for: [*Bruckner: The Symphonies*; Bernard Haitink, cond.; Royal Concertgebouw Orchestra] (Philips 442040) ♪ ♪ ♪ ♪₄

Haitink may not have the pure majesty associated with either Jochum or Karajan but his interpretations are consistently in service to the music, and his recordings with the Royal Concertgebouw Orchestra have long been a standard for Bruckner aficionados seeking a poetic yet direct approach. In this set he generally uses the Haas edition of the scores (excepting in nos. 0, 4, 7, and 9, in which he follows variations from the Nowak versions, despite what the liner notes say). Haitink's take on Bruckner's ninth symphony is one of the glories of this set, and deserves to be released on its own.

Symphony no. 4 in E-flat Major (*Romantic*)

what to buy: [Eugen Jochum, cond.; Berlin Philharmonic Orchestra] (Deutsche Grammophon 449718) ♪ ♪ ♪ ♪ ♪

Jochum's fondness for Bruckner and the legendary skill of the Berlin Philharmonic combine for a performance that revels in the composer's expansive orchestral writing. There is no conductor with the same genteel flair for Bruckner's idiosyncrasies—though Karajan has come close at times and it is unlikely that Jochum's rendition of the Nowak edition of this score will be topped anytime soon. It may seem surprising that his recording of *Night Ride and Sunrise,* the tone poem by Jean Sibelius, is included along with the Bruckner, but it is a totally agreeable performance.

what to buy next: [Georg Tintner, cond.; Royal Scottish National Orchestra] (Naxos 8.554128) ♪ ♪ ♪ ♪ ♪

Even though this is a budget-priced recording, the interpretation stands up to that of more expensive versions. Unlike Jochum, Tintner uses the Haas edition of the score, which affects changes to the scherzo and finale using Bruckner's own handwritten copy of the 1878—1880 text as a guide. That makes this recording an important alternative for Bruckner fanciers to own, even if it lacks the last bit of splendor that the other conductor coaxes from the work.

Symphony no. 7 in E Major

what to buy: [Herbert van Karajan, cond.; Vienna Philharmonic Orchestra] (Deutsche Grammophon 439037) ♪ ♪ ♪ ♪ ♪

It is fitting that Karajan's last recording displays the fruits of his fabled discipline in a work that can lose focus rather quickly if not for the firmly communicated vision of the conductor. His legendary control of orchestral textures leads to some gorgeous playing from members of the Vienna Philharmonic, creating a rewarding, unified musical force, and his handling of the composer's sublime second-movement Adagio is superb. For this performance, Karajan uses the Haas edition of the score, thus deleting the percussion found in other versions.

what to buy next: [Riccardo Chailly, cond.; Berlin Radio Symphony Orchestra] (Decca 466574) ♪ ♪ ♪ ♪ ♪

Chailly's masterful recording uses the 1954 Nowak edition of the score, which includes the percussion parts

left out of the Haas version, and his conducting strikes that elusive balance between brass and string sections that is so difficult to achieve in Bruckner. This is a patient performance, one that doesn't break any speed records but reveals an incredible sense of majesty and (in the first movement) playfulness which helped make this the composer's most popular symphony during his lifetime.

Symphony no. 9 in D Minor (unfinished)

what to buy: [Leonard Bernstein, cond.; Vienna Philharmonic Orchestra] (Deutsche Grammophon 435350) ♪ ♪ ♪ ♪ ♪

Recorded "live" in 1990, Bernstein's rendition of Bruckner's supreme orchestral statement has all the majesty, dramatic power, and spirituality one could ask for in this piece. He uses the Nowak edition of the score.

what to buy next: [Eugen Jochum, cond.; Staatskapelle Dresden, orch.] (EMI Classics 73827) ♪ ♪ ♪ ♪

Jochum also favors the Nowak edition of Bruckner's score, but he isn't afforded the kind of engineering which blesses the Bernstein performance. Still, the budget pricing is attractive for this two-disc set, and the accompanying version of the composer's eighth symphony is almost as fine a rendition as the one Jochum conducted with the Berlin Philharmonic.

Vocal
Mass no. 2 in E Minor for Woodwinds, Brass, and Chorus

what to buy: [Eugen Jochum, cond.; Bavarian Radio Symphony Orchestra; Bavarian Radio Chorus] (Deutsche Grammophon 447409) ♪ ♪ ♪ ♪ ♪

Taken as part of a two-disc set covering Bruckner's mature trilogy of masses, Jochum's version of this work is well recorded and filled with the proper reverence. It is also a better deal for those wishing to experiment in depth with the composer's choral scores than the Norrington release (see below).

what to buy next: [Roger Norrington, cond.; Philip Jones Wind Ensemble; London Schütz Choir] (Philips 455035) ♪ ♪ ♪ ♪

From a technical standpoint, Norrington's rendition of this work hews closer to the way Bruckner apparently meant it to be performed, but doesn't quite communicate the composer's spirituality with the same grace Jochum imparts to the score. In any event this is still a splendid recording, and is included as part of a sterling, budget-priced, two-disc set focusing on the composer's motets and his setting of the *Te Deum* (with Zubin Mehta conducting the Vienna Philharmonic Orchestra and Chorus). The record company has also tossed in three bonus choral works by Richard Strauss, including an impressive rendering of that composer's *Deutsche Motetette*.

Te Deum for Solo Voices, Organ, Orchestra, and Chorus

what to buy: [Maria Stader, soprano; Sieglinde Wagner, contralto; Ernst Haefliger, tenor; Peter Lagger, bass; Wolfgang Meyer, organ; Eugen Jochum, cond.; Berlin Philharmonic Orchestra; Choir of the German Opera, Berlin] (Deutsche Grammophon 457743) ♪ ♪ ♪ ♪₈

The awesome power of Bruckner's religious faith has rarely been communicated with the grace and fire of Jochum's classic account, now re-issued at mid-line price. Equally revelatory performances of the composer's *Psalm 150* and three of his motets are included in this glorious album.

what to buy next: [Joan Rodgers, soprano; Catherine Wyn-Rogers, contralto; Keith Lewis, tenor; Alastair Miles, bass; James O'Donnell, organ; Matthew Best, cond.; Corydon Orchestra; Corydon Singers, choir] (Hyperion 66650) ♪ ♪ ♪ ♪

While not as spiritually powerful a reading as that led by Jochum, Best's forces are well recorded. In that sense, the choir actually sounds much fuller than the Berlin ensemble, and their diction, much clearer. The other work on the set doesn't make for as felicitous a pairing as it could; although there is no denying the Corydon's artistry on Bruckner's Mass no. 1 in D Minor, the works accompanying Jochum's version have greater appeal for choral aficionados.

influences: Gustav Mahler, Richard Wagner, Franz Schmidt, Ludwig van Beethoven

William Gerard

Gavin Bryars
Born Richard Gavin Bryars, January 16, 1943, in Goole, Yorkshire, England.

period: Twentieth century

Gavin Bryars is one of England's most influential composers and teachers. Using elements of collage, minimalism, multimedia, and pop music, he has attained popular as well as critical acclaim for such works as *Jesus' Blood Never Failed Me Yet* and *The Sinking of the Titanic.*

Gavin Bryars started his musical career as a string-bass player. While studying philosophy and composition at Sheffield University, he began to write music in earnest. As a member of Britain's avant-garde throughout the late 1960s, he composed what became one of his signature works, *Jesus' Blood Never Failed Me Yet*. He has been on the faculties of the Portsmouth College of Art (where he conducted the Portsmouth Sinfonia, the orchestral equivalent of Florence Foster Jenkins) and Leicester Polytechnic.

A versatile and eclectic composer, Bryars has written for the theater, voice, chamber groups, electric guitar, and electronic synthesizers. His collaborators have included well-known artists such as Brian Eno, Robert Wilson (on the operatic projects *Medea* and *Civil Wars*), and Steve Reich. Choreographers like Lucinda Childs (*Four Elements*), Christine Juffs (*Sidescraper*), and Tony Thatcher (*Grey Windows*) have also used his music for their dances.

On the whole, Bryars uses traditional tonality, but in a unique context where chords do not resolve in textbook fashion. Musical or sound collages, used most notably in *The Sinking of the Titanic* and *Jesus' Blood Never Failed Me Yet,* serve to suspend time and place. While not having descended from any particular British school or tradition, his style seems to have been influenced by American composers such as Steve Reich and Philip Glass. Some of Bryars's other compositions include *My First Homage, The Vespertine Park,* and *Effarene*. His opera *Dr. Ox's Experiment,* based on the Jules Verne story, premiered at the English National Opera in 1997.

As in the case of such living composers such as Arvo Pärt, John Tavener, and Michael Nyman, Bryars's style has transcended genre classification, appealing successfully to a wide audience.

Vocal
Cadman Requiem
what to buy: [Dave Smith, cond.; Fretwork, ens.; Hilliard Ensemble, vocalists] (Point Music 462511) ♪ ♪ ♪ ♪₈

Written for Bryars's friend Bill Cadman, who died in the plane crash over Lockerbie, Scotland, in 1988, this is a work of powerful beauty. The four members of the critically acclaimed Hilliard Ensemble bring an intense intimacy to the piece, while Fretwork, the Renaissance-oriented viol consort, provides a mournful foundation for the voices. Specialists in early music, both groups achieve an appropriate purity of sound through the limited use of vibrato. Two other works by the composer, the *Adnan Songbook* and *Epilogue from Wonderlawn*, are also heard on this album in performances by the Gavin Bryars Ensemble.

Jesus' Blood Never Failed Me Yet

what to buy: [Tom Waits, singer; Michael Riesman, cond.; Hampton String Quartet; Gavin Bryars Ensemble] (Point Music 438823) ♪ ♪ ♪ ♪♪

This nearly seventy-five-minute work, written in 1971, is based on a tape loop Bryars made of an elderly homeless man in London singing the hymn of the title. The loop is played continuously over ever-changing sonorities that include string quartet, orchestra, and choir. Singer Tom Waits (who said that an earlier version of the piece was his favorite recording) joins in for the last ten minutes. The poignant sincerity of the old man's singing is moving enough, and its juxtaposition with the lush accompaniment enhances the emotional impact. Depending on your point of view, this piece can be considered a revelatory meditation or unbearably monotonous.

The Sinking of the Titanic

what to buy: [Christopher Barnett, cond.; Gavin Bryars Ensemble; Wenhasten Boy's Choir] (Point Music 446061) ♪ ♪ ♪ ♪

Bryars creates a haunting yet unlikely hypothesis: this is what the final moments of the Titanic might have sounded like under water. The strains of the band gallantly playing on, the voices of the passengers, and the clanking of metal are all captured for posterity in the chilly depths of the North Atlantic. Conceived in 1969, long before the James Cameron film phenomenon, this depiction does not convey the violent drama of the sinking but rather a sense of tragic resignation.

influences: Steve Reich, Philip Glass, Michael Nyman

Christine L. Cody and Mona C. DeQuis

Ferruccio Busoni

Born Ferruccio Dante Michelangiolo Benvenuto Busoni on April 1, 1866, in Empoli, Italy. Died July 27, 1924, in Berlin, Germany.

period: Romantic/Twentieth century

Pedagogue, performer, and composer, Ferruccio Busoni had a brilliant career as a concert pianist and conductor in Europe and America. Best known as a composer for his piano transcriptions of Bach organ pieces, he also composed sonatinas, concertos, and chamber music with piano, but is especially highly regarded for his last opera, *Doktor Faust,* posthumously completed by his student Philipp Jarnach in 1925. His published writings, among them the *Sketch of a New Esthetic of Music* (1907), reveal him as one of the most important musical minds of the early Twentieth century.

Encouraged by his parents, who were musicians, Busoni gave his first recital before his eighth birthday. After attending his Vienna debut in 1876, the influential music critic Eduard Hanslick noted that Busoni showed "no precocious sentimentality or studied eccentricity, but a naive pleasure in music." That year, the Busoni family moved to Graz, where Ferruccio studied composition with Wilhelm Mayer, and in 1883 he went to Vienna, taking the city by storm with his prodigious pianistic gifts. In 1886, on the recommendation of Brahms, he settled in Leipzig, the city of Bach, a center of music publishing and a great inspiration to the young composer, who became friends there with Gustav Mahler and Frederick Delius. In 1888 Busoni's first Bach piano transcription (the Prelude and Fugue in D major for Organ, BWV. 532) became a subject of controversy. Adapting Bach's music for the concert pianist, Busoni includes many bravura passages with double octaves, full chordal structures, and rapid scales spanning many octaves. Praised by some and loathed by others, his Bach editions and transcriptions are the work of an artist acutely aware of the compositional and dramatic structure of each fugue, prelude, or chorale, and eager to explore the tonal and dynamic range of the modern piano.

In 1890 Busoni won the first-ever Rubinstein Prize for his *Konzertstück*, op. 31a. The *Konzertstück*, a one-movement work for piano and orchestra, is constructed as a sonata-fantasia, whose scoring was influenced by romantics such as Brahms even as many of its contrapuntal passages owe a debt to Bach. The rich textures of the piano writing are also akin to those of Busoni's French contemporaries, especially César Franck. His grand transcription of Bach's Violin Chaconne in D Minor (BWV. 1004) begins in the piano's middle range before extending into the highest and lowest registers. Instead of creating a mere transcription, Busoni turned Bach's Chaconne into a technically and musically demanding piano work.

Busoni made Berlin his home in 1894 and from 1902 onward became a pioneer of twentieth-century music, presenting orchestral concerts that included world premieres of his own works and those of Bartók, Delius and Sibelius. In 1904, as part of this series, Busoni premiered his Piano Concerto in C major, op. 39, which calls for a male chorus and lasts over an hour, taxing not only the pianist but also the conductor and orchestra. The final movement is a choral setting of words by Danish poet Adam Gottlob Oehlenschläger, inspired by the story of Aladdin. One of the most important contributions Busoni made to modern music was his essay *Sketch of a New Esthetic of Music,* published in 1907 in German as *Entwurf einer neuen Äesthetik der Tonkunst.* (An English translation appeared in 1911 and was reprinted in 1962.) In it, Busoni expounds his forward-thinking humanistic views on the development of music and the arts and conveys a sense of the all-embracing quality of music that distinguishes it among the art forms. The topics covered range as widely as absolute music, transcription, harmony and tonality, composers from Bach to Richard Wagner, and his interest in music outside the Western tradition, which led him to compose pieces such as *Indianische Fantasie,* based on Native American melodies.

Music for the theater became a focus for Busoni in the last thirteen years of his life. After writing incidental music to Carlo Gozzi's play *Turandot* (first performed in 1911), he became interested in *commedia dell'arte,* writing *Arlecchino* and then expanding it into a two-act opera. Busoni's final stage work, *Doktor Faust* (based on Christopher Marlowe's play), was begun in 1916 and remained unfinished at his death. His student Philipp Jarnach completed the score in 1925, when the opera received its premiere in Dresden. Conceived as a "poem for music in two prologues, an intermezzo, and three principal scenes," *Doktor Faust,* has entered the repertory, along with Alban Berg's *Wozzeck,* and Pfitzner's *Palestrina,* as an outstanding representative of early-Twentieth century German opera.

Orchestral
Concerto in C Major for Piano and Orchestra, op. 39

what to buy: [Volker Banfield, piano; Lutz Herbig, cond.; Bavarian Radio Symphony Orchestra; Bavarian Radio Symphony Chorus] (CPO 999017) ♪ ♪ ♪♪

Providing a glimpse of Busoni the mystic and visionary of grand proportions, this Piano Concerto, featuring a male chorus in the finale, is a tour de force. Banfield brings tremendous insight into the structure of this monumental five-part work, where even the movement titles ("Prologo e Introito," "Pezzo giocoso," "Pezzo serioso," "All'Italiana," and "Cantico") are highly descriptive. The expansive orchestral and choral writing is finely interpreted by Herbig and his forces.

Turandot for Orchestra, op. 41
what to buy: [Riccardo Muti, cond.; La Scala Orchestra] (Sony Classical 53280) ♪ ♪ ♪ ♪

Busoni's *Turandot* orchestral suite is included in this compilation, with Muti leading the radiant orchestra of La Scala opera. The six movements, extracted from Busoni's incidental music to Gozzi's play, predate Giacomo Puccini's opera *Turandot.* Fragments of melodies—pentatonic, modal, or diatonic—will remind listeners of many different cultures. Works by two other twentieth-century Italians, Alfredo Casella and Giuseppe Martucci, fill out the disc.

Chamber
String Quartets
what to buy: [Pellegrini Quartet] (CPO 999264) ♪ ♪ ♪♪

Busoni's first string quartet (in C minor, op. 19), a juvenile work completed in 1881, exists in the shadow of the classical string quartet. However, his second quartet (in D minor, op. 26) shows a composer fully in command of the extreme contrapuntal textures and complex rhythmic interplay that the quartet medium can offer.

piano transcription of Bach's Chaconne in D Minor for solo violin (BWV. 1004)
what to buy: [*Jorge Bolet Live at Carnegie Hall*; Jorge Bolet, piano] (RCA Victor Gold Seal 7710) ♪ ♪ ♪ ♪♪

Bolet's performance of the piano transcription of the D minor Chaconne is grand, expansive, dramatic, and soulful. This is part of a live 1974 recording at Carnegie Hall and captures the excitement of a piano recital in progress.

various piano transcriptions

what to buy: [Ferruccio Busoni, piano; Egon Petri, piano] (Pearl 9347) ♪ ♪ ♪ ♪ ♪

Featured on this CD are two Busoni transcriptions played by the transcriber himself—a chorale prelude by Bach (BWV 734) and Beethoven's *Ecossaise*. Numerous Chopin works played by Busoni are also included here. The rest of the CD is devoted to Busoni works performed by his student Egon Petri (1881–1962), among them the third and sixth piano sonatinas, *All'Italia,* and Busoni's transcription of Franz Liszt's *Spanish Rhapsody* for piano and orchestra.

what to buy next: [Peter Rösel, piano] (Berlin Classics 1088) ♪ ♪ ♪ ♪

The piano transcriptions of Bach works included here are played by an excellent Busoni virtuoso. The choice of the Violin Chaconne in D minor, the Organ Prelude and Fugue in D major, and various organ chorale settings transports the listener to the heart of Busoni's musical world.

worth looking for: [Dinu Lipatti, piano] (EMI Classics 475172) ♪ ♪ ♪ ♪ ♪

Lipatti's sensitive playing was unique among his peers, and this recording of two Bach chorale prelude transcriptions (*Nun komm', der Heiden Heiland and Ich ruf' zu dir, Herr Jesu Christ*) are deeply spiritual. Busoni's writing here is restrained and heartfelt, the perfect medium for Bach's intricate counterpoint. These two transcriptions were recorded in July 1950, only five months before Lipatti's untimely death.

Vocal
Doktor Faust

what to buy: [Dietrich Fischer-Dieskau, baritone; Hildegard Hillebrecht, soprano; William Cochran, tenor; Karl Christian Kohn, bass; Ferdinand Leitner, cond.; Bavarian Radio Symphony Orchestra; Bavarian Radio Symphony Chorus] (Deutsche Grammophon 427413) ♪ ♪ ♪ ♪ ♪

Reissued in Deutsche Grammophon's 20th Century Classics series, this three-CD complete recording of *Doktor Faust* features a strong cast with a German orchestra keenly aware of the Busoni legacy. Recorded in 1969 but digitally remastered, this set presents

Fischer-Dieskau in his vocal and dramatic prime as Faust. The orchestra is especially moving in the performances of the *Symphonia* and the *Symphonic intermezzo*.

influences: César Franck, Carl Nielsen, Arnold Schoenberg

Joanna Lee

Dietrich Buxtehude

Born c.1637 in Oldesloe, Denmark. Died May 9, 1707, in Lübeck, Germany.

period: Baroque

Dietrich Buxtehude belongs, by most assessments, to that exclusive club of composers whose influence on the evolution of musical style remains somewhat detached from their own name and deeds. Instead, they flourish in a more vicarious manner, by way of their impact on the great masters who dominated the same period of history and whose brilliance eclipsed that of their teachers. That Buxtehude's example remains a strong ingredient in the styles of Johann Sebastian Bach, George Frideric Handel, and other Titans can hardly be questioned.

The composer's origin inspires some geographical guessing on the part of even his most ardent chroniclers. Most settle on the town of Oldesloe in Holstein (where his father, Johannes, had served as an organist and schoolmaster) as his birthplace, giving the composer what appear to be Danish roots. Even so, much evidence connects the family with their namesake village of Buxtehude in Germany prior to their relocation to the Holstein region. Within two years of his birth the family appear to have moved to Helsingborg in Sweden, where Johannes assumed the post of organist and master of music at the Marienkirche. By 1642, however, it would appear that the had family moved once more, this time to Helsingør, Denmark, where Johannes had become organist at the Olaikirche. Buxtehude probably received most of his early music education from his father and in 1658 received his first appointment as organist at Johannes's old church back in Helsingborg. He then followed his father's route to Helsingør two years later, leaving that post in 1667 upon receiving an appointment at Lübeck, where Buxtehude assumed the influential position of organist at that city's Marienkirche.

It was at Lübeck that Buxtehude's place in music history began to take firm hold. Three factors contributed to this. The first revolves around Lübeck's status at the time as a center for sacred and secular music. Buxtehude's position at one of the city's premier places of worship both obliged him and afforded him the opportunity to compose new works for the congregational worship services. These included multiple services on Sunday as well as the celebration of saints' feasts and revised parts of the Divine Office, such as vespers, offered within the Sabbath vigil. From this need sprung innumerable "geistliche Konzerte," or sacred choral works, which took the form of cantatas, chorales, and concerted settings of scripture. Another defining aspect of the Lübeck years revolved around Buxtehude offering concerts of sacred music outside of the worship service. These programs, known as Abendmusik, were originally scheduled on miscellaneous weekday evenings under his predecessors. Buxtehude not only revived them after a long dormancy but made them an extension of the Sunday calendar and presented them on four Sunday evenings throughout the year. The chosen dates usually coincided with the beginning of a new season of the church year (Advent, Lent, Pentecost, Trinity, etc.). These programs were important for the wider, non-parish audience they supplied for his music, and they soon became known and admired beyond the immediate region. The success of the Abendmusik concerts gave rise to the third and final factor supporting Buxtehude's rise to prominence, for it seems that the originality and quality of the evening offerings were enough to attract such disciples as Johann Sebastian Bach himself. Bach's visit to Lübeck in 1701 necessarily included his attendance at least one Abendmusik, introducing him first-hand to Buxtehude's writing style as well as to his exemplary organ playing. Indeed, later in life, Bach is said to have openly considered Buxtehude to be one of his greatest teachers. Other influenced "pupils" are said to include Nicolaus Bruhns, Johann Pachelbel, and Georg Fridrich Handel.

Buxtehude's most prolific compositional activity centers around the sacred repertoire. Nearly 130 vocal/choral works survive. Most follow the structure of the "sacred cantata," namely the juxtaposition of chorale, solo aria, duet, and polyphonic chorus that treats scriptural text or strophic poetic verses. Most are accompanied by a small string ensemble with organ or harpsichord continuo. Other, larger church works must by their sheer size and stylistic evolution be classified as sacred "concertos." These treat mainly psalm texts and expand the smaller

Broadway Shows as Opera:
Although music has been used to illuminate drama at least since the days of classical Greek theater, the European concept of opera as an art form really had its beginnings between the sixteenth and seventeenth centuries. Back then, the word "opera" was used to describe a play in which actors sing the text with nary a spoken word blemishing the effect. Gradually, this definition parented a number of mutations (*opera seria, opera buffa, singspiel, opéra comique, zarzuela, operetta*, etc.) all of which featured songs that helped illustrate and move the dramatic action forward but varied as to the seriousness of the plot and the amount of dialog which was sung.

The American musical theater spun away from the Viennese operetta tradition which, along with musical revues, had dominated stages in this country around the beginning of the twentieth century. Many critics point to Jerome Kern's 1927 score for *Showboat* as the catalyst for this movement, the creation of what the American music historian Mary Elaine Wallace (among others) called "Broadway Opera." Subsequent works often dealt with serious contemporary issues in fairly realistic settings; comparisons to the Italian *verismo* movement which resulted in classic operas by Giacomo Puccini (*La Bohème*), Ruggero Leoncavallo (*I pagliacci*), and Pietro Mascagni (*Cavalleria rusticana*) would not necessarily be out of place.

With that in mind, here is a listing of a few "Broadway Operas" that deserve consideration for inclusion in the regular operatic canon:

Leonard Bernstein
 Candide (Sony Broadway 48017)
 Trouble in Tahiti (Sony Classics 60969)
 West Side Story (Columbia 60724)
Jerry Bock
 Fiddler on the Roof (RCA Victor 7060)
Jerome Kern
 Showboat (Angel 49108)
Mitch Leigh
 Man of La Mancha (MCA 31065)
Cole Porter
 Kiss Me Kate (Angel 64760)
Richard Rodgers
 Carousel (Decca Broadway 157980)
 Oklahoma! (Decca Broadway 157981)
 South Pacific (Columbia 60722)
Stephen Sondheim
 A Little Night Music (Columbia 65284)
 Into the Woods (RCA Victor 6796)
 Sweeny Todd (RCA Victor 3379)
Kurt Weill
 Lady in the Dark (Sony Classics 62869)
 Lost in the Stars (Decca Broadway 110302)
 Street Scene (CBS Masterworks 44668)

Garaud MacTaggart

polyphonic chorales of the cantatas into magnificent contrapuntal masterpieces of choral writing that evoke aural sensations that at times approach the Venetian style of cori spezzati, or double chorus.

The bulk of Buxtehude's instrumental compositions are organ works. The classic northern German style of organ writing clearly finds its seminal influence here, with works that exploit the organ's natural ability to divide contrasting tonal color among the manuals of the instrument and lay heavy emphasis upon a clearly defined pedal. The works neatly divide into those that navigate along a prominent and preexistent melody acting as cantus firmus and those that are freely composed and spiral out into a polyphonic web of original material. All established forms are treated in this fashion, including the prelude, fugue, toccata, and chorale. Chamber music is also represented, no doubt an outgrowth of the Abendmusik series, and includes several sonatas for various string groupings and continuo, along with a collection of arias for solo voice and strings with continuo.

Chamber
Sonatas for Two Violins, Viol, and Harpsichord, op. 1
what to buy: [*Complete Chamber Music, Vol. 1*; John Holloway, violin; Jaap ter Linden, violin; Lars Ulrik Mortensen, harpsichord; Lars Ulrik Mortensen, organ] (Da Capo 8.224003) ♪ ♪ ♪ ♪

The ensemble responsible for these sterling interpretations proves in its minimal membership that less is truly more. Their "trio" approach to Buxtehude's music provides a clarity of line and rhythm that might well elude a larger group. It's also likely that this arrangement more closely approaches the composer's forces at the Abendmusik concerts that brought such chamber works to first light at Lübeck's Marienkirche. Clear intonation, never a sleigh ride on period instruments, seems no challenge for the group, and that singularly sweet baroque string timbre is in abundance even amid some thick and rapid counterpoint, making each work a delight.

Vocal
various sacred cantatas
what to buy: [*Geistliche Kantaten (Sacred Cantatas)*; Konrad Junghänel, cond.; Cantus Köln, ensemble] (Harmonia Mundi 901629) ♪ ♪ ♪ ♪⁔

The six works in this collection, scored for chamber choir and an assortment of period instruments, stem from the famous *Abendmusiken,* the evening concerts brought back into vogue by Buxtehude during his years as organist at Lübeck. These are precious miniatures, lasting only

a few minutes each but containing all the seminal devices that would grow into the mature cantata some decades hence: the opening instrumental sinfonia of varying textures and tempi, the polyphonic choral flourish that opens the second segment, the andante interlude in homophonic style, and the concluding antiphony between instruments and voices. Cantus Köln delivers superb performances of each cantata, replete with impeccable intonation, diction, and balance. One hearing of *Befiehl dem Engel, dass er kommt* should convince the listener that here we have some of the seventeenth century's most endearing *and* enduring music.

influences: Johann Sebastian Bach, Georg Frideric Handel, Johann Pachelbel, Johann Gottfried Walther, Nicolaus Bruhns

Frank Scinta

William Byrd
Born circa 1540, in London, England. Died July 4, 1623, in Stondon Massey, Essex, England.

period: Baroque

William Byrd, the pre-eminent composer of Elizabethan England and a Gentleman of the Chapel Royal, wrote marvelous songs, anthems, pieces for small ensembles and for keyboard. He also composed unsurpassed music for the Catholic service despite the ban against papist activities mandated by Queen Elizabeth I.

Little is known of William Byrd's early life, although there are records hinting that his father may have been a musician and employed as a Gentleman of the Chapel Royal in the mid-1500s. The first definite mention of the younger Byrd notes his position as Organist and Master of the Choristers at Lincoln Cathedral in 1563. In addition, he was reputed to have been a student of the composer Thomas Tallis and would later become his business partner. Byrd's earliest works certainly showed Tallis's influence, but they also reflected the styles of Christopher Tye, Robert White, and other well-known musicians of the period.

The time spent at Lincoln Cathedral as a performer, teacher, and composer allowed Byrd the opportunity to hone his craft and his reputation. By 1570 he was made a Gentleman of the Chapel Royal although he did not formally take up his position until a few years later. Byrd's first duties involved sharing the position of organist with his old teacher, Tallis. Byrd must have been a smooth navigator of court politics as well as a talented musician since he was known and liked by members of the nobility whose children he sometimes taught. Another sign of royal favor occurred in 1575 when Byrd, along with Tallis, received the only franchise for the printing and marketing of sheet music from the Crown. The two partners brought out the *Cantiones sacrae*, a compilation of 34 motets (17 apiece) dedicated to the Queen in appreciation of their good fortune.

It is also possible that his court connections helped keep Byrd out of prison during this period, since he was a devout Roman Catholic at a time when Queen Elizabeth was persecuting followers of his religion. Byrd's deep faith was that of an activist even though he was able to avoid many of the penalties facing his co-religionists. His willingness to promote his beliefs was especially evident after 1580 when the composer took a more active role in aiding members of the English Catholic community. One example was his setting to music the words of a flagrantly political poem lamenting the execution of Father Edmund Campion—*Why do I use my paper, ink, and pen*. Byrd also allowed his house to be used as a meeting place for his fellow Catholics and composed music for use in private worship services. Despite his willingness to promote his faith and his engagement in what would have been termed "seditious activities," Byrd also wrote material for the Anglican church and his royal patroness.

In 1585 Tallis died, which meant that Byrd was now sole controller of the publishing monopoly. What was once deemed an economic boon had not really lived up to either partner's expectations, since the only works printed up to this point were the *Cantiones sacrae* dedicated to Queen Elizabeth. This situation changed with the production of Byrd's *Psalmes, Sonnets, and Songs* in 1588, the *Songs of Sundrie Natures* and a magnificent new set of *Cantiones sacrae* in 1589, and the superb collection of keyboard works, *My Ladye Nevells Booke*, in 1591.

Byrd moved his household from London to Stondon Massey, Essex in 1593. The next works of substance from his pen were the superb masses for three, four and five voices written for use in clandestine Catholic worship services throughout England and published between 1593 and 1595. He followed these up with a pair of books for worship, the ambitious *Gradualia* of

1605 and 1607. Byrd's last published collection was a second set of *Psalmes, Songs and Sonnets* in 1611.

Chamber
various keyboard works
what to buy: [*William Byrd: The Complete Keyboard Music*; Davitt Moroney, various keyboards] (Hyperion 66551/7) ♪ ♪ ♪ ♪₄

Seven discs of solo virginal, harpsichord, and chamber organ might be a bit much for some but this collection is more for dipping into than consuming in one session. Some of Byrd's finest instrumental compositions can be found here, including *The Battle* (a programmatic bit of keyboard artistry), *The Tenth Pavan and Galliard,* and his take on the popular tune *Walsingham.*

Consort music
worth looking for: [*The Complete Consort Music*: Christopher Wilson, lute; Fretwork, viols] (Virgin Classics 45031) ♪ ♪ ♪ ♪

Fretwork is a sextet of viol players and, with lutenist Christopher Wilson, they provided a valuable service for fans of the composer by collecting all of Byrd's works for consort of viols onto one disc and performing them so well.

Vocal
Mass for five voices
what to buy: [Peter Phillips, cond.; the Tallis Scholars, choir] (Gimell 345) ♪ ♪ ♪ ♪₄

Beautifully sung and recorded by the Tallis Scholars, this version of Byrd's sublime setting of the mass goes to the top of the list. In addition to this performance, there are fine renditions of the beautiful masses for three and four voices plus fine singing in the exquisite motet, *Ave verum corpus.*

what to buy next: [David Willcocks, cond.; the King's College Choir, Cambridge] (London 452170) ♪ ♪ ♪ ♪

Before the Tallis Scholars came along, this was the top recommendation for all of the Byrd masses. Now available on a mid-priced, two disc set, along with a pair of shorter sacred works by Byrd and a wonderful version of the *Western Wynde Mass* by John Tavener, this is still pretty competitive.

[Calefax Reed Quintet] (MDG 6190745) ♪ ♪ ♪♪

This performance features an instrumental arrangement for oboe, clarinet, saxophone, bass clarinet, and bassoon of Byrd's wonderful mass setting that works surprisingly well, going beyond novelty to become a celebration of the composer's art. The album also includes three other well played arrangements of Byrd pieces with special mention going to the ensemble's take on the *Magnificat* from Byrd's Anglican *Great Service.* Five selections from the pen of Arvo Pärt round out the collection.

influences: Thomas Tallis, Thomas Morley, Thomas Weelkes, Christopher Tye

Garaud MacTaggart

John Cage

Born John Milton Cage, Jr. September 5, 1912, in Los Angeles, CA. Died August 12, 1992, in New York City, NY.

period: Twentieth Century

Like Miles Davis in the jazz world, John Cage came to value the space between the notes as much as the notes themselves—maybe even more. He spent much of his career figuring out ways to avoid harmony, or at least intentional harmony, and revolutionized music through the concept of aleatoric music, constructed using chance operations such as flipping coins and consulting the *I Ching.* He became the grand old man of the avant-garde, and influenced movements as disparate as minimalism and electronic music.

Cage studied with Henry Cowell in New York and was influenced by that composer's use of tone clusters and playing directly on the strings inside the piano. Cage's *Six Short Inventions for three or more instruments* of 1934, constructed using a technique somewhat akin to serialism, led Cowell to recommend that Cage study with Arnold Schoenberg, which he did in Los Angeles where the Austrian composer had moved after fleeing the Nazis. Cage composed using Schoenberg's 12-tone method and was greatly influenced by his teacher's dedication and example, if not necessarily his style and philosophy. When Schoenberg informed him that he had little talent for harmony and that this would hinder his

progress—harmony would be a wall between Cage and the career of composing—he vowed, "I will devote my life to beating my head against that wall." He conceived "organized sound," and prophetically wrote in 1937, "I believe that the use of noise to make music will continue and increase." Though he visualized this being done electronically in the future, in the immediate term, this meant that Cage primarily wrote for percussion.

A pivotal moment in Cage's career came while he was living in Seattle and accompanying modern dance classes. Asked in 1938 by African-American dancer Syvilla Fort to write music for the performance of the African-themed piece *Bacchanale,* Cage had to forego his usual format of massed percussion instruments because of the small size and layout of the theater, which had no pit but did have a piano. Attempting to make the piano sound African, Cage (extrapolating from Cowell's inside-the-piano technique) experimented with putting metal objects between the strings (each note on the piano has two or three strings). This affected both timbre (damping the strings, buzzing) and tuning (since it shortens the portion of the string which vibrates). Additionally, use of the piano's damper pedal (which shifts the hammers over slightly so that notes with three strings become notes with two strings—one not being struck), would change the effect of the preparations on the sound. Cage had converted the piano into a self-contained percussion ensemble controlled by a single player.

Cage moved to New York City in the early 1940s on the invitation of Peggy Guggenheim, wife of the surrealist artist Max Ernst and a generous supporter of the arts. It was there that an interest in Buddhist philosophy—fostered by the writings of Ananda Coomaraswamy and, later, courses at Columbia University taught by Zen scholar D.T. Suzuki—led Cage to the pursuit of tranquility. This strongly influenced his works, notably the extraordinary hour-long series of *Sonatas and Interludes,* the apex of Cage's composing for solo prepared piano, written between 1946 and 1948. Going even further down that path, Cage decided that the problem with music was its undue dependence on taste, or subjectivity; true tranquility would be expressed in finding the music in sound, no matter what it might be. Looking for a way around that subjectivity, Cage began shaping pieces through chance operations in 1951, using the *I Ching (Book of Changes),* an ancient Chinese ora-

John Cage

cle. His first piece so constructed was *Music of Changes* for solo piano, and the vast majority of his music for the rest of his life was determined to some extent by chance elements. Some pieces had their starts in flaws on paper being transferred onto staff paper; similarly, he would use star charts, with the *I Ching* picking out specific stars; the pattern would then be mapped out as notes. The pieces would vary in the extent of their use of chance and in the degree of strictness with which the musicians' parts were notated.

Sometimes major decisions were left up to the players in performance; in other cases, everything from the type of attack to durations and dynamics were plotted out in advance. This sometimes posed difficulties (at least psychological ones) for musicians outside the avant-garde, the most notorious example being when the New York Philharmonic was scheduled to play Cage's massive chance piece *Atlas Eclipticalis,* a work constructed using star maps and the *I Ching*, which grants the players considerable decision-making leeway. The orchestra members openly expressed their contempt for the piece, noodled away on nursery rhymes, damaged the contact mikes on their instruments, and so on, dismaying Cage not so much through their disrespect as their lack of professionalism and their gross distortion of what the audience ended up hearing. Nonetheless, this chance music—also referred to as indeterminate music or aleatoric music—greatly influenced the avant-garde, especially in Europe, where Karlheinz Stockhausen and Iannis Xenakis, among others, developed the idea still further.

The chance piece for which Cage is most famous is undoubtedly *4'33"*. He had been invited to experience an isolation chamber, and was surprised to discover that even in such an environment he could hear noise. The technicians explained to him that nothing was wrong, but that with all background noise removed people heard the sounds made by their own circulatory, respiratory, and nervous systems. This was a revelation for Cage: in practical terms, there was no such thing as silence. In *4'33"*, he took advantage of this phenomenon once again to point audiences towards his belief that noise was also music. Ostensibly *4'33"* is a piano piece in three movements, whose lengths were determined by chance, but in fact the performer remains seated at the instrument without playing for four minutes and 33 seconds, and the "music" consists of whatever ambient noise is generated during that period. The piece was premiered on August 29, 1952, by the pianist David

Tudor and was immediately controversial, with most people missing the point and thinking it was a joke or an insincere bilking of the intelligentsia by a clever charlatan. Nothing could have been further from the truth. It fit squarely into an emerging art movement known as *Fluxus,* and for a while in the 1960s Cage wrote pieces made up solely of verbal instructions, without any musical notation.

Cage was also temporarily at the forefront of electronic music. Such pieces as *Imaginary Landscape no. 5, Williams Mix, Fontana Mix,* and *HPSCHD* were created wholly or in part through this method. His interest in it eventually waned, however, partly because of how time-consuming it was to produce. Chance music certainly offered him a broad enough field to work in, with plenty of the variety he found so stimulating and necessary for composing. After the time-length pieces, he leaned towards music of indeterminate length in which specified events were not strictly placed in time. In 1987, in what proved to be the last phase of his career before he died of a stroke, Cage began writing his so-called number pieces. The titles are based on the number of performers, with multiple pieces for the same number of players differentiated by superscript numerals. Time brackets govern, without strictly determining, the placement of the musical events. *Two,* for flute and piano, was his first number piece; Cage wrote 43 of them, with 108 being the most performers used in any of them.

An articulate and provocative spokesman for his views, Cage propounded them in a number of books: *Silence, A Year from Monday, New Lectures and Writings, Notations, M: Writings '67-'72, Empty Words: Writings '63-'78, Themes and Variations,* and *X: Writings 1979-82,* as well as *I-VI* (the Charles Eliot Norton Lectures that Cage delivered at Harvard in 1988–89). The excellent *Silence* is perhaps the best introduction to his music.

[A note about the listings below: The ratings are subjective assessments not of the relative success or failure of the performances, but rather of the importance of the pieces in understanding and appreciating Cage's oeuvre.]

Orchestral
Atlas Eclipticalis
what to buy: [Petr Kotik, cond.; Orchestra of the S.E.M. Ensemble] (Wergo 6216) ♪ ♪ ♪ ♪₈

Atlas Eclipticalis is the most notorious of Cage's

aleatoric compositions, the piece which the New York Philharmonic's musicians treated with such disrespect. It calls for 86 orchestral musicians playing conventional instruments augmented by non-pitched percussion. Any number of the 86 parts can be played, the duration is unspecified, and there is considerable leeway for decision-making by the musicians in the realization of the parts. The parts themselves were constructed using star maps and the *I Ching*. Cage referred to the work as "'live' electronic music," and ideally it should be performed using contact microphones, amplifiers, and speakers. (This album also includes a performance of the Concert for Piano and Orchestra with Joseph Kubera as pianist.)

various works for piano and ensemble
what to buy: [*The Piano Concertos*; Stephen Drury, piano; Charles Peltz, cond.; Callithumpian Consort, orch.; David Tudor, piano; Ingo Metzmacher, cond.; Ensemble Modern, orch.] (mode 57) ♪ ♪ ♪ ♪ ♪

Here are works for piano and ensemble that provide a sampling of three of Cage's compositional methods. In the Concerto for Prepared Piano and Chamber Orchestra from 1951, he deploys the various timbres of the orchestra in a fashion similar to his treatment of the piano, with the orchestra as the piano's equal rather than its subordinate. This is his 1940s music on a grander scale. By contrast, the Concert for Piano and Orchestra, written in 1957–58, does give the performers material to play, but it lets the amount of time they have to play it in— and even the number of players—vary, as well as letting the performers decide how they put their parts together from those materials. With the instruments also being played using extended techniques and microtonality, the results can be dramatic and startling. *Fourteen,* from 1990, uses the methods of Cage's last period, giving a set number of players (from which the title of the piece is derived)—in this case, solo piano plus 13 instruments—specific pitches to play inside flexible time brackets, leaving note duration and dynamics up to the players. The effect is more peaceful and meditative than that of the Concert. Drury, Peltz, and the New Englanders play the Concerto and *Fourteen;* Tudor, Metzmacher, and the Ensemble Modern play the Concert.

Concert for Piano and Orchestra
what to buy: [*The 25-Year Retrospective Concert of the Music of John Cage*; David Tudor, piano; Merce Cunningham, cond.; anonymous orchestra] (Wergo 6247) ♪ ♪ ♪ ♪ ♪

Maria Callas:
American soprano Maria Callas lived as colorful a life off the stage as she did on. Her passionate relationships and glamorous, jet-setting behavior only contributed to the mystique of this gifted singing actress, ultimately elevating her to near cult status. As her career progressed she developed a reputation for storming out of rehearsals and canceling performances that made headlines throughout the media. She also had an epic on-again, off-again relationship with Aristotle Onassis, the Greek shipping magnate. Her legendary classes at the Juilliard School (1971–1972) were immortalized by Terence McNally in his play *Master Class.*

Callas and her mother moved to Greece from New York City when she was thirteen, and she soon began studying voice with Elvira de Hidalgo at the Royal Academy of Music in Athens. At age sixteen Callas made her first professional appearance in Franz von Suppe's *Boccacio.* After returning to New York in 1945, Callas auditioned for the Metropolitan Opera, but refused a contract offer in order to make her debut in Italy with Amilcar Ponchielli's *La Gioconda.* Under the guidance of conductor Tullio Serafin, Callas mastered the heavier roles of Puccini, Verdi, and Wagner, but she eventually gravitated toward the bel canto repertoire of Rossini, Bellini, and Donizetti. Many felt she possessed the dramatic temperament for such roles, but lacked the tonal quality and technical agility required to negotiate the demanding coloratura parts.

Callas appeared in many of the world's great houses before her momentous debut at the Met in *Norma* on October 29, 1956, but she ended her operatic career as Tosca at Covent Garden on July 5, 1965. She died in Paris on Sept. 16, 1977 of a heart attack and was cremated. Landmark recordings of some of her signature roles include Bellini's *Norma* (EMI Classics 56271), Cherubini's *Medea* (EMI Classics 66435), and Puccini's *Tosca* (EMI Classics 66444).

Mona DeQuis

The premiere of Concert for Piano and Orchestra came at a 1958 concert at Town Hall in New York City and was documented on this three-CD set recorded by George Avakian, a producer at Columbia Records. Tudor plays the piano part, while Cunningham is the "conductor" who acted as a human clock. In this live performance, we hear the effect Cage's then new (and still controversial) ideas had on an audience; there is laughter, booing, and derisive clapping. The playing itself is attractively pungent and lively, and the accompanying booklet is magnificent, with a score page and discussion of each piece contained in this invaluable set, along with the texts of Cage's essay *The Future of Music: Credo* from 1937 and his speech *Experimental Music* from 1957, as well as his own notes on the pieces.

Chamber
Music of Changes
what to buy: [Herbert Henck, piano] (Wergo 60099-50) ♪ ♪ ♪ ♪ ♪

Dedicated to David Tudor, the solo piano *Music of Changes* from 1951 is Cage's first *I Ching*-derived piece. In four books playing for about three-quarters of an hour, it is very strictly notated. Though its effect on listeners is not really of randomness, however, at least in its specifics the piece is unpredictable on first hearing.

Sonatas and Interludes for Prepared Piano
what to buy: [Philipp Vandré, prepared piano] (mode 50)
♪ ♪ ♪ ♪ ♪

Of crucial importance in this recording is the fact that it was made using a Steinway "O" baby grand piano, the model for which Cage wrote these 20 pieces. As his precise instructions for preparing the piano are written out in measurements from the bridge (the placement of the screws, bolts, nuts, rubber, plastic, and eraser in the strings of the piano is governed by a chart in the score, with measurements precise to within one-sixteenth of an inch), using the same model of piano (thus having the same string lengths) should result more nearly in the sounds that Cage himself heard.

what to buy next: [Aleck Karis, prepared piano] (Bridge 9081A/B) ♪ ♪ ♪ ♪ ♪

On the other hand, though Cage at first had trouble accepting that preparations on different pianos brought different results, eventually he came to terms with this aspect of indeterminacy, as he described in his book *Empty Words*. Thus, other recordings than the one listed above are equally valid. This one includes a free bonus disc with Cage reading his essay *Composition in Retrospect*.

[Nigel Butterley, prepared piano] (Tall Poppies 025) ♪ ♪ ♪ ♪ ♪

This CD is filled out with *Music for Marcel Duchamp* and *The Wonderful Widow of 18 Springs,* the latter with tenor Gerald English. *Music for Marcel Duchamp,* also for prepared piano, was originally written for a film by Hans Richter and is especially quiet and contemplative in tone.

The Perilous Night
what to buy: [Margaret Leng Tan, prepared piano] (New Albion 037) ♪ ♪ ♪ ♪ ♪

Anyone skeptical of Cage's compositional proficiency should hear this completely notated and carefully struc-

tured pair of works dating from 1944. *The Perilous Night* (played by Margaret Leng Tan) consists of six short pieces for prepared piano written before he had moved away from the idea of music as emotional expression. Its subject is loneliness. The nearly hour-long *Four Walls,* for (regular) piano with a vocal interlude (sung here by Joan LaBarbara), was written for a dance-play by Cage's friend Merce Cunningham. Using only the white keys, it is full of silences and repetitions depicting a disturbed mind.

Etudes Australes
what to buy: [Grete Sultan, prepared piano] (Wergo 6152) ♪ ♪ ♪ ♪ ♪

The four massive books of *Etudes Australes,* written for pianist Grete Sultan in 1974, consist of 32 pieces, each two pages in notated length. The notes, with no fixed durations, were derived through a combination of a star map of the sky as seen from Australia and the application of *I Ching* choices, with the etudes becoming progressively denser as the series proceeds. In addition to the played notes, Cage instructs that for each etude, notes not written in the score should be depressed (via wedges holding the keys down); their strings then vibrate sympathetically from the playing of the other notes. The average listener will not want to wade through the entire series—10 minutes shy of three hours on these three CD's—at one sitting, but in short doses, these pieces are attractive in their randomness.

various works for prepared piano
what to buy: [*Daughters of the Lonesome Isle*; Margaret Leng Tan, piano, prepared piano, and toy piano] (New Albion 070) ♪ ♪ ♪ ♪ ♪

Music for Piano #2 dates from 1953 and was composed using chance methods; the other works heard here are all from the 1940s. *Bacchanale* is the most important of them, the very first piece for prepared piano. *In the Name of the Holocaust* (Cage denied a war association for this 1942 piece and said the title was a play on *In the name of the Holy Ghost*) is for prepared piano but also uses Henry Cowell's ideas of playing the strings directly with the fingers and of clusters played with the arms. *Daughters of the Lonesome Isle* is a deeply haunting work, with the sound of the prepared piano suggesting a gamelan orchestra (though Cage denied that specific influence) because the preparing materials are exclusively metallic. *Ophelia* is full of emotional turmoil; for regular piano, it is still distinctively Cageian. Margaret

Leng Tan plays *The Seasons* more quickly than Drury, at a tempo which arguably better suits its dance origin. The Suite for Toy Piano takes Cage's interest in different piano timbres to a new level, using an instrument in which metal bars, rather than strings, are struck, making it even more percussive. At the same time, the instrument is smaller than a normal piano, with a more delicate tone. Ingenuously, it uses only nine white notes and proceeds almost entirely in stepwise motion. *In a Landscape* finds Cage moving into a more neutral style that some find reflected in the ambient music he wrote decades later; the constant use of the sustaining pedal makes the sounds blur. In this performance of the later *Music for Piano #2* the strings are bowed; Cage didn't actually call for that technique here, but Tan applies it tastefully in a few spots to vary the timbre, and Cage approved. The chance operations used to compose this piece included taking the pitches from imperfections in the staff paper; the frequency of sound events was determined through the *I Ching*. There is much space between the notes, reflecting the tranquility Cage was attempting to convey through his music at that time.

various works for two prepared pianos
what to buy: [Double Edge, pianos and prepared pianos] (CRI 732) ♪ ♪ ♪ ♪⅜

Cage wrote *Two2* for the piano duo Double Edge in 1989. It's not a time-bracket piece, though written in that period; the structure is based on the syllabic 5-7-5-7-7 structure of Japanese poetry (renga, tanka, etc.). The two piano parts are independent, yet neither pianist can proceed from one measure to the next until the other pianist is finished playing the corresponding measure, thus enforcing a degree of cooperation. The result (nearly 33 minutes here) suggests an unhurried cross between Cowell and early Morton Feldman, with a Messiaen-like celestial grandeur. Also heard here is *Experiences,* a short two-piano piece of Satie-like simplicity from 1945 and *Three Dances* for two prepared pianos. Despite its title, this last named work was not written to be danced. Dating from 1944–45, it lasts around 25 minutes and is perhaps Cage's "busiest" prepared piano piece.

various dance pieces
what to buy: [*Music for Merce Cunningham*; David Tudor, electronics; Takehisa Kosugi, pizzicato amplified violin, bamboo flute, percussion; Michael Pugliese, percussion] (mode 24) ♪ ♪ ♪ ♪ ♪

Cartridge Music, written in 1960, is another crucial and

controversial work, one of Cage's most determined efforts to reveal "noise" as music. Contact microphones capture the sounds created when phonograph cartridges (in which objects other than phonograph needles have been inserted—pipe-cleaners, wires, matches, etc.) are "played" according to intricate graphic scores interpreted independently by the performers. Open-minded listeners will be fascinated by the resulting vast array of timbres and micro-rhythms. It qualifies for this CD by virtue of Cunningham, with whom Cage collaborated intensively throughout his career, having choreographed it in 1973. *Five Stone Wind,* on the other hand, was specifically written for Cunningham in 1988; it combines two sections, *Five Stone* and *Wind.* Pugliese on clay drums; Kosugi on pizzicato amplified violin, "piezzo tree" for sound transducer (percussion), and bamboo flute; and Tudor on electronics work from a time-bracket score generated via chance. In the *Wind* section, Tudor's electronic "gate," which is processing sounds generated by vibrations, is sometimes reversed, which thus controls not the attack but rather the release of sounds, producing more sustained tones.

Vocal
Four6
what to buy: [*John Cage at Summerstage*; Joan La Barbara, soprano; John Cage, vocals; William Winant, percussion; Leonard Stein, piano, whistles, percussion, and vocals] (Music & Arts 4875) ♪ ♪ ♪ ♪⅜

This July 23, 1992 outdoor concert in New York's Central Park—an early 80th birthday celebration—includes Cage's last public performance (less than a month before his death), in the premiere of *Four6,* the main piece on this disc. Four performers choose 12 sounds with "fixed characteristics" and deploy them within flexible time brackets. Joan La Barbara (singing wordlessly, or, more accurately, making vocal sounds), percussionist William Winant, pianist Leonard Stein (a former assistant to Schoenberg), and Cage, also singing ("shocking things," as he put it), are the performers in a piece in which each sound is a major event. *Eight Whiskus,* written for La Barbara in 1984, is a series of short solo songs setting haiku-like "cut-up" texts. *Music for Three,* another piece for wordless vocal sounds, gets a 10-minute performance here by La Barbara, Winant, and Stein.

influences: Arnold Schoenberg, Henry Cowell, Erik Satie, Edgard Varèse, Lou Harrison, D.T. Suzuki, Iannis Xenakis

Steve Holtje

Elliott Carter

Born Elliott Cook Carter, Jr., December 11, 1908, in New York City, NY

period: Twentieth century

Elliott Carter's reference points start with Charles Ives and pass through Igor Stravinsky and Arnold Schoenberg before arriving at an ongoing, uniquely personal vision that plays with rhythm and timbre throughout a most complex and impressive oeuvre. His piano concerto (1967) and *Double Concerto* for Piano, Harpsichord and Two Small Orchestras (1961) were called "masterpieces" by no less a personage than Stravinsky, while the second and third of his five string quartets (1959 and 1971, respectively) won Pulitzer Prizes. Carter has a bigger following in Europe than he does in the United States, and it was in Berlin that his first opera, *What Next?*, debuted in 1999, yet another new horizon for a composer approaching age one hundred.

In the 1920s, Carter was first exposed to contemporary music by a high school teacher in New York who was friends with Charles Ives and Edgard Varèse. Once this world was opened up, Carter remained friendly with Varèse and wrote pieces for which Ives showed encouragement. Carter earned a B.A. in English and a Masters in Music from Harvard by 1932 and, because most American colleges didn't teach composition at the time he began writing music, he went to Paris to study at the Ecole Normale de Musique from 1932 to 1935. After returning to the United States, Carter served as musical director for Ballet Caravan until 1940, the year his suite from the ballet *Pocahontas* won the Publication of American Music Award from the Juilliard Foundation. His music of the late 1930s and early 1940s enjoyed moderate success and contained elements of jazz and popular music, reflecting, as he put it, a "natural desire to write something many people could presumably grasp and enjoy easily at a time of social emergency." By the end of World War II he was dissatisfied with this direction, and began exploring the distinctive characteristics of instruments themselves as his fundamental compositional resource.

Carter then broke with precedent and explored his new "metric modulation" technique, a process inspired by jazz improvisation and marked by interrelated shifts in background and foreground speeds. In 1948, he wrote his Sonata for Violoncello and Piano, a piece that introduced this new way of composing. Now considered one of the finest twentieth century cello sonatas, its success led Carter to broaden his approach to the basic materials available for musical treatment, using elements drawn from various Medieval, Oriental, and African sources to modernize his subsequent works. In 1951, at age 43, Carter jumped to the front rank of the avant-garde with his first string quartet. Inspired by a Jean Cocteau film (*Le Sang d'un poète*), Carter created this work with the help of a Guggenheim Fellowship and a grant from the National Institute of Arts and Letters. With it, he won first prize at the International Quartet Competition in 1953, the same year that he received a Fellowship to the American Academy in Rome. While there he worked on a piece commissioned by the Ford Foundation for the Louisville Symphony Orchestra, his *Variations for Orchestra*. In his second string quartet (1959) Carter would replace the individual parallelism of the four instruments, and use a more archetypal approach, assigning each instrument its own expressive character built on a repertory of musical speeds and intervals. This work won him the Pulitzer Prize and the Critics' Circle Award in 1960, and a UNESCO Prize in 1961. Later that same year, he received the Sibelius Medal and the Critic's Circle Award for his *Double Concerto,* a work which Igor Stravinsky cited as an American masterpiece.

Carter was a professor of composition at Yale from 1960 to 1962 and served as composer in residence at the American Academy in Rome the following year. He held a similar position the following year in Berlin, where he began composing his Concerto for Piano and Orchestra. More awards followed, and in 1967 Carter was enlisted for another year-long residency at the American Academy in Rome, spending some time at the Villa Serbelloni in Bellagio working on his Concerto for Orchestra—a commission from the New York Philharmonic Orchestra for its 125th anniversary. In 1971 Carter began composing his third string quartet, a work which would win him a second Pulitzer Prize in 1973. Carter also taught at the Juilliard School for twenty years, starting in 1972.

During the 1980s, Carter continued to compose a variety of chamber works including a duet for flute and clarinet, his *Canon for Four,* and the *Esprit rude/esprit doux*. One of his most captivating works from that decade, however, was his *Triple Duo*. Composed in 1983, the piece uses

Elliott Carter

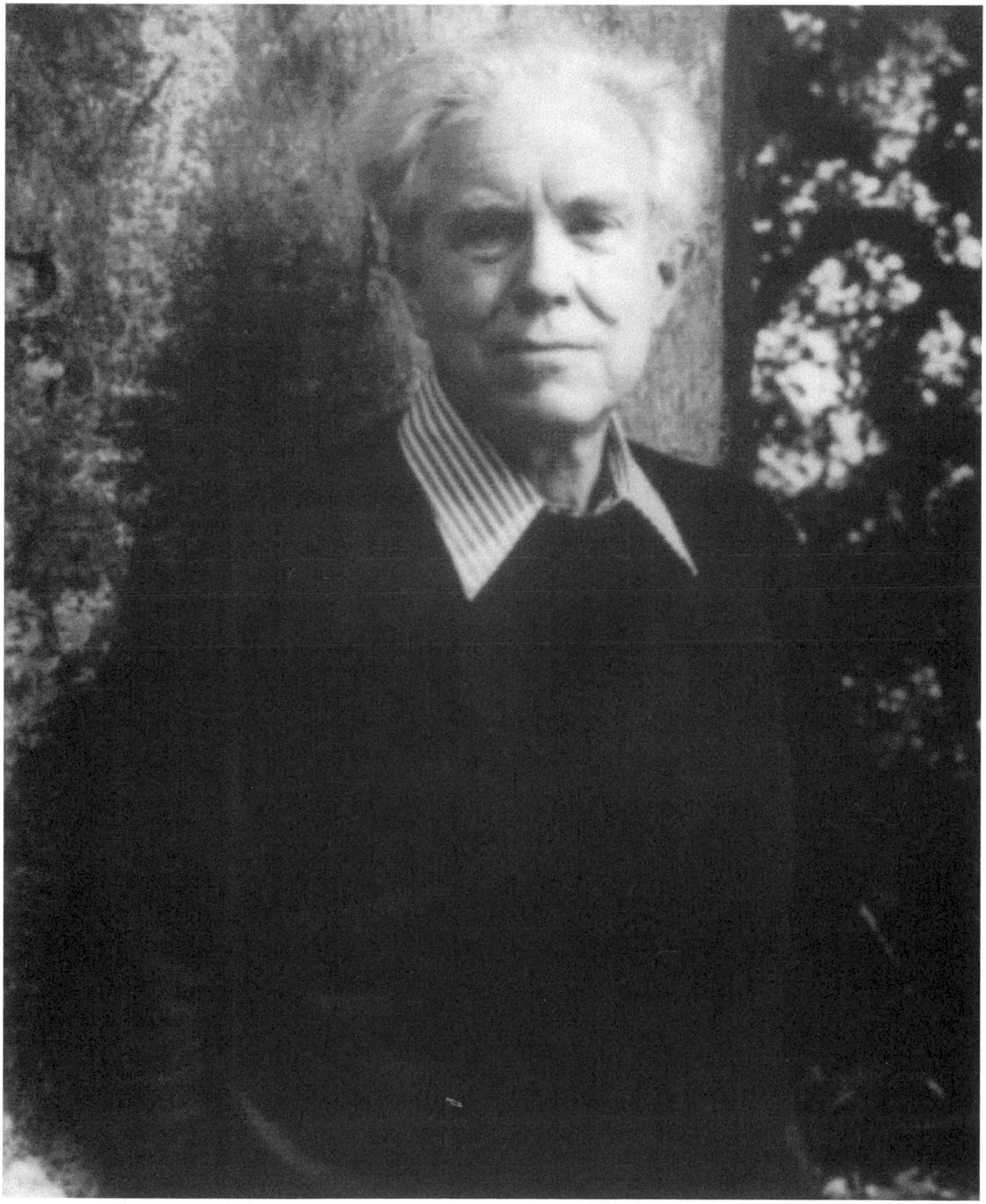

six instrumentalists divided into three pairs with each pair—flute/clarinet, violin/cello, and piano/percussion—having its own unique set of compositional materials to work with.

When he was in his late 80s, the composer was petitioned by Daniel Barenboim to write an opera. To that point Carter had resisted doing so because he felt it was difficult enough for his orchestral works to get the rehearsal time needed to perform them correctly. As he told *Opera* magazine in February 2000, "My music requires too much preparation for most opera houses." Still, Barenboim persisted and Carter finally gave in, working from 1997 to 1998 on *What Next?* (to a libretto by Paul Griffiths) and creating a short, one-act work that received its triumphant premiere in Germany at the Berlin Staatsoper Unter den Linden in September 1999. The plot revolves around a car accident and the reactions to it by a quintet of singers; the music is multi-layered in typical Carter fashion and (as of press time) there has been talk of a recording.

Orchestral
Symphonia: Sum Fluxae Pretium Spei
what to buy: [Oliver Knussen, cond., BBC Symphony Orchestra] (Deutsche Grammophon 459660) ♪ ♪ ♪ ♪♪

Barring the recording of Carter's opera, this may be the most important document of the composer's work in the 1990s. The *Symphonia* was first performed in 1998, and rewards patient listeners who are willing to thread their way through the well-recorded play of massive, volatile-sounding forces. It is paired with Carter's intriguing and surprisingly accessible 1996 Concerto for Clarinet and Orchestra, with Michael Collins as soloist and Knussen leading the London Sinfonietta.

Concerto for Piano and Orchestra
what to buy: [Ursula Oppens, piano; Michael Gielen, cond.; Cincinnati Symphony Orchestra] (New World Records 347) ♪ ♪ ♪♪

A dark, atonal piece that stabs at the listener's consciousness, this churning work is a product of its time and locale. Gielen does his best with Carter's piece, and the musicians capably master the complexities of this work that sets the piano against the orchestra in irreconcilable, violently opposed modes. While Oppens underpins much of what's happening and plays freely in isolated solos, there's not much to hold on to, except for little nuggets of melody from the strings and woodwinds

which seem to poke out of the dissonance. Still, it's an exemplary piece from this period of Carter's career, and another fine performance from twentieth century music specialist Oppens. Carter's *Variations for Orchestra,* also included on this CD, gives Gielen and the musicians the opportunity to render a splendid interpretation of this highly intriguing (and more digestible) work.

Concerto for Violin and Orchestra
worth searching for: [Ole Böhn, violin; Oliver Knusson, cond.; London Sinfonietta, orch.] (Virgin Classics 91503) ♪ ♪ ♪ ♪♪

A total attention-grabber, this stellar recording of Carter's beautiful concerto won him a 1994 Grammy Award for *Best Contemporary Composition.* Bohn premiered this work in 1990, and his performance is ear-expanding in Knusson's capable hands. Especially notable is the violinist's performance in the *Impulsiva* movement, in which it cross-cuts against the intensely swirling and churning accompaniment of the London Sinfonietta. This disc also contains Carter's challenging *Concerto for Orchestra* and the *Three Occasions for Orchestra;* a triptych of brief pieces: *A Celebration of Some 100 x 150 Notes, Remembrance,* and *Anniversary.*

Chamber
Night Fantasies for Piano
[*American Piano Music of Our Time;* Ursula Oppens, piano] (Music & Arts 4862) ♪ ♪ ♪ ♪♪

A versatile interpreter of modern music, Oppens shows amazing technique and power in her rendering of this arduous, dissonant, and intense piece. Her adroitness and confidence enhance a challenging work that scurries and jumps seemingly from one mood to another (perhaps like our nightmares). The piece contrasts sharply with some of the more tonal-leaning works by twentieth century American composers also included on this sumptuous album, which combines previously released tracks from Music & Arts 604 and 699.

Sonata for Piano
what to buy: [Paul Jacobs, piano] (Nonesuch 79248) ♪ ♪ ♪ ♪♪

Jacobs renders a virtuosic version of this revolutionary and complex two-movement work. His keyboard mastery achieves what Carter probably intended as the pianist artfully carries sustained tones, connecting one phrase to the next. This is a most passionate performance of this beautiful piece. Also included on the CD is a rendition of *The Minotaur* by the New York Chamber Symphony and two songs based on Robert Frost poems, *Dust of Snow* and *The Rose Family,* performed here by mezzo-soprano Jan DeGaetani with pianist Gilbert Kalish.

what to buy next: [*The Complete Music for Solo Piano*; Charles Rosen, piano] (Bridge 9090) ♪ ♪ ♪ ♪

Full of brawn and sensitivity, Rosen's interpretation is engaging, yet there's something lacking when compared with the Jacobs version of the sonata. The shortfall may have more to do with Rosen's particular instrument and sound production than his technique and style. This disc also includes Carter's *Night Fantasies* and *90 +* for Piano, along with a brief conversation between Carter and Rosen.

Sonata for Cello and Piano
what to buy: [Rhonda Rider, cello; Lois Shapiro, piano] (Centaur 2267) ♪ ♪ ♪ ♪ ♪

A stirring version of this early Carter work, suitably conveying its turbulence and romanticism as well as its accessible melodies. Rider's ardent passion and deep, woody tones greatly add to this recording. Shapiro is a sensitive performer who ably renders muscular or delicate passages depending on the requirements of the composition. This captivating album also contains cello sonatas by twentieth century American composers Samuel Barber and Seymour Shifrin.

Quartet no. 1 for Strings
what to buy: [Composers String Quartet, ensemble] (Nonesuch 71249) ♪ ♪ ♪ ♪ ♪

Offering a splendidly dynamic, passionately executed version of the early work that unexpectedly shot Carter to international prominence, this historic recording (made in 1970 under Carter's own musical supervision) is accompanied by liner notes from the composer. Even though they're playing divergent motifs, these musicians seem extremely well attuned to each another. The disc also contains a spectacular reading of Carter's Pulitzer-winning Quartet no. 2 for Strings.

what to buy next: [*Elliott Carter: The Four String Quartets*; Juilliard String Quartet, ensemble] (Sony Classics 47229) ♪ ♪ ♪ ♪

Sonorously pleasing, this December 1990 performance recorded at the American Academy and Institute of Arts and Letters in New York City, though also supervised by Carter, lacks the vitality and sterling sound quality of the recording by the Composers Quartet. Still, it's a praiseworthy two-disc set which also includes renderings of his other three string quartets.

Triple Duo for Flute, Clarinet, Violin, Cello, Piano, and Percussion
what to buy: [*Music of Carter, Druckman, and Davies*; Robert Black, cond.; New York Music Ensemble] (GM Recordings 2047) ♪ ♪ ♪ ♪₅

Triple Duo is one of the most interesting of Carter's compositions, a euphoric, animated piece full of puckishness and quicksilver movement. The three pairs of wind, string, and percussion instrumentalists, some doubling on additional instruments, execute this complex piece with aplomb under Black's direction. Recorded in 1991, the album is dedicated to Black, who died two years after this collection which also includes ear-tempting works by Peter Maxwell Davies (*Ave Maris Stella*) and Jacob Druckman (*Come Round*).

Vocal
Various choral works
what to buy: [Martin Amlin, piano; Frank Corliss, piano; John Oliver, cond.; John Oliver Chorale] (Koch International Classics 7415) ♪ ♪ ♪ ♪₅

Oliver leads his choir through eleven works, including *To Music,* a gorgeous, melodious work from 1937 for unaccompanied mixed chorus based on a poem by Robert Herrick. The centerpiece of this collection, however, is Carter's mature, elegant 1947 score to *Emblems* for men's chorus and piano. Constructed around an Allen Tate poem, it features beautifully blended all-male a cappella voices in the first and last sections, with spirited accompaniment from both pianists in the middle. Oliver could have done a better job of synchronizing voices in the spoken portions of *The Defense of Corinth* (based on text by Rabelais), but vocal music fans will still find this a compelling listen.

influences: Edgard Varèse, Igor Stravinsky, Roger Sessions, Charles Ives, Aaron Copland, Joel Chadabe, Alvin Curran

Nancy Ann Lee and Garaud MacTaggart

Mario Castelnuovo-Tedesco

Born April 3, 1895, in Florence, Italy. Died March 17, 1968, in Beverly Hills, California.

period: Twentieth century

Castelnuovo-Tedesco's introduction to guitar virtuoso Andrés Segovia in 1932 provided the impetus for his best-known works, including the Concerto no. 1 in D Major, op. 99 for Guitar and Orchestra. Along with concertos by Joaquin Rodrigo, Heitor Villa-Lobos, and Federico Torroba, it is among the most popular twentieth-century works written for the instrument.

Although his father was a prosperous banker in Florence, Castelnuovo-Tedesco's family roots can be traced back to Spain's Jewish community four centuries earlier. Mario's mother gave him his first piano lessons despite his father's disapproval. When the young boy demonstrated a remarkable command of the keyboard and showcased some of his budding skills as a composer, the father relented, and the son was soon enrolled at the Cherubini Royal Conservatory of Music. Studies at the Liceo Musicale of Bologna led to a degree in composition and further instruction in that discipline from Ildebrando Pizzetti.

Castelnuovo-Tedesco's introduction to Andrés Segovia at an international music festival in Venice was the singular event that would ultimately lead to the composer's greatest successes. It was there that the great guitarist asked him to compose a work for the guitar. Inspired by Segovia's skill, Castelnuovo-Tedesco wrote over three hundred pieces featuring the guitar during the next thirty-five years, including his most performed work, the Concerto no. 1 in D Major for Guitar and Orchestra, op. 99, written in 1939. By that time Italy's fascist dictator, Benito Mussolini, had forged an alliance with Germany's Adolph Hitler, putting Italian Jews in a precarious position. Shortly afterward, the young composer, his wife, and their children left Italy for the United States.

By the time Castelnuovo-Tedesco departed his homeland he was already considered an accomplished composer of songs (especially those with a Shakespearean connection) and piano music (he was fifteen when his first published work, *Cielo di settembre,* came out), as well as a card-carrying member of the Italian avant-garde. In retrospect, the latter label seems far-fetched, given his gift for melody and the kind of work he was to do in the future. In addition to the popular, smaller-scale pieces he wrote, Castelnuovo-Tedesco had tried his hand at writing larger compositions, including operas and concertos. Critical reaction to many of those efforts was mixed, but the practice he got by writing such scores served him well later in life.

Critical slights notwithstanding, the composer managed to acquire such influential advocates as the conductor Arturo Toscanini and the violinist Jascha Heifetz, who helped ease his entry into the United States. Upon his arrival, Castelnuovo-Tedesco settled his family in Larchmont, New York, a suburb of New York City. From there he arranged tours of America as a pianist and guest conductor. A year later Castelnuovo-Tedesco moved to Beverly Hills, California, where he found employment composing film scores for Metro-Goldwyn-Mayer, including the music for such popular movies as *The Yearling* and *Gaslight.* Even though he was writing for one of the biggest studios in the world, Castelnuovo-Tedesco still composed music for the concert stage. It was during this time that he composed important works for the guitar such as *Platero y Yo* (Platero and I), a quintet for guitar and string quartet, and the *24 Caprichos de Goya* for solo guitar, in addition to a wide variety of concertos, chamber pieces, and vehicles for solo instruments.

Despite his lengthy efforts to create operas, songs, and symphonic works, Castelnuovo-Tedesco is best known today for the compositions he wrote for the guitar. Like David Popper, whose cello pieces guide beginners down the road to technical proficiency, and Carl Czerny, whose keyboard exercises form the backbone of many pianists' studies, Castelnuovo-Tedesco would appear to be blessed and damned by his association with a specific instrument. The big difference is that some of Castelnuovo-Tedesco's works are still played in concert by major instrumentalists and orchestras, while Popper's and Czerny's are mainly confined to academic recitals.

Orchestral
Concerto no. 1 in D Major for Guitar and Orchestra, op. 99
what to buy: [*The Great Guitar Concertos*; John Williams, guitar; Charles Grove, cond.; English Chamber Orchestra] (CBS 44791) ♪ ♪ ♪ ♪

Williams's recording with Grove and the ECO is a bit harsher than the one by Romero and Marriner (see below), but it has been a reliable recommendation for many years. It is part of a two-CD set of guitar concertos that includes works by Mauro Giuliani, Manuel Ponce, Heitor Villa-Lobos, and Antonio Vivaldi, in addition to a classic rendition of Joaquin Rodrigo's *Concierto de Aranjuez.*

worth searching for: [Pepe Romero, guitar; Sir Neville Marriner, cond.; Academy of St. Martin-in-the-Fields, orch.] (Philips 416357) ♪ ♪ ♪ ♪♪

Romero is a stunning guitarist, and his performance on this piece may be as good as it gets. Especially felicitous is the subtle balance of guitar and orchestra heard in the slow second movement. The CD also includes fine recordings of the Villa-Lobos Concerto for Guitar and Rodrigo's two-movement *Sones en la Giralda.*

Chamber
Quintet for Guitar and Strings, op. 143
what to buy: [Stephan Schmidt, guitar; Quatuor Parish] (Auvidis/Valois 4789) ♪ ♪ ♪ ♪

Schmidt's well-played digital recording features all of the composer's works for guitar in small-group settings, including the quintet, two works for flute and guitar, and the genteel *Fantasia for Guitar and Piano,* op. 145.

what to buy next: [Andrés Segovia, guitar; members of the Quintetto Chigiano] (MCA Classics 10056) ♪ ♪ ♪♪

This monaural recording dates from 1955, but it has an undeniable authenticity to it, since Castelnuovo-Tedesco wrote the piece for Segovia. The CD also contains a stereo version of ten instrumental excerpts from *Platero y Yo,* one of the composer's major works for solo guitar and voice.

24 Caprichos de Goya for Guitar, op. 195
what to buy: [Lily Afshar, guitar] (Summit 167) ♪ ♪ ♪ ♪

These programmatic miniatures are well-composed workouts for guitar meant to illustrate a series of paintings by Francisco Goya. Afshar is a fine technician, and this recording provides a very good rendition of the complete suite.

influences: Joaquin Rodrigo, Mauro Giuliani, Agustin Barrios

Garaud MacTaggart

Canadian Brass:
The original Canadian Brass rose from its position in 1970 as the brass section for the Hamilton (Ontario) Philharmonic Orchestra to become one of the most consistently popular attractions at classical music concerts throughout the world. The earliest version of the group (trumpeters Stuart Laughton and Bill Philips, French horn player Graeme Page, trombonist Eugene Watts, and tuba player Charles Daellenbach) began their association by working with school children, playing for them, and exposing the youngsters in the Hamilton and Toronto areas to classical music. Funding from the Hamilton Philharmonic Orchestra had allowed the musicians to fulfill their outreach goals of playing in schools and putting on free or inexpensive public concerts, activities which also enabled the players to hone their lively stage presence.

The classic edition of the Canadian Brass, the one which first attracted the attention of international audiences, was the one in existence from 1972 through 1983, when Frederick Mills and Ronald Romm were filling the trumpet spots formerly occupied by Laughton and Philips. Their first recorded performances were captured by the Canadian Broadcasting Corporation and many of their programs from the 1970s are available on *CBC Radio Years* (CBC 2016), a disc which features cuts from albums that the Brass released through the CBC in addition to a selection of recordings originally meant strictly for radio broadcast. The album also provides a sampling of jazz tunes to go along with the expected classical works, documenting a non-elitist approach that became a concert hallmark of the group.

While they have recorded a number of works specifically written for brass instruments, including a delightful disc of music by Claudio Monteverdi and Giovanni Gabrielli (Sony Classics 44931), the Canadian Brass repertoire has been heavily weighted toward arrangements of scores composed for other combinations of instruments. They have recorded versions of Johann Sebastian Bach's *Art of the Fugue* (Sony Classics 89731) and *Goldberg Variations* (RCA Victor Red Seal 63610), but the group has also skirted the line between classical and popular music by covering George Gershwin's works (*Strike up the Band,* RCA Victor Red Seal 6490) and selections from Leonard Bernstein's oeuvre (*The Canadian Brass Play Bernstein,* RCA Victor Red Seal 68633), not to mention releasing albums centered around tunes by the Beatles (*All You Need Is Love,* RCA Victor Red Seal 68970), Fats Waller (*Ain't Misbehavin',* RCA Victor Red Seal 60979), and Duke Ellington (*Take the "A" Train,* RCA Victor Red Seal 63455).

As this book goes to press, Watts and Daellenbach are the sole remaining original members, working alongside trumpeters Ryan Anthony and Josef Burgstaller and horn player Jeff Nelsen, all of whom became part of the group in either 2000 or 2001.

William Gerard

Emmanuel Chabrier
Born Alexis-Emmanuel Chabrier on January 18, 1841, in Ambert, Puy-de-Dôme, France. Died September 13, 1894, in Paris, France.

period: Romantic

To the casual music lover, Chabrier is often considered a

one-trick pony, remembered for *España*, a colorful and evocative rhapsody that chronicled a trip to Spain. On closer examination, he had great influence on subsequent French composers and wrote much engaging music.

Although Emmanuel Chabrier demonstrated a marked proclivity for music, his parents were not very excited about the prospect of having their son pursue a career as a musician and composer. Dutifully, young Emmanuel complied with parental pressure and studied law in Paris. In parallel with his legal training, however, Chabrier also studied piano, harmony, and composition. Still, from the age of twenty he was employed as a regular civil servant at the Ministry of the Interior in Paris.

During his period as a government functionary, Chabrier composed a substantial number of works in a variety of genres and was caught up in the debate in France as to the merits of Richard Wagner's music. He greatly admired the work of this German master of music drama at a time when to do so was considered almost unpatriotic, as Wagner's works were viewed in some Parisian circles as the antithesis of French music. Chabrier even made a pilgrimage of sorts to Munich in 1880 with fellow composer Henri Duparc to attend performances of Wagner's music. It was while on this trip that Chabrier, at a concert featuring *Tristan und Isolde,* made the decision to pursue a full-time musical career. He finally quit his job later that year and lived off the income from his family's properties in addition to earnings from occasional positions as a vocal coach and choirmaster.

Chabrier's most famous composition, *España*, was conceived as the result of a trip to Spain with his wife in 1882, when he became infatuated with the flamenco rhythms he heard there. The orchestration of this little fantasia was unveiled a year later and was an almost instantaneous hit, generating numerous arrangements for a wide variety of instrumental forces. Prior to his success with *España*, he was considered more of a gifted amateur—a dilettante—than a serious composer, but with his credentials established, Chabrier completed two operas redolent of Wagnerian themes— *Gwendoline* and *Le roi malgré lui.* In addition he created a number of songs, plus orchestral arrangements of *Habanera* and four of the *10 pièces pittoresques* (as the *Suite Pastorale*).

Chabrier was one of the most colorful performers of his generation and good friends with the painter August Renoir and his wife Alice. A talented pianist in her own right, Alice Renoir once wrote that when Chabrier played the piano, especially a reduction of his famous *España*, it was as if a hurricane had been turned loose at the keyboard. She vowed, after hearing him play, that she would never touch the piano again, reporting that he broke several strings, inflicting severe damage to the piano action! Chabrier was also known for his ability to improvise for his friends at the piano bar when out for an evening in Paris. Upon hearing a tabloid's account of a crime, he was capable of orchestrating the action on the spot, improvising the entire scene at the piano in much the same way that a theater organist would provide a running musical commentary to a silent film—complete with an enactment of the incident, a chase scene, and finally, the capture.

For some musicologists Chabrier is seen as an important bridge between the French baroque style of François Couperin and the sultry impressionism of Claude Debussy. Others feel he was a great inspiration for Maurice Ravel, and still others point to his impact on Francis Poulenc, who wrote one of the first biographies of Chabrier. It is fair to say that his music is colorful, dynamic, and evocative, remaining essentially tuneful even when incorporating some of the chromaticism associated with Richard Wagner.

Orchestral
España for Orchestra
what to buy: [Paul Paray, cond; Detroit Symphony Orchestra] (Mercury Living Presence 434303) ♪ ♪ ♪ ♪♪

No one showcased the music of Chabrier better than Paray did when he was the conductor of the Detroit Symphony in the 1950s and '60s. This album presents a feast of Chabrier, including the *Gwendoline* overture, the *Suite Pastorale*, and three other short works by the composer. As an added bonus, there is also the Suite in F Major by Albert Roussel.

what to buy next: [John Eliot Gardiner, cond; Vienna Philharmonic Orchestra] (Deutsche Grammophon 447751) ♪ ♪ ♪ ♪

How can it be? A conductor who has specialized in early music is coupled with an Austrian orchestra in a live concert of music by a French composer and turns in a better performance than the home teams. Call the French Ministry of Culture! Gardiner has it all together, throwing in the composer's *Joyeuse Marche,* the

Larghetto for Horn and Orchestra, and five other brief works in an all-Chabrier program.

Chamber
Pièces pittoresques for Piano
worth searching for: [*Oeuvres pour Piano*; Jean-Jöel Barbier, piano] (Accord 20032) ♪ ♪ ♪ ♪

Good sound from a recording that was originally analog and has been transferred to compact disc. Four of these ten pieces (nos. 4, 6, 7, and 10) were later orchestrated by Chabrier in the *Suite Pastorale,* but the piano version, wonderfully played by Barbier, still displays a wide range of instrumental colors. Also found here are the original piano versions of the *Habanera* and the *Bourée Fantasque.*

influences: Henri Duparc, Vincent d'Indy, César Franck

Dave Wagner

George W. Chadwick
Born George Whitefield Chadwick, November 13, 1854, in Lowell, MA. Died April 4, 1931, in Boston, MA.

period: Romantic/Twentieth century

Considered to be a member of the "Boston Classicists," Chadwick was one of a group of American composers who studied in Europe and returned to the United States to pursue a career as an educator, performer, and composer. In reality, Chadwick's music was very much romantic in character, borrowing Wagnerian harmonies and such romantic forms as the concert overture and the symphonic poem, often crafted around American ideas and themes. The symphonic poem *Rip Van Winkle* and the *Symphonic Sketches* have become Chadwick's two most popular works.

George Whitefield Chadwick had a long and illustrious career that spanned more than fifty years and had a profound effect on the musical life of America. Thanks to early musical instruction from his brother, an organist, Chadwick was able to find work as a church musician. His earnings from the church and from a job clerking at his father's insurance agency enabled him to study in Boston with Eugene Thayer and Dudley Buck. On the strength of this musical training and his high school diploma, Chadwick took his first professional appointment as a music teacher at Olivet College in Michigan in 1876. While at the school, he founded the Music Teachers National Association.

In 1877, longing for more training and the prestige of a European education, he journeyed to Leipzig for classes at the conservatory there; he studied further in Munich with the renowned composer and organist Josef Rheinberger. After returning to the United States in 1880, Chadwick held a variety of positions, most notably as the organist of Boston's South Congregational Church and as a professor at the New England Conservatory of Music. By the turn of the twentieth century, he had become the director of the Conservatory, and his fame had spread because of his many works and because of the quality of students who had studied under him. He was recognized during his own lifetime for his music and teaching abilities, receiving honorary degrees from both Yale University and Tufts University.

In 1912 he composed a *verismo* opera for the Metropolitan Opera in New York titled *The Padrone,* which told the story of a group of Italian immigrants who were harassed and manipulated by a Mafia-type gangster. But the management at the Met found the subject matter too crude for its patrons, and the work was rejected. Chadwick never heard a performance of his opera while he was alive, as it was not premiered until 1995.

He did, however, live long enough to see his music go out of style. Highly romantic, chromatic, and firmly tonal, his music sounded decidedly old-fashioned, even quaint, when compared to the dynamic rhythms of Stravinsky's *Rite of Spring* and the atonal palette of Arnold Schoenberg's *Five Pieces for Orchestra.* Chadwick's music was seldom performed in the final decades of his life, although in recent years a reassessment of his contributions has been under way.

Orchestral
Symphonic Sketches in A Major for Orchestra
what to buy: [Howard Hanson, cond.; Eastman-Rochester Orchestra] (Mercury Living Presence 434337) ♪ ♪ ♪ ♪

Although it dates from 1956, this is still, hands down, the best recording of these tone poems. The original recording was made on 35-mm film, and the sonics are ready for the compact-disc age. Also included in this package are Edward MacDowell's Suite for Orchestra and Johann Friedrich Peter's Sinfonia in G Major for Orchestra.

what to buy next: [Neeme Järvi, cond; Detroit Symphony Orchestra] (Chandos 9334) ♪♪♪

Serious Chadwick fans may opt for the Jarvi recording instead of the Hanson, since this package is all Chadwick. This disc, volume seven in Chandos's American Music Series, also features the composer's Symphony no. 2 in E-flat Major, op. 21.

Rip Van Winkle for Orchestra

what to buy: Neeme Järvi, cond.; Detroit Symphony Orchestra] (Chandos 9439) ♪♪♪♪

From volume nine of Chandos's American Music Series comes this superb recording of the work that brought Chadwick his first critical acclaim in Europe and United States. Also included are a pair of his tone poems—*Tam O'Shanter* and *Melpomene*—along with Randall Thompson's Symphony no. 2. This disc is a must-have for Chadwick lovers.

influences: Dudley Buck, Horatio Parker, Arthur Foote

Dave Wagner

Marc-Antoine Charpentier

Born 1643, in or near Paris, France. Died February 24, 1704, in Paris, France.

period: Baroque

Inspired by his studies in Italy, Charpentier introduced subtle vocal shadings and dissonances into the somber world of French mass settings. Sacred music forms the bulk of his more than 500 compositions, but he is also known for providing theater music for Molière's plays and producing his most famous dramatic work, the opera *Médée*.

The details of Marc-Antoine Charpentier's early life are not well documented but it is thought that he studied music in Italy with Giacomo Carissimi during the late 1660s. When Charpentier returned to France around 1670 he introduced some of the lighter Italian-style mass settings and sacred music to those on the fringes of court circles. His own Italianate compositions may have found acceptance among these listeners as well. Soon after Charpentier's return from Italy, he was appointed music master and singer for Marie de Lorraine, Duchess of Guise. While in her employ he com-

posed at least six secular dramatic works in addition to a number of sacred works, including motets and mass settings.

Charpentier also began working with Molière's theater troupe (later to become the Comédie-Française) in 1672, writing incidental music for plays after the playwright's former partner, Jean-Baptiste Lully, abandoned the affiliation in favor of his recently won royal monopoly over music for the stage. Lully had even gone so far as to create a document (signed by Louis XIV) that expressly forbode the production of "any play set entirely to music, whether sung in French or other languages, without written permission from the aforementioned Sieur de Lully, at the risk of a fine of 10,000 livres and the confiscation of theaters, stagecraft, scenery, costumes, and other things." Given this situation, it is easy to see why Molière became upset with his former friend and sought a new partner to write music replacing the works that Lully had composed for the company. The new duo worked together for only about a year when Molière died during the initial production of their new comédie-ballet, *Le Malade imaginaire*. Charpentier, however, continued providing the company with new music through (at least) 1685.

In the early 1680s Charpentier composed several sacred and secular works for the dauphin. With his abilities and an abiding interest in liturgical music it was no surprise when he attained the high-profile post of music master at the main Jesuit church in Paris, St. Louis. There he wrote music for religious occasions celebrated at the church while also creating dramatic works for several of the Jesuit colleges in the area. In 1685, Charpentier had taken part in a contest to become music director and composer for the chapel royal but had to bow out due to ill health, before any determination could be made. The king still gave him a pension, possibly because of Charpentier's services to the dauphin's chapel.

With the death of Lully in 1687, the decks were clear for other composers to have their operas staged without fear of fiscal penalties being levied against them. Charpentier's response was the creation of two sacred dramas (operas) for the Jesuits: *Celse Martyr* in 1687 and *David et Jonathas* the following year. His operatic masterpiece, *Médée*, was staged at the Paris Opera in 1693 and received a lukewarm reception. Although Charpentier had absorbed and presented Italianate elements to good effect in his work for the Comédie-Française and in his sacred compositions, many in the

French audience didn't embrace those same elements in *Médée*.

Toward the end of his life, Charpentier composed what is widely considered to be his sacred masterpiece, the *Assumpta est Maria,* a mass celebrating the feast of the Assumption. By combining the elements of stately French religious tradition with more ornamental, Italianate figures, the composer created harmony out of diversity. In that sense he was fulfilling what he felt to be the very essence of musical composition: creating a stable yet challenging structure from disparate elements.

Vocal
Assumpta est Maria: Missa 6 vocibus cum symphonia
what to buy: [William Christie, cond.; Les Arts Florissants, vocal and instrumental ensemble] (Harmonia Mundi 901298) ♪ ♪ ♪ ♪

William Christie is, among other things, a Charpentier specialist and on this recording he allows his musicians to paint the contrasts and colors, the tension between word and melody, which so fascinated the composer. This version of the liturgy, one of two, is heard in its first complete recording. Also on the disc are *Litanies de la Vierge,* probably composed during his employ by the Duchess of Guise, and a well known piece from his association with the dauphin, the second of Charpentier's four Te Deum settings.

Médée
what to buy: [Isabelle Desrochers, soprano; Lorraine Hunt, soprano; No'mi Rime, soprano; Monique Zanetti, soprano; Mark Padmore, tenor; François Bazola, baritone; Jean-Marc Salzmann, baritone; Bernard Déletré, bass; William Christie, cond.; Les Arts Florissants, orch.] (Erato 96558) ♪ ♪ ♪ ♪

The dark and light colors of Charpentier's music are vividly shown in this recording of his only lyric opera. This was the second time Christie recorded the drama and his approach was enriched by ten years worth of experience in staging the piece. Lorraine Hunt's interpretation of Medea's complex emotions and the string section's handling of episodes ranging from delicate reflection to violent agitation, fulfill the composer's intent.

Enrico Caruso:
In terms of popularity and performance, Enrico Caruso set the standard for twentieth century tenors. Whether a particular singer rose or fell below that reference point was a matter of personal and/or critical opinion, but Caruso's singing served as a handy guide by which other male vocalists would be judged, rightly or wrongly, for much of the modern era.

Born in Naples, Italy on February 25, 1873, this future paragon of singing never began serious formal studies in his art until 1891, despite having developed into a locally prominent boy soprano/alto prior to his voice breaking. His professional debut as a tenor occurred four years later, but Caruso's reputation as a masterful singer really accelerated when he took part in a short string of prominent (at the time) world premieres, handling the primo tenor roles in Francesco Cilea's *L'arlesiana (1897)* and Umberto Giordano's *Fedora* (1898). His New York City debut on November 23, 1903 (as the Duke of Mantua in Giuseppe Verdi's *Rigoletto*) was a huge success and, along with well-received performances throughout Europe and South America, helped make him one of the most marketable singers of his generation. As such, Caruso was able to command phenomenal fees for his appearances compared to those of his contemporaries; toward the end of his surprisingly short life (he died on August 2, 1921, after suffering from a lung infection) Caruso was even reputed to have been paid $100,000 each for appearing in a pair of 1918 *silent* movies: *My Cousin* and *A Splendid Romance.*

His recording career actually began in 1902 when Caruso cut a series of discs for the Gramophone and Typewriter Company and Zonophone, but his peak earning potential really started after signing a contract with the Victor Talking Machine Company two years later. Performances of arias from the roles with which he was most closely associated, including that of Canio in Pietro Mascagni's *I pagliacci* and Rodolfo in Giacomo Puccini's *La Bohème,* were recorded multiple times and have rarely been out of print. Caruso's phenomenal tone production is still a marvel to hear, despite the vagaries of the recording process during the first quarter of the twentieth century.

Caruso: The Greatest Tenor in the World (RCA Victor Red Seal 63469) is a mid-priced, relatively easy-to-find two-disc package that features the vocalist in a variety of settings, mostly with an anonymous orchestra and sometimes with other singers. The award-winning engineer Ward Marston has restored and produced a number of well-received historical recordings, and his ongoing Caruso project for Naxos is an immaculately mastered series of budget-priced single discs. *Caruso: Complete Recordings, Vol. 1* (Naxos 8.110703) contains the early Zonophone performances he recorded in Milan amongst its twenty-seven cuts. Volume three in that series (Naxos 8.110708) covers the years 1906 to 1908 and incorporates a number of duets with outstanding divas from the era including renditions of *O soave fanciulla* with Nellie Melba and *O quanti occhi fisi* with Geraldine Farrar.

William Gerard

influences: Jean-Baptiste Lully, Giacomo Carissimi, Ignacio de Jerusalem

Kerry Dexter and Ian Palmer

Ernest Chausson

Born Amédée-Ernest Chausson on January 20, 1855, in Paris, France. Died June 10, 1899, in Limay, France.

period: Romantic

Ernest Chausson's short life and music were shaped by wealth and ease. Born into a Parisian family of means, he initially came under the spell of Richard Wagner's romanticism while a student of César Franck but later turned to a more traditional French style rooted in the music of François Couperin and Jean-Philippe Rameau. Best known for his songs and chamber music, Chausson moved toward Claude Debussy's impressionism in one of his most popular works, the song cycle *Poème de l'amour et de la mer.* His scores are generally elegiac, as in the symphonic poem *Viviane,* and passionate, as in his most popular piece, the *Poème* for Violin and Orchestra.

A unique childhood brought Chausson into the artistic salons of Paris, where he matured in the presence of the leading writers and musicians of the day. He developed the germ of his own art in this atmosphere, befriending the young Vincent d'Indy and becoming acquainted with many important musical compositions. In later life, his own home in Paris served as an artistic salon, where important figures such as Stéphane Mallarmé, Édouard Lalo, and Debussy were to meet.

Originally educated as a lawyer and admitted to the bar, Chausson never practiced law but instead entered the Paris Conservatory in 1879 to study music. Initially a composition student of Jules Massenet, he found Franck's music more to his taste and became a student of that proponent of cyclical form. As was common in the romantic atmosphere of the late nineteenth century, he also fell under the sway of Richard Wagner's music. After encountering Wagner's work in Munich in 1879, Chausson traveled to Bayreuth on a number of occasions to witness Wagner's operas, including a trip with d'Indy for the premiere of *Parsifal* in 1882. Wagner's influence on Chausson's composition is evident in his opera *Le Roi Arthus* (which shares a bond with Wagner's *Tristan und Isolde*) and in the orchestral arrangement of his song cycle *Poème de l'amour et de la mer.*

In 1886 Chausson began a ten-year tenure as secretary of the Société Nationale de Musique (SNM). Formed in 1871 by Franck, Camille Saint-Saëns, and other French composers, this nationalist movement was dedicated to the preservation and development of French music, notably through the composition of symphonies and chamber music. (Its conservative nature was later opposed by Gabriel Fauré and Maurice Ravel, who founded the Société Indépendente de Musique in 1911 with the aim of supporting modern music.) Chausson's association with the SNM influenced the form of many of his compositions—including his Symphony in B-flat Major (1889–1890) and his *Concert* in D Major for Violin, Piano, and String Quartet (1889–1891)—and brought him into the inner circle of Paris's artistic elite.

In 1888 Chausson rebelled against the influence of Wagnerian romanticism, which he described as the "red specter" that would not let him go. To de-Wagnerize his music, he sought out more traditional influences, notably the eighteenth-century French masters Couperin and Rameau, a development evidenced by his *Concert,* the very title of which denotes an eighteenth-century form. His friendship with Debussy also turned Chausson's attention to the tonal colors utilized by that younger composer and broadened his musical horizons. While Chausson's compositions abound with literary influences (the *Poème* for Violin and Orchestra, for example, was based on a short story by the Russian novelist Turgenev), most of his chamber works revolve around more abstract tendencies, as in the *Concert* and his earlier Trio for Piano, Violin, and Cello. By 1899, Chausson had matured as a composer and gained recognition. His career was cut short, however, when he died as a consequence of a fractured skull suffered in a bicycle accident.

Orchestral

Poème for Violin and Orchestra, op. 25

what to buy: [*Bernstein: The Royal Edition*; Zino Francescatti, violin; Leonard Bernstein, cond.; New York Philharmonic Orchestra] (Sony Classical 47548) ♪♪♪♪

Francescatti and Bernstein supremely capture the angst laden in this work. The violinist plays with restrained tension and passion, delicately crafting the fine details of the musical line; his trills and double stops are to die for. The piece is part of a wonderful collection of French works, including Franck's Symphony in D Minor, Fauré's *Ballade* for piano and orchestra (with pianist Robert Casadesus), and Ravel's *Tzigane* for violin and orchestra.

what to buy next: [*Great Violin Concertos*; Zino

Francescatti, violin; Eugene Ormandy, cond.; Philadelphia Orchestra] (Sony Classical 62339) ♪ ♪ ♪ ♪

This earlier monaural performance finds Francescatti more muscular in his approach, and while he plays with passion and attention to detail (as on his recording with Bernstein), the emotion of this performance does not rise to the level captured a few years later in the stereo recording. This re-mastered performance, brighter-sounding than the later Bernstein version. is part of a fabulous two-disc monaural set of violin concertos that was recorded (mainly) with Dmitri Mitropolous conducting the New York Philharmonic Orchestra.

Chamber
Concert in D Major for Violin, Piano, and String Quartet, op. 21
what to buy: [Itzhak Perlman, violin; Jorge Bolet, piano; Juilliard String Quartet, ensemble] (Sony Classics 37814) ♪ ♪ ♪ ♪

Perlman and company deliver a well-proportioned, passionate account of the *Concert,* reflecting the work's traditional eighteenth-century influences. Their "Sicillienne" truly dances, the "Grave" has an appropriate serioso quality to it, and the "Tres Anime" is a lively affair. The musicians play with emotion and finely detailed precision, making this performance stand out.

Vocal
Poème de l'amour et de la mer for Voice and Orchestra, op. 19
what to buy: [*Recital: Jessye Norman Sings Chausson*; Jessye Norman, soprano; Armin Jordan, cond.; Monte-Carlo Philharmonic Orchestra] (Erato 14073) ♪ ♪ ♪ ♪

It is hard to beat Norman's lustrous soprano in this performance, drawn from a collection of Chausson's vocal works that also includes the *Chanson perpétuelle* and various selections from the *Mélodies,* op. 2.

worth searching for: [Janet Baker, mezzo-soprano; André Previn, cond.; London Symphony Orchestra] (EMI Classics 68667) ♪ ♪ ♪ ♪

Baker delivers a strong, full-bodied account of this song cycle, lovingly accompanied by Previn and the LSO. The influence of Wagner comes through, along with hints at Mahler's orchestral songs, but the colorfully delivered second orchestral interlude (in the midst of the song "La

Mort de l'amour") beautifully smacks of Debussy's tonal palette. This well-considered performance, part of an outstanding, budget-priced two-disc recital of French and German songs, is marvelously sung by Baker.

Chanson perpétuelle for Soprano and Orchestra, op. 37
what to buy: [*La Bonne Chanson: French Chamber Songs*; Anne Sophie von Otter, mezzo-soprano; Bengt Forsberg, piano; Nils-Erik Sparf, violin; Ulf Forsberg, violin; Matti Hirvikangas, viola; Mats Lindström, cello] (Deutsche Grammophon 447752) ♪ ♪ ♪ ♪ ♪

Chausson's last completed work is radiantly sung by von Otter, with fine musical accompaniment. Slowly paced, her performance delivers the feeling of despair contained in the lyrics about lost love. This disc, comprising a unique collection of melodies by various French composers, received the 1998 Grammy Award for Best Classical Vocal Performance and is destined to be a classic.

influences: César Franck, Richard Wagner, Claude Debussy

Gerald B. Goldberg

Carlos Chávez
Born Carlos Antonio de Padua Chávez y Ramírez, June 13, 1899, in Popotla, Mexico. Died August 2, 1978, in Mexico City, Mexico.

period: Twentieth century

Carlos Chávez was an influential Mexican composer and conductor whose most familiar composition—his Symphony no. 2 (subtitled *Sinfonía Índia*)—is also the most likely symphony by any Latin American musician to show up in a modern concert program. Although he strove for a simplicity similar to that found in Native American folk culture, several years in Europe and New York City brought him into contact with many composers with whom he formed ties and exchanged ideas. While he wrote for a variety of ensembles and was considered a masterly orchestrator, some of his most popular works stress the interplay between percussion and small groups.

Carlos Chávez had already studied piano (mostly with Pedro Luis Ogazón but also briefly with Manuel Ponce) and would soon be studying harmony (with Juan Bautista Fuentes) when he completed his first symphony at the age of sixteen. This and most of the works he wrote prior to 1921 were heavily indebted to European models. He started to transcend these influences when he was commissioned by the Mexican Secretariat of Public Education to write a ballet based on themes drawn from ancient Aztec cultures. The resulting work, *El Fuego Nuevo* (The New Fire), was written in 1921 but had to wait until 1928 for its first performance, which Chávez conducted with the Orquesta Sinfónica de México.

In between the writing and performance of *El Fuego Nuevo,* Chávez lived in Europe and New York (where he formed close ties with composers Aaron Copland, Henry Cowell, and Vincent Persichetti) while shuttling back and forth to Mexico. Chávez helped establish the first permanent symphony orchestra in Mexico in 1928 when he accepted the role of principal conductor for the Orquesta Sinfónica de México, a post he would occupy until 1948. Under his direction, the orchestra adopted a wide-ranging repertoire, including several new works by Mexican composers. Also in 1928, Chávez was appointed director of the National Conservatory, an institution that became a major center for music instruction in Mexico and helped train generations of Mexican composers. After 1948, when Chávez resigned his conducting post, he began spending a great deal of time concertizing in Europe and the United States. He was even named the Charles Eliot Norton Lecturer at Harvard from 1958 to 1959.

Chávez's mature works include six symphonies, three concertos, an opera, several ballets, a variety of choral and vocal works, and a lot of chamber and piano music. Much of Chávez's early music is quite vigorous, deriving its energy from the percussive rhythms employed by the composer. An example of this is his second symphony, the *Sinfonía índia,* a 1935 work that uses native instruments amid the standard orchestra. Several of his ballets, including *Los cuatro soles, Caballos de vapor* (otherwise known as *H.P.*), and *Xochipilli* also evoke the atmosphere of pre-Columbian myth, rarely quoting actual folk material. In fact, Chávez never set about collecting folk music for use in this manner (as did Ralph Vaughan Williams in England), nor did he claim a distinctly Mexican flavor for his work. The end result, though, is something more authentic in spirit, exhibiting real musical strength. In later pieces, such as his Toccata from 1942 and *Tambuco* from 1964, the design is more

abstract, but in his symphonies, passages with a prehistoric feel can show up when one least expects them—as in the Symphony no. 6, with its sustained Indian flute call.

Orchestral
Symphonies, nos. 1–6
what to buy: [*Chavez: The Complete Symphonies*; Eduardo Mata, cond.; London Symphony Orchestra] (Vox Box 5061) ♪ ♪ ♪ ♪

This collection, recorded in 1981, includes six of the composer's seven symphonies. Mata leads the London ensemble in spirited readings, and the entire package is available at an attractive price.

Symphony no. 2—*Sinfonía índia*
what to buy: [Carlos Chávez, cond., Stadium Symphony Orchestra of New York] (Everest 9041) ♪ ♪ ♪ ♪

The composer as conductor is heard on this recording of his first, second, and fourth symphonies. Sometimes the creator of the work is not the one to bring it to life in actual performance, but Chávez was an excellent conductor. The music on this disc is energetically played, but the ensemble's performance of the *Sinfonía índia* is especially noteworthy.

Chamber
various chamber works
what to buy: [*Chamber Works*; Rodrigo Alvarado, percussion; Israel Moreno, percussion; Eduardo Mata, cond.; Tambuco Percussion Ensemble] (Dorian 90215) ♪ ♪ ♪ ♪

Here we have smaller-scale works by Chávez, stunningly played by several artists. The *Toccata* for Six Percussionists (one of the composer's most frequently performed concert pieces) is joined by *Tambuco* for Six Percussionists, *Energia, La hija de Cólquie* for Woodwind Quartet and String Quartet, and the ballet *Xochipilli.* All of the works on this recording are fine pieces, and the performances are equally good.

influences: Henry Cowell, John Cage, Lou Harrison

Frank Retzel

Luigi Cherubini

Born Luigi Carlo Zanobi Salvadore Maria Cherubini, c. September, 14, 1760, in Florence, Italy. Died March 15, 1842, in Paris, France.

period: Classical

Primarily viewed as an opera composer and lauded for his sacred choral works (especially the Requiem in D Minor), Luigi Cherubini was also an important figure in French musical history as an administrator for the Institut National de Musique and its successor, the Conservatoire. Admired by both Franz Joseph Haydn and Ludwig van Beethoven, Cherubini pointed the way towards the romantic era with scores and texts that espoused new harmonies, influencing such disparate composers as Robert Schumann and Richard Wagner.

Cherubini's exact birth date is a matter of conjecture; when he was in his late forties, he wrote that he was born on September 8, and various scholars have since taken great pains to explain why Cherubini was wrong. Even the baptismal record, dated September 14, 1760, has been called into question. It is beyond doubt, however, that his father was a harpsichordist at the Teatro alla Pergola in Florence, that Luigi was the tenth child in a dozen, and that his mother died before Cherubini was five years old.

Bartolomeo Cherubini, his father, started teaching Luigi the rudiments of musicianship when he was six and the basics of composition when he was nine. This instruction, along with lessons from other musicians, prepared him for an apprenticeship with Joseph Sarti, who taught him the mysteries of counterpoint and the elements of dramatic music. So swift was Cherubini's progress that Sarti had his young student write secondary portions of works that were attributed to the master instead of the pupil. The commission for *Il Quinto Fabio*, Cherubini's first full-fledged opera, was secured for the budding composer by Sarti, and the completed work made its debut in 1779. This modest *opera seria* received favorable reactions from regional audiences and impresarios, but the success of his next three operas—*Armida abbandonata, Adriano in Siria*, and *Mesenzio re d'Etruria*—did even more to attract a stable clientele for his talents. In 1784 he went to London, where he composed popular operas and ingratiated himself with the inner circle of the Prince of Wales.

The following year, while vacationing in Paris, he met Marie Antoinette and, through her, the cream of the French intelligentsia. Cherubini moved to France for good in 1786, creating more operas as well as miscellaneous sacred and secular works. Three years later, he became the conductor and music director of the Théâtre de Monsieur, all the while churning out incidental music for plays. The *opéra comique Lodoïska* was his first really successful work geared towards French tastes and sensibilities.

Although the Revolution and its attendant nationalism reduced Cherubini's immediate chances for income, it did give him an opportunity to shape the next generation of French musicians. In 1793 he was offered an administrative position with the newly formed Institut National de Musique, where he was able to continue composing while teaching and programming music for select ceremonial occasions. The Institut mutated into the Conservatoire two years later, and Cherubini became one of the inspectors overseeing the direction of France's musical future. Introduced in 1797, *Médée* is the opera for which Cherubini is best known to modern audiences, although one of its more straightforwardly heroic follow-ups, *Les Deux Journées, ou Le Porteur d'eau,* proved to be the biggest hit of his career.

Médée—an operatic look at the murderous, vengeful violence of Euripides' ancient Greek play *Medea*—was critically acclaimed but sparsely attended, and the show quickly closed. Cherubini and his librettist, François Benôit Hoffman, had created an intense, dramatic work accompanied by orchestral writing more symphonic in nature than the relatively episodic style usually associated with the operatic form. It remained for the German-speaking world to lengthen the life span of this intriguing character-development piece with frequent performances extending from its Berlin debut in 1800 through the early 1870s. The popularity of the work in Germany and Austria was probably the reason why Cherubini was invited to Vienna in 1805, enabling him to meet both Franz Joseph Haydn and Ludwig van Beethoven and to attend the premiere of the latter's opera, *Fidelio*.

Having returned to France, in part because of Napoleon's occupation of Vienna in 1806, Cherubini worked on *Pimmalione*, the next in a string of operas that have since faded into obscurity. The scores (other than *Médée*) that are still performed with any degree of regularity are the Requiem in C Minor, written in 1815 to memorialize the execution of Louis XVI, the Symphony in D Major (also from 1815), and the Requiem in D Minor, composed in 1836 for Cherubini's own funeral. He also wrote an important text (*Cours de contrepoint et de fugue*) with Fromental Halévy that was published in 1835.

Orchestral
Symphony in D Major
what to buy: [*The Toscanini Collection, vol. 27*; Arturo Toscanini, cond.; NBC Symphony Orchestra] (RCA Gold Seal 60278) ♪ ♪ ♪ ♪

Toscanini was a great proponent of this work, and he imbues it with a power and grandeur that few of the other recordings can touch. His rendition of the vivacious scherzo movement is a sheer joy. The sonics just aren't as good as the performance, however, and that brings the rating down a tad. The selection of overtures by Cherubini and Domenico Cimarosa provides felicitous filler.

[Howard Griffiths, cond.; Zürich Chamber Orchestra] (CPO 999521) ♪ ♪ ♪ ♪

Griffith's forces are the beneficiaries of better, more modern engineering than are Toscanini's, and the performance holds up well in comparison to the maestro's, conveying maximum excitement with a vibrant string section and a tightly organized approach to the score. The two other works on the disc are also Cherubini's—the overture to his 1791 opera *Lodoïska* and the four-part sinfonia/overture to 1786's *Il Giulio Sabino*.

what to buy next: [Donato Renzetti, cond.; Orchestra della Toscana] (Arts Music 47102) ♪ ♪ ♪ ♪

Even though this piece is written for a moderately sized orchestra, Cherubini structured the composition for an even more immediate, more intimate sound. Renzetti makes the work sound like a quintet squared, but the engineering doesn't sound much better than on the Toscanini version, even though this recording dates from 1987. Three of the composer's operatic overtures (*Medée, Ifigenia in Aulide,* and *Le crescendo*) are included.

Vocal
Médée (Medea)
what to buy: [Maria Callas, soprano; Renata Scotto, soprano; Miriam Pirazzini, mezzo-soprano; Mirto Picchi, tenor; Giuseppe Modesti, bass; Alfredo Giacomotti, bass; Tulio Serafin, cond.; Orchestra del Teatro alla Scala, Milano; Coro del Teatro alla Scala, Milano] (EMI Classics 66435) ♪ ♪ ♪ ♪

Past her prime, Callas takes a while to warm up to the task, but when she finally lets loose, there is nobody who can even approximate the ferocious impact she makes in the title role. This is hardly a surprise, since Callas used *Médée* to affirm her greatness years before 1957, when this recording was made. Fans still rave about her live recordings, but the sound on those is never that great, especially compared with this studio session.

Requiem Mass no. 1 in C Minor
what to buy: [Riccardo Muti, cond.; Philharmonia Orchestra; Ambrosian Chorus] (EMI Classics 49678) ♪ ♪ ♪ ♪

This version of Cherubini's outstanding setting of the Requiem is lean and briskly paced, with a raw, emotional power that Muti and the orchestra convey better than almost any other ensemble that has recorded this work. His impressive take on Giuseppe Verdi's Requiem is included in this fine two-disc budget set.

what to buy next: [Christoph Spering, cond.; Das Neue Orchester, orch.; Chorus Musicus Köln] (Opus 111 30–116) ♪ ♪ ♪ ♪

Spering's rendition is well recorded, with fine singing and two relatively rare Cherubini works tossed in to good effect. The *Marche Funébre* is crisp and dynamic, while *In Paradisum* is a pleasant counterweight to the solemnity of the Requiem.

Requiem Mass no. 2 in D Minor for Male Chorus and Orchestra
what to buy: [Igor Markevitch, cond.; Czech Philharmonic Orchestra; Czech Philharmonic Chorus] (Supraphon 3429) ♪ ♪ ♪ ♪

This disc may well be your one-stop shopping center for Cherubini's most important works. In addition to a finely rendered performance of the composer's final Requiem, Supraphon also includes versions of the Symphony in D Major and the overture to *Médée*, both with Josef Veselka conducting the Prague Chamber Orchestra. Buyers should be aware that Markevitch's performance is also available from Deutsche Grammophon (457744), where it is paired with Mozart's *Coronation Mass*.

what to buy next: [*Neeme Järvi: The Early Recordings, vol. 5* Neeme Järvi, cond.; Estonian Radio Symphony Orchestra; Estonian State Academy Male Chorus]

(BMG/Melodia 40723) ♪ ♪ ♪⸴

In the choral sections of this work, Melodia's budget-priced disc contains plenty of the stereotypically dark, brooding quality associated with Eastern European sources, and the engineering isn't as strong as it should be. Still, this is a performance of considerable conviction. The same forces are also heard on Dmitri Shostakovich's Ballads, op. 136, *Faithfulness*.

worth searching for: [Ricardo Muti, cond.; New Philharmonia Orchestra; Ambrosian Singers] (EMI 49301) ♪ ♪ ♪ ♪⸴

For listeners seeking the ultimate performance of this glorious and powerful work, Muti's rendition with the New Philharmonia Orchestra should fill the bill. The only problem lies with finding a copy, as it remains out of print.

influences: Ludwig van Beethoven, Daniel Auber, François Boieldieu, Fromental Halévy

Garaud MacTaggart

Frédéric Chopin
Born Fryderyk Franciszek Chopin, c. March 1, 1810, in Zelazowa Wola, Poland. Died October 17, 1849, in Paris, France.

period: Romantic

Chopin's oeuvre reflects three stages of his life: concert pianist, teacher, and salon player. In the years spent as a concert pianist, he composed his two concertos, along with his brilliant rondos and other shorter pieces for piano and orchestra. During his years as a teacher he revolutionized piano playing with his treatment of rhythm, writing études, waltzes, nocturnes, preludes, and mazurkas that were used for teaching purposes and often dedicated to specific students. Chopin's later pieces were composed for his own pleasure and these works contain some of his most inventive writing, including the Piano Sonata in B Minor, op. 58.

Despite having had piano lessons as a child, Chopin's mastery of the keyboard was essentially a self-taught one. There is also little doubt that early exposure to works by Wolfgang Amadeus Mozart and Johann Nepomuk Hummel helped him grasp some of the basics

Pablo Casals:
Pablo Casals was born in 1876 in the small town of Vendrell in Catalonia, not far from Barcelona in Spain. He had learned to play the piano, violin, and flute at an early age and sung in the church choir which his father, an organist, also directed. When young Pau (the Catalan form of Pablo) was ten years old, he requested and was given a cello. He was then enrolled at the Barcelona Municipal Music School, where he took lessons from José Garcia for three years. It was around this time that Casals discovered the Suites for Solo Cello by Johann Sebastian Bach, works which were to inspire him for the rest of his life and with which he would later make his reputation as one of the finest cellists of the twentieth century.

In 1897 Casals embarked upon the somewhat tenuous life of a cello soloist. He performed in London and Paris in 1899, and toured the United States between 1901 and 1902, becoming known for his persuasive advocacy of Bach's Suites for Solo Cello. Casals then joined with pianist Alfred Cortot and violinist Jacques Thibaud in 1905 to form one of the most impressive trios of the twentieth century.

After World War I, the cellist settled back in Barcelona and founded an orchestra, funding it out of his own earnings and conducting the musicians in addition to occasionally performing with them as a soloist. With the advent of the Spanish Civil War in 1936 Casals became increasingly distressed with the political forces driving his country toward Fascism. Casals retired in 1946, disgusted with events in Europe, and settled in Prades, France.

During this time of personal and political upheaval, the cellist went into the studio to record some of his greatest performances. First among these were his interpretations of the six Bach cello suites (Naxos 8.110915/16) and, with Cortot and Thibaud, a rendition of Ludwig van Beethoven's *Archduke* Piano Trio (EMI Classics 67001). Although Casals would later record the *Archduke* with pianist Eugene Istomin and violinist Alexander Schneider (Sony Classics 58990), the immediacy of the EMI performance outweighs the improved sonics of the subsequent version. The fabled 1939 recording of Antonín Dvořák's Concerto in B Minor for Cello and Orchestra with George Szell conducting the Czech Philharmonic Orchestra has been reissued many times. One disc pairs the performance with the cellist's 1929 playing in the *Double Concerto* by Johannes Brahms with Thibaud as violinist and Cortot conducting (Naxos 8.110930). A competing edition of the Dvořák cello concerto (Dutton Laboratories 9709) is coupled with Szell leading the CPO in a rendition of that same composer's *New World Symphony* that also dates from 1939.

Casals came out of retirement in the 1950s, organizing a festival in Prades devoted to Bach's oeuvre and concentrating more on conducting orchestras than playing the cello. After a few years he moved to Puerto Rico, using it as a new base of operations. He continued conducting there and in other countries but he also focused on leading master classes for aspiring cellists, seeking to pass his knowledge on to future generations before finally dying in 1973.

Ellen Kokko

of composition, though his three years of conservatory training in the fundamentals of theory, harmony, and counterpoint gave him an even stronger foundation. By the time he was nineteen years old, Chopin had been composing short works on his own (including some of the early *Mazurkas* and *Polonaises*, as well as the Sonata in C Minor for Piano) for nearly a dozen years, stocking his repertoire for the future while contemplating the life of a touring virtuoso.

The first international stop in his artistic journey began in Vienna, where he managed to find a publisher for his *Variations on "Lá ci darem la mano"* from Mozart's *Don Giovanni* in 1829. The following year, Chopin performed both of his piano concertos (the one in E Minor, op. 11 and the one in F Minor, op. 21) plus a rondo for piano and orchestra (*Krakowiak*) in Warsaw at the Teatr Narodowy. The rhythms of Polish folk songs dancing through his scores and the flair of Chopin's dazzling performance made him somewhat of a national hero prior to his leaving for Vienna in November. He arrived there just before news of a Polish uprising reached him, inspiring him to write a number of works based on Polish themes, including the first of his *Mazurkas* (opp. 6 and 7) to be published under his name. When concert opportunities in Vienna were not as prevalent as they undoubtedly would have been prior to the Polish rebellion, Chopin went on to his next major destination, Paris, after stops in Linz, Salzburg, Munich, and Stuttgart.

He arrived in Paris in the fall of 1831, and it became his home for the rest of his life. He soon became part of the artistic society there, joining a circle of accomplished musicians and composers that included Franz Liszt, Hector Berlioz, Vincenzo Bellini, and Giacomo Meyerbeer. Quickly becoming the most sought-after piano teacher in Paris, Chopin (possessing great charm and priding himself on impeccable dress and manners) could demand high fees which would allow him to live in the upper-class style he relished. It was also around this time that Chopin wrote one of his finest early works—the Waltz in E-Flat Major, op. 18, (a.k.a. the *Grand Waltz*)—in addition to his op. 10 *Études*, five of his haunting *Nocturnes*, the first of the *Ballades* and *Scherzi*, and the *Andante spinato*, op. 22.

This was the twenty-six-year-old who met Amandine Aurore Lucie Dupin, Baroness Dudevant (a.k.a. George Sand), the feminist writer who found him irresistible. Two years later they became lovers and she persuaded him to visit Majorca in the winter, hoping that the weather would help restore Chopin's failing health. There he completed twenty-four of his *Preludes*, (op. 28)

and began both the *Scherzo* in C-sharp Minor (op. 30) and the *Polonaise* in C Minor (op. 40, no. 2). The liaison lasted ten years, and Sand is credited with providing Chopin a sense of peace and security, encouraging the final development of his genius. Together, they spent summers at her manor house from 1839 to 1846, during which period he finished his second piano sonata (with its celebrated *Marche funèbre*), most of his *Nocturnes*, the majority of his *Waltzes*, and two prime works of genius: his *Ballade* no. 4 in F Minor (op. 52) and the Sonata no. 3 in B Minor for Piano, op. 58.

The last stage of his career began with the couple's break-up in 1847. After this, Chopin's physical state worsened and eventually illness made him unable to write effectively. With the outbreak of political instability in Paris he accepted an invitation from his rich student, Jane Sterling, to visit England in April 1848. English high society adored him and he was besieged with invitations to play in the great houses of England, including one with Queen Victoria in attendance. His last concert was at the Guildhouse in London to benefit Polish refugees, and when he finally returned to Paris in November of 1848, Chopin was too ill to teach or compose. He died on October 17, 1849, succumbing to the tuberculosis he had been fighting for years.

Orchestral
Concerto no. 2 in F Minor for Piano and Orchestra, op. 21
what to buy: [Emanuel Ax, piano; Charles Mackerras, cond.; Orchestra of the Age of Enlightenment] (Sony Classics 63371) ♪♪♪♪

The superb piano (built in 1851 in the Erard London factory), Emanuel Ax, and the Orchestra of the Age of Enlightenment are a winning combination. The incredible range of dynamic levels and nuances produced is awesome. The *Fantasia on Polish Airs* in A Major for Piano and Orchestra, op. 13, and the *Andante spianato et Grand polonaise brillante* in E-flat Major, op. 22, are also heard in this set. Ideal for those seeking both of Chopin's piano concertos in well performed, well recorded versions that will stand the test of time.

Chamber
Ballades for Piano (complete)
what to buy: [Murray Perahia, piano] (Sony Classics 64399) ♪♪♪♪

Subtle playing has been a hallmark of Perahia's performances ever since he began making a name for himself as one of the finest pianists on the international circuit. It should come as no surprise that his performances of the *Ballades* are so superb. The same holds true for the balance of the recital, which includes a wonderful version of the *Grand valse brillante* and a few other Chopin pieces.

[*Ivan Moravec Plays Chopin, vol. 2*; Ivan Moravec, piano] (VAI Audio 1092) ♪ ♪ ♪ ♪♪

Moravec is one of the finest Chopin players in history, and created a number of memorable albums for the Connoisseur Society which have since been licensed to a variety of companies, one of which is VAI Audio. The remastering is superb and the performances are beguiling. A quintet of Chopin's *Mazurkas* fills out the balance of the recital.

what to buy next: [Vladimir Ashkenazy, piano] (Decca 466499) ♪ ♪ ♪ ♪

Recorded in the mid-1960s when Ashkenazy was a young lion, these performances of the four *Ballades* have been remastered and repackaged (along with the four *Scherzi* and the Prelude in C-sharp Minor, op. 45) at an attractive price.

[*The Rubinstein Collection, vol. 45: Chopin—Ballades, Scherzos*; Artur Rubinstein, piano] (RCA Victor Red Seal 63045) ♪ ♪ ♪ ♪

For a long time Rubinstein was the de facto first choice for a Chopin recital, because of his deft handling of the themes and his ability to get to the heart of the work even if his fingers occasionally strayed from their appointed notes. These virtues have been shown anew in this remastered classic set.

Études for Piano, opp. 10 and 25
what to buy: [Maurizio Pollini, piano] (Deutsche Grammophon 413794) ♪ ♪ ♪ ♪♪

Pollini's superb technical prowess is on display in these studies, but never at the expense of their surprising charms. It is also good to hear the progress Chopin made in the space between these two opus numbers.

[Vladimir Ashkenazy, piano] (Decca 414127) ♪ ♪ ♪ ♪♪

The differences between Ashkenazy and Pollini in this material are relatively trifling, since both have a good command of these gems; the engineering for both is of a similar quality, although Ashkenazy is afforded a slightly warmer acoustic.

Études for Piano, op. 10
what to buy: [Frederic Chiu, piano] (Harmonia Mundi 907201) ♪ ♪ ♪ ♪

Chiu, born in 1965, is a dynamo, and his playing on the dozen numbers from op. 10 is exciting, ferocious, and sensitive throughout. The set also includes his versions of the Rondos from opp. 1, 5, 16, and 73.

Mazurkas for piano (complete)
what to buy: [*The Chopin Collection: The Mazurkas*; Artur Rubinstein, piano] (RCA Red Seal 5614) ♪ ♪ ♪ ♪

While not as well-known as the various waltzes and preludes, Chopin's mazurkas have their own sense of mystery and rhythm, especially in the four pieces of op. 33. The composer William Bolcom once noted that, "The Chopin mazurkas are full of wonderful lessons in tonality." Rubinstein's performances are taut, and catch the dance rhythms at the heart of these deceptively simple works.

[Frederic Chiu, piano] (Harmonia Mundi 907247/48) ♪ ♪ ♪♪

Given that Chiu is an impressive advocate for Prokofiev's piano works, with exceptionally clean, technically assured performances and an analytical approach similar to that of a young Pollini, it is pleasing to note that his Chopin playing has many of the same virtues.

Nocturnes for piano (complete)
what to buy: [Ivan Moravec, piano] (Nonesuch 79233) ♪ ♪ ♪ ♪ ♪

John Field may have created the nocturnes as a genre but Chopin elevated them to the celestial realm. Moravec's performances here are nigh unto unbeatable; his subtle phrasing in the B-flat Minor nocturne (op. 9, no. 1) is only the opening virtue in a recital full of them. These recordings are at the pinnacle of Moravec's Connoisseur Society Chopin recital, and it is a pleasure to welcome them back into the catalog.

what to buy next: [*The Rubinstein Collection, vol. 49:*

Chopin—Nocturnes; Artur Rubinstein, piano] (RCA Victor Red Seal 63049) ♪ ♪ ♪ ♪₈

Rubinstein's *Nocturnes* are widely considered peak performances. While the remastering is quite good, the original source material wasn't as well recorded as the Moravec set (see above). There is a special magic at work in Rubinstein's playing, however.

Preludes for piano, op. 28 (complete)
what to buy: [Maruizio Pollini, piano] (Deutsche Grammophon 431221) ♪ ♪ ♪ ♪₈

Pollini's technique is so formidable that it is tempting to listen just for that, but his interpretive gifts are genuinely brilliant as well. There is a single disc with all this material on it (Deutsche Grammophon 413796), but this three-CD set also includes wonderful renditions of the composer's twenty-four *Études* and the first seven of his *Polonaises*.

[*Ivan Moravec Plays Chopin, vol. 1*; Ivan Moravec, piano] (VAI Audio 1039) ♪ ♪ ♪ ♪₈

These are the legendary Connoisseur Society recordings and cover the twenty-four *Preludes* from op. 28, the first *scherzo* (in B Minor, op. 20), the *Barcarolle* in F-sharp Major, op. 60, and the seventh *Étude* (C-sharp Minor, op. 60). Moravec is an amazing Chopin player, at times ranking with Artur Rubinstein, Sviatoslav Richter, and the legendary Arturo Benedetti Michelangeli, albeit with subtle concepts and mannerisms all his own. His clean, crisp playing dances across the keyboard in strong, sensitive performances well worthy of a hearing.

what to buy next: [Martha Argerich, piano] (Deutsche Grammophon 431584) ♪ ♪ ♪ ♪

Argerich's playing is dynamic, and though her interpretations are a bit idiosyncratic, the sonics and her overall commitment are impressive. She also gets points for including all twenty-six *Preludes*—not just the twenty-four from op. 28—along with the op. 59 *Mazurkas* and the *Scherzo* no. 3 in C-sharp Minor.

Waltzes for piano (complete)
what to buy: [*The Chopin Collection: The Waltzes*; Artur Rubinstein, piano] (RCA Red Seal 5492) ♪ ♪ ♪ ♪₈

These are classic performances of keyboard poetry that helped enhance Rubinstein's reputation with the gener-

al public during the 1960s. Only fourteen of the now standardized nineteen Chopin waltzes show up here, but the playing deserves serious consideration.

what to buy next: [Vladimir Ashkenazy, piano] (London 414600) ♪ ♪ ♪ ♪

Rachmaninoff would seem the easier fit for Ashkenazy's particular predilections, but his Chopin playing is surprisingly subtle at times. The caveat for this set, as in the Rubinstein collection above, is that only the first fourteen waltzes (well-played though they may be) are included in it.

Sonata no. 2 in B-flat Minor for Piano, op. 35
what to buy: [*Complete Works of Frédéric Chopin, vol. 1: Sonatas*; Garrick Ohlsson, piano] (Arabesque 6628) ♪ ♪ ♪ ♪₈

When trekking through Chopin's three piano sonatas it is good to have Ohlsson along as a musical guide. While Ohlsson has considerable technical skills and his playing is consistently informative, it is the drama of the music you notice first—just as it should be.

what to buy next: [Maurizio Pollini, piano] (Deutsche Grammophon 415346) ♪ ♪ ♪ ♪

The noted *Marche funèbre* of the third movement receives a powerful if analytic performance from Pollini, while the balance of this impressive disc is devoted to an equally revelatory reading of the composer's third piano sonata.

Sonata no. 3 in B Minor, op. 58
what to buy: [*Great Pianists of the 20th Century, vol. 36: Emil Gilels III*; Emil Gilels, piano] (Philips 456799) ♪ ♪ ♪ ♪₈

Gilels's approach to the slow movement of this sonata is delicate, but with a force of conviction that makes one listen anew to the piece, and his powerfully articulated passagework in the finale is among the most convincing performances currently available. This two-disc set also contains solid playing in Chopin's second piano sonata and the *Étude* in F Minor (op. 25, no. 2), in addition to a piano duet by Schubert (the *Fantasy* in F Minor, with Elena Gilels); superbly played excerpts from Grieg's *Lyric*

Pieces; Clementi's op. 34, no. 1 piano sonata; the Schumann *Arabeske* in C Major (op. 18); and a lovely version of the second piano concerto by Brahms with Eugen Jochum conducting the Berlin Philharmonic Orchestra.

various piano works
what to buy: [*Great Pianists of the 20th Century, vol. 85: Artur Rubinstein I*; Artur Rubinstein, piano] (Philips 456955) ♪ ♪ ♪ ♪ ♪

The *Andante spianato,* originally composed as an introduction to the *Grand Polonaise,* is a great introduction to Chopin's early work in general. Rubinstein's delicate playing of the beautiful, improvisatory-sounding melody is sheer poetry, while his interpretation of the *Grand Polonaise* expresses the essence of the Romantic ideal with swoon-inducing energy and passion. The balance of the album is filled out with a fine performance of the second piano sonata and a well chosen selection of nocturnes, waltzes, ballades, and more.

influences: Franz Liszt, Felix Mendelssohn, Robert Schumann, Johann Nepomuk Hummel, John Field, Gabriel Fauré

Marijim Thoene and Ellen Kokko

Muzio Clementi
Born Mutius Philippus Vincentius Franciscus Xaverius Clementi, January 23, 1752, in Rome, Italy. Died March 10, 1832, in Evesham, Worcestershire, England.

Muzio Clementi was an influential composer, keyboard player, and early manufacturer of pianos who also wrote the *Art of Playing on the Piano Forte,* an important pedagogical tool whose exercises have been used by generations of pianists.

Clementi's musical skills were already apparent in his youth and he became organist for his local church when he was only 13 years old. Peter Beckford, an Englishman visiting the area, heard the lad, was suitably impressed, and prevailed upon the senior Clementi to let the boy travel back to England with him. The young keyboard wizard lived at Beckford's country estate for seven years, studying and practicing the harpsichord. Clementi moved to London around 1774 and began the life of a musician-for-hire in a crowded marketplace. His first keyboard sonatas were published in 1779 and his popularity as a performer had increased to the point where he

soon felt confident about touring Europe's cultural capitals. It was in 1781, while in Vienna, that Clementi met Mozart in a keyboard duel staged for the amusement of royalty gathered at the emperor's palace. Clementi finally returned to London in 1783, bringing his reputation as a virtuoso with him and becoming the regular keyboard player for the newly reorganized Hanover Square Concerts.

Clementi's reputation as a performer was such that by this time he was making a substantial portion of his income teaching keyboard skills to both amateurs and fellow professionals. The fortune he made from performances and teaching (he charged his students hefty fees) permitted him to invest in music publishing and the manufacture of pianos. As a publisher Clementi would later oversee the distribution of not only his own music but such major works as Haydn's oratorio *The Creation,* and compositions by Beethoven. By the end of the century the business interests of Clementi and Co. were taking up more and more of his time, although he still managed to churn out a respectable number of compositions. He also started collating his thoughts on keyboard performance into a document (the *Introduction to the Art of Playing on the Piano Forte*) which was finally published in 1801. The following year Clementi went back to the Continent in the dual role of performer and manufacturer's representative, taking John Field with him to help demonstrate pianos made by the company. It was during this journey that Clementi signed the agreement with Beethoven giving the company the right to publish his newer works. Clementi returned to London in 1810 after having made a series of profitable arrangements for the company.

In 1813 he was named one of the directors of the Philharmonic Society, which gave him an opportunity to have some of his unpublished symphonies performed in London. By then Clementi might have been thinking about posterity and his reputation as a composer, because he returned to the Continent in 1817 to conduct some of his symphonies in some of Europe's finest venues. That was also the year of publication of the first section of *Gradus ad Parnassum,* a massive collection of his piano works. The other two parts of his pedagogical magnum opus followed in 1819 and 1826.

Over a century later Clementi is remembered mostly for his treatises on keyboard playing and the many compositions he wrote illustrating technical issues of performance. This ignores the many interesting pieces filling his voluminous oeuvre, however, though some of his material has received the attention of twentieth-century virtuosi such as Vladimir Horowitz and Arturo Benedetti Michelangeli.

Chamber
Sonata for Piano in F Minor, op. 13, no. 6
worth searching for: [*The London Piano School, vol. 1: Georgian Classicists*; Ian Hobson, piano] (Arabesque 6594) ♪ ♪ ♪⁴

This is one of Clementi's greatest works, with the two and three part textures of the first movement recalling Domenico Scarlatti while the third movement is electric with soaring melodies and virtuosic scale passages. Hobson is a master technician and a soulful interpreter of the sonata's kaleidoscopic moods. His exquisite playing also graces the works by five other composers (J.C. Bach, John Burton, Thomas Busby, Jan Ladislav Dussek, and Samuel Wesley) found on this disc.

Sonata for Piano in F-sharp Minor, op. 25, no. 5
what to buy: [Nikolai Demidenko, piano] (Hyperion 66808) ♪ ♪ ♪ ♪

Demidenko's all-Clementi program is well recorded and makes a solid case for taking the composer more seriously. The four sonatas in this set display Clementi's breadth. The technical demands of this F sharp minor work, one of the composer's more frequently recorded, almost overshadow its musical value.

what to buy next: [*Piano Music*; Balázs Szokolay, piano] (Naxos 8.550452) ♪ ♪ ♪⁴

Though this is a budget disc, Szokolay is pianistically almost in the same league as Demidenko. He handles the F sharp minor Sonata with aplomb, but the real gems of the disc are his performances of the *6 Progressive Sonatinas*, op. 36, nos. 1-6.

influences: Franz Josef Haydn, John Field, Ignaz Moscheles

Marijim Thoene and Garaud MacTaggart

Aaron Copland
Born November 14,1900, in Brooklyn, NY. Died December 2, 1990, in Tarrytown, NY.

period: Twentieth century

Aaron Copland has been called the "dean of American composers" and "president of American music," titles that help define his legacy, music that speaks of the American spirit. Copland wrote in all genres, creating such popular works as the *Fanfare for the Common Man, Appalachian Spring,* and *El Salón México,* and was also active as a pianist, conductor, teacher, and writer,

Copland was the fifth child of parents who ran a department store in Brooklyn, and when not in school he spent much of his early years working there. He began taking piano lessons from his sister but moved on to more rigorous pedagogues, studying between 1913 and 1921 with Leopold Wolfsohn, Victor Wittgenstein, and Clarence Adler. From 1917 to 1921 he studied composition, harmony, and counterpoint with Rubin Goldmark, the nephew of Austrian composer Karl Goldmark. Ironically, in light of his later development, when Copland found the score for Charles Ives's Second Piano Sonata at Goldmark's studio, his teacher insisted that he not look at it, fearing that he would be "contaminated" by Ives. During this time, the young composer-to-be was also playing piano professionally, securing summer jobs in the Catskill Mountains during 1919 and 1920.

Copland finally saved enough money to go to Paris in the winter of 1920. He was greatly stimulated there by the variety of musical life and the following year began taking private lessons with the celebrated teacher, conductor and organist Nadia Boulanger, who was especially impressed by his knowledge of jazz. What endeared her to him (and to her other American students) was Boulanger's belief that American music was about to "take off," just as Russian music had done 80 years earlier. After World War I, Paris became the musical epicenter of the world, and here Copland heard works by Maurice Ravel, Igor Stravinsky, and members of *Les Six* (Francis Poulenc, Darius Milhaud, Germaine Tailleferre, Arthur Honegger, and Louis Durey). He also became acquainted with literary giants whom he met at Mlle. Boulanger's, including James Joyce, Ernest Hemingway, and Ezra Pound, as well as fellow American composers Virgil Thomson and Melville Smith. Boulanger was so impressed with Copland's talents that she asked him to write an organ composition for her American debut. The result was one of his first important works, the Symphony for Organ and Orchestra, composed in 1924 for her performances as solo organist with the New York Symphony (Walter Damrosch conducting) and Boston

Symphony Orchestras (Serge Koussevitzky conducting). After the performance in New York City, Damrosch turned to the audience and commented: "If a young man at the age of 23 can write a symphony like that, in five years he will be ready to commit murder."

Returning to the United States in 1924, Copland joined the League of Composers and co-founded (with Roger Sessions) the Copland-Sessions Concerts of 1928–31, which provided venues for works by (among others) Henry Cowell, Virgil Thomson, Walter Piston, and George Antheil, in addition to some of the duo's own scores. Carlos Chávez invited him to visit Mexico in 1932 and Copland's experiences with the country and its musical heritage resulted in the orchestral score *El Salón México*. Using American folk melodies and Mexican percussion instruments, it dazzled audiences and became the first work to bring Copland international acclaim. The recording made by Serge Koussevitzky and the Boston Symphony Orchestra prompted the publishing firm of Boosey and Hawkes to offer Copland a long-term contract for printing all of his music. He also taught at the New School for Social Research from 1927–37 and later used some of his lectures for two important books, *What to Listen for in Music* and *Our New Music*. Later, when Piston, who taught at Harvard, took leaves of absence, Copland filled in for him, and the university asked him back in 1951 to lecture as its Norton Professor of Poetics. He later distilled those lectures and published them as *Music and Imagination,* a book comparable to Paul Hindemith's classic *Composer's World*.

1938's *Billy the Kid* was the first of his three popular ballets on American themes. The legendary story and his use of cowboy songs made this a "national work." Continuing with themes drawn from the American West, Copland created *Rodeo* for Agnes de Mille in 1942 before being commissioned by the Elizabeth Sprague Coolidge Foundation two years later to write a ballet for Martha Graham. The resulting work, *Appalachian Spring*, proved to be a milestone in his career, winning him the Pulitzer Prize for Music in 1945. Although it quotes only one folksong, (the Shaker melody *Simple Gifts*), this is considered the epitome of Copland's distinctly "American" works and one of the finest of all he wrote. The fervor of patriotism during World War II resulted in one of his most popular pieces, the *Fanfare for the Common Man*, and a commission from André Kostelanetz for an orchestral work about an American hero that evolved into the *Lincoln Portrait*, a "painting in

sound" for narrator and orchestra. It uses excerpts from the president's speeches and letters, using a version of the American folksong *Springfield Mountain* and a quotation from *Camptown Races* by Stephen Foster as building blocks for the musical portion of the score. Copland also returned, in the mid-1940's, to the world of pure, non-programmatic music with his powerful Third Symphony and the Concerto for Clarinet, Strings, Harp, and Piano, a work which has since become one of the world's most performed clarinet concertos. He also wrote music for many films, transferring his gift for capturing the essence of Americana to the silver screen in adaptations of John Steinbeck's *Of Mice and Men* in 1939 and Thornton Wilder's *Our Town* in 1940. His most successful film score, however, was the one he created in 1948 for *The Red Pony,* also from a story by Steinbeck, while his largest work for the stage is the opera *The Tender Land,* about a rural American family, composed in 1952–54.

Copland's most popular music overshadows some of his more experimental works. Before 1960 only two of his scores were influenced by Arnold Schoenberg's 12-tone system: *Poet's Song* from 1927 and the Piano Quartet of 1950. He would return to serialism in 1962 with a large symphonic work called *Connotations,* commissioned for the opening of Avery Fisher Hall in Lincoln Center. His next use of the technique, 1967's *Inscape,* was the result of another commission, this time for the New York Philharmonic's 125th anniversary. After all these brief forays into the jarring and unsettling dissonance of 12-tone composition, Copland returned to writing the tonal music for which he has become best known.

Orchestral
Fanfare for the Common Man
what to buy: [Leonard Bernstein, cond.; New York Philharmonic Orchestra] (Sony Classics 37257) ♪ ♪ ♪ ♪

Bernstein was a steadfast Copland champion over the years and his recording of the famous *Fanfare* has all the *brio* one could ask for (even though the sonics are a bit dry). The record company has coupled it with other exciting Copland performances by the American maestro: the suite from *Appalachian Spring*, a passionate *El Salón México*, and the vibrant *Danzon Cubano*.

[*Music for Brass Ensemble;* David Honeyball, cond.; London Brass Virtuosi, ensemble] (Hyperion 66189) ♪ ♪ ♪ ♪

Copland is the only American on this splendid collection of brass specialties, mostly devoted to British composers (Benjamin Britten, Gustav Holst, and Ralph Vaughan Williams). The powerful first movement from Leos Janácek's *Sinfonietta* makes a worthy counterpart to the Copland and there are also fine short works by Edvard Grieg and Richard Strauss. The Hyperion sound engineering is superb.

what to buy next: [*Copland: The Music of America*; Erich Kunzel, cond.; Cincinnati Pops Orchestra] (Telarc 80339) ♪ ♪ ♪ ₰

The trumpets have great presence, refinement and sense of ensemble here in what is a virtual anthology of Copland favorites: the *Four Dance Episodes* from *Rodeo*, the suite from *Appalachian Spring, Quiet City*, and *Billy the Kid*. The energy level flags occasionally in the slow sections, but on the whole the orchestra plays with a certain rugged enthusiasm.

various ballets and concert suites
what to buy: [*Copland the Populist*; Michael Tilson Thomas, cond.; San Francisco Symphony Orchestra] (RCA Victor Red Seal 63511) ♪ ♪ ♪ ♪ ♪

Thomas's survey of Copland includes *Appalachian Spring* in addition to music from the composer's two other ballets: *Rodeo* and the suite from *Billy the Kid*. His interpretation is an invigorating alternative to the classic accounts of Bernstein (see *Fanfare* above) and Copland (see below), and better recorded to boot.

what to buy next: [*Copland Conducts Copland*; Aaron Copland, cond.; London Symphony Orchestra] (Sony Classics 42431) ♪ ♪ ♪ ♪ ₰

Copland conducts the "original" full-length version of the score for *Appalachian Spring* as opposed to the suite done by most conductors. His version of the *Lincoln Portrait* (with Henry Fonda as the narrator) is authoritative and his *Billy the Kid* stands up well against other versions. Wonderful, warm performances by the composer, albeit not as technically assured as those from Bernstein or Slatkin.

[Leonard Slatkin, cond.; Saint Louis Symphony Orchestra] (EMI Classics 47382) ♪ ♪ ♪ ♪

This release has Slatkin's recordings of the complete *Rodeo* and *Billy the Kid* ballets. The performances are solid throughout, but the main value of the two-CD set (other than the budget price) is in its completeness, giving the listener something to compare with the suite from *Rodeo* that one usually hears—there is more to the piece than the infamous (but wonderful) *Hoedown*. Also included in this set are performances of Copland scores by other conductors and orchestras. Eduardo Mata leads the Dallas Symphony Orchestra through the *Danzon Cubano* and *El Salón México* while Enrique Bátiz and the Mexico City Philharmonic Orchestra play the suite from *The Red Pony*, the *Dance Symphony*, and the ever-popular *Fanfare for the Common Man*.

Concerto for Clarinet, Strings, Harp, and Piano
what to buy: [Stanley Drucker, clarinet; Leonard Bernstein, cond.; New York Philharmonic Orchestra] (Deutsche Grammophon 431672) ♪ ♪ ♪ ♪

Drucker, the principal clarinetist of the New York Philharmonic, is a brilliant musician with phenomenal technique and control. The CD also contains a highly varied trio of other orchestral pieces by Copland (*El Salón México, Music for the Theatre*, and *Connotations*) making this a fine survey of the composer's output.

what to buy next: [*The Essential Clarinet*; Richard Stoltzman, clarinet; Lawrence Leighton Smith, cond.; London Symphony Orchestra] (RCA Victor Red Seal 61360) ♪ ♪ ♪ ₰

Stoltzman's recital is a bit more adventuresome than the all-Copland disc with Drucker. His performance of the Copland concerto is certainly in the same league although Smith isn't quite as gutsy a conductor as Bernstein, and the RCA engineers don't provide as warm a backdrop as that afforded Drucker. The other works on the album are quite interesting for clarinet aficionados, however: Igor Stravinsky's *Ebony Concerto*, John Corigliano's Concerto for Clarinet and Orchestra, and the *Prelude, Fugue, and Riffs for Clarinet and Jazz Ensemble* by Bernstein.

[Janet Hilton, clarinet; Matthias Bamert, cond.; Scottish National Orchestra] (Chandos 8618) ♪ ♪ ♪ ₰

Chandos bathes this performance by Hilton and Bamert in their typically wonderful sound and the clarinetist plays quite poetically in this most important American

clarinet concerto. An interesting historic overview of 20th-century works for clarinet and orchestra, the disc begins with the 1948 Copland piece, followed by the folk-inspired five *Dance Preludes* for Clarinet, Harp, Piano, Percussion, and Strings by Witold Lutoslawski from 1955, and ends with Carl Nielsen's wonderful Clarinet Concerto from 1928.

influences: George Gershwin, Leonard Bernstein, Virgil Thomson, Roy Harris

Marijim Thoene and Garaud MacTaggart

Arcangelo Corelli

Born February 17, 1653, in Fusignano, Italy. Died January 8, 1713, in Rome, Italy.

period: Baroque

One of Corelli's contemporaries called him "the new Orpheus of our days," and the title fits him perfectly. During his lifetime he was acknowledged as one of the most outstanding composers, performers, and teachers of his age, with compositions including solo sonatas, trio sonatas, and concertos. A brilliant violinist, Corelli's writing for his instrument brought a change in the demands placed on both the violinist and the violin. His music was emulated and borrowed by Antonio Vivaldi, Johann Sebastian Bach, and Georg Philipp Telemann, to name but a few.

Arcangelo Corelli was born into a family of wealthy, highly respected landowners, and it is probable that he received his first violin lessons from a priest based in Faenza, a town near where he lived. At the age of thirteen he went to Bologna to study violin and four years later began more formal studies at the Accademia Filarmonica of Bologna. Having developed into a formidable musician during the course of his schooling, Corelli went to Rome in 1675 to make his fortune as a composer and violinist. He soon became one of the most sought-after players in Rome, playing in the prestigious and highly visible concerts at St. Marcello and St. Luigi dei Francesi. During this time he was also employed as a performer and composer by Queen Christina of Sweden, to whom Corelli dedicated his opus 1 trio sonatas in 1681. That same year marked his leadership of the orchestra at St. Luigi. In 1684 he began playing in the Congregazione dei Virtuosi di St. Cecilia and contracting musicians to play at functions sponsored by Cardinal Pamphili, the patron of the orchestra at St.

Marcello. The cardinal hired Corelli as his music master three years later, presumably after having heard the premiere of the composer's second opus number, another set of trio sonatas. He was still doing occasional work for Queen Christina, however, directing a pair of masses in 1689 that celebrated her (brief) recovery from illness. This was also the year that Pamphili moved out of Rome and Corelli found another patron, Cardinal Pietro Ottoboni, to whom he dedicated his fourth opus, yet another set of trio sonatas, in 1694.

His fifth set of sonatas, written in 1700, marks a further, even more impressive development of Corelli's skill as a composer. He basically revolutionized violin playing, since nobody understood and realized the cantabile potential of the violin better than he. His writing for the violin demands incredible technical prowess: the violinist has not only to make the instrument sing but to effortlessly play difficult double and triple stops, fast passage work, arpeggios, cadenzas, and movements of moto perpetuo. The set of twenty-four variations concluding his fifth opus is Corelli's most challenging collection for violin. In general terms his contribution to the sonata form lies in the distinction he made between the musical architecture of the *sonata da chiesa* (the church sonata) and that of the *sonata da camera* (the chamber sonata). The former consists of four movements—slow-fast-slow-fast—while the later is a suite made up of an introduction and three or four dances. Lest one think that this was all he was writing during the 1680s, Corelli's sinfonias and concertos composed during this period attracted the attention of the German composer George Muffat, who was favorably disposed towards their handling of melodic materials and piquant rhythms. Corelli's most enduringly famous concertos, the ones in his sixth opus, were not actually published until after his death.

Unlike his contemporaries, Corelli wrote no vocal music. He is probably the first composer in Western history to acquire an international reputation based solely on his instrumental music. The sonatas from his fifth opus were his most popular works in most of Europe, with forty-two editions published by 1800, but the concertos making up his sixth opus were especially popular in England, where they were considered classics and played more than the concertos of Georg Frideric Handel.

Orchestral
Sonata de camera, op. 2
[Charles Medlam, cond.; London Baroque, orch.]

(Harmonia Mundi Musique d'Abord 1901342/43)
♪ ♪ ♪ ♪₆

Op. 2 is contained on one of the two discs in this moderately priced set, while op. 4 is contained on the other. A lush orchestral sound benefits riveting performances, with Medlam and London Baroque providing a charming propulsion, even in the slow movements.

Concerti Grossi for Two Violins, Viola, and Continuo, op. 6
what to buy: [*Concerti Grossi, Vol. 1*; Jaroslav Krcek, cond.; Capella Istropolitana, orch.] (Naxos 8.550402) ♪ ♪ ♪ ♪

Corelli's first three op. 6 concertos receive elegant performances from the Capella Istropolitana, and the transition between movements is seamless. The budget pricing for this and its companion set (see below) make the ensemble's renditions an even more attractive choice for listeners wishing to hear what Corelli's music is all about.

[*Concerti Grossi, Vol. 2*; Jaroslav Krcek, cond.; Capella Istropolitana, orch.] (Naxos 8.550403) ♪ ♪ ♪ ♪

The big hit on this disc is the famous eighth concerto, the *Fatto per la notte di Natale* (Christmas Concerto). As on its companion disc, the members of the Capella Istropolitana give excellent performances.

what to buy next: [Neville Marriner, cond.; Academy of St. Martin-in-the-Fields, orch.] (London 443862) ♪ ♪ ♪ ♪

Marriner's 1973 recording of these works still holds up very well, although the lushness of the strings may not be looked on with favor by original instrument fanciers. For those who wish to get solid performances of the complete op. 6 and who feel more comfortable with the idea of a big name conductor leading the ensemble, this is the best choice.

Chamber
Sonatas for Violin and Continuo Instruments, op. 5
what to buy: [Elizabeth Wallfisch, violin; Locatelli Trio, ensemble] (Hyperion, 66381/2) ♪ ♪ ♪ ♪

All twelve violin sonatas from this opus are included on this splendid two-disc set. Walfisch is a marvelous violinist, and her solo spot during the famous *La Folia*

sonata is brilliant.

Sonata in D Minor for Violin and Continuo Instruments, op. 5, no. 12 *La Folia*
what to buy: [*"La Folia" and Other Sonatas*; Purcell Quartet, ensemble] (Hyperion 66226) ♪ ♪ ♪ ♪

Wallfisch, the featured violinist in the complete op. 5 recordings cited above is also a member of the Purcell Quartet. This version of the twelfth concerto is a little leaner and brighter-sounding than the one on that other set, but there is also a wider variety of Corelli's compositions to listen to. The group has devised a fine program, sampling a variety of well-performed and -selected works from the composer's first four opuses.

influences: George Muffat, François Couperin, Jean-Baptiste Lully, Antonio Vivaldi

Marijim Thoene and Garaud MacTaggart

John Corigliano
Born John Paul Corigliano, February, 16, 1938, in New York City, NY.

period: Twentieth century

An eclectic contemporary composer of chamber, symphonic, and operatic works, Corigliano has written both tonal and atonal music. His 1991 opera *The Ghosts of Versailles* was immediately hailed as a success at its Metropolitan Opera premiere, and he has won Grammy Awards for recordings of his First Symphony and String Quartet. But he is perhaps best known as the composer of the technically demanding Clarinet Concerto and highly acclaimed film scores for *Altered States* (1980) and *The Red Violin* (1999).

Corigliano's mother was a pianist, and his father was concertmaster of the New York Philharmonic Orchestra from 1943 to 1966. Despite this musical background (or perhaps, because of it), his parents tried to discourage him from becoming a professional musician. It didn't work. After studying composition with Otto Luening at Columbia University—he graduated in 1959—and privately with Paul Creston, Corigliano worked in commercial radio (as a programmer and music director), for the CBS television network (as an associate producer on the influential *Young People's Concerts* series), and as a pop-music arranger for Kama Sutra and Mercury Records. In 1970, while working at Mercury Records, Corigliano composed and arranged *The Naked Carmen*, a rock album loosely based on Georges Bizet's opera whose score utilized various pop-oriented electronic elements.

Corigliano's career as a classical composer has fallen into two periods, but in each he has worked on the same principle: "I believe it is the job of the composer to reach out to his audiences with every means at his disposal." In his early period—until approximately 1975—his work is often cited as an outgrowth of an American tradition that includes Samuel Barber, Aaron Copland, Roy Harris, and Leonard Bernstein among its foremost practitioners. While primarily tonal in conception, Corigliano's music experiments with chords, meters, rhythms, and unorthodox treatments of traditional forms. Among the scores from this period are the Sonata for Violin and Piano (which won the Spoleto Festival Competition in 1964) and his Concerto for Piano and Orchestra. He was also the recipient of a Guggenheim Fellowship in 1968.

His iconoclasm and wide-ranging intellect manifest themselves even more fully after 1975. Each of the compositions from this point contain a unique "world" created by the composer for a specific performer or mode. Extremes of rhythm and orchestral coloration give a highly dramatic quality to these later works, including the *Pied Piper Fantasy*—a flute concerto commissioned for James Galway, the Concerto for Clarinet and Orchestra, the opera *The Ghosts of Versailles*, his First Symphony, and three spectacular film scores: *Altered States* (1981), *Revolution* (1985), and the Oscar-winning *The Red Violin* (1998). In 2001 he won a Pulitzer Prize for his Symphony no. 2 for String Orchestra, a five-movement revision of his 1995 String Quartet. All of these compositions are testaments to Corigliano's talent for defining mood and drama.

Perhaps the pinnacle of his vocal works, *The Ghosts of Versailles,* with a libretto by William T. Hoffman, was an immediate success for several reasons. It scored points for completing the operatic translation of Beaumarchais' trilogy of plays (the first two being *The Barber of Seville and The Marriage of Figaro:* the third play, *La Mère coupable,* forms the opera within the opera of *The Ghosts of Versailles*). Then there is Hoffman's libretto, which is canny, funny, and sharp. Last, but certainly not least in this regard, is the sumptuous score, in which beautiful arias bump up against memorable trios and

duets. William Bolcom, in an article for the magazine *Opera News,* noted that ". . . two power lines, music and words, share the current relatively equally; it is truly a play set to music." This is a treasure trove for music and voice with a great, bittersweet ending. It has been released as a video, though not, as of this book's publication, on compact disc.

Orchestral
Symphony no. 1
what to buy: [Leonard Slatkin, cond.; National Symphony Orchestra, Washington D.C.] (RCA Victor Red Seal 68450) ♪ ♪ ♪ ♪ ♪

In 1997 Corigliano received yet another Grammy award for yet another recording of his First Symphony. Where the Slatkin-conducted version may have the edge over the earlier Grammy-winning performance by Barenboim (see below) is in its inclusion of the cantata, *Of Rage and Remembrance*. Both of these works memorialize AIDS victims. For intensity, you can't beat this outpouring.

what to buy next: [Daniel Barenboim, cond.; Chicago Symphony Orchestra] (Erato 45601) ♪ ♪ ♪ ♪ ♪

Corigliano won his first Grammy for this recording, and Barenboim's conducting has a lot to do with its essential vitality. The playing time is a bit short compared to the Slatkin recording (see above), but that is relatively easy to accept, given the quality of the performance.

Concerto for Clarinet and Orchestra
what to buy: [*The Essential Clarinet;* Richard Stoltzman, clarinet; Lawrence Leighton Smith, cond.; London Symphony Orchestra] (RCA Red Seal 61360) ♪ ♪ ♪ ♪ ♪

Stoltzman's playing is revelatory, especially in the opening *Cadenzas* section where the clarinetist's occasional jazz outings have prepped him for the fluid yet swinging line demanded by the rest of the score. Interestingly, this performance is combined with Stoltzman's take on the only other American clarinet concerto to establish itself in the international repertoire, Aaron Copland's. Leonard Bernstein's *Prelude, Fugue, and Riffs* and Igor Stravinsky's *Ebony Concerto* round out this well-chosen program.

John Corigliano

what to buy next: [Stanley Drucker, clarinet; Zubin Mehta, cond.; New York Philharmonic Orchestra] (New World 80309) ♪ ♪ ♪ ♪

Commissioned for the New York Philharmonic and Drucker, with a slow movement written in memory of Corigliano's father (the former concertmaster of the orchestra), the work here receives a fine performance from all involved. That is as it should be given the circumstances of the score's creation. Samuel Barber's *Third Essay* for Orchestra fills out the disc.

various film scores
what to buy: [*The Red Violin: Music from the Motion Picture*; Joshua Bell, violin; Esa-Pekka Salonen, cond.; Philharmonia Orchestra; Shanghai Film Studio Children's Chorus] (Sony Classical 63010) ♪ ♪ ♪ ♪ ♪

The main violin theme is most attractive and Bell plays it with great sympathy. Prior to finishing his Academy Award-winning score, Corigliano began a concert piece containing themes he wanted to use in the movie. The result, his *Chaconne for Violin and Orchestra* (subtitled *The Red Violin*), is an interesting stand-alone work that is included with the soundtrack recording.

what to buy next: [*Altered States*; Christopher Keene, cond.; RCA Symphony Orchestra] (RCA Victor 3983) ♪ ♪ ♪ ♪

Although this score was nominated for an Academy Award, don't expect an easy listening experience. There are some marvelous melodies floating throughout the soundtrack (especially the *Love Theme*), but Corigliano was creating music for a disturbing movie and the bulk of the score has elements specifically crafted to build up suspense and fear—just as Herrmann's music generated for Hitchcock's *Psycho* but with modern electronic sounds woven into the process.

Chamber
Quartet for Strings
what to buy: [*The Farewell Recording*; Cleveland String Quartet, ensemble] (Telarc 80415) ♪ ♪ ♪ ♪ ♪

Here is the Grammy winner from 1997 in two categories: for *Best Contemporary Classical Work* and *Best Chamber Music Performance*. This recording also includes Joseph Haydn's String Quartet, op. 76, no. 5. While this may seem to be an odd coupling, the performances do honor to both composers.

influences: Samuel Barber, Leonard Bernstein, Paul Creston

Michael H. Margolin and Garaud MacTaggart

François Couperin, le grand
Born November 10, 1668, in Paris, France. Died September 11, 1733, in Paris, France.

period: Baroque

François Couperin, considered one of the greatest French composers between Jean-Baptiste Lully and Jean Philippe Rameau, was also a superb musician, known for his prowess on the organ and the harpsichord. He is known as *le grand* both for the quality of his music and to distinguish him from his uncle, the "other" François Couperin. The younger Couperin's compositions were admired by Johann Sebastian Bach, while later composers like Claude Debussy and Maurice Ravel often drew inspiration from his works.

Couperin was born into a family of renowned organists, and quickly became one himself. Charles Couperin, the organist at St. Gervais, was probably his son's first teacher and, after Charles died in 1679, it was decided by the church council that young François (who had already shown flashes of talent) would inherit his father's post when he turned eighteen years old. It was as organist that Couperin first gained employment at the court of Louis XIV, the "Sun King." This appointment (in 1693) was a great event in his career because it offered him improved opportunities to make a living with his music. Couperin was already composing various works for the keyboard and had published a book of organ masses but, with his royal appointment in hand, he could expect not only an increased income but mproved access to an engraver for future compositions. As part of his courtly duties, Couperin became the harpsichord teacher for the Duke of Burgundy and several other members of the royalty in addition to composing music for both the court and the royal chapel.

The composer's first book of *Pièces de clavecin* consisted of five suites for harpsichord, and was published in 1713. He published a second volume containing seven suites in 1716, the same year his *L'art de toucher le clavecin*—one of the premier instruction texts for harpsichord players—also saw print. Eight preludes from *L'art de toucher le clavecin* were appended to the reprint of the initial *Pièces de clavecin,* which also came out in 1716. Couperin's sacred choral works during this time included three of a projected cycle of nine *Leçons des Ténèbres.* If the composer ever finished the other six works in the group, they were either lost or remain to be discovered. His third and fourth books of *Pièces de clavecin* were published in 1722 and 1730.

Couperin's admiration for Archangelo Corelli's music was apparent in his efforts to meld Italian lyricism and transparent textures into a French idiom. It was a successful venture which produced music that is rich in tonal color, as Couperin exploited the extreme lower and higher ranges of the harpsichord. The results were greatly admired by Johann Sebastian Bach, who copied *Les bergeries* (from the second book of Couperin's *Pièces de clavecin*) into Anna Magdalena's notebook, and transcribed the F Major rondeau (from Couperin's trio sonata, *L'impériale*) as the *Aria in F Major* for organ, BWV 587. Claude Debussy and Maurice Ravel both considered Couperin to represent the epitome of poise and refinement in French music, with Ravel going so far as to write *Le tombeau de Couperin* in homage to the earlier genius. Other major composers affected by *le grand* Couperin include Johannes Brahms, who prepared the first complete edition of Couperin's work for publication from 1871 to 1888, and Richard Strauss, who arranged some of Couperin's harpsichord pieces in Strauss's 1922 *Dance Suite* for small orchestra.

Chamber
Les Nations for Chamber Ensemble
what to buy: [Kuijken Ensemble] (Accent 9285/86) ♪♪♪♪

Bach arranged *L'impériale* for organ but it is heard on this two-disc package as part of Couperin's impressive set of four sonatas and suites. Members of the Kuijken String Quartet and their associates do a fine job communicating the composer's genius.

Concerts royaux
what to buy: [Robert Claire, flute; Janet See, flute; Davitt Moroney, harpsichord; Jaap ter Linden, viola da gamba] (Harmonia Mundi/Musique d'Abord 1951151) ♪♪♪♪

Couperin wrote this beguiling music to entertain his king, and these wonderful, fluid performances are just the thing to brighten the spirits of anyone interested in the French Baroque era.

Pièces de clavecin, Books 1–4 (selections)
what to buy: [*Premier Livre de Clavecin;* Kenneth Gilbert, harpsichord] (Harmonia Mundi/Musique d'Abord 190351/53) ♪♪♪♪

The first four books in Couperin's cycle of works for the harpsichord are included in this fine three-disc set. Well recorded and with suitably stunning performances by Gilbert, this is one of the finest Couperin recordings available.

what to buy next: [*Music for Harpsichord, vol. 1;* Laurence Cummings, harpsichord] (Naxos 8.550961) ♪♪♪

Cummings is a very capable musician and this recital is the first in a project to completely traverse Couperin's harpsichord compositions. The playing is worth far more than the budget price would lead one to believe possible.

worth searching for: [Skip Sempé, harpsichord] (Deutsche Harmonia Mundi 77219) ♪♪♪♪

Excellent performances by Sempé garnish a well-chosen program, including representative samples from all four sets of Couperin's *Pièces de clavecin,* and six preludes from the composer's *L'Art de toucher le clavecin.*

Vocal
Leçons des Ténèbres
what to buy: [Véronique Gens, soprano; Sandrine Piau, soprano; Emmanuel Balssa, bass viol; Christophe Rousset, organ] (Decca 466776) ♪♪♪♪

Piau is heard in the first lesson, Gens in the second, which should prepare you for the virtually seamless transition between the two in the third lesson. This is beautiful, subtle, and supple singing underscored by Rousset's reflective musicianship. A trio of other works by Couperin—the *Motet de Saint Barthélemy,* the *Motet pour le jour de Pâques,* and his Magnificat—fill out this recital.

worth searching for: [Emma Kirkby, soprano; Judith Nelson, mezzo-soprano; Jane Ryan, viol; Christopher Hogwood, organ/spinet] (L'Oiseau-Lyre 430283) ♪♪♪♪

Kirkby's singing is stunningly clear in these works, and the same thing can be said for Nelson's vocals.

Couperin's three vocal pieces based on texts from the Biblical Lamentations of Jeremiah receive impeccable performances from all involved and the *Motet pour le jour de Pâques,* which takes up the balance of the disc, is an inspired pairing.

influences: Johann Sebastian Bach, Michel-Richard Delalande, Archangelo Corelli, Girolamo Frescobaldi, Louis Couperin, Jean François Dandrieu, Jean Philippe Rameau, Jean-Henri d'Anglebert

Marijim Thoene and Garaud MacTaggart

Henry Cowell

Born Henry Dixon Cowell, March 11, 1897, Menlo Park, CA. Died December 10, 1965, Shady Hill, New York, NY.

period: Twentieth century

One of the premier experimental composers in the early-to-middle years of the twentieth century, Cowell was active as a composer, pianist, and writer in the vanguard of the movement to explore new rhythmic designs and piano techniques. He was also an important advocate of American music, both traditional folk music and modern works by composers such as Charles Ives, Carl Ruggles, John Cage, and Ruth Crawford Seeger. He is best known for a short piano piece entitled *The Banshee.*

Henry Cowell embodies the American ideal of freedom of choice. With a versatility that confounds easy description, he contributed a vast catalog of works for just about all media, showing a multifaceted personality and a creative spirit. Early exposure to American folk music and Asian classical music left a permanent influence on his musical thought. A closer view of Cowell shows an enigmatic individual as traditional as he was revolutionary—an inventor, tinkerer, and experimenter with interests in every facet of creation. His main concern was "to write as beautifully, as warmly, and as interestingly as I can."

Cowell's musical talent was recognized at an early age; his initial concert performance (on violin) took place when he was seven years old. He first acquired a piano in 1912 and made his public debut as a composer-pianist that same year—although his first documented score (*Golden Legend*) was written in 1908. He began taking composition lessons with Charles Seeger in 1914, the

same year that he premiered his *Adventures in Harmony.* Seeger would later urge Cowell to write a treatise on his experimental approaches, something the young man worked on from 1916 to 1919 but didn't publish until 1930, when it was finally released as *New Musical Resources.*

A 1919 concert of his music in New York launched his international career; beginning in 1923, he made several European tours as composer-pianist. It was at these concerts that Cowell presented works that employed tone clusters, piano preparation (where objects are placed on the strings and soundboard inside the piano), and other new means of sound production. These sonic experiments would continue into the 1930s, when he collaborated with Leon Theremin to construct the "Rhythmicon," an instrument that would automatically play complex rhythms.

From his youth, Cowell took an interest in non-Western music and in the folk music of the United States, devoting much time to their study. The knowledge and understanding gained from this exposure would reveal itself in a number of his works; for example, the *Hymn and Fuguing Tune* series, *Celtic Set, Homage to Iran,* and two Concertos for Koto and Orchestra. Rhythmically inventive and harmonically adventuresome, Cowell was in the vanguard of "indeterminacy," where lengths of a composition are given over to chance or improvisation.

Cowell was also a tireless promoter of his and others' works and a teacher of some note. Besides holding a variety of academic positions, including posts at the New School for Social Research, the Peabody Institute, and Columbia University, he also taught privately, working with George Gershwin, Lou Harrison, and John Cage. Cowell lectured widely and wrote with authority on music and musicians; *Charles Ives and His Music,* which he co-authored with his wife Sidney, is a classic text. In 1927 he launched the *New Musical Quarterly,* which published the works of several American and European composers, serving as a springboard to prominence for some of them. In the 1930s he co-founded (with Edgard Varèse, Carlos Salzedo and Carlos Chávez) the Pan-American Association of Composers.

When he died, Cowell left an unequaled legacy of interest in American music and a vast catalog of compositions, many of which would wait a few more years for their premiere. William Lichtenwanger published a catalog of Cowell's works in 1986, listing over nine hundred pieces (some lost), including works for band, orchestra, and piano with orchestra; works for piano, organ, chorus, and solo voice; many chamber works, an opera, ballets, music for film, incidental music, and twenty symphonies, the last of which was completed by Lou Harrison in 1965.

Chamber
Quartet for Strings—*Euphometric*

what to buy: [*Emerson String Quartet Plays 50 Years of American Music: 1919–1969*; Emerson String Quartet] (New World 80453) ♪ ♪ ♪ ♪

This is a truly wonderful, finely played album. The Quartet is a short piece, but it is important for the rhythmic innovation alone. Along with the Cowell, you get works by Roy Harris, Gunther Schuller, Andrew Imbrie, and Arthur Shepherd. The whole recording is very strong.

Quartet Romantic for Two Flutes, Violin, and Viola

what to buy: [*Quartet Romantic*; Paul Lustig Dunkel, flute; Susan Palma, flute; Rolf Schulte, violin; John Graham, viola] (New World 80285) ♪ ♪ ♪ ♪♪

Besides the Quartet, Cowell is represented here with the seven *Paragraphs* for String Trio. Other works heard on this disc are by Wallingford Riegger, Ruth Crawford Seeger, Lou Harrison, and John Joseph Becker. There are many superb musicians in this great package of music.

various piano works

what to buy: [Henry Cowell, piano] (Smithsonian/Folkways 40801) ♪ ♪ ♪ ♪ ♪

This is the recording to buy for Cowell's piano music. It contains all of his famous (and not so famous) solo piano works, along with comments by the composer. It is a classic, fabulous recording!

what to buy next: [*Sound Forms for Piano*; Robert Miller, piano] (New World 80203) ♪ ♪ ♪ ♪

Miller's collection is wonderful, featuring three classics by Cowell (*The Banshee, Aeolian Harp,* and the *Piece Pour Piano avec Cordes*) along with works by John Cage, Ben Johnston, and Conlon Nancarrow. Miller, who died in 1981, was one of the best pianists specializing in twentieth-century music, and this recording shows him at his peak.

Classical compositions in arrangements played by jazz musicians:
Composer: Johann Sebastian Bach
Composition: Prelude and Fugue no. 10 in E Minor
Performer: Swingle Singers (*Jazz Sebastian Bach, volume 2,* Decca 54253)
Composer: Frédéric Chopin
Composition: Prelude in E Minor
Performer: Gerry Mulligan (*Night Lights,* Verve 818271)
Composer: Claude Debussy
Composition: *Prélude à l'après-midi d'un faune*
Performer: Jacques Loussier (*Jacques Loussier Trio Plays Debussy,* Telarc 83511
Composer: Antonín Dvořák
Composition: *Humoresque*
Performer: Art Tatum (*The Standard Transcriptions,* Music & Arts 919)
Composer: George Gershwin
Composition: *Rhapsody In Blue*
Performer: Paul Whiteman Orchestra (arrangement by Ferde Grofé with the composer playing piano, *The King of Jazz: Original Mono Recordings 1920–1936,* ASV Living Era 5170)
Composer: Gustav Mahler
Composition: the *Trauermarsch (Funeral March)* from Symphony no. 5 in C-sharp Minor
Performer: Uri Caine (*Primal Light,* Winter & Winter 910004)
Composer: Joaquín Rodrigo
Composition: *Concierto de Aranjuez* for Guitar and Orchestra
Performer: Miles Davis (arrangement by Gil Evans of the Adagio, *Sketches of Spain,* Columbia/Legacy 65142)
Composer: Igor Stravinsky
Composition: *Le Sacre du Printemps (The Rite of Spring)*
Performer: Hubert Laws (arrangement by Don Sebesky, *The Best of Hubert Laws,* Columbia/Legacy 45479)
Composer: Giuseppe Verdi
Composition: *Anvil Chorus* from *Il trovatore*
Performer: Glenn Miller Orchestra (*The Essential Glenn Miller,* RCA 66520)
Composer: Kurt Weill
Composition: *Bilbao Song*
Performer: Gil Evans Orchestra (*Out of the Cool,* Impulse! 186)

influences: Roger Sessions, John Cage, Conlon Nancarrow, Ben Johnston, Lou Harrison

Frank Retzel

Ruth Crawford Seeger
Born Ruth Porter Crawford, July 3, 1901, in East Liverpool, OH. Died November 18, 1953, in Chevy Chase, MD.

period: Twentieth century

Crawford Seeger was a composer and folk music specialist whose impact upon American music deserves wider recognition. Not only was she an important member of the modernist scene during the 1920s and 1930s, she (along with her husband, Charles Seeger) tran-

scribed, edited, and arranged America's disappearing folk music tradition in a series of anthologies that helped raise the appreciation of a whole generation of musicians for its musical roots.

As the daughter of a Methodist minister, Ruth Crawford's early life revolved around a succession of parsonages as the family moved from church to church—from Ohio where she was born, through various cities in Missouri and Indiana before finally settling in Jacksonville, Florida. After her father's death in 1913, Crawford's mother operated a boarding house and young Ruth began taking piano lessons. Following her earliest formal training at Jacksonville's School of Musical Art, she was admitted (in 1921) to the American Conservatory in Chicago, where she studied piano, theory, and composition. Crawford also studied piano privately with Djane Lavoie Herz (who introduced her to Henry Cowell) and became friendly with the poet, Carl Sandburg. It was during this time that she also discovered the piano works of Alexander Scriabin and Igor Stravinsky's *Rite of Spring.*

Cowell helped get her appointed to the board of the New Music Society in 1926 and two years later she also became a founding member of the International Society for Contemporary Music's Chicago branch. By this time Crawford had already written her Sonata for Violin and Piano, the two *Movements for Chamber Orchestra,* and some short piano works as well as arrangements for Sandburg's folksong collection, *The American Songbag.* She moved to New York City in 1929 (after a brief stay at the MacDowell Colony in New Hampshire) to study counterpoint with the eminent composer and musicologist Charles Seeger, who also had the distinction of being Cowell's only composition teacher.

The following year she became the first woman to win a Guggenheim Fellowship, which enabled her to study composition in Berlin (where she met Alban Berg) and Paris (where she met Maurice Ravel and Arthur Honegger). While in Europe, Crawford wrote her only string quartet, the four *Diaphonic Suites for Various Instruments,* and two of the *Three Songs* on poetry by Sandburg. Cowell later enthused to Charles Ives, that he "would rather hear [the Andante from Crawford's string quartet] than almost anything I can think of," citing it as "perhaps the best thing for quartet ever written in [the

Henry Cowell

Classical works written by jazz musicians:
Composer: Dave Brubeck
Composition: *To Hope! A Celebration* (Telarc 80430)
Composer: Jaki Byard
Composition: *European Episode* (*Jaki Byard at Maybeck,* Concord Jazz 4511)
Composer: Ornette Coleman
Composition: *Skies of America* (*Skies of America,* Columbia 63568)
Composer: Anthony Davis
Composition: *Middle Passage* (*American Piano Music of Our Time,* Music & Arts 4862)
Composer: Leroy Jenkins
Composition: *Off Duty Dryad* for String Quintet (*Themes and Improvisations on the Blues,* CRI 663)
Composer: James P. Johnson
Composition: *Yamekraw—A Negro Rhapsody* (*The Original James P. Johnson: 1942–1945 Piano Solos,* Smithsonian Folkways 40812)
Composer: John Lewis
Composition: *Original Sin* Suite for Orchestra (*Original Sin/Essence,* Collectables 6605)
Composer: Wynton Marsalis
Composition: *Blood on the Fields* (Sony Classics 57694)
Composer: Charles Mingus
Composition: *Epitaph* (Columbia 45428)
Composer: Mary Lou Williams
Composition: *Zodiac Suite* (Smithsonian Folkways 40810)

United States]." She moved back to New York City in the winter of 1931 and, after Seeger's divorce from his first wife became official, married her former teacher the following year. Her score for the *Three Songs* was chosen to represent the United States at the 1933 ISCM Festival in Amsterdam but she was already becoming involved with the next step in her creative life.

When the Seegers moved to Washington, D.C. in 1936 so that Charles could take up his new job with the music division of the Resettlement Agency, Ruth began collaborating with John and Alan Lomax at the Library of Congress, documenting musical material for the Archive of American Folk Song. Among the collections she compiled were *American Folk Songs for Children, Animal Folk Songs for Children,* and *American Folk Songs for Christmas,* the last of which was published in 1953. Her only original composition during this time was *Rissolty Rossolty,* an orchestral piece based on folk tunes that was commissioned by the Columbia Broadcasting System and first performed in 1939.

Crawford Seeger's Suite for Wind Quintet, her next and last piece in a classical vein, was written in 1952, the year before she finally succumbed to cancer. As though summing up her accomplishments over the past three decades, it contains, along with a nod to the 12-tone camp (her first ever), elements of her first score to win a modicum of acclaim (the violin sonata of 1926) and of the folk music she had studied during her years in Washington D.C.

Chamber
Suite for Wind Quintet
what to buy: [*Ruth Crawford Seeger: Portrait*; members of the Schönberg Ensemble] (Deutsche Grammophon 49925) ♪ ♪ ♪ ♪₆

This is a lovely ten-minute work for winds that may contain some of the most accessible serial music ever written. The musicianship here is technically perfect without drawing attention to itself. In addition to the quintet, Oliver Knussen has assembled a fine overview of the composer's work, including Crawford's first orchestral score (*Music for Small Orchestra*), her short, rhythmically exciting *Piano Study in Mixed Accents* (performed by Reinbert De Leeuw), the masterly Quartet for Strings, and *Rissolty Rossolty*.

what to buy next: [*Chamber Works*; Ensemble Aventure] (CPO 999670) ♪ ♪ ♪ ♪

The playing in the Suite, a bit more leisurely than the Schönberg Ensemble's, is wonderful, if not quite in the same league as the Dutch group on Deutsche Grammophon. Where the disc stands out is in its inclusion of all four *Diaphonic Suites* (for solo oboe, bassoon and cello, two clarinets, and oboe with cello respectively) and the Suite no. 2 for Piano and Strings. The Quartet for Strings is played here by the Pellegrini Quartet and stands up well against the Deutsche Grammophon performance. The acoustic surrounding these interpretations is more than acceptable, and the price of the disc makes it definitely worth investigating.

[*Music of Ruth Crawford*; Lark Quintet, ensemble] (CRI 658) ♪ ♪ ♪ ♪₆

The Lark Quintet isn't recorded quite as well as either the Schönberg Ensemble or the Ensemble Aventure, but their performance of the quintet is so good that most listeners will not complain. The album duplicates only three pieces heard on the Deutsche Grammophon disc and two from the CPO set but, it should be pointed out, CRI released these versions long before the other companies brought out theirs. What really makes this passage interesting and unique is the marvelous reading of Crawford's Sonata for Violin and Piano, with violinist Ida Kavafian and pianist Vivian Fine, and Joseph Bloch's playing of the Scriabinesque *Nine Preludes for Piano*.

Vocal
various folk song arrangements
what to buy: [*Animal Folk Songs for Children*; Kitty MacColl, Barbara Seeger, Peggy Seeger, Penny Seeger, Mike Seeger, vocals; Peggy Seeger, piano, concertina, banjo, guitar; Callum MacColl, guitar, whistle; Mike Seeger, guitar, banjo, fiddle, mando-cello, autoharp, harmonica; Penny Seeger, guitar, dulcimer, percussion; Neil MacColl, ukelele, mandolin, percussion] (Rounder 8023/24) ♪ ♪ ♪ ♪

Ruth's children (Mike, Peggy, Barbara, and Penny) and grandchildren put together this charming two-disc set drawing upon her original arrangements for voice and piano. They also adapted some of those arrangements to fit instruments more in keeping with the American folk tradition and left other songs in their natural a cappella form. The voices aren't classically trained but, then again, neither were the original performers of this material.

influences: Alexander Scriabin, Henry Cowell, Charles Ives, Charles Seeger

Garaud MacTaggart

Claude Debussy
Born Achille-Claude Debussy, August 22, 1862, in St. Germain-en-Laye, France. Died March 25, 1918, in Paris, France.

period: Twentieth century

Beginning his career when the music of the late Romantics had reached a peak of expressivity, with Richard Wagner's influence well established throughout Europe, Claude Debussy absorbed these stimuli and reacted to them in such a way as to alter the whole course of modern music. Many of the great composers of the 20th century (Béla Bartók, Pierre Boulez, Maurice Ravel, Paul Hindemith, Igor Stravinsky, and others) have acknowledged their debt to him, and works like the *Prélude à l'après-midi d'un faune, La Mer,* and his piano preludes still continually show up on concert programs and recordings.

In 1872, Debussy was admitted to the Paris

Conservatoire, where he would study for the next twelve years. After failing to win a first prize in piano, he gave up the idea of pursuing the career of a virtuoso and in 1880 joined Ernest Guiraud's composition class. He won the coveted Prix de Rome for his cantata *L'Enfant prodigue* in 1884, an award which included an extended stay in Rome for continuing his composition studies. After his return to France in 1887 he led a bohemian existence for the next few years. He visited Bayreuth during the opera seasons of 1888 and 1889 and came under the influence of Richard Wagner's revolutionary musical concepts. Another event with implications for the development of Debussy's style was his discovery of the variety of percussive sounds and harmonies produced by a Javanese gamelan (orchestra) at the Paris Exposition of 1889. While resisting the conservative approach encouraged by the conservatory, he drew inspiration from his beloved Paris and other art forms, discovered an interest in music from different cultures, and reacted to the aesthetic of Wagner's fluid tonality.

Before 1892, Debussy's compositions—a number of songs, and some chamber works, but none of any startling originality—hewed closer to the conventions of the day than he might have wanted to admit. That changed shortly after he met Ernest Chausson, a former Wagner follower who had begun to turn away from the sage of Bayreuth and explore the music of such earlier French composers as Jean-Philippe Rameau and François Couperin. This was the year when Debussy started working on his most famous orchestral score, *Prélude à l'après-midi d'un faune,* (inspired by a poem of Stephane Mallarmé), and the first version of his *Nocturnes* for Orchestra. The Impressionist paintings of his French contemporaries stressed color, fluidity, and atmosphere, and an aural equivalent can be found in Debussy's works from this time. His only string quartet, written and premiered in 1893, features a scherzo combining pizzicato and normal bowing, which would serve as a model for later 20th century composers (ex. Béla Bartók and Anton Webern) in their own quartet writing. The revolutionary *Prélude à l'après-midi d'un faune,* was first performed a year later, its continuous orchestral ebb and flow engendering a sense of weightlessness and fluidity that would become characteristic of Debussy's music from this time.

Like so many of his contemporaries, Debussy had fallen under the spell of Wagner, but unlike them he was not tempted to imitate what he admired in the German master. Rather, he dreamt "of texts which will not condemn

Van Cliburn:
In 1958, Van Cliburn returned to the United States after having been the first American to win the coveted Tchaikovsky Competition in Moscow, and doing so to nearly unanimous acclaim by Russian critics. In addition to being an impressive feat for the twenty-four-year-old pianist, it was thought to be (at least subliminally) a victory for American arts at the height of the Cold War. As such, Cliburn was treated to a ticker-tape parade in Manhattan, given a testimonial lunch with various New York City-based celebrities, and personally congratulated by President Eisenhower.

Much of the credit for Cliburn's success can be attributed to his mother, who had once taken piano lessons from Arthur Friedheim, a former pupil of Franz Liszt. Though she was not able to pursue a concert career she made sure that her son was well-tutored at their home in Kilgore, Texas, before sending him off, in 1951, to study at the Juilliard School of Music with Rosina Lhevinne. Notwithstanding the indispensable polish these studies brought, Cliburn had begun to read music when he was only three years old and made his Carnegie Hall debut in 1946. Upon graduating from Juilliard, he was already one of the most honored students in the school's history. This was topped by his winning the Levintritt Award in 1954, and a well-received performance with the New York Philharmonic Orchestra of Tchaikovsky's B-flat piano concerto, the work with which he would win the contest in Moscow. Cliburn has returned to Russia several times since his groundbreaking win at the Tchaikovsky Competition but his concertizing has tapered off in recent years, including a nearly decade-long "sabbatical" between 1978 and 1987. What he has been deeply involved with, however, is the Van Cliburn International Piano Competition, which began in 1962 and is now being held every four years in Fort Worth, Texas.

First among Cliburn's most impressive albums is his initial recording of the same Tchaikovsky piano concerto which helped vault him to fame, with Kirill Kondrashin conducting the RCA Victor Symphony Orchestra, paired with Sergei Rachmaninoff's second piano concerto, featuring Fritz Reiner leading the Chicago Symphony Orchestra (RCA Victor Red Seal 55912). For those wishing to hear Cliburn in a more intimate setting, his disc of Chopin piano music, *My Favorite Chopin* (RCA Victor Living Stereo 68813), is a good option.

William Gerard

me to perpetuate long, heavy acts, but will offer me, instead, changing scenes, varied in place and mood, where the characters in the play do not argue, but submit to life and fate." These words spoken in 1899 describe the poetic drama he was in the process of setting to music, Maurice Maeterlinck's *Pelléas et Mélisande,* in the only opera he would complete. The work was begun in 1893 and its premiere in Paris in 1902 provided Debussy with the greatest success of his career to date.

Before the success of his opera he had to undergo a series of financial travails, and composition wasn't his only source of income. He still traveled frequently, appearing as a conductor and performer of his music in

France and abroad. He also began publishing music criticism in 1901 in *La Revue blanche* and would continue writing throughout his life, often assuming the alias of "M. Croche, hater of dilettantes." Several major works date from the following years: *La Mer* and *Images* for orchestra, the ballet *Jeux,* numerous songs, piano pieces, and chamber works. He planned many other projects, which were never carried out. After his last trip abroad (to England) in 1914, he composed the *Etudes* for piano, and three sonatas for chamber ensembles (he planned six). He died in 1918 after a long bout with cancer.

Debussy could be painfully honest (perhaps undiplomatic) and clearly did not suffer fools gladly. Many young composers wanted to meet and speak with him, yet he resisted the coterie of disciples that easily could have gravitated around him. He developed no system for composition, and his music sometimes confounds analysis. He wanted it to remain magical. In 1903, Debussy wrote: "Music is a mysterious mathematical process whose elements are a part of Infinity. Nothing is more musical than a sunset! For anyone who can be moved by what they see can learn the greatest lessons in development here."

Orchestral
Images for Orchestra
what to buy: [Pierre Boulez, cond.; Cleveland Orchestra] (Deutsche Grammophon 435766) ♪ ♪ ♪ ♪ ♪

Coupled with *Prélude à l'après-midi d'un faune* and the 1887 orchestral suite *Printemps,* what a fabulous recording this is. Boulez is a master of evoking well-defined tonal colors, and this orchestra allows him to demonstrate that to the fullest.

La Mer for Orchestra
what to buy: [Pierre Boulez, cond.; Cleveland Orchestra] (Deutsche Grammophon 439896) ♪ ♪ ♪ ♪ ♪

Boulez is a wonderful conductor of Debussy, and this album shows both why and how. It also includes *Jeux,* the three *Nocturnes* and the 1911 orchestral version of the *Première Rhapsodie* for clarinet and piano. The engineering, as on other Boulez projects for Deutsche Grammophon, is marvelous.

various orchestral and vocal works
what to buy: [*Debussy: Orchestral Works*; Pierre

Boulez, cond.; Cleveland Orchestra; New Philharmonia Orchestra] (Sony Classical 68327) ♪ ♪ ♪ ♪ ♪

All the major orchestral works are represented here (including *La Mer* and *Jeux*), and lesser-known gems like *Danses sacrée et profane* (for harp and orchestra) and the *Rhapsodie* (for clarinet and orchestra) are also included. The sonics aren't quite as welcoming as Boulez's later performances on Deutsche Grammophon (see below) but the differences are relatively slight otherwise. The Cleveland Orchestra is heard only in the *Images* and *Danses sacrée et profane* with the New Philharmonia Orchestra playing the balance of the pieces in this set.

worth searching for: [*Oeuvres Orchestrales*; Daniel Barenboim, cond.; Orchestre de Paris] (Deutsche Grammophon 437934) ♪ ♪ ♪ ♪ ♪

What a set! In addition to solid performances of such Debussy standards as the *Nocturnes,* the three *Images* for orchestra, *Prélude à l'après-midi d'un faune* and *Printemps,* there is a nice sampling of vocal works featuring soloists Barbara Hendricks (singing *La Damoiselle élue*) and Dietrich Fischer-Dieskau (in a rarely heard orchestral arrangment of the three *Ballades de François Villon*).

Chamber
Quartet in G Minor for Strings, op. 10
what to buy: [Emerson String Quartet, ensemble] (Deutsche Grammophon 445509) ♪ ♪ ♪ ♪ ♪

There are so many wonderful recordings coupling the single string quartets of Ravel and Debussy, that it seemed almost a shame to elevate one above the others—at least until this one came along. The engineering is superb and the musicianship of this fine ensemble is above reproach. Especially beguiling is the group's swinging plucked-string playing in the scherzo movement.

what to buy next: [Juilliard Quartet, ensemble] (Sony Classics 52554) ♪ ♪ ♪ ♪ ♪

Taking a fairly wiry, muscular approach to this strong yet diaphanous score can work with musicians of the Juilliard Quartet's caliber. Not only Ravel's quartet is included here but also Henri Dutilleux's *Ainsi la nuit* for string quartet, a fascinating gem by a composer who deserves to be better known.

[Tokyo String Quartet, ensemble] (Sony Classics 62413) ♪ ♪ ♪ ♪

The Tokyo String Quartet's 1977 performance was one of the top recommendations for this work for years, and, if anything, time has made this rendition even more appealing by lowering the list price and coupling it not only with Ravel's quartet but Gabriel Fauré's Trio in D minor for Piano, Violin, and Cello. The Tokyo String Quartet handles the first two scores while the Roth Trio's version of the Fauré piece is solid, if not spectacular.

Preludes for Piano, Books 1 and 2
what to buy: [Walter Gieseking, piano] (EMI Classics 67262) ♪ ♪ ♪ ♪ ♪

There are times, difficult as it may be to believe in this digital age, when certain older monaural recordings *still* stand head and shoulders above the rest of the crowded field. That is the case with Gieseking's well-engineered performances from 1953 and 1954. His keyboard touch, so even and assured, reveals the musical poetry at the heart of these pieces, transforming wonderfully complete little snippets of pianistic color into otherworldly art of the highest order.

what to buy next: [Paul Jacobs, piano] (Nonesuch 73031) ♪ ♪ ♪ ♪⅛

This is a wonderful set of the complete Preludes. These performances were first-rate when they came out and remain so today. Paul Jacobs was a master!

Etudes for Piano
what to buy: [Paul Jacobs, piano] (Elektra/Nonesuch 79161) ♪ ♪ ♪ ♪ ♪

In addition to the two books of *Etudes,* this disc also includes Debussy's *En blanc et noir* for two pianos with Jacobs teaming up with another American keyboard legend, Gilbert Kalish.

Images for Piano
what to buy: [Paul Jacobs, piano] (Nonesuch 71365) ♪ ♪ ♪ ♪ ♪

Here's a budget priced recording of these delightful works that stands up well to any of the higher-priced packages. Heard here along with the two sets of *Images* (the first includes *Reflets dans l'eau* and *Hommage à Rameau*) are the *Images oubliées* from 1894, and the three *Estampes.*

Children's Corner for Piano
what to buy: [Arturo Benedetti Michelangeli, piano] (Deutsche Grammophon 415372) ♪ ♪ ♪ ♪ ♪

Unlike the Jacobs set of *Images,* (see above) Michelangeli's recording of those fine works includes a splendid performance of the *Children's Corner* but does not contain the earlier *Images oubliées* and *Estampes.* The piano is superbly recorded.

what to buy next: [Calefax Reed Quintet, ensemble] (MD & G 6190658) ♪ ♪ ♪ ♪

Raaf Hekkema, the saxophonist for this group, has created a splendid arrangement of the *Children's Corner* which honors the spirit of the suite while unveiling a whole new set of tonal colors. The band also treats Debussy's *Épigraphes antiques* and Ravel's *Le Tombeau de Couperin* with the same respect.

Vocal
Pelléas et Mélisande
what to buy: [Frederica von Stade, mezzo-soprano; Richard Stilwell, baritone; José van Dam, baritone; Ruggero Raimondi, bass; Herbert von Karajan, cond.; Berlin Philharmonic Orchestra; Chorus of the Deutsche Oper, Berlin] (EMI Classics 67168) ♪ ♪ ♪ ♪ ♪

This is certainly of one the best recordings that you can buy of this great work. Karajan's forces provide just the right amount of gloss to Debussy's impressionism and von Stade is absolutely marvelous.

[Maria Ewing, soprano; François Le Roux, baritone; José van Dam, baritone; Jean-Philippe Courtis, bass; Claudio Abbado, cond.; Vienna Philharmonic Orchestra; Vienna State Opera Chorus] (Deutsche Grammophon 435344) ♪ ♪ ♪ ♪

Comparing the singers with those in the EMI set (see above) is a bit like comparing apples and oranges, since both ensembles are magnificent in their own ways. The two casts share van Dam's lustrous baritone but Abbado's emphasis favors muscle over sheen.

various songs
what to buy: [*Complete Mélodies*; Elly Ameling, soprano; Frederica von Stade, mezzo-soprano; Michele

Command, soprano; Mady Mesplé, soprano; Gerard Souzay, baritone; Dalton Baldwin, piano] (EMI Classics 64095) ♪ ♪ ♪ ♪ ♪

Once you've discovered the wonderful world of Debussy's songs, you will want to know more and more, so why not start out with a complete edition sung by some of its finest interpreters. Baldwin is the one constant in this traversal, providing the firm base from which these superb soloists take flight.

Influences: Gabriel Fauré, Maurice Ravel, Francis Poulenc, Darius Milhaud, Igor Stravinsky, Jules Massenet, Edvard Grieg

Frank Retzel and Ian Palmer

Léo Delibes

Born Clément Philibert Léo Delibes, February 21, 1836, in Saint-Germain du Val, France. Died January 16, 1891, in Paris, France.

period: Romantic

Balletomanes are forever thankful to Léo Delibes for composing two of the most popular dance scores to emerge from the nineteenth century: *Coppélia* and *Sylvia*. His opera *Lakmé* also maintains a partial grip on modern audiences who have heard excerpts from it (particularly *Dôme épais le jasmin* a.k.a. the "Flower Duet" and *Ah! . . . Où va la jeune indoue* a.k.a. the "Bell Song") in various television commercials.

In 1876, while Piotr Tchaikovsky was in France, he paid a visit to Paris, where he picked up a piano score for the then new ballet, *Sylvia*. He would later write a note to his patron, Madame von Meck, remarking that, "I know of nothing which in recent years has really seriously captivated me except [Georges Bizet's opera] *Carmen* and Delibes' ballet [*Sylvia*]." In another letter to von Meck, Tchaikovsky wrote: "Without any false modesty I tell you that *Swan Lake* is not fit to hold a candle to *Sylvia*." This high praise from a master composer was but a hint of the accolades Delibes was receiving in France for his ballet scores.

Léo Delibes was primarily a composer for the stage whose first important lessons in composition came from his professor at the Paris Conservatoire, Adolphe Adam—a man best known today for his own ballet,

Giselle. Upon leaving the conservatory in 1853, Delibes won an appointment (with the aid of Adam) to become an organist at the Church of St. Pierre de Chaillot in Paris, but even more importantly for his future career, he also got a job as an accompanist at the Théâtre Lyrique. It was at this venue that Delibes was able to observe the more practical aspects of stagecraft, and make the kinds of influential contacts that would eventually allow him to mount a production of his very first stage piece (an operetta called *Deux sous de charbon*) in 1856. Between then and 1870 when *Coppélia* debuted, Delibes kept his position as church organist, was appointed chorus master at the Théâtre Lyrique, moved on to the same job at the Paris Opéra, and co-authored (with Louis Minkus) his first ballet, *La source*.

Coppélia, however, was the successful ballet which allowed him to leave both the organ bench and his position at the Paris Opéra in 1871 to concentrate on composing. This work was based on an E.T.A. Hoffman tale revolving around a life-like mechanical doll (the title character), her creator (Doctor Coppelius), a man who mistakenly believes that Coppélia is a real person and falls in love with her (Franz), and Swanilda, Franz's fiancé. Delibes has since been credited with creating in this ballet the first fully symphonic score which brought dance and music together to form a unified work of art. Torquato Tasso's *Aminta* provided the plot for the composer's next balletic masterpiece, *Sylvia*, in 1876. Shaped around the pastoral account of a young shepherd (Aminta) in love with one of Diana's nymphs (Sylvia), Delibes's second most popular ballet score suffers from an undistinguished storyline but makes up for it with some intermittently lovely music. However, despite the obvious charms of its most popular section (the pizzicatti from the third act), posterity, if the typical number of performances given is any indication, differs from Tchaikovsky, seeming to prefer the overall consistency of *Coppélia* (not to mention *Swan Lake*) to the variability of Delibes's later score.

The major operatic work in the composer's canon, *Lakmé,* was premiered successfully in 1883, two years after Delibes had become a composition teacher at the Conservatoire. The libretto concerns itself with the title character, the daughter of a Brahmin priest who seeks to kill the British officer with whom she is in love. There are obvious similarities to Puccini's *Madama Butterfly* in the storyline and to Bizet's operas (*Carmen* and *Les pêcheurs de perles* [*The Pearl Fishers*]) in the score, but it has maintained a relatively strong position in the repertoire (especially in France), due in part to a pair of glorious arias for the soprano voice: *Dôme épais le jasmin* and *Ah! . . . Où va la jeune indoue.*

Orchestral
Coppélia, ou La fille aux yeux d'émail
what to buy: [*Delibes: The 3 Ballets*; Richard Bonynge, cond.; National Philharmonic Orchestra] (Decca 460418) ♪♪♪♪

This admirably priced four-disc set includes not only a fine version of *Coppélia,* but an exemplary rendering of *Sylvia* (with the New Philharmonia Orchestra), and the lesser known *La source* (with the Royal Opera House Covent Garden Orchestra). Bonynge's delightfully pointed rhythms are blessed with a wonderful, spacious acoustic that almost transports the listener to the hall itself. There is less music in this set than in Mogrelia's version (see below), but the few scenes missing should only be of concern to completists.

what to buy next: [Andrew Mogrelia, cond.; Slovak Radio Symphony Orchestra] (Naxos 8.553356/57) ♪♪♪♪

The performances on this budget two-disc set are amazingly graceful and the sound quality is more than adequate. Mogrelia's steady-handed leadership in the suites excerpted from *La source* also makes this an acceptable alternative to at least part of Bonynge's survey of the three ballets (see above).

Sylvia, ou La nymphe de Diane
what to buy: [Andrew Mogrelia, cond.; Razumovsky Sinfonia, orch.] (Naxos 8.553338/39) ♪♪♪♪

No matter what Tchaikovsky may have thought about this piece, the inspiration just isn't as consistent as that found in *Coppélia,* though there are moments of near genius. That said, Mogrelia's performance of the complete *Sylvia* has the advantage over other versions of this work by virtue of playing that is far stronger than what one would think, given its budget pricing. The other plus for this two-disc set is the inclusion of the rarely heard ballet music from Camille Saint-Saëns's *Henry VIII.*

Vocal
Lakmé
what to buy: [Natalie Dessay, soprano; Patricia Petibon,

soprano; Xenia Konsek, soprano; Bernadette Antoine, soprano; Delphine Haidan, mezzo-soprano; Gregory Kunde, tenor; Charles Burle, tenor; Alain Chilemme, tenor; Franck Leguerinel, baritone; José van Dam, bass-baritone; Michel Plasson, cond.; Toulouse Capitole Orchestra; Toulouse Capitole Chorus] (EMI Classics 56569) ♪♪♪♪

Plasson conducts the first *Lakmé* of the digital era, and everything comes together quite nicely under his baton. Dessay's Lakmé is well characterized in addition to being superbly sung, but Kunde's Gerald is merely pleasant. Van Dam's prime is past but his Nilakantha is a powerfully constructed piece of acting; moreover, his faults become virtues within the context of the role. Haidan's Mallika is a good partner for Dessay in the *Flower Duet.*

what to buy next: [Joan Sutherland, soprano; Jane Berbié, mezzo-soprano; Monica Sinclair, mezzo-soprano; Gwenyth Annear, contralto; Emile Belcourt, tenor; Alain Vanzo, tenor; Claude Calés, tenor; Gabriel Bacquier, baritone; Josephte Clément, bass; Richard Bonynge, cond.; Orchestre National de l'Opéra de Monte-Carlo; Monte Carlo Opera Chorus] (Decca 425485) ♪♪♪♪

Sutherland was one of the queens of the opera when she recorded Lakmé, and her version of the popular *Bell Song* is atmospheric. Bonynge's conducting at times reduces orchestral textures to mush, however, and the rest of the cast is just adequate (although Berbié is a very competent Mallika and Bacquier is very steady as Nilakantha).

[Mady Mesplé, soprano; Bernadette Antonine, soprano; Monique Linval, soprano; Agnes Disney, mezzo-soprano; Danielle Millet, mezzo-soprano; Charles Burles, tenor; Joseph Peyron, tenor; Jean-Christophe Benoit, baritone; Roger Soyer, bass; Alain Lombard, cond.; Orchestre de Théâtre National de l'Opéra Comique; Théâtre National de l'Paris Opéra Comique Chorus] (EMI Classics 49430) ♪♪♪♪

Mesplé was a wonderful soprano, and if she didn't quite attempt the sheer variety of roles throughout her career that Sutherland did, *Lakmé* may be the one work in which she bests Sutherland, at least from an acting point of view. The production, cast, and conducting are all on a consistent level of quality in this, the first stereo recording of the opera.

influences: Adolphe Adam, Giacomo Meyerbeer,

Jacques Offenbach, Georges Bizet, Edouard Lalo, Jules Massenet, Gabriel Pierné, Piotr Tchaikovsky

Ian Palmer

Frederick Delius

Born Frederick Theodore Albert Delius, January 29, 1862, in Bradford, England. Died June 10, 1934, in Grez-sur-Loing, France.

period: Romantic/impressionist

Delius, the only major impressionist composer Great Britain ever produced, was a distinctive and fascinating figure in the revival of English music at the turn of the twentieth century. He was best when writing short evocative pieces such as *On Hearing the First Cuckoo in Spring* and *Over the Hills and Far Away.*

Julius Delius, Frederick's father, emigrated to England from Germany, forming a partnership with his brother in a business that bought and sold wool. A successful businessman, Julius did not neglect his children's instruction in the fine arts, yet despite helping to start the subscription concerts for the Hallé Orchestra, he felt that music was an unfit profession. The younger Delius did take violin lessons and managed to pick up the rudiments of piano playing, but his father saw his son's future as a member of the family business, not as a musician. Although Frederick began working in his father's wool company, he sought greater independence and eventually persuaded his father to set him up as an orange grower at Solano Grove near Jacksonville, Florida.

In Florida he took music lessons and neglected his farming duties, although he became fondly acquainted with the African-American songs sung by the plantation's workers. According to Eric Fenby, Delius's amanuensis, Julius was not happy with this turn of events but relented in his opposition to Frederick's musical pursuits, arranging for his son to begin an eighteen-month course of study at the Leipzig Conservatory in the fall of 1886. In Leipzig, Delius befriended Christian Sinding, who introduced him to the great Norwegian composer Edvard Grieg. The budding musician impressed the older man with his passion for music, leading Grieg to plead Frederick's cause with the elder Delius, finally persuading Julius to financially support his son's career choice.

In 1888 Delius moved to Paris, where he became friends with the playwright August Strindberg, the painters Edvard Munch and Paul Gauguin, and the French com-poser Florent Schmitt, whom Delius would later commission to write the vocal scores for his operas *Irmelin, The Magic Fountain, Koanga,* and *A Village Romeo and Juliet.* He also met Jelka Rosen, a young student painter from Germany, who would later abandon her own career to help further that of the young Englishman. By 1897 Delius and Rosen were living together in Grez-sur-Loing, a small village near Paris; they had moved into the house that Jelka and her mother had bought, cohabiting for several years before marrying in 1903.

Delius, whose music was first appreciated in Germany, remained virtually unknown in his native England until 1907, when the great conductor Sir Thomas Beecham became his most passionate advocate and ardent interpreter. Sadly, Delius gradually went blind and became paralyzed from the aftereffects of syphilis, even though he retained his hearing and all his mental faculties. In 1928 he was visited by an English admirer, a young musician named Eric Fenby, who ended up serving as his musical secretary, notating and transcribing all of Delius's last works. The final public event in the composer's life was a major festival of his music, organized in London by Beecham in 1929. This brought the ailing composer a great deal of critical acclaim, both in England and on the Continent.

Delius was a mostly self-taught composer who took a long time to develop. His first important works did not come until his late thirties, and he did not reach full maturity as a composer until 1901 with his beautiful opera *A Village Romeo and Juliet.* Delius's musical idiom derives from the chromaticism of Richard Wagner, filtered through his own English sensibilities and mitigated by the folk-influenced music of Grieg. He is one of the few notable composers in whose works harmony dominates and melody is secondary. His orchestrations are also strikingly individual. Just after the turn of the century, Delius read Friedrich Nietzsche's *Also sprach Zarathustra,* counting it as one of the most significant events in his life and believing that the German philosopher spoke directly to his own sensibilities. Inspired, Delius eventually produced his most ambitious work, *A Mass of Life,* which received its first complete performance in 1909 under Beecham's direction.

Delius was fond of depicting the beauty of nature, the passion of love, and the transience of worldly things in his music. This sensual element in his music is remarkable; he was at his best in pictorial or literary-influenced works but not nearly as good at dealing with conventional musical forms. His nature was closer to that of painters or poets than to the personality typically associated with musicians, and it is no accident that many people regard him as a poet in music. He spent most of his life apart from the mainstream of professional music making and is mainly remembered today for his series of exquisite orchestral miniatures.

Orchestral
various orchestral works
what to buy: [*Beecham Conducts Delius*; Thomas Beecham, cond.; Royal Philharmonic Orchestra] (EMI Angel 47509) ♪ ♪ ♪ ♪ ♪

This remarkable two-CD set of Delius's works collects all the stereo recordings made by Beecham during the 1950s and includes *Over the Hills and Far Away, On Hearing the First Cuckoo in Spring,* and *A Song Before Sunrise,* among others. Beecham's way with Delius's music has rarely been equaled and never surpassed. This magnificent set is one of the glories of the early stereo era.

what to buy next: [*Delius: Orchestral Works*; John Barbirolli, cond.; Hallé Orchestra; London Symphony Orchestra] (EMI Classics 65119) ♪ ♪ ♪ ♪

This two-disc set by Barbirolli, another fine advocate for the composer, may not capture every bit of the splendor revealed by Beecham, but it avoids duplicating most of Beecham's offering. Also included is a short excerpt of Barbirolli rehearsing his forces for a performance of *Appalachia,* revealing how humorous and exacting the conductor could be at the same time.

Concerto for Violin and Orchestra
worth searhing for: [Tasmin Little, violin; Charles Mackerras, cond.; Welsh National Opera Orchestra] (Argo 433704) ♪ ♪ ♪ ♪

The violin concerto, one of the composer's masterpieces, receives a truly inspired performance from Little and Mackerras. Also on the disc are some of Delius's purely orchestral works, including the two splendid *Dance Rhapsodies.*

Vocal
A Mass of Life
what to buy: [Joan Rodgers, soprano; Jean Rigby, mezzo-soprano; Nigel Robinson, tenor; Peter Coleman-

Alicia de Larrocha:

The Spanish pianist Alicia de Larrocha has arguably done more to popularize piano works by her compatriots than any other performer in the world, with the possible exception of Artur Rubinstein (though himself a Pole). Born in 1923, she was deemed a prodigy by the time she was four years old, and lauded for the surprising maturity of her interpretations when she made her public debut at the age of five. Since 1940, de Larrocha has been given the mantle of Enrique Granados (solidifying the symbolism, both her mother and aunt were once his students), and deemed the foremost Spanish pianist of the twentieth century by numerous critics both in Spain and abroad.

Her American concert debut took place in 1955 with the Los Angeles Philharmonic Orchestra and she gave a solo recital at Town Hall in New York City that same year. At the latter performance de Larrocha not only showcased her formidable abilities in Spanish material, playing works by Carlos Surinach, Isaac Albéniz, and Granados, but demonstrated an equally refined way with the standard repertoire, turning in what some critics raved about as "graceful yet powerful" performances of Robert Schumann's *Carnaval* and Ludwig van Beethoven's Sonata in A-flat Major for Piano, op. 110.

She has won numerous awards over the years, including the Spanish Order of Civil Merit, the Paderewski Memorial Award, and, for her initial recording of Albéniz's *Iberia*, the Grand Prix du Disque (1960). This last-named version is the one heard on the two-disc set *Great Pianists of the 20th Century: Alicia de Larrocha 1* (Philips 456883), a fine sampler devoted to her recordings of Spanish works that also includes material by Granados, Mateo Albéniz, Antonio Soler, Ernesto Halffter, and Federico Mompou. Her 1972 recording of *Iberia* (London 448191) is better-recorded, however, and includes a fine performance of Granados's *Goyescas* in addition to a rendering of *Navarra*, the work that some historians regard as the fifth book in Albéniz's *Iberia*.

Although de Larrocha's playing is often associated in many people's minds with Spanish classical music, she has reserved some of her finest performances for Wolfgang Amadeus Mozart's oeuvre, especially the piano concerti. Unfortunately, as this book goes to press, her recordings of the concertos are, for the most part, out of print. However, some of her classic versions of Mozart's piano sonatas can be found on *Great Pianists of the 20th Century: Alicia de Larrocha 2* (Philips 456886), a double CD that also features refined renditions of solo keyboard works by Johann Sebastian Bach, George Frideric Handel, Franz Joseph Haydn, and Domenico Scarlatti.

Ellen Kokko

Wright, baritone; Richard Hickox, cond.; Bournemouth Symphony Orchestra and Chorus] (Chandos 9515) ♪ ♪ ♪₄

This is Delius's most ambitious and remarkable creation. If you are interested in probing the furthest recesses of the composer's imagination, then hearing this piece is a must. Hickox's recording (paired with the composer's *Requiem*) is the best now available; even if it is not ideal in all respects, it is beautifully recorded and will have to do until somebody decides to reissue Beecham's legendary recording from the early 1950s.

Sea Drift

what to buy: [Bryn Terfel, baritone, Richard Hickox, cond.; Bournemouth Symphony Orchestra; Bournemouth Symphony Chorus] (Chandos 9214) ♪ ♪ ♪ ♪

Sea Drift, a Walt Whitman text setting, is one of Delius's greatest works. The disc also includes his choral gem *Songs of Farewell* and the *Songs of Sunset,* both of which receive wonderful performances from Hickox and the orchestra.

influences: Arnold Bax, Gerald Finzi, Hamilton Harty, Florent Schmitt

Charles Greenwell, Dave Wagner, and Garaud MacTaggart

David Diamond

Born David Leo Diamond, July 9, 1915, in Rochester, NY.

period: Twentieth century

David Diamond has been recognized throughout his prolific career as a major composer with a knack for Americana. A composer of versatility and depth whose oeuvre includes symphonies, concertos, chamber works, and vocal pieces, he is basically a traditionalist and a romantic, a fact underscored early in his career when he sought out the Viennese master Arnold Schoenberg to study twelve-tone techniques with him. Schoenberg's response was, "Why do you need to? You are a young [Anton] Bruckner." Diamond's best known and most performed composition is *Rounds* for String Orchestra.

On October 5, 1995, Diamond was awarded the Presidential Medal of Arts by President and Mrs. Clinton, crowning his career with one of the highest accolades a country can bestow—composer laureate. This honor is particularly refreshing as it came to an individual not in the forefront of revolution, innovation, or momentary fashion but rather to a man who went about his craft adhering to classical principles of composition and musical tradition. Some may label Diamond a reactionary, but it should be remembered that every musical age contains both the innovator and the traditionalist.

Diamond's talent was recognized at an early age. He taught himself to play violin and even created his own

system of notation, which he used to write his first compositions. Later, Diamond took violin lessons in public school and, when his family moved briefly to Cleveland, studied violin and theory with André de Ribaupierre at the Cleveland Institute of Music. These lessons were augmented by studies at the preparatory division of the Eastman School of Music when the family moved back to Rochester. A prolific composer from the start, Diamond wrote some one hundred compositions by the time of his high school graduation. He spent a year working with Bernard Rogers at the Eastman School of Music before leaving for New York City to study at the Dalcroze Institute with Paul Boepple and privately with Roger Sessions. One composition from 1935, *Sinfonietta,* earned Diamond a scholarship, enabling him to continue his studies.

Paris in the 1930s was a mecca for artists who sought both the inspiration and the instruction that great city provided. Diamond made a brief first visit to Paris in 1936, meeting André Gide, Albert Roussel, Maurice Ravel, and Charles Munch. The first of his compositions to bring him national attention, *Psalm for Orchestra,* was written in 1936 under the influence of his Parisian experiences and premiered by Howard Hanson and the Rochester Philharmonic when Diamond returned to the United States. He went back to Paris in 1937 and again in 1938 when the first of three Guggenheim Fellowships supported his studies with the great teacher Nadia Boulanger. Diamond returned from France surer than ever of his American heritage, a realization that would remain with him throughout his life. During the 1940s he composed a great deal, receiving many commissions and awards for his work. He won the Prix de Rome in 1942 for his first symphony and his first string quartet, and in 1946 he was honored with a special citation from the New York Music Critics' Circle for *Rounds* for String Orchestra.

Despite *Rounds'* neoclassical leanings, the gist of its themes is more American than European. Initially commissioned by Dimitri Mitropoulos and premiered by the Minneapolis Symphony in 1944, this score has become Diamond's most frequently performed work. Mitropoulos had sought a piece that would make him happy, noting the disturbing times and the fact that most of the difficult music he conducted was distressing. Olin Downes, writing for *The New York Times, described Rounds* as "admirably fashioned, joyous and vernal."

Diamond taught in Italy as a Fulbright Professor at the

University of Rome in 1951 and made his home in Florence from 1953 to 1965, returning to the United States only three times during that period. He came back for good in 1965, chairing the composition department at the Manhattan School of Music for the next two years. Even though he has taught at a variety of schools in Europe and America since then (including stints with SUNY Buffalo and the Juilliard School), Diamond has resided in Rochester, New York from 1967 onward. He is a creative force that the musical world has come to rely on, the embodiment of stability and challenge. His music shows a gift for lyricism, usually tinged with romanticism—sometimes intense and severe, always passionate and well crafted.

Orchestral
Rounds for String Orchestra
what to buy: [*David Diamond: Vol. Five*; Gerard Schwarz, cond.; Seattle Symphony Orchestra] (Delos 3189) ♪ ♪ ♪ ♪

The melodies in *Rounds* suggest American folk music, even though they are completely original. The composer himself describes them as "the essence of a style that must have been absorbed by osmosis." The set is rounded out by other Diamond works, including the *Adagio* from Symphony no. 11, *Concert Piece* for Orchestra, *Concert Piece* for Flute and Harp, and *Elegy in Memory of Maurice Ravel.* Schwarz is doing a whole series of Diamond albums for Delos (five volumes so far), and all are marvelous.

Chamber
various works
what to buy: [*David Diamond: Chamber Works*; William Black, piano; Robert McDuffie, violin; Lawrence Sobol, clarinet; Linda Moss, viola; Louise Schulman, viola; Timothy Eddy, cello; Fred Sherry, cello; Lucy Shelton, soprano] (New World 80508) ♪ ♪ ♪ ♪₆

This is a fine way to wade into Diamond's chamber music. The CD is a reissue of an earlier Grenadilla disc and contains the two Sonatas for Violin and Piano, some of the composer's fifty-two Preludes and Fugues for piano, the Quintet for Clarinet, Two Violas, and Two Cellos, and *Vocalises* for Soprano and Viola. With its consistently high level of performance, this disc is certainly one you should own.

influences: Howard Hanson, Walter Piston, Roger

Sessions, Vincent Persichetti

Frank Retzel

Vincent d'Indy
Born Paul Marie Théodore d'Indy, March 27, 1851, in Paris, France. Died December 2, 1931, in Paris, France.

period: Romantic

Known today for his *Symphony on a French Mountain Air,* Vincent d'Indy was also France's most outspoken disciple of Richard Wagner's music and a respected pedagogue who helped co-found the famous Schola Cantorum. In addition, César Franck's current reputation as an important musician, composer, and teacher reflects the public relations work undertaken on his behalf by d'Indy, his biographer and former pupil.

As the scion of a noble French household that could trace its roots back to Henri IV, d'Indy endured and was shaped by a rigorous upbringing that included strong doses of military-style discipline and a moral code that brooked few gray areas. His adherence to these qualities did not endear him to many but did win d'Indy a tempered respect from the French musical community, while his well-crafted and -organized scores attracted their own set of admirers. The wealth of his family served to insulate him from the struggles of day-to-day living; he worked brief stints as a theater musician during the early 1870s, more to get a feel for how music functioned from a practical, orchestral sense than from any need to generate income.

He had already garnered a modest reputation as a piano prodigy and (after his exposure to Hector Berlioz's classic treatise, the *Grand traité d'instrumentation et d'orchestration modernes,* in 1867) composed a number of small-scale scores by the time he met Henri Duparc in 1869. It was through Duparc that d'Indy became aware of Richard Wagner's musical theories, concepts that would continue to prove attractive for the balance of his life. The Franco-Prussian War broke out a year later, and d'Indy, along with Duparc, Camille Saint-Saëns, and a number of other Paris-based composers, joined in the defense of the city. When hostilities ceased the following year, the young musician leaped back into the cultural fray, becoming one of the initial members of the Société Nationale de Musique, a group dedicated to the encouragement and promotion of contemporary French music. There, along with Saint-Saëns, Georges Bizet,

Charles-Marie Widor, and other like-minded souls, d'Indy took part in a number of concerts that helped invigorate and reclaim a music scene whose sense of identity was being threatened by the grand-opera gestures of Gioacchino Rossini and Giacomo Meyerbeer.

D'Indy first met Franck in 1872, showing the master organist a piano quartet that met with the devastating response, "The work is not finished; in fact, you really know nothing whatever." However, Franck soon invited the young composer to enroll in his classes at the Paris Conservatoire. There d'Indy took lessons in counterpoint, fugue, and composition and was further exposed to the harmonic daring of Wagner and Franz Liszt. He became so enamored of Wagner's ideas that he made the trek to Bayreuth to see the initial production of *The Ring*. But it was *Parsifal*, the work that most fully demonstrated Wagner's palette of exquisite orchestral textures, that made the greatest impression on him after he heard a performance of that opera in 1882.

While the avowed aim of the Société Nationale de Musique was the advancement of French music, much of d'Indy's oeuvre has a Germanic flavor that stems as much from his love of Wagner's music as from the teachings of Franck, which stressed a cyclical structure and the values found in Johann Sebastian Bach's works. This curious blend of progressive and conservative values helped form d'Indy's musical priorities and explains why in 1894, six years after Franck's death, he ended up cofounding the Schola Cantorum with the choral director Charles Bordes and the organist Alexandre Guilmant.

By exploring the music of the past (Bach, Palestrina, and Gregorian chant) while seeing to it that the composers of the future had a thorough grounding in counterpoint, d'Indy and his cohorts hoped to provide a viable alternative to the education offered at the Paris Conservatoire. By 1905, however, instruction at the Schola Cantorum had become even more orthodox than at either the Paris Conservatoire or the Société Nationale de Musique. It was during his years at the school that d'Indy wrote the majority of works for which he is best known today. The most familiar of these is his *Symphonie sur un chant montagnard français* (Symphony on a French mountain air) from 1886, but *Fervall*, the Wagner-influenced opera of 1895, his Symphony no. 2 in B-flat Major from 1902, and a handful of surprisingly intense chamber works all have their admirers.

D'Indy was a prolific writer, creating biographies of

Franck and Beethoven in addition to a treatise on *Parsifal* and the scandalously anti-Semitic *Cours de composition musicale*, where he espoused the viewpoint that Jewish composers only borrowed musical ideas from the countries in which they lived and possessed no originality when it came to composition. By the end of his life, the man who began his career in search of new, more creative ways of looking at music had morphed into a conservative, denying the validity of modern works by Maurice Ravel and Claude Debussy even as he increasingly pursued his interests in folksong arrangements and promoting the veneration of Franck and Wagner.

Orchestral
Symphonie sur un chant montagnard français (Symphony on a French mountain air) for Piano and Orchestra, op. 25
what to buy: [*French Music for Piano and Orchestra*; Antonio de Almeida, piano; François-Joël Thiollier, cond.; National Symphony Orchestra of Ireland] (Naxos 8.550754) ♪ ♪ ♪

A meshing of symphonic and concerto forms, d'Indy's *Symphony on a French Mountain Air* is an admirable construction based on the folksongs he originally heard in the mountainous region where his family estates were located and where he spent many of his summers. As part of an interesting, well-chosen, pleasantly performed and recorded sampler that also contains Franck's *Symphonic Variations* and Gabriel Fauré's orchestral *Ballade*, this work receives a worthy performance that is as good as it needs to be without gussying it up into something it isn't.

worth searhing for: [*Pierre Monteux Edition, Vol. 9*; Maxim Schapiro, piano; Pierre Monteux, cond.; San Francisco Symphony Orchestra] (RCA Victor Gold Seal 61888) ♪ ♪ ♪

Monteux's conducting of this work had the composer's blessing, and the results have a "time window" feel, creating an aural snapshot of the recording and playing techniques of the early twentieth century. Ditto for the performances of d'Indy's Symphony no. 2 and the prelude to his Wagner-esque opera *Fervaal* that accompany this benchmark recording.

Chamber
String Quartet no. 2 in E Major, op. 45

what to buy: [Kodály Quartet] (Marco Polo 8.223140)
♪ ♪ ♪ ♪

While the charms of d'Indy's *Symphony on a French Mountain Air* are relatively durable, his second string quartet has an intensity that may ultimately be more rewarding. Written in 1890, at the same time he was working on *Fervaal,* this score pays homage to Beethoven's later quartets more than to either Franck's cyclical design or Wagner's grandiose tonal palette. The Kodály Quartet gives inspired readings of this and d'Indy's op. 35 quartet, making a solid case for their inclusion in current chamber music programs.

influences: César Franck, Guillaume Lekeu, Déodat de Séverac, Albert Roussel, Albéric Magnard

Garaud MacTaggart

Ernst von Dohnányi

Born Ernö Dohnányi, July 27, 1877, in Pozsony (Bratislava), Hungary. Died February 9, 1960, in New York City, NY

period: Romantic

Twinkle, Twinkle, Little Star lies at the heart of a most delightful work for piano and orchestra, Dohnányi's *Variations on a Nursery Song.* While this piece remains the composer's most frequently performed composition, there is more muscle to his music and value to his role in history than that score might lead some to believe. No less a judge of musical worth than Johannes Brahms praised some of Dohnányi's early chamber works (in particular, the Quintet no. 1 for Piano and Strings) while Béla Bartók and Zoltán Kodály owed many performances of their early compositions to his fervent advocacy.

Dohnányi attended the Royal Academy of Music in Budapest, studying piano and composition before graduating in 1897. His first notable composition, the Quintet no. 1 in C Minor for Piano and Strings of 1895, dates from his student years, and his career path seemed to lead toward a dual life as a composer and piano virtuoso. In 1898, his first international concert (as soloist in Beethoven's fourth piano concerto) received rave reviews from British critics and his Concerto no. 1 in E Minor for Piano and Orchestra won a substantial monetary prize from the Bösendorfer piano firm in 1899. Dohnányi embarked on his first tour of the United States in 1900 and, after playing a few more European concert dates, returned to the U.S. later that year. The next time

Alfred Deller:

The terms "alto" and "countertenor," despite their technical differences, are almost synonymous (in modern day usage) with use of the high male voice; in that regard, "alto" generally refers to a boy's singing voice while "countertenor" implies that an adult vocalist is producing the sound. Many of the great Baroque and Renaissance-era composers wrote music featuring the countertenor, but for some reason the practice died out in the nineteenth century. With the groundbreaking performances of harpsichordist Wanda Landowska (her first harpsichord recital was in 1903), the efforts of scholar/instrument-maker Arnold Dolmetsch (his book on the interpretation of Baroque music was published in 1915), and the enthusiasm they helped generate amongst a relatively small but vociferous band of musicians, the stage was set for Alfred Deller and the return of the countertenor in the late 1940s and early 1950s.

Deller was discovered singing in the choir at Canterbury Cathedral in 1943 by Michael Tippett, a young composer and conductor who was active in the attempt to revive the music of Henry Purcell (himself a countertenor). After hearing Deller's clear, vibrato-less voice, Tippet later recalled that "the centuries rolled back" and he ended up convincing the chorister to sing in an upcoming concert where Johann Sebastian Bach's *Magnificat* was to be presented, and then in another program which featured a performance of Purcell's great work from 1692, the *Ode for St. Cecilia's Day.* Their 1956 recording of the Purcell score (Vanguard Omega Classics 8116) is a marvelous document, even if it was laid down more than ten years after the initial performance by Deller and Tippett.

Deller shifted his base of operations to London's St. Paul's Cathedral in 1947, and moonlighted as a recitalist specializing in Elizabethan-era songs in particular and English folk songs in general. For the latter category he usually teamed up with lutenist Desmond Dupré, and a fine compilation of their work together is *The Three Ravens: Elizabethan Folk and Minstrel Songs* (Vanguard Omega Classics 8104), with most of the performances dating from 1955.

In 1950, Deller founded one of the most honored ensembles performing Baroque and Renaissance music, the Deller Consort. While this group engaged in many performances of Purcell, the lute songs of John Dowland also formed a large portion of their concert repertoire. *Ayres and Lute Lessons* (Harmonia Mundi France 1901076) and *Awake Sweet Love* (Vanguard Omega Classics 8112) are fine examples of this ensemble's way with Dowland's work.

William Gerard

he would play concerts in the United States was during the 1920–1921 season, following that up with repeat visits every year between 1923 and 1928.

His concertizing didn't stop even after he accepted a position with the piano faculty of the Berlin Hochschule für Musik in 1905. It was during his time at the Hochschule that Dohnányi composed his impressive Quintet no. 2 in E-flat Minor and the work for which he is best known today, the *Variationen über ein Kinderlied (Variations on a Nursery Song)* for Piano and Orchestra. After ten years there, however, Dohnányi resigned from the school so that he could return to Budapest, which then became his new base of operations for touring. He put on a number of concerts and also taught piano before being made President and Director of Budapest's Philharmonic Orchestra Society in 1918 and, a year later, Associate Director of the Royal Academy of Music— postings which potentially enabled him to control much of Hungary's musical life and set its course for the future. But this last position proved to be brief, when a new government took power later in 1919 and replaced Dohnányi with a malleable party hack. Still, Dohnányi was able to effect a number of changes from his position with the Philharmonic Orchestra Society (which he would hold until 1944), conducting concerts featuring compositions created by his countrymen (Béla Bartók and Zoltán Kodály among them) in addition to showcasing seldom-played works by major composers.

He was reinstated as a professor at the Academy in 1928, was made General Music Director of Hungarian Radio in 1931, and finally put back in charge of the Academy in 1934. These years of work as an administrator were vitally important to Hungary's cultural life, but they put a severe crimp in Dohnányi's time for composing. Other than a few choral works, a short orchestral work (*Szimfonikus percek [Symphonic Minutes]*), and a sextet for piano, clarinet, horn, and strings, he wrote nothing until after 1941, when he was relieved of his duties at the Academy due to his refusal to follow the anti-Semitic dictates of the Hungarian government at that time. Until 1949, when he finally settled in Tallahassee, Florida, Dohnányi would be labeled a Nazi sympathizer by his enemies for moving to Austria in 1944, and defended by his friends who were aware of the moral high ground he occupied during 1941. His opportunities to concertize during this period were few, and it was only after the threat of being deported back to Communist-ruled Hungary materialized that Dohnányi opted to flee, a decision that took him to Switzerland, Great Britain, Argentina, and, finally, the United States.

In September 1949 he arrived at Florida State University in Tallahassee, where he had been recruited to the teaching staff as pianist and composer-in-residence. He arrived with his most recent works (his second symphony, a second piano concerto, and a number of short piano pieces), and during the course of his years at the school wrote his second violin concerto, the *Concertino* for Harp

and Chamber Orchestra, a setting of the *Stabat Mater,* and his *American Rhapsody,* all orchestral works which heralded back to his glory years at the beginning of the twentieth century. Although his compositional orientation was dated, his pianistic skills were still in splendid form. In January, 1960, Dohnányi flew to New York City where he was to record some Beethoven piano sonatas and a few of his own works for Everest Records. Despite suffering from the first stages of influenza, he managed to complete the sessions for the project on February 5. He suffered a series of massive heart attacks at the hotel where he was staying and died four days later.

Orchestral
Variations on a Nursery Song for Piano and Orchestra, op. 25
what to buy: [Earl Wild, piano; Christoph von Dohnányi, cond.; New Philharmonia Orchestra] (Chesky 13) ♪ ♪ ♪ ♪⅜

Certainly bloodlines would seem to count for something here, as the grandson of the composer directs a wonderfully fluid performance from the orchestra in their role as accompanist for Wild's lively, vivid playing. The forces apply the same approach to Dohnányi's orchestral arrangement of his *Capriccio* in F Minor for Piano, and Piotr Tchaikovsky's first piano concerto, both of which complete the program of this disc.

what to buy next: [Julius Katchen, piano; Georg Solti, cond.; London Symphony Orchestra] (London 448604) ♪ ♪ ♪ ♪

Katchen was a fine pianist and one too little-known today. His performances of Dohnányi's biggest hit have always sparkled without being saccharine, and this version with Solti (one of the composer's former students) holds true to form. Included as part of an album devoted to a pair of Sergei Rachmaninoff's works for piano and orchestra (the second piano concerto and the *Rhapsody on a Theme of Paganini*), there is almost a temptation to overlook Katchen's take on this piece, and that would be a mistake.

worth searhing for: [Ernö von Dohnányi, piano; Adrian Boult, cond.; Royal Philharmonic Orchestra] (EMI Studio 63183) ♪ ♪ ♪⅜

Dohnányi's reputation as a virtuoso pianist had already been in place for fifty years when Boult and he entered into the studio to record this work in 1956. The fact that he was still able to hold his own in this delightful piece after so many decades is a tribute to focus and good genes. Malcolm Sargent leads the RPO in the accompanying version of the composer's Suite for Orchestra, op. 19.

Chamber
Quintet no. 2 in E-flat Minor for Piano and Strings, op. 26
what to buy: [Erno Szegedi, piano; Tátrai String Quartet, ensemble] (Hungaroton 11624) ♪ ♪ ♪ ♪

It is rare that the Tátrai String Quartet has ever done anything associated with Hungarian music which was not of the highest quality. That holds true here, especially in the finale of the quintet, which is almost totally in fugue. Szegedi is an interesting pianist whose (at times) edgy drive is firmly matched with that of the quartet. Also included on this disc is Dohnányi's expressive Sextet in C Major, op. 37, with Béla Kovács (clarinet) and Ferenc Tarjáni (horn) taking the place of the pianist.

what to buy next: [*The Two Piano Quintets*; Roscoe Martin, piano; Vanbrugh String Quartet, ensemble] (ASV 915) ♪ ♪ ♪ ♪

This disc is quite well played and has the added bonus of the work which caused Brahms to notice the young composer, Dohnányi's first piano quintet. The latter is a gracious, flowing piece that, while lacking the substance of the E-flat Minor quintet, is still a fine bit of youthful writing. Martin's turn in a lovely solo piano work from 1913, the *Suite in the Olden Style*, is quite pleasant.

influences: Johannes Brahms, Richard Strauss

Ellen Kokko

Gaetano Donizetti
Born Domenico Gaetano Maria Donizetti, November 29, 1797, in Bergamo, Italy. Died April 8, 1848, in Bergamo, Italy.

period: Romantic

Donizetti was the George Gershwin, Richard Rodgers, or Andrew Lloyd Webber of his day, whipping off more than seventy operas from 1818 to 1843, many of them still quite popular with audiences. One of those operas,

Lucia di Lammermoor, was at the forefront of the *bel canto* performance renaissance led by soprano Joan Sutherland and her husband, conductor Richard Bonynge, during the latter half of the twentieth century.

Realizing that Donizetti was the link between the unruffled classicism of Gioachino Rossini and the white-hot romanticism of Giuseppe Verdi helps identify his place in history. He followed Rossini in the crafting of *bel canto* ("beautiful singing") music, placing an emphasis on vocal line and high coloratura notes suspended in the air like pearls hung on a necklace, without forsaking the human element in royal personages or heroic figures. This set the stage for the *verismo* phenomenon (with its passionate and melodramatic portrayal of common people and events), which Verdi and others plunged into, moving opera into the twentieth century on waves of human emotion. But readers should not write off Donizetti as simply a link in the chain of Italian opera. Rather, see him for what he was: a prolific composer who hit high notes of his own in several of his works.

Donizetti was the fifth of six siblings whose father managed the monte di pieta, or municipal pawnshop. Early on, his talents were noted and he was admitted to the music academy in Bergamo, the place where he began his initial training as a choirboy in 1806. There Donizetti showed such promise that his teacher, Johannes Simon Mayr (a respected opera composer and pedagogue of the day), underwrote his transfer to another school, this time in the more cosmopolitan Bologna, where he studied counterpoint and attempted his first operas. He returned to Bergamo in 1817 and, a year later, produced *Enrico di Borgogna* and *Una folia*, neither of which made much of an impact with audiences or the impresario employing him at the time. His first real success didn't occur until early in 1822, when Mayr turned over one of his own commissions (from a theater in Rome) to Donizetti, with the resultant *Zoraida di Granata* leading to a contract offer for more work, this time for a theater in Naples. During these years the handsome and personable composer also acquired the syphilis which would eventually kill him.

Donizetti's work habits were impeccable and allowed him to churn out an astonishing number of operas. From 1822 to 1830 he finished at least twenty-three of them, the last being his first claim to operatic immortality, *Anna Bolena*. With this work, Donizetti broadened the markets in which his operas were presented; performances of it were scheduled in Paris and London in addition to other opera houses around Italy. Two years later, he took advantage of his increased salability and broke the contract which had bound him to the theater in Naples, so that he could offer his skills to an ever-widening audience. Things appeared to be going well for him at this point. He had found and married the love of his life (Virginia Vasseli) in 1828 and a fair number of his operas (specifically *L'elisir d'amore* from 1832 and *Lucia di Lammermoor* from 1835) were generating cash flow. This changed in 1837, when his wife died in childbirth and the composer was emotionally devastated. His relationship with Naples also changed as well. When his wife was alive and Neapolitan theaters resounded to the acclaim of his operas, life was relatively good. Now, with the death of his wife, the disappointment he felt over not being approved as director of the Naples Conservatory, and the censorship of his opera *Poliuto* (which depicted a saint's martyrdom on stage), the ties that bound him to the city were being severed.

So in 1838 he moved on to Paris, then an operatic hotbed for Italian composers like Verdi and Vincenzo Bellini as much as for those of any other nationality. There he worked with a number of talented librettists and created some of his most popular works, among them *La fille du régiment* and *Don Pasquale*. He was a star, but in 1843, while working on his final opera, *Dom Sébastien, roi de Portugal,* he had constant headaches and lapses in awareness. Thus began his descent into the final stages of syphilis. After spending more than a year in a sanitarium, Donizetti, by now paralyzed and unable to speak, was moved by his family back to Bergamo, where he finally died.

Vocal
Lucia di Lammermoor
what to buy: [Joan Sutherland, soprano; Luciano Pavarotti, tenor; Ryland Davies, tenor; Sherill Milnes, baritone; Nicolai Ghiairov, bass; Richard Bonynge, cond.; Royal Opera House Orchestra, Covent Garden; Royal Opera House Chorus, Covent Garden] (London 410193) ♪♪♪♪♪

Sutherland's phenomenal technique is the epitome of the entire bel canto style: legato, pinpoint high notes, and purity of tone. Her pairings with Pavarotti are legendary, and the recorded sound is much easier on the ears than that afforded by the Callas recording (see below).

what to buy next: [Maria Callas, soprano; Luisa Villa,

mezzo-soprano; Giuseppe di Stefano, tenor; Giuseppe Zampieri, tenor; Mario Carlin, tenor, Rolando Panerai, baritone; Nicola Zaccaria, bass; Herbert von Karajan, cond.; Berlin RIAS Symphony Orchestra; La Scala Chorus] (EMI Classics 66441) ♪♪♪♪♪

This recording marks one of the rare times when personal choice and operatic history combine: Maria Callas reinvented the bel canto tradition in the mid-twentieth century. She rescued works from obscurity by the force of her technical capacity married to a ferocious dramatic intensity (in the voice as well as on stage). As Lucia, she inhabits the character fully, and this "live" version from 1955 reflects the best of the best despite some inadequate sonics.

L'elisir d'amore
what to buy: [Joan Sutherland, soprano; Maria Casula, soprano; Luciano Pavarotti, tenor; Dominic Cossa, baritone; Spiro Maias, bass; Richard Bonynge, cond.; English Chamber Orchestra; Ambrosian Opera Chorus] (London 414461) ♪♪♪♪♪

Sutherland and Pavarotti carry the day in this warm, bumptious comedy, the first of Donizetti's great successes in Paris.

Don Pasquale
worth searhing for: [Beverly Sills, soprano; Alfredo Kraus, tenor; Alan Titus, baritone; Donald Gramm, bass-baritone; Sarah Caldwell, cond.; London Symphony Orchestra; Ambrosian Opera Chorus] (EMI Classics 66030) ♪♪♪♪⅛

This buoyant comedy nestles beautifully in the voices. Sills made her career in this repertoire, and Kraus remains one of the twentieth century's finest lyric tenors—shut out of the *Three Tenors* phenomenon allegedly because of a Luciano Pavarotti snit.

Anna Bolena
what to buy: [Maria Callas, soprano; Giulietta Simionato, mezzo-soprano; Gabriella Carturan, mezzo-soprano; Gianni Raimondi, tenor; Luigi Rumbo, tenor; Nicola Rossi-Lemeni, bass; Plinio Clabassi, bass; Gianandrea Gavazzesi, cond.; La Scala Theatre Orchestra, La Scala Theatre Chorus] (EMI Classics 66471) ♪♪♪♪⅛

Here is another strong dramatic interpretation by Maria Callas, recorded during a 1957 performance at La Scala, the site of so many of her triumphs. This was the production that essentially re-introduced *Anna Bolena* to the repertoire. The sound is a bit rough in spots, but Callas is such an overwhelming personality and the cast offers such fine support that little else need be said.

what to buy next: [Beverly Sills, soprano; Shirley Verrett, mezzo-soprano; Patricia Kern, mezzo-soprano; Stuart Burrows, tenor; Robert Tear, tenor; Paul Plishka, bass; Robert Lloyd, bass; Julius Rudel, cond.; London Symphony Orchestra; John Alldis Chorus] (Deutsche Grammophon 465957) ♪♪♪♪

Sills was quite an actress in her own right, and if her characterization of Anna Bolena lacks the last bit of pathos wrung out of the role by Callas, her singing is still glorious, and the bedrock of this production. Recorded in 1972, the sound quality benefits from Deutsche Grammophon's splendid remastering. The other singers, especially Verrett (as Giovanna/Jane Seymour) and Plishka (as Enrico/Henry VIII), add solid support to Sills's high-flying soprano.

influences: Vincenzo Bellini, Gioachino Rossini, Giuseppe Verdi

Michael H. Margolin

John Dowland

Born in London, England, 1563. Died in London, England, in 1626.

period: Renaissance

Celebrated in his day as a great lutenist with a magnificent singing voice, Dowland was also a remarkable composer whose songs are a perfect blend of melody, form, and noble, sincere sentiment. Most, but not all, of the lute pieces bearing his name appear to be derived from arrangements of his songs and consort pieces with which he may or may not have had anything to do.

Although neither Dowland's place or year of birth is known with certainty, he must have received a fairly thorough musical education in order to serve as a musician for the British ambassador to France. While in Paris, he converted to Catholicism, although that seems to have been a matter of convenience rather than deep commitment. When he returned to England around 1584, Dowland attended Oxford University, receiving his degree in music in 1588. By that time he was already

Plácido Domingo:
Domingo's grasp of the standard repertoire is surprisingly broad, though he has rarely been heard in more adventuresome twentieth century material. He seems most comfortable with nineteenth century Italian operas, but has also made inroads into Richard Wagner's canon and assayed parts in zarzuelas, the Spanish equivalent to light opera. The impressive thirty-two-disc set *Plácido Domingo: 30 Years with EMI* (EMI Classics 67449) is a treasure chest containing some of the tenor's finest performances, including his collaborations with the conductor Ricardo Muti that yielded what may arguably be the best recordings of Giacomo Puccini's *Tosca* and Giuseppe Verdi's *Otello* and *Aïda* that Domingo has ever taken part in.

Since he has recorded many operas more than once, however, there are still alternate performances of these works that contain much fine singing, including the title role with which Domingo is most closely associated, Verdi's *Otello*. The tenor has had an extremely fruitful history of working with director James Levine, and their recording of *Otello* (RCA Victor Red Seal 39501) is very good indeed. Domingo's affinity for Verdi's oeuvre is also revealed in the performance of *Aïda* that he recorded opposite Leontyne Price with Erich Leinsdorf conducting (RCA Victor Red Seal 39498). Otherwise, there are a number of Verdi arias present on *Bravo Domingo* (Deutsche Grammophon 459352), a two-disc "greatest" set that also contains famous arias from Puccini (*Nessun Dorma*) and Ruggero Leoncavallo (*Vesti la giubba*) along with examples of Domingo's refreshing advocacy of Hispanic fare by Ernesto Lara (*Granada*), Juan Carlos Cobian (*Nostalgias*), and Carlos Gardel (*El dia que me queiras*). Another of Domingo's more recent recordings displays him within the context of work by another of his favorite composers, Richard Wagner (*Wagner: Love Duets*, EMI Classics 57004). This partnership with soprano Deborah Voigt yields superb renditions of duets from *Siegfried* and *Tristan und Isolde*.

In addition to being an integral part of the Three Tenors phenomenon (along with Luciano Pavarotti and José Carreras), Domingo presently shoulders administrative burdens as the Artistic Director of both the Washington Opera and the Los Angeles Music Center Opera as well as overseeing Operalia, the vocal competition that he founded in 1993. Domingo has also embraced the art of conducting, a discipline he first learned at the Mexico City Conservatory in his youth before eventually seeking further instruction from Igor Markevitch and Hans Swarowsky. Admirers wishing to hear how well he measures up to other conductors have only a few discs available for judging, including a program of popular works by Piotr Ilyich Tchaikovsky (Seraphim 73297); a rendition of Joaquín Rodrigo's *Concierto de Aranjuez* with guitarist Manuel Barrueco (EMI Classics 56175); and a recital of Giacomo Puccini arias sung by José Cura (Erato 18838), a former prize winner at Operalia.

Ellen Kokko

acclaimed in certain quarters for the quality of his songs and the excellence of his lute playing, but his undeniable technical skills were not always enough to compensate for his prickly behavior and it was quite possibly his temperament that prevented him from becoming a lutenist in the royal household, despite his repeated applications.

There were still members of the ruling class more than willing to hire Dowland, however, and he spent most of the next 20 years wandering between the courts of Europe and winning praise from a number of contemporary sources. In 1595, while he was serving in Florence, Italy, Dowland ended up in the company of some English expatriate papists who were attempting to hatch a coup against Queen Elizabeth. It seems that he panicked when hearing of the plot and sought to distance himself from it and them by writing a note to one of the queen's privy councilors (Sir Robert Cecil) in which he described the conspiracy and the people involved. Three years later Dowland began a relatively long stint with King Christian IV of Denmark, remaining with him (except for occasional trips back to England) until 1603. With Elizabeth's death that year, the composer went back to England in yet another futile attempt at becoming a court lutenist, dedicating his *Lachrimae* to the new queen (Christian IV's sister Anne). He went back to Denmark and rejoined the royal household there before finally being dismissed in 1606. Dowland's next position was with Lord Walden, whom he served from 1609 until 1612 when he finally became a court lutenist for King James I. He then remained in London until his death.

There is a timelessness about the greatest art, and this applies to Dowland's songs. Though the language of 16th and 17th century England sounds archaic to our ears, Dowland's music is so fresh and vital that it could have been written yesterday. So many are the "hooks" in the melodies of his best songs that it seems that what makes a hit song today is not essentially different from what made a song popular four centuries ago. Dowland's musical temperament is basically melancholy and he is not one for empty-headed ditties. Though he could be merry, his feelings always run deep.

Of the 87 printed songs credited to Dowland, 84 appeared in four volumes, the three *Bookes of Songes or Ayres* and *A Pilgrim's Solace*, dating from 1597, 1600, 1603, and 1612 respectively. Dowland's son Robert was also a fine musician, and his collection *Musical Banquet* contains three more songs by the senior Dowland. Some of the better-known songs include *Come again, sweet love, Fine knacks for ladies, Flow my tears, In darkness let me dwell* and *Sweet, stay awhile*. Dowland's many solo lute pieces are often transcribed so that other instrumental combinations too may share in this beautiful music.

Chamber
Lachrimae, or Seaven Teares for Five Viols and Lute
what to buy: [*Lachrimae*; Peter Holman, cond.; Paul O'Dette, lute; The Parley of Instruments, ensemble] (Hyperion 66637) ♪ ♪ ♪ ♪♪

The original-instrument performances of Holman and his associates have more than authenticity in their favor. The playing is especially sensitive to the emotional core of these wonderful works, revelatory even if you have heard other versions.

various pieces for lute
what to buy: [*The Complete Lute Works, Vols. 1-5*; Paul O'Dette, lute] (Harmonia Mundi France 2907160) ♪ ♪ ♪ ♪♪

Probably every lutenist has been tempted by Dowland's rich body of work. Although there are hardly any bad performances among the many lute recordings, the engineering can make a crucial difference. Whether you choose the complete set or the five volumes issued separately (Harmonia Mundi 907160 - 907164), be assured that O'Dette's well-recorded efforts are among the best to be had. Also be aware however, that, as O'Dette states in his liner notes, "It is possible that none of the pieces on these CDs were conceived by Dowland as lute solos in their present form."

what to buy next: [*A Varietie of Lute Lessons*; Nigel North, lute] (Linn 97) ♪ ♪ ♪ ♪

North's performances of Dowland miscellany fill up a third of this disc, are well considered, and benefit from Linn Records' typically excellent engineering.

Vocals
various songs
what to buy: [*English Folksongs and Lute Songs*; Andreas Scholl, countertenor; Andreas Martin, lute] (Harmonia Mundi 901603) ♪ ♪ ♪ ♪♪

Scholl's voice is beautiful and his choice of material in this recital showcases it to perfection. Martin's playing is fluid, especially in the solo *The Lady Russell's Paven*. Over half the program is devoted to Dowland, but the three songs by Thomas Campion and a handful of "anonymous" and "traditional" tunes make perfect disc mates.

[*The English Orpheus*; Emma Kirkby, soprano; Anthony Rooley, lute] (Virgin Classics Veritas 59521) ♪ ♪ ♪ ♪♭

When it comes to Dowland's sensitive verse settings, a superb soprano is better than a tenor masquerading as a countertenor. Kirkby certainly has all the right credentials, having earned her outstanding reputation for early-music artistry, and Rooley is one of the finest lutenists in the world today. Their all-Dowland recital is a joy.

what to buy next: [*O sweet love*; Daniel Taylor, countertenor; Stephen Stubbs, lute; Susie Napper, viola da gamba; Margaret Little, viola da gamba] (Atma2207) ♪ ♪ ♪ ♪

Taylor is a magnificent singer with a tonal quality that should send shivers down the backs of aficionados. The album is wonderful on all counts, featuring lovely works by William Byrd and Dowland. Taylor sings only three of Dowland's songs, although his version of *Come again, sweet love* is one of the best available. There are four Dowland instrumental works, two for lute and two for viola da gamba.

[*Come again, sweet love*; Alfred Deller, countertenor; Robert Spencer, lute; Consort of Six, ensemble] (Harmonia Mundi 790245) ♪ ♪ ♪ ♪♭

Deller did much to bring this repertoire to light with his recordings. There may be "better" voices among those who have followed this trailblazer, but it is always instructive to listen to the "old masters" whose scholarly and musical aptitudes broke ground for the future. This is a fine compendium of lute songs drawn from Deller's 1950s recordings. Despite its age, it has a great sonic presence to match the heartfelt performances.

[*"The dark is my delight" and other 16th-century lute songs*; Brian Asawa, countertenor; David Tayler, lute] (RCA Victor Red Seal 68818) ♪ ♪ ♪ ♪♭

Asawa is a classy countertenor although there are some who might find his "warble" a bit over the top compared with the "purer, cleaner" tones of Andreas Scholl and Daniel Taylor. Still, he does deserve a listen, especially by those interested in further exploring Dowland's repertoire. Once again, Thomas Campion and "anonymous" songs provide the filler.

[*Flow My Teares*; Mikael Samuelson, Freddie Wadling, vocalists; Lars Åkerlund, Hållbus Totte Mattson, Roger

Tallroth, guitars; Hållbus Totte Mattson, lute, theorbo, bouzouki; Roger Tallroth, bouzouki; Forge Players, ensemble] (Atrium 22109) ♪ ♪ ♪♭

The Forge Players are five Swedish musicians (two violins, two violas, one cello) whose approach to these exquisite songs feels authentic even though a barely hidden sense of academic defiance lifts their playing into the 21st century. Split between vocal and instrumental renderings, this album is not for the faint of heart, since the sung portions of the recital are given to rock singers whose rough hewn yet professional treatment of the lyrics are more often gritty and curiously invigorating than reverent.

influences: William Byrd, Thomas Campion, Henry Purcell

Gerald Brennan and Garaud MacTaggart

Paul Dukas

Born Paul Abraham Dukas, October 1, 1865, in Paris, France. Died May 17, 1935, in Paris France.

period: Romantic/Twentieth century

Dukas would be all but forgotten today if not for Mickey Mouse! Walt Disney's movie *Fantasia* featured Mickey as *The Sorcerer's Apprentice,* who, to the accompaniment of Leopold Stokowski and his orchestra, almost re-creates the biblical Flood. A highly self-critical individual, Dukas destroyed most of his music before his death.

Paul Dukas lived and worked his entire life in the city of Paris. His early years showed much promise, and he was considered a rising musical star at the Paris Conservatoire, where he studied composition, piano, and harmony (or musical theory). Following the tradition of other European conservatories, the school awarded prizes rather than degrees, and Dukas won first prize for counterpoint and fugue in 1886. He came very close to winning the coveted *Prix de Rome* two years later for a cantata named *Velléda* but was declared runner-up. This may have contributed to Dukas's almost pathological self-doubt. From this time forward he composed very sparingly and before his death destroyed many works he deemed unworthy.

Dukas's career took a different turn as he immersed himself in education, criticism, and musicology. Along with

Camille Saint-Saëns, he edited and revised the music of the eighteenth-century French composer Jean Philippe Rameau, developing many of the tools of early-manuscript research used by later generations.

Two major works stand out as his most significant: the 1897 symphonic scherzo *L'Apprenti sorcier,* based on a poem by Goethe; and the fanfare from the 1912 ballet *La Péri,* which is now a standard feature of orchestral programming.

Orchestral
L'Apprenti sorcier (The Sorcerer's Apprentice)
what to buy: [James Levine, cond; Berlin Philharmonic Orchestra] (Deutsche Grammophon 419617) ♪ ♪ ♪ ♪

The major work on the album is the Symphony no. 3 in C Minor by Camille Saint-Saëns, but *L'Apprenti sorcier* is a fine bit of idiomatic filler. Dukas's score is afforded a crisp, clear reading, complete with more French nuances than one would normally expect from this orchestra—just the sort of thing to make the composer's music leap from the speakers.

what to buy next: [Leonard Slatkin, cond.; Orchestre National de France] (RCA Victor 68802) ♪ ♪ ♪ ♪

For listeners seeking to garner most of Dukas's important works at one fell swoop, this is your best bet. Slatkin leads the orchestra through fine if not consistently top-drawer performances of the composer's Symphony in C Major, *L'Apprenti sorcier,* and all of *La Péri,* including the fanfare.

La Péri for Orchestra
what to buy: [Yan Pascal Tortelier, cond; Ulster Orchestra] (Chandos 9225) ♪ ♪ ♪ ♪

Tortelier gives a wonderful reading, with clear orchestral sound and bright tempos. As a bonus you'll find his reading of *L'Apprenti sorcier* and two works by Emmanuel Chabrier: *España* and the *Suite pastorale.*

influences: Claude Debussy, Henri Duparc, Maurice Ravel

Dave Wagner

Marcel Dupré
Born May 3, 1886, in Rouen, France. Died May 30, 1971, in Meudon, France.

period: Twentieth century

A host of works featuring the organ make up the bulk of Marcel Dupré's compositional output, and it is upon these pieces that his reputation stands. Although his style was built around the tonal harmony and classic forms used by his teachers (Charles Marie Widor, Louis Vierne, and Alexandre Guilmant), Dupré expanded his viewpoint to include a more chromatic and polytonal harmonic language. Many of his pieces are now considered basic to the twentieth-century organ repertoire.

Dupré was born into a family of musicians—especially organists—and began studying music with his father at the age of seven. His prodigious talents quickly manifested themselves, and he was appointed to his first position as organist at St. Vivien at age twelve. Dupré entered the Paris Conservatoire in 1902 to study piano, organ, fugue, and composition. He demonstrated his growing musical mastery by winning first prizes in piano (1905), organ (1907), and fugue (1909); he was also awarded the *Prix de Rome* in 1914 for his cantata *Psyché.*

After leaving the conservatory in 1914, Dupré secured a position as organist at Notre Dame—substituting for Vierne—and engaged in a thorough study of J.S. Bach's organ oeuvre. In 1920 he became the first person to perform the complete organ works of Bach from memory, a feat he accomplished over the course of ten recitals. That December, he began an international concert career that would last for over fifty years and include over two thousand recitals. From 1926 to 1954, Dupré was professor of organ at the Paris Conservatoire, assuming the school's directorship from 1954 to 1957. In 1934 he succeeded Widor as organist at St. Sulpice, a position he maintained for the balance of his life.

Despite his stint in academia, Dupré took a practical approach to organ playing, evidenced by the various pedagogical texts he wrote during his career—including *Traité d'improvisation à l'orgue* (1925) and *Méthode d'orgue* (1927). Dupré was also skilled improviser, particularly in complicated contrapuntal structures, and this gave weight to his commentaries on the art of organ playing. As a side benefit, several of his compositions had their roots in the improvisatory process, particularly the *Symphonie-Passion* (op. 23) and *Le Chemin de la Croix* (op. 29).

Orchestral
various works

what to buy: [*The Organ Encyclopedia—Dupré: Works for Organ, Vol. 3: Complete Music for Organ and Orchestra*; Daniel Jay McKinley, organ; David Bowden, cond.; Columbus Indiana Philharmonic, orch.] (Naxos 8.553922) ♪ ♪ ♪ ♪ ♪

This marks the first time that all four of Dupré's early masterpieces for organ and orchestra (the Concerto for Organ in E Minor, op. 32; the Symphony for Organ and Orchestra in G Minor, op. 25; the *Cortège et Litanie;* and the *Poème Héroïque*) have appeared on one CD. The recording took place at the First Christian Church in Columbus, Indiana, with its fine Aeolian-Skinner organ of four manuals and eighty-one ranks, built in 1942. The performances are outstanding.

Chamber
various works

what to buy: [*Organ Music by Marcel Dupré*; John Scott, organ] (Hyperion 67047) ♪ ♪ ♪ ♪ ♪

Scott, one of today's great organists, performed these pieces on the Willis/Mander organ at St. Paul's Cathedral in London, where he has been director since 1985. The works in this recital include two of the opus 7 Preludes and Fugues, the *Esquisses,* op. 41; *Variations sur un vieux noël,* op. 20; and the Chorale and Fugue, op. 57. Scott performs these pieces in an exciting manner, taking into account the organ's characteristics and the reverberant acoustics of the church.

what to buy next: [*The Organ Encyclopedia—Dupré: Works for Organ, vol. 4*; Janette Fishell, organ] (Naxos 8.553919) ♪ ♪ ♪ ♪₈

Recorded on the fine French-influenced Casavant organ built in 1986 at St. George's Episcopal Church in Nashville, Tennessee, this disc vaults from Dupré's earliest organ works (the Three Preludes and Fugues, op. 7) to his last score (*Le Vitrail de St. Ouen,* op. 65), with some mid-period pieces tossed in for balance. All are performed by Fishell in the play-it-as-written style of which the composer would have approved.

worth searhing for: [*Dupré joue Dupré*; Marcel Dupré,

organ] (Philips 446648) ♪ ♪ ♪ ♪ ♪

In October 1965, Dupré made one of his last commercial recordings on the famous Cavaille-Coll organ (1890) at St. Ouen de Rouen. This instrument was very special to Dupré, since his father had been organist at St. Ouen de Rouen, and the organ had been dedicated by his teacher, Widor. Dupré chose to record his *Symphonie-Passion,* op. 23, and the Chorale and Fugue, op. 57 (both originally conceived as improvisations), as well as three short pieces: *Iste Confessor, In dulci jubilo,* and the Toccata on *Ave Maris Stella.* Aficionados of French organ music should not miss this recording.

influences: Maurice Duruflé, Charles Marie Widor, Jehan Alain

D. John Apple and Garaud MacTaggart

Maurice Duruflé

Born January 11, 1902, in Louviers, France. Died June 16, 1986, in Paris, France.

period: Twentieth century

Duruflé was one of the finest composer/organists of his generation, continuing the romantic tradition of his illustrious predecessors Cesar Franck and Louis Vierne rather than seeking the more exotic textures that appealed to his contemporary Olivier Messiaen.

Maurice Duruflé started his musical life when his father took him to the cathedral in Rouen, France, and enrolled him in the choir. There is little doubt that Duruflé's youthful participation in the musical and religious activities of the church had a profound effect on him. For one thing, this is where he began his lifelong fascination with Gregorian chant, whose modal harmonies were to have an important impact on Duruflé's mature compositions.

In 1919, at the age of seventeen, Duruflé moved to Paris, where he began preparing himself to take entrance exams at the world-famous Conservatoire. It was also in Paris that Duruflé studied with the two foremost living proponents of the French organ tradition, Charles Tournemire and Louis Vierne. After being accepted at the Conservatoire, Duruflé studied composition with Paul Dukas and won five first prizes in a series of competitions at the school, including awards for organ performance, accompaniment, and composition (for his *Prélude, adagio et choral varié sur le "Veni Creator,"* op. 4). Upon graduation, Duruflé aided Tournemire and Vierne as an assistant organist at their respective churches. In 1929 he was hired as church organist at St. Etienne-du-Mont in Paris, a post he held until his death. Duruflé was the featured soloist at the 1939 premiere of Francis Poulenc's Concerto in G Minor for Organ, Strings, and Timpani. In 1943 he was appointed professor of harmony at the Paris Conservatoire, a position he held until his retirement in 1969.

While teaching at the Conservatoire, Duruflé met a young organ student named Marie-Madeleine Chevalier, whom he married in 1953. It was a felicitous union, and the couple worked together as equals at St. Etienne-du-Mont. They also toured together, performing joint recitals until 1975, when they were involved in a head-on auto collision that disrupted their lives. After a long recovery, Marie-Madeleine was able to return to her performance duties at the church, but Maurice rarely left their apartment following the accident.

Despite his formidable talents as an organist, Duruflé only wrote six works specifically for his instrument. In fact, he published just fourteen different compositions in all, although many of them—including his most famous score, the beautiful Requiem, op. 9, and his last choral piece, *Notre Père,* op. 14—went through a series of extensive, ever-evolving revisions. In a 1973 interview with organist Pierre Cochereau, Duruflé seemed to attribute his small catalog of works to his responsibilities at the Conservatoire, saying he had formed "an extreme, overly developed critical sense" as a result of his teaching there.

Chamber
Prélude et fugue sur le nom d'Alain, op. 7
what to buy: [Todd Wilson, organ] (Delos 3047) ♪♪♪♪

This piece contains all the dynamics one could hope for, and Wilson's traversal of it is scintillating. The album contains the complete organ works of Duruflé and is gorgeously played and recorded. With its truly awesome sound, this CD takes full advantage of the composer's virtuoso writing and the performer's undeniable technique, making it a good first choice for audiophiles.

what to buy next: [*Maurice and Marie-Madeleine Chevalier Duruflé at the Organs of the Basilica of the National Shrine of the Immaculate Conception;* Marie-Madeleine Duruflé, organ] (Gothic 49107) ♪♪♪⁴

Although this recital was recorded in 1967 and affords a relatively decent sound picture, the results are probably of more interest to the historically oriented organ aficionado than to the casual listener. The composer performs a canon by Robert Schumann and selections by J.S. Bach and Dietrich Buxtehude and plays a duet with his wife on his own transcription of George Frideric Handel's Organ Concerto in A Major, op. 7, no. 1. Marie-Madeleine, a formidable performer in her own right, plays her husband's tribute to Jehan Alain and an improvisation by Charles Tournemire.

worth searhing for: [Herndon Spillman, organ] (Titanic 200) ♪♪♪⁴

Spillman actually studied with Duruflé and was the first artist to include all of the composer's music on one album. The organ used in this recital is mechanical, not electronic, and the clacking of stops being pulled can be heard in the quieter passages. Despite this minor caveat, Spillman's performances are impeccable. Along with the composer's complete organ music, you also get a nine-minute interview with Duruflé, conducted by the noted organist Pierre Cochereau. An English-language translation of the conversation is included in the CD booklet.

Vocal
Requiem, op.9
what to buy: [Judith Blegen, soprano; James Morris, bass; Robert Shaw, cond.; the Atlanta Symphony Orchestra and Chorus] (Telarc 80135) ♪♪♪♪

Graced with marvelous sonics and Shaw's impressive leadership, this performance will be a default choice for some listeners. The account recorded by Shaw is the large-scale rendition featured on most currently available recordings. A decent version of Gabriel Fauré's better-known Requiem is included on the same disc.

what to buy next: [Patricia Spence, mezzo-soprano; Francois LeRoux, baritone; Dennis Keene, cond.; the Voices of Ascension Chorus and Orchestra] (Delos 3169) ♪♪♪⁴

Keene's recording uses the smaller ensemble called for in Duruflé's 1961 adaptation of the score rather than the larger one utilized by Shaw. If you are looking for an all-

Duruflé program, Keene, one of Marie-Madeleine Duruflé's last students, gives more bang for the buck. In addition to the Requiem, the album includes solid performances of the *Cum Jubilo* Mass for Baritone, Male Chorus and Orchestra, op. 11 and *Notre Père*.

[George Guest, organ and cond.; St. John's College Choir, Cambridge] (London 436486) ♪ ♪ ♪ ⅜

Guest features the stripped-down version for organ and chorus that the composer wrote in between his other revisions. This version comes on a two-disc set containing some Duruflé motets and two fine, well-performed choral works by Fauré: the *Cantique de Jean Racine* and the *Messe basse*.

influences: Gabriel Fauré, Paul Dukas, Charles Tournemire, Louis Vierne

Garaud MacTaggart

Antonín Dvořák

Born Antonín Leopold Dvořák, September 8, 1841, in Nelahozeves, Bohemia. Died May 1, 1904, in Prague, Czechoslovakia.

period: Romantic/Twentieth century

Along with Bedrich Smetana and Leos Janácek, Antonín Dvořák is a member of the trinity of composers who were born in the nineteenth century and helped bring Czech music into greater prominence on the world's stages. While his best-known works (the *Slavonic Dances*, his Symphony no. 9, and the *American* string quartet) were in the spheres of orchestral and chamber music, he never really ceased his efforts to create vocal works that reflected Czech traditions.

Dvořák's early musical life revolved around the folk tunes and popular dances of his native village, where he played a surprisingly wide variety of stringed instruments in the local band. After an education that included classes in German, music theory, and organ playing, he finally finished his student years in 1859 and promptly joined an orchestra as a viola player. This gave Dvořák practical, firsthand knowledge of an orchestra's potential as he was required to play in a wide variety of compositions, including scores by Wolfgang Amadeus Mozart, Richard Wagner, and Giuseppe Verdi in addition to seminal Czech works by Smetana. While he was earning his living in this manner, Dvořák was also writing some of his earliest works.

Showing the fingerprints of Germanic composers in these initial forays, Dvořák's music began receiving performances, but nothing that would enable him to leave his primary occupation as an orchestra musician. Many of the scores he wrote before his thirtieth birthday were destroyed as he began experimenting with bringing Czech elements into his newer works. This later tactic paid off in 1875, when some of his first symphonies (he had written four by then) and a song cycle resulted in Dvořák receiving a grant from the Austrian government. Subsequent years saw similar results, but the continuing maturation of his music also caught the attention of Johannes Brahms, whose advocacy with Simrock, the German publishing house, would result in Dvořák's work being printed for the international market.

The first fruits of this relationship were the composer's *Slovanské tance (Slavonic Dances)* for piano four-hands, a huge success for both Dvořák and Simrock in 1878. The commercial and critical acclaim garnered by these lively pieces engendered a feverish demand for more material from Dvořák. Although he had already written the Serenade in E Major for String Orchestra (op. 22), nine string quartets, and his *Stabat Mater*, it was the *Slavonic Rhapsodies* (op. 49) which became Simrock's next publication in 1879. Once again Dvořák had seemingly struck a resonant chord, as orchestras around the world sought the work for their libraries, inevitably prodding the publisher to release a plethora of the composer's scores by 1880.

Dvořák was beginning to taste the fruits of his fame at home, becoming an in-demand conductor (especially of his own works) and receiving a number of commissions from civic organizations as well as requests from established musicians for works they could debut. He was also starting to be affected by the nationalist currents swirling through Europe, especially with regard to the revolutionary fervor which first exploded in Prague during the mid-nineteenth century (when Austrian forces were brought in to quell the disturbance). Despite the tensions involved in getting Dvořák's works played in Vienna, where anti-Czech feelings were running high, he was still able to secure performances in other countries, although Prague was usually the site of his premieres during this time. Such was the case for his D Major symphony (his sixth), the first of his piano quartets (op. 23), and the *Stabat Mater*, which were all first performed in Prague during 1880 or 1881.

With political tensions running high against Czech

nationalism in the cultural centers of Germany and Austria, Dvořák needed a setting for his work that was more concerned with the content of the music than the origins of the composer. In the spring of 1884, he went to Great Britain, where he was received with great acclaim from both the public and the music establishment centered around London. Repeated visits were not to dim that appreciation on either side of the composer-audience relationship, and Dvořák responded to his pleasant reception by using British venues to premiere his seventh symphony (1885), his *Requiem* (1891), and the masterful Concerto in B Minor for Cello and Orchestra (1896). In the years between his first British visit and 1892, Dvořák also managed to complete his seventh (1885) and eighth (1889) symphonies, the second set of his *Slavonic Dances* (1887), and two of his most important chamber works: the Quintet in A Major for Piano and Strings (1887) and the *Dumky* piano trio (1891).

The United States of America was another force in the composer's life during this period. In 1891, Mrs. Jeannette Meyer Thurber, a wealthy socialite and patron of the musical arts, sought to hire Dvořák as the director of the National Conservatory of Music, an academy she first opened in 1885. At first he was reluctant to sign the contract, but the salary and terms offered proved too much to resist, and Dvořák finally accepted the offer on December 23, 1891. Almost a year later, he and members of his family arrived in New York City. From then until the spring of 1895, when they returned home, the Dvořák entourage split most of their time between the East Coast and Spillville, Iowa (where there was a small Czech community). In addition to conducting concerts of his works and teaching classes, Dvořák worked on a pair of now-famous compositions inspired by American folk elements: his ninth symphony (a.k.a. *From the New World*) and his twelfth string quartet (a.k.a. the *American*).

Upon his return to Bohemia, the composer devoted much of his time to creating operas. This was an activity Dvořák had undertaken repeatedly during his career as he, like Smetana before him, attempted to create a score that would pass muster on both Czech and international stages. He had the greatest amount of luck with two of his last three operas, *Cert a Káca (The Devil and Kate)* and *Rusalka*, both of which used the Wagnerian concept of leitmotifs to define characters and crucial themes. Dvořák died shortly after the premiere of *Armida*, his last opera, and after a five-week period in

which his health seemed to fluctuate markedly. Doctors found that he had been suffering from kidney disease and cerebral arteriosclerosis.

Orchestral
Slavonic Dances, opp. 46 and 72
what to buy: [Václav Neumann, cond.; Czech Philharmonic Orchestra] (Supraphon 1959) ♪ ♪ ♪ ♪

Dvořák's orchestral arrangements for the *Slavonic Dances* are some of his most loved (and programmed) compositions. The sparkle and bounce of Neumann's performance is perfectly suited to these effervescent pieces. The orchestra is filled with Dvořák's countrymen and there is a feeling of kinship in their playing.

what to buy next: [George Szell, cond.; Cleveland Symphony Orchestra] (Sony Classics 48161) ♪ ♪ ♪♪

The Szell reading of these works set the standard for American performances when it first came out, and remains quite competitive. That isn't surprising given Szell's Czech heritage and his demanding standards.

Symphony no. 8 in G Major
what to buy: [Colin Davis, cond.; Royal Concertgebouw Orchestra] (Philips 438347) ♪ ♪ ♪ ♪♪

Despite the preponderance of recordings marking Dvořák's *New World* Symphony as the popular favorite in his oeuvre, the prior symphony is even more tuneful and exciting. This set is already recommendable for its fine recording of the ninth symphony, and Davis's version of the earlier work is even more delightful. Rounding out an excellent two-disc set is a well-played rendition of Dvořák's seventh symphony.

[Václav Neumann, cond.; Czech Philharmonic Orchestra] (Supraphon 1960) ♪ ♪ ♪ ♪♪

Neumann's performance is vibrant and exciting, although the sound isn't quite as warm as the recording afforded Davis. It is paired with a solid take on Dvořák's preceding Symphony no. 7 in D Minor, op. 70.

what to buy next: [Rafael Kubelik, cond.; Berlin Philharmonic Orchestra] (Deutsche Grammophon 447412) ♪ ♪ ♪ ♪

Kubelik is well recorded and has been a consistently appealing advocate of the composer's works for quite some time. This confluence of sound and passion makes for a wonderfully convincing performance of this piece. A very good rendition of Dvořák's last symphony rounds out the package.

[*Bruno Walter: The Edition, vol. 4*; Bruno Walter, cond.; Columbia Symphony Orchestra] (Sony Classical 64484) ♪ ♪ ♪♪

Walter's version of this work is warm without losing any of the excitement generated by the composer's propulsive score. Walter was one of the conducting greats, and a fluid, driving performance of Dvořák's *New World* Symphony is part of this wonderful memorial.

Symphony no. 9 in E Minor, op. 95—*From the New World*

what to buy: [Václav Neumann, cond.; Czech Philharmonic Orchestra] (Supraphon 2249) ♪ ♪ ♪ ♪♪

There is a swing and flow to Neumann's rendition of Dvořák's signature symphony that just feels right. Including Neumann's performance of Bedrich Smetana's symphonic poem *The Moldau* as a companion piece was a good and natural choice.

what to buy next: [Herbert von Karajan, cond.; Vienna Philharmonic Orchestra] (Deutsche Grammophon 439009) ♪ ♪ ♪ ♪♪

The sonics of Karajan's last version of the *New World* symphony are little short of awesome and the interpretation is fairly impressive, making this a first recommendation for audiophile fans. With the exception of the powerful fourth movement, however, it lacks the authoritative rhythms heard in the Davis and Neumann versions. Once again, Smetana's *The Moldau* acts as filler.

Concerto in B Minor for Cello and Orchestra, op. 104

what to buy: [Mstislav Rostropovich, cello; Herbert von Karajan, cond.; Berlin Philharmonic Orchestra] (Deutsche Grammophon 447413) ♪ ♪ ♪ ♪

Dvořák and Rostropovich both wear their hearts on their sleeves in this piece. Luckily Karajan is there to control things before they get overly schmaltzy, and the result is a performance with just the right blend of soul and technique. Tchaikovsky's lushly textured *Variations on a Rococo Theme* is a suitable partner for this program.

Antal Doráti:

Born in Budapest in 1906, the son of professional musicians, young Doráti eagerly followed in his parents' footsteps by enrolling in the Liszt Academy when he was fourteen years old. While there he studied with Béla Bartók, Zoltán Kodály, and Leó Weiner, all composers whose music he would espouse during a long career as one of the most-recorded conductors of all time and a premier orchestra-builder. He made his conducting debut with the Budapest Royal Opera in 1924, and began working as an assistant to Fritz Busch at the Dresden Opera in 1928. For the next twenty years, Doráti was on the move with various opera and ballet companies, traveling throughout Europe, Australia, New Zealand, and North America. His American reputation as an orchestra-builder began with the American Ballet Theater (1941–1945) and the Dallas Symphony Orchestra (1945–1949) and continued with the Minneapolis Symphony Orchestra (1949–1960). Doráti also maintained his ties and recording projects with European orchestras, most notably the Philharmonica Hungarica (with whom he recorded the first complete traversal of Joseph Haydn's symphonies) and the London Symphony Orchestra. From 1977 to 1981 he was the conductor of the Detroit Symphony Orchestra and made the first recordings with that outfit since the glory days of Paul Paray in the early 1960s.

Doráti was an old-fashioned disciplinarian. As a musician with the Detroit Symphony Orchestra in the late 1970s this writer was able to witness firsthand the famous Doráti outbursts when musicians did not meet his standards or something went wrong in a rehearsal. There was no questioning who was in charge when Doráti was on the podium. Doráti died in Switzerland in 1988.

More than seventy-four of his albums are still in print, but standouts include Doráti's stunning performance (with the London Symphony Orchestra) of Bartók's *Music for Strings, Percussion, and Celesta* (Mercury 434357). This particular recording was made on 35mm magnetic film and transferred well to the compact disc format. Also look for the all-Aaron Copland disc by Doráti and the Detroit Symphony Orchestra (London 430705) containing the suite from *Appalachian Spring*, *Fanfare for the Common Man*, the four *Dance Episodes* from *Rodeo*, and *El Salón México*.

Dave Wagner

[Pierre Fournier, cello; George Szell, cond.; Berlin Philharmonic Orchestra] (Deutsche Grammophon 429155) ♪ ♪ ♪ ♪

It is difficult to imagine a better budget-priced recording of this work than Fournier's and, truth to tell, there aren't really that many full-priced versions in the same league either. It is a classic performance with plenty of heartfelt playing from the cellist and superb support from Szell and the Berliners. The same orchestra, but with Alfred Wallenstein conducting, backs up Fournier in Ernest Bloch's *Schelomo*, while Jean Martinon and the Lamoureux Orchestra work with the cellist in Max Bruch's treatment of the *Kol Nidre* theme.

Serenade in E Major for String Orchestra, op. 22
what to buy: [Neville Marriner, cond.; Academy of St. Martin-in-the-Fields, orch.] (Philips 400020) ♪ ♪ ♪ ♪

This popular and seductive work for strings is often paired with Tchaikovsky's piece for the same forces but this recording is a bit different, combining two of Dvořák's tuneful serenades, including a well-judged version of the composer's Serenade in D Minor for Winds, op. 44 along with the more familiar op. 22. Marriner's performance benefits from a warmly recorded ambiance that highlights the lush string writing.

what to buy next: [Josef Suk, cond.; Suk Chamber Orchestra] (Supraphon 4136) ♪ ♪ ♪ ♪

Suk is better known as a violinist but his work as a conductor is worth noting too. Here he blends a tasteful version of the well-known serenade with the charming Serenade in E-flat Major from Dvořák's son-in-law (and the conductor's grandfather), Josef Suk. The disc is marginally less expensive than Marriner's set, but the performance has an appealing gutsiness that would be welcome at twice the price.

various symphonic poems and overtures
what to buy: [Rafael Kubelik, cond.; Bavarian Radio Symphony Orchestra] (Deutsche Grammophon 435074) ♪ ♪ ♪ ♪

Kubelik is a persuasive conductor of Dvořák's material and this two-CD set of short orchestral pieces is a winner. Particularly appealing are his versions of The Golden Spinning Wheel and The Water Goblin, but special mention should also go to his subtly swinging rendition of the Symphonic Variations on an Original Theme.

what to buy next: [Symphonic Poems; Stephen Gunzenhauser, cond.; Polish National Radio Symphony Orchestra] (Naxos 8.550598) ♪ ♪ ♪ ♪

Budget prices no longer mean inferior performances, and Gunzenhauser's single-disc set is a good example of this. These are fairly classy renditions of The Golden Spinning Wheel, The Noon Witch, and The Wild Dove.

Chamber
Slavonic Dances, opps. 46 and 72
what to buy: [Four-Hand Piano Music, vol. 2; Silke-Thora Matthies, piano; Christian Köhn, piano] (Naxos 8.553138) ♪ ♪ ♪ ♪

Dvořák's orchestral arrangements of these delightful pieces are better known, but that shouldn't stop anyone from exploring these versions, especially in such sparkling, well-recorded, splendidly△199 played performances as heard here.

Quartet no. 12 in F Major for Strings, op. 96 (American)
what to buy: [Juilliard String Quartet, ensemble] (Sony Classical 48170) ♪ ♪ ♪ ♪

Written during Dvořák's first summer vacation in America, this string quartet is the most frequently recorded of his chamber works. Despite some heavy competition, the recording by the Juilliard Quartet holds up very well. For anyone interested in pursuing Dvořák's writing for small ensemble there are two other advantages to picking up this set, since it pairs the American with an equally fine rendition of the composer's important Quintet in A Major for Piano and Strings (op. 81) featuring pianist Rudolf Firkusny.

what to buy next: [Lindsay String Quartet, ensemble] (ASV 797) ♪ ♪ ♪ ♪

This English quartet's version of the American is a little leaner-sounding than the one found on the Juilliard set, but the performances are very convincing and worth a listen. The more famous work is paired with the composer's powerful Quartet no. 13 in G Major for Strings (op. 106), a piece that deserves more attention.

[Dvořák: String Quartets, vol. 1; Vlach Quartet, Prague, ensemble] (Naxos 8.553371) ♪ ♪ ♪ ♪

This a much more romantic, broadly-envisioned performance than that given by either the Juilliard or Lindsay quartets. At the price, it is also a very good alternative to them, since the Vlach Quartet, though they are a relatively young group, provide insights into how these works used to be performed (the composer's thirteenth quartet is also included in this package).

Quintet in A Major for Piano and Strings, op. 81
what to buy: [Tucson Winter Chamber Music Festival: March 1996, vol. 2; Ralph Votapek, piano; Joseph Suk, violin; Ani Kavafian, violin; Cynthia Phelps, viola; Peter Rejto, cello] (Arizona Friends of Chamber Music 96.102) ♪ ♪ ♪ ♪ ♪

Antonín Dvořák

The artistic heat given off by this ad hoc ensemble is astounding. Suk, the composer's great grandson, and Kavafian are wonderful, as is Votapek. The same qualities carry over into the performance of the Brahms Sextet no. 1 in B-flat Major for Strings, which balances out the program.

what to buy next: [Jan Panenka, piano; Panocha Quartet, ensemble] (Supraphon 1465) ♪ ♪ ♪ ♪⁴

Panenka—whose long association with this piece began by teaming up with the fabled Smetana Quartet—and the Panocha Quartet bring a specific Czech flair to this score which makes their inspired performance of it all the more beguiling. Dvořák's earlier essay in the form, his opus 5 in the same key, is an admittedly lesser piece, but reveals its own set of charms in these musicians' hands as the work here accompanying one of Dvořák's finest compositions.

[Menahem Pressler, piano; Emerson String Quartet, ensemble] (Deutsche Grammophon 439868) ♪ ♪ ♪ ♪

Pressler, the eminence gris of the legendary Beaux Arts Trio, blends well with one of the finer young ensembles of the late twentieth century for a marvelous, albeit restrained, performance of this work. Deutsche Grammophon's engineers did a fine job of recording it, and the composer's Quartet no. 2 in E-flat Major for Piano and Strings, op. 87, is also included here.

Trio no. 4 in E Minor for Piano, Violin, and Cello, op. 90 (*Dumky*)
what to buy: [*Dvořák: Complete Piano Trios*; Beaux Arts Trio, ensemble] (Philips 454259) ♪ ♪ ♪ ♪⁴

The most famous (and last) of Dvořák's pleasant piano trio pieces, the *Dumky* draws its nickname from the folk dance that lies at the heart of the composition. Current mastering techniques have aided an already fine 1960s-era recording and there is no better performance of the work currently in catalog. It is part of a complete set of the composer's piano trios.

Vocal
Rusalka, op. 114
what to buy: [Renée Fleming, soprano; Zdena Kloubová, soprano; Lívia Ághová, soprano; Eva Urbanová, mezzo-soprano; Dolora Zajick, mezzo-soprano; Dana Buresová, mezzo-soprano; Hana Minutillo, contralto; Ben Heppner,

tenor; Iván Kusnjer, baritone; Franz Hawlata, bass; Charles Mackerras, cond.; Czech Philharmonic Orchestra; Kühn Mixed Choir] (London 460568) ♪ ♪ ♪ ♪

Although he desperately wanted to succeed as an opera composer, most of Dvořák's eleven efforts in that direction were flawed by a mediocre blend of score and libretto. Only in *Rusalka,* his ninth opera, did the composer attain the heights he sought. Fleming is a stunning singer and an ideal choice for the title role of Rusalka, a water sprite who has fallen in love with a mortal. Mackerras draws taut performances from his ensembles and the sonics are wonderful.

Stabat Mater for Soloists, Orchestra, and Chorus, op. 58
what to buy: [Edith Mathis, soprano; Anna Reynolds, contralto; Wieslaw Ochman, tenor; John Shirley-Quirk, bass; Rafael Kubelik, cond.; Bavarian Radio Symphony Orchestra and Chorus] (Deutsche Grammophon 453025) ♪ ♪ ♪ ♪

There are no light-hearted, dancing moments in this score, just a deep sense of religious conviction in every moment of this illuminating performance by Kubelik, his orchestra, and the soloists. The orchestral arrangement of Dvořák's *Legends* (op. 59) included in this two-disc set is an upbeat chaser to the solemnity, with Kubelik leading the English Chamber Orchestra.

influences: Bedrich Smetana, Leoš Janáček, Josef Suk

Ellen Kokko

Edward Elgar
Born Edward William Elgar, June 2, 1857, in Broadheath, near Worcester, England. Died February 23, 1934, in Worcester, England.

period: Romantic

One of the most popular composers ever to come out of England, Elgar was not only the finest British symphonist of his era but one of the greatest of European late-Romantic composers. He is best known to American audiences for the *Enigma Variations* for Orchestra, his cello concerto, and one of his earliest works, the Serenade in E Minor for Strings.

Largely self-taught as a composer, Elgar as a boy

learned a great deal at his father's music shop in Worcester. Originally intending to become a concert violinist, in 1885 he succeeded his father as organist at St. George's, the chief Roman Catholic church in Worcester and increasingly partook of the musical life available to him in the community, serving as violinist, conductor, and teacher. He married Caroline Roberts, one of his former piano students, in 1889, and this union was to be one of the great anchors in Elgar's life. He had found a friend, a companion, an inspiration, and a staunch supporter; until her untimely death in 1920, the two were deeply devoted to one another.

After moving to London in 1890, Elgar composed his *Froissart* Overture, which was premiered at the Worcester Festival. Although not particularly well received, it brought him his first major public recognition as a composer, but finding no real success in the capital, Elgar decided to move back to the rural setting from which he had sprung. His first really popular work, the Serenade in E Minor for Strings, was created in 1892 but his initial London success finally came in 1897 with the *Imperial March,* written for Queen Victoria's Diamond Jubilee. Then, in 1899, his *Enigma Variations* were first performed in London and put Elgar squarely on the international musical map, elevating him into the first rank of composers. His next major work began with a wedding present the Elgars had been given, a copy of Cardinal Newman's dramatic poem *The Dream of Gerontius.* Upon reading it Elgar thought immediately about turning it into an oratorio, but it was not until 1900 that he was able realize this project. Through a combination of many unfortunate circumstances its first performance was a failure, but the work has since come to be regarded as the greatest of all English oratorios.

By now, however, Elgar's career was on an upward trajectory and 1904 was a particularly good year. He had finished the five *Pomp and Circumstance* marches (begun in 1901) and, as the favorite composer of King Edward VII, was knighted. He was even popular enough with the burgeoning middle classes that an Elgar Festival was mounted for his 1898 cantata *Caractacus* and both of his major oratorios, *The Dream of Gerontius* and *The Apostles.* Elgar was also proposed as the beneficiary of an endowed professorship at the University of Birmingham, a position he reluctantly accepted later that year and was glad to relinquish in 1908.

Like Johannes Brahms before him, Elgar waited a very long time before bringing forth his first symphony, finally completing this work in 1908 when he was 50. The premiere performance created a sensation, and the ovation accorded him as he stepped onstage can only be likened to the acclaim contemporary pop singers now regularly receive. Within a year of the symphony's premiere it became his most immediately popular work, receiving nearly 100 performances, an astonishing record.

His last major works, (the Violin Concerto in B Minor, his Second Symphony, the symphonic study *Falstaff,* and the Cello Concerto in E Minor) were all completed within a span of ten years (1909–1919), but after his wife's death in 1920 he produced nothing more of importance. By this time he had everything that a composer could hope for in life: recognition, success, performances of his music around the world, and financial rewards; but during his last years, he was curiously bitter and felt that somehow he still had not been accorded his full measure of respect and acclaim.

Elgar was the first composer to bring English orchestral music into the front rank of international recognition. Of major significance is the fact that he was also the first great composer to understand and take advantage of the comparatively new recording medium. He recorded all of his major orchestral works and many minor ones with the London Symphony Orchestra at two different times and in two different processes. His first acoustic sessions were in 1914, and the last of the electrical sessions came in 1933.

Orchestral
Concerto in E Minor for Cello and Orchestra, op. 85
what to buy: [Jacqueline du Pré, cello; John Barbirolli, cond; London Symphony Orchestra] (EMI Classics 56219)
♪ ♪ ♪ ♪ ♪

This is a modern classic, featuring never surpassed performances from the 1960s in finely detailed sound. The disc also includes the great mezzo-soprano Janet Baker as soloist in Elgar's orchestral song cycle *Sea Pictures.*

what to buy next: [Pieter Wispelwey, cello; Jac van Steen, cond.; Netherlands Radio Philharmonic, orch.] (Channel Classics 12998) ♪ ♪ ♪ ♪₄

Wispelwey is, quite possibly, the most amazing cellist most North Americans have never heard of. His rendition of Elgar's masterpiece may be the only recording worth mentioning in the same breath as du Pré's. The disc also includes Wispelwey's superb, well-engineered performance of Witold Lutoslawski's Cello Concerto, a work belonging to the opposite end of the 20th century.

Concerto in B Minor for Violin and Orchestra, op. 61
what to buy: [Nigel Kennedy, violin; Vernon Handley, cond.; London Philharmonic Orchestra] (EMI Classics 63795) ♪ ♪ ♪ ♪♪

Originally dedicated to and initially performed by Fritz Kreisler, Elgar's violin concerto is one of the longest and most magnificent ever written for the instrument. Of all modern recordings of the work, this superb account still holds the palm, featuring the young Kennedy in top form, with a sensitive and impassioned accompaniment.

Enigma Variations for Orchestra, op. 36
what to buy: [Andrew Davis, cond.; BBC Symphony Orchestra] (Teldec 73279) ♪ ♪ ♪ ♪

When dealing with recordings of Elgar's major works, it is rarely possible to pinpoint a "best" or a first choice; there are simply too many good performances available. This disc gives you three of the composer's finest scores, the *Introduction and Allegro*, *Cockaigne* Overture and Serenade for Strings, in first-rate performances and splendidly engineered sound.

[Adrian Boult, cond.; London Philharmonic Orchestra] (Classics For Pleasure 69601) ♪ ♪ ♪ ♪

Boult's approach to this piece, based upon his long association with the work and the composer, is idiomatic to say the least. The sound may not be as wonderful as that heard in the Davis performance cited above, but the interpretation has a hard-won authority. Vernon Handley leads the same orchestra in performances of Elgar's five *Pomp and Circumstance* marches that make this a fine collection of the composer's most popular works.

Falstaff for Orchestra, op. 68
what to buy: [John Barbirolli, cond.; Hallé Orchestra] (EMI Classics Special Import 66322) ♪ ♪ ♪ ♪♪

Falstaff is generally considered to be Elgar's symphonic masterpiece, and while there are good recordings of the work available today, one must go to the past to find a truly definitive performance—and this is it, coupled with an equally fine performance of the great *Enigma Variations.*

Serenade in E minor, op. 20
what to buy: [*English Music for Strings*; John Barbirolli, cond.; City of London Sinfonia, orch.] (EMI Classics 47537) ♪ ♪ ♪ ♪

Elgar wrote with marvelous feeling for strings, and this collection includes the *Elegy for Strings* and *Sospiri* for Strings, Harp and Organ in luminous and inspired performances given spacious and warm recorded sound. Two of Ralph Vaughan Williams most popular works for strings, the *Fantasia on Greensleeves* and *Fantasia on a Theme by Thomas Tallis,* fill out the disc.

Symphony no. 1 in A-flat Major, op. 55
what to buy: [Adrian Boult, cond.; London Philharmonic Orchestra] (EMI Classics Import 64013) ♪ ♪ ♪ ♪♪

Boult was one of the greatest of Elgar interpreters, bringing to all of his recordings the benefit of a long association with the composer and great insight into his special musical world. There are many fine accounts of this magnificent symphony currently available, but this magisterial reading has a little something extra to it. This all-Elgar disc also includes the *Serenade For Strings* plus the *Chanson de Nuit* and the *Chanson de Matin.*

Symphony no. 2 in E flat major, op. 63
what to buy: [Vernon Handley, cond.; London Philharmonic Orchestra] (Classics For Pleasure 4544) ♪ ♪ ♪ ♪♪

Although this symphony has never been quite as popular as the First, it is equally magnificent, and in the scherzo one hears a wild, almost demonic side of Elgar which is as astonishing as it is overwhelming. This recording does full justice to this remarkable work.

worth searching for: [Adrian Boult, cond.; BBC Symphony Orchestra] (EMI Classics 63134) ♪ ♪ ♪ ♪♪

This was the first recording of this great symphony after Elgar's own, and in many respects this extraordinary 1944 performance is the finest ever put on disc. It was made in the English city of Bedford, where the orchestra had been evacuated during the bleak days of World War II, and this may have helped inspire the forces to such an exemplary reading. Well worth seeking out.

Vocal
The Dream of Gerontius for Vocal Soloists, Orchestra and Chorus, op. 38

what to buy: [Felicity Palmer, soprano; Arthur Davies, tenor; Gwynne Howell, bass; Richard Hickox, cond.; London Symphony Orchestra; London Symphony Chorus] (Chandos 8641/2) ♪ ♪ ♪

Here is Elgar's greatest choral work presented with a recorded sound and perspective which outshine all others. It is a fine performance as well, perhaps not as powerful in the climaxes as one could hope for, but for a combination of insightful performance and outstanding fidelity of sound this recording is hard to beat.

influences: Arnold Bax, William Walton, Ralph Vaughan Williams

Charles Greenwell and Dave Wagner

E

Edward Kennedy "Duke" Ellington

Born April 29, 1899, in Washington, DC. Died May 24, 1974, in New York City, NY.

period: Twentieth century

Although he is generally thought of as one of America's greatest jazz musicians and composers, Ellington also wrote suites, ballets, and incidental music for plays and movies that utilized typical symphonic elements in their construction.

African-American pianist, composer, and bandleader Edward Kennedy Ellington began his long career by playing ragtime piano in Washington, DC. He also performed with a number of bands before traveling to New York City in 1923 with what became the first of his important jazz groups, the Washingtonians.

For the next half-century, Ellington was one of the most influential forces on the American music scene. With his fertile imagination and gift for melodic invention, he could be considered America's answer to J.S. Bach. There are over one thousand pieces written by "the Duke"; he also established long-term working relationships with arrangers and performers such as Bubber Miley, Harry Carney, and especially Billy Strayhorn.

Part of Ellington's success as a bandleader lay in his

Jacqueline Du Pré:
Jacqueline Du Pré was undoubtedly one of the most dynamic and charismatic cellists of the mid-twentieth century, but after a series of ascending triumphs, multiple sclerosis robbed her first of the ability to perform as she was accustomed, and then, in 1987, of her life.

When she first began formal cello studies in 1950, Du Pré was only five years old, but had already shown a marked proficiency on the instrument. Three years later, the youngster entered London's Guildhall School of Music and Drama, where she began studying with William Pleeth, one of the finest English cellists of his day and Du Pré's most important mentor. After winning a number of important scholarships and prizes for her abilities, attending master classes led by the great Pablo Casals, and studying with the notable French cellist Paul Tortelier, her career appeared to be in full swing.

Du Pré had already taken part in many concert performances of Edward Elgar's Concerto in E Minor for Cello and Orchestra by 1965, when she entered the studio to record it with John Barbirolli conducting the London Symphony Orchestra (EMI Classics 56219). That particular performance sealed her reputation as one of the work's most perceptive interpreters. A year later she met pianist Daniel Barenboim, a felicitous pairing at a chamber music gathering that led to their marriage in 1967. Three years later, she made another recording of the Elgar concerto (Sony Classics 60789), this time with her husband leading the Philadelphia Orchestra in a concert setting that showcased Du Pré's fiery, emotional approach to the score even more than the earlier set with Barbirolli. In 1971, she took a year-long hiatus from public appearances as it became increasingly apparent that her formidable skills were eroding. After returning briefly to the public stage, Du Pré's doctors diagnosed her problems as the onset of multiple sclerosis, and she soon retired from performing.

Her recorded legacy is surprisingly skimpy for an artist of her stature, but the four-disc set *Jacqueline Du Pré Concerto Collection* (EMI Classics 67341) displays the cellist's talents with works she routinely performed in concert: concertos by Franz Joseph Haydn, Luigi Boccherini, Robert Schumann, Camille Saint-Saëns, Georg Mathias Monn, Antonín Dvořák, and Frederick Delius, in addition to Richard Strauss's tone poem for cello and orchestra, *Don Quixote*. The now-famous recording of Elgar's cello concerto with Barbirolli conducting is included in the set, but there are also a variety of other conductors and orchestras featured in support of Du Pré's artistry.

Ellen Kokko

insistence that band members be able to read music as well as to improvise. By tailoring his scores to the styles and abilities of his musicians, Ellington made his orchestra into an audio palette, enabling him to experiment with various harmonies and structural elements. This eventually cleared the way for such innovative classical-jazz hybrids as *Black, Brown, and Beige* (1943), *Liberian Suite* (1947), *Harlem Air Shaft* (1950), *Night Creature* (1955), and *In the Beginning God* (1965).

His tongue-in-cheek modesty gave Ellington a reputation for diplomatic understatement, evidenced by his response to actions taken by the Pulitzer Prize Advisory Board. In 1965, when the board's members debated giving him an award for long-term achievement but ultimately declined to do so, Ellington was quoted as saying, "Fate's being kind to me. Fate doesn't want me to be too famous too young."

Ellington, however, had garnered his share of awards and honors prior to the Pulitzer decision, and many more were to come. A short list would include the three Grammy Awards he won for his score to the movie *Anatomy of a Murder* (1959), the honorary doctorates he received from Howard University (1971) and Yale University (1967), and the Presidential Medal of Freedom he was awarded on his seventieth birthday. The last honor must have been particularly sweet, since Ellington's father had once been a domestic servant at the White House.

In 1999, the Pulitzer board, thirty-four years after denying Ellington an award, granted him a special posthumous citation "for his indelible contribution to art and culture through the medium of jazz."

Orchestral
Harlem for Orchestra
what to buy: [Neemi Järvi, cond.; Detroit Symphony Orchestra] (Chandos 9226) ♪ ♪ ♪ ♪

Ellington recalled that this piece was commissioned by Arturo Toscanini and called it "a concerto grosso for band and symphony." Järvi and the DSO combine their rendition of Ellington's work with William Grant Still's Symphony no. 2 in G Minor—*Song of a New Race*—and William Levi Dawson's *Negro Folk Symphony* for Orchestra.

worth searching for: [*The Symphonic Ellington*; Duke Ellington, cond.; Duke Ellington Orchestra and members of the Paris Symphony Orchestra] (Discovery 71003) ♪ ♪ ♪ ♪₄

This album has gone out of print three times now—twice on vinyl (for Reprise and Trend Records) and once

Edward Kennedy "Duke" Ellington

on CD (the Discovery release)—but it is still worth hunting for. In addition to *Harlem Air Shaft,* it contains three other symphonic works by Ellington, including a version of *Night Creature* that was recorded with members of the Stockholm and Paris Symphonies.

The River: Suite
what to buy: [Neemi Järvi, cond.; Detroit Symphony Orchestra] (Chandos 9154) ♪ ♪ ♪ ♪

The River, a ballet Ellington wrote in 1970, is filled with sprightly tunes. On this album it serves as a good counterweight to William Grant Still's Symphony no. 1—Afro-American.

Black, Brown, and Beige
what to buy: [Mahalia Jackson, singer; Duke Ellington, cond.; the Duke Ellington Orchestra] (Columbia 65566) ♪ ♪ ♪ ♪

Recorded in 1958, this definitive version of the 1943 suite is made all the more remarkable by the inspired inclusion of gospel singer Mahalia Jackson, whose renditions of the "Come Sunday" and "23rd Psalm" sections are beyond compare. Alternate takes, snippets of studio conversations, and otherwise unreleased cuts make this an even more valuable item.

worth searching for: [*Four Symphonic Works by Duke Ellington*; Maurice Peress, cond.; American Composers Orchestra] (Musical Heritage Society 512335T) ♪ ♪ ♪ ♪₄

In 1989, Maurice Peress orchestrated "Work Song," "Come Sunday," and "Light" from *Black, Brown, and Beige,* augmenting the string section with jazz players. Alto saxophonist Frank Wess's solo on "Come Sunday" is almost as moving as Mahalia Jackson's vocal rendition on the 1958 recording with Ellington's band. Versions of *Three Black Kings, New World A-Comin'* for Piano Solo and Orchestra, and yet another take on *Harlem* round out the album.

The Nutcracker Suite
what to buy: [*Three Suites*; "Duke" Ellington, cond.; Duke Ellington Orchestra] (Columbia/Legacy 46825) ♪ ♪ ♪ ♪₄

Ellington and Billy Strayhorn arranged Tchaikovsky's *Nutcracker Suite* (1960) and selections from Grieg's *Peer Gynt Suites* (1962) for jazz orchestra, with results that are a rare combination of charm and effectiveness. The album also contains Ellington's splendid *Suite Thursday,* (1962) completing the trilogy alluded to in the disc's title.

influences: George Gershwin, Ferde Grofé, Gil Evans, Billy Strayhorn

Gary Barton and Garaud MacTaggart

Georges Enesco

Born August 19, 1881, in Liveni Vîrnav, Romania. Died May 4, 1955, in Paris, France.

period: Twentieth century

A child prodigy on the violin, Enesco (sometimes spelled Enescu) mastered several other instruments and began composing at an early age. He also excelled as a conductor, teacher, and pianist. Enesco's amazing memory enabled him to conduct a host of works without scores—not only his own orchestral music but other large-scale symphonic works by a variety of composers. Sadly, he is only known by the public today for his first *Romanian Rhapsody.*

Georges Enesco was a naturally gifted musician. From childhood, he was filled with the sounds of Romania and its Gypsy tradition. Enesco took violin lessons from a Romanian Gypsy named Nicolas Chioru before giving his first public performance at the age of eight; by the time he was sixteen, he was giving concerts of his own works in Vienna. Enesco went to Paris in 1895 to continue his violin studies at the Paris Conservatoire and ended up studying composition with the well-known French musicians and composers Gabriel Fauré and Jules Massenet. While at the conservatory, he received a first prize in violin and pursued further studies as an organist, pianist, and cellist. Throughout his life, Enesco was able to perform publicly on these other instruments as if they had been his primary focus.

In 1901 Enesco wrote what was to become his signature piece, the *Romanian Rhapsody,* op. 11, no 1. Like the successful early works of many composers, it overshadowed the works to follow and caused its writer to loathe the "creature" as his career progressed. Enesco wanted the public to hear his later works, but fans continually requested performances of this early rhapsody. Even the composer's second *Romanian Rhapsody* (op. 11, no. 2) never approached the success of the first. Typical of

rhapsodies, these pieces feature a number of different musical themes tied together with clever transitional passages. The first rhapsody is highly evocative, with ingenious orchestral effects from harp, clarinets, and oboes and colorful aspects suggesting Gypsy fiddling.

Enesco is also known as the teacher of the renowned violin virtuoso Yehudi Menuhin; in later life, he often gave duo concerts with his famous pupil. Enesco traveled to the United States on a number of occasions, leading the Philadelphia Orchestra in a New York concert in the early 1930s and conducting the New York Philharmonic in 1937. He was warmly received by American audiences and presented a series of concerts of Romanian music at the New York World's Fair in 1938. After World War II he returned to teach in New York City, where he gave his farewell concert in 1950, almost sixty years after his debut.

Although Enesco experimented with some twentieth-century techniques, his music is firmly rooted in the late-nineteenth-century tonal tradition, with a tip of the hat to folk elements found in Romanian and Gypsy music. His tonal palette and ability to write memorable melodies is one of the reasons for Enesco's enduring popularity. His later works were certainly more daring harmonically, but they have not gained wide recognition. After his retirement from the concert stage, Enesco settled in Paris, where he suffered a stroke and spent his remaining years incapacitated. In homage to him, his hometown was renamed *Enescu,* and a street in Bucharest bears his name.

Orchestral
Romanian Rhapsody no. 1 in A Major for Orchestra, op. 11
what to buy: [Antal Dorati, cond; London Symphony Orchestra] (Mercury Living Presence 432015) ♪ ♪ ♪ ♪

Dorati really captures the spirit of the music, and these performances continue to win fans forty years after being recorded. This disc includes the orchestral arrangements by Franz Liszt of six *Hungarian Rhapsodies.*

what to buy next: [Kenneth Jean, cond; Slovak Philharmonic Orchestra] (Naxos 8.55037) ♪ ♪ ♪ ♪

From the resident conductor of the Hong Kong Philharmonic comes this outstanding disc, with great sound and precision playing. You'll also find the composer's less popular *Romanian Rhapsody* no.2, Antonín

Dvořák's *Slavonic Rhapsody* no. 2, the *Hungarian Rhapsody* no. 2 by Franz Liszt, and *Rapsodie Espagnole* by Maurice Ravel.

Symphony no. 1 in E-flat Major, op. 13
what to buy: [*Enescu: Complete Symphonic Works, Vol. 1*; Horia Andreescu, cond; Romanian Radio Orchestra] (Olympia 441) ♪ ♪ ♪ ♪

Here is a recording with good sound and interesting programming from Andreescu. The disc includes this early symphony, the 1948 Concert Overture in A Major for Orchestra, and the fourth of Enesco's early "School" symphonies.

influences: Antonín Dvořák, Bedřich Smetana

Dave Wagner

Gabriel Fauré

Born Gabriel Urbain Fauré, May 12, 1845, in Pamiers, France. Died November 4, 1924, in Paris, France.

period: Romantic

Known primarily for vocal and chamber works, and especially for his Requiem, Fauré wrote an enormous number of compositions covering all genres. Of special interest are two early works—the *Élégie* for Cello and Piano and the *Ballade* in F sharp minor for Piano—which gained "hit" status in orchestral arrangements Fauré created after their initial unveiling. His music is full of nuance, subtlety, and theatrical flair, with a verve that conveys confidence and commands the attention.

Gabriel Fauré's father was headmaster at a school when his youngest son's musical talent first manifested itself. The school chapel had a harmonium—an organ-like instrument with vibrating reeds as the source of its sound—and the young, budding organist could often be discovered playing it. When the archivist for the Paris Assemblée heard Gabriel during one of these impromptu "recitals," he suggested that the boy be sent to Paris and enrolled at the École de Musique Classique et Religieuse. Gabriel spent the next 11 years there studying to become a church choir director, immersed in the study of composition, organ, piano, theory, harmony, fugue, and counterpoint. One of his piano teachers at

the school was Camille Saint-Saëns, who broadened his pupils' horizons by adding more contemporary scores to the course work.

Part of the preparation of any music student in the French tradition included prizes to the brightest and most creative students. Fauré was among this elite group, winning awards in fugue and counterpoint, solfège (the art of singing music with pre-assigned syllables for each note of the musical scale), harmony, and piano performance. In 1865 he also won a prize in composition for his *Cantique de Jean Racine,* a work for chorus and organ, written as a graduation exercise. His first job upon leaving the school was as organist at a church in the provincial backwater of Rennes, a position that allowed the young musician the opportunity to develop his compositional craft, despite being removed from Paris, the hotbed of French artistic life.

For the next two years, beginning in 1870, Fauré led an unsettled life. After being dismissed from his rural appointment, he moved back to Paris and found himself briefly on the organ bench at Notre-Dame de Clignancourt before he enlisted in the military during the Franco-Prussian War. The next year, after being demobilized in March, he found employment as organist at Saint-Honoré d'Eylau but then fled Paris during the Commune's brief reign of terror to teach in Switzerland, finally returning in the autumn as choir organist at Saint-Sulpice. There he met up with Charles-Marie Widor, the virtuoso organist and composer, with whom he traded improvisations in a kind of musical duel during services.

Trading on his status as one of Saint-Saëns's prized pupils, Fauré managed introductions to (and friendships with) several stars of the French romantic and impressionistic movements, many of them members of the Société Nationale de Musique. This last-named organization was dedicated to the promotion of new music by French composers and counted such leading lights of the period as Vincent d'Indy, Édouard Lalo, César Franck, and Henri Duparc among its membership. Although Fauré wrote a few songs during this period and experimented with orchestral writing, he didn't really hit his stride until 1875. That was the year he wrote his first violin sonata and the first of his nocturnes for piano. From then until 1880, he seemed to produce a masterpiece or two almost every year—the first version of the Requiem (1877), the gorgeous, Italianate song, *Après un rêve* (1878), his first piano quartet and the *Ballade* for Piano (1879), and the *Élégie* for Cello and Piano (1880)—most of which he later arranged for different forces.

After his marriage in 1883, Fauré needed to concentrate on supporting his family, accepting students for piano and harmony lessons and engaging in the daily tedium of planning services for the Church of the Madeleine where he had been ensconced as chorus master since 1877. From this point until the early 1890s the only significant works coming from his pen were some songs (including *Clair de lune*), the second of his piano quartets, and the *Pavane* for Orchestra. By 1896, when he finally became chief organist at the Madeleine and succeeded Jules Massenet as composition teacher at the Paris Conservatoire, Fauré had also written two of his classic song cycles—*Cinq mélodies de Venise'* and *La Bonne chanson* (both based on texts by Paul Verlaine)—and the *Theme and Variations* in C sharp minor for Piano. Although his other duties severely limited the amount of time he could devote to composition, he still found time to travel around Europe, observing cultural events and listening to different trends in music.

In 1900, at the dawn of the 20th century, Fauré finished the re-orchestration for full orchestra of the Requiem, a project which had gone through several revisions since its first version back in 1877. This singular piece stands as one of the finest works in the choral repertoire and the composer's most performed score. He had also finished work on the incidental music to *Pelléas et Mélisande* two years earlier, and the pair of compositions formed a pivotal point in Fauré's compositional life, closing a chapter with the Requiem while looking forward to the final, mature scores he would write during the remainder of his life, including his only opera, *Pénélope,* begun in 1907 and finally completed and performed in 1913. He had also now become a well-respected teacher, his students including such important musical figures of the next generation as Maurice Ravel, Charles Koechlin, George Enescu, and Nadia Boulanger. Together with many of his former students Fauré broke away from the Société Nationale de Musique in 1909 to help form the new Société Musicale Indépendante, in part because the earlier organization had ceased to keep up with the times, becoming concerned with compositions from the immediate past to the detriment of its original mandate to promote the new and to look towards the future.

When he retired from the Conservatoire in 1920, Fauré was a respected musical elder statesman and at last able to compose without the responsibilities that had

held him back before. The fact that he was growing increasingly deaf, a complaint noticeable as far back as 1910, makes his last achievements all the more remarkable. What followed his retirement was one of the most impressive creative phases in his whole career, masterpieces including his Second Cello Sonata, the song cycle, *L'Horizon chimérique,* his Piano Trio, and finally, the String Quartet.

Orchestral
Pelléas et Mélisande for Orchestra, op. 80
what to buy: [Zubin Mehta, cond.; Israel Philharmonic Orchestra] (Sony 45870) ♪ ♪ ♪ ♪

This fine disc contains three compositions written for or based on the drama *Pelléas et Mélisande*—by Fauré, Arnold Schoenberg, and Jean Sibelius.

Ballade in F sharp minor for Piano and Orchestra, op. 19
what to buy: [*Fauré: Orchestral Works*; Kathryn Stott, piano; Yan Pascal Tortelier, cond.; BBC Philharmonic Orchestra] (Chandos 9416) ♪ ♪ ♪ ♪

Stott is one of the finest Fauré interpreters around and her playing in the orchestral version of his *Ballade* is marvelous, comparing quite well with Collard's solo piano rendition. (See below.) Chandos then surrounds this performance with a well chosen selection of the composer's works and/or arrangements for orchestra including *Dolly, Élégie, Pavane,* and the suite from *Masques et Bergamasques.*

Élégie for Cello and Orchestra, op. 24
what to buy: [Jules Eskin, cello; Seiji Ozawa, cond.; Boston Symphony Orchestra] (Deutsche Grammophon 423089) ♪ ♪ ♪ ♪

Even though the *Élégie* is a lovely work in its original chamber guise, Fauré's arrangement of it for orchestra lifts this piece to a whole new level. Eskin is a capable performer and the sonics from Deutsche Grammophon are fine here, but it's the other works on this all-Fauré disc that it so worthwhile: the *Pavane, Pelléas et Mélisande* and the orchestral arrangement of the *Dolly* suite.

Chamber
Élégie for Cello and Piano, op. 24
what to buy: [*Complete Works for Cello and Piano*;

Peter Bruns, cello; Roglit Ishay, piano] (Opus 111 30-242) ♪♪♪♪₄

This is a marvelous recording of the *Élégie* in its original form, and the other works included also show Fauré's basic affinity both for chamber music and for writing long, singing lines for the cello. The later pieces in this set—the two sonatas (opp. 109 and 117), *Papillon*, *Sicilienne*, and the *Sérénade*—all receive exemplary performances, as does Pablo Casals's arrangement of Fauré's wonderful song *"Après un rêve."*

Sonatas for Violin and Piano, opp. 13 and 108
what to buy: [*Musique de Chambre, vol. 1*; Augustin Dumay, violin; Jean-Philippe Collard, piano] (EMI Classics 62545) ♪♪♪♪

The sound is a little harsher and the playing a bit more wiry than in the Grumiaux version (below) but the performances are more than acceptable. This two-disc set includes solid versions of Fauré's complete duos for strings (or flute) and piano along with a very fine version of his Trio in D minor for Piano, Violin, and Cello, op. 120, which adds cellist Frédéric Lodéon to the mix.

worth searching for: [Arthur Grumiaux, violin; Paul Crossley, piano] (Philips 426384) ♪♪♪♪♪

More popular than Fauré's mature Second Violin Sonata (op. 108), his First Sonata op. 13 piece carries the refreshing youthful quality of its first movement all the way through to the end of the piece. Even the *Andante* is filled with freshly wrought passion. Grumiaux is an amazing violinist who captures the music's lyricism without overdoing the emotion. His superb versions of the Second Violin Sonata (a complex, driving work of art) and César Franck's Violin Sonata in A major, also included, make this one of the finest discs of 19th-century French chamber classics.

Quartets for Piano and Strings, opp. 15 and 45
what to buy: [Domus, ensemble] (Hyperion 66166) ♪♪♪♪♪

This is amazing music through and through, although the second of these quartets stands a little higher on the podium of greatness. The balance between the strings and the piano is nearly perfect and it is hard to imagine a more impressive performance.

what to buy next: [*Musique de Chambre, vol. 2*; Jean-

Philippe Collard, piano; Augustin Dumay, violin; Bruno Pasquier, viola; Frédéric Lodéon, cello] (EMI Classics 62548) ♪♪♪♪

Collard is one of the finest Fauré interpreters around, as his solo piano sets can confirm, but he is also a fine ensemble player, as exhibited in these performances of the piano quartets. For those looking to gather up all of the composer's chamber music in one fell swoop, this package and its companion (see above) make a good investment. All of the works for piano quartet and quintet can be heard here but also a suitably intense performance of Fauré's last work, the Quartet for Strings in E minor, op. 121.

Nocturnes for Piano
what to buy: [Jean-Philippe Collard, piano] (EMI Rouge et Noir 69437) ♪♪♪♪

Spread out over nine opus numbers and nearly 40 years, these deceptively simple-sounding works are filled with harmonic surprises. Collard's finely nuanced traversal of these pieces is complemented on this two-disc set by a selection of works displaying Fauré's emotional range as it developed over the years: youthful (the *Ballade* in F sharp minor, op. 19), middle-aged (the *Theme and Variations* in C sharp minor, op. 73), and valedictory (the Préludes from op. 103).

various piano works
what to buy: [Vlado Perlemuter, piano] (Nimbus 5165) ♪♪♪♪₄

Cue up Perlemuter's rendition of the first Nocturne and be amazed at the amount of poetry he unlocks from the composer's already beautiful work. Many of the pieces in this recital were performed by the then youthful pianist for the aged composer, and this gives the collection a certain cachet. Perlemuter plays magnificently in five Nocturnes, two Impromptus, the fifth Barcarolle, and the heady *Theme and Variations* in C sharp minor.

what to buy next: [Kathryn Stott, piano] (Hyperion 67064) ♪♪♪♪

Selected from Stott's traversal of Fauré's complete piano works, this tidy collection features some marvelous playing and more felicitous sound than that accorded Perlemuter. She too dips into the Nocturnes, Barcarolles, and Impromptus but also includes the wonderful *Pièces brèves* for Piano, op. 84.

Vocal
Requiem for Soprano, Baritone, Organ, Orchestra, and Chorus, op. 48
what to buy: [Caroline Ashton, soprano; Stephen Varcoe, baritone; John Rutter, cond.; City of London Sinfonia members; Cambridge Singers] (Collegium 109) ♪♪♪♪

This is probably one of the most performed and loved works in the entire choral repertoire. Rutter has created a new performing version from his research into Fauré's original instrumentation and, while there are literally dozens of recordings to choose from, this is a clean and uncluttered performance by a fine professional choir. Also featured on this CD are other smaller choral works by Fauré, including the lovely *Cantique de Jean Racine*.

[Victoria de los Angeles, soprano; Dietrich Fischer-Dieskau, baritone; André Cluytens, cond.; Paris Conservatoire Société des Concerts Orchestre; Elisabeth Brasseur Chorale] (EMI Classics 66946) ♪♪♪♪

Originally released in the early 1960s, the sonics of the album may not be as fresh as in the Rutter recording, but this is still one of the great performances of this work. The two soloists are impeccable, illustrating why they are both considered among the finest singers of the 20th century, and the choral singing is superb.

what to buy next: [Robert Chilcott, treble; John Carol Case, baritone; David Willcocks, cond.; New Philharmonia Orchestra; Choir of King's College, Cambridge] (EMI Classics Red Line 69858) ♪♪♪⁴

Willcocks's performance of the Requiem uses Chilcott's treble voice instead of a female soprano and boy choristers instead of women. The composer's *Pavane* for Flute and Orchestra, op. 50 is also included, as is one of the most famous 16th-century unaccompanied mass settings, Giovanni Pierluigi da Palestrina's *Missa Papae Marcelli*.

various songs
what to buy: [*La Chanson d'Eve*; Janet Baker, mezzo-soprano; Geoffrey Parsons, piano] (Hyperion 66320) ♪♪♪♪♪

There is the "stunning" that smacks you right between the eyes and the "stunning" that sneaks up on you with all manner of subtlety. Baker's artistry in "Après un rêve," "Mandoline," or any of the other songs on this disc puts the music first, delivering it with an artistry few have matched in this repertoire. Parsons accompanies with equal grace.

what to buy next: [Elly Ameling, soprano; Gérard Souzay, baritone; Dalton Baldwin, piano] (EMI Classics 64079) ♪♪♪♪⁴

You can buy quite worthy single-disc selections of Fauré's songs or you can take the plunge and splurge on this relatively inexpensive four-disc set of the composer's complete songs. Opting for Ameling and Souzay, two of the most formidable chanson performers in recorded history, is not a terribly difficult decision if you wish to explore these wonderful works in their entirety.

influences: Claude Debussy, Maurice Ravel, Charles Koechlin

Craig Scott Symons and Ian Palmer

Morton Feldman
Born January 12, 1926, in New York City, NY. Died September 3, 1987, in Buffalo, NY.

period: Twentieth century

Much of Morton Feldman's work adumbrated the modern minimalist/ambient approach to music, but rarely has any one practitioner of that discipline approached the sheer scale in which he operated during his last years of life. Tending towards quiet exactitude rather than orchestral blustering, his later scores are often lengthy—*For Philip Guston* runs nearly four-and-a-half hours—demanding almost as much commitment from audiences as they do from the performers.

Feldman began studying composition with Wallingford Riegger when he was only 15, continuing with Stefan Wolpe three years later. In 1949 he met John Cage, whose revolutionary ideas about what constitutes music impressed him mightily and through whom the young composer was introduced to many of the experimental painters and poets of the day. Despite his exposure to Cage's random processes, Feldman created only a few early works for piano in that style. He had developed a distaste for compositional "systems," explaining (in an article he wrote called *Conversations Without Stravinsky*) that the question for him had become "whether we will control the materials or choose instead to control the experience." In any case, rhythm was less a guide to the intricacies of his scores than a by-product of shifting (sometimes pre-determined) sonorities often (but not always) left to the discretion of the performer(s); the sounds are engaged in fluctuating combinations of timbre and density drawn from scores that assign skeletal directions to pitch and rhythm.

Much of the inspiration for his early major works had come from the avant-garde art world of the late 1940s and early 1950s when Jasper Johns, Robert Rauschenberg and Feldman's great friend, Philip Guston, were beginning to make their marks and the composer acted as a sonic associate. Pieces like *Rothko Chapel, De Kooning,* and *For Franz Kline* were inspired by the composer's fascination with graphic artists, but during the 1970s he started assigning bare-bones titles to his compositions, such as *Cello and Orchestra, String Quartet and Orchestra,* and *Voice, Violin, and Piano,* which seemed to concentrate on the time span and weight his newer works were beginning to exhibit. Feldman was increasingly concerned with the length of time a sound could be heard and the variations in pitch caused by the decay of that sound. In 1969 he had written an article that presaged these fascinations, called *Between Categories,* in which he stated that, "My obsession with surface is the subject of my music. In that sense, my compositions are really not 'compositions' at all. One might call them time canvasses in which I more or less prime the canvas with an overall hue of the music."

Rather than allow his performers the kind of freedom given them in his earlier works, Feldman started micromanaging the musicians through his scores—although it might not seem that way to the unwary listener who just hears subtle washes of sound foreshadowing minimalism. In *For Philip Guston* (composed in 1984, three years before his death), at the end of 104 oversized pages of music, he actually changes the meter in every one of the last 15 bars, dictating the pace and performance concept of the work in an almost obsessive/compulsive manner. This contrasts vividly with a 1963 work he dedicated to Guston (*Piece to Philip Guston* for Piano), which took less than three minutes to perform.

Feldman taught at SUNY Buffalo from 1972 until his death from cancer in 1987. While at the university he wrote many of his important large-scale works, including *Cello and Orchestra, Piano and Orchestra,* and *Coptic Light,* in addition to finishing *Rothko Chapel,* and creating some of his more notable scores for small ensembles—*For Frank O'Hara, For Philip Guston,* the *Quintet for Piano and Strings,* and *Why Patterns.*

Orchestral
Cello and Orchestra
what to buy: [*Hans Zender Edition, vol. 11;* Siegfried Palm, cello; Hans Zender, cond.; Saarbrücken Radio Symphony Orchestra] (CPO 999483) ♪ ♪ ♪ ♪

Zender conducted the first performance with this soloist, for whom the work was written in 1972. *Cello and Orchestra* gives periodic melodic lines to the cello over a tuneless orchestral ebb and flow. This is a powerful piece, worth repeated listening for anyone interested in exploring late 20th-century music. The three other works on this two-CD set—*Flute and Orchestra, Oboe and Orchestra,* and *Piano and Orchestra*—all date from the 1970s.

what to buy next: [*Coptic Light, etc.;* Robert Cohen, cello; Michael Tilson Thomas, cond.; New World Symphony, orch.] (Argo 448513) ♪ ♪ ♪ ♪

Despite the label's trumpeting this disc as containing *World Premiere Recordings,* none of the works heard here is actually new to the catalog. *Cello and Orchestra* receives solid (if less insightful) playing from Cohen than the Palm-powered version with Zender, but the engineering is good and Tilson Thomas is a most effective conductor, slowing the piece down to 21 minutes, a speed which Feldman himself may well have envisioned. *Piano and Orchestra,* featuring Alan Feinberg as the soloist, is also heard here.

Chamber
For Philip Guston for Flute, Alto Flute, Percussion, Piano, and Celeste
what to buy: [Dorothy Stone, flutes; Arthur Jarvinen, percussion; Gloria Cheng-Cochran, piano/celesta] (Bridge 9078A/D) ♪ ♪ ♪ ♪

The sound quality of this recording is somewhat better than that of the Hat ART release cited below, but the musicians (all members of the California EAR Unit) take the piece at a slightly faster speed, which may be a distraction for listeners used to the glacial pacing Feldman himself favored in his later works.

worth searching for: [Eberhard Blum, flutes; Jan Williams, percussion; Nils Vigeland, piano/celeste] (Hat ART 61041/2/3/4) ♪ ♪ ♪ ♪♪

Working closely with the composer for almost a decade, this trio of performers has been connected with this work since its inception. Feldman and these musicians were all based at SUNY Buffalo, often touring together to perform the composer's works. The composition grew not only out of his former relationship with Guston but his trust in the skills of these individual artists.

Piano and String Quartet
what to buy: [Aki Takahashi, piano; Kronos Quartet, ensemble] (Nonesuch 79320) ♪ ♪ ♪ ♪♪

Written in 1985 for the musicians heard here, this is another of Feldman's extended compositions—occupying nearly 80 luscious, slowed-down minutes. Since everything in the piece is marked *pianissimo,* the sound engineering is particularly important, as is the level at which the recording is played. The staff at Nonesuch did well with the first matter, and it is up to the listener to deal with the other.

The Viola in My Life (parts 1–3) for Various Instruments
what to buy: [Karen Phillips, viola; Anahid Ajemian, violin; Seymour Barab, cello; David Tudor, piano; Paula Robison, flute; Arthur Bloom, clarinet; Raymond DesRoches, percussion; Morton Feldman, cond.] (CRI 620) ♪ ♪ ♪ ♪

Released as part of CRI's *American Masters* series, this disc features Feldman conducting (in *The Viola in My Life* and *False Relationships and the Extended Ending*) and performing on piano (as part of the trio in *Why Patterns?*). With the composer's active participation, these recordings are probably as authoritative as possible. *The Viola in My Life,* written in 1970, comes from the point in Feldman's creative life when his work vacillated between freedom for the performer and the marked specificity of his later scores. In any event, this is a fine performance and worth exploring.

Vocal
Rothko Chapel for Soprano, Viola, Harpsichord, Percussion, and Chorus
what to buy: [Deborah Dietrich, soprano; David Abel, viola; Karen Rosenak, cello; William Winant, percussion; Philip Brett, cond.; University of California at Berkeley

Chamber Chorus] (New Albion 39) ♪ ♪ ♪ ♪

The engineers have done a fine job of recording what may be Feldman's easiest work to grasp (if clutching at sonic ephemera can be termed "grasping"). The aural textures seemingly float about the room at will, but a glance at the score confirms that the composer left little to chance here, directing every nuance from the printed page. *Why Patterns,* a trio for flute, piano, and glockenspiel and performed by members of the California EAR Unit is also included.

worth searching for: [Karen Phillips, viola; James Holland, percussion; Gregg Smith, cond.; Gregg Smith Singers, choir] (Columbia Odyssey 34138) ♪ ♪ ♪ ♪

Early recordings of pieces can provide a different and interesting take on the music. Feldman's aural visions are especially amenable to this sort of listening, as evidenced by this initial recording of what was to become one of his more popular (read accessible) works. This artifact of the vinyl era includes liner notes by the composer for both *The Rothko Chapel* and its accompanying piece, *For Frank O'Hara.*

influences: Pierre Boulez, Edgard Varèse, Steve Reich, Philip Glass, Pauline Oliveros

Garaud MacTaggart

John Field
Born July 26 (?), 1782, in Dublin, Ireland. Died January 23, 1837, in Moscow, Russia.

period: Romantic

In his nocturnes, this brilliant Irish pianist sought to convey a variety of emotions in small musical forms, influencing Frédéric Chopin's own nocturnes and Felix Mendelssohn's *Lieder ohne Worte (Songs without Words)* among others. He has only recently been given his due as an accomplished composer of miniatures, sonatas, and concertos for piano.

Field's father, Robert, was a violinist and his grandfather, John, an organist, and together they gave him his first music lessons. The precocious young Field made his debut as a pianist at the age of nine, astonishing the critics. The next year the family left for London where

Robert joined the Haymarket Theatre orchestra and John was apprenticed to Muzio Clementi, the great virtuoso pianist, composer, and piano manufacturer. London was a center for piano makers and players, and the synergies created there helped to bring about the transition from the old style forte-piano to the big modern grands. After writing his first piano concerto at 17, Field became a celebrated performer, and, with the publication of his first set of three piano sonatas, he was looked upon as an up-and-coming composer. In 1802 Clementi went to Paris, Vienna, and St. Petersburg, hoping to drum up some business, and he took with him John Field, whose apprenticeship with the older musician had ended. It was useful for Clementi to have a young virtuoso on hand, demonstrating pianos and playing the composer-entrepreneur's music. Field delighted audiences with his playing and when the duo ended up in St. Petersburg, Field stayed on after his employer had sailed for home. It is thought that Field served as Clementi's business agent in Russia for pianos and music publications.

Field, whose supple virtuosity was all the rage with the aristocracy, now called Russia his home, traveling between apartments in St. Petersburg and Moscow. He married one of his students in 1810 before finally settling down two years later in St. Petersburg and starting a family. During his decade there, Field published a number of his nocturnes and piano concertos in addition to venturing out on concert tours. He moved his family back to Moscow in 1821, but alcohol was starting to play a devastating role in his life and he found it difficult to write new music. While he was still able to tour as a virtuoso, Field (now bearing the nickname "Drunken John") was not always sober at concert time and his performances suffered correspondingly. By 1830 he was suffering the debilitating effects of cancer, eventually seeking treatment for it in London. Although he lived for almost six more years, even staging a comeback of sorts in various European cities, public tastes were changing. During the 1830s a new school of pianists was already taking full advantage (ironically) of the sturdy new pianos coming out of the shops. Field found his lyrical style being challenged by a group of young, strong men who played aggressively, even violently. The youthful Franz Liszt was typical in many ways of these hot bloods, and the future belonged to him and his peers.

On a more encouraging note, Field somehow managed to reconnect with his muse and began composing again, creating his last seven nocturnes (and *Midi*, often referred to as the 18th nocturne) plus a few other short piano works. On Christmas Day, 1832, Chopin attended one of Field's last concerts, the premiere of his Concerto no. 7 in C minor for Piano and Orchestra. (Reportedly he wasn't impressed by the performance but still gave his own students pieces by Field to study and play.) Field then continued what would turn out to be his last tour of the Continent, in 1834 reaching Naples where he ended up in the hospital for nine months. He finally got back to Moscow a year later with the aid of some Russian aristocrats and there composed a few more works before succumbing to his illness.

Field wrote seven piano concertos, four sonatas, various miniatures, and his beautiful nocturnes. He single-handedly invented that genre and created examples in its most basic form. They are true night pieces, with a singing melody in the right hand and an accompaniment of broken chords in the left. Exposition is the thing here, not so much development. The nocturne was the piano equivalent of a bel canto opera aria, all the rage at the time. The piano god Chopin took the nocturne to musical heaven and perfected it, but his inspiration came from the sweet and lyrical soul of John Field.

Orchestral
Concerto no. 2 in A-flat Major for Piano and Orchestra
what to buy: [Miceal O'Rourke, piano; Matthias Bamert, cond.; London Mozart Players, orch.] (Chandos 9368) ♪ ♪ ♪ ♪

Field was a miniaturist rather than someone able to expand a thought into a sentence. Given this handicap, he still manages to engender affection by the grace of his ideas. O'Rourke is a perfect pianist/advocate for the composer and his playing has the requisite energy, humor, and lightness of touch to give Field's ideas validity and power. Chandos has paired the first two (and most popular) of the seven piano concertos and Bamert's ensemble plays them as if they were masterpieces.

Chamber
Nocturnes for Piano
what to buy: [*The Complete Nocturnes*; Miceal O'Rourke, piano] (Chandos 8719) ♪ ♪ ♪ ♪

O'Rourke's admirable flexibility in these little gems makes it easy to see why they are so important historically, as precursors of Chopin's weightier, even more beautiful Nocturnes. Thhis two-disc set is the product of an expansive pianist and sympathetic engineers.

what to buy next: [John O'Conor, piano] (Telarc 80199)
♪ ♪ ♪₈

This disc offers solid, if uninspired, performances of Field's best compositions but leaves out three of the Nocturnes (nos. 3, 7, and 17), coupling them with O'Conor's less impressive recording of the composer's four piano sonatas (Telarc 80290).

[*Field: Piano Music, volume 1*; Benjamin Frith, piano] (Naxos 8.550761) ♪ ♪ ♪₈

At a budget price, this collection and its companion (Naxos 8.550762) give quite good value. If Frith is not quite the equal of O'Rourke in this material, he can certainly stand up to O'Conor, even surpassing him on occasion. Volume One contains the first nine nocturnes and the first two piano sonatas, while volume two offers the remaining nocturnes and the third of Field's early sonatas.

influences: Frédéric Chopin, Johann Nepomuk Hummel

Gerald Brennan and Garaud MacTaggart

Gerald Finzi

Born Gerald Raphael Finzi, July 14, 1901, in London, England. Died September 27, 1956, in Oxford, England.

period: Twentieth century

Gerald Finzi was a minor master who added a distinctive voice to English music during the first half of the twentieth century. He is best known for his *Ecologue* for Piano and Strings and his Christmas cantata *Dies Natalis*.

Finzi, a private person all of his life, was even educated privately—unusual for a musician at this time. His father died when Gerald was only eight years old, and the deaths in World War I of his three older brothers and his first important music teacher only intensified his introspective and pacifist nature. After teaching at the Royal Academy of Music from 1930 to 1933, Finzi married, left London, and moved to the countryside. He took to raising rare varieties of apple trees on a small farm while accumulating a large library of music and literature. Other than his agricultural chores, there were few interruptions to take him away from his compositional

labors; indeed, his only break from regular musical activity came during World War II, when he worked for the Ministry of Transport in London. In 1951 Finzi was diagnosed with a rare form of leukemia, but true to his penchant for privacy, he only told close family members of his condition and continued to work as if nothing were wrong. In 1956 he came down with chicken pox while attending the Gloucester Festival. As he was already in a weakened state, complications from the disease ended his life shortly thereafter, bringing the career of a wonderfully talented and dedicated musician to a premature conclusion.

Influences in Finzi's music spring from Edward Elgar, Ralph Vaughan Williams, and English folksongs; his works display folk-like elements without actually using folk material. Finzi had a distinctive musical voice, and even his larger works are basically intimate, with a memorably bittersweet tinge. He lived a life of total and intense dedication to his craft and exhibited a tremendous curiosity about music of all sorts and eras. He was also passionately interested in literature, poetry, and the relationship between words and music. It comes as no surprise that his vocal music is the finest part of his output. He wrote some exquisitely beautiful songs, and his Thomas Hardy-based cycle *Earth and Air and Rain* is one of the finest song cycles of the twentieth century. Finzi revived and edited a good deal of early English music, and his collection of such works from the mid-eighteenth century was considered at the time to be the finest private collection in England.

Orchestral
Concerto in C Minor for Clarinet and Strings, op.31
what to buy: [Alan Hacker, clarinet; William Boughton, cond.; English String Orchestra] (Nimbus 5101) ♪ ♪ ♪ ♪

No better introduction to this wonderful composer's music can be found than Finzi's beautiful and lyrical clarinet concerto. This outstanding disc also includes his Romance in E-flat Major for String Orchestra, op. 11; the Prelude In F Minor for String Orchestra, op. 25; and some incidental music written for a radio production of Shakespeare's *Love's Labour's Lost*.

Ecologue in F Major for Piano and Strings, op. 10**
what to buy: [Martin Jones, piano; William Boughton, cond.; English String Orchestra] (Nimbus 5366) ♪ ♪ ♪ ♪

This minor masterpiece lasts only ten minutes and was originally intended as the slow movement for a piano concerto that Finzi never completed. A beautifully atmospheric and poignant work, it gets to the heart of the composer's musical world. The disc also features music for string orchestra by Frank Bridge and Hubert Parry.

Vocal
Dies Natalis for Soprano (or Tenor) and Orchestra, op.8
what to buy: [John Mark Ainsley, tenor; Matthew Best, cond.; Corydon Orchestra] (Hyperion 66876) ♪ ♪ ♪ ♪

Finzi's two greatest vocal works are on this disc. In addition to an eloquent performance of the *Dies Natalis,* there is also a fine version (featuring the Corydon Singers) of the composer's *Intimations of Immortality* for Tenor, Orchestra, and Chorus, op. 28. The sound on both pieces is spacious and finely detailed.

worth searching for: [Philip Langridge, tenor; Richard Hickox, cond.; London Symphony Orchestra; London Symphony Chorus] (Decca 425660) ♪ ♪ ♪ ♪

Although this recording was never released in the United States, it is worth seeking out as an example of Finzi's remarkable gifts as a choral composer. The disc is a compilation of four works conducted by Hickox with either the LSO or the City of London Sinfonietta, in conjunction with either the London Symphony Chorus or the Hickox Singers. In addition to a fine *Dies Natalis,* the wonderful, short Christmas cantata *In Terra Pax* (with soprano Norma Burrowes and baritone John Shirley-Quirk) deserves special mention.

various songs
what to buy: [Martyn Hill, tenor; Stephen Varcoe, bass; Clifford Benson, piano] (Hyperion 66161/62) ♪ ♪ ♪ ♪

At his finest, Finzi was a sensitive and wholly intuitive writer of vocal scores, fitting music to words like glove to hand. This two-disc set contains the various song cycles he wrote for piano and tenor or baritone voice, including a fine performance of the marvelous *Earth and Air and Rain,* op. 15. The recorded sound has great presence and warmth.

influences: Herbert Howells, E.J. Moeran, Ralph Vaughan Williams

Charles Greenwell and David Wagner

Stephen Foster
Born Stephen Collins Foster on July 4, 1826, in Lawrenceville, PA. Died January 13, 1864, in New York City, NY.

period: Romantic

Stephen Foster became America's first truly great professional songwriter, composing over two hundred parlor ballads and minstrel songs in his tragically short life. Over the course of his career Foster became a major link between American folk and art song traditions, moving tunes from the fields into the parlors. Among his most popular works are "Oh! Susanna," "Beautiful Dreamer," "Jeanie with the Light Brown Hair," "Old Folks at Home," and "My Old Kentucky Home," that state's official song.

The child of a prominent Pittsburgh merchant, Foster showed early musical gifts but was not encouraged to develop these talents by his parents. A mostly self-taught musician who played flute, guitar, and some piano in his youth, Foster published his first song, "Open Thy Lattice Love," in 1844, when he was eighteen years old. Despite the urgings of his father and brothers to pursue a career in commerce, Foster continued writing and publishing his songs—selling his earliest ones for only a few dollars—until he became an established songwriter and was able to bargain for better prices. At the peak of his career, between 1849 and 1860, he received about $15,000 in royalties.

In 1850 Foster left Cincinnati, where he had taken a bookkeeping job in his brother's grocery, and headed back to Pennsylvania, where he married Jane Denny McDowell. He then rented an office and devoted himself to his work, writing prolifically. Foster also made an agreement with Christy's Minstrels, giving them exclusive first-performance rights to every new song he wrote. In fact, he allowed the troupe's leader, E. P. Christy, to name himself as the author of what in 1851 would become one of Foster's most successful songs, "Old Folks at Home."

The next decade was a tumultuous one. Incompatibilities in his marriage caused frequent separations, made worse when Foster's finances worsened (owing largely to the lack of copyright protection) and he was unable to support his family. From 1853 on, most of Foster's songs were published by companies in New York, where he permanently relocated in 1860. Saddened by the outbreak of the Civil War and in poor health by then, Foster signed a contract with a publisher that waived royalties in favor of a regular $800 annual fee in return for a minimum of twelve new songs. Foster went deeper into debt and started drinking heavily; he began to write mediocre songs for ready cash. On January 10, 1864, after a severe shaving accident and fall, he was taken to Bellevue Hospital from a cheap Bowery hotel. Three days later, he died while in a coma.

Foster's works were among the first popular songs that were truly American, and they swept the country via minstrel shows. He was particularly inspired by three songbook collections that evolved out of the European folk movement of the late eighteenth and nineteenth centuries: James Johnson's *Scots Musical Museum* (to which Robert Burns was a major contributor), Thomas Moore's *Irish Melodies* and George Thomson's three volumes of Scottish, Irish, and Welsh songs. Foster also drew inspiration from the bel canto melodies of European opera and from the music of African-American slaves. The minstrel dialect of Foster's songs, while politically insensitive by today's standards, represented a popular source of entertainment for both races in his day. While his earliest songs used the "Ethiopian" style adopted from stereotypical slave patois, he subsequently avoided using dialect, forbade caricatures to be used on the covers of his sheet music, and sought to humanize and make elegant what he called his "plantation songs." Although these songs were extremely popular with the public of his day, Foster's legacy resides best in the lilting melodies of his 135 ballads and romantic parlor songs.

Chamber
instrumental arrangements
what to buy: [*Mountain Songs: A Cycle of American Folk Music*; Elliott Fisk, guitar; Paula Robison, flute] (Musicmasters 7038) ♪♪♪♪

Lilting, lovely instrumental duo versions of "Beautiful Dreamer" and two other Foster tunes ("Jennie's Own Schottische" and "If You Only Have a Moustache") are contained on this 1986 recording, which includes traditional folk songs as well as works by Edward MacDowell, William Schuman, and Charles Ives.

[*Acres of Clams*; Pioneer Brass, ensemble] (Centaur 2131) ♪♪♪♪

Philip Neumann plays the reed contrabass with support from other members of the Pioneer Brass on a unique

rendering of Foster's classic "Camptown Races." Although the song was originally written for voice and piano, the band's playful arrangement will make you chuckle (doo-dah!). The enticing twenty-three-tune collection also includes clever instrumental versions of Foster's "Jeanie with the Light Brown Hair," "Old Dog Tray," and "Old Folks Quadrilles," along with works by other early American composers. Formed in 1980, the Pioneer Brass is a virtuosic group of multi-instrumentalists whose individual and collective expertise shines throughout this wonderful album.

Vocal
various songs
what to buy: [*Stephen Foster Songbook*; Robert Shaw, cond.; Robert Shaw Chorale] (RCA Living Stereo 61253) ♪♪♪♪♪

Williams and the Robert Shaw Chorale serve up an enticing twenty-song compilation recorded between 1958 and 1961. This is the only available CD containing most of Foster's popular songs, including "Old Folks at Home," "Beautiful Dreamer," "My Old Kentucky Home," "Oh! Susanna," "Nelly Bly," "Camptown Races," and "Old Black Joe." Because Shaw recorded these songs prior to any prevailing political correctness, this set remains a relative rarity for its inclusion of Foster's minstrel songs and plantation ballads.

what to buy next: [*Stephen Foster, Vol. 1*; Jan DeGaetani, mezzo-soprano; Leslie Guinn, baritone; Joan Renithaler, cond.; Gilbert Kalish, piano, melodeon; James Weaver, piano; Robert Sheldon, flute, keyed bugle; Sonya Monosoff, violin; Douglas Koeppe, piccolo, flute; Camerata Chorus of Washington] (Elektra/Nonesuch 79158) ♪♪♪♪

Guinn's stately singing, the confident accompaniment by Kalish and others, and DeGaetani's dulcet voice and heartfelt delivery make this two-volume, twenty-three-song collection delightfully appealing from start to finish. The set combines separate performances recorded with historical instruments at the Smithsonian Institution in 1972 and 1976. Not only are the tracks organized for maximum entertainment value, but the excellent musicianship in these performances makes this a highly recommended album.

Stephen Foster

[Julianne Baird, soprano; Linda Russell, alto; Frederick Urrey, tenor; John Van Buskirk, fortepiano] (Albany/Troy 119) ♪ ♪ ♪ ♪

Urrey's warm and engaging delivery, with solo piano accompaniment, is heard on "Beautiful Dreamer," one of the best tracks on this disc. Another charming track is "Old Black Joe," where each singer solos before being followed by a gorgeously blended vocal chorus. Other Foster hits are also here, including "Camptown Races" and "Jeannie with the Light Brown Hair." The distant, unamplified sound may be annoying to some listeners, but it does make you feel that you're sitting in middle of a small recital hall in Foster's day.

[*American Dreamer: Songs of Stephen Foster*, Thomas Hampson, baritone; Jay Ungar, mandolin; Molly Mason, guitar; David Alpher, piano] (Angel 54621) ♪ ♪ ♪ ♪

Hampson's lovely voice graces the classic "Beautiful Dreamer" and some of the fifteen other Foster songs here, including lesser-known but likeable ditties such as the mournful ballad "Hard Times Come Again No More" and the syncopated "My Wife Is a Most Knowing Woman." Period accompaniment makes the disc all the more enjoyable, especially on "That's What's the Matter," a perky number that adds a second male voice, banjo, and tuba to the mix.

influences: Woody Guthrie, Arlo Guthrie, Bob Dylan, Pete Seeger

Nancy Ann Lee

César Franck

Born César Auguste Jean Guillaume Hubert Franck, December 10, 1822, in Liège, Belgium. Died November 8, 1890, in Paris, France.

period: Romantic

César Franck is, arguably, the most important nineteenth century composer for the organ, and works like his *Grande pièce symphonique* and *Pièce héroïque* are cornerstones of modern organ recital programs. He didn't write exclusively for this instrument, however, and a number of his later works, written in the cyclical style with which he is most closely associated, have a harmonic and contrapuntal daring grounded in the advancements of Franz Liszt and Ludwig van Beethoven.

Franck's father, Nicolas-Joseph, sought to turn César into a virtuoso pianist, a process he evidently believed could be used to enrich the family. After his son did well in his classes at the Liège Conservatory, the head of the family decided to cash in and organized a series of concert tours which eventually hit Paris. After moving the family there in 1835, Nicolas-Joseph saw to it that his son's musical education continued—with, as always, an eye toward profiting from his progeny. César was eventually enrolled at the Paris Conservatoire and demonstrated considerable abilities on the piano and in his study of counterpoint. Ironically, the area in which he was to develop a reputation later in life, as an organist, was one in which his demonstrated competency was not up to the high standards he had achieved in the other disciplines.

In 1842, Franck left the school and went back to Belgium, which he was then supposed to use as a base of operations for the career his father had chosen for him, as a touring concert artist and a teacher to the developing bourgeoisie. Since Nicolas-Joseph had not worked at a regular job once he decided that César would be a famous musician, there was a great deal of pressure on the junior Franck to earn money. In 1846, two years after the family returned to Paris, the young man finally rebelled against his autocratic father and began to support himself by teaching and working as choir organist at the church of Notre-Dame de Lorette.

By this time he had already been composing music for his own recitals, and had also managed to secure performances of some sacred vocal works. Franck's first published piece, a piano trio, dates from 1842 and was a qualified success, but his cantata *Notre-Dame des orages* seems to have had only one performance, and the sacred oratorio *Ruth* met with blasé to bad reviews after its premiere in 1846. Orchestral scores (including a piano concerto and an early symphony) bulked up the rest of Franck's initial oeuvre. Although he continued to write music during the next few years, none of the compositions from that period seemed to strike a chord with either the public or his publishers.

Franck worked on greatly improving his playing skills and succeeded to the point where he was able to acquire a more prestigious posting in 1853, when he was appointed organist for the church of Saint-Jean-Saint-François du Marais. There Franck got the chance to perform on a relatively recent instrument (it was installed in 1846) created by legendary organ builders Aristide and Dominique Cavaillé-Coll. He also worked with the brothers, demonstrating the virtues of their instruments to prospective buyers at their factory. Five years later he was able to move on to an even more distinguished position, a recently constructed church (St. Clothilde) for which a brand new Cavaillé-Coll organ had been contracted. Once the instrument was fitted into position (in 1859), the church became Franck's main venue for the display of his talents as an instrumentalist.

While Franck was becoming known throughout Paris for his improvisatory abilities, his reputation as a teacher was steadfastly growing as well, and it was through the academic realm that his greatest impact on French music would come. This was especially true after he became a member of the Paris Conservatoire faculty as an organ professor in 1872. Franck had already finished the six pieces for organ that make up his opp. 16–21 (including the *Grande Pièce symphonique*) and written the *Messe à 3 voix* (to which he later added the famous *Panis angelicus*), and looked upon his organ class as an opportunity to disseminate his theories about composition. The methodology he taught was a cyclical process that placed short melodic lines around a single pitch and then expanded them. It was a procedure that had its roots in the works of Beethoven and Liszt, and yielded chromatic harmonies that some adherents (and detractors) likened to those of Richard Wagner. This isn't to say that Franck neglected his duties with regard to teaching the practical aspects of playing; within the first ten years of his teaching at the Conservatoire five of his students won first prize in organ.

The last eleven years of Franck's life saw the production of his most enduring compositions, including the *Pièce héroïque* and the three *Chorales* for organ; two pieces that are arguably his finest orchestral scores (the *Symphonic Variations* for Piano and Orchestra and his Symphony in D Minor); and the trio of chamber works that occupy the pinnacle of his non-organ oeuvre, his Quintet in F Minor for Piano and Strings, the Sonata in A Major for Violin and Piano, and the Quartet in D Major for Strings.

Orchestral
Symphony in D Minor
what to buy: [Pierre Monteux, cond.; Chicago Symphony Orchestra] (RCA Victor 63303) ♪ ♪ ♪ ♪♪

Despite all the advances in recording technology since, this 1961 performance has never been beaten for sheer

Arthur Fiedler:
He was known as "Mr. Pops" and conducted the Boston Pops Orchestra for a remarkable forty-nine years, from 1930 until his death in 1979. Although he didn't originate the concept of a symphony orchestra playing lighter musical fare, Arthur Fiedler expanded the concept and brought it to artistic and commercial success.

His father had been a musician with the Boston Symphony Orchestra, and after a period of study in Europe, the young Fiedler returned to the United States in 1914 and joined the BSO as a violinist before transferring to the viola section. Fiedler discovered that in addition to musical talent, he had the gift of organization. In 1925, he hired a group of colleagues from the orchestra to form the Boston Sinfonietta and eventually organized the Espalande Concerts, in which the ensemble played popular classics and light, pop-oriented material. Because of his success with this group and others, he was offered the job as conductor of the BSO's *Boston Pops* series in 1930. Fiedler expanded the scope of the Pops orchestra by playing Broadway show tunes, popular big band tunes, and finally, in the 1960s and 1970s, rock & roll. He was always daring in his programming and astute in his understanding of what would sell. The Boston Pops became a very successful money-making operation for the parent orchestra, and Fiedler-led recordings always outsold the more conservative orchestral fare. In fact, the Pops releases of the 1950s went a long way toward ensuring the financial security of the BSO, making possible other, more prestigious yet less lucrative recording projects for the organization.

Over twenty years after Fiedler's death, there are still over sixty compact discs in print, even though Fiedler only recorded through the era of the LP. A good place to start is with the *Pops Caviar* disc (RCA 68132) containing great Russian masterworks like the *Russian Easter Overture* by Nicolai Rimsky-Korsakov, the Waltz from Piotr Tchaikovsky's *Swan Lake* ballet, and highlights from Aram Khachaturian's *Gayane Ballet*, including the famous *Sabre Dance*. Also look for the all-Gershwin album (RCA 68792) featuring a killer performance of the *Rhapsody in Blue* with a young Earl Wild as piano soloist.

Dave Wagner

drive. Monteux's conception is intense and he manages to draw magnificent playing from the CSO, creating a taut, driving realization that sets an impressive benchmark for all subsequent recordings of this work. The other piece on this album, Igor Stravinsky's *Petrouchka*, is another beneficiary of Monteux's talents and the pairing makes this a most interesting offering.

what to buy next: [Paul Paray, cond.; Detroit Symphony Orchestra] (Mercury Living Presence 434368) ♪ ♪ ♪ ♪

Paray, the son of an organist, was one of the finest conductors of French repertoire during the middle part of the twentieth century, so it may be surprising to some that he made most of his best recordings in Detroit. In any event, this 1959 performance presents the music in a most natural way, emphasizing orchestral sonorities when necessary and pushing the tempo when called upon by the composer. Accompanying the Franck work is Paray's rendering of Sergei Rachmaninoff's second symphony, a good performance but one in which the conductor leads an edited version of the score, making for a somewhat leaner presentation.

Symphonic Variations for Piano and Orchestra
what to buy: [Clifford Curzon, piano; George Szell, cond.; London Symphony Orchestra] (London 425082) ♪ ♪ ♪ ♪₤

Curzon and Szell, like Monteux in Franck's Symphony, have never been bettered in this work. The sound is early stereo (1959) but, despite that caveat, the interpretation more than holds its own against newer digital releases. Curzon's fine performance of Brahms's first piano concerto accompanies the Franck piece, and on that piece the recording is admittedly a bit more dated.

[Ivan Moravec, piano; Václav Neumann, cond.; Czech Philharmonic Orchestra] (Supraphon 3508) ♪ ♪ ♪ ♪₤

Moravec's playing in this 1976 recording has a deliberate grace to it that slowly reveals the cyclical nature of the piece without belaboring how clever Franck was in working out the details of his concept. The engineers bathed the orchestra in sonic warmth; the string and woodwind sections sound positively burnished. Neumann's conducting in this and its disc-mate, Robert Schumann's piano concerto, is complimentary to Moravec's art. The pianist reveals even more of his mastery in a glorious performance of Schumann's *Kinderszenen* drawn from 1987 sessions.

what to buy next: [Pascal Roge, piano; Ross Pople, cond.; London Festival Orchestra] (ASV 769) ♪ ♪ ♪₤

Roge is a wonderful pianist better known for his playing in music by Ravel or Debussy, but his delicate touch in that material doesn't affect the power required in portions of Franck's score. Pople's conducting is fairly straightforward and the orchestra responds appropriately. The two other Franck pieces on this disc are the cello arrangement of the composer's masterful violin sonata (with Roge on piano and Pople on cello), and a good rendition of the Quintet in F Minor for Piano and Strings with Roge and Pople joined by violinists Richard Friedman and Steven Smith and violist Christopher Wellington.

Chamber
organ works
what to buy: [*Complete Works for Organ*; Michael Murray, organ] (Telarc 80234) ♪ ♪ ♪ ♪₤

For those who prefer their organ playing on the muscular side, full of bravura, distinctly virtuosic, and reveling in the massive sonorities of the "King of the Instruments," Murray is right up your alley. The *Grande pièce symphonique* is particularly impressive when given this kind of treatment.

what to buy next: [*Grandes Oeuvres pour orgue*; Marie-Claire Alain, organ] (Erato 12706) ♪ ♪ ♪ ♪

Alain recorded these works on an 1884 Cavaillé-Coll organ similar to the one Franck himself played, and her performance is solidly—not stolidly—in the French tradition.

worth searching for: [*Complete Works for Organ*; Jeanne Demessieux, organ] (Festivo 155-156) ♪ ♪ ♪ ♪ ♪

Demessieux was not only a gifted organist, she was a fine composer in her own right. These performances from 1959 showcase her superb choices in registration on one of the finest instruments ever constructed, the Cavaillé-Coll organ at the Elise de la Sainte Madeleine in Paris. Demessieux became the main organist there in 1962, following in the footsteps of other organist/composers who used to hold the post: Camille Saint-Saëns and Gabriel Fauré.

Pièce héroïque in B Minor for Organ
what to buy: [Marcel Dupré, organ] (Mercury Living Presence 434311) ♪ ♪ ♪ ♪₤

On top of being a top-notch organist, Dupré was also a well-respected composer for his own instrument. Perhaps it was due to this performer/composer duality that Dupré's insights into this short but monumental work were especially revealing when first released (the 1960s) and still hold up well today. The organist also does fine work with Franck's three glorious *Chorales*, and excerpts from the second and sixth organ symphonies by Charles Marie Widor.

Sonata in A Major for Violin and Piano
what to buy: [Kyung Wha Chung, violin; Radu Lupu, piano] (London 421154) ♪ ♪ ♪ ♪₤

Chung's playing is clear and impassioned and Lupu is a sensitive accompanist, not a soloist battling for equal time. Their approach isn't flamboyant but Franck's score creates its own excitement and the duo does a magnificent job of communicating that. Also on the same album, violinist Chung plays in two of Claude Debussy's sonatas and Maurice Ravel's gorgeous *Introduction and Allegro for Harp, Flute, Clarinet, and String Quartet.*

what to buy next: [Itzhak Perlman, violin; Vladimir Ashkenazy, piano] (London 414128) ♪ ♪ ♪ ♪

Perlman and Ashkenazy are strong-willed soloists who happen to work well together. Their virtuosity is unquestioned and even if they miss the last ounce of poetry inherent in this piece, the pairing is welcome for the power they bring to the finale's awesome canon. They close out the disc when joined by horn player Barry Tuckwell for a solid run-through of Johannes Brahms's Trio for Violin, Horn, and Piano.

worth searching for: Kaja Danczowska, violin; Krystian Zimerman, piano] (Deutsche Grammophon 2531330) ♪ ♪ ♪ ♪ ♪

Danczowka's playing is a wonderful blend of clarity and passion and Zimerman is a superb accompanist. Karol Szymanowski's *Mythes for Violin and Piano* fills out the release, and receives a sterling performance worthy of being paired with such an exemplary version of the Franck sonata.

Quartet in D Major for Strings
what to buy: [Prague String Quartet, ensemble] (Praga 250024) ♪ ♪ ♪ ♪

This is a long, complex work featuring Franck's cyclic composition style but heavily influenced by his study of quartets by Beethoven, Schubert, and Brahms. The Czech musicians properly approach this work as if it were on the cusp of the Classical and Romantic eras, giving it a grand performance worthy of the concept. The other featured piece on this disc, Franck's violin sonata, starts out the program on a high note as violinist Gidon Kremer and pianist Oleg Maisenberg perform their roles with a fair amount of passion.

[Kocian Quartet, ensemble] (Praga 250141) ♪ ♪ ♪ ♪

Fine playing and a rarely heard companion work are the

Dietrich Fischer-Dieskau:
Dietrich Fischer-Dieskau took his first formal singing lessons in 1941 when he was sixteen years old. One of his most interesting musical memories from this period (detailed in his autobiography, *Reverberations*) concerned his school concert debut, at which he sang selections from Franz Schubert's song cycle *Der Winterreise* as Allied bombs fell around Berlin. Then, during the final years of World War II, Fischer-Dieskau received his conscription notice and was sent to the Italian front, where he was eventually captured by British troops and became a prisoner of war until his release in 1947.

After his discharge, Fischer-Dieskau continued his vocal studies, finally making his professional debut as the baritone soloist in Johannes Brahms's *Ein deutsches Requiem (The German Requiem)* in 1947 and starting his operatic career as Posa in Giuseppe Verdi's *Don Carlos* in 1948. The next three decades brought him increasing fame, both in opera and as a lieder singer whose only real peer as a baritone was Hans Hotter. Fischer-Dieskau's diction is marvelous in German-language works and only slightly less so in other languages, but some critics have pointed out his tendency to stress specific words within a text at the expense of the overall meaning. Still, his is a voice to provoke wonder at times, especially in non-operatic material.

His singing of the baritone aria from Johann Sebastian Bach's cantata no. 13, *Meine Seufzer, meine Thränen (My sighs, my tears)* (EMI Classics 67202), is a splendid example of Fischer-Dieskau's craft. Most of the material heard in that recital dates from 1958 when he was in prime form, but even a session from 1971 included on the same disc yields a recitative and aria from cantata no. 123 *Liebster Immanuel Herzog der Frommen (Beloved Emmanuel, Lord of the righteous)*, with undeniable greatness at its vocal core.

Fischer-Dieskau's lieder singing has been greatly aided at times by his choice of accompanists. Pianist Gerald Moore was an integral part of an amazing sampler of Franz Schubert's songs (EMI Classics 69503), a project which includes a stunning version of *Der Erlkönig (The Erl King)* to go along with twenty other lieder. Sviatoslav Richter, one of the premier solo pianists of the twentieth century but not as well-known for his sensitive artistry as an accompanist, worked fairly frequently with Fischer-Dieskau, and the pair are best heard in a 1970 recording of Johannes Brahms's *Die Schöne Magelone* (Orfeo D'Or 490981) or in selections drawn from Hugo Wolf's *Mörike-Lieder* that are only available domestically as part of *The Fischer-Dieskau Edition* (Deutsche Grammophon 463500), a twenty-one-disc retrospective of the vocalist's art.

As an opera singer, Fischer-Dieskau has recorded works by Verdi, Wolfgang Amadeus Mozart, and Richard Strauss, but his interpretation of Kurwenal in the Wilhelm Furtwängler-led performance of Richard Wagner's *Tristan und Isolde* from 1952 (EMI Classics 56254) is probably one of Fischer-Dieskau's finest operatic accomplishments. He has also taken part in some intriguing twentieth century works, including sterling characterization of the title characters in Ferruccio Busoni's *Doktor Faust,* (Erato 25501), Aribert Reimann's *Lear* (Deutsche Grammophon 463480), and a sadly deleted rendition of Alban Berg's *Wozzeck.*

Mathilde August

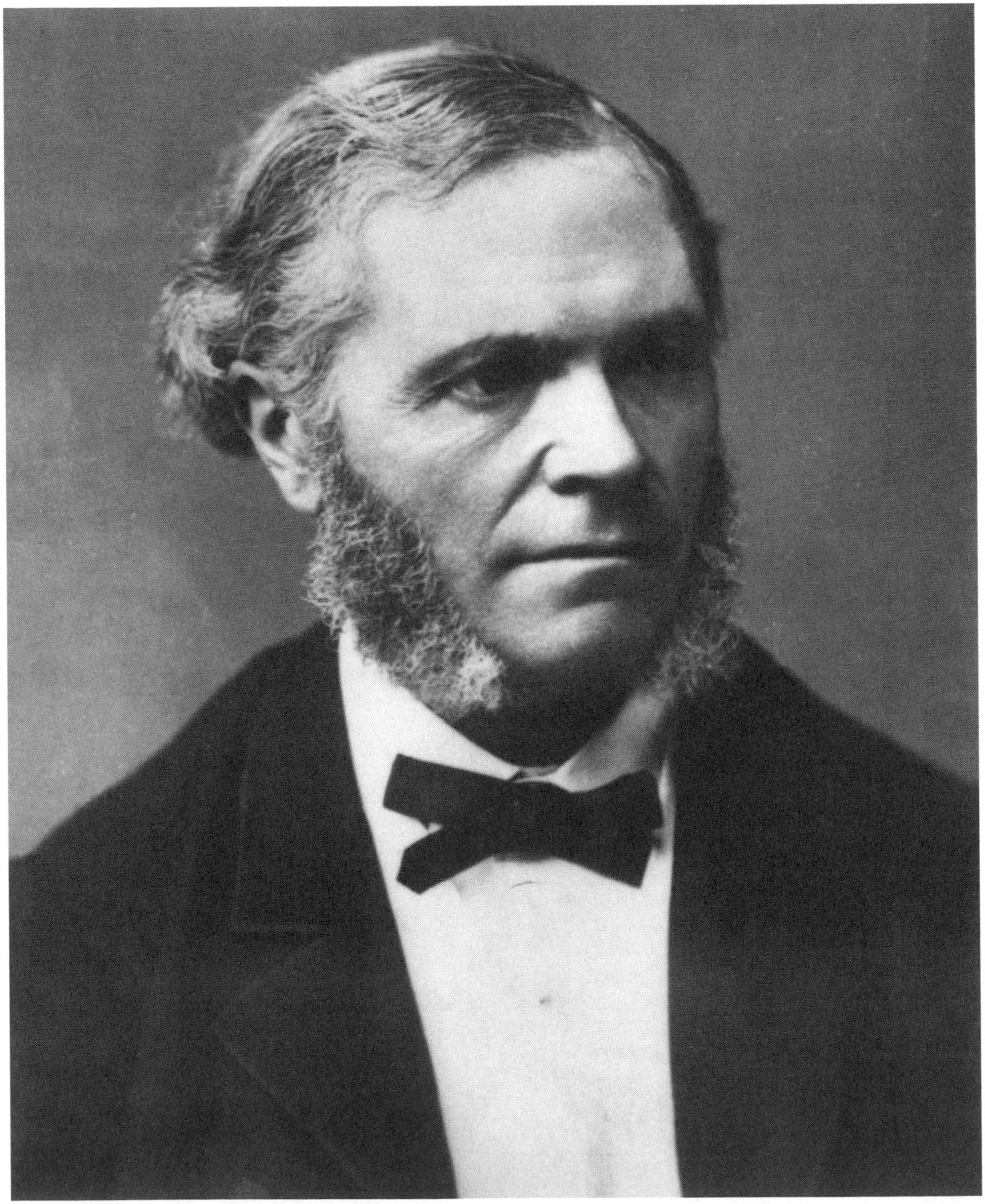

primary virtues of this particular performance. The actual differences in the way the Kocian and Prague ensembles approach this piece are relatively minimal, but the inclusion of Édouard Lalo's seldom-heard string quartet (op. 45) makes this disc a wonderful opportunity to explore a relatively hidden corner of French chamber music.

what to buy next: [Juilliard String Quartet, ensemble] (Sony Classical 63302) ♪ ♪ ♪ ♪

The Julliard Quartet's performance rewards multiple listenings, pointing up the logic and dense beauty of Franck's conception. Included on this disc, however, is a surprisingly mediocre performance of Bedrich Smetana's Quartet no. 1 in E Minor for Strings (*From My Life*).

Quintet in F Minor for Piano and Strings
what to buy: [Victor Aller, piano; Hollywood String Quartet, ensemble] (Testament 1077) ♪ ♪ ♪ ♪ ♪

The ensemble writing here is dramatic and soulful, qualities brought out in this performance by the legendary Hollywood String Quartet. As impressive as their playing is in this work, the accompanying piano quintet by Dmitri Shostakovich is even more so, making this release an easy recommendation. Aller holds up his part of the labors quite well in the putative main role, though the composer's orchestration is the real star of any well-thought-out and played performance.

what to buy next: [Michael Levinas, piano; Ludwig String Quartet, ensemble] (Naxos 8.553645) ♪ ♪ ♪ ♪

Considering the budget price, this recording has attributes that would be at home in a more expensive performance: clean playing, solid recording, and an intriguing (albeit more lightweight) companion piece: Ernest Chausson's Wagnerian-tinged string quartet.

Vocal
Panis angelicus **for Tenor, Harp, Cello, Double Bass, and Organ**
what to buy: [*O Holy Night*; Luciano Pavarotti, tenor; Kurt Herbert Adler, cond.; National Philharmonic Orchestra] (London 414044) ♪ ♪ ♪ ♪

César Franck

Every professional tenor in the universe has probably done this excerpt from Franck's *Messe à 3 voix*, but Pavarotti's Christmas album contains a perfectly gorgeous version from one of history's finest tenors, and that makes it special. The remainder of the disc is pretty decent as well, and hearing it out of season is no great, jarring hardship.

[*Sacred Songs*; Jessye Norman, soprano; Christopher Bowers-Broadbent, organ; Alexander Gibson, cond.; Royal Philharmonic Orchestra] (Philips 400019) ♪ ♪ ♪ ♪

Norman's voice is spectacular throughout this recital and her singing is a marvel of control and artistry. The disc's program also contains well-sung versions of Franz Schubert's *Ave Maria* setting and the *Sanctus* from Charles Gounod's *Messe solennelle de Sainte Cécile*, not to mention *Amazing Grace* and *Greensleeves*, two songs by that most prolific of composers, Anonymous.

[*Les Angélus: French Sacred Music for Soprano and Organ*; Margret Roest, soprano; Ben van Oosten, organ] (MD & G 3160991) ♪ ♪ ♪ ♪

The arrangement heard here is a good deal more sparse than the orchestral setting of the Pavarotti and Norman recordings, but it results in a more contemplative air totally in keeping with the subject matter. Roest is quite a good soprano but the focus of this performance is really on the excellent organist, van Oosten, and the spacious sound of his instrument. *Panis Angelicus* is the only Franck piece in this recital, but it is in good company with sacred works by Charles-Marie Widor, Charles Gounod, Francis Poulenc, and others.

influences: Vincent d'Indy, Ernest Chausson, Louis Vierne, Charles Marie Widor, Charles Tournemire, Jacques Nicolas Lemmens, Albéric Magnard, Paul Dukas, Henri Duparc

Ian Palmer

Girolamo Frescobaldi
Born September, 1583, in Ferrara, Italy. Died March 1, 1643, in Rome, Italy.

period: Baroque

Frescobaldi was one of the most famous organists of his age. As a brilliant composer of *ricercari*, fantasias, capriccios, *canzonas,* and toccatas for solo keyboard, he had a dynamic impact on the development of instrumental music in the early baroque era. His music—specifically, his toccatas, with their unbridled lyricism and dramatic intensity—had a profound influence on the work of Johann Jakob Froberger, Jan Pieterszoon Sweelinck, and Johann Sebastian Bach.

Girolamo Frescobaldi spent his childhood in Ferrara, one of the most dazzling and progressive music centers of Europe. He studied organ with Luzzascho Luzzaschi, the court organist for Duke Alfonso II d'Este (and also an influence on Carlo Gesualdo), but little is known about Frescobaldi's other influences. It is known that he owned a volume of *ricercari* by Adrian Willaert, a Netherlander who was one of the major founders of the Venetian school of composition, and that he heard Gesualdo's haunting madrigals during that composer's stay in Ferrara (1594–1597).

Frescobaldi held his first documented position as organist at Ferrara's Accademia della Morte while still in his early teens. He traveled to Rome in 1604, where he joined the Accademia di Saint Cecilia and found a patron in Guido Bentivoglio, a wealthy ecclesiastic who, upon his appointment as archbishop and nuncio to Flanders in 1607, took Frescobaldi with him. The next year found Frescobaldi back in Italy, this time under the wing of Bentivoglio's brother Enzo, who had just been appointed Ferrara's ambassador to Rome. It was probably through the influence of this new patron that Frescobaldi was elected organist of St. Peter's Basilica. He supplemented his income from St. Peter's by playing for a variety of local religious institutions in addition to performing privately for several highly placed religious functionaries.

His fame as a harpsichordist grew considerably during this period, which may have led his patrons to overlook a series of sexual indiscretions. These activities culminated in the birth of a son out of wedlock in 1612. Frescobaldi married the boy's mother nearly a year afterward, legitimizing their next child, a daughter who was born mere months later. The couple would go on to have two more sons and another daughter, making for a crowded home. Things were even more congested by 1625, when records show that the household had taken in four other souls as either students or boarders.

Between 1608 and 1628, Frescobaldi published a well-received series of fantasies, toccatas, *ricercari,* and capriccios for keyboards in which he exploited and experimented with older contrapuntal techniques, melding them with a variety of chromatic devices and a new harmonic language. One letter written by the early philologist and music theorist Giovanni Battista Doni describes Frescobaldi as "the most accomplished performer in Italy today on the organ and harpsichord and the most skillful adapter of pieces for these instruments." All harpsichordists and organists are indebted to Frescobaldi for including a how-to preface in his *Toccate E Partite, Primo Libro* of 1615. There we get a glimpse of how practical he was and how he expected the performer to be led by the muse when playing his music. "In the toccatas I have seen to it not only that they are rich in varied sections and moods, but also that one may play each section separately," Frescobaldi noted, "so that the player can stop wherever he wishes."

Shortly after he left Rome in 1628 for a new position as court organist in Florence, Frescobaldi wrote his two-volume *Arie musicali* for voice. The writing in these books foreshadowed the arrival of the baroque cantata, although his vocal works lacked the consistent level of invention heard in his keyboard music. Frescobaldi moved back to Rome in 1634, resuming his position as organist for St. Peter's. The following year he published his most famous work, the *Fiori musicali,* which consists entirely of liturgical organ music and includes three organ Masses.

By this point, Frescobaldi's fame had spread beyond Italy's borders and he was attracting students from a variety of locales. The most famous of his pupils may have been the Viennese court organist and composer Johann Jacob Froberger, who received a leave of absence from his duties in 1637 so that he could study with Frescobaldi in Rome. It was through Froberger and other admirers that Frescobaldi's music was disseminated throughout Europe. Copies of Frescobaldi's keyboard works eventually reached France, where they were studied by Louis Couperin. In Germany, J.S. Bach was known to have analyzed Frescobaldi's *Fiori musicali.* In Austria, the great theorist Johann Joseph Fux (whose *Gradus ad Parnassum* is one of the greatest texts on counterpoint of all time) hailed Frescobaldi's keyboard works as models of composition.

Chamber
various keyboard works
what to buy: *Accenni;* Jean-Marc Aymes, harpsichord] (L'empreinte digitale 13087) ♪ ♪ ♪ ♪₄

The full range of Frescobaldi's compositional prowess for keyboard is unveiled here: toccatas, fantasies, canzonas, capricci—the works. Aymes's playing is spectacularly flexible, hinting at the improvisational characteristics that made the composer one of the foremost performers of his day.

what to buy next: [*Il Primo Libro di Capricci*; John Butt, organ; Neal Rogers, tenor] (Harmonia Mundi 7907178) ♪♪♪ᵢ

Frescobaldi's musical jokes and puzzles, strewn throughout these twelve works, are of little interest to non-musicologists, so it is lucky that his basic musicality makes the various *capricci* accessible to anyone loving well-written keyboard pieces from this era. Butt, who plays these gems on a mechanical organ, is a fine musician with the kind of talent necessary to bring out the subtle shadings and characterizations contained in these scores. Rogers is heard only once on this album, in the eleventh capriccio, where he sings scales instead of text.

Vocal
Messa della Madonna
what to buy: [*Fiori musicali, Vol. 2*; Lorenzo Ghielmi, organ; Christoph Erkens, cond.; Canticum, choir] (Deutsche Harmonia Mundi 77345) ♪♪♪♪ᵢ.

The recording is outstanding, the playing is exquisite, and the Antegnati organ in the Church of San Maurizio is a perfect instrument for Frescobaldi's organ music. The choir has an unswerving sense of pitch, and the chant simply soars. The alternation of choir with organ demonstrates how the work was performed in Frescobaldi's time and is a perfect example of the composer's brilliance in melding contrapuntal techniques with a new chromatic vocabulary.

influences: Johann Sebastian Bach, Louis Couperin, François Couperin, Domenico Scarlatti, Johann Jacob Froberger, Jan Pieterszoon Sweelinck, Dietrich Buxtehude

Marijim Thoene and Garaud MacTaggart

Giovanni Gabrieli
Born c. 1554, in Venice, Italy. Died August, 1612, in Venice, Italy

period: Renaissance

Folk Music Transformed: A Few Examples:
The phrase "folk music" originally had rural connotations to it, implying anonymous origins and relatively simplistic melodies. Sophisticated arrangements of folk tunes allowed composers to musically declare their national origins, but these works could also be ways of fulfilling a perceived need in a foreign marketplace. The various *Hungarian Rhapsodies* of Franz Liszt, though they were based more on Gypsy melodies than on any true Hungarian sources, were examples of the former while settings of British songs by Ludwig van Beethoven could be counted as instances of the latter. For readers interested in exploring Beethoven's work in this regard, there is a seven-disc set that contains his adaptations of songs from a variety of countries (*The Beethoven Edition, Vol. 17: Folksong Arrangements*, Deutsche Grammophon 453786), though most of the tunes originated in Ireland, England, and Scotland.

The nationalist fervor of the nineteenth and twentieth centuries bred opportunities for research into folk music, as various ethnic groups sought to develop art music that reflected the traditions (real or perceived) of their heritage. A number of composers made lasting contributions to the cultural history of their countries by investigating and documenting music which, in many cases, was rapidly disappearing under the wheels of progress. Among the foremost of these twentieth century musicologist/composers in Europe were Great Britain's Ralph Vaughan Williams and the Hungarian pedagogue Zoltán Kodály.

Kodály and his compatriot Béla Bartók took tape recorders with them on some of their research trips, enabling them to more accurately document the manner in which the songs were performed. While Kodály adapted many of the tunes they collected for a variety of forces, he seemed particularly enamored of the piece known as *The Peacock*. It is a basis for one of his most popular orchestral works, the *Variations on a Hungarian Folk Song*, which has shown up on numerous recordings, but his related choral setting (as heard on *The Choral Music of Kodály 3*, Hungaroton 31697) is closer in spirit to the folk tune from which it is derived.

Vaughan Williams essentially planted the compositional seed in ground broken by Cecil Sharp and other British researchers, though he did engage in a fairly substantial amount of original investigation on his own. Like Kodály, he arranged many traditional songs in a variety of ways, with his treatments of *Greensleeves*—in orchestral dress as the *Fantasia on Greensleeves* and as a relatively straightforward choral piece—being among the most popular works in his catalog. A rendition of the vocal score can be heard on a program by Alfred Deller and the Deller Consort: *Folk Songs of Britain* (Vanguard Classics 8109).

The United States was also fertile territory for such musical exploration, and domestic composers ranging from Louis Moreau Gottschalk and Charles Ives to Roy Harris and John Corigliano have dipped into the American folk bag for inspiration at one time or another. One of the more notable examples in this regard was Aaron Copland, the person who transformed *Simple Gifts*, the lovely Shaker hymn, into key elements of his *Appalachian Spring* ballet and the *Old American Songs* cycle. While there are plenty of recorded versions of the ballet, the version for voice and orchestra is somewhat rarer, being best served by soloist William Warfield with the composer directing the Columbia Symphony Orchestra on *A Copland Celebration, Vol. 3: Vocal and Choral Works* (Sony Classics 89329).

Ian Palmer

The music of Giovanni Gabrieli represents the bridge between the Venetian schools of the late Renaissance and early Baroque. Its emphasis on grandiose, polychoral writing with massive, thickly textured accompaniment remains a testament to that period's embrace of the concertato style, as well as to the importance that architecture played in shaping composers' imaginations during the late sixteenth and early seventeenth centuries.

Little is known of Gabrieli's early life. His name surfaces, however, as early as 1575, when he accompanied Orlando di Lasso to Munich and served the ducal court there until 1580. By 1584 he was back in Venice, where he was acting as temporary first organist at St. Mark's, filling the vacancy left by the departure of Claudio Merulo. He assumed the position permanently in 1585 and remained there for the rest of his life. Upon the death of his uncle, Andrea Gabrieli, in 1586, the younger Gabrieli also replaced him as the church's principal composer for special ceremonies held during the liturgical year. Throughout Gabrieli's life in Venice, his fame as composer and teacher spread throughout the continent, attracting such illustrious pupils as Heinrich Schütz and Michael Praetorious.

Gabrieli's compositional style is a hybrid of late Renaissance and early Baroque forms. Whereas, for example, many of his madrigals espouse and expand upon the principles laid out in the mid-sixteenth century, others introduce new techniques such as basso continuo, cori spezzati (split choirs), and concertato treatment. All of these new mechanics clearly drew their inspiration from the fabulous acoustics and architectural layout of St. Mark's Basilica. Its traditional cruciform shape was nearly transfigured visually and sonically by the addition of multiple domes, the largest of which was located at the crossing, with other smaller versions set strategically in the transepts and nave. In addition, balconies surrounding the nave and transepts at the old "triforium" level provided superb perches from which opposing vocal and instrumental forces could play off the banquet of acoustical resonance. The beauty and uniqueness of the resulting antiphonal sound both justified this new style and encouraged an increased output of still newer works for such spaces by other composers.

Gabrieli is best known for his sacred works, among them his *Sacrae Symphoniae* (1615), which contain several motets for double choir as well as settings of various parts of the Ordinary of the Mass. These settings are few and fragmented, however, as composition for the Mass Ordinary already had reached its zenith under Giovanni Palestrina and his contemporaries. The motets, however, represent the height of the Venetian polychoral style. Gabrieli's six-part works such as *Timor et tremor* and *Beata es Virgo* especially evoke the rich texture of Venetian concertato style. Other notable motets include his *Sancta Maria* for seven voices, *O magnum mysterium,* and *Anima mea Dominum,* both for double choir.

Gabrieli also proved a prodigious composer of instrumental works, among them numerous ricercare, fantasias, toccatas, and canzoni (the prototype of the later sonata). Many are characterized by antiphonal writing, highly contrapuntal openings and closings, and highly virtuoso melodic playing in solo instrumental passages. Gabrieli also remains one of the first composers of this period to realize the full potential of early brass instruments in completing the aural fabric of polychoral compositions. Often small groupings of brass players echo the short homophonic phrases of the choir, creating a sound blend that is at once intimate and grandiose.

Chamber
various canzoni
what to buy: [*American Brass Quintet Plays Renaissance, Elizabethan, and Baroque Music;* American Brass Quintet, ensemble] (Delos 3003) ♪♪♪♪

The American Brass Quintet belongs to that exclusive club of chamber ensembles that bolsters and validates its sterling playing with that less glittery but equally needed side of good music-making: solid historical research in performance practice. Here we have not only Gabrieli in all his acoustic glory, but Gabrieli as the composer himself might have experienced it. Intelligent sound engineering keeps the usual spatial gremlins in check, allowing for a lavish sound feast. There are only two canzoni by Gabrieli in this collection but the performances are excellent. Among the other composers represented on this set are such well-known names as Johann Sebastian Bach, John Dowland, and Andrea Gabrieli.

Vocal
various choral works
what to buy: [*Gabrieli In San Marco;* E. Power Biggs, organ; Vittorio Negri, cond.; Gabrieli Consort La Fenice, orch.; Edward Tarr Brass Ensemble; Gregg Smith

Singers, choir; Texas Boys Choir] (Sony Classics 62426) ♪♪♪♪

Recorded at St. Mark's Basilica in 1967, this session by Biggs and company unveiled Gabrieli's remarkable part writing for a whole generation of listeners who would never have heard these works otherwise. For many years they served as benchmark performances, and although they have been surpassed in recent years by improved scholarship and sound engineering (the same qualities that made St. Mark's such an impressive venue for "live" music also made it a nightmare for recording purposes), the power of the music and the commitment of the musicians still come through. Works included on this disc include Gabrieli's *Beata es Virgo, Nunct dimitis,* and *Magnificat.*

influences: Giovanni Palestrina, Andrea Gabrieli, Heinrich Schütz, Michael Praetorious

Frank Scinta

Niels Gade

Born Niels Wilhelm Gade, February 22, 1817, in Copenhagen, Denmark. Died December 21, 1890, in Copenhagen, Denmark.

period: Romantic

Gade was enamored of German romanticism, both in literature and in music, and much of his music reflects his infatuation with the works of Felix Mendelssohn and Robert Schumann. Gade's first work to receive accolades in his Danish homeland was the concert overture *Efterklange af Ossian* (Echoes of Ossian). But he made his greatest impact on Danish music after his appointment in 1866 as a director of the Copenhagen Academy of Music, where he taught composition and music history to a new generation of Danish composers.

Gade's father was a versatile carpenter, crafting both cabinets and instruments, but despite his woodworking talents, he couldn't afford to provide musical instruction for his precocious son until Niels was fifteen years old. Prior to that, the younger Gade made do by picking up the violins his father made and attempting to mimic popular songs of the day. By the time Gade was seventeen, he had learned enough from his few real lessons that he joined the Royal Orchestra as a junior violinist.

Gade was introduced to contemporary German music during his tenure with the orchestra and made his first attempts at composition while under the influence of Mendelssohn and Schumann. He destroyed some of his early works shortly after their first performances because he was dissatisfied with the results; this preparation was necessary, as it showed the budding composer what was needed to create a satisfactory work. In 1840, Gade wrote his first official opus number, a concert overture called *Efterklange af Ossian* (Echoes of Ossian), which won a prize from the Copenhagen Musical Society.

After failing to find a receptive Danish audience for his Symphony no. 1, Gade sent it off to Mendelssohn, who conducted it and became a persuasive advocate for the work. Gade then received a grant to help further his studies, using some of the money to visit Leipzig, Germany, in 1843. There he met both Mendelssohn and Schumann and found things so much to his liking that he settled down and immersed himself in the musical activities of the city. He eventually led a performance of his first symphony in Leipzig and found employment at the Leipzig Academy of Music and as an assistant to Mendelssohn with the Gewandhaus Orchestra. Following Mendelssohn's death in 1847, Gade was appointed a primary conductor of the orchestra, but he left that job the next year, just as Danish and Prussian forces were massing for what would become known as the Schleswig-Holstein War.

Upon his return to Copenhagen, Gade jumped into the city's cultural leadership, reestablishing the Musical Society as an artistic force and helping supplant the ad hoc orchestras the city was used to with a more permanent ensemble. He also continued to compose music, churning out symphonies, a handful of chamber works, and a wide variety of choral music, most of which was well received not only in Denmark and Germany but in Great Britain as well. In 1866, Gade was appointed co-director of the Copenhagen Academy of Music (along with his father-in-law, composer J.P.E. Hartmann, and composer/violinist Holger Simon Paulli). His contributions to Danish arts were deemed so important by the king of Denmark that the government finally awarded him a pension in 1876.

Orchestral
***Echoes of Ossian* in A Minor for Orchestra, op. 1**
what to buy: [Ole Schmidt, cond.; Rheinland-Pfalz State Philharmonic Orchestra] (CPO 999362) ♪♪♪♪

Gade came out of the gate with a hit, and despite its relative brevity, this engaging concert overture remains his most consistently interesting work. Schmidt gives just the right Mendelssohn-ian bounce to this engaging little gem and extends the same feeling through the rest of the pleasant program of overtures (*Hamlet,* op. 37) and orchestral suites (*A Summer's Day in the Country,* op. 55 and *Holbergiana,* op. 61).

Symphony no. 4 in B-flat Major, op. 20
what to buy: [Neeme Järvi, cond.; Stockholm Sinfonietta, orch.] (BIS 338) ♪ ♪ ♪♪

If you can accept the idea of Gade as an economy-sized Mendelssohn, then you should have no problems with this work. Melodies tumble over each other in what may have been the composer's most popular symphony during his lifetime. Järvi's tempos are a tad on the quick side, but that just adds to the fun. Gade's third symphony is the accompanying work.

Vocal
Elverskud (The Elf King's Daughter) for Solo Voices, Choir, and Orchestra, op. 30
what to buy: [Eva Johansson, soprano; Anne Gjevang, contralto; Poul Elming, tenor; Dmitri Kitajenko, cond.; Danish National Radio Symphony Orchestra; Danish National Radio Choir] (Chandos 9075) ♪ ♪ ♪♪

Other than the *Echoes of Ossian* overture, this cantata was Gade's most popular composition in Denmark. Internationally, it had some legs as well, receiving performances all over Europe. The choral sections are beautiful, in a Germanic, romantic sort of way, and the recording is sterling. Other works on this album include a felicitous version of the *Echoes of Ossian* overture and Gade's *Five Songs,* op. 13.

influences: Felix Mendelssohn, Ludwig Spohr, Robert Schumann, Peter Arnold Heise, Peter Erasmus Lange-Müller

Garaud MacTaggart

Francesco Geminiani
Born Francesco Xaverio Geminiani c. December 5, 1687, in Lucca, Italy. Died September 17, 1762, in Dublin, Ireland.

period: Baroque

A baroque composer who was best known during his day as a virtuoso violinist, Francesco Geminiani was also a prolific writer on the methods for playing the violin. His most significant compositions were concerti grossi, solo sonatas for string instruments, and solo keyboard pieces.

If you have never heard of Francesco Geminiani, it may be because Antonio Vivaldi and George Frideric Handel were two of his contemporaries, and they were tough acts to follow. Thanks to a recent resurgence of interest in baroque and early music, however, worthy lesser-known composers such as Geminiani have been recognized and appreciated, taking their rightful place alongside their more famous colleagues.

During his lifetime, Geminiani was well respected as a composer, teacher, writer, and violinist. He also had friends in high places, making his career secure. Geminiani apparently had champagne tastes but a beer budget, and when he got himself into heavy debt and landed in jail, one of his influential friends bailed him out. He also befriended Handel, who was his accompanist during a performance for King George I. Geminiani spent much of his career traveling around Europe—especially Italy, France, and the Netherlands—before finally settling in England. The timing of his travels was ideal, because Italian music and musicians were all the rage throughout Europe in the early eighteenth century.

Geminiani honed his craft with two of the most prominent musicians of the day, Arcangelo Corelli and Alessandro Scarlatti. In fact, Geminiani's op. 5 concertos are adaptations of violin sonatas by his teacher Corelli. String sonatas and concertos dominate Geminiani's output as a composer, and there is a lyrical, tender quality to his compositions that is not always found in baroque music. This makes sense because he wrote so much of this music for his own performances; he was a gifted player who firmly believed in the power of musicality and interpretation. Because he possessed an extraordinary technique and composed for his own prodigious virtuosity, few of his contemporaries were willing to perform Geminiani's challenging compositions.

What is an aging virtuoso to do once those fingers start losing their agility? As the author of several treatises, Geminiani paved the way for the standardization of violin playing and baroque ornamentation. His instructional book *The Art of Playing on the Violin,* published in 1751, was a groundbreaking text on the principles of violin technique and musical interpretation. *Rules for Playing in a True Taste, A Treatise of Good Taste in the Art of Musick,* and *The Art of Accompaniment* were some of his other prominent writings, many of which included pieces composed especially to illustrate the points within.

Geminiani may be said to lack variety when compared to contemporaries such as Handel or Johann Sebastian Bach, composers who wrote in virtually every possible format, from single-instrument pieces to large-scale choral and orchestral works. Still, Geminiani made up for his dearth of diversity with a deft ability to create pleasing string sonorities.

Orchestral
12 Concerti Grossi after op. 5 of Arcangelo Corelli
what to buy: [I Musici, orch.] (Philips 438766) ♪ ♪ ♪ ♪

This two-disc recording features lovely, unpretentious violin solos and sweet, well-blended strings by one of the premier conductorless orchestras. It possesses an appropriate stylistic intimacy without the annoyingly creaky early-music sound heard on many other recordings of this vintage.

various concerti grossi
what to buy: [Jeanne Lamon, cond.; Tafelmusik, orch.] (Sony Classics 48043) ♪ ♪ ♪ ♪

Tafelmusik gives a straightforward period-instrument performance that is nevertheless full-bodied. The ensemble samples eight of Geminiani's concerti grossi, with selections from his opp. 2, 3, and 7.

influences: George Frideric Handel, Arcangelo Corelli, Antonio Vivaldi, Pietro Antonio Locatelli, Charles Avison

Suzanne Bona-Hatem

Roberto Gerhard
Born Robert Gerhard Ottenwaelder on September 25, 1896, in Valls, Catalonia, Spain. Died January 5, 1970, in Cambridge, England.

period: Twentieth century

Although working with Arnold Schoenberg had a remarkable effect on Roberto Gerhard's later scores, the earlier compositions—when the young Catalonian was drawn to rhythms found in folk-based materials—show

the profound influences of composer Manuel de Falla and musicologist/composer Felipe Pedrell. *Collages* (his third symphony) and *Epithalamion*—both from the 1960s—showcase a variety of intriguing orchestral effects, while the piano scores for *Soirées de Barcelone* (1938) and *Alegrías* (1942) hover closer to folk roots even as they demonstrate Gerhard's increasing focus on the arresting blend of tonal, bitonal, non-tonal, and twelve-tone procedures that would be representative of his compositional maturity.

Even though he went to Switzerland in 1908 and spent much of his time taking business classes (at the insistence of his parents), Gerhard managed to sneak in a few lessons in harmony and counterpoint before returning to Spain in 1915. He then moved to Barcelona, where he began taking piano lessons from Enrique Granados and studying composition with Felipe Pedrell. The latter, a former professor at the Madrid Conservatory, counted Isaac Albéniz, Enrique Granados, and Manuel de Falla among his students and helped determine the direction of Spanish music (much as Béla Bartók and Zoltán Kodály did in Hungary) by espousing the adoption of native materials into a more formal, classically oriented setting. Gerhard's only surviving works from this period are a song cycle (*L'infantament meravellós de Shahrazada*), a piano trio, and the wonderful solo piano piece *Dos Apunts*.

After Pedrell's death in 1922, Gerhard studied composition with Schoenberg in Vienna, staying with him until 1928 before moving back to Barcelona. There he began delving further into the roots of Catalonian music, building upon the lessons learned from Pedrell and doing his own original research as head of the music department of the Catalan Library (1932–1938). In 1939 he took up residence in England, partly because he was offered a research scholarship at King's College, Cambridge, but mostly as a result of Gerhard's position in 1937–1938 as a cultural adviser to the Republican government, the losing side in the Spanish Civil War.

He remained in Cambridge for the rest of his life and began a career fraught with fiscal uncertainty—that of the freelance composer. Never very prolific prior to his escape from Spanish fascism, Gerhard really got on a roll once he arrived in Great Britain, finishing the majority of works for which he is best known today. His *Homenaje a Pedrell* and the symphonic suites *Alegrías, Pandora,* and *Don Quixote* all date from the 1940s, while the five symphonies (only four of which have been published), the Concerto for Orchestra, and *Epithalamion* emerged in the 1950s and 1960s, as did his two string quartets, his only opera (*The Duenna*), and his intriguing Nonet for Wind Quintet, Trumpet, Trombone, Tuba, and Accordion. During his life in England, Gerhard also wrote a substantial amount of incidental music for films, plays, radio, and television. By the 1960s Gerhard had finally taken British citizenship and attained a relatively high level of recognition in the academic community, which translated into a demand for his services as a teacher and lecturer. In England he taught composition privately and at the summer school in Dartington, while his trips to the United States resulted in positions at the University of Michigan (as visiting professor of composition) in 1960 and at the Tanglewood Music Center in 1961. He was made a Commander of the British Empire in 1967 and was awarded an honorary doctorate by the King's College, Cambridge in 1968. The heart problems he had during the last decade of his life finally claimed him almost two years later.

Orchestral
Symphony no. 3—*Collages*
what to buy: [Matthias Bamert, cond.; BBC Symphony Orchestra] (Chandos 9556) ♪♪♪♪

Although *Collages* was originally commissioned by the Koussevitsky Foundation, its first performance (on February 8, 1961) was with Rudolph Schwarz conducting the BBC Symphony Orchestra, an earlier edition of the same organization heard on this recording. Gerhard used taped sounds as an element of his score, meshing a kinder, gentler form of the *musique concrète* espoused by Edgard Varèse (among others) into an orchestral framework. The results are both subtle and spectacular; Bamert and the BBC Symphony Orchestra are afforded a lush environment by the engineers, enhancing the overall sound. Also included are a recording of Gerhard's Piano Concerto (with Geoffrey Tozer as soloist) and a wonderful performance of his mid-1960s piece *Epitalamion*.

what to buy next: [*Roberto Gerhard: Symphonies*; Victor Pablo Pérez, cond.; Orquesta Sinfónica de Tenerife] (Auvidis/Montaigne 782113) ♪♪♪¼

Pérez conducts a rougher, more intense version of the score than does Bamert, but the results are just as valid. The rest of this two-disc set is devoted to Gerhard's three other symphonies. Pay special attention to the first of these works, since it demonstrates one of the com-

poser's initial experiments with large-scale, post-Schoenberg serialism. This same performance is also available on a single disc (Auvidis Montaigne 782103), paired with the first symphony, but the pricing for all four symphonies is the better deal.

Chamber
Leo
what to buy: [*Portraits and Horoscopes*; Ed Spanjaard, cond.; Nieuw Ensemble]

The last work written by Gerhard had plenty of serial grit to it, and the sonic effects he draws from eleven instruments and nine musicians are quite intriguing. The other pieces on this disc—*Libra*, the three *Impromptus*, the *Concert for 8*, and *Gemini*—are also well performed and recorded, making this album the best option for exploring the composer's more intimately structured, post-Schoenberg works.

what to buy: [*Piano Music (Complete)*; Jordi Masó, piano] (Marco Polo 8.223867) ♪♪♪¼

Since this album doesn't include any of Gerhard's works for two pianos, its title is a bit misleading. That said, Masó is a fairly convincing interpreter of the material, and his version of the three *Impromptus*, Gerhard's first published twelve-tone work, is among the more committed ones ever recorded. Also on this disc is a performance of the second piano sonata by Joaquim Homs, a former student (and biographer) of Gerhard.

Vocal
L'Alta Naixença del Rei en Jaume (The Noble Birth of the Sovereign Lord King James)
what to buy: [*Roberto Gerhard: Cantatas*; Anna Cors, soprano; Francesc Garrigosa, baritone; Edmon Colomer, cond.; Coral Cármina, choir; Orquestra Simfònica de Barcelona i Nacional de Catalunya] (Auvidis/Montaigne 782115) ♪♪♪♪¼

This 1932 cantata, built on a fourteen-note series, is one of the most beguiling serial scores ever constructed. Gerhard's choral writing is spectacular at times, and the soloists here are quite fine. As a bonus, there are five other large-scale works by Gerhard on this well-conceived two-disc set, including *The Plague*, *Epitalamion*, and *Cancionero de Pedrell*.

influences: Manuel de Falla, Béla Bartók, Arnold

Schoenberg, Joaquim Homs, Roger Reynolds

Garaud MacTaggart

George Gershwin

Born Jacob Gershvin on September 26, 1898, in Brooklyn, NY. Died July 11, 1937, in Hollywood, CA.

period: Twentieth century

As a composer and pianist, Gershwin is an icon of American music. He was an innovative composer of musical theater and concert works, a virtuoso pianist, and one of the few individuals able to appeal to both classical and popular audiences.

Born in Brooklyn, George Gershwin grew up on Manhattan's Lower East Side. After taking lessons from various neighborhood teachers, Gershwin studied piano with Charles Hambitzer, whom he later called "the first great musical influence in my life." Another of his teachers was Edward Kilenyi Sr., who taught the composer counterpoint, harmony, and some orchestration. Dropping out of school in 1914, Gershwin got a job as a song plugger, working for Tin Pan Alley publisher Jerome H. Remick. He published his first song, "Making of a Girl," for a revue called *The Passing Show of 1916*; he left Remick two years later when he received a contract to write for T.B. Harms, another publishing company. Meanwhile, he continued working as a rehearsal pianist and contributed his own songs to other composer's shows and revues.

The first full-length, all-Gershwin musical, *La La Lucille,* was a success in 1919, running for 104 performances. Gershwin then had a hit song when Al Jolson recorded his "Swanee" in 1920. All through the 1920s, Gershwin was a fixture on Broadway, working with lyricists such as Irving Caesar, Arthur Francis, and B.G. DeSylva. Not content with mere songwriting, however, Gershwin learned orchestration and increased his technical skills by studying with Rubin Goldmark, Wallingford Riegger, and Henry Cowell; later he would study with Joseph Schillinger. The early 1920s saw the beginning of Gershwin's career in concert music. In 1923 he accompanied soprano Eva Gauthier in a concert of art and popular song at Aeolian Hall. Early the next year, a performance on the same stage would not only launch his fame as a classical composer and performer but introduce one of the great classics of American music.

Gershwin and bandleader Paul Whiteman had discussed an idea for a large work for solo piano and orchestra in 1923. On January 4, 1924, Gershwin was surprised to read a notice announcing that he was "at work on a jazz concerto" and that it would be performed in concert on February 12. He wrote the score in two weeks, Whiteman's music director Ferde Grofé did the arrangement, and *Rhapsody in Blue* was premiered with the composer at the piano. Whiteman's concert was called *An Experiment in Modern Music*; his purpose was "to show that jazz had come to stay and deserved recognition." The afternoon concert was very long and included everything from "Livery Stable Blues," and "Yes! We Have No Bananas" to songs by Zez Confrey, Irving Berlin, and Victor Herbert. Gershwin was next to last. More importantly, the event attracted a very wide audience, including Walter Damrosch, Jascha Heifetz, Fritz Kreisler, Sergei Rachmaninoff and Leopold Stokowsky—the elite of the concert halls. The initial reviews were good, and a recording of the work came out shortly afterward. Gershwin was now to be taken seriously as a concert artist, not a small feat for the time.

Nineteen-twenty-four was truly a banner year for Gershwin. It saw not only the launching of his concert career but the start of his collaboration with his brother, Ira, which began with the London show *Primrose*. This was quickly followed by the Broadway hit *Lady, Be Good,* the first of fourteen shows that the brothers would write for Broadway. *Lady, Be Good* established the jazzy sound characteristic of musical theater in the 1920s, at the same time making Fred and Adele Astaire the leading song-and-dance team. The show had its share of hits ("Fascinating Rhythm" and "Oh, Lady Be Good!"), but surprisingly, one potential hit, "The Man I Love," was dropped before it opened. The stream of hit shows continued into the mid-1930s: *Oh, Kay* (1926), *Funny Face* (1927), *Strike Up the Band* (1930), *Girl Crazy* (1930), *Of Thee I Sing* (1931), *Pardon My English* (1933), and *Let 'Em Eat Cake* (1933). Careers were launched with their songs, as when Ethel Merman sang "I Got Rhythm" in *Girl Crazy*. And then there are the songs themselves: "Clap Yo' Hands," "Someone to Watch Over Me," "Strike Up the Band," "'S Wonderful," "My One and Only," "Embraceable You," "Bidin' My Time," "But Not for Me," "Of Thee I Sing"—the list goes on and on. Some songs are relaxed and swinging, while others are rhythmic and declamatory; the harmony is distinctive, running the gamut from diatonic to chromatic and avoiding extreme dissonances.

Along with his work in musical theater, Gershwin continued composing concert works. The Concerto in F for Piano and Orchestra was composed in 1925, and the Preludes for Piano followed in 1926. The tone poem *An American in Paris* was written in 1928 and premiered by Damrosch the same year. The year 1932 brought both the *Second Rhapsody* and the *Cuban Overture*, as well as *George Gershwin's Songbook* (the volume printed both the original sheet music and Gershwin's "party" versions), while 1934 saw the publication of *Variations on "I Got Rhythm"* for Piano and Orchestra. Gershwin's greatest undertaking, however, was the full-length opera *Porgy and Bess*, which opened at the Alvin Theatre on October 10, 1935.

Porgy and Bess is a three-act dramatic work, adapted from the 1925 novel *Porgy* by DuBose Heyward; the libretto is by Heyward, with lyrics by Heyward and Ira Gershwin. George began working on the opera in 1933, finishing it in twenty months. The original production starred Todd Duncan and Anne Brown, and its opening was considered a major event. It was not a commercial success, though, and ran for only 124 performances. Many of the solos and duets from the opera—among them "Summertime," "Bess, You Is My Woman Now," "I Got Plenty o' Nuttin'," and "It Ain't Necessarily So"—caught on and have remained as popular numbers apart from the show. Was Broadway ready for a real opera with sung recitative? Perhaps not. The work fared much better in opera houses and is now universally accepted as a true opera in the best sense of the genre. *Porgy and Bess* is also the most popular American opera.

George and Ira Gershwin worked on three movies in 1937, but this proved to be the last such work George would do. The brothers had gone to Hollywood, where they did *Shall We Dance, A Damsel in Distress,* and part of *The Goldwyn Follies* before George Gershwin died of a brain tumor. People from all over flocked to his funeral at Temple Emanu-El in New York City. The temple was full, as was Fifth Avenue, and Gershwin was already missed. The spoken and musical tributes given at his funeral attest to his being a great composer and performer, a personality, the life of any party, and a friend.

Orchestral
Rhapsody in Blue for Piano and Orchestra
what to buy: [*Gershwin and Grofé*; George Gershwin, piano; Paul Whiteman, cond.; Paul Whiteman Orchestra] (Pearl 22) ♪ ♪ ♪ ♪ ♪

This is the classic 1924 recording of *Rhapsody In Blue,* with the composer playing piano in Ferde Grofé's jazz-band arrangement. It is part of a set that features Roy Bargy playing Gershwin's Concerto for Piano in F Major in 1928 (again with Whiteman and his band) and two of Grofé's opuses, the *Grand Canyon Suite* and the *Mississippi Suite.* Even though the sonics are a bit dicey, this disc is a must-have for anyone seriously interested in Gershwin and this piece.

[James Levine, piano; James Levine, cond.; Chicago Symphony Orchestra] (Deutsche Grammophon 431625) ♪ ♪ ♪ ♪ ♪

What a stunning set this is! In addition to containing the *Rhapsody, An American in Paris,* and the *Cuban Overture,* it also includes the *Catfish Row* suite of tunes from *Porgy and Bess* that Gershwin arranged. (The last work should not to be confused with the "symphonic picture" drawn from the opera by Robert Russell Bennett.) Who could ask for anything more?

what to buy next: [*Oscar Levant Plays Gershwin*; Oscar Levant, piano; Eugene Ormandy, cond.; Philadelphia Orchestra] (Sony Classics 42514) ♪ ♪ ♪ ♪

The legendary Levant had a particular affinity for Gershwin, and his performances are a tad looser than those of his contemporaries. He was recorded in 1945 playing *Rhapsody in Blue* with Ormandy; the other pieces heard on this disc (the Piano Concerto in F Major, the *Second Rhapsody* for Piano and Orchestra, and the *"I Got Rhythm" Variations*) come from a variety of other studio sessions from that era, with either André Kostelanetz or Morton Gould conducting. Levant was one of the greatest interpreters of Gershwin's music ever, and this album shows why.

[William Tritt, piano, Erich Kunzel, cond., Cincinnati Jazz Orchestra] (Telarc 80166) ♪ ♪ ♪ ♪

This recording uses to Grofé's original 1924 jazz-band orchestration for its rendition; ditto for the version of *Rialto Ripples* heard here. Tritt and Kunzel also team up with the Cincinnati Pops Orchestra for more straightforward performances of Gershwin's *"I Got Rhythm" Variations* and the Piano Concerto.

Chamber
various piano works
what to buy: [William Bolcolm, piano] (Nonesuch

79151) ♪ ♪ ♪ ♪₄

In addition to recording Gershwin's three Preludes, Bolcom wends his way through the composer's Broadway shows, dipping into *Funny Face* for "'S Wonderful," *Strike Up the Band* for "The Man I Love," and *Lady Be Good* for "Fascinating Rhythm." There are thirty-six well-played cuts in all, most of them instrumental, although mezzo-soprano Joan Morris is featured on some songs.

what to buy next: [*Complete Piano Works*; Dag Achatz, piano] (BIS 404) ♪ ♪ ♪ ♪

The whole album is nicely done, but there is more material on the Bolcom recording. Still, there is much to recommend here, including a solo piano version of the *Rhapsody in Blue* and a number of gems like "Promenade," "Three-Quarter Blues," and the "Impromptu in Two Keys."

worth searching for: [*Gershwin: 'S Wonderful*; Ralph Grierson, Artie Kane, pianos] (EMI Classics 69119) ♪ ♪ ♪ ♪ ♪

Grierson and Kane perform a variety of two-piano arrangements from the 1930s and 1940s. The pair of brilliant pianists can be heard playing *An American in Paris,* the three Preludes, and a set of songs. This is how Gershwin and his buddies performed when they were just hanging out.

Vocal
Porgy and Bess
what to buy: [Clamma Dale, Betty Lane, Wilma Shakesnider, sopranos; Shirley Baines, Phyllis Bash, Carol Brice, Myra Merritt, mezzo-sopranos; Steven Alex-Cole, Larry Marshall Glover Parham, Alexander B. Smalls, Bernard Thacker, Mervin Wallace, tenors; Donnie Ray Albert, Hartwell Mace, Cornel Richie, Andrew Smith, baritones; Raymond Bazemore, bass; John DeMain, cond.; Houston Grand Opera Orchestra; Houston Grand Opera Chorus] (RCA Red Seal 2109) ♪ ♪ ♪ ♪ ♪

Everything is stunning! Not only was this the first complete recording of Gershwin's folk opera but the voices sound pure and the orchestra is right on the money. Definitely a recording to treasure.

James Galway:

James Galway's first instrument as a youth was the pennywhistle but he soon graduated to the flute, in which he displayed a great degree of raw talent. That quality was then honed by further studies at the Royal College of Music and the Paris Conservatoire before the young flautist began his first musical occupation, that of an orchestra member. After stints with the Sadler's Wells Opera Company, the Royal Opera House Orchestra, and the BBC Symphony Orchestra, Galway's skills and reputation had developed to the point where he was able to win appointments as principal flautist with the London Symphony Orchestra, the Royal Philharmonic Orchestra, and finally the Berlin Philharmonic Orchestra. In 1975, after a number of years proving himself within the context of an orchestra, Galway began his busy solo career.

Canny, charming, and a superb musician, Galway spreads his talents across classical and pop genres, consistently selling out concerts and generating substantial interest from mainstream audiences. While *The Man with the Golden Flute* (RCA Victor Red Seal 63807), with its program of melodic orchestral bonbons by composers both familiar (Johann Sebastian Bach, Frédéric Chopin, etc.) and unfamiliar (Benjamin Godard, Riccardo Drigo, etc.), was the flautist's first big hit with classical aficionados, he has also crossed over to a broader, more mainstream audience by mixing pop music with "light" classical material. Chief amongst this sort of fare is *Annie's Song and Other Galway Favorites* (RCA Victor 60747), an album that contains snippets of works by Claude Debussy, Fritz Kreisler, and Wolfgang Amadeus Mozart along with arrangements of traditional Irish folk tunes (*Brian Boru's March* and *Belfast Hornpipe*) and a rendition of the title tune, a piece written by pop/folk singer John Denver.

While Galway has, over the past quarter century, released a number of commercially successful variants on the *Annie's Song* programming theme, he has always returned, sooner or later, to traditional classical scores. In that capacity he has been a staunch advocate for Mozart's Concerto for Flute and Harp, both in concert and in the recording studio with harpist Marisa Robles; two notable readings are with Michael Tilson Thomas conducting the London Symphony Orchestra (RCA Victor Red Seal 61789) and with Neville Marriner leading the Academy of St. Martin-in-the-Fields (RCA Victor 68256).

Galway also features a number of works by more modern composers in his repertoire, including scores that he commissioned from John Corigliano (*Pied Piper Fantasy*), William Bolcom (*Lyric Concerto* for Flute and Orchestra), Lowell Liebermann (Concertos for Flute and Orchestra), and Lorin Maazel (*Music for Flute and Orchestra*). However, of those works, only the Liebermann (RCA Victor Red Seal 63235) and Maazel (RCA Victor Red Seal 68789) pieces are still in print.

Ian Palmer

Crazy for You
what to buy: [Beth Leavel, Stacey Logan, Judine Hawkins Richard, Paula Leggett, Ida Henry, Jean Marie, Penny Ayn Maas, Louise Ruck, Pamela Everett, Michele Pawk, Jalle Connell, Harry Groener, Bruce Adler, Geryy Burkhardt, Briarl M. Nalepka, Tripp Hanson, Hal Shane, Casey Nicholaw, Fred Anderson, Michael Kubala,

singers; Paul Gemignani, cond.; unknown orchestra] (Angel Broadway 54618) ♪ ♪ ♪ ♪

The 1992 revival/adaptation of *Girl Crazy* was a fabulous show and the cast recording is likewise. This performance is actually a pastiche and can't really be compared to the original Broadway production, since it includes music from several different musicals and is more like a revue than a scripted play with a score. Still, this disc is not to be missed.

various songs
what to buy: [*Crazy for Gershwin*; George Gershwin, Fred Astaire, Adele Astaire, Judy Garland, Helen Forrest, singers; Duke Ellington, cond.; Duke Ellington Concert Choir] (Memoir Classics 502) ♪ ♪ ♪ ♪ ♪

Although the sound quality can be a bit iffy at times, this disc features numerous singers and ensembles from the era (1922–1941) when Gershwin was king. Performances worth special mention include Gershwin singing "I Got Rhythm" and Duke Ellington conducting a concert choir in a rendition of "Sam and Delilah" from *Girl Crazy*.

what to buy next: [*Kiri Sings Gershwin*; Kiri Te Kanawa, soprano; John McGlinn, cond.; New Princess Theatre Orchestra] (EMI/Angel 47454) ♪ ♪ ♪ ♪

Here's a chance to round out your Gershwin collection with another set of well-chosen songs. The wonderful Kiri Te Kanawa makes her way through a small batch of the composer's standards, including "Love Walked In," "Summertime," "Someone to Watch Over Me," and six others. Beautiful!

worth searching for: [*Gershwin: The Man and Musician*; Unitel/London 440071211] ♪ ♪ ♪ ♪

We are in debt to the BBC for this 1987 documentary, which portrays the composer in all aspects of his life and career. It is a must-see for anyone interested in what Gershwin was really like.

influences: Cole Porter, Jerome Kern, Richard Rodgers, Leonard Bernstein, Stephen Sondheim

Frank Retzel

George Gershwin

Carlo Gesualdo
Born Carlo Gesualdo, Prince of Venosa, Count of Conza c.1561 in Naples, Italy. Died September 8, 1613, in Gesualdo, Avellino, Italy.

period: Renaissance

Although he grew up as a member of the nobility during the Italian Renaissance, Don Carlo Gesualdo was hardly a typical musical dilettante of his day. His daring use of chromaticism caused both Aldous Huxley and Igor Stravinsky to look upon him as a seminal figure.

As a child Gesualdo grew up surrounded by music, hearing professional musicians employed by his father at the family court. On one of his first visits to Naples he met the poet Torquato Tasso, and the resulting friendship led to a collaboration in which Tasso provided lyrics to Gesualdo's madrigals.

One of the most notorious events in Gesualdo's life is documented by many accounts. In 1585 he had married his first cousin, the twice-widowed, twenty-five-year-old Donna Maria d'Avalos, a woman of great beauty, charm, and accomplishment. Five years later Don Carlo became aware of his wife's torrid affair with Don Fabrizio Carafa, the Duke of Andria, and he killed both parties after supposedly catching them in bed together. For this reason, Gesualdo was often referred to as the "musician/murderer of the Italian Renaissance." Little is recorded of how Don Carlo spent the time between the murder of his first wife and his second marriage in 1594. It is known, however, that he composed two sets of rather conventional madrigal books for five voices and had built a Capuchin monastery with a chapel named Saint Maria delle Grazie. The only known portrait of Gesualdo hangs in this chapel and shows him kneeling in repentance before the Redeemer sitting in judgment. Also in the painting are his maternal uncle, Saint Carlo Borromeo (a former Archbishop of Milan), and many other saints.

A new chapter in the life of Gesualdo began with his marriage to Donna Leonora d'Este at the royal court of Ferrara. There he was surrounded by the most eminent composers of the day, a sumptuous collection of musical instruments, and virtuosic singers and instrumentalists. At this point Gesualdo abandoned his old style of composition, modeling his newer works on those of Luzzasco Luzzaschi, who was garnering fame with his madrigals for one, two, and three sopranos with a written keyboard accompaniment. Gesualdo's third and fourth books of madrigals (written in 1595 and 1596, respectively) are marked by astonishing chromaticism and harmonic surprises unique to his own work. Later on, his reputation as a composer of "new" madrigals—ones filled with a sense of waywardness and disequilibrium, with chords progressing toward other distantly related chords, creating the illusion of "floating atonality"—was solidified with the release of his fifth and sixth books of madrigals. With these works, it was Gesualdo's intent to create music derived from the text, using short poems that he could amend by repeating words or omitting lines. The lines are then declaimed according to the composer's own vision, with an intricate balance between slow, rhythmically simple passages and non-chromatic, rhythmically complex sections.

Gesualdo's sacred music consists of two categories: the *Sacrarum cantionum,* consisting of two volumes (one in five voices, the other in six and seven voices), and the *Sabbato Sancto Responsoria,* written for performance during Holy Week. In contrast to his madrigals, Gesualdo's sacred works are emotionally subdued, even though they still contain some of the strange, jarring harmonies found in his other compositions. This music was intended for Gesualdo's private use rather than at a more public venue because it did not adhere to the post-Tridentine Council formulas that were stipulated for proper church music. For example, the composer's *Tenebrae Responsories for Holy Saturday* break the rule specifying that ornamentation should be banned during Holy Week. In addition to these aforementioned works, Gesualdo composed motets in 1603, setting antiphonal, responsorial or para-liturgical texts focusing on repentance and filled with petitions of forgiveness to St. Francis and the Virgin Mary.

In the eighteenth century, Charles Burney was outraged when he heard one of Gesualdo's madrigals. Commenting on Gesualdo's *Moro, lasso, al mio duolo,* Burney called it "harsh and crude," filled with "licentious modulation" that was "extremely shocking and disgusting to the ear." Gesualdo's "shocking" chords, which failed to progress to closely related keys, paved the way for the breakdown of tonality, hinting at the techniques of Richard Wagner and twelve-tone serialism. Gesualdo's own tormented and unhappy soul was mirrored in his music. His life and music demonstrate that the line separating genius and madness is indeed a thin one.

Vocal
various madrigals
what to buy: [*Madrigaux a cinq voix*; William Christie, cond..; Les Arts Florissants Ensemble, choir] (Harmonia Mundi France 901268) ♪ ♪ ♪ ♪ ♪

Christie and his singers perform brilliantly in *Luci serene e chiare,* the first madrigal from Book IV, reflecting Gesualdo's genius for juxtaposing contrasting moods to convey the text. The CD also contains other works from Gesualdo's last three books of madrigals, including three that are beautifully performed on harp, harp with lyrone, and harp with theorbo.

Tenebrae Responsories for Holy Saturday
worth searching for: [Peter Phillips, cond.; Tallis Scholars, choir] (Gimell 454915) ♪ ♪ ♪ ♪

Especially engaging is the motet *Sicut ovis,* where the singers demonstrate Gesualdo's technique of highlighting contrasting words such as *mortem* and *vivificaret* with resplendent ease. Undergirding the excitement and intensity of the ensemble is the remarkable balance between the voices and their unswerving sense of pitch. Also included are four impeccably performed Marian motets filled with a deep sense of mystery and reverence.

influences: Luzzasco Luzzaschi, Cipriano de Rore, Luca Marenzio, Gianches de Wert, Claudio Monteverdi, Igor Stravinsky, Jehan Alain, Petr Eben, Olivier Messiaen.

Marijim Thoene

Orlando Gibbons
Born December 1583, in Oxford, England. Died June 5, 1625, in Canterbury, England.

period: Renaissance

Orlando Gibbons stands amid an illustrious gathering of sixteenth century English composers who represent the culmination of Elizabethan vocal and instrumental composition. Together with William Byrd and Thomas Tallis, Gibbons completes the triumvirate of musical genius that dominated nearly every arena of music in its day, particularly that of the Anglican Church.

At age thirteen Gibbons entered the choir of King's

College, Cambridge and later received an appointment as one of the traditional "waits" (singer/instrumentalists) at Cambridge. In 1605 he was retained as organist at the Chapel Royal, where some of his earliest compositions received their first exposure. The following year he took the Bachelor of Music degree at Cambridge, followed several years later by the awarding of the D.Mus. at Oxford (1622).

In 1623 Gibbons was elevated to the position of organist at Westminster Abbey, and in 1625 he officiated as master of music at the funeral of James I. Gibbons's sudden death at Canterbury in 1625, while in the service of Charles I as a member of the Chapel Royal, unleashed a flood of testimonials from England's musical nobility.

Considered one of the "last of the great Elizabethan composers," Gibbons was responsible for helping to elevate the already revered English polyphonic choral style to its zenith. He composed some forty church anthems, fifteen of which are considered "full," referring to the through-composed nature of the works. Here the choir sings as a unit throughout, realizing a rather constant polyphonic texture through all the voices. The remaining twenty-five works are composed as "verse anthems," a style that Gibbons largely is credited with having perfected. Here long episodes of text are sung by a soloist or semi-choir, often with accompaniment by organ continuo or viol consort. This then is answered by the full choir, often reiterating the same text or a slight variation thereof. Among Gibbons's best-known verse anthems are "This is the record of John," "Teach me, O Lord," and "O thou, the central orb of righteous love."

Gibbons's complete anthems arguably form the finest single collection of his music. They remain one of the greatest attainments in all of the choral repertoire, setting standards for polyphonic intensity and text declamation. Among his greatest such works are "Hosanna to the Son of David" (for six voices) and "O clap your hands/God is gone up" (for eight voices). He also left noted settings of the Anglican Service. Generally, they remain polyphonic, but without the highly melismatic style that characterized the services of many of his predecessors. Among the best-known are his *Short Service* for four voices, set in "full" choral style, and his *Service* for five voices, set in "verse" format. Gibbons's secular music includes a noted set of madrigals (1612), which includes such monuments as "The Silver Swan" and "Ah, dear heart." The madrigals tend toward a more sober treatment of rather serious texts revolving around the love/death archetype.

Instrumental music also receives considerable attention from Gibbons. Most noteworthy are his keyboard scores, composed primarily for virginal. Examples of popular forms such as the prelude and fantasia are attributed to him in the *Fitzwilliam Virginal Book, Benjamin Cosyn's Virginal Book,* and *Queen Elizabeth's Virginal Book.* Dance and folk forms also surface as foundations for his keyboard writing, as evidenced in the profusion of galliards, pavanes, allemandes, and courantes attributed to him. Gibbons also wrote considerably for instrumental consort, both full (all instruments of the same "family") and broken (consisting of instruments from a variety of "families"). This undoubtedly was at least in partial response to Henry VIII's preoccupation with owning and playing a large cross-section of the instruments of the day. The king's private collection of trumpets, lutes, tabors, viols, and drums no doubt had helped to keep ensemble literature in vogue. Gibbons and his generation responded with ample delicacies, mostly after dance forms with duple meters and square structural formats.

Chamber
various works for viol consort
what to buy: [*Fantaisies Royales;* Jordi Savall, soprano viol; Christophe Coine, alto viol; Sergi Casademunt, bass viol; Johannes Sonnleitner, positif organ] (Naïve 9950) ♪♪♪♪

Here we are treated to a taste of the lesser-known yet equally sublime instrumental works of one of England's greatest choral composers. The *Fantaisies Royales* comprise fourteen compositions of varying length and complexity. Often the soprano viol presents a melodic motive so lovely and "vocal" in shape and line that its contrapuntal imitation in alto and bass viols seems the most spontaneous and natural outcome imaginable. Savall's consort of viols, often with the aid of Sonnleitner's positif organ, creates moments of sweetness and delicacy, sharing the duties of rhythmic and melodic shaping with eagerness and vigor, yet always maintaining the musical intimacy required by these miniature treasures. Of particular note are the performances of *Fantaisies* III and VI, each possessing a noble rhythmic gait and lovely ornamentation.

Vocal
various choral anthems
what to buy: [*Anthems by Orlando Gibbons;* Robin

Blaze, countertenor; Stephen Varcoe, baritone; Stephen Farr, organ; Sarah Baldock, organ; David Hill, cond.; Winchester Cathedral Choir] (Hyperion 67116) ♪♪♪♪

Hill and the choir offer a splendid cross-section of Gibbons's anthems, both full and verse. Verse anthems such as the famous "This is the record of John" and the lesser-known "If ye be risen again with Christ" receive sensitive accompaniment from organists Farr and Baldock and glide seamlessly from solo passages into full choral responses. Blaze provides the solo narrative to "This is the record of John" with unblemished purity of tone and an understated dramatic elegance that draws the listener into the core of the story's events. "Hosanna to the Son of David" heads the collection of full anthems, and proceeds with the necessary rhythmic thrust to propel both text and music to a stunning climax—though in this reading, attention to diction, rhythmic phrasing, and word painting make the journey as breathtaking as the final destination. A special treat comes with the choir's rendering of Gibbons's *Second Evening Service*—its only departure from the anthem repertoire. Here the choir delves into the extended phrase lines of the *Magnificat* with close attention to the shape of both text and melody. The *Amen* that concludes both the *Magnificat* and *Nunc Dimittis* stands as a testament to both the composer's transcendent gifts and the choir's affinity for this greatest of choral repertoires.

what to buy next: [*Music by Orlando Gibbons*; Adrian Lucas, organ; George Guest, cond.; Elizabethan Consort, orch.; Choir of St. John's College, Cambridge] (Meridian 84226) ♪♪♪♪⸸

Guest directs here with a highly skilled sense of line, balance, and shading. Most notable is the manner in which he clearly defines the more intricate form of the verse anthem—works whose structure alternates between solo/duet passages and full choir responses, often with accompaniment from a full or broken consort of instruments. We hear "O Thou, the central orb," "See, the Word," and the unparalleled "This is the record of John" in their full bloom, with lovely but uncredited solo work from within the choir and marvelously understated support from organ and instruments. Full anthems also receive just representation and expert treatment, especially in "Hosanna to the Son of David" and "O clap your hands," with its rich and exuberant second half ("God is gone up") marking the high point of this disc.

influences: William Byrd, Thomas Tallis

Frank Scinta

Alberto Ginastera

Born Alberto Evaristo Ginastera on April 11, 1916, in Buenos Aires, Argentina. Died June 25, 1983, in Geneva, Switzerland.

period: Twentieth century

Alberto Ginastera, Argentina's most important twentieth-century composer, took the rhythms of his country and translated them into a ruggedly individualistic music. His creative life can be divided into three periods: the nationalist, the internationalist, and the twelve-tone, or serial. The artistic impulse to revitalize a discreet Argentinean cultural climate, combined with his own response to the vast landscapes of the grassy, treeless Pampas of his homeland, provided the seeds for each of these three periods. Even his twelve-tone works reflect Ginastera's desire to maintain his essentially South American roots.

This remarkable Argentinean composer studied piano in his youth before attending Buenos Aires's National Conservatory of Music. Like Heitor Villa-Lobos in Brazil and Béla Bartók and Zoltán Kodály in Hungary, Ginastera made himself aware of the rhythmic and melodic qualities of his country's folk music. This was evident in his first important work, the ballet *Panambí*, which had its premiere in Buenos Aires in 1937, a year before Ginastera graduated with honors from the conservatory. In 1941 he taught composition at his alma mater and was commissioned by the American Ballet Caravan to write another ballet. That same year, American composer Aaron Copland dubbed him "the white hope" of Argentinean music. His suite from the ballet *Estancia* evoked life on the farms of the Pampas and was an overwhelming success at its debut in 1943.

Although Ginastera had been awarded a Guggenheim Fellowship in 1942, he wasn't able to take advantage of the offer to come to the United States until 1945, due to travel restrictions during the Second World War. The year 1945 also marked Juan Perón's ascent to power in Argentina, and Ginastera was relieved of several academic positions because of his political affiliations. In a perverse way, his government's actions were a good thing from a creative standpoint, since they freed the composer up for his trip to the United States, where he trekked around for the next two years, visiting various universities and exposing himself to new music. After returning to his homeland in 1947, Ginastera helped create a national affiliate of the International Society for Contemporary Music and dove back into academia. His works from this period include the *Pampeana no. 1* for Violin and Piano (1947), the String Quartet no. 1 (1948), and the *Variaciones concertantes* for Chamber Orchestra (1953).

In 1956, a year after Perón was ousted, Ginastera recovered some of the academic positions he had lost almost a decade earlier. He also began another leg of his musical journey, best exemplified by the String Quartet no. 2, which had its highly acclaimed premiere in Washington, D.C., at the first Inter-American Music Festival in 1958. There followed a series of compositions that helped solidify his reputation as a composer, including four concertos—one for harp (1956), one for piano (1961), one for violin (1963), and one for orchestra (1965). Perhaps his most outrageous piece from this period was the opera *Bomarzo* (1967), a twelve-tone tour de force that evolved from a dramatic cantata of the same name written by Ginastera in 1964. In reviewing the first New York City performance (it was initially banned in Argentina), Allen Hughes wrote in the *New York Times*, "there are near approaches to both male and female nudity; there is a seduction scene in a bordello [and] a scene of lovemaking observed by a crowd of voyeurs."

By 1968 Ginastera was no longer living in Argentina, having taken up residence in New Hampshire, where he taught briefly at Dartmouth College. He then traveled to Europe, finally settling in Geneva, Switzerland, in 1971. There he composed a series of orchestral works, including the first seven movements of a projected eight-movement piece called *Popul Vuh*, inspired by the Mayan funerary guidebook, plus two more piano sonatas and the massive choral piece *Turbae ad passionem gregorianam*.

Orchestral
Estancia for Orchestra, op. 8
what to buy: [Andrzej Borejko, cond.; Poznan Philharmonic Orchestra] (Largo 5122) ♪ ♪ ♪♪

Borejko conducts Ginastera's two important early ballets and a mid-period symphonic poem on this disc. *Estancia* evokes life on the farms of Argentina's Pampas with a breathtaking third movement entitled *Malambo*. *Panambí* is a youthful piece but worth hearing, and the final selection is *Ollantay* for Orchestra, from 1947.

worth searching for: [Gisele Ben-Dor, cond.; London Symphony Orchestra] (Conifer Classics 51336) ♪ ♪ ♪♪

While the Borejko set cited above contains more of Ginastera's works, this well-recorded disc by Ben-Dor and the LSO is a bit more polished and may serve some listeners better despite its meager length. The ensemble's performance of *Panambí* displays all the sonic virtues heard in its rendition of *Estancia*.

Concerto for Piano and Orchestra
what to buy: [Hilde Somer, piano; Ernst Marzendorfer, cond.; Vienna Philharmonic Orchestra] (Phoenix USA 110) ♪ ♪ ♪ ♪ ♪

Think of the most intense roller coaster ride you ever had and then try to imagine it as a piece of music. This performance is paired with a good version of the composer's impressive first piano sonata.

Concerto for Violin and Orchestra, op. 30
what to buy: [Ruggiero Ricci, violin; Luis Herrera de la Fuente, cond.; Orquesta de las Americas] (One-Eleven 94020) ♪ ♪ ♪♪

Ricci premiered this devilishly difficult work back in 1963, but this performance was recorded live in Mexico City. The long cadenza that opens up the first movement is truly awesome. The Ginastera concerto far outshines the companion pieces on this album—a Paganini concerto and Sarasate's *Zapateado*.

Concerto for Strings, op. 33
what to buy: [*Echoes of Argentina*; New Century Chamber Orchestra] (d'Note Classics 1035) ♪ ♪ ♪♪

Ginastera based this 1965 piece on his earlier String Quartet no. 2, op. 26. Although serial techniques flavor some of it, the concerto seems to hover closer to the world of Bartók's *Divertimento* for String Orchestra than to Arnold Schoenberg's *Variations* for Orchestra. The conductorless New Century Chamber Orchestra does a marvelous job with the composer's sonic palette, and the three accompanying works by Alberto Williams, Ginastera's older and somewhat more accessible countryman, are a pleasant surprise.

influences: Carlos Chavez, Silvestre Revueltas

Gary Barton and Garaud MacTaggart

Mauro Giuliani

Born Mauro Giuseppe Sergio Pantaleo Giuliani on July 27, 1781, in Bisceglie, Italy. Died May 8, 1829, in Naples, Italy.

period: Classical

Skillful on the guitar and cello, Giuliani made his reputation in Vienna, becoming friends with Ludwig van Beethoven and many of the leading musicians of his day. His music is full of virtuosity and wonderful melodies, and two of his three guitar concertos remain popular items in today's concert repertoire.

Mauro Giuliani was born in 1781 in Italy, where guitar virtuosity had its roots in the heyday of the Renaissance court lutenists. Depending on which biographer you read, Guiliani was either totally self-taught or studied both guitar and cello for a number of years before becoming a public figure. Since he came to master two very difficult instruments, it is probably more realistic to assume (without minimizing his great talent) that he did receive some sort of formal education on string instruments. Since there was a glut of highly skilled instrumentalists in his own area, Giuliani relocated in Vienna in 1806 and remained there until 1819.

Giuliani's time in Vienna was the most fruitful professional period of his life, and he composed most of his music there. In the tradition of other virtuosos (such as Franz Liszt and Niccolò Paganini), much of Giuliani's writing was devoted to display pieces that would show off his own ample technique. While in Vienna he developed an adoring public, became close friends with many of the city's leading musicians, had a plethora of wealthy students who paid handsome sums to study with him, and gave numerous sold-out concerts. He was such a celebrity that there was even a special publication called *The Giulianiad,* a tabloid magazine that kept tabs on his activities and public performances. Some of the native Viennese musicians were resentful that Giuliani received so much fame and attention, but others were supportive. Beethoven, for example, wrote some guitar pieces for Giuliani's public concerts, and Giuliani reportedly played cello in the first performance of Beethoven's Symphony no. 7. Some biographers are at odds on this last account, with a few of them saying that Giuliani played violin in the Symphony no. 6. Since he was a cello player, however, chances are that he was on stage for the higher-numbered symphony.

In 1814 he received honors and a title from Napoleon's wife, the Empress Marie-Louise, but by 1819 he was becoming less fashionable in Austrian society and returned to Italy badly in debt. He lived in Rome, Naples, and Venice before traveling to Sicily, where he found support from various members of the local nobility. Giuliani continued teaching and giving public concerts, however, as a way of supplementing his income. During this period he, like much of the general public, came under the influence of Rossini's music, eventually paraphrasing or arranging some of Rossini's operatic themes for guitar.

Orchestral
Concerto no. 1 in A Major for Guitar and String Orchestra, op. 30
what to buy: [*Complete Guitar Concertos;* Pepe Romero, guitar; Neville Marriner, cond; Academy of St. Martin-in-the-Fields, orch.] (Philips 454262) ♪ ♪ ♪ ♪♪

Romero's recording with Marriner is first-rate, with modern instruments capturing the lightness and transparency of this music surprisingly well. As an added bonus, this two-disc set contains the composer's other two concertos for guitar plus a number of Giuliani's solo guitar pieces.

what to buy next: [John Williams, guitar; Charles Groves, cond.; English Chamber Orchestra] (Sony Essential Classics 48168) ♪ ♪ ♪ ♪

Even with a modern instrument, Williams brings out the lightness and clarity that is needed in this work. This recording is drawn from a previous two-disc CBS set; in addition to the Giuliani work, it contains Joaquin Rodrigo's popular *Concierto de Aranjuez* and Antonio Vivaldi's Guitar Concerto in D Major.

Chamber
Rossiniana for Guitar, opp. 119–124
what to buy: [Luis Orlandini, guitar] (CPO 999103) ♪ ♪ ♪ ♪

It helps that Giuliani was a virtuoso interested in exposing the various tonal colors and subtleties of the guitar, because his charming arrangements and paraphrases of Rossini's works had to stand out amid the hackwork of contemporaries who sought to cash in on that composer's fame. Orlandini's traversal of the complete cycle of six *Rossiniana* is well played and recorded, showcasing Giuliani's tune-spinning at its finest.

Rossiniana for Guitar, op. 119, no. 1
what to buy: [*Music of Giuliani*; David Russell, guitar]
(Telarc 80525) ♪ ♪ ♪ ♪ ₄

This splendid introduction to Giuliani's solo guitar works includes his most popular piece, the *Rossiniana* for Guitar no. 1, op. 119, along with his stunning *Gran Sonata Eroica*—the Sonata for Guitar in A Major, op. 150, and three other scores displaying Russell's undeniable talents.

influences: Johann Nepomuk Hummel, Antonio Salieri

Dave Wagner and Garaud MacTaggart

Philip Glass
Born January 31, 1937, in Baltimore, MD.

period: Twentieth century

One of the late 20th century's most influential composers and a leading minimalist (along with Steve Reich and John Adams), Glass has delighted, thrilled, infuriated, mesmerized, bored, and enriched audiences. In the forefront of "new" 20th-century movements, he is a post-modernist who has bridged the chasm separating classical and popular music with his *Einstein on the Beach* (an operatic collaboration with Robert Wilson) and such "pop"-oriented experiments as the *Low Symphony,* on themes drawn from a rock album by David Bowie and Brian Eno.

In the 1980s Philip Glass was a guest on the late night television show *Politically Incorrect,* did a "Profile" advertisement for Dewars scotch whiskey, and was paid a large sum to compose a short musical commercial for Swatch watches. It is precisely this notoriety, as much as his unique compositional style, that has so infuriated many of his colleagues. Some other modernist composers point to the paucity of "fresh" material in his work (in other words: he repeats himself) and his "pandering to the masses."

That kind of reaction probably couldn't have been anticipated when Glass was attending the University of Chicago. He was already a talented flutist by the time he was admitted to the university as a 15-year-old, having already studied at Baltimore's Peabody Conservatory. Majoring in math and philosophy, Glass received his B.A. in 1956 and then took off for New York City, where he studied composition with Vincent Persichetti and William Bergsma at the Juilliard School. He picked up a second B.A. and an M.A. from Juilliard by 1961 and went to Paris on a Fulbright scholarship to continue his compositional studies with renowned pedagogue Nadia Boulanger. There he was hired by Ravi Shankar, the Indian sitarist and composer, to notate his score for the film *Chappaqua,* and this exposure to Indian music and his own study of tabla rhythms (with Indian percussionist Allah Rakha) caused Glass to rethink his musical style. He adopted the rhythmic language of Indian music, along with its additive/repetitive structure and surface. So serious was he about this change of style and its meaning, that he withdrew all his compositions from before 1965. This, in a nutshell, is the origin of Philip Glass's brand of minimalism.

He has since outlined what sets his music apart from both traditional concert music and that created by other avant-garde composers: it is not only the limits of pitch and rhythm employed or the repetitive patterns played to hypnotic effect, rather, it is the non-narrative structure he favors. Glass's music requires a new mode of listening "in which neither memory nor anticipation...[has] a place in sustaining the texture, quality, or reality of the musical experience." His operas also fall outside of the genre's literary tradition and tend to relate to "a theater that comes from the worlds of painting and dance."

Since 1968, Glass has directed his own ensemble. This very tight and very successful group is made up of amplified flutes and saxophones, electric organs, and synthesizers, with the composer himself as one of the performers. He, along with co-founder Klaus Kertess, also set up his own record label (Chatham Square Productions) to document his music. Glass began attracting considerable attention during the mid-1970s, and his opera *Einstein on the Beach* put him firmly on the map after a successful performance by the Metropolitan Opera in 1976. Since then, concerts of his music have drawn large (even sell-out) crowds, with an audience ranging from more traditional classical listeners to those with a popular-music orientation.

Glass has composed a number of other operas since *Einstein on the Beach,* including *Satyagraha* (1980), *Akhnaten* (1983), *The Fall of the House of Usher* (1988), and *The Voyage* (1992). The wonderful music-theater pieces *1000 Airplanes on the Roof* (1987), and *Hydrogen Jukebox* (1990) are among his finest stage projects, and he has composed soundtrack music for television and

many films, most notably the score for Martin Scorsese's 1997 movie *Kundun*. A list of his more popular music for instrumental ensembles would cover at least two decades and include such pieces as *Music in 12 Parts* (1971-74), *Glassworks* (1981), the Concerto for Violin and Orchestra (1987), *Low Symphony* (1992), his Symphony no. 2 (1994), Symphony no. 3 (1995), and the choral Symphony no. 5 (1999).

One work by Glass deserves special mention: his opera *La Belle et la Bête* (1994). Glass took Jean Cocteau's film, removed the soundtrack, and composed an opera to be performed simultaneously with the projection of the movie. He used this technique again with Cocteau's film *Orphée* (1993), effectively inventing a new genre. As an opera, it works wonderfully, but when combined with the movie it creates a magical effect.

Orchestral
Concerto for Violin and Orchestra
what to buy: [Gidon Kremer, violin; Christoph von Dohnányi, cond.; Vienna Philharmonic Orchestra] (Deutsche Grammophon 445185) ♪ ♪ ♪ ♪

In many ways this is the orchestral composition by Glass that could bring pop and classical audiences together, even more than the *Low Symphony*. There is an abundance of melodic material here along with the composer's usual rhythmic trademarks, all within a fairly traditional three-movement format. Kremer is *the* perfect soloist for this work, despite its origin as a showpiece for violinist Paul Zukofsky. Live versions of Leonard Bernstein's *Serenade* and Ned Rorem's only violin concerto (both conducted by Bernstein with Kremer as soloist) make this all-American disc an exciting, well-programmed collection of accessible 20th-century music.

Music in 12 Parts for Chamber Ensemble
what to buy: [Michael Riesman, cond.; Philip Glass Ensemble, orch.] (Nonesuch 79324) ♪ ♪ ♪ ♪

This was one of Glass's early classics and helped to establish his innovative style. Although Riesman's recording is not the first, it is the only one available (at press time). Luckily, Riesman is an experienced Glass conductor and the engineering is top-notch.

Philip Glass

Walter Gieseking:
Born on November 5, 1895, in Lyons, France, of German parents, Walter Gieseking's childhood revealed considerable affinity for the piano, but he was also a talented amateur cellist. The family moved to Germany in 1911 just so that he could study with the noted piano pedagogue Karl Leimer at the Hanover Conservatory. Sources vary as to when Gieseking's first public concert performances were, citing either 1912 or 1915, but there is a program from the earlier date of him playing works by Johann Sebastian Bach, Felix Mendelssohn, and Ludwig van Beethoven in a recital at the Conservatory; there is also confirmation of his performance of all but two of Beethoven's thirty-two piano sonatas within the space of six concerts between November 1915 and February 1916.

Gieseking was a soldier in the German army during World War I (from 1916 to 1918), but upon the cessation of that conflict began his dual careers as concert pianist and teacher. His reputation as a superb artist really began in 1920 with a series of concerts in Berlin; tours of other European countries only added to his standing, particularly with regard to his performances of scores by Claude Debussy and Maurice Ravel. His American concert debut occurred in 1926 at Aeolian Hall in New York City.

After World War II, political controversy surrounded Gieseking's proposed American concert tour in 1949 when he was accused of cultural collaboration with the Nazi regime and forced to cancel his scheduled appearance at Carnegie Hall. An Allied Forces court cleared him of the charges and Gieseking eventually returned to the United States and made his triumphant Carnegie Hall debut in 1953. He died three years later, as the result of an automobile accident, in London; his autobiography, *So wurde ich Pianist*, was published posthumously in 1963.

Not only was Gieseking the preeminent pianist for Debussy's oeuvre during the first half of the twentieth century, he was also a gifted interpreter of works by Franz Schubert, Edvard Grieg, Robert Schumann, and Johannes Brahms. Although the bulk of his programs revolved around the music of nineteenth century composers, he sometimes included pieces by his contemporaries Arnold Schoenberg, Alfredo Casella, and Mario Castelnuovo-Tedesco. Gieseking also composed short piano works, songs, and a quintet for piano and winds.

His pre-World War II Debussy recordings for Columbia (now on two CDs, VAI 1117) have been universally acclaimed as the pinnacle of Gieseking's catalog. The Debussy *Preludes* from that era are also available as part of the *Great Pianists of the 20th Century* series (Philips 456790) in the second volume, which is devoted to Gieseking and also includes his impressive performances of Beethoven's *Waldstein* and *Appassionata* sonatas, Mozart's Sonata in C Minor (K. 457), and Ravel's *Gaspard de la nuit*.

Ian Palmer

Low Symphony for Orchestra
what to buy: [Dennis Russell Davies, cond.; Brooklyn Philharmonic Orchestra] (Point Music 438150) ♪ ♪ ♪ ♪

Now here's something different. Written in 1992, this work is based on themes by David Bowie and Brian Eno that were first used on their experimental rock album from the 1970s. It certainly is a wild piece. Glass was to continue along these lines with his 1997 *Heroes Symphony*, another work based on a rock album by Bowie and Eno.

Symphony no. 5 for Soloists, Chorus, and Orchestra—*Requiem, Bardo, Nirmanakaya*

what to buy: [Ana Maria Martinez, soprano; Denyce Graves, mezzo-soprano; Michael Schade, tenor; Eric Owens, baritone; Albert Dohmen, bass-baritone; Dennis Russell Davies, cond.; Vienna Radio Symphony Orchestra; Morgan State University Choir; Hungarian Radio/TV Children's Chorus] (Nonesuch 79618) ♪♪♪♪♪

Released in 2000, this monumental achievement is a meditative dream transcending language, culture, and religious boundaries, and looks "... at the moment of the millennium as a bridge between the past (*Requiem*), the present (*Bardo*), and culminating in *Nirmanakaya* (*Rebirth*)" (from the liner notes). The boxed set prints all texts, and the lush two-disc realization of the piece is *Music as Art* in the truest sense of both words.

Vocal
Einstein on the Beach
what to buy: [Patricia Schuman, soprano; Lucinda Childs, speaker; Gregory Dolbashian, speaker; Jasper McGruder, speaker; Sheryl Sutton, speaker; Michael Riesman, cond.; Philip Glass Ensemble, orch.] (Nonesuch 79323) ♪♪♪♪♪

With music and lyrics by Glass and design and direction by Robert Wilson, this mixed-media piece is one of the landmarks of modern musical theater and marks a shift in the composer's style. At this point Glass began moving away from using only slowly developing rhythm patterns towards a hybrid that added a more focused harmonic treatment to his standard rhythmic architecture. This 1993 recording delivers as much of the production as possible in an audio format (for the rest, you have to see/hear it). As with any Glass piece, this is an experience.

La Belle et la Bête (Beauty and the Beast)
what to buy: [Ana Maria Martinez, soprano; Hallie Neill, soprano; Janice Felty, mezzo-soprano; John Kuether, baritone; Gregory Purnhagen, baritone; Zheng Zhou, baritone; Michael Riesman, cond.; Philip Glass Ensemble, orch.] (Nonesuch 79347) ♪♪♪♪♪

This is a fabulous document of a groundbreaking work. Sadly it is not available yet in a video format, so you will miss the full force of this unique blend of opera and Cocteau's magical film.

Kundun (soundtrack)
what to buy: [Michael Riesman, cond.; anon. orch.; Gyuto Monks, choir; Monks of the Drukpa Order, choir] (Nonesuch 79460) ♪♪♪♪♪

One of Glass's more recent contributions to film scoring, *Kundun* was an ideal subject for his collaboration with Scorsese. The filmmaker found in Glass an "...artist of tremendous sensitivity whose music works from the inside of the film." The result is magnificent!

influences: Steve Reich, John Adams, Morton Feldman, John Cage

Frank Retzel and Ian Palmer

Alexander Glazunov
Born Alexander Konstantinovitch Glazunov on August 10, 1865, in St. Petersburg, Russia. Died March 21, 1936, in Paris, France.

period: Romantic

Glazunov's artistic stance as a musical conservative served him well during the Russian upheavals of 1905–1917. A man of staunch integrity, he managed, in his role as director of the St. Petersburg Conservatory, to accommodate the demands of the early Soviet state even as he defended some of his more liberal colleagues in the teaching ranks and maintained a semblance of artistic dignity within the institution. Musically, he is considered by some critics to be one of the finest Russian symphonists since Tchaikovsky. His only violin concerto has become one of the staples of the repertoire, notable for the power of its orchestration and the sheer beauty of the soloist's role. Glazunov's works for the saxophone are among the finest and most performed examples of classical music written for that instrument.

Glazunov had perfect pitch and began displaying his impressive musical abilities as an eight-year-old, when he was discovered tuning the family piano. He started formal piano studies the next year and began writing little pieces by the time he was eleven. In 1879 Mily Balakirev spoke to Nicolai Rimsky-Korsakov on Glazunov's behalf, suggesting that the master orchestrator take the young pianist on as his student. Glazunov's lessons with the composer lasted until 1881, and the results were revealed the following year with the initial performance of his first symphony. By 1885 Glazunov was traveling in high-powered circles, associating with Rimsky-Korsakov, Alexander Borodin, and Alexander Scriabin in a loosely knit cabal of composers seeking to meld the nationalist ideals of Modest Mussorgsky and Alexander Borodin with the musical advancements being manifested in the rest of Europe.

When he was appointed to a professorship at the St. Petersburg Conservatory in 1899, Glazunov had already accomplished a lot. Along with Rimsky-Korsakov, he edited and helped complete some of the scores Borodin had been working on before his death in 1887. He also carried on an active correspondence with Piotr Tchaikovsky, traveled to England (where he conducted some of his compositions), and wrote five more well-received symphonies, a pair of string quartets, a ballet, and the symphonic poem *Stenka Razin.* A popular instructor, Glazunov was also a mediator between the revolutionary and reactionary forces within the school during the political crisis of 1905. When Rimsky-Korsakov was dismissed for sympathizing with striking students, Glazunov handed his own resignation to the administration. The ensuing furor eventually caused the director of the school to resign, Rimsky-Korsakov to be readmitted to the staff, and Glazunov to be elected as the school's new director.

As the administrative head of the conservatory, Glazunov helped institute a number of reforms that strengthened the school academically and artistically. After the October Revolution of 1917, however, his defense of conservative musical virtues ran increasingly afoul of the new government. By 1928 he was tired of the constant battles to maintain what he thought was the proper course for the school, and when the chance came for him to travel abroad, he took it. Even though he journeyed through Europe and the United States, Glazunov still tried to keep tabs on what was going on back at the conservatory. Finally, in 1930, he had to give up his position as director. He moved to Paris in 1932, composing only his Concerto for Saxophone and Orchestra, the Quartet for Saxophones, and a handful of other works prior to his death in 1936 from uremic poisoning.

Orchestral
Concerto in A Minor for Violin and Orchestra, op. 82

what to buy: [Gil Shaham, violin; Mikhail Pletnev, cond.; Russian National Orchestra] (Deutsche Grammophon 457064) ♪ ♪ ♪ ♪₄

Benefiting from both fine engineering and superlative violin playing from Shaham, this disc of Russian works is very good indeed. The orchestra provides a heavy backdrop to this, Glazunov's best and most consistent score, while Pletnev is not only a sterling pianist (his other career) but a young conductor whose progress is worth keeping track of. Dimitri Kabalevsky's violin concerto and two relatively lightweight works by Tchaikovsky make up the balance of the album.

[Nathan Milstein, violin; William Steinberg, cond.; Pittsburgh Symphony Orchestra] (EMI Classics 67250) ♪ ♪ ♪ ♪₄

Milstein's association with this concerto went back to his youth, when he played it under the baton of the composer. With Steinberg conducting, the violinist made one of the most acclaimed recordings of the work, conquering its technical demands even as he developed the score's more lyrical qualities. Now available at a budget price, this disc, which includes a version of Antonín Dvořák's violin concerto and a tightly wound monaural rendition of Franz Schubert's second symphony, is a worthy addition to anyone's collection.

what to buy next: [Oscar Shumsky, violin; Neemi Järvi, cond.; Royal Scottish National Orchestra] (Chandos 8596) ♪ ♪ ♪ ♪

Shumsky is a virtuoso whom more people should be exposed to, and this is a fine place to start. Järvi provides the soloist with a taut orchestral backdrop, and the sound is quite good. The accompanying selection, Glazunov's ballet, *The Seasons,* makes this a winning choice for those wishing to experience well-played versions of both works.

Concerto in E-flat Major for Saxophone and Orchestra, op. 109
what to buy: [*Saxophone Concertos*; John Harle, alto saxophone; Neville Marriner, cond.; Academy of St. Martin-in-the-Fields, orch.] (EMI Classics 72109) ♪ ♪ ♪ ♪

Harle is a master saxophonist, and his lovely playing on this short work, one of the composer's finest, is a marvel, as are the strings of Neville's ensemble. It's all part of a well-chosen program featuring relatively conservative works for saxophone and orchestra. Other composers represented on the set include such big names as Claude Debussy and Heitor Villa-Lobos along with such lesser lights as Jacques Ibert, Ted Heath, and Richard Rodney Bennett.

influences: Mily Balakirev, Anton Rubinstein, Nicolai Rimsky-Korsakov, Mikhail Glinka

Garaud MacTaggart

Reinhold Glière

Born Reyngol'd Moritsevich Glier, January 11, 1875, in Kiev, Ukraine. Died June 23, 1956, in Moscow, Russia.

period: Romantic/twentieth century

By all accounts, Reinhold Glière was a pleasant man; even Sergei Prokofiev, a prickly rebel as a student, remembered his teacher fondly. That said, it isn't terribly surprising that Glière's compositions sound essentially pleasant. Still, when he aspires to monumental works of art based solidly on grandiose nationalist legends, filling them with big gestures and carving out impressive orchestral effects, it is readily apparent that his place in posterity is a respectable if relatively humble one. A few of his well-crafted orchestral scores still offer moments of interest, including his third symphony (*Il'ya Muromets*), his ballet *The Red Poppy,* and his Concerto for Coloratura Soprano and Orchestra.

Glière's father made wind instruments for a living and was an amateur musician of some note in Kiev. He placed his son with a local violin teacher for some rudimentary lessons, but despite Reinhold's rapid progress, the senior Glière was not enthusiastic about his son's desire to follow a musical career, preferring instead that he become a doctor or an engineer. Still, he didn't object too strenuously when it became apparent that his son was a strong enough violinist to be admitted to the Moscow Conservatory in 1894. While at the Conservatory, Glière studied harmony with Anton Arensky, polyphony and counterpoint with Sergei Taneyev, and composition with Mikhail Ippolitov-Ivanov. When he graduated in 1900, having secured a gold medal in composition, Glière started teaching. His first students included Nikolai Miaskovsky and Prokofiev, both of whom were recommended to him by Taneyev. Five years later Glière left for Berlin, where he studied composition and conducting. Although it is quite possible that he wanted to sharpen his skills in one of the world's musical capitals, it is equally possible that he felt it prudent to leave Russia after signing an open letter protesting the massacre of peaceful demonstrators in front of St. Petersburg's Winter Palace on January 9, 1905. When he returned to his homeland, he embarked upon a short-lived career as a conductor before joining the staff of the Kiev Conservatory in 1913. During this period, Glière wrote a number of works based on nationalist themes, the most prominent being his third symphony (subtitled *Il'ya Muromets*), a programmatic piece built around a legendary Russian hero.

In 1914 he was appointed director of the Kiev Conservatory; after the revolution he helped institute Soviet music policies there despite his basically apolitical mentality. After signing that protest note in 1905, he never aligned himself with controversial positions again. In 1920 Glière left Kiev and moved to Moscow, where he taught composition at the Moscow Conservatory. His next major composition—*The Red Poppy* ballet, with a story line involving revolutionary activity in China—was finished in 1927. Despite the political underpinnings of the work, it is a pleasant score with abundant melodic content, fulfilling the basic Soviet mandate by placing accessibility to the masses above rigorous intellectual substance.

For his contributions to Soviet music, Glière was awarded the Red Banner of Labor in 1937 and the Order of Honor in 1938, distinctions that stand in direct contrast to the treatment of Dimitri Shostakovich, who was accused of "formalism" during this same period. Glière was also appointed chairman of the organizing committee of the USSR Composer's Union and named People's Artist of the USSR that same year. He retired from the Moscow Conservatory in 1941 but continued composing (the Concerto for Coloratura Soprano and Orchestra of 1943 was an example of his work during this period) until his death in 1956.

Orchestral
Symphony no. 3 in B Minor, op. 42—*Il'ya Muromets*
what to buy: [Donald Johanos, cond.; Czech-Slovak Radio Symphony Orchestra, Prague] (Naxos 8.550858) ♪ ♪ ♪♭

Glière's grandest nationalist vision resulted in a work

chock full of brilliant orchestral flourishes, all quite appropriate to honor a Russian folk hero. This is the kind of excess a young romantic composer can be proud of, while an older one might lament those same traits. The disc's budget price, combined with a performance that revels in the score, should carry the day for anyone interested in exploring this work.

The Red Poppy for Orchestra
what to buy: [André Anichanov, cond.; St. Petersburg State Symphony Orchestra] (Naxos 8.553496) ♪ ♪ ♪₄

The work by Glière most likely to show up in concert halls is the *Russian Sailor's Dance*. This excerpt from the composer's most famous ballet is filled with all the exciting Slavic rhythms one could ask for and could easily be included in a concert of short Russian potboilers alongside such works as *In the Steppes of Central Asia* by Alexander Borodin, *Caucasian Sketches* by Mikhail Ippolitov-Ivanov, and the *Sabre Dance* from Aram Khachaturian's *Gayane* ballet. The rest of *The Red Poppy* is well orchestrated and filled with an abundance of catchy melodies. Anichanov's two-disc version is probably as good as you will ever need to hear, and the budget price makes it worth checking out.

Vocal
Concerto for Coloratura Soprano and Orchestra
what to buy: [Eileen Hulse, soprano; Richard Hickox, cond.; City of London Sinfonia, orch.] (Chandos 9094) ♪ ♪ ♪₄

By treating the human voice like a stringed instrument capable of sustaining a musical line without having to breathe, Glière created a technically difficult work that demands some interesting solutions. Hulse appears to have worked out the problems, leaving listeners to ponder the beauty of the music as strings and voice float along in one of the composer's loveliest, most graceful works. This is a short piece (under fifteen minutes), and its disc-mates include the composer's Concerto for Harp and Orchestra and a similar vehicle for harp written by Alberto Ginastera. Rachel Masters is the harpist in both instances.

influences: Alexander Borodin, Alexander Glazunov, Mikhail Ippolitov-Ivanov

Garaud MacTaggart

Mikhail Glinka
Born Mikhail Ivanovich Glinka, June 1, 1804, in Novospasskoye, Russia. Died February 15, 1857, in Berlin, Germany.

period: Romantic

By incorporating Russian folk themes into his work, Glinka exerted a profound influence on other Russian composers, including Mily Balakirev and Piotr Tchaikovsky. Best known for his two operatic masterpieces, *Ruslan and Ludmila* and *A Life for the Tsar,* Glinka is considered the founder and father of Russian nationalist music.

During his earliest years, Glinka was cared for by his grandmother; the only music he heard consisted of folk tunes sung by her servants and the chanting of clerics in the churches of the Smolensk area where she lived. When his grandmother died, Glinka returned to his parents' home, and it was there that he first became acquainted with Western music. Glinka's musical education was inconsistent, but after leaving school in 1822 he became a sought-after pianist on St. Petersburg's social scene, disappointing his family, who had hoped he would enter the foreign service. Most of the music he wrote in the 1820s was bland, but his adroit use of counterpoint and a budding talent for orchestration presaged subsequent developments. Perhaps feeling the need for greater depth, Glinka traveled to Italy in 1830 and Germany in 1833, exposing himself to other musical cultures. Although he undertook his only organized study of composition in Germany (with the well-respected teacher Siegfried Dehn), the chief effect of Glinka's travels was to make him miss Russia, and he started to think about incorporating his homeland's folk music into his own work.

After his father's death in 1834, Glinka returned to Russia, where he discovered the story of Ivan Susanin, a seventeenth-century peasant who saved the first Romanov tsar from death at the hands of Polish invaders. Glinka had flirted with the idea of writing an opera for some time, and this seemed to be exactly the kind of subject he had been looking for. Over the next two years he created what was basically an Italian-style opera but with several unusual characteristics, including the use of a leitmotif, or recurring theme, in association with several leading characters, especially the hero, Ivan. Glinka also broke with Russian operatic tradition by setting the text to music instead of using spoken passages to link scenes. Although the work was first called

Ivan Susanin, Tsar Nicholas's interest in the drama was so great that the title was changed to *A Life for the Tsar.* The opera was warmly received by critics and the public upon its premiere in 1836.

Encouraged by this success, Glinka immediately set about composing another opera, based this time on Pushkin's poem *Ruslan and Ludmila.* The story has inherent operatic drama, including a vanishing heroine, gallant knights, an evil dwarf, and a giant decapitated head. Unfortunately, the libretto lagged behind the music, as Pushkin died before he could work on it. Glinka went ahead with the music anyway, creating a score that experimented with a new technique even as it utilized folk elements. The new method—maintaining the basic melody line while changing the orchestral background of the tune a number of times—would prove enormously influential with later Russian composers.

Ruslan and Ludmila was not as well accepted initially as *A Life for the Tsar* had been. Depressed by this reception and by disappointments in his personal life, Glinka again left Russia, this time visiting France, Spain, and Poland. Of the pieces he wrote during these travels, the most influential and enduring is the short orchestral work *Kamarinskaya.* Based on a Russian folk song, the piece amply demonstrates Glinka's changing-background technique. Tchaikovsky was so impressed by the work that he is reported to have called it "the acorn from which all Russian [symphonic] music sprang."

Lifelong health problems finally caught up with Glinka in his later years, although he continued traveling and composing, even starting work on a third opera. He also began studying fugue with the intent of blending traditional Orthodox religious settings with the techniques of Western classical music.

Orchestral
Ruslan and Ludmilla: Overture
what to buy: [Fritz Reiner, cond.; Chicago Symphony Orchestra] (RCA Victor Gold Seal 60176) ♪ ♪ ♪ ♪

Reiner's intense conducting of Glinka's most performed work is paired with impeccable renditions of two works by Serge Prokofiev: the mighty cantata *Alexander Nevsky* and the suite from *Lieutenant Kije.*

what to buy next: [Georg Solti, cond.; London Symphony Orchestra] (Decca 460496) ♪ ♪ ♪⁴

This two-disc set of potboilers is cobbled together from various sources, with Solti leading an array of orchestras. His rendering of Glinka's big hit meshes well with the snippets of thirty-three works by Rossini, Wagner, Tchaikovsky, and others heard on this compilation.

Vocal
A Life for the Tsar
what to buy: [Alexandrina Pendachanska, soprano; Stefania Toczyska, mezzo-soprano; Chris Merritt, tenor; Boris Martinovich, bass-baritone; Emil Tchakarov, cond; Sofia National Opera Chorus; Sofia Festival Orchestra] (Sony Classical 46487) ♪ ♪ ♪⁴

Played and sung with character by Bulgarian musicians, Glinka's seminal treatment of Russian musical and historical themes is well presented here. Some of the lyrics in this version have been altered by politics—the chorus claims allegiance to the Russian state rather than to the tsar, for example—but this does not interfere with the musical drama. One of the most popular bass arias in Russian music, "They sense the truth," is handled quite well by Martinovich, although he doesn't erase memories of performances by Boris Christoff or Feodor Chaliapin.

Ruslan and Ludmila
what to buy: [Galina Gorchakova, soprano; Larissa Diadkova, mezzo-soprano; Yuri Masurin, tenor; Konstantin Pluzhnikov, tenor; Mikhail Kit, baritone; Gennadi Bezzubenkov, bass; Vladimir Ognovienko bass; Valery Gergiev, cond.; Kirov Theatre Orchestra and Chorus] (Philips 456248) ♪ ♪ ♪ ♪

For those wishing to hear the entire opera instead of just the overture, this performance is probably the best current choice. The orchestra plays with sensitivity and taste, bringing spark to the lively passages and tenderness to the meditative ones. The singers are generally good, although Netrebko, in the role of Ludmila, is particularly outstanding for the clarity and flexibility of her singing.

influences: Mily Balakirev, Piotr Illyich Tchaikovsky, Modest Mussorgsky

Kerry Dexter and Garaud MacTaggart

Christoph Willibald Gluck

Born Christoph Willibald Ritter von Gluck, July 2, 1714, in Erasbach, Germany. Died November 15, 1787, in Vienna, Austria.

period: Baroque/Classical

Christoph Willibald Gluck's music, an interesting hybrid of late Baroque and early Classical styles, has tuneful melodies and is surprisingly descriptive and dramatic. Of his many operas, it is *Orfeo ed Euridice* which still exerts a hold on modern audiences.

Gluck was one of those composers whose life spanned two historical periods in music, with some historians placing him at the end the Baroque era while others put him at the beginning of the Classical movement. We don't know very much about the early life of Gluck, except that he was the oldest of nine children and that his father was a forester in the service of various German noblemen. Despite the training in violin, cello, and clavichord he provided for Christoph, the elder Gluck was hoping to dissuade his son from a career in music and have a father-and-son forestry business. Christoph responded to the pressure by running away from home. He ended up in Prague with the local orchestra, performing operas, oratorios, and various types of orchestral music.

Christoph was inspired to write operas after spending several years in Italy (1737–1745). His first eight operas were composed in Milan, where he exhibited a preference for the unencumbered single-line melody and accompaniment. The works were popular at the time, but none of them memorable enough to have made it past the eighteenth century. Gluck then drifted to London, where he wrote a couple more Italian-style operas, spending just enough time there to make friends with—and then be insulted by—George Frideric Handel. A sweet-tempered man but not one to mince words, Handel reportedly quipped that his cook knew more about counterpoint than Herr Gluck. Since he didn't care much about writing in the Baroque contrapuntal style, Gluck just ignored the remark and moved on, eventually settling in Vienna.

In 1750 Gluck ensured his financial security by marrying the daughter of a wealthy merchant. They settled temporarily in Vienna while Gluck composed on commission and pestered the local headhunters to find a royal appointment for him. He was hired as the orchestral director for the court of Joseph Friedrich Wilhelm, Prince of Saxe-Hildburghausen—not exactly what Gluck had in mind, but it carried enough prestige that he could get his works performed in the local opera houses. By 1761 Gluck had met poet/playwright Ranieri da Calzabigi, the most important contact of his musical career. It is no understatement that Calzabigi was responsible for Gluck's dramatic turn toward opera reform. Calzabigi's libretto for *Orfeo ed Euridice* paved the road for Gluck: it was a simple approach to the expression of emotion, the drama clear-cut, the ideals of truth and nature in the forefront. Gluck rubbed his hands in delight when informing the singers that there was no room for serendipitous improvisation. He then insisted on conducting the rehearsals and performances himself, for it was no easy task to restrain the wild horses of the opera house. The resulting ecstasy was worth the agony as the performance of *Orfeo* forever changed the world of opera. One piece from the work, the ravishing flute solo *Dance of the Blessed Spirits,* has become especially popular with audiences and this sweet, tranquil selection showcases the influence of the French ballet style upon Gluck's music.

In the preface to his next opera, *Alceste,* Gluck explained, "I have striven to restrict music to its true office of serving poetry by means of expression and by following the situations of the plot . . . I have sought to divest [opera of the] abuses . . . which have made . . . the most beautiful of spectacles the most ridiculous and wearisome." Gluck's reformation of the art was as significant to the world of music as he believed, and brought him the fame and fortune he had been seeking. The successes he enjoyed in Vienna were rivaled by those he cultivated in Paris, where Gluck produced three more "reform" operas in the late 1770s. His music sparked an ongoing debate between those who adhered to the traditional forms and those who reveled in the new style.

Never one to miss an opportunity to feed his ego, Gluck let fame go to his head and developed into quite a tyrant both on and off the podium. For him, screaming at singers and instrumentalists or throwing a temper tantrum until he got the highest price for a new production was business as usual. Musicians in Paris were glad to see Gluck return to Vienna; the Viennese were twice as relieved when he traveled back to Paris. All this angst probably contributed to the series of strokes that finally killed him in 1787. Shortly before he died, Gluck gave a copy of his choral work *De Profundis* to Antonio Salieri, who conducted a performance of the work at Gluck's funeral.

Orchestral
Dance of the Blessed Spirits from *Orfeo ed Euridice*

what to buy: [*Meditations*; James Galway, flute; Charles Gerhardt, cond.; National Philharmonic Orchestra] (RCA Victor Red Seal 37731) ♪ ♪ ♪₄

Taken from Galway's breakthrough album *The Man with the Golden Flute*, this performance joins others from a variety of sources in a two-disc set that showcases his ofttimes phenomenal technique in some ofttimes woeful material. Luckily this is not always the case, since the compilers have managed to include some splendid excerpts from the oeuvre of Johann Sebastian Bach to go along with gilded arrangements of works by Frédéric Chopin, Nicolai Rimsky-Korsakov, and others.

[Christopher Hogwood, cond.; Academy of Ancient Music, orch.] (L'Oiseau-Lyre 410553) ♪ ♪ ♪₄

Hogwood leads his original-instrument ensemble through a variety of Baroque favorites that includes not only Gluck's *Dance of the Blessed Spirits* but, from the same opera, the *Dance of the Furies*. Johann Pachelbel's ubiquitous *Canon*, a pair of concertos from Antonio Vivaldi, and selections from George Frideric Handel's oeuvre fill out this well-played collection.

what to buy next: [*Adagio 2: Karajan*; Herbert von Karajan, cond.; Berlin Philharmonic Orchestra] (Deutsche Grammophon 449515) ♪ ♪ ♪₄

Galway's old boss often pulled slick, gossamer sounds from his beloved Berlin Philharmonic, and this collection contains not only Gluck's biggest hit but selections from larger scores by Georges Bizet, Antonín Dvořák, and Edvard Grieg. Listeners seeking full-length versions of those works should look elsewhere, but Karajan's rendition of the *Dance of the Blessed Spirits* has its charms.

Vocal
Orfeo ed Euridice

what to buy: [Marilyn Horne, mezzo-soprano; Pilar Lorengar, soprano; Helen Donath, soprano; Georg Solti, cond.; Royal Opera House Orchestra, Covent Garden; Royal Opera House Chorus, Covent Garden] (London 417410) ♪ ♪ ♪ ♪

Even the persnickety Gluck would have been transported to the Elysian fields with this exquisite performance of his best composition. There are many recordings of this work, but this performance surpasses them all. Marilyn Horne sings the title role in its original form, as written for alto.

influences: Niccolò Piccinni, Luigi Cherubini

Linette Popoff-Parks and Ellen Kokko

Karl Goldmark
Born May 18, 1830, in Keszthely, Hungary. Died January 2, 1915, in Vienna, Austria.

period: Romantic

This nineteenth-century composer's style mimics those of many others, but his gift for melodic writing and colorful orchestration makes his music worth hearing.

Karl Goldmark was one of over twenty children born to a Jewish cantor in Hungary. There was little money to support his musical education (or any education, for that matter), and his first violin lessons came at the hands of a local musician. Goldmark's work with the famed violinist Joseph Bohm in Vienna in the 1840s started him on the road to employment as a pit musician, where he picked up a rudimentary knowledge of composition and arranging. Goldmark was later able to support himself with occasional performing and teaching jobs, so that he could spend time pursuing his real passion—composing.

The works of Bach, Haydn, Mozart, and Beethoven were his real teachers, along with the standard composition textbooks of the nineteenth century. Goldmark's first claim to fame was his String Quartet in D Major, op. 8, written in 1860. In 1875, the Hungarian government gave him a grant to finish his first opera, *The Queen of Sheba*. The Viennese loved it, demanding forty curtain calls for Goldmark at the premiere. *Sheba*'s interesting characters and Oriental exoticism were even more popular with the highly critical Italian audiences.

Goldmark's most popular works with today's audiences—the symphonic poem *Rustic Wedding* and the Violin Concerto in A Minor—came within the next three years. The Violin Concerto was popular in its own time, remaining familiar to music lovers well into the twentieth century through performances by the great Fritz Kreisler.

Goldmark was described by music critic Max Graf as "a mushroom, a small man almost disappearing under his broad felt hat…[who] would bow with a peculiar mixture of modesty and self-consciousness." Nevertheless, Goldmark's list of acquaintances reads like a Who's Who of nineteenth-century Vienna, including Graf, critic Eduard Hanslick, Louis Spohr, Jean Sibelius (who was his student for a short time), and Hugo Wolf. Goldmark was a kindly fellow who was able to maintain friendships with such strong personalities as Johannes Brahms and Richard Wagner. In fact, Goldmark was the source of the famous Brahmsian quip "Kindly excuse me if I by chance have forgotten to offend one of your guests," spoken by a cantankerous Brahms to the hostess of a party in Vienna.

Goldmark wrote a total of six operas, two symphonies, two violin concertos, some choral works, and a modest collection of chamber pieces. His music is an amalgam of influences, based on impressions from his early life in the synagogues and his exposure to other composers' works. Beethoven, Mendelssohn, Schumann, Liszt, Wagner, and Brahms, as well as some now-obscure German composers, all had an influence on Goldmark's nebulous style. Despite their lack of stylistic focus, his scores exhibit a masterly treatment of melodic lyricism and rich orchestral color, with Spanish, Oriental, and Hungarian folk touches lending a sense of the exotic. It is a pleasant sort of music that belies its composer's desire to express his ideas in a variety of contrasting characters.

Orchestral
Violin Concerto No. 1 in A Minor, op. 28
what to buy: [Itzhak Perlman, violin; Andre Previn, cond.; Pittsburgh Symphony] (EMI 47846) ♪ ♪ ♪

Giving a tender yet dramatic performance of Goldmark's richly Brahmsian first violin concerto, Perlman makes the music sound better than it is. A reading of Erich Wolfgang Korngold's Violin Concerto in D Major, op. 35 is also included.

Rustic Wedding for Orchestra, op. 26
what to buy: [Yondavi Butt, cond.; Royal Philharmonic Orchestra] (ASV 791) ♪ ♪ ♪

There are at least four recordings available of this 1877 work, and one has to wonder why. It's pleasant enough, but…. The rating is for the music rather than the performance, which works quite well. Some of Goldmark's

Evelyn Glennie:
Born in 1965, Evelyn Glennie's career as one of the only classical percussionists to make a living from concert tours and recordings was driven by an amazing combination of will and talent. Despite having lost the bulk of her hearing before entering her teenage years, Glennie managed to secure percussion lessons at the age of twelve and then went on to join the National Youth Orchestra of Scotland. She entered the Royal Academy of Music in London when she was seventeen years old and eventually won the school's prestigious Queen's Commendation Prize. In 1984 Glennie captured the London Symphony Music Scholarship and two years later traveled to Japan, where she studied with the internationally acclaimed marimba virtuoso and composer Keiko Abe.

Much of her success stems from her acute rhythmic sense and an ability to detect differences in pitch by their vibrations. During the early years of her career, numerous stories in the media focused primarily on Glennie's profound deafness and only secondarily upon the solidity of her achievements. At first this kind of publicity tended to qualify her accomplishments in the eyes of some critics, but her busy touring and recording schedule have showcased her abilities to the point where Glennie is almost universally admired as one of the world's great contemporary percussionists. She has also written a number of film and television scores for British television in addition to authoring her autobiography (*Good Vibrations*, Century Hutchinson, 1990) and, in 1993, creating the Evelyn Glennie Award for Percussion Composition to promote the writing of music for her field of expertise.

Glennie's recording of Béla Bartók's bracingly difficult Sonata for Two Pianos and Percussion (Sony Classics 42625), with pianists Georg Solti and Murray Perahia and fellow percussionist David Coxhill, won a Grammy Award in 1988. Ten years later she was nominated for yet another Grammy, this time for her superb recording of Joseph Schwantner's Concerto for Percussion and Orchestra (RCA Victor Red Seal 68692). *Evelyn Glennie: Her Greatest Hits* (RCA Victor Red Seal 47629) is a good two-disc sampler of her art and its diversity, including some of her own compositions, scores written specifically for her, and arrangements of works by Scott Joplin, Nicolai Rimsky-Korsakov, and Camille Saint-Saëns.

Ellen Kokko

orchestral overtures are also included.

influences: Richard Wagner, Felix Mendelssohn, Ludwig Spohr

Linette Popoff-Parks

Henryk Górecki
Born Henryk Mikolaj Górecki on December 6, 1933, in Czernica, Poland.

period: Twentieth century

Górecki has long been considered one of Poland's most distinguished creative artists, at least in his homeland.

Though his music was initially overshadowed on the international scene by the work of Witold Lutoslawski and Krzysztof Penderecki, it began reaching a wider audience during the 1990s when a recording of his third symphony sold over one million copies within a three-year period.

The music of Eastern Europe has held a fascination for much of the twentieth century. Poland, in particular, attracted much attention in the years after the Second World War with the music of Lutoslawski and Penderecki. Both composers were internationally known, and quite influential for their use of avant-garde techniques. Touring never hurts either, and Penderecki traveled extensively in the 1970s as a conductor of his own music. Henryk Górecki, born only a short time after Penderecki, was a man who shunned the limelight, however, preferring to remain close to his home. Highly regarded in Poland and in avant-garde circles, Górecki was little known to the general public in the West. His Symphony no. 3 (subtitled *Symphony of Sorrowful Songs*) would change all that. Composed in 1976, the work must have seemed reactionary when it first came out, and it would take a few years for its real impact to be felt and understood. Even the composer was surprised when, years later, the score was repeatedly performed and recorded. It, and he, had become famous.

Henryk Górecki started his formal musical studies somewhat later than Lutoslawski or Penderecki. He began teaching at a primary school in 1951 but two years later enrolled as a student at the Intermediate School of Music in Rybnik. After taking classes there from 1953 to 1954, he moved to Katowice, where he entered the State Academy of Music to study composition with Boleslaw Szabelski, a former student of Karol Szymanowski. By the time he left in 1960 to continue his studies in Paris, Górecki was absorbing the post-Schoenberg serialism of Anton Webern and adapting it to his own unique vision in works like *Scontri/Collisions* for Large Orchestra and *Monologhi* for Soprano and Three Groups of Instruments. This music placed the composer among the intellectual group in vogue at such new-music hot spots as Darmstadt and Donaueschingen.

As early as 1959, with his Symphony no. 1, Górecki began to break away from that mold, however, and turn toward a newer style with a tonal language and surface closer to that of Lutoslawski and Olivier Messiaen. By 1963 his music had undergone a complete revolution, as evidenced by his *Three Pieces in the Old Style* for String Orchestra, which used a sixteenth-century Polish wedding song as part of its musical core. Here was a work that used whole-tone harmony (with a heavy reliance on the low strings) and near glacial tempos to move the music inexorably along to its conclusion. He followed this line of development through *Choros I* (1964) and *Old Polish Music* (1969) before starting on *Ad matrem* (1971), the first of his scores to include a choral group. By the 1970s there was a definite reduction of tonal material and a use of repetition that brings to mind the works of Terry Riley. The respected Polish musicologist Grezegorz Michalski wrote, "To Górecki, tone and rhythm are useful only insofar as they are capable of triggering a particular emotional resonance favorable to mystical experience, to contemplation, to total immersion in the mediated idea."

While on a fellowship to Berlin in 1974, Górecki suffered a serious illness, one that would crop up again in 1984. In between those times, he wrote his Symphony no. 3, using a fifteenth-century Polish lamentation (in which the Virgin Mary speaks to her Son dying on the cross), an inscription by a young Polish woman that was taken from the wall of a cell at a Gestapo holding center, and a Polish folk song (*Kajze mi sie podziol mój synocek mily* [*Where has he gone, my dear young son*]) as the cores around which the work's three movements were constructed. He also accepted an administrative position with the Katowice Academy of Music, only to resign in protest four years later, in 1979, over attempts by the ruling Communist Party to quash a service commemorating the martyrdom of St. Stanislaw that Pope John Paul II was scheduled to attend. Nonetheless, *Beatus Vir*, the work that the pope (while still a cardinal) had commissioned for the service, was premiered on time and with him in attendance.

This collision between Górecki's faith and a repressive government would continue throughout the 1980s. His *Miserere* for large a cappella chorus was originally written in 1981 and dedicated to the city of Bydgoszcz, a prime battleground between the forces of Solidarity reformers and the government's security forces, but it couldn't be performed until 1987. The same scenario was almost played out that same year with *Totus Tuus*, another piece for unaccompanied voices, which was composed on the occasion of the pope's third visit to Poland. Any discussion of Górecki's art and its development must consider both his Catholic faith and his commitment to Polish folk culture. Mystical experience and contemplation as a major aspect of faith's expression, especially that of the Catholic Church, can be simple and profound at the same time; with regard to Górecki, these are qualities that permeate both his sacred and secular works. His treatment of folk music materials binds contemporary music idioms to tradition in such a way that they mesh almost seamlessly. Settings that are spiritual and meditative or based on folk song are not new in and of themselves. What is new is the unique voice that Górecki has brought with his work. He is at once tied to the tradition of the Polish people and a modern sage who has seen many things.

Orchestral
Symphony no. 3 for Soprano and Orchestra—*Symphony of Sorrowful Songs*
what to buy: [Dawn Upshaw, soprano; David Zinman, cond.; London Sinfonietta, orch.] (Nonesuch 79282) ♪ ♪ ♪ ♪ ♪

There are several recordings of this work, but Upshaw's vocal splendor meshes with the lush strings in a well-engineered sound picture that makes this performance the one to beat. This is simply the best representation of Górecki's most popular work and, by virtue of selling over one million copies, the one most responsible for introducing the composer to Western audiences.

what to buy next: [Zofia Kilanowicz, soprano; Antoni Wit, cond.; Polish National Radio Symphony Orchestra] (Naxos 8.550822) ♪ ♪ ♪ ♪

While Kilanowicz doesn't quite match the high standard set by Upshaw, Wit and his team of musicians are a surprisingly worthy match for Zinman's forces. That this disc is budget-priced and includes a wonderful performance by the orchestra's string section on Górecki's *Three Pieces in the Old Style* makes it a competitive package and a worthy alternative.

Chamber
Quartet no. 1 for Strings, op. 62—*Already It Is Dusk*
what to buy: [Kronos Quartet, ensemble] (Nonesuch 79319) ♪ ♪ ♪ ♪ ♪

Fabulous playing by the Kronos Quartet brings both heat and enlightenment to Górecki's first two string quartets. The first one (subtitled *Already It Is Dusk*) was commis-

sioned by the Kronos Quartet and is a fine companion piece for the second (subtitled *Quasi una fantasia*), which was written for and dedicated to the same ensemble three years later. Neither of these pieces is particularly difficult to listen to when compared to works by Górecki's compatriots Lutoslawski and Penderecki.

Lerchenmusik, for Cello, Clarinet, and Piano, op. 53
what to buy: [Larissa Groeneveld, cello; Harmen de Boer, clarinet; Reinbert de Leeuw, piano] (Philips 442553) ♪ ♪ ♪ ♪

This work, while it has moments of contemplation, often charges ahead at full steam, creating a yin-and-yang situation that is wholly compatible with the extreme range of dynamics usually found in the composer's scores from the 1980s. One of the most interesting borrowings in this piece is the transposed quote from Ludwig van Beethoven's fourth piano concerto that appears in the finale. The accompanying work on this disc, the 1993 *Kleines Requiem für eine Polka*, op. 66, almost sounds like Kurt Weill could have written parts of it. The Shönberg Ensemble under Reinbert de Leeuw's direction gives a marvelous performance of this quirky piece.

Vocal
Miserere for Chorus, op. 44
what to buy: [John Nelson, cond., Chicago Lyric Opera Chorus] (Nonesuch 79348) ♪ ♪ ♪ ♪

This is a fine recording of the wonderful *Miserere*, a half-hour work that demonstrates the composer's grasp of choral material. It is part of a well programmed and well recorded disc of Górecki's a cappella scores that includes the *Amen* for Mixed a capella Chorus and *Euntes ibant et flebant* for Chorus (performed by Nelson and his choir), plus two works featuring Lucy Ding's Lira Chamber Chorus: *My Vistula, Grey Vistula* and *Broad Waters*.

influences: Olivier Messiaen, Arvo Pärt, Witold Lutoslawski

Frank Retzel and Garaud MacTaggart

Louis Moreau Gottschalk
Born May 8, 1829, in New Orleans, LA. Died December 18, 1869, in Tijuca, Brazil.

period: Romantic

Gottschalk is a minor American composer/pianist whose music referenced American folksongs, and foreshadowed the development of jazz and ragtime by drawing on melodies and rhythms from Creole and Cuban cultures. His popularity as a touring pianist made him the nineteenth century equivalent of a modern rock star.

Moreau, as he was called by his family, was the oldest of seven children, and a prodigy from his earliest days. Papa Gottschalk recognized his son's talent and arranged for him to study with the organist at the St. Louis Cathedral in New Orleans. He began lessons at age five, and by the time he was seven was filling in for his teacher as a substitute organist. Gottschalk's talent was very impressive, and his parents and teacher were eager to develop it further. They sent him to study in Paris, where almost everyone was equally impressed. Chopin heard the young maestro perform in 1842 and declared that Gottschalk would become "the king of pianists." Gottschalk was writing piano pieces by this time, having found his own unique voice. He had created a novel, appealing sound by fusing his native Creole music with the Chopin-esque salon pianism he discovered in Paris.

Gottschalk was all the rage in Europe by the late 1840s. He was the first to incorporate quotes from American folk tunes and utilize Creole and Cuban rhythms. The result was said to be a fascinating and almost mesmerizing concert experience. His good looks and aristocratic airs didn't hurt his popularity, either! He concertized fiendishly, traveling to other French provinces, to Switzerland, and to Spain. Eventually he returned to the United States, only to find he had to prove himself worthy of the snobbish American audiences. After three exhausting and frustrating years, he gave up and went to Cuba. He traveled extensively throughout the Caribbean, performing sporadically and trying to find a quiet refuge from the hectic world he had left in America and Europe. But soon enough he decided to make another stab at the American concert scene.

In 1862, Gottschalk gave eighty-five concerts in four months, traveling more than 15,000 miles—and kept that frenetic pace for the next two years. The American public was won over this time. Audiences fell for his flashy virtuosic technique, good looks, and "pianola style." If not for a sex scandal in San Francisco that "encouraged" him to leave the country, he might have

continued the frantic schedule. South America is where Gottschalk landed on his feet, resuming the pace he established in the United States by organizing "monster concerts" with numerous pianists performing simultaneously. He was in great demand, and continued to enjoy the lifestyle of travel and performance. It was probably a combination of his busy calendar, yellow fever, and South American heat that brought Gottschalk's life to an early end at age forty. He collapsed during a concert in Brazil and never recovered. A year later, his body was brought back to America and buried in Brooklyn, New York.

Chamber
various piano works
what to buy: [*Gottschalk: Piano Music, vol. 1*; Philip Martin, piano] (Hyperion 66459) ♪ ♪ ♪ ♪

[*Gottschalk: Piano Music, vol. 2*; Philip Martin, piano] (Hyperion 66697) ♪ ♪ ♪ ♪

[*Gottschalk: Piano Music, vol. 3*; Philip Martin, piano] (Hyperion 66915) ♪ ♪ ♪ ♪

[*Gottschalk: Piano Music, vol. 4*; Philip Martin, piano] (Hyperion 67118) ♪ ♪ ♪ ♪

This four-volume collection of Gottschalk's works for piano is beautifully played by Irish pianist Philip Martin. He performs the varied styles with meticulous attention to rhythmic aberrations, melodic quotes, and cascading, cadenza-like scales and arpeggios. This is not *great* music, but Martin's consistent interpretations seem to make it so. Specific pieces to look for: *The Banjo* from vol. 1; *La Savane* and *Souvenirs d'Andalousie* from vol. 2; *Bamboula* and *The Dying Poet* from vol. 3; and *La Gitanella* from vol. 4. These are terrifically exciting, representative works, and the most likely pieces by the composer to show up on a concert program.

what to buy next: [*The World of Louis Moreau Gottschalk, vol. 1*; Eugene List, piano] (Vanguard Classics 4050) ♪ ♪ ♪

[*The World of Louis Moreau Gottschalk, vol. 2*; Eugene List, piano] (Vanguard Classics 4051) ♪ ♪ ♪

You can get much of the more popular stuff heard on the Martin sets performed here by pianist Eugene List, who was largely responsible for the relatively recent resurgence of interest in Gottschalk's music. His interpretations, like those of Martin, are interesting and stylistically pleasing.

influences: Frédéric Chopin, Scott Joplin

Linette A. Popoff-Parks

Morton Gould

Born December 10, 1913, in Richmond Hill, NY Died February 21, 1996, in Orlando, FL.

period: Twentieth century

Morton Gould was an eclectic American composer, pianist, and conductor whose likable music mixed classical discipline with popular tastes. He once said, "I am not a purist and espouse no dogma but am curious and fascinated by the infinite variety of all kinds of musical sounds."

Gould was an incredibly gifted child prodigy who, when he was four years old, played John Philip Sousa's *Stars and Stripes Forever* on the piano after hearing it once during a band concert. His early "training" started when Gould began improvising at the piano on any music he heard in recitals, from piano rolls or on the radio. His formal musical education started (while he was still attending public school) when Gould began studying composition at the New York Institute of Musical Art— the predecessor of the Juilliard School of Music—and taking piano lessons with famed pedagogue Abby Whiteside. He was just a regular guy to his family and friends, but as Gould's talents developed, his reputation in the music world grew quickly. Even the largest music publishing house of the day—G. Schirmer—saw him as a fifteen-year-old genius whose *Three Conservative Sketches* was worthy of publication.

Like so many kids during the Depression, Gould left school (in 1930) to help support his family. The on-the-job training he received playing piano in theaters, movie houses, and radio studios was to serve him well, giving him opportunities that he would later capitalize on. By 1943, Gould had built such a strong reputation as a composer and conductor that he was appointed musical director of NBC Radio's *Chrysler Hour*, and it is in this role that much of the American public became acquainted with Gould's "style Americana." Like the composers

Aaron Copland and Charles Ives, Gould brought uniquely American touches to the concert stage. He loved jazz, boogie-woogie, spirituals, folk tunes, and parlor music—and sought to fuse them with more traditional forms and styles. One of his most popular works, the *American Salute for Orchestra,* brought the Civil War tune "When Johnny Comes Marching Home" to the ears of war-weary Americans in 1942, while his *Spirituals for Strings* consists of five starkly contrasting movements using quotes from both black and white spirituals. In Gould's words, "[The] emotions are specifically American. The songs range from ones that are escapist in feelings, or light and gay, to those having tremendous depth and tragic impact." The music is strikingly dissonant and dark, with the exception of the third movement, which uses quotes from "Shortnin' Bread," and the fifth movement, which is driven by a repetitious boogie-woogie riff.

A prolific writer, Gould created many themes for movies, television, and Broadway shows in addition to a few chamber works, some vocal pieces, and a plethora of symphonic commissions. Always one to keep abreast of the times, Gould even took on a project for the Pittsburgh Symphony Association (in 1992) called *The Jogger and the Dinosaur,* a concert piece for rapper and orchestra. Like Copland, Gould also wrote ballet scores (most of which were performed by George Balanchine's company), including a notorious piece for Agnes de Mille's troupe. This work was quite different from Copland's sweet and comparatively tame *Appalachian Spring*, since Gould's score for *Fall River Legend* was based on Lizzy Borden's infamous trial for the hatchet murders of her father and stepmother.

Among Gould's many honors were the Grammy Award he received in 1966 for his recording of Charles Ives's Symphony no. 1 (Gould was to garner twelve more Grammy nominations during his career) and, in 1995, the Pulitzer Prize in Music for his composition *Stringmusic.*

Orchestral
American Symphonette no. 2
what to buy: [*Morton Gould: A Tribute*; Kenneth Klein, cond.; London Philharmonic Orchestra] (Albany Troy 202) ♪ ♪ ♪

These are good renderings of pleasant if ephemeral music, and the pieces contain a few interesting moments of Americana, with some tunes you may recognize (though don't confuse the *Spirituals for String Orchestra and Harp* heard here with the earlier

Spirituals for Orchestra). The *Pavanne* from *American Symphonette no. 2* was a big hit at "pops" concerts led by Gould's friend Arthur Fiedler. Rounding out the album are performances of Gould's *American Salute for Orchestra* and his *American Ballads for Orchestra*.

Fall River Legend: Suite for Orchestra

what to buy: [*Morton Gould's America*; James Sedares, cond.; New Zealand Symphony Orchestra; Gould Symphony] (Koch International Classics 7380) ♪ ♪ ♪₄

This is a very good performance of the mildly interesting suite Gould created from his bizarre 1947 ballet score about Lizzie Borden's trial. The piece is rife with dissonant versions of old-time New England hymns and dances. Sedares's forces are also heard here in Gould's orchestral suite, the *Steven Foster Gallery*, while the disc's lone choral work, *Of Time and The River*, features John Daly Goodwin leading the Gregg Smith Singers, the New York Choral Society, and the New York Choral Society Orchestra.

what to buy next: [Milton Rosenstock, cond.; Brock Peters, speaker; National Philharmonic Orchestra] (Albany TROY 035) ♪ ♪ ♪

For those listeners interested in the genesis of this work, Rosenstock's world premiere recording of the complete ballet (with Peters taking the part of Speaker for the Jury) also includes a dialog between Gould and choreographer Agnes de Mille. Sedares is still the first choice for the suite.

influences: Ferde Grofé, Leonard Bernstein, Aaron Copland

Linette A. Popoff-Parks

Charles Gounod

Born Charles François Gounod, June 17, 1818, in Paris, France. Died October, 18, 1893, in St. Cloud, France.

period: Romantic

Gounod was basically a French operatic composer who happened to write several significant sacred works in

Morton Gould

Glenn Gould:

In 1945, when he was just shy of thirteen years old, Glenn Gould graduated from the Toronto Conservatory of Music, the youngest person ever to do so. His career as a concert soloist began two years later when he performed with the Toronto Symphony Orchestra. Gould eventually developed into a unique (one could justifiably say eccentric) personality whose piano playing has been alternately praised and castigated. Part of the latter in Gould's early career was undoubtedly due to his ofttimes bizarre antics on stage—particularly his insistence on playing the piano from an incredibly low position and the great, gasping breaths and humming that, for some, destroyed the flow of the composition being performed. This trait followed him into the recording studio and became even more pronounced after he suspended his concert performances in 1964.

His interpretations of works by Johann Sebastian Bach were often quite controversial, especially when considering Gould's vehement advocacy for performing them on the piano instead of the more "authentic" harpsichords, clavichords, or organ. Vladimir Ashkenazy was among those who appreciated his fellow pianist's approach to Bach, however, once defending Gould by saying that his later performances of key works in the composer's canon had "a quiet, transcendental understanding and identification with Bach's mind." The evolution of Gould's thinking about Bach can best be heard in the two versions he recorded of the *Goldberg Variations*: the youthful exuberance (if that is the proper term) of his 1958 performance (Sony Classical 38479) versus the 1981 digital remake, recorded shortly before Gould's death in 1982, which takes a deeper, more measured approach to the score. While the earlier set has its advocates and was quite revolutionary at the time of its release, the later performance shows the result of long familiarity with the music and a mature willingness to let the piece unfold.

Great Pianists of the 20th Century: Glenn Gould (Philips 456808) is a very good sampler of Gould's artistry that contains none of his Bach interpretations but instead explores the intriguing range of material performed by him over the years. In addition to his stellar way with Alban Berg's Sonata for Piano and scores by Sergei Prokofiev and Alexander Scriabin, this two-disc set also shows Gould reveling in the contrapuntal joys of Elizabethan-era composers William Byrd and Orlando Gibbons along with his playing of music by Domenico Scarlatti, Franz Joseph Haydn, Wolfgang Amadeus Mozart, Georges Bizet, and Richard Strauss.

Before he retired from the concert stage, Gould had become interested in working with the broadcast media, eventually becoming an award-winning producer of radio documentaries for the Canadian Broadcasting Corporation. Two of the projects he hosted and worked on, programs devoted to cellist Pablo Casals and conductor Leopold Stokowski (broadcast in 1971 and 1974, respectively), are now available commercially (CBC 2025), revealing yet another aspect of this most complex individual.

Ian Palmer

addition to his more secular activities. *Faust* was his single greatest achievement, though his setting for voice and piano of a prelude by Johann Sebastian Bach yielded the one work whose melody-line is familiar even to those who don't know Gounod's name—his *Ave Maria*.

Gounod began studying piano with his mother prior to attending the Lycée St. Louis for more formal classes. He passed the entrance examination for the Paris Conservatoire in 1836, and during his time there honed his skills to the point where he was able (with a cantata entitled *Fernand*) to win the Grand Prix de Rome in 1839. This enabled him to continue his studies in Rome, where he discovered the marvels of sixteenth century sacred music, particularly the masses and motets of Giovanni Palestrina.

When Gounod returned to Paris in 1843, he also brought with him a new appreciation for the works of Bach, courtesy of Fanny Hensel (Felix Mendelssohn's sister), who met the young composer in Rome. He moved in with his mother and assumed a position as organist and music director for the Missions Etrangères, a church catering to foreign diplomats. Always torn between the worlds of the sacred and the profane, Gounod then entered the Carmelite Novitiate only to earn a reputation as a philandering ecclesiastic. While he continued writing music for religious services and conducting a wider variety of sacred works than his congregation was used to, Gounod was turning gradually toward the idea of making his living with another kind of music altogether.

In 1851, upon leaving his sacred employment, Gounod gave himself over to the world of opera, composing his first work in the genre, *Sapho*. While the classical myths surrounding the subject matter were not exactly something one would expect a former aspiring clergyman to delve into, the music itself was nothing for the Parisian public to get excited about either. This was a seemingly strange lead-in to his next major work, the *Messe solennelle de Sainte Cécile,* but when one considers the duality of Gounod's impulses, an obvious devotion to the church hampered by earthy appetites, it makes perfect sense. He unveiled his second opera, *La nonne sanglante,* in 1858, but this didn't exactly turn audiences into rabid fans either. However, some incidental music he wrote for a drama (*Ulysse*) went over well enough that Gounod was hired to direct L'Orphéon de la Ville de Paris, a large male choir. *Le médecin malgré lui,* based on text originating with Molière, was his third effort in the opera genre and achieved a bit better results than the other two; Claude Debussy once declared it to be his favorite opera by Gounod.

1859 was the year in which Gounod fashioned a vocal arrangement for a short instrumental setting he had created back in 1852. This rendering of Bach's C Major prelude (drawn from the *Well-Tempered Clavier*) would come to be known as Gounod's *Ave Maria,* one of the most popular concert arias of the last 150 years. The composer's fourth opera, *Faust,* was also produced in 1859 and secured his reputation in the genre. Unlike most opera composers of the time, Gounod managed to break away from the grand opera format which dealt more with spectacle than character development. His *Faust* introduced dialog instead of declamation, subtlety instead of pomposity. The change in approach was not one that Gounod would seek to build upon in future operatic works, however, and this may be the reason why most of his later operas aren't produced very often. The closest he ever came to duplicating this kind of success for posterity was in *Romeo and Juliette,* the 1864 opera which repeated some of the virtues of *Faust* but did so without the consistent inspiration which had been a hallmark of the earlier work.

Gounod moved to England during the Franco-Prussian War (1870–1871) and stayed there until the mid 1870s, finding employment as a choral conductor and creating a plethora of vocal works (both choral and solo) and miscellaneous instrumental pieces. When he returned to France, he devoted much of his time to writing operas and masses, none of which were received with any popular enthusiasm, but he also composed his *Petite Symphony, a favorite of bands and wind ensembles to this day.*

Orchestral
Faust ballet music
what to buy: [Neville Marriner, cond.; Academy of St. Martin-in-the-Fields, orch.] (Philips 462125) ♪ ♪ ♪ ♪

French opera audiences loved their ballets and the same venues that housed opera companies often housed dance companies. This would result in composers having to create slots within their operas where dancers could exercise their art. Gounod's solution to the dictum for *Faust* resulted in some wonderful, light-textured material filled with subtle rhythms and memorable melodies. Marriner and the musicians of the Academy of St. Martin-in-the-Fields have developed quite a deserved reputation for their abilities with such string-driven works, and this performance is certainly up to their standards. Fine versions of Gounod's two symphonies fill out this delightful disc.

[*French Opera Highlights*; Paul Paray, cond.; Detroit Symphony Orchestra] (Mercury Living Presence 432014) ♪ ♪ ♪ ♪

Not only does Paray lead the DSO through a lively, sparkling performance of Gounod's tuneful ballet music, he also gets them to perform at a similarly high level throughout this program of operatic bonbons. Gounod, Camille Saint-Saëns, Georges Bizet, Hector Berlioz, and Jules Massenet are the heavyweights in this collection but contributions are also made by Ambroise Thomas, Louis Joseph Herald, and Daniel François Auber.

Chamber
Petit Symphonie for Nine Wind Instruments
what to buy: [Athena Ensemble] (Chandos 6543) ♪ ♪ ♪ ♪

The challenge of writing sans string players was set for Gounod by his good friend the flute virtuoso Paul Taffanel, and the result of the composer's labors is one of the most charming works for wind ensemble ever written. In addition to the Gounod work, this high-quality recording includes Jacques Ibert's three *Pièces Brèves* for Wind Quintet and Francis Poulenc's Sextet for Piano and Woodwind Quintet. The Athena Ensemble has created an enjoyable anthology, with the music of the twentieth century French composers highlighting the bright and joyful nature of the *Petit Symphonie*.

Ave Maria for Voice and Piano (or Orchestra)
what to buy: [*Favourite Violin Encores*; Arthur Grumiaux, violin; Istvan Hajdu, piano] (Philips 446560) ♪ ♪ ♪ ♪

Here is an exquisite instrumental arrangement of Gounod's most popular song; Grumiaux is a masterful violinist. There is a plethora of other composers represented here including Wolfgang Amadeus Mozart, Maurice Ravel, Franz Schubert, and a few other big names alongside such one-hit wonders as Franz von Vecsey, Francesco Maria Veracini, and Joseph-Hector Fiocco, all of which makes for an enjoyable, if essentially lightweight, listening experience.

[*Ceremonial Music for Trumpet and Symphonic Organ*; Rolf Smedvig, trumpet; Michael Murray, organ] (Telarc 80341) ♪ ♪ ♪ ♪

This recording's approach harkens back to the trumpet and organ arrangements of Bach himself. Murray is sur-

prisingly seductive behind Smedvig's trumpet artistry and the recital is loaded with favorites by Bach (*Jesu, Joy of Man's Desiring*), Jeremiah Clarke (*Trumpet Voluntary in D Major*), and Felix Mendelssohn (the *Wedding March*), but the other surprise success is the duo's version of the *Prayer of St. Gregory* by Alan Hovhaness.

[*O Holy Night*; Luciano Pavarotti, tenor; Kurt Herbert Adler, cond.; National Philharmonic Orchestra] (London 414044) ♪ ♪ ♪ ♪

Even though this lovely work is taken out of context when presented in orchestral dress, the soaring melody line almost overwhelms the original setting for voice and piano. Pavarotti's Christmas album includes a well-chosen, tasteful selection of works by César Franck, Franz Schubert, and others in addition to the Gounod piece.

what to buy next: [*Harmonies Célestes*; Brigitte Desnoues, soprano; Kai Gleusteen, violin; Laurent Martin, piano; Olivier Vernet, organ] (Ligia 0202011) ♪ ♪ ♪♪

Rather than separate the tune from the composer, Ligia has chosen to build a recital around Gounod's sacred works and the commendable sopranos Brigitte Desnoues and Annick Massis. The results are certainly worth hearing, not just for the interesting arrangement of *Ave Maria* featuring Desnoues but for the soprano duet in *O salutaris* and *D'un Coeur Qui T'aime* and Olivier Vernet's organ solo in the *Marche solennelle* in E-flat Major.

[*Hymn for the World, 2*; Cecilia Bartoli, mezzo-soprano; Myung-Whun Chung, cond.; Santa Cecilia Academy Rome Orchestra; Santa Cecilia Academy Rome Chorus] (Deutsche Grammophon 459146) ♪ ♪ ♪♪

The rating is more a reflection of the set from which this piece is taken than of the actual performance of the score. Everything is pleasant enough but the overall menu of this disc, including cuts featuring pop tenor sensation Andrea Bocelli and the usually tasteful baritone Bryn Terfel, smacks more of mammon than of art.

Vocal
Faust
what to buy: [Cecilia Gasdia, soprano; Brigitte Fassbaender, mezzo-soprano; Susanne Menntzer, mezzo-soprano; Jerry Hadley, tenor; Alexandru Agache,

baritone; Samuel Ramey, bass; Carlo Rizzi, cond.; Welsh National Opera Orchestra; Welsh National Opera Chorus] (Teldec 90872) ♪ ♪ ♪ ♪

An excellent recording for those willing to add a complete version of this work to their collection. Jerry Hadley as Faust and Cecilia Gasdia as Marguerite are more than adequate in their roles, but it is the stunning work of Samuel Ramey as Mephistopheles that highlights this performance.

influences: Felix Mendelssohn, Giacomo Meyerbeer, Georges Bizet

Paul Wintemute and Garaud MacTaggart

Percy Grainger

Born George Percy Aldridge Grainger, July 8,1882, in Brighton, Victoria, Australia. Died February 20, 1961, in White Plains, NY.

period: Twentieth century

Percy Grainger was one of the true originals in the history of Western music. A unique, fascinating, and somewhat controversial figure, he was misunderstood during his lifetime, but remains a remarkable pioneer whose achievements are still not fully appreciated. Grainger is best remembered today for short piano pieces and works like "A Lincolnshire Posy" and his arrangement for strings of "Londonderry Air (Danny Boy)."

Grainger originally studied piano with his mother and showed remarkable aptitude for the keyboard as a child. When he was only ten he gave a series of piano recitals which not only showcased his precocious talents, but also earned him the money to go to Germany for further studies when he was thirteen. His career as a concert pianist started in earnest in London in 1901, after which he toured Europe and elsewhere for several years. He became fast friends with the Norwegian composer Edvard Grieg, who contended that Grainger was the ideal interpreter of Grieg's world-famous piano concerto. Indeed, Grainger became closely associated with that work for most of the rest of his life. Grainger moved to New York in 1914, and made his concert debut there the following year playing—what else?—Grieg's piano concerto, receiving tremendous critical and popular acclaim.

Grainger served as a bandsman in the United States Army from 1917 to 1919. During that time he wrote many of his works for concert band, which are among the finest ever written in the genre. He became an American citizen while in the service and, after his discharge, eventually settled in White Plains, New York, the city that would be his home until his death there in 1961. In 1922 Grainger embarked on the first of a series of expeditions to collect folksongs in rural areas of Denmark. He had made similar trips throughout the English countryside in 1906, pioneering the use of the wax-cylinder phonograph to record a vanishing folk tradition. During most of the summers between 1919 and 1928 he taught piano at the Chicago Musical College and, from 1932 to 1933, he was chairman of the Music Department at New York University. He also began trying to collect much-needed funds for a museum in Melbourne which was finally established in 1938 to preserve Australian musical culture and to house his manuscripts. During the Second World War he lived temporarily in Springfield, Missouri, which he used as a base for touring on behalf of the war effort.

Grainger was largely self-taught as a composer. He was extremely prolific, and to this day the majority of his works remain in manuscript. He often created different versions or arrangements of the same piece, and pioneered the exploration of new sonorities even though his early experiments in sound were virtually ignored and unappreciated. Perhaps the most memorable part of his output is his truly remarkable and original body of folksong settings and arrangements. At their best, these settings are incomparable, and reveal the workings of an amazingly creative mind. His string orchestra arrangement of "Londonderry Air (Danny Boy)" can be considered the finest ever made of this piece. Grainger felt the study of indigenous ethnic music to be the strongest influence on his writing, and his overall philosophy of music called for the widest possible blending of peoples and styles. For most of his life he was obsessed with the idea of creating what he referred to as *free music,* that is, music free from all of the conventional restraints of harmony, rhythm, tonality, and form. He never achieved this to his satisfaction. Sadly, Grainger died a lonely and bitter man, remembered at the time only for being a brilliant concert pianist and a writer of popular folksong arrangements. Even today, his reputation lies chiefly with those light miniatures, although his total output was far more considerable. He certainly is a vastly underrated figure in twentieth century Western music.

Orchestral
Lincolnshire Posy for Band
what to buy: [*Shepherd's Hey: Wind Music of Grainger, Milhaud, Poulenc*; Denis Wick, cond.; London Wind Orchestra] (ASV White Line 2067) ♪ ♪ ♪♪

In addition to a fine version of Grainger's "Lincolnshire Posy," Wick and company give good value in their performances of the composer's "Shepherd's Hey," "Molly on the Shore," and the ever-popular *Londonderry Air (Danny Boy)*. The same applies to their take on Francis Poulenc's *Suite française after Claude Gervaise* and Darius Milhaud's *Suite française*.

worth searching for: [*In a Nutshell*; Simon Rattle, cond; City of Birmingham Symphony Orchestra] (EMI Classics 56412) ♪ ♪ ♪ ♪

"Lincolnshire Posy" is one of Grainger's finest works for wind band, and receives what is perhaps its first total realization under the hands of the extraordinary Simon Rattle and the orchestra which he led for many years. Grainger's *The Warriors* for orchestra, three pianos and percussion is also an amazing work, superbly played by Rattle and company. The balance of the disc is occupied by three additional Grainger compositions and two short pieces by other composers: an orchestration of the first of Claude Debussy's three *Estampes*, and Maurice Ravel's *Miroirs: Vallée des Cloches*.

various folksong settings
what to buy: [*Famous Folk-Settings*; Moray Welsh, cello; Philip Martin, piano; Kenneth Montgomery, cond; Bournemouth Sinfonietta, orch.] (Chandos Collect 6542) ♪ ♪ ♪♪

This is a delightful collection featuring many of Grainger's deservedly-popular folksong arrangements, including "My Robin Is to the Greenwood Gone," "Molly on the Shore," "Blithe Bells," "Handel in the Strand," and "Green Bushes." Although this set dates back to 1978, everything is well-played and well-recorded.

worth searching for: [*Folksong Arrangements*; Benjamin Britten, cond.; various soloists and ensembles) (Decca/London 425159) ♪ ♪ ♪ ♪

This is an absolutely marvelous collection of Grainger miniatures, both familiar and unfamiliar, and the performances are uniformly excellent: loving, committed, and with a great sense of atmosphere and style. A real gem!

Chamber
various piano works
what to buy: [*Percy Grainger: The Complete Piano Music*; Martin Jones, piano] (Nimbus 1767) ♪ ♪ ♪♪

The enterprising Mr. Jones has recorded all of Grainger's pieces for the keyboard, and this budget-priced five-CD set presents fine renderings of "Handel in the Strand," "The Immovable Do," "Bridal Lullaby," and "Mock Morris" among others. All are performed with great style and technical assurance, featuring bright, realistic keyboard sound.

Vocal
various folksong settings
what to buy: [*At Twilight: Choral Music of Grainger and Grieg*; Stephen Layton, cond.; Polyphony, choir] (Hyperion 66793) ♪ ♪ ♪ ♪

Lovely singing of Grainger classics like "Londonderry Air (Danny Boy)," "Mo Nighean Dubh," and "Brigg Fair" take up the lion's share of this disc, with only two works by Grieg (his *Psalms*, op. 74 and a setting of *Ave maris stella*) rounding out the program.

what to buy next: [*Grainger Edition, vol. 9: Works for Chorus and Orchestra 3*; Richard Hickox, cond.; City of London Sinfonietta, orch.; Joyful Company of Singers, choir] (Chandos 9653) ♪ ♪ ♪♪

Hickox leads his forces through a pretty mixture of instrumental and choral settings by Grainger. Chandos seems to have a real knack for recording string sections, with "Danny Boy" and "Mock Morris" being the most familiar of the tunes receiving this treatment here. The version of "Skye Boat Song" on this program benefits from some particularly lovely singing.

worth searching for: [*Danny Boy: Songs and Dancing Ballads by Percy Grainger*; John Eliot Gardiner, cond.; English Country Gardiner Orchestra; Monteverdi Choir] (Philips 446657) ♪ ♪ ♪ ♪

Grainger made folksong arrangements for different combinations of instruments and voices. This super recording features many of his choral settings, including "Brigg Fair," "The Merry Wedding," "Londonderry Air (Danny Boy)," "Mo Nighean Dubh," and "Danny Deever." Everything on this disc is performed to the hilt by Gardiner (best known as a specialist in Baroque music) and his cohorts.

influences: Frederick Delius, Hamilton Harty, Edward Elgar

Charles Greenwell and David Wagner

Enrique Granados

Born Enrique Granados y Campiña, July 27, 1867, in Lérida, Spain. Died March 24, 1916, at sea in the English Channel.

period: Romantic

Enrique Granados was a late-Romantic pianist and composer who infused his virtuosic piano works with Spanish folk melodies and rhythms. His most popular music resides in the two books of his *Goyescas,* piano pieces inspired by the paintings of Goya.

Granados did not see much of the world outside of Spain during his 49 years. Except for a couple of trips to France and Switzerland and one *really* important excursion to the United States, Granados enjoyed "the good life" of a musician in his native country. His early training took place in Barcelona where he studied piano with Joan Pujol and, less formally, with Felipe Pedrell, the important composer, pedagogue, and musicologist who advocated the study of Spanish folk traditions. At age 20 Granados went to Paris to study piano with Charles-Wilfrid Bériot. Back in Spain two years later, he tried to establish his reputation as a concert pianist while working on what would become his first successful piano score, the *Danzas españolas.* His first opera, *María del Carmen,* was unveiled in 1898 and briefly brought Granados into the limelight, but it took only a few years for it to pass out of the Spanish repertoire. He continued to write, but spent more time teaching at the music school he founded in 1901 (the *Academia Granados*) and giving recitals.

His biggest success as a composer was the piano collection *Goyescas.* This set of dance-oriented pieces, full of little rhythmic figures and melodic patterns, presents a wide variety of characters: playful, at times elegant; at others melancholic, sometimes even flirtatious. They sound more like synthesized Robert Schumann and Franz Liszt than Spanish, but an occasional Moorish melodic fragment, guitar-like ostinato rhythm, or incessantly repeating tune reminds you that you're in Iberian territory. *El fandango de candil (Dance at the oil lamp)* and *Quejas, o la maja y el ruiseñor (Complaints, or the snake and the nightingale)* are particularly appealing to those who enjoy the sensual nature of this folk-inspired art. Recall Maurice Ravel's *Bolero,* and you can imagine how enticing the composer's Spanish-Moorish flavors can be! The *Goyescas* were so popular that, in 1914, Granados was encouraged to write an opera using the material from the piano pieces and some of his songs. The European scene was involved with World War I by the time the work was finished, so he took it to the Metropolitan Opera in New York in 1916. The operatic version of *Goyescas* was politely received and shortly thereafter Granados was invited to perform at the White House for President Wilson. Because of that fateful detour to Washington D.C., Granados took a different ship back to Europe. This new, roundabout route led from the United States to Spain via England. It was his ill fortune that the *Sussex,* which was to take him to France, was torpedoed by a German sub in the English Channel. Granados reportedly dove into the water to save his drowning wife, but both perished.

Chamber
Goyescas
what to buy: [Alicia de Larrocha, pianist] (EMI Classics 64524) ♪ ♪ ♪ ♪

Originally released on Hispavox back in the mid-1960s, these delightful and virtuosic performances by de Larrocha make up the best and most valuable collection of Granados's famous piano pieces. The pianist has it all: perfect technique, gorgeous tone, rhythmic intensity, and emotional bravura. Also included on this two disc set are the six *Escenas románticas (Romantic Scenes),* the seven *Valses poéticos,* and *Seis piezas sobre cantos populares españoles (Six pieces on Spanish Folksongs).*

various piano works
worth searching for: *Grand Piano: The Composer Plays;* Enrique Granados, piano] (Nimbus 8813) ♪ ♪ ♪

The rating is for the historical value. Granados plays his own music, including selections from *Goyescas,* recorded from piano rolls the composer had cut for the Duo-Art Company. This album also includes composer/pianists George Gershwin, Sergei Prokofiev, and Igor Stravinsky playing a potpourri of their works—again via the medium of piano rolls.

influences: Isaac Albéniz, Felipe Pedrell, Manuel de Falla

Linette Popoff-Parks

Edvard Grieg

Born Edvard Hagerup Grieg, June 15, 1843, in Bergen, Norway. Died September 4, 1907, in Bergen, Norway.

period: Romantic

Grieg's music was popular among nineteenth century nationalists, especially within Scandinavia, and his international reputation was established by three works: a piano concerto and the two suites from *Peer Gynt*. The ironic fact is that these popular scores are not necessarily his best pieces.

Grieg's story began in Norway, where he was born, raised, and spent the majority of his life. His mother, Gesine, was a gifted pianist who enhanced Grieg family life by hosting many musical gatherings at their home. (She was also six-year-old Edvard's first piano teacher.) Norwegian violinist and composer Ole Bull visited the Grieg family in 1858, and was quite excited by the youngster's budding musicianship. He insisted that the Leipzig Conservatory in Germany was the only place for Edvard's talents to be cultivated, and convinced his parents to send him there. As a result, the fifteen-year-old moved to Leipzig to further develop his skills as pianist and composer.

His experiences with piano instructors were disappointing, and after a year of mind- and finger-numbing exercises Grieg changed teachers to study with E. F. Wenzel. His new teacher was a friend of Robert Schumann, and instilled in Grieg a love for Schumann's music. (Listen to Grieg's Piano Concerto in A Minor, written in the very same key that Schumann wrote his piano concerto, and you will hear many strong similarities between the two, beginning with an opening cadenza-like flourish from the solo piano.) Grieg was unhappy with the composition aspect of his Conservatory training, too. He complained that he was given rigorous composition exercises much too soon, before he had even learned the basics of musical form. Perhaps it was this stressful time that helped bring on the serious attack of pleurisy in 1860 which resulted in Grieg returning to Norway for recuperation. He spent only two more years in Leipzig after the illness had subsided before returning home for good.

Back in Norway, Grieg concertized for a bit before eventually making the decision to work on his composition skills again. He went to Copenhagen in 1863 to pick up some new ideas, and what he found there literally changed his life. First, Grieg met and worked with Niels Gade, a Danish musician who was recognized as the leader of Scandinavian Romanticism. In addition, Grieg met numerous other important cultural figures in Copenhagen, including Hans Christian Andersen, whose poetry he eventually set to music. He also met singer Nina Hagerup, a gifted soprano (and a distant cousin) whom he wasted no time in courting. They were engaged by the middle of 1864 and married three years later. Grieg's op. 5 songs—*The Heart's Melodies,* a set of short, sweet pieces based on the equally short, sweet stanzas of his new friend Hans Christian Andersen—were composed for his beloved bride.

The year 1864 was also important in the development of Grieg's compositional style. It was then that he met with Ole Bull again and discussed with him the idea of a Norwegian nationalistic "school." Another great influence on Grieg was Rikard Nordraak, a young composer already employing Norwegian folk idioms in his music; the two became very good friends, singing and playing folk songs and dances. Grieg and Nordraak were also instrumental in the founding of Euterpe, a society for the promotion of Scandinavian music.

In 1869 Grieg, accompanied by Nina and with support from the Norwegian government, took a trip to Rome that resulted in an audience with Franz Liszt. For a couple of years Grieg had been in contact with the great pianist/composer, and Liszt received the young composer's music with warmth and enthusiasm. They later became good friends and Liszt even wrote a letter of recommendation for Grieg.

After arriving back in Norway in 1870, Grieg set about conducting, concertizing, and composing. His first major work after the Liszt meetings was the incidental music for Henrik Ibsen's *Peer Gynt.* Another grant from the Norwegian government enabled Grieg to work exclusively on the piece, completing the first version of it in 1875. (It was revised twice more: in 1885 and 1888.) The suites from *Peer Gynt* consist of two sets of pieces written for choir, soloists and orchestra, and turned out to be his most popular and famous works. There is hardly anyone who has not heard fragments of *Morning Mood* or *In the Hall of the Mountain King,* even if only because of quotes used as an instrumental backdrop for cartoons.

Grieg's compositions from 1867 to 1878 are weighted toward Romanticism but begin showcasing distinct folk elements. His A Minor Piano Concerto and the early *Lyric Pieces* for piano still follow the traditional forms,

but peculiar ethnic melodic and rhythmic fragments appear here and there. Although folk elements had become increasingly pervasive within his works by the late 1890s, one can also hear influences of the French Impressionists in the pieces written after an excursion to Paris at that time. This particular trip had brought Gabriel Fauré, Claude Debussy, and Grieg together and it may have been that meeting which generated Debussy's description of the Norwegian's music as "Bonbons wrapped in snow."

Even though Grieg wrote many piano pieces, he composed few works for small ensembles. Still, his Quartet in G Minor for Strings and Sonata in G Major for Violin and Piano emerge as strong examples of Grieg's talent. (A second string quartet was left unfinished, with only the first two movements completed.) Debussy, whose own quartet in the same key came twenty years later and has strong similarities to Grieg's, acknowledged his influence. Grieg's vocal music, like his piano output, was also quite significant. His settings of poetry by Arne Garbog, Henrik Ibsen, Aasmund Olavsson Vinje, Bjornstjerne Bjornson, and other Scandinavians are quite exquisite. Ibsen's *En svane (The Swan)* and *Med en Vandlilje (The Waterlily)* are especially notable, with their rich harmonies and haunting lyricism making an indelible impression on the listener. Grieg's songs held a special place in his heart and his repertoire. In a letter to his American biographer Henry Finck, Grieg confessed, "My songs came to life naturally and through a necessity like that of a natural love, and all of them were written for her [Nina]."

Edvard's and Nina's love affair ended when he died in 1907 due to pulmonary failure. His funeral was a huge national event, as the beloved gentleman and composer was widely known and respected. Grieg's ashes are still contained in the original urn, which rests on a rock on his estate at Troldhaugen.

Orchestral
Concerto in A Minor for Piano and Orchestra, op. 16
what to buy: [Murray Perahia, piano; Colin Davis, cond.; Bavarian Radio Symphony Orchestra] (Sony Classics 44899) ♪ ♪ ♪ ♪

Edvard Grieg

Chant—Gregorian and Otherwise:
Chant is usually taken to mean liturgical music of the Medieval Christian Church, and has a vast historical importance as one of the cornerstones of Western musical tradition. Like the early church, it divided into East and West. In the East, there was Byzantine chant, and local traditions continue today in the Middle East (Armenian and Coptic) and Slavic Orthodox Churches. Western chant had numerous local expressions, but it is the Roman tradition called Gregorian (named for Pope Gregory I) that is the most known. This is the music that has remained for well over 1,000 years as the official music of the Catholic Church.

Studied for years for the beauty of its literature, performance practice, and influence, Gregorian chant (or plainsong) is always monophonic (purely melodic), sacred, and vocal. The vast repertory (approximately 3,000 pieces exist) is arranged for all times, seasons, and celebrations of the Church year. Texts are in Latin (with a few exceptions), rhythms are freely-flowing, and the range of expression and form is breathtaking.

Today, it is a very popular genre of music, but not always in ways that are predictable. There has always been an audience to savor its unique sound, but the past ten to twenty years have witnessed a resurgence totally unforeseen. In the 1980s several European rock bands began using a strange mix of Gregorian Chant and modern rhythms. One of these groups, Enigma, became known for using chant as part of its musical palette. With its album *MCMXC A.D.*, released in 1990, the band made this music of Medieval vintage a dance music of the second millennium. A further surprise was in store in 1994 when an otherwise nondescript album by the Benedictine Monks of Santo Domingo de Silos, simply titled *Chant* (EMI Angel 55138), became a best-seller on both classical and popular charts. Since then, there has been a profusion of chant recordings and even a liturgical revival. Clearly, the time of chant has come again.

Frank Retzel

Perahia creates the drama, lyricism, and poignant melancholy from Grieg's script with flawless technique and clearly defined architectural understanding. The magnificent reading makes this popular work sound more profound than it is. This performance is aptly paired with Robert Schumann's A Minor piano concerto (op. 54).

what to buy next: [Sviatoslav Richter, piano; Kiril Kondrashin, cond.; Moscow Philharmonic Symphony Orchestra] (Praga 250048) ♪ ♪ ♪ ♪

This is the closest second to Perahia's recording imaginable. Richter's insight into phrasing and tempo give this oft-performed concerto a vibrancy and excitement rarely heard in Grieg, with Kondrashin's brilliant conducting an equal partner. If it weren't for some harshness in the second movement and rushing in the third, this CD would be rated number one. The recording is taken from a live performance (August 29, 1977), so expect the usual coughs and other audience noises. The balance of this disc is devoted to Grieg's op. 13 Sonata for Violin and Piano (with David Oistrakh and Lev Oborin, respectively) and choral selections drawn from the composer's *Psalms*, op. 74, performed by the Kuhn Mixed Chorus.

Suites from *Peer Gynt,* opp. 46 and 55

what to buy: [Herbert von Karajan, cond.; Berlin Philharmonic Orchestra] (Deutsche Grammophon 419474) ♪ ♪ ♪ ♪

This budget-priced release displays a well-recorded, gorgeously played string section under Karajan's baton and may be all you need to experience this set of Grieg's most popular music. As a bonus, there are also solid performances by the same conductor and orchestra of the composer's *From Holberg's Time* (op. 40) and his suite from *Sigurd Jorsalfar* (op. 56).

Peer Gynt, op. 23 (excerpts)

what to buy: [Barbara Hendricks, soprano; Esa-Pekka Salonen, cond.; Oslo Philharmonic Orchestra; Oslo Philharmonic Chorus] (Sony Classics 44528) ♪ ♪ ♪

Just about any recording you get of the *Peer Gynt* suites will be good, but it is interesting to hear this very popular music in its original scoring for chorus and soloists. Ibsen's tragic hero's exploits are chronicled beautifully through Grieg's descriptive incidental music. A special treat in this set is soprano Barbara Hendricks's portrayal of the Gynt's savior Solvejg when she sings *Solvejg's Lullabye* with depth and tenderness.

Chamber
Lyric Pieces (excerpts)

what to buy: [Emil Gilels, piano] (Deutsche Grammophon 449721) ♪ ♪ ♪ ♪

This is a selection of favorites from the ten volumes of sixty-six piano miniatures. There is no more fluid, rich tone than that of Russian pianist Emil Gilels. Up in heaven, Grieg must have rubbed his hands in glee when Gilels recorded these twenty gems. The op. 12 *Arietta* has exquisite, Schumann-like poignancy. *Melodie* and *Norwegian Dance,* both from op. 47, consist of hauntingly beautiful melodies accompanied by pulsing harmonic accompaniments. *Kobold (Puck)* is delightfully impish, played so rapidly that you wonder if some electronic wizardry is at work.

what to buy next: [Mikhail Pletnev, piano] (Deutsche Grammophon 459671) ♪ ♪ ♪ ₄

While not as consistent a display of pianistic genius as the Gilels performances, Pletnev's rendition of thirteen *Lyric Pieces* is a solid, well-engineered complement to the older recording that doesn't give short shrift to Grieg's pianist poetics. Pletnev also includes fine versions of the composer's seven early Fugues for Piano and the surprisingly mature op. 7 Piano Sonata.

[*The Grieg Collection*; Eva Knardahl, piano] (BIS 51) ♪ ♪ ♪

Norwegian pianist Knardahl brings more drama but less introspection and tonal richness to Grieg's music than does Gilels. She performs twenty-six selections on the Bosendorfer 275, including eighteen of the *Lyric Pieces* and the second of Grieg's four harmonically and rhythmically interesting *Humoresques* (op. 6). *Wedding Day at Troldhaugen,* a delightful little work whose simple melody and rhythm portray perfectly the folksiness that is Grieg, is also included.

Vocal
various songs

what to buy: [*Grieg: Songs*; Anne Sofie von Otter, mezzo-soprano; Bengt Forsberg, piano] (Deutsche Grammaphon 437521) ♪ ♪ ♪ ♪

This is Grieg's Norwegian Romanticism at its best. 1996 Grammophone Award winner von Otter gives an exquisite performance here, breathing understanding into every word, every phrase, every note. This collection also contains the song cycle *Haugtussa (The Mountain Maid),* and settings of poetry by Heine, Goethe, Ibsen, Andersen, Bjornson, and other Nordic writers. *En svane* and *Med en Vandlilje* are absolutely stunning.

influences: Niels Gade, Robert Schumann, Claude Debussy

Linette Popoff-Parks and Ellen Kokko

Charles T. Griffes

Born Charles Tomlinson Griffes, September 17, 1884, in Elmira, NY. Died April 8, 1920, in New York City, NY.

period: Romantic

Griffes, like his fellow American Edward MacDowell, was a talented graphic artist in addition to being a fine, if underrated composer. Best known for *The Pleasure Dome of Kubla Khan* and *The White Peacock,* two works for piano that found more success in orchestral dress, Griffes's later compositions combined impressionism with oriental themes derived from Chinese, Japanese, and Javanese sources.

Although he was given his first piano lessons by his sister, it was not until Griffes began studying with Mary Selena Broughton in 1899 that his choice of career as a musician was sealed. Detecting an unusual amount of talent in her young pupil, Broughton not only suggested that he study in Europe, but she actually paid for his trip to Berlin in 1903 and supported him during his schooling there. Griffes became a student at the famous Stern Conservatory, where he developed a solid reputation as a pianist. Although he also studied composition at the conservatory, he felt the need for a teacher with a more contemporary outlook and, in 1905, began working with Engelbert Humperdinck, the Wagnerian composer of one of the finest turn-of-the-century operas, *Hänsel und Gretel.* The association did not last long, however, as Humperdinck had more pressing commitments than giving lessons to the young American. In any event, Griffes was becoming indoctrinated into the school of German Romanticism, soaking up influences ranging from Johannes Brahms to Richard Strauss, as is reflected in his early compositions. That would change within a few years of his return to the United States in 1907.

The remainder of his life was spent in Tarrytown, New York as music director of the Hackley School, a private prep school. While it provided him with a modicum of security and local prestige, the job also hampered his exposure to musical trends of the day. Griffes still managed to spend summers in New York City, however, composing and hustling his scores to publishers and visiting friends. His first printed works (a set of five songs) appeared in 1909, but not until the *Three Tone Pictures* for Piano, op. 5 did he hint at the impressionism which would color many of his works from then on: *The Lake at Evening, The Vale of Dreams,* and *The Night Winds*) were written in 1910, 1912, and 1911 respectively, with *The Night Winds* undergoing three revisions before reaching its final form in 1915, when the cycle of three pieces was published. That year he also began experimenting with oriental themes, and the stylistic combination of impressionism and orientalism would eventually result in his two most popular works, *The Pleasure*

Dome of Kubla Khan and *The White Peacock.* Although both started out as solo piano compositions, the original version of *The Pleasure Dome* remained unpublished until his death while *The White Peacock* appeared in 1917 as the first part of his *Roman Sketches,* op. 7, along with *Nightfall, The Fountain of the Acqua Paola,* and *Clouds.* Griffes orchestrated *The Pleasure Dome* in 1917 and *The White Peacock* in 1919. At the end of that year, Pierre Monteux conducted the premiere of the orchestrated *The Pleasure Dome* in Boston, while Leopold Stokowski did the honors in Philadelphia for *The White Peacock.*

Griffes's style was evolving rapidly, from the German-inspired works of his early youth to the semi-exoticism of what would be his middle period. His last works, including his only completed piano sonata, the song cycle *Three Poems of Fiona MacLeod,* and the three piano preludes of 1919 reveal him turning towards an even more complex style, which some commentators have compared with the music of the Russian composer Alexander Scriabin. Griffes was experimenting in these works with dissonance and a harmonic language at odds with most of his musical contemporaries. Sadly, he was never able to build upon these developments, another example of an artist cut down in his prime. Griffes heard the orchestral premiere of *The Pleasure Dome of Kubla Khan,* but he was already suffering from the pulmonary illness that sapped his strength and led to his early death.

Orchestral
The Pleasure Dome of Kubla Khan, op. 8
what to buy: [Seiji Ozawa, cond.; Boston Symphony Orchestra] (New World Records 80273) ♪ ♪ ♪ ♪

Not only does Ozawa deliver a wonderful performance of Griffes's most popular work, but the record company has packaged it in an ideal starter kit for introducing novices to the music of this American composer. The song cycles *Four Impressions,* (featuring mezzo-soprano Olivia Stapp) and *Three Poems of Fiona MacLeod* (with soprano Phyllis Bryn-Julson) are lovely, but Sherrill Milnes's baritone fairly explodes with tension in the *Four German Songs* and the darkly textured *Song of the Dagger.* The *Three Tone Pictures* are heard here in their guise for small orchestra, played by the New World Chamber Ensemble.

what to buy next: [*Great American Composers*; Charles

Gerhardt, cond.; RCA Symphony Orchestra] (Chesky 112) ♪ ♪ ♪♪

While Gerhardt's recording is more impressive sonically, the Ozawa performance has greater musical impact. Still, this is a fine, well recorded set that also includes the orchestral version of the composer's *The White Peacock* along with a valuable selection of works by Aaron Copland, Morton Gould, and Howard Hanson.

Chamber
The Pleasure Dome of Kubla Khan, op. 8
what to buy: [*MacDowell and Griffes: vol. 4*; James Tocco, piano] (Gasparo 234) ♪ ♪ ♪ ♪

Tocco's cleanly recorded survey of piano works by these two composers is an admirable one, and this disc deserves highest recommendation if one places a higher priority on Griffes than on Edward MacDowell. Stripped of strings, the stark yet low-key drama of *The Pleasure Dome* stands out even more, although some listeners may miss the tonal colors Griffes created in his orchestration. That also applies to the *Three Tone Pictures* that Tocco performs here. The other works on this set, MacDowell's Sonata no. 1, op. 45—*Tragica* and the *Legend, 1915* by Griffes, receive exemplary performances as well.

Sonata for Piano (1917–1918, revised 1919)
what to buy: *MacDowell and Griffes: vol. 3*; James Tocco, piano] (Gasparo 234) ♪ ♪ ♪ ♪

Griffes was moving away from the schools of romanticism and impressionism when he created this masterful piano piece. Well argued, using dissonance as well as oriental influences, it is one of those glorious works which rewards repeated listening. Tocco's survey of piano music by Griffes and MacDowell contains much of value, including this fine performance. The other two works on this album are Griffes's *De Profundis* and MacDowell's important Sonata for Piano no. 2, op. 50—*Eroica.*

what to buy next: [*Complete Piano Works, vol. 1*; Michael Lewin, piano] (Naxos 8.559023) ♪ ♪ ♪♪

Lewin is a fine musician, although the piano is recorded rather brightly and lacks the warmth given Tocco by the Gasparo engineers for his MacDowell-Griffes series. Still, this is a valuable collection that also contains several recorded "firsts," including performances of the

Prelude in B Minor, *A Winter Landscape,* and an arrangement by Griffes of the Barcarolle from Jacques Offenbach's *Tales of Hoffman.* Lewin's piano version of *The White Peacock* underscores the composer's love of the exotic.

influences: Arthur Foote, Edward MacDowell

Garaud MacTaggart

Ferde Grofé
Born Ferdinand Rudolf von Grofé, March 27, 1892, in New York City, NY. Died April 3, 1972, in Los Angeles, CA.

period: Twentieth century

Ferde Grofé was a talented violist and pianist who first gained recognition as an arranger for Paul Whiteman's Orchestra. His best known composition is the *Grand Canyon Suite,* but Grofé also arranged George Gershwin's *Rhapsody in Blue* for its 1924 premiere.

Ferde Grofé's artistic bloodlines were promising. His first music lessons came from his mother, who had studied in Europe at the Leipzig Conservatory. His father played violin with the Boston Symphony, his grandfather once worked alongside Victor Herbert, and one of his uncles was a concertmaster in Los Angeles. Despite a seeming genetic disposition to follow a classical muse, Grofé ran away from home at the age of fourteen to take up the life of a traveling musician. He roamed across the American West, playing piano in vaudeville houses, dance halls, and hotel bands. According to an article written by Grofé for the *Review of Recorded Music*), he also worked "as a bookbinder, truck driver, usher, newsboy, elevator operator, lithographer, typesetter, and steelworker."

Grofé's first significant musical job was playing viola with the Los Angeles Symphony Orchestra, but he also became known in jazz circles for his arrangements and piano playing. A jazz gig with the John Tait Orchestra led to Grofé's meeting and befriending violist Paul Whiteman. In 1919, Whiteman invited Grofé to play piano in a band he was putting together. After three years with Whiteman, Grofé became the band's full-time arranger/composer, and in this capacity he started to hit his stride.

Whiteman was known as the "King of Jazz" during the

1920s, employing such outstanding jazz musicians as Bix Beiderbecke, but the music he conducted was closer to the ballroom than the juke joint. Even though Grofé was writing charts for pop tunes by Jerome Kern (*Make Believe*), Cole Porter (*Night and Day*), and Sigmund Romberg (*Lover Come Back to Me*), he was also aiming for the highbrow with scaled-down arrangements of light classical pieces such as Fritz Kreisler's *Caprice Viennois* and Amilcare Ponchielli's *Dance of the Hours*.

This halfway position between classical and pop culture made Whiteman's band and its arranger the logical choice to present some pieces by George Gershwin, a young songwriter who was looking for a way to blend jazz with "legitimate" music. One of the first Gershwin works that Grofé arranged was *Blue Monday (135th Street)*, which received its public unveiling in 1922. It was an auspicious enough debut, but nothing could prepare Gershwin, Whiteman, or Grofé for the accolades that their next collaboration, *Rhapsody in Blue*, garnered at its 1924 premiere in New York City's Aeolian Hall.

Following the success of *Rhapsody in Blue*, Whiteman encouraged his friend to come up with another work for the orchestra, and in 1925 Grofé finished the *Mississippi Suite*. Even before completing this, his first original orchestral piece, Grofé had already sketched out the first and last movements of what would become his most famous work.

The *Grand Canyon Suite*, Grofé's magnum opus, received its first performance on November 22, 1931, at a Whiteman concert at Chicago's Studebaker Theater. It has become a classic bit of programmatic Americana, arousing idyllic images of a vacationer's Grand Canyon, with coconut shells clopping to evoke mules carrying tourists down the trail and a wind machine hinting at the onset of a rainstorm. Despite the acclaim Grofé received for this composition, he was dissatisfied. The Whiteman ensemble, although billed as an orchestra, comprised only twenty pieces, so when Grofé was appointed conductor of New York's Capitol Theater Orchestra in 1933, he leaped at the opportunity to revise the suite for a full orchestra. It is this latter version that is heard most often today.

Grofé never repeated the tremendous success he had with the *Grand Canyon Suite*, but he kept on churning out programmatic orchestral pieces for the rest of his career. These include *Tabloid Suite* (1933), *Symphony in Steel* (1935), *Hollywood Suite* (1938), *Hudson River Suite*

(1955), *Death Valley Suite* (1957), the Concerto for Piano and Orchestra in D Major (1958), *Niagara Falls Suite* (1961), and *World's Fair Suite* (1964). He also wrote film scores for a host of B movies (including Kurt Neumann's 1950 sci-fi potboiler *201 Rocketship XM*) and documentaries, in addition to punching out a considerable number of player-piano rolls and teaching orchestration at the Juilliard School of Music. Along with the images of his fellow American composers Samuel Barber, Charles Ives, and Louis Moreau Gottschalk, Ferde Grofé's visage made it onto a United States postage stamp in 1997.

Orchestral
Grand Canyon Suite for Orchestra
what to buy: [Leonard Bernstein, cond.; New York Philharmonic Orchestra] (CBS Masterworks 42264) ♪♪♪♪

While not necessarily the sonic wonder the piece deserves, this performance is about as good as it gets. Grofé's masterwork is paired with two Gershwin pieces, *Rhapsody in Blue* (featuring Bernstein in the dual role of pianist and conductor) and *An American in Paris*, for an interesting slice of jazz-inspired Americana.

what to buy next: [Erich Kunzel, cond.; Cincinnati Pops Orchestra] (Telarc 80086) ♪♪♪♪

Telarc's engineers have done a wonderful job here, bestowing a glossy sheen on Kunzel and his forces. The interpretation lacks the drive found in the Bernstein recording, but with its inclusion of a fine performance of *Catfish Row*, the symphonic suite drawn from Gershwin's *Porgy and Bess*, Kunzel's disc may be a valid alternative for some listeners.

Mississippi Suite
what to buy: [Jan Stulen, cond.; the Beau Hunks, orch.] (BASTA Audio/Visuals 30-9083) ♪♪♪♪

The Beau Hunks have recorded the finest version of this piece extant and paired it with three other well-performed Grofé rarities plus the *Cloudburst* movement from the *Grand Canyon Suite*. The orchestra sounds like a giant version of the Whiteman band, and the arrangement hovers closer to symphonic jazz than to classical music, making this recording an original-instrument rendition with a twentieth-century twist.

Death Valley Suite
what to buy: [Ferde Grofé, cond.; Capitol Symphony

Orchestra] (Angel 66387) ♪ ♪ ♪⁴

This stacks up as Grofé's finest work other than the *Grand Canyon Suite*. Filled with drama and surprisingly bleak for someone whose writing is usually fairly lush, this 1955 rendition is not only the definitive recording of the piece but the only one still available. Be aware, however, that it is paired with Felix Slatkin's constricted-sounding 1956 recording of the *Grand Canyon Suite* and his mediocre rendering of the *Mississippi Suite*.

influences: George Gershwin, Jerome Kern, Leonard Bernstein, Duke Ellington

Garaud MacTaggart

Sofia Gubaidulina

Born Sofia Asgatovna Gubaidulina, October, 24, 1931, in Chistopol, Tatar Autonomous Soviet Socialist Republic.

period: Twentieth century

Sofia Gubaidulina's music is filled with religious implications yet it should not be confused with the works of "Holy Minimalists" like Arvo Pärt, John Tavener, and Henryck Górecki. One of the most intriguing composers to come out of the former Soviet Union, her more mature works have retained the focus on rhythm which was such a strong element of her earlier, tonal compositions, while showcasing serialism and other contemporary techniques pioneered by the European and American avant-garde. This emphasis on modernity, and the adoption of Oriental philosophies and Christian symbolism as an underpinning for what is now the majority of her scores, placed Gubaidulina outside the mainstream of Soviet music. Among her most consistently impressive works are the violin concerto *Offertorium*, her symphony *Stimmen . . . verstummen. . .*, and the two versions of *In Croce*: one for organ and cello and the other for bayan (a Russian member of the accordion family) and cello.

Gubaidulina graduated from the Kazan Conservatory in 1954 before gaining admittance to the Moscow Conservatory, where she studied composition as an undergraduate with Nikolai Peiko (Dmitri Shostakovich's assistant), completing her post-graduate studies in 1962 under Vissarion Shebalin. Shostakovich sat on her examination committee and, after viewing a symphonic score she was working on, said, "My wish for you is that you should continue on your own, incorrect way." Taking that advice and generally rejecting the tenets of Socialist Realism resulted in enormous difficulties getting her most personal music performed, much as it did for her compatriots Alfred Schnittke and Galina Ustvolskaya. Like them, Gubaidulina earned much of her living during the Soviet era by composing film scores, including those for works by Rolan Bykov (*The Scarecrow*), Ida Garanina (*The Circus Tent*), and Arkadi Kordon (*Veliki Samoyed*).

It was the methodology used in her non-cinematic scores that ended up ensuring Gubaidulina's place, in 1979, as one of the seven composers (along with Edison Denisov, Vyacheslav Artyomov, Viktor Suslin, Alexander Knaifel, Dmitri Smirnov, and Elena Firsova) singled out for criticism for their avant-garde tendencies by Tikhon Khrennikov at the Fourth Conference of the Composers' Union of the Russian Federation. In an interesting twist of fate, the next year found her work for cello and organ, *In Croce,* selected for praise at the Moscow Autumn '80 Festival; it was commended by Vsevolod Zaderatsky, a dean at the Moscow Conservatory and chairman of the musicology section of the Union of Composers, for its "cosmic space." Originally dedicated to cellist Vladimir Tonkha, who debuted it on March 27, 1979, with organist Rubin Abdullin, this score was later revised by Gubaidulina, who created a version of the work for cello and bayan which was premiered November 16, 1991 by Christopher Marks and Elsbeth Moser.

By that time a host of "primitive" instruments indigenous to Russia, the Caucasus, and various Asian societies had made a significant impact on Gubaidulina's sonic palette via her participation in Astreia, an ensemble begun in 1975. Along with her co-founders Suslin and Artyomov, Gubaidulina explored the improvisatory possibilities of these ancient instruments and wrote works utilizing the timbral qualities associated with them. The bayan plays a particular role in many of her compositions, including the solo bayan showcase from 1978 *De Profundis* and her 1982 piece for cello, bayan, and strings *Sieben Worten (Seven Words),* in addition to the previously mentioned 1991 version of *In Croce* and the *Galgenlieder (à 5)* of 1996 for Mezzo-soprano, Flute, Percussion, Bayan, and Double Bass. Other unique instrumental combinations from Gubaidulina's fertile imagination include *On Tatar Folk Themes* (1977) for Domra and Piano, *. . .Early in the Morning, Right Before Waking. . .* for Seven Koto from 1993, and *Shadow of the Tree* for Amplified Koto, Bass Koto, Zheng, and Orchestra from 1998.

Gubaidulina's violin concerto *Offertorium* was premiered in 1981 and, after two more revisions, the final construct was performed in 1986. Gidon Kremer was the featured soloist in all three versions, and his consistent and powerful advocacy of the work had a lot to do with bringing an awareness of Gubaidulina's music to Western audiences. The work itself is based on the "royal theme" of Johann Sebastian Bach's *Musical Offering* and utilizes Anton Webern's arrangement as a jumping-off point. 1986, the year after Gubaidulina was allowed to leave the USSR to tour other European countries, also saw the premiere of her symphony, *Stimmen. . . verstummen. . .,* a work that has been hailed as a major addition to her already formidable canon. Her next major orchestral score, *Pro et Contra,* was commissioned by the Louisville Symphony Orchestra and premiered by them in 1989.

In 1992 Gubaidulina moved to Germany. Her more recent compositions continued to explore socio-religious themes, and now that she has gained a measure of stature within the international music community and is no longer constrained by a repressive government, some of Gubaidulina's music is, if anything, even more apocalyptic than before. Her *St. John Passion* (premiered on September 1, 2000 in Stuttgart, Germany) meshes Russian gospel texts with excerpts from the Book of Revelations in a way that, in the minds of some critics, serves as a specifically damning statement on the excesses of the Communist state and totalitarianism in general.

Orchestral
Stimmen. . .verstummen. . .
what to buy: [Gennady Rozhdeshvensky, cond.; Royal Stockholm Philharmonic Orchestra] (Chandos 9183) ♪♪♪♪♪

Featuring a large number of cymbals, tubular bells and bar percussion instruments (glockenspiel, xylophone, marimba, and vibraphone), this twelve-movement symphony is filled with surprisingly delicate, pointillistic, sounds and short-duration phrases from the string section. Rozhdeshvensky, the dedicatee, won the second of Gubaidulina's Koussevitzky International Recording Awards with this performance in 1994. The accompanying work on this disc, *Stufen (Steps),* won first prize at the Rome International Composer's Competition in 1975. Both performances make this set a key part of any collection of Gubaidulina recordings.

Offertorium for Violin and Orchestra
what to buy: [Gidon Kremer, violin; Charles Dutoit, cond.; Boston Symphony Orchestra] (Deutsche Grammophon 427336) ♪♪♪♪♪

In 1989, this authoritative performance of Gubaidulina's powerful score won the first of her two Koussevitzky International Recording Awards. Kremer, a persuasive advocate for this work, is also heard as a member of the octet supporting soprano Christine Whittlesey in the composer's *Hommage à T.S. Eliot,* a work featuring text by one of Gubaidulina's favorite poets.

Pro et Contra for Large Orchestra
what to buy: [*Orchestral Music;* Johannes Kalitzke, cond.; Radio-Philharmonie Hannover des NDR, orch.] (CPO 999164) ♪♪♪♪♪

Remarkably beautiful and haunting for vast stretches of time yet powerful, daunting, and suspenseful during other moments, this three-movement score lasts over half an hour and meshes the possibilities of the blessed with those of the damned. Gubaidulina's spirituality is an unspoken power that radiates all through this wonderfully recorded live performance. The other works on this disc maintain that high sense of commitment in their renditions of the composer's earlier *Fairytale Poem/Märchenpoem* and the *Concordanza* for Strings and Percussion.

what to buy next: [Tadaaki Otaka, cond.; BBC National Orchestra of Wales] (BIS 668) ♪♪♪♪

Otaka takes this piece at a much slower pace than does Kalitzke, coming in at one second under forty minutes as opposed to a hair under thirty-four. The extra time taken doesn't lessen the impact of the work by much (in fact it comes much closer to the length specified by Gubaidulina in the score, forty-two minutes), and the recording is quite good. While the Kalitzke disc is an all-Gubaidulina project, Otaka includes *Cassandra,* a piece commissioned from Elena Firsova by the BBC National Orchestra of Wales that seems to draw its orchestral colors from the same palette as Gubaidulina's.

Sieben Worten (SevenWords) for Cello, Bayan, and String Orchestra
what to buy: [Karine Georgian, cello; Elsbeth Moser, bayan; Thomas Klug, cond.; Deutsche Kammerphilharmonie, orch.] (Berlin Classics 0011132) ♪♪♪♪

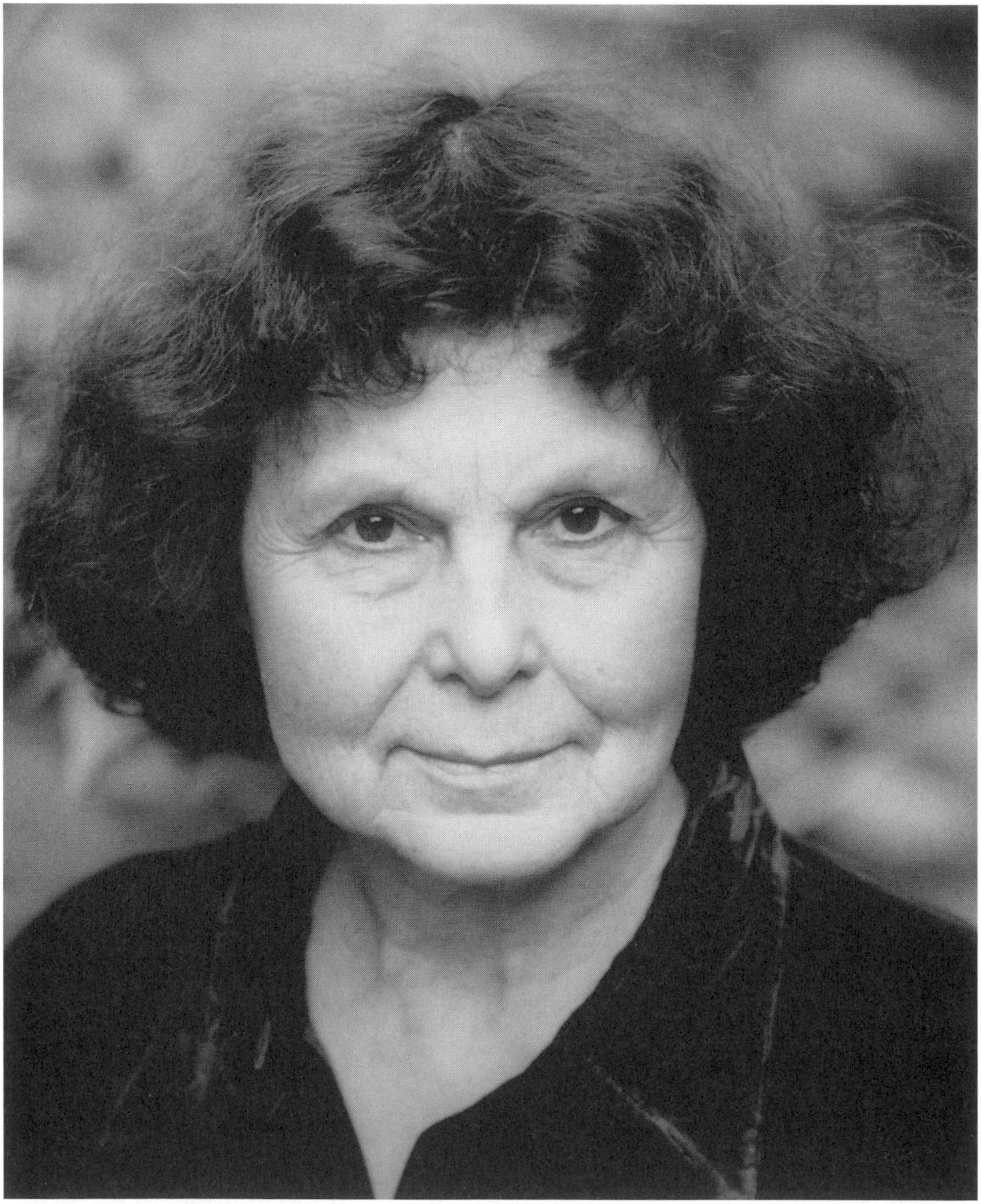

This isn't particularly easy music to listen to, even though the string writing can get downright elegiac at times. It actually makes fairly severe demands on the featured cellist in addition to the prominent role assigned the bayan player, and in the right hands the results can be powerful and moving. Georgian is marvelous, Moser is inspired, and Klug's control of the orchestra keeps a tight rein on the proceedings. The composer's *Meditation on a Bach Chorale* for Harpsichord and String Quintet is an interesting discmate, while the version of *Concordanza* heard here lacks the last ounce of tension that Kalitzke's recording gives it (see above).

what to buy next: [Maria Kliegel, cello; Elsbeth Moser, bayan; György Selmeczi, cond.; Camerata Transsylvanica, orch.] (Naxos 8.553557) ♪ ♪ ♪♪

Gubaidulina's fascination with the sound of the bayan (a little button accordion) lies at the heart of this disc's programming, and all three works heard here (*In Croce, Silenzio,* and *Sieben Worten*) feature the instrumental prowess of Moser (who played in the premiere of the cello and bayan version of *In Croce*). The budget price, clean sonics, and generally strong (but not overwhelming) performances by the orchestra make this an interesting set.

Chamber
In Croce for Cello and Organ
what to buy: [Maya Beiser, cello; Dorothy Papadakos, organ] (Koch International Classics 7258) ♪ ♪ ♪ ♪♪

Gubaidulina's initial choice of cello and organ for this work was an inspired one even though she later chose to set it for cello and bayan a decade or so later. The organ adds an appropriately sanctified (if somewhat eldritch) touch to the music that fits perfectly with the cellist's sparse bowing. Where Beiser gets a real workout is in the composer's ten *Preludes* for Solo Cello which are also included in this well-recorded album. The final piece heard here is Galina Ustvolskaya's impressive *Grand Duet* for Cello and Piano, with Beiser and pianist Christopher Oldfather as the performers.

Quartet no. 2 for Strings
what to buy: [Danish Quartet, ensemble] (CPO 999064) ♪ ♪ ♪ ♪

Sofia Gubaidulina

If you were going strictly on marketing prowess, then the Kronos Quartet version (see below) would be the way to go; however, the Danish Quartet probably gets closer to the heart of this intense, sub-nine-minute exercise. The album this performance comes from is a fine introduction to Gubaidulina's work in a particularly demanding medium. The group works on the first three of her string quartets and the Trio for Strings, in versions that stand up well against the competition.

[*Short Stories*; Kronos Quartet, ensemble] (Elektra/ Nonesuch 79310) ♪ ♪ ♪ ♪

Glowing reviews for the Kronos Quartet from around the world are quite well-deserved, and the popular ensemble often serves an important role in bringing works by modern composers to the marketplace. Clever programming is also a stock in trade for this group, and their inclusion of Gubaidulina's second quartet amidst eight short pieces by Henry Cowell (*Quartet Euphometric*) and more pop-savvy modernists like John Zorn (*Cat O'Nine Tails: Tex Avery Directs the Marquis de Sade*) and Elliott Sharp (*Digital*) will probably expose her work to a broader cross-section of the listening public. The downside of this approach is that it is harder to focus on Gubaidulina as a distinct composer than Gubaidulina as a pop offering for generalists.

influences: Alfred Schnittke, Edison Denisov, Dmitri Shostakovich, Anton Webern, Galina Ustvolskaya

Mathilde August

George Frideric Handel
Born Georg Friederich Händel, February 23, 1685, in Halle, Germany. Died April 14, 1759, in London, England.

period: Baroque

George Frideric Handel was revered by Ludwig van Beethoven, who once said, "Handel is the greatest composer who ever lived. I would bare my head and kneel at his grave." A contemporary of Johann Sebastian Bach, Georg Phillipp Telemann, and Domenico Scarlatti, Handel created works in every significant musical genre of his day, rivaling the industriousness of Wolfgang

Amadeus Mozart. He is probably best known to modern audiences for the *Messiah* oratorio, and instrumental works such as *Water Music* and the *Royal Fireworks Music.*

Handel's mother nurtured his musical talents but his father attempted to deter him from following such a problematic vocation, wanting instead for his son to become a lawyer. Eventually, his father relented and the youngster studied organ, harpsichord, and violin (as well as composition, harmony, and counterpoint) with Friedrich Wilhelm Zachow, the organist at the Liebfrauenkirche in Halle. Handel entered the University of Halle at the age of seventeen, reportedly to study law, but within a year sought to broaden his musical horizons with trips to Hamburg. When he finally moved there in 1703, Handel performed as a violinist and harpsichordist in a theater orchestra, learning, at the same time, some of the skills necessary to composing opera. His first opera score, *Almira,* was produced there in 1705 to modest success. By the next year Handel was in Italy, the center of operatic culture at that time.

While in Rome in 1707, Handel ran into a papal ban on the production of operas there which, in turn, led to the flourishing oratorio form—a de facto opera sans costumes and elaborate staging. That same year, the twenty-one-year-old composer was commissioned by Cardinal Benedetto Pamphili—who provided texts, locations, and funds—to write his first oratorio, a work that would be known as *Il trionfo del Tempo e del Disinganno (The Triumph of Time and Truth).* Although the ban on opera production in Rome was in force, that did not stop such works from being produced elsewhere. As a result, Handel's first Italian opera, *Rodrigo,* was premiered in Florence in the fall of 1707. It is likely that his dramatic cantata from 1708, *Aci, Galatea e polifemo,* received its debut outside of Rome, and it is certain that his second Italian opera, *Agrippina,* opened up in Venice in December of 1709.

In 1710 Handel went back to Germany, where he was appointed Kapellmeister to the Elector of Hanover. Because of the Elector's generous travel allowance, Handel was able to visit Düsseldorf, where he had friends, and London, where he oversaw the production of a new opera, *Rinaldo,* in the spring of 1711. Handel eventually returned to Hanover later that year, but soon left again for London. The Elector finally tired of the elusiveness of his putative Kapellmeister, and fired Handel in 1713 while he was still in England. Within five years

Handel's skills as a versatile musician, composer, and entrepreneur brought him the patronage from King George that enabled him to establish Italian-style operas at the Royal Academy of Music in London. His *Water Music*—premiered in 1717 by musicians aboard a barge accompanying the King's party down the Thames—is his most important instrumental work from this time, and probably did no harm when it came to relations with the monarch. While Handel continued premiering his own operas until 1741, Italianate operas began falling from favor with the English public as early as 1727, just about the time that his English-language oratorios, odes, and anthems began to supplant the theater works as a large part of his cash flow. His *Ode for St. Cecilia's Day* (1739) was particularly well received, but nothing like the *Messiah* would be three years later.

Considered to be Handel's greatest oratorio, this work (with a libretto by Newburgh Hamilton based on poems by Milton) was not a success initially. It didn't become widely accepted until after Handel began performing it at annual charity performances for the Foundling Hospital. Handel wrote so sensitively for each vocal register that the three-part oratorio is considered one of the best choral works in English. While Handel is not considered a religious composer in the strictest sense, the power, lyricism, seriousness, and depth of his *Messiah* make it one of the most outstanding musical creations in or out of the cannon of devotional art.

During this same period, though troubled by ill health, Handel also wrote his secular opera *Semele,* a three-act work of vital creative genius that would be followed by more pedestrian pieces. Performed as an oratorio in 1744, *Semele* featured a libretto by William Congreve that was based on Ovid's *Metamorphoses* and conveyed the story of ill-fated love between Semele and Jupiter. Handel's next big instrumental work was the *Music for the Royal Fireworks,* first performed in April of 1749 at a public celebration and, at the insistence of King George II, done without a string section, using a large orchestra of woodwinds, brass and percussion. A second version of the *Fireworks* music with strings added was presented at the Foundling Hospital on May 29, 1749.

During the last seven years of his life, Handel went progressively blind, continuing to conduct oratorio performances and revise his scores with help from his manager (and copyist) Christopher Smith and Smith's son John. When Handel died, he was buried, as per his request, at Westminster Abbey.

Orchestral
Water Music
what to buy: [Neville Marriner, cond.; Academy of St. Martin-in-the-Fields, orch.] (Argo 414596) ♪ ♪ ♪ ♪₄

The three suites comprising Handel's *Water Music* are generally recorded together and remain essential items in any classical music collection. Many versions exist but the best and most authentic usually feature period instruments. Here, Marriner's highly-regarded performances of the multi-movement suites offer ebullient, light, well-balanced, and stately playing. As with many other recordings featuring Handel's *Water Music*, his *Music for the Royal Fireworks* is also included.

what to buy next: [Alexander Gibson, cond.; Scottish Chamber Orchestra] (Chandos 8382) ♪ ♪ ♪₄

Gibson's vigor does justice to the lively and engaging suites, and his expertise at drawing the best from the orchestra musicians is obvious.

[Ton Koopman, cond.; Amsterdam Baroque Orchestra] (Erato 24243) ♪ ♪ ♪₄

This version of the complete *Water Music* offers imaginative readings that are freely and freshly rendered. The budget-priced (and bargain-value!) two-disc set also contains Handel's six Concerti Grossi, op. 3 (with Marc Minkowski conducting Les Musiciens du Louvre).

[Nicholas McGegan, cond.; Philharmonia Baroque Orchestra] (Harmonia Mundi 907010) ♪ ♪ ♪₄

The San Francisco-based Philharmonia Baroque Orchestra, led by McGegan since 1985, renders trim (but complete) period-instrument versions of these festive movements.

Royal Fireworks Music for Orchestra
what to buy: [Christopher Hogwood, cond.; Academy of Ancient Music, orch.] (L'Oiseau-Lyre 455709) ♪ ♪ ♪ ♪

Hogwood elicits a bold, brassy rendering full of the elegance and pomp one would expect from a commission to accompany a royal fireworks display. By doubling the strings (part of Handel's original scoring but not used in the 1749 Green Park performance) in this period-instrument version, Hogwood, in all likelihood, parallels the version heard a month later in the new chapel at the Foundling Hospital. This mid-priced double-CD package

also includes the *Water Music* suites, along with three concerti and a trio of other, lesser works.

Vocal
Messiah for Solo Voices, Orchestra, and Chorus
what to buy: [Heather Harper, soprano; Helen Watts, contralto; John Wakefield, tenor; John Shirley-Quirk, bass; Colin Davis, cond.; London Symphony Orchestra; London Symphony Chorus] (Philips 438356) ♪ ♪ ♪ ♪₄

Rightly considered a classic version of Handel's three-part oratorio, Davis's set was recorded in 1966, prior to the authentic-instrument craze, and features elegant singing along with instrumental solos from Ralph Downes (organ), Leslie Pearson (harpsichord), and William Lang (trumpet). Davis avoids the weightiness of many other renderings at no expense to the pieces' momentousness.

[Karen Erickson, soprano; Sylvia McNair, soprano; Alfreda Hodgson, mezzo-soprano; Jon Humphrey, tenor; Richard Stilwell, baritone; Layton James, harpsichord; Robert Shaw, cond.; Atlanta Symphony Orchestra; Atlanta Symphony Chamber Chorus] (Telarc 80093) ♪ ♪ ♪ ♪₄

This stately performance was recorded in 1983 and mirrors Handel's own occasional practice of using two sopranos. While McNair is the best known star here, the other singers possess voices resplendent enough to lure you to this version. Shaw's understanding of this passionate, sacred work (including an extra bassoon part he constructed) yields a soul-satisfying performance for listeners, especially in the solos and choruses.

what to buy next: [Karen Clift, soprano; Catherine Robbin, mezzo-soprano; Bruce Fowler, tenor; Victor Ledbetter, baritone; Martin Pearlman, cond.; Boston Baroque Orchestra; Boston Baroque Chorus] (Telarc 80322) ♪ ♪ ♪ ♪

Recorded in 1992, this version of the *Messiah* is performed on modern instruments and is based on the "Dublin" score which was used for the first performances, while incorporating Handel's later corrections. While at times the instrumentation may seem choppy and weak and the famed *Hallelujah* chorus lacks the ebullient spirit of the Davis version (see above), Clift's sweetly sonorous soloing in *He shall feed His flock like a shepherd* and *I know that my Redeemer liveth* provides some peak moments for listeners.

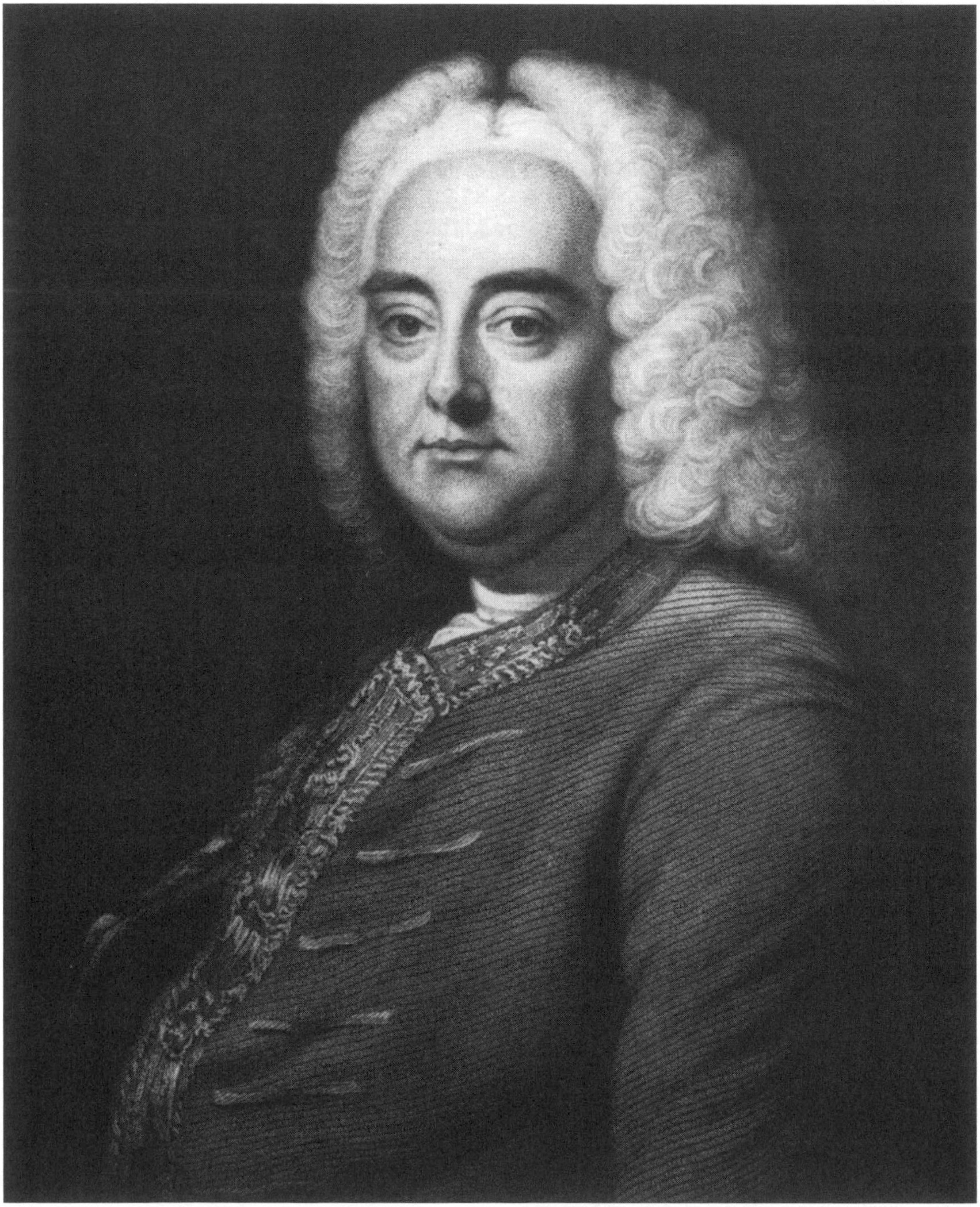

[Dorothea Röschmann, soprano; Susan Gritton, soprano; Bernarda Fink, alto; Charles Daniels, tenor; Neal Davies, baritone; Paul McCreesh, cond.; Gabrielli Players, orch.; Gabrielli Consort, choir] (Deutsche Grammophon Archiv 453464) ♪ ♪ ♪₄

This fine period-instrument version is enhanced by Röschmann's perfectly pitched, airy soprano voice and Fink's plush alto. McCreesh's conducting shows his knowledge of and respect for Handel's work in both the vocal and instrumental portions.

Ode for St. Cecila's Day
worth searching for: [Felicity Lott, soprano; Anthony Rolfe Johnson, tenor; Trevor Pinnock, cond.; English Chamber Orchestra; English Concert Choir] (Deutsche Grammophon Archiv 419220) ♪ ♪ ♪ ♪₄

Based on a 1687 ode written by John Dryden, Handel's *Ode for St. Cecila's Day* is a lush piece of work featuring some heartwarming English language arias and significant interplay between the chorus and soloists. Pinnock, in the dual role of organist and conductor, directs one of the best period-instrument versions of this beguiling score.

Semele for Solo Voices, Orchestra and Chorus
what to buy: [Kathleen Battle, soprano; Sylvia McNair, soprano; Marilyn Horne, mezzo-soprano; Michael Chance, counter-tenor; John Aler, tenor; Samuel Ramey, bass; John Nelson, cond.; English Chamber Orchestra; Ambrosian Opera Chorus] (Deutsche Grammophon 435782) ♪ ♪ ♪ ♪₄

Although you may find *Semele* listed in opera dictionaries, it is really one of the most popular and frequently staged of all Handel's dramatic oratorios. This three-CD set (with libretto) is one of the best available versions, featuring an all-star cast with American soprano Battle in the title role. Beautiful, lively arias abound, as well as harmonious quartets and choral passages, with orchestrations performed on period and modern instruments. The revelations of this reading underscore one's amazement that Handel wrote this glorious, sensuous music in only one month.

Various arias
[*Ombra mai fù*; Andreas Scholl, counter-tenor; Akademie

George Frideric Handel

für Alte Musik Berlin, orch.] (Harmonia Mundi 901685) ♪ ♪ ♪ ♪

Scholl's eleven arias and recitatives are taken from the surviving portions of operas and other vocal works Handel wrote in London between 1720 and 1736. Scholl's richly timbred, resonant, sensuous voice is delicate and graceful, naturally capturing the era between 1650 and the end of the eighteenth century when alto-tinged castrati ruled the opera world. The twelve-musician ensemble plays period instruments and is full of punch, confidence and dramatic muscle as it delivers support for Scholl or plays in any of the album's purely instrumental selections. Especially notable is the handling of the album finale, Handel's famous concerto grosso, *Alexander's Feast*.

influences: Agostino Stefanni, Henry Purcell, Domenico Scarlatti, Alessandro Scarlatti, Antonio Caldara, William Babell, Johan Helmich Roman, William Boyce, John Stanley

Nancy Ann Lee

Howard Hanson
Born Howard Harold Hanson, October 28, 1896, in Wahoo, NE. Died February 26, 1981, in Rochester, NY.

period: Twentieth century

Large orchestral and choral works form the bulk of Hanson's output. Jean Sibelius and Edvard Grieg were the major influences on his style, which combined post-Romantic elements with an interest in chorale tunes and Gregorian chant. These factors gave his music a basic tonal richness which he then combined with the rhythmic vitality of his Scandinavian roots and peppered with his own brand of American gaiety and humor. He was also an important educator, best known in that regard for his work at the Eastman School in Rochester, New York, which he directed from 1924 until 1964 and helped develop into one of the finest music schools in the United States.

Hanson studied music at Luther College in his home town, receiving his diploma when he was only 15 years old, before moving on to the Institute of Musical Art in New York City (later to become the Juilliard School of Music), where he was a student of Percy Goetschius and Frank Damrosch. Later he graduated with a B.A. from Northwestern University where he studied composition with Peter Lutkin and became a teaching assistant from 1915 to 1916. Hanson then moved to California where, during the next three years, he taught music theory and composition at the College of the Pacific. His budding administrative talents were so strong that he ended up accepting a position as Dean of the Conservatory of Fine Arts at the college in 1919. In 1921, he became the first winner of the *Prix de Rome* sponsored by the American Academy in Rome. This enabled Hanson to travel to Italy where he studied with the master orchestrator, Ottorino Respighi. While there, he wrote some of his first notable compositions, including *The Lament for Beowulf* for Orchestra and Chorus and his first symphony. Three years later, he returned to the United States and embarked on a tour, conducting many orchestras and including his own compositions in the concerts.

After conducting his Symphony no. 1 in Rochester, New York, Hanson was invited by George Eastman in 1924 to head the newly formed Eastman School of Music at the University of Rochester. As its director he guided the school to its eventual position as one of the premier musical institutions in the United States, expanding the curriculum and attracting some of the finest teachers. In 1925 he established the American Composers Orchestral Concerts to provide a venue for the performance of new music. He also was deeply involved in the recording medium, leading the Eastman-Rochester Symphony Orchestra into the studio to document works by such American composers as William Grant Still, Walter Piston, Charles T. Griffes, Charles Ives, Edward MacDowell, Leo Sowerby, and, of course, Hanson's own music. In 1934, his opera *Merry Mount* received a highly successful premiere at the Metropolitan in New York. Throughout his life Hanson's talents were recognized by a series of awards, including 36 honorary degrees, the Peabody Award, membership in the Royal Swedish Academy of Music, and a Pulitzer Prize (for his Symphony no. 4).

Orchestral
Symphony no. 2, op. 30—*Romantic*
what to buy: [Howard Hanson, cond.; Eastman-Rochester Orchestra] (Mercury Living Presence 432008) ♪♪♪♪

These recordings from 1957 and 1960 include Hanson's most popular symphony (the *Romantic*) along with his first essay in the form (the *Nordic*) and the *Song of Democracy* for Orchestra and Chorus. He was a distinguished interpreter of his own music, as this CD demon-

strates. The Eastman Theatre, where the sessions took place, does not have much resonance, making the recording fairly bright and dry.

Symphony no. 3, op. 33
what to buy: [Gerard Schwarz, cond.; Seattle Symphony Orchestra] (Delos 3092) ♪♪♪♪♪

The three compositions on this disc present a wide spectrum of Hanson's musical life beginning with his Third Symphony and continuing on to the *Fantasy Variations on a Theme of Youth* (featuring the New York Chamber Symphony Orchestra with Carol Rosenberger on piano), and concluding with his Sixth Symphony. Schwarz and his musicians bring out the music's great contrasts, emphasizing the sumptuous melodies and harmonic textures without slighting rhythmic precision and articulation. They are recorded spaciously with excellent dynamic range.

influences: Leo Sowerby, Walter Piston, Jean Sibelius, Edvard Grieg, Peter Mennin, Ottorino Respighi

D. John Apple

Roy Harris
Born LeRoy Ellsworth Harris c. February 12, 1898, in Lincoln County, OK. Died October 1, 1979, in Santa Monica, CA.

period: Twentieth century

Serge Koussevitzky, the famous conductor who premiered Roy Harris's third symphony, once said that "nobody has captured in music the essence of American life—its vitality, its greatness, its strength—so well as Roy Harris."

Roy Harris was born in a log cabin to Scots-Irish parents who had taken advantage of the Oklahoma land rush in 1889; thus he spent his earliest years on land that had been Indian Territory only two generations before. The son of hard-working farmers who did not consider music to be a practical career for their child, he later ascribed his musical abilities to his maternal grandmother, an organist. Of the Harris children, only Roy and his youngest sister, Irene, survived beyond childhood. When Harris was five years old, his family moved to a farm in California's San Gabriel Valley. Shortly afterward his father bought a piano for Roy's mother, who gave her son his first piano lessons. Upon entering high school Roy learned to play clarinet and football with equal enthusiasm, in addition to farming the ten acres his father had bought for him. Harris joined the army when he was nineteen years old, but the First World War ended by the time he completed his training. Upon his release from service, Harris sold his ten acres and enrolled at the University of California at Berkeley, where he studied music history in addition to the standard curriculum. In need of funds while attending school, he found a job working as delivery driver for a dairy.

Intrigued by his music classes, Harris decided that he needed more instruction in the basics of harmony and composition. He eventually moved to the Los Angeles area and started studying with Arthur Farwell, a composer whose own teachers had included George W. Chadwick, Englebert Humperdinck, and Hans Pfitzner. The harmonically adventurous Farwell may also have been the first American composer to respect and treat folksong sources with dignity; this viewpoint made him the perfect mentor for Harris. The young musician eventually learned enough to be able to craft an orchestral movement, which he then sent to composer/conductor Howard Hanson at the Eastman School of Music for a review. An eager advocate for American composers, Hanson saw worth in the score and added it to some of the programs he was directing. This generated enough favorable response that Harris impulsively quit his day job and headed for the East Coast. There he met Aaron Copland, who suggested that he go to Paris and study with Nadia Boulanger, the formidable French pedagogue and shaper of American composers. His initial stay in France was financed by Alma Wertheim, the wife of a banker, but Harris also managed to acquire the first and second of his three Guggenheim Fellowships to continue his studies with Boulanger. By 1929 he had written numerous works that received their premieres in Paris and was on his way to being lionized as one of America's foremost young composers. His budding reputation was enough to secure a teaching position at the Juilliard School in 1932.

During the 1930s, Harris also associated with a variety of folk singers and impresarios, including Woody Guthrie and the father-son team of John and Alan Lomax. It is quite possible that these connections influenced Harris's approach to composition just as much as his studies with Farwell and Boulanger. It was during and shortly after this period that Harris composed his greatest single work, the Symphony no. 3 (1937), and the first ver-

sion of his Symphony no. 4 for Orchestra and Chorus—the *Folksong Symphony* (1940). After his stint at Juilliard ended in 1940, Harris went on to teach at numerous colleges and universities around the country, instructing such prominent musicians as William Schuman and Peter Schickele before assuming his last academic post at the University of California at Los Angeles in 1971. He was named Composer Laureate of the State of California in 1975.

Although Harris wrote over two hundred compositions for all kinds of ensembles, his thirteen numbered symphonies and many choral works remain at the core of his oeuvre. In these scores he was able to take the folk tunes he loved and transform them for the concert hall. In one case, he took the traditional song *When Johnny Comes Marching Home* and adapted it twice, first in 1937 for mixed a cappella chorus and again in 1940 as the final movement in his *Folksong Symphony*. Harris also drew on the research of the Lomaxes (*Cowboy Songs and Other Frontier Ballads*) and Carl Sandburg (*The American Songbag*) for inspiration, in addition to helping prepare an anthology of choral music (*Singing Through the Ages*) based partly upon his own explorations of the archives at the Library of Congress. His love affair with Walt Whitman's poetry is also well documented, since it provided the texts for two of Harris's longest a cappella compositions, the *Song for Occupations* and the *Symphony for Voices*, as well as shorter choral works such as *To Thee, Old Cause* and *Freedom, Toleration*.

Orchestral
Symphony no. 3
what to buy: [*Bernstein Century: American Masters*; Leonard Bernstein, cond.; New York Philharmonic Orchestra] (Sony Classical 60594) ♪ ♪ ♪ ♪ ♪

In 1939 Bernstein was quoted in *Modern Music* saying, "Harris' *Third Symphony* is mature in every sense, beautifully proportioned, eloquent, restrained, and affecting. It greatly excited me." Capturing Harris's score with all the enthusiasm one could ask for, this performance has thankfully been reissued along with works by two other prominent American symphonists, David Diamond and Randall Thompson.

what to buy next: [Leonard Bernstein, cond.; New York Philharmonic Orchestra] (Deutsche Grammophon 419780) ♪ ♪ ♪ ♪♪

This is a splendid performance and quite well recorded, lacking only a bit of the powerful and youthful enthusiasm of Bernstein's earlier recording with the New York Philharmonic. In a nice bit of programming, the disc also includes a tautly performed version of the third symphony of one of Harris's most prominent students, William Schuman.

Symphony no. 4 for Orchestra and Chorus— *Folksong Symphony*

what to buy: [Vladimir Golschmann, cond.; American Festival Orchestra; American Festival Chorus] (Vanguard Classics 4076) ♪ ♪ ♪

While the sonics of this 1960 recording leave something to be desired, the performances led by Golschmann are perfectly idiomatic and worth hearing. Also of interest is Paul Creston's *Gregorian Chant* for Orchestra, with which the Harris symphony is paired.

Vocal
various choral works

what to buy: [*I Hear America Singing! Choral Music of Roy Harris*; Robert Shewan, cond.; Roberts Wesleyan College Choir] (Albany TROY 164) ♪ ♪ ♪

While this disc can be recommended to those wishing to get a rough idea of what Harris's choral works sound like, prospective listeners should be aware that the choir's soprano section warbles far too much and the voices aren't blended very well. While it is possible to glimpse the glories of Harris's *Symphony for Voices,* the brief *When Johnny Comes Marching Home,* and the wonderful madrigal *They Say That Susan Has No Heart for Learning,* this remains the default recommendation until something better comes along.

influences: William Schuman, Aaron Copland, Virgil Thomson, Paul Creston

Gary Barton and Ian Palmer

Karl Amadeus Hartmann
Born August 2, 1905, in Munich, Germany. Died December 5, 1963, in Munich, Germany.

period: Twentieth century

Hartmann came into prominence during the 1930s, but the rise to power of the Nazi Party in his native Germany hindered his career. After 1945, his symphonic works (particularly his eight symphonies) entered the concert repertory as representative twentieth-century contributions to the Austro-German symphonic tradition.

Hartmann's reputation in the music world rests not only on his merits as a composer but also on his role as the organizer of the first postwar new-music concert series, Musica Viva, produced for Bavarian Radio in Munich. Musica Viva became the prototype for many concert series throughout Europe and provided an environment for the development and flowering of the postwar avant-garde. Hartmann contributed a significant programming philosophy: every Musica Viva concert included works written by composers before as well as after 1945, providing a context for understanding both the modern masters (including members of the "Second Viennese School") and the generation that matured after the end of World War II.

A student of Joseph Haas and Hermann Scherchen in Munich during the mid-1920s, Hartmann won recognition by the early 1930s. His music was labeled "degenerate art" by the Nazi regime, however, and he was silent during the period between 1933 and 1945. From 1941 to 1942, Hartmann took private lessons from Anton Webern, and this link explains the intensity of his later efforts to make the music of Arnold Schoenberg, Alban Berg, and Webern accessible to the public. Despite this advocacy of the Second Viennese School, Hartmann did not employ serialism in his own compositions. Although his most prominent influences were Igor Stravinsky and Béla Bartók, his symphonic scores owe much in form, style, and content to Anton Bruckner, Gustav Mahler, and Max Reger.

Hartmann's first mature work to receive accolades was the Quartet no. 1 for Strings, which was awarded first prize at the Carillon Chamber Music Competition in Geneva in 1936. A neoclassical work, the quartet is expressive, almost bordering on romantic in the opening. The main body of the first movement, however, possesses rhythmic energy similar to that of Bartók's quartets. The forward momentum of the first and third movements is neoclassical and echoes Stravinsky's string writing, while the second movement is elegiac. The melodies tend to be long but beautifully balanced and soulful, and Hartmann's experiments with tone colors (harmonics, tremolos, and sliding pitches) are also very effective. The melancholy quality of the music reflects Hartmann's reaction to Hitler becoming chancellor of Germany in 1933.

Hartmann did not just incorporate the styles, techniques, and formal structures of his symphonic predecessors. His Symphony no. 2, in one movement, features a prominent saxophone solo in the beginning. His fifth symphony, subtitled *Sinfonia concertante,* has decidedly jazzy rhythms in the fast movements (albeit in a neoclassical style), while the slow movement shows off various wind and brass soloists in virtuosic, overlapping contrapuntal melodies.

Traces of romanticism can be found in Hartmann's symphonic output, not only in orchestral color but also in formal organization. Hartmann uses the variation procedure and mirror forms both for continuity and large-scale structure. Symphony no. 6 is in two movements, with the second identified by the composer as a *toccata variata.* The fugal sections in this movement are economically Teutonic: there are three fugues, of which the last two are variants of the first. Symphony no. 7 is also based heavily on fugal techniques, where the first movement (entitled *Introduction and Ricercare*) fuses two successive fugues, concerto and tutti, in sequence. Hartmann's eighth and final symphony quotes the composer's earlier symphonies, rounding off his oeuvre.

Hartmann also produced a chamber opera that was widely known and performed during his lifetime. *Simplicius Simplicissmus,* written between 1934 and 1935 and revised in 1955, is a collaboration with Hermann Scherchen that remains popular in Germany to this day. Unfortunately, many of Hartmann's works from the period 1933–1945 were either withdrawn by the composer or lost.

Orchestral
Symphony no. 5 for Wind Instruments, Cellos, and Double Basses—*Sinfonia concertante*
what to buy: [Ingo Metzmacher, cond.; Bamberg Symphony Orchestra] (EMI Classics 56184) ♪ ♪ ♪ ♪

The orchestra is in very good form here, especially the wind sections, and the playing is energetic, focused, and intensely neo-classical. This disc also includes the 1950 revision of the composer's second symphony and the *Symphony in One Movement* by Bernd Alois Zimmerman, a contemporary of Hartmann's.

Symphonies, nos. 7 and 8
what to buy: [Ingo Metzmacher, cond.; Bamberg Symphony Orchestra] (EMI Classics 56427) ♪ ♪ ♪ ♪ ♪

Metzmacher recorded all of Hartmann's symphonies for EMI Classics (co-produced by Bavarian Radio), and this is by far the most important recording of the series. Hartmann's last two symphonies are masterpieces—longer and more extensive (both timbrally and fugally) and employing larger orchestras. The soloists (strings, winds, and especially percussion) perform both symphonies with control, grace, and occasional bursts of emotion.

Chamber
Quartets for Strings
what to buy: [Pellegrini Quartet, ensemble] (CPO 999219) ♪ ♪ ♪ ♪

The Pellegrini Quartet provides eloquent readings of Hartmann's only two quartets, one dating from 1933 and the other from 1945–1946. These rare, deeply moving recordings display sensitivity, breadth, and tight ensemble work.

influences: Carl Nielsen, Paul Hindemith, Boris Blacher

Joanna Lee

Franz Joseph Haydn
Born March 31, 1732, in Rohrau, Austria. Died May 31, 1809, in Vienna, Austria.

period: Classical

If Joseph Haydn had not secured the stable employment he enjoyed throughout the majority of his creative life, he might not have been afforded the time necessary for the development of his particular genius. Certainly his early scores have much to recommend them, but it is really the works written from the midpoint of his life (particularly the string quartets and his latter symphonies) that provided the elegant, inventive foundation upon which Wolfgang Amadeus Mozart and Ludwig van Beethoven built their own admirable constructions.

Haydn's father Mathias was a wheelwright who loved music and played the harp at home, accompanying his own singing and that of his children. When Joseph was six years old and possessed of a clear, soprano voice, his parents entrusted his education to the husband of Mathias's stepsister, Johann Mathias Franck, the school principal and choir director of the Church of Saints Philip and James in Hainburg. Except for rare visits, the youngster, for all intents and purposes, passed out of his parent's lives.

During his time as a chorister, Haydn displayed a modicum of skill with the violin and various keyboard instruments, eventually developing an expertise that would serve him well upon his dismissal from the choir after his voice broke. When that happened (circa 1749) he was turned out (according to his earliest biographer, Georg August Griesinger) with a few items of clothing and no money. This was not an unusual occurrence for the period, and Haydn's ensuing struggle to support himself via teaching music and performing at various civil and private functions was similar to that of others who had provided voices for the greater glory of church choirs. Where he distinguished himself from his contemporaries was in the diligent study of music theory, aided in the latter stages of his life as a freelance musician/composer by Nicola Antonio Porpora, the Kapellmeister for whom he briefly served as a valet. Haydn's association with the older musician also gained him entry into the households of the nobility, where he was able to display his talents.

In 1759 he finally acquired a position as music director for Count Karl Joseph Franz Morzin, the employer for whom he wrote some keyboard sonatas, a number of his early string quartets, and the first of his symphonies. Approximately two years later, when Morzin was no longer able to support his musicians, Haydn secured employment with Prince Paul Anton Esterházy and his family, an association that would nourish and support his creativity for nearly thirty years. His first official position in that household was as vice-Kapellmeister, with the responsibility of conducting, leading, and hiring musicians for the orchestra, in addition to composing works for their exclusive use and overseeing the music library and the condition of the orchestra's instruments. When the prince died in 1762, he was succeeded by his brother Nikolaus, who had a keen interest in opera, so much so that he build a marvelous theater at his summer palace of Esterháza specifically to stage such productions.

Most of the secular dramatic works that Haydn wrote during his career were composed specifically for this venue and the separate marionette theater that was also on the estate. While Nikolaus was undoubtedly pleased with the operas and singspiels Haydn produced, they were basically rehashes of librettos which had previously been set by a number of other composers, and lacked the dramatic focus that would be brought to the form by Wolfgang Amadeus Mozart. The sacred choral scores which Haydn composed fared a little better, with the masses (the most important of which were written toward the end of his life, from 1796 to 1802) showcasing his orchestral and vocal palettes more than the cantatas but less so than in his last two oratorios—*Die Schöpfung (The Creation)* and *Die Jahreszeiten (The Seasons)*—both of which were completed after 1798.

Occupying every stage in Haydn's creative life are the more than sixty keyboard sonatas he wrote. While he broached some of the same ideas in his sonatas that he would later use in his symphonic works, Haydn's output for keyboard should not to be construed as a mere sonic scratchpad for more exalted pieces. It should instead be regarded as a group of early distillations, setting the stage for development of the form by later composers. (The recent argument against playing some of his sonatas on a piano is based on the lack of dynamics markings in all of these pieces; the ones sans direction were probably written for either the harpsichord or clavichord.)

Where Haydn truly shined was in the production of string quartets and symphonic fare. In the former he advanced the structure of the work so that it was less of a divertimento and more worthy of a composer's most intimate thoughts. This advancement first revealed itself in the six quartets of op. 20 (the *Sun* quartets) from 1772, and would culminate, in 1799, with the two works of his op. 77, although the *Lark* Quartet (op. 64, no. 5) has proven to be a favorite with modern concert audiences. Mozart was so impressed with the older composer's writing in this genre that he dedicated six of his own string quartets to Haydn and played some of them for him in 1785. It was then that Haydn is reputed to have turned to Leopold Mozart and said, "Before God and as an honest man I tell you that your son is the greatest composer known to me either in person or by name."

Of the 107 symphonies that Haydn wrote, most of the works from before 1781 can be considered relatively interesting and worth occasional listenings—especially Symphony no. 45 in F-sharp Minor. The story that goes along with the creation of that particular score (nicknamed the *Farewell* symphony), involves musicians kept too long away from their loved ones when Prince Nikolaus Esterházy decided to extend his stay at his country estate beyond that which had originally been planned. Haydn, in a subtle gesture, wrote this work which ended up with the musicians gradually filing out of the performance as their parts were finished, until only a pair of violinists were left. The prince evidently got the point and everyone ended up back home fairly quickly.

Haydn's symphonic genius really came into its fullness after 1782, specifically with the production of the *Paris Symphonies* (nos. 82–87), which were written between 1785 and 1786 as a commission from the board of directors of the Concert de la Loge Olympique, a Parisian Masonic Lodge. This set was followed by the gorgeously orchestrated Symphony no. 88 in G Major and four other symphonies before the pinnacle of Haydn's symphonic writing, the *London Symphonies* (nos. 93–104). These later items were composed between 1791 and 1795 while Haydn commuted between the Esterházy estate (Prince Nikolaus had died in 1790) and London, where he had been received with great honor. The last of his great orchestral works was the Concerto in E-flat Major for Trumpet and Orchestra, written in 1796 for Anton Weidinger, who had invented a predecessor to the valve trumpet which enabled the soloist to play all the chromatic notes between the notes of the natural series, something that was previously impossible.

Orchestral
Symphony no. 45 in F-sharp Minor (*Farewell*)
what to buy: [Iona Brown, cond.; Academy of St. Martin-in-the-Fields, orch.] (Hanssler 98.189) ♪ ♪ ♪ ♪₄

Whether the anecdote about the creation of this intriguing score is apocryphal or not, the music is splendid and Iona Brown's direction is graceful, as is the playing of the orchestra's string section. The same virtues apply to the ensemble's rendering of Haydn's symphonies nos. 44 and 49.

what to buy next: [Charles Mackerras, cond.; Orchestra of St. Luke's] (Telarc 80156) ♪ ♪ ♪ ♪

Mackerras leads a performance that is well recorded but somewhat more square from a rhythmic standpoint than Brown's with the Academy of St. Martin-in-the-Fields, yet not one that will necessarily disappoint admirers of

Thomas Hampson:
Thomas Hampson's inimitable voice, often described as being a mellow, nutty baritone, is instantly recognizable in any operatic performance. Hampson became especially identified with Wolfgang Amadeus Mozart, because, as Hampson says, "if you don't sing Mozart, you die." He has sung the roles of Don Giovanni, Don Alfonso, and notably Guglielmo in *Cosi fan tutte* (Deutsche Grammophon 423897), with James Levine leading an all-star cast. Not surprisingly, Hampson has also proved to be an ideal Figaro in Gioachino Rossini's *Barber of Seville* (EMI Classics 54863). Hampson's *Doktor Faust* in Ferruccio Busoni's neglected masterpiece has yet to be recorded; however, his role as *King Roger* (EMI Classics 56823) in Polish composer Karol Szymanowski's masterwork highlights a terrific performance conducted by Simon Rattle that might well help his gem gain a permanent spot in the standard repertoire. Contemporary composers haven't been ignored either, as Hampton has sung in works by Hans Werner Henze (*Der Prinz von Homburg*), John Adams (*The Wound Dresser*), and Conrad Susa (*Dangerous Liasons*).

For Hampson, his work in the recital hall is just as important as his work in the opera house. He has been a passionate advocate of song in both print and performance, devoting a part of every season to song recitals. In addition to well planned and beautifully sung performances of Gustav Mahler's *Des Knaben Wunderhorn* (Teldec 74726), Hampson has emerged as a leading champion of American art song. *Secrets of the Old* (Deutsche Grammophon 435867), his premiere recording (with Cheryl Studer) of the complete songs of Samuel Barber, is highly recommended, as is his Aaron Copland CD *Long Time Ago* (Teldec 77310) with Dawn Upshaw. *Night and Day* (EMI Classics 54203), Hampson's stylishly polished tribute to Cole Porter, shows us yet another side of this highly versatile artist.

Jan Jezioro

Mackerras's conducting. The companion piece to the featured work is another of Haydn's "named" symphonies, no. 31, also known as the *Hornsignal* because of the prominent role played by the instrument.

Symphonies nos. 82–87 (*The Paris Symphonies*)
what to buy: [Neville Marriner, cond.; Academy of St. Martin-in-the-Fields, orch.] (Philips 438727) ♪ ♪ ♪ ♪₄

For those listeners who seek a pared-down sound but aren't quite enamored of the period-instrument movement, Marriner's approach to these pivotal works is an excellent, well-recorded choice.

what to buy next: [Frans Brüggen, cond.; Orchestra of the 18th Century] (Philips 462111) ♪ ♪ ♪ ♪

Somewhat brisk but still admirable, Brüggen's orchestra of period instrument players delivers convincing, edgy performances, full of vim and vigor in the faster movements without neglecting the poetry inherent in the various minuets and adagios.

Symphony no. 88 in G Major
what to buy next: [Frans Brüggen, cond.; Orchestra of the 18th Century] (Philips 462602) ♪ ♪ ♪ ♪

The finest of the Haydn symphonies, bracketed by his Paris and London sets, receives a solid original-instrument performance from Brüggen, one of the foremost adherents of the practice.

Symphonies nos. 93–102 (*The London Symphonies*)
what to buy: [*Haydn: The London Symphonies, vol. 1*; Colin Davis, cond.; Royal Concertgebouw Orchestra] (Philips 442611) ♪ ♪ ♪ ♪ ♪

[*Haydn: The London Symphonies, vol. 2*; Colin Davis, cond.; Royal Concertgebouw Orchestra] (Philips 442614) ♪ ♪ ♪ ♪ ♪

Davis's steady hand at the helm of one of Europe's finest orchestras almost guarantees a good performance. This pair of two-disc sets includes the highly recommendable *Surprise* symphony and a wonderful reading of Haydn's Symphony no. 100 (*Military*).

what to buy next: [*Haydn: The Esterházy Recordings, vol. 8*; Adam Fischer, cond.; Austro-Hungarian Haydn Orchestra] (Nimbus 5200/04) ♪ ♪ ♪ ♪

Fischer's Haydn cycle is generally quite admirable, and this five-CD set of the *London Symphonies* is amongst the best in the series, filled with vibrant playing from the orchestra and quite good engineering. The budget price makes this a very competitive option to the slightly higher-priced sets led by Colin Davis.

worth searching for: [*The 12 "London" Symphonies*; Eugen Jochum, cond.; London Philharmonic Orchestra] (Deutsche Grammophon 437201) ♪ ♪ ♪ ♪ ♪

Jochum and the LPO gave a delightfully genteel sense of swing to these recordings, and it is a shame that these performances have slipped from the catalog. These "modern orchestra" renditions are highly recommended, and will probably show up on Deutsche Grammophon's reissue list someday.

Symphony no. 94 in G Major (*Surprise*)
what to buy: [Ray Goodman, cond.; The Hanover Band,

orch.] (Hyperion 66532) ♪ ♪ ♪ ♪ ♪

Goodman's troops make a good period-instrument alternative to Davis's larger, more modern orchestra. The rhythms are well-sprung and the recording is very clean, with fine performances of Symphonies nos. 93 and 95 in addition.

what to buy next: [Janos Ferencsik, cond.; Hungarian State Orchestra] (Laser Light 14007) ♪ ♪ ♪ ♪

Ferencsik was a staple of the Hungaroton label for many years, and turned out a number of fine recordings that never really received proper press coverage in the United States. His Beethoven cycle was particularly good, and the same clear-headed virtues that he applied to those symphonies are in evidence here as well. The budget pricing makes this set particularly attractive, as does the larger, more "modern" orchestra under Ferencsik's command. His version of another Haydn "name" symphony (no. 82 in C Major, *The Bear*) is also included on this disc.

Concerto no. 1 in C Major for Cello and Orchestra
what to buy: [*Haydn Concertos: Trumpet, Horn, Cello*; Mstislav Rostropovich, cello; Benjamin Britten, cond.; English Chamber Orchestra] (Decca 430633) ♪ ♪ ♪ ♪

This may be the most infectious version of this early work (written for the Esterházy court sometime between 1761 and 1765) that is still in catalog. Rostropovich does quite a virtuoso turn here, but in a way that celebrates the music, not the performer. The three other concertos on this disc are played by the Academy of St. Martin-in-the-Fields with Neville Marriner conducting: Barry Tuckwell is the soloist in the two horn concertos while Alan Stinger solos in the Concerto for Trumpet in E-flat Major.

[Yo-Yo Ma, cello; José-Luis Garcia, cond.; English Chamber Orchestra] (Sony Classics 36674) ♪ ♪ ♪ ♪

Both of Haydn's cello concertos are included in this set, and Ma's performances are very well-mannered without getting stuffy. His version of the C Major piece may not be as overtly exciting as Rostropovich's, but it is certainly in the same league from a technical standpoint.

what to buy next: [*Impressions: Jacqueline Du Pré*; Jacqueline Du Pré, cello; John Barbirolli, cond.; London Symphony Orchestra] (EMI Classics 69707) ♪ ♪ ♪ ♪

The sound in this set is adequate, and while the cellist's strong, distinctive playing may be a bit too idiosyncratic and bravura-oriented for some, it is certainly worth a listen. This two-disc set also includes her insightful rendition of the Edward Elgar cello concerto and a pair of Beethoven chamber works.

Concerto in E-flat Major for Trumpet and Orchestra
what to buy: [*Maurice André: Trumpet Concertos*; Maurice André, trumpet; Jésus López-Cobos, cond.; London Philharmonic Orchestra] (EMI Classics 69152) ♪ ♪ ♪ ♪

André has long ruled the roost when it comes to classical trumpet virtuosi and his performance here shows why. The budget-priced two-disc set it comes from has the trumpeter fronting a variety of ensembles and conductors in a host of trumpet-friendly Baroque and Classical-era standards by Handel, Telemann, Vivaldi, and others.

what to buy next: [Wynton Marsalis, trumpet; Raymond Leppard, cond.; English Chamber Orchestra] (Sony Classics 37846) ♪ ♪ ♪¼

Marsalis, a talented jazz trumpeter, proves that he has the chops to play part of the classical repertoire as well. Leppard's forces are in top shape and the other pieces on the album (trumpet concerti by Johann Nepomuk Hummel and Leopold Mozart) are agreeably lightweight.

Chamber
Piano Sonata no. 20 in C Minor (Landon 33)
what to buy: [Zoltan Kocsis, piano] (Hungaroton 11618/19) ♪ ♪ ♪ ♪

This is one of Haydn's first mature masterpieces for the piano, and Kocsis does a marvelous job of bringing out the score's nuances. Also included in this two-disc recital are some of the composer's earlier works for keyboard, including the Piano Sonata no. 18 in B-flat Major (Landon 20), in which where the pianist highlights the debt of gratitude Haydn owed to C.P.E. Bach.

Piano Sonata no. 52 in E-flat Major (Landon 62)
what to buy: [*Great Pianists of the 20th century: Alfred Brendel*; Alfred Brendel, piano] (Philips 456727) ♪ ♪ ♪ ♪¼

Brendel is one of the finest interpreters of Haydn's solo

piano music, though most of his great Haydn cycle for Philips is, sadly, out of print. Savor his performances of the great E-flat Major sonata and other works by Haydn, Franz Schubert, Wolfgang Mozart, and Robert Schumann.

what to buy next: [*Piano Sonatas, vol. 1*; Jenõ Jandó, piano] (Naxos 8.550657) ♪ ♪ ♪¼

Dating from Haydn's second trip to London, this piece is both an audio delight and a serious fingerbuster. Romping from chord to chord in a display of virtuosity, Jandó is more at home in the first-movement allegro than he is in the adagio, but his overall conception of the work is solid. The disc is part of a very good cycle of Haydn's keyboard sonatas at a budget price, and includes Sonatas nos. 49 (Landon 59) through 52 (Landon 62).

worth searching for: [*Two Great E-flat Sonatas*; Malcolm Bilson, fortepiano] (Nonesuch 78018) ♪ ♪ ♪ ♪¼

Bilson plays the score on a fortepiano—an intermediate step between the harpsichord and the grand piano—similar to the ones Haydn might have been introduced to in Vienna or London. A fine performance of the Piano Sonata no. 49 in E-flat Major (Landon 59) is also included, but there was room for more music on the disc than one ends up with.

Quartets for Strings, op. 20, nos. 1–6 (*Sun Quartets*)
what to buy: [Tátrai String Quartet, ensemble] (Hungaroton 11332/33) ♪ ♪ ♪ ♪

Haydn was in his forties when he wrote these quartets, and he was turning yet another creative corner. Other works of his from this period include the *Farewell* symphony and the Piano Sonata no. 20 in C Minor (Landon 33), all pieces exhibiting an ability to take the status quo and give it a masterly twist. The op. 20 string quartets are probably Haydn's first major artistic success with the form, and the Tátrai Quartet performs them admirably.

Quartets for Strings, op. 64, nos. 1–6 (*Tost Quartets*)
what to buy: [Tátrai String Quartet, ensemble] (Hungaroton 11838/39) ♪ ♪ ♪ ♪

Written prior to Haydn's first visit to London, these quartets mark the beginnings of a stylistic change for the composer. Certainly in the popular D Major quartet—nicknamed *The Lark*—and the E-flat Major quartet there are signs of things to come, while the other four works in this opus mark what has gone before. The Tátrai Quartet gives exemplary performances throughout the entire set.

Quartet for Strings in D Major, op. 64, no. 5 *(The Lark)*

what to buy: [*Haydn: String Quartets, vol. 2*, Lindsay String Quartet, ensemble] (ASV Quicksilva 6145) ♪ ♪ ♪ ♪

The fact that the Lindsay Quartet can play with such controlled fervor even as they let the music bloom is a tribute to their talents. Their *Lark* is clever and the reading given to the earlier Quartet in D Minor, op. 42 is fine. That they almost match the Tatrai unit (see below) for insight in the op. 76, no. 5 quartet (also included) is a further testimony to their abilities.

what to buy next: [Kodály Quartet, ensemble] (Naxos 8.550674) ♪ ♪ ♪ ♪

The last three works in op. 64 make up a well-played program for the Kodály Quartet, complete with one of the finer recordings of *The Lark* in catalog.

Quartets for Strings, op. 76, nos. 1–6 *(Erdödy Quartets)*

what to buy: [Tátrai String Quartet, ensemble] (Hungaroton 12812/13) ♪ ♪ ♪ ♪ ♪

Op. 76 contains some of the more familiar "named" quartets in Haydn's repertoire, including the *Quintenquartett,* the *Kaiserquartett,* and *L'Aurore;* the first quartet in the set is one of Haydn's finest moments in the genre.

Quartet for Strings in G Major, op. 76, no. 1

what to buy: [Kodály Quartet, ensemble] (Naxos 8.550129) ♪ ♪ ♪ ♪ ♪

Taken from a disc containing the first three quartets in op. 76, this particular performance is marvelous, giving the somewhat older Tátrai String Quartet rendition a real run for the money.

Quartets for Strings, op. 77 *(Lobkowitz Quartets)*

what to buy: [Tátrai String Quartet, ensemble] (Hungaroton 11776) ♪ ♪ ♪ ♪ ♪

There is no complete series of Haydn string quartets that outshines the one recorded by the Tátrai String Quartet for Hungaroton, and within that set a few performances especially stand out. Op. 77 features only two quartets instead of the usual six, but these are wonderful pieces and the performances are superb. While not containing anything as overtly popular as some of the "named" quartets, this disc should be included in any well-rounded collection of chamber music.

what to buy next: [Quatuor Festetics, ensemble] (Arcana 919) ♪ ♪ ♪ ♪

The Festetics Quartet are gradually releasing their journey through the Haydn Quartets and this is one of the harbingers of what looks to be an excellent cycle. Their performance of the op. 77 pieces is part of a distinguished three-CD set that also contains the opp. 75 and 76 quartets as well as the two movements from the fragmentary op. 103.

Vocal
Die Schöpfung (The Creation)

what to buy: [Gundula Janowitz, soprano; Christa Ludwig, mezzo-soprano; Fritz Wunderlich, tenor; Werner Krenn, tenor; Dietrich Fischer-Dieskau, baritone; Walter Berry, bass; Herbert von Karajan, cond.; Vienna Singverein, choir; Berlin Philharmonic Orchestra] (Deutsche Grammophon 449761) ♪ ♪ ♪ ♪

It isn't out of the question to call this performance of Haydn's greatest oratorio one of the finest things left to posterity by one of the world's most popular conductors. Karajan gloried in the sound of his orchestra's string section, creating quite a few seamless interpretations that worked well with nineteenth century composers like Mahler or Bruckner while often glossing over the wonders of earlier masters like Mozart and Bach. This rendition is splendid in every way, however, with exceptional singing (in German) from the soloists and choir.

worth searching for: [Emma Kirkby, soprano; Anthony Rolfe Johnson, tenor; Michael George, bass; Christopher Hogwood, cond.; New College Choir, Oxford; Academy of Ancient Music Orchestra] (L'Oiseau-Lyre 430397) ♪ ♪ ♪ ♪

This period-instrument version of *The Creation* is an

admirable counterweight to Karajan's larger forces. Unlike that reading (cited above), this recording is sung in English. Kirkby is in marvelous voice and Hogwood has become quite adept as a Haydn interpreter.

Mass no. 11 in D Minor (*Nelsonmesse*)
what to buy: [Elizabeth Vaughan, soprano; Janet Baker, mezzo-soprano; Neville Marriner, cond.; Kings College Choir, Cambridge; Academy-of-St. Martin-in-the-Fields, orch.] (London Jubilee 421146) ♪ ♪ ♪ ♪

Written right after the first successful performance of Haydn's oratorio *The Creation,* the *Nelsonmesse* is one of his shorter settings for the mass. Despite its brevity and the smallish size of the orchestra, this may arguably be Haydn's single greatest religious work. Marriner's version of this masterpiece is well executed and his soloists are splendid. Ditto for the rendition of Antonio Vivaldi's Gloria in D Major, which is also included in the set.

[Ann Monoyios, soprano; Svetlana Serdar, mezzo-soprano; Wolfgang Bünten, tenor; Harry van der Kamp, bass; Bruno Weil, cond.; Tölzer Knabenchor, choir; Tafelmusik, orch.] (Sony Vivarte 62823) ♪ ♪ ♪♪

This is a leaner-sounding version of the *Nelsonmesse* (by virtue of Tafelmusik's period-instrument orientation) than the one recorded by Marriner, but the strengths of the piece remain. Weil's conducting is sensitive throughout, and the choir, under the guidance of chorus master Gerhard Schmidt-Gaden, is a pleasure for the ears. Haydn's Mass no. 12 in B-flat Major—the *Theresienmesse*—is an appropriate companion on this disc, receiving all the engineering benefits enjoyed by the version of the *Nelsonmesse.*

L'anima del filosofo, ossia Orfeo ed Euridice (The Soul of the Philosopher, or Orfeo and Euridice)
what to buy: [Cecilia Bartoli, soprano; Angela Kazimierczuk, soprano; Uwe Heilmann, tenor; James Oxley, tenor; Roberto Scaltriti, baritone; José Fardilha, baritone; Ildebrando D'Archangelo, bass; Andrea Silvestrelli, bass; Colin Campbell, bass; Christopher Hogwood, cond.; Academy of Ancient Music Orchestra and Chorus] (L'Oiseau-Lyre 452668) ♪ ♪ ♪ ♪♪

The four-act *L'anima del filosofo,* the last of the operas Haydn wrote, is probably the most significant of his staged dramatic works. Partly this is due to its orchestration, which resembles that of his later symphonies,

and the presence of a larger chorus than that which he was used to working with at Esterháza. Written in 1791 for a London impresario but never performed during Haydn's lifetime, this work may be the closest he ever got to inspiration in this genre and it remains quite a pleasant diversion. Bartoli is perfect in this period repertoire, Heilmann is stupendous, and Hogwood leads his ensemble with considerable panache.

influences: Wolfgang Amadeus Mozart, Ludwig van Beethoven, Michael Haydn, Carl Philip Emanuel Bach, Ignaz Pleyel, Adalbert Gyrowetz, Johann Baptist Vanhal

William Gerard and Ellen Kokko

Michael Haydn
Born Johann Michael Haydn, c. September 14, 1737, in Rohrau, Austria. Died August 10, 1806, in Salzburg, Austria.

period: Classical

It's tough getting respect from posterity when your older sibling has essentially set the standard for nearly every genre of composition known to late-eighteenth-century Europe. However, Michael Haydn, younger brother of Franz Joseph Haydn, was a distinguished composer in his own right and, along with Johann Christian Bach, deserves a large measure of credit for influencing the work of the young Wolfgang Amadeus Mozart.

Possessed of a gorgeous voice as a child, Michael started his musical career singing in the choir at St. Stephen's Cathedral in Vienna. While churches of the time clamored for good youthful voices, offering an education covering a wide variety of disciplines in exchange for bolstering their choirs, they were also fairly ruthless about severing that relationship once a boy's voice broke. This policy applied to both of the Haydn lads, and their ensuing years were filled with struggles as they attempted to secure positions with various musical establishments. Franz Joseph's search for work led him to a precarious life as a freelance musician and teacher before he won a position with Count Morzin in 1759. Michael, five years younger, didn't begin his quest until later, but he was able to find a less prestigious post more quickly, possibly because he wasn't as ambitious as his older sibling.

Michael's initial job search ended when he was appointed Kapellmeister to the Bishop of Grosswardein in 1757. There he wrote a number of sacred choral works for performance in the chapel in addition to several orchestral scores. His talents were such that six years later Haydn was working in Salzburg as Konzertmeister for Archbishop Sigismund Schrattenbach. In Salzburg the young composer became acquainted with Leopold Mozart and his talented son, Wolfgang. There seems to have been an admiration society among the three of them, with Leopold commenting favorably on Haydn's compositions, the precocious Wolfgang writing some small works for Haydn's use, and Michael encouraging the youngster's talents.

Salzburg was a comfortable place for Haydn, and the demands on his talents were rigorous enough to ensure steady artistic progress but not stressful enough to cause him to seek employment elsewhere. He was a well-respected teacher (Carl Maria von Weber was one of his pupils), admired within the community for his abilities as a composer of vocal music. But after thirty-eight years of this life, external circumstances, specifically the seizure of Salzburg by the French army, caused Haydn and his family to seek refuge with his brother in Vienna and Eisenstadt. It wasn't long though before he returned to Salzburg, where he lived out the rest of his days.

Orchestral
Symphony no. 28 in C Major
what to buy: [Bohdan Warchal, cond.; Slovak Chamber Orchestra] (CPO 999156) ♪ ♪ ♪ ♪

It is said that the finale of this symphony impressed a young Beethoven, perhaps because of the well-thought-out fugue Haydn put at the heart of the movement. Warchal's group is skillful and finely recorded, displaying an extraordinary, seemingly instinctive flair for the rhythms of the work. Two other symphonies by the junior Haydn, included on the disc, sound nearly as delightful.

what to buy next: [*Michael Haydn: Eight Symphonies*; Harold Farberman, cond.; Bournemouth Sinfonietta] (Vox Box 5020) ♪ ♪ ♪₄

Eight symphonies, decently played, make this budget-priced two-disc set a valid option. Farberman's rendering of the Symphony no. 28 is fuller sounding but rhythmically slacker than Warchal's version. The inspiration of the performances isn't consistent throughout the package, however, and that may outweigh the allure of the low price.

Concerto no. 1 in D Major for Trumpet and Orchestra
what to buy: [*Baroque Music for Trumpets*; Wynton Marsalis, trumpet; Raymond Leppard, cond.; English Chamber Orchestra] (Sony 42478) ♪ ♪ ♪ ♪

This short concerto is one of Haydn's most recorded works, but it has a devilishly tricky role for the soloist that can trip up even the most gifted trumpeter. Marsalis, better known for his jazz playing, gives a well-shaped performance, graceful yet powerful. The balance of the program is pleasant, featuring tasteful pieces for trumpet and orchestra by Antonio Vivaldi, Georg Philipp Telemann, Johann Pachelbel, and Heinrich von Biber.

what to buy next: [*Klassische Trompeten Konzerte* (Classical Trumpet Concertos); Reinhold Friedrich, trumpet; Neville Marriner, cond.; Academy of St. Martin-in-the-Fields, orch.] (Capriccio 10436) ♪ ♪ ♪₄

For those wishing to hear both of Haydn's trumpet concertos, including the one in C Major, this disc may be the ticket. Friedrich's playing is wonderful, and the orchestra's string section plays marvelously. Trumpet concertos by Johann Nepomuk Hummel, Leopold Mozart, and Franz Joseph Haydn are also included.

Concerto in D Major for Horn and Orchestra
what to buy: [Barry Tuckwell, horn; Neville Marriner, cond.; English Chamber Orchestra] (EMI Classics 69395) ♪ ♪ ♪ ♪

Haydn's horns were valveless, capable only of notes in the natural scale. All that changed when certain virtuosos discovered that overblowing and shaping the sound in the bell of the horn with the hand could change the tones up or down as much as a step. Haydn wrote for this new type of virtuoso, and Tuckwell is more than up to the task. This performance is part of a fine budget-priced two-CD set of horn concertos featuring Tuckwell as soloist on works by Giovanni Punto, Franz Joseph Haydn, Leopold Mozart, Carl Maria von Weber, Luigi Cherubini, and Georg Philipp Telemann, in addition to the lone Michael Haydn piece.

Vocal
Requiem in C Minor
what to buy: [Ibolya Verebics, soprano; Judit Nemeth, contralto; Martin Kleitmann, tenor; Jozsef Moldvay, baritone; Helmuth Rilling, cond.; Liszt Ferenc Chamber Orchestra, Budapest; Hungarian Radio and Television

Chorus] (Hungaroton 31022) ♪ ♪ ♪ ♪⸸

Originally written as a memorial for Archbishop Sigismund Schrattenbach in 1771, this piece achieved an even greater degree of renown when it was played at the funeral of Michael's brother, Franz Joseph. Along with the *Missa Sancti Francisci*, dedicated to Saint Francis (the companion piece on this disc), and the *Missa Sancti Hieronymi* (which isn't included here), the Requiem in C Minor stands as one of the jewels in Haydn's vocal oeuvre.

influences: Franz Joseph Haydn, Wolfgang Amadeus Mozart, Leopold Mozart, Carl Maria von Weber, Anton Diabelli

Garaud MacTaggart

Hans Werner Henze

Born July 1, 1926 in Gütersloh, Westphalia, Germany.

period: Twentieth century

Despite an idiosyncratic mix of tonal and atonal material, Hans Werner Henze has occasionally written music which (relatively speaking) is accessible to the masses. At other times, however, he has composed harsh, driven scores of considerable intellectual complexity. His pair of sonatas for the guitar (*Royal Winter Music I & II*) are representative of Henze's more "populist" tendencies, while some of the settings in his song cycle *Voices* come from his more cerebral side.

According to his autobiography *Reiselieder mit böhmischen Quinten* (published in English-speaking countries as *Bohemian Fifths*), much of Henze's childhood was dominated by a mixture of music, his father's acceptance of National Socialist trappings, and his own internalized rebellion against the Nazis. Memories of receiving a copy of Anna Magdalena Bach's *Clavierbüchlein* for Christmas and listening to radio broadcasts of Mozart's music contrasted with tales of "the pale sky lit up by fires" during Kristallnacht and almost being sent to a military school for music run by the Nazis.

He was drafted into the Army in 1944 and spent much of his training being schooled as a radio operator. A year later, after Hitler's suicide, Henze was numbered amongst a group of German soldiers who eagerly surrendered to the British. Upon his release from prison

camp, Henze found work with the British army ordnance depot "loading munitions crates and other heavy objects into lorries" but, as a talented pianist and an all-around musician, he exploited his artistic competency by volunteering to be a chorus master at the Bielefeld Stadttheater, and supplemented his income by playing piano at ballet schools and military casinos. Henze had been interested in creating his own music ever since he was a child, and was finally convinced by a friend that he should get further schooling in that regard. He eventually ended up at Heidelberg's Institute of Evangelical Church Music, where he became acquainted with (and fascinated by) the music of Igor Stravinsky, Béla Bartók, and Alban Berg through the auspices of his primary teacher, Wolfgang Fortner.

Kammerkonzert, which was played at the first International Summer School for New Music (near Darmstadt) in 1946, was the first of Henze's works from this period to receive the recognition of his peers. Two years later René Leibowitz attended the Darmstadt conference and introduced Henze to the music of Arnold Schoenberg and Olivier Messiaen. Within months Henze adopted much of the serial doctrine as his own, meshing the twelve-tone row with the aspects of Stravinsky, Bartók, and (to some extent) Paul Hindemith that had already influenced the core of his art.

In 1953 Henze moved to Italy, where his first important stage works (the opera *König Hirsch (King Stag),* and *Undine,* a ballet) were composed. It was difficult to ascertain at the time of *König Hirsch's* premiere just how striking and original a piece this was, since the conductor cut several of the arias and the staging was underrehearsed. Despite Henze's fury at this tampering and the relatively poor reception of the work, he was able to salvage some of the music from the opera by using it in his fourth symphony. *Undine,* on the other hand, explored territory previously mined during the Romantic era and brought it into the twentieth century in fulfillment of a commission meant to showcase Margot Fonteyn's skills. She ended up dancing the lead role over fifty times between 1958 and 1966.

Henze's next important operas, *Die Bassariden (The Bassarids)* and *Der junge Lord (The Young Lord),* were completed within fairly close proximity of each other, during the years 1964 and 1965. The latter was conceived as an opera buffa with a satirical edge that draws inspiration from elements of Stravinsky's oeuvre even as it slips into and out of tonality. *Die Bassariden* is an adaptation of *The Bacchae* by Euripides, with text by W.H. Auden and Chester Kallman. According to Henze, "The inclusion of individual numbers such as arias, choruses and ensembles notwithstanding, the opera as a whole is based on a four-part symphonic structure which, musically and formally, spans the great conflict of this human drama and thereby holds it together." While *Der junge lord* was the greater commercial success initially, *Die Bassariden* seems to have the stronger hold on Henze's heart and may very well be his greatest opera.

From the mid-1960s on, the composer began to adopt a more political public stance, partially rooted in the antifascist attitude that characterized his reaction to World War II but definitely inspired by the socialist polemic of "Red" Rudi Dutschke and other German student radicals. In 1967 Henze was quoted in an interview with Wolf-Eberhard von Lewinski as saying, "Utopia is defined by the absence of capitalism, the absence of the dominance of men over men, the liberation of art from its commercialism." This is the ideological construct behind Henze's sixth symphony (finished in 1970 after much time spent studying and working in Cuba), a work which utilized revolutionary songs drawn from Vietnamese and Greek sources as the starting point for an intriguing, albeit difficult, score. Henze's most consistently intriguing piece from this period, however, was *Voices*. This collection of twenty-two songs for mezzo-soprano and tenor from 1973 was built around poetry from Ho Chi Minh, Bertolt Brecht, Dudley Randall, and others. The composer took his musical cues from the lyrics, as in *Prison Song,* which melded Ho Chi Minh's partisan polemic with the sounds of chains clanking.

According to Henze, the *Royal Winter Music I* developed out of Richard of Gloucester's monologue, "Now is the winter of our discontent," and was written in response to guitarist Julian Bream's request for a new piece of music. The result was premiered by Bream in 1976, and the second in the *Royal Winter Music* series debuted in 1980 with Reinbert Evers as soloist. 1976 also saw the completion of Henze's third, fourth, and fifth string quartets, small masterpieces of absolute music composed during a time when the composer was generally working on scores with agendas. From the 1980s onward, he has created some of the more arresting symphonic works of the late twentieth century, in particular his seventh (1983–1984), eighth (1992–1993), and ninth (1995–1997) symphonies and a nine-movement instrumental *Requiem*. In 1999 he composed his tenth symphony,

which at press time was scheduled to have its world premiere at the Lucerne Festival in 2002. On January 21, 2001, Henze received the Cannes Classical Award for Best Living Composer.

Orchestral
Undine
what to buy: [Peter Donohoe, piano; Oliver Knussen, cond.; London Sinfonietta, orch.] (Deutsche Grammophon 453467) ♪♪♪♪⁺

As one of the composer's first great stage works (admittedly made all the more so by Fonteyn's artistry) it is surprising that it took as long as it did for this piece to be released. Henze's orchestration for this ballet is a marvel of clarity, something that the engineers at Deutsche Grammophon and conductor Knussen have taken great care to preserve.

Symphony no. 7
what to buy: [Simon Rattle, cond.; City of Birmingham Symphony Orchestra] (EMI Classics Imports 54762) ♪♪♪♪♪

While this symphony (written between 1983 and 1984) isn't necessarily one of his most accessible works, any listener with a post-Schoenberg-ian bent should be able to absorb the sonic complexities of Henze's basic conception. Given that caveat, his dramatic seventh symphony is not a terribly long-winded score—timing out under forty minutes—but it is as dense as anything he has ever written. The 1979 *Barcarola per grande orchestra* (dedicated to Paul Dessau) that starts out Rattle's program is, from a listening standpoint, a relative breeze in comparison, albeit a darkly textured one with the composer's fingerprints all over it.

Chamber
Royal Winter Music I and II for Solo Guitar
what to buy: [David Tannenbaum, guitar] (Audiophon 72029) ♪♪♪♪⁺

Both works are (essentially) three-movement sonatas. Loosely illustrating Shakespearean characters, the two pieces have become some of the most honored works for twentieth century guitar. Tannenbaum (the dedicatee of the composer's *An eine Äolsharfe*) offers performances that are taut yet poetic, exposing Henze's lyrical streak to best advantage.

various works for guitar
what to buy: [Sabine Oehring, guitar] (Music Alliance/SFB 9601815) ♪ ♪ ♪ ♪

Oehring's take on the second *Royal Winter Music* sonata stands up well in comparison to Tannenbaum's performance, but the real advantage to this disc is its inclusion of two other major Henze works featuring the guitar: *An eine Äolsharfe* for Guitar and Fifteen Solo Instruments, and the *Carillon, Récitatif, Masque* for Mandolin, Guitar, and Harp. Oehring works with members of the Boris Blacher Ensemble in all but the album's signature piece.

Quartets for Strings, nos. 1–5
what to buy: [Arditti String Quartet] (Wergo 60114-50) ♪ ♪ ♪ ♪

The differences between Henze's first two quartets and the next three are more than just the gap of twenty-three years separating them. In the earlier works Henze was striving for a specific artistic personality, but by the time he started working on the other three he had already arrived. Henze was able to contrast experimentation with relative accessibility by then without feeling compromised, as evidenced by his fourth string quartet, in which the first two movements split the difference. The performances in this set are excellent, and unlikely to be surpassed anytime soon.

Vocal
Die Bassariden (The Bassarids)
worth searching for: [Karan Armstrong, soprano; Celina Lindsley, soprano; Ortun Wenkel, contralto; Kenneth Riegel, tenor; Robert Tear, tenor; Andreas Schmidt, baritone; Michael Burt, baritone; William B. Murray, bass; Gerd Albrecht, cond.; Radio Symphony Orchestra, Berlin; RIAS-Kammerchor, choir; Südfunkchor, choir] (Koch Schwann 314006) ♪ ♪ ♪ ♪

Henze authorized this production's excision of the third movement intermezzo, which from a textual standpoint eliminates the darker, comedic portions of this tragedy and makes the work more of a operatic symphony than an opera grafted onto a symphonic form. The vocal cast is wonderful, especially Riegel as Dionysus, and the orchestra is in fine form. Since this *was* the only extant recording of this work (the disc is now out of print), it

would have been great if Albrecht's forces had been allowed to document the whole score, yet abridged though it may be, the set is still worth seeking out.

Voices **for Mezzo-Soprano, Tenor, and Fifteen Instruments**
what to buy: [Gudrun Pelker, mezzo-soprano; Frieder Lang, tenor; Johannes Kalitzke, cond.; Musikfabrik NRW, orch.] (CPO 999192) ♪ ♪ ♪

This was the initial recording of Henze's important song cycle from 1973, but it leaves out five of the longer, more theatrical songs in the series. In that respect Kalitzke and his cohorts give the listener short shrift, but since they did their excision with the blessings of the composer, complaining about the deletions disregards some essentially good performances.

worth searching for: [Roswitha Trexler, mezzo-soprano; Joachim Vogt, tenor; Horst Neumann, cond.; members of the Leipzig Radio Symphony Orchestra] (Berlin Classics 0021802) ♪ ♪ ♪ ♪

Neumann's forces present the cycle in its entirety, but other than that fact, there is little separating this recording from the Kalitzke-led version. Both sets feature well-characterized performances, well-recorded. The higher rating is more for completeness than anything else, though *The Electric Cop* (missing from the CPO set) is a stunner.

influences: Gustav Mahler, Kurt Weill, Paul Dessau, Peter Ruzicka

Garaud MacTaggart

Bernard Herrmann
Born June 29, 1911, in New York City, NY. Died December 24, 1975, in Los Angeles, CA.

period: Twentieth century

Although Herrmann wrote a number of concert works and a full-length opera, there is little doubt that his finest, best-known, and most characteristic music is that which he wrote for motion pictures. Of the movie scores, those that he wrote for Alfred Hitchcock stand out.

The son of Russian-Jewish parents who brought him up in comfortable middle class fashion in New York City,

Hans Werner Henze

Herrmann was a precocious youngster who was curious about everything, especially music, literature, and art. He won a composition prize at the age of thirteen and studied violin for a while but, characteristically, did not get along with his teacher. Largely self-taught, Herrmann enjoyed expeditions to the New York Public Library, where he studied scores by Claude Debussy, Maurice Ravel, and Richard Wagner and read Hector Berlioz's treatise on orchestration. He also studied with Philip James, Bernard Wagenaar, and Percy Grainger at New York University and the Juilliard School of Music, but conventional academics bored him, and he never actually graduated with a degree. Instead, Herrmann decided he wanted to be a conductor and, at the age of twenty, founded his own chamber orchestra, championing the music of Charles Ives, William Walton, and Frederick Delius. In 1934 he joined the fledgling CBS radio network as a staff conductor, but his talent for contriving effective and original scores for all kinds of programs soon attracted attention. At CBS, Herrmann became associated with Orson Welles and the celebrated *Mercury Theater of the Air,* composing the music for Welles's famous *War of the Worlds* broadcast in 1938; two years later, when Welles went to Hollywood to make movies, he took the composer with him. Thus it was that Herrmann's very first motion picture score turned out to be nothing less than the legendary *Citizen Kane.* Soon afterward he won an Academy Award for *The Devil and Daniel Webster* (also known as *All that Money Can Buy*) and worked again with Welles on the ill-fated movie *The Magnificent Ambersons.*

Herrmann attempted to divide his attention among film offers, "serious" compositions, and his duties at CBS. In 1940 he composed what was, up to that time, his most ambitious concert work—a four-movement symphony. Although there was some initial interest from major orchestras, Herrmann refused to revise or shorten the piece and was unable to secure a performance. His volatile nature and inability to get along with people likewise sabotaged his ambitions to become a famous conductor. Although Herrmann's radio concerts were admired for their adventurous programming and erudition, his invitations to conduct with major American orchestras were few and far between, and such opportunities as there were usually turned out badly.

Like Orson Welles, Herrmann had a different way of doing things. This difference would arouse suspicion from the insular film community, as when he rejected the fashionably lush scoring of Erich Wolfgang Korngold and Max Steiner in favor of stark sonorities. Melody was not predominant; rather, he worked with mood and image, using harmony in a unique manner, creating motifs that conveyed the emotion of the scene in a way never heard before. His vision would paint the sonic world of many different movies, from the romantic, dreamy atmosphere of *The Ghost and Mrs. Muir* to the dizzy disorientation of *Vertigo* to the most famous musical cue in film history—the string motif for the shower scene in *Psycho.* Hitchcock himself admitted that the scene did not work until Herrmann's music was added and was grateful to his old friend for ignoring his "improper suggestion" to do the scene with no music at all. In 1948 Herrmann began work on a large-scale operatic treatment of Emily Bronte's *Wuthering Heights.* This occupied him off and on for several years, but as with the symphony, no performances were forthcoming. By the early 1950s, the demise of network radio compelled him to work almost exclusively in the movies, often at Twentieth Century Fox, where Alfred Newman greatly admired his abilities. In 1955 Herrmann wrote the music for Alfred Hitchcock's *The Trouble with Harry,* beginning a distinguished director-composer collaboration that would last a decade. In 1966 Hitchcock and Herrmann had a falling out over the score for *Torn Curtain,* with the director firing the composer after hearing only the prelude. The two men never worked together again; one wonders what *Torn Curtain* might have been like had this pair of strong-willed personalities been able to resolve their differences. Hitchcock had been under pressure to discard orchestral scoring in favor of a more contemporary sound utilizing jazz and pop elements. This was an anathema to Herrmann, who had composed music for the film using sixteen French horns, twelve flutes, nine trombones, two tubas, and strings dominated by cellos and basses. The music, which makes uncompromising use of tone clusters, is as inventive as the instrumentation, but for years the score existed only in manuscript, and it became legendary.

As the movie business and musical styles changed in the late 1960s, Herrmann, a lifelong Anglophile, became disenchanted with Hollywood and moved to London, where he made recordings of some of his works (including his symphony and *Wuthering Heights*) and took the occasional film assignment. The 1970s saw a revival of interest in Herrmann's talents, and despite his failing health, he was sought out by directors like Brian de Palma and Martin Scorsese. Herrmann returned to California to write the music for Scorsese's *Taxi Driver* in December 1975 and died in his sleep Christmas Eve, almost immediately after wrapping the final recording session.

Orchestral
film scores
what to buy: [*Jane Eyre*; Adriano cond.; Slovak Radio Symphony Orchestra] (Marco Polo 8.223535) ♪ ♪ ♪ ♪

This is the full score for Herrmann's fourth film, and this great recording was put together after painstaking research. The result is a fabulous piece of music, superbly played and recorded. It is Herrmann's longest score and his most romantic.

film score collections
what to buy: [*Citizen Kane: The Classic Film Scores of Bernard Herrmann*; Charles Gerhardt, cond.; National Philharmonic Orchestra] (RCA Victor 707) ♪ ♪ ♪ ♪₈

Here is a wonderful disc that gives a vivid portrait of Herrmann's orchestral wizardry. It contains not only selections from *Citizen Kane* (with a young Kiri Te Kanawa singing an aria from the fictional opera *Salammbo*) but also suites from such gems as *Beneath the Twelve Mile Reef* (with nine harps!), the *Concerto Macabre* from *Hangover Square,* and the terrifying "Death Hunt" (nine horns!) from *On Dangerous Ground.* And you haven't lived until you've heard *White Witch Doctor,* the percussion for which includes a brake drum from an old Volkswagen.

what to buy next: [*Bernard Herrmann: The Film Scores*; Esa Pekka Salonen, cond.; Los Angeles Philharmonic Orchestra] (Sony Classical 62700) ♪ ♪ ♪ ♪

Salonen presents a fine overview that features some of Herrmann's best film work, including selections from the scores to Hitchcock's *Vertigo, North by Northwest, Marnie, The Man Who Knew Too Much,* and *Psycho,* as well as the lovely 1967 suite from François Truffaut's film *Fahrenheit 451.* Salonen and the orchestra treat the music with the respect it deserves, and the digital sound gives this disc a slight edge over some of Herrmann's own recordings of the same repertoire, many of which have been reissued.

worth searching for: [*Bernard Herrmann: Great Film Music*; Bernard Herrmann, cond.; National Philharmonic Orchestra] (London Phase 4 443899) ♪ ♪ ♪ ♪

Most of the music heard here comes from films with a

Nikolaus Harnoncourt:
Nikolaus Harnoncourt studied cello at the Vienna Academy of Music, where he became interested in early music and old instruments, often playing the viola da gamba in various recitals. He started his professional life as an orchestral cellist with the Vienna Symphony Orchestra and performed with them from 1952 until 1969, but in 1953, with the aid of his violinist wife Alice, he founded the Concentus Musicus. This was (and is) an ensemble dedicated to performing the works of composers from the thirteenth through early nineteenth centuries in the style which they might have been accustomed to hearing. He recruited most of the members for this new group from his associates in the Vienna Symphony Orchestra, and worked with them in discovering the differences between playing instruments in a setting derived from the Romantic period (as they had been doing) and the performance practices of an earlier era.

Harnoncourt's activities in the service of early music and his research into performance practices of bygone times paralleled the efforts of like-minded souls such as David Munrow, Gustav Leonhardt, Anner Bylsma, and Frans Brüggen while following in artistic paths blazed by Wanda Landowska, Alfred Deller, Nadia Boulanger, and Arnold Dolmetsch. In an essay from 1954 entitled "Zur Interpretation historischer Musik (On the Interpretation of Historical Music)" Harnoncourt justified his approach, declaring that "works sound not only historically more correct, but also more vital, because they are performed with the means most appropriate to them, and we get an intimation of the spiritual forces which made the past so fertile. Involvement with old music in this way takes on a deep meaning, far surpassing that of purely aesthetic enjoyment." From the vantage point of a new century, however, it is apparent that not all of Harnoncourt's ideas from the 1960s and 1970s are consistent with the findings of current scholarship. This doesn't negate the concerts and recordings which he took part in during those years, since they have helped document the changing face of "period instrument performance."

Known for his performances of Johann Sebastian Bach's oeuvre, Harnoncourt has received a number of awards for his efforts in this area, including the *Deutscher Schallplattenpreis* and the *Grand Prix du Disque* for his 1968 recording of the Mass in B Minor (Teldec Das Alte Werk 95517), and the *Deutscher Schallplattenpreis* and a Grammy for his rendering of the four orchestral suites (Teldec Das Alte Werk 92174). But he was equally important in the revival of Claudio Monteverdi's works, especially for his rendition of the opera *L'Incoronazione di Poppea* (Teldec Das Alte Werk 42547). Not content to confine himself or his interests to pre-Classical era music, Harnoncourt has also conducted well-received performances of works by Wolfgang Amadeus Mozart (*Le Nozze di Figaro,* Teldec 90861), Ludwig van Beethoven (Symphonies, nos. 1–9, Teldec 46452), and Antonín Dvořák (Symphony no. 8 in G Major, Teldec 24487), confounding those listeners who would seek to label him as a strictly period-instrument performer.

Garaud MacTaggart

fantastic element in the story line. This classic recording features the composer conducting excerpts from *Day the Earth Stood Still, Gulliver's Travels, Journey to the Center of the Earth, The Seventh Voyage of Sinbad,* and *Farenheit 451.*

influences: Max Steiner, Sergei Prokofiev, Aaron Copland, Alfred Newman, Miklós Rózsa

Jack Goggin and Frank Retzel

Hildegard von Bingen
Born c. 1098, in Bermersheim, Germany. Died September 17, 1179, in Rupertsberg, Germany.

period: Medieval

One of the earliest sacred composers for whom we have both extensive biographical material and musical examples, Hildegard is also one of the earliest known female composers. She has undergone a renaissance in the past few years, with a great deal of attention given to both her life and creative output.

No other composer can claim quite the same credentials as Hildegard von Bingen. Butler writes "… the process of her canonization was twice undertaken. It was never achieved, but she is named as a saint in the Roman martyrology and her feast is kept on [September 17] in several German dioceses." (*Lives of the Saints*). Abbess, mystic, healer, herbalist, writer, and composer, this truly extraordinary woman was consulted by popes, bishops, and kings in an era when it was mostly men who received such respect. Though never canonized as noted above, she was beatified, and is frequently referred to as St. Hildegard.

Hildegard was born into a distinguished family as the tenth child of Freiherr Hiltebert von Bermersheim and Mechthild von Merxheim. She had visions from the age of three, but kept these secret until many years later. As was common for the tenth child, she was "tithed" to the church at birth and entered religious life at the age of eight. In the women's community attached to the Benedictine monastery at Disibodenberg, her education was entrusted to Mother Superior Jutta von Spanheim and, at the age of seventeen, Hildegard voluntarily chose the life of a nun. After Jutta's death in 1136, Hildegard was elected as superior of the small convent there. In 1141, Hildegard sensed a distinct change in her life when a vision gave her understanding of religious texts and a "command" to "write down what you see and hear." She sought church sanction for her visions, and wrote to St. Bernard asking his blessing. Bernard brought this to the attention of Pope Eugenius, who urged Hildegard to complete her writings. The first of these visionary writings, *Scivias* (1141), would help to spread her fame throughout Germany. She later authored two more books of this sort: *Liber vitae meritorum (Book of Life's Merits)* (1150—63), and *Liber divinorum operum (Book of Divine Works)* (1163).

The convent grew, and Hildegard moved her group in 1150 to a new monastery on the Rupertsberg near Bingen. In 1165, she also took over a monastery in Eibingen near Rudesheim, remodeling it into a Benedictine convent. Hildegard personally managed both of these institutions. From then until her death in 1179, the abbess would continue a steady stream of writings—medical texts, correspondence (with popes, emperors and princes), and musical compositions. It seems that Hildegard had a natural affinity for poetry and art, and that her musical creativity was an outgrowth of her visionary powers. In *Scivias*, she describes her visions as being permeated by light and sounds that offer praise for the saints "in harmonis symphonizans" (in harmonious unity). Hildegard titled her chants *Symphonia harmoniae caelestium revelationum (Symphony of the Harmony of Heavenly Revelation)*. Completed about 1150, they comprise a liturgical cycle of seventy-seven poems with monophonic music, observing the church year and honoring Mary, the Trinity, and a few saints. A morality play, *Ordo virtutum (Play of Virtues)*, portrayed the struggle between seventeen Virtues and the Devil over the destiny of a female soul. There is evidence that all of Hildegard's music was performed in her convent.

Having certainly been exposed to plainsong from her earliest days at Disibodenberg, all of Hildegard's work is chant-like, carrying forth the tradition of a single melodic line. Hymns, antiphons, responsories, sequences, even a Kyrie, are the familiar forms that carry the sacred texts. There is, however, a unique vision at work in Hildegard's poetry and chant. The poetry contains highly original imagery, colorful language, and sensual allusions. The music is likewise distinct. Though coming from the Roman tradition, Hildegard's chants are decidedly non-Gregorian. Her melodic lines show a tendency for tonal rather than modal organization; use of repetition; and asymmetric design. There is a preference for wide intervals, and a strong preference for melisma. Such elements infuse her music with a singular, raw power. These characteristics seem to come from an intuitive feel for music, rather than schooling in it, which it appears Hildegard did not receive. Their legacy is a creation which is both unique and prophetic.

This so-called "Sybil of the Rhine" regarded none of her work as her own creation. She lacked all "assuredness of competence," allowing herself to be a vessel for God "to make it envision wondrous things and sing of them in manifold ways." Today, over 900 years since her birth, it is generally agreed that Hildegard suffered from migraines and that her "visions" were a result. Though that conclusion can remove some of the mystique, it does not diminish the power of her achievement. That she transcended gender boundaries, overcame language and music deficiencies, and created a body of work that echoes across a millennium is testament to her stature as a great composer and thinker.

Vocal
Symphonia harmonie celestium revelationem (Symphony of the Harmony of the Heavenly Revelations) (selections)
what to buy: [*Hildegard von Bingen: Heavenly Revelations*; Jeremy Summerly, cond.; Oxford Camerata, choir] (Naxos 8.550998) ♪ ♪ ♪ ♪

This is a beautifully done selection of hymns, sequences, antiphons, responsories, and the Procession from *Ordo virtutum*.

Symphoniae: Spiritual Songs [Sequentia, ensemble] (Deutsche Harmonia Mundi 77020) ♪ ♪ ♪ ♪

Superb performances, well recorded and reasonably priced, make this a fine sampler of Sequentia's performances of this most inspirational music.

worth searching for: [M.-Immaculata Ritscher, OSB, cond.; Schola der Benediktinerinnenabtei St. Hildegard Rudesheim-Eibingen, ensemble] (Bayer Records BR 100116) ♪ ♪ ♪ ♪

This is a very loving compilation of songs from the *Symphonia* and three pieces from *Ordo virtutum*. The selections are wonderfully sung, and a booklet provides extensive notes on Hildegard's life and works.

Ordo virtutum
what to buy: [Sequentia, ensemble] (Deutsche Harmonia Mundi 77394) ♪ ♪ ♪ ♪

If you want to get the complete *Ordo virtutum*, you won't go wrong with this two-disc set from 1997. Sequentia is one of the best groups performing this type of music, and they are in top form here.

various works
worth searching for: *900 Years—Hildegard von Bingen* [Sequentia, ensemble] (Deutsche Harmonia Mundi 77505) ♪ ♪ ♪ ♪ ♪

Released to coincide with the 900th anniversary of Hildegard's birth, this eight-disc boxed compilation is as complete as possible and breathtaking in its scope. The whole of *Symphonia harmonie celestium revelationem* and *Ordo virtutum* are presented in marvelous performances. A wondrous achievement.

influences: Gregorian Chant, Minnesingers, Perotin

Frank Retzel

Paul Hindemith
Born November 16, 1895, in Hanau, near Frankfurt, Germany. Died December 28, 1963, in Frankfurt, Germany.

period: Twentieth century

One of the most important composers of the 20th century, Hindemith created a style that was dramatic, lyrical, and accessible. His teaching helped form many composers, instilling in them a delight in their craft. His own best-known orchestral works are the symphony *Mathis der Maler*, on themes from his opera of the same name, and the *Symphonic Metamorphosis on Themes by Carl Maria von Weber*.

Hindemith's music-loving father was intent on his three children becoming professional musicians, and Paul began regular violin lessons by the age of nine. In 1907 the talented boy entered the Hoch Conservatory in Frankfurt, where he would remain as a scholarship student until 1917, studying composition and becoming an accomplished performer on violin, viola, clarinet, and piano. By 1915 he was second violin in his teacher Adolf Rebner's string quartet and deputy concertmaster of the Frankfurt Opera Orchestra. Two years later he was promoted to concertmaster. He further helped supplement his family's meager income by taking part in the important series of "Museum Concerts" conducted by Willem Mengelberg. After the death of his father (as a soldier in World War I), Hindemith was drafted into the army himself and ended up serving in both a military band and a string quartet organized by his commanding officer.

After the war came the turning point in his career with a successful concert in 1919, organized by Hindemith and devoted entirely to his own music. The important firm of Schott offered to publish his works. It was to remain his publisher for life. At this time he also rejoined the Rebner Quartet (now as violist) and opera orchestra, and in 1921 he returned to the Museum Concerts, now directed by Wilhelm Furtwängler, with such distinguished guests as Bruno Walter and Fritz Busch. All three of these prominent conductors would become staunch supporters of the budding composer. Hindemith was able to indulge in his passion for performing new music as a member (from 1921–29) of the Amar-Hindemith Quartet, one of the leading chamber ensembles of its day, initially formed in order to play Hindemith's own String Quartet no.2, which had been rejected as too difficult by the group originally scheduled to perform it. Although his compositions were already being heard more widely and frequently, it was the introduction of the Second Quartet in 1921 at the influential Donaueschingen Festival for contemporary music and the *Kammermusik no. 1* for small orchestra at the following year's festival that firmly established Hindemith's reputation as Germany's leading young composer. This period also saw the initial version of his song cycle *Das Marienleben (The Life of Mary)* for soprano and piano, based on poetry by Rainier Maria Rilke.

His successes led to Hindemith's appointment to teach composition at the Berlin Hochschule für Musik in 1927. He also taught an evening course for amateurs at the Volksmusikschule Neu-Kölln, which gave him a heightened sense "of the danger of an esoteric isolationism in music." His solution: *Gebrauchsmusik*—music composed with a specific purpose. "Utility music," "workaday music," however translated, it means music designed for practical use by amateurs (*Hausmusik*). The composer contributed works in every conceivable setting and for players (and perhaps listeners) of varying abilities, in the hope that he could reduce the gap between amateur and professional.

With the coming to power of the National Socialist party in 1933, the composer's days in Germany were numbered. Although Hindemith was not Jewish, his wife and many of his close associates were. Furtwängler, who had conducted the premiere of *Mathis der Maler* in 1934, was enraged by the official boycott of Hindemith's music announced earlier that year and came to the composer's defense, but to no avail. Hindemith then had to endure a forced "leave of absence" from the Hochschule in 1935. With the Nazis working vigorously to "purify" music by driving out "undesirables" (read: Jews and

modernist composers), Hindemith and his family emigrated to Switzerland in 1938 before moving to New York City in 1940. Europe's loss was America's gain as Hindemith made the rounds of universities, finally settling for more than a decade (1940–53) at Yale where he taught composition, harmony, and theory, and directed the Yale Collegium Musicum. He also held the Charles Eliot Norton chair at Harvard from 1949–50, and his lectures there were published as the now classic *A Composer's World*. In 1951, he divided his teaching between Yale and Zurich universities, finally moving permanently to Switzerland in 1953. After 1955 he devoted himself to composing and conducting.

In the three volumes of *Unterweisung im Tonsatz*, (the first two volumes of which were published in English as *The Craft of Musical Composition*), Hindemith developed a theory and method for composition, and revised many of his early works to make them conform to his concept of "broadened tonality." For all of his teaching and theories, however, he did not establish a "school of composition" in the sense of Arnold Schoenberg and the legions of his serialist followers. But Hindemith's unique feeling for harmony and consonance-dissonance relationships, craftsmanship, and neoclassic sensibilities would influence many—both those who studied with him and those who became entranced by his style. By the time of his death in 1963, many of his works were considered classics. Compositions such as the symphony from *Mathis der Maler*, the *Symphonic Metamorphosis of Themes of Weber*, *Ludus tonalis*, *Das Marienleben*, and many of his sonatas and chamber works have remained in the repertory of major orchestras and chamber ensembles even as the composer's influence has been eclipsed.

Orchestral
Mathis der Maler for Orchestra
what to buy: [*Paul Hindemith: Orchestral Works, Vol. 5*; Werner Andreas Albert, cond.; Sydney Symphony Orchestra] (CPO 999008) ♪ ♪ ♪ ♪¼

Marvelous playing is the hallmark of this recording and the entire series of Hindemith works on CPO. The album also includes the composer's *Symphonia Serena* and the prelude to his requiem based on Walt Whitman's text, *When Lilacs Last in the Dooryard Bloom'd*.

worth searching for: [Herbert von Karajan, cond.; Berlin Philharmonic Orchestra] (EMI Classics 69242) ♪ ♪ ♪ ♪ ♪

Here is an earlier recording of this masterpiece, coupled with Béla Bartók's *Music for Strings, Percussion and Celesta*. Both compositions are stunning and Karajan and the Berlin Philharmonic play them for all they're worth!

Symphonic Metamorphosis on Themes of Carl Maria von Weber

what to buy: [*Paul Hindemith: Orchestral Works, Vol. 1*; Werner Andreas Albert, cond., Queensland Symphony Orchestra] (CPO 999004) ♪ ♪ ♪ ♪⅛

This is another in the fine series of performances under Albert's direction. Included in this volume are a few more Hindemith gems: two ballets (*Amor und Psyche* and *Nobilissima Visione*), along with a set of orchestral variations, the *Philharmonische Konzert*.

Chamber
Ludus tonalis for Piano

what to buy: [John McCabe, piano] (Hyperion 66824) ♪ ♪ ♪ ♪

Hindemith's cycle of twenty-four preludes and fugues is in the same vein as those by Johann Sebastian Bach as well as works by Frédéric Chopin and Dmitri Shostakovich. McCabe's playing is very fine indeed, with a sure touch and sense of abandon. The album also includes the Suite for Piano, op. 26—*1922*.

Sonata in F Major for Viola and Piano, op. 11, no. 4

what to buy: [*Sonatas for Viola/Piano and Solo Viola*; Kim Kashkashian, viola; Robert Levin, piano] (ECM 21330) ♪ ♪ ♪ ♪

Hindemith the violist is at the heart of this music. The score is filled with challenges for the performer but it doesn't neglect the ears of the listener either. Kashkashian and Levin are admirable advocates for this and the other works on this two-disc set. Especially wonderful are the four sonatas Hindemith wrote for solo viola, pieces in which Kashkashian luxuriates without sacrificing their essential muscularity.

Vocal
Das Marienleben, op. 27

what to buy: [Roxolana Roslak, soprano; Glenn Gould, piano] (Sony Classical 52674) ♪ ♪ ♪ ♪⅛

This cycle (after Rilke) is utterly charming, and the per-

Jascha Heifetz:
A former student of the noted Russian pedagogue Leopold Auer, Jascha Heifetz supplanted Fritz Kreisler as the virtuoso with whom all other early twentieth century violinists were compared. While Kreisler's interpretive strengths (particularly with regard to tonal production) often outweighed his technical handling of the materials, Heifetz's oft-lauded technical skills sometimes blinded listeners to his interpretive abilities even as they praised the speed of his vibrato and his impressive command of the bow.

Heifetz first concertized in the United States on October 29, 1917, when he was sixteen years old. On his program that evening were Henryk Wieniawski's formidable Concerto no. 2 in D Minor for Violin and Orchestra, the last of Nicolò Paganini's twenty-four *Caprices* for solo violin, and a number of other technically challenging works. In a post-concert review by Richard Aldrich of the *New York Times*, it was noted that "Mr. Heifetz produces tone of remarkable beauty and purity; a tone of power, smoothness, and roundness, of searching expressiveness, of subtle modulation in power and color."

Valuing, as he did, Ludwig van Beethoven's violin concerto and Wolfgang Amadeus Mozart's five essays in the form, it is surprising that he did not record them more frequently. As it is, Heifetz's 1940 performance of the Beethoven concerto with Arturo Toscanini conducting the NBC Symphony Orchestra (Naxos 8.110936) is to be preferred over the stereo rendition cut in 1955 with Charles Munch leading the Boston Symphony Orchestra (RCA Living Stereo 68980), while Heifetz's 1934 rendition of Mozart's *Turkish* concerto (no. 5 in A Major, K. 219) with John Barbirolli conducting the London Philharmonic Orchestra (Naxos 8.110941) is very impressive.

In many ways, the biggest bang for the buck comes with the five-CD set *Heifetz: The Concerto Collection* (RCA Victor Gold Seal 61779), which contains not only the Beethoven concerto with Munch but a battery of performances dating from 1959 through 1970 that include Heifetz's truly impressive version of Jean Sibelius's concerto (with Walter Hendl and the Chicago Symphony Orchestra) and similar works by Piotr Tchaikovsky, Johannes Brahms, Felix Mendelssohn, Sergei Prokofiev, Max Bruch, Henrí Vieuxtemps, Johann Sebastian Bach, and, to top it off, Mozart's *Sinfonia concertante*.

Heifetz was also a consummate chamber music player and, with Artur Rubinstein and Gregor Piatigorsky, created one of the great piano trios of the mid-twentieth century. Their vintage 1950 performances of the Ravel and Tchaikovsky trios (*Rubinstein Collection: Vol. 25*, RCA Victor Red Seal 63025) are quite arresting.

Mathilde August

formance matches its wide range of expression. Listen also to the fine songs by Ernst Krenek and Richard Strauss that are also included.

influences: Richard Strauss, Igor Stravinsky, Aaron Copland, Benjamin Britten

Frank Retzel and Garaud MacTaggart

Gustav Holst

Born Gustavus Theodore von Holst, September 21, 1874, in Cheltenham, England. Died May 25, 1934, in London, England.

period: Twentieth century

Holst was a highly original composer and influential teacher who made a substantial contribution to music-making in England during the first 30 years of the 20th century. While he is best known for his symphonic suite *The Planets,* many of his other works have something of the visionary qualities found in Ralph Vaughan Williams's output, although Holst's fascination with Hindu philosophy and literature served to distinguish him from his great friend and contemporary.

Gustav Holst originally intended to become a concert pianist, but severe neuritis in his right arm compelled him to abandon this idea, and he eventually took up the trombone. He entered the Royal College of Music in London in 1893, although he already had practical experience as an instrumentalist and conductor through working with small choirs around his native Cheltenham. In that same year he met Ralph Vaughan Williams and the two budding composers became lifelong friends and colleagues. Partly as a result of this friendship, Holst became deeply interested in English folksong, which was to be a great influence on his later works, particularly his setting of words to music. Meanwhile, he had developed into a fine trombonist and supported himself in his student days by playing in various theaters and music halls.

The aspiring composer finally began his illustrious teaching career in 1903, just two years prior to becoming Music Master at the St. Paul's School for Girls in west London, a position Holst was to hold for the remainder of his life. He also joined the staff of London's Morley College (in 1907) and eventually returned to the Royal College of Music as a teacher (in 1919). His pioneering teaching methods, including the revival of English choral and vocal traditions, were still influential in many English schools at the middle of the 20th century, and, as an outgrowth of his practical outlook, he wrote a great deal of music for his students to sing and play.

His suite for large orchestra, *The Planets* (the work by which Holst is still best known), was first performed privately in an unfinished form at the Royal College of Music under Adrian Boult in 1918. Two years later the work received its first complete public performance. It was an immediate and enormous triumph, and its popularity has not waned to this day. Holst was always bewildered by this success, as he felt he had written far finer pieces, including *The Hymn of Jesus* and *Ode to Death.* His fame began to wane a bit towards the end of the 1920s, and even though many of his compositions from this time were greeted with a certain reserve by some friends and admirers (Vaughan Williams among them), Holst was writing music that anticipated a number of the trends embodied by the next generation of composers. In many ways the years from 1927 to 1933 were (for him) his best time as a composer: his music was by then no longer in vogue, and freed from the pressures of popularity he could relax, contemplate, and pursue other interests.

Throughout his career Holst tended to write for large instrumental and choral forces, composing little in the way of chamber music. There is also no doubt that his great interest in Hindu philosophy and literature served a double duty, inspiring a variety of fascinating operas and choral works and influencing his remarkable ability to write slow, contemplative music which can seem almost timeless.

Orchestral
The Planets for Orchestra, op. 32
what to buy: [Charles Dutoit, cond.; Montreal Symphony Orchestra; Montreal Symphony Choir] (Penguin Classics 460606) ♪ ♪ ♪ ♪

With so many fine recordings of this amazing work available, any choice is bound to be highly subjective, but for a combination of inspired, idiomatic conducting and stunning recorded sound, this disc is hard to beat. Toss in the fact that this is available at a budget price, and it becomes even more attractive.

Suites for Symphonic Band, op. 28
what to buy: [Frederick Fennell, cond.; Cleveland Symphonic Winds] (Telarc 80038) ♪ ♪ ♪ ♪♪

These two wonderful suites are among the finest works ever created for band, and this is arguably the finest recording of them ever made, aided by truly hair-raising, knockout sound. Handel's *Music for the Royal Fireworks* and an arrangement of part of Bach's organ Fantasia in G major (BWV 572) round out the program.

Vocal

The Hymn of Jesus for orchestra, female semi-chorus and chorus, op. 37

what to buy: [Richard Hickox, cond.; London Symphony Orchestra; London Symphony Chorus] (Chandos 2406) ♪ ♪ ♪♪

This is Holst's greatest choral work, and it is presented here alongside a fine selection of his other works in the genre, including the premiere recording of his *The Cloud Messenger*, op. 30 with mezzo-soprano Della Jones in the solo spotlight. The performances under Hickox's direction are impassioned and powerful, and the sound of this double-disc set is full, rich, and finely detailed.

influences: Frederick Delius, Hamilton Harty, Ralph Vaughan Williams

Charles Greenwell and Dave Wagner

Arthur Honegger

Born March 10, 1892, in Le Havre, France. Died November 27, 1955, in Paris France.

period: Twentieth century

Even though he was born and died in France, Arthur Honegger (along with Frank Martin) is considered Switzerland's most important twentieth-century composer. His most notable works—the short and powerful orchestral movement *Pacific 231*, the dramatic oratorio *Le Roi David*, and the third of his five symphonies—display a rigorous intellect and a slowly developing sense of power and grace.

Both of Honegger's parents were Swiss citizens from Zurich, even though they were living in France at the time of his birth. While the bulk of his early musical training took place in France, Honegger also spent two years at the Zurich Conservatory before returning in 1911 to complete his studies at the Paris Conservatory. During the First World War, Honegger—along with Georges Auric, Germaine Tailleferre, Francis Poulenc, Louis Durey, and Darius Milhaud—was involved with Eric Satie and Jean Cocteau in efforts to promote new music. They were dubbed "Les Six" by the writer Henri Collet in 1921, but besides their youth, their French residency, and their sense of musical adventure, the similarities among these six young composers were few. Honegger was probably the most serious-minded of the group, musically speaking and otherwise, and his relationship with Satie, whose well-developed sense of irony was foreign to the young Swiss's sensibilities, foundered. By 1923, Honegger was composing music substantially different from that created by the rest of Les Six.

Even though his training was basically French (Charles-Marie Widor and Vincent d'Indy were among his teachers), Honegger's writing reflected a heady blend of German (Richard Strauss and Max Reger) and French (Claude Debussy and Gabriel Fauré) influences. In 1923 he finished two of his most enduring compositions, the dramatic oratorio *Le Roi David* and the short but powerful *Pacific 231*. The former work was based on incidental music he had written in 1921 for a play based on the biblical King David, while the score for *Pacific 231* is thought by some to depict a steam locomotive gradually moving from zero to full speed and back to zero again. In an interview with Bernard Gavoty, Honegger noted the disparity between what people believed and what he actually intended. According to Honegger, "So many, many critics have so minutely described the onrush of my locomotive across the great spaces that it would be inhuman to disabuse them!" Even though he named the piece after a locomotive, he said he had merely meant to give "the impression of a mathematical acceleration of rhythm, while the movement itself slowed." While the oratorio has plenty of musical merit, it was the six-and-a-half-minute *Pacific 231* that became Honegger's single most performed score, often diverting attention away from his larger-scaled works.

A pacifist by nature, Honegger was deeply affected by the horrors of World War II. His second symphony (commissioned by Paul Sacher, founder of the Basel Chamber Orchestra) was a somber piece for string orchestra written in 1941 during the Nazi occupation of Paris. The next symphony (subtitled *Liturgique*) was finished in 1946 and, according to Honegger, reflects "a drama in which three actors play happiness, unhappiness and man." Sacher also commissioned the composer's fourth symphony, a work Honegger completed the same year as the more tragic third symphony. Loosely based on folk tunes he heard while vacationing in Switzerland, Honegger's pleasant melodies provide a contrast with the war-torn fabric of the composer's other symphonies.

Orchestral

Pacific 231

what to buy: [Leonard Bernstein, cond.; New York

Arthur Honegger

Philharmonic Orchestra] (Sony Classical 62352) ♪ ♪ ♪ ♪

Bernstein's interpretations usually have plenty of drive, making his take on this little power bonbon a natural. Other pieces on the album include Albert Roussel's Symphony no. 3, Milhaud's incidental music for *Les Choëphores,* and the second of Honegger's three *Mouvement symphonique* pieces, "Rugby."

what to buy next: [David Zinman, cond.; Tonhalle-Orchester, Zürich] (Decca 455352) ♪ ♪ ♪ ♪

Zinman is blessed with better sonics than Bernstein, and that makes his version of this orchestral powerhouse seem even more intimidating. All three of the *Mouvement symphonique* works are heard here, but they are sandwiched around solid interpretations of Honegger's Symphony no. 2, *Monopartita,* and the *Pastorale d'été.*

Symphony no. 3—*Liturgique*
what to buy: [Herbert von Karajan, cond.; Berlin Philharmonic Orchestra] (Deutsche Grammophon 447435) ♪ ♪ ♪ ♪₄

Disciplined, dense and dynamic are three good ways to describe this performance, and it is difficult to imagine a better version of Honegger's most intense work. This disc also includes a fine rendition of the composer's second symphony (a place where the BPO string section can really shine) and a rhythmically charged take on Igor Stravinsky's Concerto in D Major for String Orchestra.

worth searching for: [Paul Sacher, cond.; Basler Sinfonie-Orchester] (Pan Classics 510053) ♪ ♪ ♪₄

Sacher's association with the composer gives this all-Honegger recording extra cachet, but the string section isn't quite as polished as von Karajan's. Still, this is a credible set, and the accompanying works (*Chant de*

Joie and *Horace Victorieux*) are worth adding to your library.

Vocal
Le Roi David
what to buy: [Jean Desailly, narrator; Simone Valere, narrator; Christine Eda-Pierre, soprano; Jeannine Collard, contralto; Eric Tappy, tenor; Charles Dutoit, cond.; Ensemble Instrumental, orch.; Chorale Philippe Caillard, choir] (Erato 45800) ♪ ♪ ♪ ♪

Dutoit and his musicians get right to the heart of this piece. The pacing is superb, the choir is great, and the orchestral playing is top-notch. The use of a boy sopra-no for the brief role of David as a youth is a wonderful dramatic touch that's missing from other recordings of this work.

what to buy next: [Lambert Wilson, narrator; Yvette Théraulaz, narrator; Brigitte Fournier, soprano; Felicity Palmer, contralto; John Elwes, tenor; Michel Corboz, cond.; Gulbenkian Orchestra and Chorus] (Cascavelle 1017) ♪ ♪ ♪⅔

The female soloists here outshine those on any other recording of this piece, but everyone else is merely good, and that isn't enough to give this disc a top rec-ommendation. Still, Corboz is a decent conductor, and the orchestra-chorus combination is solid.

influences: Frank Martin, Albert Jenny, Bernard Schulé

Gary Barton and Ian Palmer

Alan Hovhaness
Born Alan Hovhaness Chakmakjian, March 8, 1911, in Somerville, MA. Died June 21, 2000, in Seattle, WA.

period: Twentieth century

Self-taught and prolific are probably the best words to describe Alan Hovhaness. Although he studied music at the New England Conservatory of Music and Tanglewood, he never acquired an academic degree, ultimately preferring to find his own way in the musical world. His interest in pan-Asian musical forms and the rhythms of his Armenian heritage guided him in a total-ly new direction, meshing principles from the Western classical music tradition with elements from the East to create a unique, personal synthesis.

Hovhaness started composing when he was four years old, picking out tunes on the family harmonium. He wrote a lullaby for violin and piano when he was 11, revising it four years later and including it in his budding oeuvre as op. 1. After graduating from high school in 1929, he attended Tufts University for two years before going to the New England Conservatory of Music. It was around this time that he changed his middle name to Hovaness (in honor of his grandfather), then dropped Chakmakjian, his last name, and (for unknown reasons) added an "h" to his new patronymic.

At the New England Conservatory he took composition and theory classes with Frederick Converse, a respected American composer who had studied in Europe with Joseph Rheinberger in 1896 but in his later years was beginning to experiment with jazz rhythms, bitonality, and dissonant chords. Hovhaness then received a schol-arship to the Berkshire Music Center at Tanglewood, where he worked briefly with the great Czech composer-in-exile, Bohuslav Martinu but ran afoul of Aaron Copland and Leonard Bernstein, both of whom vigorous-ly disparaged a performance of Hovhaness's First Symphony. This last event affected the young composer deeply, and he decided to destroy a great many of his early compositions and start anew. Back in Boston, while working at a series of jobs including jazz arranger with the Works Progress Administration and organist for a local Armenian church, he began studying non-European music. He was fascinated by the rhythms, col-ors, and melodic contours he heard in the Armenian, Jewish, and Asian traditions, and these would continue to intrigue him become a major influence in his scores.

A pivotal moment came about with his introduction to the Armenian folk singer, Yenouk Der Hagopian, in the early 1940s. After destroying (for the second time) much of the music he wrote during the 1920s and 1930s, Hovhaness managed to secure performances of a new batch of compositions in 1944, including his opera *Etchmiadzin* and the *Armenian Rhapsody no. 1*. He left Boston and attempted to make a living in New York City, fulfilling a commission from Martha Graham for music to a ballet (*Ardent Song*) but generating little else in the way of income. Returning to Massachusetts, he man-aged to get a job teaching at the Boston Conservatory of Music in 1948.

During the next decade Hovhaness began to find recognition, securing two Guggenheim Foundation fellowships and a commission from the conductor Leopold Stokowski for what would turn out to be one of his most popular works, his Symphony no. 2, *Mysterious Mountain*. In 1959, Hovhaness was the beneficiary of a Fulbright Research fellowship which enabled him to travel to India where he studied South Indian music; he also visited Japan and made an extensive investigation of Gagaku orchestral music and learned to play a variety of traditional Japanese instruments.

By the late 1960s Hovhaness had produced an amazing number of compositions, most of them not given opus number until the conductor Leopold Stokowski suggested that he do so. Numbers were given to most of the surviving early scores approximating their order of composition, with some unfortunately being assigned more than once. A piano piece from 1930 (*Dance Gazhal*) ended up as op. 362, while the 1961 arrangement of *The Lord's Prayer* was designated op. 35. Not until the late 1970s were his compositions more accurately numbered.

It is difficult to assess the entire Hovhaness canon properly since its sheer bulk (over 60 symphonies, a multitude of sonatas for different instruments, a veritable plethora of songs and choral works, etc.) is the product of a man driven, since the 1930s, to compose in abundance. His ability to turn out music in vast quantities may indeed be unparalleled in modern times. That much of it still sustains interest today is a tribute to his art.

Orchestral
Symphony no. 2, op. 132—*Mysterious Mountain*
what to buy: [Fritz Reiner, cond.; Chicago Symphony Orchestra] (RCA Victor 61957) ♪ ♪ ♪ ♪₵

"Definitive" is a word that should not be used lightly but in this case it applies. Reiner's version of this seductive score, recorded in the late 1950s, is unlikely to be bettered. The sound in this recording and in the accompanying works by Igor Stravinsky (*The Fairy's Kiss: Divertimento*) and Sergei Prokofiev (the suite from *Lieutenant Kijé*) is top-notch and belies its age.

what to buy next: [Gerard Schwarz, cond.; Seattle Symphony Orchestra] (Delos 3157) ♪ ♪ ♪₵

This all-Hovhaness disc includes his most popular scores and is well recorded and played by Schwarz and the SSO. Not only is there a good version of *Mysterious Mountain*, but you get exemplary performances of his *Celestial Fantasy*, the *Prayer of St. Gregory* (with Charles Butler as the trumpet soloist), *and* the environmentalist favorite from 1970, *And God Created Great Whales*, which weaves recorded whale songs into an orchestral tapestry.

[John T. Williams, cond.; London Symphony Orchestra] (Sony Classics 62729) ♪ ♪ ♪₵

Film composer and pops conductor John Williams gives an admirable, if briskly paced, performance of the Hovhaness symphony, but the main work on this disc is Williams's own Bassoon Concerto, *The Five Sacred Trees*, marvelously played by soloist Judith LeClair. The other music heard here is by Toru Takemitsu (*Tree Line*) and Tobias Picker (*Old and Lost Rivers*).

Prayer of St. Gregory for trumpet and string orchestra, op. 626
what to buy: [*Celestial Gate*; Benny Wiame, trumpet; Rudolf Werthen, cond.; I Fiamminghi, orch.] (Telarc 80392) ♪ ♪ ♪ ♪₵

Setting a fluid trumpet solo against gossamer string writing, Hovhaness created this short but beautiful work as an intermezzo for a religious opera, and, at the very least, it cries out for use in a soundtrack. The playing of I Fiamminghi throughout this album is lush, especially on the *Alleluia and Fugue* for string orchestra, the Concerto no. 7 for orchestra, and what may be the definitive version of the composer's sixth symphony, *Celestial Gate*.

what to buy next: [John Wilbraham, trumpet; Alan Hovhaness, cond.; Polyphonia Orchestra] (Crystal 807) ♪ ♪ ♪₵

The composer as conductor doesn't linger over this work's beauty, bringing it in at 4:22—more than a minute faster than Werthen. While Wilbraham is a knockout trumpeter with a well-deserved reputation as a virtuoso, Hovhaness's tempos leave him sounding hurried. Werthen and Schwarz are preferable. Although all the performances on this disc sound under-rehearsed, those of Symphony no. 25 (*Odysseus*) and Symphony no. 6 (*Celestial Gate*) are quite satisfactory.

Concerto for Harp and String Orchestra, op. 267
what to buy: [*Music of Alan Hovhaness*; Yolanda Kondonassis, harp; Rudolf Werthen, cond.; I Fiamminghi, orch.] (Telarc 80530) ♪ ♪ ♪₵

The only orchestral work on this lovely album is a splendid, atmospheric addition to the harp and orchestra catalog. The rest of the program is devoted to the composer's more intimate settings for the harp including *The Garden of Adonis* for flute and harp (with Eugenia Zukerman), the engaging Sonata for Harp, op. 127, *Upon Enchanted Ground* (a piece for flute, cello, tam-tam, and harp), and the world premiere of *Spirit of Trees,* a sonata for harp and guitar (with David Leisner). The only thing missing here is Hovhaness's Suite for Harp, op. 270—a piece that Kondonassis recorded on her album, *Sky Music* (Telarc 80418).

influences: Lou Harrison, Dominick Argento

Ian Palmer

Herbert Howells

Born Herbert Norman Howells, October 17, 1892, in Lydney, Gloucestershire, England. Died February 24, 1983, in Oxford, England.

period: Twentieth century

Herbert Howells was a much-loved composer, teacher, and writer who at one time held great promise as a composer. He is regarded today as a distinguished minor master in the great English pastoral tradition, a composer more respected than performed. Howells's best known compositions are choral works such as the *Hymnus Paradisi* and the Fantasia for Cello and Orchestra.

In 1912, Howells received a scholarship to the Royal College of Music in London, where he studied composition with Charles Stanford. His talents were such that only months after his enrollment, a major Mass setting of his was performed in Westminster Abbey; within a year, his First Piano Concerto received its initial hearing. After graduation, Howells was appointed to a position as organist at Salisbury Cathedral, but a serious illness kept him from performing his duties. For a time, family and friends feared he would die, but Howells recovered and returned to the Royal College in 1920 as a teacher of composition, a post he would hold for over half a century. From 1936 to 1962, he was also director of music at the prestigious St. Paul's Girls' School in the West London district of Hammersmith, succeeding another famous English composer/teacher, Gustav Holst. In 1950, he was appointed King Edward VII Professor of Music at London University.

Until 1935, Howells was widely considered to be potentially the next great English composer, but his life was devastated by tragedy that year when his nine-year-old son died of spinal meningitis. Howells never recovered, either personally or professionally, and no matter how fine his later compositions may have been, something substantial was missing. Three years later, in an attempt to come to terms with his grief, Howells produced what is generally considered to be his greatest work, the *Hymnus Paradisi*. The piece is an intense, deeply moving requiem of extraordinary depth and power. Howells withheld the work for many years, first allowing it to be performed in 1950 at the urging of his friend, the great composer Ralph Vaughan Williams. In 1964, Howells wrote another unusual requiem, an a cappella motet entitled *Take Him, Earth, for Cherishing,* mourning the death of President John F. Kennedy.

Howells's musical idiom is an amalgam of English styles and influences from the late nineteenth to the mid-twentieth century. It is essentially a pastoral, nature-based idiom in the tradition of Edward Elgar and Ralph Vaughan Williams; the bulk of his output is for chorus, strongly influenced by the great English choral tradition. Given his predilection for vocal writing, it is not surprising that his melodies were vocal in character, even when written for instruments. Howells's music, while unfailingly eloquent, is often subtle and restrained, with some of his later works exhibiting an almost mystical undertone. The majority of his church music was written relatively late (in the 1940s and early 1950s), and many of the other choral works for which he is most highly regarded were written after that. Howells has one other minor distinction: he was one of the only twentieth-century composers anywhere to write for the early keyboard instrument known as the clavichord. In some of the little miniatures written for that obsolete instrument, he seems to be paying homage to English composers and performers of the Elizabethan era.

Orchestral
Fantasia for Cello and Orchestra.
what to buy: [*Orchestral Works, Vol. 1*; Moray Welsh, cello; Richard Hickox, cond.; London Symphony Orchestra] (Chandos 9410) ♪ ♪ ♪

All the essential elements of Howells's music can be found in this lovely collection, which contains six of his short orchestral works. Included, along with a fine performance of the Fantasia for Cello and Orchestra, are several first-ever recordings. All the pieces here are performed affectionately and recorded with a warm, glowing sound.

Vocal
Hymnus Paradisi for Soprano, Tenor, Orchestra, and Chorus
what to buy: [Julie Kennard, soprano; John Mark Ainsley, tenor; Vernon Handley, cond.; Royal Liverpool Philharmonic Orchestra; Royal Liverpool Philharmonic Chorus] (Hyperion 66488) ♪ ♪ ♪ ♪

This is arguably the finest recording ever of the *Hymnus Paradisi,* which Handley and his forces interpret with great compassion and tenderness, beautifully bringing out the pathos and mysticism inherent in the work. Also included is Howells's *An English Mass.* The recorded sound on both works is beautifully balanced and immediate.

Requiem for Solo Voices, Orchestra, and Chorus
what to buy: [Matthew Best, cond.; Corydon Singers] (Hyperion 66076) ♪ ♪ ♪♪

Best gives us a fine recording that, in addition to the Requiem, also includes Howells's motet on the death of President John F. Kennedy (*Take Him, Earth, for Cherishing*) and two choral works by Vaughan Williams: the Mass in G Minor and the Te Deum in G Major. Listeners will enjoy the fine, clear sound made possible by remarkably refined acoustics.

worth searching for: [*Sacred Choral Works*; Nicholas Cleobury, cond.; Choir of King's College, Cambridge] (London 430205) ♪ ♪ ♪ ♪

This superb disc presents a number of Howells's liturgical works, sequenced as they would be performed in an actual service. These pieces, all inspired by the King's College Choir, will provide a rewarding experience even for those who don't normally listen to Anglican church music.

influences: Gerald Finzi, George Butterworth, Ralph Vaughan Williams

Charles Greenwell and David Wagner

Johann Nepomuk Hummel
Born November 14, 1778, in Pressburg, Austria. Died October 17, 1837, in Weimar, Germany.

period: Classical

Johann Nepomuk Hummel was a brilliant pianist and generally regarded as the last great composer of the Classical era, but he was also a prominent teacher whose students included such pianistic luminaries of the day as Sigismund Thalberg and Adolf Henselt. While he was a prolific writer of operas, choral works, chamber music and symphonic fare, Hummel's current claim to fame rests with his popular Concerto in E-flat Major for Trumpet and Orchestra, although his piano concertos and chamber music are generally more representative of how his music bridged the gap from Franz Joseph Haydn and Wolfgang Amadeus Mozart to Frédéric Chopin and Ludwig van Beethoven.

Hummel studied with some of the greatest names in music. He was one of Mozart's favorite piano pupils, and there were also organ studies with Franz Joseph Haydn (who warned that too much organ playing would ruin his piano technique!), vocal lessons with Antonio Salieri, and counterpoint courses from Johann Albrechtsberger (Beethoven's teacher). Having thus embraced (and been embraced by) the elegance and balance typifying the works of Haydn and Mozart, Hummel could not find it within himself to break with the classical tradition and follow the more radical compositional path being trod by Beethoven at that time.

He began his career as a child prodigy at the age of nine and, a couple of years later, embarked on a highly successful concert tour of Britain, the Netherlands, and Germany. By 1803, Hummel was a fairly popular piano teacher and was attempting to learn the art of composition. It was about this time that Haydn recommended his former student for the position of Konzertmeister with the Esterházy court at Eisenstadt, Hungary. Despite this steady employment, Hummel's years with the Esterházys were not happy ones. Part of the problem was his writing scores for a variety of outside interests when the Prince was under the impression that Hummel's works were to remain with the Esterházys. Hummel's contract was finally terminated in 1811, freeing the composer from those responsibilities and enabling him to seek his fortune in Vienna.

Hummel's time there was concurrent with the emergence of Beethoven, whose powerful personal and musical presence severely tested Hummel's self-confidence. A rivalry between the two men was eagerly established by the Viennese musical establishment.

However, the two were generally able to maintain friendly contact throughout their lives, with Hummel even performing as a percussionist in 1814 for the first performance of Beethoven's *Wellington's Victory*. That was also the year that Hummel returned to an active concert career; his playing once again caused a sensation that catapulted him into celebrity. Following a highly successful series of recitals and a short and unhappy stay in Stuttgart as Hofkapellmeister (1816—1818), Hummel landed a very secure position as Kapellmeister in the Grand Ducal estates at Weimar. Financial security was finally his in this new position, and he settled into a comfortable bourgeois existence which provided him with the plentiful musical resources of Weimar and three months of the year off for composing and touring. It was also there that Hummel became the most highly paid teacher in Europe. Using an excellent business sense, he was instrumental in reforming the copyright laws in Austria and Germany, encouraging musicians and composers to organize and protect their interests. It is interesting to note at this juncture that Hummel's greatest fiscal success came not through his ventures as a composer or performer, but rather through the publication of his three-volume piano method, *Ausführlich theoretisch-practische Anweisung zum Piano-forte Spiel (Detailed Theoretical and Practical Instruction in Pianoforte Performance)*, which sold more than a thousand copies during its first week on sale.

A series of concert tours in the 1830s confirmed that Hummel's musical and pianistic skills were in decline; when he died in 1837, his funeral featured a performance of Mozart's *Requiem,* a tribute not only to him but, some say, to the passing of the classical era.

**Concerto for Trumpet and Orchestra in E-flat Major
what to buy:** [Gerard Schwarz, trumpet; Gerard Schwarz, cond.; New York Chamber Symphony Orchestra] (Delos 3001) ♪ ♪ ♪ ♪₄

A big, full, resonant sound marks Schwarz's playing in this most frequently performed Hummel concerto. Everything that you would expect of a sturdy classical concerto, complete with the required double exposition of the first movement, is here. This recording is coupled with Haydn's legendary Trumpet Concerto, which he wrote for Anton Weidinger—who later rewrote the Hummel Concerto and transposed it to E Major!

what to buy next: [Maurice André, trumpet; Herbert von Karajan, conductor; Berlin Philharmonic Orchestra]

Paul Hillier:
Scholar, conductor, singer, and founding member of the Hilliard Ensemble and the Theatre of Voices—two of the finest choral ensembles of the late twentieth century—Paul Hillier's musical interests span the ages with aplomb. It appears that he is as comfortable with the works of the Elizabethan genius William Byrd as he is with those of the early American composer William Billings or the minimalist excursions of Steve Reich. As this book goes to press, Hillier is not only the Director of the Early Music Institute at Indiana University but Artistic Director and Principal Conductor of the Estonian Philharmonic Chamber Choir, and Artistic Director of the Theatre of Voices.

The Hilliard Ensemble, the assemblage with which Hillier first achieved a modicum of renown, derived its name from that of Nicholas Hilliard, an Elizabethan painter of miniatures. Hillier and David James, the like-minded co-founder of the group, started the vocal quartet back in 1974, with the dual purpose of exploring pre-Baroque era music and investigating the opportunities offered by contemporary choral works and their composers. Although early music was the group's initial focus, both men had an appreciation for modern idioms, perceiving similarities in the way that some modern composers approached spiritually-oriented choral music and the way specific modes were utilized during the Medieval era. Among the many fine recordings of Medieval and Renaissance music that Hillier made with the Hilliard Ensemble were their renditions of Guillaume de Machaut's *Messe de Notre Dame* (Hyperion 66358) and, with an augmented version of the regular quartet, explorations of works by the twelfth century French choir director Pérotin (ECM 837351) and the Italian nobleman Carlos Gesualdo (*Tenebrae,* ECM 843867). In 1987, they recorded *Arbos* (ECM 831959), the initial album in a series devoted to Arvo Pärt's oeuvre.

Hillier left the group in 1980 and moved to the United States, where he taught at universities in California and Massachusetts and, in 1990, began forming the Theatre of Voices, another choral group. While not neglecting his early-music roots—as demonstrated by his recording, with the Theatre of Voices, of William Byrd's Mass for Four Voices (ECM 439172)—Hillier expanded his traversal of important twentieth century choral works to include John Cage's *Litany for the Whale* (Harmonia Mundi 907187) and Pärt's *Berliner Messe* (Harmonia Mundi 907242). In 1996 Hillier moved to Bloomington, Indiana, where he became director of Indiana University's esteemed Early Music Institute. The next year saw the publication of his biography/study of Pärt (Oxford Press, 1997), the twentieth century Estonian composer for whose work Hillier has long been an advocate.

Mathilde August

(EMI Classics 66961) ♪ ♪ ♪ ♪

Bright, cheery, and well recorded, this performance of Hummel's most popular work headlines an album featuring André—arguably one of the finest trumpeters of all time—in fine form playing concertos by Leopold Mozart, Antonio Vivaldi, and Georg Phillipp Telemann. The BPO under Karajan had a string section second to none.

[Wynton Marsalis, trumpet; Raymond Leppard, cond.; National Philharmonic Orchestra, London] (Sony Classics 37846) ♪ ♪ ♪ ♪

It's always tempting to think jazz musicians can't really play classical music and vice versa, but that isn't a fact carved in stone, as proven with Marsalis's recording here. Leppard is a marvelous conductor as well, and the two of them do a fine job of performing one of the most popular pieces for trumpet and orchestra. Leopold Mozart's one big hit is here too, as well as Franz Joseph Haydn's essay in E-flat Major for the same forces. The Haydn piece is really the most interesting work on the disc, but the Hummel concerto is more up Marsalis's alley.

Concerto in B Minor for Piano and Orchestra, op. 89

[Stephen Hough, piano; Bryden Thomson, cond.; English Chamber Orchestra] (Chandos 8507) ♪ ♪ ♪ ♪

what to buy: This is a more adventurous piece than the companion work on this set—Hummel's Piano Concerto in A Minor, op. 85—and Hough makes a fairly convincing case for its being heard more often. His technique in the finger-busting *Finale: Vivace* covers all the bases seemingly without strain, while in the *Larghetto* Thomson manages the composer's surprisingly subtle interplay between horns and piano with aplomb and turns this into one of the most moving moments in all of Hummel's scores. The A Minor concerto is a typical pianistic showpiece from the composer with a very effective first movement *Allegro moderato,* but the balance of the work is less than inspiring despite Hough's obvious talents. The set is extremely well recorded.

what to buy next: [Hae-won Chang, piano; Tamás Pál, cond.; Budapest Chamber Orchestra] (Naxos 8.550837) ♪ ♪ ♪

The tempos in this recording are more relaxed than in the Hough/Thomson set and it is also a more approachable performance, relying less on virtuosity (though Chang is more than capable in that regard) and more on the music itself. Despite this disc being a mirror image of the other album from a programming standpoint, the sound quality of the Chandos release outclasses this set while Naxos has a distinct price advantage and sonics which really aren't that bad.

Chamber
Septet in D Minor for Piano, Flute, Oboe, Horn, Viola, Cello, and Double Bass, op. 74

what to buy: [Nash Ensemble] (CRD 3344) ♪ ♪ ♪ ♪

The English-based Nash Ensemble gives a fluent, bright reading of this wonderfully balanced music, with crisp tempos and very gentle dynamic changes. Also included in this recording is the Septet in B-flat Major by Franz Berwald, who has been called the "Swedish Mozart."

what to buy next: [Capricorn, ensemble] (Hyperion 66396) ♪ ♪ ♪ ♪

The effervescent first movement *Allegro* of this work is a fine ear-catcher, but the heart of the composition lies in the second and third movements, in which Hummel allows talented musicians (like those in Capricorn) to meld their disparate instruments into a unified work of wonder. His later *Septet Militaire* (op. 114) is also featured here, but despite the best efforts of the ensemble the piece never really jells in the same way.

influences: Franz Berwald, Wolfgang Amadeus Mozart, Franz Joseph Haydn, Franz Berwald

Sharon L. Hoyer and Dave Wagner

Engelbert Humperdinck
Born September 1, 1854, in Siegburg, Germany. Died September 27, 1921 in Neustrelitz, Germany.

period: Romantic

Humperdinck worked in the shadow of the great German opera composers Richard Wagner and Richard Strauss, adopting elements of their styles and crafting them to suit his own quite different purposes. Besides composing orchestral and chamber works and much vocal music (including his enormously popular opera, *Hänsel und Gretel*), Humperdinck was also a well-respected teacher, critic, and editor.

Although Humperdinck started taking music lessons at an early age and as a schoolboy in Paderborn sang in the cathedral choir—even attempting to write operas and songs on his own—his father wanted him to pursue a more stable, lucrative profession and tried to steer him towards a career in architecture. In 1872 he rebelled against parental authority and enrolled at the Cologne Conservatory, where he studied harmony, composition, piano, cello, and organ—soaking up as much musical knowledge as he could. After completing his studies in Cologne, Humperdinck attended the Royal Music School in Munich, taking classes in counterpoint and fugue from the noted organist-composer Joseph Rheinberger. Munich was also where he first came under Wagner's spell, listening to and performing his music as a member of a club dedicated to the Bayreuth master's art, the *Order of the Grail.*

In 1878, Humperdinck was awarded the Berlin Mendelssohn Prize which enabled him to study for a year in Italy. It was there that he met Wagner, who invited the young composer to assist him in preparing the premiere of *Parsifal* at Bayreuth, where Wagner had built a theatre dedicated to the performance of his works. A close friendship developed between the two which would last for years, even if it was understood that Wagner was the genius and Humperdinck the acolyte. Leading a relatively peripatetic life after his experiences with Wagner, Humperdinck traveled to Paris, Spain, and Morocco, usually working as a teacher, before finally finding himself back in Cologne in 1886, where for a short time he taught and directed the choir at the Conservatory. The following year he moved to Mainz to edit scores for a music publisher, finally, from there eventually going to Frankfurt to join the staff of the Hoch Conservatory in 1890. By this time he had composed a great number of songs and choral works, honing his vocal writing for his next great task.

Hänsel und Gretel began as a song cycle based on the Grimm fairy tale before mutating into a singspiel and, finally, an opera. The work makes use of several folksongs, which are set to Wagnerian harmonies and orchestration to create a series of charming arias for several singers in addition to well-defined character roles he helped shape (with his sister and librettist, Adelheid Wette) for the two children. 1893 was Humperdinck's watershed year, with the initial production of *Hänsel und Gretel* being entrusted to (and conducted by) the *other* giant of German modernism, Richard Strauss. Although he was to follow this opera with nine more, none of the others have entered the active repertory. *Königskinder,* a tale constructed around a young prince, a haunted forest, and a wicked witch, went through the same evolutionary process as *Hänsel und Gretel*—from singspiel to opera—and was the closest he came to repeating the success of the earlier opera.

Humperdinck continued teaching at the Hoch Conservatory until 1897, when he retired to devote himself to composing. By 1900 he had moved to Berlin and began a stint teaching composition at the Academy of Arts (one of his students, briefly, was the American composer Charles Tomlinson Griffes) until 1920 when deteriorating health forced him to retire.

Vocal
Hänsel und Gretel
what to buy: [Elisabeth Schwarzkopf, soprano; Elisabeth Grümmer, soprano; Anny Felbermayer, soprano; Maria von Ilosvay, mezzo-soprano; Else Schürhoff, mezzo-soprano; Josef Metternich, baritone; Herbert von Karajan, cond.; Philharmonia Orchestra; Loughton High School Chorus; Bancroft's School Chorus] (EMI Classics 67145) ♪ ♪ ♪ ♪

Here is a critically praised version in which Schwarzkopf and Grümmer are expressive as well as technically adept and Karajan is fully in sympathy with the music. Although the monaural sound of this set dates from the 1950s, the quality of remastering and the immediacy of the performance are first class—and at mid-price.

influences: Otto Nicolai, Richard Wagner

Michael H. Margolin and Garaud MacTaggart

I

Jacques Ibert
Born Jacques François Antoine Marie Ibert, August 15, 1890, in Paris, France. Died February 5, 1962, in Paris, France.

period: Twentieth century

Ibert's music is consistently urbane, witty, brilliantly scored, and utterly French in its outlook. His most famous composition, *Escales (Ports of Call),* was an early orchestral travelogue that clearly established him as an heir to the orchestral color of Claude Debussy and Maurice Ravel. He also made his mark in his fluid writing for wind instruments, creating several works (the flute concerto and his *Pièces Brèves* for Wind Quintet in particular) that have become part of the standard repertoire.

Jacques Ibert studied at the Paris Conservatoire from 1910 to 1913, taking classes in harmony, counterpoint, and composition. Of these three subjects, the one most important to him was probably counterpoint, not so much because of the topic but because of who taught it: André Gédalge. Since Ibert had showed the requisite diligence and promise, Gédalge included him in a private class on orchestration (along with fellow classmates Arthur Honegger and Darius Milhaud). This not only helped Ibert progress substantially in his application of technique but also introduced him to Honegger, who would become one of his closest associates in the community of composers.

Ibert left school to serve in the navy during World War I, but soon after receiving his discharge he resumed his studies and, in 1919, won the Prix de Rome with his cantata *Le Poèt et le Fée (The Poet and the Fairy)*. Although he wrote several well-received compositions during his stay at the Villa Medici—where winners of the Prix de Rome were housed—it was the score for his *Escales (Ports of Call)* that solidified his reputation as a composer when it was premiered in 1924. The three movements of this lusciously orchestrated piece were finished in 1922 and inspired by his honeymoon trip with his wife Rosette Veber, during which he became intrigued with the sights and sounds of various ports in Italy, Africa, and Spain.

After his success with *Escales,* it looked for a while like Ibert would find his livelihood in the theatrical arts, composing operas, incidental music for plays, and ballet scores, since much of the music he was writing during the later half of the 1920s showed up at the Opéra. Ibert continued in this vein during the 1930s, when he collaborated with Honegger on two operas (*L'aiglon* and *Les petites cardinal*) and worked with film directors G. W. Pabst (*Don Quichotte*), Maurice Tourneur (*Les deux orphelines*), and Julien Duvivier (*Les cinq gentlermen maudits*) on film scores. (His greatest achievement in this field, however, would be reserved for Orson Welles's 1948 film, *Macbeth*.) The composer's works for wind ensembles also took flight during the 1930s. The Concerto for Flute and Orchestra, the *Concertino da camera* for Saxophone, the *Pièces Brèves* for Wind Quintet, and the *Cinq Pièces en trio* all date from this time period and have graced many a recital since then.

Ibert's bent for academic administration came into focus when, in 1937, he was made director of the Académie de France at the Villa de Medici, the first musician ever appointed to that post. He stayed in it until 1960 except for the years of the Second World War, when he vacillated between France and Switzerland while the Vichy government was in power. After the war, however, Ibert returned to Paris, where he became assistant director of the Paris Opéra. He also visited the United States in 1950, serving on the faculty of the Berkshire Music Center at Tanglewood during the summer before returning to France. Five years later he also headed the Réunion des Théâtres Lyriques Nationaux (briefly) and was elected to the Académie des Beaux-Arts.

Orchestral
Escales (Ports of Call) for Orchestra
what to buy: [Paul Paray, cond.; Detroit Symphony Orchestra] (Mercury Living Presence) ♪ ♪ ♪ ♪₄

This is essentially an album of Maurice Ravel's works with Ibert's *Escales* tacked on at the end. Paray (who conducted the premiere of *Escales* in 1924 with the Orchestre des Concerts Lamoureux) was conductor of the DSO during its first great blossoming and his approach to Ravel's work was of the highest order, delicate or robust depending on the demands of the score. In that sense, what was good for the great (Ravel) is fine for the good (Ibert). In addition to *Escales,* Paray leads his forces through the *Rhapsodie espagnole, La valse, Le tombeau de Couperin, Pavane pour une infante defunte,* and *Alborada del gracioso.*

what to buy next: [Eduardo Mata, cond.; Dallas Symphony Orchestra] (Dorian 90181) ♪ ♪ ♪ ♪

Evocative playing from the woodwinds and strings makes this a marvelous rendition of the composer's most popular orchestral work. This album also contains well-performed versions of Ibert's *Divertissement* and Ernest Chausson's Symphony in B-flat Major, op. 20.

Concerto for Flute and Orchestra
what to buy: [*20th Century Flute Masterpieces*; Jean-Pierre Rampal, flute; Louis de Froment, cond.; Lamoureaux Concerts Association Orchestra] (Erato 45839) ♪ ♪ ♪ ♪₄

Premiered in 1934 by its dedicatee Marcel Moyse, Ibert's concerto, with its shimmering orchestral backdrop, explores the full range of flute techniques without ever getting bogged down in virtuosity for virtuosity's sake. Absolutely lovely performances by a master of his instrument spark this intriguing two-disc set of works for the flute. Although Frank Martin's *Ballade* or Carl Nielsen's concerto are not part of the program, the concertos by Ibert, Aram Khachaturian, and André Jolivet, along with sonatas from Bohuslav Martinu, Paul Hindemith, Francis Poulenc, and Sergei Prokofiev, all justify the album's title.

Chamber
Pièces Brèves for Wind Quintet
what to buy: [*Favorite Works for Wind Quintet*, Frösunda Quintet, ensemble] (BIS 136) ♪ ♪ ♪ ♪₄

This Danish group has put together a wonderful program of music, some of which many listeners have never heard before. Their take on the Ibert set is very recommendable, while the reading of Carl Nielsen's Quintet for Winds is superb, Malcolm Arnold's three *Shanties* is lively as all get-out, and the *Antique Hungarian Dances* by Ferenc Farkas is delightful.

what to buy next: [Athena Ensemble] (Chandos 6543) ♪ ♪ ♪₄

Ibert's three little gems for wind ensemble receive fine performances here and the album contains a pair of other typically French works for the same lineup: Charles Gounod's wonderful *Petit Symphonie* for Nine Wind Instruments, and the interesting Sextet for Piano and Woodwind Quintet by Francis Poulenc.

influences: Claude Debussy, Maurice Ravel, Gabriel Fauré, Gabriel Pierné

Ian Palmer

Mikhail Ippolitov-Ivanov
Born Mikhail Mikhaylovich Ippolitov-Ivanov on November 19, 1859, in Gatchina, Russia. Died on January 28, 1935, in Moscow, Russia.

period: Romantic

Ippolitov-Ivanov's positions in academia and as director of various opera companies gave him ample opportunity to write dramatic orchestral scores, operas, and programmatic pieces. Though most of his output consists of choral music, his most recognizable composition today is a short movement, the "Procession of the Sardar," drawn from his orchestral suite *Caucasian Sketches*.

Heinz Holliger:
Heinz Holliger was born in Switzerland, studying oboe and piano before undertaking composition course work with Sándor Veress (a Hungarian immigrant to Switzerland who once studied with Béla Bartók) in 1955. Holliger then went to Paris, where he continued his oboe and piano studies prior to taking further lessons in composition, this time from Pierre Boulez. Holliger's earliest works stem from the time he spent with Veress, and reveal not only the influence of his teacher but that of the early serial composers, especially Alban Berg. After his period of instruction with Boulez ended in 1963, Holliger's compositional style eased away from the tone row as he eventually began experimenting more with the idea of musical disintegration in his pieces from the mid-1970s onward.

Although he has received a number of commissions as a composer, Holliger's present-day reputation is based more upon his undeniable skills as an oboist. He has, from a technical standpoint, expanded the possibilities of the instrument beyond what had previously been the norm and, as such, benefited as the dedicatee of many contemporary scores including Luciano Berio's *Sequenza VII* for solo oboe (Aura Classics 171) and various works by Hans Werner Henze (Deutsche Grammophon 449864).

Despite these modernist credentials, much of Holliger's recorded legacy deals with pre-twentieth century music. He has taken part in a number of excellent performances of concerti by Johann Sebastian Bach (Philips 412851), Georg Phillipp Telemann (Philips 412879), and Wolfgang Amadeus Mozart (Philips 411134), and—perhaps most importantly—done much to advance knowledge about the Baroque Bohemian composer Jan Dismas Zelenka, whose Trio Sonatas for Two Oboes and Continuo were recorded twice by Holliger-led groups (Deutsche Grammophon 423937 and ECM 1671/72). A fairly decent, mid-priced sampler that displays both his musicianship and his skill as a composer is *The Artistry of Heinz Holliger* (Denon 8006). Included along with works by Telemann, Bach, and Mozart are a pair of the oboist's own pieces: *Studie über Mehrklänge* and *Lied for Electric Flute*.

Garaud MacTaggart

Although his early training seems unremarkable, Ippolitov-Ivanov later made much of his education. He attended the local school for choir boys from age thirteen until his admission to the St. Petersburg Conservatory at age sixteen; he graduated from the instrumental class at age twenty and the composition class at age twenty-two. Upon graduation he moved to Tbilisi, Georgia, where he directed both the academy and the local branch of the Russian Music Society even as he was conducting the local opera company. In 1893 he became a professor at the Moscow Conservatory, where he served for the rest of his life. Following a pattern of multiple jobs and responsibilities he first exhibited in Tbilisi, Ippolitov-Ivanov worked as a conductor at the Russian Choral Society from 1895 to 1901, overlapping his 1898–1906 conducting tenure at the Mamontov Opera. In 1905 he also became Director of the Moscow Conservatory, a post he held until 1922. Life at the conservatory (and outside of it) was increasingly busy for Ippolitov-Ivanov. Not only was he teaching classes in harmony, composition, orchestration, and opera at the Moscow Conservatory, he also taught composition classes at the Tbilisi Conservatory during the years 1924–1925.

While working at the Mamontov Opera, Ippolitov-Ivanov conducted performances of many works by Nikolai Rimsky-Korsakov, including the scores for *The Tsar's Bride* and *The Legend of Tsar Saltan*. This connection gives us a clue to his compositional preferences: like Rimsky-Korsakov's, Ippolitov-Ivanov's music is largely nationalistic in tone, utilizing folksong melodies, legends, and country scenes as the basis for his scores. His last conducting post, at the Bolshoi Theater, started in 1925 and let him immerse himself deeper in the nationalist style, as evidenced by his staging a revival of Modest Mussorgsky's *Boris Godunov*. Most of Ippolitov-Ivanov's works are operas, large choral scores, and short orchestral pieces, although he did compose a few chamber works. His most famous composition, however, remains the "Procession of the Sardar" from his *Caucasian Sketches*. Here the influence of Rimsky-Korsakov and the rest of the nationalist movement shows most clearly, both in the use of folk themes and in the lush orchestration.

Orchestral
Caucasian Sketches **Suite no. 1, op. 10— "Procession of the Sardar"**
what to buy: [*The Royal Edition: Russian Orchestral Music*; Leonard Bernstein, cond.; New York Philharmonic Orchestra] (Sony Classical 47607) ♪ ♪ ♪ ♪

Bernstein's collection is a double handful of Russian orchestral bonbons that includes not only Ippolitov-Ivanov's excerpted claim to musical posterity but another slice of his opus 10 ("In the Village"), plus short works by Alexander Borodin, Reinhold Glière, Modest Mussorgsky, Sergei Prokofiev, and Dmitri Shostakovich. All the performances are as exciting as one has any right to expect, and the engineering is fairly clear.

what to buy next: [*Class Brass on the Edge*; Empire Brass, ensemble] (Telarc 80305) ♪ ♪ ♪ ♪

This arrangement for brass quintet is very well recorded and gives the composer's exciting little charmer a lot of oomph. The balance of the set is taken up by fourteen more short "hits" by Leonard Bernstein, Jacques

Offenbach, Aram Khachaturian, Georges Bizet, and others. It only goes to show that Ippolitov-Ivanov and the other composers represented on this set created perfect small gems for "pops" programming.

influences: Nikolai Rimsky-Korsakov, Mily Balakirev

Melissa M. Stewart

John Ireland
Born John Nicholson Ireland, August 13, 1879, in Bowdon, Cheshire, England. Died June 12, 1962, in Rock Mill, Washington, Sussex, England.

period: Twentieth century

While he wrote in most genres, John Ireland's strict self-criticism reduced the number of works he was willing to see published. Still, the scores that made the cut are well crafted—often tinted with folk melodies and a hybrid Celtic-Germanic mysticism of the kind popular during the early years of the twentieth century—without breaking new ground. Ireland's best work seems reserved for smaller forces—chamber works and songs predominate on any list of Ireland's more important pieces—but his Piano Concerto is still highly regarded in England.

Both of Ireland's parents were writers, but his father was also part-owner, publisher, business manager, and editor of the *Manchester Examiner*, a man who counted Ralph Waldo Emerson and Thomas Carlyle among his friends. The young Ireland started taking piano lessons when he was eight years old and progressed rapidly, passing the audition for the Royal College of Music when he was only thirteen. His parents died within fourteen months of his admission, and though they left a fairly sizable estate, the majority of it went to his older brother and sisters. Ireland was able to continue his schooling, however, since he received a small allowance from a trust fund. As a way of supplementing his allowance and gaining practical experience, he played organ at various churches around London. He began studying composition with Charles Stanford in 1897, hoping to hone his skills with the most influential teacher in Great Britain, and finally received his Bachelor of Music degree in 1905.

Ireland spent the next twenty years as an organist and choir director, although he did devote a substantial amount of time to composing. His finest works from this period include the third of his piano preludes, "The Holy Boy" (a Christmas piece that, through a proliferation of arrangements for different-sized forces, became one of his most popular works); the song cycles *Five Poems by Thomas Hardy, Mother and Child,* and *Songs of a Wayfarer;* the two violin sonatas; and the symphonic rhapsody *Mai-Dun.* From 1923 to 1939, Ireland put his composing experience to use as an academic, teaching composition at his alma mater, where E. J. Moeran and Benjamin Britten were among his students. He also continued writing music, including the Sonatina for Piano, another song cycle (the *Songs Sacred and Profane*), his lone piano concerto, *Legend* for Piano and Orchestra, and the *Downland Suite* for brass band. After retiring from teaching in 1939, Ireland continued composing, but few of the pieces from his last years have made an impact on the standard repertoire, even in England.

Orchestral
Concerto in E-flat Major for Piano and Orchestra
what to buy: [Eric Parkin, piano; Bryden Thomson, cond.; London Philharmonic Orchestra] (Chandos 8461) ♪ ♪ ♪

Ireland wasn't necessarily at his most inspired when writing for orchestral forces, but he did manage to pack a few melodies into this piece, even if it sounds like it would be more at home on a soundtrack than in a concert hall. Parkin makes the most of his role, and the recording is spacious and complimentary. Ireland's early symphonic rhapsody *Mai-Dun* and the slight yet pleasing *Legend* for Piano and Orchestra are also included.

Chamber
Sonata no. 2 in A Minor for Violin and Piano
what to buy: [*Chamber Works*; Lydia Mordkovitch, violin; Ian Brown, piano] (Chandos 9377/78) ♪ ♪ ♪ ♪

In this particular work, Ireland melded the typical sonata structure with a cyclical form that allowed specific folk-oriented themes to crop up throughout the piece. Mordkovitch is a wonderful violinist who makes the most of this work and its earlier sibling in D Minor. Also on this two-disc set are the composer's Cello Sonata, the *Fantasy Sonata* for Clarinet and Piano, the *Phantasie Trio,* a pair of Ireland's piano trios (nos. 2 and 3), and the cello and piano arrangement for "The Holy Boy."

Vladimir Horowitz:
Born in 1903 and Raised in Kiev, Russia, Vladimir Horowitz took his first piano lessons from his mother, a professional pianist. When his talents outstripped her abilities as a teacher, he went to the Kiev Conservatory. Horowitz's debut public recital occurred when he was sixteen years old, and shortly thereafter young Vladimir became the chief breadwinner for the family, supplementing a household income that had been decimated when his father, an engineer, lost most of his financial holdings during the Russian Revolution. Horowitz left Russia for his first official international concert tour in 1925 and then didn't return to the land of his birth for more than sixty years.

American impresario Arthur Judson heard the pianist at a concert in Paris and offered Horowitz a contract to play in the United States. He eventually made his American debut in 1928, playing Piotr Ilyich Tchaikovsky's first piano concerto with the New York Philharmonic Orchestra. After marrying Wanda Toscanini (the daughter of Arturo Toscanini) in 1933, Horowitz entered the first of his withdrawals from concertizing and moved to Switzerland. There he mostly remained out of the public eye until 1938, when he gave a recital in Zürich and followed it the next year with a program in Paris.

Horowitz took up residence in the United States in 1940, becoming an American citizen in 1944. The next of his periodic "retirements" occurred in 1953 and lasted until 1965; when he gave a highly anticipated recital at New York City's Carnegie Hall. Further concerts followed, but so too did periods of retreat from the stage. Horowitz's absence from the concert hall did not prevent him from making recordings, however, and it is essentially the studio performances of the 1950s and 1960s which document the pianist at the height of his powers.

Pride of place among his many notable recordings of that period belongs to *Horowitz Plays Rachmaninoff* (RCA Victor Gold Seal 7754). The composer and pianist were friends and admirers of each other's work, Horowitz playing Rachmaninoff's third piano concerto frequently and the composer, a formidable piano virtuoso in his own right, professing himself overwhelmed by the quality of the resulting performances. Nonetheless, on this recording Horowitz's accompanying performance of Rachmaninoff's Sonata no. 2 in B-flat Minor for Piano almost steals the show from the flashier concerto. The concerto performance, led by Fritz Reiner conducting the RCA Victor Symphony Orchestra, is also part of a two-disc set (*Great Pianists of the 20th Century: Vladimir Horowitz III,* Philips 456841) which features the pianist and Reiner teaming up in Beethoven's *Emperor* concerto too, along with Horowitz tackling a fine array of Frédéric Chopin's solo piano works.

Other noteworthy recordings by the pianist include *Horowitz Plays Scriabin* (RCA Victor Gold Seal 6215), a collection of various *Preludes* and *Études* by Alexander Scriabin that also features a fine performance of the composer's Sonata no. 5 in F-sharp Major for Piano; and *Horowitz in Moscow* (Deutsche Grammophon 419499), a recital that was recorded in 1986 at the Great Hall of the Tchaikovsky Conservatory and marked the first time the pianist played in Russia since his departure over sixty years before. Horowitz made his final recording on November 1, 1989, four days before he suffered a fatal heart attack. The resulting album (*Horowitz: The Last Recording,* Sony Classics 45818) won a Grammy Award in 1990.

William Gerard

what to buy next: [Albert Sammons, violin; John Ireland, piano] (Dutton Laboratories 7103) ♪ ♪ ♪₄

The presence of the composer as pianist gives this performance an undeniable air of authenticity, as does the playing of Sammons, the work's dedicatee. Remastered from the original 78 rpm records by Michael J. Dutton, this disc also includes the first of Ireland's violin sonatas (with Ireland and Frederick Grinke), in addition to the *Phantasie Trio* for Violin, Piano, and Cello (with Grinke, Kenneth Taylor, and Florence Hooton) and an arrangement of the ubiquitous "Holy Boy" for piano and cello (with Hooton and Lawrence Pratt).

worth searching for: [*Violin Sonatas*; Yfrah Neaman, violin; Eric Parkin, piano] (Lyrita 64) ♪ ♪ ♪ ♪₄

Parkin has a long history of persuading audiences that Ireland's music is better than average through performances that are sympathetic without being overly dramatic. His colleague here, Yfrah Neaman, nails every phrase with just the right amount of conviction. The resulting versions of Ireland's two violin sonatas deserve to be reissued.

Vocal
Songs Sacred and Profane
what to buy: [*The Songs of John Ireland*; John Mark Ainsley, tenor; Graham Johnson, piano] (Hyperion 67261/2) ♪ ♪ ♪ ♪

This is one of the finest song cycles in the English language, and it is good to hear the six pieces bound together as a unit instead of sprawled across many different albums. Ainsley's interpretation of *The Salley Gardens*, while not quite up to the exalted level of Dame Janet Baker's classic but now out-of-print rendition, has much to offer discerning listeners. The other songs on this two-disc set display Ireland's impressive songwriting skills and are split fairly evenly between Ainsley, soprano Lisa Milne, and baritone Christopher Maltman, with Johnson's marvelous piano playing heard throughout the program.

"Sea Fever"
what to buy: [*"The Vagabond" and Other Songs*; Bryn Terfel, bass-baritone; Malcolm Martineau, piano] (Deutsche Grammophon 445946) ♪ ♪ ♪ ♪

Terfel's marvelously deep, rolling tones are well suited

for this mini-masterpiece. While it might be too much to hope to hear him in an all-Ireland recital, the three Ireland songs on this disc—"Sea Fever," "The Vagabond," and "Bells of San Marie"—are in good company, with tunes by Ralph Vaughan Williams, Gerald Finzi, and George Butterworth filling out the set.

influences: Edward Elgar, Arnold Bax, Charles Stanford, E.J. Moeran

Garaud MacTaggart

Charles Ives
Born Charles Edward Ives on October 20, 1874, in Danbury, CT. Died May 19, 1954, in New York, NY.

period: Twentieth century

In his music, Charles Ives sought to blend the sublime with a constant drive to expand human potential and test its limits. An insurance agent by trade, Ives drew upon his background as a church organist and bandmaster's son to produce a number of groundbreaking polytonal works, often based on familiar American tunes. His "orchestral set" *Three Places in New England* is a fine example of Ives's use of hymn tunes and patriotic songs in a polytonal setting.

His father's versatility as a bandmaster and teacher (especially of music theory) gave Ives an ideal environment for learning the basics of his craft, but even more important for his musical development was his father's continual urging to do more, to expand what he knew. The older Ives believed that "man as a rule didn't use the faculties the Creator had given him" and urged his sons to sing in one key and accompany themselves in another on the piano. This introduction to (and sanctioning of) a much broader tonal universe than the diatonic system undoubtedly had as much to do with Ives's later success as learning basic scales and harmony, giving him a kind of post-graduate training in compositional theory even before he entered music school. At age twelve he was already composing and playing drums in his father's band. He was also engaged in his own musical experiments, playing various rhythm patterns on the piano (which foreshadowed his later experiments with polyrhythms) and creating dissonant chords for these rhythms, even at this early stage showing his interest in non-tonal pitch relations.

When he was only fourteen, Ives was engaged as organist of the Danbury Baptist Church, making him the youngest church organist in Connecticut. In 1893 he became the organist at St. Thomas Episcopal Church in New Haven, where the style of singing biblical texts during the service probably inspired Ives during the summer of 1894 to begin a series of psalm settings. These might be called the beginnings of his mature style. He returned to them often, repeatedly reworking some of them throughout his entire life. *Psalm 90* in particular was being rewritten as late as 1924, and Ives later said it was the only one of his works with which he was happy. Another important element in Ives's style, musical quotation, is also evident from his very earliest pieces. Though they could seem to suggest a lack of originality, these devices were in fact necessary ingredients for Ives in the creation of tonal pictures that are often scenes from his own boyhood. The *Variations on America* for organ, written in 1892, take the familiar melody through a series of transformations—from a military band to a church chorale, to an out-of-tune amateur performance, even to a Spanish dance hall. Some of the titles acknowledge the music's programmatic content, though not all are meant to describe a specific scene. But all of Ives's music struggles with the problem of trying to encompass a three-dimensional world in the medium of sound. One could almost think of him as a musical cubist, seeking to transcend the two-dimensional constraints of traditional music in order to include every detail of the sound-picture he had imagined.

In 1894 Ives entered Yale, and during his four years at the university he met two figures who would become important for his development as a composer: John Cornelius Griggs, the choirmaster at Centre Church, and Horatio Parker, a composer and Yale music professor. Griggs remained Ives's friend and supporter for his entire life, while Parker's attention to the basic craft of composition helped Ives give his First Symphony (1895–98) a quality of restraint that balances the exuberance of his new ideas. Upon graduation from Yale, through a cousin of his father's, Ives got a day job got as an actuary for the Mutual Insurance Company. In 1899, he was asked to fill in for the vacationing Julian Myrick, and upon Myrick's return the two worked together finding new ways to present insurance to businesses. They functioned well together, each balancing the other's strengths and weaknesses, and remained partners for the rest of their very successful business careers.

Ives was still working as an organist as well as compos-

Sol Hurok:
Solomon Israelovich Hurok arrived in the United States from Russia in 1906, with no money but plenty of ambition, moxy, and commitment to social justice. That last quality came to the fore in 1907 when he began raising money for various labor organizations by booking musicians to play at their meetings. His first success as a concert promoter was when the young violin virtuoso Efrem Zimbalist agreed to perform at a worker's gathering in Brooklyn.

By the 1930s Hurok was famed for the quality of the dancers, musicians, and singers whose careers he managed and promoted. Among the most prominent of these artists in the early years were the dance divas Anna Pavlova and Isadora Duncan and the groundbreaking choreographers Katherine Dunham and Martha Graham. A number of notable classical music performers also had portions of their careers guided or aided by Hurok, including Marian Anderson, Maria Callas, Andrés Segovia, Artur Schnabel, Artur Rubinstein, Roberta Peterson, Isaac Stern, and Rudolf Serkin.

In 1939 Hurok fought the "whites only" policy of the Daughters of the American Revolution when they refused to book Anderson into Washington, D.C.'s Constitution Hall (which they controlled), with Hurok securing access to the Lincoln Memorial from the Department of the Interior and presenting an Easter Sunday concert outdoors with (as he noted in his 1946 autobiography, *Impresario*) 75,000 people in attendance. Three years later he promoted the very first jazz concert ever held at Carnegie Hall, an event which headlined Benny Goodman but also featured musicians from the bands of Duke Ellington and Count Basie.

During the late 1950s Hurok was largely responsible for the cultural exchange that enabled American audiences to see Soviet artists, setting up engagements for the Bolshoi Ballet, David Oistrakh, and Feodor Chaliapin. After Hurok sold his company in 1969, he still managed artists and produced shows. Perhaps one of the most memorable, from a musical oddity standpoint, occurred in 1970, when he promoted a concert featuring the premiere of Gershon Kingsley's Moog quartet with arrangements of works by Giovanni Gabrieli, George Frideric Handel, and the Beatles.

Though Hurok was ever-quotable, his most telling remark may have been that "the arts are a major part of my life, and to be without them is to starve, no matter what other wealth one may achieve."

Ellen Kokko

ing in his spare time; from 1898 to 1900 he was organist at the First Presbyterian Church in Bloomfield, New Jersey, and from 1900 to 1902 at Central Presbyterian Church in New York City. During this period he composed a number of pieces, most notably his Second Symphony and a seven-movement cantata entitled *The Celestial Country*. In June of 1902, Ives resigned his post as organist in order to have more time for composition. Without church work to restrain his creativity, his music now began to show a more experimental bent, although he also continued to use hymn tunes and fragments, as in the Third Symphony and *Thanksgiving*.

1905 was a banner year for Ives. He began an extended courtship of Harmony Twichell (who become his wife in 1908) and composed some of his most important music—especially the orchestral movements *The Unanswered Question* and *Central Park in the Dark.* These works demonstrate his characteristic juxtaposition of opposites using two orchestras—one with atonal music in the foreground and one with tonal in the background for the first movement, then reversed for the other movement. Ives's compositional life as a whole was showing a similar duality, as his experimental pieces contrasted with songs written to please Harmony and her family. Many of his best-known works were written during the next few years: the *Emerson Overture* (later to become a movement of his second piano sonata, known as the *Concord Sonata*) was sketched in 1907; the First Piano Sonata and *Washington's Birthday* in 1909; and the *First Orchestral Set* (also known as *Three Places in New England*), *Decoration Day,* the *Second Orchestral Set,* and *Holidays,* were all composed during the period between 1905 and 1916, when Ives's enthusiasm for the war effort and health problems may have lowered his compositional stamina. His family life was equally productive—he bought a farm in West Redding, Connecticut, and in 1915 he and Harmony began inviting families to stay at the farm through the Fresh Air Fund. When the United States entered the war against Germany in 1917, Ives became active in the Red Cross. He had just convinced the administrators to sell Liberty Loans in smaller shares (Baby Bonds) so that more Americans could participate, when he had a serious heart attack and spent two of the winter months of 1918 in Asheville, North Carolina. There he began putting his music in order and published a collection of over 100 songs.

After the war, Ives finished a few pieces, including the set of three quarter-tone pieces for two pianos, and re-composed his setting of *Psalm 90,* but following the song *Sunrise* in 1926, he lost confidence in his work and virtually stopped composing. He retired from business in 1930 and in 1931 went on a two-year tour of Europe with the musicologist-conductor Nicolas Slonimsky and the Boston Chamber Orchestra, who performed Ives's music to great acclaim. In 1932 his songs were performed at the first Yaddo Festival for contemporary American music at Saratoga Springs, NY, and, as the reviews became more and more favorable, Ives was recognized as a composer worthy of scholarly attention. He won the Pulitzer Prize in 1947 for a performance of his Symphony no. 3 (with the composer Lou Harrison con-

ducting), and younger composers began adopting some of his techniques. With his reputation now at last on the rise, Ives's constitution, damaged by diabetes, grew weaker; he died from a stroke on May 19, 1954.

Orchestral
Contemplations no. 1: The Unanswered Question for Orchestra
what to buy: [Gerhard Samuel, cond.; Cincinnati Philharmonia Orchestra] (Centaur 2205) ♪ ♪ ♪ ♪ ♪

This is a superb recording of *The Unanswered Question,* probably Ives's best-known composition. But you also get the highly representative *Orchestral Set no. 2,* and his *Universe Symphony,* sketched (and mostly lost) between 1916 and 1928. The performance of the symphony, now reconstructed and heard here in a world-premiere recording, is outstanding. The recording quality is good, but it is the orchestral playing that shines in these performances.

Holidays for Orchestra
what to buy: [Michael Tilson Thomas, cond.; Chicago Symphony Orchestra; Chicago Symphony Chorus] (Sony Classics 42381) ♪ ♪ ♪ ♪

This is a fine, clean recording. The Chicago orchestra is known for its brilliant virtuosity, and Tilson Thomas gets the very last drop of polish here, in clarity and in dynamics, both so important in Ives. Included in this set are versions of *The Unanswered Question* and *Central Park in the Dark.* Only the lack of variety in the program prevents this disc from being rated above the Strickland recording (see below).

worth searching for: [William Strickland, cond.; Iceland Symphony Orchestra; Finnish Radio Symphony Orchestra; Tokyo Philharmonic Orchestra; Gothenburg Symphony Orchestra] (CRI 6014) ♪ ♪ ♪ ♪

This is a veritable hodgepodge of Ives's pieces and varying instrumentation. Along with the patchwork *Holidays* it includes the Fourth Violin Sonata, with the legendary Joseph Szigeti on violin and Andor Foldes on piano in a wonderful performance from 1942, *Three Outdoor Scenes,* with Strickland and the Olso Philharmonic, and *Six Songs* with baritone Mordecai Bauman and pianist Albert Hirsch. All the performances are good, but the

Charles Ives

recording quality leaves something to be desired. Still, the broadly varied program alone makes it a good sampler.

Chamber
Sonata no. 2 for Piano—*Concord, Mass., 1840-1860*
what to buy: [Gilbert Kalish, piano; Samuel Baron, flute; John Graham, viola] (Nonesuch 71337) ♪ ♪ ♪ ♪

The composer's whimsical and groundbreaking approach to the "piano sonata" is exemplified by his incorporating a brief passage for viola in the *Emerson* movement and a somewhat larger role for the flute in the *Thoreau* movement. Kalish's recording has made a successful transition from vinyl to CD and the performance still stands up well against the competition. The record company could, however, have filled out the playing time of less than 50 minutes with some of the composer's songs or a few other little Ives bon-bons, but that is a minor quibble when considering the overall quality of the music making.

Emerson Overture
what to buy: [*Ives Plays Ives*; Charles Ives, piano] (CRI 810) ♪ ♪ ♪ ♪

The composer plays piano transcriptions from his aborted *Emerson Overture* project in this recording whose studio dates span the period from 1933 to 1943. Much of the material heard here would end up in the first movement of Ives's Second Piano Sonata (he also plays bits and pieces of the sonata's *Hawthorne* movement), but there are also studies for *The Anti-Abolitionist Riots* and the somewhat corny *They Are There!* The recording is obviously far from state-of-the-art, but hearing the composer play and improvise on his adventurous scores is fascinating and more than reason enough to justify this disc's existence.

influences: Aaron Copland, John Cage, Conlon Nancarrow, Elliot Carter

Melissa M. Stewart

J

Leoš Janáček
Born Leoš [Leo Eugen] Janáček, July 3, 1854, in Hukvaldy, Moravia [now in the Czech Republic]. Died August 12, 1928, in Moravská-Ostrava, Moravia.

period: Twentieth century

Like Olivier Messiaen later, Janáček was enthralled by nature: by birdsong, but also by the sounds of flowing water, the wind in tall pines, and the rhythmic implications of animal movement. This fascination extended to the melodic and rhythmic qualities of human speech and Moravian folk music which he then incorporated into works of late-blooming genius. His greatest works—the four late operas *Kát'a Kabanová, The Makropulos Case, The Cunning Little Vixen* and *From the House of the Dead,* the *Glagolitic Mass,* the Sinfonietta, his wind sextet *Mládí (Youth),* and two string quartets—were all finished after his sixty-fifth birthday.

Leoš Janáček was born into a family of village musicians and teachers but received much of his early musical training as a choirboy at a monastery in Brno, the Moravian capital. It was there that he acquired his love of the human voice and its possibilities. One of the results of his affiliation with the monastery was a continued association with various choral groups throughout his career. He began directing the monastery choir in 1872 and in that position developed a reputation for the depth and variety of his programs, including in the services works by such Renaissance masters as Lassus and Palestrina as well as the standard repertoire by Haydn, Mozart, and Beethoven, and music by contemporary Czech composers. His adventurousness led to Janáček's appointment in 1873 as choirmaster of a working-men's choral society, for whom he wrote some of his first choral music. By using folk tales and songs as the basis of many of these pieces, Janáček was providing a vent for the expression of nationalist yearnings in one of the few Czech cultural institutions allowed to flourish under Austrian rule. He was also building a musical foundation for his own future.

1872 also found the young composer and chorus master passing his final exams at the Czech Teachers' Institute, which required him, as a condition of the scholarship he had received, to teach for two years without pay. After serving this period at a school established by the Institute, in 1874 Janáček went to study for a year at the Prague Organ School, where he met and became friends with Antonín Dvořák. For the next few years he moved between Brno, where he had returned as a choir director and to teach, and Prague, for yet another (short) stint at the Organ School. He also went to Leipzig and Vienna where he studied composition briefly at their respective conservatories. Janáček finally received his teaching certificate from the Czech Teachers' Institute in 1880.

By this time he had written a few works for string orchestra, some chamber works, and several vocal pieces, but nothing that brought him attention as a composer. In 1881 he created, with the aid of a committee, an organ school in Brno that eventually blossomed into a full-fledged conservatory. Janáček also founded a journal of musical criticism (*Hudební listy*) which lasted four years. The other major change in his life that year was his marriage to Zdenka Schulzová, the daughter of his former superior at the Teachers' Institute. It was to be a tumultuous relationship that afforded neither party the emotional stability they sought. The composer's fiery personality and nationalist leanings clashed repeatedly with Zdenka's immaturity (she married just before her 16th birthday) and middle-class, Germanic background, resulting in periods of separation and reconciliation.

Janáček embarked on his first attempt at creating an opera (*Sarka*) in 1887, about the time he began an intense study of Moravian folk music—an endeavor he would continue to pursue for the next decade. The initial results of his studies could be heard in a series of pleasantly undistinguished orchestral suites and some fairly conventional stage works. *Jenufa*, his earliest successful opera, was premiered in 1904. This was the first score in which he used the rhythms and accents of the Czech language to shape the melodic contours. His next operas (*Osud [Fate]* and *Výlet pana Broučka do mesíce [The Excursion of Mr. Brouček to the Moon]*) marked further steps in the highly individual instrumental style that Janáček was developing, but they were hampered by inept librettos and met with tepid responses from a number of potential venues. Although he was respected in Brno as the founder of the organ school and the poverty of his early years was erased by the perceived comforts of a middle-class existence, Janáček was not to enjoy his breakthrough as a composer until 1915 when the Prague National Theatre finally accepted *Jenufa* for production. It was premiered to rave reviews during the 1916 season; the Vienna firm of Universal Edition approached Janáček about publishing the score; and the opera even traveled well, winning favorable audience response in Vienna and Berlin, two of Europe's foremost cultural centers.

This success (and the subsequent creation of the Czechoslovak republic in 1918) stimulated Janáček to create his two most popular orchestral works: *Taras Bulba* (1918) and the Sinfonietta (1926). The other inspi-

ration for his new flurry of compositional genius was a more personal one involving his love for a married woman (Kamila Stösslová) thirty-five years his junior. The results of this more intimate passion include the fine song cycle *Zápisník zmizelého (The Diary of One Who Disappeared)*, one of his greatest operas (*Kát'a Kabanová*), the wind sextet *Mládí (Youth)*, and the second of his two superb string quartets.

Orchestral
Sinfonietta for Orchestra
what to buy: [Vaclav Neumann, cond.; Czech Philharmonic Orchestra] (Supraphon 111965) ♪ ♪ ♪ ♪⸴

The incredible playing by the Czech Philharmonic brass in this recording, much of it an absolute avalanche of emotionally driven sounds, has yet to be surpassed. On the same disc is a fine performance of Janáček's orchestral rhapsody, *Taras Bulba*, and two relative rarities that the composer only sketched during his last year of life: the incidental music from Gerhart Hauptmann's play *Schluk und Jau* and the composer's violin concerto, *Putování dušičky (Pilgrimage of the Soul)*, with soloist Josef Suk.

what to buy next: [Charles Mackerras, cond.; Vienna Philharmonic Orchestra] (London 448255) ♪ ♪ ♪ ♪

If the Neumann recording weren't in print, this would be an easy first choice, especially when one considers its impeccable engineering. Mackerras has a solid grip on the nuances of the score, the VPO is a top-notch band, and their version of *Taras Bulba* is even more exciting. This mid-priced two disc set also includes one of Janáček's finest chamber works, the sextet *Mládí (Youth)*, and four other works in fine performances by a variety of artists.

Chamber
Quartet no. 1 for Strings—*The Kreutzer Sonata*
what to buy: [Janáček String Quartet, ensemble] (Supraphon 3460) ♪ ♪ ♪ ♪ ♪

Taking his cue from Leo Tolstoy's tale *The Kreutzer Sonata*, Janáček wrote an intensely moving work that places huge demands on its performers. His challenges were met in full when this ensemble went into the studio and set the standard for all other recordings to follow. Supraphon has meshed this magnificent performance with the ensemble's equally impressive rendering of Janáček's second quartet and tossed in their version

of the op. 35 quartet by Vitezslav Novák, his somewhat younger contemporary, for good measure.

what to buy next: [Talich String Quartet, ensemble] (Calliope 9699) ♪ ♪ ♪ ♪

The Talich Quartet lacks only the very last scintilla of commitment that makes the version by the Janáček Quartet such a monumental recording. Their excellent performance of the composer's second string quartet is also included in the set.

[Guarneri Quartet, ensemble] (Philips 456574) ♪ ♪ ♪ ♪

The hushed, suspenseful opening of Janáček's first quartet leads into a series of desperately intense moments and the Guarneri Quartet is more than up to the task. Their version of *Listy důvěrné (Intimate Letters)*, the second of the composer's works in this genre, is even better.

[Vlach Quartet, Prague, ensemble] (Naxos 8.553895) ♪ ♪ ♪

Bargain-priced recordings are sometimes great value and such is the case here. Well-played versions of both of Janáček's string quartets are coupled with solid performances of the composer's Sonata for Violin and Piano and the rarely heard *Pohádka (Fairy Tale)* for Cello and Piano.

Vocal
Glagolská mše (Glagolitic Mass) for soloists, chorus, orchestra, and organ
what to buy: [Libuše Domanínská, soprano; Vera Soukpová, alto; Beno Blachut, tenor; Eduard Haken, bass; Jaroslav Vodrázka, organ; Karel Ančerl, cond.; Czech Philharmonic Orchestra; Czech Philharmonic Chorus] (Supraphon 1930) ♪ ♪ ♪ ♪

Ančerl has this music in his bones and the orchestra plays its heart out in this, the benchmark against which all other recordings of the piece must be judged. Blachut, in the extremely difficult tenor part, is especially notable and the choral work is stunning. An impressive pair of pre-minimalist scores by Miloslav Kabeláč (*The Mystery of Time* and *Hamlet Improvisations*) fill out the disc.

Leoš Janáček

what to buy next: [Elisabeth Söderström, soprano; Drahomira Drobková, alto; Frantiček Livora, tenor; Richard Novák, bass; Jan Hora, organ; Sir Charles Mackerras, cond.; Czech Philharmonic Orchestra; Czech Philharmonic Chorus] (Supraphon 103075) ♪ ♪ ♪ ♪

Despite the fact that Supraphon includes no other works on this disc, leaving it at a paltry 40 minutes, Mackerras's leadership makes this one of the finest performances of Janáček's choral masterpiece currently available. The sonics are far better than those afforded Ancerl and the interpretation is much stronger than anything recorded by Mackerras's contemporaries.

[Christine Brewer, soprano; Marietta Simpson, mezzo-soprano; Karl Dent, tenor; Roger Roloff, bass; Norman MacKenzie, organ; Robert Shaw, cond.; Atlanta Symphony Orchestra; Atlanta Symphony Chorus] (Telarc 80287) ♪ ♪ ♪

Shaw was a marvelous choral conductor, whose disciplined approach to music making was a joy to hear. That said, the singers in this recording lack just the last bit of Slavic authenticity in their diction that would put this effort on a par with Mackerras's forces. The engineering is superb, as one would expect from Telarc, and Dvořák's intermittently glorious *Te Deum* is the coupling.

Kát'a Kabanová
what to buy: [Gabriela Benačková, soprano; Dagmar Pecková, mezzo-soprano; Martina Bauerová, mezzo-soprano; Dana Buresová, mezzo-soprano; Eva Randová, alto; Peter Straka, tenor; Miroslav Kopp, tenor; Jozef Kundlák, tenor; Zdenek Harvánek, baritone; Ludek Vele, bass; Sir Charles Mackerras, cond.; Czech Philharmonic Orchestra; Prague National Theater Chorus] (Supraphon 3291) ♪ ♪ ♪ ♪

Arguably the greatest opera in the composer's canon, *Kát'a Kabanová* is filled with heart-rending drama and astounding vocal and instrumental writing. Mackerras has recorded this opera before, but this time he uses Universal Edition critically revised (1993) version of the score. He also has the noted Czech soprano Gabriela Benačková in the title role: her beautifully controlled voice and superb acting ability help bring out the tragedy at the heart of the story.

influences: Zoltán Kodály, Bedrich Smetana, Bohuslav Martin, Antonín Dvořák, Vítzslav Novák

Gary Barton and Garaud MacTaggart

Joseph Jongen

Born Marie Alphonse Nicolas Joseph Jongen, December 14, 1873, in Liège, Belgium. Died July 12, 1953, in Sart-lez-Spa, Belgium.

period: Romantic/Twentieth century

His trusted friend and fellow Belgian, the violinist/composer Eugène Ysaÿe, thought that Jongen was a great composer, a notion that was probably colored by the close relationship between the two musicians. A truer appraisal would place him in the first tier of composers known for their organ works (notably the *Symphonie concertante,* op. 81, and the *Sonata heroïca,* op. 94) and relegate him to the minor leagues for his other scores.

Jongen's father was a cabinetmaker with a love of music who also conducted a small choir in Liège. When he was almost eight years old, Jongen was admitted to the Liège Conservatoire, where he was awarded first prize in solfège when he was only twelve. By the time he graduated, he had won all the major awards the school could give. Jongen started composing regularly in 1890, a year before he was appointed to the staff of his alma mater as a teacher of harmony and counterpoint. Jongen's reputation as an organist was already secure in his hometown when he won the Belgian Grand Prix de Rome in 1897. The award provided him with a four-year scholarship, allowing him to pursue his studies in Berlin, Paris, and Rome and to display his impressive performance skills to a wider audience. On his return to Belgium in 1902, he was again appointed to the teaching staff of the Liège Conservatoire, remaining at that post until the outbreak of World War I, when he and his family moved to London. After the war he returned to Belgium and assumed the directorship of the *Concerts spirituels,* premiering works by Kodaly (the *Psalmus Hungaricus*), Honegger (*Le Roi David*), and others. Shortly afterward he became a professor at the Brussels Conservatory and in 1925 was appointed director of that institution.

Although he had taken on an increased administrative burden, Jongen continued to perform and compose. In 1926, when he was commissioned to write a work for the inauguration of a revamped organ at the Wanamaker Auditorium in Philadelphia, Jongen created the score for which he is best known, the *Symphonie concertante* for Organ and Orchestra, op. 81. Four years later he composed what many organists feel is his greatest work for solo organ, the *Sonata heroïca,* op. 94. He formally retired from his directorship on July 31, 1938 and, upon the outbreak of World War II, left for France. Returning to Belgium after the war, Jongen learned that his son had died in the concentration camp at Buchenwald. His wife's mental state was deteriorating, and he was suffering an erosion of confidence in his abilities as a composer, despite an almost yearly unveiling of new works. However, Jongen was still sought after as an adviser on the construction of new organs and the revamping of instruments that had fallen into disrepair. He finally died at his estate in 1953 from an intestinal problem that may or may not have been cancer.

Orchestral
Symphonie concertante for Organ and Orchestra, op. 81
what to buy: [Michael Murray, organ; Edo de Waart, cond.; San Francisco Symphony Orchestra] (Telarc 80096) ♪ ♪ ♪ ♪

While this is a virtuoso work for organ and orchestra, it isn't likely to overwhelm anyone who isn't an organist or an organ aficionado. Yet in many respects, this is Jongen's signature work, and he managed some skillful orchestration here, blending the organ into the whole instead of assigning an overtly massive role to the solo instrument. Murray is as overt a virtuoso as one could hope for, however, and the recording is very impressive. Two of César Franck's solo showpieces for the organ (the *Fantaisie* in A Major and the *Pastorale* in E Major, op. 19) round out the album.

what to buy next: [Hubert Schoonbroodt, organ; Rene Defossez, cond.; Liège Symphony Orchestra] (Koch/Schwann 315012) ♪ ♪ ♪ ♪

Schoonbroodt is a very good organist, and the orchestral colors are well handled by Defossez and the other musicians on this 1975 recording. However, the accompanying works by Jongen—the Suite for Viola and Orchestra and the *Allegro appassionato* for Viola and Orchestra—are marvelous little gems, worth the price of the album by themselves. Violist Therese-Marie Gilissen and the Belgian-French Radio-TV Symphony Orchestra under the guidance of Brian Priestman give totally committed performances that showcase Jongen as more than just a composer for his own instrument.

Chamber
Sonata heroïca for Organ, op. 94
what to buy: [*Great French Virtuosic Organ Music*; Todd Wilson, organ] (Delos 3123) ♪ ♪ ♪ ♪

By utilizing the sonic strength associated with the "king of instruments" without neglecting the organ's surprising subtleties, the composer wrote what is possibly his finest organ work. Wilson is more than capable of dealing with Jongen's devilish technical problems and delivers one of the finer performances of this score. As part of an admirable sampler of gorgeous music, the *Sonata heroïca* fits in well with Charles-Marie Widor's mighty Symphony no. 10 for Organ (the *"Romaine"*) and shorter works by Jean Langlais, Marcel Dupré, Joseph Bonnet, and Jeanne Demessieux.

influences: César Franck, Camille Saint-Saëns, Marcel Dupré, Charles-Marie Widor

Garaud MacTaggart

Scott Joplin

Born November 24, 1868, in Marshall, TX, or Shreveport, LA (sources differ). Died April 1, 1917, in New York, NY.

period: Romantic/twentieth century

Known as the King of Ragtime, Scott Joplin was one of the most successful African-American composers of his day. Through his many piano rags, Joplin brought ragtime out of the dance halls and into middle-class parlors, legitimizing the form and paving the way for classic jazz artists such as James P. Johnson and Duke Ellington.

The son of a former slave and a freeborn black woman, Joplin began life with few advantages. He spent his boyhood in Texarkana, on the Texas-Arkansas border, and received his early musical training at home. He learned several musical instruments, probably from family members, and turned professional while still a youngster, singing in a quartet and giving lessons on piano, guitar, and mandolin. Sometime between 1884 and 1888 he left Texas and began a twelve-year stint as a traveling musician, playing piano and singing. In 1890 he seems to have gone to St. Louis, where he met Tom Turpin, the famous ragtime performer; in 1893 he attended the World's Columbian Exhibition in Chicago, where he led a band and played cornet. In 1895 he went to Syracuse, New York, as a singer with the Texas Medley Quartette; that same year he published his first two waltz songs, "A Picture of Her Face" and "Please Say You Will."

In 1896, Joplin settled in Sedalia, Missouri, where he enrolled at the George R. Smith College for Negroes and taught piano and composition to other rag composers. It was here that he met John Stark, who was to publish a third of all Joplin's works and would later arrange many of his rags for larger ensembles. In 1899, through Stark, Joplin published his first two piano rags—"Original Rags" and his most famous and best-selling composition, "Maple Leaf Rag." Although it was not an overnight success, "Maple Leaf Rag" sold a half-million copies by 1909, making Joplin famous as well as dignifying ragtime by putting a copy on the parlor piano of every fashionable home. Although his career seemed successful, Joplin was not satisfied. He wanted to be recognized as a serious composer and hoped to do so by meshing ragtime mannerisms with classical forms. In his piano rags, Joplin paid meticulous attention to detail, giving careful consideration to voice leading, strong bass lines, and a solid formal foundation. In a way, his piano rags are almost extensions of classical minuets and rondos, using the peculiar syncopations and harmonies of dance-hall rags.

Joplin used other classical forms as well. In 1901 he moved to St. Louis and formed the Scott Joplin Opera Company, which in 1903 presented his first opera, *A Guest of Honor,* to little acclaim. In 1907, now possessing considerable fame and a comfortable income, Joplin moved to New York City, where he redoubled his efforts to have his ragtime compositions regarded as serious music. He published a pedagogical manual, *School of Ragtime,* and in 1911 published his second opera, *Treemonisha.* He could not find a backer to stage it, though, so in 1915 he personally financed a single performance at the Lincoln Theatre in Harlem.

Although the fame he desired as a serious composer did not come during his lifetime, Joplin's compositions have endured. During the 1970s most of his works were reissued, due in some degree to the use of his rag "The Entertainer" in the movie *The Sting. The Red Back Book,* a nickname for the book containing piano rags by Joplin, Joseph Lamb, James Scott, and others in arrangements by John Stark, was loaned to the New England Conservatory Ragtime Ensemble in the 1970s, and that group performed them at the Smithsonian Institution in 1973. Formally titled *Fifteen Standard High-Class Rags,* these pieces are arranged for combinations of eleven instruments. The NEC Ragtime Ensemble recorded the Joplin pieces in 1973, and the recording was reissued on CD. *Treemonisha* was finally staged in 1972 by the Houston Opera Company and recorded in 1975. The fol-

lowing year Joplin was posthumously awarded the Pulitzer Prize, granting him the "legitimate" acclaim that eluded him during his lifetime.

Chamber
various rags
what to buy: [*The Red Back Book*; Gunther Schuller, cond.; New England Conservatory Ragtime Ensemble] (EMI 47913) ♪ ♪ ♪ ♪♪

This historic 1973 recording features excellent performances by the NEC Ragtime Ensemble that more than adequately show off John Stark's arrangements. In addition, there are two solo piano performances—"The Entertainer" and "Sun Flower Slow Drag." It's a live performance, recorded in Jordan Hall at the New England Conservatory, so there's a little extra noise, but the overall quality is good.

what to buy next: [*Thompson Plays Joplin*; Butch Thompson, piano] (Daring Records 3033) ♪ ♪ ♪ ♪♪

This is a nice buy if you prefer these piano rags in their original format. The rendition of "Maple Leaf Rag" is a little unemotional, but "Solace: A Mexican Serenade" is performed with just the sort of careless introspection the music seems to call for. "The Cascades," especially, shows off Thompson's skillful articulation. This is a very enjoyable disc to listen to, either as background music or as the main attraction.

Vocal
Treemonisha
what to buy: [Carmen Balthrop, Cora Johnson, sopranos; Betty Allen, mezzo-soprano; Curtis Rayam, Kenneth Hicks, tenors; Dorceal Duckens, baritone; Willard White, Edward Pierson, bass-baritones; Raymond Bazemore, bass; Ben Harney, Dwight Ransom, singers; Gunther Schuller, cond.; Houston Grand Opera Orchestra] (Deutsche Grammophon 435709) ♪ ♪ ♪♪

There are times when this work seems more like a revue than an opera, but Schuller and the Houston company do their best to give Joplin's scoring the weight and heft it deserves. As a precursor to James P. Johnson's *Yamecraw* and Duke Ellington's *Harlem Airshaft*,

Scott Joplin

Treemonisha has plenty of historical value.

influences: James Scott, Joseph Lamb, James P. Johnson, Edward "Duke" Ellington, Hubert "Eubie" Blake, William Bolcom, William Albright

Melissa M. Stewart

Josquin des Prez (or Desprez)
Born c. 1440/1455 in France. Died August 27, 1521, in Condé-sur-l'Escaut, France.

period: Renaissance

Josquin, as he is known, was the most honored composer of the late fifteenth and early sixteenth centuries; his supple mastery of text and score provided a model for generations of musicians to follow. Decades after Josquin died, the Florentine historian Cosimo Bartoli wrote: "Just as there has been no one who approaches Josquin in his compositions, so Michelangelo is alone and peerless among those who practice his arts. Both men have opened the eyes of those who delight in these arts, now and in the future."

History doesn't yield many facts about Josquin's early life. The location and date of his birth are suspect, as some documents hint that Josquin was born in Belgium while others imply French roots. There is even some controversy over his name. Most music history texts refer to him as Josquin, without attaching a surname. The "des Prez" often appended to Josquin could refer to his birthplace or it could be a family name, but there is no hard evidence for either conjecture. There is also speculation that he may have been a student of Johannes Ockeghem, the great Flemish composer. In fact, one of Josquin's most moving works is his memorial to the older musician, the *Deploration sur la Mort d'Ockeghem* (Lamentation on the Death of Ockeghem).

Much of Josquin's musical training probably occurred in Italy, since he spent much of his professional life prior to 1500 working and living in that country. His exposure to the most fertile music scene in Europe may have started when he was a singer at the Milan Cathedral, but some recent scholarship suggests that it was another Josquin who was mentioned in the roles of that time. There is little doubt, however, that he had attached himself to the staffs of various powerful Italian families before the mid-1470s and that he undertook a stint in Cardinal Ascanio's household after the latter's exile from Milan.

Josquin's Italian stay produced some of his finest works, including the great *Missa "La sol fa re mi,"* the dynamic *Missa Gaudeamus,* and the motet *Absalom fili mi,* a setting of the biblical King David's lament for his son.

After leaving Italy circa 1500, Josquin next appeared in France, where he worked briefly as a singer and composer for Louis XII. He returned to Italy in 1503 and associated himself with Ercole d'Este, the Duke of Ferrara, but this period of employment was lasted only a year at most. Josquin then went back to France, finally settling in Condé-sur-l'Escaut, where he served as provost of the Collegiate Church of Notre-Dame. It was during his final years in France that Josquin created his magnum opus, the intensely wrought *Missa Pange lingua.*

Chamber
various transcriptions
what to buy: [*Josquin des Prez: Sixteenth-Century Lute Settings*; Jacob Heringman, lute] (Discipline Global Mobile 0006) ♪ ♪ ♪ ♪

Josquin's vocal works were often transcribed for other instruments by admiring composers and musicians, ensuring the wider dissemination of his ideas. Heringman did extensive research on these materials, finally selecting arrangements by such Renaissance notables as Valentin Bakfark, Hans Newsidler, and Alonso Mudarra for this well-recorded, well-played collection. The results are stunning in their clarity and presentation, giving the listener an aural window into another time and place.

Vocal
Missa Pange Lingua
what to buy: [Bernard Fabre-Garrus, cond.; A Sei Voci, choir] (Auvidis Astrée 8639) ♪ ♪ ♪ ♪

This recording of what is arguably Josquin's finest work is a fine addition to Fabre-Garrus's ongoing survey of the composer's oeuvre. As in the version by the Tallis Scholars (see below), the plainchant that served as the foundation for this Mass is included on the disc, a nice scholarly touch that works well artistically, too. Here and in the other examples of plainchant included on this set, Fabre-Garrus gives way to Bertrand Lemaire, who leads a somewhat larger choir, the Maitrise des Pays de Loire, through the material. The engineers bless these performances with lush acoustics.

worth searching for: [Peter Phillips, cond.; Tallis Scholars, choir] (Gimell 009) ♪ ♪ ♪ ♪

The singing of the Tallis Scholars is distinguished and fluid under Peter Phillips's direction. The plainchant that served as inspiration for this work is sung here by the Tallis Scholars, with a sound more austere than on the performances led by Fabre-Garrus. Instead of the trio of motets that make up the balance of the Fabre-Garrus album, the Tallis Scholars include an impressively sung performance of Josquin's earlier *Missa "La sol fa re mi."*

various vocal works
what to buy: [*Motets and Chansons*; Paul Hillier, cond.; Hilliard Ensemble, choir] (Virgin Classics Veritas 61302) ♪ ♪ ♪

This budget-priced collection includes a good mix of Josquin's secular and sacred songs, including the moving memorial to his older Flemish contemporary *La Deploration de Johannes Ockeghem.* Unlike Philips or Fabre-Garrus, Hillier uses an all-male choir, working the authenticity angle that rules out female voices in performances of this material.

influences: Johannes Ockeghem, Jacob Obrecht, Adrian Willaert, Antoine Busnois

Garaud MacTaggart

Dmitri Kabalevsky
Born Dmitri Borisovich Kabalevsky, December 30, 1904, in St. Petersburg, Russia. Died February 14, 1987, in Moscow, Russia.

period: Twentieth century

Though he was one of the most popular composers in Soviet Russia, Kabalevsky was respected more for his pedagogical works and for his contribution to Soviet musical education. Most of his works are harmonically conservative, since he was trying to reach a wider audience while spending his life in the shadow of Sergei Prokofiev and Dmitri Shostakovich, the two Titans of twentieth-century Russian music.

Music history will look upon Dmitri Kabalevsky as the only significant composer of Soviet Russia to escape censure by the feared Central Committee of the Communist Party. This was the organization that charged the country's greatest composers with "formalism," a vague word that instilled fear in the Soviet musical establishment up to and after the death of Josef Stalin. Kabalevsky managed to satisfy the party's desire that the country's spirit be expressed through art and music in direct and nationalistic terms. His music is tuneful, lyrical, often folk-like and simple, and many of his works were based on propaganda subjects, including the Symphony no. 1 in C-sharp Minor, op. 18, commemorating the fifteenth anniversary of the October Revolution. Symphony no. 3 in B-flat Minor, subtitled *Requiem* and scored for chorus and orchestra, was created as a tribute to Lenin.

Kabalevsky first studied composition at the Moscow Conservatory with the prolific Russian symphonist Nicolai Myaskovsky. In 1930, shortly after graduation, he became a professor of composition at that esteemed institution. He also devoted time to music criticism and edited the influential publication *Soviet Music*. The composer's first success abroad was the Symphony no. 2 in C Minor, a patriotic work urging active participation in the reconstruction of society, a concept that was certainly in line with Soviet thinking. Kabalevsky's toeing of the party line came to disgust those composers searching for honest expression, and his music began to be viewed by his contemporaries as academic and utilitarian. Although these criticisms may be valid, Kabalevsky was able to command a melodiousness that eluded many of his colleagues.

Kabalevsky's biggest success, the opera *Colas Breugnon,* was based on the novel by Romain Roland and inspired by French folk songs. Although the work entered the Russian repertoire shortly after its premiere in 1938, it was soon forgotten. Kabalevsky then fashioned a suite from the opera, and it was this piece that made his name in the West. The tuneful overture from *Colas Breugnon* is without question his most popular piece.

Highly prolific, Kabalevsky composed in many forms—songs, operas, ballets, symphonies, concertos, piano pieces, film scores, and assorted chamber music, including string quartets. His most lasting contribution may have been the many studies and exercises he wrote for children, which remain in use by aspiring young pianists the world over.

Neeme Järvi:

One of the busiest conductors on the international scene today is Neeme Järvi, the music director of the Detroit Symphony Orchestra since 1989. In the age of global travel, Järvi is also principal conductor of the National Orchestra of Sweden in Gothenburg, chief guest conductor of the Japan Philharmonic in Tokyo, and conductor laureate of the Royal Scottish Orchestra. A native of Estonia, Järvi studied at the St. Petersburg Conservatory and was first music director of the Estonian Radio and Television Orchestra. He left the Soviet Union in 1980 and settled in the United States.

What sets Järvi apart from many other current conductors is his amazing recording career, with over 350 discs to his credit. His discography includes complete symphonic cycles of Swedish composers Wilhelm Stenhammar and Hugo Alfvén, and Estonian composers Arvo Pärt and Eduard Tubin. There is a fine all-Stenhammar two-disc set (Deutsche Grammophon 445857) featuring the first two symphonies, the Serenade in F Major, and the symphonic overture *Excelsior!*. Also particularly interesting is the all-Pärt disc (Chandos 9134) featuring *Summa* for Orchestra, the composer's second symphony, *Fratres* for eight cellos, and four other works.

One of Järvi's most ambitious projects has been the internationally recognized *American Series* (with the DSO and on the Chandos label) featuring the works of Samuel Barber, Amy Beach, Charles Ives, and George Chadwick, as well as music by the African-American composers Duke Ellington, William Grant Still, and William Levi Dawson. Check out Chandos 9154 with the *Afro-American Symphony* by Still and the symphonic suite *The River* by Ellington, and Chandos 9226 with Still's second symphony and Ellington's symphonic poem *Harlem*.

Look for the Järvi name on recordings for years to come. His son Paavo is principal guest conductor of both the Stockholm Philharmonic and the City of Birmingham Symphony Orchestra in Birmingham, England; son Krisjan is the founder and conductor of the Absolut Ensemble in New York City, and an assistant conductor at the Los Angeles Philharmonic Orchestra; and daughter Maarika is principal flutist with the Orquesta Sinfonica de RTVE in Madrid, Spain.

Dave Wagner

Other than a handful of scores—the Second Piano Concerto in G minor, *Colas Breugnon,* and the orchestral suite from *Komedianti* (The Comedians)—few of Kabalevsky's compositions are remembered today except for his scholarly work and his children's pieces. The best of his music is characterized by a certain melodic resourcefulness and harmonic simplicity, but not by a striking originality.

Orchestral
Komedianti **(The Comedians) for Small Orchestra, op. 26**
what to buy: [Kiril Kondrashin, cond; RCA Victor Symphony Orchestra]] (RCA 63302) ♪ ♪ ♪₄

Finally reissued on a resplendent-sounding CD, this classic recording features the great conductor Kiril Kondrashin in a piece for which he seems to have a natural affinity. The suite from Aram Khachaturian's incidental music to *Masquerade* is the headline work for the album, however, and versions of Tchaikovksy's *Capriccio Italien* and Rimsky-Korsakov's *Capriccio Espagnol* make up the balance of the disc.

what to buy next: [*Kabalevsky, Vol. 10*; Walter Mnatsakonov, cond; Russian Cinematographic Symphony Orchestra] (Olympia 593) ♪ ♪ ♪

Mnatsakonov conducts a strong account of this lively work, coupled here with the first piano concerto and three other short orchestral pieces by the composer.

influences: Nicolai Myaskovsky

Sean Hickey

Jerome Kern

Born Jerome David Kern, January 27, 1885, in New York City, NY
Died November 11, 1945, in New York City, NY.

period: Twentieth century

Considered to be the "father of modern American musical theater," Jerome Kern is most widely known for writing (with lyricist Oscar Hammerstein) the musical *Show Boat*. He is also credited by some critics with inventing the first Tin Pan Alley jazz melodies, steering popular music in new directions while maintaining strong links to the old operetta conventions. He never fully embraced the jazz tradition as did George Gershwin, but many of Kern's songs have become jazz classics on their own due to harmonies and melodies that lend themselves well to the improvised art form.

Born to an upper middle-class New York family, Kern showed an early interest in music, and studied at New York College of Music. Despite his father's wishes for Kern to follow in the family piano-sales business, Kern eventually followed his own inclinations and went to Germany to study at Heidelberg University, returning with a Master of Music degree. Back in New York City by 1904, he worked as a pianist and marketed songs for a music publisher before working for Charles Frohman as a music editor. In 1915 he teamed with librettist Guy Bolton for *Very Good Eddie* and then added lyric-writer P.

G. Wodehouse for 1917's *Have A Heart*, a minor hit that preceded the triumvirate's first big success, *Oh Boy!* with its centerpiece song "'Til the Clouds Roll By."

By the mid-1920s, Kern was experiencing a low point in his composing career. Few of his shows were huge hits and critics were carping about the general lack of great melodies. Kern had originally focused on dance rhythms—polkas, fox trots, waltzes, and two-steps—as the basis for his tunes, but with his 1924 score for *Sitting Pretty* his adherence to his previous standards began to change. He featured longer melodies demanding an increased vocal range, and started making slow tunes as prevalent as spirited ones. Kern began moving away from the revue approach with this musical, a change in methodology which would eventually lead to *Show Boat*, his best-known work.

Based on Edna Ferber's novel, *Show Boat* had a superior dramatic score that meshed words and music in ways which had never been accomplished before. In gems such as "Make Believe," "Ol' Man River," "Can't Help Lovin' That Man," "Why Do I Love You," and "Bill," Kern's spectacular melodies and the lyrics of Oscar Hammerstein II made it a classic show that still holds up well today. The story is set in a period that stretches from the mid-1880s to 1927 and the main plot involves the love between Magnolia Hawks (daughter of Cap'n Andy Hawks, who runs the showboat *Cotton Blossom*) and the dapper gambler Gaylord Ravenal. A secondary (and tragic) plot concerns Magnolia's friend, Julie, a young woman whose "mulatto" heritage is revealed by a disgruntled suitor. The story is backgrounded by the tribulations of blacks as deeply expressed in the character Joe's poignant rendering of "Ol' Man River."

Kern would continue to write music for shows such as *The Cat and the Fiddle* (1931) and *Music in the Air* (1932), but *Roberta* (1933) had the longest legs of all. With a thin plot and fabulous songs ("Smoke Gets In Your Eyes," "All the Things You Are," and "Yesterdays"), *Roberta* was almost tailor-made for the movies. Like many composers in the 1930s, Kern was lured to Hollywood to try his hand at scoring music for films, and he left New York for California in 1934. While *Show Boat* was first made into a movie in 1929, the series of films that followed it contained new classics from the composer's fertile imagination. *Roberta*, filmed in 1935, was a prominent example, with the songs "I Won't Dance" and "Lovely to Look At" added to the score. The film *Swing Time* in 1936 brought classics such as "A Fine

Romance" and "The Way You Look Tonight" to the silver screen, while the 1941 film version of *Lady Be Good* by Kern's contemporary, Gershwin, contained one Kern song, "The Last Time I Saw Paris," with lyrics by Hammerstein. Kern returned to New York City in 1945 to start writing for a new musical, *Annie Get Your Gun,* but died of a heart attack before he could begin. He was succeeded by Irving Berlin.

Vocal
Showboat
what to buy: [Teresa Stratas, soprano; Frederica von Stade, soprano; Paige O'Hara, soprano; Karla Burns, mezzo-soprano; Jerry Hadley, tenor; David Garrison, tenor; Bruce Hubbard, baritone; John McGlinn, cond.; London Sinfonietta, orch.; Ambrosian Chorus] (Angel 49108) ♪ ♪ ♪ ♪

Probably the best version of *Showboat* is this critically-acclaimed performance. It's a scholarly edition containing all the songs from the original 1927 score, plus ones which were added to later productions and the 1936 film version, along with a couple written for the original show but never performed. Included in the three-CD package are notes and text.

what to buy next: [Kathryn Grayson, singer; Annette Warren, singer; Ava Gardner, singer; Marge Champion, singer; Gower Champion, singer; Howard Keel, singer; William Warfield, singer, MGM Studio Orchestra; MGM Studio Orchestra Chorus] (Rhino 71998) ♪ ♪ ♪ ♪

Containing a collection of tunes from the soundtrack of the 1951 film remake, this CD reissue offers extra takes by Ava Gardner of songs that were originally sung in the movie by her vocal double, Annette Warren. Don't confuse the Rhino version with the lackluster Columbia/Sony recording, on which William Warfield also appears. Also be advised that much of the score as heard in these performances was revised and some of the original music was cut.

Various songs
what to buy: [*Silver Linings: Songs by Jerome Kern*; Joan Morris, mezzo-soprano; William Bolcom, piano] (Arabesque 6515) ♪ ♪ ♪ ♪ ♪

Morris's exquisite phrasing gets to the real heart of the songs, avoiding any trace of facile, lounge-style crooning, while Bolcom, a composer in his own right, provides loving support from the keyboard.

what to buy next: [*Jerome Kern: Lost Treasures*; Anne Sciolla, soprano; Brian Kovach, piano] (Centaur 2371) ♪ ♪ ♪ ♪

This wonderful twenty-four-song collection represents Kern's early years, between 1905 and 1914. Capably supported by sensitive accompaniment from Kovach, Sciolla captures the lively, impish wit of Kern's melodies with her sparkling soprano voice, evoking laughs with the very first song, "I Want to Sing in Opera," written by Kern in 1911. Other songs here deserve new life today, especially "Take Care," syncopated gems such as "Katy Was a Business Girl," and the floating romanticism of "Ballooning."

influences: George Gershwin, Richard Rodgers, Harold Arlen, Arthur Schwartz, Robert Russell Bennett

Nancy Ann Lee and Michael H. Margolin

Aram Khachaturian
Born Aram Il'yich Khachaturian June 6, 1903, in Tbilisi, Georgia. Died May 1, 1978, in Moscow, Russia.

period: Twentieth century

One of the most popular composers from the former Soviet Union, Aram Khachaturian achieved prominence under a regime noted for its strict control of the arts. During his career, Khachaturian wrote successful ballets, film scores, and songs utilizing various folk elements, proving himself to be a Soviet-realist tunesmith of the first order. His list of works is extensive, including such famous compositions as the violin concerto he wrote in 1940 and the suite drawn from his ballet *Gayane*. This last set piece may actually be his most popular work, since it contains the *Sabre Dance*, a crowd-pleasing staple of concert programs around the world.

Khachaturian was born in the Georgian capital Tiflis (now called Tbilisi), but he was an Armenian, not a Georgian. At the invitation of his brother, he moved to Moscow in 1921, where he passed the entrance exam at Moscow University, enrolling in biology classes. A year later he entered the Gnessin Musical Technical School, where he studied cello and took courses in composition with Reinhold Gliere. He continued his musical education at the Moscow Conservatory from 1929 to 1934, studying composition (with Nikolai Miaskovsky and Mikhail Gnessin), orchestration, and harmony. After graduating with honors, he pursued post-doctoral courses until 1936.

Soon afterward, Khachaturian achieved international success with his piano concerto, following that with a violin concerto. He received more accolades for his ballet *Gayane* in 1942 and his second symphony in 1943. The symphony received warm praise from Dmitri Shostakovich, but it was the ballet (with a plot centered on an Armenian collective farm) that solidified his fame for the century, if only because specific individual movements have achieved great popularity. Both the *Dance of the Rose Maidens* and the pulse-pounding *Sabre Dance* still sound thrilling. Other works, including a cello concerto and his third symphony, soon followed.

Despite having received most of the awards that the Soviet Republic could bestow upon a composer, Khachaturian was not able to escape criticism in the cultural purges of the 1940s. In 1948, he became part of a group censured for "following an anti-popular, formalistic trend"; the list of composers condemned in this manner also included Miaskovsky, Shostakovich, and Sergei Prokofiev. If Khachaturian's 1940s works could be considered "formalistic," several written after the purge (including the *Funeral Ode in Memory of Lenin* and the film score to *The Battle of Stalingrad*) were meant to please the regime.

From 1950 on, Khachaturian spent time in academia teaching composition, first at the Gnessin School and later at the Moscow Conservatory. He also conducted his own music and continued composing. The wildly successful ballet *Spartacus* (centered around a slave revolt in Rome circa 73 b.c.) made its debut in 1954, and the suites for concert performance that followed proved to be among Khachaturian's most popular orchestral sets. His later works include more ballets and incidental music, the concerto-rhapsodies for violin, cello, and piano (composed in the 1960s), and the solo sonatas for unaccompanied cello, violin, and viola (from the 1970s). At the time of his death, Khachaturian was a professor at the Moscow Conservatory.

Music from any period in Khachaturian's working career has always been solid, well crafted, and well developed, with sparkling orchestration helping to make his scores

exciting. His gift for melody and rhythm was such that, had he chosen to go to the West, he could have had a career as a Broadway composer. He likewise had a flair for drama, an element that served him well in his film scores, ballets, and symphonies.

Orchestral
Gayane
what to buy: [Yuri Temirkanov, cond.; Royal Philharmonic Orchestra] (EMI Classics 47348) ♪♪♪♪♪

The album includes the bulk of Khachaturian's best known compositions—selections from the *Spartacus* and *Gayane* ballets. They remain fine and thrilling works, and you will enjoy them as Temirkanov puts the RPO through its paces.

Symphony no. 2 in E Minor—*The Bell*
what to buy: [Neeme Järvi, cond.; Royal Scottish National Orchestra] (Chandos 8945) ♪♪♪♪♪

Järvi presents this work in its pre-revision state, as the composer originally intended it. Included along with the symphony are four selections from the *Gayane* ballet, including the ever-popular *Sabre Dance*. A wonderful, exciting recording.

Concerto in D Minor for Violin and Orchestra
what to buy: Lydia Mordkovitch, violin; Neeme Järvi, cond., Royal Scottish National Orchestra] (Chandos 8918) ♪♪♪♪♪

Khachaturian's famous Violin Concerto is paired here with Dimitri Kabalevsky's effort along the same lines. Both are wonderful works that feature Mordkovitch, a convincing soloist with just the right blend of technical assurance and over-the-top emotionalism. The recording by Chandos's engineers is very good.

worth searching for: [David Oistrakh, violin, Aram Khachaturian, cond., Philharmonia Orchestra] (EMI Classics 55035) ♪♪♪♪♩

One of the finest albums in EMI's Composers in Person series, this disc showcases the composer as conductor, working with the man who premiered the work and wrote the fiery first-movement cadenza—the legendary violinist David Oistrakh. There are also performances of suites drawn from *Gayane* (including *Dance of the Rose-*

Maidens and *Sabre Dance*) and a suite from Khachaturian's ballet *Masquerade*. The whole package makes for great listening, since the remastering of the original 1954 recordings is handled quite well.

influences: Sergei Prokofiev, Dmitri Shostakovich, Dmitri Kabalevsky, Igor Stravinsky

Frank Retzel

Zoltán Kodály
December 16, 1882, in Kecskemét, Hungary. Died March 6, 1967, in Budapest, Hungary.

period: Twentieth century

Zoltán·Kodály is often overshadowed by the genius of his countryman Béla Bartók, but that comparison is unfair because it often ignores Kodály's contributions to Hungarian music as a musicologist and educator in addition to his gifts as a composer. Even though his orchestral suite from *Háry János* is deservedly popular, potential listeners should be aware that Kodály's gutsy and searching Sonata for Solo Cello is worth mentioning in the same breath as Bach's Suites and his superbly crafted choral music is arguably more impressive than that of Bartók's.

Kodály's father played violin in an amateur string quartet, and his mother and sister were both talented pianists. Growing up in a house where music was such an important part of family life, young Zoltán not surprisingly chose to become a musician and took lessons in piano, violin, viola, and cello in addition to singing in a church choir and following a regular academic course at the village school. All of these studies went into the formation of a scholarly mind whose early exposure to the folk music of the Galánta region (where he spent many years of his youth) and the sacred choral works of Haydn, Mozart, and Beethoven (especially his Mass in C Major) would have a lasting impact on his own work.

By the time Kodály moved to Budapest in 1900 to enroll as a student in the Franz Liszt Academy of Music, he had already had two of his earliest works performed: an orchestral overture and a string trio. In addition to his musical studies, he also pursued classes at Budapest University, eventually taking a degree in Hungarian and German and, later, earning a Ph.D. in linguistics. Meanwhile, back at the Academy, he had also received diplomas in composition and teaching along with a doc-

Jazz Influences on Classical Music:
It is hardly surprising that twentieth century composers would look to the most enduring American musical legacy not only as a source of inspiration, but as a wellspring of musical gestures. From its roots in blues and the rhythmic exhortations of work songs and spirituals, jazz came to represent the collective consciousness of black America. By the early 1920s, its popularity was felt across the world and classically trained composers began to assimilate many of its elements. Syncopation, the shifting of accents from one beat to another; "swing" feeling, a hard-to-describe rhythmic inflection; improvisation (more or less spontaneous composition); and instrumentation were all ingredients in the stew of jazz borrowed by the world's great composers.

Though Igor Stravinsky's *Rag-Time* of 1918 is often acknowledged as the first notated composition to incorporate jazz elements, Darius Milhaud's 1923 ballet *Le Creation du Monde* was the first extensive work to make novel use of the idiom, integrating syncopated rhythms and the flattened fifth, or "blue" note, with jazz instrumentation. The exportation of jazz was advanced as the "Roaring '20s" of America spread to Europe, particularly to cosmopolitan Paris, where the joyous optimism and exuberance of the decade found a sympathetic audience tired of war. Nods to jazz and music-hall abound in the works of Frenchman Francis Poulenc, and even the fastidious Maurice Ravel was enamored enough to utilize syncopation and jazz instrumentation in his 1931 Concerto in G Major for Piano and Orchestra.

In Germany, the autodidact Paul Hindemith fell under the spell with his *Ragtime* for orchestra (built on a "swung" Bach fugue subject), but it was his countryman Ernst Krenek who brought jazz into the opera house with his wildly successful *Jonny spielt auf* (1925–1926), an opera that set off a musico-dramatic movement that portrayed contemporary subjects and glorified new technology. Later, in Nazi Germany, jazz was considered to be a product of American imperialism and decadence, and therefore banned. Soviet composers were subject to a similar form of censorship, and jazz works such as Dmitri Shostakovich's *Suites for Jazz Orchestra* risked being labeled "formalist," a Stalinist catch-all for anything un-Soviet.

But obviously, it was skilled American composers who did much to bring jazz to the concert-going public. Bursting with shifting accents and swinging rhythms, Aaron Copland's youthful Concerto for Piano from 1926 is but one early and important example. As the country's preeminent vaudeville and Broadway songwriter, George Gershwin brought the sound of jazz to classical concert-goers with the unforgettable clarinet wail that opens his *Rhapsody in Blue,* a staple of the repertoire. The work was commissioned and premiered by bandleader Paul Whiteman, himself a fervent advocate of the fusion of jazz and European art music. The indefatigable Leonard Bernstein was a tireless champion of jazz and made liberal use of syncopation and kindred elements in his numerous works for the theater and concert hall. Gunther Schuller pioneered a further amalgamation with his "third stream music."

Today the overlap between jazz improviser and classical composer is both less novel and less prominent. With jazz supplanted in preeminence by rock and subsequent pop forms in American culture, its adoption is of less interest to classically-trained composers abroad.

Sean Hickey

torate based on his early research into Hungarian folksong. It was during the course of those cultural investigations that Kodály met and became friends with Béla Bartók. The two men explored the countryside, recording facets of a vanishing tradition in much the same way that England's Ralph Vaughan Williams and Brazil's Heitor Villa-Lobos did, all eventually merging the results of their various musicological studies with a genuine flair for composition. The duo's first collection of traditional tunes, *Erdélyi magyarság: népdalok (The Hungarians of Transylvania: folksongs)*, was published in 1923 and proved to be an important survey of Hungary's gradually disappearing folk culture and a way of preserving it for posterity.

Kodály was appointed to a professorship at the Academy, teaching theory and composition, in 1907. There he began training a new generation of musicians (among them Antal Doráti and László Lajtha) to absorb many of the technical advancements being made in the main European cultural centers (particularly the music of Claude Debussy) and infuse them with indigenous folksong to create a distinctly Hungarian idiom. Within a dozen years Kodály had developed into one of Hungary's most important musical forces. Not only was he influencing the direction its music would take during the next few decades through his teaching and research, he was developing his own compositional language, one based on folksong and away from the Germanic model which had been a feature of Hungarian music since the days of Franz Liszt. While he tended to concentrate on choral music, a genre to which he would always return, Kodály had also created (in 1915) his first masterpiece, the Sonata for Solo Cello, op. 8, the greatest work for unaccompanied cello since Johann Sebastian Bach's set of six suites.

By 1923 he had survived the revolutionary hurly burly of the short-lived Hungarian Republic of Councils (1919) and an attempt to besmirch his reputation as a composer and pedagogue by enemies in the new government. He had also signed a publishing contract in 1921 with Universal Edition in Vienna which assured the wider dissemination of his music. All this led up to the creation of the *Psalmus Hungaricus,* an oratorio for tenor voice, orchestra, and chorus, composed to celebrate the 50th anniversary of the union of Buda, Pest and Óbuda to form Budapest. Not only was it a success at home, but

Zoltán Kodály

Herbert von Karajan:
The Austrian-born Herbert von Karajan's professional debut as a conductor came at the Ulm Musical Theatre (where he was Germany's youngest general music director), leading a performance of Wolfgang Amadeus Mozart's *Le Nozze di Figaro (The Marriage of Figaro)* in 1927. After seven years there, Karajan moved on to Aachen, where he became music director of the opera and symphony orchestras. He also applied to join the Austrian Nazi Party around this time, a fact he later ascribed to his desire for the music directorship in a period when the National Socialists were tossing non-affiliated civil servants out of office. After the end of World War II, Karajan was interrogated about his relationship with the Third Reich and eventually cleared of being anything more than a glorified civil servant. He then began a truly remarkable run of appointments and recordings that would solidify his reputation as one of the premier conductors of the twentieth century. At one point during the mid-1950s he held concurrent positions with the Berlin Philharmonic Orchestra, the Vienna State Opera, the London Philharmonia Orchestra, and the Salzburg Festival, causing some critics to speak of his musical "empire."

At his commercial peak in the 1960s and 1970s, Karajan was one of the world's most famous conductors, and his recordings sold better from a global standpoint than just about any of his immediate contemporaries. His status as music director for life of the Berlin Philharmonic Orchestra, which he acquired in 1967, rewarded him for developing a uniquely polished platform upon which to construct his artistic vision, one that required a disciplined corps of musicians willing to forego their own musical opinions and submit to his. The resulting sound of the orchestra was distinct, featuring a string section of uncommon unity, but was often accused of being too mannered in its presentation. Still, there were undeniable moments when aural magic was being made, before members of the orchestra revolted, in 1982, against their music director's wish to hire the clarinetist Sabine Meyer as the first non-probationary, female member of the ensemble. This defiance only heralded Karajan's increasing problems imposing his will upon the orchestra, a situation that, combined with an accelerating array of health problems, led to his eventual retirement in 1989, mere months before he died.

Karajan's recorded legacy is vast and includes a number of works that he recorded more than once or twice. Although he went into the studio to create four complete sets of Ludwig van Beethoven's symphonies, Karajan's 1963 edition with the Berlin Philharmonic Orchestra is, with the exception of a surprisingly weak rendition of the *Pastoral* symphony, one of the finest surveys of the composer's symphonies that can be had (Deutsche Grammophon 453701). One of the best albums detailing Karajan's work with the London-based Philharmonia Orchestra finds him and the orchestra providing the backdrop for horn player extraordinaire Dennis Brain in a recital that includes all four of Wolfgang Amadeus Mozart's horn concertos (Angel 66950). Given Karajan's predilection for eighteenth and nineteenth century works, it may have shocked some listeners when he recorded a trio of pieces by the core triumvirate of twelve-tone music, Arnold Schoenberg, Alban Berg, and Anton Webern (Deutsch Grammophon 457760). Still, this album is one of the cornerstones of Karajan's recorded oeuvre and can serve as a splendid introduction to the scores of these three Viennese giants.

Mathilde August

it was also performed throughout Europe and raised Kodály's standing among international audiences. Three years later, in 1926, he unveiled his opera (technically a Singspiel, with spoken dialogue. in five scenes) *Háry János,* based on the story of a Hungarian folk anti-hero whose braggadocio was the military equivalent of Baron von Munchausen's. Kodály concert suite drawn from *Háry János* became his most performed work.

Although he would continue writing music up until 1966, including such fine orchestral scores as the *Dances of Marosszék* (1930), *Dances of Galánta* (1933), and *Variations on a Hungarian Folksong* (1939)—also known as the *Peacock Variations*—Kodály's greatest achievement after his compositions of the 1920s lay with his work as an educator and ethnomusicologist. His decades of field work (with and without Bartók), combined with his continual striving to improve music education in Hungary, has affected generations of musicians and proven the potency of his methods to the world.

Orchestral
Háry János: Suite
what to buy: [Antal Doráti, cond.; New Philharmonia Orchestra] (London 443006) ♪ ♪ ♪ ♪

Here is a very good orchestral sampler of Kodály's larger-scaled works including the aforementioned suite and two rhythmic works with great melodic inspiration—the *Galanta Dances* and the *Peacock Variations*—performed by Doráti and the Philharmonica Hungarica.

what to buy next: [Iván Fischer, cond.; Budapest Festival Orchestra] (Philips 462824) ♪ ♪ ♪₄

In addition to the suite and some rarely recorded incidental music from the *Háry János* Singspiel, Fischer also conducts fine performances of the composer's *Dances of Galánta* and *Dances of Marosszék.* The bonus selections making this collection a solid choice are three of Kodály's choral works sung by two children's choirs—a nice way of experiencing yet another of the composer's strengths. The sonics are very clear, almost disturbingly so in the choral selections.

[George Szell, cond.; Cleveland Orchestra] (Sony Classics 48162) ♪ ♪ ♪₄

Added almost as an afterthought to sterling renditions of Sergei Prokofiev's *Lieutenant Kijé* suite and Maurice Ravel's orchestral arrangement of Modest Mussorgsky's

Pictures at an Exhibition, Szell proves the Hungarian flair to be at least as powerful and dynamic as the Russian one. The album's programming is ideal for anyone wanting to pick up three well-performed "hits" at a bargain price.

Chamber
Sonata for Solo Cello, op. 8
what to buy: [*Starker Plays Kodály,* Janos Starker, cello] (Delos 1015) ♪ ♪ ♪ ♪ ♪

Given that the piece is a masterpiece worthy of being considered in the same class as Johann Sebastian Bach's efforts for the instrument, Starker gives one of those legendary performances which illuminate a work so well that everyone interested in classical music should have access to it. Kodály's *Duo for Violin and Cello* (with Josef Gingold joining Starker) is a worthy program-mate on the disc and Hans Bottermund's *Variations on a Theme by Paganini* (transcribed by Starker) is a nice icebreaker placed before the great sonata.

what to buy next: [Yo-Yo Ma, cello] (Sony Classics 64114) ♪ ♪ ♪ ♪

It is good to hear this superstar cellist in material that avoids the grand gesture and dwells on the soul. Here he does a splendid job technically, if not quite up to Starker's standards interpretively. Still, this is a recording that is hard to fault, not only for the diversity of its programming (works by Kodály, Alexander Tcherepnin, David Wilde, Bright Sheng, and bluegrass fiddler, Mark O'Connor) but in its attempt (via the artist's mainstream acceptance) to put challenging music before a wider audience.

[Miklos Perényi, cello] (Hungaroton 31046) ♪ ♪ ♪ ♪

While Perényi may not have the exalted technique of Yo-Yo Ma, he does have enough of that quality to go along with his Hungarian soul, making this performance (especially at mid-price) a good second choice. It is part of an all-Kodály disc that includes the composer's *Sonata for Cello and Piano* (with pianist Jenö Jandó) and the *Serenade for Two Violins and Viola.*

Vocal
Psalmus Hungaricus for Tenor, Orchestra, and Chorus, op. 13

what to buy: [József Simándy, tenor; Antal Doráti, cond.; Hungarian State Orchestra; Budapest Chorus; Hungarian Radio and Television Children's Chorus] (Hungaroton 11392) ♪ ♪ ♪ ♪

Simándy is in fine voice although his Magyar warble may be a bit off-putting to some listeners. Doráti's forceful, disciplined conducting keeps the orchestral forces on their toes but the strings never really reach the glossy heights attained by some of their Western European counterparts. The singing throughout is quite good and the version of Bartók's *Cantata Profana* included on the album means that the two most important Hungarian choral works of the 20th century can be found in solid performances on a single disc.

worth searching for: [Endre Rosler, tenor; Zoltán Kodály, cond.; Hungarian Concert Orchestra; Budapest Chorus] (Artia 152) ♪ ♪ ♪

When the composer conducts a work, there is an assumption that listeners will hear how it was intended to sound. Given that dictum, this recording is more of a "classic" for what it attempts than for what it actually accomplishes. Make no mistake, Doráti was a better conductor than Kodály (see above), but this record still has plenty of heart and a solid version of the composer's *Te Deum* as a coupling. The sonics are constricted yet serviceable, but the historical importance of the album is greater than the actual performance.

various choral works
what to buy: [*An Ode For Music: Choruses for Mixed Voices*; Aurél Tillai, cond.; Chamber Choir of Pécs] (Hungaroton 31524) ♪ ♪ ♪ ♪

Here are 18 examples here of a writer secure in the ability to write for massed human voices without instruments. Gorgeous harmonies look back more to an Italian Renaissance tradition than a Hungarian-drenched romanticism—although Kodály's setting of the 18th-century French Advent anthem *O come, O come, Emmanuel* is a fine exception to the rule. Tillai's choir also performs *Tœrót eszik a cigány (See the gypsies)*, and it is interesting to contrast this version featuring adult voices with the children's choir rendition heard on the Iván Fischer disc (see orchestral, above).

influences: Béla Bartók, Antal Doráti, László Lajtha, Miklós Rózsa

Garaud MacTaggart

Charles Koechlin
Born Charles Louis Eugène Koechlin on November, 27, 1867, in Paris, France. Died December 31, 1950, in Le Rayol Canadel, France.

period: Twentieth century

Koechlin lived on the cusp of great French music, having studied with Jules Massenet and Gabriel Fauré, maintained a friendship with Eric Satie, orchestrated Claude Debussy's ballet *Khamma* (at the composer's request), and taught Maurice Ravel. His most frequently performed orchestral scores were inspired by Rudyard Kipling's *Jungle Books,* while piano pieces and compositions featuring the flute dominate his chamber works.

Charles Koechlin was born into a wealthy family who derived their income from the textile firm founded by his maternal grandfather. His father had envisioned a military career for his son, and three years after the senior Koechlin died, Charles attempted to enter the French naval college before finally gaining admission to the École Polytechnique in 1885. After contracting tuberculosis, which ruled out any sort of naval career, Koechlin recuperated in Algeria before finally enrolling at the Paris Conservatory in 1890. There he studied composition with Massenet and Fauré and developed a lifelong fascination with counterpoint and the works of Johann Sebastian Bach. His classes with Fauré heavily influenced the budding composer, although Koechlin never seemed to develop the self-editing process adopted by his instructor. Fauré must have thought highly of him, however, since he delegated Koechlin to drill his classmates (including Maurice Ravel) in fugue and counterpoint whenever Fauré was away. In 1898 Koechlin also aided his mentor in the initial orchestration of the incidental music to Fauré's *Pelléas et Mélisande.*

In 1909, Koechlin, Ravel, and Fauré became co-founders of the Société Musicale Indépendante, an organization dedicated to performing the new music of the day. Financial troubles were beginning to disturb the relatively comfortable life that Koechlin had been able to lead until then, and he undertook parallel professions as a teacher, lecturer, and critic, in addition to his composing career. Even though he wrote several important pedagogical texts and worked with a variety of students (including Cole Porter and Francis Poulenc), Koechlin still found time to compose well over three hundred scores, assigning opus numbers to 224 of them. Most of his compositions before 1920 dealt with the human voice or were written for small instrumental groupings, although Koechlin occasionally used his expertise in orchestration to write scores for larger forces.

He had read Rudyard Kipling's *Jungle Books* in 1899 and soon started composing the first of a five-part cycle based on his impressions of the text, never really completing the massive orchestral project until forty years later (with his symphonic poem, *Les Bandar-Log,* op. 176). Four of the five works Koechlin wrote around Kipling's classic tales are orchestral compositions, while the song cycle that started the series, *Trois poèmes du "Livre de la Jungle,"* op. 18, is based on three extracts from the first *Jungle Book.* It consists of *Berceuse phoque* for soprano and female choir; *Chanson de nuit dans la jungle* for alto, baritone, and female choir; and *Chant de Kala Nag* for tenor, with an optional chorus of tenors.

During the 1930s, Koechlin became enamored of movies, working musical portraits of several actors' screen personas into his scores. In 1933 Koechlin created a suite of themes based on the film stars he admired and called it the *Seven Stars Symphony.* This intriguing mélange included an Ondes Martenot, an early electronic instrument, in the score. The most impressive segment of the work—the closing movement devoted to Charlie Chaplin—is more than twice as long as the other sections and contains themes spelling out Chaplin's name in a surprisingly musical exercise. The British actress Lilian Harvey was a particular font of inspiration for Koechlin, and he composed over one hundred works specifically relating to her. The two books of *L'Album de Lilian,* opp. 139 and 149, date from 1934 and 1935, respectively, and mix flute, piano, and soprano vocals in a variety of ways, although only the piano has movements all to itself. Again Koechlin includes the Ondes Martenot in his score, designing a duet between that instrument and the harpsichord in the sixth movement of the second book, the *Sicilienne de rêve.*

The last decade of Koechlin's life saw no serious deterioration in his ability to crank out score after score. He published the last two entries in his *Jungle Book* series (*La loi de la jungle,* op. 175, and *Les Bandar-Log,* op. 176), a batch of short works showcasing various wind instruments (including two books of solo flute pieces entitled *Les chants de Nectaire* and the *Stèle funéraire*), some fine choral scores, and still more orchestral works.

Orchestral

Le livre de la jungle (The Jungle Book), opp. 18, 95, 159, 175, and 176

what to buy: [Iris Vermillion, mezzo-soprano; Jacque Trussel, tenor; Vincent LeTexier, baritone; Steuart Bedford, cond.; Orchestre Philharmonique de Montpellier Lanquedoc-Roussillon; Chœur des Opéras de Montpellier, choir] (Naïve 34101) ♪ ♪ ♪ ♪

Like David Zinman in his now-out-of-print account, Bedford and company present the entire cycle of five opus numbers that make up Koechlin's musical images of Kipling's *Jungle Books.* The two conductors even share the same mezzo-soprano. This is a concert recording, however, and the audience, although relatively restrained, is a factor missing from the Zinman project. The magic of a wonderful performance, with all the thrills and chills of the live experience, make this the version to get, at least until the Zinman sessions are reissued.

what to buy next: [Leif Segerstam, cond.; Rheinland-Pfalz Philharmonic Orchestra] (Marco Polo 8.223484) ♪ ♪ ♪

Segerstam only includes the last four opus numbers in his survey of Koechlin's Kipling cycle, addressing the meat of the issue while skipping the appetizer and putting the project all on one platter. His *Les Bandar-Log* (op. 176) handles the composer's stylistic mockery with all the verve it needs, but he misses some of the wonder inherent in the op. 159 *Meditation of Purun Bhagat.*

worth searching for: [Iris Vermillion, mezzo-soprano; Johan Botha, tenor; Ralf Lukas, baritone; David Zinman, cond.; Berlin Radio Symphony Orchestra; RIAS Chamber Choir] (RCA Victor Red Seal 61955) ♪ ♪ ♪ ♪

Zinman is at his best in *The Meditation of Purun Bhagat,* where the low-key, rhapsodic introduction for strings mutates into some harmonically adventurous dissonances, and in the last movement of op. 95 (*The Spring Running*), which features still more inventive string writing. The often-recorded (relatively speaking) *Les Bandar-Log* receives a solid performance overall, even if it misses the last ounce of irony found in Koechlin's satire of the then-modern schools of musical thought.

Les Heures Persanes (Persian Hours), op. 65

what to buy: [Leif Segerstam, cond.; Rheinland-Pfalz Philharmonic, orch.] (Marco Polo 8.223484) ♪ ♪ ♪ ♪⅓

What a wonderful, atmospheric score this is! In its original 1913 piano version, this work delves into all kinds of interesting harmonies, but Koechlin's 1921 orchestral arrangement of his sixteen-piece suite magnifies the effect with lush string writing that hints at exotic Oriental mysteries. Segerstam's interpretation, far more interesting than his take on the *Jungle Book* series, is worthy of investigation by anyone interested in this composer.

Chamber
various piano works
what to buy: [*Piano Works*; Deborah Richards, piano] (CPO 999054) ♪ ♪ ♪ ♪

L'Ancienne maison de campagne, Koechlin's relaxed twelve-movement audio flashback to youthful pastimes at his grandfather's lakeside estate, is a deceptively simple piece, filled with delightful melodies and harmonic surprises, and *Paysages et marines* has the same hazy, impressionistic feel that Claude Debussy's later piano pieces do. The most interesting of the three works on the album, however, might be the *Nocturne chromatique* (originally written in 1907 for a chromatic harp or piano), which features chord sequences that hang suspended in space and time until the next set of phrases melts gently into place.

Les Heures Persanes (Persian Hours)
worth searching for: [Herbert Henck, piano] (Wergo 60 137-50) ♪ ♪ ♪ ♪ ♪

Henck, who is known for recordings of works by adventurous composers like John Cage, Charles Ives, and Karlheinz Stockhausen, displays the hazy yet crystalline textures of this work in its primordial form. There is no way to overstate the skill with which he conveys Koechlin's ideas and reveals this bare-bones structure to be worthy of consideration as one of the great piano works of the twentieth century.

influences: Gabriel Fauré, Claude Debussy, Francis Poulenc, Germaine Tailleferre, Henri Sauguet

Garaud MacTaggart

Kim Kashkashian:
Antonín Dvořák and Paul Hindemith were violists, Wolfgang Amadeus Mozart often played the viola, and Hector Berlioz wrote *Harold in Italy* for Nicolò Paganini when the famous violinist wanted a piece to play on the viola. Still, it is an instrument that doesn't seem to get the respect it warrants, partly because, as master violist William Primrose once noted in an interview (with David Dalton in his book *Playing the Viola*), the viola is often "the liaison voice between the cello and the upper voices…the violins."

Despite being considered one of the finest performers on her instrument, it has proven too difficult for Kim Kashkashian to forge an exclusive career as a viola soloist, and she has opted to use academia as a base of operations. As a result, Kashkashian has done a fair amount of teaching, including stints at Mannes College of Music, Indiana University, the Hochschule für Musik in Berlin, and the New England Conservatory.

Kashkashian has also worked closely with a number of prominent contemporary composers to broaden the limited repertoire featuring her instrument. In that regard she has premiered works by Arvo Pärt, Luciano Berio, Barbara Kolb, John Harbison, Linda Bouchard, and Peter Eötvös, while remaining a worthy advocate for twentieth century masterpieces of the viola repertoire by Béla Bartók, Paul Hindemith, and Dmitri Shostakovich. She seems especially enamored of compositions by György Kurtág and Giya Kancheli, and has recorded splendid examples of their oeuvre on ECM New Series 465420 (*Movement* for Viola and Orchestra) and 437199 (*Liturgy* for Viola and Orchestra) respectively.

Hindemith's Sonatas for Viola and Piano and Viola Alone (ECM New Series 833309) are major twentieth century works for the instrument and Kashkashian's playing in the solo sonatas is especially marvelous, worthy of comparison to great performances of the past by viola luminaries Walter Trampler and Samuel Rhodes. *Elegies* (ECM New Series 827744) features a fine program of works by Benjamin Britten, Ralph Vaughan Williams, and Franz Liszt for viola and piano with Robert Levin accompanying Kashkashian. The duo is also featured playing a pair of sonatas that were originally written for clarinet and piano by Johannes Brahms (ECM New Series 457068) in a recording which was nominated for a Grammy Award as the Best Chamber Music Performance in 1999 and won the Edison Prize that same year.

Ellen Kokko

Erich Wolfgang Korngold
Born May 29, 1897, in Brno, Czechoslovakia. Died November 29, 1957, in Hollywood, CA.

period: Twentieth century

One of the most brilliant child prodigies in music history, Korngold achieved worldwide fame as a composer while still in his teens. Later, when his work was proscribed by the Nazis, he made a successful switch to American movies, where his lush, late-romantic style became the Hollywood norm. Although Korngold's concert and operatic output outweighs his motion picture work, the best introduction to his music is probably still to be found in film scores like *The Sea Hawk* and *The Adventures of Robin Hood.*

The son of Vienna's most powerful newspaper music critic, Erich Wolfgang Korngold showed extraordinary musical gifts at a very early age. On the recommendation of Gustav Mahler, he was educated privately and studied composition with Robert Fuchs and later Alexander Zemlinsky. It was Zemlinsky who orchestrated the thirteen-year-old Korngold's ballet-pantomime *Der Schneemann* (The Snowman) when it was performed before the Emperor Franz Josef in 1910.

Chamber and orchestral pieces began to flow from Korngold's pen. His music was championed by Artur Schnabel, Bruno Walter, and Felix Weingartner, and Richard Strauss and Giacomo Puccini pronounced the youngster a genius. By the time he was seventeen, Korngold had written a pair of popular one-act operas, *Der Ring des Polykrates* (The Ring of Polycrates) and *Violanta.* Drafted into the Austrian army during World War I, Korngold escaped injury and, after being mustered out of the military, completed work on his most famous opera, *Die Tote Stadt* (The Dead City), in 1920. Simultaneously premiered in Hamburg and Cologne, this lush, romantic stage work eventually made its way to the Metropolitan Opera in New York, where it served as the vehicle for the American debut of Maria Jeritza.

In the 1920s Korngold worked on a series of Johann Strauss Jr. operetta revivals and completed his fourth opera, *Das Wunder der Heliane* (The Miracle of Heliane), which he always considered to be his finest stage work. Near the end of the decade the composer began his association with the well-known director and theatrical impresario Max Reinhardt, producing a Strauss pastiche called *Waltzes from Vienna,* which later became popular in America as *The Great Waltz.*

It was Reinhardt who brought Korngold to Hollywood in 1934 to arrange Felix Mendelssohn's music for the Warner Brothers movie version of Shakespeare's *A Midsummer Night's Dream.* The studio was so impressed with the composer's work that it offered him a lucrative contract to write original scores, and after considering the worsening political climate in Europe, Korngold accepted. Almost immediately he became the most famous musician in Hollywood, winning Academy Awards for the music to *Anthony Adverse* (1936) and *The Adventures of Robin Hood* (1938). Although he wrote fewer than twenty film scores during his decade in the movies, Korngold was enormously influential, and his quasi-operatic idiom became widely imitated.

After dividing his time between Europe and California, Korngold eventually settled in Hollywood and became an American citizen. Following World War II, he stopped writing film scores and tried to resume his prewar eminence as a composer for the concert stage, writing a Violin Concerto (premiered by Jascha Heifetz), a Serenade for Strings (intended for Furtwangler), and a Symphony in F-sharp, only to run into a wall of vituperative critical opposition. Musical fashion had changed, but Korngold had not, and the onetime wunderkind was no longer on the cutting edge. Plagued by poor health, Korngold wrote very little in the last years of his life and died of a heart attack in 1957, convinced that he had somehow failed to live up to his potential and that his music would be forgotten. He was wrong, and it was a record of his film music conducted by Charles Gerhardt that turned things around.

Orchestral
various film scores
what to buy: [*The Sea Hawk: The Classic Film Scores of Erich Wolfgang Korngold*; Charles Gerhardt, cond.; National Philharmonic Orchestra] (RCA 60863) ♪ ♪ ♪ ♪

When this magnificent recording burst on the scene in the early 1970s, it not only started a successful series (the twelve-album *RCA Classic Film Scores*), it began a revival of interest in Korngold's music that's still going on today. Gerhardt leads the orchestra with a conviction that only someone who passionately loves this music can attain. Music from *The Sea Hawk, Kings Row, The Adventures of Robin Hood, The Constant Nymph,* and *Escape Me Never* were recorded beautifully in London by legendary engineer K. E. Wilkinson.

Violin Concerto in D Major, op. 35
what to buy: [Gil Shaham, violin; Andre Previn, cond.; London Symphony Orchestra] (Deutsche Grammophon 439886) ♪ ♪ ♪♪

If you liked the movie music, the next step is this beautiful violin concerto, which was actually based on motifs from some of Korngold's film scores. The first movement contains themes from *Another Dawn* and *Juarez,* the second movement quotes the love theme from *Anthony*

Adverse, and the rollicking finale is taken from *The Prince and the Pauper*. Also included is Korngold's early suite for *Much Ado about Nothing*, op. 11, and a very fine recording of Samuel Barber's Concerto for Violin and Orchestra, op. 14.

influences: Richard Strauss

Jack Goggin

Edouard Lalo

Born Edouard Victoire Antoine Lalo on January 27, 1823, in Lille, France. Died April 22, 1892, in Paris, France.

period: Romantic

Along with Georges Bizet, Emanuel Chabrier, and Camille Saint-Saëns, Edouard Lalo sought to reinvigorate French music and lead it away from the perceived excesses of composers who were overly infatuated with grand opera. The irony is that Lalo, who greatly advanced the cause of chamber music through his participation in one of the most important string quartets of his day, met his greatest personal disappointments at the hands of those who repeatedly rejected his operatic creations. Lalo is best known today for a masterly cello concerto and his exciting score for violin and orchestra, the *Symphonie espagnol*.

While Lalo showed remarkable talent in his youthful violin and cello studies, his father felt that his career should be in the military. When Edouard was sixteen years old, he took matters into his own hands by running away from home and going to Paris. Somehow he managed to find his way into the Paris Conservatory, where he sat in on one of the violin classes. Lalo also took private lessons in composition at this time and ended up living the life of a struggling freelance violinist and music teacher for a few years while he worked at perfecting his craft. He also took up the cause of chamber music, a genre that French composers of the day had seemingly banished. To that end, Lalo became one of the founding members of the Armingaud-Jacquard Quartet, a pioneering ensemble that sought to bring performances of the great string quartets by Franz Joseph Haydn, Ludwig van Beethoven, and Wolfgang Amadeus Mozart to French audiences. His attempts to stimulate the creation

King's Singers:
Established in 1968, this sextet was originally made up of former students at King's College, Cambridge University, who had each gained admittance to the school's choral program, passing a rigorous audition that made them part of the elite fourteen-person college choir. They initially called themselves Six Choral Scholars from King's College, but later amended their name and made their London debut with the popular orchestra conducted by Neville Marriner, the Academy of St. Martin-in-the-Fields. Despite the fact that none of the original members of the group are associated with it, the King's Singers are still an ongoing concern. Technically speaking, every version of this group has featured fine singing, using little vibrato and producing a smoothly fashioned tone with impressive dynamic range despite a trademark tendency to dwell on the brighter side of the sonic picture.

The ensemble's embryonic foray into the world of the recording studio has been reissued (*Original Debut Recording*, Chandos 6562), and is an interesting sampling of the traits which would make the King's Singers not only one of the world's top choral groups but one of the most popular crossover "bands" of the late twentieth century. The programming for that project——mainly older English folk fare like *Scarborough Fair, Cherry Ripe*, and *The Oak and the Ash*, but also including songs by Burt Bacharach (*Wives and Lovers*) and George Gershwin (*Summertime*)——foreshadowed much of what has been heard on the group's albums and recitals over the following decades. It should be noted, however, that while Piotr Ilyich Tchaikovsky's *None but the Lonely Heart* is the only nod toward standard classical repertoire included in that set, the King's Singers have, over time, also developed an extensive repertoire of Medieval, Renaissance, and Baroque works and many of their finest albums have dwelt exclusively on music from that era.

Of particular interest is the King's Singers approach to the music of Thomas Tallis and William Byrd, the great composers of the Elizabethan era (*English Renaissance*, RCA Victor Red Seal 68004), but there is also much to appreciate in *Annie Laurie: Folksongs of the British Isles* (EMI Classics 54904), which features eighteen well-sung selections, either a cappella or with accompaniment (Manuel Barrueco on guitar and/or flautist Nancy Hadden). A favorite with Gilbert and Sullivan aficionados is *Here's a Howdy Do!* (RCA Victor Red Seal 61885), a tribute album with songs from *H.M.S Pinafore, The Mikado*, and *Pirates of Penzance* filling up the bulk of the set.

The group has also commissioned scores from Toru Takemitsu (*Handmade Proverbs*), Peter Maxwell Davies (*Sea Runes*), Gyorgi Ligetti (*Nonsense Madrigals*), Krysztof Penderecki (*Ecloga VIII*), and Ned Rorem (*Pilgrim Strangers*), though few of these works are still in print. *Street Songs* (RCA Victor Red Seal 63175), the King's Singers' collaboration with percussionist Evelyn Glennie, explores the somewhat melodic music of South African composer Peter Klatzow, and may be the most consistent option for those seeking to hear the group in more adventurous material.

William Gerard

of modern French chamber music began with his own efforts in the 1850s, when he composed a pair of piano trios, a violin sonata, a cello sonata, and a string quartet. Of these, the Sonata in A Major for Cello and Piano

(1856) and the Quartet in E-flat Major for Strings (1859) were the most accomplished, with the cello score being particularly notable for the beauty of its themes and its clever use of enharmonic tones.

While Lalo had written some early orchestral works, he destroyed them later and didn't really experiment in that direction until the late 1860s, when he was persuaded to begin work on his first grand opera, *Fiesque,* and enter it into a contest sponsored by the Théâtre-Lyrique. Based on a play by Friedrich Schiller (whose "Ode to Joy" appears in the finale of Beethoven's Ninth Symphony), the libretto by Charles Beauquier was evidently quite clumsy and not worthy of the music Lalo set it to. Although this score was never performed during his lifetime, the favorable response he drew from various opera houses should have given him cause for celebration; instead, he was embittered when he didn't win the competition. All was not lost, however, since he later cannibalized portions of that score to aid in the creation of his only symphony and at least six other orchestral pieces. The practical orchestration lessons he obtained from occasional orchestra jobs and his work on *Fiesque* would reap dividends by the following decade.

In the early 1870s, Lalo (along with Camille Saint-Saëns, Vincent D'Indy, and Ernest Chausson) was a member of the Société Nationale de Musique Française, an organization initially dedicated to the promotion of French music in spheres other than grand opera. That this association would later fracture into pro- and anti-Wagnerian factions doesn't negate its impact on the French music scene of that time. It was because of his affiliation with this group that Lalo began his association with violin virtuoso Pablo de Sarasate, a relationship that resulted in the premieres of two of Lalo's orchestral works—a violin concerto in 1874 and the *Symphonie espagnole* in 1875. The latter piece was, for all intents and purposes, a violin concerto with Spanish-flavored melodic content, and it supposedly inspired Piotyr Tchaikovsky to write his own violin concerto. It has since become one of the most popular works for violin and orchestra in the repertoire.

In 1875, Lalo again turned his attention to opera, working on the score for *Le roi d'Ys* before receiving yet another disappointment when he couldn't find a venue willing to stage it. Thirteen years later, it received its first performance and became his last great success. Lalo's next compositions to gain entrance into the concert hall were the Concerto in D Minor for Cello and

Orchestra in 1877 and the ballet score *Namouna* from 1881. The Wagnerian aspects of this ballet so excited Claude Debussy when he first heard it that he became overly raucous and was kicked out of the concert. In 1880, in between the concerto and the ballet, Lalo created what may be the pinnacle of his chamber works, the Trio no. 3 for Piano, Violin, and Cello, op. 26. The composer later orchestrated the scherzo from this piece, and that version is more familiar to French audiences. Lalo also started another opera, *La jacquerie,* but he only completed part of the first act before he died in 1892.

Orchestral
Symphonie espagnole for Violin and Orchestra, op. 21
what to buy: [Vadim Repin, violin; Kent Nagano, cond.; London Symphony Orchestra] (Erato 27314) ♪ ♪ ♪ ♪

Repin plays this florid orchestral bonbon with a blend of technique and heart that is complemented perfectly by Nagano's sympathetic conducting. Ernest Chausson's *Poème* and Maurice Ravel's *Tzigane* also receive commendable performances from these exemplary musicians.

[Zino Francescatti, violin; Andre Cluytens, cond.; Columbia Symphony Orchestra] (Pearl 9250) ♪ ♪ ♪ ♪

Passionate performances guided by a formidable musical intellect were Francescatti's forte, and this recording documents his unique flair and fire. Unusual as it may seem, Lalo's *Symphonie espagnole* is the orchestral centerpiece for this recital, while a glorious rendering of César Franck's violin sonata (with pianist Robert Casadesus) provides a different picture of Francescatti's art. The balance of the disc consists of short works by Johann Sebastian Bach, Robert Schumann, Dmitri Shostakovich, Giuseppe Tartini, and Henryk Wieniawski.

what to buy next: [Marat Bisengaliev, violin; Johannes Wildner, cond.; Polish Radio Orchestra, Katowice] (Naxos 8.550494) ♪ ♪ ♪

Naxos has been developing quite a reputation for providing well-thought-out, solidly performed discs at a budget price, and this one is no exception. Bisengaliev delivers a totally credible version of this work, and the program, with renditions of Ravel's *Tzigane,* Camille Saint-Saëns's *Havanaise,* and Pablo de Sarasate's *Zigeunerweisen,* is a good sampling of showpieces for violin and orchestra.

Concerto in D Minor for Cello and Orchestra

what to buy: [Pierre Fournier, cello; Jean Martinon, cond.; Orchestre Lamoureux, Paris] (Deutsche Grammophon 457761) ♪ ♪ ♪ ♪♪

For years, Fournier and Martinon's recording has been a benchmark for other performances of this work, and it is a joy to have it back in the catalog. While they capture the essential elegance of this score and the A Minor concerto by Saint-Saëns (as well as some of the passion informing Max Bruch's *Kol Nidre*), Fournier's rendering of *Schelomo* by Ernest Bloch, with Alfred Wallenstein conducting the Berlin Philharmonic Orchestra, may be the actual highlight of the program.

[Janos Starker, cello; Stanislaw Skrowaczewski, cond.; London Symphony Orchestra] (Mercury Living Presence 432010) ♪ ♪ ♪ ♪♪

Starker's big, woody tone is muscular but not musclebound, imparting mass to the solo lines without destroying the delicate balance between cello and orchestra. Skrowaczewski leads the LSO through its paces, compelling the players to provide a taut backdrop for Starker's superb performance. The same forces can also be heard on this disc in exemplary renditions of cello concertos by Robert Schumann and (with Antal Dorati substituting for Skrowaczewski) the A Minor, op. 33, by Saint-Saëns.

what to buy next: [Maria Kliegel, cello; Michael Halasz, cond.; Nicolaus Esterhazy Sinfonia, orch.] (Naxos 8.554469) ♪ ♪ ♪♪

Kliegel follows the same interpretive path blazed by Starker, with a full-bodied way of playing that bodes well for her future as a soloist. For those listeners seeking a more complete understanding of Lalo's output for cello, this may be the way to go, because Kliegel (ably assisted by pianist Bernd Glemser) also gives moving performances of two of the composer's compositions for cello and piano—the Cello Sonata in A Minor (with a marvelous opening allegro moderato marking) and the somewhat slighter *Chants russes*.

influences: Gabriel Fauré, Georges Bizet, Camille Saint-Saëns, Claude Debussy

Ian Palmer

Fritz Kreisler:
Kreisler's legend starts in 1875, the year of his birth, and before he was just another one of those child prodigies populating classical music success stories. Tales of him being admitted to the Vienna Conservatory as a seven-year-old, studying violin with Leopold Auer, and taking theory lessons from Anton Bruckner hint at the special kind of virtuoso Kreisler would become. Around 1890 he opted out of music for the world of medicine, taking four years of medical studies (while dabbling in art in Rome and Paris) before serving in the military. Kreisler opted for music again when he left the army, eventually trying to join the Vienna Opera Orchestra as a violinist in 1896. He was turned down and went on to become one of the twentieth century's foremost artisans of the bow. This isn't to say that his life was all peaches and cream post-1896. After all, he was living at a time of change in Europe, when boundaries shifted as governments sought either advantage or stasis. Still, composers like Edward Elgar wrote works for him, his concerts were well-attended, and his recordings sold phenomenally once his reputation was established.

Another stage of Kreisler's success happened when he put pen to paper, creating works that he would pass off as a "lost" or "forgotten" work by an older composer. When he revealed the origin of the tunes, Kreisler alienated quite a few critics (and some members of his audience), but he had also written many little gems by then. Tunes like *Liebesfreud*, the *Tambourin Chinois*, and his arrangement of Antonin Dvorák's *Humoresque* still pepper the recitals of violinists.

Recordings of Kreisler often reveal the artist/composer at work, weaving aural magic with body and mind. *Original Compositions and Arrangements* (EMI Classics 64701) is a fine example of truth in labeling. Ditto for *Kreisler Plays Kreisler* (RCA Gold Seal 68448). Both discs showcase Kreisler in his multiple role as performer and composer/arranger; the first set was remastered from 78 rpm discs recorded from 1930 to 1938, while the later album covers a wider period of time (1910–1946), with a corresponding improvement in technology over that span.

Garaud MacTaggart

Orlando di Lasso

Born in Mons, Flanders, c. 1532. Died June 14, 1594, in Munich, Germany.

period: Renaissance

Although Flemish by birth, Orlando di Lasso (also known as Orlande de Lassus) stands as one of the chief figures among the "international" composers of Germany in the latter half of the sixteenth century.

Lasso's fame and enduring popularity are largely a function of his place in the pantheon of composers of sacred music. Nevertheless, his total output also ranks him among the greatest madrigalists of his generation. Lasso arguably stands at the very forefront of the development of the sixteenth-century Italian-style madrigal, along with Philippe da Monte and Giaches de Wert. Although Lasso's travels and cultural exposure throughout his career easily surpass those of any of his contemporaries, his employment, ironically, remained stable and long-term. His most significant journey was from his native Antwerp to Munich to enter into service at the court of Duke Albert V of Bavaria in 1556. By 1563 he was in charge of all music for the ducal chapel. In 1570 he was knighted by Maximilian II and remained at court in Munich until his death.

Lasso's work influenced a number of European national styles. He is credited with being one of the primary forces behind the insinuation of the Dutch-Italian style of secular madrigal writing into sixteenth-century France. His mentoring of Andrea Gabrieli also helped bring that composer's Venetian choral identity to full maturity, largely as a result of their journeys together through Bavaria and Bohemia. Lasso's secular writing embraces nearly every popular form of the period, including the German lied, Italian madrigal, and French chanson. His seven collections of German lieder depart from the earlier pattern of placing an existing secular tune in the tenor. Instead, they are set in a more madrigal-like manner, with a declamatory style tracing its way through all voices. "Ich armer Mann was hab ich than" stands as a brilliant example of such reformist writing. Most of Lasso's chansons set French texts and come wrapped in a tight polyphonic texture that adds great rhythmic energy. Mostly imitative, they feature sudden shifts in rhythm and metrical groupings that successfully mirror the emotional tone of the text. Other chansons are set in more thoughtful, homophonic textures, closer to the style of the traditional Parisian chanson. "Bon jour mon coeur" remains a prime example of this approach.

Lasso also ranks high among late-sixteenth-century composers of sacred music. The difference between Lasso and such contemporaries as Giovanni Palestrina and Tomás Luis de Victoria is that he successfully spread his efforts along both sacred and secular lines, while Palestrina and Victoria excelled primarily within the realm of church music. In addition, Lasso's efforts focused on the motet, while Palestrina produced an abundance of Mass settings and a relatively small but superb motet collection. Unlike Palestrina's restrained, elegantly classical treatments, Lasso's motet settings reflect a dynamic, impulsive, and emotional approach,

characterized by unexpected melodic jumps and jarring dissonances. They are less melismatic than their earlier models and thus shorter in length. Lasso shares less of Palestrina's predilection for plainsong characteristics and more of a thirst for dramatic, almost pictorial treatments of texts. Lasso's twelve-volume *Magnum Opus Musicum,* published ten years after his death, contains the bulk of his sacred output, including 516 motets for ensembles ranging from two to twelve voices. Among the most celebrated of these are *Surrexit Pastor bonus, Videntes stellam magi, Tristis est anima mea,* and *Quam pulchra es.* Some twelve works for two voices appear without text and were perhaps intended for instrumental performance.

Vocal
Passio Domini nostri Jesu Christi secundum Mattheum (St. Matthew Passion) for Five Voices
what to buy: [Paul Elliott, tenor; Paul Hillier, cond.; Theater of Voices, choir] (Harmonia Mundi 907076) ♪ ♪ ♪ ♪₈

Paul Hillier and his Theater of Voices bring us superlative vocal sounds in this performance of a musical monument; their a cappella balance, blend, diction, and general corporate identity prove perfect for the needs of Lasso's music and St. Matthew's exalted text. As in most Passion settings of the late Renaissance and baroque periods, we are presented with a form of early "readers' theater," where the musical forces are charged with conveying both the narrative and its accompanying dramatic tension. What often turns out to be an exercise in listening tedium, due to the performers' lack of imagination or skill, instead becomes a feast for both ear and soul. Lasso sets only Christus and the Evangelist as solo roles, again following convention. The plainsong statements respectively proclaimed by Hillier and Elliott are melodically rich and vocally centered, while the choral interpretation of the *turba* (crowd) and other smaller roles is nothing short of superb. Also included are fine performances of Lasso's briefer *Visitation* and his *Exsultet coelum mare,* paraphrased from the great proclamation for the vigil of Easter.

Lagrime di San Pietro (The Tears of St. Peter)
what to buy: [Bo Holten, cond.; Ars Nova, choir] (Naxos 8.553311) ♪ ♪ ♪ ♪

Here, Holten and Ars Nova convince the listener that the madrigals of Lasso are indeed the groundbreaking works that most music historians have always claimed them to be. From the first musical volley, the singers emphasize Lasso's harmonic and melodic adventurousness, handily navigating the composer's seven-voice texture to reveal a brilliant text that lesser ensembles would have gulped like swimmers succumbing to heavy surf. Those words, from Tansillo's *Lagrime di San Pietro,* express with vivid grief the remorse felt by Peter following his renunciation of Christ prior to the Passion and Crucifixion.

influences: Andrea Gabrieli, Giovanni Palestrina, Tomás Luis de Victoria

Frank Scinta

Franz Lehár
Born Ferencz Lehár, April 30, 1870, in Komáron, Hungary. Died October 24, 1948, in Bad Ischl, Austria.

period: Twentieth century

The Hungarian-born Viennese bandmaster Franz Lehár was the leading twentieth-century composer of operettas. He is mainly associated with his farcical 1905 stage piece *Die lustige Witwe* (The Merry Widow), with which he revived the waning art form. His serious musical nature and a changing musical landscape led Lehár to revise operetta's basic identity from lighthearted comedy to a more realistic representation of its characters' relationships, a change observed chiefly in his 1929 operetta *Das land des Lächelns* (The Land of Smiles).

Principally associated with "light" music, Franz Lehár was a well-trained musician with extensive experience both as a violinist and a conductor. The son of an Austro-Hungarian army bandmaster, Lehár took lessons in violin and piano from his father prior to entering the Prague Conservatory, where he studied violin with Antonín Bennewitz and theory with Josef Bohuslav Foerster. He subsequently took private composition lessons with Zdenek Fibich and also received advice from Antonín Dvořák upon presenting the composer with the scores for two piano sonatas in 1887.

Lehár began his musical career as a theater violinist a year later but then joined the army and played in his father's band, assisting as conductor. He advanced to the position of bandmaster in 1890 and directed army bands in various localities. He left the military six years later, shortly before the production of his first operetta, *Kukuschka,* but returned to the army when the production failed, serving as a bandmaster in Trieste, Budapest,

Gidon Kremer:
Latvian violinist Gidon Kremer, born in 1947 into a family of violinists, studied with David Oistrakh and initially established his reputation by winning the Queen Elisabeth Competition in 1967, the Paganini Competition in 1968, and the Tchaikovsky Competition in 1970. Kremer moved to Western Europe where, in 1981, he started a summer chamber music festival at Lockenhaus, Austria. There he encouraged musicians to explore new compositions while rediscovering standard works. Renamed the Kremer ATA Musica in 1992, the festival has continued to investigate new paths and issued a number of recordings drawn from its concerts. Continuing in his chosen role of teacher and explorer, Kremer recently assembled a new group, Kremer ATA Baltica, made up of very young musicians from the three Baltic countries. Astor Piazzolla's *Tango Ballet* (Teldec 22661) and Latvian composer Peteris Vasks's *Distant Light, Voices* (Teldec 2260) showcase both the range and the superbly versatile musicianship of Kremer and his young players.

Kremer has an enormous repertoire, in which he uses a highly expressive tone that, while not overly sensuous, is full of expressive shadings. Even though he has recorded traditional repertoire—his all-Schubert CD (Deutsche Grammophon 453665) is a good example of his original treatment of works by well-known composers—Kremer has perhaps become best-known for his ceaseless exploration of the works of contemporary composers, especially those from the former Eastern Bloc. He has recorded works by Arvo Pärt as well as lesser-known composers such as Edison Denisov, Georgs Pelecis, and Giya Kancheli. His long association with Alfred Schnittke, who dedicated his Concerto no. 4 for Violin and Orchestra (Teldec 26866) to Kremer, did much to popularize the music of the late Russian composer. Kremer's recording of Sofia Gubaidulina's exquisite *Offertorium* (Deutsche Grammophon 427336), which is both a violin concerto and a set of variations on the theme from Johann Sebastian Bach's *Musical Offering,* helped introduce this very original composer to a wider audience.

Jan Jezioro

and Vienna. Lehár's band and theater experiences in Vienna influenced his musical direction, leading him to compose a series of popular marches and waltzes, most notably the waltz "Gold und Silber" ("Gold and Silver"). He finally left the army for good in 1902, having been engaged to conduct in Vienna, at both the Venedig in Wien summer theater and the esteemed Theatre an der Wien.

During this period Lehár composed a number of operettas, with varying success, but it wasn't until 1905 that his operetta *Die Lustige Witwe* (The Merry Widow) brought him to international prominence. The great success of this frothy romp had as much to do with the high quality of the libretto as with Lehár's music. The story was adapted by the Viennese writers Leo Stein and Victor Léon from a French novel, *L'attaché d'ambassade,* by Henri Meilhac (known for his opera librettos to *Carmen* and *Manon*). Although Lehár was the second choice to compose the musical score (the then-prominent Richard Hueberger proved unequal to the task), his infectious melodies and dance-like rhythms made *The Merry Widow* the rage from Vienna to Buenos Aires. This first major success, premiered the same year as Richard Strauss's modernist *Salome*, proved to be Lehár's most enduring work, and its popularity resulted in the revitalization of the waning operetta form. In the years following *The Merry Widow*, other Lehár operettas, such as *Der Graf von Luxemburg* (The Count of Luxemburg) and *Zigeunerliebe* (Gypsy Love), failed to gain wide popularity. But the music of Claude Debussy, Richard Strauss, and Giacomo Puccini, as well as social changes following the First World War, had an impact on Lehár's work, leading him transform the operetta from a lighthearted musical revue to a more dramatic work.

This new development was unveiled in a series of Lehár operettas for the tenor Richard Tauber, works more serious in tone than the composer's earlier efforts. In *Paganini* (1925) and *Frederike* (1927), Tauber portrayed historical characters such as Goethe, but it was Lehár's bittersweet *Das Land des Lächelns* (The Land of Smiles), from 1929, that departed most sharply from the traditional operetta. This was reflected in its more serious music, its dramatic character relationships, and its departure from the traditional happy ending. *The Land of Smiles* proved to be Lehár's second major success and contained his most beloved song, "Dein ist mein ganzes Herz" ("You Are My Heart's Delight"), reworked from an instrumental passage in an earlier operetta. The great success of these later works, premiered mainly in Berlin, led to an important commission from the Vienna State Opera for the composition of what was to be Lehár's last operetta, *Giuditta* (1934). By that time, Lehár's music had become so popular that the premiere of *Giuditta* was broadcast across Europe by 120 radio stations. Retiring from composition following the production of *Giuditta*, Lehár turned around and built his own music publishing business so that he could control the copyrights to his own works.

Lehár remained in Austria during the years of Nazi occupation. Pressured by the grave danger to his Jewish wife, he revised *The Merry Widow* at Hitler's suggestion, adding an overture. This spared him and his wife from the fate of several friends and collaborators, but it also opened him up to later criticism. Following the Second World War, Lehár relocated to Switzerland due to his health, only returning to Austria shortly before his death in 1948.

Vocal
Die Lustige Witwe (The Merry Widow)
what to buy: [Elisabeth Schwarzkopf, soprano; Emmy Loose, soprano; Nicolai Gedda, tenor; Otakar Kraus, baritone; Erich Kunz, baritone; Otto Ackermann, cond.; Philharmonia Orchestra; Philharmonia Chorus] (EMI Classics 69520) ♪ ♪ ♪ ♪

Here is a *Merry Widow* for posterity, capturing the joy of this Viennese classic. Lovingly sung by soloists associated with the Vienna Opera, this outstanding 1953 performance is truly idiomatic. Though the album was recorded in monaural sound with some unfortunate cuts, the singing and authenticity are so formidable that they make this mid-priced disc worthy of serious consideration.

what to buy next: [Elisabeth Schwarzkopf, soprano; Hanny Steffek, soprano; Nicolai Gedda, tenor; Eberhard Wächter, baritone; Lovro von Matacik, cond.; Philharmonia Orchestra; Philharmonia Chorus] (EMI Classics 47177) ♪ ♪ ♪ ♪

This outstanding 1963 performance is a classic, and Viennese to the core. While Schwarzkopf is not in such fine voice as on her earlier effort with Ackermann, this is still a wonderful performance, captured in good stereo sound. Sadly, this set was issued on two discs when it easily would have fit onto one.

Das Land des Lächelns (The Land of Smiles)
what to buy: [Anneliese Rothenberger, soprano; Renate Holm, soprano; Nicolai Gedda, tenor; Harry Friedauer, tenor; Willy Mattes, cond.; Graunke Symphony Orchestra; Bavarian Radio Chorus] (EMI Classics 65372) ♪ ♪ ♪ ♪

Here is a *Land of Smiles* that would make even Lehár smile. Gedda is in fine voice, and Rothenberger and Holm sing marvelously on this robust 1967 performance, recorded in full-bodied stereo.

various songs
what to buy: [*Fritz Wunderlich: The Great German Tenor*, Melitta Muszely, soprano; Liselotte Schmidt, soprano; Lisa Otto, soprano; Pilar Lorengar, soprano; Anneliese Rothenberger, soprano; Edith Mathis, soprano; Elisabeth Grummer, soprano; Sieglinde Wagner, contralto; Friz Wunderlich, tenor; Rudolf Schock, tenor; Hermann Prey, baritone; Marcel Cordes, baritone; Frick Gottlob, bass; various conductors; various orchestras]

(EMI Classics 62993) ♪ ♪ ♪ ♪ ♪

This three-disc opera/operetta set contains only ten Lehár songs, but Wunderlich's wonderful voice and no-holds-barred delivery make it an outstanding collection, well worth buying, particularly at its bargain price. Notable among the Lehár selections are "Freunde, das Leben ist lebenswert" from *Giuditta* and "Von apfelbluten einen Kranz" from *The Land of Smiles*. The many other opera and operetta gems in this set are just as delightful, forming a testament to one of the twentieth century's truly great tenors.

what to buy next: [*Dein ist mein ganzes Herz*, Lucia Popp, soprano; Anneliese Rothenberger, soprano; Ursula Reichart, soprano; Sari Barabas, soprano; Erika Koth, soprano; Brigitte Fassbaender, mezzo-soprano; Fritz Wunderlich, tenor; Nicolai Gedda, tenor; Heinz Hoppe, tenor; Peter Seiffert, tenor; Rudolf Schock, tenor; Rene Kollo, tenor; Harry Friedauer, tenor; Ernst Schutz, tenor; various conductors; various orchestras] (Capriccio 10727) ♪ ♪ ♪ ♪

Containing a generous sampling of eight Lehár songs, as well as a unique selection of songs from other operetta composers, this is a wonderful collection. Notable is the singing of Peter Seiffert, whose delivery of "Freunde, das Leben ist lebenswert" from *Giuditta* and the title song from *The Land of Smiles* is incomparable.

worth searching for: [*Elisabeth Schwarzkopf Sings Operetta*; Elisabeth Schwarzkopf, soprano; Otto Ackermann, cond.; Philharmonia Orchestra; Philharmonia Chorus] (EMI Classics 47284) ♪ ♪ ♪ ♪ ♪

This 1959 collection is a treasure, with a sampling of Lehár songs from *Der Graf von Luxemburg*, *Giuditta*, and *Der Zarewitsch*, in addition to works by other composers. Schwarzkopf sings wonderfully, her idiosyncratic style providing the ring of authenticity and conveying all the charms of Viennese operetta.

influences: Jacques Offenbach, Johann Strauss II, Sigmund Romberg, Imre Kálmán, Oscar Straus,

Gerald B. Goldberg

Ruggero Leoncavallo
Born March 8, 1857, in Naples, Italy. Died August 9, 1919, in Montecatini, Italy.

Kronos Quartet:
After hearing a radio broadcast of George Crumb's *Black Angels,* violinist David Harrington resolved to form a group capable of playing the work. The new ensemble (formed in 1973) would place Harrington as first violin, John Sherba as second violin, Hank Dutt on viola and Joan Jeanrenaud on cello. (Jeanrenaud left the ensemble in 1999 and was replaced by Jennifer Culp.) From the beginning, the Kronos Quartet was unique. They approached their varied repertory with a passion and energy few ensembles could match. Dispensing with many of the usual niceties (such as formal attire), Kronos created their own avant-garde, adding listeners who crossed musical lines in ways previously unthinkable. While other string quartets performed an exclusively classical repertory (often pre-twentieth century), Kronos often chose its selections from modern times, bridging the gap between the spheres of classical, jazz, rock, and world music.

Though they had been recording since the late 1970s, their 1985 album *Monk Suite*, with classical performances of works by Thelonious Monk—now available, along with their tribute to Bill Evans, as part of *The Complete Landmark Sessions* (32 Jazz Records 32011)—was their first project to cause a stir among jazz and pop record buyers. Kronos then debuted on the Nonesuch label in 1986 with an album (Nonesuch 79111) that included a cover version of Jimi Hendrix's "Purple Haze" in addition to works by Philip Glass, Conlon Nancarrow, Peter Schulthorpe, and Aulis Sallinen.

Unpredictable, eclectic, ever one step ahead of their contemporaries, the Kronos Quartet has remained committed to all types of modern music. The ensemble has commissioned 400 works by a wide range of composers (including Philip Glass and John Zorn), and performed compositions by the likes of Arvo Pärt, Sofia Gubaidulina, Henryk Górecki, Steve Reich, tango innovator Astor Piazzolla, and jazz visionary Ornette Coleman. They have gone back to the time of Guillaume de Machaut (*Early Music*, Nonesuch 79457) and traveled to Africa (*Pieces of Africa,* Nonesuch 79275), always delivering music with the polish, zest, and freshness that so characterizes real modern expression. That standard of quality, delight in discovery, and unprejudiced view of art is the twenty-first century. And it is the Kronos Quartet.

Frank Retzel

period: Romantic

I pagliacci (The Clowns) was not Leoncavallo's first or last opera, but it has certainly proven to be his most celebrated. Heard frequently in tandem with Pietro Mascagni's *Cavalleria rusticana*, a large part of this work's acclaim centers on *Vesti la giubba (Put on the costume)*, the popular aria that has proven to be a staple of tenor recitals from Enrico Caruso and Beniamino Gigli through Luciano Pavarotti and the current generation of stars.

Ruggero Leoncavallo's upbringing as the child of a Neapolitan police magistrate was one of relative wealth and privilege. He was also talented enough to gain entry into the Naples Conservatory in 1866, studying piano and composition there until 1876 when he switched over to Bologna University. There Leoncavallo came under the influence of the poet Giosuè Carducci and, through him, Richard Wagner's music. After leaving Bologna in 1877 (sans degree) he eventually attempted to make his living by teaching music and playing piano recitals in Paris. He was finally commissioned to write an opera (*I Medici*) by Giulio Ricordi, the famous music publisher, but never actually finished it until 1893 and, because of legal difficulties with Ricordi, ended up giving it to Eduardo Sonzogno to publish.

Part of the reason why Sonzogno may have gotten the nod over Ricordi in this matter could have been the success his company had with Pietro Mascagni's *Cavelleria rusticana* in 1890. It was Sonzogno who sponsored the contest that Mascagni's one-act opera won, and it was Sonzogno and Mascagni who profited mightily from the sale of *Cavelleria rusticana* scores and arrangements once that opera became a massive hit. All of a sudden "verismo" operas were the rage, with composers attempting to outdo each other in their presentation of realistic people going through relatively realistic problems in naturalistic settings. Leoncavallo saw his chance to jump on the bandwagon with a plot supposedly inspired by one of his father's court cases; not only did he write the music, he also authored the libretto.

The basic storyline for *I pagliacci* revolves around a double murder involving the leader of a troupe of actors who is insanely jealous over his wife's supposed infidelity. When her unfaithfulness proves rooted in reality, he (Canio) stabs her (Nedda) and her lover (Silvio), but he does so within the context of a play-within-a-play, a farce gone mad. Canio acts out the role of the clown (Pagliacci) in love with Columbine (Nedda) who refuses to tell her husband the name of her lover. The aria *Vesti la giubba* comes about as the tormented Canio, dressed as the clown, has the dreadful, tormented epiphany that will result in lives lost. The opera was not subtle in its music or its storyline, and that may actually be why it was and has remained such a big hit with opera audiences.

After the success of *I pagliacci,* Leoncavallo tried his hand at other operas (fifteen more completed, five unfinished), including a setting of the very story (*Scènes de la vie de Bohème*) that Puccini would later use for one his most famous operas. While Leoncavalo had middling triumphs with his version of *La bohème* and its follow-up,

Zazà, there was nothing that he could do to repeat the overwhelming mastery of *I pagliacci*. He did manage to write a few popular songs, including *Mattinata,* a tune he wrote in 1904 that Enrico Caruso recorded soon after, and a small handful of piano works, choral scores, and orchestral pieces, but his most creative post-*pagliacci* exercise appeared to be the sheer bulk of paperwork that he and his publishers generated in their lawsuits against each other.

Vocal
I pagliacci
what to buy: [Barbara Frittoli, soprano; José Cura, tenor; Charles Castronovo, tenor; Adrian Folea, tenor; Carlos Alvarez, baritone; Simon Keelyside, baritone; Gert-Jan Alders, bass; Ricardo Chailly, cond.; Royal Concertgebouw Orchestra; Netherlands Radio Choir; Het National Kinderkoor, choir] (Decca 467086) ♪ ♪ ♪ ♪₄

Cura is a powerful Canio and Chailly's direction keeps things on pace quite well, making this the finest version of this opera to have been recorded on the cusp of the twenty-first century, and one which stands up well to the classic performances that have gone before it.

what to buy next: [Teresa Stratas, soprano; Placido Domingo, tenor; Florindo Andreolli, tenor; Alberto Rinaldi, baritone; Juan Pons, bass-baritone; Georges Prêtre, cond.; Orchestra del Teatro alla Scala di Milano; Coro del Teatro alla Scala di Milano, choir] (Philips 454265) ♪ ♪ ♪ ♪

This performance is the soundtrack of Franco Zeffirelli's cinematic rendering of the opera, as is the accompanying version of Mascagni's *Cavalleria rusticana. It was nominated for a Grammy Award as Best Opera Recording* in 1985. Stratas is truly a Nedda to die for and Domingo, though acting may not be his strong suit as Canio, gives up a soulful *Vesti la giubba,* proving once again why he is one of the more favored tenors of the modern era. The VHS video version of this performance is available thru Philips Classics (070204).

Vesti la giubba (Put on the costume)
what to buy: [*Il Mitl Dell'Opera: 23 "Vesti la giubba";* Enrico Caruso, tenor; Antonio Paoli, tenor; Giovanni Zenatello, tenor; Amedeo Bassi, tenor; Hermann Jadlowker, tenor; Fernand Ansseau, tenor; Jussi Björling, tenor; Mario Chamlee, tenor; Miguel Fleta, tenor; Beniamino Gigli, tenor; Giacomo Lauri-Volpi, tenor; Hipolitio Lazaro, tenor; Giuseppe Lugo, tenor;

Giovanni Martinelli, tenor; Lauritz Melchior, tenor; Francesco Merli, tenor; Aureliano Pertile, tenor; Nico Piccaluga, tenor; Helge Rosvaenge, tenor; Joseph Schmidt, tenor; Georges Thill, tenor; Alessandro Valente, tenor; Marcel Wittrisch, tenor; various conductors; various orchestras] (Bongiovanni 1071) ♪ ♪ ♪

Strictly for lovers of Leoncavallo's most famous tenor aria, this album digs into the vaults for some great and some not-so-great performances dating as far back as the dawn of recording. The sound is not necessarily the best but the excitement (however brief) of giants like Caruso, Gigli, and Björling is formidable, and matched surprisingly by Paoli and Pertile. There are a few clunkers here (Zenatello has a tendency to square his phrases), but it is interesting to trace at least part of the performance history belonging to this gem of an aria.

influences: Pietro Mascagni, Giacomo Puccini

Ellen Kokko

György Ligeti

Born György Sándor Ligeti on May 28, 1923, in Dicsöszentmárton (now Târnarveni), Transylvania, Romania.

period: Twentieth century

Ligeti is one of the leading living composers of the Western classical tradition; since the 1960s his experimental works have met with public interest worldwide. From his rise to prominence in Western Europe in the late 1950s to his present-day masterpieces, Ligeti's output has spanned electronic music, atonal music, microtonal works, and the dissection of language and syntax (whether in words or music). The innovative technique of tone clusters and the timelessness created in *Apparitions* and *Lux aeterna*—both featured in Stanley Kubrick's 1969 film *2001: A Space Odyssey*—catapulted the composer's career. His opera, *Le Grand Macabre,* is now a repertory piece at major international festivals and venues.

Now residing in Germany, György Ligeti was born of Hungarian-Jewish parents and began composition lessons with Ferenc Farkas in 1941. During the Second World War he was sent into forced labor, but as soon as the war ended he resumed his musical studies with Farkas and Sándor Veress at the Franz Liszt Academy in

Erich Kunzel:
A native New Yorker, Erich Kunzel has continued in the great "Pops" conducting tradition established by Arthur Fiedler to become the most successful Classical recording artist in history, outselling even the famed Boston ensemble that defined the Pops format.

After attending Dartmouth College, where he received a Bachelor of Music degree in 1957, Kunzel went on to graduate studies at Harvard and Brown University and worked with conductor Pierre Monteux. His association with the Cincinnati Symphony Orchestra began in 1965, when he became an assistant to Max Rudolf. Kunzel became associate conductor of the orchestra two years later and also served, at various times, as conductor of the Cincinnati Opera and the Cincinnati Ballet.

It is his role as conductor of the Cincinnati Pops, however, that has brought Kunzel and this orchestra the most fame. Kunzel's discography with this ensemble follows in the tradition of Fiedler by touching on all forms of American popular music in addition to more venerable masterworks. A typical program could contain show tunes, gospel songs, soundtracks to Disney films, and scores by George Gershwin, Aaron Copland, Ferde Grofé, Stephen Foster, John Williams, and Irving Berlin, as well as classics from the Strauss Family, Piotr Tchaikovsky, Modest Mussorgsky, and Giuseppe Verdi. Kunzel, who has a great interest in jazz, also gave the world premiere of Dave Brubeck's oratorio *The Light in the Wilderness.*

Kunzel began recording with the Cincinnati Pops in the fall of 1978 and has outsold every other Pops ensemble in the period since, with more than eight million records sold. The all-Copland album *Music in America* (Telarc 80339) won the 1997 Grammy Award for Best Engineered Classical Album, with a gorgeous reading of *Appalachian Spring* that is worth of price of the album alone. It also contains *Quiet City, Fanfare for the Common Man,* and the ballet score to *Billy the Kid,* plus selections from *Rodeo.* A personal favorite is *The Fantastic Stokowski Transcriptions for Orchestra* (Telarc 80338) featuring marvelous arrangements by Leopold Stokowski, who was conductor of the Cincinnati Symphony before he took over the Philadelphia Orchestra.

Dave Wagner

Budapest. After graduating in 1949, Ligeti spent a year collecting folk music, following a tradition established by Béla Bartók and Zoltán Kodály. In 1950 he returned to the Liszt Academy as a teacher of harmony, counterpoint, and analysis. During the Hungarian uprising in 1956, Ligeti fled Budapest for Vienna, where he became acquainted with European avant-garde composers and their music. Karlheinz Stockhausen and Herbert Eimert befriended him and arranged an invitation for Ligeti to join the electronic music studio at the West German State Radio station in Cologne. *Artikulation* is the most notable of Ligeti's electronic pieces from that time. Ligeti also became a frequent participant at the Darmstadt Summer School for New Music, exchanging ideas and sharing his music with Stockhausen, Pierre

Boulez, Bruno Maderna, and Mauricio Kagel, among others.

In 1960, Ligeti's international reputation was established with the memorable premiere of *Apparitions* at the International Society for Contemporary Music festival in Cologne. This work offered an alternative to post-Webern serialism, exploring orchestral clusters and creating a new sense of timelessness in music. Other works from this period (*Atmosphères* for orchestra and *Volumina* for solo organ) provide new textures—what the composer calls "micropolyphony," where orchestral or instrumental colors are so rich that individual lines cannot be heard in isolation and traditional distinctions such as rhythm, melody, and harmony are dissolved in the listening experience. A year later, Ligeti received a commission to write a vocal chamber piece (*Aventures*), which was premiered in the North German Radio new-music series *das neue werk* in 1963. *Aventures* and its companion piece, *Nouvelles Aventures,* break down the spoken and sung text into phonemes. Ligeti even chooses to use international phonetic symbols in the score to create a dramatic scenario at once fantastic and nonsensical. This dissection of language is parallel to the composer's innovative treatment of musical syntax. Subsequent choral works (*Requiem* and *Lux aeterna*) brought the composer even more accolades. When Stanley Kubrick used four of Ligeti's works (*Aventures, Requiem, Lux aeterna,* and *Atmosphères*) in his movie *2001: A Space Odyssey,* it made Ligeti's music known to a worldwide audience.

Other orchestral works composed in the late 1960s and early 1970s (among them *Ramifications, Chamber Concerto, Melodien,* and *San Francisco Polyphony*) continually challenge the listener's aural imagination. *Ramifications* is written for a string orchestra in which half of the players tune their instruments a quarter-tone apart from the other half, while *Melodien* explores not only melodic fragments superimposed upon one another but polyrhythms as well. Also among Ligeti's experimental works from that period are witty commentaries on contemporary musical trends. Satire plays a part in *The Future of Music* (subtitled "musical provocation for lecturer and audience"), since the lecturer does not speak to the audience. Obviously, this composition had Ligeti poking fun at the performance art of the era, specifically that of John Cage and his followers. Another work,

György Ligeti

Katia and Marielle Labèque:
The piano duo of sisters Katia and Marielle Labèque purvey an art usually reserved for the parlor and rarely heard in the concert hall. This is actually surprising given the amount of music written and/or arranged for piano four-hand or two pianos by famous composers, including important works by Antonín Dvořák (the *Slavonic Dances,* opp. 46 and 72), Johannes Brahms (his *Waltzes,* op. 39), and Francis Poulenc (the Concerto for Two Pianos and Orchestra).

Born in France nearly two years apart (Katia in 1950 and Marielle in 1952), they took their first piano lessons from their mother, a fairly well-known piano teacher who had herself studied with the noted pedagogue Marguerite Long. This fairly rigorous instruction prepared them for entry into the Paris Conservatoire, where they received the kind of training necessary to hone their already considerable talents into those of touring virtuosos. Since their graduation in the late 1960s, the pair has toured all over the globe, performed in a variety of venues, and played with some of the world's finest orchestras.

While many of their recordings as a duo are out of print, there are still enough available to reveal the breadth of their repertoire. They've covered arrangements of Leonard Bernstein's works in *West Side Story, Symphonic Dances, and Songs* (Sony Classics 45531) and performed Olivier Messiaen's *Visions de l'amen* on an album otherwise devoted to the composer's orchestral works (Erato 91707). Another disc, *En Blanc et Noir: The Debussy Album* (Philips 454471), includes the title work as well as the *Petite Suite* and arrangements of Claude Debussy's first two *Nocturnes* for Orchestra, plus *Lindaraja* and the six *Épigraphes antiques.* Katia and Marielle have also recorded a jazz album called *Love of Colours* (Sony 47227), which features works by Thelonious Monk, Miles Davis, John McLaughlin, and others.

Katia has indeed developed an additional career as a jazz pianist. After having worked throughout the 1980s as an integral part of guitarist John McLaughlin's band, she eventually formed a touring ensemble specifically geared toward that end of the musical spectrum. She also released her own solo jazz album (*Little Girl Blue,* Dreyfus 36186) in 1996, a project which features her in piano duets with prominent jazz keyboard players including Chick Corea, Herbie Hancock, and Joe Zawinul.

Ian Palmer

the *Poème symphonique,* is a "musical ceremonial" for one hundred metronomes played by ten musicians directed by a conductor. Within this work are tremendous rhythmic complexities. Ligeti's only opera to date, *Le Grand Macabre,* (written between 1975 and 1977 and first performed in 1978 in Stockholm) is a fantastic story about the end of the world. This work, based on the play *La Balade du Grand Macabre* by Michel de Ghelderode, borders on the brink of total absurdity but allows the composer to take his audience on true flights of fancy. The Salzburg Festival presented a revised version of this opera in 1997, and the Covent Garden Opera reopened its opera house with it in 1999.

A self-professed fan of the Beatles, Ligeti has put a great deal of swing and rhythmic energy into his many keyboard works. His *Hungarian Rock* for harpsichord (written in 1978) is at once a witty and a serious composition in the form of a chaconne, while his series of *Études,* (begun in 1985) and his Piano Concerto are recognized by critics and pianists alike as twentieth-century masterpieces. Of similar stature are the composer's Cello Concerto from 1966 and his Violin Concerto of 1990.

Chamber
Quartets for Strings, nos. 1 and 2
what to buy: [*György Ligeti Edition 1*; Arditti String Quartet, ensemble] (Sony Classics 62306) ♪ ♪ ♪ ♪₄

This first volume of the *Ligeti Edition* (supervised and approved by the composer) was recorded in 1994, many years after the String Quartets were premiered. The polish and poise of the Arditti String Quartet are tremendous, and the technical recording expertise is first rate. The first string quartet (subtitled *Metamorphoses nocturnes*) was written by the composer in 1954, before his departure for the West, while the second was finished in 1968, after he had established himself as part of the avant-garde. The change in the musical language is inevitable, considering the cultural and temporal gaps between the two works, but the sense of drama and the mastery of proportion can easily be traced from the earlier to the later quartet. World premiere recordings of early Ligeti chamber pieces for violin duet and string quartet are also included.

various chamber works for winds
what to buy: [*György Ligeti Edition 7*; London Winds, ensemble] (Sony Classics 62309) ♪ ♪ ♪ ♪₄

Both of the wind quintet scores heard here (the six *Bagatelles* and the ten *Pieces*) are seminal works that are popular in the new-music concert repertory. Ligeti's highly successful Trio for Violin, Horn, and Piano from 1982 is also included here, performed by violinist Saschko Gawriloff, French horn player Marie-Luise Neunecker, and pianist Pierre-Laurent Aimard.

various works
worth searching for: [Jane Manning, soprano; Mary Thomas, mezzo-soprano; William Pearson, bass; Pierre Boulez, cond.; Ensemble Intercontemporain; Helmut Franz, cond.; North German Radio Chorus; La Salle String Quartet, ensemble] (Deutsche Grammophon 423244) ♪ ♪ ♪ ♪₄

This is the most representative single recording of Ligeti's major chamber and vocal works of the 1960s, capturing the range and breadth of the composer's oeuvre during that decade. The playing and singing are crisp and the interpretations sound. Included in the set are his *Chamber Concerto, Lux aeterna, Aventures* (with vocalists Jane Manning, Mary Thomas, and William Pearson), *Ramifications,* and Quartet no. 2 for Strings. The performance of the La Salle Quartet in the string quartet (recorded in 1970, when the work was new) is especially touching.

Vocal
Le Grand Macabre
what to buy: [*György Ligeti Edition 8*; Laura Claycomb, Sibylle Ehlert, sopranos; Charlotte Hellekant, Jard Van Nes, mezzo-sopranos; Derek Lee Ragin, countertenor; Graham Clark, Steven Cole, tenors; Marc Campbell-Griffiths, Michael Lessiter, Richard Suart, Martin Winkler, baritones; Willard White, bass-baritone; Frode Olsen, bass; Esa-Pekka Salonen, cond.; Philharmonia Orchestra; London Sinfonietta Voices, choir] (Sony Classical 62312) ♪ ♪ ♪ ♪₄

Le Grand Macabre, premiered in 1978, is superbly performed in this live recording at the Théâtre du Châtelet, co-produced with the Salzburg Festival during the 1997–1998 season. Sung in English and based on revisions made by the composer in 1997, this version has a clarity (in the orchestral textures and the vocal dexterity of the soloists) that is an improvement on the earlier recording of the opera.

what to buy next: [Eirian Davies, Penelope Walmsley-Clark, sopranos; Olive Fredericks, Christa Puhlmann-Richter, mezzo-sopranos; Kevin Smith, countertenor; Peter Haage, tenor; Johann Leutgeb, Laszlo Modos, Ernst Salzer, Dieter Weller, baritones; Ude Krekow, bass; Herbert Prikopa, speaker; Ernst Leopole Strachwitz, speaker; Elgar Howarth, cond.; Austrian Radio Symphony Orchestra; Arnold Schoenberg Choir] (Wergo 6170) ♪ ♪ ♪₄

This concert recording of the original 1977 version of *Le Grand Macabre,* sung in German, was made in 1987. For those interested in comparing the 1997 and 1977 versions, this is the only recorded document of the original.

Nonsense Madrigals
what to buy: [*György Ligeti Edition 4*; King's Singers, choir] (Sony Classics 62311) ♪ ♪ ♪ ♪

The versatile *Nonsense Madrigals,* composed from 1988 through 1993, were written for a cappella chorus. Paying homage to the Renaissance genre, Ligeti created new sound worlds and vocal idioms, serving wit and wisdom simultaneously as he embraced and synthesized various influences. In addition to the *Nonsense Madrigals,* this disc includes Ligeti's *Aventures* and *Nouvelles Aventures,* recorded anew in 1995 by Ligeti vocal specialists Phyllis Bryn-Julson, Rose Taylor, and Omar Ebrahim. Instrumentalists for this recording were selected from the Philharmonia Orchestra, conducted by Esa-Pekka Salonen.

influences: Pierre Boulez, Karlheinz Stockhausen, Luigi Nono

Joanna Lee

Franz Liszt

Born Ferenc Liszt, October 22, 1811, in Raiding, Hungary. Died July 31, 1886, in Bayreuth, Germany.

period: Romantic

One of the most important musical figures of the nineteenth century Romantic period, Franz Liszt led an active life as a traveling virtuoso, composer, and teacher. His best-known works include a healthy number of solo piano compositions, two piano concertos, and volumes of transcriptions. He indeed may have been the greatest pianist of all time, creating works that often defy the talents of even the most gifted modern players. Liszt is often also credited with the invention of the symphonic poem, and of his twelve pieces in this form it is *Les Preludes* that is best-known and most-played today.

If ever a musician embodied the spirit of the "Artist as Bohemian" theme of the nineteenth century, it was certainly Franz Liszt. A powerful and dynamic individual who always seemed divided between worldly interests and those of the spirit, Liszt fathered all of his children with two aristocratic women he never married, had numerous affairs and mistresses, and traveled the world as a piano virtuoso, casting the feminine members of his audiences under a spell with his powerful personality. Yet he yearned for a spiritual connection throughout his life and on more than on occasion wanted to dedicate himself to the priesthood of the Roman Catholic Church. Although he did take Holy Orders with the Franciscans late in life and was known as the "Abbé Liszt," he always carried a walking stick that showed the dual per-

Wanda Landowska:

Wanda Landowska, the person most responsible for making the harpsichord a viable instrument in twentieth century compositions, did so from her position as the foremost interpreter of Baroque works for her instrument. She started out playing the piano, studying in her native Warsaw before moving on to Berlin. Her next stop was Paris, where she landed in 1900 and started her intense research into performance practices of the seventeenth and eighteenth centuries. All during this time she was performing Bach in the customary arrangements for piano. Her studies converted her to the idea of performing Bach's compositions on the harpsichord, the instrument that she was convinced they were meant for.

It wasn't until 1903 that she first played the harpsichord in public, exposing music that was conceived for a different time and a different manner of playing. It was a worthy cause but a slowly developing one, and Landowska was on the front lines; playing, writing, teaching people to react to Bach and his brethren with the kind of joy they normally reserved for Beethoven and Brahms. She was fairly successful in that regard, garnering respect for her artistic point of view and the way she played, while also becoming somewhat of a pop phenomena in certain circles. In an article she wrote titled "About Music of the Past and Us," Landowska expresses some weariness tempered with disgust when she says,

"The gluttony with which the public rushes to buy tickets to hear *The Goldberg Variations* saddens and discourages me. Is it through love for this music? No, they do not know it. They are prompted simply by the base curiosity of seeing a virtuoso fight with the most difficult work ever written for keyboard."

Over time, however, she prevailed: There was a whole new crop of harpsichordists out there; musicologists were delving further into "original instruments" and historic playing methods; and every one of them and their successors has probably been influenced in some way and at some time by the actions she took on behalf of the music. Almost immediately after Landowska made the above statement, she also noted, "And to think that my only dream is to play beautiful and noble music!"

As to the record of her achieving this dream, the sound may be a tad boxy, but her approach to Bach's *Goldberg Variations* can be sampled with the 1934 recordings on EMI 7610082; or you can experience her take on *The Well-Tempered Clavier,* Books 1 and 2, on RCA Red Seal 6217 and 7825, respectively.

Garaud MacTaggart

spectives of his personality; on its head were carved the images of St. Francis of Assisi and Mephistopheles!

A child prodigy who began his formal musical studies at the age of seven, Liszt later studied piano with Carl Czerny; Antonio Salieri was his initial instructor in theory and counterpoint and when Liszt was twelve years old, his father hired Antoine Reicha to teach him theory and Ferdinando Paer to instruct him in composition. Liszt also met Ludwig van Beethoven early in his career and there is a story, probably apocryphal, that Beethoven

was so impressed with his musical ability that he affectionately kissed the young man on the forehead after hearing him perform. Liszt later remarked that he took this act as a sign of divine direction that his life was to be dedicated to music.

Liszt spent a good portion of his early adult life in Paris as the darling of various aristocratic circles. It was in the French capital that he began one of his more serious love affairs in 1835 with the Countess Marie d'Agoult, who left her husband for the pianist and over the course of a four-year affair bore him three children. Their initial attempts at avoiding the scandal led them to Switzerland in 1835, and two years later they toured Italy, actions which Liszt later turned into three books of musical reminiscences, the *Années de pèlerinage*. After the birth of their third child, the pianist and the countess began going their separate ways, with Liszt embarking on an intensive virtuoso career that took him all over Europe, into the arms of other women, and out of Marie's life by 1844.

Touring and concertizing took Liszt back to Hungary in 1840, at which time he reacquainted himself with the Gypsy songs and folk melodies of his homeland, tunes which later showed up in re-harmonized form as the *Hungarian Rhapsodies*. Until the pioneering musicological research of Béla Bartók and Zoltán Kodály in the twentieth century revealed the real roots of that country's musical soul, Liszt's civilized hybrid arrangements were what people tended to think of when the subject of Hungarian music came up.

The second most important relationship in Liszt's adult life was with the Princess Carolyn Sayn-Wittgenstein, whom he met in 1847. This was the liaison that would most effect him for the rest of his life, for the Princess encouraged Liszt to give up touring and concentrate on composition. Their emotional involvement grew and, in 1848, the Princess left her husband to take up residence with Liszt in Weimar. It was while living in Weimar that Liszt may have made his biggest impact on music, through his development of the symphonic poem and his advocacy of the coming generation of progressive composers, including Hector Berlioz and Richard Wagner.

In this last capacity, Liszt organized festivals featuring Berlioz's music and even conducted the premiere of

Franz Liszt

Mario Lanza:
Born Alfredo Arnold Cocozza in Philadelphia, Pennsylvania, Mario Lanza's stage name came about when he adapted his mother's maiden name (Maria Lanza) to fit his own gender. Before that occurred, however, he was working as a truck driver and singing in his spare time. A tremendous fan of Caruso's recordings, he took some voice lessons from Irene Williams and she convinced him to audition for Serge Koussevitzky, the conductor of the Boston Symphony Orchestra. Impressed by the young man's potential, Koussevitzky then arranged for Lanza to study at the New England Conservatory of Music in 1942. Drafted into the armed forces a year later, Lanza ended up in a choir, entertaining the troops instead of fighting in the war. After being released from service, he worked for a while as a day laborer before finally going out on tour in 1947 as part of the Bel Canto Trio along with George London and Frances Yeend. The next year found him appearing as Pinkerton in two performances of Giacomo Puccini's *Madame Butterfly*—the only opera he was ever to perform in—with the New Orleans Opera. 1948 was also the year that he sang at the Hollywood Bowl, after which he was signed to a movie contract with MGM Studios.

Lanza made his first film (*That Midnight Kiss*) in 1949, but his motion picture career really took off with the following year's release, *The Toast of New Orleans*, which contained the one song that would forever be associated with Lanza, "Be My Love." In 1951, Lanza appeared in the role which was probably closest to his heart, *The Great Caruso*. This movie showcased his clear, limpid tenor to its best advantage and proved to be the biggest cinematic hit he would ever have. He continued to make movies for the next few years, but grew increasingly dissatisfied with his life in the United States and moved to Italy in 1957. There Lanza starred in two more films and had even made arrangements to appear in Giuseppe Verdi's *Tosca* at the Rome Opera House in 1960, when he suffered a heart attack, dying on October 7, 1959, at the age of thirty-nine.

Lanza sings *Vesti la giubba* from Ruggero Leoncavallo's *I pagliacci*, along with arias by Verdi, Georges Bizet, and Pietro Mascagni, on *The Mario Lanza Collection* (RCA Victor 60889), but roughly two and two-thirds of this three-CD set is devoted to pop fare like "Be My Love," "Lady of Spain," and "Arrivederci, Roma." Those looking to hear Lanza in a program devoted more to classical selections should search out a copy of *The Great Caruso* (RCA Victor 60049), which contains eight songs from the film along with a dozen other works associated with Caruso. The singer is a bit off-pitch on some of the material, but his charisma is for the most part still intact.

William Gerard

Wagner's opera *Lohengrin*, but it was as a composer that he really hit his stride. By condensing the sonata form into one movement and then rearranging its internal structure, Liszt's symphonic (or tone) poems changed the way future composers would think of orchestral music, influencing Richard Strauss and other musicians unborn at the time of his innovations. Of these pioneering works, however, only *Les Préludes* shows up on concert programs with any frequency. Other major scores that emerged from Liszt's Weimar years include the

Faust-Symphonie and the great Sonata in B Minor for Piano.

He left Weimar in 1861 and moved to Rome, then back to Weimar, with occasional trips to Budapest filling out the triumvirate of places he was to live for the balance of his life. When Carolyn's husband died in 1864 the way seemed clear for the composer and the princess to be married, but instead Liszt took the four minor orders of the Catholic Church the following year. It should come as no surprise that the majority of his sacred compositions date from this time forward, including the oratorio *Christus,* which some scholars have thought influenced Wagner's music for *Parsifal.*

The effect of Liszt's personality cannot be underestimated. He was truly a superstar performer and a very charismatic individual who changed the place of the piano in the world of the concert stage. Before his time, pianists would be heard only as part of a larger varied musical program, sharing the stage or playing in combination with other instrumentalists. It was Franz Liszt who was the first to present the solo piano recital and to play consistently from memory, a demand that has been a standard feature of the pianist's performance to this day. He also insisted that the piano be placed on the stage with his right side facing the audience so that the ladies in attendance could admire his profile! Up until this point, pianists often played with their back to the audience. His very large hands and long, slender fingers made reaching the interval of tenth very easy for him, and Liszt was able to get amounts of sound from the instrument that astounded audiences and critics alike. Liszt was lavish in his praise of other composers and musicians, would give musical instruction for free to deserving individuals, and did his best to promote and support the works of talented young individuals by playing their music or arranging concerts on their behalf. Liszt also had a strong social conscience, and often gave benefit performances for causes in which he believed, or simply generously gave of his money.

Orchestral
Concerto no. 1 in E-flat Major for Piano and Orchestra
what to buy: [Martha Argerich, piano; Claudio Abbado, cond.; London Symphony Orchestra] (Deutsche Grammophon 449719) ♪ ♪ ♪ ♪₄

If there is an embodiment of the bravura style of playing that Liszt must have presented, then it certainly must be

Martha Argerich. A musician known to take chances and blessed with an incredible technique, Argerich blazes through this music with a passion and conviction that is truly amazing. Also on this disc is the E Minor, op. 11 Piano Concerto of Frédéric Chopin.

[Van Cliburn, piano; Eugene Ormandy, cond.; Philadelphia Orchestra] (RCA Gold Seal 7834) ♪ ♪ ♪ ♪₄

For many people this is the recording to have of the Piano Concerto no. 1 by Liszt. Here is Van Cliburn at the height of his powers, playing with all of the skill and verve that guaranteed his stunning win of the 1958 Tchaikovsky Competition in Moscow that electrified the world. Also on this disc is Edvard Grieg's one and only Piano Concerto, which was a concert favorite for years but is seldom played on stage today.

Concerto no. 2 in A Major for Piano and Orchestra
what to buy: [Boris Berezovsky, piano; Hugh Wolff cond.; Philharmonia Orchestra] (Ultima 21092) ♪ ♪ ♪ ♪₄

This double-disc set is a fine collection featuring Liszt's two popular piano concertos in bold, exuberant performances. Wolff's direction is right in sync with Berezovsky's interpretation of this full-blooded, sprawling music. We also get to hear these two dig into the *Totentanz (Dance Macabre)* with a *Dies Irae* that will send shivers down your spine. The second disc is devoted to the composer's solo piano works and features pianist Elisabeth Leonskaya in her readings of the mighty Sonata in B Minor for Piano and three selections from the second book of Liszt's *Années de pèlerinage: Sonetto 104 del Petrarca, Sonetto 123 del Petrarca,* and the majestic *Après une lecture du Dante: Fantasia quasi sonata.*

Hungarian Rhapsodies (orchestral arrangements)
what to buy: [Antal Dorati, cond.; Budapest Symphony Orchestra] (Mercury 432015) ♪ ♪ ♪ ♪₄

This recording is still the one to have after all these years, for it contains the six *Hungarian Rhapsodies* that were transcribed for orchestra from the original nineteen works for piano. This album also contains a well performed and recorded version of the first of Enesco's two *Roumanian Rhapsodies,* making it a truly outstanding value.

Les Préludes Symphonic Poem no. 3 for Orchestra
what to buy: [*Liszt: Orchestral Works*; Herbert von

Karajan, cond.; Berlin Philharmonic Orchestra] (Deutsche Grammophon 453130) ♪ ♪ ♪ ♪₎

Here is another outstanding recording with the type of repertoire that Karajan did best. Of the dozen symphonic poems by Liszt, this one is the best known and it is given an expansive and warm reading by the Berliners. Also on this two-disc set are a bevy of the composer's most beloved orchestral scores including the second, fourth, and fifth of his *Hungarian Rhapsodies* and the *Mephisto Waltz.*

Chamber
Sonata in B Minor for Piano
what to buy: [*Liszt: "Liebesträum"—Favourite Piano Works* Jorge Bolet, piano] (London 444-851) ♪ ♪ ♪ ♪₎

Many a pianist has died on the Sonata in B Minor hill, but Bolet makes it look like the first book of a beginner's piano method. He is in his element here, turning in a spirited performance that sails through the third movement fugato with seamless legato. This two-CD set also includes such Lisztian favorites as *Liebesträum,* the *Mephisto Waltz,* and *La Campanella (The Little Bell).* There are also some of his famous transcriptions and arrangements of works by other composers: two songs by Schubert (*Die Forelle* and *Der Erlkönig*), and themes drawn from operas by Mozart (*Don Giovanni*) and Verdi (*Rigoletto*).

what to buy next: [*My Favorite Liszt*; Van Cliburn, piano] (RCA 63613) ♪ ♪ ♪ ♪

Cliburn not only turns in a bravura performance of the Sonata in B Minor but tenderly presents such favorites as two of the six *Consolations* (nos. 3 and 5), the *Mephisto Waltz,* the *Sonetto 123 del Petrarca,* the third of Liszt's *Concert Éßtudes* (*Un sospiro*), and *Liebesträum* no. 3.

Hungarian Rhapsodies for Piano
what to buy: [Gyorgy Cziffra, piano] (EMI Classics 67555) ♪ ♪ ♪ ♪₎

Cziffra seems to have these works in his bones, because he certainly plays them with the barely contained ferocity which they deserve and rarely seem to get. The only reason this particular disc doesn't get the top rating is because it doesn't include the full complement of Liszt's *Hungarian Rhapsodies.*

Gustav Leonhardt:
Within the context of the early-music movement, the Dutch musician, conductor, and teacher Gustav Leonhardt is sometimes condemned for his deliberate approach to the score, a seeming unwillingness to impart more to the aural experience than what he deems to be the intentions of the composer, an approach that could, by all rights, lead to dry, unfeeling performances. In reality, Leonhardt's skills are such that what emerges from the keyboard he plays or the orchestra he conducts is a subtle, rhythmically nuanced sound picture, colored by impeccably-conceived, well-thought-out ornamentation that is far removed from the strict, metronomic methodology adopted by many of his predecessors and contemporaries in the "period instrument" camp.

Leonhardt studied at one of the initial bastions of the early-music crusade, the Schola Cantorum in Basel, Switzerland. After graduating from there in 1950 he went to Vienna, where he made his professional debut as a harpsichordist by playing Johann Sebastian Bach's *Die Kunst der Fuge (Art of the Fugue).* He also delved further into the study of historical performance practices, a discipline to which he had been exposed while still at the Schola Cantorum. Leonhardt's own activities as a teacher began in 1952 when he became a professor of harpsichord at the Vienna Musikhochschule. From there he went on to teach at the Amsterdam Conservatory, a post he took in 1954 and kept until 1988. It was shortly after he began working in Amsterdam that he founded the Leonhardt Consort, one of the many groups with which he would perform over the ensuing years and thus disseminate his conception of how the music of seventeenth and eighteenth century masters should be played.

Perhaps the single grandest recording project that Leonhardt ever involved himself with was one he undertook with Nikolaus Harnoncourt, acting as guiding forces in one of the first attempts to record all of Bach's sacred cantatas with period instruments and in a style approximating what the composer might have heard in his day. While present-day advances in scholarship have called into question some of the methodology used, their cantata cycle for Telefunken (now Teldec) is still considered a landmark event by many musicologists.

As a conductor, Leonhardt's collection of symphonies and cello concertos by Carl Philipp Emanuel Bach (Virgin Veritas 61794, with the Orchestra of the Age of Enlightenment) may very well be one of the better performances in his voluminous catalog. The same could also be said of his continuo playing as a member of the Quadro Amsterdam (along with violinist Jaap Schröder, cellist Anner Bylsma, and recorder player Frans Brüggen) in a superb rendition of Georg Philipp Telemann's *Paris Quartets* (Teldec Das Alte Werk 92177). Listeners curious about Leonhardt's abilities as a soloist can find good examples of his harpsichord playing in Bach's *Art of the Fugue* (Virgin Classics 2011), and of his skills as an organist in *The Organ in the Renaissance and Baroque* (Sony/Seon 60364), a two-disc set containing works by Johann Pachelbel and a fine array of lesser-known composers.

Ellen Kokko

what to buy next: [*Liszt: The Complete Works for Solo Piano, vol. 57*; Leslie Howard, piano] (Hyperion

67418/19) ♪ ♪ ♪₄

Howard's impressive traversal of Liszt's dauntingly difficult works for solo piano includes this two-disc set of performances. He plays quite well and includes all of the composer's *Hungarian Rhapsodies,* but seems to lack the fire in the belly that drives Cziffra in his playing of these pieces. Despite that caveat, Howard is eminently recommendable and well recorded.

Années de pèlerinage: 2nd year for Piano—Italy
what to buy: [*Années de pèlerinage: I-III (complete),* Alfred Brendel, piano; Zoltán Kocsis, piano] (Philips 462312) ♪ ♪ ♪ ♪₄

In this two-disc, mid-priced set, Brendel plays the first two books of the *Années de pèlerinage* while Kocsis plays the third. Brendel's performances are the product of his vaunted intellect married to a sterling technique. There is enough poetry in his playing here (especially in the three *Sonetti de Petrarca*) to beat back the critics who sometimes complain of the pianist being overly analytical.

what to buy next: [Louis Lortie, piano] (Chandos 8900) ♪ ♪ ♪ ♪

Lortie is a young pianist and has a tendency to glory in the technical aspects of playing Liszt's devilishly difficult music. That he hits all the notes is a plus; that he does so in a well-produced sound picture is also a bonus. He'll need a bit more seasoning, however, before he can approach the heights reached by Brendel, Horowitz, or Richter.

[Jenó Jandó, piano] (Naxos 8.550549) ♪ ♪ ♪₄

Attractive pricing and a solid performance from Jandó make this an easy recommendation for budget-minded listeners, even though this disc will never be a first choice overall.

Sonetti de Petrarca
what to buy: [John Browning, piano] (Delos 3022) ♪ ♪ ♪ ♪₄

The three *Sonetti de Petrarca* (47, 104, and 123) are the most played elements in the second of Liszt's *Années de pèlerinage,* and the highly romantic feel embodied in these pieces makes their popularity no mystery.

Browning's approach luxuriates in the moment, stretching the music almost to the breaking point, with a result that may infuriate some listeners by its pacing and beguile others with its soulfulness. The pianist applies the same artistic mannerisms to Liszt's Sonata in B Minor and the *Après une lecture du Dante: Fantasia quasi sonata.*

influences: Hector Berlioz, Nicolò Paganini, Charles-Valentin Alkan, Richard Wagner, Richard Strauss

Dave Wagner and Garaud MacTaggart

Andrew Lloyd Webber
Born March 22, 1948, in London, England.

period: Twentieth century

Love him or hate him, Andrew Lloyd Webber has been a major force in changing the face and structure of musical theater in the twentieth century. Broadening the musical composer's palette to include influences from rock and various ethnic styles while blending musical theater with operatic tradition, Lloyd Webber has, for better or worse, introduced legions of new fans to the genre.

Andrew Lloyd Webber's father, William, was a well known composer and organist, and his brother, Julian, is a cello soloist and professor at the Guildhall School of Music. Within this familial framework, young Andrew grew up absorbing classical music, but not to the exclusion of the rock music he heard in London during the 1960s. From childhood, however, his main interest was in composing and playing his own melodies, and while still attending Magdalen College in Oxford, he became acquainted with Tim Rice, a young law student and lyricist who shared his eclectic musical tastes.

Their initial forays into to pop songwriting met with limited success until they composed a brief cantata for a boys' school in 1967. *Joseph and the Amazing Technicolor Dreamcoat* applied a blend of rock, pop, country, calypso, and operatic stylings to the biblical story of Joseph. It received favorable notices and was expanded into a full-length stage piece a few years later. In 1971, after writing a couple of film scores (*Gumshoe* and *The Odessa File*), Lloyd Webber teamed with Rice again and achieved a breakthrough success with another work that lifted a story line from the Bible. With *Jesus Christ Superstar,* the duo extended the musical range for stage productions by including rock elements, creating one of the first rock operas. They also sold the drama with a strategy Lloyd Webber was to find useful more than once—creating an album and releasing singles from it before finding a producer to stage the play. From the CD buyer's point of view, this means that recordings listed as cast albums may not include all the actors found in the original staged versions. Lloyd Webber and Rice next found success in 1976 with *Evita,* a musical about the larger-than-life Argentinean figure Eva Peron. With music combining Hispanic folk themes and modern rock influences (some in symphonic dress), this pop extravaganza won seven Tony Awards. Rice and Lloyd Webber parted ways after *Evita.*

In 1977, Lloyd Webber wrote *Variations* (a work for cello soloist and rock band that was based on a theme by Paganini) as a showpiece for his brother, Julian; he arranged it for cello and orchestra a year later. He then experimented with several other musicals and collaborators before returning to Broadway and West End stage success in 1981 with *Cats,* a musical based on the poetry of T. S. Eliot. The show had no plot, and it relied as much on staging, dance, and costuming for its impact as it did on the music. That's a point that has often been made about Webber's productions, and despite the lush music and operatically based score, it's one that could also apply to what is perhaps his most successful musical, *Phantom of the Opera* (1986). By applying his flair for drama and exaggeration to a wildly romantic Victorian melodrama, Lloyd Webber created a show that broke all previous ticket sales and attendance records. The production also came the closest of all his scores to melding the operatic and musical theater worlds. In 1993 he also tackled a stage remake of the Billy Wilder film *Sunset Boulevard,* another work featuring a larger-than-life character (silent screen star Norma Desmond) as its heroine. As with many composers of wildly popular entertainment, the judgment of future generations about Lloyd Webber's work may differ from that of contemporary critics and audiences. Nevertheless, it is probably true that somewhere in the world, a piece composed by Andrew Lloyd Webber is being performed every hour of every day.

Vocal
Requiem
what to buy: [Sarah Brightman, soprano; Placido Domingo, Paul Miles-Kingston, tenors; James Lancelot,

organ; Lorin Maazel, cond.; English Chamber Orchestra; Winchester Cathedral Choir] (Decca 448616) ♪ ♪ ♪

First performed in 1985 and constituting his most defined excursion into classical composition, this group of settings from the Mass for the Dead was composed in memory of Lloyd Webber's father. This particular recording won the Grammy Award for Best Classical Composition in 1986. While perhaps not showing as distinctive a style in this genre as he does in his pop scores, Lloyd Webber nevertheless provides vocal challenges to which this trio of accomplished singers is well suited.

Evita
what to buy: [*American cast*; Patti LuPone, Bob Gunton, Mandy Patinkin, singers; Rene Wiegert, cond.] (MCA 1107) ♪ ♪ ♪

American stage and television star Patti LuPone brings a sultry and sensuous touch to her intense rendering of Eva Peron's character. Of those performers who have appeared in the role (including Elaine Page, who starred in the original London production, and Madonna, who did the film version), LuPone most directly conveys the balance of passion and power at the center of Evita's character.

Cats
what to buy: [*Broadway cast*; Betty Buckley, Ken Page Terrence V. Mann, Timothy Scott, Anna McNeely, Bonnie Simons, singers; Rene Wiegert, cond.; Stanley Lebowsky, cond.] (Polydor 314521463) ♪ ♪ ♪

The songs are stronger than the story line in this plotless musical, which in performance relies as much on costume and dance as it does on the score. There is a structure to the work, though, and its heart is captured in the reflections of the aging cat Grizabella's show-stopping song "Memory," performed here by Betty Buckley.

Phantom of the Opera
what to buy: [*London cast*; Sarah Brightman, soprano; Michael Crawford, tenor; Steve Barton, John Savident, Rosemary Ache, David Firth, Mary Millar, John Aron, singers; Rudy Montague Mason, cond.] (Polydor 831273) ♪ ♪ ♪

The lush and dramatic story of Beauty and the Beast, played out in the Opera House of Victorian Paris, is given full operatic treatment by the fine voices of Sarah Brightman and Michael Crawford, who played the leads on both the London and New York stages. In addition to song lyrics, the accompanying booklet gives dialogue and stage directions, adding to the re-creation of the theatrical event.

Various selections
what to buy: [*The Premiere Collection: The Best of Andrew Lloyd Webber*, Yvonne Elliman, Murray Head, Paul Nicholas, Sarah Brightman, and others, vocals] (MCA 6284) ♪ ♪ ♪♪

This is the equivalent of a greatest-hits collection, containing selections from the first two decades of Lloyd Webber's work, including "Memory" from *Cats*, "I Don't Know How to Love Him" from *Jesus Christ Superstar*, and "Don't Cry for Me Argentina" from *Evita*. These songs illustrate his flair for melody and adaptation, reasons why so many fine singers have been drawn to his work. The performers here are the signature singers who first recorded the pieces. There is a second collection (*The Premiere Collection, Encore*) that extends the idea, but this set has the stronger selection of songs.

influences: Johann Strauss Jr., Carlisle Floyd, Richard Rodgers, Cole Porter, George Gershwin

Kerry Dexter

Pietro Locatelli
Born Pietro Antonio Locatelli on September 3, 1695, in Bergamo, Italy. Died March 30, 1764 in Amsterdam, the Netherlands.

period: Baroque

Locatelli was by all accounts a masterly violinist, but despite his well-crafted, tuneful music, he was considered by many of his contemporaries to be a secondary composer. That this opinion still holds today should not dissuade potential listeners from giving his graceful, charming scores a hearing. Full of virtuoso passages for his instrument, Locatelli's best-known pieces are the Concerti Grossi, op. 1, and the *L'arte del violino,* op. 3, but the Sonatas for Flute and Continuo from op. 2 have also achieved a modicum of fame.

Not much is known of the early life of Pietro Locatelli or the economic status of his family, but it has been assumed that they were well-off because his parents were buried in private graves—a final resting place

reserved for those with social standing and monetary resources. Locatelli studied violin and composition in Rome as early as 1711, and many biographers report that he may have been a student of the famous Arcangelo Corelli. We do not know whether it was Locatelli himself who later asserted that he was Corelli's student, but it is more likely that he studied with a musician named Giuseppe Valentini, himself a former student of Corelli's. While in Rome, Locatelli made his living as a freelance musician, but he was also employed as a salaried player in a number of important churches and developed a reputation for his skillful playing. In 1729, Locatelli moved permanently to Amsterdam, where he found work as a virtuoso violinist, teacher, publisher, and businessman. He seems to have begun selling violin strings when he took over the business of an Italian violin dealer named Aurelli. This came about through the urging of Aurelli's widow, who became Locatelli's business partner and later his mistress.

There were some innovations in Locatelli's music; he was one of the first composers to write out cadenzas in his concertos. While this was a common practice for romantic composers, these solo flurries were always improvised by baroque-era musicians. Many of his sonatas also abandon the multi-movement form of the baroque sonata and settle on the three-movement forms of the later classical period. Finally, from the French tradition, Locatelli borrowed the idea of including complete viola parts in his early concertos. His compositions and playing received distinctly mixed reviews, however, and the well-known traveler, music critic, and correspondent Charles Burney said his music was more "surprise than pleasure," meaning that technical displays masked empty musical rhetoric and often-faulty compositional technique. Despite these criticisms, Johann Sebastian Bach felt so positive about Locatelli's music that he copied out an entire concerto for use with his Leipzig Collegium Musicum. Locatelli's *Caprices* for the violin (from his op. 3) were also said to be the inspiration for Niccolo Paganini's famous *24 Caprices* for solo violin.

Orchestral
Concerti Grossi for Two Violins, One (or Two) Violas and Continuo, op.1
what to buy: [Jaroslav Krecek, cond; Capella Istropolitana, orch.] (Naxos 8.553445 and 8.553446) ♪ ♪ ♪♪

These are solid recordings from the Naxos budget label, which divides the twelve concerti grossi from Locatelli's opus 1 between two discs. Fine playing from this conductor and his orchestra proves that a cheap price doesn't necessarily mean mediocre performances.

Concerto Grosso no. 6 in E-flat Major—*Il Pianto d'Arianna*
what to buy: [Fabio Biondi, cond; L'Europa Galante, orch.] (Opus 111 30104) ♪ ♪ ♪ ♪

Biondi conducts an all-Locatelli sampler that includes the first, second, and twelfth concertos from opus 1, plus the composer's *Sinfonia funebre*. The music is beautifully played and afforded exceptional sound.

Chamber
various sonatas
what to buy: [Schönbrunn Ensemble Amsterdam] (Globe 5134) ♪ ♪ ♪ ♪

With clear sonics and dynamic playing from this Dutch group, this album presents a nice selection of Locatelli's music, including two sonatas from the op. 2 set for flute and continuo. You'll also find a pair of sonatas for two violins from the opus 8 set, a sonata for two flutes from opus 5, and a chamber sonata in D Minor from op. 6.

influences: Arcangelo Corelli, Giuseppe Tartini

Dave Wagner

Jean-Baptiste Lully
Born Giovanni Battista Lulli, November 28, 1632, in Florence, Italy. Died March 22, 1687, in Paris, France.

period: Baroque

During his days as master of music to the royal family at the court of Louis XIV, Lully was considered to be the best and most representative of French composers. Although he wrote a number of sacred motets, his many *comedies-ballets* and *tragedies-lyriques* (an invention of Lully's that foreshadowed tragic opera) remain the best examples of his compositional style.

The life of Jean-Baptiste Lully could easily be called a study in contrasts. The son of an Italian miller, he rose from humble beginnings to become the main stylistic and compositional influence on the French courts. His fame and his influence with the royal family cannot be denied, yet he was unpopular with many other French musicians and critics of the time. His compositional style ran the gamut from the fashionable to the sacred. Finally, at the height of his power, he was brought down in the lowliest fashion by one of his own inventions.

Much of what we know of Lully's early life is hearsay, as might be expected, since no one expected this lower-class child to become great and his training to be worth documenting. We do know he studied guitar and violin as a boy and by 1644 had become sufficiently well known as a guitarist that he was asked to travel to France as a page for Mlle. de Monpensier (also known as Mlle. d'Orleans, niece of the Chevalier de Guise). While at her court, he studied theory and became better known as a violinist; he also had the opportunity to hear the *Grande Bande des 24 violons du Roi*. In 1652 he was released from service at that court and through his acquaintance with Louis XIV was appointed to the post of *compositeur de la musique instrumentale* for the king's household. In his new role he was responsible for the music in the royal court ballets. During the next two years he made his first attempts at composing for the ballet, and in 1656 the king named him leader of a smaller version of the *Grande Bande*. Lully paid such attention to detail and quality of technique that the smaller group soon rivaled the larger ensemble.

In 1660 he composed the first of his most famous ballets (*Xerxes*) and his first sacred motets. The following year, he was named the first *surtendant* of royal music and became a French citizen. For the next ten years, he continued writing ballets and motets, but he also began a fruitful collaboration with the great French playwright Molière, which lasted until their ballet *Le bourgeois gentilhomme* was composed in 1670. In 1672 Lully received the sole right to form an Academie Royal de Musique, which gave him control of any vocal music heard at the court. Just after the performance of his first opera (*Cadmus et Hermoine*) and shortly after Molière's death in 1673, Lully received the right to take over his theater in the Palais Royale at no cost. From this time until the end of his life, Lully composed an average of one opera per year with his new librettist, Philippe Quinault. In keeping with the style of the time, all of these were set to ancient myths and legends. Lully's innovations in French opera, such as the use of ballets within the operas, and his adaptations of Italian opera, including replacing the solo recitative with an accompanied recitative, have marked him as the stylistic founder of French national opera. In addition, he developed the format for the stylistic prelude known today as the "French overture," including three parts—slow, fast, and a repeated slow section. Finally, he is known anecdotally as the inventor of the conducting baton, although his invention, unlike our modern sticks, was a large staff that he used to bang out the time on the floor. It was this staff that brought about his demise when he accidentally missed the floor and smashed his foot instead. When he would not let his doctors amputate his infected toe, gangrene set in, and Lully soon died of blood poisoning, an ignominious end for such a successful person.

Orchestral
Le Bourgeois Gentilhomme
what to buy: [*L'Orchestre du Roi Soleil: Symphonies, Ouvertures, and Airs à jouer,* Jordi Savall, cond.; Le Concert des Nations, orch.] (Alia Vox 9807) ♪ ♪ ♪ ♪♪

The music for *Le Bourgeois Gentilhomme* makes a marvelous suite that conveys all the glory and decadence associated with court life during the Sun King's reign. Savall's forces play this disarming yet pompous music with great skill, and the recording is clear. The conductor also includes *Le Divertissement Royal* and a suite from *Alceste,* making this the place to start for those interested in exposing themselves to Lully's art.

selections from various ballet scores
what to buy: [*Ballet Music for the Sun King,* Kevin Mallon, cond. Aradia Baroque Ensemble, orch.] (Naxos 8.554003) ♪ ♪ ♪ ♪

This disc contains some fine performances of Lully's ballet music, arranged in suites. There are movements from *Le bourgeois gentilhomme, Alcidiane et Polexandre, Xerxes, L'amour malade, Le Ballet des Temps,* and *Le Ballet des Plaisirs,* all given good treatments on period instruments. The budget price makes it a bargain.

Vocal
Atys
what to buy: [Agnes Mellon, soprano; Guillaumette Laurens, mezzo-soprano; Guy de Mey, tenor; Jean-Francois Gardeil, baritone; William Christie, cond. Les Arts Florissants, ensemble] (Harmonia Mundi 901257/59) ♪ ♪ ♪ ♪

It may not be Lully's best-known opera, but this modern premiere performance is not to be missed. William Christie is an expert on French vocal music of this period, and this is a fine recording. The program notes (in English as well as French) contain interesting historical

anecdotes in addition to the libretto.

influences: Jean-Philippe Rameau, Marin Marais, Marc-Antoine Charpentier

Melissa M. Stewart

Witold Lutoslawski
Born Witold Roman Lutoslawski on January 25, 1913, in Warsaw, Poland. Died February 7, 1994, in Warsaw, Poland.

period: Twentieth century

Lutoslawski's music is hard to pigeonhole. His finest compositions range from the folk-inspired Concerto for Orchestra, his first great work, to those utilizing the unique hybrid he once described as "aleatory counterpoint" (a method he adopted for his Quartet for Strings and the powerful Concerto for Cello) and finally to ones using a distinctive process he termed "chain form," in which two strands of harmonic patterns alternated with or overlapped each other.

At the beginning of World War I, Witold Lutoslawski's father was involved in the nationalist struggle to secure Poland's liberty. The family was living in Moscow at the time, and the senior Lutoslawski was attempting to aid his native country in its fight against German occupation by raising funds for the resistance while simultaneously advocating Poland's freedom from Russian domination. When his allegiances brought him into conflict with the Bolsheviks, he was imprisoned and, in 1918, executed. His wife (a physician) and their three sons (Witold was the youngest) then moved back to Warsaw, where they set about making a new life for themselves, including lots of musical activities. Soon young Witold was taking piano lessons and developing into a child prodigy. Despite his flair for the piano, he was more fascinated by the violin and eventually took instruction on that instrument as well. He began studying composition in 1928 and in 1932 was admitted to the Warsaw Conservatory, where his composition teacher, who had become a professor at the school, convinced him to drop his violin studies and concentrate on the piano. By 1937, when Lutoslawski graduated with degrees in piano and composition, he had already written a few scores and begun a promising career as a pianist.

Immediately upon graduating, however, he was conscripted into the army. After a year he was demobilized and made plans to study with Nadia Boulanger in Paris, but with the outbreak of World War II he was reassigned to a radio communication installation. Shortly thereafter he was captured by German forces and held in a prisoner-of-war camp before escaping. Making his way back to Warsaw, he found the conservatory taken over by Polish collaborators and most cultural life at a standstill. He was able to survive as a musician, teaming up with his friend and fellow composer Andrzej Panufnik in a piano duo performing arrangements of works by Wolfgang Amadeus Mozart, Franz Schubert, and other composers in the city's cafés. Lutoslawski also continued writing music, although only his *Variations on a Theme of Paganini* for Two Pianos was completely finished during this period, and he had to wait until after the war to complete his first symphony. Using rhythms and themes closely associated with Polish folk music, he also wrote a series of songs for the Polish underground that were circulated anonymously.

Following the war, much of Lutoslawski's material (which had displayed ambiguous tonal relations ever since his last days at the conservatory) didn't find favor with the authorities at the Ministry of Culture and the Arts. To make a living, he ended up working for Polish Radio, writing various "functional" pieces, including incidental music for radio plays, until 1960. While many of these works received awards from the government, Lutoslawski was also writing music that would challenge the Soviet-realist model adopted by the state. First among these compositions would be the Concerto for Orchestra, which he started in 1950 and finished in 1954. While folk elements are an integral part of the score, Lutoslawski's approach was closer Béla Bartók's than it was to that of Poland's great turn-of-the-century composer Karol Szymanowski. Lutoslawski's next major work was written in 1958, during one of Communist Poland's periodic cultural thaws. His *Musique funèbre* was dedicated to Bartók, but it used serial methods in a highly personal manner that aligned the composer more with the twelve-tone experiments of Igor Stravinsky than those of Arnold Schoenberg or Anton Webern.

Lutoslawski's stylistic evolution continued after he heard a performance of John Cage's Concerto for Prepared Piano and Orchestra—music that piqued the composer's interest in aleatory procedures. Lutoslawski sought to deal with these random elements by putting them within a specific context, a tactic that veered away from a strict adherence to Cage's precepts and would evolve into another of Lutoslawski's highly original conceptions. The most intriguing works from this phase include the Concerto for Cello and Orchestra (1970) and *Mi-parti* for Orchestra (1976). The composer's final stylistic turn involved what he called "chains"—linkages of rhythmic and melodic fragments, best exemplified by *Chain 1* for Chamber Orchestra, *Chain 2* for Violin and Orchestra, *Chain 3* for Orchestra, and the Partita for Violin and Piano.

Orchestral
Concerto for Cello and Orchestra
what to buy: [Pieter Wispelwey, cello; Jac van Steen, cond.; Netherlands Radio Philharmonic] (Channel Classics 12998) ♪ ♪ ♪ ♪

Wispelwey's disc meshes cello concertos from opposite ends of the twentieth century for an intriguing look at how musical culture has progressed from the Victorian elegance of Edward Elgar's time until the post-World War II tumult that shaped modern masterpieces by Bartók, Schoenberg, Cage, and Lutoslawski. While the cellist does a marvelous job with the Elgar concerto (also heard in this set), Lutoslawski's powerful mix of methods and sounds brings out Wispelwey's best performance. Even though his recording isn't as consistently inspired as the Rostropovich rendition (see below), it ranks as the best performance currently in catalog and a solid introduction to one of the most important twentieth-century works for cello and orchestra.

worth searching for: [Mstislav Rostropovich, cello; Witold Lutoslawski, cond.; Orchestre de Paris] (EMI Classics 49304) ♪ ♪ ♪ ♪

Lutoslawski, a fine conductor in his own right, wrote this piece for Rostropovich, and the pairing of the composer and the cellist makes this the benchmark against which all other recordings of this work must be judged. Rostropovich's warm tone and overall playing strength stand up well in the give-and-take measures, which pit the cello against driving brass choruses. Lutoslawski's conducting maintains a sense of orchestral balance, allowing all the voices to come through with clarity. The work is paired with Henri Dutilleux's cello concerto (featuring the same orchestra under the baton of Serge Baudo), a very complementary, somewhat more accessible piece with a palpable air of mystery.

Concerto for Orchestra
what to buy: [Yan Pascal Tortelier, cond.; BBC

Philharmonic Orchestra] (Chandos 9421) ♪ ♪ ♪ ♪

Tortelier's well-programmed disc covers Lutoslawski's early, folk-inspired Concerto for Orchestra along with two other important works from the composer's catalog—the twelve-tone *Musique funèbre* and the partially aleatory *Mi-parti*. The resulting performances rival the composer's own authoritative recordings, tracing Lutoslawski's compositional development toward his own unique maturity.

Partita for Violin, Orchestra, and Obligato Piano
what to buy: [*Mutter Modern*; Anne-Sophie Mutter, violin; Phillip Moll, piano; Witold Lutoslawski, cond.; BBC Symphony Orchestra] (Deutsche Grammophon 445487) ♪ ♪ ♪ ♪

Mutter is an astounding violinist with a special affinity for twentieth-century scores, particularly Lutoslawski's. *Partita* and *Chain 2* are works with specific ties to her: the former was arranged for orchestra from a duo for violin and piano after Lutoslawski heard her performance of his *Chain 2*. Both of those extremely seductive compositions are part of this amazing three-disc set, which also includes outstanding renditions of concertos by Bartók, Stravinsky, and Alban Berg, in addition to a pair of works by lesser-known composers Wolfgang Rihm (*Gesungene Zeit*) and Norbert Moret (*En rêve*).

Chamber
Quartet for Strings
what to buy: [Kronos Quartet, ensemble] (Nonesuch 79255) ♪ ♪ ♪ ♪

This recording is easier to find than the one by the Wilanow Quartet (see below), but there are no other works included on the disc, which makes this a suspect buy despite the undeniable strength of the performance. However, if you only want Lutoslawski's quartet, this is the way to go.

worth searching for: [*Musique de Chambre*; Wilanow Quartet, ensemble] (Accord 201142) ♪ ♪ ♪ ♪

Missing only the *Dance Interlude* for Clarinet and Piano, this disc gives you not only a fine performance of Lutoslawski's early quartet but equally valid takes on the composer's other major chamber music scores—the violin and piano version of *Partita* and the impressive *Grave* for cello and piano (both of which feature pianist Maciej Paderewski and members of the Wilanow Quartet). The

clearly articulated performance by the ensemble matches up quite well with that of the better-known Kronos Quartet (see above).

influences: Béla Bartók, Andrzej Panufnik, Krzysztof Meyer

Garaud MacTaggart

Edward MacDowell
Born Edward Alexander MacDowell on December 18, 1861, in New York, NY. Died January 23, 1908, in New York, NY.

period: Romantic

Chances are good that every late-nineteenth-century American household with a piano in its parlor had a little sheaf of sheet music with MacDowell's "To a Wild Rose" in it. The second of his piano concertos was the first American work of its kind to enter the international repertoire. His reputation as a composer was such that MacDowell was able to found an arts colony in New Hampshire, an establishment that has proven to be a crucible for new American music in the twentieth century.

MacDowell grew up in a Quaker household, where he demonstrated a marked aptitude for drawing and painting despite the general familial opinion that such pursuits were frivolous. When he was eight years old, MacDowell began studying piano, applying himself so assiduously that he was admitted to the Paris Conservatory by the time he was sixteen. Two years later he was in Frankfurt, Germany, taking piano lessons from Carl Heymann and studying composition with Louis Ehlert. MacDowell formally entered the Hoch Conservatory in the spring of 1879 and ended up studying composition with Joachim Raff. A month after his enrollment, he played in a piano recital that Franz Liszt attended; a year later he left the conservatory to begin teaching piano privately. One of his first students was Marian Griswold Nevins, an American pianist whom he married in 1884. He was hired to teach piano at the Darmstadt Conservatory in 1881 but left after a year because he felt that his responsibilities at the school were encroaching on his time for composition. This was a theme that would be repeated throughout his life: although he needed to work as a teacher or performer in order to support his family, he would abandon these positions when he felt that his need to compose was getting short shrift.

In 1882, Liszt heard MacDowell play a piano reduction of his first piano concerto and pronounced it good. On Liszt's recommendation, the Breitkopf and Härtel publishing house printed some of his scores, and performances of MacDowell's works were soon heard throughout Europe and America. Despite this apparent success, however, the budding popularity of his music didn't translate into a steady income. He continued teaching privately and even aspired to be appointed to England's Royal Academy of Music, but in 1888 he moved back to the United States with Marian. Arriving in Boston, MacDowell realized that he needed to pursue a gainful profession. He began performing as a composer/pianist at venues throughout the Boston area, gradually introducing new compositions into his recitals. Prior to the unveiling of his second piano concerto in 1889, MacDowell had been just another in a group of good but not necessarily great young composers. This new work generated almost immediate response, not just from American conductors and audiences but in Paris and other European capitals. Between 1889 and 1896, MacDowell received rave notices for his concerts, taught piano to a fairly large number of students, and still managed to devote time to composition. These were the years when many of his major piano pieces were being written: his twelve *Virtuoso Etudes,* his second piano sonata (the *Sonata Eroica*), and his *Woodland Sketches.* It was this last set of little essays that contained what would become MacDowell's most popular piece ever, "To a Wild Rose."

His reputation was so solid by this time that Columbia University in New York City offered to make him its first-ever professor of music and, in 1896, MacDowell accepted the offer. The position lasted until 1904, but during that time he also taught piano, conducted and led the Mendelssohn Glee Club, edited music, toured North America as a concert pianist, and in the summers, wrote even more music. The most impressive works to come from his pen during this time were his third and fourth piano sonatas, the *Norse* and *Keltic,* respectively. After a series of arguments with Columbia's president, Nicholas Murray Butler, MacDowell handed in his resignation. Although he continued to teach piano and work with a variety of arts-related organizations, things soon

started to go downhill for the composer. He had been hit by a cab in the spring of 1904 and by the winter of that year began exhibiting signs of mental deterioration. His illness was to continue with only a few breaks until his death in January 1908.

Just before he died, Marian MacDowell turned the couple's summer home in Peterborough, New Hampshire, into an artists colony, complete with residence halls, a library, dining and recreation halls, and a large number of studios, all situated on more than four hundred acres of woods and meadows. Composers who have used the MacDowell Colony to work on various projects include Leonard Bernstein, Aaron Copland, Roy Harris, Ned Rorem, and Virgil Thomson.

Orchestral
Concerto no. 2 in D Minor for Piano and Orchestra, op. 23

what to buy: [Donna Amato, piano; Paul Freeman, cond.; London Philharmonic Orchestra] (Olympia 353) ♪ ♪ ♪ ♪₆

Amato plays both of MacDowell's piano concertos in this set, and if not for the earlier Cliburn recording, hers would have to be considered the top recording of this score. Not only is her playing consistently well thought out and executed, but Freeman and the London Philharmonic Orchestra provide admirable support on both concertos.

what to buy next: [André Watts, piano; Andrew Litton, cond.; Dallas Symphony Orchestra] (Telarc 80429) ♪ ♪ ♪

If you never heard the versions of this work by Amato or Cliburn, you might think this was a nice recording of a good but not great Brahms-inspired piano concerto. Watts does well, Litton and the orchestra are OK, and the engineers at Telarc have done their usual fine job. The performers do much better on the MacDowell piece, where there is less competition, than they do on the two Liszt concertos with which the MacDowell is paired. The performances are satisfactory, not revelatory.

worth searching for: [Van Cliburn, piano; Walter Hendl, cond.; Chicago Symphony Orchestra] (RCA Gold Seal 60420) ♪ ♪ ♪ ♪ ♪

Everything seems to have gone right in this performance: the pacing is impeccable, the orchestra is in top form, and most of all, Cliburn achieves a level of poetry in this work that no one else appears to have attained. His solo piano take on "To a Wild Rose" is as inspired as can be. People who bought this disc for Cliburn's fine rendition of Robert Schumann's piano concerto (with Fritz Reiner conducting the Chicago Symphony Orchestra) must have been very pleasantly surprised. Stunning is an adjective that would not be out of place here.

Chamber
Woodland Sketches for Piano, op. 51
what to buy: [*Piano Music, Vol. 1*; James Barbagallo, piano] (Naxos 8.5559010) ♪ ♪ ♪ ♪

This suite of piano pieces contains one of the simplest, most beautiful minute-and-a-half moments in keyboard literature, "To a Wild Rose." On hearing it, there should be no doubt as to why this little gem was such a parlor favorite. It has the same timeless quality that Beethoven's *Für Elise* has, and it is deceptively easy to play. The other nine parts of the suite also have their charms, and Barbagallo does his utmost to bring them out. The balance of the set constitutes a solid introduction to MacDowell's oeuvre, as it contains most of the composer's popular piano suites, including the eight *Sea Pieces*, the six *Fireside Tales*, and the ten short *New England Idyls*.

Sonata no. 4 in E Minor for Piano, op. 59—*Keltic*
what to buy: [*Piano Music, Vol. 3*; James Barbagallo, piano] (Naxos 8.559019) ♪ ♪ ♪ ♪

Dedicated to the Norwegian composer Edvard Grieg, MacDowell's fourth piano sonata may be his most important piece for solo piano. Then again, some folks might opt for the composer's twelve *Virtuoso Etudes* for Piano, op. 46. Both factions can find happiness with this disc, which features both works—along with the early *Forgotten Fairytales,* op. 4, and the six mid-period *Poems After Heine,* op. 31—in fine, understated, well-recorded performances by Barbagallo.

influences: Edvard Grieg, Charles Tomlinson Griffes, Arthur Foote, George W. Chadwick

Garaud MacTaggart

Guillaume de Machaut
Born c. 1300, in Rheims, France. Died c. April 1377 in Rheims, France.

period: Medieval

Guillaume de Machaut remains the greatest example of that singular medieval hybrid, the poet-musician, and represents the full embodiment of the fourteenth century Ars Nova in France. The music of this period can seem foreign to the twentieth-century ear and requires great attention to such intangibles of performance practice as proper declamation of ancient texts, correct vocal timbre and placement, and even the appropriate spacing of the performance within the most accurate acoustical surrounding.

The Ars Nova movement, which allowed the style of vocal composition to evolve beyond the narrow confines of the thirteenth century "conductus" style of Léonin and Pérotin, was both defined and chronicled by the composer Phillipe de Vitry in his treatise *Ars Nove* (c. 1325). It generally is agreed that Machaut's innovative compositional style signals the realization and fruition of de Vitry's earlier proposals.

Machaut was born in Rheims and seems to have received his early education and musical training there. Little else is known about his youth until 1323, when his name appears on the service ledgers of John of Luxembourg, King of Bohemia. There he filled multiple posts, first as composer and later as clerical adviser and secretary to the King. Machaut's name continues to surface in various accounts of court life through John's death in 1346. The composer's later years in Rheims remain delineated more by compositional than personal milestones, but his very last years are even sketchier, with little trace of either his day-to-day activities or his compositional efforts. Yet his death in 1377 elicited numerous poetic and musical testimonials from his contemporaries, most notably the equally prolific Francesco Landini.

There is no doubt that Machaut's great and tender facility with verse evolved from the tradition of the *trouveres,* whose telling tales of romance flooded the European continent and brought depth and definition to the otherwise ephemeral ideal of courtly love. Though nimble with text, he excelled at delivering these poems via a transfigured musical style that illuminated the text with unique brilliance. Of all his works, Machaut's *Messe de Notre Dame* most clearly underscores the composer's fidelity to the precepts of the Ars Nova. One of the earliest polyphonic settings of the Ordinary, it is a mature work scored for four voices in a declamatory style that reminds both performer and listener of Machaut's poetic roots.

Vocal
Messe de Notre Dame
what to buy: [Jeremy Summerly, cond.; Oxford Camerata, choir] (Naxos 8.553833) ♪ ♪ ♪ ♪

Here we have yet another attempt by an early music ensemble not only to re-create the music of the period but also to supply the aural and spatial ambiance within which the music's true soul awakens. The happy difference is that Jeremy Summerly's Oxford Camerata, unlike so many other well-intentioned ensembles, succeeds admirably on so many levels. The *Messe de Notre Dame* constitutes the major offering on this album, which also includes the composer's *Songs from "Le Voir Dit."*

influences: Phillipe de Vitry, Francesco Landini

Frank Scinta

Gustav Mahler
Born July 7, 1860, in Kalischt, Bohemia [now Kaliště, Czech Republic]. Died May 18, 1911, in Vienna, Austria.

period: Twentieth century/Romantic

Gustav Mahler, the Austrian composer and conductor, has been characterized as a colossus astride the 19th and 20th centuries. His works, described as modernist and introducing a "new Romanticism," were often incomprehensible to critics and listeners of his time. Today, he is identified primarily as the composer of nine large-scale (albeit very personal) symphonies and of often haunting orchestral songs. While his tonal language found its origins in the Romantic era, Mahler transformed the symphony and loosened its dependence on the traditional sonata form.

Mahler was originally admitted to the Vienna Conservatory (in 1875) as a piano student but also studied composition with Franz Krenn and harmony with Robert Fuchs. He won the Conservatory's prizes for piano performance and for composition, the latter for a scherzo for piano quartet (1876, lost). After receiving his diploma in 1878, he stayed in Vienna, and his intellectual and musical development were shaped by what would

become his life-long spiritual home. There he became familiar with the music and ideas of Richard Wagner (who would be one of his primary influences) as well as an assortment of the pan-German and socialist views popular in Austria at that time. Entering the University, he enrolled in history, philosophy, and literature classes, and attended Anton Bruckner's lectures. While later contending that he was never Bruckner's student, Mahler was greatly influenced by him and developed a close friendship with him, even making a reduction for two pianos of Bruckner's Third Symphony that received the older composer's approval.

In order to support himself while composing, Mahler pursued conducting rather than a career as a pianist, for which he had actually trained. He was appointed to a succession of increasingly important theater posts including Kassel (1883-85), the German Theater in Prague (1885-86), and Leipzig (1886-88). While at Kassel, Mahler's unhappy love affair with Johanna Richter, a singer at the theater, inspired the composition of his first orchestral song cycle, *Lieder eines fahrenden Gesellen (Songs of a Wayfarer)*. These musical settings of his own texts expressed a sadness and estrangement from the world, capturing the theme of lost love in ways reminiscent of Franz Schubert's *Winterreise (Winter's Journey)*. In Leipzig, he became acquainted with an anthology of folk poetry edited by Achim von Arnim and Clemens Brentano and published under the title *Des Knaben Wunderhorn (The Youth's Magic Horn)*. It provided the spur to much of his early composition, furnishing texts for his Second, Third, and Fourth Symphonies in addition to several songs with piano and his orchestral song collection actually entitled *Des Knaben Wunderhorn*.

In 1888 he moved to Budapest (where he had been appointed to the conductorship of the Royal Opera) during a period of intense Hungarian resentment towards Austrian domination. Mahler was able to transform the ailing opera company, improving the quality of its singers and orchestra to create a national theater in line with prevailing sentiments. He even recruited Hungarian singers and had operas translated into and sung in Hungarian, rather than given in multi-language performances, as had been done in the past. Notwithstanding these beneficial changes, Mahler was forced to resign his post in 1891 when the administrator was succeeded by an anti-Semitic aristocrat. While in Budapest, the composer premiered his Symphony no. 1, the most lyrical and accessible of his symphonic works, to the condemnation of local critics who called it a crime against law and order. This score, which quoted generously from Mahler's own *Songs of a Wayfarer*, also incorporated a funeral march parodying the famous round *Bruder Martin*—also known in French as *Frère Jacques*. Mahler also completed his first *Wunderhorn* songs and started on his Second Symphony.

After serving as first conductor at the Municipal Theater in Hamburg (1891-97)—where he completed his Second and Third Symphonies—the Jewish Mahler had himself baptized as a Roman Catholic in order to qualify for a post at the Vienna Court Opera, the most prestigious European musical establishment at that time. Initially appointed as a conductor in 1897, he was promoted to director the following year. During his tenure at the Opera (until 1907), Mahler also took over directorship of the Vienna Philharmonic concerts. With these duties limiting the time available for his own creative work, he found a balance in his career by composing during his summer holidays. He closed out the 19th century with his Fourth Symphony (the last of his *Wunderhorn* inspired compositions) and entered the 20th century with three abstractly conceived symphonies—his Fifth, Sixth, and Seventh—which, unlike the preceding three, contain no vocal movements. These scores, along with Mahler's two haunting orchestral song cycles—the *Rückert Lieder* and *Kindertotenlieder (Songs on the Death of Children)*—contain certain autobiographical references to the composer and his family (he married Alma Schindler in 1902), but far less blatantly than do Richard Strauss's *Ein Heldenleben* and *Symphonia domestica*. In 1906, Mahler composed his unique Symphony no. 8, incorporating settings of the old Latin hymn *Veni Creator Spiritus* and the final scene from Johann Wolfgang von Goethe's *Faust*. Known as the *Symphony of a Thousand* for its large orchestral and vocal forces, it reflected the influence of Johann Sebastian Bach in its intensive polyphonic writing and was the first predominantly vocal symphony. Its premiere in Munich in 1910 would remain the single greatest triumph of Mahler's career.

Mahler's tenure in Vienna, like all his earlier posts, was controversial, mixing great success with great conflict. On one hand, he was praised for his meticulously prepared opera productions, for improving the livelihood of his stage hands, and for strengthening his orchestral and vocal ensembles. On the other, a series of dismissals and disciplinary problems at the Opera created resent-

ments and a hostile campaign against him by members of the anti-Semitic press. This increasingly vitriolic movement criticized him for his authoritarian measures, his conducting style, his revisions and "corrections" of the Austro-German orchestral repertoire (most notably in his treatment of Ludwig van Beethoven's symphonies), his compositions, and finally, his increasing absence from the Opera to conduct his own music. Mahler was forced to relinquish his leadership of the Philharmonic concerts in 1901, and in 1907, faced with mounting hostility and attracted by an offer from the Metropolitan Opera in New York City, he felt compelled to tender his resignation from the Opera and leave Vienna. Shortly after he made this decision, his beloved older daughter died from scarlet fever and he himself was diagnosed with an incurable heart ailment. Though it was not immediately life-threatening, Mahler was advised to avoid strenuous physical activities and interpreted his condition as a death sentence.

Mahler was at the Metropolitan Opera from 1907 until 1909 before leaving, again prompted by conflict with the administration, to take over the directorship of the New York Philharmonic Orchestra. His American conducting seasons were relatively short and he returned to Europe to compose during the extended summer holidays. Following the premiere of his Symphony no. 7 in Prague (1908), Mahler composed *Das Lied von der Erde (The Song of the Earth)*, a setting for two solo voices and orchestra of Hans Bethge's German adaptations of ancient Chinese poems, which amalgamates song with symphonic form. Written in anticipation of his death, it evokes both the joy and anguish of life and Mahler's fear of not living to see another spring. He superstitiously avoided designating *Das Lied von der Erde* as his Ninth Symphony in an attempt to trick fate, mindful that Beethoven and Bruckner had not lived long enough to compose more than nine symphonies. Returning to Europe during the summer of 1909, Mahler finally composed his Ninth Symphony. It was his last completed work and perhaps his most self-indulgent and transcendent score. In it, Mahler expressed not only the wrenching conflicts in his life, but also a resignation to death. During the 1911 New York Philharmonic season, he was diagnosed with a heart infection, causing him to return to Europe for treatment. He died in Vienna within a month of his arrival.

Gustav Mahler

Orchestral

Symphony no. 1 in D Major—*Titan*

what to buy: [Bruno Walter, cond.; New York Philharmonic Orchestra] (Sony Classical Masterworks 63328) ♪ ♪ ♪ ♪ ♪

Bruno Walter, Mahler's assistant and close friend, had an intimate knowledge of the composer's music. This lively, unexaggerated 1954 issue offers an idiomatic, insightful account of Mahler's most accessible symphonic work. Superbly transferred to a mid-priced disc, this performance is well worth exploring. Johannes Brahms's *Variations on a Theme by Haydn* is the companion piece on this album.

what to buy next: [Rafael Kubelik, cond.; Bavarian Radio Symphony Orchestra] (Deutsche Grammophon 449735) ♪ ♪ ♪ ♪

For those who prefer stereo recordings, Kubelik's lyrical account is lively and well-shaped, with an entrancing account of the funeral march. It is combined with Dietrich Fischer-Dieskau's famous performance of the *Lieder eines Fahrenden Gesellen (Songs of a Wayfarer).* The same coupling is also available as a budget recording on Penguin Classics 460654.

Symphony no. 2 for Soprano, Mezzo-soprano, Orchestra, and Chorus—*Resurrection*

what to buy: [Barbara Hendricks, soprano; Christa Ludwig, mezzo-soprano; Leonard Bernstein, cond.; New York Philharmonic Orchestra; Westminster Choir] (Deutsche Grammophon 423395) ♪ ♪ ♪ ♪ ♪

Bernstein's long-lined account, detailed and emotionally involved, storms heaven like no other. Christa Ludwig's heart-achingly slow performance of the vocal fourth movement evinces a rare commitment and the conductor shapes the performance with a profound depth of feeling.

what to buy next: [Elisabeth Schwarzkopf, soprano; Hilde Rössl-Majdan, mezzo-soprano; Otto Klemperer, cond.; Philharmonia Orchestra] (EMI Classics 67255) ♪ ♪ ♪ ♪

Mahler acknowledged Klemperer's understanding of this work when Klemperer played his piano reduction for the composer. This grasp of the score comes through in an idiomatic, nicely detailed performance, with unexaggerated tempos that probably come close to Mahler's own.

This is an outstanding buy in its newly re-mastered incarnation.

Symphony no. 3 for Mezzo-soprano, Orchestra, and Chorus

what to buy: [Christa Ludwig, mezzo-soprano; Leonard Bernstein, cond.; New York Philharmonic Orchestra] (Deutsche Grammophon 427328) ♪ ♪ ♪ ♪ ♪

Bernstein shapes a profound, powerful account of this long and complex work. With severely restrained tempos, detailed phrasing, and outstanding orchestral and vocal contributions, this is a memorable performance.

Symphony no. 4 for Soprano and Orchestra

what to buy: [Judith Raskin, soprano; George Szell, cond.; Cleveland Orchestra] (Sony Essential Classical Classics 46535) ♪ ♪ ♪ ♪

Szell's lyrical rendition is a wonderfully classical performance, and Raskin finely realizes the heavenly life of Mahler's *Wunderhorn,* in a setting that forms the symphony's last movement. At bargain price, with a performance of the *Gesellen Lieder* by Frederica von Stade (with Andrew Davis conducting the London Philharmonic Orchestra) filling out the disc, this offers outstanding value.

what to buy next: [Elisabeth Schwarzkopf, soprano; Otto Klemperer, cond.; Philharmonia Orchestra] (EMI Classics 67035) ♪ ♪ ♪ ♪

Schwarzkopf's vocal depiction of the heavenly life is angelic, with a wonderful articulation of the text and an attention to detail that finely matches that of conductor and orchestra. This classic performance is newly re-mastered at mid-price and also includes Schwarzkopf with Klemperer and his forces in three of the *Rückert Lieder* and two songs from *Des Knaben Wunderhorn.*

Symphony no. 5

what to buy: [Leonard Bernstein, cond.; Vienna Philharmonic Orchestra] (Deutsche Grammophon Panorama 469154) ♪ ♪ ♪ ♪ ♪

Stretching his tempos to the breaking point, Bernstein never loses control or lets this performance lag, creating one of the most visceral, engaging accounts of this symphony. The VPO performs admirably in a magnificent rendition like no other. Deutsche Grammophon's reissue also offers Bernstein leading performances of Mahler's

First Symphony and the *Gesellen Lieder* (sung by Thomas Hampson).

Symphony no. 6 in A Minor—*Tragic*
what to buy: [Leonard Bernstein, cond.; Vienna Philharmonic Orchestra] (Deutsche Grammophon 427697) ♪ ♪ ♪ ♪ ♪

This is a powerful, thoughtful performance with outstanding orchestral detail. Bernstein and the VPO are relentless in this most "autobiographical" of Mahler's works. The opening Allegro energico is electrically charged, while the ensuing Andante is perhaps the most unashamedly romantic rendition on disc. Bernstein and the orchestra also join with Thomas Hampson in a fine version of the composer's *Kindertotenlieder*.

Symphony no. 7—*Song of the Night*
what to buy: [Leonard Bernstein, cond.; New York Philharmonic Orchestra] (Sony Classics 60564) ♪ ♪ ♪ ♪ ♪

This admirably paced and well-shaped account is resplendent, with an undeniable emotional commitment from all concerned. On a single, mid-priced disc, this performance is the apotheosis of Romanticism.

Symphony no. 8—*Symphony of a Thousand*
what to buy: [Arleen Augér, soprano; Heather Harper, soprano; Yvonne Minton, mezzo-soprano; Lucia Popp, mezzo-soprano; Helen Watts, mezzo-soprano; Rene Kollo, tenor; John Shirley-Quirk, bass-baritone; Martti Talvela, bass; Georg Solti, cond.; Chicago Symphony Orchestra; Vienna Singverein; Vienna State Opera Chorus; Vienna Boys Choir] (Decca Legends 460972) ♪ ♪ ♪ ♪ ♪

Composed around orchestral settings of the hymn *Veni, Creator Sanctus* and the final scene from Goethe's *Faust*, this unique piece finds the key to its realization in its singing. This fine account, boasting an outstanding group of vocal soloists admirably accompanied by Solti and the CSO, perfectly balances voices and orchestra, allowing both to shine.

what to buy next: [Erna Spoorenberg, soprano; Gwyneth Jones, soprano; Gwenyth Annear, contralto; Anna Reynolds, contralto; Norma Procter, contralto; John Mitchinson, tenor; Vladimir Ruzdjak, baritone; Donald McIntyre, baritone; Hans Vollenweider, organ; Leonard Bernstein, cond.; London Symphony Orchestra; London Symphony Chorus; Leeds Festival Chorus; Orpington Junior Singers; Highgate School Boys Chorus; Finchley Children's Music Group] (Sony Classics 61837) ♪ ♪ ♪ ♪

The close recording of the soloists and chorus allows a clear realization of the vocal line in this wonderful performance. With memorable singing by Gwyneth Jones and a beautifully realized Part II, this memorable recording is a bargain at mid-price. As a bonus, the record company has included a rendition of Mahler's *Kindertotenlieder* with Janet Baker as the soloist and Bernstein conducting the Israel Philharmonic Orchestra.

Symphony no. 9
what to buy: [Bruno Walter, cond.; Vienna Philharmonic Orchestra] (EMI Classics 63029) ♪ ♪ ♪ ♪

This is the benchmark recording of Mahler's Ninth Symphony. Recorded in 1938 shortly before the Nazi Anschluss, it vitally captures both Mahler's face-to-face encounter with eternity and Walter's own profound sadness at the coming demise of a great culture. The extraneous noise and sound limitations of this older recording are transcended by what is arguably the best performance of this symphony.

what to buy next: [Pierre Boulez, cond.; Chicago Symphony Orchestra] (Deutsche Grammophon 457581) ♪ ♪ ♪ ♪

While it is difficult to find a modern recording that delivers a well-realized, all-around account of this work, Boulez and the CSO deliver one of the finest recorded performances of Mahler's great swan song. Boulez doesn't conjure the profound awe at the mystery of the universe, the standing at the abyss, characteristic of Bernstein's wonderfully self-indulgent Deutsche Grammophon account but he captures the composer's great sadness and resignation in a performance that objectifies this most subjective work.

Vocal
Lieder und Gesänge aus der Jungendzeit (Songs of Youth) for Voice and Piano
what to buy: [*Bernstein Century: Mahler Lieder*, Dietrich Fischer-Dieskau, baritone; Leonard Bernstein, piano] (Sony Classical 61847) ♪ ♪ ♪ ♪ ♪

Fischer-Dieskau delivers dramatic accounts with unsurpassed character in ten selections from the early *Wunderhorn* and other piano-accompanied songs. The duo also delivers fine performances of selections from the *Songs of a Wayfarer* and *Rückert Lieder*.

[Anne Sofie von Otter, mezzo-soprano; Ralf Gothoni, piano] (Deutsche Grammophon 423666) ♪ ♪ ♪ ♪ ♪

Von Otter's six selections sparkle, helped by Gothoni's fine accompaniment. This delightful album also samples *Des Knaben Wunderhorn,* in addition to selections from Hugo Wolf's *Goethe Lieder* and *Mörike Lieder.*

Des Knaben Wunderhorn (The Youth's Magic Horn) for Voice and Orchestra
what to buy: [Elisabeth Schwarzkopf, soprano; Dietrich Fischer-Dieskau, baritone; George Szell, cond.; London Symphony Orchestra] (EMI Classics 67256) ♪ ♪ ♪ ♪ ♪

This is the classic account of Mahler's famed *Humoresken.* The vocal and expressive detail of the soloists is unsurpassed for purity of tone, dramatic delivery, and textual articulation, while the orchestral sound sparkles in its full bloom. This attractive recording is deservedly reissued in EMI's *Great Recordings of the Century* series, now re-mastered at mid-price.

Das Lied von der Erde (The Song of the Earth) for Solo Voices and Orchestra
what to buy: [Christa Ludwig, mezzo-soprano; Fritz Wunderlich, tenor; Otto Klemperer, cond.; Philharmonia Orchestra; New Philharmonia Orchestra] (EMI 66944) ♪ ♪ ♪ ♪ ♪

One of the great recorded Mahler performances, this vital reading, with its high level of emotional commitment, vocal detail, and orchestral playing, strongly conveys the composer's emotional range and lust for life in the face of his anticipated death. The performances of Ludwig and Wunderlich are unsurpassed for their lustrous tone, outstanding articulation, and dramatic involvement. This is essential listening.

what to buy next: [Kathleen Ferrier, contralto; Julius Patzak, tenor; Bruno Walter, cond.; Vienna Philharmonic Orchestra] (Decca 466576) ♪ ♪ ♪ ♪ ♪

While Walter premiered this work and gives one of its great recorded performances, it is for Ferrier's *Abschied* that this account is most memorable. Many, reared on a more recent crop of singers, will find it difficult to warm to her, but Ferrier, already dying from cancer, became the embodiment of Mahler's anguish in the face of death. Three of the *Rückert Lieder* are also sung here by Ferrier with Walter conducting the VPO.

various orchestral songs
what to buy: [Dietrich Fischer-Dieskau, baritone; Rafael Kubelik, cond.; Bavarian Radio Symphony Orchestra; (in the *Lieder eines Fahrenden Gesellen*) Karl Böhm, cond.; Berlin Philharmonic Orchestra (in the *Kindertotenlieder* and the *Rückert Lieder*)] (Deutsche Grammophon 415191) ♪ ♪ ♪ ♪ ♪

In these classic performances of Mahler's most haunting orchestral songs, Fischer-Dieskau does a fine job of depicting Mahler's range of emotional color: from contentment, to anguish, to shouting at the moon. While perhaps not in as fresh voice as on his earlier EMI recordings, Fischer-Dieskau's singing is wondrous, and Deutsche Grammophon offers up the *Rückert Lieder* in the glorious orchestral version.

influences: Anton Bruckner, Richard Wagner, Richard Strauss

Gerald B. Goldberg

Marin Marais
Born May 31, 1656, in Paris, France. Died August 15, 1728, in Paris, France.

period: Baroque

A prodigious talent on the bass viol even as a child, Marin Marais became the most prominent composer and performer on the bass viol in all of France. He spent most of his creative life in royal service, and his huge output (over five hundred pieces in the viol collections alone) comprises most of the body of bass viol music still extant. A 1992 film by Alain Corneau—*Tous les matins du monde* (The mornings of the world)—presented a fictionalized account of the relationship between Marais and his teacher, Sainte-Colombe; it won five César Awards (including Best Score) from the French Academie des Arts et Techniques.

Renewed interest in early music and historically correct performance has opened the door to composers whose works had previously been familiar only to scholars. Often these were immensely popular musicians in their own time, but their music was written for instruments that, until very recently, had become all but extinct. Marais is one such composer, having written almost all of his huge body of compositions for the bass viol (also known as the viola da gamba), an instrument that is enjoying renewed popularity and familiarity thanks to the early-music explosion of the past quarter century. Prior to this revival, his best-known work was a set of variations on *Les Folies d'Espagne,* which was often performed as a violin solo.

During the late seventeenth and early eighteenth century, bass viol playing enjoyed great popularity and renown in Paris as the very pinnacle of musical taste and achievement. Marais began his viol studies as a child and soon became proficient enough to take lessons with Sainte-Colombe, the best-known viol teacher at the time. He also studied composition with Jean-Baptiste Lully and began writing music that he could perform on the bass viol. By the time Marais turned twenty years old, he had earned a reputation as a virtuoso and become a member of the royal orchestra at the Paris court. In 1676 he was appointed *Ordinaire de la chambre du Roi pour la viole,* remaining in this post until his retirement three years prior to his death. It was at court that Marais wrote his most important scores, five collections for the bass viol spanning almost forty years (1686–1725) and containing over five hundred pieces—a few for two or three viols but most for one viol with figured bass. As was customary, the pieces were arranged in suites, but Marais varied the number of movements in each suite from seven to forty-one. Most of the suites contain dance movements such as minuets and sarabands, but Marais also included what he called "character pieces," program music that depicted specific scenes or situations. Some scholars believe that the subject of one such evocation was the composer's own (non-anesthetized) gall bladder operation. For this piece, a note in the score describes the operation in great detail.

While the viol pieces are by far Marais most prominent works, he is also known for his *Pièces en trio pour les flutes, violon, et dessus de viole* (1692), which may represent the first appearance of trio sonatas in France. Marais also wrote four operas, perhaps in homage to Lully, his friend and teacher. Certainly one can trace his association with that composer in these works, since their similarities are striking. Just as in Lully's operas,

there are five acts, and the one fully realized score available shows the same unusual five-part scoring for strings that Lully used. Lully's son Louis even contributed the libretto to *Alcide,* one of Marais's operas. *Alcione,* another of his operas, was still being performed at the court as late as 1771.

Chamber
Pièces de viole
what to buy: [*Pièces de viole du second Livre, 1701;* Jordi Savall, viola da gamba; Anne Gallet, harpsichord; Hopkinson Smith, theorbo] (Auvidis Fontalis 7770) ♪ ♪ ♪ ♪ ♪

When one mentions viol music to connoisseurs, Jordi Savall's tonal clarity and pleasantly sensitive performances immediately spring to mind. This disc includes the famous *Les Folies d'Espagne* mentioned above; the recording is blessed with exceptional sonics, as exemplified by clear, well-balanced miking and just the right atmosphere.

what to buy next: [*Pièces a deux violes du premier Livre, 1686;* Jordi Savall, Christophe Coin, viola da gamba; Ton Koopman, harpsichord; Hopkinson Smith, theorbo] (Auvidis Fontalis 7769) ♪ ♪ ♪ ♪ ♪

While this recording is every bit as good as the one above, it contains quite a bit of Glenn Gould-type humming. If that doesn't bother you, give this one five bones as well.

La Gamme et autres morceaux de symphonie
what to buy: [Boston Museum Trio, ensemble] (Centaur 2129) ♪ ♪ ♪ ♪

This is an excellent recording and performance, although the pieces here are not among the composer's best known. These works are a bit lighter in character, and the playing (recorded at Slosberg Recital Hall at Brandeis University) has a spontaneity that suits them well.

various works
what to buy: [*Tous les matins du monde;* Jordi Savall, viola da gamba; members of the Concert des Nations, ensemble] (Auvidis Valois 4640) ♪ ♪ ♪ ♪

This is the soundtrack album that helped spark the miniboom in Marais recordings. It contains seven selections for viola da gamba drawn from books one, three, and four, plus "La Sonnerie de Sainte Geneviève du Mont à Paris" from the composer's *La Gamme et autres morceaux de symphonie*. Since the premise of the movie is the relationship between Marais and his teacher, Savall also includes four compositions by Sainte-Colombe, in addition to one work apiece by Lully and François Couperin.

influences: Jean-Baptiste Lully, Jean-Philippe Rameau

Melissa M. Stewart

Frank Martin

Born September 15, 1890, in Geneva, Switzerland. Died November 21, 1974 in Naarden, the Netherlands.

period: Twentieth century

Frank Martin and Arthur Honegger are generally considered the greatest Swiss composers of the twentieth century. Martin's own personal style emerged when he was in his forties, but he didn't achieve international fame for another decade. Martin was a prolific composer in a number of genres, and his scores are generally characterized by singing melodies and a deep sense of spirituality.

The son of a Calvinist minister and the youngest of ten children, Martin began composing at age eight. When he was ten years old he heard a performance of J.S. Bach's *St. Matthew Passion* and was fascinated with the harmonies. By the time he was sixteen Martin knew he wanted to be a musician, but to appease his parents he studied mathematics and physics at the University of Geneva (although he never finished the course). In 1918 he regularly attended concerts of the Orchestre de la Suisse Romande in Geneva, where he heard Ernest Ansermet conduct music by Claude Debussy and Igor Stravinsky.

In 1926, Martin established the Société de Musique de Chambre de Genève, which he directed for ten years while also acting as the group's harpsichordist and pianist. That same year, he met Emil Jaques-Dalcroze at a music education conference and was impressed enough to study rhythmic theory for two years at the Jacques-Dalcroze Institute prior to becoming a teacher

there. During this time he was also a lecturer on chamber music and the director of a private music school, the Technicum Moderne de Musique. Martin moved to the Netherlands in 1946, living first in Amsterdam and then in Naardem, where he would spend the balance of his life. From 1950 to 1957 he taught a class in composition at the Cologne Hochschule für Musik before finally giving up teaching altogether and devoting himself to composing. He interrupted his work only to go on chamber music tours or to accept invitations as a guest conductor of his own works.

The most dramatic and clearly identifiable influence on Martin's mature writing was the twelve-tone music of Arnold Schoenberg, which he discovered at age forty. Before that, his compositions reflected the mixture of French impressionism and German romanticism that was common in Switzerland. Serial techniques permeated the music Martin wrote in the 1930s without diluting his reliance on harmony as the basic building material of his compositions. His stance was explained in this quote: "I can say that at one and the same time I was influenced by Schoenberg and yet set myself against him with all my musical feeling." The first important piece to demonstrate his mastery at blending twelve-tone techniques with his own harmonic vocabulary (and to bring him a modicum of international renown) was the secular oratorio *Le vin herbé*, written in 1941. Martin's 1945 concerto grosso, the *Petite symphonie concertante*, is his most popular work, illustrating his penchant for composing scores utilizing unique combinations of instruments. The use of harp, piano, and harpsichord as solo vehicles for the *Petite symphonie concertante* is truly captivating and ingenious.

Orchestral
***Petite symphonie concertante* for Harp, Harpsichord, Piano, and Two String Orchestras**
what to buy: [Ernest Ansermet, cond.; Orchestre de la Suisse Romande] (London Classics 448264) ♪ ♪ ♪ ♪

Ansermet had a long association with Martin's music, and the results heard here reflect the comfortable intimacy that comes with time. This performance is part of a catchall collection that binds various conductors, orchestras, choirs, and soloists into a fairly decent Martin sampler. Other pieces on this two-disc set include the Concerto for Winds, the Violin Concerto, the Etudes for String Orchestra, the Passacaglia for Large Orchestra, and the oratorio *In Terra Pax*.

worth searching for: [Armin Jordan, cond.; Orchestre de la Suisse Romande] (Erato 45694) ♪ ♪ ♪ ♪ ♪

This piece is a gem of shining elegance. The orchestra is superb, and the three solo instrumentalists play with such brilliance and sensitivity that one wishes the work were much longer. On the same disc, Jordan conducts Martin's Concerto for Winds and the six *Monologues aus "Jedermann"* with equal grace.

Etudes for String Orchestra

what to buy: [Stuart Canin, violin; Stuart Canin, cond.; New Century Chamber Orchestra] (New Albion 86) ♪ ♪ ♪ ♪

Stuart Canin is an exquisite violinist and a great conductor, and this is one of those rare performances capable of transporting the listener to a magical place. Included in this all-Martin set is the composer's Concerto for Violin and Orchestra (with the Berkeley Symphony Orchestra) and the *Maria-Triptychon* for Soprano, Violin, and Orchestra (with the same ensemble). The last work, based on three Marian texts, showcases Martin as a master of orchestral tone painting, featuring soloists Sara Ganz and Canin.

Vocal
Mass for Double Chorus

what to buy: [James O'Donnell, cond.; Westminster Cathedral Choir] (Hyperion 20017) ♪ ♪ ♪ ♪♪

Although it was more or less finished by 1922, Martin's score had to wait until 1963 to receive its first performance. His only a cappella work, the Mass is a profoundly moving piece and a testament to the composer's craftsmanship. O'Donnell and the disciplined choir from Westminster Cathedral are impressively recorded and treat this music with all the respect due a true work of art. The Requiem by Ildebrando Pizzetti, an Italian contemporary of Martin's, is the other featured work on this disc.

worth searching for: [*Messes A Capella*; Michel Corboz, cond.; Lausanne Vocal Ensemble, choir] (Cascavelle 1025) ♪ ♪ ♪ ♪

Corboz pairs Martin's early masterpiece (written prior to the composer's exposure to twelve-tone methods) with a mass by Claudio Monteverdi, with interesting results. A Swiss choir, singing music by one of their country's most important native sons, gives this recording a special

Neville Marriner:
Born in 1924, Neville Marriner began studying the violin with his father before winning a scholarship to the Royal College of Music (RCM) in London. His training there was interrupted by service in the British military toward the end of World War II, but after demobilization Marriner continued his studies at the RCM, before going to France and enrolling at the Paris Conservatoire. Upon completing his academic training, Marriner taught briefly at Eton and at the RCM in addition to playing in a few chamber music groups; the most important part of that last activity was his partnership with the keyboard player and musicologist Thurston Dart. The pair were quite interested in Baroque music, and both ended up working with the groundbreaking countertenor Alfred Deller on some of his recordings of music by Claudio Monteverdi and Henry Purcell. During this time, however, Marriner's main employers were (first) the London Philharmonic Orchestra and (next) the London Symphony Orchestra.

In 1956 Marriner and a number of London's finest string players founded the chamber orchestra known as the Academy of St. Martin-in-the-Fields (ASMF), named in honor of the church where the organization started. Although he originally directed this ensemble from his position as concertmaster—a fact totally in keeping with the Baroque music that the group was known for at this time—Marriner began conducting it from the podium upon the recommendation of maestro Pierre Monteux. Gradually the orchestra and its fledgling conductor began building a reputation for their performances, both in concert and in the recording studio, where they churned out a surprising number of decently selling albums.

Marriner's own increasing popularity was in direct proportion to the record sales of the ASMF, and brought him an offer to leave his violin behind and bring his baton with him to take the reins of the newly formed Los Angeles Chamber Orchestra in 1968. After ten years as music director there—in addition to continuing his duties with the Academy—Marriner moved on to conduct the Minnesota Orchestra (1979–1986) and the South German Radio Symphony Orchestra (1986–1989) as well as engagements with other orchestras around the world. Further honors eventually came his way, including the Commander of the Order of the British Empire in 1979 and knighthood in 1985.

The ASMF and Marriner first came to fame via their performances of Baroque composers, and some of their finest early recordings include renditions of Antonio Vivaldi's quartet of concertos from his eighth opus, the *Four Seasons* (London 466232), and an edition of Johann Sebastian Bach's six *Brandenburg Concertos* (Philips 426088 and 426089) that was prepared by Thurston Dart. Marriner was also music director for the Academy Award-winning film *Amadeus*, and put together a soundtrack collection of snippets from the title composer's oeuvre (Fantasy 4403) that won a Grammy Award. Lest one think that the conductor is stuck in a pre-twentieth century mode, it should also be noted that Marriner has broadened his sonic palette to include works by such modern icons as Béla Bartók, Ralph Vaughan Williams, and Igor Stravinsky. One of the finest albums that Marriner and the ASMF put together featured a collection (Argo 417818) of American compositions by Samuel Barber (the *Adagio for Strings*), Aaron Copland (*Quiet City*), Henry Cowell (*Hymn and Fuguing Tune no. 10*), Paul Creston (*A Rumour*), and Charles Ives (Symphony no. 3).

William Gerard

interpretive oomph. The overall sonics are good but not as special as this piece deserves.

influences: Aaron Copland, Paul Hindemith, Samuel Barber

Marijim Thoene and Garaud MacTaggart

Bohuslav Martinu

Born Bohuslav Jan Martinu on December 8, 1890, in Policka, Bohemia. Died August 28, 1959, in Liestal, Switzerland.

period: Twentieth century

Bohuslav Martinu, one of the most fruitful composers of the twentieth century, was world-renowned during the last thirty years of his life. Despite the enormous volume of compositions that he churned out, Martinu's level of craftsmanship was always high, even when the inspiration might have been suspect.

By the time Martinu entered the Prague Conservatory as a violin student in 1906, he had already written some short pieces and developed a reputation as an indifferent student. This dubious distinction was confirmed when he was finally kicked out of school in 1910. At various times during his career, Martinu would attempt to rectify the shortcomings he and others found in his composition techniques, but each academic fling met with Martinu's basic unwillingness to conform to the demands of schooling. Fortunately, his brief experiments with formal studies in harmony and counterpoint did not hinder Martinu's ability to teach violin—which he did for several years—or his talent for writing highly individual works. He was later to write (for David Ewen's anthology *The New Book of Modern Composers*) that "the technique comes out of the work itself; not the work from the technique. Music is not a question of calculation."

He moved to Paris in 1923, studying briefly with Albert Roussel, who helped Martinu get his music performed. For the next seventeen years he lived in France, writing prolifically and building his reputation among that country's musical elite. Works written during this period include an ample number of chamber pieces, eight ballets, ten operas, and over twenty scores for large-scale instrumental forces, among them the Double Concerto for Piano, Timpani, and Two String Orchestras. By 1940 the political climate in Paris had changed, and the Nazi

sympathizers were in charge. The notorious Munich agreement of 1938 and the German army's subsequent occupation of Bohemia and Moravia a year later made Martinu's continued safety in France a concern. On June 10, 1940, he and his wife left their apartment carrying only a few personal possessions, leaving behind Martinu's manuscripts and most of their belongings. They were able to find space on an unscheduled train that Martinu happened upon while wandering the rail yards. The couple finally managed to board a ship bound for the United States in 1941, after nine months spent working their way across France and into Portugal. Once they landed in New York, the couple was quickly embraced by that city's musical community.

Martinu managed to find some music paper while waiting to escape Europe and had already written a few new pieces, some of which were performed soon after the composer reached America. His stay in the United States resulted in a veritable flood of material, including all six of his symphonies. After the Second World War, a communist government took power in Czechoslovakia, causing Martinu to give up his hope of returning there. He ended up residing in the United States, France, Switzerland, and Italy during the next decade. Among Martinu's notable postwar works are his cantata *The Epic of Gilgamesh*, his opera *The Greek Passion*, and his Piano Trio, no. 2. He died while in Switzerland and was initially buried in Liestal, a suburb of Basel. When Czechoslovakia eventually regained its independence, Martinu's remains were finally returned to his beloved homeland.

Orchestral
Double Concerto for Piano, Timpani, and Two String Orchestras
what to buy: [Jíri Belohlávek, cond.; Czech Philharmonic Orchestra] (Chandos 8950) ♪ ♪ ♪ ♪₄

Arguably Martinu's greatest single work, this piece is crammed with ideas. Despite this abundance of content, the composer stamps his personality on each phrase, using sonic textures as building blocks to create a marvelous musical structure. These qualities are made wonderfully apparent on this superb recording by Belohlávek, who is rapidly becoming the premier modern-day conductor of Martinu's oeuvre. The concerto is the major work on the album, but there is also a solid performance of the composer's first symphony.

Symphonies for Orchestra (complete)
what to buy: [Vaclav Neumann, cond.; Czech Philharmonic Orchestra] (Supraphon 110382) ♪ ♪ ♪ ♪₉

If you want a complete set of Martinu's symphonies, Neumann's 1970s recordings of these complex, intellectually gratifying works are the way to go. While there may be better individual performances of these works by other forces, the consistent level of intensity and unified vision of Neumann and company are appealing and rewarding.

Symphony no. 6—*Fantaisies symphoniques*
what to buy: [Jíri Belohlávek, cond.; Czech Philharmonic Orchestra] (Chandos 8897) ♪ ♪ ♪ ♪₉

Belohlávek follows in Neumann's footsteps with a tautly played performance in Martinu's most interesting and challenging symphony. The recording is excellent, and the companion pieces on this disc, Leoš Janáček's *Sinfonietta* and Josef Suk's *Fantasticke Scherzo*, are exciting Czech soul mates.

Chamber
Nonet for Wind Quintet and Piano Quartet
what to buy: [Dartington Ensemble] (Hyperion 22039) ♪ ♪ ♪ ♪₉

This is a stunning two-CD sampler of Martinu's chamber music, ranging from the *La Revue de Cuisine* ballet of 1927 through the various "madrigals" he set from 1937 through 1948. It also contains one of the finest versions of his lovely Nonet ever recorded.

influences: Leoš Janáček, Igor Stravinsky, Albert Roussel

Gary Barton and Garaud MacTaggart

Pietro Mascagni
Born December 7, 1863, in Livorno, Italy. Died August 2, 1945, in Rome, Italy.

period: Romantic

Pietro Mascagni composed in the verismo style, fitting intense music to the dramatic situations of everyday folk played out on the stage. Even though several other operas by him exist, his reputation rests solely upon the torrid one-acter, *Cavalleria rusticana,* written when he was only twenty-six years old. Mascagni, with the wisdom of hindsight, later admitted that his early hit was an act he couldn't follow, noting that "I was crowned before I was king."

By the time Mascagni was eighteen years old, he had already tasted a modicum of success with his cantata *In filanda,* a work which received rave reviews at the Casino San Marco. He passed the entrance exam for the Milan Conservatory in October 1882, and left in March 1885 without a degree after engaging in a raucous dispute with the director about whether one of his scores should or should not be performed. His first positions as a professional musician were with touring opera companies, with whom he served as either an assistant conductor or music director. Mascagni met his wife when she was singing with one of the companies. They were married in 1888, the year that a competition for one-act operas was being sponsored by Sonzogno, a music publishing company. Mascagni decided to enter this contest and was fully prepared to submit the fourth act of his already completed full-length opera *Guglielmo Ratcliff,* but his wife had already turned in his recently completed *Cavalleria rusticana.* One of three winners, it received a wildly enthusiastic first performance on May 17, 1890, and it has not been out of the repertoire since.

The basic plot of *Cavalleria rusticana* takes about an hour to reach a climax, with Santuzza being spurned by Turridu in favor of a now-married former love, Lola. The duo argues, he mistreats her, he challenges Lola's husband to a duel, and is killed offstage. Cue the reaction of Santuzza and the crowd. Often paired in performance with Ruggero Leoncavallo's *I pagliacci,* another one-act opera, each work received its limited measure of fame by strumming the heart-strings, telling of inflamed passions, and featuring violent death. No gods or royalty here: the folks populating these tales toil for a living, providing the very soul of "verismo" (realism) through their connections with reality. By creating the first verismo opera ever and garnering rapid success with it, Mascagni inspired hordes of imitators, including *I pagliacci,* Puccini's *Il tabarro,* and Jules Massenet's *La Navarraise.*

Mascagni's next opera, *L'amico Fritz,* was written speedily in an attempt to cash in on the notoriety of *Cavalleria rusticana.* Even though it stretched a relatively thin libretto over three acts, the music was deemed good enough at its premiere in Rome (1891) that it received more than thirty curtain calls. Mascagni, with his experience directing small opera companies at the beginning of his career, was now in demand to lead performances of not only his two hit operas, but works by other composers as well. That was fortunate because most of the vocal scores he wrote after *L'amico Fritz* avoided the verismo genre and fell short of its financial rewards. When he finally did dip back into the verismo well in 1895, Mascagni came up with *Silvano,* a rather tepid imitation of his first hit.

In that same year, his reputation was still fairly solid and he was appointed Director of the Liceo Musicale at Pesaro. While Mascagni had been an indifferent student back in his days at the Milan Conservatory, his stints as a professional conductor and composer would serve him in good stead as he sought to turn the student orchestra into one of the finest performing units of its day. Mascagni's frequent conducting commitments undermined his ability to be an effective administrator for very long, however, and he regularly butted heads with the committee in charge of the school's finances. After an extended (and disastrous) tour of North America ended in 1903, so too did his stewardship of the Liceo Musicale. However, Mascagni was offered the directorship of the Rome Scuola Nazionale di Musica later that year, holding the position until 1911.

The quality of his reputation as a conductor diminished when he took over some of Arturo Toscanini's duties at La Scala in 1929. This came about when Toscanini resigned in protest over the fascist regime of Benito Mussolini. Mascagni, whose relationship with Mussolini went back to the mid-1920s when the composer proved to be a rabid nationalist advocate for Italian opera, began each performance with the fascist hymn and was adopted by the regime as its official composer. By the time he died in 1945, Mascagni's reputation as a composer rested solely on *Cavelleria rusticana,* but his character was sullied by his association with fascism—a cause he may not have agreed with inherently but one which he allowed to co-opt his morals for the sake of convenience.

Vocal
Cavalleria Rusticana
what to buy: [Zinka Milanov, soprano; Carol Smith, mezzo-soprano; Jussi Björling, tenor; Robert Merrill, baritone; Renato Cellini, cond.; RCA Victor Symphony Orchestra; Robert Shaw Chorale] (RCA Victor Gold Seal 6510) ♪♪♪♪♩

Milanov had the deep, lustrous soprano desired for this role while Björling's tenor always meant refined excitement. The basic sonics of the performance are a bit constricted, due both to age and recording techniques, but the singing outshines these limitations.

what to buy next: [Jessye Norman, soprano; Martha Senn, mezzo-soprano; Rosa Laghezza, mezzo-soprano; Giuseppe Giacomini, tenor; Dmitri Hvorostovsky, baritone; Semyon Bychkov, cond.; Orchestre de Paris, orch.; Chœurs de Orchestre de Paris, choir] (Philips 432105) ♪♪♪♪

If you are seeking the best Santuzza currently on the market, then Norman gives a very convincing performance, perhaps even ranking among the best of all time. When she isn't on stage, though, the cast and conductor drop down about a bone.

influences: Ruggero Leoncavallo, Giacomo Puccini

Michael H. Margolin and Garaud MacTaggart

Jules Massenet
Born Jules Émile Frédéric Massenet, May 12, 1842, in Montaud, France. Died August 13, 1912, in Paris, France.

period: Romantic

Although Jules Massenet wrote in a number of genres, the bulk of his fame comes from the twenty-six completed operas he completed between 1867 and his death in 1912. *Manon, Werther,* and *Thaïs* are the main works that still show up on stage, though the *Méditation from "Thaïs"* for violin and orchestra, with its soaring melodic lines, probably has the most active concert life of all Massenet's works.

In 1851, three years after taking his initial piano lessons with his mother, Massenet passed the entrance examination for the Conservatoire National de Musique (according to his autobiography, *Mes souvenirs*) by playing two or three pages of the finale to Beethoven's Sonata for Piano, op. 29. Other sources have placed his admittance to the Conservatoire anywhere from 1852 through January 10, 1853, and noted that the Beethoven piece played was probably one of the three sonatas from his op. 31 which had been circulated with a misprint labeling them as op. 29. The bottom line, however, is that young Jules played well and that, after admission, he would study at the school through 1863 when he won the Prix de Rome (on his second try) with the cantata *David Rizzio.* In the years between entering and finally leaving the Conservatoire, Massenet studied piano, solfège, and composition (with Ambroise Thomas). By 1858 his musicianship was of a high enough quality that he was able to take on a few piano students and hire on as a timpanist with the orchestra at the Théâtre Lyrique. It was during his stint as an orchestral percussionist that he met Charles Gounod and Richard Wagner, becoming particularly entranced with the latter's musical concepts during a performance of *Tannhäuser.*

Unlike other prominent winners of the Prix de Rome (Hector Berlioz and Claude Debussy, for instance), Massenet actually enjoyed his time at the Villa Medici in Rome, composing a few works (as required), traveling around Italy, and meeting the woman who would become his wife, Louise Constance de Gressy. Upon returning to Paris in 1866, he earned money teaching piano and sought to find a publisher for some of his works—songs and slight piano pieces that he had created with the salons in mind. One year later, the opportunity to compose a one-act opera for a guaranteed performance at the Opéra Comique resulted in *La grand' tante.* While this wasn't Massenet's first opera (he had tried at least six times before), it was as close to success as he had yet come, despite a number of lukewarm reviews from critics. After the hostilities of the Franco-Prussian War were resolved, Massenet began to slowly build a catalog of well-regarded works (instrumental and otherwise) that would attain its first peak with the triumphant production of his opera, *Le roi de Lahore,* in 1877. He was appointed professor of composition at the Conservatoire a year later and, in 1882, began toiling over what would become the first of the scores for which he is best known to modern audiences, *Manon.*

The story of Manon Lescaut, as written by Abbé Prévost, intrigued many nineteenth century composers, including Daniel Auber, Jacques Halévy, and, most famously, Giacomo Puccini. Massenet's take on the storyline was massaged in the libretto by Henri Meilhac and Philippe Gille, who took care to clean up much of the novel's imagery, creating an essentially pure heroine despite the impetuous, self-serving, and sensual nature ascribed to her in the original tale. After the work's premiere in 1884, Massenet was catapulted into the ranks of the greatest French composers of the day, a position he

never really ceded during his lifetime. After the production of his next opera (*Le Cid,* in 1885) he began work on what would become the second of his massive triumphs, *Werther.*

Massenet's *Werther* took its basic plot from the second edition of Johann Wolfgang von Goethe's novel, *Die Leiden des Jungen Werthers (The Sorrows of the Young Werther).* Massenet turned it over to his librettists (Edouard Blau, Paul Milliet, and George Hartmann), who then re-shaped the storyline to make it more palatable to the French opera-going public. They did this by turning Charlotte from an innocent, unaware of Werther's all-too-consuming attraction to her, into someone who eventually reciprocates the hero's affections, albeit reluctantly due to her prior commitment to marry Albert. The storyline was (not surprisingly) deemed too depressing for a premiere at the Opéra Comique, and received its first performance in Vienna, Austria in 1892.

Three years earlier, Massenet had met the American singer Sybil Sanderson and was impressed enough by her singing and beauty to create two of his next four operas (*Esclarmonde* and *Thaïs*) specifically for her. While *Esclarmonde* was fairly successful at its premiere in 1889, the next two works were either never heard during the composer's lifetime (*Amadis*) or passed quickly from the repertoire (*Le mage*). It remained for *Thaïs* to recapture Massenet's magic touch at its premiere in 1894. The libretto for the opera began with Anatole France's story about a reformed Egyptian courtesan who eventually abandons her role as a priestess of Venus for life as a saintly Christian. Louis Gallet, Massenet's librettist, downplayed the anti-clerical stance of the original in favor of a less politically charged outline, although the monk Athanaël (Paphnuce in France's narrative) still abandons his faith to profess his forbidden, sinful love even as the heroine, dying, focuses on the seraphim waiting to take her to heaven. The entrancing *Méditation from "Thaïs"* occurs between the second and third acts and has gone on to become one of the most famous operatic excerpts of the nineteenth century.

Massenet's projects were still welcomed at European venues toward the end of his life, and he completed working on *Cléopatre,* his thirty-ninth opera, three months before succumbing to cancer.

Orchestral
***Méditation from "Thaïs"* for Violin and Orchestra**

what to buy: [*Carmen Fantasy*; Anne-Sophie Mutter, violin; James Levine, cond.; Vienna Philharmonic Orchestra] (Deutsche Grammophon 437544) ♪ ♪ ♪ ♪

In the opera, this is the musical interlude where Thaïs undergoes a spiritual transformation from pagan to Christian. The poignant, melancholy intensity of this theme has been a violin bonbon for decades, and its essentially bittersweet nature is played up here without getting too cloying. It is included in a fine collection of short violin favorites by Pablo de Sarasate, Gabriel Fauré, Maurice Ravel, Giuseppe Tartini, and Henryk Wieniawski.

[*Tortelier's French Bonbons*; Yuri Torchinsky, violin; Yan Pascal Tortelier, cond.; BBC Philharmonic Orchestra; Royal Liverpool Philharmonic Choir] (Chandos 9765) ♪ ♪ ♪ ♪

Tortelier's program puts this piece into a more felicitous context than does the album featuring Mutter. The orchestra is quite responsive and well-recorded, and the wordless chorus behind the violinist (who only solos in this piece) is a nice touch. Peter Dixon is the cello soloist in Massenet's *Mélodie-Elégie* from *Les Érinnyes*, while the only other time that the choir appears is in the *Entr'Acte et Barcarolle* from Jacques Offenbach's *The Merry Wives of Windsor*. The balance of the disc showcases short instrumental set pieces by Charles Gounod, Ambroise Thomas, Emmanuel Chabrier, and others.

various ballets
what to buy: [*Jules Massenet: Ballet Suites*; Neville Marriner, cond.; Academy of St. Martin-in-the-Fields, orch.] (Capriccio 10569) ♪ ♪ ♪ ♪

French opera audiences had to have their ballet interludes. Even such master composers as Richard Wagner, Giuseppe Verdi, and Carl Maria von Weber bowed to this inevitability and wrote balletic addendums for insertion into French productions. Most of the time Massenet, since he was basically writing for Gallic audiences in the first place, provided such dance pieces automatically. This doesn't change the fact that the suites from *Thaïs*, *Le Cid*, and *Cendrillon* included in this set are quite pleasant, and a good introduction to the composer's works for those who don't feel up to tackling his greatest operas.

Jules Massenet

Chamber
Méditation from "Thaïs" for Violin and Piano
what to buy: [*Souvenirs*; Kyung Wha Chung, violin; Itomar Golan, piano] (EMI Classics 56827) ♪ ♪ ♪ ♪♭

This arrangement is a lovely aperitif or chaser, depending upon where it's put in the program. Here, Chung serves up a nice, well-recorded rendition of the *Méditation,* with similar arrangements and works by Johann Sebastian Bach, Antonín Dvořák, Fritz Kreisler, and others—eighteen cuts in all.

Vocal
Manon
what to buy: [Victoria de los Angeles, soprano; Liliane Berton, soprano; Raymonde Notti, soprano; Marthe Serres, soprano; Henri Legay, tenor; René Hérent, tenor; Michel Dens, baritone; Jean Vieuille, baritone; Jean Borthayre, bass; Pierre Monteux, cond.; Orchestre du Théâtre National de l'Opéra Comique; Chœurs du Théâtre National de l'Opéra Comique] (Testament 3203) ♪ ♪ ♪ ♪ ♪

Recorded for EMI in 1955, this performance has never been surpassed, a fact that can be attributed specifically to the drop-dead gorgeous singing of de los Angeles in the title role and the magnificent support given her by Monteux. Borthayre is magnificent as Le Comte des Grieux but Legay sounds a bit strained at times in his role as La Chevalier des Grieux. This is, however, a minor quibble when weighed against the undeniable virtues of the set. As a bonus, Testament includes de los Angeles singing Debussy's *La damoiselle élue* and Berlioz's *Les Nuits d'été* accompanied by Charles Munch and the Boston Symphony Orchestra.

what to buy next: [Angela Gheorghiu, soprano; Anna Maria Panzarella, soprano; Sophie Koch, soprano; Susanne Schimmack, mezzo-soprano; Roberto Alagna, tenor; Gilles Ragon, tenor; Nicolas Rivenq, baritone; Earle Patriarcho, baritone; José van Dam, bass-baritone; Nicolas Cavallier, bass; Antonio Pappano, cond.; Orchestre Symphonique de la Monnaie; Choeurs de la Monnaie] (EMI Classics 57005) ♪ ♪ ♪ ♪

Gheorghiu is, at times, quite credible as the heroine but the consistent technical demands of the role seem to strain her abilities. Alagna, on the other hand, always focuses on the character (La Chevalier des Grieux), which makes occasional vocal lapses forgivable because they fit within the context of the role. Van

Dam's voice is not the glory it once was, but he is such a master of his craft and surmounts difficulties with such aplomb that they are barely noticeable.

Werther
what to buy: [Victoria de los Angeles, soprano; Mady Mesplé, soprano; Nicolai Gedda, tenor; Andre Mallabrera, tenor; Jean-Christophe Benoit, baritone; Roger Soyer, bass; Georges Prêtre, cond.; Orchestre de Paris; French Radio and Television Orchestra Childrens Choir] (EMI Classics 63973) ♪ ♪ ♪ ♪♪

Werther is, arguably, the greatest of Massenet's operas; the orchestration is masterful and the characterization of even the most menial roles is developed with great care. De los Angeles is a wonderful Charlotte, certainly among the best on record, and Gedda is also in fine form. While Prêtre's direction is not particularly inspired, he keeps things on an even keel so that the singers can take flight.

what to buy next: [Angela Gheorghiu, soprano; Patricia Pétibon, soprano; Roberto Alagna, tenor; Jean-Paul Fouchécourt, tenor; Thomas Hampson, baritone; Jean-Marie Frémeau, baritone; Jean-Phillipe Courtis, bass; Anthonio Pappano, cond.; London Symphony Orchestra; Tiffin Children's Choir] (EMI 56820) ♪ ♪ ♪ ♪

Alagna is superb as Werther and Hampson's Albert is well characterized. Gheorghiu, as the conflicted Charlotte, caught between the two men, is quite good, though she doesn't reach the level of consistency attained by Victoria de los Angeles in the same role. When all is said and done, however, this relatively recent performance is one of the finest currently on the market.

Thaïs
what to buy: Renée Fleming, soprano; Elisabeth Vidal, soprano; Marie Devellereau, soprano; Isabelle Cals, mezzo-soprano; Enkelejda Shkosa, mezzo-soprano; Giuseppe Sabbatini, tenor; Thomas Hampson, baritone; David Grousset, baritone; Stefano Palatchi, bass; Yves Abel, cond.; Orchestre National Bordeaux Aquitaine; Chœur de l'Opéra de Bordeaux] (Decca 466766) ♪ ♪ ♪ ♪♪

Fleming's acting as the troubled prostitute is quite good, as is her undeniably luscious singing. Hampson is a bit over the top at times, but his Athanaël is quite convincing on the whole and sung with considerable flair. It is

difficult to imagine this performance being bettered anytime soon.

influences: Charles Gounod, Ambroise Thomas, Gustave Charpentier, Léo Delibes, Reynaldo Hahn

Ian Palmer

(Sir) Peter Maxwell Davies
Born September 8, 1934, in Manchester, England.

period: Twentieth century

Peter Maxwell Davies was one of the prototypical "bad boys" of classical music during the 1950s and 1960s, experimenting with theatrical pieces owing as much to medieval church music as they did to Anton Webern and Arnold Schoenberg. Of late, the prolific composer has departed somewhat from this flamboyant stance in his series of *Strathclyde Concertos* and symphonies, but compositions like his 1990 children's piece *Dinosaur at Large* and the short orchestral work from 1997 *Mavis in Las Vegas* mark a relatively restrained return to the theater of the mind, but employing his trademark wit and piquant instrumental colors to full effect.

While Davies was attending the Royal Manchester College of Music during the early 1950s, he was part of a pack of upstart, budding, avant-garde composers that included Harrison Birtwistle and Alexander Goehr. Although they were conveniently lumped together later as the Manchester Group, all of these composers developed in quite different ways. Davies is perhaps the most conservative of them, striving for accessibility while experimenting with serialism and even techniques derived from medieval and Renaissance music.

In 1957 he went to Italy to study with Goffredo Petrassi on an Italian government scholarship. When he returned to Britain, Davies already had an award for the orchestral piece *Prolation* to his credit and a newly burnished reputation of exciting young composer on the rise. He was appointed music director at Cirencester Grammar School in 1959. There the need to create music for musicians of limited technical ability forced him to simplify his style without abandoning its framework. This resulted in a series of works (such as the *Five Klee Pictures* for Orchestra), which could be performed by student ensembles.

In 1962 he went to the United States on a Harkness Foundation scholarship to study with Roger Sessions, Earl Kim, and (less pleasantly, according to Davies) with Milton Babbitt at Princeton University. Davies worked on his first opera *Taverner* (about the 16th-century English composer John Taverner) at the same time that Sessions was writing his opera *Montezuma*. The two frequently compared notes and often found themselves conversing as equals rather than teacher and student. This had to do partly with the reputation Davies had already established in Britain and partly with the two composers' genuine admiration for each other's work.

When he returned from the United States in 1964, convinced by his experience that composing must be his core occupation, Davies signed a contract with the music publishers Boosey and Hawkes that put him on an annual retainer for the right to print his scores. He received the first of his many commissions from the British Broadcasting Corporation and moved to a cottage in the country in Dorset to escape the noises of urban life. Later (in 1970) Davies moved even further away from urban existence by taking up residence in the Scottish islands of Orkney.

The first of his many published theater pieces, *Revelation and Fall,* was started in 1965; the next year saw Davies accepting a year-long appointment as Composer-in-Residence at the University of Adelaide in Australia. When he finally returned to Britain in 1967, he was instrumental in the formation of the Pierrot Players (along with his "Manchester Group" cohort Birtwistle). This ensemble, either as the Pierrot Players (until 1970) or as the Fires of London (from 1970 onwards), premiered the majority of his dramatic (non-operatic) works from the late 1960s and throughout most of the 1970s. Perhaps the most important was *Eight Songs for a Mad King,* a work from 1969 whose storyline features an insane King George III trying to teach his birds to sing, and whose staging literally puts the instrumentalists in cages. Davies finally finished *Taverner* in 1970 (it premiered in 1972) before being commissioned by film director Ken Russell to provide the music for *The Devils* and *The Boy Friend*. Davies was living in the remote Orkneys by that time, and many of his compositions since then have become, if not mellow, but more reflective—filled with a sense of grace but maintaining the acerbic wit and intellectual strength that characterize so many of his earlier scores. This is especially apparent in the series of ten *Strathclyde Concertos* he has worked on since 1987, and the later symphonies.

Wynton Marsalis:
Best known for his work in jazz settings, Wynton Marsalis and his brothers (saxophonist Branford, trombonist Delfeayo, and drummer Jason) grew up under the tutelage of their father, New Orleans pianist and educator Ellis Marsalis. The paterfamilias made sure that his sons had a solid technical grounding in their respective instruments, including not only the ability to read music, but instruction in the analysis of scores and an appreciation for classical music. Wynton, the most famous of the children, played in marching bands as he grew up, but he also performed trumpet concertos with the New Orleans Philharmonic Orchestra prior to attending the Juilliard School of Music in 1979, when he was seventeen years old. Readers interested in Marsalis's career as a jazz musician are advised to consult the entry on him in *MusicHound Jazz,* or read selections from his book, *Sweet Swing Blues on the Road*.

In 1983, Marsalis won a classical Grammy Award for *Best Instrumental Soloist With Orchestra* for his performance of Leopold Mozart's trumpet concerto on an album that also featured works by Franz Joseph Haydn and Johann Nepomuk Hummel (Sony Classics 37846). He repeated that feat the next year with a set devoted to arrangements of works for trumpet by Henry Purcell, George Frideric Handel, and others (*Baroque Music for Trumpet,* Sony Classics 39061). On a more adventurous note, Marsalis was later featured on an album playing twentieth century trumpet concertos by André Jolivet (among other periods and composers) with Esa-Pekka Salonen conducting the London Philharmonia Orchestra (Sony Classics 44726).

Not content to be just a crossover musician adept at playing in jazz and classical idioms, Marsalis also had aspirations toward creating classical works on the same scale as that attempted decades earlier by his idol, Edward "Duke" Ellington. The two men shared a tendency to write for instrumentalists whose manner of playing would influence the specific demands of the scores, a trait not uncommon among jazz or classical composers. While Marsalis first revealed his compositional impulse in works featuring jazz musicians (*In This House, on This Morning* and his dance score to *Citi Movement/Griot New York*), his first real piece of music written for traditional classical music forces was his String Quartet no. 1, otherwise known as *At the Octoroon Balls*. Originally debuted at Lincoln Center (where Marsalis headed the jazz programming), this work showed up on disc shortly thereafter (Sony Classics 60979), played by the group that performed at the premiere, the Orion String Quartet, and paired with the suite from *A Fiddler's Tale,* Marsalis's musical reaction to Igor Stravinsky's *A Soldier's Tale*. Marsalis also wrote an impressive three-and-a-half-hour-long oratorio about slavery called *Blood on the Fields* (Sony Classics 57694), which won a Pulitzer Prize in 1997.

Ian Palmer

Davies had a unique arrangement with the label Collins Classics that allowed him to conduct and record most of his newer works, but the project ended with the beginning of the 21st century. Thus (as we go to press) much of his music is now available only in remainder bins and used CD shops, although it is still possible to acquire some of these recordings through outlets that have taken up residence on the Internet.

Orchestral
Symphony no. 5
worth searching for: [Peter Maxwell Davies, cond.; Philharmonia Orchestra] (Collins Classics 1460) ♪ ♪ ♪ ♪

The symphonic music of Sibelius has had a great impact on Davies and hovers in the background of this large-scale, single-movement symphony. It has the same sort of orchestral density one finds in the Finn's later works but the little stabs of dissonance, the quirky percussion passages, and an undeniable flair for playing the brass against the string section, clearly mark this as a Davies piece. Some of the basic material for the symphony was drawn from *Chat Moss,* a short work also included here. The other two scores on the disc are the fanciful *Cross Lane Fair,* complete with pipers and frame drums, and an expanded version of *Five Klee Pictures* that has its roots back in the composer's tenure at Cirencester Grammar School.

Strathclyde Concerto no. 9 for Woodwinds
worth searching for: [*Strathclyde Concertos*; David Nicholson, piccolo; Elizabeth Dooner, alto flute; Maurice Checker, English horn; Josef Pacewicz, E flat clarinet; Ruth Ellis, bass clarinet; Alison Green, contrabassoon; Peter Maxwell Davies, cond.; Scottish Chamber Orchestra] (Collins Classics 1459) ♪ ♪ ♪ ♪

The ten "Strathclyde Concertos" were commissioned for the principal players of the Scottish Chamber Orchestra. By the time Davies reached number nine there were some instruments unrepresented in the series. That led him write this most inventive piece, in which he uses the thematic transformation methods that had informed his works for decades, meshing the six soloists with the orchestra and generating truly marvelous results. The accompanying series finale, *Strathclyde Concerto no. 10* for Orchestra is substantially darker, right up until the last movement which is downright sprightly in spots, with distorted dance rhythms propelling woodwinds, plucked strings, and timpani. *Carolisima* for Orchestra is a lovely serenade and makes a well-deserved encore for the disc.

Vocal
Eight Songs for a Mad King for Baritone and Ensemble

what to buy: [Julius Eastman, baritone; Peter Maxwell Davies, cond.; Fires of London, ensemble] (Unicorn 9052) ♪ ♪ ♪ ♪

Think of this work as an updated version of Arnold Schoenberg's *Pierrot Lunaire* but with a few decades of 20th-century madness tacked on for good measure. Their similarities extend to the instruments used but Davies's take on dementia blurs even more the line separating reality from a dream state. The accompanying *Miss Donnithorne's Maggot,* a similarly dramatic work for soprano and ensemble, also demonstrates the composer's eccentric humor, with the Fires of London and singer Mary Thomas proving to be ideal interpreters.

influences: Roger Sessions, Alexander Goehr, Benjamin Britten

Garaud MacTaggart

(Sir) Paul McCartney
Born James Paul McCartney, June 18, 1942, in Liverpool, England.

period: Twentieth century

Primarily known as a pop composer and musician, McCartney was a member of the groundbreaking group the Beatles, which helped liberate rock music from simplistic three-chord structure and predictable boy-meets-girl lyrics. After the Beatles disbanded in 1970, he performed variously as a solo artist and leader of his own band, Wings, and in the 1990s extended his melodic gifts into the realm of classical music.

McCartney, the son of a former ragtime pianist, grew up in the port city of Liverpool, England. Recordings of American popular music, including those of Elvis Presley, were plentiful there, and it was Presley's influence that first led McCartney to pick up a guitar. By the time he met John Lennon, at about age fourteen, he was able to teach the older boy a few new chords. Thus began a friendship, and one of the most successful songwriting partnerships in the history of popular music.

As a Beatle, McCartney played bass guitar, keyboards, and other instruments. He also shared songwriting credits with Lennon on everything he wrote, although the actual amount of collaboration varied considerably. Many of the pop and rock songs with the strongest

McCartney influence were among the ones most covered by other artists. A few examples include "Yesterday," "Hey Jude," "Eleanor Rigby," "Let It Be," "And I Love Her," and "Here, There, and Everywhere." He showed himself capable of a variety of styles, from bubblegum pop ("Love Me Do") to rockers ("I Saw Her Standing There"); from quiet ballads ("Yesterday") to soul-influenced songs ("Got to Get You into My Life").

The Beatle years also brought McCartney into close contact with classical music and musicians for the first time. He acquainted himself with classical composers, took some music lessons, and in 1966 made his first foray into large-scale instrumental composition with the soundtrack to the film *The Family Way*. Since McCartney, a self-taught musician, had never learned to read or write musical notation, Beatles producer George Martin served as arranger for the soundtrack. McCartney found the ability of classically trained musicians to play on demand fascinating—the Beatles were often more dependent on mood and perceived inspiration (one reason the "documentary" approach of the *Let It Be* recording sessions worked against them, since they had to play for the cameras regardless of whether they felt like it). On occasion he took the baton himself, as he did during the recording of *Sergeant Pepper's Lonely Hearts Club Band* in 1967.

More than twenty years passed before McCartney tackled a large, independent work in the classical mode. His *Liverpool Oratorio*, written with composer/conductor Carl Davis and first performed in 1991, commemorates the 150th year of the Royal Liverpool Philharmonic Orchestra. Although "oratorio" conjures thoughts of Bach and Handel, with McCartney the sound lies somewhat closer to Broadway, and the theme is primarily secular rather than religious. It is an autobiographical work, covering his life from birth during World War II, to school, to marriage and parenthood. Serious critics faulted the *Liverpool Oratorio* for sentimentality and for sounding like a melange of many other composers, among other drawbacks, while acknowledging McCartney's tunefulness as a point in its favor. Orchestras, however, have found it more appealing—more than one hundred of them have performed the work since its premiere. Record-buyers sent the original recording to the top of the classical charts—perhaps a greater testament to the ongoing power of Beatlemania than to the work's intrinsic merits. With its emphasis on solo voices and lyrics that tell stories, the *Liverpool Oratorio* represents a fairly modest departure from

McCartney's familiar pop modes; certainly much less than later works.

McCartney's next classical compositions were shorter pieces. *Stately Horn, Inebriation, Spiral,* and *A Leaf* were written as "practice" to prepare him for an even greater challenge: in 1993 EMI Classics commissioned him for a work celebrating its centenary year. McCartney decided to make it a symphony. With the symphonic poem *Standing Stone* McCartney abandoned lyrics almost entirely, making the chorus one more instrument in the mix. The work begins with a cacophonous evocation of the earth's creation and proceeds through lyrical and dramatic passages chronicling the mythical adventures of an early man, closing with a melodic affirmation of love. (McCartney wrote a long free-verse poem to help tell the story, which is included in the EMI Classics recording.) While McCartney is credited as sole composer of this work, he had the help of four other professionals in getting his keyboard sketches and improvisations transcribed and orchestrated. Again critics praised his use of melody, particularly as expressed in the final soaring love duet, but judged the piece weaker in its more experimental passages.

Orchestral
Standing Stone for Orchestra and Chorus
what to buy: [Lawrence Foster, cond.; London Symphony Orchestra; London Symphony Chorus] (EMI Classics 56484) ♪ ♪₄

This rambling seventy-seven-minute symphonic poem for orchestra and chorus will likely startle McCartney's usual fans with its atonal, dissonant passages, but it also contains lyricism befitting one of pop's longest-reigning hitmakers. It sounds a bit like a moody soundtrack to a movie you've never seen. Oddly, the lavish boxed package does not include the lyrics to the closing love theme; a pity, since it is easily the most memorable part of the composition.

Chamber
various arrangements
what to buy: [*Working Classical: Orchestral and Chamber Music by Paul McCartney,* Loma Mar Quartet, ensemble] (EMI Classics 56897) ♪ ♪ ♪₄

As in *Standing Stone* and the *Liverpool Oratorio,* other hands arranged the basic materials provided by McCartney, the composer (and executive producer). His strength is in the short form, and pop classics like *Maybe I'm Amazed* and *My Love* translate well from song to string quartet. Three of the pieces heard on this disc (*A Leaf, Spiral,* and *Tuesday*) are in orchestral dress with either Lawrence Foster or Andrea Quinn conducting the London Symphony Orchestra.

Vocal
Liverpool Oratorio for Vocal Soloists, Orchestra, and Chorus
what to buy: [Kiri Te Kanawa, soprano; Sally Burgess, mezzo-soprano; Jerry Hadley, tenor; Willard White, bass; Carl Davis, cond.; Royal Liverpool Philharmonic Orchestra; Royal Liverpool Philharmonic Choir; Liverpool Cathedral Choristers] (EMI Classics 54371) ♪ ♪♪

Here we have over an hour and a half (on two discs) of McCartney lyrics exploring the lives of an ordinary family, sung by soloists and choir. Both leading soloists (Te Kanawa and Hadley) earn kudos for their performances; the recording also features boy soloist Jeremy Budd.

influences: Aaron Copland, Edward Elgar, Charles Ives, Ralph Vaughan Williams

Polly Vedder

Nicolai Medtner
Born Nicolai Karlovitch Medtner, January 5, 1880, in Moscow, Russia. Died November 13, 1951, in London, England.

period: Twentieth century/romantic

Nicolai Medtner was a Russian-born descendant of German immigrants. Although he was a piano virtuoso of the first order, his music hews closely to a melodic line, often foregoing showy effects for contrapuntal exercises that reveal their considerable charms slowly. His first scores reflect the influences of Robert Schumann and, to some extent, Piotr Tchaikovsky, while his later works eschew the trappings of Russian nationalism as espoused by Mily Balakirev or Anatoly Liadov. Instead, they display a Teutonic bias, placing Johannes Brahms above the work of Medtner's international contemporaries Igor Stravinsky and Béla Bartók.

Medtner was a product of the Moscow Conservatory, where he thrived under a series of demanding teachers, including Anton Arensky. He had taken piano lessons

from the age of six, displaying a preference for keyboard pieces by Johann Sebastian Bach, Wolfgang Amadeus Mozart, and Domenico Scarlatti. Medtner entered the conservatory in 1892 and won a gold medal for his final recital before graduating in 1900. He also studied composition and counterpoint with Sergei Taneyev, who encouraged the young pianist to devote his life to composing. Three years later, Medtner's first works, the eight *Stimmungsbilder* (Mood Pictures), were published. Despite his resolution to pursue composing, he continued an active career as a concert pianist, returning briefly in 1909 to his alma mater, where he taught piano for a year before resigning. Medtner was also on the editorial board of the *Russian Musical Press* and was developing a mini-career as a critic when he was introduced to Sergei Rachmaninoff, who would become one of his closest friends and supporters.

Written in 1911, the Sonata in E Minor, op. 25, no. 2, is the first real example of Medtner's specific genius. It was dedicated to Rachmaninoff, who was thoroughly astounded by its scope at a 1916 performance and, according to Medtner, "applauded until the lights were put out." The remarkable British pianist-composer Kaikhosru Shapurji Sorabji wondered "whether any other work in the same genre, of more than forty years of age, retains its impressive power, its assertion of itself as one of the major pianistic masterpieces of modern times." In 1913, the critic Grigory Prokofiev noted, "The sonata is powerfully and strongly constructed, and it is not even saturated with scholasticism or academicism, but the composer's eyes are set on such far distances that almost no one will follow him there." These reactions are typical of the way Medtner's music has been received throughout the twentieth century. On one hand, aficionados of form are rewarded for following the composer's musical arguments, while other listeners can admire the craft involved without getting the point of the exercise.

From 1910 until 1914, most of Medtner's time was spent either composing or touring. When he returned to a teaching position at the Moscow Conservatory in 1914, it was more to maintain a steady income than from any deep-seated need to impart wisdom. After the First World War broke out, Medtner, due to his German heritage, was increasingly isolated from most of his colleagues at the school, although his family had lived in Russia for four generations. With the coming of the October Revolution, Rachmaninoff and other like-minded artists left Russia, but Medtner stuck it out until 1921.

He continued working at the conservatory after it was brought under state control and, with Alexander Glazunov and others, even joined the advisory board to the People's Commissariat of Public Education. He finally emigrated in 1921, due to his essential disagreements with the revolutionary political system. After traveling through Europe and over to the United States, he and his wife settled near Paris in 1925. He continued touring, finding British audiences particularly amenable not only to his performances but to his compositions, which he would always include in his concerts. In 1935, Medtner left France to live near London.

In 1942, his deteriorating health forced him to stop touring, putting a pinch on the family finances that wasn't alleviated until the Maharajah of Mysore sent a letter authorizing the formation of a Nicolas Medtner Society in 1945. By bankrolling this organization, he not only contributed mightily to the composer's living standard but helped document his artistic legacy by financing recording sessions in which the composer played his own works for posterity. Six years later, after recording a substantial number of his compositions and working on some songs and his final score (the Quintet in C Major for Piano and Strings), Medtner died.

Orchestral
Concerto no. 2 in C Minor for Piano and Orchestra, op. 50
what to buy: [*The Romantic Piano Concerto, Vol. 2*; Nikolai Demidenko, piano; Jerzy Maksymiuk, cond.; BBC Scottish Symphony Orchestra] (Hyperion 66580) ♪ ♪ ♪ ♪ ♪

From the staggered opening rhythms of a mighty toccata through the sweet, seductive *romanza* of the second movement and on through the sparkling divertimento that closes this marvelous work, Demidenko is in top form. Dedicated by Medtner to Rachmaninoff (who in turn dedicated his fourth piano concerto to Medtner), this is a virtuosic work that cries out to be performed and heard more often. The accompanying work, the composer's third and final piano concerto, was created more than fifteen years after its predecessor. Presenting a more fluid, almost fantasia-like backdrop for the pianist's phrases, this and his lone piano quintet were Medtner's final instrumental compositions.

what to buy next: [Nicolas Medtner, piano; Issay Dobrowen, cond.; Philharmonia Orchestra] (Testament 1027) ♪ ♪ ♪ ♪

On Medtner's 1947 monaural recording of this powerful concerto (underwritten by the Maharajah of Mysore), there is a curiously relaxed, almost contemplative air to his playing in the toccata, while the second movement romance is recorded rather harshly. On the whole, however, this is an admirable counter to the more virtuosic, better-recorded version by Demidenko and deserves to be explored by people who love the work. Medtner's third piano concerto and two solo piano pieces—the Arabesque in A Minor, op. 7, no. 2, and the Tale in F Minor, op. 26, no. 3—complete the program.

Chamber
Sonata in E Minor for Piano, op. 25, no. 2—*Night Wind*
what to buy: [*The Complete Piano Sonatas*; Marc-André Hamelin, piano] (Hyperion 67221/4) ♪ ♪ ♪ ♪ ♪

Even though this four-disc set has a fairly steep price tag, the music is definitely worth the money, especially for those seeking a masterly performance of Medtner's most important work for solo piano. That Hamelin surveys not only the composer's nine essays in the form but also includes the first two books of *Forgotten Melodies* (opp. 38 and 39) in well-recorded performances of distinction is more than a bonus—it is a triumph.

what to buy next: [*Piano Works, vol. 4*; Geoffrey Tozer, piano] (Chandos 9618) ♪ ♪ ♪ ♪

For those folks unwilling to shell out for Hamelin's set, this is a worthy alternative, lacking only the last possible scintilla of excitement. Tozer's album is also well recorded and duplicates Hamelin's program for the *Sonate-Idylle* (op. 56), *Fairy Tale Sonata* (op. 25, no. 1), and the awesome *Night Wind,* but it also tosses in a pair of Medtner's early works—the first of his *Two Fairytales* (op. 14, no. 1) and the second of his three *Dithyramben* (op. 10, no. 2).

influences: Robert Schumann, Johannes Brahms, Sergei Rachmaninoff

Garaud MacTaggart

Felix Mendelssohn
Born Jakob Ludwig Felix Mendelssohn-Bartholdy, February 3, 1809, in Hamburg, Germany. Died November 4, 1847, in Leipzig, Germany.

period: Romantic

While Mendelssohn's glorious E Minor violin concerto and Symphonies nos. 3 (*Scottish*) and 4 (*Italian*) have maintained their hallowed places in the standard orchestral repertoire, the one work for which he is best known by the general public, one which sparks recognition even if they don't remember the composer's name, is the *Wedding March* from Mendelssohn's incidental music (op. 61) to the Shakespeare play *A Midsummer Night's Dream*.

Although Felix Mendelssohn descended from a line of prominent Jewish intellectuals, his father had forsaken the family faith and converted to Protestantism. Whether this was a matter of real religious conviction or a matter of convenient practicality (given the consistent persecution of Jews in Europe), it resulted in a household where religious tolerance was practiced and philosophical concepts from both camps were discussed. When considered against that backdrop, Mendelssohn's later advocacy for the works of Johann Sebastian Bach and the creation of his own masterful Old and New Testament oratorios (*Elijah* and *Paulus*) only make sense.

Prior to all that, however, was the preternatural development of instrumental genius which young Felix displayed by 1818 when, with Fanny, his beloved and talented older sister, he performed in his first public piano recital. In addition to an impressive scholastic regimen which included lessons in Latin, French, and Greek, Mendelssohn was also learning to play the violin, singing in a prestigious choir, and gradually being exposed to the works of Bach and George Frideric Handel. The first of his compositions of which there is any record was premiered in 1819, shortly after Mendelssohn's initial lessons in music theory had begun. This action more or less opened the floodgates, since the following year saw the creation of three operettas (Singspiels), some songs, a pair of choral works, half a dozen symphonies for strings, and a number of other, smaller scores. His most important youthful concert, however, may have been the one in 1821 where Mendelssohn played his own compositions and various works by Bach, Beethoven, and Mozart on the piano for Johann Wolfgang von Goethe and various members of the Weimar court. By this time, his reputation as a virtuoso was being vouched for by seasoned professionals like Johann Nepomuk Hummel, Louis Spohr, and Frédéric Kalkbrenner.

All of the instrumental scores that Mendelssohn wrote prior to October 1825—the string symphonies, his Concerto in E Major for Two Pianos and Orchestra, the three piano quartets, numerous keyboard works—were pleasant preparatory exercises leading up to his first major piece, the Octet in E-flat Major for Strings, op. 20. Unlike Ludwig Spohr, who wrote music for double quartet, Mendelssohn's octet treats the combined forces with an orchestral flourish that makes the piece less of a hybrid and more of a separate, unified foundation for future composers to build and expand upon. The next important work that Mendelssohn composed was the overture to *A Midsummer Night's Dream*, op. 21, which received its public premiere in February, 1827, just months before the composer entered the University of Berlin. It was also about this time that his study of Bach's works began to intensify, an endeavor that resulted in Mendelssohn conducting a performance of that composer's *St. Matthew Passion* in 1829 and the composition of two sacred cantatas inspired by Bach's efforts in that genre.

1829 was also the year that Mendelssohn visited Great Britain for the first time, taking part in concerts (both as a conductor and a pianist) and touring Scotland, where he found the inspiration for one of his most famous concert overtures, *The Hebrides (Fingal's Cave)*. He also finished his op. 12 string quartet, a work in E-flat Major that shows Beethoven's influence, especially in the first movement. The next year saw the completion of Mendelssohn's *Reformation* symphony—even though it is listed in Mendelssohn's canon as the fifth of his symphonies—as well as the beginning of a lengthy visit to Italy where he wrote a number of choral works. He left there in 1830 and traveled to Switzerland before venturing to France in December 1831 and back to London in the spring of 1832. All during the time Mendelssohn was away from Germany, he sent numerous letters back to family members and friends, detailing his experiences in foreign lands and the famous musicians (Mikhail Glinka, Giacomo Meyerbeer, and Frédéric Chopin among them) he had met.

Mendelssohn took a position as music director at Düsseldorf, Germany in the fall of 1833, after mulling over a competing offer from the London Philharmonic Society, conducting the premieres of his *Italian* (no. 3) and *Reformation* symphonies, and overseeing the publication of the first volume of his short piano works, the *Lieder ohne Worte (Songs without Words)*. In

Düsseldorf, Mendelssohn led a number of operatic works but concentrated much of his efforts in an attempt to revive the oratorio format, conducting major scores in that genre by Josef Haydn and George Frideric Handel.

Dissatisfied with the management at Düsseldorf, Mendelssohn then left for Leipzig to take control of the Gewandhaus Orchestra in 1835, a position he was to hold for the next dozen years. 1836 and 1837 saw the premiere of his debut oratorio *Paulus (St. Paul)*, marriage, and the composition of his second piano concerto and the first of his op. 44 string quartets. As a conductor, Mendelssohn continued his advocacy of Bach's works, but he also led the first public performance of Franz Schubert's ninth symphony and the debut of Robert Schumann's first symphony, while turning the Gewandhaus concerts into some of the most notable and polished showcases for music in Europe. Mendelssohn premiered his *Scottish* symphony there in 1842 and also played an important role in the establishment of the Leipzig Conservatory, the educational institution which opened its doors in 1843. He also wrote some incidental music for *A Midsummer Night's Dream* (op. 61) which premiered in 1843 and is now often paired with the overture (op. 21) that he debuted in 1827. Mendelssohn's justly famous Concerto in E Minor for Violin and Orchestra was finished in 1844, the same year that he completed the first draft of his masterful oratorio, *Elijah*.

When Mendelssohn died in 1847 (after a series of strokes), he was mourned all over Europe, especially in Great Britain where his oratorios *Paulus* and *Elijah* were extremely popular. Within a few years, however, there was a backlash against his music, partly as a response to his classical tendencies in an era drenched in romanticism and the ensuing orchestral innovations of Hector Berlioz and Richard Wagner. Then too, his music was also tarred by anti-Semitism, with Wagner being the most prominent of initial denigrators while the National Socialists of Adolph Hitler continued the process in the twentieth century. Despite these ugly, unwarranted ideological attacks, Mendelssohn's graceful and at times powerful music has survived and provided pleasure to generations of musicians and listeners.

Orchestral
Concerto in E Minor for Violin and Orchestra, op. 64
what to buy: [*Favorite Violin Concertos*; Arthur Grumiaux, violin; Bernard Haitink, cond.; Royal

Concertgebouw Orchestra] (Philips 442287) ♪ ♪ ♪ ♪

Musical poetry runs all through this piece and Grumiaux makes the most of it. He doesn't shirk the pyrotechnics, however, and the famous last movement has plenty of fireworks without forgetting the essential grace of the work. This two-disc set features Grumiaux playing very recommendable versions of violin concerti by Ludwig van Beethoven, Johannes Brahms and Piotr Tchaikovsky as well.

what to buy next: [Itzhak Perlman, violin; André Previn, cond.; London Symphony Orchestra] (EMI Classics 69863) ♪ ♪ ♪ ♪

Even though Perlman recorded this concerto two other times—with conductors Bernard Haitink and Daniel Barenboim—this is the version that sings. This budget-priced CD finds Mendelssohn's concerto paired with a very good rendition of Max Bruch's Violin Concerto no. 1 in G Minor.

[Kyung-Wha Chung, violin; Charles Dutoit, cond.; Montreal Symphony Orchestra] (Decca 460976) ♪ ♪ ♪ ♪

This is a more substantial album from a programming standpoint than the Perlman set, but the differences are minimal from one of technique, though the Chung set is a tad less hard-edged. Rudolph Kempe leads the Royal Philharmonic Orchestra in the other pair of showpieces for the violin, Bruch's first violin concerto and *Scottish Fantasy*.

[Jascha Heifetz, violin; Charles Munch, cond.; Boston Symphony Orchestra] (RCA Victor Living Stereo 68980) ♪ ♪ ♪ ♪

Heifetz is a speed demon and if his undoubtable technical expertise is for you, then you should love this. Otherwise, the recording is a tad stiff and the interpretation lacks the last bit of tenderness that Grumiaux, Perlman and Chung give. The Beethoven Violin Concerto in D Major with which the Mendelssohn work is paired is much more worthy of Heifetz's hallowed reputation.

Concerto no. 2 in D Minor for Piano and Orchestra, op. 40
what to buy: [Murray Perahia, piano; Neville Marriner, cond.; Academy of St. Martin-in-the-Fields, orch.] (Sony Classics 42401) ♪ ♪ ♪ ♪

Perahia treats this pleasant, well-thought-out work with genteel respect and tons of technique. Ditto for Mendelssohn's somewhat slighter piano concerto and the three solo piano pieces that are included in the same package.

what to buy next: [*The Romantic Piano Concerto, vol. 17;* Stephen Hough, piano; Lawrence Foster, cond.; City of Birmingham Symphony Orchestra] (Hyperion 66969) ♪ ♪ ♪ ♪

Hough is almost in Perahia's class as far as pianism goes, but the orchestra isn't quite in the same bracket as Marriner's. Still, this is a very solid offering combining well-played versions of both piano concerti plus three other Mendelssohn works for piano and orchestra, the *Capriccio brillante,* the *Rondo brilliant,* and the *Serenade and Allegro giocoso.*

Ein Sommernachstraum (A Midsummer Night's Dream), opp. 21 and 61
what to buy: [Miranda van Kralingen, soprano; Iris Vermillion, mezzo-soprano; Hans Vonk, cond.; Cologne Radio Symphony Orchestra; Cologne Radio Chorus] (Capriccio Records 10407) ♪ ♪ ♪ ♪ ♪

The recording is altogether lovely and the performances have just the right audio sparkle, bounce, and lift. Vonk's singers and chorus are nigh unto perfect in *Ye spotted snake,* and the popular scherzo and *Wedding March* show off the conductor and his orchestra to full advantage.

what to buy next: [Edith Wiens, soprano; Sarah Walker, mezzo-soprano; Andrew Litton, cond.; London Philharmonic Orchestra; London Philharmonic Chorus] (Classics for Pleasure 4593) ♪ ♪ ♪ ♪

Ye spotted snake is sung in English and, depending upon which side of the "original language" debate you occupy, that may or may not make a difference for you. All things being equal however, Litton's conducting of a substantial portion of Mendelssohn's incidental music is relatively pointed; not quite as sharp as Vonk (see above) and not as loose as Previn (see below).

[Lillian Watson, soprano; Delia Wallis, mezzo-soprano; André Previn, cond.; London Symphony Orchestra; Finchley Children's Music Group, choir] (EMI Angel 47163) ♪ ♪ ♪ ♪

Previn's take on the overture is a bit slack but the scherzo bounces along quite nicely and the *Wedding March* is likely to disappoint no one. That said, the main thing Previn has going for him is the completeness of this recording; it has more of the incidental music from this play than just about any other recording currently on the market.

Symphony no. 3 in A Minor, op. 56 (*Scottish*)
what to buy: [Otto Klemperer, cond.; Bavarian Radio Symphony Orchestra] (EMI Classics Imports 66868) ♪ ♪ ♪ ♪

Klemperer's adherents loved his usually firm grasp of the score and the way he kept the tension up even at tempos that would sound flabby in a less skilled conductor's hands. His detractors generally had problems with his deliberate pacing. Everything that his fans loved applies to this magnificent performance of Mendelssohn's third symphony. Ditto for his take on Franz Schubert's great *Unfinished* Symphony (no. 8) that fills up the balance of this disc.

[*Complete Symphonies, vol. 1;* Bernard Haitink, cond.; London Symphony Orchestra] (Philips 456071) ♪ ♪ ♪ ♪

A mid-line price hides a splendid performance of Mendelssohn's third symphony, good versions of the first two numbered symphonies (the second symphony is conducted by Riccardo Chailly), and a solid rendition of the overture *The Hebrides (Fingal's Cave).*

[Claudio Abbado, cond.; London Symphony Orchestra] (Deutsche Grammophon 427810) ♪ ♪ ♪ ♪

The pacing is a bit quicker here than in the Haitink or Klemperer recordings, but it still works well from an interpretive standpoint. Abbado includes a very good version of the composer's fourth symphony (the *Italian*), and that may help you choose between the three.

Symphony no. 4 in A Major, op. 90 (*Italian*)
what to buy: [Christoph von Dohnányi, cond.; Vienna Philharmonic Orchestra] (Decca 460239) ♪ ♪ ♪ ♪

Of all the Mendelssohn symphonies, this is the most immediately appealing, with a sprightly opening that is consistently ingratiating. Relaxed without being slack,

Felix Mendelssohn

this performance of the *Italian* is graceful and well mannered, agile rather than peppy. In that sense, Dohnányi's direction here is, in many ways, a throwback to the way Otto Klemperer used to conduct this piece, steady and with a keen feeling for its architecture. The same values work well in his treatment of the third and fifth symphonies, with a pair of familiar overtures (*The Hebrides [Fingal's Cave]* and *Calm Sea and Prosperous Voyage*) and two excerpts from the incidental music to *Athalie* completing this good-sounding, reasonably-priced, two-disc set.

what to buy next: [John Eliot Gardiner, cond.; Vienna Philharmonic Orchestra] (Deutsche Grammophon 459156) ♪ ♪ ♪ ♪

Gardiner's performance here is quite good, but what makes it stand out from all the other *Italian* symphonies on the market is his inclusion of the revised edition of this work. Since Mendelssohn didn't muck around with the first movement, Gardiner leads his orchestra through the rendition which has served generations as the "real" thing, before sliding into a pleasant concert recording of the fifth (*Reformation*) symphony, and then closing the disc out with the last three movements of the *Italian* that the composer reworked. With a programmable CD player you can play the first movement and then skip to the last three "revised" movements to get an idea of how the piece was probably meant for posterity. The revisions themselves resolve a number of loose ends and tighten the musical argument considerably, but it will probably take most listeners quite a few sittings to get comfortable with the changes Mendelssohn intended for this beloved symphony.

[Herbert Blomstedt, cond.; San Francisco Symphony Orchestra] (London 433811) ♪ ♪ ♪ ♪

Blomstedt captures that bounce and spring so needed in performances of this piece, and matches this work up with a very worthy take on the composer's third symphony. The record company could have fit an overture or two on here but, for whatever reasons, they didn't.

Chamber
Lieder ohne Worte (Songs without Words)
what to buy: [Daniel Barenboim, piano] (Deutsche Grammophon 453061) ♪ ♪ ♪ ♪

Robert Schumann praised these works, calling them "most beautiful," and it would be difficult to find fault

with his observation. Many pianists include various elements from the *Songs without Words* in their recitals, but there are no complete cycles that can compare with Barenboim's. These little gems contain some lovely tunes, and Barenboim makes more of them than just about anyone else.

Quartet no. 1 in E-flat Major for Strings, op. 12
what to buy: [Eroica Quartet, ensemble] (Harmonia Mundi USA 907245) ♪ ♪ ♪

Despite the earlier opus number, this lovely piece was actually written a couple years after the op. 13 string quartet (A Minor) that is also on this disc. The last work heard here is the posthumously premiered quartet dating from 1823 and in the same key as the later op. 12 piece. The Eroica Quartet is a marvelous recent group and, if their playing on this set is any indicator, they will long be an ensemble to watch.

Quartet no. 3 in D Major for Strings, op. 44, no. 1
what to buy: [Guarneri String Quartet, ensemble] (Arabesque 6714) ♪ ♪ ♪

While Mendelssohn's gift for melody is apparent all through this composition, there is a virtuoso first movement which presages some of the fireworks he would later unleash in his violin concerto. The long-lived Guarneri String Quartet pushes the energy of this work for all it is worth, but their accompanying recording of the youthful Octet (augmented by the Orion String Quartet) isn't as felicitous as either performance of that piece by the Academy of St. Martin-in-the-Fields Chamber Ensemble (see below).

[Talich Quartet, ensemble] (Calliope 9302) ♪ ♪ ♪ ♪

Despite occasional intonation flaws (as in the last movement of the D Major quartet) the Talich Quartet's survey of all three op. 44 quartets is a nobly intentioned one, played with plenty of vigor and heart and decidedly recommendable.

Octet in E-flat Major for Strings, op. 20
what to buy: [Academy Chamber Ensemble] (Philips 420400) ♪ ♪ ♪ ♪

This is a fine performance of one of the most beguiling and artistically satisfying pieces in the composer's oeuvre and his first acknowledged masterpiece. A well-played version of his Quintet no. 2 in B-flat for Strings, op. 87, makes a wonderful pairing for the octet. The group playing this is an early version (1978) of the Academy of St. Martin-in-the-Fields Chamber Ensemble with Iona Brown as one of the violinists.

what to buy next: [Academy of St. Martin-in-the-Fields Chamber Ensemble] (Chandos 8790) ♪ ♪ ♪ ♪

Only cellist Roger Smith and violinist Malcolm Latchem are left over from the group that recorded this piece in 1978 (see above), but the same uniformity of purpose that made the other disc such a joy to listen to can be heard here as well—just not as felicitously. The recording is quite good, just what one expects from the engineers at Chandos, but the pairing (Joachim Raff's Octet in C Major for Strings, op. 176) isn't as involving as the Mendelssohn works in the prior version. Still, it is an interesting program from a historical standpoint and the disc is a bit easier to find than the 1978 set.

Vocal
Elijah, op. 70
what to buy: [Renée Fleming, soprano; Patricia Bardon, mezzo-soprano; John Mark Ainsley, tenor; Bryn Terfel, bass-baritone; Paul Daniel, cond.; Edinburgh Festival Chorus; Orchestra of the Age of Enlightenment] (London 455688) ♪ ♪ ♪ ♪

Other than Handel's *Messiah,* this was the most popular oratorio in England during the nineteenth century. Terfel is an outstanding Elijah, with the kind of vocal presence a prophet of doom needs. Fleming and Ainsley are very good in their roles and Daniel's direction is solid throughout.

Paulus (St. Paul), op . 36
what to buy: [Melanie Diener, soprano; Annette Markert, mezzo-soprano; James Taylor, tenor; Matthias Görne, bass-baritone; Philippe Herreweghe, cond.; La Chapelle Royale, choir; Collegium Vocale, choir; Orchestre des Champs Élysées, orch.] (Harmonia Mundi 901584/85) ♪ ♪ ♪ ♪

This well-recorded "live" version of Mendelssohn's first oratorio is filled with gorgeous themes and melodies. While not as overtly powerful as *Elijah* this is a work that deserves respect and, with Herreweghe's performers, gets it.

influences: Robert Schumann, Ludwig Spohr, Niels Gade, Carl Maria von Weber, Wolfgang Amadeus Mozart, Ludwig van Beethoven

Garaud MacTaggart

Gian Carlo Menotti
Born July 7, 1911, in Cadegliano, Italy.

period: Twentieth century

Although he may stick in many people's minds as the composer of *Amahl and the Night Visitors*—a television opera from 1951 that was broadcast every Christmas season for years—Menotti wrote in a variety of genres. Vocal works dominate his oeuvre, however, with *Amahl* remaining his most consistently popular composition despite his having created two other stage works—*The Medium* and *The Consul*—that rank among of twentieth-century America's greatest operas.

Menotti's works lean heavily toward opera, a predilection first exhibited in the two stage works he wrote before his thirteenth birthday. By that time, Menotti had already received his first music lessons (from his mother) and was primed to enter the Milan Conservatory. After studying there, he came to the attention of Arturo Toscanini, who saw the young musician's potential and recommended that Menotti further his studies at the Curtis Institute in Philadelphia. In 1927, the budding composer left his homeland for the United States, where he would make his reputation and spend most of his life. While at the Curtis Institute, he met Samuel Barber, beginning a friendship (and occasional business relationship) that would last for decades.

After receiving his degree in 1933, Menotti started working on his first mature opera, *Amelia al ballo* (Amelia goes to the ball), which had its English-language premiere in 1936 under the direction of Fritz Reiner. Its success was solid enough that the National Broadcasting Company (NBC) commissioned him to write a radio opera, *The Old Maid and the Thief.* As with *Amelia al ballo* and his other operas, Menotti wrote not only the music but the libretto. Next came *The Island God,* written for somewhat larger forces, which met with indifference on the part of critics and audiences. Menotti's first great triumph was *The Medium,* a violence-filled two-act tragic opera about the gray area between illusion and reality, which premiered in 1946. The next year saw the production of *The Telephone,* a

lighter-hearted one-act stage work that has since often been paired with *The Medium* as a curtain-raiser. *The Consul,* Menotti's first full-length opera, received its debut in 1950; for this work, which dealt with the problems of refugees bumping up against an implacable bureaucracy, Menotti received the first of his two Pulitzer Prizes.

Amahl and the Night Visitors was commissioned by NBC as a television opera and scheduled for a Christmas Eve broadcast. The tale of the young lad and his encounter with the Three Wise Men resonated with the viewing audience, and the original cast recording remained a holiday staple for many years. Its simple melodic structures stand in marked contrast to the grim libretto and dramatic score of *The Consul.* Vying with *The Medium* for consideration as the composer's greatest work, *The Consul* should also be thought of as one of the greatest (and most accessible) American operas, putting it right up there with Leonard Bernstein's *West Side Story* and Stephen Sondheim's *Sweeny Todd.* The tale of an attempted escape from a police state thwarted by the uncaring bureaucracy of another country has Orwellian and Swiftian overtones. Menotti regarded his next opera, *The Saint of Bleecker Street,* as his best work, and it won him his second Pulitzer Prize, along with a Drama Critics Circle Award and a Music Critics Circle Award. This last work marked the tail end of Menotti's most creative period, although he has written at least a dozen more operas and/or stage works, along with a host of compositions in other genres.

Menotti's talent for combining his own taut, skillfully fashioned librettos with well-constructed (if basically conservative) scores makes his operas among the most easily assimilated vocal stage works for beginning listeners. Menotti also contributed librettos to Samuel Barber's two operas, *Vanessa* and *A Hand of Bridge,* and to Lukas Foss's *Introductions and Goodbyes.* In addition, he helped found the famous Festival of Two Worlds in Spoleto, Italy, in 1958 and its counterpart in Charleston, South Carolina, in 1977. The Kennedy Center honored him in 1984 for "lifetime achievement in the arts."

Vocal
Amahl and the Night Visitors
what to buy: [Chet Allen, boy soprano; Rosemary

Kuhlmann, soprano; Andrew McKinley, tenor; Davis Aiken, baritone; Leon Lishner, bass; Thomas Schippers, cond.; NBC Symphony Orchestra; NBC Symphony Chorus] (RCA Victor Gold Seal 6485) ♪ ♪ ♪ ♪♪

These are the musical forces behind the original broadcast production of *Amahl and the Night Visitors.* Their recording of Menotti's score still sells steadily every Christmas, even though current broadcasts of the work are rarer than during its heyday. Schippers was a marvelous conductor, and the performance remains definitive in many respects.

The Medium
what to buy: [Patrice Michaels Bedi, soprano; Diane Ragains, soprano; Joyce Castle, mezzo-soprano; Barbara Landin, mezo-soprano; Joanna Lind, singer; Peter Van DeGraff, bass-baritone; Lawrence Rapchak, cond.; Chicago Opera Theater Orchestra] (Cedille 34) ♪ ♪ ♪ ♪

The Medium is a highly charged piece that demands both good singing and good acting. While they don't give a perfect performance by any means, Rapchak and his Chicago-based ensemble are more than adequate, conveying all the drama of this tightly wound work with a high degree of musicality.

The Consul
what to buy: [Susan Bullock, soprano; Victoria Livengood, mezzo-soprano; Jacalyn Kreitzer, contralto; Louis Otey, baritone; Herbert Eckhoff, baritone, Charles Austin, bass; Richard Hickox, cond.; Spoleto Festival Orchestra] (Chandos 9706) ♪ ♪ ♪ ♪♪

Recorded at the 1998 Spoleto Festival, this performance of Menotti's work is cinematic in its sweep and at the same time intensely focused, making a good argument for a future film noir treatment. Musically, this is one of the composer's most dramatic and intense scores—a fit partner for his own topical, darkly textured libretto. Bullock and Otey are effective in their primary roles, acting as much as singing, communicating Menotti's concept and not just intoning the music.

influences: Giacomo Puccini, Samuel Barber, Ned Rorem, Ermanno Wolf-Ferrari

Gian Carlo Menotti

Garaud MacTaggart

Saverio Mercadante

Born Giuseppe Saverio Raffaele Mercadante c. September 17, 1795, in Altamura, Italy. Died December 17, 1870, in Naples, Italy.

period: Romantic

Mercadante was one of the most important composers of Italian opera in the mid-nineteenth century, beginning with a style that emulated Gioacchino Rossini and ending with a much more romantic and personal sound that looked forward to Giuseppe Verdi. Although he wrote more than sixty operas, few have remained in the repertoire of even minor opera companies. It is his instrumental music, particularly his writing for flute, that is heard most often in modern concerts and recordings.

Mercadante was an illegitimate child, which caused him much shame and which he tried to hide by insisting in his later years that he was born in Naples. In reality he had moved to Naples at the age of ten or eleven to be with his father. Young Saverio had displayed musical talent prior to moving to Naples, but the local conservatory wouldn't admit him on a scholarship unless he was younger than ten years old and a native Neapolitan. So his father falsified the necessary information to help his son gain admission to the Collegio di S. Sebastiano, causing confusion among later musicologists as to his date of birth.

At the conservatory, Mercadante studied flute and violin, in addition to the usual classes in harmony, counterpoint, and composition. He wrote two complete symphonies and a number of works for string quartet before he turned twenty-three. Rossini, who was to remain a lifelong friend, noted that the young man had much talent and envisioned a bright future for him. It is ironic, based upon his future success as a composer of vocal works, that Mercadante concentrated almost entirely on writing instrumental music until the age of twenty-four, when he turned his attention to operas.

In 1821 he created his first truly successful opera, *Elisa e Claudio,* which led to performances of his work across Europe. He continued churning out scores (averaging over two operas a year) with varying degrees of success through 1840, when he became the dominant Italian operatic composer by default. (Rossini had stopped writing by 1830, Vincenzo Bellini died in 1835, Gaetano Donizetti was delivering his best work to Parisian and Viennese opera houses, and Verdi had not yet written his first big hit, *Nabucco.*) The year 1840 was also when

Mercadante accepted the position of music director at his alma mater, where he remained until his death in 1870. He also took on the music directorship at the cathedral at Novara in 1861, at which time he began experiencing vision problems. By 1862 he was completely blind, but he kept composing by dictating his music to students, who would carefully copy down his instructions note for note. After his death, production of Mercadante's operas virtually ceased, and today they are rarely performed in public.

Orchestral
Concerto in E Minor for Flute and Orchestra, op. 57
what to buy: [*Concertos Romantiques Pour Flute*; Jean-Pierre Rampal, flute; Claudio Scimone, cond.; I Solisti Veneti, orch.] (Erato 45838) ♪ ♪ ♪ ♪

Since flutists Jean-Pierre Rampal and James Galway (see below) play with the same conductor and orchestra in their respective renditions of this concerto, the differences between them are slight, with Rampal giving a marginally stiffer performance than the more vivacious Galway. Rampal's version of the Mercadante piece is packaged with concertos by two other composers (Carl Reinecke's op. 283 and Bernard Romberg's op. 17).

worth searching for: [*Mercadante: Flute Concertos*; James Galway, flute; Claudio Scimone cond.; I Solisti Veneti, orch.] (RCA Victor Red Seal 61447) ♪ ♪ ♪ ♪

Galway is at his very best on this disc, which features three complete concertos from Mercadante's prolific pen, including one in E Major and another in D Major. Galway also tosses in a delightful little cavatina from the composer's opera *Caritea, regina de Spagna,* which he transcribed for flute and orchestra. Be aware, however, that Galway's performance of the op. 57 concerto is the only piece from this album that is still available. You can get it as part of a suitably pricey fifteen-disc retrospective of Galway's career (*60 Years 60 Flute Masterpieces,* RCA Victor Red Seal 63432).

Chamber
various chamber works for flute
what to buy: [*Mercadante: Duetto Concertante, Serenades, Trios*; Andrea Adorján, Aurèle Nicolet, Marianne Hendel, flutes; Julius Berger, cello; Dieter Salewski, English horn; Han-An Liu, harp] (Tudor 763) ♪ ♪ ♪ ♪

Here is a delightful all-Mercadante set containing a fine selection of lightweight works fashioned around the sound of flutes. Not only are there a pair of bouncing duets for Adorján and Nicolet, but Hendel joins them for the composer's *Serenade for Three Flutes.* The disc also includes Mercadante's Fantasia for Flute, played by Adorján, and a quintet, *La Serenata* for Flutes, Harp, English Horn, and Cello.

influences: Vincenzo Bellini, Gaetano Donizetti, Giacomo Meyerbeer

Dave Wagner

Olivier Messiaen

Born Olivier Eugene Prosper Charles Messiaen, December 10, 1908, in Avignon, France. Died April 28, 1992, in Paris, France.

period: Twentieth century

One of the pre-eminent composers of organ music in the twentieth century, Messiaen created his own style of composition through the use of specific modes (scales) and birdsongs that he studied. The major works for which Messiaen is known are the *Turangalîla-symphonie,* the *Quatuor pour la Fin du Temps (Quartet for the End of Time),* and the seven books of the *Catalogue d'oiseaux* for piano, though he also wrote several masterworks for his own instrument, the organ.

Messiaen's father, Pierre, was a Shakespearean scholar and English teacher, while his mother, Cècile Sauvage, was a poet. His formal musical training began at the Paris Conservatoire when he was eleven years old and he studied the usual array of musical subjects—harmony, theory, counterpoint, history, and, of course, composition—with his most notable teacher, Paul Dukas. In 1930, because of his outstanding talents, Messiaen won the Premier Prix in all those disciplines and left the Conservatoire to become organist for La Trinité Church in Paris.

When World War II broke out in 1939, he was drafted into the army but declared unfit for active duty and relegated to a medical auxiliary. His life took a turn for the worse when he was taken prisoner by German forces in 1940 and held at a prison camp in Görlitz, Silesia (now Poland). It was during this period that Messiaen composed one of his most famous works, the *Quatuor pour la fin du temps,* utilizing the instruments and performers available to him at the camp: a violinist, a cellist, and a clarinetist, with the composer himself playing the piano part on a beat-up, vaguely in-tune, upright piano. The work was first performed in 1941 before an audience of 5,000 prisoners and Messiaen was freed from the camp later that year. Upon his release, he resumed his position at La Trinité and took an appointment to teach harmony at the Paris Conservatoire, a capacity in which he was to serve for the next forty years.

Labeling Messiaen's compositional style is not easy, and it is most often regarded as a form unto itself. Early in his career, he designed a set of modes of limited transposition. These scale-like modes can only be transposed by half-steps a few times before the original notes begin to reappear. Several recurring elements also play a dominant role in the composer's musical language, including the Hindu rhythms he studied in *Salgîta-Ratnâkara* (a thirteen century resource), and birdsong. Like his modes of transposition, Messiaen carefully organized the Hindu-based rhythms into several categories which signified their religious, philosophical, and rhythmic elements and, being an avid ornithologist, he found a way to transcribe the various birdsongs using conventional musical notation rather than a recording device. He had the opportunity to pass many of his ideas on to a new generation of musicians when he was allowed to teach a class in musical analysis at the Conservatoire in 1947.

It was also during this period that Messiaen was working on the *Turangalîla-symphonie,* a massive work originally commissioned by Serge Koussevitzky, that included an ondes martenot—an electronic keyboard/oscillator hybrid—as a key element in the unique sonorities the composer was attempting to construct. The inventor of the instrument, Maurice Martenot, managed to convince the Conservatoire to conduct classes for his invention in the same year that Messiaen started teaching his musical analysis course, so it is possible that there was some artistic cross-fertilization going on. Still, other composers (Darius Milhaud, Arthur Honegger, and André Jolivet, to name three) had used the instrument within their works, and Messiaen may have been exposed to its unique qualities prior to Martenot's association with the school. In any case, the *Turangalîla-symphonie* is an extravagant summing-up piece, lasting well over an hour and filled with the Hindu rhythms and adventurous harmonies Messiaen was experimenting with during his first great cycle of composition.

The birdsongs also became the basis for many of his works, including his 1956 composition for piano and orchestra *Oiseaux exotiques* and the solo piano cycle from 1958, *Catalogue d'oiseaux*. The way in which Messiaen weaves these birdsong ideas into his music is fascinating. The intricate details of putting into notation the different birdsongs and aligning the desired harmonic or melodic phrases may not have been as difficult for the composer as it is for the performer. Very often, music of the twentieth century is more a matter of conveying a mood or sensation than striving for accuracy of notes in performance. Because of the demands of music notation editors, sometimes notes and/or chords end up being more structured on the page than the composer intended them to be. Messiaen's music, fortunately, has not fallen into this trap.

It is possible, however, that his greatest musical contributions may be heard in his compositions for organ, not a particularly surprising fact since it was Messiaen's primary instrument. Throughout his music for the organ, he employs modes of limited transposition, birdcalls, and driving rhythms. From the ethereal *Le Banquet celeste* of 1928, to the monumental *Livre du Saint Sacrement* of 1984, all of his music requires attention to detail and rewards careful study.

Orchestral
Turangalîla-symphonie for Piano, Ondes Martenot, and Orchestra
what to buy: [Yvonne Loriod, piano; Jeanne Loriod, ondes martenot; Myung-Whun Chung, cond.; Bastille Opera Orchestra] (Deutsche Grammophon 431781) ♪ ♪ ♪ ♪

This monumental symphony gives one an idea of the intricate nature of Messiaen's music. Who better to help interpret it than his wife, pianist Yvonne Loriod? The sonic depth of the strings, and the woodwind section's fiery sounds, are captured extremely well on this recording.

Oiseaux Exotiques for Piano and Orchestra
what to buy: [Yvonne Loriod, piano; Karl Anton Rickenbacher, cond.; Bavarian Radio Symphony Orchestra] (Koch Schwann 311232) ♪ ♪ ♪ ♪

With great whoops from the winds, tinkling percussion, and bird-like flourishes from the keyboard, Messiaen's work for piano and orchestra, heavily weighted toward percussion, reed, and brass sections (with only token output from the strings), gets under way. The instrumental colors of this piece are glorious but it may not be the

place for neophytes to start. Loriod is marvelous throughout this performance and Rickenbacher draws fine, taut playing from his orchestra. The rest of the program on this album features *Un Sourire, Un Vitrail et des Oiseaux, La Ville d'en-Haut,* and the half-hour-long *Et Exspecto Resurrectionem Mortuorum.*

what to buy next: [Peter Donohoe, piano; Reinbert de Leeuw, cond.; Netherlands Wind Ensemble, orch.] (Chandos 9301) ♪ ♪ ♪ ♪

Donohoe and de Leeuw have a firm, if somewhat speedy, grasp on this relatively short composition, taking it almost a minute faster than Loriod and Rickenbacher's 15:35. The sonics are a little less forgiving as well, but the set is still of value to Messiaen fans and neophytes. The balance of this two-disc, all-Messiaen program duplicates all of the Loriod disc (see above) except for *Un Sourire* (which is supplanted by *Sept Haïkai*) and *Couleurs de la Cité Céleste.*

Chamber
Quatuor pour la Fin du Temps (Quartet for the End of Time)
what to buy: [Claude Desurmont, clarinet; Luben Yordanoff, violin; Albert Tétard, cello; Daniel Barenboim, piano] (Deutsche Grammophon 423247) ♪ ♪ ♪ ♪

The vibrancy and intensity shown by the performers on this recording is astounding. Although released in 1979, this is still one of the finest performances available. The German import of this disc (Deutsche Grammophon 445128) can occasionally be found and, besides the quartet, includes a fine rendition of the composer's *Theme and Variations* for Violin and Piano with violinist Gidon Kremer and pianist Martha Argerich.

what to buy next: [Tashi, ensemble] (RCA Victor Gold Seal 7835) ♪ ♪ ♪ ♪

Much of the public's awareness of this piece came from this recording, with a young Richard Stoltzman playing the important clarinet part and Peter Serkin directing traffic from the piano bench. The album served as an easy introduction for "hip" record buyers seeking entrance to the world of classical music post-Schoenberg. Time has not dimmed its wonders perceptibly, and many people may actually prefer this recording to the one with Barenboim, et al.

[Paul Meyer, clarinet; Gil Shaham, violin; Jian

Wang, cello; Myung-Whun Chung, piano] (Deutsche Grammophon 469052) ♪♪♪₄

This ad hoc ensemble of talented musicians doesn't quite grasp the art of balancing their individual voices. As a result, the best performances are the intensely moving violin and piano duet in the closing movement (*Eulogy to the Immortality of Jesus*) and the solo sections for clarinet (*Abyss of the birds*) and cello (*Eulogy to the Eternity of Jesus*). When the quartet plays together, as in the brief *Intermède,* things get rather perfunctory.

Catalogue d'oiseaux for Piano
what to buy: [Håkan Austbø, piano] (Naxos 8.553532/34) ♪♪♪♪₄

Austbø is a Norwegian who has spent most of his life in France studying at the Paris Conservatoire and won first prize in the *Olivier Messiaen Competition for Contemporary Music*. This three-CD set also includes not only a totally idiomatic performance of the seven books that make up this cycle, but a fine rendition of 1985's *Petites esquisses d'oiseaux* for Piano.

various organ works
what to buy: [*Organ Works*; Olivier Messiaen, organ] (EMI Classics 67400) ♪♪♪♪♪

When looking into the world of a composer as deep as Messiaen, it's always wonderful hearing what the composer himself intended a work to sound like. This four-CD set preserving his own performances on CD allows one to do just that, and is well worth the relatively inexpensive price.

worth searching for: [*Messiaen: Complete Organ Music*; Gillian Weir, organ] (Collins Classics 7031) ♪♪♪♪♪

It may be blasphemous for some to suggest that a composer's works are often better played by a non-composing virtuoso musician than by the creator himself but, in all honesty, no one understands or plays this music better than this English virtuoso. Possessed of not only a great technique but a great musical understanding, Wier makes the music come through her joyful interpretations. Highly recommended if you want the entire enchilada, seven discs' worth in this case.

Messe de la Pentecôte
what to buy: [*Things Visible and Invisible*; Catherine

Crozier, organ] (Delos 3147) ♪ ♪ ♪ ♪ ♪

Crozier and her late husband Harold Gleason defined the contemporary approach to organ-playing in their landmark textbook, now in its eighth edition. More than just a pedagogue, Crozier plays (on the new Manuel Rosales organ in Portland, Oregon's Trinity Episcopal Church) one movement from this suite—*Things Visible and Invisible*—and matches it with the *Trois Danses* by Jehan Alain and Jean Langlais's *Trois Paraphrases*.

influences: Claude Debussy, Igor Stravinsky, Pierre Boulez, Pierre Henry

Craig Scott Symons and Dave Wagner

Giacomo Meyerbeer

Born Jakob Liebmann Meyer Beer, September 5, 1791, in Vogelsdorf, Germany. Died May 2, 1864, in Paris, France.

period: Romantic

Taking his cue from prevailing ideas about romantic realism and historical dramas, Giacomo Meyerbeer tended to see opera as a whole work, not just musical flesh hung on a skeletal libretto. *Robert le diable, Les Hugenots,* and *Le Prophète* (along with its ballet music, *Les Patineurs*) were his biggest hits, and the orchestral effects he created for these works, seeking to draw his audiences into a vast, scenic concept, may have influenced some of Richard Wagner's earlier operas.

In 1810 Meyerbeer went to Darmstadt where he became a student of Abbé Georg Joseph Vogler, a marvelous organist and the premier music theorist in Germany. Two years later, Meyerbeer left Darmstadt with the intention of making his mark as a concert pianist and composer, traveling to Munich, Vienna, Paris, and London in his quest. He went to Italy in 1816, hoping to hone his writing for the human voice; he found such a hospitable reception for his operatic efforts that he ended up staying there for nine years and writing six operas. While Meyerbeer had developed quite an audience in Rome, Venice, and Milan, his efforts to have those same works mounted in Germany were rebuffed. Despite the rejection his Italian operas received in his homeland, the success (in 1824) of his heroic melodrama *Il crociato in Egitto* emboldened the young composer to seek his fortune in Paris.

It was there that Meyerbeer made the acquaintance of Eugène Scribe, a dramatist who had already cobbled together librettos for Gioachino Rossini (*Le comte Ory*) and Daniel Auber (*La muette de Portici*) and was interested in creating historical settings for characters that would embrace both visual spectacle and emotional situations. Together the pair would go on to help lay the foundation for what would become known as grand opera. Their first collaboration, *Robert le diable,* started out as an *opéra comique* but by the time of its public unveiling had evolved into a full-fledged, prototypical grand opera. Over the course of five acts, Meyerbeer lessened the importance of solo arias from the main characters, in favor of a unified approach that developed the orchestral portions of the score into equality with the vocal sections, advancing the dramatic elements of the opera in a way that broke ground for the later achievements of Richard Wagner. It was an unprecedented success at its premiere in 1831, generating all sorts of positive responses from critics of the day and bringing Meyerbeer a series of honors that ranged from his being made a Chevalier of the Légion d'honneur in 1832 to his appointment in 1834 as a member of the French Institute.

Les Huguenots, the next project for Meyerbeer and Scribe, featured a plot set around the St. Bartholomew's Day Massacre of 1572, in which French Protestants were slaughtered by the Catholic nobility. The French government got wind of the storyline and censors demanded a series of restrictions, including the excision of the character known as Cathérine di Medici and the scene where the daggers are blessed. Despite governmental meddling and the aggravation it caused for the author and composer, the opening night's performance (February 29, 1836) was yet another success. Hector Berlioz was so enamored of *Les Huguenots* that he declared the work to be packed with "enough musical riches for twenty successful operas." It is still considered by many to be the definitive example of French grand opera for its blend of historical and romantic subject matter, dramatic orchestration, and (of course) broad spectacle.

The thirteen years that lay between the opening of *Les Huguenots* and Meyerbeer's next opera, *Le Prophète,* were filled with delays—often due to the challenge his compositions placed upon their singers. For instance, work on *L'Africaine* was begun in 1837 and interrupted the following year when Meyerbeer's choice for the lead role lost her voice and a suitable replacement could not be found. The composer was also forced to rewrite the tenor part of *Le Prophète* almost ten years after its completion when no singer capable of properly handling the role could be found. *Le Prophète* was finally produced in 1849 and enjoyed the same accolades that *Robert* and *Les Huguenots* received. The critics who had been skewering Meyerbeer over this lengthy delay between works now sang his praises, taking particular note of the ballet scene where dancers used roller skates to mimic the act of ice skating. Much of the music from that tableau, along with melodies taken from his opéra comique, *L'Etoile du Nord,* were crafted into a suite (*Les Patineurs*) by Constant Lambert in 1937. *Le Prophète* also featured the *Krönungsmarsch (Coronation March),* music illustrating the point in that opera at which the title character has led a revolt by the Annabaptists and had himself crowned as their divine prophet. Aside from the passage's significance as a turning point within the opera (it is all down hill from here for the "prophet"), the well-crafted tunes have proven resistant to the disappearing act most of Meyerbeer's music has suffered during the twentieth century, turning up as a frequently programmed orchestral bonbon in much the same way that the *Grand March* from Giuseppe Verdi's *Aida* or Georges Bizet's *March of the Toreadors* do.

During the final years of his life, Meyerbeer attempted to finish work on *L'Africaine* but always seemed to be sidetracked. In this case his work on a pair of well-received comic operas, incidental music to various plays, and various choral works occupied much of his time. The debut of *L'Africaine* was further delayed when Scribe died on February 20, 1861. Still, Meyerbeer completed the basic framework for the opera by November 1863. After he died a few months later, the raw elements of *L'Africaine* were then edited by François-Joseph Fétis, a Belgian musicologist, and prepared for the work's posthumous premiere on April 28, 1865.

Orchestral
Krönungsmarsch (Coronation March) from *Le Prophète*
what to buy: [*Music For Festive Occasions*; Michail Jurowski, cond.; Hanover Radio Philharmonic Orchestra] (CPO 999168) ♪♪♪♪

Where Jurowski's well-played version of this gem differs from that heard on other recordings is in its setting amidst other celebratory works by the composer, including the *Fest-Overture* he wrote for the London World Exhibition in 1862, the *Festmarsch* for the centenary of

Schiller's birth, and four dances created for Prussian royal weddings.

[*Bernstein Century: Great Marches*; Leonard Bernstein, cond.; New York Philharmonic Orchestra] (Sony 63154) ♪♪♪♪

Bernstein's energy level never really seemed to dip, ranging from the flamboyant to the intensely probing. No matter what else you may have thought of his style, there is relatively little doubt that he invested much of his emotions into his conducting. Such is the case here in this cleverly selected batch of orchestral marches that includes an exciting rendition of Meyerbeer's hit in addition to works by John Philip Sousa (*Stars and Stripes Forever!*), the first of Edward Elgar's *Pomp and Circumstance* marches, and a rousing version of *Le Marseillaise.*

what to buy next: [*Marches and Overtures à la Française*; Paul Paray, cond.; Detroit Symphony Orchestra] (Mercury 434332) ♪♪♪♪

Paray was a great conductor in his day and these recordings showcase his splendid command of the Detroiters. The well-recorded program dates from 1959 and is a pretty straightforward recitation of short, punchy works by Jacques Offenbach, Camille Saint-Säens, Charles Gounod, and others that is almost guaranteed to perk up the average listener's ears.

Les Patineurs
what to buy: [Michail Jurowski, cond.; Hanover Radio Philharmonic Orchestra] (CPO 999336) ♪♪♪♪

Jurowski and his German orchestra give a solid (not stolid) rendition of these graceful melodies, and package them alongside a skillful interpretation of the prelude to *L'Africaine* and incidental music that Meyerbeer wrote for his youngest brother's play *Struensee.*

Vocal
Le Prophète
what to buy: [Renata Scotto, soprano; Marilyn Horne, mezzo-soprano; James McCracken, tenor; Jerome Hines, baritone; Henry Lewis, cond.; Royal Philharmonic Orchestra; Ambrosian Opera Chorus] (Sony Classics 34340) ♪♪♪♪

This is probably the most complete version of this work that you can buy through regular commercial outlets. In this 1977 production Scotto is a fair-to-middling Berthe but Horne produces a benchmark performance of Fidés against which (despite the singing not being in peak form) other versions must be judged.

Les Huguenots

what to buy: [Joan Sutherland, soprano; Giulietta Simionato, mezzo-soprano; Fiorenza Cossotto, mezzo-soprano; Franco Corelli, tenor; Nicolai Ghiaurov, bass-baritone; Giorgio Tozzi, bass-baritone; Vladimiro Ganzarolli, bass-baritone; Gianandrea Gavazzeni, cond.; L'Orchestre del Teatro alla Scala; Coro del Teatro alla Scala, chorus] (Gala 100.604) ♪ ♪ ♪

This may be the best version of *Les Huguenots* to get, but the buyer should be aware that there were some major adjustments made in Act II (when the duet between Margarite and Raoul was changed to a solo for Sutherland), and cuts inflicted on Act V (where Raoul's aria, a potential showpiece for Corelli, was eliminated).

influences: Louis Spohr, Christoph Willibald Gluck, Hector Berlioz, Richard Wagner

Sharon L. Hoyer and Louise Cohen

Darius Milhaud

Born September 4, 1892, in Aix-en-Provence, France. Died June 22, 1974, in Geneva, Switzerland.

period: Twentieth century

Milhaud was one of the most prolific composers of the twentieth century. Known for his frequent use of polytonality, he composed music characterized by melodic straightforwardness, folk-like simplicity and rhythmic playfulness, tinged with Latin American colors and illuminated by the Mediterranean sun of his beloved Provence. During the 1920s he was a member of the Paris-based group of young composers known as *Les Six.*

Darius Milhaud was a simple man with an insatiable passion for writing music. Moving to Paris from France's colorful south, Milhaud entered the Paris Conservatory in 1909, where he studied composition with Vincent d'Indy and orchestration with Paul Dukas. His early works showed great signs of originality, but it wasn't until 1917, when he became secretary and cultural attaché to the poet Paul Claudel at the French legation

in Rio de Janeiro, Brazil, that his fervent imagination was let loose. Milhaud quickly absorbed several Latin American idioms, particularly the samba and other dance rhythms of the tropics, as well as the region's varied folk elements. The most successful piece he wrote in Brazil, the ballet *L'homme et son désir,* is a nocturnal evocation of the tropical forest, scored for a percussion-heavy chamber ensemble and vocalists. The popular *Saudades do Brasil,* composed after his return to France in 1918, is the composer's fond remembrance of his time in South America. It is also one of the most successful of his experiments in bitonality, which he had used in the earlier *Protée* and *Les choëphores.*

Milhaud began exploring the superimposition of chord upon chord, saying that "they began to satisfy my ear more than the normal ones, for a polytonal chord is more subtly sweet and violently potent." The rambunctious ballet *Le boeuf sur le toit,* a series of stylized Latin American dances linked by a snappy rondo, was composed upon Milhaud's return to Paris. It became a huge success, due partly to the ceaseless promotion efforts of the dynamic Jean Cocteau. In addition to being one of Milhaud's major collaborators over the years, Cocteau possessed a keen ear for originality and turned everything he became involved with into a spectacle.

A Paris newspaper article at this time linked Milhaud's name with those of several other young French-based composers—Francis Poulenc, Arthur Honegger, Louis Durey, Georges Auric, and Germaine Tailleferre—and christened the group "Les Six." At first, although each composer's style was quite distinct from the others, the group benefited from the label applied by the press. They began organizing group concerts before growing tired of the implied association and going their separate ways. But this was Paris in the 1920s, a time of ebullience and artistic fruitfulness; the witty, spirited music of this period, as well as the wonderful collaborations across disciplines, echoed these qualities. Milhaud fraternized and worked closely with many of the great painters, sculptors, poets, playwrights, and choreographers of the day, all the while penning modernist miracles and carefree trifles.

A trip to New York in 1922, where the composer experienced jazz in Harlem nightclubs, resulted in the piece on which Milhaud's fame largely rests, the ballet *Le créa-*

Darius Milhaud

tion du monde. Written before George Gershwin's *Rhapsody in Blue,* this work is widely regarded as the first concert or stage piece to incorporate the lively syncopations and improvisatory freedom of American jazz.

He continued churning out a formidable body of work, though by the time he settled in America during World War II, much of his youthful vigor had left him. Still, the composer found a new home for his talents as a widely respected teacher at Mills College in Oakland, California, where Steve Reich, William Bolcom, and Dave Brubeck were among his students.

Milhaud composed in all genres, turning out symphonies, operas, songs, choral music, several concertos, a monstrous volume of works for solo piano, and copious amounts of chamber music (including his fourteenth and fifteenth string quartets, which can be played together as a contrapuntal octet). Even if all Milhaud's scores are marked by a pronounced tunefulness, some, particularly the symphonies, seem to be mere note spinning. His more notable works include the popular *Scaramouche* for two pianos, the orchestral *Suite provençale,* the *Suite française* for wind band, the operas (*Maximilien, Christophe Colomb,* and *Bolivar*—each on a historic figure), the delightful wind quintet *La cheminée du roi René,* several sacred works on Jewish subjects, *La muse menagère* for piano and narrator, and the joyous *Le carnaval d'Aix* for piano and orchestra. Though his output was uneven, the best of Milhaud's music possesses a classical simplicity and clarity as well as a baroque sense of motion and a refreshing lack of pretentiousness. But despite his various experiments and the scandalousness of his music from the 1920s, melody continued to be the core of his work throughout his long career. Milhaud's wit, charm, and melodic ease shine though his vast catalogue.

Orchestral
Le création du monde for Orchestra, op. 81
what to buy: [Leonard Bernstein, cond; Orchestre National de France] (EMI Classics 47845) ♪ ♪ ♪♪

Bernstein seems to really swing this ballet, which remains Milhaud's biggest success. The album also includes the orchestral version of the *Saudades do Brasil*—a good example of the potency of bitonality—and *La boeuf sur le toit* for Orchestra, op. 58

what to buy next: [Kent Nagano, cond; Lyon Opera

Orchestra] (Erato 45820) ♪ ♪ ♪

Nagano delivers a decidedly jazzy reading of *La création du Monde,* coupled with a fun take on the frivolous *Le boeuf sure le toit* and Milhaud's Concerto for Harp and Orchestra.

Chamber
La cheminée du roi René for Wind Quintet, op. 205
what to buy: [*Milhaud: Music for Wind Instruments*; Athena Ensemble] (Chandos 6536) ♪ ♪ ♪♪

An infectiously tuneful piece with sprightly rhythms, this charming work is accompanied by the composer's other forays into the wind quintet format.

Vocal
Les choëphores for Narrator, Solo Voices, Orchestra, and Chorus, op. 24
what to buy: [Vera Zorina, narrator; Virginia Babikian, Irene Jordan, sopranos; McHenry Boatwright, baritone; Leonard Bernstein, cond; New York Philharmonic Orchestra; Schola Cantorum New York, choir] (Sony Classical 62352) ♪ ♪ ♪♪

Based on the second play in Aeschylus's *Oresteia* trilogy, this curious work is beautifully served by Bernstein, who held it in the highest regard. The 1961 performance is marvelously captured, with great singing by each soloist. Two short pieces by Arthur Honegger (*Pacific 231* and *Rugby*) and Albert Roussel's Symphony no. 3 complete the program.

influences: Erik Satie, Francis Poulenc, Arthur Honegger

Sean Hickey

E.J. Moeran
Born Ernest John Moeran, December 31, 1894, in Heston, Middlesex, England. Died December 1, 1950, in Kenmare, County Kerry, Ireland.

period: Twentieth century

E. J. Moeran is considered a minor British composer but a fine craftsman whose refined technique was equaled by few of his contemporaries. His best known work is the Symphony in G Minor, which he wrote between 1934 and 1937.

His father was a clergyman, and Moeran's first connection with music came through the hymnals his father's congregation used. He learned to play the violin while attending secondary school and made some early attempts at composition. By this time Moeran had started collecting and arranging folk songs, whose melodies were to prove a strong influence throughout his life.

He enrolled in the Royal College of Music in London in 1913 but enlisted in the army upon the outbreak of World War I. He was seriously wounded in action, and when he was released from service in 1919 he returned to his old secondary school as Master of Music. In the early 1920s his music was beginning to be heard at public concerts, and his name began to be better known. His musical style and propensities seemed best suited to smaller pieces, and throughout the 1920s and early 1930s these are essentially all he wrote. In 1926, Moeran turned down a commission to write a symphony because he did not feel ready to deal with that kind of larger form. At the time he was influenced by Frederick Delius and John Ireland, with whom he had studied after returning from the army, as well as by his contemporaries. As he matured however, these influences became subservient to his own individual idiom.

In 1933, Moeran moved to the countryside, mainly to reassess his musical style and to expand his abilities in technique and form. Although his musical language did not change much, he now found himself able to work in larger forms and finally produced a symphony—his only one—in 1937. This is a fine work and a considerable achievement for a man who until then was essentially a writer of shorter pieces. It took him three years to complete the symphony, the time involved perhaps indicative of just how much effort it took to change his basic compositional nature. From then to the end of his life he wrote mainly in larger forms and produced only a few of the smaller pieces that used to dominate his oeuvre. He was fishing in a stream in Ireland in late 1950 when he suffered a heart attack, fell in the water, and drowned.

Moeran's best music is down-to-earth, honest, and direct, and the strong folk influence makes it very appealing. Most authorities agree that the best of his output is in his vocal writing, but precious little of it has been recorded—a bewildering and inexplicable gap in the documentation of British music from the first half of the twentieth century.

Orchestral
Symphony in G Minor
what to buy: [Vernon Handley, cond.; Ulster Orchestra] (Chandos Enchant 7106) ♪ ♪ ♪⅛

Surely Moeran's finest work, this can stand alongside the best British symphonies of the twentieth century. Handley's performance could hardly be bettered, and the recorded sound is absolutely superb. Also included on this disc is the Rhapsody for Piano and Orchestra in F-sharp Minor, with Margaret Fingerhut as the soloist.

Concerto for Violin and Orchestra
what to buy: [Lydia Mordkovich, violin; Vernon Handley, cond.; Ulster Orchestra] (Chandos 8807) ♪ ♪ ♪⅛

Strongly influenced by folk song and the composer's love of Ireland, this is a beautiful and haunting work that, although it is in the usual three movements, is constructed in a highly unusual and individual fashion. The performance leaves little to be desired, and the sound quality is outstanding. Included on this disc are two short tone poems, "Lonely Waters" and "Whythorne's Shadow."

influences: Gerald Finzi, Peter Warlock, Frederick Delius, John Ireland

Charles Greenwell

Federico Mompou
Born April 16, 1893, in Barcelona, Spain. Died June 30, 1987 in Barcelona, Spain.

period: Twentieth century

It is for his singularly reflective piano music that Mompou is most remembered outside his native country. He dedicated himself to subtle explorations of piano timbre and excelled as a miniaturist. His pieces sometimes lack meters or even barlines, and virtuosity is shunned in favor of finding profundity in simplicity. Mompou also wrote a number of songs for solo vocalist and piano, several of which have been orchestrated by himself or others, and a few lengthier works.

Mompou was born to a Catalan father and a French mother; in life and music he moved between Paris and Barcelona. His grandfather had a bell foundry, and the composer-to-be acquired a love for bells that could be said to later mark his conception of the piano. First musically educated at the conservatory attached to the Barcelona opera house, Mompou made his piano debut in 1908. But hearing Fauré playing his own music in 1909 inspired Mompou to pursue composition. In 1911 he moved to Paris and studied at the Conservatoire (piano with Isidor Philipp; composition with Samuel Rousseau) in a period when there was quite a creative ferment in that city. After two years Mompou returned to Barcelona; in 1921 he moved back to Paris and became a small but significant part of the city's musical life, friendly with most of the major French composers and achieving praise for his own distinctive works. Mompou continued to live in Paris until the Nazi occupation in 1941, when he returned to Barcelona permanently.

He had a period of creative drought in the 1930s; he composed only eighteen minutes of music (the *Variations sobre un tema de Chopin*) during the whole decade. He snapped out of it after returning to Barcelona, where he met his wife-to-be while judging a piano competition she had entered. Mompou was appointed to the Real Academia de Bellas Artes de San Jordi in 1952, the same year he wrote the first book of piano pieces entitled *Música Callada*. At that time he described his music as having "neither air nor light," saying "it doesn't ask to reach more than a few millimeters into space, but rather penetrate the great profundities of our soul and the most secret regions of our spirit." Mompou had a distinguished career until a cerebral hemorrhage in 1978 confined him to a wheelchair and prevented him from playing piano. Fortunately, in 1974 he made a series of recordings of his piano music for the Spanish label Ensayo. They have flitted in and out of print but have reappeared recently, offering priceless insight into his style and frequently supplying definitive renditions.

Chamber
Música Callada
what to buy: [*Mompou Plays Mompou, vol. 1*; Federico Mompou, piano] (Ensayo 9716) ♪ ♪ ♪ ♪ ♪

It's surprising that this set of twenty-eight short solo piano pieces, Mompou's most typical yet distinctive statement, is not more frequently recorded. In them, time seems suspended, and the sounds hang weightlessly in the air, shimmering mysteriously, as appropriate for "music of silence." Nobody has yet surpassed the composer in providing exactly the right touch and mood:

slightly dry, carefully nuanced in timbre, and never pushy.

what to buy next: [Herbert Henck, piano] (ECM 1523) ♪ ♪ ♪ ♪

Henck plays these pieces faultlessly from a technical point of view, but without quite the same hushed fervor as the composer himself. The biggest problem is not Henck's fault: the recorded sound is more unrealistically "wet" than piano purists will prefer, by a wide margin. However, collectors having difficulty locating Mompou's version will find the music speaks in this version more appealingly than in the other alternatives.

Cançons i danses nos. 1–12, 14
what to buy: [*Mompou Plays Mompou, vol. 2*; Federico Mompou, piano] (Ensayo 9725) ♪ ♪ ♪ ♪ ♪₄

Mompou's longer solo piano cycles tended to accrue gradually over the course of many years rather than being conceived as integral sets—the fourteen *Cançons i danses*, his best-known works (ideal encores, some have shown up in the repertoires of Artur Rubinstein and Arturo Benedetti Michelangeli), were composed from 1921 to 1963. These works are meant to be paired (no. 13 is omitted in this recording as it is for guitar rather than piano), and are Mompou's most popular pieces, yet his most atypical. Mostly based on Catalan themes, they have a gentle yet undeniable rhythmic liveliness to them. While de Larrocha (see below) is a notch above the composer as a pure pianist, Mompou's own take on this cycle is also quite noteworthy. This disc also includes his invaluable readings of *Canción de cuna*, *Cants màgics*, and *Paisajes*.

worth searching for: [*Spanish Songs and Dances*; Alícia de Larrocha, piano] (RCA Victor 62554) ♪ ♪ ♪ ♪ ♪

Alícia de Larrocha has long been an advocate of the music of her compatriot—one of Mompou's preludes is dedicated to her—and this is a most flavorful program that also includes persuasive readings of *Preludes* nos. 5–7 and 11. Her authority in the rhythmic snap of the *Cançons i danses* is unsurpassed.

various works for piano
what to buy: [*Mompou Plays Mompou, vol. 3*; Federico Mompou, piano] (Ensayo 9726) ♪ ♪ ♪ ♪ ♪

The most compelling set of *Préludes* since Debussy's is best played by the composer (the top-line pianists who have taken an interest in Mompou's music having only chosen to play selections). His exquisitely modulated touch and subtle variations of timbre make each of his eleven *Préludes* a world unto itself. His *Variations sobre un tema de Chopin* is also an important work in his oeuvre, the twelve developments of the theme (from Chopin's Prélude no. 7 in A Major) being quite imaginative. Also included on this disc are his *Trois variations, Dialogues,* and *Souvenirs de l'Exposition.*

what to buy next: [Stephen Hough, piano] (Hyperion 66963) ♪ ♪ ♪ ♪ᵢ

This talented young British pianist alternates six of the *Songs and Dances* (nos. 1, 3, 5, 7–9) and six of the *Préludes* (nos. 1, 5–7, 9–10) with five distinct and complete sets of other miniatures: *Cants Mágics, Charmes, Trois Variations, Dialogues I and II,* and *Paisajes.* Hough's pellucid tone and thoughtful manner are well-suited to this music, and he never lets his outstanding technique overwhelm or distort the music. The resulting graceful ease allows these works their proper weightlessness.

[*Mompou Plays Mompou, vol. 4*; Federico Mompou, piano] (Ensayo 9727) ♪ ♪ ♪ ♪ᵢ

Impresiones Íntimas was Mompou's first set of piano pieces, produced during his first period in Paris and strongly related to French examples. The suite *Suburbis (Suburbs),* by contrast, is redolent of everyday observations of life on the outskirts of Barcelona, though still rife with Impressionist influence. *Fêtes lointaines (Distant Festivities)* from 1920 initiates Mompou's fascination with things faintly heard and remembered, setting the stage for his highly atmospheric and evocative mature style. Also included here are *Scènes d'enfants, Pessebres (Nativity Scenes),* and *Charmes.*

Vocal
Los Improperios **for Soprano, Baritone, Orchestra, and Chorus**
worth searching for: [Virgínia Parramon, soprano; Jerzy Artysz, baritone; Josep Pons, cond.; Orquestra de Cambra Teatre Lliure; Cor de Valencia, choir] (Harmonia Mundi 901482) ♪ ♪ ♪ ♪

The most significant work on this out-of-print collection, valuable for shedding light on areas beyond Mompou's

solo piano pieces, is the twenty-five-minute *Los improperios.* Part of the Good Friday liturgy, it sets the words of Jesus on the cross. This 1963 composition was one of the few commissions Mompou accepted, and his harmonies prove just as gorgeous for choir as for piano. The other three works on this set are orchestrations (by Manuel Rosenthal, Alexandre Tansman, and Mompou himself) of the song cycle *Combat del somni* (originally for soprano and piano) and of two piano cycles: *Suburbis* and *Scènes d'enfants.*

influences: Erik Satie, Claude Debussy, Maurice Ravel, Francis Poulenc, Alexander Scriabin

Steve Holtje

Meredith Monk
Born Meredith Jane Monk November 20, 1942, in Lima, Peru.

period: Twentieth century

A respected figure in the world of performance art, Meredith Monk successfully combines elements of dance, music, and innovative vocal techniques into impressive theatrical experiences. Her opera, *Atlas,* was commissioned and performed by the Houston Grand Opera in 1991.

Born into a musical family and raised in Queens, New York and Connecticut, Monk's childhood included lessons in piano, voice, and eurythmics—the study of music and movement. Upon graduation from high school (in Bucks County, Pennsylvania) she enrolled at Sarah Lawrence College where, besides studying the Merce Cunningham dance technique, she took courses in composition, chamber music, and opera. After graduating in 1964, Monk took up with the Judson Dance Theater, a New York-based experimental theater group. In 1968, Monk founded *The House,* a company committed to multimedia performance, making her one of the most prominent forces in New York's downtown avant-garde scene. Monk's first "theater cantata," *Juice* (a work for two violins and eighty-five performers who sang and played jew's-harps), was performed at the Guggenheim Museum in 1969. She has received the prestigious Obie Award for both *Vessel: An Opera Epic,* in 1972, and *Quarry: An Opera,* in 1976, evidence of her steadily growing reputation in the theater community. Having been previously occupied with the solo voice, she formed the Meredith Monk Vocal Ensemble in 1978. The works that followed the creation of her new group were

Dolmen Music in 1979, *The Games* in 1983, and the film *Book of Days* in 1988.

While she has been compared to Steve Reich stylistically, Monk's music is difficult to categorize. Influenced by minimalism, she uses fragmentation and repetition to dramatic effect and often there is an ostinato or sustained pedal point underneath an unfettered, uninhibited vocal line. There is a sense of total emotional exposure in the voice, and this unique use of the voice is referred to as "extended vocal technique." Monk's choice of instruments ranges from the conventional to shawms, bagpipes, and dulcimers. Elements of jazz and pop music can be heard, with a striking affinity for music of other cultures. Hers is an art form that has crossed many of the tried and true barriers between genres, with enthusiastic followers among devotees of classical music, new age, jazz, world, and alternative musics. Monk's hallmark has been to challenge the traditionally held view of theater every step of the way. She has staged works in unconventional venues and placed audiences at unique vantage points. Time, space, movement, and sound take on new meanings, while the human voice explores uncharted territory. With several recordings, commissions, grants, and awards, Monk is one of the most honored and popular performance artists living today.

Among the numerous awards Monk has garnered are a MacArthur Foundation fellowship in 1995, two Guggenheim Fellowships, the 1986 National Music Theatre Award, sixteen ASCAP Awards for Musical Composition, and the 1992 *Dance* Magazine Award. She also received the German Critics Prize for Best Records of 1981 and 1986 for *Dolmen Music* and *Our Lady of Late: The Vanguard Tapes.*

Vocal
Dolmen Music
what to buy: [Meredith Monk and Vocal Ensemble] (ECM New Series 825459) ♪ ♪ ♪♪

Ever wonder what you would get if you put Joni Mitchell, the Bulgarian Women's Chorus, Tibetan Monks, Philip Glass, and Yma Sumac in a room together? Listen to this recording and stop wondering. There is a little bit of pop, world music, art song, and hardcore minimalism. Written in 1981, *Dolmen Music* is an excellent introduction to Monk's work.

Atlas: An Opera in Three Parts

what to buy: [Shi-zheng, soprano; Dana Hanchard, soprano; Robert Een, vocalist; Stephen Kalm, baritone; soloists; Meredith Monk, vocalist; Wayne Hankin, cond.; various soloists] (ECM New Series 437773) ♪ ♪ ♪ ♪

Atlas was commissioned by the Houston Grand Opera in 1991. This recording was made one year later and requires twenty-nine performers. The consistent technique found here, as in many of Monk's pieces, is the use of repetitive vocal sounds on one pitch alternating with very lyrical melodic lines. This is usually juxtaposed over a repeated ostinato fragment in the instrumental accompaniment. The text becomes subservient to the creation of pure sound, as feeling and sensation take precedence over meaning.

influences: Philip Glass, Steve Reich, Laurie Anderson

Christine L. Cody and Mona C. DeQuis

Claudio Monteverdi
Born c. May 15, 1567, in Cremona, Italy. Died November 29, 1643, in Venice, Italy.

period: Renaissance

Claudio Monteverdi and his music form a pivotal turning point in vocal composition between the classical ideals of the Italian High Renaissance and the passion and expressiveness of the early Baroque. Armed with unique new devices of vocal performance and practice and guided by the period's emerging attention to the concept of human *affections,* Monteverdi transformed late sixteenth century monody and polyphony into true music drama, fusing evocative texts with a melodic style that penetrated each word's core of emotion. The evolution of the solo song under Monteverdi eventually led to the birth of opera, and reaffirmed the role of vocal music as humanity's most potent and immediate means of artistic expression.

Known for centuries as one of Italy's centers for music and the manufacture of stringed instruments, Cremona provided Monteverdi with fertile ground in which to cultivate his early education in the arts. His earliest music studies were under the renowned Marc Antonio Ingegneri, who served the cathedral of Cremona as organist and choirmaster. Monteverdi studied counterpoint and more than likely began to play both viol and organ under the master. This is evidenced by a journey to Milan in 1589, during which he gained employment as a musician.

Monteverdi's coming of age, however, must be assigned to his arrival in Mantua in 1590, where he entered into the service of the Gonzaga family, principally Vincenzo I, Duke of Mantua. By 1594 Monteverdi had produced his third book of madrigals, a collection that most scholars agree firmly established the composer's name and popularity throughout northern Italy. In 1601 he accepted appointment as maestro di cappella at Mantua, following in the line of his second great mentor, Giaches de Wert, and Benedetto Pallavicino. By this time Monteverdi's madrigal output had established him as Italy's leading proponent of dramatic expression in text, a practice largely fueled by the Camerata, a collection of artists and intellectuals who met in irregular session at the Bardi palace in Florence to discuss and articulate the movement toward greater expression and lyricism in music. Musical luminaries such as Vincenzo Galilei, Peri, and Caccini joined the period's great poets, among them Tasso and Rinuccini, to develop and refine new expressive musical devices. In the forefront of these stood the *accompanied recitative*, in which words would be sung in the same declamatory style as dramatic speech.

Monteverdi's residence at Mantua remained productive for the next seven years, during which he published his fourth and fifth books of madrigals as well as his first opera, *L'Orfeo* (1607). The illness of his wife, however, required his return to Cremona, and her death in 1607 slowed the composer's output and delayed his return to the court at Mantua due to grief and depression. His ultimate return to court marked the beginning of a reversal of fortune and, due to an erosion in relations with the court, the composer began to seek another post. The subsequent death of Vincenzo I, followed by the composer's summary dismissal by Duke Francesco, hastened Monteverdi's job search. It ended in 1613 with his appointment at St. Mark's in Venice. The arrangement pleased him greatly, as he had been welcomed earlier in Venice on the occasion of performances of his music. More importantly, Venice by this time held a virtual monopoly on music printing, beginning earlier with Petrucci's press, and Monteverdi now was in possession of another yet-unpublished book of madrigals as well as numerous miscellaneous works.

Monteverdi's first task at St. Mark's was to rebuild the flagging choir and music program. Here his considerable

organizational skills enabled him to recruit new and capable members as well as secure full-time residency for a collection of instrumental players. Thus St. Mark's began to enjoy a reinstitution of its earlier music traditions, including sung masses and elements of the Divine Office and concerts outside of the liturgy. Listeners were treated to a judicious blend of the older masters such as Palestrina and Lassus and the newest sacred offerings of the maestro di cappella. Monteverdi remained at Venice until his death in 1643, completing an opus as varied and sizable as it was unique in style.

Above all, Monteverdi remains the master of early opera and monodic song of this period. He built upon the earlier innovations of Peri and Caccini to refine a solo song style known for its deep emotional expressiveness. Among the finest from this genre are his 1608 *Lament d'Arianna* (the sole remnant of the opera *Arianna*), *Se i languidi* (1619), *Tempo la cetra* (1619), and *Ohime ch'io cado* (1624). All follow the principle of *affections,* in which the expressive nature of both text and music must be equal in intensity. Examples of free rhythms, concertato style, and remnants of earlier *gorgia* practice are found throughout. In addition, his seven books of madrigals (containing many monodic songs as well) trace a maturing style that begins in a rather formulaic manner and ends with highly expressive lines in all voices with rhythm and interval motifs that magnify texts based on unrequited love, death, and revenge.

Monteverdi's operas represent the full flowering of that idiom's first stage of development. In *L'Orfeo* (1607), his first major dramatic work, the composer reveals the dramatic intensity of Striggio's poem. Set in five acts, the opera employs vocal forms such as strophic song, duet, choral madrigal, variation, and accompanied recitative. Numerous instrumental interludes, or sinfonias, divide and define dramatic episodes of the story, and the opera's grand overture achieves new heights in orchestral coloring. Other operas of note include *Il Ritorno d'Ulisse in patria* (1641) and *L'incoronazione di Poppea* (1642). The latter, Monteverdi's last opera, was composed at age seventy-four and remains one of the great masterpieces of operatic literature.

Vocal
L'incoronazione di Poppea
what to buy: [Danielle Borst, soprano; Lena Lootens, soprano; Guillemette Laurens, mezzo-soprano; Jennifer Larmore, mezzo-soprano; Axel Kohler, countertenor;

Michael Schopper, bass; René Jacobs, cond.; Concerto Vocale, ensemble] (Harmonia Mundi 901330/32) ♪ ♪ ♪ ♪

The initial swell of the consort, complete with lightning-like solo viol interpolations, convinces the listener early on that Monteverdi's "other" opera may very well be in the hands of the muses themselves. Jacobs drives this reading forward with measured intensity and superior attention to balance, line, and rhythmic integrity. The result is a most credible and touching narration of Poppea's tale. Both instruments and singers display remarkable command of Baroque performance practice and style. They sound genuinely excited to be performing this confection of 1642. Each miniature section moves with seamless grace and energy from recitative to aria to duet and beyond, creating a sense of expectation often lacking in lesser renderings of this wondrous music drama.

Vespro della Beata Virgine for Six Voices and Six Instruments (1610)

what to buy: [Jill Gomez, soprano; Felicity Palmer, soprano; James Bowman, countertenor; Robert Tear, tenor; Philip Langridge, tenor; John Shirley-Quirk, baritone; Michael Rippon, bass; Nicholas Kraemer, harpsichord; Malcolm Hicks, organ; Alastair Ross, organ; Robert Spencer, lute; Jennifer Ward Clarke, cello; John Eliot Gardiner, cond.; Philip Jones Brass Ensemble; David Munrow Recorder Ensemble; Monteverdi Orchestra; Monteverdi Choir; Salisbury Cathedral Boys Choir] (London 443482) ♪ ♪ ♪ ♪

Monteverdi's great *Vespers* are in very good hands in this expertly engineered recording. The performance gives us bright sonorities, energetic tempi, orchestral sounds attuned to Mahler as much as Monteverdi, and a choral sound and blend that, although top-drawer, seems more conducive to music of the nineteenth century masters than it does to the Italian Baroque. Nevertheless, Gardiner bravely pursues and captures the contrapuntal and motivic drive of the work from the very opening tenor proclamation of the *Deus in Adjutorium meum intende*. The instrumental *intrada* that follows along with the chorus sets the dynamic and rhythmic pace for the rest of the work, with punctuated instrumental and choral entrances, driving ensembles (e.g., *Laetatus sum*), and duet passages that demonstrate remarkable technique and vocal pliancy (sopranos Gomez and Palmer sing as virtually one voice).

influences: Heinrich Schütz

Frank Scinta

Leopold Mozart

Born Johann Georg Leopold Mozart, November 14, 1719, in Augsburg, Germany. Died May 28, 1787, in Salzburg, Austria.

period: Classical

Chiefly remembered today as the sometimes shameless promoter of his child prodigy son, Wolfgang Amadeus, the elder Mozart was a fine composer in his own right and left many well-crafted compositions. Most popular today are his Trumpet Concerto in D Major, the *Musical Ride,* and the *Toy Symphony.*

The son of a bookbinder in the city of Augsburg, Leopold Mozart was first introduced to music as a choirboy there. Although it was thought that he would have some sort of civil service career, his prodigious musical talents finally led him to one as a violinist, teacher, conductor, and composer. Leopold studied at the Benedictine University and received a degree in philosophy there but was later expelled because of poor attendance. Eventually he found work as a violinist in the court orchestra of his hometown, where he rose from the ranks to become assistant music director. During his own musical career, which he would later totally abandon to manage the affairs of his genius son, he also taught keyboard and music to the choirboys at the Cathedral in Salzburg. What made Leopold famous in his own time, however, were not his musical compositions, but a method book on how to play the violin, the *Versuch einer gründlichen Violinschule.* Published when he was thirty-seven years old, this tome has been a valuable reference in the twentieth century on the early classical approach to violin, and by extension, orchestral playing.

The event that changed Leopold's life and would essentially end his career as an active composer was the birth of his son in 1756. Even though he was at the height of his musical powers in 1762, it seems that the elder Mozart cared little for his own career and composing, spending all of his time in the service of his only two surviving children, Maria Anna (known as Nannerl) and the boy genius Wolfgang Amadeus.

Music historians have not been very kind to the memory of Leopold Mozart, calling him a crass promoter of his children who dragged them across Europe to perform in all of the important aristocratic circles as if they were trained circus animals. Even though the promotion of his children could appear crude to the casual observer, there is no doubt that Leopold was truly devoted to them and was particularly astute in identifying, almost immediately, the superior talents of his only surviving son. In Leopold's favor, history has him to thank for carefully preserving his son's music (often in the original manuscripts) and for cataloguing Wolfgang's work from the earliest compositions. It is through the father's efforts that the younger Mozart's scores appeared in print as early as 1775. Like many overbearing parents, however, Leopold tried to interject himself into all aspects of his young son's life, being overprotective and constantly criticizing his son's spending habits, choice of friends, and finally his marriage to the young Constanze Weber. Although the younger Mozart was very devoted to his father, this constant meddling strained their relationship. The elder Mozart, whose wife predeceased him, died alone in 1787, about which the son felt a great deal of guilt in his final years.

One of the ironies of musical history is that some of Wolfgang Amadeus's early music was attributed to his father in the belief that one so young could not possibly write such mature music. Conversely, after both of their deaths, some music written by Leopold was attributed to his more famous son. Finally, it was discovered that the renowned *Toy Symphony*, which was once thought to have originated with Franz Joseph Haydn, came from the pen of Leopold Mozart!

Orchestral
Concerto in D Major for Trumpet and Orchestra
what to buy: [Maurice André, trumpet; Herbert von Karajan, cond.; Berlin Philharmonic Orchestra] (EMI Classics 66961) ♪ ♪ ♪ ♪₇

This disc was reissued as part of EMI's *Great Recordings of the Century* series and for many listeners it is still the performance to beat due to the exceptional playing of André in his prime. Even though the orchestra is too large by the present-day standards of original-instrument performances, this disc is outstanding, and also includes Johann Nepomuk Hummel's Concerto in E-flat Major for Trumpet and Orchestra and trumpet concertos by Georg Phillipp Telemann and Antonio Vivaldi.

what to buy next: [*Klassische Trompeten Konzerte*;

Meridian Arts Ensemble:
There just aren't that many compositions created specifically for brass quintets, one reason why the Canadian Brass and the Empire Brass make such heavy use of arrangements, especially settings of music from past decades and centuries. While these two outfits are the overwhelming commercial giants of this mini-category, there is still room in the world's concert halls for a group willing to take chances in their approach to developing a repertoire. The various members of the Meridian Arts Ensemble are just the folks to do that, having won the 1995 Chamber Music America/ASCAP Award for Adventurous Programming with a set-list that included works by Johann Sebastian Bach, Domenico Scarlatti, Frank Zappa, Witold Lutoslawski, and the Brecker Brothers, persuasively traveling between centuries and genres with surprising ease.

One of their first appearances on an album was when they played Otto Luening's *Divertimento for Brass Quintet* on a set devoted to that composer's works (*No Jerusalem but This*, CRI 600). The first release under their own banner, however, was a disc containing performances of twentieth century scores by Lutoslawski (*Mini Overture*), Paul Hindemith (*Morgenmusik*), and four other, more contemporary, composers (Channel Crossings 2191), essentially duplicating the program with which the Meridian Arts Ensemble won First Prize at the 1990 Concert Artists Guild New York Competition.

Their second album (*Smart Went Crazy*, Channel Classics 4192) came out in 1992 and is, in many ways, the model for most of their releases since then. Much of the disc was taken up with seriously considered arrangements (mostly by trumpeter Jon Nelson) of work by rock musician Frank Zappa, an approach aided in part by direct contact with the composer and input from him as to how the music could be performed. Whereas the composer/conductor Pierre Boulez has occasionally expanded Zappa's work to fill an orchestral canvas, the Meridian Arts Ensemble operated on a smaller scale but with similarly sterling results. *Prime Meridian* (Channel Crossings 8195), *Anxiety of Influence* (Channel Crossings 9796), and their latest (1996) release *Ear Mind I* (Channel Crossings 11898) follow roughly the same pattern as *Smart Went Crazy*, meshing Zappa material with that of Don Van Vliet (Captain Beefheart), Igor Stravinsky, Milton Babbit, and works by newer composers (including various of the group's own members).

Visions of the Renaissance (Channel Classics 6594), their third album, was released in 1994 and contains works by Johann Sebastian Bach, Carlos Gesualdo, Domenico Scarlatti, and Orlando Gibbons in tasteful arrangements, but it stands apart from the bulk of their catalog, as does *Five* (Channel Crossings 8195), which harkens back to the programming heard on their debut album, being more of a straight-ahead twentieth century avant-garde recital with both pre-existing works and those commissioned by the group.

Ian Palmer

Ludwig Güttler, trumpet; Max Pommer, cond.; Leipzig New Bach Collegium Musicam, orch.] (Capriccio 10010) ♪ ♪ ♪ ♪₇

For ears interested in the more transparent sounds of smaller ensembles and earlier instruments, the Güttler disc delivers all that is needed and more. This all-digital recording includes Joseph Haydn's famous Trumpet Concerto in E-flat Major, and a concerto by the Baroque master Johann Melchior Molter.

Cassation in G Major (*Toy Symphony*)
what to buy: [Hans Stadlmair, cond.; The Munich Chamber Orchestra] (Tudor 737) ♪ ♪ ♪ ♪

Not the greatest piece in the world but fun to hear, the *Toy Symphony* was created for home use with reduced musical forces. The publisher not only sold the score but the toy instruments as well, including a small drum, a toy trumpet, and a whistle! This good musical entertainment is played by the Munich Orchestra with tongues firmly in cheek. Also heard on this program devoted to works by the elder Mozart are the Symphony in D Major, the Sinfonia da caccia in G Major, and the famous *Muiskalische Schlittenfahrt (Musical Sleigh Ride)*, a piece often heard during the winter holidays

influences: Antonio Salieri, Joseph Haydn, Wolfgang Amadeus Mozart

Dave Wagner

Wolfgang Amadeus Mozart
Born Johann Chrysostom Wolfgang Amadeus Mozart, January 27, 1756, in Salzburg, Austria. Died December 5, 1791, in Vienna, Austria.

period: Classical

Wolfgang Amadeus Mozart, along with the older Franz Joseph Haydn and the younger Ludwig van Beethoven, brought the Viennese Classical style to its pinnacle. A brilliant and hard-working composer, he started early and wrote more high-quality work in a couple of decades than most other composers could do in a lifetime. He composed more than 626 scores (including operas, masses, symphonies, concerti, sonatas, and string quartets), working in just about every genre known to Western composers of that era.

Johann André Schacter, a court trumpeter at Salzburg, wrote a letter to Wolfgang's beloved older sister Maria Anna (nicknamed "Nannerl") upon her brother's death and noted some details about the great composer's early life. He recalled Wolfgang's absolute pitch by telling how, in 1763, the youngster observed that Schacter's

violin was "half a quarter of a tone lower than mine, that is, if it is tuned as it was, when I played on it last." Young Wolfgang's first attempts at composition are reputed by Schacter to have happened when he was four years old, though the first completed scores—some small keyboard works—date from 1761. By the next year Leopold Mozart, a composer and musician in his own right, judged both his offspring to be good enough musicians that he felt comfortable promoting their skills at the keyboard via a four-month-long series of concerts in Vienna. While there Wolfgang and Nannerl played before various heads of state and members of the nobility, garnering praise, lucre, and requests to put off their return to Salzburg.

Although the trio returned home in January 1763, their stay would be relatively brief as they began a lengthy, multi-year tour in June of that year which took them to the music capitals of Europe, not only displaying the children's talents to the cultured multitudes but exposing the siblings to some of the finest music and musicians. It was while on this tour that Wolfgang published two pairs of sonatas for keyboard and violin in Paris, the first of his music to appear in print. In the years between their first European tour and 1772, when the last of his three trips to Italy was undertaken, Wolfgang had furthered his reputation as one of the finest keyboard musicians of his day in addition to creating masses, symphonies, serenades, concert arias, and a few works for the stage including his first opera, *La finta semplice*.

1773 found Mozart back in Salzburg, just in time to witness a cultural upheaval that affected nearly every arts-oriented establishment in the city. The Archbishop of Salzburg had just died and his successor had curtailed much of the financing for most of the musical organizations under his control. Despite this potential drawback, Mozart engaged in a protracted flurry of compositional activity during the next four and a half years that saw the creation of numerous symphonies in addition to concertos, divertimentos, sacred choral works, and string quartets and quintets. Leopold and Wolfgang were both employed by the new Archbishop but a personal antipathy between master and servants eventually resulted in the Mozarts' dismissal in 1777, and an ensuing attempt to secure more satisfactory postings or lucrative commissions. Wolfgang and his mother then traveled to courts in Munich and Mannheim, where they met with polite but definite refusals to hire. These factors then led to a trip to Paris, where some of Mozart's works were performed and, sadly, where his mother expired from what the death certificate called "heart disease."

This death adversely affected relations between the father and son at first, as Leopold sent Wolfgang a series of notes blaming him for not taking better care of his mother. Eventually the rift healed as the senior Mozart seemingly realized the irrationality of his position. Wolfgang then stayed on in Paris for another few months before receiving word from Leopold that the position of court organist had opened up in Salzburg, for which his father urged him to return. When he finally arrived and attained the position, Mozart evidently dove into his work, composing four enduring sacred masterpieces in C Major for the Salzburg Cathedral: two Masses (K. 317 and K. 337), the *Vesperae de Dominica* (K. 321) and his *Vesperae solennes de confesore* (K. 339).

Somewhere along the way, however, the Archbishop became dissatisfied with his organist, perhaps as a result of Mozart's increasing number of secular works, which may have been perceived as cutting into the labors rightfully due his employer. Among these "outside" endeavors are some of the composer's finest early works including the opera *Idomeneo,* his Sinfonia concertante (K. 364) and the *Posthorn* Serenade (K. 320). In any event, neither employee nor employer were satisfied with the other and a parting of the ways occurred in 1781, when Mozart was severed from his relatively safe and secure job to begin a more tenuous life as a freelance teacher, musician, and composer. He then moved to Vienna and, during the next decade, created a series of exceptional works comprising nearly everything for which he is best known. A letter Mozart wrote to his father after his confrontation with the Archbishop revealed that the young musician had no qualms about his choice, stating, "I am so certain of success here [Vienna] that I might have resigned even without a cause."

The acclaim and fiscal rewards Mozart was so sure of seemed quite possible, as he was soon considered one of the finest keyboard players in the city, and the first of his operas from this period—*Die Entführung aus dem Serail (The Abduction From the Seraglio)*—was a great success at its premiere on July 16, 1782. Other important works in Mozart's canon had their beginnings during this time, including the *Haffner* Symphony no. 35 in D Major (K. 385) and the six string quartets dedicated to Franz Joseph Haydn (K. 387, K. 421, K. 428, K. 458, K. 464, K. 465). Things must have looked so good to him

that he felt like he could afford to get married, and despite the wishes of Leopold, who only grudgingly gave his permission for the union, Wolfgang and Constanze Weber were wed August 4, 1782. For a while it appeared that the young composer was happy in his marriage, successful as a performer and teacher, and on the right track from a compositional standpoint. The piano sonatas in A Major (K. 331) and F Major (K. 332) date from this period, as does his *Linz* Symphony no. 36 in C Major, the Concerto no. 20 in D Minor for Piano and Orchestra, and the Concerto no. 21 in C Major for Piano and Orchestra.

On the fiscal front however, Mozart's handling of money was notably atrocious, and there were constant loans from Peter to pay Paul or visits to the pawn shop where he would exchange various personal items for cash. Humiliated as he may have been on a personal level by these circumstances, he seemingly did little to change his habits. Having set up his own household and taken hold of his own financial well-being sans the somewhat wiser counsel of his father, Mozart was living beyond his means; this was a predilection which he had already exhibited in the period between his mother's death and his return to Salzburg, when he alienated some people who would have been his friends if he had only taken care to repay their loans.

Leopold died in May 1787 right about the time that Wolfgang's receipts from concertizing in Vienna dried up, and two years later the junior Mozart embarked on a brief tour of German cities to shore up his finances to some degree. These setbacks on personal and business fronts actually marked the beginning of Mozart's greatest period of achievement as a composer, though his personal life would go further into decline.

Mozart's Serenade no. 13 in G Major (*Eine kleine Nachtmusik*), perhaps his best-known instrumental work, was finished in 1787, after the premiere of his opera, *Le nozze di Figaro (The Marriage of Figaro),* and just about the same time he finished working on *Don Giovanni.* His symphonies no. 39 in E-flat Major, no. 40 in G Minor, and no. 41 in C Major were all finished within the space of three months in 1788, while his opera *Così fan tutte (Thus Do All Women)* was premiered in January 1790 and his last three string quartets (K. 575, K. 589, and K. 590) were finished by June of that year. 1791 saw the completion of his last two stage works (*Die Zauberflöte [The Magic Flute]* and *La clemenza di Tito [The Clemency of Titus],*) the Concerto no. 27 in B-flat Major for Piano and Orchestra, and the Concerto in A Major for Clarinet and Orchestra—all major scores within his oeuvre.

Mozart's final illness (he was bedridden for fifteen days with what was later diagnosed as rheumatic inflammatory fever) prevented him from completing the *Requiem* which he had been commissioned to compose by Count Walsegg-Stuppach—a nobleman and dilettante composer/musician who sought to memorialize his deceased wife by passing off a work by Mozart as his own. The *Introitus* had been completely orchestrated at the time of the composer's death, with the balance of the scoring only sketched out. Mozart's assistant for most of 1791, Franz Xavier Süssmayr, ended up finishing some of the orchestrations in the *Kyrie* (Franz Jakob Freystädtler contributed to all but the trumpet and kettledrum parts) in addition to completing the *Lacrimosa* and composing the *Santus, Benedictus,* and *Agnus Dei* according to the plan laid out by Mozart.

Orchestral
Serenade no. 7 in D Major for Violin and Orchestra (K. 250/248b) (*Haffner*)
what to buy: [Oldrich Vlech, violin; Charles Mackerras, cond.; Prague Chamber Orchestra] (Telarc 80161) ♪ ♪ ♪ ♪

This is one of Mozart's most popular serenades and Mackerras, a renowned Czech music specialist, reminds one by the very lightness of this orchestra's textures that the composer spent a fair amount of time in Prague. The same forces wend their way through the equally charming version of the *Serenata notturna* (K. 239).

what to buy next: [Isaac Stern, violin; Jean-Pierre Rampal, cond.; Franz Liszt Chamber Orchestra] (Sony Classics 66270) ♪ ♪ ♪⸝

This 1995 version is recommended purely for the performance by Stern, who renders an exquisite execution of this well-known Mozart work. The composer's March in D Major for Orchestra is the filler on this disc.

Serenade no. 13 in G Major for Strings and Continuo (K. 525) (*Eine kleine Nachtmusik*)
what to buy: [Christoph von Dohnányi, cond.; Cleveland Orchestra] (London 443175) ♪ ♪ ♪ ♪ ♪

This is a stunning, impeccably produced rendering. The

disc also includes Mozart's Concerto for Flute, Harp and Orchestra in C Major (K. 299) with flautist Joshua Smith and harpist Lisa Wellbaum, plus the Sinfonia Concertante in E-flat for Violin, Viola, and Orchestra (K. 364) with violinist Daniel Majeske and violist Robert Vernon. Combining these works on one CD works very well and you'll find the nearly seventy-nine minutes of resplendent music by this world-class orchestra and its astounding soloists exceptionally satisfying.

[*Mozart: Great Serenades*; Neville Marriner, cond.; Academy of St. Martin-in-the-Fields, orch.] (Philips 464022) ♪ ♪ ♪ ♪ ♪

Marriner's version is part of safe, reliable, well-produced and reasonably-priced two-disc set. The orchestra has long been known for the quality of its string section and this performance bears that reputation out. For someone looking to acquire the four most popular serenades (*Serenata Notturna, Haffner, Posthorn,* and *Eine kleine Nachtmusik*) this may be the best bet.

what to buy next: [Nikolaus Harnoncourt, cond.; Vienna Concentus Musicus, orch.] (Teldec 44809) ♪ ♪ ♪ ♪⸝

Harnoncourt has been an advocate for period-instrument performances for decades and his take on Mozart's popular serenade is proof of the validity of his artistic commitment. The accompanying Divertimento no. 11 in D Major for Oboe, Two Horns, and Strings doesn't fare as well, however, as the tempos set by the conductor make the music seem brittle rather than flexible. *Eine musiklaischer Spass* (K.522), the last work on Harnoncourt's program, is interesting primarily for its relative rarity on disc.

[Christopher Hogwood, cond.; Academy of Ancient Music, orch.] (L'Oiseu-Lyre 411720) ♪ ♪ ♪ ♪

Although this performance does not quite hold the energetic appeal of the Dohnányi, Marriner, or Harnoncourt readings (see above), it is an attractive period-instrument recording. Disc-mates include the Serenade no. 6 in D Major for Orchestra (K. 239) (*Serenata notturna*) and the *Notturno* in D Major for Four Orchestras (K. 286/269a).

Concerto no. 20 in D Minor for Piano and Orchestra (K. 466)
what to buy: [Murray Perahia, piano; Murray Perahia,

cond.; English Chamber Orchestra] (Sony Classics 42241) ♪ ♪ ♪ ♪ ♪

You can't go wrong with *any* recording featuring top Mozart maven Murray Perahia. His exquisite performance here beautifully conveys the piece's fury and romanticism. Mozart's final piano concerto, no. 27, in B-flat Major (K. 595) is the other piece in this splendid package. Both performances can also be found in Perahia's fine multi-disc set of all twenty-seven Mozart piano concertos. (Sony Classics 46441)

what to buy next: [Rudolf Serkin, piano; Claudio Abbado, cond.; London Symphony Orchestra] (Deutsche Grammophon 431278) ♪ ♪ ♪ ♪ ♪

Perahia's playing is a tad more delicate and refined when compared to Serkin's, while the latter seems to be a bit more analytical in his approach. Abbado is a far more masterful conductor than Perahia, however, and the LSO is larger than the ECO, which gives the Serkin performance more of a sonic backdrop. The qualification here is that the bigger ensemble may not be as "authentic" as the smaller one. Serkin's disc does include a very good performance in the twenty-first piano concerto, however, and that may tip the balance his way.

Concerto no. 21 in C Major for Piano and Orchestra (K. 467) (*Elvira Madigan*)
what to buy: [Mitsuko Uchida, piano; Jeffrey Tate, cond.; English Chamber Orchestra] (Philips 416381) ♪ ♪ ♪ ♪ ♪

Uchida matches Perahia's performances, showing flawless keyboard technique and passionate sensitivity, especially in the Andante movement, which was featured in the soundtrack for the Swedish film *Elvira Madigan*. Her rendition of Mozart's Concerto no. 20 for Piano and Orchestra is a worthy alternative to the Perahia and Serkin sets (see above).

Concerto in A Major for Clarinet and Orchestra (K. 622)
what to buy: [Richard Stoltzman, clarinet; Alexander Schneider, cond.; English Chamber Orchestra] (RCA Victor Red Seal 60723) ♪ ♪ ♪ ♪ ♪

Stoltzman is a stellar soloist and serves up mellifluous and deep-toned perfection, especially in his beautiful rendering of this work's luscious Adagio. The disc also contains the composer's Quintet for Clarinet in A Major

(K. 581), which matches Stoltzman with the Tokyo String Quartet.

[Antony Pay, clarinet; Christopher Hogwood, cond.; Academy of Ancient Music, orch.] (L'Oiseau-Lyre 414339) ♪ ♪ ♪ ♪ ♪

Pay, Hogwood, and the Academy of Ancient Music have created a viable and enjoyable original-instrument performance as an alternative to the more "traditional" forces employed by Stoltzman (see above) and Meyer (see below). Their rendition is paired with a well-executed version of Mozart's Concerto in C Major for Oboe and Orchestra (K. 271k) with Michel Piguet as soloist.

what to buy next: [Sabine Meyer, clarinet; Claudio Abbado, cond.; Berlin Philharmonic Orchestra] (EMI Classics 56832) ♪ ♪ ♪ ♪

Meyer's tone is absolutely gorgeous and Abbado has proven himself to be a very good Mozartean. When teamed with the Berliners, the combination can be hard to resist. What may hold this performance back in the minds of some potential listeners is the idea of going from Mozart, to Claude Debussy (*Premiere Rhapsodie* for Clarinet and Orchestra), to Toru Takemitsu (*Fantasma/Canto*), composers whose sound world is markedly different from the one inhabited by Mozart. Still, this could be an interesting way to broaden one's musical horizons.

Concerto no. 1 in G Major for Flute and Orchestra (K. 313/285c)
what to buy: [Susan Palma, flute; Orpheus Chamber Orchestra] (Deutsche Grammophon 427677) ♪ ♪ ♪ ♪ ♪

If you favor the flute, these light and lovely interpretations by Palma constitute a fetchingly lyrical listen. The album also includes attractive performances of the Andante in C Major for Flute and Orchestra (K. 315) and adds harpist Nancy Allen for the Concerto in C Major for Flute, Harp, and Orchestra (K. 299/297c).

[Emmanuel Pahud, flute; Claudio Abbado, cond.; Berlin Philharmonic] (EMI Classics 56578) ♪ ♪ ♪ ♪ ♪

Pahud's lighter touch and Abbado's quicker, flowing tempos make this piece and others on the disc an appealing alternative to the Palma set. The modest-sized orchestra matches Pahud's virtuosic yet tender style. Also included on this disc are Mozart's Concerto no. 2 in D Major for Flute and Orchestra (K. 314/285d) and the Concerto in C Major for Flute and Harp (K. 299/297c) with Marie-Pierre Langlamet playing as harpist.

what to buy next: [Eugenia Zukerman, flute; Pinchas Zukerman, cond.; English Chamber Orchestra] (Sony 62424) ♪ ♪ ♪ ♪

Eugenia Zukerman's willowy smooth, sweetly-rendered flute solos thrill the ears on this classic recording made in 1977. Pinchas Zukerman extracts a sensitive performance from the ECO that doesn't tread on the soloist's toes in both this piece and the second flute concerto (K.314/285d). The last work featured on this disc—the Concerto in A Major for Clarinet and Orchestra (K. 622)—was recorded in 1961 with George Szell conducting the Cleveland Orchestra and clarinet soloist Robert Marcellus.

Concertos for Horn and Orchestra (K. 412/386b, 417, 447, 495)
what to buy: [Dennis Brain, horn; Herbert von Karajan, cond.; Philharmonia Orchestra] (EMI Classics 66950) ♪ ♪ ♪ ♪ ♪

A car accident robbed the world of the greatest horn player of the twentieth century, Dennis Brain. These performances remind the listener of just how large a loss that was. Brain's control of this unwieldy instrument was nearly uncanny and Karajan's conducting had an ingratiating bounce to it that contrasted the almost too serious aspect he would adopt in later years. In addition to the four concertos, EMI also includes the Dennis Brain Ensemble in a performance of Mozart's Quintet for Piano and Winds in E-flat Major (K. 452).

what to buy next: [Lowell Greer, natural horn; Nicholas McGegan, cond; Philharmonia Baroque Orchestra] (Harmonia Mundi 907012) ♪ ♪ ♪ ♪

This period-instrument recording offers spirited versions of various pieces for horn, which the internationally-acclaimed Greer polishes off with aplomb under McGegan's direction. This disc includes all of Mozart's horn concertos and both rondos for horn and orchestra: the more popular work in E-flat Major (K. 371) and the one in D Major (K. 514), which was completed by Herman Jeurissen.

[Eric Ruske, horn; Charles Mackerras, cond; Scottish Chamber Orchestra] (Telarc 80367) ♪ ♪ ♪ ♪

A world-class performer who had already won international acclaim and been named associate principal horn of the Cleveland Orchestra by age thirty, Ruske (also a member of the Empire Brass) is coaxed by Mackerras into fine, warm-toned renderings of these concertos. Ruske's technical virtuosity glistens especially in the *Rondo* of the Concerto in E-flat major (K. 417). The set also includes baritone Richard Suart singing a short vocal version of the final movement of Mozart's fourth Horn Concerto (K. 495) with witty lyrics (Gilbert and Sullivan-style) about a musician who cannot find his French horn.

Concerto for Violin and Orchestra no. 1 in B-flat Major (K. 207)
what to buy: [*The Five Violin Concertos*; Gidon Kremer, violin; Nikolaus Harnoncourt, cond.; Vienna Philharmonic Orchestra] (Deutsche Grammophon 453043) ♪ ♪ ♪ ♪ ♪

Kremer plays with agility and fervent expressiveness on this spirited, spellbinding concerto. The same holds true for the four other concertos (K. 211, K. 216, K 218, K. 219) and the Sinfonia Concertante in E-flat major (K. 364) on this two-disc set.

what to buy next: [Mela Tenenbaum, violin; Richard Kapp, cond.; Czech Philharmonic Chamber Orchestra] (ESS.A.Y. 1070) ♪ ♪ ♪ ♪

Tenenbaum is a masterful, emotional soloist in this agreeable performance astutely conducted by Kapp. Sound quality may be a tad bright but, overall, the balances are well maintained between soloist and orchestra. Also on this CD are two other Mozart violin concertos: no. 2 in D Major (K. 211) and no. 3 in G Major (K. 216).

[Cho-Liang Lin, violin; Raymond Leppard, cond.; English Chamber Orchestra] (Sony Classics 42364) ♪ ♪ ♪ ♪

This performance is as appealing as the Kremer version (see above), with Lin's passion and vitality matching his. The main difference between the recordings lies in the timbral qualities of their instruments, with the nimble Lin's violin sounding sweeter in the upper-to-mid-registers while Kremer evokes richer tones in the lower register. The progam also contains Mozart's fifth violin concerto (K. 219) and the Adagio in E Major for Violin and Orchestra (K. 261).

Symphony no. 29 in A Major (K. 201)

what to buy: [Charles Mackerras, cond.; Prague Chamber Orchestra] (Telarc 80165) ♪ ♪ ♪ ♪₈

Mackerras is an excellent interpreter of Mozart symphonies, and yields a pitch-perfect, passionate reading of this graceful, light and airy work in both the strings-sweetened Allegro moderato and the frolicsome third movement. This disc also includes fine performances of Symphony no. 25 in G Minor (K. 183) and Symphony no. 28 in C Major (K. 200).

Symphony no. 38 in D Major (K. 504) (*Prague*)

what to buy: [John Eliot Gardiner, cond.; English Baroque Soloists, orch.] (Philips 426283) ♪ ♪ ♪ ♪₈

The richness, vigor, and detail of Gardiner's 1988 period-instrument performance makes this reading a standout. His conducting of the Symphony no. 39 in E-flat Major (K. 543) adds further listening pleasure to the album.

what to buy next: [Benjamin Britten, cond.; English Chamber Orchestra] (London 444323) ♪ ♪ ♪₈

Britten was not only one of the major English composers of the twentieth century, he was usually a fairly solid conductor as well. While his conducting in the four Mozart symphonies heard here (nos. 25, 29. 38, and 40) is not necessarily consistent in its quality, the *Prague* gets a very good reading, as does the early and delightful no. 29. The pacing in the great *Jupiter* symphony is a bit brisk at times, but nothing that listeners can't adjust to.

[Charles Mackerras, cond.; Prague Chamber Orchestra] (Telarc 80148) ♪ ♪ ♪₈

Mackerras gives a reading that, with the help of the string section, is passionate and pleasing. The disc also contains Mozart's Symphony no. 36 in C Major (K. 425) (*Linz*).

Symphony no. 40 in G Minor (K.550)

what to buy: [*The Last 5 Symphonies*; Neville Marriner, cond.; Academy of St. Martin-in-the-Fields, orch.] (Philips 438332) ♪ ♪ ♪ ♪₈

Marriner leads his orchestra through a marvelously

Midori:

Midori (birth name: Goto Mi Dori) was born in Japan and took her first violin lessons with her mother, Goto Setsu. In 1981, when Midori was eleven years old, the two of them moved to the United States, where, after playing at the Aspen Music Festival, Midori soon began studying violin with the noted pedagogue Dorothy DeLay at the Juilliard School of Music. In 1982, the young violin prodigy made her New York City debut, playing a concerto by Nicolò Paganini with the New York Philharmonic Orchestra under the direction of Zubin Mehta.

Midori left the Juilliard School when she was fifteen years old and had graduated from high school (at the Professional Children's School). She soon began working with a management company (ICM Artists) and booking appearances with orchestras as a soloist in addition to developing her recital repertoire. Despite displaying considerable poise early in her career and generating plenty of favorable reviews in the mainstream press, Midori's playing often left veteran critics praising her technique even as they questioned the depth of her interpretations, a perfectly natural discrepancy given her age. The first album she released, a 1988 rendition of Paganini's twenty-four *Caprices* (Sony Classics 44944), was the work of a prodigy and not of the gradually maturing artist Midori was working toward becoming.

Her 1991 recording with pianist Robert McDonald, *Live At Carnegie Hall,* (Sony Classics 46742), was a step in the right direction, but a better indicator of her maturity (at least from a non-performance standpoint) came in the next year when she started the Midori Foundation (Midori and Friends), an organization that has, in the presence of reduced federal and state funding for such programs, sought to introduce elementary school children in New York City to the performing arts by supplying workbook materials and audio-visual aids to twenty to twenty-five public schools per year. In this way Midori, with the assistance of such musical luminaries as pianist Emanuel Ax and the Manhattan Brass Quintet, aims to broaden the horizons of children through an interdisciplinary method that combines music with art, history, and writing projects led by the individual school's teaching staff.

With regard to her artistic growth, Midori's more recent interpretations seem to lean away from the technical perfection that characterized earlier performances in favor of a slightly broader tone and a harder-edged attack that heralds a more personal approach to the instrument. This tactic is one that is still in development, however, and the results can often be a bit uneven. Midori's 1998 concert recording of Dmitri Shostakovich's Concerto no. 1 for Violin and Orchestra (Sony Classics 68338) is a case in point, showcasing a tautly-constructed conception (ably aided by the Berlin Philharmonic Orchestra conducted by Claudio Abbado) that is paired with a relatively safe, clean, and uninspiring performance of Piotr Ilyich Tchaikovsky's lovely violin concerto.

Mathilde August

shaded rendition of this symphony. The Academy is especially effective in the Andante and the Menuetto, where the playing has a lovely Viennese lilt to it. The one problem with this set lies more in the way it is programmed than anything else: In order to fit all five of Mozart's last symphonies into one release, the record company split Symphony no. 39 between two discs.

what to buy next: [Trevor Pinnock, cond.; The English Concert, orch.] (Deutsche Grammophon 447048) ♪♪♪♪

Pinnock's surprisingly graceful and dramatic performance of Mozart's Symphony no. 40 is the mainstay of this disc and the reason for its recommendation. His opening Molto Allegro is controlled, not constricted, and the third movement Menuetto is brisk but effective. The accompanying version of Mozart's *Jupiter* symphony features tempos that are a bit speedy, lessening the punch of this powerful work.

[Bruno Walter, cond.; New York Philharmonic Orchestra] (Sony Classics 64477) ♪♪♪♪

Exquisitely played performances with fairly decent sound, at a reasonable price. Walter was one of the great conductors of the twentieth century and his work here in the last three Mozart symphonies (nos. 39—41) is top-drawer all the way. The burnished sound he draws from the strings and winds in no. 40 is both a marvel and a model for other conductors.

Symphony no. 41 in C Major (K. 551) (*Jupiter*)
what to buy: [Otto Klemperer, cond.; Philharmonia Orchestra] (Testament 1093) ♪♪♪♪♪

Klemperer had a unique way with Mozart, imparting a grandeur through (generally) slower tempos than many of his contemporaries, but maintaining such tension that, as in the case of the finale here, the emotional force of the music becomes overwhelming. The remastering of this marvelous 1954 monaural performance is spectacular, and the inclusion of Klemperer's takes on *Eine kleine Nachtmusik* and the graceful Symphony no. 29 make this a Mozart disc to treasure.

worth searching for: [*Toscanini Collection, vol. 11*; Arturo Toscanini, cond.; NBC Symphony Orchestra] (RCA Gold Seal 60285) ♪♪♪♪♪

Although this version combines recordings made on June 22, 1945, and March 11, 1946 (with sound quality that's acceptable considering the source materials), the great Toscanini gives consistent import and color to his performance of this work.

various opera overtures
what to buy: [Bruno Weil, cond.; Tafelmusik, orch.] (Sony Classics 46695) ♪♪♪♪♪

Weil achieves ardent, authoritative, and detailed period-instrument performances from the expanded orchestra as they perform overtures from *Idomeneo* (K. 366), *Die Entführung aus dem Serail* (K. 384), *Der Schauspieldirektor* (K. 486), *Le nozze di Figaro* (K. 492), *Don Giovanni* (K. 527), *Così fan tutte* (K. 588), *La Clemenza di Tito* (K. 621), and *Die Zauberflöte* (K. 620). Highly recommended, this album also contains a fine rendition of *Eine kleine Nachtmusik*, filled with sensitivity, detail, enthusiasm, and authority.

Chamber
Quartets for Flute and Strings
what to buy: [Jean-Pierre Rampal, flute; Isaac Stern, violin; Alexander Schneider, viola; Leonard Rose, cello] (Sony Odyssey 42601) ♪♪♪♪♪

On this soothing budget recording, Rampal and his colleagues deliver brilliant readings of all three Mozart flute quartets (K. 285, 285a, and 298) plus K. 285b, the one accredited to him despite some scholars' doubts as to its authenticity.

what to buy next: [Susan Milan, flute; Levon Chililingirian, violin; Louise Williams, viola, Philip de Groote, cello] (Chandos 8872) ♪♪♪♪♪

Excellent sound quality adds to the spirited, passionate rendering of this piece. Milan is a confident player whose fluidity, verve, and skillful technique make this budget-priced CD a must-add attraction to your collection. Particularly arresting is her delicate, heartwarming reading of the Adagio in K. 285.

various chamber works for winds
what to buy: [members of the Nash Ensemble] (Virgin Classics Veritas 61448) ♪♪♪♪♪

For people seeking a well-chosen, splendidly played selection of Mozart's chamber works for winds, this budget-priced two-disc set is a worthwhile listen. Frank Lloyd shows considerable skill by generating a fluid, precise, warm-toned horn solo in the Quintet in E-flat Major for Horn and Strings (K. 407/386c), the piece-de-resistance of this all-Mozart set. Other scores heard here include the Trio in E-flat Major for Clarinet, Viola, and Piano (K. 498), the *Adagio and Rondo* in C Minor for Flute, Oboe, Viola, Cello, and Piano (K. 617), the Quartet in E-flat Major for Oboe, Violin, Viola, and Cello (K. 370), and the quartets for flute and strings.

Sonata no. 11 in A Major for Piano (K. 331) (*Alla Turca*)

what to buy: [*Great Pianists of the 20th Century: vol. 76*; Maria João Pires, piano] (Philips 456928) ♪ ♪ ♪ ♪

Portuguese pianist Pires doesn't have many releases on the market currently, which makes this two-disc collection one to be cherished all the more. In addition to her superb handling of this delicate masterwork, she performs three other Mozart sonatas (K. 282, K. 333, and K. 545) plus the Piano Concerto no. 14 in E-flat Major (with Claudio Abbado conducting the Vienna Philharmonic Orchestra) and a fine selection of works by Johann Sebastian Bach, Frédéric Chopin, Franz Schubert, and Robert Schumann.

what to buy next: [Alfred Brendel, piano] (Philips 462903) ♪ ♪ ♪ ♪

Recorded in concert for the BBC, this performance deals well with the poetry and mischief of this piece, especially in the third movement which gives the work its nickname, *Alla turca*. Two of the other three works on this disc, the Rondo in A Minor (K. 511) and the majestic Sonata in B-flat Major (K. 570), were also recorded "live"; only Brendel's performance of the Sonata in C Major (K. 330) was done in the studio.

Sonata no. 12 in F Major for Piano (K. 332)
what to buy: [Moises Knoll Luria, piano] (Centaur 2093) ♪ ♪ ♪ ♪

A young Venezuelan pianist-composer trained at Juilliard, Moises Knoll-Luria has a gorgeously light keyboard touch and shows great sensitivity on this solo piano piece, as well as on the Sonata in D Major (K 311). As demonstrated in a standout performance of the brisk and brawny Allegro Assai, Knoll-Luria's playing certainly rivals that of more popular artists who have recorded this piece. He also turns in an elegant performance of the Concerto no. 26 in D Major for Piano and Orchestra (K. 537), with Paul Freeman conducting the London Symphony Orchestra.

Quartets for Strings, nos. 14–19 (the *Haydn*

Sherill Milnes:

Sherill Milnes was considered by many listeners to be one of the finest Verdi baritones during the last half of the twentieth century and perhaps the best American baritone since Leonard Warren, high praise when one considers the route from the farmhouse to the Metropolitan Opera stage that Milnes traveled. Although his childhood on an Illinois dairy farm involved the usual chores of any agrarian homestead, the musically inclined Milnes somehow found time to gain a modicum of proficiency on the piano, violin, clarinet, tuba, and other instruments before entering college, where he took pre-med classes with the aim of becoming a doctor. He had sung in a church choir, but Milnes didn't really study voice formally until he gave up the idea of someday establishing a medical practice and decided to follow his muse, opting to take music courses at Drake University and working toward getting a job as a music teacher. After receiving his Bachelor's and Master's degrees in music education from Drake, Milnes did some postgraduate work at Northwestern University's School of Music. During this period, he worked at different music-related jobs—singing with bands, in some commercials, and as a member of the Chicago Symphony Chorus. He finally got his first big chance when he passed an audition for a touring opera company in 1960. Five years later he debuted at the Metropolitan Opera as Valentin in Giuseppe Verdi's *Faust.*

Despite his obvious talents, it took Milnes a while before he was able to control his vocal shadings to the point where communication and characterization meshed with the tremendous vocal prowess he was capable of. While he could reach high notes with relative ease, he also had a tendency to play havoc with diction, especially in non-Italianate repertoire, a factor that the mature Milnes was able to correct. In 1981, just as he was coming into what would normally be thought of as his prime years, Milnes suffered from capillary hemorrhages on one of his vocal chords, essentially curtailing his career for a considerable length of time. When his contract at the Metropolitan Opera eventually came up for renewal, the administration let it lapse, for all practical purposes cutting Milnes loose from the venue which he had come to consider his home base.

After a few years, Milnes began to mount a comeback, exploring his options as a conductor, a teacher, and finally, a singer. In addition to presiding over master classes at schools in North America and Europe, Milnes was the subject of *Sherril Milnes at Juilliard: An Opera Master Class* (Homevision, 1986), which won an award for Best Instructional Music Tape from the American Film Institute in 1989. He also began singing the more mature roles that his experience and reconstructed approach to his craft best suited, including, in 1991, his first attempt at the lead role in Verdi's *Falstaff.*

While Milnes has taken more to singing in recitals than treading the stage in operatic finery, there are few good recorded examples of him in the former setting. The best of the lot finds him vocalizing on five songs as part of an album dedicated to works by the American composer Charles Tomlinson Griffes (New World 80273). Milnes at his peak of Verdi as an interpreter can be heard singing splendid duets with Placido Domingo in *La forza del destino* (RCA Victor Red Seal 39502), or soloing in the aria *Per me orafalale* from Act II of *Il trovatore* as part of a cast that also included Domingo and Leontyne Price (RCA Victor Red Seal 39504).

Ellen Kokko

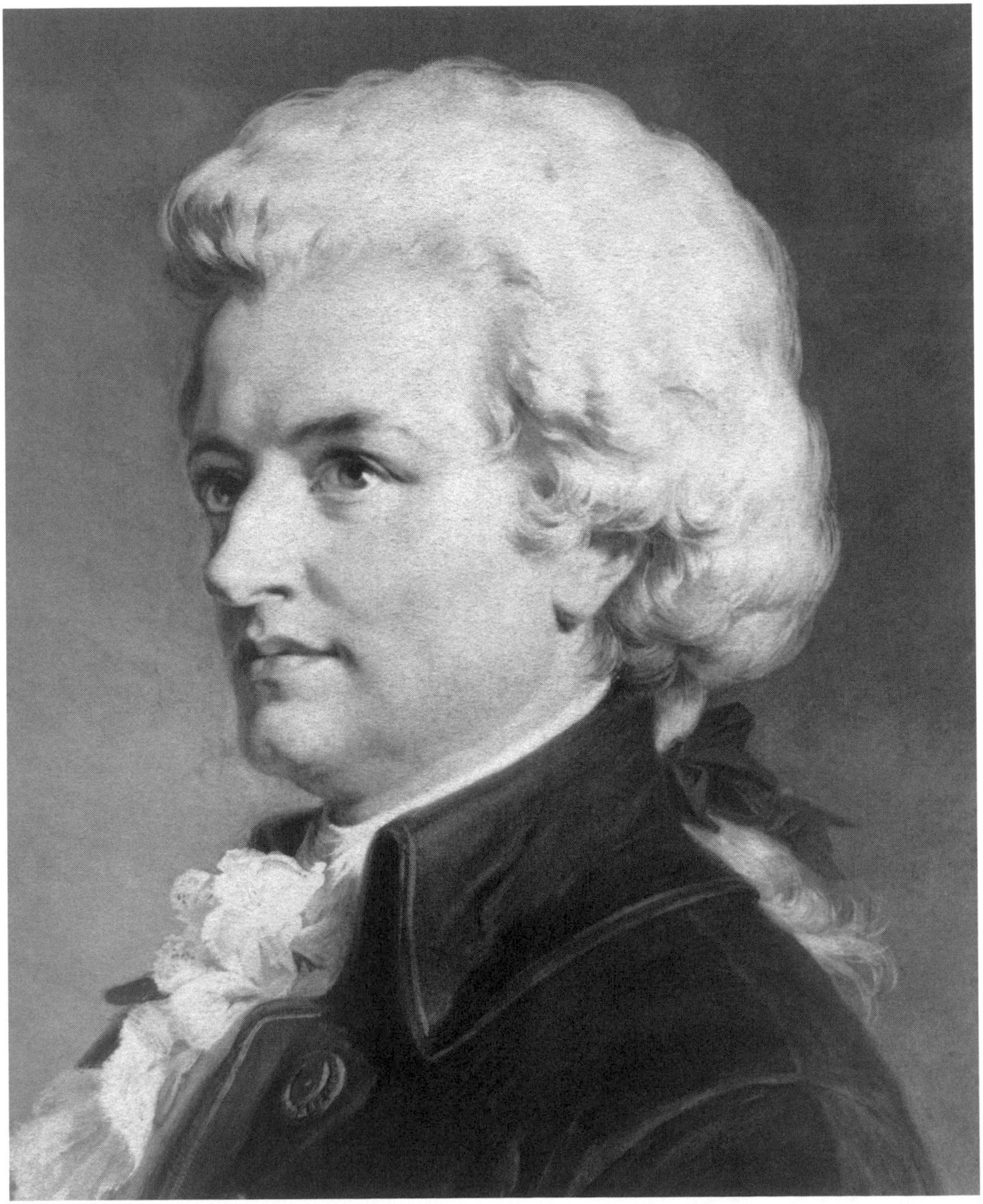

Quartets [K. 387, K. 421, K. 428, K. 458, K. 464, K. 465])

what to buy: [*Complete Mozart Edition, vol. 12: String Quartets*; Quartetto Italiano, ensemble] (Philips 422 512) ♪ ♪ ♪ ♪ ♪

The six *Haydn Quartets* and the four following them stand in the front ranks of Mozart's instrumental music, serving as influences to Ludwig van Beethoven and just about every one of the Romantic-era composers following him. The Quartetto Italiano gives eminently civilized renditions of these masterworks without negating any of the distilled emotion at their core; the group's performances of the last two quartets are particularly effective. This eight-CD box contains all of Mozart's string quartets and may seem like an expensive proposition to some, but given the quality of the playing, to others it will be a bargain.

what to buy next: [Talich Quartet, ensemble] (Calliope 3241/3) ♪ ♪ ♪ ♪ ♪

Not quite as fluid and graceful as the Quartetto Italiano, the Talich Quartet still manages to convey a powerful artistic impression by virtue of their intensity, especially in the C Major (*Dissonance*) Quartet (K. 465) where rhythm and chromatics mesh to create an intriguing whole.

[Juilliard String Quartet, ensemble] (Sony Odyssey 45826) ♪ ♪ ♪ ♪

At a budget price, the strongly characterized performances are indeed a bargain, containing a find blend of verve and intellect. The sound is a bit constricted, but not enough to hinder one's appreciation of the group's performances.

Vocal

Requiem in D Minor for Soloist, Orchestra, and Chorus (K. 626)

what to buy: [Lynne Dawson, soprano; Jard van Nes, contralto; Keith Lewis, tenor; Simon Estes, bass; Carlo Maria Giulini, cond.; Philharmonia Orchestra; Philharmonia Chorus] (Sony Classics 45577) ♪ ♪ ♪ ♪ ♪

The voices of Dawson and Lewis blend beautifully

Wolfgang Amadeus Mozart

throughout, but the pinnacle of their pairing comes in their attention-getting rendering of the *Recordare*. Giulini's sensitive conducting adds to the compelling performance. In softer passages such as the familiar *Lacrimosa* (finished by Mozart's assistant, Süssmayr) both the chorus and orchestra are captured with incredible clarity. While other recordings of the *Requiem* often become muddy as dynamics build, one attractive point of this recording is the satisfying sonorities, well-balanced even when the dynamics are at full power. An impeccably produced recording.

[Arleen Augér, soprano; Cecilia Bartoli, mezzo-soprano; Vinson Cole, tenor; Rene Pape, bass; Sir George Solti, cond; Vienna Philharmonic Orchestra; Vienna Philharmonic Choir] (London 433688) ♪ ♪ ♪ ♪ ♪

Solti extracts a performance capturing all the power and majesty of this piece. Fine soloists and spectacular chorus work make this 1991 recording an engaging, uplifting listen throughout.

[Sibylla Rubens, soprano; Annette Markert, contralto; Ian Bostridge, tenor; Hanno Müller-Brachmann, baritone; Philippe Herreweghe, cond.; Orchestre des Champs Élysées; La Chapelle Royale, choir; Collegium Vocale, choir] (Harmonia Mundi 901620) ♪ ♪ ♪ ♪ ♪

A lean, taut rendition of the *Requiem* by Herreweghe and company goes to the fore of more recent recordings. He uses the Süssmayr edition of the score for the most part, and although he does include some changes in the interest of clarifying Süssmayr's orchestral textures, they are not drastic. The soloists are all quite good, with special mention going to the male half of the quartet. Mozart's *Kyrie* (K. 341) is included in this program to good effect.

what to buy next: [Barbara Bonney, soprano; Anne Sofie von Otter, contralto; Hans Peter Blochwitz, tenor; Willard White, bass; John Eliot Gardiner, cond.; English Baroque Soloists, orch.; Monteverdi Choir, London] (Philips 420197) ♪ ♪ ♪ ♪

In its entirety, this is a splendid rendering, although the voices of Bonney and Blochwitz don't blend quite as well as those of Dawson and Lewis on the Giulini recording (see above). Still, Gardiner's conducting achieves the melancholy best from the instrumentalists, and the choral parts are also well performed.

Missa in C Minor (K. 427) (*The Great Mass*)
what to buy: [Sylvia McNair, soprano; Diana Montague, mezzo-soprano, Anthony Rolfe Johnson, tenor; Cornelius Hauptmann, bass; John Eliot Gardiner, cond.; English Baroque Soloists, orch.; Monteverdi Choir, London] (Philips 420210) ♪ ♪ ♪ ♪ ♪

More often recommended than Mozart's *Coronation Mass* (see below), this version of K. 427 is clinched by McNair's mellifluous performances throughout, as well as Gardiner's tasteful conducting. Crisp, clear, well-produced chorus parts add beauty.

Missa in C Major (K. 317) (*Coronation Mass*)
what to buy: [Emma Kirkby, soprano; Catherine Robbin, mezzo-soprano; John Mark Ainsley, tenor; Michael George, bass; Christopher Hogwood, cond.; Academy of Ancient Music, orch.; Winchester Cathedral Choir; Winchester College Choristers] (L'Oiseau Lyre 436585) ♪ ♪ ♪ ♪₅

This period-instrument performance of K. 317 simmers with grace and beauty, with Hogwood minding tempos and paying attention to detail. Among many highlights, the deliciously slow tempo of the *Agnus Dei* is highlighted by Kirkby's sweet solo. The disc also contains an equally magnificent performance of *Vesperae solennes de confessore* (K. 339), further enhanced by the brightly resonant boy's choir.

worth searching for: [Sylvia McNair, soprano; Delores Ziegler, mezzo-soprano; Hans Peter Blochwitz, tenor; Andreas Schmidt, baritone; James Levine, cond.; Berlin Symphony Orchestra; Berlin RIAS Chamber Choir] (Deutsche Grammophon 435853) ♪ ♪ ♪ ♪ ♪

Better soloists all around plus brighter, crisper sound quality, with satisfactory separation even in the softest choral passages, earn this version a half-bone advantage over the Hogwood set cited above. The 1991 recording also contains Haydn's Mass in C Major (*Mass in Time of War*), a powerful composition that rivals the Mozart work in grace and tone.

Exsultate, jubilate in F Major for Soprano and Orchestra (K. 165)
what to buy: [Kiri Te Kanawa, soprano; Colin Davis, cond.; London Symphony Orchestra] (Philips 412873) ♪ ♪ ♪ ♪

Te Kanawa's glorious reading of this radiant piece is the crowning achievement capping off a full program of Mozart's sacred works. The only real drawback to this project occurs in the *Vesperae solennes de confessore* (K. 339), which features contralto Elizabeth Bainbridge, tenor Ryland Davies, bass Gwenny Howell, and the LSO Chorus, here poor remastering makes the choral sections sound a tad muddy.

what to buy next: [*Kathleen Battle Sings Mozart*, Kathleen Battle, soprano; André Previn, cond.; Royal Philharmonic Orchestra] (EMI Angel 47355) ♪ ♪ ♪ ♪

Soprano Battle is in exquisite voice on this flawless presentation, including the reverent *Exulatate, jubilate* and a lush rendering (performed with solo violinist Barry Griffiths) of the aria *L'amero, saro costante* from *Il re pastore* (K. 208). Battle delivers the seven works in this program with exquisite precision, ardent passion, and awesome drama.

various sacred works
[Carolyn Dill Smith, soprano; Marianna Busching, mezzo-soprano; Gene Tucker, tenor; Peter Fay, baritone; Haig Mardirosian, cond; St. Thomas Moore Cathedral Orchestra; St. Thomas Moore Cathedral Chorus] (Centaur 2074) ♪ ♪ ♪ ♪

Completist Mozart collectors may want to pick up this CD containing three seldom-recorded compositions dating from Mozart's Salzberg years. While *Vesperae de Dominica* in C Major (K. 321), *Missa Brevis* in D Major (K. 194), and *Tantum ergo* in D Major (K. 197) are not nearly as wildly popular as Mozart's *Great Mass* or *Coronation Mass*, they are beautiful and spiritually uplifting in this 1989 performance conducted by Mardirosian. He draws the best from the choir, orchestra, and splendid soloists—especially robust soprano Smith, who excels with her gorgeous solo in the *Laudate dominum* from K. 321.

Le nozze di Figaro (The Marriage of Figaro) (K. 492)
what to buy: [Charlotte Margiono, soprano; Barbara Bonney, soprano; Ann Murray, mezzo-soprano; Petra Lang, mezzo-soprano; Philip Langridge, tenor; Christoph Spath, tenor; Thomas Hampson, baritone; Anton Scharinger, baritone; Kurt Moll, bass; Kevin Langan, bass; Nikolaus Harnoncourt, cond.; Royal Concertgebouw Orchestra; Netherlands Opera Chorus] (Teldec 90861) ♪ ♪ ♪ ♪

Harnoncourt achieves a performance full of sturdy solos (though not quite as cleverly characterized as the Marriner version; see below). Barbara Bonney's exquisite voice is enough to win you over completely, though Scharanger's smooth and tonally rich singing and performance still fail to match those of the robust José van Dam on the Marriner version. Exalted, powerful tutti passages add considerable appeal, to make this version a serious contender.

worth searching for: [Lucia Popp, soprano; Barbara Hendricks, soprano; Felicity Palmer, soprano; Agnes Baltsa, mezzo-soprano; Ruggerio Raimondi, tenor; Jose van Dam, bass-baritone; John Constable, harpsichord; Neville Marriner, cond.; Academy of St. Martin-in-the-Fields, orch.; Ambrosian Opera Chorus] (Philips 416370) ♪♪♪♪♪

There are abundant recordings of this highly popular Mozart opera, but the soloists in this all-star cast are well-suited to their parts and render performances that glitter under Marriner's leadership. In addition to flawlessly passionate and precise technical performances (sung in Italian), the soloists achieve characterizations appropriately ripe with dramatic appeal.

Don Giovanni (K. 527)
what to buy: [Elisabeth Schwarzkopf, soprano; Joan Sutherland, soprano; Graziella Sciutti, soprano; Luigi Alva, tenor; Eberhard Wächter, baritone; Piero Cappuccilli, baritone; Gottlob Frick, bass; Giuseppe Taddei, bass; Carlo Maria Giulini, cond.; Philharmonia Orchestra; Philharmonia Chorus] (EMI Classics 56232) ♪♪♪♪♪

The pairing of the older, more experienced Schwarzkopf and the young, still untried Sutherland was an unexpected stroke of genius when this recording first appeared, and has now passed into legend. The rest of the cast is marvelous (especially Taddei) and Giulini keeps everybody on the same glorious page.

what to buy next: [Felicity Lott, soprano; Christine Brewer, soprano; Nuccia Focile, soprano; Jerry Hadley, tenor; Alessandro Corbelli, baritone; Boje Skovhus, baritone; Umberto Chiummo, bass; Charles Mackerras, cond.; Scottish Chamber Orchestra; Scottish Chamber Chorus] (Telarc 80420) ♪♪♪♪

Among the plethora of recordings of Mozart's most romantic opera, this appealing version ranks high if only

for the elegantly rich voices and well-matched timbres of Lott (Donna Elvira), Skovhus (Don Giovanni), and Hadley (Don Ottavio). The entire cast sparkles and the convincing dramatic tension created by the young team of singers stands out admirably. It's a credit to Mackerras, who extracts a fine performance from all concerned.

Così fan tutte (K. 588)
what to buy: [Véronique Gens, soprano; Bernarda Fink, soprano; Graciela Oddone, soprano; Werner Gura, tenor; Marcel Boone, baritone; Pietro Spagnoli, baritone; René Jacobs, cond.; Concerto Köln, orch.; Köln Chamber Choir] (Harmonia Mundi 951663) ♪♪♪♪♪

This 1999 release received rave reviews not only for the magnificent performances from all under Jacobs' brilliant direction, but because the three-CD box set contains a separate, interactive CD-ROM with seven chapters about the creation of this opera and its characters, as well as a bilingual libretto, an interview with Jacobs, and more. As for the performance itself, voices of the principals are gorgeously exhilarating—well-matched in ensemble work, outstanding in solos, and exquisite with the chorus and orchestral passages. In case you don't have a computer to access the CD-ROM, a 255-page booklet with libretto translations in English, French, Italian, and German is included.

what to buy next: [Felicity Lott, soprano; Marie McLaughlin, soprano; Nuccia Focile, soprano; Jerry Hadley, tenor; Alessandro Corbelli, baritone; Gilles Cachemaille, bass-baritone; Charles Mackerras, cond.; Scottish Chamber Orchestra; Edinburgh Festival Chorus] (Telarc 80360) ♪♪♪♪

Mackerras extracts an expressive and lively performance from the wonderful soloists, chorus, and orchestra that is just a few minutes longer than the Jacobs account cited above. If that set is too pricey for your budget, this version represents a satisfying second choice.

Die Zauberflöte (The Magic Flute) (K. 620)
what to buy: [Irmgard Seefried, soprano; Wilma Lipp, soprano; Sena Jurinac, soprano; Emmy Loose, soprano; Anton Dermotta, tenor; Erich Majkut, tenor; Peter Klein, tenor; Erich Kunz, baritone; George London, bass-baritone; Ludwig Weber, bass; Harald Pröglhöf, bass; Ljubomir Pantscheff, bass; Herbert von Karajan, cond.; Vienna Philharmonic Orchestra; Vienna Singverein,

choir] (EMI Classics 67165) ♪ ♪ ♪ ♪ ♪

One of Karajan's finest moments as an opera conductor is this vintage recording of Mozart's penultimate singspiel. The folks at EMI have done a great job of remastering this set and letting the full vocal flowering of Seefried's Pamina and Lipp's Queen of the Night come through. Dermotta is a magnificent Tamino and Kunz's Papageno is more than adequate. The playing of the VPO string section is disciplined without being stiff, glorying in Mozart's orchestration.

what to buy next: [Gundula Janowitz, soprano; Lucia Popp, soprano; Elisabeth Schwarzkopf, soprano; Marga Höffgen, soprano; Ruth-Margret Putz, soprano; Christa Ludwig, mezzo-soprano; Nicolai Gedda, tenor ; Walter Berry, bass-baritone; Gottlob Frick, bass; Otto Klemperer, cond.; Philharmonia Orchestra; Philharmonia Chorus] (EMI Classics 55173) ♪ ♪ ♪ ♪ ♪

The sound may be a bit dated (1964) but the performances are top-notch, about what you should expect given such a stellar lineup of talent. Janowitz is a fine Pamina, Gedda is a very good Tamino, and Berry's bird/man (Papageno) is one of the best on disc.

[Dawn Upshaw, soprano; Beverly Hoch, soprano; Catherine Pierard, soprano; Anthony Rolfe-Johnson, tenor; Guy de Mey, tenor; Olaf Bär, baritone; Andreas Schmidt, bass; Cornelius Hauptmann, bass; Roger Norrington, cond.; London Classical Players, orch.; Heinrich Schütz Choir, London] (Virgin Classics Veritas 61384) ♪ ♪ ♪ ♪

The stage work calls for superb comedic characterization and glorious singing, something that Upshaw, Rolfe-Johnson, and Schmidt do quite well. Hoch's singing in the famous Queen of the Night aria is quite wonderful.

[Barbara Hendricks, soprano; June Anderson, soprano; Ulrike Steinsky, soprano; Jerry Hadley, tenor; Thomas Allen, baritone; Robert Lloyd, bass; Charles Mackerras, cond.; Scottish Chamber Orchestra; Scottish Chamber Chorus] (Telarc 80302) ♪ ♪ ♪ ♪

Crackling thunder and other special sound effects enliven an effervescent performance, brilliantly conducted by Mackerras. Hadley's Tamino is one of his best performances ever.

influences: Franz Josef Haydn, Michael Haydn, Ludwig van Beethoven, Johann Sebastian Bach, Franz Schubert, Johannes Brahms, George Frideric Handel, Frédéric Chopin, Antonín Dvořák, Piotr Illych Tchaikovsky

William Gerard and Nancy Ann Lee

Modest Mussorgsky

Born Modest Petrovich Mussorgsky, March 21,1839, in Karevo, Russia. Died March 28, 1881 in St. Petersburg, Russia.

period: Romantic

Although Modest Mussorgsky's most famous composition, *Pictures at an Exhibition,* began life as a solo piano suite, it has become familiar to most concert audiences via the orchestral arrangement that Serge Koussevitzky commissioned from Maurice Ravel in 1922. Of the true handful of orchestral works that Mussorgsky actually composed, only the short, exciting *St. John's Night on the Bare Mountain* is programmed with any frequency. His powerful song cycles, *Sunless* and *Songs and Dances of Death,* are rarely heard, and his masterpiece, *Boris Godunov,* may be the greatest Russian opera in history but it is infrequently performed.

Mussorgsky's background was as part of the noble, landed gentry, but his heritage was also a military one. It was this factor that guided his father when he enrolled Modest and his older brother in the Cadet School of the Guards in 1852, despite a demonstrated interest and talent in music on the part of Modest that included his playing a piano concerto by John Field when he was only nine years old. Mussorgsky managed to study some music history at the school, in addition to continuing private piano lessons that he had begun with Anton Herke prior to his enrollment, and garnered favor with his fellow students through his abilities as a pianist. Upon graduation in 1856, Mussorgsky entered the Preobrazhensky Regiment, an elite part of the Imperial Guard. There, according to one of his biographers (Nikolai Kompaneysky), he "strutted like a rooster, dressed smartly, spoke excellent French, danced even better, played the piano splendidly and sang beautifully, and even learned how to get drunk . . . ." He also came in contact with the young doctor/chemist Alexander Borodin later that year when both were assigned to the same military hospital.

In 1857 Mussorgsky met established composer Alexander Dargomïzhsky and César Cui, a young military officer who, like him, dabbled in composition. Through them he made the acquaintance of Mily Balakirev, whom he eventually persuaded to give him lessons with the aim of becoming a better composer. The two of them undertook this task by playing piano four-hand versions of works by Ludwig van Beethoven, Franz Schubert, and Mikhail Glinka, and attempting to analyze their structure. Nicolai Rimsky-Korsakov once wrote that Balakirev was "an excellent pianist, a superior sight reader of music, [and] a splendid improviser" but also noted that Balakirev "had never had any systematic course in harmony and counterpoint and had not even superficially applied himself to them." Despite this apparent drawback, Rimsky-Korsakov, Mussorgsky, and the others in the group that would later become known as the "Mighty Five" often deferred to the elder musician because they felt that "he was a marvelous critic, especially a *technical* critic." During this period, Mussorgsky began to write songs and a number of piano works as exercises for Balakirev.

Mussorgsky succumbed to a kind of mental malaise in 1858 during which he resigned his commission; he claimed that a "laziness and indolence" had came over him, and later that year Cui noted Mussorgsky's tendency to spend "half a day thinking about what he will do tomorrow and the other half about what he did yesterday."

In 1861, Rimsky-Korsakov joined the circle of composers around Balakirev, which by then also included Borodin in addition to Cui and Mussorgsky. The emancipation of serfs at that same time resulted in Mussorgsky spending most of the next two years helping to manage the family estate. This formidable task proved more than he could handle and he ended up entering the civil service, working for the Ministry of Communications until he was dismissed in 1867. His compositions from 1859 until 1863 totaled a few piano pieces, the incidental music to *Oedipus in Athens,* and a few songs. Mussorgsky also began working on the libretto for an opera based on Gustave Flaubert's *Salammbô*, a project which occupied him off and on through the summer of 1866 before he finally abandoned it. After he lost his job, Mussorgsky spent the summer of 1867 at his brother's country house, Minkino Farm, where he wrote his first important orchestral work, *St. John's Night on the Bare Mountain.*

Early in 1869 Mussorgsky re-entered government service and, living with old friends under more settled con-

Medieval Liturgical Dramas: Taking the Mystery Out of Mystery Plays

During the ninth century, as a way of instructing an illiterate peasantry who did not understand the Latin of the church service, certain portions of the Bible were acted out by clergy. The first of these rudimentary "plays" was either the scene at the tomb on Easter Sunday, or the story of the Magi bringing gifts at Christmas time. These little performances (often with chant or added music, called tropes) later evolved into plays and music dramas that were held out on the porch of the church or in an area next to the church. By the sixteenth century, various guilds of potters, weavers, and carpenters had been given the responsibility of producing many of these plays.

"Mystery plays" were usually based on scripture and recounted a Biblical story, with favorite topics including Noah's Flood and Daniel being thrown into the lion's den; "miracle plays" found their inspiration in the lives of particular saints and the deeds they accomplished. Noah Greenburg recorded *The Play of Daniel* with New York Pro Musica (MCA 10102) back in the 1950s, and the CD repackaging also offers *The Play of Herod* for those wishing to experiment with both mystery plays and miracle plays. Andrew Lawrence-King and the Harp Consort (Deutsche Harmonia Mundi 77395) feature more up-to-date sonics and just *The Play of Daniel.*

"Morality plays," on the other hand, featured newer texts (relatively speaking) and concerned themselves with topics like the struggle between good and evil. One of the most interesting of the morality plays was written by the Abbess Hildegard von Bingen in the twelfth century. In her *Ordo Virtutum (The Book of Virtues),* the virtues contend with the Devil for the deliverance of the human soul and eventually win, just like the white hats used to do in Westerns. The German ancient-music group Sequentia has recorded this work twice, with their most recent version (Deutsche Harmonia Mundi 77394) receiving a fair number of awards. By the way, the only speaking part in the play is reserved for the Devil, who is not allowed to sing a note.

Dave Wagner

ditions, managed to complete the full score for the original version of *Boris Godunov* by December. The piece was eventually rejected by the Mariinsky Theatre, and Mussorgsky set out to drastically revise it. Although excerpts of *Boris Godunov* would be subsequently performed in various settings, in 1872 the work was again rejected, this time by the opera committee of the Imperial Theatres. In 1873, following a benefit performance for the stage manager of the Mariinsky Theatre, that opera committee finally accepted the work and a successful production was mounted at the theater in February 1874.

Though Mussorgsky changed living quarters a couple of times, he meanwhile began work on another historical opera, *Khovanshchina*. Progress on the score was interrupted partly because of Mussorgsky's unsettled housing circumstances at the time, but more due to his heavy drinking, which left him incapable of sustained creative effort. Several additional compositions belong to this period, including the song cycles *Bez solntsa (Sunless)* and *Pesni i plyaski smerti (Songs and Dances of Death)* and the cycle of piano pieces, *Karttinski s vïstavki (Pictures at an Exhibition)*—a brilliant and bold series inspired by a memorial exhibition of architectural drawings, stage designs, and watercolors by his friend Victor Hartmann. Mussorgsky also began to pursue his idea for a comic opera based on a story by Gogol, an activity that competed with his work on *Khovanshchina*. He eventually tucked *St. John's Night on the Bare Mountain* into his subsequent opera *Sorochintsï Fair* after he was unable to arrange a first performance of the orchestral work. Based on Russian folk tales about witches and Satan, *Bare Mountain* was extracted from the opera by Rimsky-Korsakov, who then edited it and published it under the title by which it is known today. Both *Khovanshchina.* and *Sorochintsï Fair*, however, remained unfinished at Mussorgsky's death.

During the earlier part of 1878 Mussorgsky seems to have led a more respectable life, and in 1879 his employer at his latest state job even gave him leave for a three-month concert tour with the contralto Darya Leonora. After he was obliged to leave government service again in January 1880, Leonora helped provide him with employment and a home. After a series of seizures he was taken to the Nikolayevsky Military Hospital on February 26, 1881, and though his health rallied temporarily, chronic alcoholism finally took its toll when he died there a month later.

Orchestra
Karttinski s vïstavki (Pictures at an Exhibition) (arranged by Maurice Ravel)
what to buy: [Lorin Maazel, cond.; Cleveland Orchestra] (Telarc, 80042) ♪ ♪ ♪ ♪₎

This 1978 recording by Maazel and the Cleveland Orchestra is among the many top-notch versions of Ravel's orchestration. The conductor captures all of the work's detail and drama in a crisp-sounding yet sensitive interpretation. Leading off the program is Mussorgsky's bold, brassy *St. John's Night on the Bare Mountain*.

[Claudio Abbado, cond.; London Symphony Orchestra] (Penguin Classics 460633) ♪ ♪ ♪ ♪₎

Abbado's rendition of the Ravel arrangement would be a prime recommendation at full-price and is an even better one in this mid-priced edition. The pairing is particularly felicitous, with three of Ravel's other works acting as filler: the composer's torrid orchestral bonbon, *Bolero,* the popular *Rhapsodie espagnole,* and *La Valse.*

what to buy next: [Leonard Bernstein, cond.; New York Philharmonic Orchestra] (Sony Classics 36726) ♪ ♪ ♪ ♪

This grandiose Bernstein interpretation of the Ravel version invites you to crank up the volume, but lacks some of the sophistication of the Maazel and Abbado versions. *St. John's Night on the Bare Mountain* follows *Pictures* and works almost as a continuation of the other piece, with similar boldness and light, dancing strings.

[Valéry Polyansky, cond.; Russian State Symphony Orchestra] (Chandos 9497) ♪ ♪ ♪ ♪

Polyansky has developed quite a reputation as one of Russia's finest conductors, especially in later twentieth century scores by Alfred Schnittke and Dmitri Shostakovich. His conducting in this somewhat earlier piece is suitably dark, deliberate, and majestic. Mussorgsky provides the base for the other works here as well: Rimsky-Korsakov's arrangement of the *Three Symphonic Choruses* and Vissarion Shebalin's 1932 treatment of Act 3, no. 2 from the opera *Sorochintsï Fair.*

Chamber
Karttinski s vïstavki (Pictures at an Exhibition)
what to buy: [John Browning, piano] (Delos 1008) ♪ ♪ ♪ ♪₎

Browning's disc is an all-Mussorgsky recital, with only Rachmaninoff's arrangement of *Hoska* from *Sorochintsï Fair* to detract from its purity. The *Pictures* heard here is one of the finest available, musically unpretentious and well recorded. The composer's crafty *Sonata in C Major for Piano Four Hands* features an overdubbed Browning, and the *Impromptu Passioné* which closes out the set deserves to be heard more often.

[*The Sofia Recital 1958*; Sviatoslav Richter, piano] (Philips 464734) ♪ ♪ ♪ ♪₎

Richter's performance is sterling, if sabotaged by a noisy audience even modern remastering was not able to adjust for. If you can ignore this then the depth and consistency of the pianist's interpretive powers is of the highest order. The balance of the disc is taken up with works by Schubert, Liszt, and Rachmaninoff.

[Vladimir Horowitz, piano] (RCA Victor Gold Seal 60449) ♪ ♪ ♪ ♪₂

Recorded at a concert in 1951, Horowitz plays his own version of *Pictures,* one that luckily enough doesn't veer too far from that of the composer's. His playing is magnificent throughout, especially in *The Great Gate of Kiev* sequence. The other major work on this attractively priced disc is Horowitz's rendition of Tchaikovsky's first piano concerto, with Arturo Toscanini conducting the NBC Symphony Orchestra.

what to buy next: [Alfred Brendel, piano] (Vox Classics 7203) ♪ ♪ ♪ ♪

It is rare to find such a compelling performance at such a low price. Brendel recorded this back in 1955 and his playing was powerful and exciting, if not quite as cerebral as it would later become. As to the remainder of the disc, his rendition of Balakirev's *Islamey* is one of the finest on record, though Stravinsky's three-movement suite from *Petrouchka* has been better served by Shura Cherkassky and Mauricio Pollini.

[Nikolai Demidenko, piano] (Hyperion 67018) ♪ ♪ ♪₂

The combination of virtuoso piano playing and good engineering heard in Demidenko's performance makes his version of *Pictures* a technical tour de force if not a first choice. Had Richter been given this kind of engineering support and a less colicky audience, he would have had an unbeatable recommendation. A lack of poetry in *Gnomus* and *The Old Castle* eventually gives way to more sympathetic playing, and by the time Demidenko reaches *The Great Gate of Kiev* his performance has evolved considerably. Selections by Sergei Prokofiev (the Toccata for Piano in D Minor, op. 11, and the ten *Pieces for Piano* from *Romeo and Juliet,* op. 75) are admirable adjuncts to the recital.

Vocal
Songs and Dances of Death for Voice and Piano
what to buy: [Lina Mkrtchyan, contralto; Yevgeny Talisman, piano] (Opus 111 30-235) ♪ ♪ ♪ ♪₂

Mkrtchyan's luxurious, low tones convey a multitude of

Michael Murray:
No musical instrument has engendered such devotion or scorn as the pipe organ. To paraphrase an old musical joke, "Many people don't like organ music, but they like the noise it makes." In the early days of long-playing recordings, those who wanted a performance influenced by scholarship would turn to E. Power Biggs. Those who wanted to just bathe in the sheer sound of the instrument and appreciate an emotional, personal interpretation would find Virgil Fox their musical patron saint. It seemed at one time that that divide would never be bridged by any one individual.

Times have changed, however, and in the person of the American organist Michael Murray, these two seemingly irreconcilable approaches meet on more neutral ground. With a love of French Romantic organ literature and studies with two of its most distinguished proponents (Marcel Dupré and Jean Langlais), Murray's music-making is also a consummation of the two traditions represented by Biggs and Fox.

Murray first burst on the musical scene performing an all-Bach recital in 1968, and followed that with a series of all-Franck recitals in 1970. Though Murray truly loves the music of Johann Sebastian Bach, the French Romantic school of César Franck, Louis Vierne, Charles Tournemire, and Dupré is where his heart is. There are more than thirty recordings to Murray's credit, but in particular look for his specialty on a fine recording of the *Complete Masterworks of César Franck* (Telarc 80234). Here Murray's thorough understanding of the music is displayed on one of the original Cavaillé-Coll organs at Saint Sernin Basilica of Toulouse, making this repertoire sing as if the Belgian master composer himself were seated at the *grand orgue.*

You will find a loving portrait by Murray of his teacher in *Marcel Dupré: The Work of a Master Organist* (Boston University Press). Murray has also written a book on the musical life of Albert Schweitzer (*Albert Schweitzer, Musician,* Scholar Press), and recently completed one on the French organ school of the nineteenth and twentieth centuries (*French Masters of the Organ,* Yale University Press).

Dave Wagner

emotions and work wonders in Mussorgsky's most important song cycle. Her characterizations in this quartet of tunes are most convincing, and with the translated lyrics included, it is easy to follow the compact dramas underlying each piece. *Marfa's Song,* an aria from *Khovanshchina,* is also part of the program, as is Georgi Sviridov's song cycle *Russia Adrift.*

what to buy next: [Dmitri Hvorostovsky, baritone; Valery Gergiev, cond.; Kirov Orchestra, St. Petersburg] (Philips 438872) ♪ ♪ ♪ ♪

On Dmitri Shostakovich's orchestral arrangement of Mussorgsky's song cycle, Hvorostovsky displays one of the deepest, richest baritones to come out of Russia in the later stages of the twentieth century. The combination is nigh unto unbeatable. While the *Songs and Dances of Death* remains the principle reason for picking this program up, the rest of the material—arias from Russian operas by Rimsky-Korsakov, Borodin, Sergei Rachmaninoff, and Anton Rubinstein—reveals Hvorostovsky to be a singer capable of lustrous tone production and fine characterizations.

[Marjana Lipovsek, mezzo-soprano; Graham Johnson, piano] (Sony Classics 66858) ♪ ♪ ♪ ♪

This is a wonderful collection that features Mussorgsky's three important song cycles: his early *The Nursery,* the impressive *Sunless,* and the richly textured *Songs and Dances of Death.* If Lipovsek is not as convincing a singer as Mkrtchyan in the *Songs and Dances of Death,* there have been few who were. The inclusion of the other song cycles makes this a good buy for the (relatively) economy-minded.

Boris Godunov
what to buy: [Valentina Valente, soprano; Marjana Lipovsek, mezzo-soprano; Liliana Nichiteanu, mezzo-soprano; Yevgenia Gorokhovskaya, mezzo-soprano; Elena Zaremba, mezzo-soprano; Philip Langridge, tenor; Sergei Larin, tenor; Helmuth Wildhaber, tenor; Alexander Fedin, tenor; Sergei Leiferkus, baritone; Albert Shagidullin, baritone; Wojciech Drabowicz, baritone; Anatoly Kotcherga, bass; Samuel Ramey, bass; Gleb Nikolsky, bass; Mikhail Krutikov, bass; Claudio Abbado, cond.; Berlin Philharmonic Orchestra; Berlin Radio Chorus; Slovak State Philharmonic Chorus; Tölz Boys Choir] (Sony Classics 58977) ♪ ♪ ♪ ♪

Kotcherga's Boris is a powerfully characterized one, if a tad over the top, and Langride is a delightfully evil Shuisky. Where this recording most shines, however, is in Abbado's handling of the orchestra rather than in the vocal portions of Mussorgsky's score.

[(1869 version) Olga Trifonova, soprano; Liubov Sokolova, soprano; Evgenya Gorochovskaya, contralto; Zlata Bulycheva, alto; Viktor Lutsuk, tenor; Nikolai Gassiev, tenor; Konstantin Pluzhnikov, tenor; Evgeny Akimov, tenor; Yuri Laptev, tenor; Nikolai Putilin, baritone; Vassily Gerello, baritone; Evgeny Nikitin, bass-baritone; Grigory Karassev, bass-baritone; Nikolai Ohotnikov, bass; Fyodor Kuznetsov, bass; Valery Gergiev, cond.; Kirov Opera Orchestra; Kirov Opera Chorus]

[(1872 version) Olga Trifonova, soprano; Liubov

Sokolova, soprano; Evgenya Gorochovskaya, contralto; Zlata Bulycheva, alto; Vladimir Galusin, tenor; Nikolai Gassiev, tenor; Konstantin Pluzhnikov, tenor; Evgeny Akimov, tenor; Yuri Laptev, tenor; Yuri Schikalov, tenor; Vladimir Vaneev, baritone; Vassily Gerello, baritone; Evgeny Nikitin, bass-baritone; Grigory Karassev, bass-baritone; Nikolai Ohotnikov, bass; Fyodor Kuznetsov, bass; Valery Gergiev, cond.; Kirov Opera Orchestra; Kirov Opera Chorus] (Philips 462230) ♪ ♪ ♪ ♪

This five-CD set lets you see the "before" and "after" of Mussorgsky's own *Boris.* First up is the 1869 version, a shorter, more succinct one in some ways but lacking in the dramatic buildup afforded the 1872 reworking. Nikolai Putilin is Boris in the earlier rendition and Vladimir Vaneev takes over the role in the later version, while Viktor Lutsuk and Vladimir Galusin split the role of Grigory, the Pretender. Otherwise the casting remains the same, with Olga Trifonova as Xenia, Konstantin Pluzhnikov as the villainous Shuisky, and Nikolai Ohotnikov as Pimen. For those listeners who are already acquainted with this opera and love it dearly, this recording will give critical insights into Mussorgsky's creative process as they hear the changes worked upon the score and the characters. Of particular note is the development of Grigory from fanatic to power-mad Pretender.

what to buy next: [Galina Vishnevskaya, soprano; Catherine Dubosc, soprano; Mira Zakai, contralto; Matthew Adam Fish, alto; Vyacheslav Polozov, tenor; Misha Raitzin, tenor; Kenneth Riegel, tenor; Nicolai Gedda, tenor; Thomas Booth, tenor; Michael Pastor, tenor; Ruggero Raimondi, baritone; Lajos Miller, baritone; Stefan Szkafarowsky, baritone; Jacques Trigeau, baritone; Malcolm Smith, bass-baritone; Richard Cowan, bass-baritone; Paul Plishka, bass; Nikita Strorojev, bass; Romuald Tesarowicz, bass; Mstislav Rostropovich, cond.; National Symphony Orchestra; Choral Arts Society of Washington, choir; Oratorio Society of Washington, choir; Chevy Chase Elementary School Chorus] (Erato 45418) ♪ ♪ ♪ ♪

Raimondi's characterization is more impressive than his tonal quality, a matter for consideration if you are looking more for a superbly acted Boris than a powerfully sung one. The real standout from both a singing *and* dramatic standpoint in this production is Vishnevskaya's Marina, who smolders before bursting into flames. Rostropovich utilizes the 1872 Mussorgsky revision and turns in one of his better performances from the podium.

[Halina Lukomska, soprano; Bozena Kinasz, mezzo-soprano; Stefania Toczyska, mezzo-soprano; Wiera Baniewicz, mezzo-soprano; Nicolai Gedda, tenor; Bohdan Paprocki, tenor; Kazimierz Pustelak, tenor; Paulos Raptis, tenor; Andrzej Hiolski, baritone; Martti Talvela, bass; Leonard Andrzej Mróz, bass; Aage Haugland, bass; Kazimierz Sergiel, bass; Wlodzimierz Zalewski, bass; Jerzy Semkow, cond.; Polish Radio National Symphony; Polish Radio Chorus, Krakow; Boys's Chorus from Krakow Philharmonic Chorus] (EMI 54377) ♪ ♪ ♪⅛

This performance by Semkow and company was the first-ever complete recording of Mussorgsky's 1872 scoring, and deserves a place of honor for that. Talvela's Boris is well sung, as is Gedda's Grigory/Dimitri, but the field is a bit more crowded nowadays and the competition has gotten tougher.

influences: Nikolai Rimsky-Korsakov, Alexander Borodin, Sergei Rachmaninov, Dmitri Shostakovich, Alfred Schnittke

Nancy Ann Lee and Mathilde August

Conlon Nancarrow
Born October 27, 1912, in Texarkana, AR. Died August 10, 1997, in Mexico City, Mexico.

period: Twentieth century

When Fats Waller or George Gershwin cut piano rolls, they sought to play their songs as you would hear them in live performance. Conlon Nancarrow took the player piano one giant (but logical) step further, using the programming possibilities of the instrument to create his own personal computer/orchestra and programming it with metrical concepts that put his scores beyond the reach of human pianists. For instance, his early *Toccata* was originally scored for violin and piano, but Nancarrow rearranged it for player piano because he wanted the music played faster and cleaner, closer to the actual tempo markings than any flesh-and-blood pianist was capable of. His monumental, ever-evolving *Studies for Player Piano* may turn out to be one of the most important musical documents of the twentieth century.

Conlon Nancarrow's unique musical vision may have

originated in an article that Henry Cowell published in 1930 called "New Musical Resources," in which Cowell posed the idea of dividing a whole note into five, six, and seven equal parts and meshing the three resulting tempos together. In a later article Cowell asked, "Why not hear music from player piano rolls on which have been punched holes giving the ratios of rhythms of the most exquisite subtlety?" There is evidence that Nancarrow read "New Musical Resources" in 1939 but scant information as to whether he ever saw the second essay. Nevertheless, it is almost indisputable that Cowell had articulated the vision that helped set Nancarrow on his own peculiar creative journey.

Early musical influences in the Nancarrow household revolved around the player piano, which was stocked with rolls of music by Frédéric Chopin and Edward MacDowell. Young Conlon was more interested in learning jazz trumpet at the time, however, attempting to reproduce the performances of his hero, Louis Armstrong. In 1930, while attending the Cincinnati College Conservatory of Music and playing trumpet in various groups around the city, Nancarrow heard Igor Stravinsky's *Le Sacre du printemps* and was mesmerized by the rhythmic complexities of the score. He moved to Boston in 1934, where he studied composition and counterpoint with Nicolas Slonimsky, Walter Piston, and Roger Sessions, and conducting with Arthur Fiedler. He then went to Europe for two months in 1936 as part of a jazz band, returning there the following year to fight fascism as a member of the Abraham Lincoln Brigade in the Spanish Civil War.

When he came back to the United States in 1939, Nancarrow's socialist views made him persona non grata with the American government, which refused to grant him a passport. He moved to New York City, where he tried his hand as a critic for *Modern Music* and met fellow composers Elliott Carter, Aaron Copland, and Wallingford Riegger. Some of his compositions were already in print, including *Sarabande and Scherzo* (1930), *Blues for Piano* (1935), and *Toccata* (1935), but this was not enough to keep him in the United States after his request for a passport was denied. Instead, Nancarrow moved to Mexico in 1940, establishing residency in Mexico City and finally becoming a Mexican citizen in 1956.

Some critics believe that Nancarrow's turning to the player piano was a consequence of his moving to Mexico and away from the classical music hub of New York City, while others point to his frustration with the limitations of musicians and their inability to play music at the precise tempos he desired. He didn't abandon more conventional means at first, since he wrote a Septet in 1940 and continued creating music for conventional forces through the mid-1940s. All the while, however, he was pondering Cowell's ideas, finally moving to realize his own vision of those concepts when he visited New York City in 1947 to purchase his own player piano, along with a machine to punch out the requisite piano rolls. With his newly acquired equipment, Nancarrow laboriously proceeded to compose over fifty *Studies for Player Piano.*

Six of his early *Studies* were choreographed by Merce Cunningham in 1960, and by the late 1970s recognition of his abilities and ideas had spread beyond a small circle of admirers. This phenomenon was aided by the publication of some of his studies by Soundings Press and by recordings of those works on 1750 Arch Records, a small company devoted to esoteric music. In 1982 he received a "genius grant" of $300,000 as a MacArthur fellow, which led adventurous musicians to seek Nancarrow out. This led to his writing *Two Canons for Ursula,* commissioned for Ursula Oppens by the Composers Forum in 1988, and the Quartet for Strings, no. 3, commissioned by the Arditti Quartet the same year. The flurry of recognition led him to teach classes at Mills College and to journey around the world to speak about his musical ideas and attend performances of his works. In 1990 he received an honorary doctorate from the New England Conservatory.

Orchestral
Studies for Player Piano (arranged by Yvar Mikhashoff)
worth searching for: [*Studies*; Ingo Metzmacher, cond.; Ensemble Modern, orch.] (RCA Victor Red Seal 61180) ♪ ♪ ♪ ♪♪

With the composer's approval, pianist Mikhashoff made orchestral arrangements of eleven of Nancarrow's earliest *Studies for Player Piano,* with results that can be heard on this remarkably accessible album. *Study no. 3c,* for which Nancarrow suggested the instrumentation, reveals the jazz trumpeter he once was, with swinging blue notes on trumpet suggesting the young Miles Davis as arranged by Gil Evans or Oliver Nelson. Mikhashoff also provides charts for *Tango?* and *Toccata,* but the rest of the disc includes early works for more conventional instrumentation, such as the *Piece no. 2 for Small Orchestra, Trio,* and Nancarrow's earliest surviving composition, the *Sarabande and Scherzo* from 1930.

Chamber
Studies for Player Piano, Vols. 1–5
what to buy: [Conlon Nancarrow, player piano] (Wergo 6907) ♪ ♪ ♪ ♪ ♪

Recorded in 1988 on Nancarrow's own custom-altered 1927 Ampico reproducing piano, this five-CD set is authoritative and unlikely to be duplicated anytime soon. While it's not as accessible as the Ensemble Modern recording, the same jazz-inflected rhythms pop up all over the place. So do some amazing sonic effects, especially when the work is scored for two player pianos. This set is a must for anybody interested in the composer.

Two Canons for Ursula

what to buy: [*American Piano Music of Our Time*; Ursula Oppens, piano] (Music & Arts 862) ♪ ♪ ♪ ♪₄

After gaining some notoriety for his player-piano works, Nancarrow created a few human-powered pieces, including this set for Ursula Oppens. Her benchmark performance of these striking scores is part of a two-disc compilation that also features Nancarrow's *Tango?* and works by William Bolcom, Elliott Carter, John Adams, and other twentieth-century composers.

various works

worth searching for: [*Conlon Nancarrow: Lost Works, Last Works*; Conlon Nancarrow, player piano; Trimpin, pianola; Trimpin, "Conloninpurple" instrument] (Other Minds 1002) ♪ ♪ ♪ ♪₄

Not all of Nancarrow's works for player piano are accounted for in the excellent Wergo set, and this collection displays some of those missing pieces, as well as a two-minute bit of musique concrète he created in the 1950s. The disc also includes an interview Nancarrow did with Charles Amirkhanian in 1977, in which he discusses the making of his hole-punching machine, favorite jazz artists, canons, and other topics. Trimpin, the German-born engineer who invented machines capable of translating Nancarrow's piano rolls into MIDI files, is responsible for roughly half of this material being salvaged. Kyle Gann, who authored the definitive Nancarrow biography, wrote the liner notes, putting the music into perspective. This album is available from Other Minds, 333 Valencia Street, Suite 303, San Francisco, CA 94103-3552.

influences: Henry Cowell, Charles Ives, Igor Stravinsky, Roger Sessions, Milton Babbitt, Pierre Boulez, Karlheinz Stockhausen, Iannis Xenakis, György Ligeti

Garaud MacTaggart

Alfred Newman

Born March 17, 1901, in New Haven, CT. Died February 17, 1970, in Los Angeles, CA.

period: Twentieth century

Probably the finest all-around musician who ever worked in Hollywood, Newman was a brilliant conductor and a superb executive, arranger, and judge of talent. He was also a first-rate composer for films, with an eclectic style that enabled him to write for everything from Westerns to religious epics.

A child prodigy, Newman became the sole support of his family while still in his teens; by the 1920s he was already a veteran theater conductor who had worked with such Broadway luminaries as George Gershwin, Irving Berlin, Al Jolson, and the team of Rodgers and Hart. It was Berlin who brought Newman to Hollywood in 1930 to arrange and conduct a musical called *Reaching for the Moon.* Newman performed a similar function for Charlie Chaplin's *City Lights,* a silent film with a recorded musical soundtrack.

Newman never went back to New York. He threw himself into the movie business, working first at United Artists and then for 20th Century Fox, where in 1939 he became the General Music Director, a position he held until 1960. (Newman's single most famous composition may well be the 20th Century Fox fanfare, still in use today.) After leaving Fox, he worked as a freelance composer and conductor; his last completed work was for the film *Airport.*

Although he preferred to conduct, Newman wrote a great deal of original music during his Hollywood career, much of it under murderous deadline pressure. (It was reputedly Newman who coined that famous movie music quote, "They don't want it good, they want it Thursday.") As head of the Fox music department, he was responsible for budgets and assignments, hiring and firing, and maintaining the studio's musical organization. In this capacity his influence was instrumental in furthering the careers of composers whose work he admired, including Bernard Herrmann, David Raksin and Hugo Friedhofer.

Newman was perhaps the most honored musician in Hollywood history. He worked on approximately 230 films, was nominated for forty-five Academy Awards, and actually won the Oscar nine times, in various categories. His first Oscar for Best Original Score came in 1943 for *The Song of Bernadette,* an assignment he got after Igor Stravinsky withdrew from the project.

Newman was also the senior member of a remarkable musical family. His younger brothers Emil and Lionel joined him in California before going on to successful conducting and composing careers. His sons, David and Thomas, are among the most talented composers working in Hollywood today. And Randy Newman, the well-known pop musician who has also done a number of film scores, is Alfred's nephew.

Orchestral
various film scores
what to buy: [*Captain from Castille: The Classic Film Scores of Alfred Newman*; Charles Gerhardt, cond.; National Philharmonic Orchestra; Band of the Grenadier Guards; Ambrosian Singers, choir] (RCA Victor 0184) ♪ ♪ ♪₄

This is one of the outstanding albums in RCA's Classic Film Score series and a fine introduction to Newman's work, showcasing his chameleonic ability to adapt to any genre. From the bluesy, Gershwinesque *Street Scene* to the soaring romanticism of *The Robe* and the stupendous march from *Captain from Castille* (which USC football fans will recognize), this recording shows that Newman was a composer for all seasons.

what to buy next: [*Wuthering Heights: A Tribute to Alfred Newman*; Richard Kaufman, cond.; New Zealand Symphony Orchestra] (Koch International Classics 7376) ♪ ♪ ♪

In addition to featuring a lovely *Wuthering Heights* suite, this excellent disc includes some never-before-available music from such fine scores as *Prince of Foxes, Dragonwyck, Brigham Young,* and *The Prisoner of Zenda* (which was used twice—once in 1937 and again in 1952 when MGM remade the film in color).

influences: Max Steiner, Franz Waxman, Bernard Herrmann

Jack Goggin

Otto Nicolai
Born Carl Otto Ehrenfried Nicolai, June 9, 1810, in Königsberg, Prussia. Died May 11, 1849, in Berlin, Germany.

period: Romantic

Once thought to be a compositional "one trick pony" for the opera *Die lustigen Weiber von Windsor (The Merry Wives of Windsor)*, recent research has revealed Nicolai as a musicologist, virtuoso keyboard performer, chorale conductor, and orchestral coach/founder.

An immensely talented composer filled with undeserved self-doubts, Otto Nicolai missed the fame and fiscal rewards that *The Merry Wives of Windsor* could have brought him if his life had not been cut short by a stroke at the age of thirty-nine. His formative years were not happy ones. While he was still a child, his mother and father (a professional musician himself) saw the musical gifts of their young son and hoped to benefit financially by displaying their offspring as a prodigy. The younger Nicolai chafed under the harsh treatment of his father and successfully ran away from home at the age of sixteen. He then came under the protection of a civil servant named August Adler, who took him in and eventually secured the funds enabling Nicolai to study music in Berlin. He finally completed his training, mostly in the vocal arts, at the Royal Institute for Church Music in 1830.

Once he had graduated, Nicolai quickly established himself as a teacher, singer, pianist, and organist. One of his first coups as a performing artist occurred when he appeared in the role of Jesus during an early revival of Johann Sebastian Bach's *St. Matthew Passion.* Even though he fit in well among the wide range of musical organizations in Berlin, Nicolai was the prototypical "starving young artist." He managed to get some early compositions published, but this was no guarantee of cash flow either. He finally became organist of the Prussian embassy chapel in Rome in 1833, and quickly found himself in demand as an underpaid keyboard player for a variety of state functions.

It was in Italy that Nicolai first became interested in older music, eventually becoming somewhat of an expert in the work of Giovanni Palestrina and of the Gabrielis (Andrea and Giovanni). It was, however, the attraction of the theater that turned his attention away from musical scholarship to composition. When he wrote a funeral cantata on the occasion of Vincenzo Bellini's death, his introduction to the world of the theater was underway. After failing to find funding to support the writing of his first opera, Nicolai moved to Vienna, where he established himself as a singing teacher and choir master at the Hoftheater in 1837. He returned to Italy a year later and finally got the chance to stage his first opera, a melodrama called *Enrico II.* After mixed responses to his next three operas, Nicolai shifted his base of operations back to Vienna, where he eventually found employment as the principal conductor with the Vienna Hofoper in 1841. The very next year he booked a successful series of concerts devoted to Ludwig van Beethoven's symphonies. By 1844 it appeared that Nicolai's star was finally rising, but this too proved illusory. He was offered the position of Director of Music at a cathedral in Berlin after Felix Mendelssohn declined to accept the appointment, but Nicolai turned down this opportunity, hoping instead that he would be offered a similar position with the Berlin Opera. When this didn't materialize, he went back to the Hofoper and resumed his conductorial slot until 1847. This was the year that his initial concept for *The Merry Wives of Windsor* was rejected and he resigned from the company. With this rejection he thought of emigrating to either London or St. Petersburg to try his luck as a composer, but his fortune changed for the better in 1848. In that year he went back to Berlin and took over the leadership of both the cathedral choir and the opera company. He worked on and finally completed *The Merry Wives of Windsor* for an initial production on March 9, 1849, just two months and two days before he suffered a major stroke while conducting the choir in a special concert. Nicolai died on the same day that he was awarded membership in the Royal Academy of Arts, and never realized the financial and artistic rewards generated by his operatic masterpiece.

Orchestral
Die lustigen Weber von Windsor: Overture
what to buy: [*The Royal Edition: Opera Overtures*; Leonard Bernstein, cond.; New York Philharmonic Orchestra] (Sony Classics 47601) ♪ ♪ ♪ ♪

Bernstein conducts with all the flair of his younger days and the bold sound of the New York Philharmonic to match his mood. Also on the disc are overtures by Bedrich Smetana (*The Bartered Bride*), Wolfgang Amadeus Mozart (*Le nozze di Figaro*), Johann Strauss, Jr. (*Die Fledermaus*), and more.

Kirchliche Festovertüre über "Ein feste Burg," op. 31
what to buy: [Max Jurowski, cond.; Cologne West German Radio Symphony Orchestra] (Capriccio 10592) ♪ ♪ ♪ ♪

Here is an all-Nicolai disc, with this very interesting yet seldom-heard church festival overture (based on the Lutheran chorale *A Mighty Fortress Is Our God*) and the

Fantasie et variations brillantes sur "Norma" for Piano and Orchestra, plus overtures from his operas *The Merry Wives of Windsor, Il templario,* and *Die Heimkehr des Verbannten*. This is a great recording and well worth having.

Vocal
Die lustigen Weber von Windsor (The Merry Wives of Windsor)
what to buy: [Edith Mathis, soprano; Helen Donath, soprano; Hanna Schwarz, mezzo-soprano; Peter Schreier, tenor; Bernd Weikl, baritone; Karl Moll, bass; Siegfried Vogel, bass; Bernard Klee, cond.; Berlin Staatskapelle, orch.; Berlin German Opera Chorus] (Berlin Classics 2115) ♪ ♪ ♪ ♪ ♪

This is the same 1976 recording that used to be available on Deutsche Grammophon, and is still the one to beat. Blessed with superb sound and wonderfully cast voices, this is a truly stunning performance by all concerned, Mathis in particular.

influences: Engelbert Humperdinck, Felix Mendelssohn, Charles Gounod

Dave Wagner

Carl Nielsen
Born Carl August Nielsen, June 9, 1865, in Sortelung, Denmark. Died October 3, 1931, in Copenhagen, Denmark.

period: Romantic

A powerful symphonist whose career as an orchestra violinist and conductor gave him a keen insight into orchestral textures and colors, Nielsen towers over the Danish musical landscape in much the same way that his friend Jean Sibelius dominates the Finnish scene. His most frequently performed scores date from his maturity and include the third, fourth, and fifth symphonies, his Concerto for Clarinet and Orchestra, and the impressive Quintet for Winds.

The rural backdrop of Nielsen's early life includes a father who worked as a painter but brought extra money into the meager family coffers by playing violin and cornet for a variety of village functions and a mother who sang while working around the homestead. The son picked up his first music lessons from his father and was soon proficient enough to play in his father's band. Nielsen's first experience with classical music came from his exposure to a local amateur orchestra that played a variety of simpler works by eighteenth and nineteenth century composers. Upon adding the cornet to his musical arsenal, he joined a military orchestra, where he picked up the rudiments of music theory, taught himself to play piano, and played in a string quartet. Nielsen also dabbled in composition at this time, although he was yet to have any formal compositional training.

In 1884 he entered the Copenhagen Conservatory on what amounted to a scholarship, as he was financially backed by some admirers from his days in the military band. Although he appeared to be a mediocre student, his time at the school enabled him to further his studies in theory, music history, and violin playing, and he left two years later with a degree. During his postgraduate years, the budding musician held a series of temporary positions as a violinist in a number of Copenhagen-based orchestras while continuing his studies outside the confines of the school. Nielsen began studying composition in earnest in 1886, creating a few rudimentary works. His first piece to make an impact, the *Little Suite in A Minor for String Orchestra*, premiered in 1888 and marked the beginning of Nielsen's slow but sure development as a composer. The next year found him employed as a second violinist in the royal chapel under the direction of Johan Svendsen, a prominent conductor and composer of Norwegian descent, whose rural background was similar to Nielsen's and who took a keen interest in his works.

Nielsen's travels around Europe began with trip to Germany in 1890 to study Richard Wagner's music. A year later he went to Paris, where he met and married Anne Marie Brodersen; he then ventured on to Italy before returning to Denmark. By this time the young composer had already written his first symphony, in addition to a handful of chamber works. Over the next decade he embarked upon a maturing creative process that wound its way through operas (*Saul and David* and *Makarade*), songs, more chamber works, and yet another symphony. In 1910 he inaugurated his mature period with his third symphony, the *Sinfonia Espansiva*.

Nielsen had quit his post at the royal chapel in 1905 so that he could concentrate on composition, but he accepted the offer to succeed Svendsen as conductor at the Royal Theater in 1908. While this latter office had its

own set of demands, it secured Nielsen a steady income and a position of power within the Danish musical community without cutting too deeply into his composing time. Still, he wasn't cut out for the administrative politics of his new office, and even though he managed to write another pair of symphonies, he resigned in 1914. He renewed his association with the Copenhagen Conservatory the following year, progressing from teaching theory and composition to becoming director of the school in 1931, just before he died. Nielsen's major works during this time included the Quintet for Winds and the Concerto for Clarinet and Orchestra. He is still ranked as Denmark's greatest composer.

Orchestral
Symphony no. 5, op. 50
what to buy: [Leonard Bernstein, cond.; New York Philharmonic Orchestra] (Sony Classics 47598) ♪ ♪ ♪ ♪ ♪

Combining rhythmic power with the composer's unique orchestral voicings and thematic evolution, this is *the* work of genius for Nielsen, forming the cornerstone of any collection of his music. Bernstein understands this, delivering the mysterious opening, with woodwinds floating over a hushed orchestral backdrop, into the snare-drum-driven passages percolating through a string section tinged with Orientalisms. He works a similar magic with Nielsen's *Sinfonia Espansiva,* the composer's third symphony, where the soprano Ruth Guldbæk and the tenor Niels Møller intone the wordless lines that weave through the second movement. Bernstein also conducts the Royal Danish Symphony Orchestra in the *Sinfonia Espansiva.*

what to buy next: [Herbert Blomstedt, cond.; San Francisco Symphony Orchestra] (London 421524) ♪ ♪ ♪ ♪

While Blomstedt's performance of Nielsen's towering fifth is really quite good, the orchestral playing doesn't have the snap that Bernstein gets out of his New York players. That said, the accompanying work (Nielsen's fourth symphony, the *Inextinguishable*) benefits from an absolutely marvelous interpretation by Blomstedt and company that may be the best on the market.

Concerto for Clarinet and Orchestra, op. 57
what to buy: [Janet Hilton, clarinet; Matthias Bamert, cond.; Royal Scottish National Orchestra] (Chandos 8618) ♪ ♪ ♪ ♪

This work can be compared to Nielsen's fifth symphony in its use of a snare drum to break up the flow and act as an impetus for change. There is also a series of conflicting key relationships that makes this piece one of the composer's more challenging works. Still, Hilton's command of her instrument, combined with a sympathetic orchestra and conductor, makes this piece fit in well as part of an intriguing program that includes weighty twentieth-century works for clarinet and orchestra by Aaron Copland and Witold Lutoslawski.

what to buy next: [Walter Boeykens, clarinet; Jan Caeyers, cond.; Beethoven Academy, orch.] (Harmonia Mundi 7901489) ♪ ♪ ♪₈

A slightly smaller-scale rendition of Nielsen's concerto is the main focus of this all-Nielsen disc, but Boeykens is a major performer on clarinet and can hold his own with just about any of the other stars of his instrument. The other pieces on this disc are lighter in nature and serve as a pleasant counterbalance to the concerto. They include the composer's first big "hit," the *Little Suite,* as well as the overture to *Amor and the Poet* and the delightful *Pan and Syrinx.*

Chamber
Quintet for Winds, op. 43
what to buy: [*Favorite Music for Wind Quintet,* Frösunda Wind Quintet, ensemble] (BIS 136) ♪ ♪ ♪ ♪ ♪

This is a truly wonderful performance, part of a well-thought-out recital for winds that includes Jacques Ibert's pleasant if lightweight *Pièces Brèves* for Wind Quintet, three of Malcolm Arnold's lively essays for winds, and the *Antique Hungarian Dances* by Ferenc Farkas.

what to buy next: [Bergen Wind Quintet, ensemble] (BIS 428) ♪ ♪ ♪ ♪₈

For those seeking a deeper appreciation of Nielsen's chamber music, this might actually be a better choice than the recording by the Frösunda Wind Quintet. The playing is still high-quality, and the disc includes the composer's other major work for winds, the *Serenata in vano,* along with the *Canto serioso* for Horn and Piano, selections from the incidental music Nielsen created for *The Mother,* and a pair of early works centering respectively on oboe and clarinet.

influences: Johan Svendsen, Jørgen Bentzon, Robert Simpson

Garaud MacTaggart

Michael Nyman
Born Michael Laurence Nyman, March 23, 1944, in London, England.

period: Twentieth century

The first person to apply the term "minimalism" to music was British composer, critic, and scholar Michael Nyman. He didn't stop there, however, changing his own particular methodology from (as he put it) "a kind of Hindemith-Shostakovich style" to one more closely aligned with this newly-named concept. His most popular piece of music was the soundtrack score he wrote for *The Piano,* but there are brighter nuggets than that in his expansive oeuvre.

Nyman's educational background would seem to have destined him for life as an academic composer instead of a commercially viable one; he studied composition at the Royal Academy of Music and musicology at King's College, London. Thurston Dart, the renowned musicologist and Baroque music scholar, was an important early influence on Nyman, introducing him to the works of Henry Purcell and encouraging him to explore the folk music of Romania—each of which he would later adapt for his own purposes. Swirling around London at the same time Nyman was studying there were rock-and-roll currents that swept up the young composer (and nearly every other budding musician of the day). During much of this time Nyman consorted with other musicians attempting a hybridization of traditional classical music and the newer, hipper attitudes typified by such bands as the Beatles. In that regard he often worked with experimental outfits like the Flying Lizards and unvarnished classical satirists like the Portsmouth Sinfonia. He was also a member of the working press, writing critiques of diverse musics for a number of publications. It was in one of these articles, a review of a piece by Cornelius Cardew, that Nyman introduced the term "minimalism" to the modern musical lexicon. One of his biggest achievements as a writer occurred in 1974 when his seminal text on the direction of classical music, *Experimental Music—Cage and Beyond,* was published.

Already versed in Baroque forms through his study of

Purcell, Nyman received an invitation in 1976 from the composer Harrison Birtwistle (at that time, the Director of Music at the National Theatre) to arrange some eighteenth century music for a "street band" that included typical Baroque instruments in addition to a banjo and saxophones. This event led to the formation of the Michael Nyman Band, a loose-knit organization with varying formations, for which the composer would create much of his later music. The core of this group features a string quartet, a trio of saxophonists, a bass guitarist, and a piano, but instruments (including a full-blown orchestra) can be added or subtracted based upon the demands of the score being played. Purcell's music also played a role in the score which Nyman wrote for the 1982 Peter Greenaway film, *The Draughtman's Contract*, since it provided him with source material that he could quote and reshape by means of repetition and superimposition.

The partnership with Greenaway was a fruitful one that resulted in a number of well-received film scores: *A Zed and Two Noughts* (1985), *Drowning By Numbers* (1988), *The Cook, the Thief, his Wife and Her Lover* (1989), and *Prospero's Books* (1990). Without a doubt, however, Nyman's biggest fiscal success in cinema came with his soundtrack to Jane Campion's Oscar-winning 1992 film *The Piano*. For this work, he adapted some Scottish folk songs and attempted to create music that would echo the nineteenth century setting of the movie without turning into something that was a "pastiche and obviously written in 1992." The resulting album sold well over a million copies and brought the composer increased income and notoriety. With regard to his role as a writer of film scores, Nyman said, in an interview with the BBC, "I think I've managed in the films that I've done to retain my individuality and integrity, while satisfying the demands of the film and satisfying the demands of the director." Since *The Piano*, he has written scores for *Carrington* (1994), a new production of *The Diary of Anne Frank* (1995), and the science fiction film *Gattaca* (1997), to name just a few, plus a fair amount of music for various television shows and commercials.

The process of quotation and self-quotation is a time-honored tradition that dates back centuries, and it shows up repeatedly in Nyman's oeuvre. His musicological studies in the 1960s yielded rewards decades later when he adapted a tenth century text of the Book of Lamentations and some Armenian and Romanian folk songs into a striking choral work, *Out of the Ruins* (1989), which he then customized further in creating his

superb third string quartet (1990), and again for his soundtrack to *Carrington; The Piano* begot the Concerto for Piano and Orchestra (1993); elements of *Prospero's Books* turned up in three arrangements of *Ariel Songs* (1992) and a concert suite (1994); his work for solo violin, *Yamamoto Perpetuo* (1993), was used as the first violin part for his fourth string quartet (1995). He hasn't been shy about lifting material from the masters either, with *In Re Don Giovanni* quoting from Wolfgang Amadeus Mozart while Nyman's wonderful chamber opera, *The Man Who Mistook His Wife for a Hat,* used the whole of *Ich grolle nicht* (from Robert Schumann's song cycle *Dichterliebe*) as a key element in the story-line.

Orchestral
The Piano (soundtrack)
what to buy: [*The Piano*; Michael Nyman, piano; John Harle, saxophones; David Roach, saxophones; Andrew Findon, saxophones; Andrew Findon, flutes; Michael Nyman, cond.; members of the Munich Philharmonic Orchestra] (Virgin Records America 88274) ♪ ♪ ♪♪

This was the soundtrack that helped Michael Nyman's reputation as a film composer to skyrocket. While detractors may call it "minimalism lite," the truth of the matter lies in its effectiveness as a musical vehicle supporting the action in the movie. From that standpoint, this music is a success, especially in the most memorable tune from the score, *The Heart Asks Pleasure First*.

Concerto for Piano and Orchestra
what to buy: [Kathryn Stott, piano; Michael Nyman, cond.; Royal Liverpool Philharmonic Orchestra] (Argo 443382) ♪ ♪ ♪♪

Stott breathes life into a score that skirts the saccharine. While fans of *The Piano* will recognize elements of that music in the first and fourth movements, it is really the swift-moving passages of the third section that bring out Stott's virtuosity to the fullest. The composer and his band are heard in *MGV (Musique a grande vitesse)*, an electric-powered suite that gives further meaning to the words "commercial filler."

Where the Bee Dances for Soprano Saxophone and Orchestra

Michael Nyman

what to buy: [*The Piano Concerto*; Simon Haram, soprano saxophone; Takuo Yuasa, cond.; Ulster Orchestra] (Naxos 8.554168) ♪ ♪ ♪♪

While John Lenehan's solidly-played rendition of the piano concerto, with its cinematic associations, may draw some listeners to this budget disc, it is really the mellifluous 16:36 of *Where the Bee Dances* that should keep them coming back. A short, one-movement concerto for saxophone and orchestra inspired by the same Shakespearean works that Nyman drew upon for *Prospero's Books* and *Noises, Sounds, and Sweet Airs,* this work is played fluidly by all involved, though the sonics are a bit constricted at times.

worth searching for: [*Saxophone Works*; John Harle, soprano saxophone; Ivar Bolton, cond.; Bournemouth Sinfonietta, orch.] (Argo 433847) ♪ ♪ ♪ ♪

Harle is the dedicatee of this work and it is hard to imagine anyone doing a better job interpreting it than he. The other pieces on this disc were also crafted with Harle in mind and come from Gavin Bryars (*The Green Ray*) and Mike Westbrook (*Bean Rows and Blues Shots*).

Chamber
Quartet no. 3 for Strings
what to buy: [*String Quartets 1–3*; Balanescu Quartet] (Argo 433093) ♪ ♪ ♪ ♪♪

Of the four "traditional" string quartets that Nyman has written to date (not counting *In Re Don Giovanni,* which was written for amplified string quartet, or *The Piano Sings,* for soprano and string quartet), it is his third that seems most likely to pass the test of time. The other two works on this disc are interesting as well, just not *as* interesting. The first quartet is the longest and features a segment where Nyman shows off his rock-and-roll heart by reworking the Righteous Brothers' "Unchained Melody" in one of the movements; the second quartet was originally crafted as a dance piece and bears the subtitle *Miniatures/Configurations.*

Songs for Tony
what to buy: [*First and Foremost*; Apollo Saxophone Quartet, ensemble] (Argo 443903) ♪ ♪ ♪ ♪

This graceful, sixteen-minute-long suite was written as a memorial to Nyman's friend and business partner Tony Simmons, whose death from cancer greatly affected the composer. It seems to have become part of the standard

repertoire for saxophone quartets these days, but the Apollo Saxophone Quartet premiered it. Their performance here is quite lovely, and it makes an admirable counterweight for the other material on this disc: works by "Chick" Corea, David Bedford, Ray Powell, and Will Gregory.

what to buy next: [*Faces*; Quartz Saxophone Quartet, ensemble] (Black Box 1024) ♪ ♪ ♪♪

The programming on this set is actually more interesting than that heard on the Apollo Saxophone Quartet disc, but this young group doesn't quite pull off Nyman's relatively simple score with the aplomb of the older musicians. That said, the differences are not monumental at best and the works by Gary Carpenter, John Buckley, Alexander Levine, and Graham Fitkin are all worthy additions to the rapidly growing catalog of music available for this configuration.

Vocal
The Man Who Mistook His Wife for a Hat
what to buy: [Sarah Leonard, soprano; Emile Belcourt, tenor; Frederick Westcott, baritone; Michael Nyman, cond.; Michael Nyman Band, orch.] (Sony Classics 44669) ♪ ♪ ♪ ♪

Based on a medical/psychiatric case study by Oliver Sacks, this moving tale makes a surprisingly effective libretto. In it, Dr. P (a respected singer and teacher) and his wife use music to help circumvent the peculiar problems arising from his neurological difficulties. The psychiatrist (Dr. S) makes his diagnosis of the problem through their mutual love for Robert Schumann's song cycle, *Dichterliebe*. Westcott's Dr. P is quite moving, as is Leonard's portrayal of the wife, and the scoring, while lean, is quite effective.

influences: Brian Eno, Philip Glass, Steve Reich, John Adams, Graham Fitkin, Michael Torke

Ian Palmer

Johannes Ockeghem
Born c. 1410, in Saint Ghislain, Belgium. Died February 6, 1497, in Tours, France.

period: Medieval

Johannes Ockeghem stands as one of the fifteenth century's foremost exponents of the Franco-Flemish school of sacred choral music.

Although Ockeghem's name is similar to that of a village in his native Flanders, his birthplace is generally placed at Tours in the first decade of the century. Little is known of the composer's childhood and early music training, although it is presumed his family's social standing allowed him the advantage of church schooling in theology and singing from an early age. Ockeghem's name first arises within professional circles as a member of a small collection of singers in the service of Charles I, Duke of Bourbon, in the mid-1440s. His activities centered around the city of Moulin which, at that time, served as the seat of the Bourbon court. These posts generally carried with them a semi-clerical status, conveying with them titles such as "singer chaplains."

As his reputation as a composer to the court spread, Ockeghem received numerous invitations to travel abroad. Following these excursions, he was elevated to the Chapel Royal of Charles VII of France. Attached to this position were various non-musical administrative obligations at the church of St. Martin-de-Tours, of which Charles VII was titular abbot. Here Ockeghem's compositional work for the chapel was supplemented by fiscal oversight of the church community as well as attending to material needs of his fellow clerics. This variety of tasks and obligations continued well into the 1460s and the reign of Louis XI, during which Ockeghem was named "premier chapelain." Ockeghem's earlier visits to Paris Cathedral (Notre Dame) apparently left enough of an impression with that music center's power-elite to gain him appointment there as canon. There he worked from 1463 until 1470, producing some of his most notable sacred works, including several polyphonic settings of the Mass. Upon completing his tenure at Paris, Ockeghem is believed to have traveled with an ambassadorial delegation to Spain. Within the entourage he served as both composer and ambassador, fulfilling certain duties of state. Journeys to Bruges to assist in negotiating certain treaties between the throne and Flanders and Ghent are chronicled in or around 1484. Bruges also was the home of the composer Gilles Binchois, largely credited by Ockeghem himself as having been his greatest teacher and mentor. Such a bond suggests that he enjoyed an earlier and close familiarity with the city, perhaps during previous training under the master. Ockeghem's death in 1497 is documented less by public record and more by the canonizing odes in his honor offered by the great writers of the day. Guillaume Crétin's *deploration* remains the model of eulogies for a musician, referring to the composer's exceptional vocal gifts and creative genius.

Ockeghem's sacred works form the bulk of his opus. Pre-eminent among them are his motets and his settings of the Mass. These settings, in keeping with the normal practice, treat primarily what is known as the *Ordinary*, or the body of prayers that remain the same in each daily celebration of the Eucharist.

As was the custom in the Franco-Flemish school, the Mass settings fall largely into two distinct groupings. The first includes settings based on pre-existent thematic material. Various plainsong melodies, contemporary hymns, or even secular works such as the rondeau and chanson would serve as the melodic groundwork upon which the polyphony builds itself. Other Mass settings build upon original rather than borrowed material, most notably Ockeghem's own chansons. Perhaps Ockeghem's most lasting legacy to the liturgical canon is his setting of the Requiem also known generically as the *Missa pro Defunctis*. Other than Dufay's setting, of which only fragments are extant, Ockeghem's Requiem remains the earliest known setting of the Mass for the dead. Here the composer "enthrones" the original chants of the *Missa pro Defunctis* within the highest voice, allowing them to sing out above the polyphony and color the overall texture with appropriate grandeur and sobriety. Ockeghem's motets number fewer than his Masses yet reveal an astonishing kinship with this shorter form. In these he digresses from the more formulaic liturgical grid and uses both original and borrowed material to craft highly polyphonic treatments of texts well known at the time. Most notable among these are the motets that set three of the four traditional Marion antiphons: *Ave Maria, Salve Regina,* and *Alma Redemptoris Mater.*

Vocal
Requiem
what to buy: [Bo Holten, cond.; Musica Ficta, choir] (Naxos 8.554260) ♪ ♪ ♪ ♪₄

From the start of this CD, the voices treat Ockeghem's fragile lines with delicate accuracy but never fail to supply the energy that his spiraling polyphonic lines need and deserve. The Requiem sets the haunting text of the

Missa pro Defunctis with reverence and a fitting sense of calm and denouement. Also included in this set is the *Missa Prolationum,* in which the voices alternate skillfully between long, full choral statements and brief gems sounded by one voice on each part.

what to buy next: [Marcel Pérès, cond.; Ensemble Organum, choir; Les Pages de la Chapelle, choir] (Harmonia Mundi 901441) ♪ ♪ ♪ ♪

A far more "formal" yet nevertheless lovely rendering of this great work. This is a very small group, mostly performing with one voice on a part, extracting the germinal sound of the plainsong lines upon which Ockeghem's polyphony rests. All of it is elegant and profound in its severity. The end result of hearing the Requiem in its fullest context is the sense that one has enjoyed the supreme benefit of having shared the process as well as the product.

Missa "L'homme arme"
what to buy: [Jeremy Summerly, cond.; Oxford Camerata, choir] (Naxos 8.554297) ♪ ♪ ♪ ♪

Summerly's veteran forces treat the *Missa "L'homme arme"* with agility and attention to the jaunty paean to St. Michael upon which the work is based. Superb diction waits behind every new phrase in the model hymn and carries over into the main body of the Mass. The *Gloria* stands out in particular for its attention to textual detail, such as the choir's swelling at "Deus Pater omnipotens" and its supplicant "Qui tollis peccata mundi." Lovely settings of two of the four Marion antiphons (*Ave Maria* and *Alma Redemptoris Mater*) round out this recording.

influences: Guillaume Dufay, Josquin Desprez, Jacob Obrecht, Gilles Binchois

Frank Scinta

Jacques Offenbach
Born Jakob Eberst on June 20, 1819, in Deutz (near Cologne), Germany. Died October 5, 1880, in Paris, France.

period: Romantic

A favorite operatic composer in Paris during the 1860s, Offenbach wrote more than one hundred works for the musical stage. His music was simple, clear, and direct;

Gioachino Rossini called Offenbach the "Mozart of the Champs Elysées." Often thought of as the king of the Parisian musical stage, he could aptly be regarded as the Andrew Lloyd Webber of his day. Richard Wagner, however, had a very different view of music by this "citizen of the boulevards," describing it as "a dung heap on which all the swine of Europe wallowed."

Jacques Offenbach was the son of a synagogue cantor who had changed the family name from Eberst to Offenbach (Offenbach am Main being the town where the family originated). After initial studies on the violin, his early musical training focused on the cello. Offenbach entered the Paris Conservatory in 1833 but failed to complete his studies because he could not afford the tuition. He struck out on his own in 1834, working as a cellist in the orchestra of the Opéra-Comique in addition to touring as a soloist and conducting theater orchestras. He wrote a series of works for cello and his first, relatively unsuccessful operetta, *L'alcôve* (The Alcove). By the early 1850s, the romantic operetta was in vogue in Paris, but Offenbach's flair for theater wasn't recognized by the Opéra-Comique, which rejected several of his works. In response, he opened his own venue in 1855, which he named the Bouffes-Parisiens; there he produced his first major work, *Orphée aux enfers (Orpheus in the Underworld)* in 1858.

The 1860s shaped Offenbach's fortunes, as his operettas formed the backbone of popular music in Paris, providing the public with lively, identifiable melodies mixed with satirical, irreverent plot lines. The Second Empire of Napoleon III, with its decadence and intrigue, also helped foster the appeal of Offenbach's music. During this decade, he teamed up with librettist Ludovic Halévy to produce a series of classic operettas that would pack enthusiastic audiences into the theaters: *La Belle Hélène* in 1864, *La Vie Parisienne* in 1866, *La Grande-Duchesse du Gérolstein* in 1867, and *La Périchole* in 1868. However, Offenbach's musical fortunes fell into decline after the collapse of the Second Empire. The Franco-Prussian War was a turning point in French life, and the public tired of Offenbach's social satire. By 1873 he had bankrupted the theater he was managing, and in 1876 he toured the United States in an effort to reestablish himself financially. (His first concert in New York City featured an orchestra whose concertmaster was a young violinist named John Philip Sousa.) While these

Jacques Offenbach

concerts were not critically successful, Offenbach did return to Paris with a fair amount of money and managed to write a book *(Offenbach en Amérique: Notes d'un musicien en voyage)* about his adventures in America.

In his last years, Offenbach began writing *Les Contes d'Hoffmann* (Tales of Hoffman), a serious operatic work that he believed would establish his reputation as one of the finest composers of his day. The libretto was by Jules Barbier and Michel Carré (also the librettists for Charles Gounod's *Faust*), with a story that featured a force-of-destiny characterization recurring throughout the opera. The work captured the mood of the new Third Republic of France, demonstrating that Offenbach was now back in tune with the times, but he died four months before the first performance, and portions of the opera were finished by Ernest Guiraud. Hoffman remains part of the standard operatic repertory today. In 1938, Emmanuel Rosenthal arranged several of Offenbach's works into the score of Léonide Massine's ballet *Gaîté Parisienne* for the Ballets Russes de Monte Carlo,

Orchestral
Gaîté Parisienne for Orchestra
what to buy: [André Previn, cond.; Pittsburgh Symphony Orchestra] (Philips 442403) ♪ ♪ ♪♪

The Rosenthal arrangement for the ballet (incorporating the famous *Can Can* from *Orphée aux enfers*) receives a solid yet sensitive performance from Previn and the Pittsburgh Symphony. To fill up the disc, the record company has grafted on more music by Offenbach—including selections from *Le Voyage dans la lune* (Voyage to the Moon) and still more excerpts from *Orphée aux enfers*—in performances from the Philharmonia Orchestra led by Antonio de Almeida.

worth searching for: [Charles Dutoit, cond.; Montreal Symphony Orchestra] (London 447532) ♪ ♪ ♪♪

This particular recording should be acquired by anyone seeking a satisfactory and intelligent performance of only the Rosenthal arrangement.

Vocal
Les Contes d'Hoffmann (Tales of Hoffman)
what to buy: [Joan Sutherland, soprano; Placido Domingo, Hugues Cuénod, tenors; Gabriel Bacquier, baritone; Richard Bonynge, cond.; Orchestre de Suisse

Romande; Radio Chorus de Suisse Romandeb; Lausanne Pro Arte Chorus; Du Brassus Chorus] (London 417363) ♪ ♪ ♪ ♪

Still considered the ultimate recording of the *Tales of Hoffman,* this album features the glorious voice of Dame Joan Sutherland singing all of the heroine roles. Placido Domingo, as Hoffman, is a match for Sutherland, while the force-of-destiny roles, played by Gabriel Bacquier, are as powerfully foreboding as Offenbach intended. It should be noted that the conductor has opted for spoken dialogue between arias as opposed to the recitative written by Guiraud.

influences: Andrew Lloyd Webber, Léo Delibes, Adolphe Adam

Paul Wintemute

Carl Orff
Born July 10, 1895, in Munich, Germany. Died March 29, 1982, in Munich, Germany.

period: Twentieth century

Although best known as the composer of *Carmina burana,* one of the twentieth century's most popular choral works, Carl Orff's major musical contributions can be found in the field of music education.

Orff's career was centered in his birthplace of Munich, from his early studies in composition at the Munich Academy of Music to his later years teaching at the Staatliche Hochschule für Musik. He wrote his first opera *(Gisei)* in 1913, while still at the academy. This work, like others from the same period, was marked by the influences of Claude Debussy and Richard Strauss. Orff would later be drawn more to the music of Igor Stravinsky and Arnold Schoenberg among the moderns, while using Claudio Monteverdi as a reference point in his choral works. Upon graduating in 1914, he began a career as a conductor, which took him to other parts of Germany, including Mannheim and Darmstadt. After spending two years in the military, Orff went back to Munich, where he began teaching. During this time he also undertook studies in early music with Heinrich Kaminski, with particular emphasis on the music of sixteenth and seventeenth century Italian madrigalists. Orff completed his first arrangement of Monteverdi's *Orfeo* in 1925 and, continuing his work in early music, led the Munich Bach Society from 1930 to 1933.

Orff first became fascinated with the concept of blending music and movement during the early 1920s. He had already worked with dancer Mary Wigman (a former student of Émile Jaques-Dalcroze, the Swiss composer and teacher who developed eurythmics as a way of blending the rhythmic aspects of music with a form of gymnastics) in an attempt to formulate strategies that would combine the two disciplines. He then met Dorothee Günther, an artist involved in another new approach to physical education called Mensendieck gymnastics; after discovering their mutual interest in sound and motion, the pair opened up the Günther School of Munich in 1923. Together they created a unique form of music education for children incorporating the study of rhythm through movement and improvisation. Orff and his associate Gunild Keetman evolved the basic texts for a series of musical exercises they called "Schulwerk" and published them between 1930 and 1935. Orff also saw to it that his students had specially constructed percussion instruments (mostly balaphones inspired by Indonesian gamelans), many of which are still in use today among music teachers in the elementary grades.

Until the 1937 staging of the scenic oratorio *Carmina burana* in Frankfurt, Orff was relatively unknown. The text, based on thirteenth-century poems discovered in a Bavarian monastery, ranges from the sacred to the profane. The driving rhythms and folk-like melodies have put *Carmina burana* near the top of the classical hit list. Originally conceived to include pantomime, dance, and scenery, this work embodies Orff's ideal of "total theater" and can be seen as an outgrowth of the same interests that drove his groundbreaking music-education efforts. Similar techniques are found in *Catulli carmina* and *Trionfo di Afrodite,* the second and third parts of Orff's trilogy based on ancient texts. Although he preferred these simple, Stravinsky-inspired musical dramas, Orff also wrote traditional operas. These include his *Antigonae* of 1949 and *Oedipus der Tyrann* of 1959 (based on works by Sophocles), as well as *Der Mond* from 1938 and *Die Kluge* from 1942 (with texts from fairy tales by the Grimm brothers).

Vocal
Carmina burana for Soprano, Tenor, Baritone, Orchestra, and Chorus
what to buy: [Lynn Dawson, soprano; John Daniecki, tenor; Kevin Macmillan, baritone; Herbert Blomstedt, cond.; San Francisco Symphony Orchestra; San Francisco Symphony Chorus; San Francisco Girls and

Boys Chorus] (London 430509) ♪ ♪ ♪ ♪

Scored for three vocal soloists, children's and adult choirs, and full orchestra, Carl Orff's *Carmina burana* is a sonic spectacle. Used in numerous films, this "secular cantata" is represented by many fine recordings, but perhaps the best is London's "demonstration quality" recording with Blomstedt and the San Francisco Symphony. The choral work is superb, with excellent characterizations from all three soloists.

[Gundula Janowitz, soprano; Gerhard Stolze, tenor; Dietrich Fischer-Dieskau, baritone; Eugen Jochum, cond.; Berlin Deutsche Oper Orchestra, Berlin Deutsche Oper Chorus; Schoneberger Sangerknaben, choir] (Deutsche Grammophon 447437) ♪ ♪ ♪ ♪

Jochum's historic 1968 account of this work was recorded with the composer present, acquiring an air of authenticity unmatched by other recordings. It is now available as a carefully remastered and moderately priced release.

what to buy next: [Christiane Oelze, soprano, David Kuebler, tenor; Simon Keenlyside, baritone; Christian Thielemann, cond.; Orchestra of the German Opera, Berlin; Chorus of the German Opera, Berlin; Knabenchor, Berlin] (Deutsche Grammophon 453587) ♪ ♪ ♪ ♪

The latest contender in the Orff-a-thon is Thielemann's 1999 release, with virtually the same chorus and orchestra used by Jochum over thirty years ago. While the chorus does not deliver the same immediacy as Blomstedt's, Thielemann brings forth an energetic and beautifully contrasted performance. Baritone Simon Keenlyside deserves special mention.

Schulwerk (excerpts)
what to buy: [*Orff-Schulwerk, Vol. 1: Musica Poetica*; Marina Koppelstetter, mezzo-soprano; Godela Orff, voice; Carolin Widmann, violin; Sabina Lehrmann, cello; Markus Zahnhausen, recorders; Karl Peinkofer Percussion Ensemble] (Celestial Harmonies) ♪ ♪ ♪ ♪

Now translated into eighteen languages, Orff's *Schulwerk* is based on the traditional music and folklore of each country where it is used; the vocal performances here are in German. Of the forty-two cuts on this album, Keetman's works, including the delightful "Gassenhauer nach Hans Neusiedler," generally revolve around recorders and percussion, while Orff's pieces include some vocals in addition to a wider range of instruments—encompassing little gems for violin and cello plus the recorders and percussion instruments that form the core of any *Schulwerk* performance.

influences: Igor Stravinsky, Paul Hindemith, Zoltán Kodály

Christine L. Cody, Mona C. DeQuis, and Garaud MacTaggart

Johann Pachelbel

Born c. September 1, 1653, in Nuremberg, Germany. Died c. March 9, 1706, in Nuremberg, Germany.

period: Baroque

One of the most important composers of the baroque era, Pachelbel was a highly inventive and prolific musician who had a profound impact on the keyboard style of Johann Sebastian Bach. Never totally forgotten after his death, Pachelbel has gained fame in the United States since 1960 for his Canon in D Major, which has been used as theme music in a number of feature films, including *Ordinary People* and *The Elephant Man.*

Johann Pachelbel came from a humble background but through talent and persistent hard work made a name for himself as one of the most brilliant keyboard virtuosos of his time. His parents were of modest means and could not afford to send him to the university at Regensburg, but he nonetheless distinguished himself academically and in 1670 won a full scholarship. By this time Pachelbel was already a virtuoso player; while still attending the university, he began his career as an organist by working for a number of area churches. In 1673, at the age of twenty, he was appointed assistant organist at St. Stephen's Cathedral in Vienna, even though he was a practicing Lutheran. It was during his four-year tenure in Vienna that he learned the techniques and mannerisms of southern German and Italian organists, later meshing their unique styles with the traditions of northern German keyboard players.

After the death of his principal patron's brother in 1678, Pachelbel's situation eroded to the point that, with his employer's assistance, he sought a more stable position. Consequently, part of his career was spent in Erfurt and

Eisenach, where he became a close friend of Ambrosius Bach, the father of Johann Sebastian; at one point the elder Bach even asked Pachelbel to act as music instructor to his son, Johann Christoph. With the untimely death of Ambrosius Bach and his wife, young Johann Sebastian went to live and learn music from his older brother Johann Christoph, establishing a direct historical connection between Bach's musical instruction and Pachelbel's methodology.

Pachelbel also had a number of talented children. One daughter, Amalia, earned fame as a painter, while two sons, Wilhelm Hieronymus and Charles Theodore, became composers in their own right. Charles Theodore emigrated to the United States and became a musical fixture in Boston before moving on to Newport, Rhode Island; New York City; and finally, Charleston, South Carolina.

Pachelbel eventually returned to Nuremberg, where he became organist of St. Sebald's Church in 1695. When such a major position opened up, it was customary to hold a series of examinations for musicians aspiring to the post. So anxious were the authorities to have Pachelbel as their organist, however, that they not only offered him the position without an examination but also paid a portion of his moving expenses. He remained as the church's organist until his death in 1706.

Even though he never traveled very far from his hometown of Nuremberg, his fame was known throughout Europe, due to the publication of his music; during Pachelbel's lifetime, more of his music was published than Johann Sebastian Bach's during his own lifetime.

Today, Pachelbel's Canon is one of the most performed and arranged pieces of baroque music, having won a permanent place in the hearts and minds of new brides throughout the Western world. One can only hope that it inspires some listeners to explore more of his works.

Orchestral
Canon and Gigue in D Major for Three Violins and Continuo
what to buy: [*Orchestral Favorites, Vol. 1*; William Boughton, cond.; English Chamber Orchestra] (Nimbus 7019) ♪ ♪ ♪ ♪♪

It seems only natural these days that most conductors have led performances of the Canon at some point in their careers. This particular rendering is packaged with the famous Adagio in G Minor ascribed to Tomaso Albinoni, Gustav Holst's *St. Paul's Suite,* Edvard Grieg's *Holberg Suite,* and portions of Peter Warlock's *Capriol Suite.* All of these works are played on modern instruments, with impeccable performances and gorgeous sound.

what to buy next: [Jean-Francois Paillard, cond.; Jean-Francois Paillard Chamber Orchestra] (Erato 98475) ♪ ♪ ♪ ♪

Old-time record collectors might remember this performance, released by the Musical Heritage Society in 1968. Although Paillard adds violas here, the effect is valid for many listeners. Trumpeter Maurice André is one of the featured soloists in the accompanying Concerto in D Major for Trumpet, Two Oboes, Strings, and Continuo by Johann Friedrich Fasch, a contemporary of Johann Sebastian Bach.

Chamber
Toccata in C Major
what to buy: [*Complete Organ Works, Vol. 2*; Joseph Payne, organ] (Centaur 2306) ♪ ♪ ♪ ♪ ♪₈

Payne is an English organist who studied in Vienna and now makes his home in the United States. Little known, since he hardly performs publicly, he is a wonderful player who has recorded the complete organ works of Pachelbel. The clear sound of this Texas-based organ really captures the clarity of the silvery southern baroque sound. Also included here are eleven of the *Magnificat Fugues,* the *Chaconne in D Major,* and some of the older German chorales, many of which were also treated by Johann Sebastian Bach as chorale preludes.

influences: Johann Sebastian Bach, Dietrich Buxtehude, Johann Frederick Fasch

Dave Wagner

Niccolò Paganini
Born October 27, 1782, in Genoa, Italy. Died May 27, 1840, in Nice, Italy.

period: Romantic

Probably the most venerated violinist in history, Niccolò Paganini's virtuosity set a standard for playing the

instrument that remains in force today through his six violin concerti and, in particular, his twenty-four frighteningly difficult *Caprices* for Solo Violin, op. 1.

By the time he was twelve years old Paganini was already a talented sight reader, and often employed in Genoese church orchestras. Having exceeded the abilities of his local teachers to instruct him further, he mounted a concert in 1795 that was meant to generate enough cash for him to take lessons with mentors who would provide more challenge. After spending a year in Parma studying violin with Gaspare Ghiretti and composition with Ferdinando Päer, Paganini returned home, for all intents and purposes a fully-formed musician trained in counterpoint and composition in addition to having honed his violin playing.

After Paganini toured Northern Italy from 1797 to 1798, his father (who had given him his first music lessons and guided his career to this point) kept the young virtuoso near their home outside of Genoa, partly because of his desire to keep tabs on the family meal-ticket and partially because of the Napoleonic wars affecting Italian commerce at that time. Upon the completion of a short concert tour that took Paganini to Lucca and Pisa in 1801, he finally managed to break away from his father, further his reputation as a soloist, and eventually assume his first professional post as first violin with the newly founded National Orchestra in 1805. However, these years also saw Paganini experimenting with harmonics—especially with regard to extending the range of the G string to more than three octaves—and composing a number of scores that were often variations on thematic material drawn from operas. This last set of activities assured him of a specific, highly personalized oeuvre (including the twenty-four *Caprices* and some works for violin and guitar) for the solo career he embarked upon in 1810.

The next two decades were a time of increasing fame and fortune for the violinist, both as a performer and as a composer. His first five violin concertos as well as the string quartets and guitar quartets date from this period, as does the publication of his technical tour de force, the twenty-four *Caprices.* Paganini also met and became friends with Gioachino Rossini, suffered the vicissitudes of venereal disease, sired a son, toured most of the art capitals of Europe, and amazed concert audiences and fellow virtuosi (Franz Liszt among them) with the seeming ease of his technical artistry. What naysayers there were (including fellow violinist and composer Ludwig

Spohr) focused on Paganini's flamboyant manner of playing and the liberties he took with a score. From 1830 until 1837, he kept up a heavy schedule of touring, primarily in France and Great Britain, despite increasing bouts of ill health. It was during this time that Paganini (who could also play the guitar) became interested in the viola. He even went so far as to ask Hector Berlioz to write a work for him that featured the instrument but, when presented with an initial draft of the score for *Harold in Italy,* spurned it as unchallenging.

In 1837, Paganini embarked upon an ill-advised undertaking with a friend: the establishment of a Parisian venue called Casino Paganini where he would play and draw crowds. Since he was not in good physical shape for much of his last five years, even being unable visit Rome in 1836 to accept an honorary membership in the society of St. Cecilia, Paganini was not able to fulfill the contractual obligations imposed upon him by the venture. This would result in a lawsuit that led him to leave Paris for Marseilles toward the end of 1838; upon losing his appeal he then went to Nice, Italy (in 1839), where he would live out the balance of his days. Before he left, however, Paganini managed to attend a concert where the completed *Harold in Italy* was performed. According to Berlioz (who recounted the scene in his *Mémoirs*), Paganini was incapable of sustained speech by this time and had to communicate via his son, but managed to note that "in the whole of his life he (had) never been so deeply impressed at a concert." He later sent Berlioz a check for 20,000 francs. Once Paganini was settled in Italy, he didn't have long to live, finally dying of tuberculosis in 1840.

Orchestral
Concertos for Violin and Orchestra (complete)
what to buy: [*Paganini: The 6 Violin Concertos*; Salvatore Accardo, violin; Charles Dutoit, cond.; London Philharmonic Orchestra] (Deutsche Grammophon 437210) ♪ ♪ ♪ ♪

Accardo's performances of these works are not only consistently rewarding, they are the only readily available complete cycle of Paganini's virtuoso showpieces for violin and orchestra. The sound quality is quite good and the pricing is fairly decent.

Concerto no. 1 in D Major for Violin and Orchestra, op. 6
what to buy: [Itzhak Perlman, violin; Lawrence Foster, cond.; Royal Philharmonic Orchestra] (EMI Classics

47101) ♪ ♪ ♪ ♪ ♪

Perlman handles the difficulties of this piece with considerable aplomb, but he also invests his playing with the same kind of poetry that distinguished classic accounts by Yehudi Menuhin, Artur Grumiaux, and Henryk Szeryng. When combined with Pablo Sarasate's *Carmen Fantasy* and a mid-line price, this is a difficult recording to find flaws with, especially if you are looking for violin fireworks.

what to buy next: [Ilya Kaler, violin; Stephen Gunzenhauser, cond.; Polish National Radio Symphony Orchestra] (Naxos 8.550649) ♪ ♪ ♪ ♪

Every violin virtuoso seems to tackle this score, but seldom do any of the newer crop of technicians play with this much understanding of the passion behind the music. Kaler is a talent to look for in the future and his budget-priced performance is a valid alternative to Perlman's, even if the orchestra is not quite in the same league as the RPO. The same forces also do a wonderful job with Paganini's second violin concerto, a.k.a. *La Campanella.*

Chamber
Caprices for Solo Violin, op. 1
what to buy: [Itzhak Perlman, violin] (EMI Classics 67257) ♪ ♪ ♪ ♪ ♪

Bearing in mind that these works should be sampled gradually instead of listened to in one fell swoop (unless you are a rabid fan of solo violin), Perlman's vision and technique are at the full service of the music. It is difficult to think of a more impressive approach to these devilish pieces.

what to buy next: [Salvatore Accardo, violin] (Deutsche Grammophon 429714) ♪ ♪ ♪ ♪

While Accardo's tone is not as sweetly singing as Perlman's, his gutsy reading of Paganini's exercises has its own rewards. It makes a fine adjunct to his concerto cycle too.

[James Ehnes, violin] (Telarc 80398) ♪ ♪ ♪ ♪

Ehnes is one of the newer violin virtuosi on the touring circuit and won the very first *Ivan Galamian Memorial Award* in 1994. These performances have a surprising delicacy to them even as they shine with technical brilliance. It all augurs well for the future.

influences: Pietro Antonio Locatelli, Eugène Ysaÿe, Pablo de Sarasate, Henryk Wieniawski, Henri Vieuxtemps

William Gerard

John Knowles Paine

Born January 9, 1839, in Portland, ME. Died April 25, 1906, in Cambridge, MA.

period: Romantic

John Knowles Paine, the dean of nineteenth-century American composers, was one of the first Americans to achieve an international reputation in classical music. He was the first professor of music at an American university (Harvard), where he taught a generation of prominent composers including Arthur Foote and John Alden Carpenter.

Paine began his musical education in Portland before leaving for Berlin, Germany, in 1858 to attend the Hochschule für Musik, where he studied orchestration, organ, and composition. While in Europe he gave recitals in Germany and England, once even playing for Clara Schumann. Returning to America, Paine settled in Boston in 1861 and was named assistant professor of music at Harvard University a year later. In 1875 he was appointed to a full professorship, the first person to hold this type of position at an American university. Through his writings and lectures, Paine was able to communicate a strong belief that music should be an integral part of a good liberal arts education; in so doing, he was instrumental in making Boston an important center for American classical music.

A cultural pioneer, Paine led a life filled with firsts. As an active organ recitalist, Paine helped introduce the organ works of J. S. Bach to American audiences; he was also involved in establishing the American Guild of Organists. His *Saint Peter,* premiered in 1867, was the first major oratorio composed in America, and his *Mass in D Major,* premiered in Berlin, was the first large work by an American to be performed in Europe. Later, his Symphony no. 2 became the first American symphonic work to be published in full score. In 1867, both Paine and Richard Wagner were asked to compose works for the Philadelphia Exposition. As this was the one-hundredth anniversary of the signing of the Declaration of Independence, Paine received much attention for his *Centennial Hymn,* scored for chorus, organ, and orchestra.

As the oldest member of the so-called Second New England School, Paine inspired many American composers who followed. Basically, this school was a group of composers, teachers, and performers who studied the "cultivated" European style of composition and whose models were the abstract compositional forms of Beethoven, Mendelssohn, Schumann, and Brahms. Paine's creative output—including operas, incidental music, songs, chamber music, orchestral pieces, solo keyboard works, and pieces for chorus—hued closely to those values. There are hints of Liszt and Wagner to be found in his later scores, as his works became more programmatic and chromatic. Although his music is not widely performed today, Paine, in his roles as composer, teacher, and performer, helped create an academic and creative tradition that set the stage for the twentieth century.

Orchestral
Symphony no. 2 in A Major, op. 34—*Im Frühling (In Springtime)*
what to buy: [Zubin Mehta, cond.; New York Philharmonic] (New World Records 80350) ♪ ♪ ♪ ♪₈

Paine's symphonies mark the beginning of the American symphonic tradition. A programmatic work that depicts the transformation of winter into spring, his second symphony clearly shows the influence of Robert Schumann. The third movement looks ahead in time with a hint of Mahler: pizzicato strings, embellished melodic turns, interval skips, a beautiful second theme in minor, and an abrupt shift from major to minor. Written four years after Paine's first symphony, this work is more chromatic in nature. Mehta and the orchestra provide a deeply committed performance, making it even more difficult to understand why this work has been so neglected.

Vocal
Mass in D Major for Solo Voices, Organ, Orchestra, and Chorus, op. 10
what to buy: [Carmen Balthrop, soprano; Joy Blanchett, contralto; Vinson Cole, tenor; John Cheek, baritone; Gunther Schuller, cond.; St. Louis Symphony Orchestra; St. Louis Symphony Chorus] (New World Records 80262) ♪ ♪ ♪ ♪

Paine's Mass is a large work scored for soprano, contralto, tenor, and bass soloists, mixed chorus, full orchestra, and organ. Overall, the choral writing shows the influence of Mendelssohn, with dramatic moments reminiscent of Verdi's operatic sounding Requiem. While not quite in the ranks of Beethoven's *Missa Solemnis* or Mendelssohn's *Elijah,* there are moments of true beauty in the "Sanctus" and power and dignity in the work's "Osanna." Gunther Schuller and company are to be applauded for this valuable addition to the catalog.

influences: George Whitefield Chadwick, Horatio William Parker, Arthur Foote

Mona C. DeQuis

Giovanni Paisiello

Born May 9, 1740, in Roccaforzata, Italy. Died June 5, 1816, in Naples, Italy.

period: Classical

Even though he was a prolific writer of both comic and serious operas, very few of Giovanni Paisiello's musical theater works are ever staged today. In the late eighteenth and early nineteenth centuries, however, he was one of the most popular opera composers in Europe, influencing even the young and impressionable Wolfgang Amadeus Mozart. There has been a recent resurgence of interest in Paisiello's music, but his choral and instrumental works find greater representation on disc than do his many operas.

Despite his parents' initial desire that their only son become a lawyer, Paisiello demonstrated such a beautiful singing voice that they were persuaded by a nobleman to send him to Naples for musical instruction. In 1763, after receiving his education at the Conservatorio di Sant'Onofrio a Capuano (where his teachers included Francesco Durante, Girolamo Abos, and Carlo Cotumacci), Paisiello obtained his first position with a newly formed opera theater created by Don Giuseppe Carafa. His skills rapidly improved and he started taking independent commissions, embarking on a career as a freelance composer. After producing more than fifty operas, to general acclaim, he was offered a position as court composer by Catherine II of Russia in 1776. He was paid very well during his stay in Russia and left the country a wealthy man, but his situation there was not to his liking. Not only did he have to reduce the scale of his operas from three acts to two (since the empress could not abide any production that lasted more than two hours), but there were constant intrigues at court, punctuated by conflicts with theater managers and temperamental performers. Paisiello used the excuse of his wife's illness to get permission to return to Italy, but Catherine was so distressed at the thought of his permanent departure that she offered him a paid leave of absence for a year. After agreeing to this proposal, Paisiello, once he was safely out of the country and beyond Catherine's considerable reach, never went back.

Returning to Italy in 1784, Paisiello took a position as court composer with the king of Naples, Ferdinand IV. A year later, the appreciative king granted his musical minion an annual pension. All this came to nothing in January 1799, when Ferdinand was overthrown by a populist rebellion. Still, Paisiello proved adept at treading political waters, managing to stay on in a similar position as *maestro di cappella nazionale* after cleverly distancing himself from the old regime. Incredibly, after the reinstatement of the king later that year, the composer appealed for clemency and was returned to royal favor after an investigation cleared him of complicity in the revolt.

Paisiello was a favorite of Napoleon Bonaparte's, and in 1802 Bonaparte himself negotiated his release from the service of King Ferdinand and brought him to Paris. There the composer was essentially double dipping—drawing a healthy sum from Napoleon while still collecting his annual pension from Ferdinand. This lasted until 1804, when Paisiello, at his own request, was released from Napoleon's service so that he could return to Italy. Back in Naples, the composer witnessed yet another transfer of power when Napoleon's brother Joseph ousted Ferdinand in 1806. Paisiello's luck continued to hold when Joseph prevailed upon him to become the music director for his court. When Ferdinand overthrew Joseph and retook the throne in 1815, it seemed likely that Paisiello would be stripped of his position and any benefits he had accrued, but instead he was spared under a blanket amnesty issued by Ferdinand. Paisiello died almost a year later from complications associated with hepatitis.

Orchestral
Concerto no. 2 in F Major for Piano and Orchestra
what to buy: [*Giovanni Paisiello: Complete Piano Concertos, Vol. 1*; Mariaclara Monetti, piano; Stephanie Gonley, cond.; English Chamber Orchestra] (ASV 872) ♪ ♪ ♪ ♪

With this all-Paisiello disc, you can sometimes close your eyes and think you are listening to Mozart. There is plenty of wonderful playing here by Monetti and the orchestra, who perform with admirable clarity and precision. Drawn from Monetti's complete set of Paisiello piano concertos, this album also contains the composer's third, fourth, and sixth essays in the form.

Vocal
Mass for the Coronation of the Empress Josephine
what to buy: [*Coronation Music for Napoleon I*; Vladislav Tchernushenko, cond.; St. Petersburg Capella Orchestra; St. Petersburg Capella, choir] (Koch Schwann 312082) ♪ ♪ ♪ ♪₄

There are two major works represented here—the mass and a setting of the *Te Deum* text—both written when Paisiello was in the employ of Napoleon. Also included is music by two of Paisiello's contemporaries—Nicolas Roze and Jean-François Le Sueur.

influences: Franz Joseph Haydn, Wolfgang Amadeus Mozart, Antonio Salieri, Niccolo Piccini, Dominic Cimarosa

Dave Wagner

Giovanni Palestrina
Born Giovanni Pierluigi da Palestrina c. February 1525 or 1526 in Palestrina, Italy. Died February 2, 1594, in Rome, Italy.

period: Renaissance

Palestrina was one of the preeminent composers of the Renaissance. His sacred works, particularly the *Missa "Papae Marcelli,"* exemplify the pinnacle of choral music in the late sixteenth century.

There is no evidence to prove it, but it is possible that Giovanni Pierluigi da Palestrina was born in Palestrina, a small town outside of Rome. Most of his life was spent in Rome, however, and there is no doubt that he received his early musical training in Rome as a choirboy at Santa Maria Maggiore. In 1544 he went to Palestrina, where he became organist and music teacher at Saint Agapit. In 1551 he moved permanently to Rome to become choirmaster for the Julian Chapel at Saint Peter's Basilica. Four years later, Palestrina was admitted to choir of the Sistine Chapel, the official chapel of the

pope. Palestrina's appointment was controversial, as Pope Julius III had waived both the entrance examination and the requisite vote of the other singers. Just three months into this new appointment, however, Julius III died and was replaced by Marcellus II, who died suddenly after only three weeks. Marcellus's successor, Pope Paul IV, began his zealous efforts to reform the Roman Catholic Church. The new pope removed Palestrina from the Sistine Chapel in the fall of 1555, citing the previously neglected rule of celibacy. Palestrina quickly accepted the choirmaster position at Saint John Lateran, a post once held by his contemporary Orlando di Lassus. In 1561 he found himself once again at Santa Maria Maggiore, where composed some of his most important works, including his masterpiece, the *Missa "Papae Marcelli."* In 1571 he accepted a secular position from Cardinal d'Este to direct music at his summer villa. He then returned to the Julian Chapel at Saint Peter's Basilica, where he remained until his death in 1594.

An extremely prolific composer, Palestrina wrote hundreds of masses, motets, madrigals, and other types of sacred and secular vocal works. His most famous piece, the *Missa "Papae Marcelli,"* dedicated to Pope Marcellus II, has acquired legendary status. It is believed that Palestrina composed it to discourage the Council of Trent (convened in response to the Protestant Reformation) from abolishing the use of polyphony, or counterpoint, in church music. According to the council, the music in the church was becoming secular in nature; the council members believed that the musical trends of the Renaissance, such as elaborate counterpoint, chromaticism, and dissonance, were corrupting forces. The use of polyphony (independent melodic lines moving simultaneously) made the text hard to understand. Palestrina wanted to prove that a Mass in six voices utilizing the polyphonic style could be spiritually appropriate. The result is a clarity that faithfully serves the meaning of the words. Hardly a musical pioneer, Palestrina embraced the conservative ideals of the Counter Reformation. In his scores, the melodic lines are gently curving and primarily stepwise, the use of dissonance is subtle, and intervals are small. The well-crafted simplicity and directness of Palestrina's compositions served as models for the generations that followed.

Vocal
Missa "Papae Marcelli"
worth searching for: [Peter Phillips, cond.; Tallis Scholars, choir] (Gimell 454939) ♪ ♪ ♪ ♪ ♪

The Tallis Scholars and their visionary leader, Peter Phillips, present a beautifully selfless performance of Palestrina's Mass. Through their near-perfect intonation they allow the work's essential spirituality and humility to shine through. This recording also includes exquisite performances of William Mundy's *Vox Patris caelestis*—written at almost exactly the same time as *Palestrina's Mass*—and Gregorio Allegri's Miserere. The recording is warm and full, without a loss of clarity.

Missa "Viri Galaei"

what to buy: [James O'Donnell, cond.; Westminster Cathedral Choir] (Hyperion 66316) ♪ ♪ ♪ ♪

Each motet on this disc is heard before its reworking as a Mass, so we can meet the stylistic differences head on. Palestrina's motet writing is somewhat freer, and he shows the influence of some of his contemporaries. The larger choir of Westminster's boys and men serves as a good contrast to the smaller adult forces of the Tallis Scholars, while the Westminster Cathedral provides sumptuous acoustics entirely appropriate for this music. Also included is Palestrina's *Missa "O Rex gloriae."*

influences: Josquin Desprez, Orlando di Lassus, William Byrd

Christine L. Cody and Mona C. DeQuis

Horatio Parker

Born Horatio William Parker, September 15, 1863, in Auburndale, MA. Died December 18, 1919 in Cedarhurst, Long Island, NY.

period: Romantic

One of the most celebrated American composers and teachers of the late nineteenth century, Parker is perhaps best known for his stint as dean of the Yale School of Music, where Charles Ives and Roger Sessions were among his pupils.

Horatio William Parker started his musical studies with his mother and later studied composition with Charles Whitefield Chadwick (1854–1931). In 1880 Parker began a successful lifelong career as an organist and choir director, spelled by a brief time out when, following Chadwick's example, Parker went to Germany to study with Josef Rheinberger at the Hochschule für Musik in Munich from 1882 to 1885.

Upon his return to America in 1886, Parker took a series of church and teaching positions that included a job at the National Conservatory of Music in New York. In 1893 he wrote what proved to be his masterwork, the oratorio *Hora novissima*. The success of this piece established Parker's reputation in the United States and abroad, especially in England, where *Hora novissima* enjoyed a number of performances. Parker was so popular there that he received numerous commissions and an honorary music degree from Cambridge University. Parker also became an important force in the musical life of New Haven, Connecticut, when he accepted the position of music theory professor at Yale University in 1894. One year later he founded the New Haven Symphony Orchestra, which he conducted until 1918. Most significantly, Parker became dean of the Yale School of Music in 1904, serving in that capacity until his death in 1919. He is best remembered as the academician who brought the Yale School of Music to international prominence.

Parker was part of a group of influential late-nineteenth-century composers, teachers, and performers known as the Second New England School, which also included John Knowles Paine, Arthur Foote, Amy Beach, Edward MacDowell, Charles Whitefield Chadwick, and others. The name distinguishes them from an earlier group of singing schoolmasters or "Yankee tunesmiths" of the eighteenth century, of whom William Billings is the most famous. Members of the Second New England School were thoroughly trained in the European musical tradition of harmony, form, orchestration, and counterpoint. They believed in the use of abstract forms such as sonatas, with Beethoven, Schumann, and Brahms as their models. However, there was a concerted effort by these composers to create a distinctively American classical tradition.

Although Parker was primarily a composer of vocal works such as oratorios, cantatas, operas, songs, hymns, and anthems, he also wrote instrumental music. In addition to a number of chamber pieces and works for piano and organ, he composed scores like *A Northern Ballad* and the Concerto for Organ and Orchestra (which Parker performed with the Boston Symphony in 1902 and the Chicago Symphony Orchestra in 1903). His opera *Mona* won a prize from the Metropolitan Opera Company and received four performances in 1912. Other prestigious ensembles in Philadelphia, Cincinnati, and Los Angeles performed Parker's compositions during his lifetime. He died of pneumonia in the West Indies in 1919.

Orchestral
A Northern Ballad for Orchestra, op. 46
what to buy: [Julius Hegyi, cond.; Albany Symphony Orchestra] (New World Records 80339) ♪ ♪ ♪ ♪

A Northern Ballad can be considered a symphonic tone poem in form, although Parker provided no extramusical program. Fans of late Schumann, Brahms, and Dvořák will find it very satisfying; it also hints of the dark richness of Sibelius. The Albany Symphony gives an excellent performance, with some particularly nice playing from the winds. This is the only commercially available recording of this unjustifiably neglected gem; the disc also includes George W. Chadwick's Symphony no. 2.

Vocal
Hora novissima for Solo Voices, Orchestra, and Chorus, op. 30
what to buy: [Anna Soranno, soprano; Julie Simson, mezzo-soprano; Kent Hall, bass-baritone; Duane Andersen, bass-baritone; John Levick, cond.; Nebraska Chamber Orchestra; Abendmusik Chorus; Nebraska Wesleyan University Choir] (Albany TROY 124/5) ♪ ♪ ♪₅

At one time *Hora novissima* was the most famous and most performed choral work in America. Deeply rooted in the European romantic style, with flowing melodies, subtle use of chromaticism, and fugal passages, it is also reminiscent of the British choral tradition of Charles Hubert Parry and Edward Elgar. Parker's Concerto in E-flat Minor for Organ and Orchestra, with soloist Stephen Krahn, is also included in this set. These solid performances, led by conductor Levick, are highly valuable, as the album is the only commercially available recording of Parker's most significant compositions.

influences: John Knowles Paine, George Whitefield Chadwick

Christine L. Cody and Mona C. DeQuis

Hubert Parry
Born Charles Hubert Hastings Parry, February 27, 1848, in Bournemouth, England. Died October 7, 1918, in Rustington, Sussex, England.

period: Romantic

Parry's prolific output encompasses all musical genres of his day, each work encoded with the nationalism prevalent in the nineteenth century and representative (along with works by Edward Elgar and Charles Villiers Stanford) of what modern listeners consider distinctly English in character. Parry was also an important scholar, influencing a number of eminent British composers through his positions as professor and director at the Royal College of Music.

Born into the landed classes, Parry grew up in a life of relative ease. His father was not only a landowner but a patron of the arts, with an impressive collection of paintings and a host of literary and musical friends. As a student at Eton, the younger Parry studied composition with George Elvey and participated in concerts of the Musical Society as pianist, violinist, organist, and composer. His earliest published compositions, the anthems *Blessed Is He* and *Prevent Us O Lord,* date from this period, but it was his cantata, *Oh Lord Thou Hast Cast Us Out,* which enabled him, in 1866, to become the youngest candidate ever to be awarded a Bachelor of Music degree from the school. He then enrolled at Exeter College, Oxford, where, in 1870, he graduated with a Bachelor of Arts degree. This gave way to a distinctly unmusical position as an underwriter at Lloyds Register of Shipping, though Parry continued post-graduate study in piano with Edward Dannreuther, who introduced him to the music of Wagner, and counterpoint with George MacFarren, head of the Royal Academy of Music.

Parry kept composing songs and a variety of piano works during the next decade, but it was a set of poems he wrote that served as introduction to Sir Charles Grove, who published them and then sought Parry's abilities as a knowledgeable contributor to a forthcoming *Dictionary of Music and Musicians.* Parry ended up helping Grove edit the undertaking and furthering his scholarly credentials. He began achieving a measure of success as a composer in 1880, after performances of his piano concerto were staged at the Crystal Palace and a cantata with a distinctly Wagnerian flavor (*Scenes from Prometheus Unbound*) was unveiled at the Gloucester Festival. As a result of these successes Parry was commissioned to write choral works for a variety of festivals, and some of his instrumental works were performed. In 1883, the Royal College of Music was just opening and Grove asked him to join the staff there as a professor.

As a teacher and scholar, Parry influenced the lives of a whole generation of young British composers including

Ralph Vaughan Williams, Gustav Holst, Herbert Howells, and George Butterworth. He also wrote and/or edited a series of texts (*The Music of the Seventeenth Century, Studies of Great Composers,* and a critical biography of Johann Sebastian Bach) and collected doctorates from Cambridge (1883) and Oxford (1884) in addition to a knighthood (1898).

Orchestral
Symphony no. 3 in C Major (*The English*)
what to buy: [Matthias Bamert, cond.; London Philharmonic Orchestra] (Chandos 8896) ♪ ♪ ♪ ♪ ♪

Parry's third symphony, influenced by similar compositions from Felix Mendelssohn and Robert Schumann, was the most performed symphony written by any English composer until Elgar's efforts in that medium. Paired with Bamert's recording of Parry's Symphony no. 4 in E Minor, this disc is part of an exemplary series devoted to Parry's orchestral and large choral compositions which makes one wonder why these works have been neglected. The sound quality is impeccable, realistic, and very British.

Concerto for Piano and Orchestra in F-sharp Major
what to buy: [*The Romantic Piano Concerto, vol. 12*; Piers Lane, piano; Martyn Brabbins, cond.; BBC Scottish Symphony Orchestra] (Hyperion 66820) ♪ ♪ ♪ ♪ ♪

This composition made Parry famous in England, and helped raise the general level of music composition to a point not seen since that of Purcell some 200 years before. This first recording of the work balances the piano with the orchestra and blends well throughout. While this piece will not replace other nineteenth century piano concertos in popularity, it is clear that it deserves to be part of the repertoire. Also on this CD is the first recording of Stanford's Concerto no. 1 in G Major for Piano and Orchestra, op. 59.

Vocal
various choral works
what to buy: [*I Was Glad: Cathedral Music by Parry*; Roger Judd, organ; Christopher Robinson, cond.; St. George's Chapel Choir, Windsor] (Hyperion 66273) ♪ ♪ ♪ ♪

This recording contains most of Parry's major choral works sans orchestral accompaniment, including *I Was*

Glad and the six *Songs of Farewell.* Several of these are considered staples of (and set the style for) the English cathedral anthem literature. This choir of men and boys renders credible performances while the overall sound from the moderately reverberant chapel at Windsor Castle is recorded realistically and pleasantly.

influences: Charles Villiers Stanford, Gustav Holst, Herbert Howells, Ralph Vaughan Williams

D. John Apple

Arvo Pärt
Born September 11, 1935, in Paide, Estonia.

period: Twentieth century

Arguably the most consistently rewarding of the so-called "Holy Minimalists" (John Tavener and Henryck Górecki being the other major figures so dubbed), Pärt went through several stylistic phases, including serialism, before arriving at the repetitive yet intricate methods which characterize his mature work. Though minimalist in effect, his sparely constructed, quietly reverential music is also grounded in the same sort of complex working out of patterns that characterizes serialism, a study of Medieval and Renaissance polyphony, and deep religious belief. Strictly speaking, Pärt's music is not so much repetitive—though it can seem that way—as starkly simple in its motivic material. In his vocal music, the stop-start motion of strings of short notes framed by longer notes recalls chant without copying its shape or methods.

Pärt studied composition with Heino Eller at the Tallinn Conservatory, graduating in 1963. From 1958 to 1967 he worked as a recording engineer for Estonian Radio, also cranking out around fifty soundtracks. He started as a neo-classicist, but was mostly an avant-gardist (and frequently a serialist) until 1968, when he began a period of transition. He also had a penchant for Alexander Schnittke-like collage and quotation and a Pendereckian regard for colorful orchestral sonorities, with a willingness to go to unusual lengths or sources for special effects; his second symphony includes a squeaking rubber toy in its instrumentation. His 1963 composition *Perpetuum mobile* (dedicated to Italian avant-gardist Luigi Nono) garnered him some attention in the West. Serialism was not looked upon favorably by the Soviet government, however, and Pärt was the first Estonian serialist; he got away with it in 1960 by dedicating

Nekroloog, his first work in the idiom, to the victims of Fascism.

In 1962 he won first prize in the All-Union Young Composers' Competition for his children's cantata *Meie Aed (Our Garden),* and his oratorio *Maailma samm (The World's Stride).* His 1968 composition *Credo,* on the other hand, was banned due to its religious content. He was a musical puzzle, too. His serial or collage compositions could be harshly dissonant, even violently so, and unusually complex, yet his 1964 choral work *Solfeggio* uses the notes of the C Major scale to produce shimmeringly euphonious tone clusters through sustained tones. It anticipates the restful mood and surface simplicity of his later work, if not especially its methods. It was apparently Pärt's own dissatisfaction with serialism that led him into experimenting with collage technique. *Collage on BACH,* with its references to Baroque forms (the three movements are Toccata, Sarabande, and Ricercar) is his classic work in collage style and was written in 1964. After the condemnation of *Credo,* also a collage piece, he apparently found it wise to temporarily cease composing. At that point, Pärt rethought his style and cut back on his productivity. He studied Medieval and Renaissance polyphony intently and extensively, absorbing the methods of Guillaume de Machaut, Johannes Ockeghem, Josquin Desprez, and others, along with chant. His 1971 Symphony no. 3—at twenty-five minutes, longer than his previous symphonies—was among his first major works to show this influence, complete with strong tonality (or modality).

Still not satisfied, he again took a composing sabbatical; when he emerged from it in 1976, he was a vastly different composer. He had developed something he called tintinnabuli—Latin for "little bells." It was insistently triadic, yet not in a normal tonal manner; rather, a triad could sound throughout an entire piece with no harmonic changes or modulations. The deliberate simplicity which this enforced was reinforced with square rhythms; virtuosity, both in performance and writing, was abandoned. The short piano piece *Für Alina* was the beginning of a flood of works in this new style, which recalls the sound and texture of minimalism (though less rhythmically charged) and its concern for process. Three pieces from the following year, *Fratres, Cantus in Memoriam Benjamin Britten,* and *Tabula Rasa,* show Pärt using the tintinnabuli technique on a greatly expanded scale. There's a certain Spartan lyricism to these works which many musicians in the avant-garde realm found refreshing, violinist Gidon Kremer being

---

Luciano Pavarotti:

During the last quarter of the twentieth century Luciano Pavarotti was considered one of the greatest operatic tenors in the world, and was certainly the most commercially successful. When Pavarotti, Plácido Domingo and José Carreras banded together for an appearance during the 1990 World Cup soccer match in Rome (*The Three Tenors In Concert,* London 430433), a popular phenomenon was unleashed that would drag several similar groups ("Three Irish Tenors," "Three Mo' Tenors," "Three Counter-Tenors," "Three Sopranos," etc.) into the marketplace.

Pavarotti's success resulted from a confluence of heredity and years of hard, dedicated training. Pavarotti's father was a baker who also sang tenor and owned a number of recordings by Giuseppe di Stefano, the young singer's initial idol. This enthusiasm helped guide him toward a detailed study of *bel canto* singing, with an eye toward developing a well-focused sound and an ability to string words together in a long, elastic line. In 1961, when he was twenty-six years old, Pavarotti impressed local critics during his debut as Rudolfo in a production of Giacomo Puccini's *La Bohème* at the Teatro Municipale in Reggio Emilia. By 1965 he was touring Australia with the noted soprano Joan Sutherland, a match that would later produce some of the finest, most lauded modern performances of the *bel canto* repertoire. The first concert pairing of these two magnificent voices occurred in Gaetano Donizetti's *La fille du regiment,* a successful outing that led to their acclaimed studio recording of the opera (London 414520).

Pavarotti initially concentrated on roles that would preserve his voice for future years, singing the major tenor roles in Giacomo Puccini's *Madama Butterfly* (London 417577) and *La Bohème* (London 421049) in addition to performing as the Duke of Mantua in Giuseppe Verdi's *Rigoletto* (London 414269). As he matured and his voice darkened, Pavarotti broadened the range of parts he would attempt, tackling roles in Verdi's *Otello* (London 433669), *Il trovatore* (Bella Voce 7216), and *Un ballo in maschera* (Bella Voce 7236).

For those listeners seeking a solid, all-around introduction to his artful singing while avoiding the expense of a full-length opera recording, an easy recommendation is *Arias—Airs—Arien* (London 400053), which features classic arias by Ruggiero Leoncavallo (*Vesti la giubba*), Puccini (*Nessun dorma!*), Verdi (*Celeste Aïda*), and more. Pavarotti also created a set of albums filled with popular Neapolitan songs after initial success with the genre on *O Sole Mio* (London 410015). However, it looks as though many of his finest releases are disappearing from print while newer titles offer an unwelcome contrast, as Pavarotti's aging vocals pale in comparison to the best of his earlier years.

William Gerard

---

among the high-profile supporters who began performing Pärt's music (and eventually recording it).

Pärt left Estonia in 1980. Theoretically, he was to move to Israel with his wife and two children, but instead he spent a year and a half in Vienna (becoming an Austrian citizen) before moving to West Berlin. After this relocation, his tintinnabuli compositions became less mechanical in construction, requiring more compositional decisions and resulting in a less stark sound—mirroring a similar move in American minimalism made earlier by composers such as Steve Reich and Philip Glass, though again in a different manner. Once away from the strictures of Soviet bureaucrats, he could finally set religious texts fearlessly and, ever since, choral works have poured prolifically from the pen of a man whose stern visage, full beard, and bald pate fit the image of an Old Testament prophet.

Three conductors in particular have championed Pärt's music repeatedly on recordings: Paul Hillier (on ECM and Harmonia Mundi), Neeme Järvi (on Melodiya, Chandos, Delos, BIS, and Deutsche Grammophon), and Tõnu Kaljuste (on ECM and Virgin Classics). In fact, Pärt's current popularity is inconceivable without recordings, most notably the many on the ECM label of Manfred Eicher, who started the imprint's *New Series* in 1984 so that the previously jazz-oriented company could issue recordings of Pärt's music. Also notable is that Hillier, an esteemed choral conductor, wrote a book, published in 1996, about Pärt's music for the Oxford University Press's composer series.

Orchestral
Tabula Rasa for Violin, Prepared Piano, and String Orchestra
what to buy: [Gidon Kremer, violin; Tatiana Grindenko, violin; Alfred Schnittke, prepared piano; Saulus Sondeckis, cond.; Lithuanian Chamber Orchestra] (ECM 1275) ♪ ♪ ♪ ♪ ♪

This 1984 release was most people's introduction to Pärt's music, instantly propelling him from avant-garde obscurity to the attention of a much broader audience. All the pieces on it were composed in 1977 and are in Pärt's tintinnabuli style. Having fellow Soviet composer Schnittke play the piano part of *Tabula Rasa* is quite apt considering that his Concerto Grosso no. 1 for Two Violins, Piano, Harpsichord, and Strings dates from the same year and the pieces were programmed together in concert. The other works here have varying personnel: *Fratres II* for Violin features an arrangement for violin and piano with Gidon Kremer and Keith Jarrett respectively; *Fratres III* for Cello is arranged specifically for the twelve cellists of the Berlin Philharmonic Orchestra; *Cantus in Memoriam Benjamin Britten* for Bell and String Orchestra finds Dennis Russell Davies leading the

Stuttgart Radio Symphony Orchestra.

what to buy next: [Gil Shaham, violin; Adele Anthony, violin; Erik Risberg, prepared piano; Neeme Järvi, cond.; Gothenburg Symphony Orchestra] (Deutsche Grammophon 457647) ♪ ♪ ♪ ♪

Listeners not persuaded by Gidon Kremer's astringent violin tone on *Fratres* or *Tabula Rasa* (see above) may respond more positively to the voluptuous sound of Gil Shaham. Whether that sound, and Shaham's more Romantic approach, are appropriate to the music is debatable and a matter of taste. (Completists should note that this *Fratres* is a 1992 revision for violin, string orchestra, and percussion). Järvi's second recording of the composer's Symphony no. 3 included in this package has a more profound impact than the first (see below), with his new reading broader and in more spatial sound.

Symphony no. 3
what to buy: [Neeme Järvi, cond.; Bamberg Symphony Orchestra] (BIS 434) ♪ ♪ ♪ ♪

Conductor Neeme Järvi, like Pärt, is Estonian and studied in Tallinn; the two have known each other for many years, and Pärt dedicated his Symphony no. 3 to Järvi. This 1989 recording is therefore not only an important look at Pärt's overly neglected early style, but also filled with a long-term understanding of where he came from and where he has gone since. Also on this disc are the composer's first two symphonies in addition to his cello concerto (*Pro et Contra*) with cellist Frans Helmerson, and the orchestral *Perpetuum mobile*.

Chamber
various organ works
what to buy: [Christoph Maria Moosmann, organ] (New Albion 074) ♪ ♪ ♪ ♪

Along with premiere readings of pieces by John Cage and Giacinto Scelsi, this disc contains all of Pärt's solo organ works to the date of recording (1996). *Pari intervalli* and *Trivium I—III* are both from 1976 and the first moves into the tintinnabuli style, which is well-suited to a cathedral organ and the space's reverberation. *Annum per annum* and *Mein Weg hat Gipfel und Wellentäler* fill out the Pärt organ works in the collection.

Vocal
Kanon Pokajanen for Chorus

what to buy: [Tõnu Kaljuste, cond.; Estonian Philharmonic Chamber Choir] (ECM 1654/55) ♪♪♪♪♪

This is Pärt's longest work—an eighty-three-minute setting of the Church Slavonic text of the *Canon of Repentance* by St. Andrew of Crete (c.660–740). Pärt bases the rhythms on the text, and more than in his setting of Latin texts, this music draws on some of the effects familiar from Russian Orthodox choral writing, though quiet sections are prototypically Pärt-like.

Litany for Solo Voices, Orchestra, and Chorus

what to buy: [David James, alto; John Potter, tenor; Rogers Covey-Crump, tenor; Gordon Jones, bass; Tõnu Kaljuste, cond.; Tallinn Chamber Orchestra; Estonian Philharmonic Chamber Choir] (ECM 1592) ♪♪♪♪♪

Litany is something of a precursor to *Kanon Pokajanen*. Though in English translation, it also uses a Church Slavonic text, in this case of the famous Liturgy of St. John Chrysostom. While it's clearly a concert work—the orchestral accompaniment and the English words prevent it from being used liturgically—the angular melody lines recall the pre-European-influence *znamenny* chant of Russian Orthodoxy. The orchestral compositions *Psalom* and *Trisagion,* with Saulus Sondeckis conducting the Lithuanian Chamber Orchestra, follow the choral work.

Berliner Messe (Berlin Mass) for Organ and Chorus

what to buy: [*Te Deum*; Tõnu Kaljuste, cond.; Tallinn Chamber Orchestra; Estonian Philharmonic Chamber Choir] (ECM 1505) ♪♪♪♪♪

The *Berlin Mass* is more ornate than the *Missa sillabica,* with more passing tones and melismas. It's also, therefore, more lush in harmony, showing how much Pärt's tintinnabuli style had developed in the decade since he moved to the West. It's heard here with a string orchestra accompaniment rather than the original 1990 version with organ. The sonorous a cappella *Magnificat* for Chorus is also absolutely essential; it may rank as Pärt's most frequently programmed work, since its level of performance difficulty lies comfortably within the abilities of top-flight amateur choirs. The *Te Deum* (for which the CD is titled) is, like the *Berlin Mass,* a fairly colorful work by Pärt's standards. Also included is *Silouans Song,* which, despite its title, is a purely orchestral work.

what to buy next: [Christopher Bowers-Broadbent, organ; Paul Hillier, cond.; Theatre of Voices, choir; Pro Arte Singers, choir] (Harmonia Mundi 907242) ♪♪♪♪♪

This newer album features a more recent revision of the *Berlin Mass,* back to chorus and organ but with the organ part more fleshed out as it incorporates aspects of the string accompaniment of the previous version; some tastes may prefer it to the version with strings, and certainly this is how it's more likely to be performed. It's given a superb reading by Hillier and his forces. The disc is filled out with five shorter works by Pärt, three exclusive to this CD as this is written.

Magnificat for Chorus

what to buy: [*De Profundis*; Christopher Bower-Broadbent, organ; Paul Hillier, cond.; Theatre of Voices, choir] (Harmonia Mundi 907182) ♪♪♪♪♪

The Theatre of Voices is a much larger group (twenty-two singers) than the one-voice-to-a-part Hilliard Ensemble Paul Hillier used to conduct and sing in, and also lacks the sometimes annoying habit some of the Hilliard men have of dynamically inflecting each note to the detriment of the overall phrase. In the repertoire on which the groups overlap, the fuller, more mellifluous Theatre of Voices performances are preferable. In addition to their superb *Magnificat,* the choir delivers other Pärt choral works: the seven *Magnificat Antiphons, De Profundis,* the *Missa sillabica, Solfeggio, Cantate Domino, Summa,* the *Beatitudes,* and *And One of the Pharisees.*

Stabat Mater for Vocal Ensemble

what to buy: [*Arbos*; Gidon Kremer, violin; Vladimir Mendelssohn, viola; Thomas Demenga, cello; Dennis Russell Davies, cond.; Hilliard Ensemble, choir] (ECM 1325) ♪♪♪♪♪

The main work on this disc is the ethereal *Stabat Mater,* perhaps the most gentle setting of that great text ever composed. For three soloists and a trio of violin, viola and cello, it shifts textures just enough to not blur together. *An den Wassern zu Babel* and *De Profundis* are also well-known texts, set here for choir and organ (with percussion on the second piece). *Summa* is the Latin Credo, for four voices, showing the tintinnabuli style at its most methodical. The non-religious *Es sang vor langen Jahren* (text by Romantic poet Clemens Brentano) is for alto, violin, and viola. Two instrumental works are included for variety: the fanfare-like *Arbos* for brass (twice), and the soothing solo organ piece *Pari Intervallo*.

influences: John Tavener, Henryk Górecki, Alfred Schnittke

Steve Holtje

Harry Partch

Born June 24, 1901, in Oakland, CA. Died September 3, 1974, in San Diego, CA.

period: Twentieth century

Largely self-taught, Harry Partch is considered an important if iconoclastic composer who zealously explored microtonal music by creating a new set of scales that included forty-three tones per octave. He also built his own original instruments and developed a unique kind of performance art.

Partch was the son of missionary parents who, fleeing the Boxer Rebellion, returned to the United States from China shortly before he was born. Growing up in isolated areas of the American Southwest, he formed his musical tastes during his preteen years, drawing inspiration from Christian hymns, Chinese lullabies, Yaqui Indian ceremonies, and "Okie" songs heard in California vineyards. Partch began writing serious music at the age of fourteen and in the following years composed a quartet, a symphonic poem, and many short pieces. By the time he was twenty-eight, however, Partch had grown frustrated with orthodox Western musical culture; his fury increased until he burned all his scores, emancipating himself from the old ways. In order to bring his new ideas to fruition, however, Partch realized he would have to construct his own instruments. Luckily, he was handy with woodworking tools and other common implements. Using his original concepts about scales (forty-three tones per octave) and the unique instruments necessary to play them, he wrote a series of novel works. From 1932 to 1934, Partch performed these pieces for small groups and in various San Francisco and New York City clubs. Then, in 1935, he received a grant from the Carnegie Corporation of New York that permitted him to travel to the British Museum, Ireland, Italy, and Malta. When he returned to a jobless America, he took on a series of menial positions to support himself, hung out with hobos, and went through hard times—experiences

that influenced his work during the early 1940s.

In 1943, a Guggenheim Fellowship afforded Partch the opportunity to complete his first major piece, *The Wayward*. Written between 1941 and 1943, its four movements include "U.S. Highball: A Musical Account of a Transcontinental Hobo Trip," "San Francisco: A Setting of the Cries of Two Newsboys on a Foggy Night in the Twenties," "The Letter: A Depression Message from a Hobo Friend," and "Barstow: Eight Hitchhiker Inscriptions from a Highway Railing at Barstow, California." As the most substantial of these elements, "U.S. Highball" features the thoughts and experiences of a lone hobo on a long journey, with Partch including a backdrop of freight-train sounds and the conversational musicality of hobos (all based on inscriptions in a journal he kept during this time). Partch's next important work, a ten-scene suite called *The Bewitched: A Dance-Satire*, was completed in 1955. The lengthy satire was premiered by the University of Illinois Musical Ensemble at the Festival of Contemporary Arts in 1957 and contains movements wittily entitled "The Romancing of a Pathological Liar Comes to an Inspired End," "A Court in Its Own Contempt Rises to a Motherly Apotheosis," and "The Cognoscenti Are Plunged into a Demonic Descent While at Cocktails." Partch's first composition to directly combine dance-theater with music, it included clarinets, piccolo, and cello in addition to his specially made instruments, all of which were placed on risers as part of the performance staging.

From 1963 to 1966 Partch toiled over *And on the Seventh Day Petals Fell in Petaluma*, a piece consisting of one-minute verses performed by duets, trios, quartets, quintets, and a septet. Although it ranks among the most concise and complex of Partch's works, it may be the easiest for the average listener to absorb. It is certainly the best example within a single composition of his abilities as a composer and instrument builder. Partch's last major composition, a theater piece called *Delusion of the Fury: A Ritual of Dream and Delusion*, was also his most successful. The first act of the work is based on an eleventh-century Japanese story, while the second act is based on an African folk tale; much of *Petaluma* was also incorporated into this extremely complex score. All of Partch's accumulated instruments (except his adapted viola) were used at some point in the performance, which required the costumed musicians to become dancers or actors.

Partch's array of instruments developed gradually; they

are astonishing for the increasing complexity of their construction and their eccentric nomenclature. Five of the six "harmonic canons" constructed since 1945 contain two planes of forty-four strings each; moveable bridges can be placed under the strings, which are then plucked by fingers and picks or struck with sticks. Two "chromelodeons," dating from 1945, are reed pump organs tuned to the complete forty-three-tone octave, with total ranges of more than five octaves. (All other instruments in a typical Partch ensemble are tuned to the chromelodeons.) The "spoils of war" consists of artillery-shell casings, Pyrex jars, a high woodblock, a low marimba bar, spring-steel flexitones called "whang guns," and a guiro. The "cloud-chamber bowls," built of Pyrex jars cut in half, suspended on a rack, and hit on sides and tops with soft mallets, is the most fragile of all Partch's instruments. The NewBand, a music ensemble founded in 1977 by composer Dean Drummond and flutist Stefani Starin, has received custodianship of the original Harry Partch instrument collection and continues to perform and record Partch's works in addition to compositions by other modern composers.

Vocal
Delusion of the Fury: A Ritual of Dream and Delusion
what to buy: [Victoria Bond, soprano; John Stannard, tenor; Paul Bergen, bass; Danlee Mitchell, cond.; various musicians] (Innova 406) ♪ ♪ ♪ ♪ ♪

Delusion of the Fury, Partch's last large-scale piece, is considered by many to be his masterwork. It was originally recorded on a Columbia Records album that included an extra LP on which the composer described each of his instruments. The Innova release includes all the material heard on that first issue with the exception of Partch's descriptions. A short essay by Partch, a note by Eugene Paul (who produced the Columbia set), and additional liner notes by Danlee Mitchell provide welcome insight into the composer's trials and tribulations in getting this work produced.

"U.S. Highball" for Solo Voices, Original Instruments, and Chorus
what to buy: [*The Harry Partch Collection, Vol. 2*; Jack McKenzie, cond.; The Gate 5 Ensemble] (CRI 752) ♪ ♪ ♪ ♪₆

"U.S. Highball" is (at over twenty-five minutes) the most substantial and attention-getting of the four movements in the complete performance of *The Wayward* heard here; the fourth section ("Barstow: Eight Hitchhiker

Inscriptions from a Highway Railing at Barstow, California") is the most performed of Partch's works. This CD also contains a fascinating performance of his all-instrumental work, *And on the Seventh Day Petals Fell in Petaluma.*

Eleven Intrusions for Voices and Original Instruments
what to buy: [*The Harry Partch Collection, Vol. 1*; Harry Partch, vocals; Harry Partch, cond.; various instrumentalists; various vocalists] (CRI 751) ♪ ♪ ♪ ♪₆

This CD is a good starting point if you are just beginning to explore Partch's oeuvre. Recorded in the 1950s and 1960s, it chronicles the composer's works, preserving elements of the Partch sound exceptionally well. *Eleven Intrusions* features intoned voice and uses ten of Partch's unique instruments, including cloud-chamber bowls, bass marimba, and various woody-sounding percussion instruments. You may also hear the influences of Partch's earliest musical inspirations, especially Asian music. Other pieces splendidly performed here by Partch and friends include selections from his *Plectra and Percussion Dances* and *Ulysses at the Edge of the World.*

The Bewitched for Solo Voice and Instrumental Ensemble
what to buy: [*The Harry Partch Collection, Vol. 4*; Freda Schell, singer; John Garvey, cond.; University of Illinois Musical Ensemble, orch.] (CRI 754) ♪ ♪ ♪ ♪

This recording documents the first performance of this dance-satire, featuring eighteen musicians playing many of the instruments Partch designed. Melodious, dramatic, and filled with intriguing vocal/instrumental sounds and colorful percussive splashes, the performance wholly captures your interest, even though you'll need to follow scene descriptions in the liner booklet to know what's going on.

influences: Danlee Mitchell, Dean Drummond, Lou Harrison, John Zorn

Nancy Ann Lee

Krzysztof Penderecki
Born November 23, 1933, in Debica, Poland.

period: Twentieth century

Penderecki started out as a Polish ultramodernist but later turned his back on the avant-garde. Subsequent periods have witnessed his quest to find an original voice through principles of the past, resulting in a unique fusion of the modern and traditional.

Krzysztof Penderecki is that rare creature in the annals of twentieth-century music—a composer who successfully infuses the avant-garde with raw emotion and expressive power to create a beautifully fashioned whole. Using fifty-two stringed instruments playing a quarter-tone apart to amass a solid wall of sound, the chilling *Threnody for the Victims of Hiroshima* took the music world by storm in 1961 and established Penderecki's name among modernists. The conjured screams of victims and the shrieks of air-raid sirens in this short piece are truly horrifying. Penderecki's fascination with historical and religious subjects continued with the stirring *St. Luke Passion* and powerful *Miserere*, and later the *Polish Requiem* and the *Dies Irae*, composed for the fortieth anniversary of the Warsaw ghetto uprising.

Penderecki's earliest works, the most notable being the Sonata for Violin and Piano from 1953, display a thorough understanding of contemporary techniques. But it wasn't until the *Threnody* that we hear a complete break with the past; many people in musical circles eagerly waited to see how far the radical young composer would push things. Instead, after the cluster-filled *Magnificat*, Penderecki toned down his austere style in the mid-1970s; critics were baffled, but the general public liked the romantic tone of his works from this period. (It is worth noting that Penderecki wasn't the only Polish composer to turn an abrupt about-face on musical complexity. Henryk Górecki, his exact contemporary, felt that stringent modernism could go no further and completely streamlined his harmonic language.) Penderecki's opera *Paradise Lost* and his second and third symphonies, also from this period, sound a bit like leftovers from the previous century, marked by the motivic development and symphonic proportions that were the bane of modernists.

By the 1980s, starting with the Concerto for Cello and Orchestra no. 2, Penderecki seemed to achieve a stylistic synthesis of modern and traditional elements, making for a more satisfying and cohesive unit. The Concerto for Viola and Orchestra, from 1983, is a great example; the humanistic *Polish Requiem, Agnus Dei,* and *Veni Creator* apply these principles to religious subjects. This period

also witnessed an outpouring of the composer's chamber music, including the String Trio and the well-crafted Quartet for Clarinet and Strings.

Those who have seen Stanley Kubrick's movie *The Shining* (with *The Awakening of Jacob, De Natura Sonoris II,* and excerpts from *Utrenja* on the soundtrack) or William Friedkin's *Exorcist* (featuring *Polymorphia*) have already heard Penderecki's early sonic collages. There is something to appreciate in each stylistic period, though many listeners may find the neo-romantic works from the middle period a bit unsatisfying; indeed, many of these pieces don't seem to leave a lasting impression. Nonetheless, Penderecki has consistently composed works of great emotional immediacy and clarity through the decades, proving himself to be one of the giants of European music in the turbulent second half of the twentieth-century.

Orchestral
Threnody for the Victims of Hiroshima for Orchestra
what to buy: [*Orchestral Works, Vol. 1*; Antoni Wit, cond.; National Polish Radio Symphony Orchestra, Katowice] (Naxos 8.55449) ♪ ♪ ♪ ♪

There is a good deal of variety in this package, including the successful Symphony No. 3, *Flourescences,* and the *De natura Sonoris II* for Orchestra, along with the *Threnody.* The budget price makes it a great deal.

worth searching for: [Szymon Kawalla, cond.; Polish Radio and Television Symphony Orch.] (Conifer 168) ♪ ♪ ♪

A molten *Threnody* and a poignant interpretation of the Concerto for Viola and Orchestra (with Grigori Zhislin as soloist) are combined with another postmodern work on the subject of urban disaster, Nancy Van de Vate's *Chernobyl.*

Concerto no. 2 for Violin and Orchestra— *Metamorphosen*
what to buy: [*Violin Concerto no. 2: Metamorphosen*; Anne-Sophie Mutter, violin; Krzysztof Penderecki, cond.; London Symphony Orchestra] (Deutsche Grammophon 453072) ♪ ♪ ♪

Though this one-movement work can sound a bit derivative, it certainly receives a fluid performance at the hands of Mutter (to whom it is dedicated) on this Grammy-winning 1998 recording. The second of Béla Bartók's violin sonatas is also included, with Mutter accompanied by pianist Lambert Orkis.

various works
what to buy: [*Penderecki Gala*; Jadwiga Gadulanka, soprano; Jean-Pierre Rampal, flute; Sharon Kam, clarinet; Vladimir Viardo, piano; Grigori Zhislin, Christoph Poppen, violins; Kim Kashkashian, viola; Boris Pergamenschikow, cello; Krzysztof Penderecki, Henryk Wojnarowski, conds.; Sinfonia Varsovia, orch.; Warsaw National Philharmonic Choir] (Sony Classics 66284) ♪ ♪ ♪

This Penderecki potpourri contains a few works not available elsewhere, including the "Lacrimosa" for Soprano, Chorus, and Orchestra (from the *Polish Requiem*) and the Concerto for Flute and Chamber Orchestra, featuring Jean-Pierre Rampal. The composer conducts most of the works heard here, including the Sinfonietta for Strings, the Concerto for Flute and Chamber Orchestra, the "Lacrimosa" for Soprano, Chorus, and Orchestra, and the "Song of the Cherubim," while Wojnarowski leads the choir through the "Benedicamus Domino." Zhislin and Viardo team up in the Sonata for Violin and Piano, with Kam, Poppen, Kashkashian, and Pergamenschikow rendering the Quartet for Clarinet and Strings. This set is only for those interested in Penderecki's works of the 1980s and 1990s.

Chamber
various works
what to buy: [*Chamber Music: Ensemble Villa Musica*] (MDG 3040917) ♪ ♪ ♪

Here is a splendid and diverse collection of Penderecki's chamber music, ranging from the very early Sonata for Violin and Piano to works of the early 1990s. The program includes the composer's Trio for Strings, the *Prelude for Clarinet Solo, Per Slava* for Solo Cello, the *Cadenza* for Solo Viola, and the Quartet for Clarinet and Strings.

Vocal
Stabat Mater
what to buy: [*Complete Sacred Works for Chorus A Cappella*; Juha Kuivanen, cond.; Tapila Chamber Choir] (Finlandia 98999) ♪ ♪ ♪₄

The Period Instrument Debate: Pros and Cons
The *New Harvard Dictionary of Music* defines "authentic" this way: "In performance practice, instruments or styles of playing that are historically appropriate to the music being performed." The devil is in the details, however, and a key issue at the heart of the debate over such practice is whether anyone really has the right to designate what is or is not historically appropriate. As musicologist Howard Mayer Brown put it in a 1988 symposium, "Should we play music in the way the composer intended it, or at the very least in a way his contemporaries could have heard it (bearing in mind that these are not always the same thing)?"

Nikolaus Harnoncourt voiced his thoughts on the subject in an essay from 1954 entitled "Zur Interpretation historischer Musik (On the Interpretation of Historical Music)," declaring that "works sound not only historically more correct, but also more vital, because they are performed with the means most appropriate to them, and we get an intimation of the spiritual forces which made the past so fertile. Involvement with old music in this way takes on a deep meaning, far surpassing that of purely aesthetic enjoyment."

The perception of a historically faithful manner of performance by musicians does not guarantee the quality of the interpretation to the listener, however. As Gustav Leonhardt, one of Harnoncourt's compatriots in the movement, has noted, "If one strives only to be authentic, it will never be convincing. If one is convincing, what is offered will leave an authentic impression." Raymond Leppard, a conductor who did much to advance the cause of Claudio Monteverdi and other Renaissance-period composers, once railed against those who swore blind adherence to the concept of historical authenticity, calling them a cult "that is as offensive to the art of music as it is inhibiting and unattractive at a human level."

Casual listeners seeking confirmation of whether "original instrument" performances are better than those using more modern instruments are advised to take the whole matter with a grain of salt. The bottom-line value of a performance or recording is strictly a personal matter of whether the one hearing the music actually likes what is being played. With that in mind, there is definitely value in comparing at least two different takes on a particular piece of music; it helps listeners determine for themselves what it is about an interpretation that they like and don't like. Moreover, there is always the possibility that they may actually appreciate both of these contrasting approaches, or that the recordings will give them the parameters necessary to eventually find a performance they prefer above all others.

Ellen Kokko

Penderecki's outpouring of sacred music is key to understanding the composer. This program finds Kuivanen's forces performing nine exquisite and emotive works from four decades, including the composer's *Stabat Mater*, the *Veni Creator*, and the "Song of the Cherubim."

Polish Requiem for Solo Voices, Orchestra, and Chorus

what to buy: [Jadwiga Gadulanka, soprano; Jadwiga Rappe, contralto; Zachos Terzakis, tenor; Piotr Nowacki, bass; Krzysztof Penderecki, cond.; Royal Stockholm Philharmonic Orchestra, Royal Stockholm Philharmonic Chorus] (Chandos 9459/9460) ♪ ♪ ♪

This is the composer's most ambitious humanitarian statement, coupled here with the beguiling *Als Jakob erwachte* (The Dream of Jacob) from 1974.

St. Luke's Passion

worth searching for: [Krzysztof Penderecki, cond; National Radio Symphony Orchestra; Warsaw National Philharmonic Chorus] (Argo 430328) ♪ ♪ ♪ ♪

The composer is also an esteemed conductor; this import disc finds him directing his complex and monumental choral opus.

influences: Henryk Górecki, Witold Lutoslawski, Luciano Berio, Karol Szymanowski

Sean Hickey

Giovanni Battista Pergolesi

Born January 4, 1710, in Iesi, Italy. Died March 16, 1736, in Pozzuoli, Italy.

period: Baroque

Despite his death at the age of twenty-six, Pergolesi played a major role in developing Italian comic opera with what is arguably his most popular composition, *La Serva Padrona*. He also wrote numerous sacred works, among them a genuine masterpiece, his setting of the Stabat Mater.

Pergolesi studied composing at the Conservatorio dei Poveri di Gesù Cristo in Naples during the early 1720s. After completing his formal musical education, he secured a series of freelance commissions and served as a musician at various public and church-related functions. While he had written a number of sacred vocal works at the conservatory, including some religious operas, his first serious opera, *Salustia,* wasn't written until 1731. The next year, he was offered a position with a nobleman attached to the court of the Viceroy of Naples. Pergolesi was already a violinist of some note and had started to be recognized for his work as a com-

poser of vocal scores, but it was during the last five years of his life that he wrote his most important compositions. His first brush with fame grew out of a contract he received from the City of Naples. An earthquake had devastated the city in 1731, and the town fathers approached the young musician to write a mass and some other sacred music commemorating the event. Encouraged by the reception to his work, Pergolesi began dabbling in opera again.

The biggest hit he had in that field was with an opera within an opera. In 1733, he was commissioned to write a dramatic opera, *Il Prigionier Superbo,* wrapped around a lighthearted intermezzo called *La Serva Padrona.* This last work has since become the most frequently performed piece in Pergolesi's catalog, although it didn't seem to excite as many people when it was initially staged as it did in the years after he died. The basic story line involves a scheming servant girl plotting to marry her master and the hoops she jumps through to accomplish her goal. There is one other character in this mini-opera, a mute who briefly masquerades as her fiancé, but the arias are essentially reserved for the lead roles.

Pergolesi wrote a few more works after that, generally getting a good reception from his audiences until 1735, when his opera *L'Olimpiade* utterly bombed in Rome. He then moved into a Franciscan monastery and returned to writing music for the church. One of his last works was a splendid setting of the *Stabat Mater,* which has since been acclaimed as his masterpiece. This work was carefully studied and transcribed by no less than Johann Sebastian Bach, and nearly two centuries later the young composer's music would capture the fancy of Igor Stravinsky, whose *Pulcinella* was inspired by several Pergolesi melodies. It was said that the failure of *L'Olimpiade* was a contributing factor to his declining health, and in 1736 he succumbed to tuberculosis.

Vocal
Stabat Mater in F Minor for Soprano, Alto, Organ, and Strings

what to buy: [June Anderson, soprano; Cecilia Bartoli, mezzo-soprano; Charles Dutoit, cond.; Montreal Sinfonietta, orch.] (London 436209) ♪ ♪ ♪ ♪ ♪

Gorgeous vocals combine with Dutoit's wonderful handling of this superb score to create a very special recording. The inclusion of *Salve Regina* settings by Pergolesi and Alessandro Scarlatti only serves to make this an even better program.

[Gillian Fisher, soprano; Michael Chance, countertenor; Robert King, cond.; The King's Consort, orch.] (Hyperion 20294) ♪ ♪ ♪ ♪₈

The meshing of soprano to countertenor has never been carried out so well, and this should undoubtedly be the first choice of those wishing to hear this work in as close to an original setting as possible. The conductor also plays the chamber organ on this set, adding further to the intimate sonics this performance is blessed with. The composer's *Salve Regina* in A Minor and *In coelestibus regnis* are delightful additions to the whole package.

what to buy next: [Emma Kirkby, soprano; James Bowman, countertenor; Christopher Hogwood, cond.; Academy of Ancient Music, orch.] (L'Oiseau Lyre 425692) ♪ ♪ ♪₈

Here's a case where the austere sound of the Academy's authentic instruments and performance practices is entirely appropriate to the subject matter. Kirkby and Bowman make a fine duo in a moving performance of Pergolesi's masterpiece.

La Serva Padrona for Soprano, Bass-Baritone, and Orchestra
what to buy: [Patrizia Biccire, soprano; Donato Di Stefano, bass; Sigiswald Kuikjen, cond.; La Petite Bande, orch.] (Accent 96123) ♪ ♪ ♪₈

Kuijen's "band" is a well-versed original-instrument ensemble, and its 1996 live performance at the Luna Theater in Brussels, Belgium, contains all the fire and spunk audiences could hope for when hearing this seminal work. Biccire is fine as the shrewish maid, and Di Stefano has that burly quality one seeks for his role.

what to buy next: [Isabelle Poulenard, soprano; Philippe Cantor, baritone; Gilbert Bezzina, conductor; Nice Baroque Ensemble, orch.] (Pierre Verany 795111) ♪ ♪₈

The principals certainly seem to be enjoying themselves in this comic romp; Poulenard's soprano is a joy, and Cantor's emphatic bass adds just the right amount of bluster to his character. Unfortunately this recording suffers from a somewhat distant miking and an orchestral balance that is at times uneven, qualities that can impede a listener's enjoyment of this classic opera buffa.

worth searching for: [Rosanna Carteri, soprano; Nicola Rossi-Lemeni, bass; Carlo Maria Giulini, cond.; La Scala Orchestra] (Angel 35279) ♪ ♪ ♪ ♪

La Scala veteran Carteri is a versatile singer/actress who can act out the flighty portions of the libretto without sacrificing the basic musicality of the role. Rossi-Lemeni is a good match for her, and Giulini's conducting is uniformly fine. If there is any caveat to the recording, it lies with the orchestra's string section, which is a tad ragged at times but not enough to affect the good overall impression of the cast.

influences: Francesco Durante, Igor Stravinsky

Chris Felcyn and Garaud MacTaggart

Allan Pettersson
Born Gustav Allan Pettersson, September 19, 1911, in Västra Ryd, Sweden. Died June 20, 1980, in Stockholm, Sweden.

period: Twentieth century

Pettersson's oeuvre leans towards the symphonic, although his most important early composition—the *Barfotasånger* (Barefoot Songs)—is a song cycle for voice and piano. In the large-scale pieces (such as his Symphony no. 7, the work that brought him to the attention of an international audience) he can be heard imparting his own dark, textured vision to the music, mixing orchestral dissonances with folkloric elements to create an intense, passionate, idiosyncratic body of work, with nary a hint of serialism or other modern trends. He is without a doubt the most important Swedish symphonist of the twentieth century.

Born poor and raised in a slum district of southern Stockholm, with a brutal, alcoholic, blacksmith for a father and a religious mother (the memory of her hymn singing was to form an important element in many of his later compositions), Allan Pettersson retained a basic sympathy for the downtrodden throughout his creative life. While his firsthand insight into social injustice didn't lead him into the arms of Communism, it certainly provided him with a healthy class awareness and a palpable sense of anger and despair (along with a strong persecution complex) that would be evidenced in many of his later works.

For Pettersson, music came to be a way of escaping, if only for a moment, the poverty surrounding him. By selling Christmas cards, he was able to save enough money to purchase a violin and proceeded to teach himself how to play. He was soon good enough to join local ensembles in a variety of settings, honing his abilities and furthering his improbable dream of entering the Stockholm Royal Conservatory. He finally achieved this goal in 1930 after two unsuccessful attempts, later attributing his pair of failed auditions to his economic background and the prejudice against the lower classes held by the school's administrators. In a interview with Göran Bergendal, Pettersson admitted that, "Perhaps [my music] is a protest against predestination, cruelty towards the individual, the individual without a chance."

He studied at the conservatory until 1939, taking classes in violin, viola, theory, and composition. While at the school, Pettersson played in the Swedish premiere of Arnold Schoenberg's *Pierrot Lunaire*. His hard-won experience paid off with a Jenny Lind Fellowship in 1938, which enabled him to study in Paris the following year. It was a short-lived venture, however, as the German invasion of France compelled Pettersson to return to Stockholm; there he joined the Stockholm Konsertföreningen (now the Stockholm Philharmonic Orchestra) as a viola player, a position he held until 1950. During his years as an orchestral musician, he continued to study the basic elements of composition, working with Karl-Birger Blomdahl, Tor Mann, and Otto Olsson. A product of these efforts was Pettersson's 1945 song cycle, *Barfotasånger* (Barefoot Songs), which was not publicly performed until the late 1960s. The first concert performances of Pettersson's works took place in 1948 (the *Fugue for Woodwind Instruments*) and 1949 (the Concerto no. 1 for Violin and String Quartet), but both premieres were unsuccessful. Convinced that he needed to sharpen his composing skills, Pettersson went back to Paris in 1950, joining Arthur Honegger's class at the Paris Conservatoire and dabbling briefly in serialism with René Leibowitz.

When he finally returned to Stockholm in 1953, Pettersson embarked upon a serious career as a composer, although he still played viola until 1964, when crippling rheumatoid arthritis (which first manifested itself in 1953) finally put an end to his days as a performer. He began receiving critical acclaim from

Swedish critics, winning the 1963 Expressen Music Prize for his Symphony no. 5 (the last work he was to score in his own script) and the 1968 City of Stockholm Award of Honor for his Symphony no. 6. But his first real brush with international success came when Antal Doráti conducted the maiden performance of Pettersson's Symphony no. 7 in the fall of 1968. By this time, his disease had severely limited Pettersson's ability to write his own scores, and his attempts to travel were hindered by the number of steps leading up to the small, cramped fourth-floor apartment where he had lived with his wife since 1946. Although the Swedish government granted him an income guarantee similar to the one Finland awarded Jean Sibelius, his medical expenses were mounting. Further physical maladies would strike in 1970, when his kidneys were seriously bruised. Confined to a hospital bed for nine months, Pettersson still kept working on his musical ideas, sketching out the concepts that would eventually culminate in his tenth and eleventh symphonies.

In the mid-1970s, the Swedish government gave Pettersson a state-owned house to move into, and he was awarded various financial prizes for his musical contributions. The last years of his life would be more comfortable than any he had experienced before. The works from this final period included his Symphony no. 16 (a score that originated as an alto saxophone concerto), his unfinished Symphony no. 17, and his Concerto no. 2 for Violin and Orchestra. In May 1980 he was admitted to the hospital for the last time, dying a month later.

Orchestral
Symphony no. 7
what to buy: [Antal Doráti, cond.; Stockholm Philharmonic Orchestra] (Swedish Society Discofil 1002) ♪ ♪ ♪ ♪

A massive-sounding single-movement work, this is a symphony of taut emotions, with little light breaking through the aural storm clouds. During Doráti's tenure at the head of the Stockholm Philharmonic, he recorded this classic performance, bringing an awareness of Pettersson's peculiar genius to an international audience. He then programmed it frequently in Swedish concerts and elsewhere, doing more to raise the composer's banner than anyone before or since. Paired with this seminal work is a performance of Pettersson's last completed symphony, the Symphony no. 16, conducted by Yuri Ahronovitch and featuring Frederick L. Hemke playing the prominent saxophone part.

what to buy next: [Gerd Albrecht, cond.; Hamburg State Philharmonic Orchestra] (CPO 999190) ♪ ♪ ♪ ♪

Albrecht's recording of this work is slightly easier to find than Doráti's, and the performance is quite good, just missing the awesome power generated on the earlier set. Still, this is a worthy rival to the Doráti recording, with very good sonics and an interpretation that reinforces Pettersson's reputation as a major symphonist.

Symphony no. 8
what to buy: [Thomas Sanderling, cond.; Berlin Radio Symphony Orchestra] (CPO 999085) ♪ ♪ ♪ ♪ᵢ

Most of Pettersson's symphonies consist of one massive movement, but this work is constructed from two nearly equal halves. First there is the dramatically introspective first movement; then the tension of the second half explodes, subsides, and regains momentum before fading into an uneasy peace. Despite the bleak aural picture painted by the composer, this may actually be the most listener-friendly of his symphonies. Sanderling is a sympathetic conductor whose orchestral leadership helps control Pettersson's magnificent pathos.

worth searching for: [Sergiu Comissiona, cond.; Baltimore Symphony Orchestra] (Deutsche Grammophon 2531176) ♪ ♪ ♪ ♪ᵢ

Comissiona gave the American premiere of this work, and his recording of the symphony (originally released on Polar Records in 1980) was the best available at the time. That this remnant of the vinyl age holds up so well two decades later is a tribute to both the composer and the forces involved.

Vocal
Barfotasåanger **(Barefoot Songs) for Voice and Piano**
what to buy: [*Complete Songs*; Monica Groop, mezzo-soprano; Cord Garben, piano] (CPO 999499) ♪ ♪ ♪ ♪

These are among the most outwardly conventional works in Pettersson's canon, but they also form one of the finest twentieth century song cycles. The composer wrote the lyrics and music for these twenty-four songs prior to his Parisian studies, and their basic, folk-like melodies are most beguiling, as Groop's beautifully controlled vocals make clear. Also included on this disc are

Itzhak Perlman:
One of the most popular and technically adept violinists in the world today, Itzhak Perlman was born in Tel Aviv, Israel, in 1945, and stricken with polio when he was four years old. Perlman had evinced an interest in playing the violin prior to the onset of his physical travails, and eventually showed enough promise that he was admitted to the Tel Aviv Academy of Music. He had begun performing at various recitals throughout the area when the American television impresario Ed Sullivan visited Israel in 1958 to scout out talent for his variety show. Suitably impressed, Sullivan made arrangements to ensure the youngster's debut performance in America. Following Perlman's appearance on the Sullivan show, he visited the United States a few more times before moving to New York City, where he began studying with Ivan Galamian and Dorothy DeLay at the Juilliard School of Music. Within a few years, he attracted the attention of Isaac Stern (who would become his friend and mentor), won a scholarship from the Israel-American Foundation, signed a management contract with Sol Hurok, and won the Leventritt Award for 1964.

Since that time, Perlman has become acknowledged as the greatest violinist of his generation and one of the finest of the twentieth century. Like Stern, he has also developed into a mentor for a number of musicians, including fellow violinist Gil Shaham. Perlman and his wife Toby have even established the Perlman Summer Music Program, a school for musically gifted children that occasionally features the violinist in the role of teacher and conductor. In addition, Perlman joined the faculty at Juilliard in 1999 and teaches there when he is not out concertizing or fulfilling other commitments.

His recordings with pianist Vladimir Ashkenazy are among the most impressive in Perlman's massive discography. Pride of place belongs to their performance of Ludwig van Beethoven's *Kreutzer* and *Spring* sonatas for violin and piano (Decca Legends 458619). These are also available as part of Perlman and Ashkenazy's complete survey of the composer's ten sonatas for that configuration (Decca Jubilee 421453). Another fine set by the duo is their recording of Johannes Brahms's three violin sonatas (EMI Classics 66945), though as this book goes to press, an even finer disc by them, a performance of César Franck's violin sonata (London 414128), has recently been deleted from the catalog. Perlman and Ashkenazy have also delivered an excellent rendering of Piotyr Illyich Tchaikovsky's Trio for Piano and Strings in A Minor (EMI Classics Special Imports 47988) with cellist Lynn Harrell.

As an orchestral soloist, Perlman has recorded most of the standard repertoire, but a few recordings stand out. Among these are his performances of Alban Berg's lone violin concerto with Seiji Ozawa conducting the Boston Symphony Orchestra (Deutsche Grammophon 447445), and the Concerto no. 3 in B Minor for Violin and Orchestra by Camille Saint-Saëns (Deutsche Grammophon 445549) with Daniel Barenboim leading the Orchestre de Paris. Perlman has also released a few albums for the crossover market that are worth investigating. Notable in this regard are his two discs of klezmer music (*In the Fiddler's House*, EMI Angel 55555, and *Live in the Fiddler's House*, EMI Angel 56209), a set of compositions and arrangements by Fritz Kreisler (*My Favourite Kreisler*, EMI Classics 47467), and an album devoted to Scott Joplin's rags (*The Easy Winners*, EMI Classics 47170).

Ellen Kokko

Pettersson's only other works for voice and piano—the six songs he wrote when he was twenty-five years old.

influences: Jean Sibelius, Dmitri Shostakovich, Gustav Mahler, Vagn Holmboe

Garaud MacTaggart

Gabriel Pierné

Born Henri-Constant Gabriel Pierné, August 16, 1863, in Metz, France. Died July 17, 1937, in Ploujean, France.

period: Romantic/Twentieth century

Pierné was a well-respected composer and conductor whose craftsmanship often outshone his inspiration. Although he wrote for a variety of forces and forms, creating delightful ballets and pleasant songs, Pierné's best work came later in his career, when he devoted more of his compositional efforts toward chamber music.

As a result of the Franco-Prussian War, France had to give up the province of Lorraine, a geopolitical fact that resulted in Pierné's family leaving there when he was seven years old and moving to Paris. His parents were both musicians, and taught their son well enough that he was able to enroll at the prestigious Paris Conservatoire in 1871. While there, Pierné studied organ with César Franck and composition with Jules Massenet, with each eventually exerting a strong influence on the young composer. The young man proved to be a gifted and hard working student and won a number of awards from the school including first prize for piano (1879), counterpoint (1881), and organ (1882) prior to winning the coveted Prix de Rome in 1882. This last prize was added to Pierné's trophy case for composing a cantata titled *Edith,* and enabled him to study in Italy.

He was apparently in no great hurry to return to France after his Italian sojourn, but he came home anyway and taught piano and singing. He was offered the opportunity to succeed his mentor Franck as organist at St. Clotilde in 1890, took it, and remained in that position until 1898. During this time, Pierné wrote pleasant, well-constructed songs, ballets, and light operas during his vacations but his lone piano concerto (op. 12) has proven to be the most durable of the earlier works. In addition to his career as an organist and composer, Pierné developed into a highly respected conductor and champion of his country's new music. This last portion of his reputation was forged at the Concerts Colonne where he start-

ed out as a deputy conductor in 1903, becoming principal conductor seven years later. It was in this last capacity that he led the premieres of Igor Stravinsky's *Firebird,* Claude Debussy's *Ibéria, Images,* and *Jeux,* and Maurice Ravel's *Tzigane.* Pierné finally retired from his position with the Concerts Colonne in 1933.

While some critics have voiced the criticism that Pierné's own music sounds a little too much like a sampler of his contemporaries at the Conservatoire, there is also broad agreement on the craft and polish of his compositions. Massenet's teachings can be most clearly heard in Pierné's orchestral works, which tend toward light, well-constructed pieces that engage the ear more than the mind. One such work worth investigating is his scintillating *Concertstück* for harp and orchestra (op. 39), which he finished composing in the same year he was appointed deputy conductor at the Concerts Colonne. Although he wrote for nearly every genre, a better gauge of Pierné's skills as a composer can probably be found in his chamber works. Good, solid orchestration can cover a multitude of sins, but small-scale pieces leave the architecture of a composition exposed and here Pierné, with his customary attention to detail and the open nature of the medium, is concerned with both mind *and* ear. While he felt that his piano quintet (op. 41) was among his finest achievements, that and his marvelous violin sonata (op. 36) both show Franck's stylistic fingerprints more than they do Pierné's. A truer test of his merit as a composer can be found in the cello sonata (op. 46) that he wrote in 1919.

Orchestral
Concerto in C Minor for Piano and Orchestra, op. 12
what to buy: [Dag Achatz, piano; Jacques Houtmann, conductor; Lorraine Philharmonic] (BIS 381) ♪ ♪ ♪ ♪

Even on first hearing, much of this music may sound strangely familiar, particularly to fans of Camille Saint-Saëns's second piano concerto. It has virtuosic runs, sparkling orchestration, and a score full of wit and grace. This recording features a terrific performance from Achatz and Houtmann. Pierné's two colorful and rarely-heard suites from *Ramuntcho* are also incorporated into the program.

Concertstück for Harp and Orchestra, op. 39
what to buy: [*French Harp Concertos*; Isabelle Moretti, harp; Karl Arp, conductor; Southwest German Radio Symphony Orchestra, Baden-Baden] (Koch Schwann

311422) ♪ ♪ ♪ ♪

Moretti and Arp deliver all the rich detail of Pierné's lovely *Concerstück* in a performance of glittering clarity. Also included are harp works scored by François-Adrien Boïeldieu and Saint-Saëns.

Chamber
Sonata for Cello and Piano, op. 46
what to buy: [Mats Lidström, cello; Bengt Forsberg, piano] (Hyperion 66979) ♪ ♪ ♪ ♪

This is an extraordinary sonata, one that deserves an important place among the many other distinguished examples in the cello literature. Lidström delivers a powerfully engaging performance, beautifully supported by Forsberg at the piano. The French cello music theme continues with a pair of attractive works from Charles Koechlin: his *Chansons Bretonnes sur d'Anciennes Chansons Populaires,* op. 115, and the Sonata for Cello and Piano, op. 66.

influences: Jules Massenet, Gabriel Fauré, Maurice Ravel, César Franck, Paul Dukas, Camille Saint-Saëns

Chris Felcyn and Garaud MacTaggart

Walter Piston
Born Walter Hamor Piston, Jr., January 20, 1894, in Rockland, ME
Died November 12, 1976, in Belmont, MA.

period: Twentieth century

A modern American Neo-Classical composer who wrote primarily in traditional forms such as the symphony, concerto, and sonata, Piston also authored several important, highly respected textbooks (all of which remain in widespread use) on various aspects of composition.

Even as a young boy, Walter Piston had a clear image of his future: he wanted to be an architect. At the age of eleven, his family moved to Boston at the urging of one of his father's business acquaintances. There he graduated from the Mechanic Arts High School, where he picked up the skills necessary to work as a draftsman for the Boston Elevated Railway Company. When he was eighteen years old he enrolled at the Massachusetts Normal Art School so that he could further hone his skills, taking classes in architectural drawing that should have eventually led to his becoming an architect.

Somewhere along the way, however, Piston had also developed an interest in music, teaching himself to play the violin and the piano. During World War I he ended up enlisting in the Navy, where he joined a navy band and learned to play the saxophone. By the time the war was over and he had finished his service, music had begun to take over his plans. With the musical skills Piston now possessed, he was able to procure a modest income by playing in various theater orchestras and dance bands. He had other ambitions, however, and these soon came to the fore.

At the age of twenty-five, he began a lifelong association with Harvard University, graduating *summa cum laude* in 1924. His academic achievement earned him a fellowship to continue his studies, so Piston decided he would make a pilgrimage to Paris to study composition and counterpoint with Nadia Boulanger (as did many of his contemporaries). He also spent some time at the Ecole Normale de Musique, where his composition teacher was Paul Dukas, his violin teacher was Georges Enescu, and he played viola in the school orchestra. After two years of breathing the heady atmosphere of the Parisian artistic community (and being exposed to much of the era's newest music), he returned to Boston in 1926 and accepted a position on the faculty at Harvard—an institution which would provide him a comfortable artistic home for the rest of his career.

Piston also benefited from his proximity to one of the most effective champions of twentieth century music: these were the years when Serge Koussevitzky reigned as music director of the Boston Symphony Orchestra, and through the older man's sponsorship Piston began a relationship with the BSO that would result in eleven premières between 1927 and 1971. The one major work by which Piston is best known, the ballet *The Incredible Flutist,* was written in 1938 and performed by the BSO that year. It marked a breaking away from the more abstract, Stravinsky-influenced scores he had written since his days in Paris, and was actually composed in response to a request by Arthur Fiedler for a ballet that could be performed by Hans Wiener's dance troupe and the Boston Pops spin-off of the BSO. It irked Piston, a composer of "absolute" music, that one of the only two programmatic works he wrote (*Three New England Sketches* is the other) would become his most popular score. Incidentally, those expecting a flute concerto may be surprised at the relatively brief role played by the solo flute in this suite. In the plot of the original ballet it was the flutist's powerful ability to enchant a young woman

as much as his musicianship that made him incredible.

During most of this same period the composer continued teaching music theory at Harvard, rising from full professor in 1944 to his appointment in 1951 as the Walter W. Naumberg Professor of Music. Before he retired from Harvard in 1960 Piston collected an impressive array of awards, including a Guggenheim Fellowship (1935), Pulitzer Prizes for his Symphony no. 3 (1948) and Symphony no. 7 (1961), and eight honorary doctorates. As an educator, his students included Elliot Carter, Irving Fine, and Leonard Bernstein, and the textbooks Piston wrote—particularly *Harmony* (1941), *Counterpoint* (1947), and *Orchestration* (1955)—are highly regarded and still in wide use today.

Orchestral
The Incredible Flutist for Orchestra
what to buy: [Scott Goff, flute; Gerard Schwarz, conductor; Seattle Symphony Orchestra] (Delos 3126) ♪ ♪ ♪ ♪

Schwarz and his Seattle colleagues provide a beautiful sound, in a performance full of both tenderness and flair. The entire album presents a solid picture of Piston's oeuvre, including not only this work but his Concerto for String Quartet, Wind Instruments, and Percussion; his Suite no. 1 for Orchestra; the *Psalm and Prayer of David* (a setting of Psalms nos. 86 and 96, which was Piston's only religious work); and the *Fantasy* for English Horn, Harp, and Strings.

what to buy next: [*An American Tapestry*; Jean Weger Larson, flute; Andrew Litton, conductor; Dallas Symphony Orchestra] (Dorian 90224) ♪ ♪ ♪♪

Although they have some serious competition, Litton and the DSO deliver a fine performance that significantly tightens the race. The CD is further enhanced by excellent sound captured by Dorian's engineers, demonstrating why the Meyerson Symphony Center's vivid acoustics are so highly regarded. The balance of the program is filled out by a fine selection of works by Charles Ives, Alan Hovhaness, Charles Tomlinson Griffes, and William Schuman.

New England Sketches for Orchestra

Walter Piston

what to bsuy: [Gerard Schwarz, cond.; Seattle Symphony Orchestra] (Delos 3106) ♪ ♪ ♪ ♪♪

Within the extensive series of Piston recordings issued by Schwarz and the Seattle Symphony, this CD may well be their best. Included are excellent performances of the three *New England Sketches* and the *Serenata* for Orchestra, along with what is easily one of Piston's most attractive symphonic scores, the Symphony no. 4. This last work dates from 1951, a time during which Piston felt his music was becoming "more relaxed . . . more flowing, less angular and nervous."

Chamber
Quintet for Piano and String Quartet
what to buy: [Leonard Hokanson, piano; Portland String Quartet] (Northeastern 232) ♪ ♪ ♪ ♪

Written in 1963, Piston's quintet is a good example of twentieth century counterpoint—full of textures more than melodies, but with flavors of Johannes Brahms, Gabriel Fauré, and Igor Stravinsky. Particularly striking is the furious finale, which is syncopated, jazzy, and fun to listen to. Hokanson is also heard here in the composer's early Sonata for Piano (Piston was fresh from his studies with Boulanger and Dukas when he wrote this work—the score is marked "Paris, 1926"). Hokanson's performance on this disc is a marvel of control, from the percussive chords of the first movement, through the delicacy of the second, right through the intricate, brooding fugal writing of the finale. He plays with confidence and great skill, maintaining a crystal clear sound no matter how crowded the score gets.

influences: Aaron Copland, Howard Hanson, Leonard Bernstein, Samuel Barber

Chris Felcyn

Manuel Ponce
Born Manuel María Ponce on December 8, 1882, in Fresnillo, Mexico. Died April 24, 1948, in Mexico City, Mexico.

period: Twentieth century

Manuel Ponce is considered by many historians to be the father of modern Mexican classical music. A composer, conductor, critic, and teacher, Ponce was a scholar of his country's folk themes who, along with Carlos Chávez and Silvestre Revueltas, did much to mesh

European orchestral concepts with Mexican rhythms and melodies.

The twelfth child in a large middle-class family, Ponce began taking piano lessons from one of his sisters when he was six years old. When he was nine years old and recovering from the measles, he wrote what may have been his first composition, *La Marcha del Sarampión* (The March of the Measles). A year later Ponce joined the choir of the San Diego Aguascalientes church, where one of his brothers was a priest; he progressed from the choir loft to positions as assistant organist (1895) and principal organist (1897).

By this time it became obvious to members of his family that Manuel was eager to pursue his musical training but had exhausted the limited resources of his hometown. In 1900, another of his brothers put up the money for Ponce to study piano with Vicente Mañas at the Conservatorio Nacional in Mexico City. Unhappy with the quality of instruction there, Ponce returned home in 1902 to teach at the local music academy, give concerts, write concert reviews for the local newspaper, and compose small pieces for solo piano. Eventually, feeling hemmed in by rampant provincialism, he sold his piano and left home to embark on a concert tour of North America in order to raise enough money to travel to Europe. Once overseas, Ponce studied in Bologna, Italy, and Berlin, Germany, but was eventually convinced by some of his German friends to study the rhythms and intricacies of Mexican folklore rather than ape European conventions. Inspired and low on funds, he finally headed back to Mexico and in 1908 began teaching in Mexico City at the same Conservatorio Nacional that he had left in disgust six years earlier.

Ponce engaged a few tours after his stint at the conservatory and by 1910 opened his own piano studio, where one of his first students was the preteen Carlos Chávez. He also began to create his first important compositions—a piano concerto in 1912 and an original song, "Estrellita" (The Little Star), that was published in 1914 as part of his *Canciones Mexicanas* for piano. That small tune would become extremely popular across Latin America, but like other young, naive composers, Ponce had given up all rights to the song to his publisher, resulting in years of lost royalty payments. He continued touring, sojourning in Cuba for a few years before venturing to New York City, where a concert of his original works failed miserably at the box office. Ponce moved back to Mexico in 1917, getting married and conducting

the Orquesta Sinfónica Nacional that same year. Two years later he was editing and writing articles for a journal called *Revista Musical de México,* including essays on Mexican folk songs and the music of Claude Debussy, Maurice Ravel, and Richard Strauss.

In 1923 he attended a recital of a prominent Spanish guitarist who was playing Mexico City for the first time. Ponce was mightily impressed with the performance and said so in the review he wrote. This marked the beginning of a warm relationship between Ponce and Andrés Segovia, which would prove mutually beneficial for years to come. The following year his wanderlust struck once more, and Ponce left for Paris to study composition and orchestration with Paul Dukas. He also struck up an acquaintance with the Brazilian composer Heitor Villa-Lobos. These two composers, with their emphasis on the folk music of their respective countries, had a powerful influence on Ponce. Upon his return to Mexico in 1933, he began writing music inspired by Mexican folk themes, one of the best examples of which is the set of three symphonic sketches, *Chapultepec.*

Ponce's last major work was a violin concerto written for Henryk Szeryng, who premiered it in 1943. On the podium was Carlos Chávez, by now a prominent composer and pedagogue in his own right. A few minutes into the second movement, Ponce quotes a familiar theme so briefly that its significance was probably lost on many in the audience. But to the keen-eared, and of course to Szeryng and his fellow musicians, the reference was unmistakable. It was just a few measures of *Estrellita,* that "little star" of Ponce's early years, which by 1943 had become the most popular art song in Latin America. Four years later Segovia performed an all-Ponce concert, including the composer's *Concierto del Sur,* a work that was dedicated to the master guitarist.

Orchestral
Concierto del Sur for Guitar and Orchestra
what to buy: [Alfonso Moreno, guitar; Enrique Batiz, cond.; Mexican State Symphony Orchestra] (ASV 952) ♪ ♪ ♪ ♪

There is a real sense of urgency and spontaneity in this excellent performance by Moreno. His playing is very engaging, providing a reading that rivets the listener's attention. The other two works on the disc include Ponce's Concerto for Violin and Orchestra played by the dedicatee, Henryk Szeryng, and the composer's early

Concerto for Piano and Orchestra, the score of which is essentially virtuosity in search of a mission.

what to buy next: [*Great Guitar Concertos*; John Williams, guitar; André Previn, cond.; London Symphony Orchestra] (Sony Classics 44791) ♪ ♪ ♪

Williams and Previn turn in a reasonably well-played account but fail to let their hair down. A little less restraint might have served better. The rest of this two-disc set contains well-known works by Joaquin Rodrigo, Antonio Vivaldi, Heitor Villa-Lobos, Mario Castelnuovo-Tedesco, and Mauro Giuliani.

Chamber
various guitar sonatas
what to buy: [*The Legendary Andrés Segovia: Vol. VI*; Andrés Segovia, guitar] (MCA 42072) ♪ ♪ ♪ ♪

These three sonatas (*Sonata Romantica, Sonata Clasica,* and *Sonata Mexicano*) contain some of the most intricate and sophisticated serious music ever written for the classical guitar. All it takes to play them is someone with three hands—or one Segovia.

various guitar works
what to buy: [*Guitar Music, Vol. 1*; Adam Holzman, guitar] (Naxos 8.553832) ♪ ♪ ♪ ♪

This fine collection showcases Ponce's gift for writing attractive melodies and Holzman's gift for playing them. Included is the famous song *Estrellita,* the twenty-four Preludes, *Tres Canciones Populares Mexicanas,* and many selections—forty-seven tracks in all.

influences: Paul Dukas, Heitor Villa-Lobos, Silvestre Revueltas, Carlos Chávez, Mario Castelnuovo-Tedesco

Chris Felcyn

Cole Porter
Born Cole Albert Porter, June 9, 1891, in Peru, IN Died October 15, 1964, in Santa Monica, CA

period: Twentieth century

Porter was an American songwriter responsible for some of the most admired songs and musicals in Broadway history. He made his mark on the stage with shows like *Anything Goes* and *Kiss Me, Kate,* and on the screen with *High Society,* to name but a few.

One of the more unsung figures in the history of the American musical may have been the Dean of the Harvard Law School in 1914—it was he who advised a second year law student named Porter to consider transferring to the school of music (fun though it may be to imagine what a legal brief written by Cole Porter might have sounded like). Porter, who had been taking law classes upon the insistence of his wealthy grandfather, was already well-known at both Harvard and Yale for his literate and very clever songs. Only two years after taking the dean's advice, his first Broadway show was ready to take the boards. Unfortunately *See America First,* described as "a patriotic comic opera," was a runaway flop. The show, complete with patter songs reminiscent of those written by Gilbert and Sullivan, closed after just fifteen performances. Its composer marked the occasion by leaving town, for Paris.

While the City of Light may not have been everyone's first choice for a getaway at the time (it was the middle of the First World War), Porter made the best of it. Apparently he served briefly with the French Foreign Legion, until the Armistice. While in Paris, Porter kept developing the blend of well-crafted, farcical wordplay and witty, sophisticated music that he would later become famous for. He played his material in the various salons of the time and garnered a number of influential adherents among the expatriate community there. On a trip back to the States to see his family, Porter was overheard playing one of his songs ("An Old Fashioned Garden") on a shipboard piano by a theatrical agent. Sensing the composer's talents, the agent, Raymond Hitchcock, contracted Porter to help put together some songs for a revue called *Hitchy-Koo of 1919,* paving the way for "An Old-Fashioned Garden" to become Porter's first big hit, generating substantial royalties for the budding hit-maker.

With his increased income and augmented by a larger allowance from his family, Porter felt comfortable enough to get married. He did so with a woman fifteen years his senior and with whom he led the life of the sophisticated expatriate, traveling across the Continent to various heady, fashionable locales. First, however, Porter spent two years studying harmony, counterpoint, and orchestration at the Schola Cantorum in Paris. This classical grounding no-doubt added to the inherent sophistication of Porter's music, although it never completely displaced the jazz and ragtime elements for which he would become known, or his appreciation for the Gilbert and Sullivan oeuvre.

Just as the Roaring '20s were hitting their stride, Porter's music started to take off, first in Great Britain and then back in the States. He penned a string of great tunes that would become standards: "Let's Do It" (for the 1928 revue *Paris*), "Night and Day" (first heard in *Gay Divorce* from 1932 and then in the 1934 movie *The Gay Divorcée*), "You're the Top" (only one of the hits from the landmark musical of 1934, *Anything Goes*), and "Begin the Beguine" (included along with "Just One of Those Things" in 1935's *Jubilee*).

A serious riding accident in 1937 cost Porter the use of his legs and left him with chronic pain. It became increasingly harder to write hit songs. For ten years the success he'd known eluded him and he suffered self-doubts. When Bella Spewack came to him with the book for a new musical based on Shakespeare's *The Taming of the Shrew*, Porter wasn't interested. His last two shows had failed, and he wasn't anxious to add to the string. But Spewack persisted, Porter finally relented, and on opening night the critics gushed. Brooks Atkinson, writing for the *New York Times,* wrote that the new show had "a remarkable melodious score with an occasional suggestion of Puccini, who was a good composer too." The show was *Kiss Me, Kate* and it took five Tony awards in 1949, including one for Porter for best score. After that, he had successes on Broadway (with *Can-can* in 1953) and in Hollywood (the soundtrack to *High Society* in 1956), but never quite delivered anything else with the punch of his tunes from the 1930s.

Vocal
Anything Goes
what to buy: [Patti LuPone, singer; Rex Everhart, singer; Steve Steiner, singer; Howard McGillin, singer; Bill McCutcheon, singer; anonymous conductor; anonymous orchestra; anonymous chorus] (RCA 7769) ♪ ♪ ♪ ♪₄

This recording features terrific voices, masterful accompaniment and utterly committed performances which enrich this 1987 Broadway revival. You get the feeling that this must be what Porter heard in his head when he was creating these wonderful songs.

Kiss Me, Kate
what to buy: [Kathryn Grayson, soprano; Ann Miller, singer; Howard Keel, baritone; Keenan Wynn, singer;

James Whitmore, singer; Tommy Rall, singer; André Previn, cond.; MGM Studio Orchestra; MGM Studio Chorus] (Rhino 72152) ♪ ♪ ♪ ♪

It's hard to resist the energy and sheer pizzazz in this Hollywood soundtrack. Grayson, Miller, and Keel are terrific, Previn's direction is polished, and Whitmore and Wynn nearly steal the show with "Brush up Your Shakespeare."

[Alfred Drake, singer; Patricia Morison, singer; Lisa Kirk, singer; Harold Lang, singer; Annabelle Hill, singer; Lorenzo Fuller, singer; Aloysius Donovan, singer; Alexis Dubroff, singer; Bob Sands, singer; Ray Drakely, singer; Pembroke Davenport, cond.; anonymous orch.; anonymous chorus] (Angel 64760) ♪ ♪ ♪ ♪

Porter's masterpiece premiered in 1948 with Drake and Morison in the leading roles, and in 1959 they went into the studio to cut this stereo recording. This is a reading full of wit, energy, and style, and one that is much more intimate than the movie soundtrack. It is good to hear tunes like "Wunderbar," "Too Darn Hot," and "So in Love" in something approaching their original context.

High Society
what to buy: [Bing Crosby, singer; Frank Sinatra, singer; Celeste Holm, singer; Grace Kelly, singer; Louis Armstrong, singer; Louis Armstrong, trumpet; Louis Armstrong Band; Johnny Green, cond.; MGM Studio Orchestra] (Polydor 814079) ♪ ♪ ♪ ♪₄

Just hearing Bing and Frank vamp through Porter's "Well Did You Evah?" is worth the price of this movie soundtrack. Add Celeste Holm more than holding her own with Sinatra on "Who Wants to Be a Millionaire?" not to mention Louis Armstrong and his band and you've got a marvelous artifact of American bel canto at the twilight of the Hollywood musical. Originally released through Capitol Records, this recording is now part of a box set that also includes the soundtracks to Porter's *Can-can* and Rodgers and Hart's *Pal Joey*.

various songs
what to buy: [*Ella Fitzgerald Sings the Cole Porter Song Book*; Ella Fitzgerald, singer; Buddy Bregman, cond.; Buddy Bregman's Orchestra] (Verve 537257) ♪ ♪ ♪ ♪₄

Vocal collections showcasing Porter's flair for witty, erudite lyrics and sophisticated melodies are the best way to appreciate his craft. Here are thirty-five irresistible, thoroughly convincing performances by a truly formidable jazz artist. Each word of Porter's precious text is presented like a jewel on velvet by the First Lady of Song. Highlights include "Anything Goes," "Let's Do It," "You're the Top," the wry "Miss Otis Regrets," and the heartbreaking "Love for Sale."

what to buy next: [*Cole Sings Porter*, Cole Porter, singer; Cole Porter, piano] (Koch 7171) ♪ ♪ ♪ ♪

This is a fascinating collection of rare and unreleased songs from *Can-can* and *Jubilee*. Many of these tunes were recorded in Porter's Manhattan apartment as a document of the composer's intentions while these musicals were being developed. Though never intended for public release and somewhat crudely recorded (you can frequently hear pages rustling, little asides like "now the refrain," etc.), there is a raw spontaneity here that makes these performances a real find.

influences: George Gershwin, Jerome Kern, Irving Berlin, Stephen Sondheim, Kurt Weill

Chris Felcyn and Garaud MacTaggart

Francis Poulenc

Born January 7, 1899, in Paris, France. Died January 30, 1963, in Paris, France.

period: Twentieth century

During his life Poulenc was well-known as a concert pianist. As a composer, his early scores are direct and filled with crisp writing and Gallic wit while his mature choral works include some of the most important examples of twentieth century sacred music.

Francis Poulenc's father was a successful pharmaceutical manufacturer (the company still exists today as part of Rhône-Poulenc), and provided his family with a comfortable lifestyle. The youngster began taking piano lessons from his mother at the age of five, and within three years had advanced enough to study with Boutet de Monvel (a niece of César Franck) with whom Poulenc discovered the works of Claude Debussy and Franz Schubert. Paris was an exciting place for music in those days; over at the Ballets Russes, Serge Diaghilev had just begun a series of legendary collaborations with Igor Stravinsky; the *Firebird* premiered when Poulenc was eleven and three years later the infamous furor over the *Rite of Spring* was the talk of the town. Then one day, on a trip to the local *Maison Pathé* in Paris, Poulenc dropped a coin into a nickelodeon and was rewarded with piano music by Emmanuel Chabrier. The experience was revelatory. "A harmonic universe opened up before me," he would later write, "and my music has never forgotten that first loving kiss."

His next important musical influence was the pianist Ricardo Viñes, whom Poulenc met in 1915 and began taking lessons from soon after. Viñes, who had already premiered such important piano works as *Gaspard de la Nuit* by Maurice Ravel (1908) and the first book of Claude Debussy's *Images* (1905), was the perfect person to help develop Poulenc's unique artistic sensibilities, having had firsthand experience with some of the most celebrated artists and performers of the day. By 1918, Poulenc's score for the three *Mouvements Perpétuels* (written during World War I while he was serving in an anti-aircraft unit of the military) became quite popular among amateur pianists across Europe.

Poulenc saw the need for increased formal training and, upon Darius Milhaud's recommendation, undertook studies in harmony and counterpoint with Charles Koechlin in 1921. Soon, Poulenc's music would attract the attention of Stravinsky and Diaghilev at the Ballet Russes. The resulting ballet score of Poulenc' own, *Les Biches,* had its triumphant premiere in 1924 and, though his music was still regarded by some critics as a bit lightweight, helped to establish his international reputation. After the initial performance of his next ballet (*L'Éventail de Jeanne: Pastourelle*) in 1927, Poulenc met harpsichordist Wanda Landowska at a salon presided over by Princess Edmond de Polignac. Landowska had just finished a performance of Manuel de Falla's *El Retable del Maese Pedro* (the first time a harpsichord had been used within a modern orchestral context), and proceeded to talk with Poulenc about writing a harpsichord concerto for her to perform. The resulting *Concert Champêtre* for Harpsichord and Orchestra was premiered in the spring of 1929, with Landowska in the solo role and with Pierre Monteux conducting the Paris Symphony Orchestra. The composer's last big orchestral work of the decade was *Aubade,* a ballet that premiered in the summer of 1929 with Poulenc playing the piano part and choreography by Nijinsky.

While Princess de Polignac was only peripherally involved with the creation of the *Concert Champêtre*, she took a more active role when she commissioned two more of Poulenc's finest works, the Concerto in D Minor for Two Pianos and Orchestra (1932) and the Concerto in G Major for Organ, Strings, and Timpani (1938). Between the production of those last two works, however, a series of events occurred which would set Poulenc on a new path. In 1936, while planning for a working holiday, he contemplated a visit to the chapel of the Black Madonna in Rocamadour. Before the trip however, word reached him of the sudden, violent car accident that resulted in the death of his friend and fellow composer Pierre-Octave Ferroud. Later, at Rocamadour, Poulenc was awestruck by the humble chapel cut out of the rocky mountainside and had a renewed religious awakening. In a burst of inspiration, he began writing *Les Litanies à la Vierge Noire*, completing it in a matter of days.

Sacred music would occupy a major portion of Poulenc's output for the rest of his life, resulting in such modern masterpieces as his *Gloria* and the *Stabat Mater*, but also playing a substantial role in the formation of his Concerto in G Major for Organ, Strings, and Timpani—in *Entretiens avec Claude Rostand* Poulenc observed, "If one wants an exact idea of the serious side of my music, he must look here, as well as in my religious works." Part of the reason for that, he noted, was that by "limiting the orchestra to strings alone and three timpani, I made performance in a church possible."

During most of World War II, Poulenc remained in and around Paris, composing, performing as a pianist, and organizing concerts dedicated to French music. After the war, Poulenc made several tours of the United States (where he premiered his Concerto for Piano and Orchestra in 1950 and witnessed the debut of his *Gloria* in 1961) and across Europe, often appearing in song recitals as an accompanist to his close friend, the singer Pierre Bernac. His last major choral composition was the *Sept Répons de Ténèbrè*, commissioned (in 1961) and premiered (on April 11, 1963) by the New York Philharmonic Orchestra in celebration of its opening season in the Lincoln Center for the Performing Arts. Poulenc's last completed works were the Sonata for Clarinet and Piano (1962) and the Sonata for Oboe and Piano (also 1962).

Orchestral
Concert Champêtre for Harpsichord and Orchestra
what to buy: [George Malcolm, harpsichord; Iona Brown, conductor; Academy of St. Martin-in-the-Fields, orch.] (London 448270) ♪ ♪ ♪ ♪

A wonderful meeting of terrific musicians out for a romp.

The music cannot fail to make you smile. Included on this budget-priced two-CD set is a first-rate performance of Poulenc's Concerto for Organ, Strings, and Timpani (with Malcolm playing organ), the Concerto for Piano (featuring Pascal Rogé), a sparkling rendition of the Concerto for Two Pianos and Orchestra (with soloists Bracha Eden and Alexander Tamir), the Sextet for Piano and Wind Quintet, the Sonata for Two Pianos, and Poulenc's gorgeous choral work, the *Gloria* in G Major. Different orchestras and conductors are featured throughout the package.

worth searching for: [Francis Poulenc, piano; Dimitri Mitropoulos, conductor; New York Philharmonic Orchestra] (New York Philharmonic Special Editions 9701) ♪ ♪ ♪ ♪

Part of the New York Philharmonic's extensive ten-CD collection of radio broadcasts, this 1948 performance preserves the only appearance Poulenc ever made with the orchestra. Interestingly, just three years after the *Concert Champètre*'s premiere, it was the composer himself who first performed it using a piano instead of the harpsichord.

Concerto in D Minor for Two Pianos and Orchestra
what to buy: [*Great Pianists of the 20th Century*, Lyubov Bruk, piano; Mark Taimanov, piano; Arnold Katz, cond.; Leningrad Philharmonic Orchestra] (Philips 456736) ♪ ♪ ♪ ♪

Bruk and Taimanov aren't as well-known as other pianists of the Soviet era, but their performances stand up well, especially in the two-piano arena. Their performance of Poulenc's dynamic showpiece reveals more of the work's basic musicality, something that often gets lost in the desire to show off technique. Katz is a solid conductor, creating a blend that allows the pianos to breathe while keeping the string section on its toes. Other composers represented on this revelatory two-CD set include Arensky, Busoni, Chopin, Milhaud, Rachmaninoff, and (the only real clinker of a rendition in the batch, and that due mostly to Lazar Gozman's conducting) Mozart.

worth searching for: [Sylviane Deferne, piano; Pascal Rogé, piano; Charles Dutoit, conductor; Philharmonia Orchestra] (London 436546) ♪ ♪ ♪ ♪♪

Another spectacular recording that has it all: power, wit, grace, great sound, and terrific artists. The deciding factor may be the inclusion here of equally fine performances of the Piano (with Rogé) and Organ (with Peter Hurford) Concertos.

Chamber
various chamber works
what to buy: [James Levine, piano; Ensemble Wien-Berlin] (Deutsche Grammophon 427639) ♪ ♪ ♪ ♪♪

Here is a thoroughly enchanting all-Poulenc CD focusing on his works for wind instruments, with magnificent playing anchored by Levine's outstanding performances at the piano. Compositions included in the set include the Sextet for Piano and Woodwind Quintet, the Sonata for Clarinet and Piano, Sonata for Flute and Piano, the Trio for Oboe, Bassoon, and Piano, and the *Élégie* for Horn and Piano.

[*The Complete Chamber Music*; Nash Ensemble] (Hyperion 67255/56) ♪ ♪ ♪ ♪♪

It is so nice when, after shelling out for a two-CD set, you find that all of the performances are of such high quality that there is *almost* no need for duplication. The playing in the piano sextet is wonderful, the clarinet sonata is a gem, and the *Élégie* (written as a memorial to the brilliant horn player Dennis Brain) is suitably moving. There are also short little audio bonbons included here—specifically the *Villanelle* for Piccolo and Piano and the *Sarabande* for Solo Guitar—that would be throwaways under normal circumstances, but receive performances that grant them grace.

what to buy next: [*Poulenc d'après Poulenc*; Francis Poulenc, piano; Suzanne Peignot, soprano; Claire Croiza, soprano; Walther Straram, cond.; L'Orchestra de Concerts Straram] (Pearl 9311) ♪ ♪ ♪ ♪

This is a wonderful collection of recordings made between 1928 and 1934 featuring the pre-Rocamadour Poulenc performing his own music. Included are *Aubade*, the three *Mouvements Perpétuels,* and several songs.

Vocal
Gloria in G Major for Soprano, Orchestra, and Chorus
what to buy: [Kathleen Battle, soprano; Seiji Ozawa, conductor; Boston Symphony Orchestra; Tanglewood Festival Chorus] (Deutsche Grammophon 427304) ♪ ♪ ♪ ♪ ♪

Pleyel:
Ignaz Pleyel was an Austrian student of Franz Joseph Haydn from 1772 to 1777 and wrote over sixty orchestral pieces, more than ninety chamber works, two operas, and a host of scores in other genres. He eventually moved to Paris in 1795, and set up a publishing house that printed and distributed not only his own scores and that of his son Camille, but those of Ludwig van Beethoven, Johann Nepomuk Hummel, and Haydn. While this was a fairly successful enterprise initially, by 1813 a series of legal suits drained his capital severely and he sought to sell the business. Luckily Pleyel had begun another company in the meantime, one which was equally important from a historical standpoint and certainly longer-lasting.

He had started his piano factory in 1807 and it was soon manufacturing about one hundred instruments per year. Pleyel was inspired to some extent by the pianos being built by John Broadwood and Robert Wornum and hired Jean-Henri Pape, a gifted technician who would later be responsible for many of the advances made in piano construction, as foreman. By 1829, Camille had taken over the company from his father and, with the famous pianist/composer Frédéric Kalkbrenner as a partner who concertized on Pleyel's pianos, began increasing the business's market share, eventually becoming the number two manufacturer of pianos in France (after the company begun by Sébastian Érard).

Pleyel pianos were played by many of the prominent pianist/composers of the nineteenth and twentieth centuries including Franz Liszt, Claude Debussy, and Igor Stravinsky. Frédéric Chopin performed on one at his Paris debut in 1832 and greatly preferred its trademark "singing tone" to that of other companies' models. The firm continued making instruments under its own name until 1961, when it merged with the Érard-Gaveau company, which in 1971 was itself bought out by Schimmel, which manufactured the pianos until 1994. The firm was revived shortly thereafter and is now back in business under its own name in Paris, France.

William Gerard

Here's a *Gloria* to knock your socks off. Incredibly vivid sound coupled with a performance that is utterly secure under Ozawa's leadership. The capper is Battle's gorgeous voice, which soars through this wonderful music. Also included is Poulenc's setting of the *Stabat Mater*, a piece that is often more dreamy than dolorous and (nonetheless) one of his most attractive and moving vocal scores.

what to buy next: [Donna Deam, soprano; John Rutter, conductor; City of London Sinfonia, orch.; Cambridge Singers, choir] (Collegium 108) ♪ ♪ ♪ ♪ ♪

Rutter and the Cambridge Singers have provided a long list of very fine choral recordings, and this one has much to offer, containing some of Poulenc's motets as well as a tender and poignant reading of *Litanies à la Vierge Noire*, the work that began his exploration of sacred vocal music. Rutter's judicious use of an orchestra (instead of the customary organ accompaniment) is very effective, and the female voices of the Cambridge Singers are lovely, as usual.

[Danielle Borst, soprano; Michel Piquemal, conductor; Orchestre de la Cité, orch.; Choeur Régional Vittoria d'Ile-de-France] (Naxos 8.553176) ♪ ♪ ♪♪

Here's an attractive performance at an unbeatable price. Piquemal's leadership is precise and well-balanced, although the choral forces have a tendency to sound slightly muddled in the Salle Pleyel's acoustics. By including the composer's *Stabat Mater* and *Litanies à la Vierge Noire,* Piquemal's set offers a valid alternative to Ozawa and Rutter for those just wishing to dabble respectably in the lower end of the economic pool.

various songs
what to buy: [*Mélodies*; Elly Ameling, soprano; Nicolai Gedda, tenor; Michel Senechal, tenor; Gerard Souzay, baritone; William Parker, baritone; Dalton Baldwin, piano] (EMI Classics 64087) ♪ ♪ ♪ ♪

When art-song lovers can get a well-sung four-disc set of Poulenc's delectable *Mélodies* (perhaps the most charming French songs of the twentieth century) at a relatively inexpensive price, it becomes a bargain beyond compare. Ameling, Gedda, and Souzay are particularly accomplished, justifying their high reputations, and Baldwin is an effective accompanist.

influences: Igor Stravinsky, Erik Satie, Arthur Honegger, Darius Milhaud, Olivier Messiaen, Serge Prokofiev

Chris Felcyn and Ellen Kokko

Michael Prætorius
Born Michael Schultheiß Prætorius, c. February 15, 1571, in Creuzberg an der Werra, Germany. Died February 15, 1621, in Wolfenbüttel, Germany.

period: Renaissance

Prætorius was a very prolific German composer and musicologist whose three-volume musical encyclopedia *Syntagma Musicum* is a priceless resource on the instruments and performance practices of the late Renaissance.

The son of a conservative Lutheran pastor, Michael Prætorius would become known as an astonishingly meticulous and hard-working figure in early seventeenth century music. His musical education came mainly from the Lateinschule in Torgau (near Leipzig) and the University of Frankfurt. By 1587 his skill as an organist was sufficient to land him a position at St. Marien in Frankfurt. In 1595 Duke Heinrich Julius of Brunswick awarded Prætorius a prestigious appointment as organist to his court in Wolfenbüttel. It only took a few years before Prætorius so had proven his worth to the Duke that, in 1602, he was given a promotion and a raise sufficient to establish a household of his own. His career continued to advance, and two years later he succeeded Thomas Mancinus, the court's retiring Kapellmeister. Although Prætorius would essentially spend the rest of his artistic life in service to the court, his talent was much in demand and he was a frequent contributor to the musical vitality of Prague and Copenhagen as well. After Duke Heinrich died in 1613, Prætorius spent a few years at Dresden as deputy Kapellmeister, meeting Heinrich Schütz and becoming acquainted with the Italian-style music that Schütz—who had studied in Italy with Giovanni Gabrieli—was bringing to the Dresden court.

Volume One of *Musae Sioniae*, Prætorius's first published work, came out in 1610. The complete collection was issued over the next five years, and included nine parts containing more than 1,200 hymns for the Protestant Church. While he composed primarily sacred music, Prætorius was keenly interested in the secular music of the day as well. In 1612 he published *Terpsichore, musarum aoniarum quinta*, another huge collection consisting of 312 arrangements of French popular dances. Companion volumes of English, Italian, and German secular music were planned, but never completed. His attention was also taken up with the writing, printing, correcting, and publishing of his own pedagogical and theoretical texts. Easily the most important of these was the *Syntagma Musicum*. Written between 1614 and 1618, this collection consists of a three-volume text on then-current musical theory, complete with an appendix containing forty-two pages of engravings picturing Renaissance musical instruments. (Prætorius originally planned a fourth volume, but one was never published.) His prolific output came at a price, however; Prætorius was quickly working himself to exhaustion. Absences and declining health became enough of a problem by 1620 that he was replaced as Wolfenbüttel's Kapellmeister. He died the following year, but his legacy lives on in an incredible wealth of surviving material that is keeping scholars occupied to this day, a life's work that provides a vivid window into the music of his time.

Orchestral
excerpts from *Terpsichore* for Chamber Ensemble
what to buy: [David Munrow, cond.; London Early Music Consort, orch.] (Virgin Classics Veritas 1289) ♪♪♪♪

From the day of its original release in 1974, Munrow's sparkling collection of dances from *Terpsichore* has been prized by collectors, largely for the infectious spontaneity he imparts to this Renaissance jukebox. It requires a very special talent indeed to take music that is nearly four centuries old and make it sound like it was written yesterday. Also included are six of the composer's motets.

what to buy next: [*Dances from Terpsichore*; Lena Hellström-Färnlöf, soprano; Bertil Färnlöf, cond.; Ensemble Bourrasque, orch.; Westra Aros Pijpare, ensemble] (Naxos 8.553865) ♪♪♪♪

Bertil Färnlöf's approach to this material falls somewhere between exuberance and refinement. A welcome addition is a spirited (if all-too-brief) appearance by soprano Lena Hellström-Färnlöf in performances of songs by two of Prætorius's near-contemporaries (Adriaen Valerius and Orazio Vecchi) and one of his predecessors (Pierre Certon).

Vocal
Magnificat for Chorus
what to buy: [Paul van Nevel, conductor; Huelgas Ensemble] (Sony Classics 48039) ♪♪♪♪

A very attractive showcase of Prætorius's choral gifts. This collection contains not only the *Magnificat*, but beautifully rendered performances that range from his first published collection in 1605 to the *Psalm of David*, completed just before he died in 1621.

Polyhymnia Caduceatrix et Panegyrica for Chorus
worth searching for: [Roland Wilson, cond.; Cologne Musica Fiata, ensemble; La Capella Ducale, choir] (Sony Classics 62929) ♪♪♪♪

Wilson and his cohorts serve up a generous two-disc helping of the massive *Polyhymnia*, subtitled by the composer *Festive Concert of Peace and Joy*. The first CD is filled with very appealing music intended for the Christmas season while the balance of the recording is equally fine and full of variety.

influences: Heinrich Schütz, Samuel Scheidt, Martin Luther

Chris Felcyn

Sergei Prokofiev
Born Sergei Sergeyevich Prokofiev, c. April 27, 1891, in Sontzovka, Ukraine. Died March 5, 1953, in Moscow, Russia.

period: Twentieth century

Along with his somewhat younger contemporary Dmitri Shostakovich and the somewhat older Igor Stravinsky, Sergei Prokofiev was one of the true giants of twentieth century Russian music, composing masterpieces in nearly every genre as well as being one of finest pianists of his time. Generally speaking, he is remembered today for his symphonic works, his concertos, and his ballet scores. Prokofiev's solo piano music (including a substantial body of sonatas), while well-regarded, has not really entered the basic international recital repertoire, though with the regular reassessment of scholarly consensus, this too may change.

Misunderstood early in his career (like Igor Stravinsky) and labeled as a kind of musical "wild man," Prokofiev is now seen more correctly as a continuation of the Russian symphonic tradition of Piotr Tchaikovsky. Less of an innovator than Stravinsky, and perhaps less profound than Shostakovich, Prokofiev followed a middle path, avoiding the loss of touch with the broad audience that often dogged the former and the almost pathological pessimism that marks much of the work of the latter.

Prokofiev grew up in the last days of the old czarist regime and showed extraordinary talent at a very early age. His first piano lessons were taken from his mother and he soon progressed to composition, writing a rudimentary opera when he was only nine years old. By the time he was eleven the young Prokofiev was taking lessons in harmony and theory from Reinhold Gliere. Admitted to the St. Petersburg Conservatory in 1904 at the age of thirteen, he studied with such eminent teachers as Anatol Liadov for composition, Anna Essipova for piano, Nikolai Tcherepnin for conducting, and the great Nicolai Rimsky-Korsakov for orchestration. Because he was so young when he started his formal studies, Prokofiev spent a long time at the Conservatory, finally graduating in 1914. There is little doubt that his graduation evoked sighs of relief from some of the more conservative faculty members, who had difficulty getting the headstrong youth to follow the rules. Prokofiev characteristically broke precedent by winning the Anton Rubinstein Prize for piano performance by playing his own Piano Concerto no. I, cheerfully handing out copies of the score to the jury who were probably expecting something by Mozart or Beethoven. Perplexed though they might have been, they had to admit he played it well enough to take home the prize.

Prokofiev continued to further his reputation as an iconoclast who delighted in upsetting traditionalists. His music was full of dissonances, strange harmonies, and unusual rhythmic combinations that struck many of his older contemporaries as purposeless noise. So extreme was his reputation that when the premiere of the *Scythian Suite* (arranged from an unperformed ballet score) was announced for a concert in Moscow, one of the critics wrote a scathingly detailed review of the piece, only to find out afterward to his embarrassment that the suite had been canceled at the last minute and no performance had taken place. Even as a strident young innovator, however, Prokofiev was still capable of writing totally accessible works, such as his first symphony (a.k.a. the *Classical Symphony*) or the pleasantly lyrical Violin Concerto no. 1. Later in life this softer, more romantic and traditional side of his creativity became even more evident.

In 1918, shortly after conducting the premiere of his first symphony in Petrograd, Prokofiev left Russia by way of Siberia and Japan, eventually making his way to the United States. He may have been something of a musical revolutionary, but political upheavals were something else altogether and Prokofiev recognized that he would be better off elsewhere. Eventually he settled in Paris, where he wrote ballet scores for Diaghilev including *The Buffoon, Le Pas d'acierand, The Prodigal Son.* His comic opera *The Love for Three Oranges* (the one with the famous little march) was produced in Chicago in 1921, and Prokofiev continued to make appearances as a piano virtuoso, playing the premiere of his Piano Concerto no. 3 in Chicago that same season. Nostalgia for his homeland, combined perhaps with a sense of frustration over the failure of some of his most ambitious projects in the West (like the opera *The Flaming Angel*, which was never performed in its entirety while

he was alive), led Prokofiev to return to Russia for a couple of concert tours in the late 1920s. He was so well received that he decided to go back for good a few years later. Almost immediately his compositional activity increased. While the totalitarian society of Josef Stalin's Soviet Union would not appear to be the best atmosphere for creativity, apparently Prokofiev found it congenial enough, because many of his finest works were written during this period. These include *Peter and the Wolf*, his fifth symphony, the ballets *Romeo and Jullet* and *Cinderella*, and the landmark film score *Alexander Nevsky*.

Prokofiev's last years were an ironic combination of artistic success and personal disaster. The privations of World War II and physical problems precipitated by a bad fall soon after the premiere of his Symphony no. 5 caused many disruptions in the composer's routine and made work very difficult. To make matters worse, in the late 1940s Prokofiev fell afoul of Soviet officialdom and was denounced for the "decadence" and "formalism" exhibited in his music. Around this time he separated from his Spanish-born wife (Lina), and went to live with a woman (Myra Mendelson, a writer) who was more politically correct and who helped him with the libretto of his gargantuan operatic version of Tolstoy's *War and Peace*. Prokofiev died on March 5,1953, the same day as Stalin, an event which so overshadowed his passing in the Soviet media that observers in the West didn't find out until days later.

Orchestral
Symphony no. 1 in D Major, op. 25 (*Classical Symphony*)
what to buy: [Neeme Järvi, cond.; Royal Scottish National Orchestra] (Chandos 8400) ♪ ♪ ♪ ♪₄

A brilliant synthesis of late eighteenth century and early twentieth century style, this work is brash, witty, and dynamically propulsive; pure Prokofiev, in spite of its Haydn-esque clothing. Järvi's version is stunningly recorded and coupled with a rarely-performed revision of the composer's fourth symphony that he made in 1947.

worth searching for: [Gennady Rozhdestvensky, cond.; USSR Radio-TV Large Symphony Orchestra] (Consonance 81-5007) ♪ ♪ ♪ ♪

Sergei Prokofiev

Rozhdestvensky downplays the more classical aspects of this piece and concentrates on placing it within a modern context. His recording of the composer's seventh symphony and two smallish orchestral works (*Autumnal Sketch* and *Dreams*) fill out the disc quite admirably.

Symphony no. 5 in B-flat Major, op. 100

what to buy: [Leonard Slatkin, cond.; St. Louis Symphony Orchestra] (RCA Gold Seal 61350) ♪ ♪ ♪ ♪♪

This work is, without a doubt, Prokofiev's symphonic masterpiece, and Slatkin's wonderfully sharp and clear reading of it (which won a Grammy) carries the day here. His version of Prokoviev's first symphony also receives a fine performance, wherein the conductor brings a lighter touch to the material than does Rozhdestvensky (see above).

Concertos for Piano and Orchestra

what to buy: [*Prokofiev: The Five Piano Concertos*; Vladimir Ashkenazy, piano; André Previn, cond.; London Symphony Orchestra) (London 452588) ♪ ♪ ♪ ♪ ♪

Most of Prokofiev's piano compositions (including all of his five concertos except the fourth) were written with his own athletic, muscular technique in mind. This two-CD set is one of those rare, wonderful collaborations between a soloist, an orchestra, and a conductor whose collective affinity for the work of a particular composer results in definitive recordings. The fact that these recordings are now available at a reduced price just makes them an even greater value.

Concerto no. 2 in G Minor for Violin and Orchestra, op. 63

what to buy: [Maxim Vengerov, violin; Mstislav Rostropovich, cond.; London Symphony Orchestra] (Teldec 13150) ♪ ♪ ♪ ♪

Rostropovich has made great strides as a conductor and Vengerov is a talent worth looking out for. Together, they make the most of Prokofiev's lyrical yet fiery work for violin and orchestra. Their performance of Dmitri Shostakovich's second essay in the form is a perfect partner for the Prokofiev.

worth searching for: [Itzhak Perlman, violin; Eric Leinsdorf, cond.; Boston Symphony Orchestra] (RCA Gold Seal 61454) ♪ ♪ ♪ ♪

Perlman was a young maverick in those days, full of fire.

Leinsdorf was just the soul to harness all that energy and draw a marvelously nuanced performance out of the budding virtuoso. The pairing of Perlman and Ashkenazy on the accompanying Prokofiev violin sonatas is a gem as well.

Peter and the Wolf for Narrator and Orchestra, op. 67

what to buy: [John Gielgud, narrator; Richard Stamp, cond.; Academy of London Orchestra] (Virgin Classics 61137) ♪ ♪ ♪ ♪

Recordings of this work clog up record store bins around Christmas time but this performance, with Gielgud in his best storytelling mode, is the most listener-friendly version out there. The rendition of Camille Saint-Säens's *Carnival of the Animals* included in this package is a splendid child- (and adult-) friendly bonus.

what to buy next: [André Previn, narrator; André Previn, cond.; Royal Philharmonic Orchestra] (Telarc 80126) ♪ ♪ ♪♪

Previn is charming and effective in this work. Telarc's sonics are a bit bright, but not enough to take away from one's enjoyment of the performance. His version of Benjamin Britten's *Young Person's Guide to the Orchestra* is an apt pairing for the Prokofiev chestnut.

Romeo and Juliet, op. 64

what to buy: [André Previn, cond; London Symphony Orchestra] (EMI Classics 68607) ♪ ♪ ♪ ♪

Previn has always had an affinity for Prokofiev, and his warm, sympathetic approach to the star-crossed lovers in *Romeo and Juliet* is surely the way to go. This two-disc set (recorded in 1973) covers the complete ballet and is well worth listening to in its entirety.

what to buy next: [Michael Tilson Thomas, cond.; San Francisco Symphony Orchestra] (RCA Red Seal 68288) ♪ ♪ ♪♪

For those who lack the patience to sit through the entire ballet, this 1995 disc of highlights from the score is almost as good as the Previn set and has the added advantage of digital sound.

Cinderella, op. 87

what to buy: [André Previn, cond; London Symphony Orchestra] (EMI Classics 68604) ♪ ♪ ♪ ♪

This superb fairytale score also deserves to be heard in its entirety, and once again the old Previn recording (available at a budget price!) is the best overall. Included is the conductor's solid version of Prokofiev's first symphony.

what to buy next: [Neeme Järvi, cond.; Scottish National Orchestra] (Chandos 8511) ♪ ♪ ♪₄

For a single disc of highlights from the ballet, this recording is fine, and more up-to-date sonically than the Previn set. It also has a programming advantage; the composer's popular *Peter and the Wolf* with Lina Prokofiev's narration is the accompanying performance.

Lieutenant Kijé Suite for Orchestra, op. 60
what to buy: [Fritz Reiner, cond.; Chicago Symphony Orchestra] (RCA Victor Living Stereo 61957) ♪ ♪ ♪ ♪₄

Reiner's fiery interpretation was recorded in 1957, but the budget price and the re-mastering of this performance give it an edge over a crowded field. *Mysterious Mountain* by Alan Hovhaness (the definitive recording, no less) and Stravinsky's *Divertimento* from *The Fairy's Kiss* fill out the disc quite well.

what to buy next: [Claudio Abbado, cond.; Chicago Symphony Orchestra] (Deutsche Grammophon 447419) ♪ ♪ ♪ ♪

Many conductors go for high-powered gloss with this orchestral showpiece but Abbado plays it straight, with well-judged tempos that let the natural power of the composer's score come through. The same qualities apply to the takes on Prokofiev's *Scythian Suite* and *Alexander Nevsky* in this decently-priced two-disc set.

[George Szell, cond.; Cleveland Orchestra] (Sony Classics 48162) ♪ ♪ ♪ ♪

The qualities that Szell brought to almost all of his performances included drive and impeccable musicianship. Such is the case here. Prokofiev's popular piece is often combined with other orchestral potboilers, and Szell's version is no exception to this marketing scheme. Luckily his takes on the suite from Zoltán Kodály's *Háry János* and Maurice Ravel's orchestration of Modest Mussorgsky's *Pictures at an Exhibition* are textbook examples of the conductor's virtues.

Leontyne Price:
American soprano Leontyne Price has led a career of historic proportions. Like contralto Marian Anderson, she towers not only in the world of classical music but also civil rights. Honored by two presidents and participant in many world premieres, she has earned her status as a national treasure.

Price was born Mary Violet Leontyne Price in Laurel, Mississippi, on February 10, 1927. She studied voice with Catherine Van Buren at the College of Education and Industrial Arts in Wilberforce, Ohio, receiving a B.A. in 1948. A scholarship to the Juilliard School presented Price the opportunity to study with Florence Page Kimball. Composer Virgil Thomson saw Price in a workshop production of Verdi's *Falstaff* and asked her to join the 1952 Broadway revival of his opera *4 Saints in 3 Acts*. This led to a two-year tour of Gershwin's *Porgy and Bess* in America and one year in Europe. Charles Munch conducted the Boston Symphony when Price premiered Samuel Barber's *Prayers of Kirkegaard* in 1954. She stirred up controversy in the next year when, as an African-American woman, she performed the title role in *Tosca* on television, but performances of Verdi's *Aïda* in San Francisco, Vienna, and Covent Garden solidified her growing success. In 1959, she became the first black woman to perform at La Scala in Milan. An auspicious debut at the Metropolitan Opera as Leonora in Verdi's *Il trovatore* followed in 1961, making her a favorite with that company. Price also originated the role of Cleopatra in Samuel Barber's *Antony and Cleopatra* for the 1966 opening of the new Met at Lincoln Center. She gave her final opera performance at the Met as well in 1985 as *Aïda*, but continued to appear in recital to great acclaim. Highlights of her discography include Verdi's *Aïda* (RCA Victor Red Seal 39498) and *Il trovatore* (RCA Victor Red Seal 39504), Bizet's *Carmen* (RCA Victor Red Seal 39495), Barber's *Knoxville: Summer of 1915* (Sony Classics 46727), and the eleven-disc box set *The Essential Leontyne Price* (RCA Victor Gold Seal 68153).

Mona DeQuis

Chamber
Sonata no. 7 in B-flat Major for Piano, op. 83
what to buy: [Maurizio Pollini, piano] (Deutsche Grammophon 447431) ♪ ♪ ♪ ♪ ♪

With fingers of steel mounted on springs of titanium, Pollini powers into this keyboard monster with technique and finesse to spare. This performance has been the benchmark for quite some time and little has changed since its initial release. The only caveat might be the accompanying works by Pierre Boulez, Igor Stravinsky, and Anton von Webern, which provide an interesting overview of twentieth century piano directions but little in the way of mental comfort.

what to buy next: [*Complete Piano Music, vol. 2*; Boris Berman, piano] (Chandos 8881) ♪ ♪ ♪ ♪

Not only does this disc contain a fine version of Prokofiev's fiendishly difficult seventh piano sonata, but Berman's accompanying rendition of the *Visions Fugitives* is almost worth the price of admission itself.

Sonatas for Piano, nos. 1–9 (complete)
[*Complete Piano Music, vol. 1*; Gyorgy Sandor, piano] (Vox Box 3500) ♪ ♪ ♪ ♪

The sound quality of this budget set may not be up to the standards afforded Pollini or Berman, but Sandor's interpretations are consistently fine and there may be no better complete cycle of Prokofiev's piano sonatas than this. The set also includes the two Sonatinas from op. 54 and an additional batch of short, well-crafted pieces from the composer's pen.

Vocal
Alexander Nevsky for Mezzo-soprano, Orchestra, and Chorus, op. 78
what to buy: [Linda Finnie, mezzo-soprano; Neeme Järvi, cond.; Scottish National Orchestra; Scottish National Chorus] (Chandos 8584) ♪ ♪ ♪ ♪

The choice between Abbado's version (see above) and this one is a toughie. Both are well recorded and performed but the nod goes to Järvi for a chorus that is slightly more Slavic-sounding. The *Scythian Suite* fills out the rest of the disc.

worth searching for: [Larissa Avdeyeva, mezzo-soprano; Yevgeny Svetlanov, cond.; USSR Symphony Orchestra; RSFSR Russian Chorus] (Melodiya/Angel 40010) ♪ ♪ ♪ ♪

Talk about your basic Russian interpretation! From the halcyon days of vinyl comes this totally idiomatic rendition of Prokofiev's cantata. Great chorus vs. semi-muddy sonics but worth every minute.

influences: Dmitri Shostakovich, Igor Stravinsky, Nicolai Rimsky-Korsakov

Jack Goggin and Garaud MacTaggart

Giacomo Puccini
Born Giacomo Antonio Domenico Michele Secondo Maria Puccini, December 22, 1858, in Lucca, Italy. Died November 29, 1924, in Brussels, Belgium.

period: Romantic/Twentieth century

Although he wrote some sacred music, a few songs, and a handful of chamber works, Giacomo Puccini is better known for carrying the Italian opera tradition of Gioachino Rossini, Gaetano Donizetti, Vincenzo Bellini, and Giuseppe Verdi into the twentieth century. He wrote a dozen operas, three of which—*Madama Butterfly, Tosca,* and *La Bohème*—are among the most frequently performed operas in the world. Despite the assertions of many critics that Puccini wrote only of victimized women, citing some of his more tragic heroines (the precious Butterfly, the hapless bohemian Mimi), a few of his female characters—Minnie in *La fanciulla del West (The Girl of the Golden West),* Floria in *Tosca,* and the Princess Turandot—are strong, gutsy women who give orders, not take them.

Puccini has been dubbed a *verisimo* (realistic or true) composer by some and a shameless sentimentalist by others. The reality is somewhere between the two, and in no way diminishes the greatness of what he accomplished. He was a talented musical craftsman whose technique grew impressively, especially his gift for comedy and his sense for the theatrical. He also had an uncanny gift for gorgeous, sumptuous melody and was more lyrical and selective in style than many of his contemporaries. All those qualities have contributed to the lasting appeal of Puccini's work.

A slow starter, his two earliest operas, *Le Villi* and *Edgar,* were not very popular. Then, in 1893, *Manon Lescaut* (his opera based on the novel by Abbé Prevost), became a success, helping to establish a personal style that became even more apparent in his next three masterpieces. Working with librettists Luigi Illica and Domenico Oliva on that opera, as well as with Illica and Giuseppe Giacosa on *La Bohème* (1896), *Tosca* (1900), and *Madama Butterfly* (1904), Puccini established himself as the leading Italian composer of his generation. He did this by constantly assessing his work, seeking ways to make the production better and, when it comes right down to it, working harder and smarter than some of his contemporaries—men like Ruggero Leoncavallo (*I pagliacci*) and Pietro Mascagni (*Cavalleria rusticana*), who wrote one verismo hit and then struggled to recapture the kind of magic that Puccini seemed to consistently generate. When *Manon Lescaut* premiered, the composer took note of what the audience responded to and what seemed not to work within the context of a live performance. He then went about refining the score and, at Illica's suggestion, changing the ending he had written for Act I; when the revised opera was first performed (February 7, 1894) it was an even bigger success.

Puccini's next opera, *La Bohème,* took four years to come to the stage, starting out as an option in 1892 (he could have done an opera based on Giovanni Verga's *La lupa*), confirmed as a definite project two years later, completed in December 1895, and, finally, premiered three months later. The work itself straddles the fence between comedy and tragedy, with a plot drawn from *Scènes de la vie de Bohème* (by Henry Murger) and influenced by Puccini's own experiences as an impoverished student. Taking place in 1830s Paris, the action revolves around two pairs of lovers—the more serious Rodolfo/Mimi relationship alongside that of the painter Marcello and the flamboyant Musetta—with the latter duo providing comedic counterpoint. The final heartrending scene takes place in winter, before Rodolfo's friends can return with medicine for Mimi who is ill with consumption. She dies in Rodolfo's arms, creating one of the most emotional scenes in all of opera.

Tosca remains one of Puccini's most popular operas despite having once been referred to as "a shabby little shocker." There is little doubt that this particular score rivals that of *La Bohème* for popularity, but it is also one of the composer's most technically accomplished works. First performed in Rome on January 14, 1900, *Tosca* received its North American debut at New York's Metropolitan Opera in February of the following year. The plotline is pure soap opera in many respects, but Puccini's warm, emotional music makes this opera about passion, jealousy, betrayal, and revenge believable. All the action evolves from the point where the heroine (Tosca) and her lover, an artist and republican loyalist (Cavaradossi), aid the escape of a political fugitive (Angelotti). Toss in a chief of police (Scarpia) who lusts after Tosca and all the elements for death and tragedy are in place.

The inspiration for *Madama Butterfly* came from a performance of David Belasco's play that Puccini saw in June 1900. Intrigued by the exotic elements of the setting and the clash of cultures that drove the storyline, the composer sought to bring the account of a Japanese geisha's tragic love for an American naval officer onto the musical stage. Although the opera's premiere at La Scala, Milan was a resounding flop, Puccini revised and recast the score, removing some of the detailed Japanese local color and adding new material for

Pinkerton, the naval officer. Three months later, the resulting changes were enthusiastically received.

By now, Puccini was a renowned composer able to secure performances of his operas all over the world. As follow-ups to *Madama Butterfly* he wrote *La fanciulla del West (The Girl of the Golden West)* (which premiered at the Metropolitan Opera in New York City), *La Rondine* (a work written for the Vienna Karltheater), and an interesting trio of one-act operas, *Il Tabarro, Suor Angelica,* and *Gianni Schicchi.* This last work, a farce involving a con-man, a corpse, a will, and an attempt to change the terms of said document, is the most popular element in the trilogy.

Puccini had been dead for almost a year and a half by April 15, 1926, when his opera *Turandot* (based on Carlo Gozzi's play) was heard for the first time. The plot takes place in legendary China and involves the cruel Princess of Peking (Turandot), who will marry the man who is able to answer her three riddles. Left unfinished by the composer, who died in Brussels after undergoing treatment for cancer, the last two scenes of the opera were eventually completed by Franco Alfano on the basis of Puccini's sketches.

Vocal
La Bohème
what to buy: [Victoria de los Angeles, soprano; Lucine Amara, soprano; Jussi Björling, tenor; William Nahr, tenor; Robert Merrill, baritone; John Reardon, baritone; George del Monte, baritone; Thomas Powell, baritone; Giorgio Tozzi, bass; Fernando Corena, bass; Thomas Beecham, cond.; RCA Victor Symphony Orchestra; RCA Victor Chorus; Columbus Boy Choir] (EMI Classics 56236) ♪ ♪ ♪ ♪

Made in 1956, all the artistic elements—the balance between orchestra and vocals, the conducting, the artists' voices—came together to produce a classic. You should be aware, however, that this is a monaural recording, and the performance far outshines the engineering used to preserve it.

[Mirella Freni, soprano; Elizabeth Harwood, soprano; Luciano Pavarotti, tenor; Gernot Pietsch, tenor; Michel Sénéchal, tenor; Gianni Maffeo, baritone; Rolando Panerai, baritone; Hans-Dietrich Pohl, baritone; Nicolai Ghiaurov, bass; Herbert von Karajan, cond.; Berlin Philharmonic Orchestra; Berlin Deutsche Opera Chorus] (London 421049) ♪ ♪ ♪ ♪

Recorded in October, 1972, this version of *La Bohème* ranks among the best, with eloquent, well-matched performances from stars Pavarotti (Rodolfo) and Freni (Mimi). Their initial encounter in Act I is so dramatically tender and sonorous that it carries the listener smoothly through the more than two hours of Puccini's lush masterpiece.

what to buy next: [Cynthia Haymon, soprano; Marie McLaughlin, soprano; Dennis O'Neill, tenor; Peter Hall, tenor; Mark Milhofer, tenor; Alan Opie, baritone; Andrew Shore, baritone; William Dazeley, baritone; Alastair Miles, bass; David Parry, cond.; Philharmonica Orchestra; Geoffrey Mitchell Choir] (Chandos 3008) ♪ ♪ ♪ ♪

For listeners desiring an English-language version of the opera, this one strikes a good balance between the dramatic skills of the performers and the clarity of singing. While it's not recommended as one's only purchase, it makes a fine supplement to the Italian renderings. Haymon as Mimi steals the show and, with the possible exception of O'Neill's inconsistent performance as Rodolfo, the rest of the cast is quite proficient.

Tosca

what to buy: [Maria Callas, soprano; Alvaro Cordova, treble; Giuseppe di Stefano, tenor; Angelo Mercuriali, tenor; Tito Gobbi, baritone; Melchiorre Luise, bass-baritone; Franco Calabrese, bass; Dario Caselli, bass; Victor de Sabata, cond.; La Scala Theatre Orchestra; La Scala Theatre Chorus] (EMI Classics 56304) ♪ ♪ ♪ ♪ ♪

Here Maria Callas, the great soprano, is recorded in 1953 in one of her showcase roles.

what to buy next: [Nelly Miricioiu, soprano; Giorgio Lamberti, tenor; Miroslav Dvorsky, tenor; Silvano Carroli, baritone; Jozef Spacek, baritone; Andrea Piccinni, bass; Stanislav Benacka, bass; Jan Durco, bass; Andrea Piccinni, bass; Alexander Rahbari, cond; Czecho-Slovak Radio Symphony Orchestra (Bratislava); Slovak Philharmonic Chorus] (Naxos 8.660001) ♪ ♪ ♪ ♪

Rahbari extracts the passionate best from singers and orchestra on this two-disc version that launched the affordable Naxos Opera Series in the early 1990s. Showcasing impeccable performances from Miricioiu and Lamberti, this exceptional rendering matches versions featuring better-known stars such as Callas or Freni. The only drawback is an enclosed libretto which

contains Italian text but no English translation.

Madama Butterfly

what to buy: [Renata Tebaldi, soprano; Fiorenza Cossotto, mezzo-soprano; Lidia Nerozzi, mezzo-soprano; Carlo Bergonzi, tenor; Angelo Mercuriali, tenor; Enzo Sordello, baritone; Virgilio Carbonari, bass; Paolo Washington, bass; Tullio Serafin, cond.; St. Cecilia Academy Orchestra, Rome; St. Cecilia Academy Chorus, Rome] (London 452594) ♪ ♪ ♪ ♪♪

Renata Tebaldi, like Callas, inspired adulation from opera-goers. Here, in a 1958 studio performance with tenor Carlo Bergonzi, is one of the recognized classics of Italian opera recording. Butterfly begins as a girl before becoming a woman and a heroine—Tebaldi brings it all to life.

[Mirella Freni, soprano; Christa Ludwig, mezzo-soprano; Luciano Pavarotti, tenor; Michel Sénéchal, tenor; Robert Kerns, baritone; Hans Helm, baritone; Wolfgang Schneider, baritone; Siegfried Rudolf Frese, bass; Herbert von Karajan, cond; Vienna Philharmonic Orchestra] (London 417577) ♪ ♪ ♪ ♪♪

How can you go wrong by pairing Freni and Pavarotti? This version is exceptionally well done from start to finish. You'll be enraptured with wonderful interchanges between Pavarotti and Kerns, and by Freni whose clear, sweet soprano voice is pure listening pleasure. Karajan extracts magnificent performances from all.

what to buy next: [Maria Callas, soprano; Lucia Danieli, mezzo-soprano; Luisa Villa, mezzo-soprano; Nicolai Gedda, tenor; Mario Carlin, tenor; Mario Borriello, baritone; Renato Ercolani, baritone; Enrico Campi, bass; Plinio Clabassi, bass; Herbert von Karajan, cond.; La Scala Orchestra; La Scala Chorus] (EMI Classics 56298) ♪ ♪ ♪ ♪

This impeccably remastered version of Puccini's two-act opera is a reissue of the 1955 monaural recording. Conductor Karajan achieves an agreeable reading of this work and the singers are all well-suited to their parts. Gedda and Callas, in the major roles, are elegantly superb.

Turandot

what to buy: [Birgit Nilsson, soprano; Renata Scotto, soprano; Franco Corelli, tenor; Angelo Mercuriali, tenor; Piero de Palma, tenor; Franco Ricciardi, tenor; Giuseppe

Morresi, bass-baritone; Bonaldo Giaiotti, bass; Guido Mazzini, bass; Francesco Molinari-Pradelli, cond.; Rome Opera Orchestra; Rome Opera Chorus] (EMI Classics 69327) ♪ ♪ ♪ ♪ ♪

Birgit Nilsson has the correct heft and timbre for the title role and she is majestically malevolent. The all-too-short career of Franco Corelli is regrettable; here his wild and brilliant sound are suited to the role and a young Renata Scotto is perfect as the slave girl, Liu.

what to buy next: [Joan Sutherland, soprano; Montserrat Caballé, soprano; Luciano Pavarotti, tenor; Peter Pears, tenor; Piero de Palma, tenor; Tom Krause, baritone; Pier Francesco Poli, baritone; Nicolai Ghiaurov, bass; Sabin Markov, bass; Zubin Mehta, cond.; London Philharmonic Orchestra; John Alldis Choir; Wandsworth School Boys Choir] (London 414274) ♪ ♪ ♪ ♪₆

The teaming of Joan Sutherland and Luciano Pavarotti, two of the greatest voices of the twentieth century, is something to hear—especially since Pavarotti was magnificent in 1972 (before he sang it on stage) and Sutherland never sang the Ice Princess in performance. Brawny, brassy tutti passages, full of sweeping pathos, add to the dark, dramatic flavor of Puccini's work.

various arias
what to buy: [*Puccini Arias*; José Cura, tenor; Placido Domingo, cond.; Philharmonia Orchestra] (Erato 18838) ♪ ♪ ♪ ♪₆

Cura opens with a thrilling, goose-bumps-inducing version of the familiar *Nessun dorma!* from Act III of *Turandot,* and continues to offer nineteen more stunning performances. If this splendid, ultra-handsome tenor were to receive the same promotional pitch afforded Andrea Bocelli, there is a chance that he might enjoy comparable popularity with the crossover crowd. This is a highly recommended album for fans desiring to explore the newest generation of opera stars.

influences: Amilcare Ponchielli, Umberto Giordano, Pietro Mascagni, Ruggero Leoncavallo, Leoni Franco, Giuseppe Verdi

Nancy Ann Lee and Michael H. Margolin

Henry Purcell
Born c. September 10, 1659, in London, England. Died November 21, 1695, in London, England.

period: Baroque

An English court composer, musician, and singer, Henry Purcell was a master of counterpoint and by far the most noteworthy English composer until George Frideric Handel left Germany for London and swept the stage. Though he had a short life, Purcell produced a great deal of important and distinctive music for the English court and theater, including *Dido and Aeneas,* the first true opera to be written in Great Britain.

There is no doubt that young Henry was a prodigious musical talent. He became a chorister in the Chapel Royal at an unusually early age, perhaps as young as six. It was there that he also learned to play the lute, violin, and organ. By the time he was eight, he had already begun to compose music of his own. His singing career suffered a bit of a setback in 1673 when his voice broke, but he managed to keep himself occupied by assisting John Hingeston, caretaker of the king's keyboard and wind instruments. Here again Purcell proved to be gifted. About a year later he'd become so skilled in the intricate mechanics of the baroque pipe organ that he earned the prestigious appointment of tuner for Westminster Abbey. His new position provided him routine access to a splendid instrument, and more importantly to the Abbey's organist, John Blow.

Under his mentor's guidance, Purcell's skill as an organist grew, and he began to mature as a composer as well. Before long, the music coming from this rising star of Westminster attracted some royal notice. In 1677, Charles II appointed him Composer of the King's Violins. Purcell's responsibilities grew further when his mentor stepped aside as organist at Westminster Abbey, affording the former pupil a shot at his most important post yet; it also put him in charge of the same instrument he been hired to maintain only a few years earlier. In 1683 Charles added Court Composer to Purcell's growing list of royal appointments; that same year saw the publication of the first book devoted solely to his own compositions, the *Sonatas of 3 Parts.* Later in 1683, the Musical Society of London began the tradition of observing the name day of St. Cecilia. Purcell wrote his ode *Welcome to all the Pleasures* for the occasion, the first of several works he would create celebrating the patron saint of music.

Purcell's second royal employer was James II, who assumed the throne following the death of Charles II in 1685. Though as a statesman James had some decidedly mixed results in his brief reign, he did have the sense to renew all of Purcell's appointments. By 1689 King James had lost the throne to one of Great Britain's most celebrated royal couples; William III, also known as William of Orange, shared the throne (and its power) with his royal consort, Queen Mary II. Fortunately the new tenants of Windsor Castle were quite satisfied with Purcell's abilities, and like James, renewed all of his appointments. The reign of William and Mary was graced by some of Purcell's most important work. Just a few weeks after the coronation, Purcell furnished music for a grand celebration honoring the Queen's birthday. Despite a typically overwrought text from one of the court poets, Purcell's music was a great success. In the years to come, between Mary's great popularity and Purcell's music, April thirtieth became one of the most important dates on the British social calendar.

Less successful was Purcell's only attempt at full opera, *Dido and Aeneas*. This time he had a good libretto to work with, one provided by Nahum Tate, who would go on to become poet laureate. Although full-sung opera had been a great success in Italy for years, apparently English audiences weren't yet ready for it, and one of Purcell's most important masterpieces was not also a hit. Much more popular was a curious English mix of spoken word and song, or "semi-opera." Purcell would write several of these hybrids which were quite well received, including *The Fairy Queen* and *King Arthur*. By now, Purcell was a real celebrity, and though barely in his thirties, he was by far England's most important composer.

In 1694, just six years into her reign, Mary II succumbed to smallpox. She was laid to rest with an extremely poignant and solemn state funeral in Westminster Abbey. Purcell himself would acquire a life-threatening illness a year later. He was known to frequent the local tavern, often staying out quite late. According to the (apocryphal) story, his wife, unhappy with Purcell's chronic carousing, had ordered the servants to lock the doors at midnight. One late rainy night, Henry, like countless bingeing husbands before and since, found himself locked out of his house. He contracted a cold and over the next several months his health deteriorated. He died on November 21, 1695, the day before St. Cecilia's Day, and was interred in the north aisle of Westminster Abbey, next to the organ. The music played at his funeral was the same music he had written for Queen Mary's burial.

Chamber
Fantasias for Viols
what to buy: [*Fantasias for the Viols: 1680*; Jordi Savall, cond.; Hespèrion XX, ensemble] (Auvids Astrée/Naïve 9922) ♪ ♪ ♪ ♪

The six viols of Hespèrion XX are led through one of Purcell's most original and moody collections by Savall, arguably the greatest viol player on the planet. The music is often very poignant, and listening to it can feel as intimate as glancing through a stranger's diary. Apparently never intended for public distribution, these fifteen brief pieces weren't published until 1927, nearly 250 years after they were written.

Vocal
Dido and Aeneas
what to buy: [Anne Sofie von Otter, soprano; Lynne Dawson, soprano; Elisabeth Priday, soprano; Sarah Leonard, soprano; Kim Amps, soprano; Carol Hall, mezzo-soprano; Nigel Rogers, tenor; Stephen Varcoe, baritone; Trevor Pinnock, cond.; English Concert, orch.; Choir of the English Concert] (Deutsche Grammophon/Archiv 427624) ♪ ♪ ♪ ♪

This is a beautifully rendered recording with noteworthy contributions from all the participants. Particularly fine are von Otter as Dido and Dawson as her confidante Belinda; their solos are wonderful and their duets are exquisite. The rest of the cast is very fine indeed with impressive support from the Choir of the English Concert, all presided over by Pinnock's sure hand.

[Janet Baker, soprano; Patricia Clark, soprano; Eileen Poulter, soprano; Catherine Wilson, soprano; Dorothy Dorow, soprano; Monica Sinclair, mezzo-soprano; John Mitchinson, tenor; Raimund Herincx, baritone; Anthony Lewis, cond.; English Chamber Orchestra; St. Anthony Singers, choir] (Decca 466387) ♪ ♪ ♪ ♪

Janet Baker's acting and singing are at their best here; her characterization of Dido has so many dramatic shades to it that the merest change in inflection reveals worlds. Lewis does a splendid job of keeping his forces on task and Herincx is a fine Aeneas. This has been the standard by which all other performances have been judged for quite some time and it will probably remain so.

what to buy next: [Emily van Evera, soprano; Janet Lax,

soprano; Hanne Mari Ørbaek, soprano; Kate Eckersley, soprano; Lucie Skeaping, soprano; Sara Stowe, soprano; Haden Andrews, tenor; Ben Parry, baritone; Andrew Parrott, cond.; Taverner Players, ensemble; Taverner Choir] (Sony Classics 62993) ♪ ♪ ♪ ♪

There is a real and spontaneous theatricality to this performance, creating an unusually vivid rendition of this seventeenth century masterpiece. Van Evera and Parry shine in the title roles, and Andrews is particularly entertaining as the Sorceress, played with a twinkle in his eye and a tongue in his cheek.

The Fairy Queen
what to buy: [Barbara Bonney, soprano; Sylvia McNair, soprano; Elisabeth von Magnus, soprano; Michael Chance, countertenor; Laurence Dale, tenor; Robert Holl, bass; Anthony Michaels-Moore, bass; Nikolaus Harnoncourt, cond.; Vienna Concentus Musicus, orch.; Arnold Schoenberg Choir] (Teldec 97684) ♪ ♪ ♪ ♪ ♪

Harnoncourt doesn't indulge in the eccentricities that blighted some of his earlier recordings, taking a measured approach that lets Purcell's music bloom on its own. The cast is marvelous and understands the importance of diction (or, as in the first-act scene with the drunken poet, the struggle to maintain one's dignity while stuttering). Teldec's engineers provide a spacious (but not overwhelmingly so) acoustic.

what to buy next: [Kym Amps, soprano; Diane Atherton, soprano; Helen Parker, soprano; Angus Davidson, countertenor; Robin Doveton, tenor; John Bowen, tenor; David van Asch, bass; Adrian Peacock, bass; David van Asch, cond.; Scholars Baroque Ensemble; Scholars Baroque Choir] (Naxos 8.550660) ♪ ♪ ♪ ♪

Purcell's take on *A Midsummer Night's Dream* is a romp under the leadership of van Asch. Each of the soloists is a delight but van Asch's own drunken poet is unforgettable. The ensemble work is precise and nimble, making an attractive case for one of Purcell's more entertaining "semi-operas."

Hail, Bright Cecilia for Solo Voices, Chamber Ensemble, and Chorus
what to buy: [*Gardiner: Purcell Collection*; Jennifer Smith, soprano; Ashley Stafford, countertenor; Brian Gordon, countertenor; Paul Elliott, tenor; Stephen Varcoe, baritone; David Thomas, bass; John Eliot

Gardiner, cond.; English Baroque Soloists, orch; Monteverdi Choir] (Erato 96554) ♪ ♪ ♪ ♪

Gardiner's somewhat reserved reading of Purcell's most celebrated ode is delivered with plenty of care, but unfortunately not much spark. The voices of the soloists are certainly pleasant enough, and the musicians are clearly accomplished, but on the whole they're never really allowed to show their stuff.

worth searching for: [Norma Burrowes, soprano; James Bowman, countertenor; Charles Brett, countertenor; Robert Lloyd, bass; David Munrow, cond.; Early Music Consort of London, ensemble] (Virgin Classics 61333) ♪ ♪ ♪ ♪

Excellent soloists well-supported by Munrow's Consort make for a most pleasurable royal celebration. Burrowes and Lloyd shine, particularly in the intricate counterpoint of their climactic duet in *Come ye sons of art*, "See nature, rejoicing."

various songs
what to buy: [*O Solitude: Songs and Airs*; Nancy Argenta, soprano; Nigel North, lute; Nigel North, guitar; Richard Boothby, viola da gamba; Paul Nicholson, harpsichord; Paul Nicholson, organ] (Virgin Veritas 59324) ♪ ♪ ♪ ♪

Argenta's soaring soprano is lovely, and particularly poignant on the title track, *O Solitude*. Her able colleagues provide sonically-varied which makes this a very pleasant collection.

various anthems and odes
what to buy: [*Anthems, Incidental Music, Songs*; James Bowman, countertenor; Nigel Rogers, tenor; Max von Egmond, bass; Gustav Leonhardt, cond.; Leonhardt Consort, ensemble; David Willcocks, cond.; King's College Choir, Cambridge] (Teldec Das Alte Werk 77608) ♪ ♪ ♪ ♪

An important and fascinating two-disc collection of early, lesser-known works by Purcell. On the first CD, Willcocks's selection of seven choral anthems written for the Anglican church paints an impressive portrait of an extremely gifted and inventive young composer, barely in his twenties. All of the purely instrumental pieces in this set, ranging from keyboard solos to viol trios and quartets, are performed by Gustav Leonhardt and his Leonhardt Consort.

[Mary Thomas, soprano; Alfred Deller, countertenor; Mark Deller, countertenor; Maurice Bevan, baritone; Alfred Deller, cond.; Deller Consort, ensemble; Oriana Concert Orchestra; Oriana Concert Choir] (Vanguard 8115) ♪ ♪ ♪ ♪

Here the Deller Consort serves up a very appealing and attractive performance, full of life and good humor. It's also a real treat to hear the great Alfred Deller perform *Sound the Trumpet* from *Come ye sons of art* with his son Mark. Vanguard caps off a fine release with very bright and rich sound.

what to buy next: [Felicity Lott, soprano; Charles Brett, countertenor; John Williams, countertenor; Thomas Allen, bass; John Eliot Gardiner, cond.; Equale Brass Ensemble; Monteverdi Orchestra; Monteverdi Choir] (Erato 96553) ♪ ♪ ♪♪

This is a rather satisfying performance, with enthusiastic soloists and first-rate ensemble playing and singing, but on the whole it falls just a notch below the recordings mentioned above. Purcell's *Funeral Music for Queen Mary* fills up the bulk of the disc.

influences: John Bull, Matthew Locke, Johann Sebastian Bach, George Frideric Handel

Chris Felcyn and Ellen Kokko

Johann Joachim Quantz

Born Johann Joachim Quantz on January 30, 1697, in Oberscheden, Hanover, Germany. Died July 12, 1773, in Potsdam, Germany.

period: Baroque

Quantz was a musician, composer, and teacher who, though skilled with many instruments, achieved his greatest fame as a flutist and composer. With over three hundred concertos for his instrument to his credit, Quantz bridged the stylistic gap between the late baroque and early classical periods. An interesting footnote to his career is that King Frederick the Great of Prussia, a flute player and amateur composer, was one of Quantz's students.

If not for a twist of fate, Johann Joachim Quantz might have followed his father into the blacksmithing trade, but the elder Quantz died when Johann was ten. Instead of shoeing horses for a living, he became apprenticed to his uncle, a town musician. A natural performer, Quantz quickly became proficient on several instruments, including the double bass, trumpet, and oboe, and jumped into the life of a professional musician. In 1718 he was able to secure a position playing the oboe in the chapel of King Augustus II of Poland. Although his employer maintained courts in both Warsaw and Dresden, the ambitious Quantz soon realized that his prospects for advancement were limited as an oboist, so he took up the more glamorous flute. Barely three years later he had become one of the leading flutists in Europe. In 1726 he was granted a leave of absence to tour Paris and London, where he was a sensation. George Frederick Handel tried to get him to stay in England, but Quantz sensed that better opportunities awaited him back home and returned to Dresden, where he was made a member of the regular court band.

In 1728 Quantz and several other court musicians accompanied King Augustus on a state visit to Berlin. While Augustus discussed politics with King Frederick Wilhelm I, Quantz crossed paths with the sixteen-year-old Frederick, Crown Prince of Prussia. The Prussian King was not exactly a lover of music (he considered the profession unmasculine and inappropriate for a head of state). His son, however, was quite impressed with Quantz, who agreed to give discreet flute lessons to the Prince, journeying to Berlin every six months to tutor the future King. In 1733 Prince Frederick offered his teacher a permanent position with the Prussian court, but Berlin was still a musical backwater in those days, and the Dresden orchestra, with Quantz as one of its most esteemed players, was the leading ensemble in Europe. The Prince's offer was politely declined, and Quantz remained in service to the Dresden court until 1740. By then Prince Frederick had succeeded his father to the throne of Prussia and, as King Frederick, was able to entice Quantz with a proposal he couldn't refuse. The terms included several unique perks: Quantz would report directly to the king, would be exempt from duties in the opera orchestra, and would be given a generous salary for life, with additional bonuses for creating new compositions and making new flutes. In 1741 Quantz moved to Berlin, where he would spend the rest of his career writing and performing music for the Prussian court, all the while enjoying the singular generosity of his royal student.

Orchestral
Concerto for Two Flutes and Orchestra in G Major
what to buy: [*Music from the Dresden Court*; Jed Wentz, flute; Marion Moonen, flute; Reinhard Goebel, cond.; Musica Antiqua Köln, orch.] (Archiv 447644) ♪ ♪ ♪ ♪₄

A score brimming with baroque ornamentation and executed with breathtaking precision and brilliant sound can make for a thrilling experience. Goebel and the Musica Antiqua fill the bill on this elegant collection of concertos written for the Dresden court at a time when it arguably had the most influential orchestra in the world. In addition to the Quantz piece, there are works by such formerly renowned composers as Francesco Maria Veracini, Charles Dieupart, Johan Friedrich Fasch, and Johann Georg Pisendel. Buyers should look for an album ballyhooing Johann David Heinichen, since he wrote two of the scores heard here and his name gets the biggest play on the cover.

various flute concertos
what to buy: [Rachel Brown, flute; Roy Goodman, cond.; Brandenburg Consort] (Hyperion 66927) ♪ ♪ ♪₄

Supported by the vintage instruments of her cohorts, Brown's period flute has a sound somewhere between the recorder that preceded it and today's modern flute. These performances are considerably more delicate than their modern counterparts.

worth searching for: [James Galway, flute; Jörg Faerber, conductor; Württemberg Chamber Orchestra of Heilbronn] (RCA Victor Red Seal 60247) ♪ ♪ ♪ ♪

Quantz spent a good part of his life improving the flute and would likely have been very interested in hearing today's instrument. Galway's typically silky, confident playing is beautifully set off by Faerber's elegant accompaniment in these four concertos.

Chamber
various flute sonatas
what to buy: [Rachel Brown, flute; Mark Caudle, cello; James Johnstone, harpsichord] (Chandos Chaconne 0607) ♪ ♪ ♪ ♪

These eight sonatas are among the hundreds of pieces Quantz produced for the amusement of his royal patron. The simple purity of Brown's period flute is wonderfully evident against the filigreed backdrop of her partners.

influences: George Friderick Handel, Georg Philipp Telemann, Carl Philipp Emanuel Bach, Jan Dismas Zelenka, Johann Georg Pisendel

Chris Felcyn

Sergei Rachmaninoff
Born Sergei Vasil'yevich Rachmaninoff, c. April 1, 1873, in Oneg, Russia. Died March 28, 1943, in Beverly Hills, CA, USA.

period: Romantic

Though he was still composing as late as 1940, the music of Sergei Rachmaninoff has much more in common with the nineteenth century than it does with the middle of the twentieth. His beloved *Rhapsody on a Theme of Paganini,* for example, was actually written twenty-one years *after* that infamous Parisian riot over Stravinsky's *Rite of Spring.* In addition to the tremendous popularity of his music, Rachmaninoff was in constant demand as a concert artist. He was an accomplished conductor and his formidable gifts at the keyboard made him one of the all-time great classical pianists.

Rachmaninoff was born into a wealthy Russian family, but by 1882 young Sergei's father had blown the family fortune through a combination of mismanagement and profligate spending. After selling the last of their properties, the Rachmaninoffs moved to St. Petersburg, where further tragedies awaited them. Soon after relocating, Sergei's parents separated and his sister died during a diphtheria epidemic. If there was a silver lining amongst all this personal tragedy it was the scholarship he received to the St. Petersburg Conservatory, where the young Rachmaninoff studied piano and harmony. Aided by a near-photographic memory, music came easily to him and he didn't have to work as hard at it as many of his colleagues. He apparently didn't work on anything else, either; his academic studies began to suffer and after failing all his general subjects one term, his mother decided to ship him to the Moscow Conservatory under the strict tutelage of Nikolai Zverev.

Rachmaninoff's new teacher imposed a tough regimen but there were perks too. These included frequent concerts and encounters with the many musical luminaries who were always stopping by Zverev's flat (where

Rachmaninoff was boarding). Among the visitors was the dean of Russian composers, Peter Ilyich Tchaikovsky, who was very impressed with young Sergei's musical abilities. After living with Zverev and some fellow pupils for a while, Rachmaninoff began writing music and, failing to find the quietude he needed to hone his craft, eventually moved in with some relatives where he could have more privacy. After taking his piano and composition finals (for which he wrote his first opera, *Aleko*) in 1891, he graduated with the highest possible honors.

Soon the new graduate had a contract with a publisher and an international hit, his *Prelude* in C-sharp Minor, op. 3, no. 2 (actually the second of the *Morceaux de fantasie,* op. 3). He had already composed a number of piano works in addition to scoring his first piano concerto and a symphonic poem toward the end of his student days, but now the twenty-two-year-old composer poured his heart into what he thought of as his first major orchestral composition: the Symphony no. 1 in D Minor, op. 13. It bombed at its premiere in 1895. Three years followed in which, suffering from a deep depression, Rachmaninoff wrote little of consequence, though he did manage to fall into a third career path (conducting) during this time. Finally, at the suggestion of some close friends, he sought help from Dr. Nikolai Dahl, a man who had studied some of Dr. Franz Mesmer's hypnotic techniques and sought to apply them in the healing of troubled minds. His treatments seemed to have a positive affect on Rachmaninoff, as the young musician began composing more, finishing off a few short pieces before starting work on what was to become one of his most beloved scores, the Concerto no. 2 in C Minor for Piano and Orchestra. The work received its first complete performance in 1901.

The years up to the outbreak of the First World War were filled with activity for Rachmaninoff. He got married, started a family, was appointed to conduct a number of operas at the Bolshoi Theatre, and found only a little, harried time which he could devote to composition. The principal completed works during this period were his third piano concerto, the two sets of *Preludes* (opp. 23 and 32), *The Bells,* and his second piano sonata. With the outbreak of World War I, followed by the death of his admired friend the composer/pianist Alexander Scriabin in 1915 and the Bolshevik coup two years later, Rachmaninoff felt the need to leave his homeland. Just before Christmas of 1917, he packed up his family and left Russia, never to return.

The need for income to support his family was now of paramount importance since just about everything they had owned was back in Russia. After spending a brief time in Sweden and Denmark, the Rachmaninoffs left for New York City; the most numerous and lucrative offers for performing and recording were coming from the United States. After the war had ended, the family divided their time between Europe, where Rachmaninoff was to do the bulk of his concertizing, and the United States. Among the pieces written after he left Russia were his third symphony, the *Rhapsody on a Theme of Paganini,* and the *Symphonic Dances,* adding to what was, and remains today, some of the most popular repertoire ever to fill a concert hall. In 1943, at the height of World War II, he became an American citizen, just two weeks before he died from cancer.

Orchestral
Concerto no. 2 in C Minor for Piano and Orchestra, op. 18
what to buy: [Vladimir Ashkenazy, piano; André Previn, conductor; London Symphony Orchestra] (Penguin Classics 460632) ♪ ♪ ♪ ♪

This is an amazingly crisp collaboration between Ashkenazy, Previn and the LSO, full of fire and passion without a trace of cloying sentimentality. Also featured on this disc is an exceptional *Rhapsody on a Theme of Paganini,* op. 43. The price is extremely attractive.

what to buy next: [Sviatoslav Richter, piano; Stanislaw Wislocki, cond.; Warsaw Philharmonic Orchestra] (Deutsche Grammophon 447420) ♪ ♪ ♪ ♪

Like Horowitz, Richter is a powerful and exciting pianist who keeps his audience (and probably his conductors) on the edge of their seats. The pairing here is Tchaikovsky's Piano Concerto no. 1 in B-flat Minor, op. 23, with Herbert von Karajan conducting the Vienna Symphony Orchestra.

[Gary Graffman, piano; Leonard Bernstein, cond.; New York Philharmonic] (CBS 36722) ♪ ♪ ♪ ♪

Part of the "Great Performances" series, this recording provides some very fine music and an excellent value. Included on this disc is a first-rate performance of the *Rhapsody on a Theme of Paganini,* op. 43.

Sergei Rachmaninov

Concerto no. 3 in D Minor for Piano and Orchestra, op. 30
what to buy: [Vladimir Horowitz, piano; Fritz Reiner, cond.; RCA Victor Symphony Orchestra] (RCA Victor Gold Seal 7754) ♪ ♪ ♪ ♪

After attending a concert where Rachmaninoff heard Horowitz play this concerto, he was so bowled over he vowed never to play it in public again. The pianist recorded this concerto several times, and while his later performance with Eugene Ormandy is somewhat more refined, this hair-raising recording is loaded with thrills that are just too good to pass up. Four of Rachmaninoff's works for solo piano, including the Sonata no. 2 in B-flat Minor, serve as warm-ups for Horowitz's performance of the concerto.

[*Rachmaninoff Plays Rachmaninoff*; Sergei Rachmaninoff, piano; Eugene Ormandy, cond.; Philadelphia Orchestra] (RCA Red Seal 5997) ♪ ♪ ♪ ♪

Rachmaninoff's own performance of this stratospheric concerto still gives Horowitz a run for his money. Despite the somewhat wooly sound of this 1940 recording, Rachmaninoff's explosive power as a concert pianist is evident, particularly in the finale. A long and warm personal association with the composer informs Ormandy's fine direction. The composer also plays his second piano concerto on this disc, with Leopold Stokowski conducting the Philadelphia Orchestra.

what to buy next: [Byron Janis, piano; Antal Dorati, cond.; London Symphony Orchestra] (Mercury Living Presence 432759) ♪ ♪ ♪ ♪

In a field crowded with fine recordings, Janis and Dorati's collaboration ranks with the very best of the lot. Technically secure and full of passion, this performance would enhance any collection. The CD includes yet another notable recording of the composer's second piano concerto.

Rhapsody on a Theme of Paganini for Piano and Orchestra, op. 43
what to buy: [*The Rubinstein Collection, vol. 35: Rachmaninoff*; Artur Rubinstein, piano; Fritz Reiner, cond.; Chicago Symphony Orchestra] (RCA Victor Red Seal 63035) ♪ ♪ ♪ ♪

As always, Rubinstein sustains a glittering, brilliant technique full of warmth and exquisite taste, and Fritz

Reiner gets drop-dead gorgeous music out of an orchestra. This set has reappeared on the market as part of a carefully remastered edition dedicated to the pianist's performances. In addition to this piece and the third concerto, Rubinstein and Reiner are also heard in the composer's second piano concerto and the pianist takes a solo turn with Rachmaninoff's immortal *Prelude* in C-sharp Minor.

Symphony No. 2 in E Minor, op. 27
what to buy: [André Previn, cond.; London Symphony Orchestra] (EMI Classics 66997) ♪ ♪ ♪ ♪

Long out of print, this recently reissued performance has yet to be surpassed. The program also includes two instrumental excerpts from the composer's opera *Aleko* and a fine version of *Vocalise,* op. 34, no. 14.

what to buy next: [Eugene Ormandy, cond.; Philadelphia Orchestra] (Sony Classics 63257) ♪ ♪ ♪

This music demands a crack string section, and at the time this recording was made one of the best sections in the world was in Philadelphia. Included on this two-CD set are all three of Rachmaninoff's symphonies as well as the famous *Vocalise,* an attractive package made virtually irresistible by its bargain price.

Chamber
Preludes, **opp. 23 and 32**
what to buy: [Vladimir Ashkenazy, piano] (London 443841) ♪ ♪ ♪ ♪

Ashkenazy would seem to have been the perfect Rachmaninoff player in his younger days. It would certainly be hard to argue against his recordings (from the mid-1970s) of that composer's music. This two-disc set contains fine, near-definitive performances of the two proper sets of *Preludes* plus the ever-popular *Prelude* in C-sharp Minor and a fine version of the Sonata no. 2 in B-flat Minor for Piano, op. 36.

what to buy next: [*Rachmaninov: The Complete Solo Piano Music, vol. 4*; Ruth Laredo, piano] (Sony Classics 48471) ♪ ♪ ♪ ♪

While Laredo did an absolutely superb job of recording Alexander Scriabin's piano sonatas, her traversal of Rachmaninoff's solo piano oeuvre, though very good, doesn't have quite the impact of Ashkenazy's performances. Still she has valuable insights into these pianistic gems, and can't by any means be faulted for her inter-pretations; anyone looking for a single-disc survey of the composer's *Preludes* should welcome Laredo's set.

Sonata no. 2 in B-flat Minor for Piano, op. 36
what to buy: [Earl Wild, piano] (Chesky Classical 114)
♪ ♪ ♪ ♪₄

An audiophile recording of a gifted, insightful pianist playing this powerful work was a great idea that, in Wild's talented digits, was executed to near perfection. His interpretation is on a par with that of either Horowitz or Ashkenazy and, in the poetic *Non Allegro* movement, may even be preferred. Wild also plays the ten *Preludes* of op. 23 with considerable panache and concludes the program with the first eight of the op. 32 set.

various solo piano works
what to buy: [*A Window in Time*; Sergei Rachmaninoff, piano] (Telarc 80489) ♪ ♪ ♪ ♪ ♪

Here is the result of a remarkable digital reconstruction based on Ampico piano rolls made by Rachmaninoff in the early 1920s and '30s, and played via a computer-controlled Bosendorfer piano that is vividly recorded by Telarc's engineers. The playing is simply extraordinary, ranging from the pyrotechnics of the *Prelude* in G Minor, op. 23, no. 5, to the irresistible charm and wit of Fritz Kreisler's *Liebesfreud*. It is a powerful collection and one of the most exciting Rachmaninoff recordings to be released in a long time.

[*Horowitz in Moscow*; Vladimir Horowitz, piano] (Deutsche Grammophon 419499) ♪ ♪ ♪ ♪ ♪

Only three pieces by Rachmaninoff are included on this historic 1986 recording: the preludes in G Major (op. 32, no. 5) and in G-sharp Minor (op. 32, no. 12) and the *Polka on a Theme by W.R.* The drama of the Horowitz home-coming, in front of a spellbound audience in the same Moscow Conservatory where the young Rachmaninoff honed his craft, is just overwhelming. Scriabin, Chopin, and Liszt are the next most-featured composers, but the pianist also turns his hand to works by Mozart, Schumann, Moszkowsky, and Domenico Scarlatti.

what to buy next: [John Browning, piano] (Delos 3044)
♪ ♪ ♪ ♪

This is a very well-chosen sampler, including a half-dozen *Preludes*, three of the *Études-tableaux*, and the

formidable Sonata no. 2 in B-flat Minor for Piano (op. 36). Browning's playing is immensely appealing, particu-larly in the more lyrical pieces such as the Prelude in G major (op. 32, no. 5) and the lesser-known *Daisies*, op. 38, no. 3.

Vocal
The Bells for Soprano, Tenor, Baritone, Orchestra, and Chorus, op. 35
what to buy: [Yelizaveta Shumskaya, soprano; Mikhail Dovenman, tenor; Alexei Bolshakov, baritone; Kiril Kondrashin, cond.; Moscow Philharmonic Orchestra; Russian Republican Capella, choir] (RCA Gold Seal 32046) ♪ ♪ ♪ ♪₄

Based on a text by Edgar Allen Poe, Rachmaninoff con-sidered *The Bells* to be his finest work. The piece is often called a choral symphony and is filled with some of Rachmaninoff's most sparkling orchestration. Under Kondrashin's direction, the formidable forces required deliver a thrilling performance, with an astonishing spontaneity not heard elsewhere. The composer's *Symphonic Dances* is the other work on the disc.

[Suzanne Murphy, soprano; Keith Lewis, tenor; David Wilson-Johnson, baritone; Neeme Järvi, cond.; Scottish National Orchestra; Scottish National Chorus] (Chandos 8476) ♪ ♪ ♪ ♪₄

This is another in a growing string of fine recordings fea-turing the Scottish National Orchestra led by Neeme Järvi. They are joined here by a trio of superb soloists. A most welcome bonus is the inclusion of two works by Tchaikovsky and Suzanne Murphy's exquisite perform-ance of Rachmaninoff's *Vocalise* in E Minor for Soprano, op. 34/14.

influences: Peter Ilyich Tchaikovsky, Nikolai Rimsky-Korsakov, Nikolai Medtner, Alexander Scriabin

Chris Felcyn and Mathilde August

Jean-Philippe Rameau
Born c. September 25, 1683, in Dijon, France. Died September 12, 1764, in Paris, France.

period: Baroque

Self-taught as a composer, organist and harpsichordist, Jean-Philippe Rameau was probably the greatest musical genius of eighteenth century France. He was also known as a theoretician on acoustics and authored important books on harmony and accompaniment.

Little is known about the childhood and early teens of Rameau, but we do know that he was the son of a church organist and that his parents enrolled him in the Jesuit Collège des Godrans, where they hoped he would study law. Instead, the young Rameau turned out to be an inattentive student who devoted most of his time to musical pursuits before finally leaving the school after four years without completing a specific course of education. Around 1702 he visited Italy briefly, but it appears that he may have then shown up in the south of France as a violinist with an opera troupe from Lyons. This last engagement has not been proven with any degree of certainty, but what is known for sure is that he began his long tour of organ postings in important French cathedrals that same year, with a temporary appointment at Notre-Dame des Doms in Avignon. From there it was on to Clermont-Ferrand, where he remained ensconced on the organ bench for four years. His next position, as organist at the Collège Louis-le-Grand, was held simultaneously with a similar slot at the church of the Pères de la Merci, both in Paris. The first of his important scores, the *Premier livre de pièces de clavecin,* dates from this time (1706). Three years later he went back to Dijon as his father's successor but he abandoned that posting within a few years to move to Lyons. There he became organist for a Dominican convent in 1714, leaving to go back to Clermont-Ferrand a year later.

Despite Rameau's seeming unwillingness to be tied to any one spot for longer than convenient, it is apparent that his skills as an organist were strong enough to overcome some of the objections which reasonable congregations might have raised to his appointments. It is also clear that Rameau was developing his craft as a composer, writing the bulk of his motets and cantatas during this time, and enhancing his reputation as a remarkable keyboard player. In 1722 Rameau published his famous *Traité de l'harmonie (Treatise on Harmony)* to rave reviews and moved to Paris. Further pedagogical texts (the *Noveau système de musique théorique* and his *Dissertation sur les différentes méthodes d'accompagnement pour le clavecin, ou pour l'orgue*) were to follow during the next few years, but so too were his first orchestral compositions (usually as incidental music to plays) and books of music for the keyboard. He was also developing quite a reputation as a teacher.

It is interesting to note that Rameau did not write an opera (*Hippolyte et Aricie*) until he was fifty, but when he did, there was an almost immediate split between Rameau's fans and those who still held Jean Baptiste Lully as the ultimate opera composer. Rameau's antagonists felt that the music was too complex and Italianate, vigorously protesting the work's harmonic daring. Proponents were excited by the possibilities that Rameau was offering them, and just as vigorously hailed the advancements. This duality of opinion was to follow the production of Rameau's next major work, a wonderful opéra-ballet called *Les Indes Gallantes* (1735), and continue through his great tragédie en musique, *Dardanus* (1739). By the time the latter score was produced, however, the best argument that Rameau's opponents could raise had more to do with the quality of the libretto, a factor that the composer would address in 1744 with a well-thought-out revision. When the opera was revived yet again (in 1760), Rameau was already being acknowledged as France's greatest composer and his enemies had diminished powers.

Around the mid-1730s, an influential patron of the arts, Monsieur La Pouplinière, hired Rameau to be his music director. The composer stayed in that position until 1753, when his employer took up with a mistress whose prickly temperament clashed with Rameau's equally pointed opinions and caused his departure. While he was still in his patron's good graces, though, Rameau was appointed *Compositeur du cabinet du roy* in 1745, a position that included a sizable pension. He also staged and revived a number of his theater works in addition to publishing yet another major theoretical work, his *Démonstration du principe de l'harmonie,* in 1750. Rameau's last years were absorbed in teaching and working on further pedagogical concepts. He was finally made a member of the nobility mere months before his death.

Orchestral
various overtures
what to buy: [Christophe Rousset, cond.; Christophe Rousset, harpsichord; Les Talens Lyriques, orch.] (L'Oiseau Lyre 455293) ♪ ♪ ♪ ♪♪

Rousset has put together a well-chosen, well-recorded compilation devoted to Rameau's overtures for various dramatic projects. In addition to the intro for *Les Indes Galantes*, which seems to show up on just about every album devoted to the composer's orchestral works, this disc also includes overtures for *Zaïs, Castor et Pollux, Platée,* and more.

Chamber
Les Indes galantes (transcriptions by the composer)
what to buy: [Kenneth Gilbert, harpsichord] (Harmonia Mundi/Musique d'Abord 1901028) ♪ ♪ ♪ ♪ ♪

Rameau created a suite for harpsichord from the music he used for his popular opéra-ballet including the overture, the *Air pour les Esclaves Africains,* and the *Tambourin* nos. 1 and 2. Gilbert is a master of his craft and brings undeniable familiarity with this oeuvre to the project since he worked on a modern edition of Rameau's keyboard works.

Pièces de clavecin en concert (1741)
what to buy: [Sigiswald Kuijken, violin; Wieland Kuijken, viola da gamba; Barthold Kuijken, flute; Robert Kohnen, harpsichord] (Accent 9493) ♪ ♪ ♪ ♪ ♪

This is an excellent introduction to Rameau's music for small ensemble from a group of long-time practitioners whose skills are beyond question.

Vocal
Les Indes Galantes
what to buy: [Claron McFadden, soprano; Sandrine Piau, soprano; Isabelle Poulenard, soprano; Noemi Rime, soprano; Miriam Ruggeri, soprano; Howard Crook, tenor; Jean-Paul Fouchecourt, tenor; Nicolas Rivenq, baritone; Jerome Corréas, bass; Bernard Delétré, bass; William Christie, cond.; Les Arts Florissants, orch.] (Harmonia Mundi France, 901367/69) ♪ ♪ ♪ ♪

If you liked the overtures from the operas, why not take the plunge? This opéra-ballet is filled with delicious melodies and is, with good reason, the most popular of Rameau's vocal scores. Christie has been a steady, longtime advocate of material from this period and brings out wonderful performances from his associates.

Dardanus
what to buy: [Véronique Gens, soprano; Mireille Delunsch, soprano; Françoise Masset, soprano; Magdalena Kozená, mezzo-soprano; John Mark Ainsley, tenor; Jean-François Lombard, tenor; Laurent Naouri, baritone; Russell Smythe, bass-baritone; Jean-Philippe Courtis, bass; Jean-Louis Bindi, bass; Marcos Pujol, bass; Marc Minkowski, cond.; Les Musiciens du Louvre, orch.; Chœur des Musiciens du Louvre, choir] (Deutsche Grammophon/Archiv 463476) ♪ ♪ ♪ ♪

Blessed with a strong cast and sensitive direction, this set was one of the nominees for *Best Opera Recording* at the forty-third Grammy Awards. Minkowski not only conducted the performance, but also prepared the edition used, choosing (for the most part) to work from the 1739 score but supplementing it with an important and artistically viable change to the (almost terminally bad) libretto that was added in 1744: the scene where Dardanus is imprisoned. Ainsley is a suitably heroic Dardanus while Gens and Delunsch are close to perfect in their roles as Iphise and Venus, respectively.

influences: François Couperin, Claude-Benigne Balbastre, Louis-Claude Daquin

Gerald Brennan and Garaud MacTaggart

Einojuhani Rautavaara
Born October 9, 1928, in Helsinki, Finland.

period: Twentieth century

One of the principal leaders of the post-Sibelius musical renaissance in Finland, Rautavaara has been able to successfully synthesize various elements including Romanticism, mysticism, twelve-tone procedures, and birdsong in his music to create a powerfully individual compositional voice.

After initial studies at the Helsinki Academy and with other teachers in continental Europe, Rautavaara traveled to the United States to continue studying with Aaron Copland, Roger Sessions, and Vincent Persichetti. Early compositions—like the String Quartet no. 1 from 1952—more than flirted with modernistic tendencies, but it became clear that the composer owed a lot to his European predecessors. This was particularly true in the symphonies—five of which were composed in the late 1950s and early 1960s—in which influences from the great symphonic genius of Anton Bruckner, Gustav Mahler, and Dmitri Shostakovich could be felt. Nonetheless, these compositions were of great originality, combining modernistic elements with a clear Romantic bent, as best defined in the works composed during the 1970s beginning with the early piece for brass, *A Requiem in Our Time.*

Cantus Arcticus, perhaps the composer's best-known work, is scored for pre-recorded birds and orchestra. Here he evokes a hazy and sunless tundra by combining tape with live instruments, a technique used by numerous postwar composers, but none so successfully or programmatically expressive as Rautavaara. Later compositions made use of strict twelve-tone procedures, most successfully in the String Quartet no. 2 of 1958, though in all cases harsh dissonance is balanced by a remarkable use of instrumental color and dramatic pacing. The mysticism pervading Rautavaara's more recent compositions stems from his fascination with religious texts and metaphysical subjects, something that was gradually incorporated into each musical utterance. The "Angel Series" is one such example, comprising *Angels and Visitations, Angel of Dusk* (a double bass concerto), and *Angel of Light,* the subtitle for his Symphony no. 7, a work of concentrated, hymn-like serenity. However, when commenting on this cherubic obsession, Rautavaara states that the word or word groupings were inspiration for the aforementioned works, yet each piece is not to be construed as programmatic. Mystic elements are perhaps best appreciated in his deft setting of the all-night Orthodox divine service, the powerfully emotive *Vigilia.*

Rautavaara's excursions into vocal music include numerous songs and several works for the stage, of which the opera *Vincent,* based on the life of Vincent van Gogh, is his best-known. In addition to a formidable body of expressive works for mixed chorus, he has composed a large amount of chamber music and two fine piano concertos, fusing the virtuosically muscular with the arcane and mysterious.

As a professor of composition at Helsinki's Sibelius Academy from 1976 to 1991, Rautavaara's impact on recent Finnish musical life has been significant, and many non-established composers were numbered among his students. His best music displays elements of modernism, even strict serialism, with a reverent, airy quality that hints at the music of the so-called "Holy Minimalists"—Arvo Pärt, John Tavener, Henryck Gòrecki—but with little of the modal meanderings and undisciplined, quasi-religious drama of that group. Rautavaara's fusion of past, present, and future, tempered by an obvious Nordic solemnity, makes for some truly original music, music that reveals greater riches upon repeated listening.

Orchestral
Cantus Arcticus for Birds and Orchestra, op. 61
worth searching for: [Max Pommer, cond.; Leipzig Radio Symphony Orchestra] (Catalyst 62671) ♪ ♪ ♪♪

A beguiling work, and the perfect introduction to the composer's sound world. The taped recording of birds is particularly ethereal, and this disc is coupled with the Symphony no. 5 and the String Quartet no. 4, op. 87, for an effective juxtaposition of genres.

Symphony no. 7 (*Angel of Light*)
what to buy: [Leif Segerstam, cond.; Helsinki Philharmonic Orchestra] (Ondine 869) ♪ ♪ ♪♪

The Finnish Segerstam proves a sympathetic conductor for this colorful, dream-like piece filled with hymns and flowing, pastel-colored passages. The Concerto for Organ, Brass Group and Symphonic Wind Orchestra (*Annunciations*) is the accompanying piece.

Vocal
Vigilia for Unaccompanied Chorus, op. 57
what to buy: [Timo Nuoranne, cond.; Finnish Radio Chamber Choir] (Ondine 910) ♪ ♪ ♪ ♪

In many ways, Rautavaara seems to feel most at home with choral music. Scored for mixed choir and soloists, *Vigilia* is music of great sweep and emotional intensity, all placed in the framework of the Orthodox liturgy. The Vespers and Matins make up the work's two sections.

influences: Jean Sibelius, Allan Pettersson, Aare Merikanto, Rued Langgaard, Kalevi Aho, Olli Kortekangas

Sean Hickey

Maurice Ravel
Born Maurice Joseph Ravel, March 7, 1875, in Ciboure, Basses-Pyrénées, France. Died December 28, 1937, in Paris, France.

period: Twentieth century

Maurice Ravel, the quintessential twentieth century French composer best known for his exciting dance scores *La Valse* and *Boléro,* was a brilliant orchestrator whose compositions are often noted for their sensuousness, shimmering tone color, virtuosity, and mood. While often characterized as an "impressionist," Ravel's early works evoke extra-musical themes and the sense of an intangible, remote past as he continually experimented with simplifying his scores, highlighting melody at the expense of harmony. However, with his exposure to Igor Stravinsky's *Le Sacre du Printemps* and Arnold Schoenberg's *Pierrot Lunaire,* he struck off into new compositional territory. Even though he was always operating within the bounds of tonality, Ravel explored its outer borders to achieve works that remain a major foundation of twentieth century music.

Born near France's border with Spain, Ravel moved to Paris shortly after his birth. Of Swiss and Basque decent, his heritage ofttimes influenced the utilization of Spanish and Basque melodies in his compositions, and even though he spent most of his life in Paris, Ravel was to continually look southwards, toward Spain, for inspiration.

Ravel was admitted to the Paris Conservatoire in 1889, where he studied composition with Gabriel Fauré in 1897. Ravel's analyses of compositions by Franz Liszt, Robert Schumann, Frédéric Chopin, and Emmanuel Chabrier were important in the development of his musical technique, while contemporary influences on his artistic growth included the eccentric Eric Satie (whom Ravel befriended outside of the Conservatoire) and Claude Debussy (who was generally admired in Ravel's artistic circle). In 1895, his first published works, the piano compositions *Menuet Antique* and *Habanera,* were released. 1899 saw his initial success with the popular *Pavane pour une Infante Défunte (Pavane for a Dead Princess)* for piano, a work greatly influenced by Chabrier and Fauré. While the musical imitation of cascading water from 1901, *Jeux d'Eau (Fountains),* was considered Ravel's first truly original work, the influence of Debussy remained discernible in both the masterful Quartet in F Major for Strings and the song cycle, *Schéhérazade,* that followed.

Ravel achieved a number of successes while at the Conservatoire, including a second place prize in the prestigious Prix de Rome competition of 1901 for his cantata *Myrrha.* During the 1905 competition, however, Ravel was disqualified by judges objecting to his modernist compositions, thus prompting the young composer to leave the Conservatoire without benefit of a diploma. Following his departure from the school, Ravel

orchestrated many of his earlier piano pieces and, in 1908, produced his first major orchestral composition, the *Rapsodie Espagnole.* This was followed shortly thereafter by the radiant *Gaspard de la Nuit,* Ravel's great virtuosic piano score, whose three movements were inspired by an Aloysius Bertrand poem. The formation of Serge Diaghilev's Ballets Russes in Paris engendered a commission for Ravel in 1909 to score the ballet *Daphnis et Chloe.* Conceived on a grand symphonic scale and inspired by the ancient Greece of eighteenth century French paintings, *Daphnis et Chloe* was Ravel's orchestral masterpiece, and his arrangement of the score into two suites secured its continued place in the orchestral repertoire. A founding member of the Société Indépendente de Musique (SMI), an organization established in 1911 to support new music, Ravel premiered his *Valses Nobles et Sentimentales* (a set of piano pieces inspired by Franz Schubert's *Valses Nobles*) on a SMI concert program that year. Further Diaghilev commissions were to follow soon after, including the partial re-orchestration (in collaboration with Igor Stravinsky) of Mussorgsky's opera *Kovanshchina* (1913) and the ballet *La Valse* (1919). Though rejected by Diaghilev as too symphonic, *La Valse* remains one of Ravel's major achievements.

The 1913 collaboration with Stravinsky opened Ravel's eyes to broader musical possibilities. Stravinsky introduced Ravel to his ballet *Le Sacre du Printemps* and the song cycle *Japanese Lyrics,* along with Schoenberg's *Pierrot Lunaire.* As a result, Ravel's work began to take on a new austerity and edge. His three *Poèmes de Stèphane Mallarmè* (1913) bore the inescapable influence of Schoenberg's *Pierrot Lunaire,* and the Trio in A Major for Piano, Violin, and Cello (1914), completed at the outbreak of the First World War, showed an unusual severity and passion. With his enlistment in the ambulance service and duty at the front lines, Ravel personally felt the impact of the war. Discharged for ill health, Ravel completed his *Le Tombeau de Couperin* and dedicated each of its six sections to a different friend killed in the conflict. Though he remained patriotic, Ravel refused to endorse a ban in France on the performance of music by composers from the enemy countries, citing his admiration for the works of Schoenberg, Béla Bartók, and Zoltán Kodály.

Important commissions following the war immortalized Ravel's reputation as an orchestrator. Serge Koussevitsky's commissioning of an orchestration of Mussorgsky's *Pictures at an Exhibition* (1922) forever linked Ravel's name with that popular work while Ida Rubinstein's request for the ballet *Boléro,* the composer's 1928 tour de force, was to set the musical world on its ear and make Ravel's name a household word. By the 1920s, Ravel's writing had taken on a new stringency. In works such as the Sonata for Violin and Cello (1920–1922) and the three *Chansons Madècasses* (1925–1926), Ravel abandoned the charm characteristic of prior works and exhibited an extreme paring down of compositional elements, exploring the limits of his tonal writing. In the Sonata for Violin and Piano (1923–1927) and his two piano concertos—the Concerto in G Major for Piano and Orchestra and the Concerto in D Major for Piano (Left Hand) and Orchestra—Ravel lavishly employed elements of the jazz idiom, which had become popular in Europe and which he had come to love. The latter concerto, commissioned by the Austrian pianist Paul Wittgenstein—who had lost his right arm in the war—is terse, intense, and jazzy, with skillful writing disguising the fact that the solo piano role is scored for one hand. For all intents and purposes Ravel abandoned composing in 1932, though he had completed an orchestration of one of his earlier songs (*Ronsard à son âme*) in that year, and died in 1937 following brain surgery.

Orchestral
Boléro for Orchestra
what to buy: [Pierre Boulez, cond.; Berliner Philharmonic Orchestra] (Deutsche Grammophon 439859) ♪ ♪ ♪ ♪

Boulez relentlessly drives his forces in this orchestral tour de force that defines the art of musical repetition and augmentation. The BPO plays magnificently under the measured, unrushed hand of a master who steadily builds the intensity of this musical house of cards until its collapse in an exciting final crescendo. Boulez's rendition of the *Rhapsodie Espagnole,* also heard on this disc, doesn't smile to the extent of Reiner's (see below), but it creates a generous splash of color, characteristic of Ravel's orchestration. Sharp, clear sound and a generous helping of other well-performed and spaciously recorded works, including a gorgeous *Ma Mère l'Oye,* make this disc a gem.

what to buy next: [Herbert von Karajan, cond.; Berlin Philharmonic Orchestra] (Deutsche Grammophon 427250) ♪ ♪ ♪ ♪

Von Karajan and the BPO deliver a powerful, distinguished, sexy performance. With outstanding recordings

of the second *Daphnis et Chloe* suite and Debussy's *La Mer* and *Prèlude à l'après-midi d'un faune,* this mid-priced disc is a real bargain.

Rhapsodie Espagnole for Orchestra
what to buy: [Fritz Reiner, cond.; Chicago Symphony Orchestra] (RCA Gold Seal 60179) ♪ ♪ ♪ ♪ ♪

Ravel's great orchestral homage to Spanish music, audaciously filled with color and sunshine, comes alive with the fabulous playing of the CSO under Reiner's baton. This outstanding mid-priced collection also contains the composer's *Alborada del gracioso, Pavane pour une Infante Défunte,* and *La Valse,* along with one of the finest performances of Debussy's *Iberia* on disc.

Daphnis et Chloe
what to buy: [Pierre Boulez, cond.; Berlin Philharmonic Orchestra; Berlin Radio Choir] (Deutsche Grammophon 447057) ♪ ♪ ♪ ♪ ♪

The Berlin Philharmonic is vibrant with color under a master of Ravel's finest orchestral score. In the accompanying *La Valse,* the Schubert and Strauss-inspired waltz melodies are well paced and the two crescendos are strong and convincing. Boulez conveys the necessary sense of dancers at an imperial court being pulled into the final abyss.

what to buy next: [Charles Munch, cond.; Boston Symphony Orchestra; New England Conservatory Chorus; Alumni Chorus] (RCA Victor 61846) ♪ ♪ ♪ ♪ ♪

Early stereo doesn't diminish this dynamic reading and, though not afforded every advantage of modern sound, Munch's recording is vibrant and alive, as heard in his bright brass and fine chorus. Not to be missed; this is a bargain at mid-price.

Concerto in G Major for Piano and Orchestra
what to buy: [Martha Argerich, piano; Claudio Abbado, cond.; Berlin Philharmonic Orchestra] (Deutsche Grammophon 447438) ♪ ♪ ♪ ♪ ♪

Argerich's shimmering color and carefree abandon make this concerto come alive. It is paired with a sizzling *Gaspard de la Nuit,* in which her performance brims with vitality and virtuosity, and Serge Prokofiev's third piano concerto.

worth searching for: [*Ravel: Orchestral Works*; Pascal

Rogé, piano; Charles Dutoit, cond.; Montreal Symphony Orchestra] (London 421458) ♪ ♪ ♪ ♪₄

The middle *adagio assai,* patterned on Mozart, has the warmth of a summer day, and Rogé's heart-achingly slow tempo brings out that quality to the extreme. While his performance crafts the movement more like Eric Satie's *Gymnopédies* than Ravel, this is music-making that should not be missed. Be aware, however, that this performance is but one part of a four-disc set of Ravel's orchestral works (albeit reasonably priced).

Concerto in D Major for Piano (Left Hand) and Orchestra

what to buy: [Krystian Zimerman, piano; Pierre Boulez, cond.; London Symphony Orchestra] (Deutsche Grammophon 449213) ♪ ♪ ♪ ♪₄

Zimerman's opening in the Wittgenstein-inspired concerto is stunning, and he and Boulez take the slow passages with a severe restraint that is pregnant with anticipation. The two also work their magic on the accompanying G Major Piano Concerto, this time accompanied by the Cleveland Orchestra. Here, the outer jazz-tinged movements are played with verve, hints of Gershwin's *Rhapsody in Blue* and Stravinsky's later *Ebony Concerto* adding the right spice.

what to buy next: [*Complete Piano Music*; Robert Casadesus, piano; Eugene Ormandy, cond.; Philadelphia Orchestra] (Sony Masterworks Heritage 63316) ♪ ♪ ♪₄

Casadesus, who performed with the composer on legendary concert tours, delivers this work with idiomatic flair. Besides the concerto, this two-disc collection contains Ravel's major piano output, wonderfully rendered. Of special note is the pianist's take on *Gaspard de la Nuit,* in which his "Scarbo" is thrilling, though he lacks the intensity of Argerich (see above) in "Ondine" and "Le Gibet." That may simply be playing characteristic of earlier times, however.

Chamber
Quartet in F Major for Strings

what to buy: [Lindsay Quartet, ensemble] (ASV 930) ♪ ♪ ♪ ♪

Thanks are owed Debussy, whose own string quartet inspired Ravel and who admonished him not to change a note of this powerful work. The Lindsay Quartet's performance is dynamic and well-crafted, delivering the full

Jean-Pierre Rampal:
Rampal's father Joseph was a fairly well-known flautist and teacher in Marseilles, France, when Jean-Pierre was born in 1922. Even though Joseph gave him flute lessons when he was thirteen years old, the father still tried to discourage him from pursuing a musical career. This seemed to work for a while, especially when Jean-Pierre enrolled at the Thiers-facultes des Sciences et Medicine de Marseille with an eye toward becoming a doctor. At the same time, however, the younger Rampal was taking flute lessons at the Marseilles Conservatoire.

During the German occupation of France in 1939, Rampal was called upon for military service by the Nazi sympathizers in the government but fled to Paris instead, where he eventually continued his flute studies at the Paris Conservatoire. After German troops were driven out of Paris, he was employed by the Vichy and Paris Opera House Orchestras. In 1946 he combined his work in the orchestra pit with a career as a flute soloist, recording his first session that year (flute quartets by Franz Joseph Haydn and Wolfgang Amadeus Mozart) with the Pasquier Trio. Rampal also began working closely with keyboard player Robert Veyron-Lacroix, performing with him often during the next few decades. A good example of the superbly polished interplay between them can be found on an album of flute sonatas by Johann Sebastian Bach (Erato 45830).

Although Rampal had traveled all over the world as a soloist, it was the critical praise following his concert at the Library of Congress in 1958 which seemed to set the stage for the phenomenal career he enjoyed from that point. On that occasion he was playing Francis Poulenc's Sonata for Flute and Piano, which Rampal had previously premiered at the Strasbourg Festival. Other twentieth century composers who wrote works specifically tailored to Rampal's gifts include Aram Khachaturian, who asked Rampal to arrange his violin concerto for the flute; Luciano Berio (*Sequenza 1* for Solo Flute); and André Jolivet (Concerto no. 2 for Flute and Orchestra). The Poulenc sonata and the Jolivet and Khachaturian concertos can be heard on an exemplary two-disc set (*20th Century Flute Masterpieces,* Erato 45839) along with music by Jacques Ibert, Bohuslav Martinu, Paul Hindemith, and Sergei Prokofiev.

Rampal has also recorded a number of albums that have reached across national and musical borders to find commercial success. The best among these include a piece he recorded with Indian sitar virtuoso Ravi Shankar (*Morning Love*, Angel 69121) and some arrangements of Japanese folk songs performed with harpist Lily Laskine (*Japanese Melodies for Flute and Harp*, Denon 8115). Without a doubt, however, Rampal's most popular album is the one he released with French jazz pianist Claude Bolling, the *Suite for Flute and Jazz Piano Trio* (Milan 35645).

Ian Palmer

potential of this great score. Debussy's Quartet for Strings also makes an appearance on this set, as does Igor Stravinsky's three *Pieces for String Quartet.*

what to buy next: [Juilliard Quartet, ensemble] (Sony Classical 52554) ♪ ♪ ♪ ♪

The Juilliard Quartet's slow approach to this score delivers an intense feeling. Well recorded, with good ambiance and sound, this fine performance is accompanied by equally rich treatments of works for quartet by Debussy and Henri Dutilleux.

worth searching for: [Alban Berg Quartet, ensemble] (EMI Classics 67551) ♪ ♪ ♪ ♪

The crisp, clear pizzicatti of the second movement stand out notably in the Berg Quartet's exciting treatment. Their performances of Debussy's lone quartet and three works in the format by Igor Stravinsky (the three *Pieces for String Quartet*, the *Double Canon for String Quartet*, and the *Concertino for String Quartet*) are worthwhile as well.

Sonata for Violin and Piano in G Major
what to buy: [*Un Cœur en Hiver: Music from the Film*; Jean-Jacques Kantorow, violin; Jacques Rouvier, piano] (Erato 45920) ♪ ♪ ♪ ♪ ♪

Ravel's employment of the jazz idiom gives the Sonata its distinctive flavor. The restrained violence with which Kantorow attacks the pizzicatti of the second "Blues" movement makes this performance unforgettable. In the film *Un Cœur en Hiver,* Emmanulle Beart's acting out of a performance of the "Blues" over this recording by Kantorow created what may be the most exciting musical scene in cinema history. This disc contains additional fine performances of Ravel's Trio in A Minor for Piano, Violin, and Cello, and the Sonata for Violin and Cello.

Tzigane
what to buy: [Gil Shaham, violin; Gerhard Oppitz, piano (Deutsche Grammophon 429729) ♪ ♪ ♪ ♪ ♪

A potpourri of Gypsy melodies arranged for the Hungarian violinist Jelly d'Aranyi—to whom Bartók dedicated two violin sonatas—this bravura violin piece gets fiery, virtuosic treatment from Shaham. Accompanying fine performances of the Camille Saint-Saëns and César Franck violin sonatas make this an attractive disc.

Vocal
Poèmes de Stéphane Mallarmé **for Voice and Ensemble (or Piano)**
what to buy: [*La Bonne Chanson: French Chamber Songs*; Anne Sofie von Otter, mezzo-soprano; Peter Rydström, flute/piccolo; Andreas Alin, flute; Lars Paulsson, clarinet; Per Billman, clarinet/bass clarinet;

Nils-Erik Sparf, violin; Ulf Forsberg, violin; Matti Hirvikangas, viola; Mats Lindström, cello; Bengt Forsberg, piano] (Deutsche Grammophon 447752) ♪ ♪ ♪ ♪ ♪

While they were influenced by Stravinsky's *Pierrot Lunaire*, the warmth and charm of French "melodie" inherent in the *Poèmes* is fully realized by von Otter's beautiful, clear, finely crafted singing. This disc, containing a unique collection of French chamber songs by Ravel, Ernest Chausson, Gabriel Fauré, Francis Poulenc, and others, is destined to be a classic.

what to buy next: [Sarah Walker, soprano; Nash Ensemble] (Virgin Classics 61427) ♪ ♪ ♪♪

Walker's performance is well-delivered, but lacks the charm of von Otter's recording. Still, this is a wonderful collection of Ravel and Debussy chamber works, including Ravel's impressive vocal chamber piece *Chansons Madècasses*. With two discs for the price of one, this set is a nice buy.

influences: Claude Debussy, Gabriel Fauré, Ralph Vaughan Williams, Maurice Delage, William Walton

Gerald B. Goldberg

Max Reger
Born Johann Baptist Joseph Maximilian Reger, March 19, 1873, in Brand, Bavaria. Died May 11, 1916, in Leipzig, Germany.

period: Romantic

Reger produced a large number of compositions during a working life of only twenty-six years, a feat unparalleled by most of his contemporaries. His love for the music of Johann Sebastian Bach helped him produce some of the most complex contrapuntal structures since the Baroque period, while his use of chromaticism heralded the coming of Arnold Schoenberg and the Second Viennese school.

Reger's father was a schoolmaster and an amateur musician who played the oboe, clarinet, and double bass. He had also published a text on harmony which was used fairly frequently within the German school system. Although Reger was encouraged to play instruments, and had even helped his father rebuild an organ that was scrapped, he was not given formal music training until he was past the first blush of childhood. His first music lessons (after those he received from his mother) were given by Adalbert Lindner, the town organist and teacher at Weiden, where the Reger family had lived since 1874. During their lessons, Lindner introduced the youngster to the music of Johann Sebastian Bach and Johannes Brahms, engendering a lifelong passion for the works of these masters in his protege. In 1888, Reger attended performances of Richard Wagner's *Die Meistersinger von Nürnberg* and *Parsifal* at the Bayreuth Festival, and came away with a resolve to devote himself to music. Lindner sent an overture that Reger had composed (under the influence of his Bayreuth journey) to Hugo Riemann, who took him on as a student and, later, as a teacher's assistant in Wiesbaden. Despite his exposure to Wagnerian concepts, Reger never fully adopted that composer's methodology, remaining enthralled by the "absolute music" of his heroes Bach and Brahms.

After undergoing an obligatory period of military service (where he suffered mental problems and became an alcoholic in training), Reger returned to Weiden in 1898 to recuperate. At this time, he started the academic career which would provide him with income, but he also began composing a healthy number of works devoted to the organ, most notably the *Chorale Fantasia "Ein feste Burg is unser Gott"* (op. 27) and the *Fantasia and Fugue on B-A-C-H* (op. 46). After moving to Munich in 1901, he continued his teaching but he also began attracting attention as a piano accompanist, supporting various artists in performances throughout Germany, Austria, and Switzerland. Reger's compositions were beginning to divide the critics as well, with his (at times) belligerent attitudes toward those who would abandon the art of "absolute music" for Lisztian and Wagnerian excess showcasing an abandonment of diplomacy in defense of his own concepts. His first large-scale theoretical writing, *Beiträge zur Modulationslehre,* was published in 1903 and sidestepped some of the teachings of his former mentor, Riemann. While this earned Reger no points with Riemann, it undoubtedly helped enhance his academic standing, to the point that he ended up securing a position teaching theory, composition, and organ at the Munich Akademie der Tonkunst a year later. In 1907 he accepted an offer from the University of Leipzig to become director of music and, in the process, left behind a battery of local critics.

In Leipzig, Reger somehow found the inspiration necessary to write the first of his important orchestral works, the *Variations and Fugue on a Theme of J.A. Hiller* (op.

100), as well as his Concerto for Violin and Orchestra (op. 101) and the *Symphonic Prologue for a Tragedy* in A Minor for Orchestra (op. 108). His reputation spread further as he gained success as a composer, conductor, and soloist through concert tours to the Netherlands, Belgium, Austria, Hungary, Russia, and England. In 1911, Reger won an appointment to conduct the court orchestra in Meiningen. There he created his most popular orchestral score, the *Variations and Fugue on a Theme by Mozart* (op. 132), in addition to the four *Tondichtungen nach Arnold Böcklin* (op. 128). His most mature chamber music scores date from this period as well, including the last of his string quartets (op. 121), the three suites for solo cello (op. 131c), and his masterful piano work, *Variations and Fugue on a Theme of G.P. Telemann* (op. 134). Due to ill health, Reger resigned the Meiningen position in 1915, and went to Jena; he died in Leipzig from a heart attack while returning from a concert tour of the Netherlands.

Orchestral
Variations and Fugue on a Theme by Mozart for Orchestra, op. 132
what to buy: [Leif Segerstam, cond.; Norrköping Symphony Orchestra] (BIS 771) ♪ ♪ ♪ ♪♪

Written in 1914, this set of variations is a wonderful example of Reger at his non-pedantic best. The melodies just flow into one another with incredible ease, and time seems to pass far too quickly. Segerstam gets his orchestra to play far better than one would expect a regional ensemble to, and the results are felicitous to say the least. Reger's powerful, majestic *Symphonic Prologue for a Tragedy* in A Minor for Orchestra (op. 108) isn't played very often, which makes the other part of this program of particular value.

what to buy next: [Heinz Bongartz, cond.; Staatskapelle Dresden, orch.] (Berlin Classics 2177) ♪ ♪ ♪ ♪

Once again, price has little real meaning when confronted with a very good performance. Such is the case with this mid-priced version of Reger's most popular orchestral work. The orchestra is well-recorded and Bongartz's direction is just fluid enough to lend a lilt to the proceedings. Good too, is the rendition of the composer's *Tondichtungen nach Arnold Böcklin (Tone Poems)* for Orchestra, op. 128, with harmonic influences clearly derived from Claude Debussy's sonic world.

[Horst Stein, cond.; Bamberg Symphony Orchestra] (Koch Schwann 311412) ♪ ♪ ♪₄

The pairing on this disc is Reger's orchestral arrangement of his own *Variations and Fugue on a Theme of Beethoven* for Two Pianos (op. 86) in a felicitous performance by Stein and company. While the playing on this CD is very good overall, the real value of the project lies in its combination of Reger's two most popular orchestral pieces. Both are performed well enough to provide a viable, economical alternative to buying them separately.

Chamber
String Quartets, opp. 54 (nos. 1 and 2), 74, 109, 121, and the D Minor (1889)
what to buy: [*Complete String Quartets*; Berner String Quartet] (CPO 999069) ♪ ♪ ♪ ♪ ♪

These six quartets were composed at a time when such things were considered dated, but intrepid listeners will be rewarded for their efforts with this three-CD set. The Berner Quartet performs these scores with virtuosity and great emotional contrast, and they are recorded so clearly that the listener can hear the individual musical lines and still experience the power of the whole ensemble.

Suites for Cello Solo, op. 131c, nos. 1–3
what to buy: [Erling Blondal Bengtsson, cello] (Danacord 372) ♪ ♪ ♪ ♪₄

Bengtsson gives a rich, full-blooded performance of these works that exposes the debt Reger owes to J.S. Bach's own masterful suites. Along with similar scores by Zoltán Kodály and Benjamin Britten, Reger's solo cello pieces are among the finest ever written for that instrument during the twentieth century. Bengtsson's recital also includes Eugene Ysäye's Sonata for Solo Cello (op. 28), an interesting work that isn't heard very often.

what to buy next: [Pieter Wispelwey, cello] (Channel Classics 9596) ♪ ♪ ♪ ♪

Wispelwey is a consistently talented cellist and there is little to separate his recording of these works from Bengtsson's except for the accompanying pieces. This is an all-Reger disc that includes the composer's transcriptions of his pieces for violin and piano (*Wiegenlied*, op. 79d, no. 1 and the *Aria*, op. 103a, no. 3) plus the short *Kleine Romanze*, op. 79e, no. 2, and the *Caprice*, op. 79e,

no. 1, all with pianist Paolo Giacometti accompanying Wispelwey.

Variations and Fugue on a Theme of J.S. Bach for Piano, op. 81
what to buy: [Marc-André Hamelin, piano] (Hyperion 66996) ♪ ♪ ♪ ♪ ♪₄

The variations at the heart of this work are based upon a theme from Bach's Cantata BWV 128, *Auf Christi Himmelfahrt allein ich meine Nachfahrt gründe*. Hamelin, one of the world's finest pianists, does a wonderful job of exposing the details of the awesome fugue which closes out one of Reger's most important and continually arresting scores. Ditto for his performance of the *other* big work for piano, the *Variations and Fugue on a Theme of G.P. Telemann*, op. 134, and the five earlier *Humoresques* for Piano, op. 20.

various organ works
what to buy: [*Die Grosse Sauer-Orgel Im Berliner Dom*; Michael Pohl, organ] (Motette 11781) ♪ ♪ ♪ ♪ ♪

Reger's later organ pieces are sampled in this album (the *Toccata and Fugue* in D Minor from op. 129 and three of the chorales from op. 135a among them), along with works by Bach, Felix Mendelssohn, and Josef Rheinberger; a varied and interesting program, to be sure. The large Sauer organ, built in 1905, represents the end of the orchestral organ from the high Romantic period. Reger's music, with very small to very large sounds, comes alive through the expansive tonal design of this organ and the cathedral's resonant acoustics. Pohl, a student of Kastner (see below), performs with conviction and the sound is superb.

what to buy next: [*Max Reger: Organ Works, volume 2*; Ludger Lohmann, organ] (Naxos 8.553927) ♪ ♪ ♪ ♪

Lohmann delves into a trio of Reger's opus numbers, with the mighty *Introduction, Passacaglia, and Fugue* in E Minor, op. 127 being perhaps the most overwhelming of the three. This is one of those pieces that organists love, especially when played with the superb awareness of tonal color that Lohmann displays. The ten short choral preludes from op. 135a are delightful, and the excerpts from the composer's op. 129 (especially the brief Kanon in E Minor) are quite lovely. Still, this is not the place to begin listening to Reger's oeuvre despite the disc's budget price and overall worthiness.

worth searching for: [Hannes Kastner, organ] (Ars Vivendi 2100187) ♪ ♪ ♪ ♪ ♪

This recording, made in 1972, is one of the best collections of Reger's organ music. It was recorded on the Sauer organ, built in 1889 with additions in 1903 and 1908, at St. Thomas Church, Leipzig. Kastner, organist at St. Thomas from 1951–1984, was a student of Gunther Ramin (organist-cantor there from 1918–1956), who in turn was a student of Karl Straube (organist-cantor there from 1902–1938). As part of this lineage, Kastner performs these works (drawn from Reger's opp. 59, 65, and 129) with great sensitivity. The recording captures the sound of this period organ very well.

influences: Richard Wagner, Sigfrid Karg-Elert, Richard Strauss, Gustav Mahler, Ferruccio Busoni

D. John Apple and Garaud MacTaggart

Steve Reich

Born Stephen Michael Reich, October 3, 1936, in New York City, NY

period: Twentieth century

An early pioneer in tape music and American minimalism, Reich has been internationally recognized as one of the world's foremost living composers. Throughout the course of his career, Reich has embraced aspects of Western forms of classical music as well as the structures, harmonies, and rhythms of non-Western and American popular music, especially jazz. From early works in the 1960s such as *It's Gonna Rain* and *Come Out,* to grand-scale, multimedia works such as *The Cave* from 1993, his spellbinding, original compositions have dazzled music critics and fans alike.

Usually categorized with other "first generation" minimalist composers including Philip Glass and La Monte Young, and more recently with younger composers such as John Adams, Reich has produced music characterized by a strong, steady pulse and strictly diatonic and tonal harmonies. His music, with its unrelenting pulse and short, repeating melodic figures, has often been compared to rock-and-roll and be-bop jazz. In contrast to Glass and Adams, Reich's work has commanded a generally wider variety of vocal types, with strong concerns in the area of manipulating speech rhythms, qualities

which date from his earliest pieces. His strict, tonal melodic style has brought him much critical acclaim, even from a general public that is often distrustful of "new music." He has, in many ways, led the charge toward establishing in contemporary music the accessible and almost anti-academic fulmination of advanced developments. Yet, like other minimalist composers, Reich's music is considerably influenced by other European forms and techniques that grew out of the largely academic, elitist climate of New Music in the 1950s and '60s.

Born in New York and raised partly there and partly in California, Reich received some piano instruction as a child before developing an interest in jazz drumming. At age fourteen, he began formal instruction as a percussionist, continuing on this path right up until he enrolled at Cornell University in 1953. While there he concentrated his studies on philosophy and music, graduating with honors in philosophy in 1957. He then studied composition with Hall Overton, a composer/arranger best known for his work with jazz musicians in general and the Thelonious Monk Big Band in particular. Reich's next stop was the Juilliard School of Music, where he continued his education in composition with William Bergsma and Vincent Persichetti before transferring out to Mills College in Oakland, California, and coming under the tutelage of Darius Milhaud and Luciano Berio. He finally received his M.A. in Music from Mills in 1963.

While living in the San Francisco Bay area Reich produced his early taped-speech pieces such as *Come Out* and *It's Gonna Rain.* For the latter work, he recorded the voice of a young black Pentecostal preacher ("Brother Walter") along with pigeons and traffic in Union Square in downtown San Francisco. Later at home, Reich began playing with tape loops of the preacher's voice, and by accident discovered the process of allowing two identical loops to go gradually out of phase with each other. By measuredly increasing from two to eight voices in a kind of "controlled chaos," *It's Gonna Rain* was the first piece ever to use his process of gradually shifting phase relationships between two or more identical repeating patterns. This same procedure was later incorporated into several pieces for traditional acoustic instruments (or instruments and tape), such as *Piano Phase* and *Violin Phase,* both composed in 1967. In addition to his phasing, Reich also introduced (especially in *Violin Phase*) the feeling of "found" or "resulting" patterns which involved new melodic figures created from the overlapping voices of the original theme.

Reich joined the faculty of New York's New School for Social Research in 1969 and, with a grant from the Institute for International Education, began studying drumming at the Institute for African Studies at the University of Ghana a year later. The composer started incorporating rhythmic processes derived from these studies into an original style of composition that was driven by a pronounced, ever-evolving pulse. His next major work, *Drumming*, was created upon his return to New York in 1970. The new score translated into an hour-long elaboration of a single rhythmic cell, developed and re-orchestrated through four distinct sections. After this composition began his delving into processes derived from African drumming techniques, he added the percussive sounds of Balinese gamelan music to his repertoire, by studying Balinese Semar Pegulingan and Gamelan Gambang at the American Society for Eastern Arts in Seattle, Washington, in the summers of 1973 and 1974. Two years later he continued adding to his knowledge base by analyzing the traditional forms of cantillation (chanting) as applied to the Hebrew scriptures. During this period, he also wrote *Music for 18 Musicians,* his largest, most complex piece to that time, and other non-percussion-oriented works such as *Music for a Large Ensemble* and *Octet.*

A co-commission by West German Radio, Cologne, and the Brooklyn Academy of Music, *The Desert Music* (based on poems by William Carlos Williams), was begun in September 1982 and called for an orchestra of eighty-nine musicians and a chorus of twenty-seven voices. Reich also reverted to using the voice or speech recordings occasionally, as in *Tehillim* (a setting of Psalm texts in Hebrew), *Different Trains* for string quartet and tape, and in his successful venture into theater, *The Cave.* Each of these works explores the pitch of taped and sequenced voices, and then uses those pitches as melodic material in the accompanying instrumental ensemble. His piece *Different Trains* was hailed by *The New York Times* as "a work of such astonishing originality that 'breakthrough' seems the only possible description. . . possesses an absolutely harrowing emotional impact." *The Cave,* a five-screen, eighteen-musician production consisting of edited documentary video footage timed with live and sampled music, was a collaborative work with Reich's wife, video artist Beryl Korot. This towering theater piece about Arab-Jewish relations explores the Biblical story of Abraham, Sarah, Hagar, Ishmael, and Isaac and further develops Reich's overriding interests in speech rhythm and rhythmic organization. Of Reich's most recent major concert

works, *City Life* and *Proverb* have received widespread acclaim. Commissioned by the Ensemble Modern, the London Sinfonietta, and the Ensemble Inter Contemporain, *City Life* utilizes sampled sounds of a metropolis (such as car horns, air brakes, subway chimes, pile drivers, car alarms, heartbeats, boat horns, and sirens) as part of the musical mix. *Proverb,* scored for six voices, two keyboards, and two percussions, is set to text by Ludwig Wittgenstein. Forthcoming from Reich and Korot is *Three Tales,* a full-evening music-theater piece on the theme of technology and its consequences. The first act, *Hindenburg,* premiered at the Spoleto USA Festival in May 1998. Two other parts of the trilogy, *Bikini* and *Dolly,* examine atomic bomb testing and the cloning of an adult sheep, respectively, and were scheduled to premiere as part of the completed *Three Tales* by the end of 2002.

Orchestra
City Life for Ensemble and Tape
what to buy: [Bradley Lubman, cond.; Steve Reich Ensemble, orch.] (Nonesuch 79430) ♪ ♪ ♪ ♪♪

A stirring work that conveys the various moods of a large metropolis, this hip, melodious five-movement piece not only features the musicians in his ensemble but a wide variety of urban-based sounds which Reich taped in New York City on the day of the 1993 World Trade Center bombing. The stark intensity of the middle movement (*It's been a honeymoon—Can't take no mo'*) will remind some listeners of Reich's early tape pieces *It's Gonna Rain* and *Come Out.* Though others have recorded this work, this version is the obvious masterpiece. The album also contains Reich's *Proverb* and *Nagoya Marimbas.*

Chamber
Different Trains for String Quartet and Pre-Recorded Tape
what to buy: [Kronos Quartet, ensemble] (Nonesuch 79176) ♪ ♪ ♪ ♪ ♪

In 1990 Reich received a Grammy Award for Best Contemporary Composition for *Different Trains,* and this was the recording that clinched the deal. One of Reich's most captivating and compelling works for voice and instruments, the three-part piece uses tape loops of American and European train sounds from the 1930s and 1940s, and repeated patterns of some at times poignant vocal vignettes. A dark shift of mood occurs in *Part II,*

Europe—During the War as the piece recalls Nazi concentration camp trains. A performance of Reich's *Electric Counterpoint* by guitarist Pat Metheny completes the disc, but *Different Trains* is unequivocally the outstanding piece.

Drumming

what to buy: [Steve Reich, cond.; Steve Reich and Musicians, ensemble] (Nonesuch 79170) ♪ ♪ ♪♪

Divided into four parts (performed without pause) for a total time of about fifty-six minutes, this is the longest piece Reich composed and if you make it through the 17:30 minutes of Part I, which contains only varying hand-drum patterns fading in and out, your attentiveness is supreme and you'll be rewarded as other instruments and vocalese are added. *Drumming* may have been revolutionary when first introduced, and important in terms of developing his ideas, but Reich's later works are far more interesting.

Vocal
It's Gonna Rain for Tape

what to buy: [*Early Works*; Brother Walter, voice; tape loops] (Nonesuch 79169) ♪ ♪ ♪ ♪♪

Hallelujah! Amen! What Reich does with these early tape loops featuring the voice of a black preacher (Brother Walter) will thrill your ears with its musicality and rhythmic intensity. His serendipitous discovery while experimenting with the tapes yields an eerie, two-part piece that begins with a single voice that doubles to two, four, and finally a cacophonous, oscillating eight. This album of Reich's revolutionary early works also includes *Come Out, Piano Phase,* and *Clapping Music.* This CD would be the best starting point if you desire to trace the development of Reich's music.

Music for 18 Musicians for Voices and Ensemble

what to buy: [Steve Reich Ensemble, orch.] (Nonesuch 79448) ♪ ♪ ♪ ♪ ♪

A jolting, colorful crossover piece when it was first released in 1978 by ECM (selling 100,000 LPs in the first year), this 1996-recorded version (eleven minutes longer than the original) again demonstrates how brilliantly Reich balances both Western conventions (harmony, meticulous orchestration) and his modernist concepts. Reich has said this fourteen-movement score changed his life, and as one of his most ear-enticing, landmark works, it certainly helped alter the course of Western

music. One listen to this ravishing example of minimalism and you'll understand why.

Tehillim for Winds, Strings, Percussion, and Voices

what to buy: [Barbara Borden, soprano; Tannie Willemstijn, soprano; Yvonne Benschop, mezzo-soprano; Ananda Goud, mezzo-soprano; Reinbert de Leeuw, cond.; Schönberg Ensemble, orch.; Percussion Group The Hague] (Nonesuch 79295) ♪ ♪ ♪ ♪

Written for voices and ensemble, this 1981 four-movement piece is remarkable in that it uses no repeated melodic patterns and is more musical and flowing than some of Reich's other works to that point. The four soprano voices act as the core of the piece and are lightly supported by the instrumental ensemble. Also included on this disc is a fine rendering of Reich's *Three Movements* for Orchestra, performed by the London Symphony Orchestra with Michael Tilson Thomas conducting.

The Cave

what to buy: [Cheryl Rowe Bensman, soprano; Marion Beckenstein, soprano; James Bassi, tenor; Hugo Munday, baritone; Paul Hillier, cond.; Steve Reich Ensemble, orch.] (Nonesuch 79327) ♪ ♪ ♪ ♪ ♪

This contemplative, tantalizing piece—a new type of musical theater based on videotaped documentary sources—gives us a glimpse of what opera might be like in the next millennium. Certainly you'd want to see this grand-scale piece performed on stage, but this two-disc set (with 105-page booklet) resplendently conveys the Biblical story of the cave Abraham bought as a burial place for his wife. The three-act opera (with video and text by Beryl Korot) unfolds through the mixture of taped interviews, sung text, and instrumental scoring by Reich. Speech becomes melody, doubled and harmonized by the instruments, and the four singers perform in the non-vibrato manner of Reich's earlier pieces while referencing Medieval and Renaissance styles. It's an ambitious project and one of Reich's best large-scale works.

The Desert Music for Large Orchestra and Small Amplified Chorus

what to buy: [Michael Tilson Thomas, cond.; Brooklyn Philharmonic Orchestra; Brooklyn Philharmonic Chorus] (Nonesuch 79101) ♪ ♪ ♪ ♪♪

Thomas is an expert conductor who extracts superior performances from everyone on the five movements of this gorgeous forty-eight minute work of art. Recorded in 1984, the piece begins with a steady, fast pulse and gradually unfolds to an exhilarating finish. A complex, sensuous work of many colors, it is beautifully executed and manipulated by the producers (Reich and Rudolph Werner) and engineers.

influences: Philip Glass, Terry Riley, La Monte Young, John Adams

Nancy Ann Lee

Ottorino Respighi

Born July 9, 1879, in Bologna, Italy. Died April 18, 1936, in Rome, Italy.

period: Romantic/Twentieth century

Ottorino Respighi was one of Italian music's dominant creative forces in the early twentieth century—a champion of Romanticism in the face of what he called "chaos," and a restorer of the symphonic tradition to an Italy that had been obsessed with opera. In 1932, near the end of his career and after his most popular compositions were behind him, Respighi signed a manifesto extolling the virtues of personal, emotional expression. Part of his criticism against the emerging modernists said, "We are against this art that cannot have and does not have any human content and desires to be merely a mechanical demonstration and a cerebral puzzle . . . . The Romanticism of yesterday will again be the Romanticism of tomorrow." This belief is clearly articulated in Respighi's Roman trilogy (*Fontane di Roma, Pini de Roma,* and *Feste romane*) and the three suites he called *Ancient Airs and Dances.*

Respighi initially studied violin and composition in his home town of Bologna before leaving Italy for Russia in 1900. While in St. Petersburg he got a job as first violist with the Opera Theater Orchestra and briefly spent some time studying with Nikolai Rimsky-Korsakov, a defining event in Respighi's life as a composer/arranger. He then went to Berlin, Germany, but after a relatively unrewarding series of lessons with Max Bruch in 1902 decided to go back to Bologna. There he earned his living as an orchestral musician, playing violin and viola. He had been composing various songs, short orchestral works, and chamber music scores during this time, but nothing that attracted much attention from the public.

Then, in 1906, Respighi began exploring seventeenth and eighteenth century music, finding works by Antonio Vivaldi, Claudio Monteverdi, and others, which he transcribed and rearranged to great response from Berlin audiences when he returned there two years later. This time Respighi stayed in Germany for about a year, took a job as accompanist for a voice class, and managed to come under the spell of Richard Strauss, the other great musical influence in his life.

Once back in Italy, Respighi joined a quintet and managed to secure a production of *Semirâma,* an opera that he had been working on since 1908. This was followed by performances of other works and a stint as a teacher at the Bologna Liceo Musicale. 1913 found him settling down in Rome, where he had found a job on the staff of the Liceo di Saint Cecilia (later the Conservatorio di Santa Cecilia). The first compositions by which he is remembered, *Fontane di Roma (Fountains of Rome),* the initial set of *Ancient Airs and Dances,* and the ballet score based on music by Gioachino Rossini (*La boutique fantasque*), were written during his years at the school. By 1923 he was appointed director there, although he would resign three years later in order to further pursue a career as a composer and conductor.

Audiences around the world responded to Respighi's orchestrations and compositions with a mixture of delight and cold, hard cash that enabled the composer to travel around the world. Unburdened by academic considerations, he took a trip to the United States in 1925 and heard Arturo Toscanini conduct the American premiere of Respighi's *Pini de Roma.* Two years later he returned to give a chamber music concert at the Library of Congress and was inspired to write *Trittico botticelliano (Three Botticelli Pictures),* based upon paintings he had seen there. Inspiration was to strike again when he took a trip with his wife to Brazil later that same year. While he was mainly there to spend a few months in the sun, he ended up absorbing some of the local music. Upon his return to Rome, Respighi began working on his *Impressioni brasiliane (Brazilian Impressions),* returning to Rio de Janeiro the next year to conduct the work's premiere to an enthusiastic audience. The United States was also where the last of his really popular scores, *Feste romane,* would receive its world premiere, with Toscanini conducting the orchestra at Carnegie Hall in 1929.

The last years of Respighi's life were relatively comfortable ones despite the presence of a Fascist regime. The composer's music was favored by many in the government but he was basically an apolitical, non-confrontational type of personality—though, to his credit, he supported his good friend Toscanini when the latter refused to play the fascist anthem (*Giovinezza*) at a concert, thus inflaming local dignitaries and sparking an ugly demonstration.

Orchestral
Fontane di Roma (Fountains of Rome)
what to buy: [*Immortal Toscanini, vol. 10: Italian Orchestral Music*; Arturo Toscanini, cond.; NBC Symphony Orchestra] (RCA Victor Red Seal 72374) ♪ ♪ ♪ ♪

Toscanini was a great champion of Respighi, and their temperaments blended well. This disc, containing the entire Roman Trilogy, features splendid music-making, but the recording is rather cramped and dry. Most of the other composers heard in this collection (including Gioachino Rossini, Gaetano Donizetti, and Giuseppe Verdi) are represented by famous overtures from their operas.

[Charles Dutoit, cond.; Orchestre Symphonique de Montréal] (Decca 410145) ♪ ♪ ♪ ♪

While it doesn't quite pack the excitement of the Toscanini performance (see above), the sound is a couple of steps above that disc's vintage RCA sonics. Like the Toscanini set, Dutoit includes the complete trilogy, and the performances are quite good.

what to buy next: [*Dorati Conducts Respighi*; Antal Dorati, cond.; Minneapolis Symphony Orchestra] (Mercury Living Presence 432007) ♪ ♪ ♪♪

The sound is also much better on the Dorati disc than it is in Toscanini's version. Included along with *Fontane di Roma* is Dorati's rendition of *I Pini di Roma (The Pines of Rome)* (with the Minneapolis Symphony Orchestra), and two other Respighi pieces played by Dorati leading the London Symphony Orchestra: *Brazilian Impressions* and *Gli Uccelli (The Birds)*.

Ancient Airs and Dances
what to buy: [Antal Dorati, cond.; Philharmonica Hungarica, orch.] (Mercury Living Presence 434304) ♪ ♪ ♪♪

Respighi arranged sixteenth and seventeenth century

lute pieces into three orchestral suites, binding them together under the blanket title *Ancient Airs and Dances*. Dorati's vision of these works is most felicitous and the recording, dating from the 1960s, holds up amazingly well.

[Orpheus Chamber Orchestra] (Deutsche Grammophon 437533) ♪ ♪ ♪ ♪♪

While this conductor-less ensemble only includes the first and third of Respighi's *Ancient Airs and Dances* on this set, they give marvelous, totally recommendable performances that are deliciously pointed and danceable. They give extra value in their renditions of the composer's *Gli Uccelli* and the *Three Botticelli Pictures* as well.

what to buy next: [Richard Hickox, cond.; Sinfonia 21, orch.] (Chandos 9415) ♪ ♪ ♪♪

Hickox directs a very acceptable version of the three suites, but this is more of an alternative performance to one you might already have on hand. The case for picking this set over the hordes of other ones on the market lies in what it offers above and beyond the *Ancient Airs and Dances*—in this case, very respectable performances of two lesser-known works by Respighi: the *Berceuse* for Strings and the *Aria* from his Suite for Flute and Strings.

influences: Heitor Villa-Lobos, Mario Castelnuovo-Tedesco, Nikolai Rimsky-Korsakov

Gerald Brennan and Ellen Kokko

Silvestre Revueltas
Born Silvestre Revueltas Sanchez, December 31, 1899, in Santiago Papasquiaro, Durango, Mexico. Died October 5, 1940, in Mexico City, Mexico.

period: Twentieth century

Silvestre Revueltas, born on the last day of the nineteenth century, is perhaps one of the few composers who lived a life as colorful as his music. One of Latin America's boldest and most original composers, this eccentric Mexican helped shape the world view of Mexican concert music with a group of strikingly individual, often witty works.

Trained as a violinist, Revueltas's first works were

strongly influenced by Claude Debussy, whose music he came in contact with when living in Chicago during the 1920s, and later when playing violin in a San Antonio, Texas theater orchestra. In 1929 Revueltas went to Mexico City at the request of the dean of Mexican music, Carlos Chávez, to become assistant conductor of the newly-formed Orquesta Sinfónica Nacional. He held that post until 1936 but also taught violin at a local conservatory. Revueltas went to Spain in 1937, where he fought on the Republican side during the Spanish Civil War before returning to Mexico. While turning out some vividly unusual and original works in the last ten years of his life, Revueltas was to die young (and poor) as a result of his particular fondness for alcohol. He wandered in and out of mental institutions and was, to quote the composer, "born with a regrettable inclination toward music and loafing."

What is most striking to most listeners is not Revueltas's use of Mexican folk elements but his wry and playful humor. Nowhere is this better exemplified than in the oddly-titled *Ocho x Radio*, a brief and deftly-scored chamber work that sounds about as un-European as one can imagine. His most popular work, *Sensemayá* (in its version for full orchestra) has found its way into the repertoire. Beginning with a barely audible ostinato in 7/8 and maintaining this time signature throughout, *Sensemayá* showcases Revueltas's rhythmic bombast and unique use of instrumental color. The belligerent brass and percussion exhortations are truly brutal and the effect, when well-executed, is entirely memorable. Those interested in Aaron Copland's explorations into Latin American rhythms and gestures will certainly have something to discover here.

Written in homage to a murdered Spanish poet, the *Homanaje a Federico García Lorca* is one of the composer's most successful compositions. Blending folk elements of his native country (echoes of mariachi bands) with overt polytonality and an earthy audacity, this is a work that could not have been written by any other composer. The splendidly evocative *La Noche de los Mayas* captures the spirit of a pagan Indian ritual in Mexico before the Spanish conquest. Bold, daring, startling, succinct: all words that describe the music of this puzzling and overlooked figure of twentieth century music.

Orchestral
various works
what to buy: [*Centennial Anthology: 15 Masterpieces*; various cond.; various orch.] (RCA Victor Red Seal 63548)

♪ ♪ ♪ ♪

This two disc album is probably the best introduction to Revueltas. Certainly it is the most comprehensive recording of his works currently in catalog, containing performances by a wide variety of forces including two versions of *Sensemayá*: one with Eduardo Mata conducting the New Philharmonia Orchestra, and an older rendition by Leopold Stokowski leading his own hand-picked band of musicians.

Sensemayá
what to buy: |Eduardo Mata, cond.; Simón Bolívar Symphony Orchestra] (Dorian 90178) ♪ ♪ ♪ ♪

The late Eduardo Mata conducts probably the most visceral interpretation of this popular work. Revueltas's *Redes* is also part of the program, along with pieces by Alberto Ginastera (the *Pampeana no. 3*) and Julián Orbón (his Concerto Grosso for String Quartet and Orchestra).

what to buy next: [*Sensemayá: The Unknown Revueltas*; Enrique Arturo Diemecke, cond; Camerata de las Américas, orch.] (Dorian 90244) ♪ ♪ ♪

This recording features numerous works not found elsewhere, including some delightful songs and the original chamber version of *Sensemayá*.

influences: Manuel de Falla, Carlos Chávez, Heitor Villa-Lobos, Aaron Copland, Juan Esquivel

Sean Hickey

Joseph Rheinberger
Born Joseph Gabriel Rheinberger on March 17, 1839, in Vaduz, Liechtenstein. Died November 25, 1901, in Munich, Germany.

period: Romantic

Josef Rheinberger was an underrated romantic composer known principally for his organ-related works. He is the only classical composer of distinction ever born in Liechtenstein, a tiny country situated on the border between Austria and Switzerland. But to note Rheinberger only for that would be a disservice to him, to music history, and to curious listeners who might not explore his oeuvre otherwise.

Rheinberger's biography is not very exciting, since it is

totally devoid of scandal or high living, yet listening to his music provides much pleasure. After lessons in piano and organ, the precocious Rheinberger amazed everyone by becoming organist in a Vaduz church at age seven. By the time he was twelve years old, his father was convinced to let him attend the conservatory in Munich, the city where he would live for most of his life. While still in his teens, Rheinberger held organ posts in several churches and accumulated a sizable roster of private students. In his early twenties, Rheinberger began to attract notice for his compositions, while also filling a number of conducting posts. In 1867 he became a professor at the Munich Conservatory and married his former pupil Franziska von Hoffnaass, a gifted poet whose writings Rheinberger would often set to music. The marriage domesticated the composer and kept him happily centered in Munich.

Upon his death Rheinberger was considered of importance primarily as a pedagogue, having taught such prominent musicians as Englebert Humperdinck, Ermanno Wolf-Ferrari, Horatio Parker, and Wilhelm Furtwängler. But organists and, to a somewhat lesser degree, choral directors knew a good thing when they heard it and kept his name alive by playing his twenty organ sonatas, his sacred choral music, and other works from his extensive output. Eventually, Rheinberger's chamber, orchestral, and vocal works began to earn respect. In the 1950s, with the proliferation of LP recordings, his virtues could at last be appreciated beyond the inside ranks of musicians.

Orchestral
Concerto no. 1 in F Major for Organ and Orchestra
what to buy: [Michael Murray, organ; Jahja Ling, cond.; Royal Philharmonic Orchestra] (Telarc 80136) ♪ ♪ ♪ ♪

This is a work of genial yet robust character, with flowing melodies, warm harmonies (somewhat reminiscent of an easygoing Johannes Brahms), and a flag-waving finale that invites standing ovations. Also included is Murray's performance of Marcel Dupré's Symphony in G Minor for Organ and Orchestra, op. 25, a work whose essentially French character nicely contrasts Rheinberger's Germanic influences.

Chamber
Sonata for Organ no. 16 in G-sharp Minor, op. 175
what to buy: [Bruce Stevens, organ] (Raven OAR 220) ♪ ♪ ♪♪

This is one of the best of Rheinberger's twenty organ sonatas, works that are characterized by an amazing evenness of lyrical inspiration and by the fact that they "lie so well" for the organ. Stevens gives a fine performance on an organ of eminently suitable disposition. You also get his takes on the composer's seventeenth and twentieth organ sonatas.

Vocal
Mass in E-flat for Eight Voices, op. 109—*Cantus Missae*
what to buy: [*Rheinberger: Sacred Choral Music*; Helen Cole, harp; Christopher Monks, organ; Geoffrey Webber, cond.; Gonville and Caius College Choir, Cambridge] (ASV 989) ♪ ♪ ♪ ♪

While this a cappella work captures the feel and vaulted cathedral spirit of Giovanni Palestrina, Rheinberger cloaks it in beautiful, indisputably nineteenth-century chromatic harmonies. Also on this disc is the composer's Requiem in D Minor, op. 194; the hymn *Ave Regina caelorum*; and a work for solo organ.

The Star of Bethlehem, op. 164
worth searching for: [Rita Streich, soprano; Dietrich Fischer-Dieskau, baritone; Robert Heger, cond.; Graunke Symphony Orchestra; Bavarian Radio Chorus] (Carus 83.111) ♪ ♪ ♪ ♪♪

Texts to this Christmas cantata were supplied by the composer's wife, who died immediately after the work's initial public unveiling. It became very popular in Germany, but Rheinberger was so distraught that he could not bring himself to attend any of the subsequent performances. It is a very beautiful, uplifting work for soloists, chorus, and orchestra, deserving exposure but probably still awaiting its North American premiere. While it may be hard to find, this recording is well worth trying to ferret out.

influences: César Franck, Horatio Parker, Dudley Buck

Herman Trotter

Terry Riley
Born Terry Mitchell Riley on June 24, 1935, in Colfax, CA.

period: Twentieth century

Terry Riley, one of the godfathers of minimalism, created one of that genre's seminal works, *In C,* in 1964. This composition, utilizing constantly reappearing musical patterns without any melody lines laid over them, helped introduce the concept of repetition as a valid ingredient in Western music. Riley is also a masterly pianist who blends classical tradition with influences drawn from the discipline of North Indian ragas and the improvisatory flair of American jazz. His hypnotic, multi-layered, polymetric, brightly orchestrated, Eastern-tinged compositions and improvisations helped set the stage for much of the New Age music heard today.

Terry Riley is a multi-instrumentalist who learned to play the violin, piano, and saxophone at an early age. During the late 1950s these talents, and his fascination with jazz, helped support him and his young family when, as a student at San Francisco State University, he got a job playing ragtime piano in a bar at night. His love of jazz improvisation was shared by his friend La Monte Young, another key figure in the development of minimalism.

In 1960 Riley and Young became graduate students at the University of California at Berkeley, where they ran into other like-minded musicians. Inspired by his friend's slow-moving jazz improvisations (in a style Riley once likened to "being on a space station and waiting to get to the next planet"), Riley began experimenting with similarly sustained ideas, forming an improvisation group with composition classmates Pauline Oliveros and Loren Rush. Riley and Young also worked with choreographer Anna Halprin, using tape loops and the technology of the day to create works for her dance company. After Riley obtained his M.A. degree in composition, he spent two years in Europe with his family—living in Spain, visiting Morocco, and participating in "happenings," street theater, and jazz concerts throughout Scandinavia. During this time he was not composing much, a circumstance that would change in 1963 when he received increased access to the ORTF (Office de Radiodiffusion-Television Française) recording studios. There he began experimenting with tape loops in earnest and in the process working out his theory of "pattern fields"—the simultaneous sound of identical, tonal, highly rhythmic musical phrases that shift against one another in a pulsating field of sound.

All of this sonic experimentation piqued Riley's interest in moving beyond theory and trying his concepts with live musicians, using repetition and musical fragments to create an abstract fabric of sound in a concert situation. Upon his return to the United States in 1964, he

began examining the possibilities of electro-acoustic music even further. *In C* evolved out of the composer's ideas about musical constructs based on layers of repetitive patterns that shift constantly even while weaving around each other. Although the piece is notated, it doesn't specify the instrumentation; all performances of *In C* include elements of improvisation as directed by the score, factors that change the shape of the piece every time it is played. Riley achieved this by setting up patterns that should be repeated and directing the performers to choose the number of repetitions they will play, thereby allowing the architecture of the work to shift each time it is performed. When *In C* was premiered on November 1, 1964, at the San Francisco Tape Music Center, the group playing it included such late-twentieth-century heavyweights as Oliveros, Morton Subotnick, Jon Gibson, Steve Reich, and the composer.

Since then, *In C* has proved to be a highly adaptable and popular example of minimalism, with successful performances given by percussion ensembles, guitar groups, a Chinese traditional orchestra, and a microtonal band. It not only had an impact upon contemporary classical composers such as Steve Reich, Philip Glass, and John Adams, but the initial album documenting the piece (released by CBS Records in 1968) also influenced rock bands such as the Who, Soft Machine, and Tangerine Dream. By the time *In C* was finally released on vinyl, Riley had already composed (in 1967) *A Rainbow in Curved Air* for electronic keyboards and percussion. The original album containing that piece and *Poppy Nogood and the Phantom Band* (composed for overdubbed saxophones, electric organ, and a "time-lag accumulator") turned out to be yet another relatively commercial hit for the young composer when it was released in 1969.

After his work on *In C,* Riley went to hear Indian musicians Ravi Shankar and Alla Rahka in concert, an event that impressed him because he was able to hear an ancient cultural form that included elements of improvisation within a clearly defined structure—the same kinds of things that he was interested in doing with tape loops and other electronic paraphernalia. In 1970 Riley met North Indian raga singer Pandit Pran Nath and subsequently became his disciple, making numerous trips to India to study with this master.

Riley's academic career began in 1971 (despite having been associated with the Center for Creative and Performing Arts at SUNY Buffalo four years earlier), when he taught North Indian raga and music composition at Mills College. There Riley met fellow faculty member David Harrington, the founder and leader of the San Francisco-based Kronos Quartet. They began a long association that has produced a number of string quartets, a keyboard quintet (*Crows Rosary*), and a concerto for string quartet, *The Sands,* which was the Salzburg Festival's first-ever new music commission. The Kronos Quartet's album *Cadenza on the Night Plain,* comprising four of Riley's compositions, was selected by *Time and Newsweek* magazines as one of the ten best classical albums of 1985. The quartet's 1988 recording of Riley's epic five-quartet cycle, *Salomé Dances for Peace,* was selected as the number one classical album of the year by *USA Today* and was nominated for a Grammy Award.

In 1992 Riley formed a small theater company, The Travelling-Avantt-Gaard, to perform his chamber opera *The Saint Adolf Ring.* This work is based on the drawings, poetry, writings, and mathematical calculations of Adolf Wölfli, an early-twentieth-century Swiss artist who suffered from schizophrenia and created his entire output while confined in a mental institution. Riley's fascination with Wölfli also yielded *The Heavenly Ladder,* a series of piano suites, in 1994. Riley regularly performs solo piano programs of his works and often appears in duo concerts with Indian sitarist Krishna Bhatt, saxophonist George Brooks, and Italian bassist Stefano Scodanibbio.

Orchestral
In C for Saxophone and Instrumental Ensemble
what to buy: [*In C: 25th Anniversary Concert*; Loren Rush, cond.; Terry Riley, cond.; various musicians, orch.] (New Albion Records 071) ♪ ♪ ♪ ♪

Riley considers this recording to be "a document of the best *In C* performance ever." At nearly twice the length of the original CBS album, this version of the work is also more richly scored, with a variety of percussion instruments creating dense non-Western polyrhythms underneath layers of guitars, synthesizers, and saxophones.

Chamber
The Harp of the New Albion for Piano
what to buy: [Terry Riley, piano] (Celestial Harmonies 14018) ♪ ♪ ♪ ♪

The composer performs the ten movements of this piece

for nearly two hours. While it's not one of his widely heralded major works, Riley's brilliant performance illustrates the story behind the music—the legend of a harp brought to the New World and left behind on the shores of "New Albion." Although each movement is defined by composed elements, Riley improvises throughout and—using just intonation, shifting tonal clusters, and a meritorious keyboard technique—capably evokes the constantly changing, swimming sounds of the harp, especially in the swirling third movement, "Riding the Westerleys."

Cadenza on the Night Plain for String Quartet
worth searching for: [Kronos Quartet, ensemble] (Gramavision 79444) ♪ ♪ ♪ ♪ ♪

This piece has been hailed as one of Riley's best works, maybe even second to his seminal *In C.* Each player is spotlighted at one point in the thirty-seven minute piece, and together the quartet captures the inherent spirituality of Riley's adventurous score. This is a work that conveys the aura of an Indian raga, touches of folksiness, and aspects of the composer's personality at the same time as it expresses the minimalism for which he's best known. The all-Riley fare on this rapturous album (certainly among this ensemble's best) includes *Sunrise of the Planetary Dream Collector, G Song,* and *Mythic Birds Waltz.*

Salomé Dances for Peace for String Quartet
what to buy: [Kronos Quartet, ensemble] (Nonesuch 79217) ♪ ♪ ♪ ♪♪

On this two-disc set, the Kronos Quartet renders a passionate, elegant performance of this beautiful five-part Riley work. Listeners will hear influences of jazz, blues, North Indian raga, Middle Eastern scales, minimalist patterns, and traditional Western art music. Kronos sensitively allows Riley's penchant for storytelling to shine through on this masterly (nearly two-hour) performance.

influences: LaMonte Young, Steve Reich, John Adams, Philip Glass

Nancy Ann Lee and Garaud MacTaggart

Nikolai Rimsky-Korsakov
Born Nikolay Andreyevich Rimsky-Korsakov, c. March 18, 1844, in Tikhvin, Russia. Died c. June 21, 1908, in Lyubensk, Russia

period: Romantic

The last of the *Mighty Handful*, Rimsky-Korsakov was a master orchestrator attracted to fantastical and pagan themes, a predilection that can be seen in his symphonic piece, *Scheherazade,* and several of his operas. Despite his fascination with opera and his many attempts at composing them, few of his efforts have made an impact on international stages. He did, however, provide a bridge for Russian nationalist music to enter the twentieth century by influencing many composers to follow in his footsteps, particularly his student, Igor Stravinsky.

As he was a staunch supporter of the revolutionary fervor of late nineteenth century Russia, the music of Nikolay Rimsky-Korsakov (like that of his contemporaries) is constructed on Russian nationalistic idioms; however, his particular bent for pantheistic subjects and his consequent bright and sprightly orchestration distinguishes him from fellow nationalists Modest Mussorgsky and Alexander Borodin. While Rimsky-Korsakov had harbored a love of music since early childhood, particularly for the scores of Mikhail Glinka, much of his youth was spent pursuing a naval career. It was not until his introduction to Mily Balakirev in 1861 that his passion for composition was sparked. Inspired by Glinka and encouraged by Balakirev, Rimsky-Korsakov finally embarked on a musical career in 1865. The first work he subsequently finished was one which positively identified his compositional strengths: a flair for orchestral colors and a highly individual manner of layering rhythms and sounds. This was *Antar,* his second symphony, first performed in 1868 (and revised twice more, in 1875 and 1897). Despite limited formal training and a lack of theoretical knowledge, Rimsky-Korsakov was recognized by his contemporaries as a master of orchestration and, in 1871, accepted a position as instructor of composition at the St. Petersburg Conservatory. In 1873 his first grand opera, *The Maid of Pskov,* was produced.

Rimsky-Korsakov took a hiatus from serious composition for the next few years to dedicate time to his newly acquired job and, more importantly, to study techniques of instrumentation and counterpoint. It was not until 1878 that he returned to composition with *May Night,* a light-hearted, folklore-inspired opera. Shortly after that the composer reached a peak of enthusiasm for pagan and fantastical themes with his composition of *The*

Nikolai Rimsky-Korsakov

Snow Maiden. He spent the summer of 1880 in the countryside, where he found plentiful inspiration for his pantheistic opera, enraptured by the beauty and magic of the natural world. He composed quickly and enthusiastically and, when finished, took another two-year respite from original composition as he became submerged in the task of polishing and publishing the posthumous manuscripts of his good friend Mussorgsky—including the score to *Night on the Bare Mountain*—as well as shouldering the new post of assistant musical director (to Balakirev) of the imperial chapel.

From 1883 to 1887 (aside from a few songs, a movement for a string quartet, and a textbook on harmony) Rimsky-Korsakov underwent a barren period from which he emerged dissatisfied with his own work and disenchanted with music in general. A phase of fervent revision began; none of his early works (pre-1880) were left in their original form. By 1888, however, he seemed to be working himself back into form, finishing the *Capriccio espagnol, Sheherazade* (an orchestral suite that owed its origins to *Tales of the Arabian Nights*), and the *Russian Easter Overture*—a trio of works which would later become his best-known, most popular scores. The next year, Rimsky-Korsakov saw the four operas comprising Richard Wagner's *Der Ring des Nibelungen* and was impressed enough by the orchestration that he would end up changing elements of his own style. Challenges were on the horizon, however, particularly in his private life, where he experienced a series of personal tragedies between 1890 and 1893: the deaths of his mother and two youngest children along with the serious illness of his wife and another of his sons.

After a hiatus imposed by these vicissitudes, Rimsky-Korsakov returned to music upon one more: the death of Piotr Tchaikovsky in 1893. His friend's passing inspired him to tackle a story by Gogol with which he had long been fascinated and which Tchaikovsky had adapted for his own opera, *Vakula the Smith.* This was "Christmas Eve," a tale infused with mystical subjects that had always been close to Rimsky-Korsakov's heart. While working on turning the story into an opera, he was inspired with a flood of ideas for his next project, *Sadko,* in which the composer utilized some of the Wagnerian concepts he had first heard back in 1889. *Sadko* was finally completed in 1896, and produced two years later by a wealthy railroad baron and arts patron. The year 1898 saw the completion of a new opera (*The Tsar's*

Bride) and the near-completion of *The Tale of Tsar Saltan*, a hearkening back to stylistic characteristics originated in *The Snow Queen*. Rimsky-Korsakov's successive works were relative commercial failures; however, he found a revived enthusiasm for pantheism when he worked on *The Tale of the Invisible City of Kitezh* in 1903. This too was put on the back burner when he became deeply involved in the political upheavals of the period. Rimsky-Korsakov vocally supported the cause of student protesters and was consequently dismissed from the Free School of Music. (He was, however, invited back later when Alexander Glazunov was elected the new director.) The remainder of Rimsky-Korsakov's life was focused on the frustrating task of producing his last opera, *The Golden Cockerel*. He was plagued by censorship of his libretto and, having suffered worsening heart troubles, did not live to see its debut performance in 1909.

Orchestral
Scheherazade for Orchestra, op. 35
what to buy: [Charles Mackerras, cond.; London Symphony Orchestra] (Telarc 80208) ♪ ♪ ♪ ♪ ♪

It is difficult to imagine a recording of this work that is so well-balanced that you hear the glories of Rimsky-Korsakov's orchestration without thinking about the actual musicians playing it. This is an ideal performance in every way and, with the composer's *Capriccio espagnol* tossed in for good measure, you can get his two most popular orchestral works in one fell swoop and be mightily satisfied.

what to buy next: [Herbert von Karajan, cond.; Berlin Philharmonic Orchestra] (Penguin Classics 460618) ♪ ♪ ♪ ♪₅

Well-played and well-recorded, this performance by Karajan and his BPO may strike some as a bit too slick, but it could be argued that the high-powered gloss applied to this score by Karajan and company is exactly what it needs. Everything is in its place, including the pulse that makes Rimsky-Korsakov's melodies sing. Alexander Borodin's *Polovtsian Dances* is an inspired pairing and the budget pricing makes this a fine choice.

Capriccio espagnol in A Major for Orchestra, op. 34
what to buy: [Antál Dorati, cond.; London Symphony Orchestra] (Mercury Living Presence 434308) ♪ ♪ ♪ ♪

Despite the vintage of the recording (1959), the sound is amazingly good in superb transfers that feature Dorati and the LSO in peak form. The programming is quite felicitous as well, especially for listeners who don't need *Scheherazade* but covet the *Capriccio espagnol*, the suite from *The Golden Cockerel*, and the *Russian Easter Overture*. The excitement continues with a fine performance of Alexander Borodin's pulse-pounding *Polovtsian Dances*.

Flight of the Bumble Bee
what to buy: [*Russian Festival*; Anthony Bramall, cond.; Czech-Slovak Radio Symphony Orchestra] (Naxos 8. 550085) ♪ ♪ ♪₅

This relatively slight (but popular) piece is taken from Rimsky-Korsakov's opera *The Tale of Tsar Saltan* and provides the instrumental backdrop for that point in the storyline where Prince Guidon (the hero) is transformed into a bee so that he can sting his wicked aunts and the old witch who helped them plot against his birthright. Because of its brevity, there probably isn't a whole lot of need to spend a lot to get a decent version of this little gem. Bramall includes the work as part of a budget-priced compilation featuring music from a high-powered batch of Russian composers: Rimsky-Korsakov, Glinka, Borodin, Aram Khachaturian, and Reinhold Glière.

influences: Mikhail Glinka, Alexander Glazunov, Igor Stravinsky, Sergei Prokofiev

Sharon L. Hoyer and David Wagner

George Rochberg
Born July 15, 1918, in Paterson, NJ.

period: Twentieth century

A leader of the postmodernist movement in mid-twentieth-century music, composer and teacher George Rochberg turned his back on the atonal tradition of the Second Viennese School represented by Arnold Schoenberg, Alban Berg, and Anton Webern and the aleatory, or chance, method espoused by John Cage. Although Rochberg's early compositions reflect the influences of Igor Stravinsky, Bela Bartok, and Paul Hindemith, his 1965 chamber work *Music for the Magic Theater* represents Rochberg's signature technique of using musical quotation, collage, and elements of neoclassicism.

The son of Ukranian-Jewish immigrants, George Rochberg began composing at age ten. He graduated from Montclair State Teacher's College in his home state of New Jersey in 1939 and then enrolled in the Mannes School of Music, where studied counterpoint and composition with George Szell. Drafted into the army shortly after his marriage to writer Gene Rosenfeld in 1941, Rochberg was seriously wounded and received the Purple Heart. Following the war, he studied theory and composition with Gian Carlo Menotti at the Curtis Institute in Philadelphia. In 1948 he obtained a graduate degree from the University of Pennsylvania and returned to Curtis as a faculty member, remaining until 1954. Rochberg became a music editor for the Theodore Presser Company in 1951 and was later promoted to director of publications, a position he held until 1960. Rochberg was then appointed chairman of the music department at the University of Pennsylvania, finally stepping down from that post in 1968 to become a professor of music at the school.

In 1950, while in Rome as a Fulbright and American Academy fellow, Rochberg befriended Italian serialist composer Luigi Dallapiccola, who exposed this method of composing music to his new friend. The serial, or twelve-tone, technique—music using a preordained series of notes—was the primary compositional method of mid-twentieth century academics, and Rochberg, as a composer and teacher, embraced it wholeheartedly. During this period he published his first important serial pieces: the *12 Bagatelles for Piano* (1952), his Symphony no. 2 (1955–56), and the *Cheltenham Concerto* (1958). Following the untimely death of his twenty-year-old son Paul in 1964, Rochberg dramatically reevaluated a musical aesthetic he felt was emotionally limited. Rejecting the restrictions of intellectually oriented serialism and the almost mechanistic detachment of aleatory music, Rochberg rocked the very foundation of musical academia, launching a debate that is still with us today. He sought a language that could communicate his unbearable loss, feeling that the tenets of the twelve-tone system were no longer adequate.

Contra mortem et tempus and *Music for the Magic Theater,* both written in 1965, represent the beginning of this search. Rochberg directly quotes the work of other composers within the fabric of these pieces. The result is a suspension of time, juxtaposing past and present. The change in style included a return to tonality and an acceptance of earlier musical forms, elements that found their culmination in three string quartets written

during the early 1970s. Branded a reactionary and a traitor, Rochberg was severely criticized for "retrenching." Critics said these pieces were nostalgic and gimmicky, but his contribution to the musical discourse was nothing less than a revolution. His search for a more meaningful way to create and communicate challenged the classical canon so prevalent in American universities and conservatories at the time. A need to transcend the intellectual and reconnect with an alienated audience is the legacy he passed on to postmodernist composers such as Steve Reich, Philip Glass, William Bolcom, John Corigliano, Joan Tower, and Ellen Taaffe Zwilich.

As significant a force in the academic world as he was

in the composing arena, Rochberg finally retired from teaching in 1983. Throughout his distinguished career, he has been the recipient of numerous awards and honorary degrees, including first prize in the Kennedy Center Friedheim Awards for his String Quartet no. 4 and awards from the National Endowment for the Arts and the Guggenheim Foundation.

Orchestral
Symphony no. 2
what to buy: [*American Masters: George Rochberg,* Werner Torkanowsky, cond.; New York Philharmonic Orchestra] (CRI 768) ♪ ♪ ♪ ♪

Composed in 1955 and 1956, Rochberg's second symphony received its premiere with George Szell and the Cleveland Orchestra on February 26, 1959. The four uninterrupted movements, written using the twelve-tone method, show that Rochberg was a very adept disciple of serialism. On the whole, he successfully merges this rigid compositional technique with the large scale of the symphonic form. Other works on this disc are his String Quartet no. 1 and *Contra mortem et tempus,* a quartet for violin, flute, clarinet, and piano.

Music for the Magic Theater
what to buy: [Stephen Rogers Radcliffe, cond.; New York Chamber Ensemble, orch.] (New World Records 80462) ♪ ♪ ♪ ♪

After his renunciation of serialism and his return to tonality, Rochberg explored the use of musical quotation. Here he incorporates passages from Mozart, Beethoven, Mahler, Webern, Varèse, Stockhausen, Miles Davis, and his own previous works. The result is a surrealistic collage of styles, as music from various times and places emerges, only to quickly dissipate. Also included is one of his later works, Octet for Strings and Winds—*A Grand Fantasia,* written in 1980.

Chamber
String Quartet no. 4
what to buy: [Concord String Quartet] (New World Records 80551) ♪ ♪ ♪ ♪ ♪

This is the first in a group of three pieces that some critics believe is the real start of the anti-serialist revolution, with Rochberg alternating atonal movements with overt tonal expressionism. The second movement is an excellent example of the neo-romanticism Rochberg

began employing. This two-disc set also includes his third, fifth, and sixth string quartets in extremely well-performed versions by the ensemble for which they were originally written.

influences: Charles Ives, Anton von Webern, William Bolcom

Mona C. DeQuis and Christine L. Cody

Joaquín Rodrigo
Born November 22, 1901, in Sagunto, Spain. Died July 6, 1999, in Madrid, Spain.

period: Twentieth century

A most distinctive composer of guitar-oriented scores, Rodrigo's gifts earned him status as a Spanish national treasure, and his *Concierto de Aranjuez* has brought him world renown and esteem. Miles Davis and Gil Evans even released a jazz album (*Sketches of Spain*) flavored by Rodrigo's catchy melody. While that work, by virtue of its subtle tunesmithing and Spanish rhythms, is certainly deserving of its fame, Rodrigo's oeuvre is deeper than that. In Spain, his piano pieces and songs are well-thought-of, while the *Fantasia para un gentilhombre* for Guitar and Orchestra has also made inroads on international concert stages.

Joaquín Rodrigo was born on St. Cecilia's Day, the name day for the patron saint of music. At the age of three, Rodrigo almost completely lost his sight as a result of an epidemic of diphtheria. With healthy ears, a very young Joaquín was struck by the color and vigor of Spanish music and, at age eight, began his first musical studies. He later took lessons in composition with Francisco Antich, which ended up predisposing him toward a Neo-Classical stance, as evidenced by his first orchestral work to receive attention from Spanish audiences, *Juglares.* In 1927 Rodrigo went to Paris, where he enrolled in the Schola Cantorum and began studying with Paul Dukas. Eventually this led to a meeting with Victoria Kamhi, a Turkish pianist whom he married in 1933. Victoria became amanuensis to the blind composer, as well as collaborator on his autobiography in 1986.

After years spent in France and Germany with only intermittent journeys back to Spain, Rodrigo finally returned in 1939 and took up residence in Madrid. He brought with him a work for guitar and orchestra that he had written the previous year while living in Paris, the

Concierto de Aranjuez. Prior to this, his most appreciated score was a symphonic poem, *Per la Flor del Lliri Blau (By the Flower of the Blue Lily),* which he had written in 1934 and based on a folk song from Valencia. This all changed with the enormously successful premiere of the *Concierto de Aranjuez* in 1940. It seemed as if he had found the perfect formula and would spend the rest of his life attempting to duplicate this early hit. The basic construction for his future orchestral works revolved around three movements: the outer portions unveiled a typically generic Spanish rhythm while the central section highlighted the basic tune of the work with little touches of orchestral coloring, providing a backdrop for the (usually) lovely solo line.

Fantasía para un gentilhombre, Rodrigo's next most popular composition, was written in 1954 and based on themes by the seventeenth century Baroque guitar master Gaspar Sanz. Rodrigo wanted to compose something for Andrés Segovia which would adapt the music of Sanz to the modern guitar, thus bringing together two great Spanish musicians. In between the creation of *Concierto de Aranjuez* and the *Fantasia para un gentilhombre,* Rodrigo tried applying his formula to works for other instruments and orchestra: the *Concierto heroico* for Piano and Orchestra, the *Concierto de estío* for Violin and Orchestra, the *Concierto galante* for Cello and Orchestra, and the *Concierto serenata* for Harp and Orchestra. Some of these works were quite pleasant, especially the *Concierto serenata,* but the formula didn't seem to work as well for other instruments as it did for the guitar. Thus, Rodrigo went back to the tried-and-true. He was familiar with the exploits of Celedonio Romero and his three sons and created the *Concierto andaluz* for Four Guitars and Orchestra for them in 1967. A year later he finished his *Concierto Madrigal* for Two Guitars and Orchestra, and dedicated it to the Presti/Lagoya duo. In between then and 1982, Rodrigo created some songs and a few works for solo guitar, but went back to the guitar and orchestra combination when he composed the *Concierto para una fiesta* for Pepe Romero and, in 1991, the *Rincones de España* for Angel Romero. Perhaps Rodrigo said it best when he noted, "Even though my glass may be small, I still drink from my own glass."

Orchestral
Concierto de Aranjuez for Guitar and Orchestra
what to buy: [Carlos Bonell, guitar; Charles Dutoit, cond.; Montreal Symphony Orchestra] (London 430703) ♪ ♪ ♪ ♪

Bonell's recording with Dutoit has been placed above all other attempts as far as the *Concierto de Aranjuez* is concerned. This recording fulfills the demand for passion written in Rodrigo's melodies. The sweeping Adagio makes you close your eyes and imagine yourself at court with the nobles at the Aranjuez of many years ago.

Manuel de Falla's great work for piano and orchestra, *Noches en los jardines de España (Nights in the Gardens of Spain)*—with pianist Alicia de Larrocha and soprano Juguette Tourangeau joining Dutoit's ensemble—is the main pairing on this disc, followed by the ballet music for Manuel de Falla's *El amor brujo.*

what to buy next: [John Williams, guitar; Daniel Barenboim, cond.; English Chamber Orchestra] (Sony 33208) ♪ ♪ ♪ ♪

Though the reserved style of the English can be detected in this recording, the vivacity of the basic tune comes shining through and Williams brings brilliant flair and fluidity to his role. The Concerto for Guitar and Orchestra by Heitor Villa-Lobos, another popular staple of the guitar-and-orchestra repertoire, is included on this set and receives a similarly well-thought-out performance.

Concierto de Aranjuez (arranged for harp and orchestra)
what to buy: [Isabelle Moretti, harp; Edmon Colomer, cond.; Real Orquesta Sinfónica de Sevilla, orch.] (Auvidis Valois 4815) ♪ ♪ ♪ ♪

In 1974, the great Spanish harp virtuoso Nicanor Zabaleta wrote an arrangement of the *Concierto de Aranjuez* showcasing his own instrument. The felicitous melodies are still there, but the delicacy of the harp gives them a particularly sprightly character. Moretti is one of the finest young performers on her instrument and gives full value here. Two works by Rodrigo which were written specifically with Zabaleta in mind, the *Concierto Serenata* and *Sones en la Giralda,* are also included, in performances that would do either of the masters proud.

Fantasía por un gentilhombre for Guitar and Orchestra
what to buy: [Pepe Romero, guitar; Neville Marriner, cond.; Academy of St Martin-in-the-Fields, orch.] (Phillips 432828) ♪ ♪ ♪ ♪

The engineering for this set is quite good and Romero is

even better. The strings of Marriner's ensemble are suitably lush, and the pairing on this all-Rodrigo disc makes this a strong contender for listeners who want to pick up the bulk of the composer's "hits" in one package. Romero gives a truly poetic performance in this account with Marriner, but then, he has lived with this work almost since its inception. Ditto for his rendition of the *Concierto de Aranjuez* with the same forces. Also on the disc, Pepe's brother Angel joins with him for the all-too-rarely heard *Concierto Madrigal* for Two Guitars and Orchestra.

influences: Manuel de Falla, Mario Castelnuovo-Tedesco, Joaquín Turina, Miguel Llobet

Lori Lee Smith and Ian Palmer

Ned Rorem
Born October 23, 1923, in Richmond, IN

period: Twentieth century

Throughout his lifetime, Ned Rorem has enjoyed a colorful and dynamic career as composer, author, lecturer, and performer. His *Air Music* for Orchestra won a Pulitzer Prize in 1976, but he is best known in America for his vocal works. In addition to Rorem's musical output, he has published over a dozen books and diaries and, in fact, is better known in Europe as a diarist than he is as a composer.

Rorem's early musical development began at age seven after the family moved to Chicago and he started piano lessons. In one of his diaries he recounts that, at age ten, one of his piano teachers introduced him to the works of Claude Debussy and Maurice Ravel, an experience which "changed my life forever." When he was fifteen, Rorem took lessons in piano and composition from Leo Sowerby, Director of Music and organist at the Cathedral of St. James in Chicago. A relatively indifferent student, he later recalled being allowed to enter Northwestern University at the age of seventeen purely on the basis of his "creative potential." He studied music there and two years later received a scholarship to the Curtis Institute of Music in Philadelphia, where Gian Carlo Menotti was one of the instructors. Rorem moved to New York City in 1944 and entered the undergraduate program at the Juilliard School of Music. His parents had cut off his allowance and, to raise cash, he spent time as a copyist for composer and music critic

Virgil Thomson and took on work as a rehearsal pianist while completing his degrees: a B.A. in 1946 and an M.A. in 1948.

In 1949, Rorem moved to France on a Fulbright Scholarship to study with Arthur Honegger, remaining there (except for a two-year residency in Morocco) until 1958. While he was in Europe, Rorem's energetic lifestyle won him many friends and his music became more widely known. One reason for this increased notoriety arose from the determined advocacy of a wealthy and influential arts patroness, the Vicomtesse Marie Laure de Noailles. She operated a salon where many of France's intellectual elite came to visit, and was the first one to encourage his habit of writing in a diary. His diaries are now considered an important part of his overall oeuvre and the early ones, chronicling the trials and tribulations of composing music in the pre- and post-war years, caused quite a commotion when they were first printed. Part of the reason for outrage in some quarters was that Rorem's homosexuality was a prominent feature of these tomes, with descriptions of drunken encounters and one-night stands often accompanying his recorded experiences with famous composers and literary figures.

Since his return to the United States in 1958, Rorem's focus has been on music for solo voice, particularly the female voice. In that regard, he has made an indelible mark on repertoire for the recital stage and been deemed one of the American masters of song. His gift for weaving intricate vocal melodies and sumptuous harmonies has made him one of the most-commissioned composers of the twentieth century. Not relying on any one style of composition, Rorem's music has evolved over his lifetime, just as all composers' styles tend to do. In the beginning of his compositional career, his music was less dense and filled with simpler harmonies. Later, he ended up toying with more complex ideas, sometimes, for instance, creating compositions with serial elements, the kinds of things that are more often associated with composers like Arnold Schoenberg and Anton von Webern. Above all, though, Rorem seems obsessed with tonal colors, a factor that has remained constant in all his compositions since his years in France.

Orchestral
Concerto for Piano Left Hand and Orchestra
what to buy: [Gary Graffman, piano; André Previn, cond.; Curtis Institute of Music Symphony Orchestra]

(New World 80445) ♪ ♪ ♪ ♪♪

This is a stunning performance of an incredible work. The notion of playing a concerto is impressive enough, but adding the restriction of only using one of your hands (as Maurice Ravel did in his magnificent work for Paul Wittgenstein) makes it all the more enticing. Also included on this disc are the eleven *Studies for Eleven Players,* an intriguing set of pieces for chamber ensemble.

Concerto for Violin and Orchestra
what to buy: [Gidon Kremer, violin; Leonard Bernstein, cond.; New York Philharmonic Orchestra] (Deutsche Grammophon 445185) ♪ ♪ ♪ ♪

In the liner notes to this set Rorem wrote that he conceives "all non-sung pieces as though they were songs—like settings of words that aren't there." If you look at it that way, it explains why this score (on the whole) is so lyrical; with the only real exception in the six-movement work being the section *Toccata-Chaconne,* in which the timpani spring to the fore. Also included on this disc are a fine performance of the Philip Glass violin concerto and a solid rendition of Bernstein's own *Serenade.*

Chamber
Bright Music for Flute, Piano, and String Trio
what to buy: [Marya Martin, flute; André-Michel Schub, piano; Ani Kavafian, violin; Ida Kavafian, violin; Fred Sherry, cello] (New World 80416) ♪ ♪ ♪ ♪

Rorem's writing for the string ensemble allows his strength as a master of melodic line to shine brightly in the two excellent works showcased on this disc. *Bright Music* was written for Marya Martin and first performed in 1988, while *Winter Pages* is another quintet (substituting the clarinet and bassoon for the flute and cello of *Bright Music*) based on Rorem's life in Nantucket, where he spends most of his summers.

Vocal
Nantucket Songs for Voice and Piano
what to buy: [*American Masters: Ned Rorem*; Phyllis Bryn-Julson, soprano; Ned Rorem, piano] (CRI 657) ♪ ♪ ♪ ♪ ♪

Each individual work within this song cycle is a piece that stands on its own as well as being a pillar within the whole. Bryn-Julson has been a close friend of Rorem and premiered many of his works, including the first performance of this set of songs. The other song cycles on this disc are either written for voice and piano (*Women's Voices*) or a trio of voices and piano (*Some Trees*). All are wonderfully compact works of art.

Motets for the Church Year
what to buy next: [*Sing My Soul: The Choral Music of Ned Rorem*; David Westfall, piano; Richard Coffey, cond.; CONCORA-Connecticut Choral Arts, choir] (Albany TROY 307) ♪ ♪ ♪ ♪♪

CONCORA sings with great mastery and verve on one of the few recordings available that cover Rorem's choral music. Particularly beautiful is their version of *"Sing, my soul, His wondrous love"* from the seven *Motets for the Church Year,* but they also include a host of Rorem's other sacred music, making this an important collection.

various songs
what to buy: [*Songs of Ned Rorem*; Susan Graham, mezzo-soprano; Malcolm Martineau, piano; Oriol Ensemble] (Erato 80222) ♪ ♪ ♪ ♪♪

Graham's approach to Rorem's songs marks her as one of his supreme interpreters and this set was deservedly praised in a number of quarters for its breadth of programming. She dips into the *Nantucket Songs* for *Ferry Me across the Waters,* delivers a stunningly tasteful version of *I Am a Rose,* and carries a whole host of virtues into each of the other songs in this recital. The engineering showcases the singing most elegantly.

influences: Gian Carlo Menotti, David Diamond, Stephen Sondheim

Craig Scott Symons and Ian Palmer

Gioachino Rossini
Born Gioachino Antonio Rossini, February, 29, 1792, in Pesaro, Italy. Died November 13, 1868, in Passy, France.

period: Romantic

At the age of thirty-seven, the man who once said "Give me a laundry list and I'll set it to music" virtually stopped composing. Behind him were nearly three dozen operas while ahead of him lay nearly forty years of high-profile social life. Even though Rossini composed chamber music and a famous choral work (his setting of the *Stabat Mater*), his reputation has been inextricably linked to his operas and their overtures. One of the latter, the overture to *William Tell,* can be whistled or hummed by most of us when we hear three words: *The Lone Ranger.*

Both of Rossini's parents were musicians with a regional opera (his mother, a singer, and his father, a horn player) and it seemed perfectly natural for him to spend time in and around the theater, where he could often be found singing and playing music. His father had taught him to play the French horn when Rossini was around ten years old, and a local clergyman gave him his first singing lessons about the same time. When the family finally moved to Bologna, young Gioachino had already demonstrated a remarkable singing ability, one that allowed him to enter the Liceo Filharmonica when he was only fourteen years old. By the age of fifteen he had learned to play not only the horn but also the violin and harpsichord, with similar achievements on the cello and piano following within the next year. While Rossini wrote relatively little during his student days (generally speaking, only what was required for his classes), he actually composed at least part of an opera (*Demetrio e Poblio*) sometime before 1809.

After reaching puberty, he was unable to continue his singing, a source of income for the family. However, Rossini moved quite easily into the role of accompanist, then conductor. His youthful compositions by that time included choral works and five string quartets, but in 1810 he officially began his career as an opera composer upon receiving a commission to provide music for a one-act farce, *La cambiale de matrimonio.* For the next twenty years, he would devote many of his working days to creating new operas. Those two decades fall, roughly, into two periods in Rossini's output. There was the Italian period, when Venice, Milan, and Naples saw and heard his tireless effects and when he began to make changes which would affect subsequent Italian opera. And then there was the Parisian period; less fruitful, but producing some near masterpieces nonetheless.

While most of his earliest operas fluctuated in quality and audience response, the generally solid appeal of Rossini's scores kept commissions coming in. He started developing an international reputation with the Venetian productions, in 1813, of *Tancredi,* an *opera seria* (dramatic opera), and *L'italiana in Algeri,* an *opera buffa*

(comedic opera). Rossini wrote five more operas (of which only *Il turco in Italia* maintains any fascination for modern audiences) before 1816, when he produced the score to *Il barbiere di Siviglia (The Barber of Seville)* in a torrid sixteen days of writing. This achievement seems amazing, even considering that he rarely rewrote and casually borrowed from himself, yet the outpouring of shining, lyrical music combined with a plot that is clockwork impeccable is wondrous; its admirers included not only Giuseppe Verdi, but Ludwig van Beethoven.

Two other operas separated *La Cenerentola,* Rossini's next hit, from *Il barbiere di Siviglia,* even though all four were written within the space of a year and a half. Audiences of the day still supported Rossini's music for the next dozen years, despite the fact that the composer would not write another theater score after his last effort, *Guillaume Tell (William Tell),* received its initial production in the fall of 1829. His work in other areas, specifically the compositions he wrote in the last years of his life, generally deal more with heavenly matters. These scores include his marvelous setting of the *Stabat Mater* (initially performed in 1832 but revised in 1841), a fairly large selection of cantatas and secular songs, a few instrumental works, and the intensely moving (if sometimes overly florid) *Petite messe solennelle,* a piece which Rossini did not allow to be published during his lifetime.

As insouciant—even lazy—as he may have appeared in later life, Rossini had followed his natural bent toward the theater house and successfully challenged many of the conventions of the day. Through the directness and immediacy of his scoring he succeeded in bridging the gap between the Classical period and the emerging Romantic period, doing away with unaccompanied recitative and, for the first time, making opera a continuous musical form. He wrote out the embellishments for the singers, furthering the overriding presence of the composer, but he was also ridiculed by some critics for the typical "Rossini Crescendo," whereby a theme is repeated, each time at a higher pitch with a larger orchestral accompaniment. In any case, all these elements, buoyed by an effortless treasure trove of melody, helped make him a success as an opera composer.

Orchestral
various overtures
what to buy: [*Rossini Overtures*; Roger Norrington, cond.; London Classical Players, orch.] (EMI Classics 54091) ♪ ♪ ♪ ♪ ♪

Rossini had a way with overtures and many of them stand alone as buoyant, elegant, and often witty musical pieces. Norrington and his ensemble stick close to the style of the time and this collection contains the most famous of the composer's openers (from *The Barber of Seville* and *William Tell*) while including the overtures to *Scala di Seta* and *La Gazza Ladra,* among others. The playing also provides an insight into the composer's splendid orchestrations, in particular the use of the trademark Rossini Crescendo.

what to buy next: [Leonard Bernstein, cond.; New York Philharmonic Orchestra] (Sony Classics 47606) ♪ ♪ ♪ ♪

While not as well-recorded or idiomatic as the Norrington set (see above), Bernstein's heart-on-sleeve conducting works quite well in the more "traditional" framework of this album. He too includes overtures from the "Big Two" (*The Barber of Seville* and *William Tell*) and duplicates most of Norrington's recital, but the bravura performances may be more appealing to some listeners in these works.

Vocal
Il Barbiere di Siviglia (The Barber of Seville)
what to buy: [Maria Callas, soprano; Luigi Alva, tenor; Tito Gobbi, baritone; Carl Maria Giulini, cond.; La Scala Orchestra; La Scala Chorus] (Melodram 20038) ♪ ♪ ♪ ♪ ♪

This is a rootin' tootin' version of the opera buffa. It has the exciting sounds as well as the exquisite ebullience. This is a monaural concert recording from 1956, however, and the sound is not as felicitous as that granted some of the newer renditions of this work. But the issue here is less one of sonics than style, and on that frontier Callas rules!

what to buy next: [Teresa Berganza, mezzo-soprano; Luigi Alva, tenor; Hermann Prey, baritone; Paolo Montarsolo, bass; Claudio Abbado, cond.; London Symphony Orchestra; London Symphony Chorus] (Deutsche Grammophon 457733) ♪ ♪ ♪ ♪ ♪

Since the role of Rosina was written for a mezzo-soprano, it seems only fair to recommend this fine set as well, despite the excision of the tenor aria in Act II.

La Cenerentola
what to buy: [Cecelia Bartoli, mezzo-soprano; Fernanda Costa, mezzo-soprano; Gloria Banditelli, contralto;

Paul Robeson:
Paul Robeson had dabbled in acting while still in college, working in *Shuffle Along,* the all-Negro revue by Noble Sissle and Eubie Blake. Robeson's big acting break came when, in 1924, he was asked to join the cast of Eugene O'Neill's play *All God's Chillun Got Wings,* giving a performance that only hinted at the greatness he would achieve in a production of O'Neill's *The Emperor Jones* one year later. Robeson's 1928 appearance in London as part of the ensemble for Jerome Kern's *Showboat* found him delivering a rendition of "Ol' Man River" that was one of the high points of the musical. Robeson later played the title role in *Othello.*

The singing portion of his career began with memberships in various choral groups and occasional gigs at one of Harlem's leading jazz venues, the Cotton Club. The rich quality of his deep voice later attracted a packed house to New York City's Greenwich Village Theater in 1925, when Robeson made history as the first black vocal soloist to perform in a recital devoted to African-American songs. Another reason for the success of the concert was Robeson's pianist, Lawrence Brown, who adapted the songs to fit the vocalist's relatively constricted vocal range.

Robeson began living in Europe in 1928, using London as a base of operations from which he gave concerts, acted in plays and movies, and explored Russia and Africa. It was during a trip to Russia that Robeson began publicly empathizing with the perceived goals of Socialism though he never actually joined the Communist party. In 1939, when he returned to live in the United States, Robeson became involved with various organizations for social change. One song from this period, "Ballad for Americans," became closely associated with Robeson and was featured at many of his concerts. His recording of this tune appears on a two-disc set, *Ballad for Americans* (Vanguard 117/118).

Songs of Free Men: A Paul Robeson Recital (Sony Masterworks Heritage Vocal Series 63223) also documents the kind of material he was singing during the 1940s. There are eight tunes performed with the Columbia Concert Orchestra, while the rest of the set is excerpted from six concerts in which he was accompanied by Brown. Many of the songs heard here also turn up on *Paul Robeson Live at Carnegie Hall: The Historic May 9, 1958 Concert* (Vanguard 72020). The breadth of styles covered therein offers an amazingly succinct summation of the man's musical career to that point, including *Balm in Gilead,* "Joe Hill," and Johann Sebastian Bach's *Christ lag in Todesbanden* along with monologues from William Shakespeare's *Othello* and Modest Mussorgsky's *Boris Godunov.*

In the climate of the Cold War, any perceived association with Communism or its ideals became an open invitation for persecution. Robeson's outspoken attitudes in this regard resulted in his passport being revoked by the State Department in 1950. Five years later Robeson found himself accused by the House Committee on Un-American Activities of being a secret member of the Communist Party. By 1958, he finally got his passport back and left the United States to live in Europe, shuttling between Russia, East Germany, and Great Britain before returning to America in 1963 and dying there in 1976.

Mathilde August

William Matteuzi, tenor; Alessandro Corbelli, baritone; Enzo Dara, baritone; Michele Pertusi, bass; Ricardo Chailly, cond.; Bologna Teatro Communale Orchestra; Bologna Teatro Communale Chorus] (London 436902) ♪♪♪♪

Cenerentola is the Cinderella story, and while Rossini's reworking is less magical than the original folktale—no mice, just the usual love at first sight and vindication—the music is quite lovely. The wondrous Cecelia Bartoli is well suited for this part, combining all the qualities needed to bring off the role: timbre, coloratura capacity, and temperament.

Tancredi

what to buy: [Sumi Jo, soprano; Anna Maria di Micco, soprano; Lucretia Lendi, mezzo-soprano; Ewa Podles, contralto; Stanford Olsen, tenor; Pietro Spagnoli, baritone; Alberto Zedda, cond.; Collegium Instrumentale Brugense, orch.; Capella Brugensis, chorus] (Naxos Opera Classics 8.660037) ♪♪♪♪♪

The musical world has been waiting for this recording. First, it is a true chamber ensemble playing within parameters which, increasingly, purists and others are asking for. And then there is the palpable star quality of Podles, matched with the very wonderful Korean soprano Sumi Jo.

Stabat Mater for Voices, Orchestra, and Chorus

what to buy: [Helen Field, soprano; Della Jones, mezzo-soprano; Arthur Davies, tenor; Roderick Earle, bass; Richard Hickox, cond.; City of London Sinfonia; London Symphony Chorus] (Chandos 8780) ♪♪♪♪♪

The *Stabat Mater* is a sacred text in the Roman Catholic liturgy but Rossini treated it as an opportunity for vocal showmanship and, in the words of one anonymous reviewer, it is "almost indecently tuneful." This recording, under Hickox's careful tutelage, brings out the blending of voices as well as the sheer range and power of individual solo parts.

what to buy next: [Krassimira Stoyanova, soprano; Petra Lang, mezzo-soprano; Bruce Fowler, tenor; Daniel Borowski, bass; Marcus Creed, cond.; Academie für Alte Musik, Berlin, orch.; RIAS-Kammerchor, choir] (Harmonia Mundi 901693) ♪♪♪♪

While the soloists in this performance are good, it is the choral singing that really stands out here. Creed's direc-

tion is quite flexible throughout, something that works well in the climaxes. The orchestra usually specializes in period-instrument performances of the eighteenth century, which generally gives an almost Haydn-esque sound to the proceedings, though the arrangement places this work squarely in the Romantic camp.

Petite messe solennelle for Voices, Piano, Harmonium, and Chorus

what to buy: [Lucia Popp, soprano; Brigitte Fassbaender, mezzo-soprano; Nicolai Gedda, tenor; Dmitri Kavrakos, bass; Katia Lebèque, piano; Marielle Lebèque, piano; Stephen Cleobury, cond.; King's College Choir, Cambridge] (EMI Classics 68658) ♪♪♪♪

Here is a work which was intended for chamber performances, is very accessible, and has developed a devoted following. This recording, though without the harmonium called for in the original score and with modern pianos substituted, nonetheless receives a very sympathetic treatment. These are top-of-the-line vocalists, and the sisters Lebèque on the pianos are in touch with the core of the composition. This budget-priced double disc pairs the mass with a version of the *Stabat Mater* conducted by Riccardo Muti which features Catherine Malfitano, Agnes Baltsa, Robert Gambill, and Gwynne Howell as the vocal soloists.

influences: Giuseppe Verdi, Wolfgang Amadeus Mozart

Michael H. Margolin and Garaud MacTaggart

Albert Roussel

Born Albert Charles Paul Marie Roussel, April 5, 1869, in Tourcoing, France. Died August 23, 1937, in Royan, France.

period: Twentieth century

Despite his relatively late start as a composer, Roussel passed quickly through a fruitful, early impressionist period to find (especially in his ballet scores and last two symphonies) his own highly rhythmic, compact style. The methods used in these later scores involve an advanced harmonic language and increased experimentation in bitonality. His output was not large, but it was evenly balanced between music for the stage, orchestral compositions, vocal works, and chamber music.

Orphaned at the age of seven, Roussel was raised first by his grandfather and then by his aunt. Early piano studies gave way to a desire for a naval career, and Roussel gained entry into the Ecole Navale as a cadet in 1887. The musical urge never really left him, however, and he attempted to educate himself by studying Emile Durand's *Traité d'harmonie (Treatise on Harmony)* during one of his tours of duty. He managed to secure the first public performance of one of his compositions (an andante for string trio and organ which was later destroyed) in Cherbourg, on Christmas, 1892. Encouraged by friends and plagued by poor health, he decided, after a long voyage to the Orient, to resign from the Navy in 1894. Roussel then settled in Paris, where he began four years of instruction in piano and organ playing, harmony and counterpoint with the organist Eugène Gigout—a former classmate of Gabriel Fauré, who based his instruction methods on the music of Bach, Handel, Mozart, and Beethoven. In 1898, Roussel commenced a ten-year course of study in composition, orchestration, and music history with the composer Vincent d'Indy at the newly created Schola Cantorum. D'Indy, an effective teacher, was both a fervent nationalist and a fervent Wagnerite—not an easy position to maintain in *fin de siecle* France. He showed his appreciation of Roussel's ability by putting him charge of the counterpoint class (in 1902) where he eventually instructed, among others, Edgard Varèse and the eccentric Erik Satie.

Roussel formally graduated from the Schola Cantorum in 1908 when he was almost forty years old. He had already composed a variety of works, but he subsequently destroyed many of them. One work which survived his student days, the *Divertissement* for Wind Quintet and Piano (1906), was an early success, and uses the percussive and harmonic possibilities of the piano in a way that doesn't alter the essential woodwind ensemble character. *Le Festin de l'araignée (The Spider's Feast)*, a ballet-pantomime from 1913, represents the culmination of Roussel's impressionist phase. Ironically, while *Festin* became his greatest success, his later works of generally equal or superior quality were often criticized or dismissed for being unlike it. In 1914, after a return trip to the Orient (this time as a relative newlywed), Roussel resigned his position at the Schola Cantorum to devote more time to composing, working on *Pâdmavatî*, a score influenced by Hindu scale forms and commissioned by Jacques Rouché for the Théâtre National de l'Opera.

With the onset of the First World War a year later, Roussel went back into military service, as an artillery

Clara Rockmore:

Leon Theremin invented an instrument without which Clara Rockmore might not have found her specific niche in musical lore, for she was history's foremost virtuosa on the theremin. This apparatus was essentially a plain-looking cube filled with circuitry and vacuum tubes that featured a pitch antenna rising from the top, right-hand side of the box, a volume antenna shooting out from the left-hand side of the box, and a batch of knobs. A humming sound would emanate from the attached speakers when hands approached or drew back from either of the two electronic appendages.

Originally Rockmore had set her sights on being a concert violinist, but muscle and joint problems would soon force her to rethink that option. She met Theremin while still in her teens and soon became his prize student and chosen soloist. Her first concert promoting the theremin took place at the Town Hall, in New York City, on October 30, 1934. Standing behind her instrument, virtually motionless except for small, precise gestures with her hands, Rockmore exerted more control over the instrument than anyone prior to her. Even though the theremin is best remembered now for providing the musical backdrop to bad bug-eyed-monster flicks during the 1950s and 1960s, the eerie hum emanating from the instrument was tamed by Rockmore's hands into something that could perform an arrangement of César Franck's Violin Sonata without sounding like total kitsch. The sound of the theremin under Rockmore's guidance can almost be mistaken for a wordless human vocal at times, and is an interesting reminder of the steps electronic music took in its search for mass acceptance during the pioneering days of the mid-twentieth century.

In 1976, electronic music pioneer Robert Moog recorded Rockmore in conversation and in performance for *Clara Rockmore: The Greatest Theremin Virtuosa*, which was finally released on video in 1998 by Big Briar Video. The only CD out there which really documents the Rockmore phenomena to any great length, however, is *The Art of the Theremin* (Delos 1014). On it, she plays arrangements of Rachmaninoff's *Vocalise*, Stravinsky's *Berceuse*, and Tchaikovsky's *Valse sentimentale* (along with nine other relatively familiar works) aided by her piano accompanist (and sister) Nadia Reisenberg.

Garaud MacTaggart

officer. He finally finished *Pâdmavatî*, an important work that further expanded his experiments in harmonic and melodic chromaticism, in 1918, after leaving the armed forces yet again. Three years later he completed his second symphony, a score that, with its prominent rhythmic ostinato technique, marks the final turning point in Roussel's evolution. From this point on, his music became, in his own words, ". . . more pruned, more distilled, more schematized." The Suite in F Major for Orchestra (1926) was premiered by the Boston Symphony Orchestra conducted by Serge Koussevitsky, who also commissioned the composer's third symphony for the orchestra's 50th anniversary in 1930. The lushly composed ballet *Bacchus et Ariane* dates from the same year, and ensured that Roussel's reputation as a composer for the theater would equal his reputation as a symphonist.

Roussel's last years saw the composition of various chamber works (including his only string quartet) along with other orchestral works. In 1935, his Symphony no. 4 in A Major (the only handicap of which is that it follows the magnificent third symphony) was followed by *Aeneas,* another ballet on a classical theme, and the 1936 Concertino for Cello and Orchestra. Suffering from ill health for many years, Roussel still managed to organize the important International Society for Contemporary Music Festival in 1937, while typically refusing to allow his own fourth symphony to be played so that some younger, less known musician would get an opportunity to have a work performed. He died later that year after a heart attack.

Orchestral
Bacchus et Ariane for Orchestra, op. 43
what to buy: [Yan Pascal Tortelier, cond.; BBC Philharmonic Orchestra] (Chandos 9494) ♪ ♪ ♪ ♪

The most exciting of Roussel's three ballets, *Bacchus et Ariane* is given a sonically superb performance by the forces of the BBC Philharmonic led by Tortelier. The clean lines and strong rhythms of Roussel's fully harmonic neo-classical style are ideally suited to the mythic subject matter. The CD also contains an excellent reading of the ballet *Le Festin de l'araignée,* op. 17, the work of Roussel's that was most successful during his lifetime.

what to buy next: [Charles Dutoit, cond.; Orchestre de Paris] (Erato Ultima 24240) ♪ ♪ ♪

This is a nicely priced, two-disc anthology binding Roussel's biggest hits into one package. Good performances of *Bacchus et Ariane* and the Suite in F Major for Orchestra by Dutoit and company are combined with performances by Jean Martinon leading the Orchestre National de l'O.R.T.F (*Aeneas,* the *Petite Suite, Pour une fête de printemps,* and *Le Festin de l'araignée*) and Jean-François Paillard conducting his own Orchestre de Chambre Jean-François Paillard (the Sinfonietta).

Symphony no. 3 in G Minor, op 42
what to buy: [Charles Dutoit, cond.; Orchestre National de l'O.R.T.F.] (Erato Ultima 21090) ♪ ♪ ♪↕

Dutoit leads a strongly accented performance of Roussel's most compact and dynamic symphony. All four of the symphonies, including the rarely recorded nos. 1 and 2, are included on this well performed, reasonably priced two-disc set.

worth searching for: [Leonard Bernstein, cond.; Orchestre National de France] (Deutsche Grammophon 445512) ♪ ♪ ♪↕

Bernstein again demonstrates his affinity for French music in this 1986 recording. For someone who is only seeking a version of Roussel's most popular symphony, it should be noted that this release also had an excellent rendition of César Franck's Symphony in D-Minor. Amazingly enough, the performance of this symphony's third movement is still in print, as part of a set called *Leonard Bernstein: The Artist's Album* (Deutsche Grammophon 457691).

influences: Claude Debussy, Maurice Ravel, Igor Stravinsky, Bohuslav Martinu

Jan Jezioro

Miklós Rózsa
Born April 18, 1907, in Budapest, Hungary. Died July 27, 1995, in Los Angeles, CA.

period: Twentieth century

Without a doubt, Miklós Rózsa was the most honored and fiscally successful composer for the cinema from the early 1940s until the early 1960s. Best known for providing award-winning music for films like *Spellbound* (1945) and *Ben-Hur* (1959), he also composed a fair number of compositions for the concert hall, including an exciting violin concerto that was premiered by Jascha Heifetz in 1956.

Although Rózsa began playing the violin and composing when he was only five years old, his father, an industrialist, preferred him to study chemistry. The dutiful son enrolled at the University of Budapest and worked toward a chemistry degree, but he also took music classes on the side at the local conservatory. His father eventually gave in, and Rózsa went to Germany, where he began studying violin and taking composition classes with Hermann Grabner at the Leipzig Conservatory. He moved to Paris in 1931, but though he was able to secure performances of some of his chamber works and a few orchestral scores rooted in the folk music of his native Hungary, he was not able to make a living as a composer. That changed in the mid-1930s when he met film producer Alexander Korda, who suggested that Rózsa come to London and score some of the films being released by *London Film Productions,* the company Korda and his brothers had founded.

Although he had no idea of the processes necessary to compose soundtracks, Rózsa bought some books on writing for the cinema, saw a few films, and wrote music for *Knight Without Armor,* a 1937 film starring Marlene Dietrich and Robert Donat. That led to further work for Korda's British studios before the young composer followed the producer to Hollywood in 1940. Rózsa found plenty of work in Hollywood, first as an independent contractor and then as a staff composer for MGM Studios. He finished work on *The Thief of Baghdad* (which he'd started in England) and began an incredible streak of Academy Award nominations—at least one per year from 1940 to 1948. Two smaller streaks followed, from 1952 to 1954 and from 1960 to 1962. Rózsa actually won the Oscar in 1946 for the Alfred Hitchcock thriller *Spellbound,* in 1948 for *A Double Life,* and in 1960 for *Ben-Hur.*

Rózsa's film scores can be divided into specific periods. At first he composed for movies such as *The Thief of Baghdad* and *The Jungle Book* that needed music with an exotic, Oriental flavor. In the 1940s he did a lot of work in film noir, creating innovative, Oscar-nominated scores for Billy Wilder's *Double Indemnity* and *The Lost Weekend* and introducing the theremin to herald danger and strangeness. His epic period began in the 1950s, when he scored such MGM blockbusters as *Quo Vadis, Ben-Hur, King of Kings,* and *El Cid.* Throughout these decades, however, Rózsa's cinema music often belied attempts to pigeonhole him into a specific period. The year before he worked on *Quo Vadis,* he wrote the soundtrack to *The Asphalt Jungle,* and the year before that he created the music for *Madame Bovary.* His last two film scores (both from 1981) were for Steve Martin's deranged comedy *Dead Men Don't Wear Plaid* and the gripping *Eye of the Needle.*

While Rózsa was working for the film industry, he also wrote concert works like his violin concerto from 1956; sometimes he adapted themes from his soundtracks into pieces such as the *Spellbound Concerto* for Piano and Orchestra or the *Jungle Book Suite.* All in all, Rózsa

Los Romeros Guitar Quartet:
Although there are some musicologists who would make a case for the Munich Guitar Quartet, which was formed in 1907, Los Romeros are generally considered to be the first professional guitar quartet of the twentieth century. Their roots begin with Celedonio Romero, who was born in Cuba on March 2, 1913 to a Spanish architect and his wife and returned to Spain with his family a few years later. While in Spain, Romero demonstrated a remarkable affinity for the guitar, and eventually began carving out a career for himself as a guitar soloist and composer. After marrying and starting a family, he moved with his wife and children to southern California in the late 1950s, and it was there that he and his three sons (Celin, Pepe, and Angel) began working the concert circuit as a guitar quartet. Over the decades, Los Romeros has become known as one of the finest ensembles of its type in the world, and garnered numerous awards and accolades.

In 1959 Celedonio recorded an album of short works for the guitar (*Spanish Guitar Music,* Contemporary 14069) with Celin, his eldest son, which is still available, but the earliest obtainable recordings of the Romeros as a quartet can be found on *The Royal Family of the Spanish Guitar* (Mercury Living Presence 434385), a broad sampler of their art. It is filled with material recorded during the early 1960s and features various combinations of the Romeros displaying their remarkable talents sans orchestral backdrop. Most of the scores heard here are transcriptions of works meant for other instruments, but there are also some excerpts from compositions by Heitor Villa-Lobos, Francisco Tárrega, and Fernando Sor which were written for the guitar, in addition to a pair of works composed by Celedonio.

Perhaps the most arresting album in their catalog, however, is the one (Mercury Living Presence 434369) on which they are accompanied by Victor Alessandro and the San Antonio Symphony Orchestra in recordings of two concertos by Joaquín Rodrigo: the famous *Concierto de Aranjuez* for Guitar and Orchestra features Angel as the soloist, but Los Romeros play as a unit in the *Concierto Andaluz* for Four Guitars and Orchestra, which the composer dedicated to them.

The current edition of Los Romeros (Angel left the group in 1990 to pursue a dual career as soloist and conductor and Celedonio died in 1996) still tours frequently and features Celin and Pepe along with Celin's son Celino and Angel's son Lito.

Ian Palmer

delivered intense, well-crafted scores, filled with rhythm and suspense, no matter what the genre.

Orchestral
Concerto for Violin and Orchestra, op. 24
what to buy: [*The Heifetz Collection, Vol. 21*; Jascha Heifetz, violin; Walter Hendl, cond.; Dallas Symphony Orchestra] (RCA Gold Seal 61752) ♪ ♪ ♪ ♪♪

Recorded in 1956, this is a work filled with fire in the opening Allegro, honeyed gold in the second movement, and cinematic drama at the close. Rózsa's typical Hungarian flavoring runs all through the score, and Heifetz, who premiered this work with the same orchestra and conductor heard here, is masterly. Also heard in this set is Rózsa's "Theme and Variations for Violin and Cello, Op. 29a" (actually a re-orchestrated version of the second movement from his Sinfonia Concertante for Violin, Cello, and Orchestra, op. 29), with Heifetz and cellist Gregor Piatigorsky in the solo roles. Rounding out the program are fine performances of Franz Waxman's *Carmen Fantasy* and Erich Wolfgang Korngold's violin concerto.

Spellbound Concerto for Piano and Orchestra
what to buy: [Danielle Laval, piano; László Kovács, cond.; North Hungarian Symphony Orchestra, Miskolc] (Valois 4841) ♪ ♪ ♪♪

Like Richard Addinsell's *Warsaw Concerto*, the *Spellbound Concerto* is a brief, one-movement piece designed to cash in on the success of the film from which the music is drawn. Skillfully cobbled together, it presents material from the movie *Spellbound* in the best light-classical tradition. The other Rózsa pieces on this set are meatier, among them the suite he made from the *Ben-Hur* film score (complete with the rousing "Parade of the Charioteers") and the highlight of the disc, a genuine piano concerto. Laval is the soloist in both the *Spellbound* piece and the Concerto for Piano and Orchestra, op. 31. She has power to burn in what may be Rózsa's second-most-substantial concert piece, just behind the Concerto for Violin and Orchestra, op. 24.

various film scores
what to buy: [*Spellbound*; Charles Gerhardt, cond.; National Philharmonic Orchestra, London; Ambrosian Singers] (RCA Victor 0911) ♪ ♪ ♪ ♪

Gerhardt did a marvelous job of choosing which of Rózsa's many soundtrack themes to use in this program. Some people may have preferred a recording of the complete *Spellbound* score, but the individual scenes showcased here ("The Dream Sequence" and "The Mountain Lodge") represent the most effective parts of the soundtrack, including the suspenseful theremin passages. The balance of the album contains musical selections from *The Lost Weekend, The Thief of Bagdad, Double Indemnity,* and five other films.

what to buy next: [*The Epic Film Music of Miklós Rózsa*; Kenneth Alwyn, cond.; City of Prague Philharmonic, orch.; Crouch End Festival Chorus] (Silva Screen Records 1056) ♪ ♪ ♪♪

The brawny, heroic music Rózsa created for such blockbuster films as *King of Kings, Quo Vadis,* and *Ben-Hur* is the focus of Alwyn's disc. Well recorded and containing such glorious moments as the violin solo in the "Love Scene" from *El Cid* (played by Josef Kroft) and the brassy fanfares of the "Parade of the Charioteers" from *Ben-Hur,* the album is a florid paean to a lush, over-the-top era of movie making. Other scores represented here include *The Golden Voyage of Sinbad, Sodom and Gomorrah, All the Brothers Were Valiant, Beau Brummell,* and *Madame Bovary.*

influences: Franz Waxman, Bernard Herrmann, Erich Wolfgang Korngold, Max Steiner

Garaud MacTaggart

Carl Ruggles
Born Carl Sprague Ruggles on March 11, 1876, in East Marion, MA. Died October 24, 1971, in Bennington, VT.

period: Twentieth century

One of the century's least prolific composers, Carl Ruggles spent most of his life fashioning just a few works of roughhewn and dissonant austerity. Although his ultramodern music received few performances in his lifetime, his influence on other American composers is well documented, as is his reclusiveness.

At a concert of Ruggles's music, during which a hostile audience was responding to the grinding dissonance with loud irritation, Charles Ives, a near contemporary to Ruggles, stood up and shouted at the unruly crowd, "Stand up and use your ears like a man!" Like Ives's, Ruggles's musical training was exclusively American, though most teachers at the time advocated the nineteenth-century Germanic tradition. He took lessons in music theory from Josef Claus and studied composition privately with John Knowles Paine while undertaking studies in English at Harvard.

Ruggles's fame rests on a single orchestral composition, *Sun-treader,* completed in 1931 after five years of working and reworking. *Sun-treader* is generally considered to be a modernist masterpiece; indeed, its foreboding introductory march, led by loud timpani, seems to underscore what the composer must have surely felt was the dark ages of music. Ruggles believed that no tone should be repeated until it had faded from the listener's memory, generally allowing nine or ten notes to intervene. He was aware of similar atonal experiments being done in Europe by members of the Second Viennese School even as he was working to free himself from the tyranny of tonality. His solution to the problem was quite different, however. Long, arching lines of wide intervals, extremes of register, grating dissonances, and a dense, wild counterpoint characterize his music, with *Sun-treader* being the prime example. Rugged and audacious yet compact, it is Ruggles's longest completed composition, lasting less than fifteen minutes.

The granitic *Men and Mountains* was a reworking of earlier material that Ruggles had found unsatisfactory. A new shuffling of movements from the earlier *Men and Angels* allowed this inexorable piece—as well as the taut *Angels,* scored for six trumpets—to come to fruition. His later works, no less severe, include the *Polyphonic Composition* for three pianos, the piano suite *Evocations* (his only solo piano work), and the orchestral *Organum.* The scrutiny with which he viewed his music was legendary; at one point he burned the score of an opera (*The Sunken Bell*) he had been working on for several years.

His career included time spent founding and conducting both the Winona Symphony Orchestra in Winona, Minnesota, and an orchestra at the Rand School in New York City, as well as teaching composition at the University of Miami in Florida. He spent his final years on a farm in Vermont, painting watercolors in rural isolation.

Though the American element in Ruggles's music comes from a distinct individuality that discarded European musical models, there are none of the folksong quotations, flagrant patriotism, or programmatic evocations of American life that so fascinated his friend Ives. Ruggles is best remembered for *Sun-treader,* whose title was taken from Robert Browning's reference to Percy Bysshe Shelley. His tough, uncompromising approach paved the way for subsequent generations of composers who viewed themselves as voices in the desolate wilderness of modern music.

Mstislav Rostropovich:
Rostropovich initially studied with his father (Leopold Rostropovich, a professor of the instrument at the Gnesin Institute in Moscow and a former student of noted cellist Pablo Casals) before entering the Moscow Conservatory in 1943 at the age of sixteen. There he not only broadened his knowledge of cello techniques but studied composition with Sergei Prokofiev and Vissarion Shebalin and instrumentation with Dmitri Shostakovich. After taking part in various competitions in Eastern Bloc countries, Rostropovich was able to list a number of impressive wins on his resume before assuming a teaching position at the Moscow Conservatory in 1953, a professorship there in 1959, and a professorship at the Leningrad Conservatory in 1961.

That year also marked Rostropovich's initial appearance as a conductor, but his most important debut on the podium occurred in 1968, when he led a production of Piotr Ilyich Tchaikovsky's opera *Eugene Onegin* at the Bolshoi Theatre. He accepted a position as chief conductor of the National Symphony Orchestra in Washington, D.C. in 1976, and was appointed artistic director of the Aldeburgh Festival a year later. Ever since the beginning of his stay with the NSO, Rostropovich's conducting style has been criticized by some listeners for its tendency to stretch phrases beyond what is written in the score, while others have praised the heartfelt content of his performances. Rostropovich has defended his mannerisms by saying, "I believe that if an artist has a feeling for the music...then he will have faith in what he's doing and it will sound right." He evidently feels a special kinship with the works of Tchaikovsky, and regards many of his recordings of that composer's scores among his best efforts as a conductor. One of the finest in that regard is his relatively recent disc with violinist Maxim Vengerov and the London Symphony Orchestra, which features a traversal of Tchaikovsky's lovely *Sérénade mélancolique* and concertos by Igor Stravinsky and Rodion Shchedrin (EMI Classics 56966).

Among the finest works written specifically for Rostropovich as a performer are a pair of cello concertos by Hénri Dutilleux and Witold Lutoslawski (EMI Classics Imports 749304). The two-disc set entitled *Mstislav Rostropovich: Russian Years* (EMI Classics Imports 72295) is also worth seeking out, in part due to the intense, visceral performances by the cellist in three Shostakovich works: the two masterful cello concertos (opp. 107 and 126) and, with the composer playing piano, the Sonata in D Minor for Cello and Piano, op. 40. The concertos are concert performances with Gennady Rozhdestvensky conducting the Moscow Philharmonic Symphony Orchestra in no. 1 and Yevgeny Svetlanov leading the USSR State Symphony Orchestra in no. 2. Other important composers represented in this package include Benjamin Britten, Richard Strauss, Heitor Villa-Lobos, and Arthur Honneger, but there are a few Soviet composers as well.

Mathilde August

Orchestral
Sun-treader
what to buy: [Christoph von Dohnányi, cond.; Cleveland Orchestra] (London 443776) ♪ ♪ ♪ ♪

London's vivid recording brings out the depth and immediacy of this riveting piece. The album also includes the seldom-heard *Men and Mountains* alongside works by Ives (*Three Places in New England* and *Orchestral Set no. 2*) and Ruth Crawford Seeger (*Andante for Strings*).

influences: Charles Ives, Roger Sessions, Elliot Carter

Sean Hickey

John Rutter

Born John Milford Rutter, September 24, 1945, in London, England.

period: Twentieth century

John Rutter (along with John Tavener, James McMillan, Arvo Pärt, and Stephen Paulus) has helped to establish the beginnings of a twenty-first century school of sacred choral composition, characterized by attention to new and unconventional sources for texts and the use of ancient forms and styles as foundations for new compositional structures. He has also gained worldwide acclaim as a respected conductor and lecturer, working throughout Great Britain as well as in Europe, North America, Scandinavia, and Australia.

Rutter received his early education at Highgate School, London. There he served as chorister and supplemented his traditional course of study with training in several areas of music. He continued his education at Clare College, Cambridge, where his talents as conductor and composer began to come into clear focus. His early compositional efforts included two children's operas, several orchestral works, and numerous shorter choral pieces. Rutter returned to Clare College as its music director in 1975 and remained in that position until 1979. He founded the Cambridge Singers in 1981, intending to foster an ensemble dedicated to scholarly interpretations of a cappella choral music; his efforts resulted in a choir of incomparable artistic quality that has garnered international attention and critical acclaim. Demand for recordings of the group resulted over time in the establishment of its own recording label, Collegium Records, and the issuance of over thirty choral CDs to date.

Rutter's music has been characterized both as avantgarde and retrospective in style. His compositions range in genre from the choral anthem to small and large orchestral works, as well as several large works for chorus and orchestra. Among his most celebrated larger scores is the *Requiem*, composed in 1985 and set for vocal and instrumental soloists, chorus, and orchestra. Just as in the *Requiem* settings of Maurice Duruflé and Gabriel Fauré, Rutter's rendering uses the ancient Requiem Mass (*Missa pro defunctis*) merely as a thematic touchstone, otherwise abandoning its strict liturgical structure for a more poetic and meditative form that includes not only contemporary treatments of Psalms 130 and 23 but references to the *Anglican Burial Service* from the *Book of Common Prayer.*

His approach opens with the traditional statement of the *Requiem aeternam,* inspired in part by the highly melodic style, if not the tune, of the original plainsong Introit. The low, brooding winds and strings speak first, accompanied by the slow, steady pulse of the timpani. They are joined by the haunting tone clusters of the choir, receding finally into consonant harmonies of celestial lightness. The full strings then introduce a plaintive, contemporary line delivered in sweet unison first by the women, and then by the full choir. *Out of the deep* continues along this same soundscape with solo string bass and cello introducing a monotone lament that evokes its *de profundis* origin. Some blues-like melodic material follows, nearly conjuring the funeral scenes of the Old South. *Pie Jesu* aptly flies to the upper vocal and instrumental registers as the touching soprano solo entrances are supported by lovely choral interpolations of the same text.

Choral works beyond the *Requiem* feature a variety of textual themes and prayers as their foundations. Among the best-known of this repertoire are *A Gaelic Blessing* (evoking the ancient Celtic benediction), *God be in my head, Open thou mine eyes,* and *The Lord bless and keep you*—all representing common texts within English culture and its worship experience. Other anthems favor younger singers and/or the small choir, such as the charming *All things bright and beautiful* and *For the beauty of the earth.* Larger choral works in addition to the *Requiem* include his *Magnificat* (1990) and *Psalmfest* (1996). In addition to his work as composer, conductor, and lecturer, Rutter remains an editor of note, helping to compile and edit the *Oxford Choral Classics, Carols for Choirs,* and *European Sacred Music.*

Vocal
Requiem
what to buy: [Rosa Mannion, soprano; Stephen Layton, cond.; Bournemouth Sinfonietta, orch.; Polyphony, choir] (Hyperion 66947) ♪ ♪ ♪ ♪♭

Rutter's *Requiem* assumes a unique structural form and receives an equally unique and lovely performance under Stephen Layton's direction. From its first measures, the *Requiem* establishes an atmosphere of meditation upon the mystery and miracle surrounding the dual theme of death and eternal life. There are other high points in this all-Rutter disc as well. Among them are his uplifting *Hymn to the Creator of Light,* a highly chromatic paean to the God of sun, light, and life that is scored for double choir. Rutter's well-known and oft-performed anthems are also represented, among them *A Gaelic Blessing, Open thou mine eyes,* and *The Lord bless you and keep you.* Here Polyphony and the Bournemouth Sinfonietta offer interpretations that should act as performance models for all choirs studying these gems of liturgical music.

various choral works
what to buy: [*Treasures of English Church Music*; John Rutter, cond.; The Cambridge Singers, choir] (Collegium 302) ♪ ♪ ♪ ♪♪

Although there is only one Rutter composition (*Loving Shepherd of thy sheep*) on this remarkable two-disc, forty-six-anthem anthology, his careful preparation of the materials showcases his abilities as a conductor and the Cambridge Singers' talents as a choir. High points include Richard Farrant's *Lord, for thy tender mercy's sake* for the ultimate in choral phrasing and John Amner's *Come, let's rejoice* for a lesson in contrapuntal precision. Other composers represented in this collection include Elizabethan stalwarts Thomas Tallis, William Byrd, and Orlando Gibbons, but the twentieth century is also featured via material from Ralph Vaughan Williams, Benjamin Britten, and John Tavener.

influences: John Tavener, James McMillan

Frank Scinta

S

Camille Saint-Saëns
Born Charles Camille Saint-Saëns, October 9, 1835, in Paris, France. Died December 16, 1921, in Algiers, Algeria.

period: Romantic

By all accounts a brilliant organist, Camille Saint-Saëns

Artur Rubinstein:
In 1894, when he was eight years old, Artur Rubinstein performed for Johannes Brahms's great advocate, violinist Joseph Joachim, who was so impressed with the youth's talents that he largely assumed responsibility for Rubinstein's musical education for the next eight years. Rubinstein's debut as a solo pianist took place in Berlin when he was eleven years old, performing Wolfgang Amadeus Mozart's Piano Concerto no. 23 in A Major (K. 488) with Joachim conducting the orchestra.

Rubinstein's American debut occurred in 1906 where he played the Piano Concerto no. 1 in E Minor by Frédéric Chopin with the Philadelphia Orchestra. Rubinstein first visited Spain and Mexico ten years later and began featuring works by a number of important contemporary Hispanic composers in his recitals, including music by Federico Mompou and Manuel de Falla. (In particular, he made a superb arrangement of de Falla's *Ritual Fire Dance*.) Brazilian composer Heitor Villa-Lobos was another beneficiary of Rubinstein's advocacy, especially when his suite for piano, *A Prolé do Bébé (The Child's Dolls),* began showing up on the pianist's programs. (Villa-Lobos would show his appreciation for Rubinstein's efforts in 1930, dedicating the lengthy and challenging *Rudepoêma* to him.)

Despite the accolades that Rubinstein was receiving from audiences during this period, by 1932 he felt (and many critics seemed to agree) that he was experiencing personal triumphs more because of his flamboyant manner of playing than for the surety of his technique. He then began a serious period of reevaluation and practice, which eventually helped rid him of the technical deficiencies which were getting in the way of how he felt the music should sound. Three years later, the pianist emerged from his studies with a semblance of the technique he would have had earlier had he not coasted on his natural abilities instead of practicing diligently.

The transition period encompassing Rubinstein's technical adjustments of the early 1930s can be best heard on a five-CD set of recordings from 1928–1939 (EMI Classics 64933). In addition to his performances of Chopin's two piano concertos here (with John Barbirolli conducting the London Symphony Orchestra), Rubinstein works his way through the *Nocturnes, Mazurkas, Scherzi,* and *Polonaises* in addition to a few other short works. The artistic difference between those performances and the ones heard on Rubinstein's set of Chopin *Nocturnes* from 1965 to 1967 (*Rubinstein Collection, Vol. 49: Chopin—Nocturnes,* RCA Victor Red Seal 63049) is remarkable, benefiting from the pianist's advanced interpretative skills and the various technological improvements in studio engineering that occurred in the decades after his EMI recordings.

William Gerard

is best known to modern audiences for *Carnival of the Animals*—a charming work he never meant to have published—as well as tone poems, his third symphony, and concertos for piano, violin, and cello. He also composed operas, a large number of works for piano, and a wide variety of chamber music, using Classical models combined with great skill, sense of form, and clarity of orchestration.

Saint-Saëns was the son of an audit clerk (who died a few months after the child's birth) and an amateur artist. Frail and afflicted with tuberculosis, the young Camille began piano studies with his aunt when he was two and one-half years old. His enormous musical gifts, including perfect pitch, made him an obvious prodigy, and he proceeded to prove his talents by composing his first piano piece shortly after his third birthday. At the age of seven, he began studies in composition and organ and started performing in public. In 1848, he entered the Paris Conservatoire as an organ student; in 1851, he continued as a composition student with Fromental Halévy, although the lessons were rather haphazard and, according to Saint-Saëns in his autobiography, "He came only when he had time." In 1853 Saint-Saëns completed his first published symphony (op. 2) and, after serving as organist at St. Severin for a few months, became organist of St. Merry. From then until he accepted a position as organist at the Madeleine in 1858 he composed relatively little, concentrating instead on his duties and studying scores of older composers, including Johann Sebastian Bach, Wolfgang Amadeus Mozart, and Jean Philippe Rameau. Once he was ensconced in his post at the Madeleine, Saint-Saëns used this prominent venue to dazzle many of the finest musicians of his day with the stunning variety and quality of his improvisations on the organ. Franz Liszt, for one, heard him and declared him to be the greatest organist in the world, while Hector Berlioz gave him a left-handed compliment when he said, "He knows everything but lacks inexperience."

Perhaps Berlioz had it right. Everything seemed to come easily to Saint-Saëns, and while there is grandeur in some of his music, there is also little to hint at grand problems wrestled with until hard-won solutions have been chosen. Technique and a modicum of inspiration, combined with good work habits, resulted in a relatively tidy art for this composer. Up to the time he resigned from his post at the Madeleine (1877), he had composed a healthy number of songs and choral works, some small piano pieces, and a few chamber works, few of which rise beyond adequacy. He fared much better with the Concerto no. 2 for Piano and Orchestra (1868), his impressive Concerto no. 1 for Cello and Orchestra (1872), and the potboiler tone poem *Danse Macabre* (1874). For part of his tenure at the Madeleine he worked concurrently (from 1861 to 1865) as a teacher at the École Niedermeyer, where Gabriel Fauré was one of his students.

Saint-Saëns, surprisingly enough given his keen interest in Baroque composers, was also a fairly active supporter of contemporary music during his younger days. Not only did he promote works by Liszt, Robert Schumann, and Richard Wagner, he helped to found the Société Nationale de Musique for the encouragement and performance of new music by French composers, such as Fauré, Caésar Franck, Édouard Lalo, Emmanuel Chabrier, Paul Dukas, and Maurice Ravel. In later years, however, his conservative streak came to the fore, and he looked askance at the innovations of Claude Debussy and many others in the Impressionist camp, while the initial performance of Igor Stravinsky's *The Rite of Spring* simply horrified him.

Saint-Saëns resigned from church work in 1877 to devote himself to composition, conducting, and performance. The most impressive scores to come from this period belong to his opera *Samson et Dalila* (1877), the fiery third violin concerto (1880), his compelling Symphony no. 3 with its important role for the organ (1886), and the utterly charming *Carnival of the Animals* (also 1886). After his mother's death in 1888, he traveled on concert tours or on vacation to Europe, Russia, Africa, England, and America. In 1891, he established a museum in Dieppe, his father's birthplace, to which he gave his manuscripts, paintings, and art objects. It was there that he gave his last piano recital in 1921.

Orchestral
Carnival of the Animals for Two Pianos and Orchestra
what to buy: [Pascal Rogé, piano; Cristina Ortiz, piano; Charles Dutoit, cond.; London Sinfonietta, orch.] (London Jubilee 430720) ♪ ♪ ♪ ♪

This has become Saint-Saëns's most famous work, despite his not permitting a public performance during his lifetime. This recording uses a larger string ensemble than the composer envisioned, but the solo instruments are clearly brought out in the recording. A bonus in this budget reissue is a good recording of his third symphony, with Dutoit, organist Peter Hurford, and the Montréal Symphony. The same performance can also be found on London 41440 in a package that includes the composer's popular *Danse Macabre* and two other short orchestral tone poems by him: *Phaéton* and *La Rouet d'Omphale*.

what to buy next: [*Children's Classics*; Leonard Bernstein, narrator; Leonard Bernstein, cond.; New York

Philharmonic Orchestra] (Sony Classics 37765) ♪ ♪ ♪♪

Ogden Nash wrote some clever poetry to mesh with this music and the resulting product has become a mainstay of concerts focusing on music for youngsters. Bernstein had a flair for this kind of orchestral evangelism, as witnessed in his legendary *Young Peoples Concerts,* and this performance is both a fine example of his outreach programming and a decent rendition of the score. Another youth favorite, Sergei Prokofiev's *Peter and the Wolf,* can also be found on this disc.

Symphony no. 3 in C Minor for Organ and Orchestra, op. 78 (*Organ Symphony*)
what to buy: [Marcel Dupré, organ; Paul Paray, cond.; Detroit Symphony Orchestra] (Mercury Living Presence 432719) ♪ ♪ ♪ ♪♪

There are many recordings of this, the best-known piece for organ with orchestra, but there are few that capture the Gallic spirit of Saint-Saëns as well as this one. Early in his life, Dupré served as registrant (pulling stops and turning pages) to Saint-Saëns while the composer played the organ in a performance of this piece. Even though one would desire a more lively acoustic setting than Ford Auditorium, the orchestra and Aeolian-Skinner organ are fully up to the task of giving a memorable performance. The conductor's own *Mass for Joan of Arc* fills out the disc.

what to buy next: [Jean Guillou, organ; Eduardo Mata, cond.; Dallas Symphony Orchestra] (Dorian 90200) ♪ ♪ ♪ ♪

This recording captures the memorable acoustics of the Meyerson Hall and the virtuosic performance of this orchestra. Guillou uses the organ to good effect, in spite of some uncharacteristic stop choices. This is coupled with a not-to-be-forgotten performance of the *Symphonie Concertante* by Joseph Jongen.

[Simon Preston, organ; James Levine, cond.; Berlin Philharmonic Orchestra] (Deutsche Grammophon 419617) ♪ ♪ ♪ ♪

Preston is a fine organist and the engineering is marvelous, making this a viable alternative for those to whom sonics are more important than slight differences in performance. Paul Dukas's *L'Apprenti sorcier* is an interesting programming choice as filler and actually works well.

Anna Russell:
During the 1940s, 1950s, and on into the early 1960s, Anna Russell was the preeminent comedienne in classical music circles, preparing the way for the inspired zaniness of Peter Schickele's P.D.Q. Bach with her music-history "lectures" and skewed "analysis" of popular works. Russell was born in London, England in 1911 and moved to Canada in 1939 after completing her course work at the Royal Conservatory of Music—where she was a student in one of Ralph Vaughan Williams's composition classes. Although she took part in a variety of "straight" musical roles, Russell also attempted careers as a folk singer and in the English music-hall tradition before finally launching her first one-woman show as a parodist in 1942. This was the perfect occupation for Russell, since she had a solid education in traditional classical performance coupled with a natural flair for entertaining (and the knowledge that her voice was *not* going to cut it in the world of lieder, chanson, and song.) She became a Canadian citizen in 1943 and used Toronto as a base of operations for her concertizing before changing her citizenship once more, becoming an American in 1955. This last event occurred only eight years after her Carnegie Hall debut, and during the same year as her successful Broadway run with *Anna Russell's Little Show.* She recorded a series of albums for Columbia Records that featured many of her concert-tested routines, filled with a variety of outrageous puns and malapropisms that would cause classical buffs and neophytes alike to double up in mirth. Her autobiography, *I'm Not Making This Up, You Know,* appeared in 1985, the year before she officially retired. Two of her greatest routines, "How to Write Your Own Gilbert and Sullivan Opera" and the hilarious analysis of Richard Wagner's *The Ring of the Nibelung* ("…the only grand opera that comes in the giant economy size"), show up on *The Anna Russell Album* (Sony 47252), the perfect introduction to her art.

Garaud MacTaggart

Concerto no. 1 in A Minor for Cello and Orchestra, op. 33
what to buy: [Yo-Yo Ma, cello; Lorin Maazel, cond.; French National Orchestra] (Sony Classical 35848) ♪ ♪ ♪ ♪ ♪

Providing strong, delicate, and graceful performance, these musicians are a wonderful fit in this material. The cello playing is everything that one could ask for and the conducting is some of Maazel's best work. If there is a weak spot to this disc, it can be heard in Édouard Lalo's accompanying cello concerto, of which there are better versions available.

what to buy next: [Janos Starker, cello; Antal Doráti, cond.; London Symphony Orchestra] (Mercury Living Presence 432010) ♪ ♪ ♪ ♪♪

Combining cello concertos by Saint-Saëns, Lalo, and Robert Schumann, this disc by one of the twentieth century's finest cellists is a good sampler combining clever programming and top-notch performances. Starker's Lalo is among the best currently in catalog, the

Schumann rendition is pretty good, and the Saint-Saëns is the finest of the lot. Recorded in the 1960s, the sonics still hold up very well and the pricing is fairly decent.

Concertos for Piano and Orchestra, opp. 17, 22, 29, 44, and 103

what to buy: [Aldo Ciccolini, piano; Serge Baudo, cond.; Orchestre de Paris] (EMI Classics 69443) ♪ ♪ ♪ ♪ ♪

These concertos were composed over almost four decades and are significant in French musical literature for their piano writing and orchestration. This two disc set—winner of France's *Grand Prix du Disque*—was recorded in the 1970s. It is still highly regarded today because of its interpretation and performance.

Concerto no. 2 in G Minor for Piano and Orchestra, op. 22

what to buy: [Idel Biret, piano; James Loughran, cond.; Philharmonia Orchestra] (Naxos 8.550334) ♪ ♪ ♪ ♪

A budget recording of a Cadillac performance is always worth searching out, and here is a fine example of what can be had. The price, surprisingly clean sonics, and Loughran's usual dependability all give this disc a good shot at being a high recommendation, but Biret's artistry is the important ingredient that ensures the results. The same forces also wend their way through the composer's fourth piano concerto.

Concerto no. 3 in B Minor for Violin and Orchestra, op. 61

what to buy: [Itzhak Perlman, violin; Daniel Barenboim, cond.; Orchestre de Paris] (Deutsche Grammophon 429977) ♪ ♪ ♪ ♪₴

Digging into the challenge right from the opening solo, Perlman's interpretation has all the fire one would expect (and hope for) in a piece dedicated to the great Spanish violinist Pablo de Sarasate. Originally released in 1983, these performances have been reissued as a budget disc with Perlman's persuasive rendition of Lalo's classic violin showpiece, the *Symphonie espagnole* for Violin and Orchestra.

what to buy next: [Gil Shaham, violin; Giuseppe Sinopoli, cond.; New York Philharmonic Orchestra] (Deutsche Grammophon 429786) ♪ ♪ ♪ ♪

Shaham's performance is one of contained heat; not quite as overtly flamboyant as Perlman's version yet not lacking in intensity, Shaham's interpretation has much to recommend it. Including Niccolò Paganini's first violin concerto as part of the package offers the violinist yet another piece upon which to work his magic.

[Philippe Graffin, violin; Martyn Brabbins, cond.; BBC Scottish Symphony Orchestra] (Hyperion 67074) ♪ ♪ ♪₴

Graffin's performance in the third concerto is acceptable but not quite as "in control" as either Perlman or Shaham. The recording is quite good and Graffin is actually more fun to listen to in the composer's earlier essays in the form than he is in the final one. That said, the inclusion of all three Saint-Saëns violin concertos is valuable for illustrating the growth of the composer's abilities, as the youthful brio of the initial concerto in C Major (the first he wrote even if it is given a later opus number than the designated no. 1) gives way to the intense mastery of the no. 3 in B Minor.

Havanaise in E Major for Violin and Orchestra, op. 83

what to buy: [Itzhak Perlman, violin; Zubin Mehta, cond.; New York Philharmonic Orchestra] (Deutsch Grammophon 423063) ♪ ♪ ♪ ♪

The honor role for this set also includes: the *Intro and Rondo capriccioso* by Saint-Saëns, Ernest Chausson's *Poéme*, Maurice Ravel's *Tzigane*, and Pablo de Sarasate's *Carmen Fantasy*. Mehta can be a bit staid at times but he manages to keep the orchestra's playing sparkling more than he usually does. Perlman is stunning in his virtuosity.

Chamber
The Carnival of the Animals

worth searching for: [Michel Béroff, piano; Jean-Philippe Collard, piano] (EMI Classics 47543) ♪ ♪ ♪ ♪₴

This recording is unusual in presenting the original chamber version of this work. Each part is heard distinctly, probably in much the same way as the composer and his private audiences initially heard it. When Franz Liszt requested of Saint-Saëns to hear the piece, this is the version he heard. Composed a few years earlier than *Carnival of the Animals* and at the request of a friend, the disk's accompanying piece, the Septet in E-flat Major, is for an unusual combination of string quartet, piano, and trumpet.

influences: César Franck, Franz Liszt, Gabriel Fauré, Charles Gounod

D. John Apple and Garaud MacTaggart

Antonio Salieri

Born August 18, 1750, in Legnago, Italy. Died May 7, 1825, in Vienna, Austria.

period: Classical

Salieri's character was assassinated in retrospect when *Amadeus,* Peter Shaffer's play (and Milos Forman's movie), created an evil, petty, personality with the composer's name attached to it and then let this jealous doppelganger attempt to wreak havoc on Wolfgang Amadeus Mozart's life. All this because Salieri was a tad delirious while lying on his deathbed and "confessed" to poisoning the great man, an account that was doubted at the time because of the composer's diminished mental capacity. In reality, he had carved out a decent life for himself as a well-respected conductor, composer, and teacher who counted Ludwig van Beethoven (who dedicated his op. 12 violin sonatas to Salieri) among his students.

Salieri had already begun taking violin and harpsichord lessons by the time he was orphaned in 1765. Luckily, one of his father's friends took the budding musician into his household and saw to it that Salieri's musical education continued. A year later, Florian Gassman, a Bohemian composer ensconced in Austria as a theater conductor for Emperor Franz I, took Salieri to Vienna, where Gassman oversaw the balance of his studies in counterpoint and other musical disciplines. When his teacher died in 1774, Salieri was appointed to fill the court composer slot. His chief responsibility became the production of operas in the Italian manner, a task he already had some experience in, having previously churned out ten such works within a six-year period. The bulk of his oeuvre from that point on revolved around the vocal arts, whether opera, sacred choral works, or pieces based on secular texts, although he did create a small number of instrumental works for a variety of forces.

By this time he had already struck up a close friendship with his fellow composer Christoph Willibald Gluck. This relationship provided extra benefits for Salieri, and not just because the two composers genuinely admired each other. When Gluck bowed out of a commitment to write an opera for the 1778 opening of the Teatro alla Scala in Milan, Salieri wangled a two-year leave of absence from Emperor Joseph II (the successor to Franz I) in order to create *L'Europa riconosciuta.* Before he returned to his Viennese post, Salieri wrote and premiered four more operas in Italy, fortifying his reputation as a composer of Italianate stage works. Gluck, who was already popular in Paris, also bowed out of a production there in 1784, and once again Salieri stepped in with another opera (*Les Danaïdes*) to fill the contractual gap. This time, however, the theater managers presented it as a work by Gluck (with the putative composer's compliance), and it wasn't until much later that the rightful creator received his due. This bit of subterfuge served to bolster Salieri's stock with the theater owners, and after one more opera that opened under his own name and tanked (*Les Horaces,* from 1786), he finally achieved a modicum of success in Paris with the production of his *Tarare* in 1787. Ironically, Gluck died five months after Salieri's accomplishment.

With regard to the legend at the heart of *Amadeus,* Mozart and Salieri evidently knew each other. Both composers even had operas presented at the Austrian court at the same time, an event that occurred in 1786 when, at Joseph II's command, Mozart's *Der Schauspieldirektor* shared the bill with Salieri's *Prima la musica e poi le parole.* The two composers were at least cordial to each other a fair amount of the time, with Mozart once noting that his *Die Zauberflöte* received a favorable response from the older (by six years) composer.

Salieri was appointed Kapellmeister of the Austrian court in 1788 and tendered his resignation as court composer in 1790 upon the death of Joseph II and the ascension of Leopold II to the throne. This didn't mean that he would cease composing altogether, just that he would no longer have to create operas on such a regular basis and could devote more time to the administrative tasks of his post as Kapellmeister and to the composition of other (mainly sacred choral) works. He was also able to concentrate more on pedagogical undertakings, including working with Franz Schubert, Carl Czerny, Franz Liszt, Johann Nepomuk Hummel, and Ludwig van Beethoven on the art of composition. When Salieri finally died, he was one of the most honored musicians in the history of Vienna, remembered for his musical contributions as a composer and his work as an educator and administrator.

Orchestral
various overtures
what to buy: [Michael Dittrich, cond.; Czecho-Slovak Radio Symphony Orchestra] (Naxos 8.554838) ♪ ♪ ♪⸕

The twelve light and lively overtures included in this budget-priced collection could serve as pleasant concert openers for just about any program revolving around late classical or early romantic composers. Of the operas represented here, only *Axur, Re d'Ormus* (a refashioning of *Tarare* with a new libretto) is currently represented in the catalog, and though that work was one of Salieri's greatest Parisian successes, the overture is probably all that non-specialists would ever want to hear. The orchestral playing throughout the album is quite accomplished under Dittrich's steady direction, and the sonics (from the early 1990s) are very clear.

influences: Christoph Willibald Gluck, Johann Nepomuk Hummel, Carl Czerny

Garaud MacTaggart

Pablo de Sarasate
Born Pablo Martín Melitón de Sarasate y Navascuéz, March 10, 1844, in Pamplona, Spain. Died September 20, 1908, in Biarritz, France.

period: Romantic

Sarasate's success and acclaim as a violin player often got in the way of his life as a composer for the instrument. Although the bulk of his oeuvre is made up of technical showpieces with little in the way of formal structure, Sarasate still managed to create several challenging pieces for the violin virtuoso that have remained in the repertoire to this day. His most popular works, *Zigeunerweisen (Gypsy Airs)* and the lively and colorful *Carmen Fantasy*, make good use of stereotypical Spanish folk rhythms.

Sarasate's father was a military bandleader who encouraged his precocious son's desire to play the violin. Queen Isabella of Spain heard the twelve-year-old violinist at a recital and was very impressed. As a sign of her regard for Sarasate's budding talents she gifted him with a Stradivarius violin and helped pay for further studies at the Paris Conservatoire. While at the prestigious school Sarasate won several performance-related awards, and in 1859 felt sure enough of his technique to

begin a career as a touring virtuoso.

Though he started with a series of moderate successes, he soon won over critics and audiences alike with his assured interpretations of works by Johann Sebastian Bach, Frédéric Chopin, and Johannes Brahms. Some prominent composers of his day were impressed enough by his skillful interpretations that they wrote works specifically taking advantage of his skills: Max Bruch wrote both his second violin concerto and the *Scottish Fantasy* with Sarasate in mind; Camille Saint-Saëns composed two of his three violin concertos for the young Spaniard; and Édouard Lalo dedicated his *Symphonie espagnole* to him.

While Sarasate didn't engage in the pyrotechnics common to many of his competing contemporaries, he was loved for the apparent ease of his playing and the sweetness of tone he drew from his two Stradivarius violins. As a composer, Sarasate is best known for the *Zigeunerweisen*, a technically challenging piece that demands impressive control from the soloist, and the equally ingenious and devilishly difficult *Carmen Fantasy*, which used themes from Georges Bizet's Spanish-themed opera, *Carmen*.

Orchestral
Carmen Fantasy for Violin and Orchestra, op. 25
what to buy: [*Carmen-Fantasie*; Anne-Sophie Mutter, violin; James Levine, cond.; Vienna Philharmonic Orchestra] (Deutsche Grammophon 437544) ♪ ♪ ♪ ♪

Mutter is a phenomenal violinist, and this album shows off her skills in a variety of short works. In addition to the Sarasate piece that gives the album its name, there is a nice handful of violin bonbons from the pens of Gabriel Fauré, Jules Massenet, Maurice Ravel, Giuseppe Tartini, and Henryk Wieniawski.

what to buy next: [Itzhak Perlman, violin; Lawrence Foster, cond.; Royal Philharmonic Orchestra] (EMI Studio 63533) ♪ ♪ ♪⸕

For a budget price you get Perlman performing a whole lot of Sarasate including not only the *Carmen Fantasy* but *Zigeunerweisen*, the *Caprice basque*, and six of the composer's *Spanish Dances* for Violin and Piano. Four short pieces by Isaac Albéniz, Ernesto Halffter, Enrique Granados, and Manuel de Falla are tossed in almost as an afterthought, something usually reserved for Sarasate's scores.

Zigeunerweisen (Gypsy Airs) for Violin and Piano, op. 20 (orchestrated)

what to buy: [Gil Shaham, violin; Lawrence Foster, cond.; London Symphony Orchestra] (Deutsche Grammophon 431815) ♪ ♪ ♪ ♪

Shaham has grown into a marvelous violinist. His sure-handed way with this piece brings out the poetry inherent in Sarasate's music, making this performance a most interesting companion for the two violin concertos by Wieniawski.

influences: Édouard Lalo, Henryk Wieniawski, Max Bruch, Camille Saint-Saëns

Kerry Dexter

Erik Satie

Born Erik Alfred Leslie Satie, May 17, 1866, in Honfleur, France. Died July 1, 1925, in Paris, France.

period: Twentieth century

Satie was an influential French composer whose eccentricities, acerbic wit, and gift for gentle sarcasm are often revealed in the titles of his works. Hc, along with writer/filmmaker Jean Cocteau, was a catalyst for the budding musical avant-garde movement of his day, aiding in the development of the young composers known as "Les Six": Darius Milhaud, Arthur Honegger, Francis Poulenc, Georges Auric, Germaine Tailleferre, and Louis Durey.

The Satie family held a prominent position in Honfleur, a maritime town on the coast of Normandy. Erik's lineage was closely tied to the sea and included a paternal great-grandfather who was an officer in the French navy during Napoleon's reign, and a grandfather, father, and uncle who were ships' brokers. While most of the family consisted of hard-working souls, Erik's uncle was, reportedly, a bit of an eccentric and a kindred free spirit for the young Satie to admire and emulate.

When his mother died in 1872, Satie went to live with his grandparents, staying there until his father remarried in 1878. His new stepmother had some modest musical training and attempted to guide her stepson along established pedagogical pathways, but was rebuffed at nearly every turn by the recalcitrant lad. In 1879 Satie was sent away to the Paris Conservatoire, where he studied harmony and piano with a leisurely attitude that

Johann Peter Salomon:

If Johann Peter Salomon had not invited Franz Joseph Haydn over to London and commissioned twelve symphonies from him, it is doubtful that Salomon would be anything more than a minor footnote in the history of Western music. As it is, this feat, combined with his numerous vocal and instrumental compositions, his notoriously skillful violin playing, and his undeniable importance as an impresario who competed with other prominent concert promoters of the day, only adds to the footnote's length.

Born in 1745, Salomon was installed as musical director to Prince Heinrich of Prussia by the time he was nineteen years old and spent much of his artistically formative years in service to that household. There he developed the abilities for which he would become famous later on, and took advantage of the numerous opportunities he was afforded to meet many of the musical luminaries of the day, including Carl Philipp Emanuel Bach. It was this distinguished composer who introduced Salomon to the solo violin sonatas and partitas of Johann Sebastian Bach; the disciplined and thoughtful performance of those works was to help bring the young violinist a modicum of fame, especially after Salomon moved to England a few decades later.

Haydn's visits to London (1791–1795) generated the dozen symphonies (nos. 93–104) that crown his symphonic output and are now known as either the *London* symphonies or the *Salomon* symphonies. These compositions were all originally performed at Salomon's concerts in the Hanover Square Rooms and at the Theatre Royal, Haymarket. The impresario retained the autograph copies of nos. 95 and 96, but also kept duplicates of the others that were made from Haydn's autograph scores prior to the composer's return to Austria. In the case of no. 93, the autograph for the symphony was lost and Salomon's copy is the earliest version of that score currently in existence.

Despite the mountain of publicity engendered by Haydn's presence and the generally positive reception of the music by the public, Salomon didn't really escape bathing in red ink until the concerts of 1793. Part of this might have owed to the fact that his productions were not supported by subscriptions from the upper classes like those of rival organizations; Salomon preferred garnering his funding from the developing middle class and, to fill up the venue, selling single tickets to members of the public who had not subscribed to the series. Salomon also employed many foreign musicians for his concerts, paying them less than what the typical English musician was getting while upgrading the perceived quality of the entertainment. By 1793 his efforts seemed to have paid off, as a contemporary critic in *The Morning Herald* noted that "instrumental music, under his leading, and with his band, seems to have acquired powers with which we were unacquainted before."

Ian Palmer

failed to impress his instructors. His lackadaisical career at the school was shortened in 1882 when Satie was kicked out for failing to attain an acceptable level of scholarship. This didn't stop him from continuing his rather desultory approach to learning, however, and he enrolled in further classes in harmony and piano per-

formance. Satie was also spending much of his time in the library at the Notre Dame Cathedral, studying texts on Gothic art and Gregorian chant.

Satie's father had started a music-publishing business and, in 1886, after Erik's brief stint in the French infantry, published some songs written by his son. The younger Satie followed up these initial efforts by writing some of first important works for piano, including *Ogives* (1886), *Trois Sarabandes* (1887), the *Trois Gymnopédies* of 1888, and the *Gnossiennes* from 1890. These scores experimented with harmonies in a way that presaged developments found in the later works of Claude Debussy (whom Satie met and became close friends with in 1891) and Maurice Ravel. During this period Satie also grew interested in Rosicrucianism, an artistic and religious movement led by Joséphin Péladan who, according to Satie's biographer Rollo H. Myers, succeeded in reviving an old Christian cult and draping it "with all the appropriate medieval flummery with which it used to be surrounded." Satie wrote some ceremonial music for the group before breaking away from the Rosicrucians in 1892 and creating his own satirical vision of religion—the Metropolitan Church of the Art of Jesus the Conductor—of which he was the head and sole member. This small detail did not prevent him from excommunicating individuals who met with his artistic disapproval, however.

Two of the *Trois Gymnopédies* were finally published in 1895, and Debussy's orchestration of those pieces followed shortly thereafter. By this time, however, Satie was starting to run though the small bequest left to him after his father's death, and needing to generate some income, he became a cabaret pianist. He also entered the Schola Cantorum for a few years, studying with Vincent d'Indy and Albert Roussel in an attempt to pick up some of the techniques he had neglected to learn while enrolled at the Paris Conservatoire.

It wasn't until 1915 that Satie was to meet his most important adherent and publicist, the young writer Jean Cocteau. Together they collaborated on a variety of artistic projects including their most infamous endeavor, the ballet *Parade*. This particular composition, based on a theme suggested by Cocteau with music by Satie and set and costume design by Pablo Picasso, was first performed in 1917 by Serge Diaghilev's Ballets Russes with

Erik Satie

Ernest Ansermet conducting the orchestra. By incorporating typewriters, sirens, and propellers within the score, Satie and Cocteau almost guaranteed the critical outrage that followed the ballet's inaugural production. *Parade* placed the composer in the spotlight as a focus for the day's avant-garde, including the young musicians who would later become lumped together as "Les Six": Darius Milhaud, Arthur Honegger, Francis Poulenc, Georges Auric, Germaine Tailleferre, and Louis Durey. Satie would reap the rewards of his new notoriety until his death from sclerosis of the liver in 1925. However, he wrote a wide variety of works in this final period, including *Socrate* (a cantata based upon Plato's *Dialogues*) and two more ballets, *Mercure* and *Relâche*.

Orchestral
Gymnopédies, nos. 1 and 3 (orchestrated by Claude Debussy)
what to buy: [Leonard Slatkin, cond.; St. Louis Symphony Orchestra] (Telarc 80059) ♪ ♪ ♪ ♪ ♪

Debussy's arrangements of these short piano compositions are part of a well-chosen program of lush orchestral works by Samuel Barber, Gabriel Fauré, Percy Grainger, and Ralph Vaughan Williams.

what to buy next: [*Pavane*; Orpheus Chamber Orchestra] (Deutsche Grammophon 449186) ♪ ♪ ♪ ♪

This is a more intimate performance by a smaller ensemble than the one conducted by Slatkin, and the leaner textures emphasize the architecture of the pieces most appealingly. The album from which these performances are taken highlights French Impressionism, and this explains the presence of compositions by Maurice Ravel and Gabriel Fauré in addition to the Debussy arrangements of Satie's keyboard works.

Parade for Orchestra
what to buy: [Antal Dorati, cond.; London Symphony Orchestra] (Mercury 434335) ♪ ♪ ♪ ♪

Although there is also a version of this score for piano four-hand, the orchestral setting gives the listener an aural peek at what early twentieth century audiences considered outrageous. Dorati's clean-limbed rendition of Satie's piece fits well on an album of short works by Milhaud, Auric, Françaix, and Fetler.

Chamber
Trois Gymnopédies
what to buy: [*Satie: The Early Piano Works*; Reinbert de

Leeuw, piano] (Philips 462161) ♪♪♪♪♪

Pacing is the key to these performances since de Leeuw takes much slower tempos on these little gems when compared to just about any other pianist. Listen to this album enough times and you might wonder why everyone else is in such a hurry. This two-disc collection contains Satie's other major set pieces for piano, the six *Gnossiennes*, in addition to the other noteworthy cycles *Ogives, Sonneries de la Rose-Croix,* and *Piéces froides.*

what to buy next: [*Satie: 3 Gymnopédies & other piano works*; Pascal Rogé, piano] (Decca 410220) ♪♪♪♪

Rogé's splendid, well-recorded performances of *Trois Gymnopédies, Gnossiennes,* and the other selections on this album are a treat to the ears.

various piano works
what to buy: [*Satie: The Four-Handed Piano*; Pascal Rogé, piano; Jean-Philippe Collard, piano] (Decca 455401) ♪♪♪♪

Rogé and Collard do a fine job of collaborating on the four-hand version of *Parade; Trois Morceaux en forme de poire* (a work in seven sections, not three); *La Belle Excentrique;* and three others. Rogé also plays three solo piano pieces and is joined by violinist Chantal Juillet in Satie's only work for that duo, *Choses vues à droite et à gauche (sans lunettes).*

what to buy next: [*Satie: Piano Works*; Aldo Ciccolini, piano] (EMI Classics 67282) ♪♪♪♪

Drawn from Ciccolini's pioneering set of Satie's complete works for piano, this two-disc collection duplicates some of the material found on the de Leeuw and Rogé albums but also covers some compositions not touched upon by either of the others. The performance of *Trois Gymnopédies* lacks the last ounce of grace but the album as a whole is more than acceptable. Satie's wry humor and harmonic adventurousness are evidenced in pieces like *Jack in the box, Peccadilles importunes (Inconvenient trifles),* and *Embryons desséchés (Desiccated embryos).*

influences: Claude Debussy, Maurice Ravel, Francis Poulenc, Charles Koechlin

Gary Barton and Mathilde August

Alessandro Scarlatti
Born Pietro Alessandro Gaspare Scarlatti, May 2, 1660, in Palermo, Italy. Died October 22, 1725, in Naples, Italy.

period: Baroque

An Italian composer especially important in the development of opera, Alessandro Scarlatti is considered the founder of the so-called "Neopolitan School." Of his 115 operas about seventy survive, but he also wrote oratorios and masses (including several settings of the *Stabat Mater*) as well as forty motets, more than 600 solo cantatas with basso continuo, and various chamber cantatas, serenatas, and madrigals.

Although little is known for sure about his early musical education, it is thought that Scarlatti took lessons from Giacomo Carissimi (the putative father of the modern oratorio) when the youngster was sent to Rome by his parents in 1672. If that was the case their association was relatively limited, since Carissimi died within one and a half years of Scarlatti's arrival. The first mention of Scarlatti as a composer relates to a Lenten oratorio he was commissioned to write, but his earliest known work was an opera (*Gli equivoci nel sembiante*) which was initially performed in 1679 to rave reviews. It was also about this time that he entered the service of Queen Christina of Sweden as her maestro di cappella, in charge of the household's musical activities. Naples was his next stop when he was asked to assume a similar position with the Marquis del Carpio, the Spanish ambassador to the Vatican who became Viceroy of Naples in 1683. Scarlatti was to function in that capacity with the Viceroy until 1702.

Scarlatti's Neapolitan years were not exactly the happiest ones, as he was subjected to (and undoubtedly took part in) a host of domestic intrigues. But he also churned out at least thirty-five operas (scholars are still debating the true authorship of a number of others credited to him). Most of these works (authentic or otherwise) derived their librettos from mythological and pseudo-historical sources, a practice which was to continue for centuries to come. But Scarlatti's specific musical innovations in this genre resulted from his mutation of the basso continuo, changing the bottom end of a score to a more harmonically charged one than what had gone before. He also expanded the role of the overture and, for better or worse, the use of accompanied recitative.

By 1702, the War of the Spanish Succession was about

to throw Europe into turmoil and political unrest was already creating concerns for the viceroys in Naples. Since Naples was officially ceded to Austria when the war reached its conclusion in 1713, it is apparent that their fears were totally justified. It is also easy to see why Scarlatti might have wanted to leave town. He managed to obtain a leave of absence from his employer and, in June of 1702, left Naples for Florence, taking his young son, Domenico, along. The composer had hoped to find a new patron in that city, but when things didn't work out he returned to Naples. His search for a new position was eventually rewarded when he finally secured a posting in Rome as an assistant music director at a church toward the end of 1703. Once he arrived in Rome, he complained about the lack of support for his art but he still managed to hook up with the Arcadian Academy, an outgrowth of Queen Christina's palace academy, in 1706. The following year Scarlatti received a promotion at the church, becoming its music director. He still faced a multitude of problems in Rome and by 1708 probably appreciated the offer (after considerable lobbying on his part) to work for Cardinal Grimani, the Austrian Viceroy in Naples.

While Scarlatti spent the next decade there he still maintained contact with powerful friends in Rome. This would gain him entry to the nobility, but by 1718 he probably came to the unwelcome realization that the style of opera which made him such a formidable force on the cusp of the century made him a relic in a newer era. Roman patrons were still hospitable to him, however, and he sought to produce most of his newer works there. Finally Scarlatti spent his remaining years as a Neapolitan in quiet retirement, composing only a few scores before his death.

While he was known during the early part of his career for the quality and quantity of his operas and is still considered to be a pivotal figure in the development of Italian opera, Scarlatti's role as a composer of church music yielded works that have more appeal to modern audiences than his recitative-laden stage works. Of particular interest are the numerous cantatas, motets, and oratorios he wrote during the period from his first days in Naples until the start of his association with Cardinal Grimani in 1708.

Vocal
various cantatas
what to buy: [Deborah York, soprano; James Bowman, countertenor; Crispian Steele-Perkins, trumpet; Robert

King, cond.; King's Consort, orch.] (Hyperion 66875) ♪♪♪♪

This delightful disc contains three cantatas by Alessandro Scarlatti (two secular and one sacred) plus settings of the *Salve Regina* by Alessandro's son Domenico and Johann Adolph Hasse. Bowman was one of the world's finest countertenors, but his vocal quality has deteriorated somewhat over the years and the results of that can be heard in his singing of *Infirmata, vulnerata*. York, on the other hand, is superb in both *Su le sponde del Tebro* and the one sacred cantata heard here, *O di Betlemme altera povertà*. Domenico's piece will surprise those who only know him through the keyboard works, while Hasse's composition is solid but not quite in the same league as the other pieces.

***Dixit Dominus* for Soloists, Strings, and Continuo worth searching for:** [Nancy Argenta, soprano; Ingrid Attrot, soprano; Catherine Denley, contralto; Ashley Stafford, alto; Stephen Varcoe, bass; Trevor Pinnock, cond.; English Concert, orch.; English Concert Choir] (Deutsche Grammophon/Archiv 423386) ♪♪♪♪♪

Bright and lively in its opening violin passages, this performance is an uplifting listen enhanced by the beautiful voices of the chorus and soloists, as well as the period instrumentation. Everyone deftly navigates this work, which is more animated and intricate in contrapuntal detail than Antonio Vivaldi's *Gloria* in D Major, also included on the album.

influences: Domenico Scarlatti, Johann Adolph Hasse, Marc-Antoine Charpentier

Nancy Ann Lee and Ian Palmer

Domenico Scarlatti
Born Guiseppe Domenico Scarlatti on October 26, 1685, in Naples, Italy. Died July 23, 1757, in Madrid, Spain.

period: Baroque

Born the same year as Johann Sebastian Bach and George Frideric Handel, Italian composer Domenico Scarlatti—the son of prolific opera composer Alessandro Scarlatti—is best known for his keyboard sonatas. Any classical collection should contain selections from his more than 500 sonatas, and many of the best recordings are those performed by leading virtuosos on the harpsichord, an instrument Scarlatti had mastered in his youth.

Scarlatti was more famous early in his career than toward the end. His father took him along on trips to find work among the aristocracy of Florence, Rome, and Venice when he was only seven years old. Domenico had been vigorously schooled in the sacred vocal composition tradition, mastering both the strict, polyphonous Renaissance style and the more modern one that allowed for independent instrumental parts and solo vocal writing. By the time he was sixteen, the younger Scarlatti was working under his father (the maestro di cappella) as an organist and composer at the court of the Viceroy of Naples and, by age nineteen, had two of his operas (*L'Ottavia ristituita al trono* and *Il Giustino*) produced there. It was about this time that he met George Frideric Handel during one of the latter's tours of Italy and the two became close friends, fully aware of each other's prodigious skills at the keyboard.

Scarlatti's first important position—as maestro di cappella for Maria Casimira, the exiled Queen of Poland—began sometime between 1709, when she commissioned him to write the music for an oratorio (*La conversione di Clodoveo*), and 1711, when the score to his opera *L'Orlando* was published. He then moved on to the Basilica Giulia as assistant to the director in 1713, only to be appointed maestro di cappella a year later when the director died. The majority of Scarlatti's church music dates from the years he worked there, including his *Stabat Mater*, a twenty-six-minute liturgical choral work for ten parts, that was written around 1715. Impressive for its grace, lyricism, harmoniousness, and amazing modernity, it demonstrates Scarlatti's early expertise and has proven to be the most popular of his non-keyboard works.

His descent into relative obscurity began when he resigned from this post in 1719 and, rather than entering the musically competitive realm of Rome, took a secure position with the Portuguese royal family in Lisbon, a city far from the major music centers of the day. When his pupil, Princess Maria Barbara, married the Spanish Crown Prince Fernando, Scarlatti accompanied her to Spain, the then-unfashionable country which remained his home until his death in 1757. While he kept writing sacred and secular vocal music, the main focus of his years on the Iberian peninsula was a remarkable series of keyboard sonatas. Scarlatti's early mastery of Italian harpsichord styles had affected his entire sound-world

and he continued composing for this favored instrument with its bright colors, quick delivery, and penetrating, melodious tone. This is not to say that his life in Spain was unaffected by the everyday music which surrounded him, since there is evidence, in some of his later sonatas, of folk tunes and effects amazingly similar to those utilized by guitarists. His sonatas feature sparse textures and quirky phrases, switches from major to minor keys, crazy leaps and hand-crossings, dynamic harmonies and explosive accompaniments—all elements which, in combination, make his ingenious, joyous works uniquely his own.

The sheer volume of Scarlatti's keyboard sonatas poses its own problems for listeners and performers who wish access to specific pieces. The most commonly used catalogs for his works were compiled by Alessandro Longo (published in 1908) and Ralph Kirkpatrick (published in facsimile in 1970). The Longo numbering appears to be relatively arbitrary in its sequencing while the Kirkpatrick system makes an attempt to order the works by date. Older recordings of Scarlatti's sonatas will often note a Longo number (L.) but not a corresponding Kirkpatrick number (K.). Newer performances will sometimes include both numbering systems.

Chamber
various keyboard sonatas
what to buy: [*The Complete Masterworks Recordings, vol. 2: The Celebrated Scarlatti Recordings*; Vladimir Horowitz, piano] (Sony Classics 53460) ♪ ♪ ♪ ♪♪

Horowitz features a series of impeccably selected and recorded keyboard sonatas, at a total time of seventy-two minutes. After a self-imposed twelve-year exile from public life Horowitz signed a long-term contract with Columbia Masterworks, and from the very first recording which grew out of this alliance both public and critics were won over by the pianist's outstanding virtuosity, warmth, and maturity. The works here were recorded in the CBS studio in New York City on six separate dates in 1964 between April 23 and September 28, and demonstrate the pianist's deft keyboard mastery.

[John Gibbons, harpsichord] (Centaur 2177) ♪ ♪ ♪ ♪♪

Expertly recorded in 1992 at Pilgrim Congregational Church in Lexington, MA, John Gibbons displays loose, unstrained demeanor as well as flawless technique polished as resident harpsichordist of the Musical Instrument Collection at Boston's Museum of Fine Arts and through worldwide performances. No information is given about the particular instrument he plays, but it has a very robust, pleasing sound that enables Gibbons to confidently convey with impassioned, flowing artistry and fleet fingering the complex, textural nature of these fourteen sonatas. If you didn't favor the harpsichord before, Gibbons's astounding executions here should win you over.

[*Scarlatti Sonatas*; Colin Tilney, harpsichord] (Dorian 90103) ♪ ♪ ♪ ♪₈

Colin Tilney is a world-class harpsichordist who proves his fleet-fingered finesse on nineteen complex sonatas performed here. His animated performance on the Presto in D Minor (K. 18) will especially amaze you, as you imagine his fingers flying over the keyboard of the brass-strung Italian-made instrument. In addition to Tilney's virtuosic performance, it is the rich sound of this particular instrument (thought to be crafted around 1730) and its suitability to Scarlatti's flamboyant keyboard writing that makes this recording an exceptionally attractive listen.

[*12 Sonatas*; András Schiff, piano] (Hungaroton 11806) ♪ ♪ ♪ ♪₈

If the sound of a harpsichord is not to your liking, try this recording by Schiff, who renders magnificent, multi-layered solo piano performances of twelve emotionally rich and rosy Scarlatti sonatas. The pianist deftly masters technical problems generally found in these works: gradual runs, scale-play, broken chords, passages of thirds and sixths, tone repetitions, leaps, and crossed hands.

what to buy next: [*Domenico Scarlatti: Keyboard Sonatas, vol. 1*; Etero Andjaparidze, piano] (Naxos 8.553061) ♪ ♪ ♪ ♪

This pianist born in the Republic of Georgia performs seventeen sonatas on a modern grand piano. A highly qualified musician who has won numerous prestigious awards and performed with major orchestras, she does a splendid job throughout, especially in the spirited pieces that focus on the upper register such as the Sonata in F Minor (K. 184).

Vocal
Stabat Mater **in C Minor for Organ, Continuo, and Two Choirs**
what to buy: [Timothy Farrell, organ; Anthony Pleeth,

cello; Francis Baines, double bass; John Poole, cond.; BBC Singers, choir] (Sony Classics 48282) ♪ ♪ ♪ ♪

A fine rendering of this sacred masterpiece. The compilation disc of religious music also contains a pair of Vivaldi choral works (the *Stabat Mater* in F Minor, RV. 621, and *Dixit Dominus* in D Major, RV 594) with the English Bach Festival Choir and Orchestra conducted by Jean-Claude Malgoire. All recorded in the 1970s, these works by Baroque composers are similar in tone and style, making this CD a seamless listen.

worth searching for: [Anthony Pleeth, cello; Chi-Chi Nwanoku, double bass; Timothy Byram-Wigfield, organ; Francis Grier, cond.; Christ Church Cathedral Choir, Oxford] (Hyperion 66182) ♪ ♪ ♪ ♪₈

A beautiful version of this deeply expressive work recorded in the acoustically fine Christ Church Cathedral, Oxford. Grier and company capably capture the composer's rich contrapuntal textures and serendipitous harmonies of the ten voices and continuo, achieving a chiaroscuro impact by effectively varying the dynamics. The album also contains five of Scarlatti's sonatas arranged for organ played by Grier, and the composer's *Salve Regina* performed by Charles Harris (treble), Nicholas Clapton (alto), and organist Timothy Byram-Wigfield, with Grier conducting.

influences: Johann Sebastian Bach, Carlos Seixas, Antonio Soler, Felix Maximo Lopez, Sebastian Albero

Nancy Ann Lee

Franz Schmidt
Born December 22, 1874, in Pressburg (then Pozsony), Hungary. Died February 11, 1939, in Perchtoldsdorf, Austria.

period: Romantic/twentieth century

For most of his life Franz Schmidt was virtually unknown outside of Austria. A teacher, administrator, and composer whose scores reflected some of the same post-romantic concepts espoused by Anton Bruckner and Gustav Mahler, he also admired Arnold Schoenberg and Paul Hindemith without necessarily understanding their works. Even though he played cello during the inaugural performance of Schoenberg's *Verklärte Nacht* and admired that composer's *Gurrelieder* and *Pierrot Lunaire*, his own scores were more conservative. Schmidt's finest works are the oratorio *Das Buch mit sieben Siegeln (The Book with Seven Seals)* and his deeply moving Symphony no.4.

Schmidt was born in an area whose borders were often in flux, at the mercy of political dynamics within the Austro-Hungarian empire and the fortunes of war. Growing up in a household that took pride in its Magyar heritage, the youngster spoke German, Hungarian, or (when speaking to household servants) Slovakian. His father played a variety of wind instruments, and his mother gave her son his first piano lessons. His next teachers, Rudolf Mader and Ludwig Burger, were hired to help him develop his technique, although the latter's methodology failed to impress Schmidt; in a later autobiographical sketch, he referred to Burger as "a peacock" who played "the part of the neglected German artist, condemned to go to wrack and ruin in this land of barbarians." It remained for Felizian Josef Moczik, a Franciscan monk whose piano technique was rudimentary compared to his pupil's, to make the biggest impression on young Franz, leading him through exercises in music theory and harmony that stayed with him for the rest of his life.

Schmidt embarked on a career as a child prodigy after his abilities attracted the attention of the Archduke Frederick of Hapsburg. By the time he was thirteen years old, the family had moved to Vienna, and in 1890 Schmidt was admitted to the conservatory of the Gesellschaft der Musikfreunde (Philharmonic Society), where he easily passed the entrance examination to Anton Bruckner's composition class. Schmidt never became the great composer's pupil, however, since Bruckner had taken a leave of absence due to illness and eventually retired without ever having taught the youngster. At the conservatory, Schmidt's piano studies took a temporary back seat to cello lessons with Karl Udel and Ferdinand Hellmesberger. Despite his contempt for Hellmesberger's teaching methods, Schmidt eventually developed sufficient cello skills that, after graduating with honors in 1896, he ended up winning an audition over thirty-nine other cellists to take a chair in the Vienna Court Opera Orchestra, an adjunct of the mighty Vienna Philharmonic Orchestra.

His experience in the pit with other musicians was valuable despite his realization that "even in the world's foremost orchestra real artistry is not at all required, that purely mechanical precision and safety is the most

important requirement, and everything else is superfluous and not desired." He was still a member of the orchestra in 1897 when Gustav Mahler was appointed its conductor and director. Many times during Mahler's tenure, Schmidt was called upon to fill the role of principal cellist, although he was never compensated appropriately for the task or appointed to the position. In fact, the cellist was caught up in the throes of orchestral politics until he left the ensemble in 1912.

Schmidt began teaching cello at his alma mater in 1901 but had already begun writing music in earnest, completing his first opera, his first symphony, and a handful of chamber works, most of which he destroyed when he was older. In contrast to his career as an orchestral musician, Schmidt's tenure in academia progressed fairly well, from his position as the school's cello teacher to a stint as piano instructor and on through his appointment as professor of counterpoint and composition. He finally became privy councilor of the Musikhochschule in 1926 before resigning a year later due to repeated illnesses. Despite that, the teaching staff conferred the title of vice chancellor upon him as a reward for his past achievements, a title he held until 1931, when he stepped down to teach a composition class and a special class in modern piano literature.

A year later, his beloved daughter Emma died while giving birth, and this calamity devastated Schmidt. Pouring all the grief he felt into composing, he created the single most moving and shattering work in his oeuvre—his Symphony no. 4. Again and again in this autobiographical, one-movement work, Schmidt seems to have worked through his bleak despair, only to have his hopes dashed, repeatedly and with ever-greater intensity, on the rocks of destiny. Completed six years before he died, this work expresses a loneliness that is awesome in its eloquence.

Schmidt's other major composition, the oratorio *Das Buch mit sieben Siegeln (The Book with Seven Seals)*, was written in 1938, a year before his death, and is considered by many to be his crowning achievement. Dedicated to the Philharmonic Society on its 125th anniversary and based on the biblical Apocalypse, this is a concentrated piece of post-Wagnerian power and romanticism that shines with artistic brilliance.

Orchestral
Symphony no. 4
what to buy: [Zubin Mehta, cond.; Vienna Philharmonic

Orchestra] (Decca 440615) ♪ ♪ ♪ ♪♪

This early 1970s recording is *the* version of Schmidt's most important work. The degree to which the composer's heart was broken by his daughter's death is evident in the performance heard here. Mehta's recording is aptly paired with his performance of Mahler's Symphony no. 2—*Resurrection,* which will pull you back out of the depths in a glorious manner.

Vocal
Das Buch mit sieben Siegeln (The Book With Seven Seals)
what to buy: [Sylvia Greenberg, soprano; Carolyn Watkinson, contralto; Peter Schreier, tenor, Thomas Moser, tenor; Robert Holl, bass; Kurt Rydl, bass; Lothar Zagrosek, cond.; Vienna State Opera Chorus; Austrian Radio Symphony Orchestra] (Orfeo 143862) ♪ ♪ ♪♪

Here we have a great piece, a very good performance, and mediocre sonics. Schreier is the most impressive soloist, but the overall strength of the music is what carries the day.

influences: Anton Bruckner, Gustav Mahler, Hans Pfitzner, Max Reger

Gary Barton and Garaud MacTaggart

Alfred Schnittke
Born Alfred Garriyevich Shnitke, November 24, 1934, in Engels, German Volga Republic. Died August 3, 1998, in Hamburg, Germany.

period: Twentieth century

Alfred Schnittke first started receiving his due in the Western world just as the Iron Curtain started to lift; prior to that he eked out an existence writing soundtracks for Soviet-era films and teaching. His later compositions feature a non-cloying spirituality that can hide a harder, serialist edge at times. In that respect Schnittke's music can be compared to scores by Sofia Gubaidulina and Edison Denisov, other Russian composers who were once condemned by their own government for their striking non-conformism.

In 1946, when his father was stationed in Vienna as a translator and interpreter with the Soviet Army, young

Adolphe Sax:
In 1815, when Adolphe Sax (born Antoine-Joseph Sax) was one year old, his father started a factory in Brussels, Belgium that made various brass and woodwind instruments. This development eventually gave Sax an understanding of the processes by which such devices were made. When he was twenty-six years old, and after studying flute and clarinet at Brussels Conservatoire, Sax began work on what would become the saxophone. His primary goal was to create an instrumental sound that could bridge the winds and strings in the orchestra and, incidentally, replace the quieter double reeds that were used in French military bands of the day.

Controversy surrounded his most important innovations; Sax's modifications to the bass clarinet were so extreme that most musicians referred to it as a new instrument, and his use of the piston valves in brass instruments was received cooly. This reaction may have been partially influenced by the established instrument companies, who didn't want to see a newcomer entering their territory; there were legends of attempts on Sax's life, and the burning of his factory was allegedly funded by some of his major competitors.

A great promoter of his own products, Sax organized events at which bands with his instruments would compete against other manufacturers in order to see which group was loudest (his always won.) There were also advertising campaigns claiming that the playing of saxophones improved one's health. His miraculous recovery from mouth cancer was occasionally ascribed to this phenomenon. After obtaining a monopoly for supplying the French army with instruments, Sax's company won various medals at the Expositions of 1844, 1849, 1851, 1855, and 1867. He also went bankrupt twice (in 1856 and 1873) because of constant legal challenges to his patents. In all, Sax's inventions include over sixty instruments, yet despite his hard-won successes, he abandoned his businesses in 1877 and died penniless in 1894.

While modern listeners are more apt to associate the saxophone with jazz than with classical music, it is important to note that a number of composers have written pieces placing the instrument within a variety of settings. Claude Debussy wrote his *Rhapsodie* for Saxophone and Orchestra, while Alexander Glazunov composed not only his Concerto in E-flat Major for Alto Saxophone and Orchestra (op. 109) but arranged it for saxophone quartet. More recent composers who have written for the instrument include Luciano Berio (*Sequenza VIIb* for Soprano Saxophone), Paul Creston (Sonata for Saxophone and Piano, op. 19), and Philip Glass (Concerto for Saxophone Quartet). A listing of prominent classical saxophone soloists in the twentieth century would have to include Sigurd Rascher, Marcel Mule, Paul Brodie, and John Harle, while the Rova Saxophone Quartet, the Amherst Saxophone Quartet, and the Vienna Saxophone Quartet are among the multitude of current groups featuring the instrument.

Kevin Kazmierczak and Garaud MacTaggart

Alfred Schnittke began studying music seriously. After returning to Russia with his family, he continued these studies, finally gaining admittance to the Moscow Conservatory in 1953 and attaining a postgraduate degree in 1961. By that time he had also written his first big composition, *Nagasaki,* an oratorio with atonal elements which attracted the attention of Soviet-era critics at the Union of Composers who condemned it in 1958 for his experimental leanings.

After his graduation, Schnittke began teaching at his alma mater, creating scores for the Soviet film industry, and writing essays on music that dealt mainly with issues closely associated with modernist tendencies. He also began a deeper, more independent-minded study of contemporary Western composing techniques, including the serialism in which he had only dabbled during his Conservatory years. The initial results of Schnittke's experiments in this direction—the Sonata no. 1 for Violin and Piano (1963) and the Concerto for Violin and Orchestra (1966)—once again engaged the ire of official state music journals and other adherents of "Socialist Realism."

Despite the criticism, he continued his explorations, poring over scores by members of the Second Viennese School (Schoenberg, Berg, and Webern in particular) as well as those by the Russian expatriate, Igor Stravinsky. The end result was a gradual weaning from serial procedures, though Schnittke would never abandon them totally. His Sonata no. 2 for Violin and Piano (*Quasi una Sonata*) dates from 1968 and unveils some of the approaches he would employ in future compositions, meshing aleatory elements with quotation techniques that drew upon the music of the past.

When Schnittke's mother died, he was consumed with grief and, in 1975, composed the first of his large-scale choral works, a Requiem Mass that was a fundamentally tonal score. The Quintet for Piano and Strings (1976) is another important work from this period, one which would further detail the composer's mourning process when he arranged and expanded the score to create *In Memoriam . . .* in 1978. Schnittke's music after that appeared to become even more emotional, affecting a darker orchestration that seemed obsessed with adding a historical and religious context to an essentially modern viewpoint. In that sense, his second symphony (subtitled *St. Florian*) can be seen as a further advance into this sonic territory. Commissioned in 1979 by the BBC, it was originally meant to be paired in a program with Anton Bruckner's Mass in E Minor; Schnittke actually visited the church at St. Florian (Austria) where Bruckner had been organist and was buried, in search of inspiration. Schnittke would later refer to this work as "a mass embedded in a symphony."

During the 1980s he expanded his palette into ever more personal and religious areas following his conversion to Roman Catholicism in 1982. Schnittke began by including Medieval and Renaissance church music into the structure of his second and third string quartets (1980 and 1983), delving into ancient Russian chant for his fourth and fifth symphonies (1983 and 1985), and drawing upon the vocal tradition of the Russian church for the *Concerto for Chorus* of 1985 and the twelve *Penitential Psalms* from 1987.

Schnittke, in 1985, experienced the first of the heart attacks which would sap his strength and eventually kill him. Under the eased travel restrictions of the Gorbachev era he moved to Germany in 1990 and began teaching composition at the Hochschule für Musik und Theater, but suffered a heart attack the following year. Upon his recovery, a sense of mortality probably affected the composition of his last four symphonies (nos. 6–9), causing him to write in an ever leaner, more austere manner. At the time of writing there is no recording of Schnittke's ninth symphony, a work from 1997 that was written after his third heart attack and is purported to contain some of his most severe orchestral thoughts.

Orchestral
Concerto no. 2 for Cello and Orchestra
what to buy: [Alexander Ivashkin, cello; Valéri Polyansky, cond.; Russian State Symphony Orchestra] (Chandos 9722) ♪ ♪ ♪ ♪ ♪

Even though Schnittke played the piano he displayed a marked preference for string instruments in his scores, appreciating their tonal freedom. Such is the case with this large-scale, almost Mahler-esque concerto he wrote for Mstislav Rostropovich in 1990. Ivashkin's control over his instrument rivals that of the older virtuoso, and the engineers have created a sonic environment that casts the deep, woody tones of the cello into the thorny thickets of Schnittke's music with nary a problem. The composer's sardonic sense of humor comes to the fore in the accompanying *(K)ein Sommernachtstraum (Not A Midsummer Night's Dream),* which was written more than ten years after his *Suite in the Old Style* and takes its basic joke/premise even further by twisting Mozartean lines into dissonant territory.

what to buy next: [Mstislav Rostropovich, cello; Seiji Ozawa, cond.; London Symphony Orchestra] (Sony Classics 48241) ♪ ♪ ♪ ♪

In some ways this might be a better introduction to the piece than the Ivashkin performance (see above), especially when you have the dedicatee playing cello, and sonics which display the well-delineated lines of the LSO. If you try this rendition of the work first and like it, then the Ivashkin rendering, darker, heavier, and somehow more "Russian," may be even more appealing. The best interpretation on the disc is actually reserved for *In Memoriam . . .*, with Rostropovich conducting the LSO in a piece for which the orchestra's clarity and subtle tone-production work are even finer.

In Memoriam . . . for Orchestra
what to buy: [Valéri Polyansky, cond.; Russian State Symphony Orchestra] (Chandos 9466) ♪ ♪ ♪ ♪♪

Polyansky's cycle of Schnittke's orchestral works is turning out to be the benchmark for all future performances. Certainly this large-scale outgrowth of the composer's most tautly argued chamber work (the Quintet for Piano and Strings) deserves the kind of well-recorded production Chandos has given it. Interpretively speaking, Polyansky slows down the pace when compared to Rostropovich (see above) and the results, especially in the deranged little waltz of the final movement, are hard to argue with. The disc also displays a fine mix of the composer's other material including a chamber work for trombone and organ from 1983 (*Sound and Resound*) and first recordings of the early *Music for Piano and Chamber Orchestra* (with Gennady Rozhdestvensky conducting) and the Septet of 1982 (played by soloists from the Bolshoi Theatre Orchestra).

Chamber
Sonata no. 2 for Violin and Piano (*Quasi una Sonata*)
what to buy: [Mark Lubotsky, violin; Ralf Gothoni, piano] (Ondine 800) ♪ ♪ ♪ ♪♪

By meshing ideas from soundtracks he wrote during the 1960s, Schnittke created the *Suite in the Old Style* for Violin and Piano in 1972, a piece of striking simplicity and charm that harkens back to early nineteenth century drawing rooms. Lubotsky and Gothoni play this most accessible work right after traversing the twelve-note rows of the composer's Sonata no. 1 for Violin and Piano and the even more forbidding Sonata no. 2 for Violin and Piano. This last work marked a stylistic turning point in Schnittke's development, and uses space and phrasing to chilling effect. From this point on, the composer's serious works, which were never terribly light in the first

place, became even more intense—and, ultimately, rewarding.

Quintet for Piano and Strings
what to buy: [Gary Graffman, piano; Lark Quartet, ensemble] (Arabesque 26707) ♪ ♪ ♪ ♪ ♪

This may very well be the most important piano quintet of the late twentieth century. It is certainly one of the finest chamber works written in the last fifty years, packed with slow-release emotion that builds and builds before resolving in an eerily calm movement marked *Moderato pastorale*. Graffman is spectacular in his deceptively simple role while the Lark Quartet provide their own highlight moments. Schnittke's second and third string quartets (also heard here) are the most-performed of his four essays in that medium, and the Larks handle the challenges proposed by the composer quite well.

worth searching for: [Constantine Orbelian, piano; Moscow String Quartet, ensemble] (Russian Disc 10031) ♪ ♪ ♪ ♪♪

The solo piano intro is a harbinger of the glacially slow tempos favored in this recording, taking 2:40 as opposed to Graffman's 2:00 (see above). Instead of feeling slack, however, this performance has a tension to it which, while it doesn't quite supplant Graffman and the Lark's reading, is quite effective. An argument can be made that the strings, if anything, are even more convincing in this rendition. Pairing Schnittke's quintet with the lone piano quintet by Dmitri Shostakovich (in G Minor, op. 57) is an inspired bit of programming that is carried through by taut, well-thought-out performances in both works.

Vocal
Concerto for Chorus
what to buy: [Valéri Polyansky, cond.; Russian State Symphonic Cappella, choir] (Chandos 9332) ♪ ♪ ♪ ♪

Using the *Book of Lamentations* by a tenth century Armenian poet as a starting point, Schnittke also delved into the past to touch upon the Russian Orthodox chants of the late nineteenth century for musical inspiration. The resulting work is a deeply moving testament to faith in hard times and Polyansky's choir members are convincing advocates for it.

what to buy next: [Stefan Parkman, cond.; Danish

National Radio Choir] (Chandos 9126) ♪ ♪ ♪♪

Lacking the last bit of Slavic heft to make this recording a first choice for the concerto, Parkman and company have included a fine performance of Schnittke's 1981 choral piece *Minnesang* almost as a way of making amends. This score is a work for seven vocalists split into two groups which draws its inspiration from thirteenth century German troubadours and, as such, is a splendid companion for the main attraction.

influences: Sofia Gubaidulina, Dmitri Shostakovich, Edison Denisov, Olivier Messiaen

Mathilde August

Arnold Schoenberg

Born Arnold Franz Walter Schönberg, September 13, 1874, in Vienna, Austria. Died July 13, 1951, in Los Angeles, CA.

period: Twentieth century

More influential as a revolutionary theorist and teacher than as a writer of music, Arnold Schoenberg sought to break away from the constraints of tonality. The result was a method using a specific series of twelve notes (and their derivatives) as the basis for his compositions. This twelve-tone, or serial, technique was employed by Schoenberg starting in the 1920s and influenced generations of composers after him.

Schoenberg learned to play the violin and began composing short chamber works before he entered his teens. He left school in 1891 after his father died and began working as a bank clerk to help support the family. Schoenberg did not desert his muse, however, and soon taught himself to play cello, picking up the rudiments of music theory by reading basic texts on harmony. Alexander von Zemlinsky, the conductor of an amateur orchestra that Schoenberg joined in 1894, became a seminal influence on the younger man, tutoring him in counterpoint and other formal compositional techniques.

By 1896 Schoenberg had left his position at the bank; he spent the rest of his life attempting to make a living with music. He began by directing small choral groups, arranging operettas for theater performances, and working in cabaret ensembles. Schoenberg's composing slowly started to evolve, but before he found his own, highly original voice, his works (like those of many of his

contemporaries) were heavily impacted by Richard Wagner's treatment of harmony. This was apparent in Schoenberg's first semi-mature piece—the sextet version of *Verklärte Nacht* (Transfigured Night) from 1899, which was drenched in Wagnerian colors.

In 1901 Schoenberg married Zemlinsky's sister and moved to Berlin, where he managed to show Richard Strauss sections of his latest works-in-progress—the secular oratorio *Gurrelieder* and the lushly scored tone poem *Pelleas und Melisande.* Strauss was suitably impressed and recommended the young composer for a teaching post at the Stern Conservatory in Berlin. Shortly after starting his new position, Schoenberg completed *Pelleas und Melisande,* but it took nearly a decade before *Gurrelieder* was fully orchestrated and performed.

Meanwhile, he returned to Vienna in 1903, met Mahler (whom he loved and admired), and began teaching in earnest. In 1904 two students who were later to find their own paths to greatness—Anton Webern and Alban Berg—joined Schoenberg's composition class. He also began working with the Rosé Quartet, who later gave the premieres of both his first string quartet and his first chamber symphony. Around 1908 Schoenberg hit the wall of conventional tonality and could go no further. He began writing pieces without a tonal center, but when audiences heard the first fruits of his new style, they reacted badly. His music was almost universally despised, and only his little band of close supporters (including Webern and Berg) remained true. Schoenberg had also begun codifying his ideas in the *Harmonielehre* (Manual of Harmony), the first in a series of texts he would write on various musical building blocks.

In 1911 Schoenberg and his family moved back to Berlin, where he rejoined the Stern Conservatory. Public reaction to his compositions was still unkind for the most part, but Schoenberg continued probing and expanding his musical frontiers. Things appeared to change for the better in 1912, when the first performance of *Pierrot lunaire* (Moonstruck Pierrot) received generally favorable reviews. This momentary good fortune changed with the outbreak of World War I, which necessitated another move back to Vienna for Schoenberg's family. In December 1915 Schoenberg joined the armed forces, but due to his asthma he was released from duty in October 1916.

The next few years proved to be an artistic crucible for

the composer. From the time he left the army until 1930, despite physical and fiscal hardships, he pressed on toward a totally new method of working, further honing the concepts expressed in *Harmonielehre* and creating a veritable revolution in music. The initial results of Schoenberg's efforts could be heard in the five *Pieces for Piano*, op. 23, and the Serenade, op. 24, where conventional tonality was abolished and replaced with a system relying on the twelve tones of an octave and their relationships. Once he had the basic process formulated, Schoenberg proceeded to write some of his most groundbreaking music, including the Wind Quintet, op. 26, Variations for Orchestra, op. 31, and portions of the opera *Moses und Aron*.

At the same time Schoenberg's artistic life was going through transformations, his personal reality was changing as well. His first wife died in 1923, and Schoenberg remarried the following year. By 1925 he had taken a position at the Prussian Academy of Arts in Berlin, but the rise of Adolf Hitler and the Nazi Party would make life in Germany intolerable for the composer and his family. The German Ministry of Education announced the impending removal of Jewish "elements" from the Academy in 1933, and Schoenberg rightly assumed that he was among the targets. The family left Berlin that year and, after a brief stay in France, moved to the United States.

The Malkin Conservatory in Boston was the first school to offer the new exile a position, but Schoenberg would move to Los Angeles in 1934 to take up teaching posts, first at the University of Southern California and two years later at the University of California at Los Angeles. The balance of his life was spent in academia, where he continued to teach despite his worsening health. Schoenberg's works from this period include his fourth string quartet, the String Trio, the Violin Concerto, the Piano Concerto, and *A Survivor from Warsaw*, a piece for narrator, orchestra, and male chorus. He also revised some of his earlier scores, tinkering with the *Five Pieces for Orchestra*, originally completed in 1909, and the second Chamber Symphony, begun in 1906.

Schoenberg became an American citizen in 1941, received the Award of Merit from the National Institute of Arts and Letters in 1947, and was elected honorary president of the Israel Academy of Music in 1951, just before he died. He was the most influential theorist and teacher of the twentieth century, and his ideas are still with us today. Schoenberg once said, "The tempest

Peter Schickele:
Peter Schickele was the son of an agricultural economist and spent most of his teenage years growing up in Fargo, North Dakota. He and his younger brother were both huge admirers of Spike Jones, the comedic bandleader whose skewed arrangements of classics featured bells, whistles, and other extraneous noises. Those antics inspired the youngsters to model the music played by their own basement quartet (Jerky Jens and His Balmy Brothers) after that of Jones's groups. Other early influences on Schickele's humor (at least as it relates to classical music) included Gerard Hoffnung, Anna Russell, and Victor Borge.

In 1957 Schickele managed to gain admission to the Juilliard School of Music, where he studied composition with Vincent Persichetti and William Bergsma, aiming toward eventually making a living as a college professor. Two years later he became a composer-in-residence in the Los Angeles school system, writing music for high school ensembles under the auspices of a Ford Foundation grant. He returned to Juilliard in 1961, joining the faculty there and moving up the academic ladder from working in the school's extension division to instructing the regular and pre-college divisions. Schickele finally gave up his career as a teacher in 1965, starting a new one as a freelance musician and arranger.

One of the first things he did, with the aid of his friend the conductor Jorge Meister, was rent Town Hall in New York City and put on the initial public concert featuring the music of the last and least offspring of Johann Sebastian Bach, his putative son P.D.Q. Bach. The idea for the character was an outgrowth of Schickele's fascination with the pompousness associated with many classical music concerts. In 1959, he and some of his friends at Juilliard started a five-year run of concerts spoofing these pretensions by using P.D.Q. Bach as the vehicle for their good-natured satire. After the Town Hall show was finished, the results were released as an album (*An Evening With P.D.Q. Bach*, Vanguard 79195), unleashing a franchise that would support Schickele for decades to come.

Other albums followed, including a hilarious takeoff on classical radio programming (*P.D.Q. Bach on the Air with Professor Peter Schickele*, Vanguard 79268) which included spurious works along the lines of the *Echo Sonata for Two Unfriendly Groups of Instruments* and the entertaining parody *What's My Melodic Line?* Schickele revisited this topic in 1991 with his Grammy Award-winning *WTWP, Classical Talkity-Talk Radio* (Telarc 80295), which lampooned public radio mainstays *(Pledge Plea)* and mounted musical caricatures like *Four Folk Song Upsettings* and the *"Safe" Sextet*. In a case of life imitating art, there is now a real radio program called *Schickele Mix*, which is distributed by Public Radio International.

While Schickele is best known among the general public for his comedic activities, he has managed to engage in more serious-minded ones as well. At the same time he was springing P.D.Q. Bach upon the art music world, Schickele was also writing film scores (*Crazy Quilt*), music for theater projects (the notorious, nude, off-Broadway production of *Oh, Calcutta!*), and arrangements for folk singers Joan Baez and Buffy Sainte-Marie. Those wishing to hear Schickele in a more straightforward, non-farcical context should look for performances of his first and fifth string quartets by the Audubon String Quartet (Centaur 2505), or sample the second string quartet, Sextet for Strings, and Quintet no. 2 for Piano and Strings found on *Schickele on a Lark*, (Arabesque 6719).

Garaud MacTaggart

raised about my music does not rest upon my ideas, but exists because of the dissonances. Dissonances are but consonances that appear later among the overtones." Though it is only recently that we have become aware of other, equally valid ways to accomplish the same ends he sought, Schoenberg let the genie out the bottle, and it will never be put back in.

Orchestral
Verklärte Nacht (Transfigured Night) for String Sextet (or String Orchestra), op. 4
what to buy: [Herbert von Karajan, cond.; Berlin Philharmonic Orchestra] (Deutsche Grammophon 457721) ♪ ♪ ♪ ♪₈

Schoenberg's lush writing for strings in this early masterpiece is complemented by the Berlin Philharmonic's legendary string section under the guidance of von Karajan. For years, this performance has been the standard-bearer by which all other orchestral renditions of this score must be judged. Equally fine is the recording of the composer's impressive *Pelleas und Melisande* that completes this great disc of pre-serial Schoenberg.

what to buy next: [Orpheus Chamber Orchestra] (Deutsche Grammophon 429233) ♪ ♪ ♪₈

Here this conductorless orchestra gives one of the best overviews of Schoenberg's orchestral craft, with three high-quality works (*Verklärte Nacht* and the two Chamber Symphonies) from three different periods in Schoenberg's career.

Pelleas und Melisande for Orchestra, op. 5
what to buy: [Christoph Eschenbach, cond.; Houston Symphony Orchestra] (Koch International Classics 7316) ♪ ♪ ♪₈

Schoenberg's early scores are surprisingly ripe and luxurious to modern ears, although they initially caused quite a ruckus among audiences. Balancing out the album is Anton Webern's *Passacaglia*, a rich, romantic essay that predates his falling under Schoenberg's spell.

Chamber
Verklärte Nacht (Transfigured Night) for String Sextet (or String Orchestra) op. 4
what to buy: [members of the Ensemble InterContemporain] (Sony Classical 48465) ♪ ♪ ♪ ♪

This is the surprisingly lush-sounding sextet version of

Verklärte Nacht, an apt counterweight to the orchestral account by the Orpheus Chamber Orchestra above. The other pieces on the album—the Suite op. 29 and the *Three Pieces for Chamber Orchestra*—also feature performances by the full Ensemble InterContemporain, this time conducted by Pierre Boulez.

what to buy next: [Walter Trampler, viola; Yo-Yo Ma, cello; Juilliard String Quartet] (Sony Classical 47690) ♪ ♪ ♪₈

While this ad hoc grouping has not worked as long or consistently with this score as the Ensemble InterContemporain may have, their performance has an admirable tautness and intensity that reflects their own hard-won skills. They have paired this work with Schoenberg's later masterwork, the String Trio op. 45, and that may tempt some folks to opt for this set rather than the other one.

various piano works
what to buy: [Maurizio Pollini, piano] (Deutsche Grammophon 423249) ♪ ♪ ♪ ♪

Pollini, master technician of the piano that he is, tackles these works as if they were beautifully constructed engineering problems. His approach to Schoenberg's scores, especially with the six *Little Pieces for Piano*, op. 19, where the composer was attempting to create a new method of building his musical structures, and the five *Pieces for Piano,* op. 23, one of the first of his twelve-tone works, is entirely valid. There is important poetry here, albeit poetry that not everyone will find to their liking.

what to buy next: [Paul Jacobs, piano] (Nonesuch 71309) ♪ ♪ ♪₈

These are solid performances of important music, and viable alternatives to the Pollini set. Jacobs was an impressive pianist, especially at home in Debussy's world, and that perspective—strange as it may seem—informs his playing here.

Vocal
Pierrot lunaire (Moonstruck Pierrot) for Speaker and Instruments, op. 21

Arnold Schoenberg

what to buy: [Christine Schäfer, narrator; Pierre Boulez, cond.; Ensemble InterContemporain, orch.] (Deutsche Grammophon 457630) ♪ ♪ ♪ ♪♪

Written during one of the most productive periods of Schoenberg's life, *Pierrot lunaire* is a stage piece of considerable power and one that Boulez has had considerable experience with over the years. This is a much more lived-in performance than the one on his earlier collaboration with Yvonne Minton and an all-star cast of musicians (still available on Sony 48466). Schäfer does a wonderful job of hovering in that particular Schoenbergian world between song and speech (sprechgesang), and the recording is truly splendid, allowing every instrumental nuance to come through to full effect. The rarely heard *Herzgewächse,* based on a poem by Maurice Maeterlinck, and Schoenberg's setting of Lord Byron's angry polemic *Ode to Napoleon Bonaparte,* are fitting companion pieces to *Pierrot lunaire.*

what to buy next: [Jan DeGaetani, narrator; Alexis Weisberg, cond.; Contemporary Chamber Ensemble, orch.] (Elektra/Nonesuch 79237) ♪ ♪ ♪♪

DeGaetani gives a very good performance here and also does fine work (with pianist Gilbert Kalish) on the composer's song cycle *Das Buch der hängenden Gärten* (Book of the Hanging Gardens), op. 15, that completes the album.

Gurrelieder for Solo Voices, Orchestra and Chorus
what to buy: [Werner Klemperer, narrator; Jessye Norman, soprano; Tatiana Troyanos, mezzo-soprano; James McCracken, tenor; Kim Scown, tenor; David Arnold, baritone; Seiji Ozawa, cond.; Boston Symphony Orchestra; Tanglewood Festival Chorus] (Philips 412511) ♪ ♪ ♪ ♪♪

Ozawa's "live" recording of Schoenberg's oratorio won all sorts of awards when it came out in the late 1970s, and it still serves as a rebuttal to those who don't believe that the composer ever wrote a beautiful score.

influences: Anton von Webern, Alban Berg, Roberto Gerhard, Nikos Skalkottas

Gerald Brennan and Garaud MacTaggart

Franz Schubert
Born Franz Peter Schubert on January 31, 1797, in Vienna, Austria. Died November 19, 1828, in Vienna, Austria.

period: Romantic

Franz Schubert ranks among the greatest melodists of music. Despite a shockingly short life (he died at age thirty-one), he was extremely prolific from his teens onward, especially in the writing of lieder and other sorts of songs. Schubert's two great lieder cycles—*Die schöne Müllerin* and *Winterreise*—and such unconnected masterpieces of song as the vividly evocative *Erlköng* and *Gretchen am Spinnrad* were what he was most admired for during his life, offering tunefulness, rich piano accompaniments, ideal proportions, and concision of expression. After his death, his symphonies and chamber music gradually earned attention from subsequent generations.

Franz Schubert was born in what was then a suburb of Vienna to a Moravian peasant schoolteacher and a Viennese cook. He was the twelfth of fourteen children, though only five lived past infancy. At the age of eleven, he joined the court chapel choir at the Imperial and Royal Seminary as a mezzo-soprano, and received his education there as well. In 1814 he began five years of working for his father at the little school which was run out of the Schubert home. That same year he composed the much-admired and highly original lied *Gretchen am Spinnrade;* the fertile year of 1815 (when he turned eighteen) brought 145 songs, most notably the brilliant *Der Erlkönig.*

Influenced by Beethoven in some respects, and certainly inspired by him, Schubert nonetheless very much went his own way. Conscious of laboring in the shadow of Beethoven, he often squeezed his intensely lyrical and spontaneous works into sonata-allegro form, which they didn't always fit. In longer works, he had a penchant for rambling structures. While he was not known as a symphonic composer, in Vienna (arguably the musical capitol of Europe at the time) Schubert became much admired as a composer of songs, thanks in no small part to the advocacy of baritone Johann Michael Vogl, who frequently programmed Schubert's works.

Of Schubert's two great song cycles, *Die schöne Müllerin (The Fair Maid of the Mill)* is the more immediately appealing and approachable. It sets twenty poems of Wilhelm Müller relating the romantic tale of a simple man who falls in love and then commits suicide in despair. Müller's original set of poems included a prologue and an epilogue that Schubert omitted, preferring to forego their arch condescension towards the main character and instead take his plight seriously, adeptly depicting his shifting moods. The cycle ends up, in some respects, being almost as much about the brook that's a constant in the scenery and imagery of the poems—and the instrument of the protagonist's death.

Much darker, more psychologically profound, and vastly more personal to the composer, is *Winterreise (Winter Journey)*, also setting poems of Wilhelm Müller. Few connoisseurs of song will argue with the contention that this is the greatest of all song cycles, but the way the music amplifies its dark emotions upset Schubert's circle of friends and admirers when they heard it; such intensity in this form was then unheard of. In the twenty-fourth and final song, the heartbroken protagonist comes across an old man, shunned by people and beset by growling dogs, playing a hurdy-gurdy with stolid determination. The image of music as eternal solace for the lonely offers a final glimmer of hope, or at least peace, in an otherwise bleak cycle. Even within the dominant mood of despair mingled with resigned resolution, Schubert finds enough variety to give each song individual characterization. He does this not only with the harmonies and melodies and tempos, but also the style of the piano accompaniment; the pianist is practically an equal partner with the singer.

The tales of Schubert's poverty were blown out of proportion. He certainly was far from rich, and sometimes had to rely on his friends' support, but over the last twelve years of his life his published works brought him over $12,000—more than subsistence money back then. After leaving his father's school for good in 1818, he worked almost entirely as a composer, leading a Bohemian lifestyle of composing, socializing, and concertizing at the private evening performances devoted to his music; these were organized by his circle of admirers and known as Schubertiads. The major exceptions to these activities were his two stints of teaching (1818 and 1824) at the Esterházy estate in Hungary—also the only trips he made far from Vienna.

Similarly, it's widely believed he suffered from syphilis (some say from a prostitute, others from an Esterházy serving girl while teaching); it's also strongly averred by some (most famously by Maynard Solomon) that he was homosexual. No insurmountable proof of either of these positions is available, and some accounts seem to contradict them. Certainly he didn't die of venereal disease; it was typhoid fever that ended his life.

After his death, Schubert was venerated by the following generation of composers. Schumann hailed him while moonlighting as a music critic; Liszt was fascinated by the *"Wanderer" Fantasy* and based the structure of his lone piano sonata on it. This enthusiasm did not particularly spread to the public at large until later, however; the focus of concerts at that time was still largely on living composers (the iconic Beethoven being the major exception). Schubert's Symphony no. 9 in C Major (*The Great*) had to be rediscovered. Its posthumous premiere by the Leipzig Gewandhaus Orchestra in 1839 was not followed up on until eleven years later in Vienna because the work was considered too long and difficult.

In 1865 the conductor Johann Herbeck discovered the two completed movements of Schubert's "Unfinished" Symphony in the private collection of the composer Anselm Hüttenbrenner (to whom Schubert had apparently given them in gratitude for having received a Diploma of Honorary Membership in the Music Society of Graz), they caused a great stir after their Vienna premiere that Autumn, thirty-seven years after Schubert's death. It turned out that he left a great many works incomplete, often for unfathomable reasons, but given his prolific nature, it perhaps seemed to him to be of no import if all his loose ends were not tied up. This ended up fueling his legend, though it's worth pointing out that the assumption that his eighth symphony was interrupted by death was long ago disproven, as it was actually written in 1822. Certainly it is true that Schubert achieved far greater fame in death than he did in life, which is why musicologists are so fascinated by those loose ends, and occasionally attempt to tie them up themselves. Schubert is now seen as one of the pillars of the Romantic era.

Orchestral
Symphonies nos. 1–6, 8–9 (complete)
what to buy: [Karl Böhm, cond.; Berlin Philharmonic Orchestra] (Deutsche Grammophon 419318) ♪ ♪ ♪ ♪₇

This four-CD set, recorded at various points in the 1960s and '70s, follows a mainstream approach. Böhm is sterner than some, but warm and flexible compared to most. The playfulness and lightness of the early works is honored if not indulged, and the Eighth and, especially, the Ninth rank among the finest recordings of those oft-heard works. The Berlin Philharmonic sounds wonderfully rich and full (no cutting down on the string sections here!) yet quite precise enough to offer clarity.

Symphonies nos. 3, 5–6
what to buy: [Thomas Beecham, cond.; Royal Philharmonic Orchestra] (EMI Classics 66999) ♪ ♪ ♪ ♪

The genial charm of Beecham in these early works is so great that it's hard not to forgive his tinkering with the text (he makes some small cuts). With the RPO playing at its peak, these 1955–1959 recordings have been classics of Schubertian grace—if not without a certain gravitas—since they were released.

Symphony no. 8 in B Minor (*Unfinished,* D. 759)
what to buy: [Bruno Walter, cond.; New York Philharmonic Orchestra] (Sony Classical 64487) ♪ ♪ ♪ ♪ ♪

This 1958 recording captures this famous work's mercurial moods vividly. The strings are plush without slipping into syrupiness, and if there are tiny slips in orchestral execution, Walter's vision of the piece is so gripping, his speeds so perfect, that they are easily overlooked. In Walter's hands, the *Unfinished* sounds complete. The package includes a Fifth that some will find too relaxed (and a fine reading of Beethoven's third *Leonore Overture*).

what to buy next: [Herbert von Karajan, cond.; Berlin Philharmonic Orchestra] (EMI Classics 66105) ♪ ♪ ♪ ♪ ♪

Only this CD of Karajan's four-CD traversal of nos. 1–6 and 8–9 is currently in EMI's U.S. catalog, alas (the rest can be found on import and are worth seeking out, if not on this level of excellence). He clearly aims for emotionally shattering transcendence, and collectors sympathetic to his trademark glossy Berlin sound will find it unparalleled. The piece comes with a fine Ninth featuring dramatic third and fourth movements—recommendable to those who enjoy a Beethovenian interpretation.

Symphony no. 9 in C Major (*The Great,* D. 944)
what to buy: [Wilhelm Furtwängler, cond.; Berlin Philharmonic Orchestra] (Deutsche Grammophon 447439) ♪ ♪ ♪ ♪ ♪

The sonic deficiencies that usually scare non-fanatics away from classic Furtwängler performances are absent

from this 1951 studio recording, and neither does his dislike of studio recording show here. This performance is the epitome of the grand, Romantic interpretive style in this work, mastering its tricky structure with superbly balanced proportions and offering riveting expressiveness. It's paired with an equally revelatory reading of Franz Joseph Haydn's Symphony no. 88. There are several other superb Furtwängler readings of this favorite work, including two compellingly urgent wartime concert recordings, but for once the "official" release is preferable.

what to buy next: [Charles Mackerras, cond.; Orchestra of the Age of Enlightenment] (Virgin Classics Veritas 61806) ♪ ♪ ♪ ♪

Mackerras offers the best period-instrument performance, and also takes a rather brisk approach. It's invigorating rather than merely hectic, tempo relationships being quite convincing, and the change in balance between the strings and other sections is refreshing. Mackerras also leads his forces through Schubert's *Unfinished* and fifth symphonies as well as the ballet music from *Rosamunde*.

[*Bruno Walter Edition*; Bruno Walter, cond.; Columbia Symphony Orchestra] (Sony Classical 64478) ♪ ♪ ♪ ♪

Walter's is definitely the friendliest reading of this epic piece. For some, it may lack sufficient intensity, but others will find its warmth most attractive. The 1959 sound is a bit muddy, but adequate. As filler, there are three monaural excerpts from the incidental music to *Rosamunde*.

worth searching for: [Sergiu Celibidache, cond.; Munich Philharmonic Orchestra] (EMI Classics 56527) ♪ ♪ ♪ ♪

Schumann famously referred to the Ninth's "heavenly length," and as led by Celibidache it truly fits that description. He favors broad tempos (though not to the extreme of his Bruckner recordings with the same orchestra) and luminescent orchestral tone, and this concert recording is most effective, and less eccentric than some of his efforts.

incidental music to *Rosamunde* (D. 797)
what to buy: [Ileana Cotrubas, soprano; Willi Boskovsky, cond.; Staatskapelle Dresden, orch.; Leipzig Radio Choir] (Berlin Classics 9004) ♪ ♪ ♪ ♪

Schubert had little success writing for the stage; ironically, the only such work to cling to the fringes of the repertoire is not one of his operas, but incidental music for a play. Most orchestras only play three or four of the purely instrumental movements, but on this complete performance, Cotrubas and the Leipzig Radio Choir make fine contributions to the rarely programmed movements. With few classic recordings of the complete score, this less ballyhooed reading suffices quite nicely. As filler for the program, there is the Overture to *Die Zauberharfe* (D. 644) that is sometimes substituted for the *Rosamunde* Overture.

Chamber
Octet in F Major for Winds and Strings, op. 166 (D. 803)
what to buy: [Vienna Octet, ensemble] (Decca 466580) ♪ ♪ ♪ ♪

Though Schubert was depressed when he composed the Octet in 1824, one would never guess it from the cheeriness of most of the music—the lovesick aura of the Adagio being the exception. For clarinet, horn, bassoon, two violins, viola, cello, and double bass, it's over fifty minutes long, and the time has never passed so sweetly as in this classic 1958 recording with violinist Willi Boskovsky leading a prototypical Viennese reading. The pairing is Ludwig Spohr's Octet, op. 32.

Piano Quintet in A Major for Piano and Strings, op. 114 (*The Trout*, D. 667)
what to buy: [Jenö Jandó, piano; István Tóth, double bass; members of the Kodály Quartet] (Naxos 8.550658) ♪ ♪ ♪ ♪

This is a bright, exuberant reading of Schubert's most popular chamber work. It's played with such verve by Naxos house pianist Jandó and his cohorts that one can practically see the water sparkling and the fish jumping. The substantial *Adagio and Rondo Concertante* in F Major for Violin, Viola, Cello, and Piano (D. 487) makes for a nice filler, and if the timing seems a bit short at fifty-three minutes, it's budget-priced.

worth searching for: [*Marlboro Festival 40th Anniversary*; Rudolf Serkin, piano; Jaime Laredo, violin; Philipp Naegele, viola; Leslie Parnas, cello; Julius Levine, double bass] (Sony Classical 46252) ♪ ♪ ♪ ♪ ♪

Captured at Marlboro in 1967, these world-class musicians play this piece as naturally as breathing. Serkin's

pianism is scintillating, the group overall exhibits the spontaneity of a concert performance, string tone is richly vibrant and alive, and balances are good. The equally classic coupling finds clarinetist Harold Wright, violinists Alexander Schneider and Isidore Cohen, violist Samuel Rhodes, and cellist Parnas delivering an affecting version of Mozart's Quintet in A Major for Clarinet and Strings (*Stadler*, K. 581).

Quintet in C Major for Strings, op, 163 (D. 956)
what to buy: [*The Casals Edition*; Isaac Stern, violin; Alexander Schneider, violin; Milton Katims, viola; Pablo Casals, cello; Paul Tortelier, cello] (Sony Classical 58992) ♪ ♪ ♪ ♪

This vintage classic may have slightly dim sound, but the Old World radiance of the playing is timeless. The famous Scherzo (Presto) is played with great vim, while the contrasting Trio (Andante sostenuto) stops time with its weightlessness. The coupling is of Casals leading the Prades Festival Orchestra in a mellow 1953 reading of Schubert's fifth symphony (B-Flat Major).

what to buy next: [Heinrich Schiff, cello; Alban Berg Quartet, ensemble] (EMI Classics 66942) ♪ ♪ ♪ ♪

The Berg Quartet and regular collaborator Heinrich Schiff take an expansive view of this work in the first two movements, especially the Adagio, then tighten up a bit for the final two movements. Their sound is warmly Viennese, though not without bite at crucial moments. Some may find them so polished and precise as to (paradoxically) be distracting, but accusations of coldness are unfounded. The lack of any coupling, however, makes for a 47:33 timing, rather ungenerous even at mid-price.

String Quartets nos. 12–15
what to buy: [Juilliard String Quartet, ensemble] (CBS Odyssey 45617) ♪ ♪ ♪ ♪

These 1980s recordings date from before the precipitous decline of this ensemble (though violinist Robert Mann's vibrato is perhaps wider at times than some tastes enjoy, his intonation was still strong). These late quartets—the only ones with much of a foothold in the repertoire, the posthumously published No. 14 in D Minor (*Death and the Maiden*) being by far the best-known—actually benefit from the Juilliard's lean approach. It gives the contrasting moods their due, but the transitions don't become jagged, and for an

American group, the sound is relatively emotional. This two-fer is a fine value.

Quartet no. 14 in D Minor for Strings (*Death and the Maiden,* D. 810)
what to buy: [Vienna Philharmonic String Quartet] (Penguin Classics 460650) ♪ ♪ ♪ ♪ ♪

There are more burningly intense readings of the *Death and the Maiden* Quartet, but none more warmly Viennese than this 1964 release. Violinist Willi Boskovsky, long the first chair of the Vienna Philharmonic, leads three colleagues through an interpretation that balances lightness and interior fire with supernal grace. The sound here is superb, which cannot quite be said for the coupling, a 1958 *Trout* Quintet played (rather eccentrically at some points) by Clifford Curzon with Boskovsky and a different assortment of Viennese players.

Trios for Piano, Violin, and Cello, opps. 99 (D. 898) and 100 (D. 929)
what to buy: [*Isaac Stern: A Life in Music*; Eugene Istomin, piano; Isaac Stern, violin; Leonard Rose, cello] (Sony Classics 64516) ♪ ♪ ♪ ♪ ♪

These three celebrated players, one of the most empathic chamber music combinations America has produced, deliver sparkling, extroverted Schubert entirely appropriate to these bubbly masterpieces of the piano trio repertoire. Stern was still at his considerable peak, Istomin plays with grace and pizzaz, and Rose is the elegant anchor. The piano could be a tad less recessed in the soundstage, but otherwise there are no complaints. This two-CD set also includes the same personnel in Haydn's Piano Trio in E-flat Major (Hob. XV: 10) and Stern, Istomin, violinist Milton Katims, and cellist Mischa Schneider in Mozart's Quartet in E-flat Major for Piano and Strings (K. 493).

Piano Sonatas (complete)
what to buy: [*Schubert: The Piano Sonatas*; Wilhelm Kempff, piano] (Deutsche Grammophon 463766) ♪ ♪ ♪ ♪

The executional failings that mark Kempff's Beethoven sonata cycles are not a worry here, leaving one to marvel at his organic, perceptive yet unforced interpretations in these 1965—69 recordings. With Schubert, the question of completeness is debatable; there are sets with more sonatas than these, but by keeping the frag-

ments to a minimum, Kempff's seven-CD set presents Schubert in a better light and provides a more enjoyable listening experience. Quite sensibly, the programming starts with the final works and moves backwards.

various piano sonatas
what to buy: [Artur Schnabel, piano] (Pearl 9271) ♪ ♪ ♪ ♪ ♪

[Artur Schnabel, piano] (Pearl 9272) ♪ ♪ ♪ ♪ ♪

This pair of two-CD sets contain arguably the most incisive and pointed Schubert playing any pianist has committed to posterity. It was Schnabel's determined advocacy that moved Schubert's piano sonatas from obscurity to prominence, and the stern nobility and taut energy he brings to them is invigorating. The late-1930s sound is hissy and has little depth, but the close recording provides clarity, body, and tone. Among the other solo works included, the most important are the six *Moments musicaux* (D. 780), and there are also many duo tracks with Karl Ulrich Schnabel (Artur's son).

Sonata in A Minor for Piano, op. 143 (D. 784)
what to buy: [Stephen Hough, piano] (Hyperion 67027) ♪ ♪ ♪ ♪ ♪

This three-movement work has been called the first of Schubert's mature piano sonatas. The pianist here, the articulate Stephen Hough, is of the opinion that Schubert composed it (in 1823) after learning he was seriously ill. With its dark textures and lengthy first movement, it certainly shows the direction in which he was to move in this genre, while yet showing the influence of Beethoven. The resulting mix of introverted statements interrupted by extroverted gestures is emotionally disturbing, and Hough accents this effect dramatically. This well-filled CD also includes fine reading of the Sonata in B-flat Major (D. 960) and the short, fragmentary two-movement Sonata in C Major (D. 613).

Sonata in D Major for Piano, op. 53 (D. 850)
what to buy: [Sviatoslav Richter, piano] (Music & Arts 957) ♪ ♪ ♪ ♪ ♪

This 1956 Prague concert performance is in surprisingly good sound, documenting one of those once-in-a-lifetime musical moments in which one very slight fumble in the finale can't detract from the overall thrill ride Richter has taken us on. He turns the work from a pleasant piece on the cusp of Romanticism into a raging force of nature. The pairing is a fine reading of the Sonata in C Minor for Piano (D. 958) from a 1958 Budapest concert.

Sonata in C Minor for Piano (D. 958)
what to buy: [Mitsuko Uchida, piano] (Philips 456579) ♪ ♪ ♪ ♪

Though Uchida, as is her wont, leans toward the lyrical side of Schubert, power is not lacking where required. Certain phrases erupt from this expansive, deeply introspective reading like emotional outbursts, lending it the drama required to offset and contextualize the quiet passages in which Uchida, with her delicate touch, excels. It's paired with a fine reading of the Sonata in A Major (D. 959).

Piano Sonatas in A major, D.959; in B-flat major, D.960
what to buy: [Alfred Brendel, piano] (Philips 456573) ♪ ♪ ♪ ♪ ♪

Rethinking these career-capping works in concert, Brendel gives them a spontaneity missing from his previous recordings, which were sometimes more mannered. They emerge as Olympian statements, not note-perfect but close enough, noble but kinetic. This new two-CD set also includes performances of the Sonatas D.575 and D.894 that, if not quite as revelatory as the two later works, still exhibit fine pianism and many insights.

Sonata in B-flat Major for Piano (D. 960)
what to buy: [Murray Perahia, piano] (CBS Masterworks 44569) ♪ ♪ ♪ ♪

Perahia doesn't receive recorded sound that does full justice to his pearl-like tone, but this is still a gorgeous performance. Arpeggios and runs flow like quicksilver, but where weight is required, Perahia provides it. The pairing is Robert Schumann's Sonata for Piano, op. 22 (albeit in brittle sound).

what to buy next: [*Sviatoslav Richter in Prague, vol. 9*; Sviatoslav Richter, piano] (Praga 254032) ♪ ♪ ♪ ♪.

In a 1972 Prague concert, Richter once again delivers a transcendent performance. The other Schubert work heard here is the Impromptu in G-flat major, op. 90, no. 3 (D.899), but Franz Liszt's *Polonaise* no. 2 in E Major is also included.

Fantasie in C Major, op. 15 (*"Wanderer" Fantasy*, D. 760)
what to buy: [Sviatoslav Richter, piano] (EMI Classics 64429) ♪ ♪ ♪ ♪ ♪

The first Schubert work Richter learned was the four-movement *"Wanderer" Fantasy*. In this 1963 studio performance he takes risks from the very beginning, yet this is a technically secure reading. Passionately fiery or quietly intimate as the music demands, this interpretation lives on the edge, and makes the work's influence on Liszt easy to hear. Currently this classic reading is on a CD with Richter's fine studio recording of Antonín Dvořák's piano concerto.

[*The Rubinstein Collection: vol. 54*; Artur Rubinstein, piano] (RCA Red Seal 63054) ♪ ♪ ♪ ♪ ♪

Rubinstein played this work throughout his career, and professed a great love for Schubert's music even though he recorded very little of it. By the 1960s he was seemingly less excitable in the studio, but in this 1965 recording there is plenty of his old Romantic bravura, yet also great sensitivity and creamy piano tone. Delectable too are his performances here of the final Piano Sonata (D. 960) and the third and fourth *Impromptus* from D. 899.

what to buy next: [Murray Perahia, piano] (CBS Masterworks 42124) ♪ ♪ ♪ ♪.

Perahia can sometimes seem to be whispering his way through a piece, showing off his finely gradated control of tone and dynamics, but not here. While he could hardly be said to be banging, or even aggressive, this is a highly dramatic reading that yet retains the most estimable characteristics of Perahia's art. It's paired with Schumann's Fantasie, op. 17.

Impromptus, op. 90 (D. 899) and op. 142 (D. 935)
what to buy: [Murray Perahia, piano] (Sony Classical 37291) ♪ ♪ ♪ ♪

This or that pianist may play one or two of these pieces better than Perahia, but for one beautiful CD containing both sets of four, this is hard to beat. Their intimacy and spontaneity shine through most alluringly, on challenging passages delivered with seeming (and, in these works, essential) ease, and lyrical melodies delivered with breathtaking songfulness.

Sonatas for Violin and Piano (complete); Violin Sonatas, D. 384–5, 408, 574; Fantasie, D. 934
what to buy: [Szymon Goldberg, violin; Radu Lupu, piano] (Decca 466748) ♪ ♪ ♪ ♪₆

Also known as Sonatinas, the Violin Sonatas (with piano accompaniment of equal importance) are nowhere near as venerated as some of the Piano Sonatas. However, they are quite a varied foursome, all quintessentially Schubertian yet each with a distinct mood. The much later four-movement Fantasie for Violin and Piano (D. 934) is a big, overtly virtuosic work. Goldberg and especially Lupu capture the characters of these works well in sonically sparkling 1978–1979 recordings. The filler on the second CD in this two-fer is a 1952 recording by cellist Maurice Gendron and pianist Jean Françaix of the *Arpeggione* Sonata (D. 821).

Vocal
Masses nos. 4 in C Major (D. 452); 5 in A-flat Major, (D. 678); 6 in E-flat Major (D. 950)
what to buy: [Helen Donath, soprano; Lucia Popp, soprano; Brigitte Fassbaender, mezzo-soprano; Francisco Araiza, tenor; Adolf Dallapozza, tenor; Peter Schreier, tenor; Dietrich Fischer-Dieskau, bass-baritone; Wolfgang Sawallisch, cond.; Bavarian Radio Symphony Orchestra; Bavarian Radio Symphony Choir] (EMI Classics 73365) ♪ ♪ ♪ ♪₆

Schubert's later Masses, much loved by choirs yet somehow falling outside the attention of mainstream listeners, offer an opportunity to hear him operating on a large public scale surpassed only by the Ninth Symphony. Extroverted and stirring, full of gorgeous melodies even by Schubert's high standard, they have many juicy solo parts but also much excellent choral writing, and the orchestral accompaniments emphasize their symphonic dimensions. These 1980–81 recordings (now on two CDs for the cost of one, extracted from a larger set no longer available in the U.S.) raised the bar for these works, with superb soloist teams and masterful shaping of the flow by Sawallisch. As filler, *Tantum ergo* (D. 962) and *Offertorium* (D. 963) are included.

Die schöne Müllerin (The Fair Maid of the Mill) (D. 795)
what to buy: [Dietrich Fischer-Dieskau, baritone; Gerald Moore, piano] (EMI Classics 66959) ♪ ♪ ♪ ♪₆

Fischer-Dieskau made four studio recordings of this cycle; this 1961 reading gets the nod for its relatively

unexaggerated emphases of diction and dynamics. In 1961, his voice still had a brightness and agility it would lose somewhat in the following decade. Fischer-Dieskau starkly focuses attention on the words, but here that is rarely allowed to interfere with beautiful, effectively emotional singing. His voice caresses each word, conveying a wide gamut of human emotion as the cycle progresses. Pianist Gerald Moore reveals as much beauty and profundity in the piano part as the baritone does in the vocal line. Fischer-Dieskau recites the prologue and epilogue to frame the cycle, but they can easily be skipped over.

Winterreise (Winter Journey), op. 89 (D. 911)
what to buy: [Hans Hotter, baritone; Gerald Moore, piano] (EMI Classics 67000) ♪ ♪ ♪ ♪ ♪

This 1954 recording is monaural, but it's crisp and clean—and interferes not a bit with Hotter's careful shadings of timbre. His dark baritone is perfect for these shadowed poems, and he spins out the long line with great beauty of tone. This is not to say that he doesn't offer moment-to-moment characterization of the words, but Hotter achieves intensity without seeming hectoring or fussy in his phrasing. Not that he sings in an undifferentiated manner: his tone always matches the mood of the text. Nearly a half-century on, Hotter's approach remains exquisitely refreshing. Moore is ideally supportive in his articulation and phrasing, and comes forward to set the mood astutely in many of the songs. Moore's attentive accompaniment (and the better sound quality) result in this version receiving the nod over Hotter's November 1942 recording with the marginally less insightful (and less sympathetically miked) pianist Michael Raucheisen, even though Hotter was at his absolute peak of vocal perfection then. That Deutsche Grammophon recording, now available on Music & Arts CD-1061, makes a fine supplement to the EMI, however.

what to buy next: [Dietrich Fischer-Dieskau, baritone; Jörg Demus, piano] (Deutsche Grammophon 447421) ♪ ♪ ♪ ♪₆

Fischer-Dieskau's approach offers a clear alternative to Hotter's, with a lighter vocal tone and more micromanaging of the vocal line in the younger baritone's more text-focused style. Choosing between Fischer-Dieskau's ten (!) recordings of this cycle is not easy. The main studio contenders feature accompanists Daniel Barenboim in 1979 (Deutsche Grammophon 463501), Jörg Demus in 1965, and Gerald Moore in 1962 (EMI

Classics 83087, imported but fairly easily tracked down). If the 1965 version takes the honors, it is only by the slimmest of margins; all are quite rewarding. The intensity Fischer-Dieskau finds with Demus is positively riveting without becoming overstated, conveying all the emotionally shattering nuances with a jagged sharpness that's cathartic.

Schwanengesang (D. 957)

what to buy: [Hans Hotter, baritone; Gerald Moore, piano] (EMI Classics 65196) ♪ ♪ ♪ ♪ ♪

Hotter's tone is ideal for the Heine settings in this collection, and these readings are arguably unsurpassed. Of the other nine assorted lieder filling out this disc, *An die Musik* (D. 957), *Meeresstille* (D. 216), *Im Frühling* (D. 882), *Am Bach im Frühling* (D. 361), *Gruppe aus dem Tartarus* (D. 583), and *Wandrers Nachtlied* I & II (D. 224 & 768) date from a 1949 session, while *Geheimes* (D. 719), *Sei mir gegrüßt* (D. 741), and *Im Abendrot* (D. 799) come from a 1957 session. Throughout, Hotter's subtle insights and glorious voice combine in a lieder-lover's dream. These are perfectly good monaural recordings that shouldn't scare away any collectors.

what to buy next: [Dietrich Fischer-Dieskau, baritone; Gerald Moore, piano] (EMI Classics 67559) ♪ ♪ ♪ ♪₄

Fischer-Dieskau has exactly the proper gravity for the six Heine settings of *Schwanengesang*, and while some might find him a bit too pointed in the ReslIstab poems, the effect is to make this collection seem more like a coherent cycle. The 1950s recordings are monaural, and the piano is slightly more recessed than would be ideal, but the singer's voice was at its peak at this time. There are only four lieder filling out the program: a separate recording of the cycle's *Ständchen, Der Erlkönig* (D. 328), *Nacht und Träume* (D. 827), and *Du bist die Ruh* (D. 776).

worth searching for: [Dietrich Fischer-Dieskau, baritone; Gerald Moore, piano] (Deutsche Grammophon 463503) ♪ ♪ ♪ ♪ ♪

This 1972 recording has no sonic problems and of course is in stereo. It's part of the twenty-one-CD *Fischer-Dieskau Edition* box set that Deutsche Grammophon released in 2000 for the singer's seventy-fifth birthday, but the CDs are now available individually in Europe and can be found so in the U.S. as imports. The more modern recording allows full appreciation of, for instance, Moore's complexly shaded piano part in *Die Stadt*. Also,

the filler is more generous than on the (less expensive) EMI disc cited as a "buy": recordings made from 1966 to 1972 of nine assorted lieder—*Vollendung* (D. 579A), *Die Erde* (D. 579B), *An die Musik* (D. 547), *An Silvia* (D. 891), *Heidenröslein* (D. 257), *Im Abendrot* (D. 799), *Der Musensohn* (D. 764), *Die Forelle* (D. 550), and *Der Tod und das Mädchen* (D. 531). Several of these are among the most popular, and the last two are famous for their instrumental use in Schubert's two chamber music masterpieces of those titles.

various lieder
what to buy: [*Franz Schubert: 21 Lieder*, Dietrich Fischer-Dieskau, baritone; Gerald Moore, piano] (EMI Classics 69503) ♪ ♪ ♪ ♪ ♪

The 1958 and 1965 recordings on this mid-price CD feature some of the most famous Schubert lieder, including an aptly urgent but well-proportioned, well-acted, and never-overwrought reading of *Der Erlkönig* (D. 328). On some other songs, Fischer-Dieskau floats his most enticingly restrained soft notes, even while foregoing none of his trademark pointing of details (though more subtly than at other times in his career).

what to buy next: [Janet Baker, mezzo-soprano; Gerald Moore, piano; Geoffrey Parsons, piano] (EMI Classics 69389) ♪ ♪ ♪ ♪ ♪

This budget two-fer offers the opportunity to hear Schubert sung expertly and movingly by a beloved mezzo-soprano, with the majority of these forty-two songs not normally essayed by male vocalists. Moore is the accompanist on the three-quarters of the set recorded in 1970; Parsons takes his place for the 1980 items. No texts, alas.

[*An die Musik: Favorite Schubert Songs*; Bryn Terfel, baritone; Malcolm Martineau, piano] (Deutsche Grammophon 445294) ♪ ♪ ♪ ♪ ♪

Terfel's dark, heavy voice on *Gruppe aus dem Tartarus* (D. 583), the first track of this CD, is entirely appropriate, but one worries that it portends a standard approach that would be wearing on the ear over the course of this seventy-minute recital. Not to worry: Terfel is musically sensitive, frequently displays wonderful soft singing, and never slips into the bull-in-a-china-shop approach his public image sometimes verges on suggesting. He offers a distinct alternative to Fischer-Dieskau's lieder hegemony, like Hotter but with impeccable digital recording. The program, which includes excerpts from *Schwanengesang*, fits the CD's title both on the first track and beyond.

[Dietrich Fischer-Dieskau, baritone; Sviatoslav Richter, piano] (Orfeo 334931) ♪ ♪ ♪ ♪ ♪

Except for *Der Schiffer* (D. 536) this 1977 recital recorded live at the Salzburg Festival finds Fischer-Dieskau largely avoiding inappropriately punched-out accents, something he was becoming occasionally prone to by

this point in his career. Richter's accompaniments are so ravishingly beautiful that even if the singing weren't so admirable, this disc would be worth acquiring just to hear the Russian render the piano parts with his silken touch. The twenty-three lieder selected for this program are mostly on the quiet, lyrical end of the spectrum, which certainly helps the baritone avoid strain.

influences: Wolfgang Amadeus Mozart, Franz Joseph Haydn, Ludwig van Beethoven, Hugo Wolf

Steve Holtje

William Schuman
Born William Howard Schuman, August 4, 1910, in New York City, NY Died February 15, 1992, in New York City, NY

period: Twentieth century

While Schuman would probably have been considered a significant force even if he had only stuck to composing, the fact that he was one of the finest, most innovative music educators and administrators of the twentieth century makes him an even more important figure in the history of American music.

William Schuman's career as a composer began slowly since music was not a major factor in his upbringing, hovering around the periphery of family life instead. True, the family did have regular Sunday evening song sessions, in which tunes from popular stage works of the day played a big part, and 78 rpm discs by Enrico Caruso and other classical artists could sometimes be heard in the home, but the violin lessons he took while going to elementary school were tolerated rather than enjoyed. There was a slow shift in his perceptions as he made his way toward and through his high school years, capped when he began writing pop tunes and leading his own jazz band—Billy Schuman and His Alamo Society Orchestra. After graduation Schuman initially enrolled at New York University's School of Commerce with an eye toward a career in advertising, but this changed as the lure of Tin Pan Alley started leading him away from his studies.

Frank Loesser—a boyhood chum who would later go on

to provide the music for *Guys and Dolls* and *How to Succeed in Business without Really Trying* and create pop standards like "Praise the Lord and Pass the Ammunition" and "On a Slow Boat to China"—collaborated with Schuman on a few songs which they then managed to foist on various vaudeville acts. As these tunes all failed to develop into hits, Schuman decided that he needed some lessons in harmony. He also started attending concerts at Carnegie Hall, where he was first exposed to standard orchestral repertoire, and at the Metropolitan Opera. He then began taking lessons in counterpoint and composition, all of which finally caused him to embark upon the biggest musical journey of his life to that point: enrolling in the Juilliard School of Music's summer sessions in 1932 and 1933. Soon he went to Europe, where he took some conducting courses at the Salzburg Mozarteum; upon his return to the United States, he started studying composition with Roy Harris at Juilliard. During this time, Schumann also began preparing for a career as a teacher, taking classes at Columbia University (and graduating with a B.A. in 1937) even as he was teaching music at Sarah Lawrence College—a position he would hold from 1935–1945.

This relatively brief period of intensive experience had longstanding impact upon Schuman's subsequent career development. His work with Harris was of particular importance because it helped shape Schuman's basic approach to composition, introducing him to Renaissance-style polyphony and causing him to focus even more on counterpoint studies. Harris was also a valuable advocate for his pupil, lobbying for him with the noted conductor Serge Koussevitzky, who then inserted Schuman's second symphony into the program for the Boston Symphony's season in 1939. Two years later Schuman's Symphony no. 3 won the first New York Critic's Circle Award. Meanwhile, his work at Sarah Lawrence was providing him with a laboratory for testing educational methods, the kinds of ideas he was further able to put into action when he accepted a position as president of the Juilliard School in 1945, which he was to hold until 1962. These years, from the premiere of his third symphony until his retirement from Juilliard, were fairly fertile from a compositional standpoint as well, seeing the creation of five symphonies, two string quartets, a violin concerto, the *New England Triptych* (probably his most popular work), an opera (*The Mighty Casey*, a one-acter built around the classic poem about a baseball player), and a host of choral music, including the frequently performed *Carols of Death*. He also won the very first Pulitzer Prize for Music (in 1943) for his

choral cantata with orchestra, *A Free Song*.

In 1962 Schumann became president of Lincoln Center in New York City, where he aided in the commissioning and performance of new works by American composers and instituted a series of outreach programs designed to bring classical music into city schools. Despite his busy schedule he managed to keep writing new material, including another symphony and an arrangement of Charles Ives's *Variations on "America."* When he finally stepped away from music administration in 1970, Schumann wrote his last symphony (no. 10), a short series of chamber works revolving around wind and brass instruments, the quirky *Mail Order Madrigals* (based on an 1897 Sears Roebuck catalog), and even more vocal works. By the time he died, Schuman had written over seventy different compositions in a variety of genres, received over twenty-five honorary degrees from various colleges and universities, won two Pulitzer Prizes (the second was for lifetime achievement), and made significant contributions to the teaching of music.

Orchestral
Symphony no. 3
what to buy: [Leonard Bernstein, cond.; New York Philharmonic Orchestra] (Deutsche Grammophon 419780) ♪ ♪ ♪ ♪

It is interesting to compare the work of the teacher (Roy Harris) with that of the student (Schuman) on this disc since Bernstein's performances let the individual strengths of each shine to their best advantage. Harris's third symphony is more raw-boned, more overtly emotional, and packed into one movement, while Schuman's third leans toward the theoretical, building a structure upon older forms (passacaglia, fugue, chorale, toccata) contained within two sections. Both works are among the best American scores written during the first half of the twentieth century, and this is a particularly apt pairing.

New England Triptych for Orchestra
what to buy: [*A Tribute to William Schuman*; Gerard Schwarz, cond.; Seattle Symphony Orchestra] (Delos 3115) ♪ ♪ ♪ ♪

Recorded and released just prior to Schuman's death, this set is a solid partner to the Bernstein disc of the composer's third symphony. The *New England Triptych* is an instrumental setting of three William Billings hymns and, along with Schuman's arrangement of Charles

Ives's *Variations on "America"* heard here, is loaded with brassy flourishes. These then serve as distinct contrasts to the rest of the material filling up this well-recorded and performed album: the more rigorous yet tune-filled Symphony no. 5 (a.k.a. the *Symphony for Strings*) and *Judith,* the "dance concerto" he wrote for choreographer Martha Graham.

influences: Roy Harris, Walter Piston, Vincent Persichetti, George Perle

Garaud MacTaggart

Clara Schumann
Born Clara Josephine Wieck, September 13, 1819, in Leipzig, Germany. Died May 20, 1896, in Frankfurt, Germany.

period: Romantic

Clara Schumann-Wieck started out as a child prodigy and developed into one of the leading pianists of the nineteenth century. Her piano compositions (most of which were written before her marriage to Robert Schumann) and performances greatly inspired both her husband and Johannes Brahms, her long-time friend and admirer. Although she was considered more of a concert artist during her lifetime—premiering works by her husband, Brahms, and Frédéric Chopin—she was also a gifted and respected teacher.

As a young child, Clara Wieck was assumed to be hard of hearing, because she didn't speak her first words until she was nearly five years old. However, just as she began speaking and communicating, her parents divorced. Clara's father, Friederich Wieck, retained custody of her and made sure she spent nearly every waking moment practicing the piano or learning languages and social skills that would allow her to communicate in countries where he planned to showcase her talents. He recognized her prodigious musical talents and made it his mission to mold her into the best pianist of her time. Her first public concert occurred when she was nine years old, followed by her debut on international stages two years later when her father booked concerts that took her to Paris and other important venues abroad. An important feature of Clara's concerts was her improvisations on opera themes and popular tunes of the day, displays of technique that won the admiration of Franz Liszt and Frédéric Chopin among others.

By this time Professor Wieck had accepted a new piano student, Robert Schumann, who came to live with the family in 1830. Although he was nine years her senior, Schumann soon became enamored of young Clara, and she of him. A passionate believer in the Romantic ideal, Robert's influence expanded her musical horizons and she began adding works by contemporary composers to her concert programs. She had already written and published her first piano scores, the *Four Polonaises,* op. 1, and the *Caprice en forme de Valse,* op. 2, before dedicating her third opus, the *Romance varié,* to Schumann in 1833. Her lone completed piano concerto (op. 7) was started that same year and finished in 1835. After Robert proposed the idea of marriage to the senior Wieck in 1937, the couple had to take her father to court for permission to marry. Clara was not only her father's pride and joy, but she also provided his reason for living and means of making one. Although he liked Schumann, Friederich wasn't about to allow him to interfere with Clara's bright future, especially since the young pianist/composer didn't appear to have any real earning power. Accordingly, the father began placing rancorous roadblocks on the path to matrimony. The courts felt differently, however, ruling in the plaintiffs' favor, and the pair were married on September 12, 1840.

Because both Schumanns already had careers, they encountered some problems early in their marriage. While Robert understood, from an intellectual standpoint, his wife's need to perform, he felt that such activities were secondary to the raising of their offspring (eight children in fourteen years). Both taught at the Leipzig Conservatory but Robert didn't allow his wife to play the piano at home when he was attempting to compose music, a factor which, along with tending to their children, seriously hampered her own ability to compose and to practice piano technique. Since her concerts still brought in the most income, Clara often found it necessary to break away from the homestead and go out on tour, a fact that Robert had to accept since he had no steady source of funding. Thus, she would often leave him and their children behind, performing to sold-out concerts and rave reviews throughout Europe. During this time she proved a worthy advocate for her husband's piano scores but was able to write little in the way of her own music, with the most prominent of her compositions emerging from this period being a set of three songs based on texts by Friedrich Rückert (1841) and her piano trio (1847).

Meanwhile, Robert, who was known to have led a profligate lifestyle prior to marrying, had contracted syphilis somewhere along the way. Slowly, the disease revealed itself, affecting his mind and his music, often sending him into violent mood swings that stifled his creativity and wreaked havoc on their homelife. In 1853 Clara met Johannes Brahms, a young composer from whom her husband predicted great things, and who would later become her greatest admirer and one of her truest friends. The next year, after an unsuccessful suicide attempt, Robert was placed in a mental institution. Clara's visits upset him to the point that she was advised to stay away, and she didn't lay eyes on him again until a few days before he died in 1856. Brahms, however, was allowed to see her husband, and he relayed reports on Robert's condition to Clara after each visit.

To cope with the loss of her beloved, Clara turned to her piano for solace and continued performing. She engaged in a rigorous concert schedule until 1873 and did not fully give up touring until she was in her seventies. During this time she also kept up a steady correspondence with Brahms and the two of them passed a great deal of time together despite her workload and his increasing fame. She also spent fourteen years of her later life as a piano teacher at the Hoch Conservatory in Frankfurt, where she taught, among others, the American composer Edward McDowell. She was considered an excellent teacher, insisting that her students master technique, pay attention to the most minute details, and interpret the music exactly as the composer had intended it. In 1990 the German government put her picture on the 100 Deutschmark banknote, the only musician so honored.

Orchestral
Concerto in A Minor for Piano and Orchestra, op. 7
what to buy: [*The Women's Philharmonic*; Angela Cheng, piano; JoAnn Falletta, cond.; Bay Area Women's Philharmonic, orch.] (Koch International Classics 7169)
♪ ♪ ♪ ♪

Clara Schumann's concerto is the most substantial work on this program, but everything here is worth more than a couple listenings. Pianist Angela Cheng is winning the hearts of audiences around the world and JoAnn Falletta (currently with the Buffalo Philharmonic Orchestra) is a consistently solid force on the podium. The other works in this collection, all written by women, include Lili Boulanger's *D'un soir triste* and *D'un matin de printemps*, an overture by Fanny Mendelssohn-Hensel, and Germaine Tailleferre's Concertino for Harp.

Chamber
Sonata in G Minor for Piano
what to buy: [Yoshiko Iwai, piano] (Naxos 8.553501)
♪ ♪ ♪ ♪

Iwai's performances are a perfect match for Eickhorst's (see below) since she is a fine pianist and there is relatively little duplication in the material covered. What is repeated (the *Soirées musicales,* op. 6 and the *Variations on a theme by Robert Schumann,* op. 20) is the sort of music that can only be illuminated further by differing interpretations. The biggest deal in this set is the piano sonata, a work which is reflective of its era and perfectly able to stand alongside ones by Schumann or Chopin in a recital program.

various piano works
what to buy: [Konstanze Eickhorst, piano] (CPO 999132)
♪ ♪ ♪ ♪

These are lovely performances of beguiling music and Eickhorst's playing of the *Variations on a theme by Robert Schumann* (which Clara wrote after Robert's death) is a marvel of clarity, worth the price of the disc alone.

influences: Robert Schumann, Fanny Mendelssohn-Hensel, Johannes Brahms

Steve Coghill and Garaud MacTaggart

Robert Schumann
Born June 8, 1810, in Zwickau, Germany. Died July 29, 1856, in Endenich, Germany.

period: Romantic

Robert Schumann helped set the tone for the Romantic era, not only through the high caliber of his piano and vocal scores but through his music criticism. He was co-founder of *Neue Zeitschrift für Musick (The New Journal for Music),* which quickly became one of the most important music journals in Europe, and his essays on the music of Frédéric Chopin and Johannes Brahms helped launch the careers of both composers.

Schumann's father, a bookseller, instilled in him a life-long love for poetry and literature. He also saw to it that his son took piano lessons starting when he was six years old. Schumann developed into a fairly talented pianist by the time he entered his teenage years, inspired, in part, by a performance by the great pianist Ignaz Moscheles he had witnessed in 1819. A few years afterwards, at his mother's insistence (and against his own desires), he studied law at the University of Leipzig and later Heidelberg University before eventually giving it up to pursue a livelihood in music.

He didn't really start to hit his stride until after 1828, when he began studying piano with the renowned pedagogue Friedrich Wieck. This was a pivotal time for the young Schumann, since he was intent on pursuing a career as a piano virtuoso despite his mother's wishes. By 1830 he had moved to Heidelberg (ostensibly to continue his schooling), where he traveled in artistic circles and practiced playing the piano for up to seven hours a day. With the grudging assistance of Wieck, who didn't have faith in the consistency of Schumann's temperament, the aspiring young pianist managed to convince his mother that there was a real future for him as a concert artist. With this reprieve from his legal studies, Schumann moved back to Leipzig where he was to live with the Wiecks.

He had met Wieck two years earlier after hearing Clara, the music teacher's daughter, give a piano recital. Schumann, who had promised to give up his profligate ways, was reneging, and earning the somewhat stern Wieck's further disapproval. In turn, the young pianist/composer was experiencing some dissatisfaction with Wieck, who was more concerned about his daughter's career than he was about instructing Schumann. While Clara and her father were off on concert tours, Robert sought instruction from other sources (including Johann Nepomuk Hummel) before finally beginning his studies with Heinrich Dorn, the conductor at the Leipzig theater. By 1832 Dorn had also given up on the idea of Schumann as a worthy student and the young man attempted to study theory on his own, using a book (*Abhandlung von der Fuge*) and examining Johann Sebastian Bach's *Das wohltemperirte Clavier*.

Schumann's career as a promising concert pianist ran into problems when he began experiencing an increasing weakness in his right hand. Some scholars have believed the debility was caused by a contraption he built for his hand that would supposedly help him extend the range he could cover on the keyboard, but current historians lean toward blaming the medication he was taking for a sexually transmitted disease. It is perhaps

Sequentia:
Barbara Thornton and Benjamin Bagby met while studying Medieval performance practice with the renowned musicologist Thomas Binkley at the Schola Cantorum Basiliensis in Basel, Switzerland. Upon the conclusion of their course work in 1977, Thornton and Bagby formed Sequentia, an ensemble devoted to exploring the traditions of Medieval vocal and instrumental music, and moved their base of operations to Cologne (Köln), Germany.

One of the first recorded projects that Sequentia involved themselves with was *Vox Iberica*, a set of three albums devoted to Spanish music drawn from eleventh, twelfth, and thirteenth century texts, for which they won the 1993 Deutsche Schallplattenpreis. Unfortunately, this trio of discs (*Donnersöhne: Sons of Thunder* [Deutsche Harmonia Mundi 77199], *Las Huelgas Codex* [Deutsche Harmonia Mundi 77238], and *El Sabio: Alfonso X* [Deutsche Harmonia Mundi 77173]) is out of print as this book goes to press.

In 1982, at a time when, as Thornton later noted, Abbess Hildegard von Bingen's works were considered "something less sophisticated than Gregorian chant or less transcendental," Sequentia became the first ensemble to perform Hildegard's Medieval morality play *Ordo virtutum (Play of Virtues)* in a historically accurate way. *Symphoniae* (Deutsche Harmonia Mundi 77020) was the group's first album devoted to Hildegard, and was recorded in the early 1980s, prior to their complete traversal of the Abbesses's oeuvre. That project began with *Canticles of Ecstasy* (Deutsche Harmonia Mundi 77320), nominated for a Grammy Award in 1996 though it was made in 1993. Sequentia finished recording all of Hildegard's works by 1998, including another rendition of the *Ordo virtutum*, the more recent of which (Deutsche Harmonia Mundi 77394) is more assured than the earlier one and benefits from Thornton and Bagby's increased expertise with the vocal style necessary to perform Hildegard's magnificent music.

Unfortunately, Thornton died on November 8, 1998 due to an inoperable brain tumor. Bagby and the scholarly journal *Early Music America* have since set up the Thornton Scholarship Fund, aimed at providing monies to worthy students seeking to broaden their knowledge of Medieval music and the relevant performance characteristics. Sequentia as an entity has also continued its mission of exploring early music. Bagby, who plays the six-stringed Medieval harp in addition to singing, has developed a poetic staging of the *Beowulf* saga and spearheaded Sequentia's exploration of the *Edda* (Deutsche Harmonia Mundi 77381), a Medieval Norse/Icelandic manuscript that details the activities of the gods, heroes, and villains that would later show up in different forms in Richard Wagner's operatic cycle *Der Ring des Nibelungen (The Ring of the Nibelung)*.

Garaud MacTaggart

no coincidence that Schumann, who had been composing on and off for years, now began focusing on his writing for the piano. In 1833 he started writing the fourteen short pieces that were to make up his *Carnaval* (op. 9), and from then until 1838 the world saw the creation of some of his finest piano scores: the *Symphonic Études* (op. 13), *Davidsbündlertänze* (op. 6), *Kinderscenen* (op. 15), and *Kreisleriana* (op. 16). Schumann, who had been

writing critiques and other articles for a small number of musical journals, also began working with some of his associates to create a new periodical, *Neue Leipziger Zeitschrift für Musik,* with its debut issue published in April 1834.

During his time at the Wieck household, Schumann fell in love with Clara, who was nine years younger. After a courtship that lasted five years—much to the dismay of Friederich, who refused to give Schumann Clara's hand in marriage—Schumann was finally allowed by the courts to wed Clara in 1840. He was now with the woman of his dreams and deeply in love. As a result, the following year turned out to be one of Schumann's most productive. He wrote more than a hundred songs for voice and piano, many of them settings of poetry by Johann Wolfgang von Goethe, Heinrich Heine, and Joseph Eichendorff. The most important song cycles from this period include the two sets of *Liederkreis* (opp. 24 and 39) and *Dichterliebe* (op. 48).

In 1841 Schumann wrote the first of his symphonies, a work subtitled *Spring,* which he created as a way of celebrating life, love, and new beginnings. Felix Mendelssohn conducted the debut performance of the score at the Leipzig Gewandhaus and the relative success of this concert encouraged Schumann to write more works for orchestra. One of the first compositions in this mode was a symphony in D Minor which would later be designated as his Symphony no. 4 (op. 120), but the next year saw Schumann turning to chamber music, composing three string quartets, a piano quintet, and a piano quartet. Clara and Robert went on a concert swing through Russia for the first five months of 1844, on which she played before Czar Nicolas I and Robert's first symphony and piano quintets received performances. Schumann was demonstrating symptoms of depression all during the tour and continued to throughout most of the year, only starting to recover (to some extent) by January 1845. The following year he began getting back into the flow of composing, completing his wonderful piano concerto and beginning work on the C Minor symphony (later known as his "second" symphony). This relatively small stream of compositions trickled on into 1847, when he wrote a few vocal works and finished off the *Genoveva Overture.* Two years later, however, Schumann began another impressive run of scores, completing the *Phantasiestücke* for Clarinet and Piano (op.

Robert Schumann

73), the twenty-eight songs in the *Lieder-Album für die Jungend* (op. 79), and the *Concertstück* for Four Horns and Orchestra (op. 86).

Before he married Clara, Schumann's reputation for drinking, partying, and sexual promiscuity was well-deserved, and the latter activity had led to syphilis. Medication failed to curb the symptoms of the disease, and around 1850 he began hearing voices in his head. He was still able to compose music on a sporadic basis (his *Rhenish* Symphony dates from this period), but four years later, after much suffering and the deterioration of his ability to compose, he asked to be taken to an insane asylum. His doctor refused and told him to get some rest; soon after, in a fit of severe depression, Schumann threw himself from a bridge into the Rhine River. He was rescued by fishermen and placed in a mental institution, where he remained until his death in 1856.

Orchestral
Symphonies nos. 1–4 (complete)
what to buy: [*Schumann: Complete Symphonies*; John Eliot Gardiner, cond.; Orchestre Révolutionaire et Romantique] (Deutsche Grammophon/Archiv 457591) ♪ ♪ ♪ ♪

Schumann didn't write his symphonies to be performed by large orchestras. Rather, he wrote them for orchestras of about fifty players. This is the size of the Revolutionary and Romantic Orchestra on this recording, and the result is an exciting contrast to other tried-and-true recordings of these symphonies. Gardiner's three-disc set also includes the 1841 edition of Schumann's fourth symphony (in addition to the 1851 version), the *Zwickau* Symphony in G Minor, the *Konzertstük* in F Major for Four Horns and Orchestra, and the *Overture, Scherzo, and Finale,* op. 52.

[*Schumann: 4 Symphonien*; Herbert von Karajan, cond.; Berlin Philharmonic Orchestra] (Deutsche Grammophon 429672) ♪ ♪ ♪ ♪

For people who prefer their performances of these problematic works in the "traditional" large-band format, Karajan's well-recorded, superbly-judged readings, should fill the bill.

what to buy next: [Leonard Bernstein, cond.; Vienna Philharmonic Orchestra] (Deutsche Grammophon 453049) ♪ ♪ ♪ ♪

Bernstein's second run-through of the symphonies (the first one happened with the New York Philharmonic Orchestra) is the product of his increased artistic maturity and an orchestra with a long and distinguished pedigree. The engineering is good if not spectacular, and Bernstein tends toward speed in his tempos though not enough to lose sight of Schumann's Romantic vision.

[Paul Paray, cond.; Detroit Symphony Orchestra] (Mercury Living Presence 462955) ♪ ♪ ♪

These 1950s-vintage performances, full of sparkle and verve, reveal Paray as a marvelous conductor able to get every last ounce of polish out of his orchestra. Their playing in Symphony no. 1 in B-flat Major (*Spring*) is a joy, and in the *Rhenish* (no. 3 in E-flat Major) they treat the opening movement *Lebhaft* with suitable power and dignity. The fourth symphony (in D Minor) is the only monaural recording in the set, but the playing is such that only diehard stereophiles are likely to complain.

Symphony no. 3 in E-flat Major, op. 97 (*Rhenish*)
what to buy: [Christian Thielemann, cond.; Philharmonia Orchestra] (Deutsche Grammophon 459680) ♪ ♪ ♪ ♪

Schumann's last large-scale orchestral work (his fourth symphony was actually written before this one) demands a performance that can handle its rhythms without tripping over its own feet. Thielemann is a young conductor who is fast becoming a force to be reckoned with, and well-recorded versions of the composer's *Genovena Overture* (op. 81) and the *Overture, Scherzo, and Finale* (op. 52) prepare the way for Thielemann's *Rhenish*.

Concerto in A Minor for Piano and Orchestra, op. 54
what to buy: [Murray Perahia, piano; Claudio Abbado, cond.; Berlin Philharmonic Orchestra] (Sony 64577) ♪ ♪ ♪ ♪

Released in late 1997, this Grammy-nominated recording is an exciting performance of Schumann's only piano concerto. Written soon after his marriage to Clara, the concerto reflects the blossoming of love in Schumann's life and another feather in his cap as he pursued the lofty ideals of composers like Beethoven and Schubert. Perahia also includes the *Concertstück*, op. 92, and the *Introduction and Allegro* for Piano and Orchestra, op. 134, in this recital.

what to buy next: [*Great Pianists of the 20th Century: Artur Rubinstein II*; Artur Rubinstein, piano; Josef Krips, cond.; RCA Victor Symphony Orchestra] (Philips 456958) ♪ ♪ ♪

Poetry abounds in the pianist's interpretation, and the engineering is one of the better RCA efforts from the late 1950s. This two-disc set also includes Rubinstein in concertos by Edvard Grieg, Camille Saint-Saëns (his second), Frederic Chopin (his second), and Piotr Tchaikovsky (his first).

[Maria João Pires, piano; Claudio Abbado, cond.; Chamber Orchestra of Europe] (Deutsche Grammophon 463179) ♪ ♪ ♪ ♪

The orchestra is smaller than what one normally hears in this work but Abbado and Pires are able to turn that to their advantage, presenting a surprisingly intimate version of this score that still contains plenty of power. Pires, who records far less than other pianists of her stature, is marvelous throughout, and her playing on the other piece on this disc, Schumann's Quintet in E-flat Major for Piano and Strings (op. 44), is consistently charming.

worth searching for: [Van Cliburn, piano; Fritz Reiner, cond.; Chicago Symphony Orchestra] (RCA Gold Seal 60420) ♪ ♪ ♪ ♪

Cliburn's approach is more muscular than Rubinstein's version, but then again his manner at the keyboard is a better match for Reiner's somewhat speedier tempos than it would be for Krips's more even pacing. Not that the performance lacks subtlety, because it certainly does have lovely moments, but this is Schumann as Romantic virtuoso instead of Schumann as mere Romantic musician. Cliburn's performance here is paired with a really wonderful recording of Edward MacDowell's second piano concerto with Walter Hendl conducting.

Concerto in A Minor for Cello and Orchestra, op. 129
what to buy: [Yo-Yo Ma, cello; Colin Davis, cond.; Bavarian Radio Symphony Orchestra] (Sony Classics 42663) ♪ ♪ ♪ ♪

Schumann wrote this concerto in just two weeks in 1850, intending it to be a showpiece for the cello with orchestral accompaniment, and what better way to show off the cello than to have one of the world's finest cellists, Yo-Yo Ma, as soloist. Colin Davis leads the Bavarian Radio Symphony in a clear, precise, and powerful accompaniment role. This is an all-Schumann disc that also features his arrangements for cello and piano of the *Adagio and Allegro* in A-flat Major and the *Fantasiestüke* (op. 73), in addition to his five *Stüke im Volkston* for Cello and Piano, with Emmanuel Ax accompanying Yo-Yo Ma.

what to buy next: [Janos Starker, cello; Stanislaw Skrowaczewski, cond.; London Symphony Orchestra] (Mercury Living Presence 432010) ♪ ♪ ♪♪

Starker is a masterful performer possessed of a strong, powerful, almost brawny sound that still manages to convey the delicacy of the composer's lovely second movement. The cellist also supplied the cadenza heard in the finale and it proves to be an altogether interesting alternative to the way Yo-Yo Ma plays the movement. Skrowaczewski leads the LSO through their paces, compelling them to provide a taut backdrop for Starker's superb performance. These same forces can also be heard on this disc in exemplary renditions of cello concertos by Édouard Lalo and (with Antal Dorati taking the place of Skrowaczewski) the first cello concerto, op. 33, by Saint-Saëns.

Chamber
Carnaval for Piano, op. 9
what to buy: [*Great Pianists of the 20th Century: Arturo Benedetti Michelangeli II*; Arturo Benedetti Michelangeli, piano] (Philips 456904) ♪ ♪ ♪ ♪

The earliest of Schumann's great piano cycles gets a marvelous performance here that transcends the engineering processes available to Michelangeli when he recorded it in 1957. While there are several recordings of these scores by the pianist available, these are the most accessible and the most consistent. This two-disc set also includes worthy performances of works by Beethoven, Brahms, Chopin, and Mompou in addition to three excerpts from Schumann's *Album für die Jungend*.

Symphonic Études for Piano, op. 13
what to buy: [Murray Perahia, piano] (Sony Classics 34539) ♪ ♪ ♪ ♪♪

Perahia plays with the right mixture of grandeur and subtlety to bring out all of the nuances Schumann packed into this magnificent score. The earlier *Papillons* (op. 2) is a pleasant set of sonic bonbons that the pianist

includes in contrast to the weightier work.

what to buy next: [Wilhelm Kempff, piano] (Deutsche Grammophon 447977) ♪ ♪ ♪ ♪

Kempff was a maddeningly erratic pianist but when he was in top form, as on this recording, he gave glorious readings of consummate artistry. Included on this disc is his performance of Schumann's *Fantasie in C Major,* a wonderful piece but not one which Kempff delivers with the quality of inspiration heard in his rendition of the *Symphonic Études.*

worth searching for: [Vladimir Ashkenazy, piano] (London 414474) ♪ ♪ ♪ ♪

Schumann might be surprised to know that his Symphonic Études are now among his most well-loved and well-respected compositions, since he originally intended for the études to be simple variations on a funeral march. What he created instead was a set of pieces that explore the possibilities of the piano's sound. Ashkenazy is highly qualified to lead the exploration.

Kinderszenen for Piano, op. 15
what to buy: [*Ivan Moravec Plays Schumann and Franck*; Ivan Moravec, piano] (Supraphon 3508-2 011) ♪ ♪ ♪ ♪

Moravec is known more for his Chopin and Debussy playing, but it makes perfect sense for him to record one of Schumann's most delightful piano cycles. The results are quite lovely indeed and worth seeking out, especially at the relatively inexpensive price point this album was assigned. Moravec also displays a canny grasp of Schumann's piano concerto on this disc. Although the tempos are a bit quick, nowhere are they merely facile. Václav Neumann conducts the Czech Philharmonic Orchestra in support of the pianist in both the Schumann concerto and César Franck's *Symphonic Variations* for Piano and Orchestra.

[*Piano Music of Robert Schumann*; Antonin Kubalek, piano] (Dorian 90116) ♪ ♪ ♪ ♪

Czech pianist Antonin Kubalek became a profound admirer of Schumann after hearing the great Russian pianist Sviatoslav Richter perform a selection from the composer's *Kinderszenen.* This disc also contains worthy renditions of two other popular piano works by Schumann, the *Carnaval* cycle and the three

Fantasiestüke for piano, plus the composer's later masterpiece, *Gesänge der Frühe* for Piano (op. 133). Kubelik displays great precision and control in these performances.

Kreisleriana for Piano, op. 16
what to buy: [Andras Schiff, piano] (Teldec 14566)
♪ ♪ ♪ ♪

On a purely technical level *Kreisleriana* is similar in complexity to Johann Sebastian Bach's intricate keyboard music of the early eighteenth century. Schumann, always the romantic, also builds upon Bach's controlled musical language and provides a great deal of passion in this work, from unrestrained emotion to quiet introspection. Pianist Andras Schiff seems to put himself inside the mind of Schumann and gives a moving performance on this recording.

Vocal
Dichterliebe for Voice and Piano, op. 48
what to buy: [Dietrich Fischer-Dieskau, baritone; Alfred Brendel, piano] (Philips 416352) ♪ ♪ ♪ ♪

Brendel is known more as a solo artist but the pairing with Fischer-Dieskau on this recording is felicitous to say the least. It may not erase memories of the singer's earlier versions of *Dichterliebe* with either Christoph Eschenbach or Jörg Demus, but this older, wiser version of the great baritone (despite the occasional break in his voice) is still hard to beat. The duo's take on Schumann's *Liederkreis* (op. 39) stands up to the competition as well.

[Fritz Wunderlich, tenor; Hubert Giesen, piano] (Deutsche Grammophon 449747) ♪ ♪ ♪ ♪

Wunderlich has a secure reputation for his operetta recitals (particularly in works by Franz Lehár), and possessed one of the sweetest tenors of his day. This 1962 recording shows that he was also a more than capable interpreter of Schumann's finest song cycle. To make things even more interesting, the disc includes four lieder from Ludwig van Beethoven and nine songs by Franz Schubert, richly rounding out this delightful, mid-priced set.

what to buy next: [*The Songs of Robert Schumann, vol. 5: "Dichterliebe" and other Heine settings*; Christopher Maltman, baritone; Graham Johnson, piano] (Hyperion 33105) ♪ ♪ ♪ ♪

Maltman's voice has a darker coloring to it than either Fischer-Dieskau or Wunderlich, and his phrasing lacks the last ounce of finesse that maturity will undoubtedly bring to it. Still, this is an admirable entry in Hyperion's Schumann cycle, and one that takes on more value upon repeated listenings. Part of this has to do with the other settings of twenty Heinrich Heine texts in this release, pieces in which Maltman does exemplary work. The accompanying booklet contains 119 pages' worth of notes with translated lyrics and fine essays about the cycle, which only aids in the appreciation of this recital.

worth searching for: [*Deutsche Grammophon Centenary: Vol. III, 1948–1957*; Dietrich Fischer-Dieskau, baritone; Christoph Eschenbach, piano] (Deutsche Grammophon 459067) ♪ ♪ ♪ ♪ ♪

Fischer-Dieskau and Eschenbach give an intimate performance of these songs which almost makes it seem as if Schumann wrote them for this duo. Schumann's love of poetry and his skill for creating beautiful melodies are never more evident than in these songs of love and nature. The one problem is that this performance is now only available on a ten-CD set with many other artists doing material by a bevy of other composers.

Liederkreis, op. 39
what to buy: [Margaret Price, soprano; Graham Johnson, piano] (Hyperion/Helios 55011) ♪ ♪ ♪ ♪

The first of Schumann's great song cycles receives an exemplary performance from Price. This stands as a wonderful mirror image to the Fischer-Dieskau version cited above (with the Brendel-powered *Dichterliebe* interpretation), both in pacing and nuances. Price also gives a worthy rendition of the dozen lied in the composer's *Gedichte* (op. 35).

influences: Johannes Brahms, Clara Schumann, Johann Nepomuk Hummel

Steve Coghill and Ian Palmer

Heinrich Schütz
Born c. October 9, 1585, in Köstritz, Germany. Died November 6, 1672, in Dresden, Germany.

period: Baroque

Schütz is widely considered to be the most influential composer of Germany's middle-baroque period. Along with his countrymen Johann Hermann Schein and Samuel Scheidt, Schütz deserves credit for the transfer of the Italian *concertato* style to the choral music of the German Lutheran Church in the first half of the seventeenth century. Schütz's prodigious output of concerted choral music helped establish the modal framework for the late-baroque cantatas of Johann Sebastian Bach as well as the oratorios of George Frideric Handel and others.

Schütz's early university education centered on the law, but music theory and composition eventually took precedence, and Schütz traveled to Venice to study, first under Giovanni Gabrieli (from 1609 to 1612) and later with Claudio Monteverdi. In Venice, alongside the two masters of the Italian baroque, Schütz gained firsthand exposure to the dramatic *concertato* style that had as its central characteristic the highly expressive interpretation of text. Both Gabrieli and Monteverdi had successfully applied this style to their sacred choral music, and Monteverdi used it as a primary ingredient in his monody. Schütz's first set of five-part madrigals in the Italian style appeared during this period. Aside from his Venetian sojourn, Schütz, like many of his German contemporaries, traveled relatively little and occupied only a few musical positions during his career. By far the most significant of these was his tenure as Kapellmeister to the Elector of Saxony in Dresden, the seat of the imperial court and an important European cultural center. His appointment was granted in 1617 and lasted until his death in 1672. The only interruptions came as a result of the Thirty Years War, when he labored as court composer and conductor in Copenhagen and when he briefly returned to Italy in 1628, at which time he renewed his acquaintance with Monteverdi and the Venetian court.

Although Schütz is known to have written instrumental works and even opera-like compositions, most of this very small repertoire is either lost or of questionable authorship. The composer's reputation as a leader of the German baroque movement rests on his vast sacred vocal/choral oeuvre, which contains a treasury of compositions following virtually every form of the period. His *Psalmen Davids* (1619) consists of twenty-six settings for single and double choruses, soloists, and instrumental continuo. Each setting applies the expressive Venetian style in a passionate treatment of the German text. The treatments vary from immense choral sonori-

ties to intimate solo passages in the monodic style. Schutz's *Cantiones Sacrae* (1625), an apparent extension of Monteverdi's *concertato* motet style, includes forty motets in the Venetian manner. Each voice part helps propel the other three parts forward as it simultaneously collides rhythmically and harmonically with them. The three collections of *Symphonie Sacrae* were published in 1629, 1647, and 1650 and range from works requiring only a few performers to major offerings in six parts with continuo accompaniment. Changing meters, steep melodic ascents and descents, and jarring harmonic episodes characterize what remains Schütz's greatest single collection of sacred choral works. The composer's smaller works include the intimate *Kleine Geistliche Konzerte* (1636–1639), set for between one and five solo voices. All of these *Konzerte* employ straightforward organ accompaniment in primarily homophonic texture, with little counterpoint.

Schütz stands as one of the baroque era's earliest successful experimenters with the maturing oratorio form. Indeed, his oratorios are a worthy foundation for the later perfection of the form under Bach and Handel. His *Seven Last Words of Christ on the Cross* (1645) includes episodes of expressive monody under both the narrations and Christ's quotes, all with a spare accompaniment of strings with continuo. Symmetry also comes into focus in the work, with an opening and closing sinfonia and chorus that give the work a circumspection that its stunning text truly deserves. The *Christmas Oratorio* (1664) also evokes a singularly dramatic style, with accompanied choruses at both start and finish. Within the body of the work, the major plot elements are conveyed via recitative, while commentary is delivered by way of choruses and solos in the monodic style. All this points to the strong influence of early opera and the "crossover" application of its stylistic elements to the unstaged yet increasingly dramatic sacred oratorio. The three *Passions* were composed in or around 1666 and follow the gospel narratives of Matthew, Luke, and John. Each work is unaccompanied throughout, offering the words of Jesus and other characters in an austere quasi-plainsong style while representing the *populi* (multitude) in a cappella four-part polyphony.

Vocal
Cantiones Sacrae **for Solo Voices and Continuo, op. 4**
what to buy: [Mona Spägele, soprano; Ralf Popken, alto; Rogers Covey-Crump, John Potter, tenors; Peter Kooj, bass; Thomas Ihlenfeldt, chitarrone; Manfred

Cordes, organ; Manfred Cordes, cond.] (CPO 999405) ♪ ♪ ♪ ♪₈

The superb work of these musicians under Manfred Cordes's direction makes this performance of Schütz's greatest choral music a revelation to even the most seasoned disciple of this baroque master. The ensemble correctly chooses to retain the accuracy of Schütz's original sonic design by placing only one voice on each choral part. Such treatment provides a translucent clarity to each melodic line and an aura of pious sincerity to each phrase of the text. The blend, balance, and continuity of each line as it slips from one part to another are all superb, making this a performance for the ages.

Psalmen Davids for Continuo and Chorus, op. 2
what to buy: [Konrad Junghänel, cond.; Concerto Palatino, ensemble; Cantus Cölln, choir] (Harmonia Mundi 901652/53) ♪ ♪ ♪ ♪

Junghänel's forces achieve a stylistic and acoustic revisitation of Venetian soil through the crisp and youthful treatment of each motet. Clearly articulated phrases of melody and text are hallmarks throughout, especially in moments of highly contrapuntal movement and sharp shifts in rhythm, meter, and tempo. This performance vehicle handles such curves with superb control and foresight. Here is ample testimony to Schütz's role as the "anonymous Venetian" of the German mid-baroque.

influences: Claudio Monteverdi, Giovanni Gabrieli, Johann Hermann Schein, Samuel Scheidt

Frank Scinta

Alexander Scriabin
Born Alexander Nikolayevich Skryabin, January 6, 1872, in Moscow, Russia. Died April 27, 1915, in Moscow Russia.

period: Romantic/20th century

Alexander Scriabin's skill as a pianist has become the stuff of legend, and the ecstatic works written by the Russian composer towards the end of his brief life nearly skate off the tonal map, presaging some of the stylistic features in music by Alban Berg and Olivier Messiaen.

Scriabin was brought up and hopelessly spoiled by a doting aunt, grandmother, and great-aunt after his own mother died and his father abandoned him to become an interpreter at the Russian Embassy in Turkey. The feminine triumvirate made him the center of their universe and, by extension, the axis around which his entire world would revolve. In a life governed by egocentricity and expediency, the one area with a modicum of discipline was music. His mother had been one of the finest pianists in Russia, and his aunt, also a pianist, gave him his first lessons. Scriabin received further musical training from Georgy Konyus and Sergei Taneyev before entering the Moscow Conservatory in 1888 and studying piano with Vassili Safonov. He soon demonstrated his brilliance as a virtuoso, winning a second prize (his fellow student Sergei Rachmaninoff won the first). An opportunity arose to show some of his compositions to a publisher, and Scriabin's self-confidence in his own music was validated when five of his piano works were published in 1893.

It was around this time that Scriabin began reading the first of the philosophical treatises which would make a profound impression on his thought and art: Arthur Schopenhauer's *Die Welt als Wille und Vorstellung (The World as Will and Representation)*. His cultural horizons were further broadened through travel, particularly to Paris, where he played at a number of fashionable salons and wrote a number of his early Preludes and Etudes before returning to Russia in 1896. That year he composed his only piano concerto, and a year later he married Vera Ivanova Isakovich, a talented pianist in her own right. By the time he joined the piano teaching staff of the Moscow Conservatory in 1898, Scriabin had composed his second and third piano sonatas and had met a young woman, Tatyana Schloezer, for whom he would eventually abandon Vera.

When he resigned from his post in 1902, he had completed two symphonies, toyed with the idea of writing an opera, and been buoyed by the reception at the first concert devoted exclusively to his piano and orchestral works. His style was becoming increasingly individual, further removed from the influence of earlier Russian and Romantic composers; this tendency can already been seen in his next major works, the Third Symphony (the *Divine Poem*) and Fourth Piano Sonata. Joining a philosophical society, he became acquainted with the existentialist works of Friedrich Nietzsche and infatuated (like Richard Wagner before him) with the relation of concepts such as the "will to power" and the *Übermen-*

sch (Superman) to the arts. He left Russia in 1904, taking up residence first in Switzerland, then in Paris where he managed to secure a performance of the *Divine Poem* in 1905.

By this time Vera had found out about Tatiana and returned to Russia with their four children. A year later, he moved with his young paramour, now pregnant, to Italy, and it was there that he first became acquainted with Helena Petrovna Blavatsky's theosophical writings, concepts which subsumed the Nietszchean denial of a universal morality through her argument for reconciling "all religions, sects, and nations under a common system of ethics, based on eternal verities." This potpourri of mystical tenets found fertile ground in the self-involved Scriabin and greatly influenced the grandiose musical ideas upon which his last works would be based. He also became fascinated by colors and scents and how they could be related to music.

The first works to emerge in this new creative phase—the Fifth Piano Sonata in 1907 and a tone poem for large orchestra (sometimes called his Symphony no. 4) the following year, both based on Scriabin's poem entitled the *Poem of Ecstasy*—were meant to convey "harmonies of sounds, harmonies of colors, harmonies of perfume!" That they were to do so within a radically revamped sonata form built out of continually evolving motifs and themes that was almost incidental to the philosophical underpinnings Scriabin associated with his work. From then on he would assign colors to specific keys and emotions, with the eventual aim of constructing a piece that would be the fulfillment of his philosophies. The next step on this path was *Prometheus, Poem of Fire,* completed in 1910, which calls for an enormous orchestra augmented by a solo piano, chorus, and light effects—the first large-scale multi-media composition of the 20th century But Scriabin had even grander plans, envisioning a pair of works he called the *Prefatory Action* and *Mysterium*. These "events" (for surely they were conceived as such) were meant to vault the listeners out of the physical universe and into a higher consciousness. While he was working out the processes involved in this colossal undertaking, Scriabin also wrote his most innovative piano sonatas (nos. 6-10) and the ecstatic *Vers la flamme* for piano. He did not live to finish either the *Prefatory Action* or the *Mysterium* however, but succumbed to blood poisoning at the age of 43 as a result of attempts to remove an infected carbuncle.

Orchestral
Concerto in F-sharp Minor for Piano and Orchestra, op. 20

[Roland Pöntinen, piano; Leif Segerstam, piano; Stockholm Philharmonic Orchestra] (BIS 475) ♪ ♪ ♪ ♪

Pöntinen is a marvelous, subtle pianist, something readily apparent from his handling of the *Andante* in Scriabin's early showpiece for piano and orchestra. Segerstam is a thoroughly capable conductor in this and the composer's Third Symphony (*Divine Poem*) but both are sabotaged by acoustics which at times threaten to obliterate the music's architectural details. The performance of the concerto by Boulez and Ugorski (see below), is graced with much better sonics and may be a better buy if you are looking specifically for that work.

Symphony no. 4, op. 54—*Poem of Ecstasy*
what to buy: [Mikhail Pletnev, cond.; Russian National Orchestra] (Deutsche Grammophon 459681) ♪ ♪ ♪ ♪

Pletnev has moved from the piano bench to the podium with surprising ease, leading the orchestra with considerable aplomb, and reveling in Scriabin's lush orchestral textures. His performances of the *Poem of Ecstasy* and the accompanying *Divine Poem* are almost ideal.

what to buy next: [Igor Golovschin, cond.; Moscow Symphony Orchestra] (Naxos 8.553583) ♪ ♪ ♪

The conductor's tempos are expansive to say the least. Although the work never really loses its shape and there is something to be said for Golovschin's vision of this score as a slow burgeoning force of nature, those who want a truly revelatory performance of this work are invited to try the Pletnev (see above) or Boulez (see below) recordings. The budget price of this set (which also includes the *Divine Poem*), however, makes it a viable alternative.

Symphony no. 5, op. 60—*Prometheus, Poem of Fire*
what to buy: [Pierre Boulez, cond.; Anatol Ugorski, piano; Chicago Symphony Orchestra; Chicago Symphony Chorus] (Deutsche Grammophon 459647) ♪ ♪ ♪ ♪ ♪

The engineers have outdone themselves here, allowing Boulez (always a stickler for clarity) to bring out the inner details of the score, something that has eluded many other recordings of this work. The same applies to

Ugorski's performances of Scriabin's Piano Concerto and the CSO's playing in the third piece on this disc, the *Poem of Ecstasy.*

Chamber
Sonatas for Piano (complete)
what to buy: [Ruth Laredo, piano] (Nonesuch 73035) ♪ ♪ ♪ ♪♪

Originally released by Connoisseur Society, Laredo's performances of the complete sonatas have been benchmarks for many years now. The two-CD set is also an excellent place to begin a traversal of Scriabin's other piano works, as Laredo's exemplary program also includes a sampling of the etudes and the extraordinary *Vers la flamme.*

what to buy next: [Marc-André Hamelin, piano] (Hyperion 67131/32) ♪ ♪ ♪ ♪

Hamelin's technique tends to overwhelm at times and various critics have called into question his rapid-fire approach to these sonatas. Bearing all that in mind however, these are still magnificently crafted performances, showcasing what will perhaps be the next step in the evolution of how Scriabin's piano works are played, full of intellectual fire but not much fury.

Sonata no. 5 in F sharp major for Piano, op. 53—
Poem of Ecstasy
what to buy: [*Svjatoslav Richter In Prague: Frédéric Chopin*; Sviatoslav Richter, piano] (Praga 254056) ♪ ♪ ♪ ♪ ♪

Hidden away towards the end of a very good Chopin recital from 1988 (five etudes, two nocturnes, and the *Polonaise-Fantaisie*) are excellent versions of Scriabin's second and fifth piano sonatas. The Fifth, with its quick mood shifts, is particularly devastating, especially abrupt and shattering conclusion. This 1972 vintage concert recording is sonically undistinguished, but the performance is so elemental and powerful that Czech Radio's workmanlike engineers of the time couldn't possibly spoil it.

what to buy next: [*Horowitz Plays Scriabin*; Vladimir Horowitz, piano] (RCA Victor Gold Seal 6215) ♪ ♪ ♪ ♪

The piano sound is a bit "clanky" in Horowitz's "live" 1953 recording but the fire of his performance combines with the relative availability of the disc and the budget

price make this a strong recommendation. Adding to its attractiveness is the bounty of other superbly played Scriabin pieces, including the Third Piano Sonata (*Etats d'âme*), a number of the composer's beguiling Preludes, and three of the Etudes. The uneven sound quality is the result of a variety of sources, spanning the period from 1953 to 1982.

influences: Franz Liszt, Richard Wagner, Karol Szymanowski, Olivier Messiaen, Vissarion Shebalin

Mathilde August

Roger Sessions
Born Roger Huntington Sessions on December 28, 1896, in Brooklyn, NY. Died March 16, 1985, in Princeton, NJ.

period: Twentieth century

There may have been no more important composer/teacher in the United States than Roger Sessions. His students, including Milton Babbitt, David Diamond, Conlon Nancarrow, and Ellen Taafe Zwilich, have helped shape American classical music in the last half of the twentieth century. His own scores show a progressively individual voice that commands attention from both performer and audience.

Even though Sessions received many honors in his life, they didn't translate into popular success. This may be largely attributed to his natural academic bent, which ensured his admission to Harvard University when he was only fourteen years old. Sessions remained in academia for the rest of his life, as a student, researcher, or teacher. It seems he never felt a call to interact with the non-scholarly world and was content to work out his own unique compositional style without regard to whether his works sold or not.

After graduating from Harvard in 1915, Sessions went on to Yale, where he studied composition with Horatio Parker before forming his important relationship with Ernest Bloch. The older composer acted as a mentor to Sessions, hiring him as his assistant. The influence on Sessions of Bloch's essentially rhapsodic approach is most clearly seen in works like the incidental music for *The Black Maskers* (1923) and the Symphony no. 1 (1927). By this time Sessions was showing such potential that he was awarded two Guggenheim Fellowships, a Fellowship of the American Academy in Rome, and a

Carnegie Fellowship, which together underwrote his studies in Europe from 1925 to 1933. Despite his European residence, Sessions entered into a partnership with Aaron Copland to present concerts of contemporary music in New York City between 1928 and 1931. Their first program included music by Virgil Thomson, Carlos Chávez, and Walter Piston, but Olin Downes, the influential critic of the *New York Times,* wrote the evening off as too conservative, calling the music "of such poor, weak, and childish character as to afford no justification for public performance." Still, the series served as an important forum for American composers of that era, and the first season's concerts also presented works by Henry Cowell, George Antheil, and Ruth Crawford Seeger, in addition to two movements from Sessions's first piano sonata.

Sessions returned to the United States in 1935 to resume teaching, wending his way through Princeton, the University of California at Berkeley, Harvard, and the Juilliard School while instructing many of America's finest post-World War II composers. From 1915 through 1970, he wrote and edited for the *Harvard Music Review* and *Modern Music* and published a number of books, including a textbook (*Harmonic Practice* from 1951) and collections of lectures (*The Musical Experience of Composer, Performer, Listener* from 1950 and *Questions about Music* from 1970). During the same period, Sessions only managed to compose nine symphonies, four concertos, a few songs and choral pieces, two operas, less than a dozen chamber works, and a handful of smaller works for orchestra. Meanwhile, his music evolved from a neo-Stravinskian style to serialism, as he developed a highly individual voice that critics deemed thorny but unimpeachable. Sessions wrote that "the key to the understanding of contemporary music lies in repeated hearing; one must hear it till it sounds familiar, until one begins to notice false notes if they are played." Certainly that advice applies to his opera *Montezuma,* which took the composer more than twenty years to compose and received only three productions, even though *Time* magazine once deemed it "12-tone music's finest hour on the operatic stage." Sessions was honored with a Pulitzer Prize in 1974 for his life's work and received another Pulitzer in 1982 for his last completed piece, the Concerto for Orchestra.

Orchestral
Black Maskers Suite
what to buy: [Paul Zukofsky, cond.; Juilliard Orchestra] (New World 80368) ♪ ♪ ♪₆

Written in 1928, this may be the composer's most accessible piece and certainly should be heard by anyone wishing to sample his oeuvre. Based on the incidental music Sessions wrote for Leonid Andreyev's play of the same title, this score hovers close to models provided by Ernest Bloch and Igor Stravinsky. Even though a student orchestra performs the piece here, they are the equal of many professional ensembles. The other works on this disc, William Schuman's *In Praise of Shahn* and Aaron Copland's *Connotations,* are worth checking out as well.

worth searching for: [Walter Hendl, cond.; Vienna Symphony Orchestra] (Desto 6404) ♪ ♪ ♪ ♪

Despite the disappointing "bisonic stereo"—essentially fake stereo from reprocessed monaural tapes—Hendl's version of this score has plenty of emotional impact. The accompanying rendition of Roy Harris's third symphony isn't as convincing as Leonard Bernstein's, but Hendl's version of William Schuman's *American Festival Overture* (also included) is a gem.

Concerto for Orchestra
what to buy: [Seiji Ozawa, cond.; Boston Symphony Orchestra] (Hyperion 66050) ♪ ♪ ♪ ♪

Written specifically for this BSO, Sessions's Concerto for Orchestra was his last completed work and won him a Pulitzer Prize in 1982. Like much of the composer's oeuvre, it is not a terribly easy listen, but it provides its own set of intellectual challenges and rewards. Andrzej Panufnik's Symphony no. 8—*Sinfonia Votiva* fills out the program nicely.

Chamber
Sonata no. 3 for Piano—*Kennedy*
what to buy: [Robert Helps, piano] (New World 80546) ♪ ♪ ♪ ♪₆

Not an easy piece to love but certainly an important one, this sonata is the essence of distilled intensity, with a heartbreaking final movement designated "In memoriam: November 22, 1963"—the day President John F. Kennedy was assassinated. Helps's playing is marvelous and convincing throughout. Sessions's Sonata no. 2 for Piano is also found on this disc, but the performance by Randall Hodgkinson is not as moving, although the pianist does provide an interesting take on Donald Martino's *Fantasies and Impromptus* to finish out the set.

worth searching for: [*The Three Piano Sonatas*; Rebecca La Brecque, piano] (Opus One 56/57) ♪ ♪ ♪⁴

La Brecque gives solid performances on all three of Sessions's piano sonatas. The bonus on this limited-edition vinyl set, however, is her rewarding, insight-filled conversation with Sessions about these works, which is included right after her version of the third sonata.

Vocal
When Lilacs Last in the Dooryard Bloom'd
what to buy: [Esther Hinds, soprano; Florence Quivar, mezzo-soprano; Dominic Cossa, baritone; Seiji Ozawa, cond.; Boston Symphony Orchestra; Tanglewood Festival Chorus] (New World 296) ♪ ♪ ♪

Sessions had played with the idea of working Walt Whitman's poetry into this kind of score as far back as the mid-1920s, but it took him until 1970 to complete this project, which is based on Whitman's famous elegy to Abraham Lincoln. As Ozawa's 1977 recording proves, the results are impressive, riding the edge of serialism but concerned with how the human voice can work within Sessions's unique, contrapuntal stylings. Until somebody records his opera *Montezuma,* this cantata will remain Sessions's most important vocal work to be released on disc.

influences: Ernest Bloch, Arnold Schoenberg, Milton Babbitt, David Diamond, John Harbison, Ellen Taafe Zwilich

Garaud MacTaggart

Dmitri Shostakovich
Born Dmitri Dmitriyevich Shostakovich, c. September 25, 1906, in St. Petersburg, Russia. Died August 9, 1975, in Moscow, Russia.

period: Twentieth century

Although many of Dmitri Shostakovich's works paid lip service to the Russian State and their ideal of "socialist realism" (as defined by the Stalinist regime), his finest scores avoided the guidelines established by the government, instead creating music of great individuality and invention that would sometimes cause communist critics to brand his music as "anti-proletariat." In addition to his impressive symphonic writing, Shostakovich also composed one of the finest string quartet cycles of the twentieth century.

After the Bolshevik coup of 1917 and the ensuing Civil War (1918–1921), Shostakovich's family went from being fairly well-off to scrabbling for enough money to buy bread and other sustenance. When Dmitri's father died in 1922, his mother was not able to generate sufficient income to meet the needs of herself and the three children (Mariya, Dmitri, and Zoya), which meant that the elder members of the trio (Mariya and Dmitri) needed to find some way to help support the family. Alexander Glazunov—director of the Petrograd Conservatory, where Shostakovich had been studying piano, violin, and conducting in addition to composition—even made a pitch to the authorities, attempting to secure an increase in rations for his gifted pupil's family due to Dmitri's poor health. In 1924, Shostakovich eventually secured a job at a cinema providing background music for silent films by playing piano.

On the academic front, the young man was engaged in finishing his first symphony, the graduation exercise which would bring him his initial round of renown. He finished orchestrating it in 1925 and the first complete performance of the work (May 12, 1926) was a success. Despite this achievement, Shostakovich still needed to help support his family and, like many other Soviet-era composers, wrote a number of film scores and incidental music, few of which reflected the direction he would take later. He also improved his scant cash flow with a number of piano recitals, a modicum of publishing royalties, and teaching. From a compositional standpoint, Shostakovich was starting to explore some of the innovations made by Western composers, in particular Alban Berg, who had praised Shostakovich's first symphony and whose opera *Wozzeck* had its Leningrad premiere in 1927. Sergei Prokofiev, whom Shostakovich met that same year, also offered encouragement to the young composer.

The music which would precipitate the first of his crises with the Soviet government had its roots in the period from 1927 to 1932. These works were his first two operas, *Nos (The Nose)* (op. 3) and *Ledi Makbet Mtsenskogo uyezda (Lady Macbeth of the Mtsensk District)* (op. 29). At its premiere, *The Nose* brought charges of "formalism" against Shostakovich from ideological government critics, compelling him to backtrack publicly from his adventurous stance to one more in support of the Stalinist doctrine of "socialist realism." The scores which appeared in-between the pair of operas

varied in their acceptability to the government critics—a process that depended on the changeable tides of official opinion (which were, in turn, governed by the plethora of political show trials characterizing the Stalin regime), and on Shostakovich's tendency to see how much he could get away with. Thus the relatively innocuous *Tahiti Trot* for Orchestra (op. 16) and *Two Pieces by Scarlatti* for Wind Orchestra (op. 17) were passed fairly easily, while his ballets *Bolt* (op. 27) and *Zolotoy vek (The Golden Age)* (op. 22)—despite the political correctness of the storylines the scores were illustrating—provoked blistering reviews from the state-controlled media for their lack of music that the proletariat could easily assimilate.

All of this presaged the firestorm of criticism from organs of the state which he would receive for *Lady Macbeth* after the initial popular and critical acclaim of its 1934 premiere; especially unkind was a later editorial ("Muddle Instead of Music" in the January 28, 1936 edition of *Pravda*) which condemned the opera for its lack of political commitment and sympathetic proletarian characterizations, and the incompatibility of his music with the "universally proclaimed" official style.

Other works written by Shostakovich around this time, including a cycle of twenty-four *Preludes* (op. 34) for piano and the driving yet lyrical Concerto no. 1 in C Minor for Piano, Trumpet, and Orchestra (op. 35), were received more kindly by Soviet critics, but his fourth symphony (written under the influence of his studies of Gustav Mahler scores) remained unperformed until 1961 (according to Maxim, the composer's son, after an initial orchestra rehearsal the musicians were "nervous because of the difficulty" and Shostakovich decided to withdraw it).

His fifth symphony was debuted in 1937 and was termed "a Soviet artist's practical creative reply to just criticism." There is some doubt as to whether the phrase came from the pen of a journalist as has been bandied about or from the composer's mind as a way of heading off critical challenges. In 1940, Shostakovich said, "the finale of the symphony resolves the tragic, tense elements of the first movements on a joyous, optimistic level." In *Testimony: The Memoirs of Dmitri Shostakovich* (compiled by Solomon Volkov, published in 1979, and trashed by Tikhon Khrennikov, then chairman of the state-run Composers' Union, as "this vile falsification") Shostakovich was quoted as saying that "The rejoicing is forced, created under threat . . . ." In any

case, his fifth symphony has since become the most performed orchestral work within his oeuvre after receiving both audience and critical acclaim at its premiere.

1937 was also the beginning of his on and off career as a teacher at the Leningrad Conservatory. His first stint there lasted until 1941 when it was interrupted by the siege of Leningrad. (Shostakovich's seventh symphony was written during this time as a way of memorializing the citizens who fought for their homes and eventually repulsed the invading German troupes after many deaths and serious hardships.) He then resumed his position in 1943, until his next major run-in with the government in 1948 when Shostakovich was accused of formalism once again; his setting of the song cycle *Iz yevreyskoy narodnoy poeziy (From Jewish Folk Poetry)*, a piece that came at a time of anti-Semitic activity on the part of the state, might have been a contributory factor. During those eleven years Shostakovich continued to churn out a number of film scores and incidental music but he also wrote his sixth through ninth symphonies, his stunning first violin concerto, the most impressive piano quintet of the twentieth century, and the first three of his string quartets.

In order to reestablish himself in the good graces of the state, Shostakovich turned to political hack work, a demeaning tactic that had served him well in the past, saving him from the death camps which Stalin and his sycophants had set up for troublesome artists, some of them friends and coworkers of the composer. He created songs and choral pieces to texts glorifying aspects of Russian public policy, whipping out more soundtracks and other dramatic works meant for approved public redemption even as his chamber music scores became an increasingly important way for him to vent more forbidding, private thoughts and explore other artistic avenues than those sanctioned by the government.

This was the period when Shostakovich, taking his cue from the preludes and fugues of Johann Sebastian Bach's *Well-Tempered Clavier*, responded (in 1951) with his own set of twenty-four preludes and fugues and created the magnificent sequence of short keyboard works that make up his opus 87. His tenth symphony (arguably his finest) was completed and premiered in 1953 and built upon many of the ideas of this piano cycle. Some Western critics have called this last work his most "Mahlerian," but the incredibly moving string writing throughout it is distinctly Slavic, hovering around tonality as a response to the dictates of the Party but still invested with the composer's own distinctive personality. Two other great pieces of music date from this time of tribulation for Shostakovich: the first cello concerto (1959), which he wrote for Mstislav Rostropovich, and the most overtly impressive of his string quartets, the eighth (1960).

Shostakovich's next major projects included the 1962 setting of texts by the poet Yevgeni Yevtushenko for his thirteenth symphony (*Babi Yar*). Those stanzas commemorated the 1941 massacre of thousands of Jews in a Ukranian ravine and probably caused a great deal of "official" distress as the chorus shouts, during the first movement, "Let the *Internationale* thunder out when the last anti-Semite on the earth has been finally buried." He balanced this strong work of conscience with the total revamping of his earlier opera, *Lady Macbeth of the Mtsensk District,* in 1963. He transformed it into *Katerina Izmaylova,* but still received a modicum of official criticism despite changing the heroine from a strong, passionate merchant woman motivated by love and cupidity to a gifted woman oppressed by her husband, father-in-law, and the civil bureaucrats of pre-Revolutionary Russia.

The music of Shostakovich's final years includes the balance of his fifteen string quartets and fifteen symphonies, as well as the second concertos he wrote for cello and violin in addition to another symphonic choral work setting text by Yevtushenko, *Kazn/Stepana Razina (The Execution of Stepan Razin)*. He finally died from cancer after years of ill health.

Orchestral
Symphony no. 5 in D Minor, op. 47 *(Revolution)*

what to buy: [Bernard Haitink, cond.; Concertgebouw Orchestra] (Decca 425066) ♪ ♪ ♪ ♪ ♪

Stunning in execution from both performance and engineering standpoints, this recording deserves to be heard by anyone interested in Shostakovich. This disc also contains a very good rendition of the composer's ninth symphony performed by Haitink and the London Philharmonic.

what to buy next: [*Leonard Bernstein: The Royal Edition*; Leonard Bernstein, cond.; New York Philharmonic Orchestra] (Sony Classical 44903) ♪ ♪ ♪ ♪

This is the composer's single most popular symphony and Bernstein dug into it with a powerful conception that his orchestra executed to the fullest. Accompanying this version is Yo-Yo Ma's well-played (but not necessarily top-shelf) recording of the composer's Concerto no. 1 in E-flat Major for Cello and Orchestra, with Eugene Ormandy conducting the Philadelphia Orchestra.

[Maxim Shostakovich, cond.; USSR Symphony Orchestra] (RCA Gold Seal 32041) ♪ ♪ ♪ ♪

Dmitri's son leads a Russian orchestra in performances that are idiomatic to say the least. He imbues the opening *Moderato* marking with that odd mixture of winsome brutality and genteel pathos which makes so many of his father's orchestral scores memorable, and continues onward with an interpretation that vies with Bernstein's. The polka from the *Age of Gold* ballet suite and incidental music for the film *Michurin* round out the disc.

worth searching for: [Mstislav Rostropovich, cond.; National Symphony Orchestra of Washington, D.C.] (Deutsche Grammophon 410509) ♪ ♪ ♪ ♪

Cellist and conductor Mstislav Rostropovich was a close friend of the composer and has an insider's perspective on the music. Unlike the composer, the cellist fled to the West in order to make a living as an artist, leaving the Soviet Union and vowing to make his friend's music known to the entire world. This was one of Rostropovich's best efforts. Sergei Prokofiev's Suite no. 1 from *Romeo and Juliet* is the accompanying work.

Symphony no. 10 in E Minor, op. 93
what to buy: [Herbert von Karajan, cond.; Berlin Philharmonic Orchestra] (Deutsche Grammophon 439036) ♪ ♪ ♪ ♪ ♪

The knock on Karajan has been that he sometimes values precision more than heart, but this recording shows that the two are not mutually exclusive, as the conductor brings out all the dark, bitter pain that Shostakovich invested in this score while not neglecting its warped but majestic beauty.

what to buy next: [Bernard Haitink, cond.; London Philharmonic Orchestra] (Decca 425064) ♪ ♪ ♪ ♪₈

Haitink's performance with the LPO is well-recorded and gives very good value, both in the musicianship displayed and in the pairing of Shostakovich's intense tenth with his second symphony, *To October—a symphonic dedication*. In some ways this earlier work is a more overtly experimental piece, responding to the "decadent" orchestral innovations and mannerisms espoused by Igor Stravinsky and Alban Berg despite its inclusion of a politically-correct second-movement choral paean that champions the heroes of the October Revolution.

[André Previn, cond.; London Symphony Orchestra] (EMI Classics 73369) ♪ ♪ ♪ ♪

Previn treats the work like a safety valve for the composer's emotions, allowing the music to build without bursting its boundaries. It is a remarkably clear-headed rendition drawn from the conductor's traversal of the symphonies and is paired (in a particularly apt move by the record company) with Shostakovich's searing indictment of Soviet anti-Semitism, the Symphony no. 13 in B-flat Minor, op. 113. This two-disc set is attractively priced and the performances stand among the best currently in catalog.

Symphony no. 13 in B-flat Minor, op. 113 (*Babi Yar*)
what to buy: [Anatoly Kotscherga, bass; Neeme Järvi, cond.; Gothenburg Symphony Orchestra; National Male Choir of Estonia] (Deutsche Grammophon 449187) ♪ ♪ ♪ ♪₆

In many ways this work is more an orchestral song cycle than a symphony, but despite the setting of Yevtushenko's poems (one per movement), the construction of the work vindicates the composer's right to call it a symphony. Järvi is blessed with a very good bass in Kotscherga, and the choral passages are most moving throughout. The engineers at Deutsche Grammophon are to be commended for their work as well. The liner notes are relatively informative and, along with the inclusion of the poems lying at the core of this piece, greatly aid the listener's appreciation for one of the composer's most heartfelt, moving compositions.

what to buy next: [Marius Rintzler, bass; Bernard Haitink, cond.; Concertgebouw Orchestra; Concertgebouw Men's Chorus] (Decca 425073) ♪ ♪ ♪ ♪

Haitink's Shostakovich cycle is an admirable one, filled with uniformly fine performances in exemplary recordings at a fairly decent price. This is the case here, though the playing and singing are not as idiomatic as Järvi's Estonian forces in the top-rated disc.

Concerto no. 1 in A Minor for Violin and Orchestra, op. 77
what to buy: [David Oistrakh, violin; Evgeny Mravinsky, cond.; Czech Philharmonic Orchestra] (Le Chant du Monde 7250052) ♪ ♪ ♪ ♪ ♪

Taken from a 1957 radio broadcast not too long after Oistrakh recorded the revision of this work with Mitropoulos (see below), this performance has a taut, edgy quality that serves the score extremely well. The monaural sound is quite clear, communicating the basic power of Oistrakh's playing and Mravinsky's disciplined orchestra. The other work on the program is the composer's second violin concerto with soloist Jirí Tomásek fronting Charles Mackerras and the Prague Radio Symphony Orchestra. This last piece doesn't have quite the fireworks found in the first concerto, but anyone interested in the composer's later works should hear this score too. Tomásek's performance, in this stereo radio broadcast from 1982, is masterful.

Concerto no. 1 in A Minor for Violin and Orchestra, op. 99 (revision of op. 77)
what to buy: [David Oistrakh, violin; Dimitri Mitropoulos, cond.; New York Philharmonic Orchestra] (Sony Classics 63327) ♪ ♪ ♪ ♪₆

Although this was recorded in 1956 when the revision to this work was fairly new, Oistrakh, who was also the dedicatee, displays the raw-boned virtuosity that virtually defined the Russian school of violinists during the Stalinist era. The pairing for the disc is also felicitous, with Mstislav Rostropovich playing cello alongside Eugene Ormandy and the Philadelphia Orchestra in the debut recording of Shostakovich's first cello concerto. The sonics have been cleaned up fairly well and the results deserve to be on everyone's shelf of Shostakovich performances.

what to buy next: [Midori, violin; Claudio Abbado, cond.; Berlin Philharmonic Orchestra] (Sony Classics 68338) ♪ ♪ ♪ ♪

It is almost a given that Midori, a talented violinist, would hit all the right notes in this most demanding score. What surprises is how well the young artist gets to the emotional core of the work in this concert recording, negotiating the difficulties of the cadenza with aplomb while not neglecting to effectively communicate the composer's more dramatic elements. The accompanying version of Tchaikovsky's D Major violin concerto is up against strong competition and doesn't fare as well.

worth searching for: [Itzhak Perlman, violin; Zubin Mehta, cond.; Israel Philharmonic Orchestra] (EMI Classics 49814) ♪ ♪ ♪ ♪ ⅛

Perlman's level of intensity is matched by Mehta and the orchestra in this concert recording and the results are very impressive. Not only is this an emotion-packed performance, it is a technically gifted one that will stand the test of time, especially Perlman's traversal of the fiendish *Scherzo* and his handling of the cadenza. The same forces also do a fine job with Alexander Glazunov's one magnificent essay for violin and orchestra.

Concerto no. 1 in E-flat Major for Cello and Orchestra, op. 107
what to buy: [Pieter Wispelwey, cello; Richard Tognetti, cond.; Australian Chamber Orchestra] (Channel Classics 15398) ♪ ♪ ♪ ♪ ⅛

Wispelwey's grasp of the score is more impressive than just about anyone else's, arguably exceeded only by that of the dedicatee, Mstislav Rostropovich. His playing in the six-minute-long cadenza is packed with a rare combination of intellect and emotion, boding well for the other work on this impressive disc, a stellar performance of Zoltán Kodály's astounding Sonata for Solo Cello, op. 8.

what to buy next: [Maria Kliegel, cello; Antoni Wit, cond.; Polish National Radio Symphony Orchestra (Katowice)] (Naxos 8.550813) ♪ ♪ ♪ ⅛

The only drawback to this recording is an acoustic picture that places the orchestra in a position of dominance more often than it needs to be. That is too bad since Kliegel is an outstanding cellist in many ways and, as evidenced by her playing in the cadenza, one whose career promises much. Notwithstanding the aforementioned reservation, the orchestra's playing is quite impressive. The budget pricing of this set makes Kliegel the first choice for those wishing to have both of Shostakovich's cello concertos in totally recommendable performances.

Concerto no. 1 in C Minor for Piano, Trumpet, and Orchestra, op. 35
what to buy: [Yefim Bronfman, piano; Thomas Stevens, trumpet; Esa-Pekka Salonen, cond.; Los Angeles Philharmonic Orchestra] (Sony Classics

60677) ♪ ♪ ♪ ♪ ⅛

Bronfman is a powerhouse pianist but the technical aspects of his playing rarely interfere with the music, at least in this case. The interplay between piano and trumpet is a joy to hear and Salonen's directing keeps everybody on pace. Shostakovich's second piano concerto, also included, isn't as immediately accessible as his first, but the rewards are there for patient listeners. The last work on this all-Shostakovich disc is the composer's exquisite Quintet in G Minor for Piano and Strings, which finds Bronfman in the company of the Juilliard String Quartet.

[Dmitri Shostakovich, piano; Ludovic Vaillant, trumpet; André Cluytens, cond.; Orchestre National de la Radiodiffusion Française] (EMI Classics Imports 54606) ♪ ♪ ♪ ♪ ⅛

Don't let the vintage 1958 monaural recording dissuade you from this amazing performance. Shostakovich was a masterful pianist and he was a very persuasive advocate for his own works, especially in this concerto where he plays portions of the work at a surprisingly speedy pace. Vaillant was an impressive trumpeter who had a successful career as a teacher after he decided to retire from full-time playing, and he is a totally compatible partner for Shostakovich. The composer's piano artistry is also on display in his second piano concerto, the three early *Fantastic Dances*, op. 5, and a selection of *Preludes and Fugues* from op. 87.

Chamber
Preludes and Fugues, op. 87
what to buy: [Tatiana Nikolayeva, piano] (Hyperion 66441/3) ♪ ♪ ♪ ♪ ♪

Shostakovich wrote this cycle under the influence of Bach and for the pianist playing it on this recording. Nikolayeva premiered the set in 1950, and every decade since then (this three-disc set was recorded in 1990) has increased her familiarity with the score, revealing new insights with each performance. While they can be dipped into enjoyably, Shostakovich's preludes and fugues are even better appreciated when listened to in one fell swoop, a task that would last over two and one-half hours but that would never fail to impress the listener with the composer's consistent level of invention. Although there are other renditions that approach these Olympian performances, the blend of technique and poetry found here is unlikely to be bested.

what to buy next: [Vladimir Ashkenazy, piano] (London 466066) ♪♪♪♪₆

Ashkenazy comes as close to the mountaintop experience of Nikolayeva's recording as anyone has since Roger Woodward's splendid (but deleted) set on RCA Victor. The sound is quite good and Ashkenazy's set puts everything on two discs instead of Nikolayeva's three, which makes his performances a viable, well-thought-out alternative to hers.

[*Shostakovich Plays Shostakovich, vol. 3*; Dmitri Shostakovich, piano] (Revelation 70003) ♪♪♪♪₆

Not all performances by a composer are authoritative, but Shostakovich was such a persuasive piano virtuoso in his own right that these recordings make a wonderful addition to any collection of piano music. The composer can be heard playing seven of his twenty-four preludes on this set (nos. 16–18, 20, and 22–24) and eleven more (nos. 1–8 and 12–14) on a companion disc (Revelation 70001), with both discs featuring cleanly remastered recordings from the 1950s. The three *Fantastic Dances*, op. 5, written when Shostakovich was sixteen years old, fill out the album.

String Quartets (complete)
what to buy: [Fitzwilliam String Quartet, ensemble] (London 455776) ♪♪♪♪♪

High skill, good sonics, and reasonable price combine with the Fitzwilliam String Quartet's sheer level of intensity in landmark performances of Shostakovich's most impressive block of compositions. Spread over six discs, this set has few peers, with only the cycles by the Emerson String Quartet and the Borodin Sting Quartet approaching it (see below).

[Emerson String Quartet, ensemble] (Deutsche Grammophon 463284) ♪♪♪♪♪

This reasonably-priced five-disc set was drawn from concert recordings at the Aspen Music Festival, and packs all the excitement of a well-executed "live" performance into every moment. These are not note-perfect renditions but it almost seems silly to quibble about that when the sheer emotive powers of Shostakovich's scores (especially in nos. 8, 13, and 15) comes through with such poignant force.

Robert Shaw:
When Robert Shaw, the son and grandson of ministers, enrolled at Pomona College in 1934, he began studying comparative religion, philosophy, and English Literature, with an eye toward entering the ministry. Having grown up singing in church choirs, it was only natural for him to gravitate toward the college glee club, the group he was conducting in 1937 when Fred Waring first saw him. The veteran chorus master was suitably impressed with the young man's handling of the choir and praised him. A year later, when Shaw wrote Waring inquiring about the possibility of making a career out of music, he was invited to join Waring's organization.

Although Shaw was employed by Waring from 1938 through 1945, he also worked with choirs at the Berkshire Music Center, ran the choral department at the Juilliard School of Music, and formed the Collegiate Chorale, a partially amateur outfit that frequently appeared with orchestras in New York City. This last-named chorus then gave way in 1944 to the all-professional ensemble known as the Robert Shaw Chorale. Arturo Toscanini supposedly admired Shaw's abilities so much that he considered him the finest choral director he had ever worked with, utilizing the choir in many of his recordings with the NBC Symphony Orchestra. Among the finest examples of Shaw's work with Toscanini were their recordings of Ludwig van Beethoven's Symphony no. 9 in D Minor and Giuseppe Verdi's *Requiem*, both of which are available on *The Immortal Arturo Toscanini, Vol. 3* (RCA Victor Red Seal 55837).

Shaw toured the world with his Chorale throughout the 1950s and 1960s, in addition to working as a conductor with the San Diego Symphony Orchestra and with George Szell in Cleveland as an associate conductor of that city's orchestra. Shaw then moved to Atlanta in 1966 and became co-conductor of the Atlanta Symphony Orchestra, before accepting the position of musical director there a year later. He presided over the enlarging of both the orchestra and the Atlanta Symphony Orchestra Chorus, guiding both units into world-class status and a recording contract with Telarc Records. His twenty-one years at the helm in Atlanta produced a number of award-winning albums, including six Grammy Awards for Best Choral Performance. His recordings of Benjamin Britten's *War Requiem* (Telarc 80157) and the two *Requiems* of Gabriel Fauré and Maurice Duruflé (Telarc 80135) are among the most moving albums that Shaw created during his stay with the Atlanta Symphony Orchestra and Chorus.

When he retired from his day-to-day activities there in 1988, Shaw concentrated his energies on the Robert Shaw Choral Institute and a series of workshops dealing with the art of a cappella singing. Before he died in 1999, Shaw had been given the first Guggenheim Fellowship ever awarded to a conductor, gotten the George Peabody Medal for outstanding contributions to music in America, and received the National Medal of Arts, to name but a few such well-earned honors.

William Gerard

what to buy next: [*Complete String Quartets*; Borodin String Quartet, ensemble] (BMG/Melodiya 40711) ♪♪♪♪₆

The price is right and the sound is good (if not in the same league as the Fitzwilliam or Emerson sets), all of which is great for those longtime aficionados who swear that no one has ever bettered the legendary group in this material. As an added bonus the set includes the composer's Quintet in G Minor for Piano and Strings, op. 57, with Sviatoslav Richter joining the quartet in a fiery performance.

Quartet no. 8 in C Minor for Strings, op. 110
what to buy: [St. Petersburg String Quartet, ensemble] (Hyperion 67154) ♪ ♪ ♪ ♪₄

This group is working their way through Shostakovich's string quartet cycle and this disc is one of their finest efforts to date, containing a forceful, well-shaped eighth, an interesting albeit darkly-textured sixth, and the lively, folk-inspired rhythms of the all-too-little-played fourth. Their energetic second movement *Allegro molto* is a masterpiece of controlled hysteria while the disturbing drone underlying the beginning of the fourth movement *Largo* is most affecting.

what to buy next: [Rosamunde Quartet, ensemble] (ECM New Series 457067) ♪ ♪ ♪ ♪₄

If their playing in Shostakovich's masterful eighth quartet is any indication, a traversal of the composer's quartet oeuvre by this group would be a welcome addition to the catalog. Well recorded and lean in texture, these are admirable adjuncts to the fine performances listed in the complete sets recommended above. A surprisingly romantic treatment of Anton Webern's *Langsamer Satz* and the intriguing fourth quartet by Emil Frantisek Burian are the other works on this program.

Quintet in G Minor for Piano and Strings, op. 57
what to buy: [Victor Aller, piano; Hollywood String Quartet, ensemble] (Testament 1077) ♪ ♪ ♪ ♪₄

One of America's greatest string quartets brought power, flair, and a surprising Slavic quality to what is arguably the finest piano quintet of the twentieth century. Their speed and accuracy in the *Scherzo* is amazing, but they also have the poetry in their fingers to make the most out of the poignant *Intermezzo*. Their performance in the piano quintet by César Franck is also of a high order.

what to buy next: [Dmitri Shostakovich, piano; Beethoven String Quartet, ensemble] (Vanguard Classics 8077) ♪ ♪ ♪ ♪

These players present a performance of conviction and authenticity in this most moving piece. If Shostakovich's playing lacks the total package of power and delicacy that Richter brings to his version with the Borodin String Quartet (see "string quartets" above), the composer still imparts telling emotional accuracy to the bleak austerity residing in the *Fugue*. The accompanying work is a very good performance of Shostakovich's second string quartet, but it pales beside that of the quintet.

influences: Gustav Mahler, Alban Berg, Sergei Prokofiev, Alfred Schnittke, Sofia Gubaidulina, Vissarion Shebalin, Boris Tishchenko, Galina Ustvolskaya

Mathilde August and Steve Coghill

Jean Sibelius
Born Johan Julius Christian Sibelius, December 8, 1865, in Hämeenlinna, Finland. Died September 20, 1957, in Järvenpää, Finland.

period: Twentieth century

Orchestral works, including tone poems, symphonies, and a magnificent violin concerto, are at the core of Sibelius's reputation, with much of his music running toward the dark and earthy in an austere yet passionate embrace. Finland's national folk epic, the *Kalevala,* was the prime inspiration for many of his most famous pieces, and it is unlikely that *Finlandia, The Swan of Tuonela,* or the *Karelia Suite for Orchestra* would have existed without it.

Even though he became closely associated with Finnish culture, Sibelius was never completely comfortable with the language until after his college years. He was born into the Swedish-speaking elite as the son of an army surgeon and didn't really come into full contact with the Finnish language until 1873, when he went to a grammar school and became immersed in it. By this time the young Sibelius had already shown some musical aptitude and taken piano lessons. In 1879 he started studying the violin with an eye toward a career as a virtuoso musician, and a few years later began creating a handful of youthful chamber works.

It wasn't until 1885, when Sibelius entered the University of Helsinki as a law student, that his interest in the *Kalevala* grew into an obsession. Finland was part of the Russian Empire at that time, dating back to 1808 when Russia invaded the country and severed the connection to its former ruler, Sweden. A fever of nationalism was sweeping Europe during the approach of the twentieth century and Finland was not immune. All over the continent, universities were serving as intellectual breeding grounds for nationalist ideals, some of which related to rediscovering the folk roots of a national culture. Elias Lönnrot had already collected much of his research into the *Kalevala* and, in 1836, published his results. Many young Finnish composers were to draw inspiration from this work, most notably Robert Kajanus, whose symphonic poem *Aino* was unveiled in 1885 and made a powerful impact on the young Sibelius when he heard it later, at a performance in Berlin.

After a year in law school, Sibelius switched to the music department at the Helsinki Conservatory, where he studied composition with Martin Wegelius and played second violin in a string quartet. He also met Feruccio Busoni, who was teaching at the university then, and became lifelong friends with him. In 1889 Sibelius went abroad and studied counterpoint in Berlin with Albert Becker and composition in Vienna with Karl Goldmark before returning to Finland in 1891. It was around that time that Sibelius realized he wasn't cut out to be a virtuoso violinist and devoted himself to creating music for others to play. The first real fruits of this decision could be heard in *Kullervo,* a symphonic poem for vocal soloists, chorus, and orchestra, that was based on the tragic anti-hero of the *Kalevala* and first performed in 1892. It was a big success and Kajanus, who was a noted conductor as well as a composer, commissioned the tone poem *En Saga* that same year because he was so impressed with Sibelius's work. The composer's personal life was starting to solidify as well when he married Aino Järnefelt shortly after the premiere of *Kullervo.* The next year found Sibelius employed as a theory teacher at the Helsingfors Conservatory. His next major work, the *Four Legends from the Kalevala* for Orchestra, was finished in 1895.

By 1897 the Finnish government took the unprecedented step of awarding Sibelius with an annual pension (later increased in 1926 by the newly independent Finland) that should have enabled Sibelius to devote more time to composition. The young composer was a profligate spender, however, having developed a love of alcohol and the high life during his trips to Berlin and Vienna. This constant drain on the family finances forced Sibelius to take on students and, later in life, churn out a batch of piano works that, while pleasant, amounted

to hackwork. The composer later acknowledged that he was cashing in on his reputation just so he could generate further funding.

Another banner year for Sibelius was 1899, when he completed work on both his first symphony and the tone poem *Finlandia.* By the end of 1901 he had revised *En Saga,* started working on his second symphony, and quit his teaching job in Helsingfors. Over the course of the next three decades, Sibelius finished the rest of the published work upon which his reputation is based. Included among those pieces were his violin concerto, the balance of his seven symphonies, a handful of tone poems, and an impressive, if too little performed, string quartet, *Voces intimae.* 1929 was the last year that any new composition was released by Sibelius. From then until his death in 1957, Sibelius rarely ventured from his home in Järvenpää. He did mention to Olin Downes that his eighth symphony was finished, and the first movement actually made it to a copyist in 1933, but no other works were forthcoming.

Orchestral
Concerto in D Minor for Violin and Orchestra, op. 47
what to buy: [Anne-Sophie Mutter, violin; André Previn, cond.; Staatskapelle Dresden, orch.] (Deutsche Grammophon 447895) ♪ ♪ ♪ ♪₄.

While Itzhak Perlman has the bigger reputation, his outing with Previn doesn't have the bite that Mutter's newer rendition does. The recording is excellent, the performance is exciting and technically secure, and the three filler pieces consist of other works for violin and orchestra by Sibelius.

[Jascha Heifetz, violin; Walter Hendl, cond.; Chicago Symphony Orchestra] (RCA Victor Red Seal 61744) ♪ ♪ ♪ ♪₄.

This has been a benchmark recording of the concerto for quite some time and there is no reason to stop recommending it now. Heifetz was a musical and technical giant whose playing, while sometimes erring toward the cerebral, never lacked for emotion in all the right spots. The rating is for the performance, not the sonics. Violin concertos by Alexander Glazunov and Sergei Prokofiev (no. 2) are also included in this set.

what to buy next: [Zino Francescatti, violin; Leonard Bernstein, cond.; New York Philharmonic Orchestra]

(Sony Classical Essential Classics 63260) ♪ ♪ ♪ ♪

Francescatti was an intense musician, matching Bernstein's legendary flair with a reading that deserves to be heard. The violinist favors a concept in which density of feeling has the edge on speed in this vintage item from the 1960s. The recording itself is unremarkable, but the relatively cheap price and fiery performance more than make up for any minor sonic shortcomings. When the record company tossed in performances of the first two symphonies (impressively led by Leopold Stokowski and Thomas Schippers, respectively), *The Swan of Tuonela, Finlandia,* the *Valse Triste,* and the *Karelia Suite,* they made this disc an almost unbeatable buy.

[Nadja Salerno-Sonnenberg, violin; Michael Tilson Thomas, cond.; London Symphony Orchestra] (EMI Classics 54855) ♪ ♪ ♪ ♪.

Her interpretation is a little more flexible than one normally hears, but Salerno-Sonnenberg performs with such icy power that the results are more than credible. Her recording of the *Poeme for Violin and Orchestra* by Ernest Chausson is an interesting contrast to the Sibelius piece.

Finlandia for Orchestra, op. 26
what to buy: [*Finlandia*; Vladimir Ashkenazy, cond.; New Philharmonia Orchestra] (Decca Double Decker 452576) ♪ ♪ ♪ ♪♪

Ashkenazy's versions of the tone poems on this two-disc set—*En Saga, Tapiola* and *Finlandia*—are much better than his recordings of the symphonies would lead one to believe. He also conducts a more than passable version of *Luonnotar* (with Elisabeth Söderström as the featured soprano) and the *Karelia Suite.* Horst Stein conducts the Orchestre de la Suisse Romande in the three remaining works heard here, *Nightride and Sunrise, Pohjola's Daughter,* and the *Lemminkäinen Suite.*

what to buy next: [Herbert von Karajan, cond.; Berlin Philharmonic Orchestra] (Deutsche Grammophon 439010) ♪ ♪ ♪ ♪.

The legendary Karajan was a powerful advocate for Sibelius's vision, and this recording shows just how well the composer was served by the master conductor. In addition to *Finlandia,* Karajan leads his orchestra through *The Swan of Tuonela, Valse Triste,* and the two *Peer Gynt* suites and *From Holberg's Time* by Edvard Grieg.

[Eugene Ormandy, cond.; Philadelphia Orchestra] (Sony 48271) ♪ ♪ ♪♪

If everything Ormandy did were as focused as this performance, he would have an even more enduring reputation. This budget-priced compilation also includes most of the same works found on the other sets, but the forces playing them are divided between Ormandy and his Philadelphians and Bernstein with the New York Philharmonic Orchestra.

Four Legends from the Kalevala for Orchestra, op. 22
what to buy: [Paavo Järvi, cond.; Royal Stockholm Philharmonic Orchestra] (Virgin Classics 45213) ♪ ♪ ♪ ♪

The *Lemminkäinen Suite* listed on the disc jacket is an alternate name for the *Four Legends,* so don't be misled. The third movement—otherwise known as *The Swan of Tuonela*—is a lovely piece often performed outside of its original context, but when heard as part of the suite it helps form a consistent whole. Järvi also includes fine readings of two lesser-known tone poems, *Nightride and Sunrise,* op. 55, and *Luonnotar,* op. 70.

what to buy next: [Leif Segerstam, cond.; Helsinki Philharmonic Orchestra] (Ondine 852) ♪ ♪ ♪♪

Segerstam has done a fine version of the suite, but the real reason for picking this disc up is probably the best recording of *Tapiola,* op. 112, the last great tone poem that Sibelius wrote.

various tone poems
what to buy: [Neeme Järvi, cond.; Gothenburg Symphony Orchestra] (Deutsche Grammophon 457654) ♪ ♪ ♪ ♪

The senior Järvi has proven himself, over time, to be a fine Sibelius advocate and this recording is certainly a solid entry in his catalog. The *Tapiola* isn't quite as revelatory as Segerstam's (see above) and his version of *En Saga* lacks some of the dramatic tension that Ashkenazy works up (see above), but the performances on this disc are quite good nonetheless. Fine renderings of *The Bard* and *Spring Song* are also included, but the real find here is the inclusion of four excerpts from the composer's incidental music to *Kuolema,* with Järvi's *Valse triste* standing among the better-recorded versions.

Symphony no. 1 in E Minor, op. 39
what to buy: [Colin Davis, cond.; Boston Symphony Orchestra] (Philips 446157) ♪ ♪ ♪ ♪

Davis's well-judged performances are part of a two-disc set that includes solid renditions of the second and fifth symphonies plus a very good version of the fourth.

what to buy next: [Alexander Gibson, cond.; Royal Scottish Symphony Orchestra] (Chandos 6555) ♪ ♪ ♪₄

Blessed by the Chandos engineers with very good sound, Gibson can be a little brass-heavy at times, but that is the only caveat. His version of the fourth symphony, also on this disc, is solid.

Symphony no. 2 in D Major, op. 43
what to buy: [Osmo Vänskä, cond.; Lahti Symphony Orchestra] (BIS 862) ♪ ♪ ♪ ♪₄

Introspective is the wrong word for this interpretation, and so is pensive. Somewhere in-between is a phrase for the kind of intense, inward-looking emotion that Vänskä brings to this surprisingly warm reading and that of the composer's Symphony no. 3.

what to buy next: [Charles Mackerras, cond.; London Symphony Orchestra] (IMP 927) ♪ ♪ ♪ ♪

Strings are the thing in Sibelius's second symphony, and Mackerras's players are among the best in the world. His version of *The Swan of Tuonela* is one of the better performances currently on the market, which makes this budget recording a double treat.

Symphony no. 4 in A Minor, op. 63
what to buy: [Osmo Vänskä, cond.; Lahti Symphony Orchestra] (BIS 861) ♪ ♪ ♪ ♪ ♪

It doesn't lessen the impact of what had gone before to say that with this symphony Sibelius hit his stride as a highly individualistic painter of orchestral colors. It is hard to imagine a better modern recording of this work than the one by Vänskä. BIS pairs this performance with a sterling, if somewhat speedy, rendition of the composer's first symphony.

what to buy next: [Colin Davis, cond.; London Symphony Orchestra] (RCA Red Seal 68183) ♪ ♪ ♪ ♪

His earlier set of Sibelius symphonies with the Boston

Symphony Orchestra is still one of the finest complete cycles in the catalog, but Davis's new recording of the composer's fourth symphony outshines his previous effort with Boston.

Symphony no. 7 in C Major, op. 105
what to buy: [Colin Davis, cond.; Boston Symphony Orchestra] (Philips 446160) ♪ ♪ ♪ ♪₄

This is an intense, brooding, bleak work that rewards the effort of a committed listener. Davis and the orchestra are very strong throughout. The performance is part of a fine two-disc set that includes good recordings of the third and sixth symphonies, a solid rendition of the violin concerto with Salvatore Accardo as the soloist, and very good versions of *Finlandia* and *The Swan of Tuonela*.

Chamber
Quartet in D Minor for Strings, op. 56 (*Voces intimae*)
what to buy: [Juilliard String Quartet] (Sony Classical 48193) ♪ ♪ ♪ ♪₄

The Juilliards are masters of programming in addition to turning out uniformly good recordings. This holds true for their pairing of this intensely moving work with Verdi's only piece for quartet.

[Melos Quartet] (Harmonia Mundi 901671) ♪ ♪ ♪ ♪₄

With the same pairing on this recording as on the Juilliard one, the comparisons between the two should be easier, but they are not. It comes down to the listener's preference for the lean muscularity of the Americans or the beefy muscularity of the Germans, who are blessed with a somewhat warmer acoustic. Both performances should satisfy their respective purchasers.

what to buy next: [Sibelius Academy String Quartet] (Finlandia 95851) ♪ ♪ ♪₄

While this is a well-played version of this masterpiece, it isn't quite as strong as that of either the Juilliard String Quartet or the Melos Quartet. However, the scale-tipper for this two-disc set may be its inclusion of good, solid interpretations of all the works Sibelius wrote for string quartet, something that is unlikely to be duplicated in the near future.

Vocal
Finlandia-hymni
what to buy: [*Mieskuorolaulut: Songs for Male Voice Choir*, Matti Hyökki, cond.; Helsinki University Chorus] (Finlandia 205) ♪ ♪ ♪ ♪

Sibelius's tone poem *Finlandia* was turned into a song with patriotic lyrics by V.A. Koskenniemi during the Winter War of 1939 to 1940. It is now the de facto national anthem of Finland and often paired with the official anthem, *Maamme*. The choir heard here has a long association with Sibelius's material, having performed his *The Boat Journey* (also heard on this album) as far back as 1893.

influences: Richard Wagner, Richard Strauss, Leevi Madetoja, Toivo Kuula, Joonas Kokkonen, Einojuhani Rautavaara

Garaud MacTaggart

Bedrich Smetana
Born March 2, 1824, in Litomysl, Bohemia. Died May 12, 1884, in Prague, Czechoslovakia.

period: Romantic

It is fair to say that Bedrich Smetana, by virtue of having written the first Czech-language operas to have maintained a hold on the stages of his homeland, should be deemed the first great Czech composer of the nineteenth century. However, his most important instrumental works—an orchestral cycle of six tone poems called *Má Vlast (My Fatherland)* and a pair of string quartets—are actually performed far more often in international venues than are his operas. Two of the tone poems from *Má Vlast—Vlatava (Moldau)* and *Z ceskych luhu a háju (From Bohemia's Fields and Groves)*—show up fairly frequently on public programs, and the overture to his comic opera *Prodaná nevesta (The Bartered Bride)* is a sprightly favorite at pops concerts.

Bedrich Smetana, a talented pianist and violinist who had written some small piano works and a handful of chamber music pieces, moved to Prague in 1843. He was relatively unschooled compared to most of the top-notch musicians living there, but improved his status somewhat by taking lessons in music theory and composition from Josef Proksch, a respected teacher who was

friendly with Robert Schumann, Hector Berlioz, and Franz Liszt. Almost simultaneously Smetana secured a position as piano teacher to Count Leopold F. Thun's family, a relatively stress-free job which afforded him sufficient time for studying harmony and orchestration. He left the Thun household in 1847 to pursue a career as a piano virtuoso, but the disastrous reception of his first few attempts convinced him to fall back upon the idea of starting his own music school. After writing a letter to Liszt in which he more or less begged for a loan to get the project off the ground, Smetana managed to secure enough funding to open the doors. Although Liszt lent him no money, the older composer did recommend Smetana's *Six Characteristic Pieces* for Piano (op. 1) to Franz Kistner, a Leipzig-based music publisher, who in 1851 included it in his company's offerings. After the surprisingly successful start of his music school, Smetana married Katerina Kolarová on August 27, 1849.

The years when Smetana began to strike out on his own coincided with political revolution in Europe. Insurrection in France spread to Austria and then, inevitably, to Prague, where Czech nationalists staged a brief uprising (June 11–16, 1848) against their Austrian rulers. This last event undoubtedly contributed greatly to Smetana's political awareness as a Czech and led him to consider composing works which, to some extent, reflected his countrymen's yearning for a free Bohemian state. It was a process that would eventually yield a series of operas with Czech themes, but not before he would leave his homeland (in 1856) to accept a better-paying position as a music teacher in Göteborg, Sweden. Money wasn't the only reason he left Prague, however. What probably tipped the balance was the seeming inability of Czech audiences to accept his music; Italian and French operas were the rage in Prague theaters and the works of German composers (no matter that he was friends with some of them) seemed to be monopolizing recital programs. In Sweden, Smetana began conducting and programming concerts, including his own scores as well as a number of contemporary works.

The confluence of his wife's ill health (she died from tuberculosis in 1859) and the opening of a theater in Prague which would be devoted to Czech works and artists helped drive Smetana's thoughts toward Bohemia. He married again (Bettina Ferdinandi) in 1860 and finally moved back to Prague a year later. Once there, Smetana dove into the cultural life of the city, organizing concerts of his music, starting up yet another music school, working as a chorus master, and writing concert reviews for a newspaper. Finally, in 1862, he became the principal conductor at the Royal Provincial Czech Theatre, the very venue he had first read about when he was still employed in Göteborg. It is from his stint at the theater that Smetana's first operas date.

Branibori v Cechách (The Brandenburgers in Bohemia), his first dramatic opera, premiered in 1866 and was not well-received by local critics. Smetana's second effort at musical stagecraft, the comedic *Prodaná nevesta (The Bartered Bride),* contains melodies reminiscent of Bohemian folk song and underwent four revisions before achieving success in 1870. *Dalibor,* his next offering, only underwent two revisions but it was bracketed by the third and fourth versions of *The Bartered Bride* and had a more problematic reception after critics leveled charges against what they deemed Smetana's Wagnerian tendencies. Since then, however, these works and, to some degree, his other five operas have become the pillars of the Czech opera tradition even though they haven't traveled well on the international circuit.

In 1872 he began work on a series of six symphonic poems depicting various aspects of Czech legend, history, and scenery. Together the six poems became known as *Má Vlast (My Fatherland).* They depict the course of the river Vltava (or Moldau), beginning from its sources and flowing through Bohemian forests and meadows, past cliffs where castles, mansions and ruins rise up, before finally disappearing in the distance as it flows into the Elbe. As Smetana was writing *Má Vlast* he began to experience syphilitic symptoms, including a high-pitched ringing in his ears. He said that the sound was really "A-flat Major, the interval chord of the sixth to the octave" although it was represented by a sustained E Major in the final movement of his first string quartet, *From My Life.* By 1874 Smetana was completely deaf but six years later he managed to complete *Má Vlast.* In 1882 he began working on his second string quartet, a piece he subtitled *Out of My Life* and finished in 1883. Little more than half the length of his first effort in that medium, this score was meant to continue the storyline of *From My Life*—as he characterized it, "after the catastrophe." His mental state was deteriorating at an increased pace by now and the moments of lucidity were farther and farther apart. In April 1884 he was finally taken to an asylum in Prague, where he died the following month.

Beverly Sills:
Whether on the opera stage or in the executive boardroom, soprano Beverly Sills has been a tireless advocate for the arts in America, as well as a singer of the highest caliber. "Bubbles"—a nickname that has endured her whole life—showed performing abilities as a very young child, working in radio commercials and as part of the company for *Major Bowes' Amateur Hour,* even singing in a movie (*Uncle Sol Solves It*) before she hit her teen years. She made her operatic debut in Philadelphia as Frasquita in Georges Bizet's *Carmen* in 1947. A series of tours with various companies led to performances with the San Francisco Opera and New York City Opera in the mid-1950s. It was her 1958 appearance in the title role of Douglas Moore's *Ballad of Baby Doe* at the New York City Opera that secured her position as one of America's finest singers. Prestigious appearances in Vienna, Buenos Aires, Covent Garden, and La Scala preceded her official Metropolitan Opera debut in Gioachino Rossini's *La Siège de Corinthe* in 1975. As well as possessing a virtuoso vocal instrument, she displayed depth and intelligence.

A skilled and thoughtful administrator, Sills became general director of the New York City Opera in 1979, and bid farewell to performing the following year. She has been an enthusiastic promoter and crusader for the performing arts ever since. It can be argued that she has made an even greater contribution to the future of classical music in her life after opera. Highly regarded the world over, Sills holds a number of honorary degrees and she has been very active in support of a number of worthy causes, perhaps owing to the fact that one of her children is hearing-impaired and the other mentally retarded. A sampling of her impressive discography reveals an artist of great range: Jules Massenet's *Manon* (EMI Classics 69831); George Frideric Handel's *Giulio Cesare (Julius Caesar)* (RCA Victor Gold Seal 6182); Moore's *The Ballad of Baby Doe* (Deutsche Grammophon 465148); Giuseppe Verdi's *La Traviata* (EMI Classics 69827); and *The Three Queens* (Deutsche Grammophon 465967), containing Gaetano Donizetti's *Anna Bolen, Maria Stuarda,* and *Roberto Devereux.* (The last three operas are also available separately as Deutsche Grammophon 465957, 465961, and 465964, respectively.)

Mona DeQuis

Orchestral
Má Vlast (My Fatherland)
what to buy: [Charles Mackerras, cond.; Czech Philharmonic Orchestra] (Supraphon 3465) ♪ ♪ ♪ ♪ ♪

Mackerras studied in Prague with Vaclav Talich, and during the last few decades has been such a persuasive advocate for Czech music that his performances have gained a unique aura of authority. His concert recording of this hallowed cycle showcases the music as few others have been able to do, and is one of the best-recorded versions at any price point.

what to buy next: [Vaclav Talich, cond.; Czech Philharmonic Orchestra] (Supraphon 1896) ♪ ♪ ♪ ♪ ♪

This 1954 recording is a good companion disc to the Mackerras release, displaying his teacher's ability to wring every last bit of emotion from a score even as he communicates the majestic drama underlying some of these pieces. Talich's handling of *Tábor's* brass flourishes amidst the strings is a testament to his formidable skills as a clarifier of orchestral textures.

[Rafael Kubelik, cond.; Boston Symphony Orchestra] (Deutsche Grammophon 429183) ♪ ♪ ♪ ♪ ♪

For a long time, Kubelik's version of these works with the BSO was an automatic recommendation, blessed with fine, fiery playing from a top-notch orchestra guided by the baton of a conductor who knows these pieces inside and out. The budget pricing makes this a compelling alternative to either Mackerras or Talich.

The Bartered Bride: Overture
what to buy: [James Levine, cond.; Vienna Philharmonic Orchestra] (Deutsche Grammophon 427340) ♪ ♪ ♪ ♪

Levine's tautly played collection of Smetana's more popular works serves as a fine introduction to the composer's orchestral writing. In addition to the overture from *The Bartered Bride* there are dances from the opera and two of the symphonic poems from *Má Vlast: From Bohemia's Fields and Groves* and *Vysehrad*.

Chamber
Quartet no. 1 in E Minor for Strings (*From My Life*)
what to buy: [Panocha Quartet, ensemble] (Supraphon 0179) ♪ ♪ ♪ ♪ ♪

One of the Panocha Quartet's finest recorded achievements was their Antonín Dvořák string quartet cycle, and that probably makes their recording of his famous *American* string quartet (no. 14) the primary focus of this disc. Too bad, because the version of *From My Life* heard here compares favorably to the excellent rendering done by the Smetana Quartet back in 1976.

what to buy next: [Prazák Quartet] (Praga 250128) ♪ ♪ ♪ ♪

The steady mental deterioration of the composer is documented most heart-rendingly in these performances by

one of the finer quartets on the international circuit. While not as finely detailed in their interpretation as either the Smetana Quartet (see below) or the Panocha Quartet (see above), the Prazák Quartet still gives an exemplary interpretation of *From My Life.* Where the value of this recording increases is in the group's finely detailed performance of Smetana's follow-up quartet *Out of My Life,* and the more lighthearted duet for violin and piano *From My Homeland,* with the ensemble's first violinist Václav Remes ably accompanied by pianist Sachiko Kayahara.

worth searching for: [Smetana Quartet, ensemble] (Denon 7339) ♪ ♪ ♪ ♪ ♪

These are fine, well-engineered recordings of both string quartets that should serve as the benchmark against which all other performances are compared. However, the only way to get them, now that this Denon release is out of print, is in a six-CD box set (Supraphon GEMS 0076) devoted to some of the group's finest musical moments. In addition to their namesake's two essays in the form are impeccable renditions of both of Leos Janácek's impressive quartets, Antonín Dvořák's famous *American* string quartet, four works by Ludwig van Beethoven (including the *Grosse Fuge*), a pair of Wolfgang Amadeus Mozart's quartets, and pieces by Josef Suk, Jirí Jaroch, and Vitezslav Novák.

Trio in G Minor for Piano, Violin, and Cello, op. 15
what to buy: [*Smetana: Chamber Works, vol. 2;* Guarneri Trio, ensemble] (Supraphon 3449) ♪ ♪ ♪ ♪ ♪

Totally idiomatic in its conception and playing, the Guarneri Trio is one of the finest piano trios in the world and this performance is just about as good as it gets. The other short scores on this set, Smetana's *Fantasie sur un air bohemien* and *From My Homeland*, are pleasant, agreeable makeweights that do no harm to the composer's reputation.

what to buy next: [Golub/Kaplan/Karr Trio, ensemble] (Arabesque 6661) ♪ ♪ ♪ ♪

While Smetana's intensely focused, heart-on-the-sleeve trio is the real emotional core of the disc, more people are likely to buy it up for its pairing, the Trio in A Minor for Piano, Violin, and Cello by Piotr Tchaikovsky, a work which receives a stunning performance by this trio.

[Joachim Trio, ensemble] (Naxos 8.553415) ♪ ♪ ♪ ♪

This muscular performance is the primary reason for picking up this budget-priced disc, but listeners will also discover worthy works for piano trio by Josef Suk and the altogether underrated Vitezslav Novák.

influences: Antonín Dvořák, Leoš Janáček, Vitezslav Novák, Franz Liszt, Hector Berlioz

Ellen Kokko and Steve Coghill

Antonio Soler

Born Antonio Francisco Javier José Soler-Ramos on December 3, 1729, in Olot, Spain. Died December 20, 1783, in El Escorial, Spain.

period: Baroque

While living within the imposing gray stone monastery walls of El Escorial, Padre Antonio Soler wrote some of the most exuberant music of the eighteenth century. He composed nearly five hundred works in various genres but is best known today for his 150 keyboard sonatas, most of which were intended for harpsichord. Soler's knowledge of music theory and history is exhibited in his daring 1762 treatise on modulation, *Llave de la Modulación.*

Antonio Soler probably received his first music lessons from his father (a regimental bandsman) prior to entering the choir school at the monastery of Montserrat when he was six years old. There he studied composition and organ, using the music of Juan Cabanilles, Miguel López, and José Elias as primers. When he was only fifteen he was appointed organist at the cathedral in Seo de Urgel; at age twenty-one he was appointed *maestro de capilla* (choirmaster) at Lérida. In 1752 Soler entered the community of Jeronymite monks at El Escorial, a year before being ordained as a priest. In addition to his monastic duties, he was responsible for training five separate choirs, providing choral music for the services, and furnishing music for the royal family during their visits to El Escorial. He composed and worked with ferocious intensity, leading one of his fellow monks to comment that Soler usually only slept four hours, working until midnight or one o'clock before resting, only to rise at four or five o'clock in the morning to say Mass.

The frequent visits to El Escorial of King Ferdinand VI and Queen Maria Bárbara had a great impact on Soler, because they brought with them their court musician,

Domenico Scarlatti. On these visits, Soler studied with Scarlatti and picked up some of the concepts he would later use. When the family visited, Soler also tutored the talented Infante (Prince) Don Gabriel, using some of the eight organs found within the walls of El Escorial as instruments on which to practice. There were two large organs at the sides of the transept, four portable organs, and a pair of organs in the choir. The colorful, unique, and unusual pieces Soler wrote for these instruments, many of them dedicated specifically to the Infante, remain a part of the popular recital repertoire today— filled with guitar-like strumming effects, echo passages, and dazzling virtuoso passage work.

His secular music was probably written to entertain the royal family when they visited, and there is little doubt that some of his 128 *villancicos* were written for this purpose. In his time, this peculiarly Spanish art form had evolved into a new genre—a sort of mini-musical drama, dramatic cantata, or playlet. His most popular *villancicos* were designed to be performed in the church to celebrate Christmas: the soloists assumed the role of the characters in the story, while the chorus provided narration. A small chamber orchestra accompanied the voices and provided instrumental interludes.

Chamber music
various harpsichord sonatas
what to buy: [*Sonatas for Harpsichord, Vol. 1*; Gilbert Rowland, harpsichord] (Naxos 8.553462) ♪ ♪ ♪ ♪

Gilbert Rowland delivers masterly interpretations with unflagging energy on this first volume of Naxos's complete set of Soler's sonatas for harpsichord. All the sonatas here are played on a French two-manual harpsichord built by David Rubio—an ideal instrument for Soler's style. There is great resonance in the bass, and the richly contrasting manuals are perfect for the echo passages.

Concertos for Two Keyboard Instruments
what to buy: [Bernard Brauchli, Esteban Elizondo, keyboards] (Titanic 152) ♪ ♪ ♪♪

The interplay between Brauchli and Elizondo is beguiling, as is their choice of who is to play which notes. The instrumental colors are captivating, and the acoustics set them off to advantage. The first and second concertos are performed on subtle clavichords, the third and fourth present dueling organs, and the final pair feature Elizondo as organist and Brauchli on harpsichord.

worth searching for: [E. Power Biggs, organ; Daniel Pinkham, organ] (Columbia 7174) ♪ ♪ ♪ ♪

While there are several recordings of Soler's six concertos on two organs, this vinyl set is one of the best. The dialogues between the instruments are sizzling, and the exuberance of the playing is like champagne bubbles. The instruments are ideal for this performance: one is a small cabinet organ built in Gouda by the eighteenth-century Dutch builder Hendriks Hermanus Hess, and the other was built by D.A. Flentrop and housed in the Busch-Reisinger Museum at Harvard University.

Vocal music
Ciego Y Lazarillo **(The Blind Man and Lazarillo)**
worth searching for: [*Los Villancicos*; Pierre Catala, tenor; Luis Alvarex, baritone; Jean-Michel Hasler, cond.; Ensemble Baroque Pygmalion, orch.; Escolania de la Abadia de Santa Cruz del Valle de los Caidos, choir] (Jade 39429) ♪ ♪ ♪ ♪♪

This Christmas *villancico* is kaleidoscopic in its variety of sounds, ranging from a plaintive bagpipe playing at the gates of Bethlehem to foot-tapping folk songs. The disc contains other Christmas playlets: *Little Boy, Poet, and Priest, Visit to the Prisons, Angel, Joseph, and Our Lady, Anton and Gila, Anton and Pascual,* and *An Angel and the Devil.* While the orchestra and choir are superb, the boy soprano soloist is especially delightful. The acoustics in the Benedictine Abbey of Santa Cruz (where this album was recorded) greatly enhance the sound.

influences: Antonio de Cabezón, Domenico Scarlatti, José Elias

Marijim Thoene

Fernando Sor
Born Joseph Fernando Macari Sors c. February 14, 1778, in Barcelona, Spain. Died July 10, 1839, in Paris, France.

period: Classical

The Catalan composer and virtuoso guitarist Fernando Sor wrote ballets, operas, and vocal music, but his most vivid legacy is contained in the more than sixty-five pieces he wrote for solo guitar and in his instructional book on guitar technique, the *Méthode pour la guitarre.*

Sor's opera *Telemaco nell'isola di Calipso* received its premiere at the Barcelona Opera House in 1796 when he was only eighteen years old, but it did not indicate the direction the composer's life was to take. At first he held a number of administrative positions in the Barcelona area, but he managed to compose a number of works in a variety of genres while developing his skills as a guitarist. When the French invaded the Iberian Peninsula in 1808, Sor initially joined the resistance and wrote a number of patriotic songs. By 1810, when it appeared that the occupying forces had solidified their hold on the government, he switched sides and took his administrative talents with him. This flexible attitude toward national loyalty resulted in Sor's evacuation to Paris when the French were driven out of Spain in 1813. Two years later, he relocated to London, where he wrote some well-received vocal works in addition to a small number of scores for piano and guitar. By this time he had developed a reputation as a guitar virtuoso and teacher, and he capitalized on it by publishing his *Twelve Studies,* (op. 6). Although he had previously published a number of his guitar works, this was the first time that any of his guitar studies appeared in print.

Besides his guitar compositions, which reinforced his reputation as an instrumentalist, Sor also composed a series of ballets, the most popular of which—*Cendrillon,* based on the Cinderella story—was premiered in London in 1822 before being performed in Paris and at the grand opening of the Bolshoi Theater in Moscow in 1823. Sor traveled to Russia with the ballet company and stayed there until 1826, composing and performing. He eventually moved back to Paris, where he resumed his career as a guitar virtuoso, playing concerts and composing more material for his instrument. In 1830 he published his magnum opus, the *Méthode pour la guitarre,* which became a standard text on the art of guitar playing and remains so today. After its publication, Sor kept on writing and performing, sometimes in duo recitals with Dionisio Aguado, a younger guitarist who had made a big impact on Parisian audiences while Sor was in Russia.

Since there are no extant copies of Sor's original guitar studies, musicians and scholars have had to rely on the numerous editions of these works published during and after the composer's lifetime. The most famous twentieth-century collection is the *Twenty Sor Studies* created in 1945 by Andrés Segovia, but not even that one can claim total authenticity, since it introduces tempos different from those in earlier editions compiled by the composer's own students—in particular, that of

Napoléon Coste. Sor's own text in the *Méthode pour la guitarre* seems to address his critics rather than define a path of instruction for students to follow, deferring in some cases to the approach first laid down in 1820 by his friend Dionisio Aguado in Aguado's own *Colección de estudios para guitarra.* The biggest difference between the two methods appears to be that Aguado favors playing with the fingernails for clarity of sound while Sor prefers playing with the fingertips for more power.

Chamber
Variations on a Theme by Mozart, op. 9
what to buy: [*An Evening of Guitar Music*; Celedonio Romero, guitar] (Delos 1004) ♪ ♪ ♪ ♪

This composition dates from Sor's years in London, illustrating his interest in larger forms of music as well as songs and ballades. The theme on which he built his variations was taken from Mozart's opera *Die Zauberflöte* (The Magic Flute). Sor liked to compose concert pieces that showed off his technique, but Romero's playing pays respect to the natural, intimate qualities of the guitar as well. Romero also showcases two of Sor's guitar sonatas (opp. 15b and 25), in addition to a pair of works by Mauro Giuliani and three by Francisco Tárrega.

Fantaisies for Guitar
what to buy: [Adam Holzman, guitar] (Naxos 8.553450) ♪ ♪ ♪ ♪₆

Holzman's artistry is worth more than the price of admission to this most enjoyable recital. In addition to the opp. 52 and 56 *Fantaisies,* the guitarist includes the six wonderful *Valses et un Galop* from op. 57 and the delightful two-movement *Morceau de Concert.*

what to buy next: [Luis Orlandini, guitar] (CPO 999199) ♪ ♪ ♪₆

This three-disc set covers all of Sor's *Fantaisies* for solo guitar and tosses in the composer's *Variations on Rossini's "Nel cor più non mi sento"* and Ernesto Lecuona's *Diary of a Child* for good measure. Orlandini may not have the name recognition that Julian Bream, Christopher Parkening, or any of the Romeros (Celedonio, Celín, Angel, and Pepe) have, but his talent is undeniable.

influences: Mauro Giuliani, Juan Cabanilles, Federico Moretti, Dionisio Aguado, Francisco Tárrega, Miguel Llobet, Emilio Pujol, Napoléon Coste

Kerry Dexter and Ian Palmer

John Philip Sousa
Born November 6, 1854, in Washington, DC USA. Died March 6, 1932, in Reading, PA, USA.

period: Twentieth century

Although he was a violinist, composed numerous operettas and suites, led the United States Marine Band, and conducted theater orchestras, Sousa was best-known for writing magnificent patriotic marches. Some of his most popular ones include *The Stars and Stripes Forever, The Washington Post, Semper Fidelis,* and *El Capitan.* The distinguished American composer William Schuman once noted that "The marches of Sousa are as thoroughly American as the waltzes of Strauss are thoroughly Viennese."

The third of ten children born to immigrant parents—a father from Spain, who became a trombonist in the United States Marine Band, and a mother from Bavaria—John Philip Sousa began taking music lessons around age six, studying voice, violin, piano, and a variety of reed and wind instruments. He was also exposed to music theory at an early age and even became something of a violin prodigy, performing as a soloist at age eleven. During the American Civil War years, Washington, D.C. was abuzz with the chaotic sounds of war and, in addition to visiting the wounded in area hospitals, Sousa heard many military bands, claiming in his autobiography to have "loved all of them, good and bad alike." In 1868 while studying composition, theory, and harmony with George Felix Benkert (a conductor and pianist who lead and orchestra in which Sousa performed on violin), Sousa was offered the post of bandleader with a visiting circus. Before the youngster could accept the position, his father intervened and enlisted his son as an apprentice violinist in the Marine Band. Young Sousa remained with the Marine Band until 1875 when his father left.

After leaving military service on a special discharge at age twenty, Sousa played in various theater orchestras and touring bands. In 1876 he moved to Philadelphia, where he served as violinist in an orchestra formed to play at the Philadelphia Centennial Exposition under the

direction of visiting conductor Jacques Offenbach. Remaining in Philadelphia for four years, Sousa received his first exposure to the most popular band in the country at that time, the one led by Patrick S. Gilmore. He also worked in theaters as a violinist and taught arranging and composing. In 1879, during rehearsals for the Gilbert and Sullivan operetta *H.M.S. Pinafore,* Sousa met Jane van Middlesworth Bellis and they married later that same year. While on tour with a production of *Our Flirtations* in 1880, he was invited to take over the reins of the United States Marine Band, thus becoming the first American-born bandmaster of that organization and the one who would eventually boost the band's celebrity status.

When he left the military again in 1892, Sousa formed his own civilian band, employing many players from the Gilmore band. With this new organization, he was able to shape both the music and the musicians to his own needs. One of his innovations involved the development of the quick-step march form. When Sousa wrote a new march, he heavily orchestrated the parts and the resulting music was published with an eye toward outdoor marching performances. However, Sousa's own band was a concert unit that performed in theaters and opera houses, and the leader would announce alterations on the spot to his players, making Sousa's performances of his own music most unique. Throughout the years the traditional scores were used, but veteran Sousa band instrumentalists would pass the Sousa style along by word-of-mouth to new members.

While he wrote about 135 marches, his most famous one, *The Stars and Stripes Forever,* was written in 1896 on a return voyage from vacation in Europe, and earned him more than $300,000 in his lifetime. Recorded more times than any other single piece of music in history, this popular composition has become the official march of the United States. Sousa's most successful operetta, *El Capitan,* premiered in New York in 1896 and in London in 1899; he would take two pieces from the operetta to compose his well-favored march also titled *El Capitan.*

With America's entry into World War I, Sousa (at age sixty-two) re-enlisted, joining the United States Naval Reserve Force. Lieutenant Sousa formed a huge band of over 300 players and toured the country in parades which raised millions of dollars for the war effort. After

John Phillip Sousa

his last stint in the military Sousa returned to leading his own band, a venture which remained profitable until the Great Depression years when his band finally broke up. He also wrote *Marching Along,* an autobiography that was first published in 1928. Four years later, while rehearsing the Ringgold Band in Reading, Pennsylvania, Sousa suffered a heart attack and died at age seventy-seven. He was buried in Washington, D.C. The Hollywood film version of Sousa's life, *Stars and Stripes Forever,* was loosely based on his autobiography and released in 1952; it featured many of his more popular marches and starred Clifton Webb, Robert Wagner, and Debra Paget.

Orchestral
various marches
what to buy: [*A Grand Sousa Concert*; Timothy Foley, cond; Great American Main Street Band, orch.] (EMI Angel 54130) ♪ ♪ ♪ ♪⁸

Along with one of the best-recorded versions of *Stars and Stripes Forever,* this well-produced album contains the splendid mixture of harmonious orchestration, brassy pizzazz, and sprightly sparkle one expects from Sousa marches. It's one of the more enjoyable collections of its kind and includes some of his most popular pieces, including *The Washington Post, El Capitan,* and more. Trained at Oberlin College Conservatory of Music and a former conductor of the United States Marine Band, Foley gets the best from this outfit.

what to buy next: [*The Original All-American Sousa!*; Keith Brion, cond.; New Sousa Band, orch.] (Delos 3102) ♪ ♪ ♪ ♪

The disc contains thirteen selections with Keith Brion conducting the exceptional New Sousa Band, a concert ensemble originally formed for a 1986 PBS TV special, *The New Sousa Band on Stage at Wolf Trap.* What makes this release special, however, are the seven rare recordings (vintage 1929–1932) of Sousa leading his own band through such favorites as *The Stars and Stripes Forever* and *The U.S. Field Artillery March.*

worth searching for: [*Semper Fidelis: Music of John Philip Sousa*; "The President's Own" United States Marine Band] (Marine Corps Heritage Foundation, no number available) ♪ ♪ ♪ ♪⁸

Although this compilation CD is currently out of print,

various public radio stations and libraries may have copies on file. The band performs a variety of American music and this CD is a worthy listen if you encounter it anywhere. You may also wish to check the Marine Band website at www.marineband.usmc.mil for touring information and news.

The Dwellers in the Western World

what to buy: [*Sousa for Orchestra*; Richard Kapp, cond.; Philharmonia Virtuosi of New York, orch.] (ESS.A.Y. Recordings 1003) ♪ ♪ ♪ ♪ ♪

While today's political correctness has probably made this work taboo, Kapp does a first-class job of bringing out all the nuances (and musical stereotyping) of Sousa's three-part orchestral piece (*The Red Man, The White Man,* and *The Black Man*). The album also contains *Teddy and Alice,* a compilation of Sousa music which Kapp helped select and/or "co-composed" for an unsuccessful Broadway musical about the special relationship between Teddy Roosevelt and his daughter Alice.

[*John Philip Sousa: At the Symphony*; Keith Brion, cond.; Razumovsky Symphony Orchestra] (Naxos 8.559013) ♪ ♪ ♪ ♪

In addition to *The Dwellers in the Western World* this album contains the ever-popular *Stars and Stripes Forever* and *Semper Fidelis* plus a pleasant variety of light classics. As on the other two albums (Naxos 8.559020 and 8.559029) in his excellent three-disc survey of Sousa material, Brion offers one of the best and most comprehensive overviews of the composer's exceptional talents.

influences: Richard Wagner, Jacques Offenbach, Arthur Sullivan, Herbert L. Clarke

Nancy Ann Lee

Louis (Ludwig) Spohr

Born April 5, 1784, in Brunswick, Germany. Died October 22, 1859, in Kassel, Germany.

period: Classical

Louis Spohr, also known as Ludwig Spohr, was an important violin virtuoso (rivaled only by Niccolò Paganini), pedagogue, and conductor, whose use of leitmotif and chromatics in his later works helped break ground for Robert Schumann, Richard Wagner, and other romantic composers. He was also one of the first conductors to use the baton to guide the orchestra, applying this innovation to revivals of music by Johann Sebastian Bach and for performances of works by many of his contemporaries. Somehow, between tours and teaching, Spohr found time to write nine operas, nine symphonies (a tenth was incomplete), fifteen violin concertos, and thirty-six string quartets. However, the works for which he is best known today—the clarinet concertos and his utterly delightful Nonet in F Major for Strings and Winds—stem from the early part of his career.

When Spohr was fifteen years old, his talents as a violinist had already developed to the point that he was considering a career as a touring virtuoso, a fanciful option that gave way to practicality when, upon the failure of concerts booked for him in Hamburg, he joined a group of household musicians employed by Duke Karl Wilhelm Ferdinand of Brunswick. There he honed the technical aspects of his playing even further before being granted permission by his employer to make a more successful venture onto the concert trail in 1802.

By 1805, Spohr was considered to be one of the finest violinists in Germany, with skills that led to his being offered a position as concertmaster in Gotha. His search for job security eventually took him to Vienna (where he directed the orchestra of the Theater an der Wien), Frankfurt am Main (again as opera director), Dresden, and finally Kassel, where he accepted the post of Kapellmeister in 1822. During these years he also embarked on concert tours with his first wife, the harpist Dorette (née Scheidler), that took him to London, Paris, Rome, and virtually all the other cultural capitals of Europe. This was also the time when Spohr was maturing as a composer, creating his first four operas, two symphonies, ten violin concertos, three clarinet concertos, the charming Nonet in F Major, and more than half of his surviving string quartets. In addition, he wrote a number of works for violin and harp, intending them for concerts with his wife. One of the lesser-known yet influential scores from the pre-Kassel period was his setting of an a cappella mass for double chorus in ten parts that experimented with chromaticism to such an extent that its first performance was deemed too difficult to complete. Spohr made a series of revisions to it, unveiling the simplified version of the score at a concert in Leipzig in 1822.

It seems strange that Spohr would end up in Kassel,

since his political leanings were heavily influenced by the Enlightenment and the same ideals of Freemasonry that inspired Mozart—concepts totally at odds with those held by the autocratic ruler of Kassel, Elector Wilhelm II. Political censorship was strict, the Continental reactionaries typified by the Austrian chancellor Metternich were in power, the elector was more interested in the reputation of his musical establishment than in the actual content of the music, and the orchestra was in need of an upgrade in personnel. Despite these drawbacks, Spohr took a pragmatic approach that favored art above politics, hiring and firing musicians in a manner that would reshape the elector's orchestra into one of the finest organizations of its kind in Europe. Conveniently enough, this also gave the composer a well-honed ensemble with which to try out his own scores.

One of the first fruits fostered by the improved musicianship was *Jessonda,* Spohr's most accomplished and popular opera, a work that has maintained a semblance of popularity in Germany but faded from the rest of the world's repertoire. Four more operas followed, along with a variety of secular and sacred vocal works, symphonies, and a host of other scores for diverse forces. As prolific and influential as he was in his day, however, Spohr would come to be seen as a transitional figure, overshadowed by the burgeoning romantic movement represented by Schumann. Even though composers such as Felix Mendelssohn, Frédéric Chopin, and Johannes Brahms took up Spohr's cause, posterity seems for the most part to have shelved his name and oeuvre, deeming only a few of his works worthy of attention.

Orchestral
Concerto no. 4 in E Minor for Clarinet and Orchestra
what to buy: [Ernest Ottensamer, clarinet; Johannes Wildner, cond.; Slovak Radio Symphony Orchestra, Bratislava] (Naxos 8.550689) ♪ ♪ ♪ ♪

Ottensamer deserves recognition as one of today's finest clarinet soloists. The string section of the Czech orchestra has a deep, dark, rich sound that is especially suited to the concerto's opening Allegro vivace markings and the pulsing rhythms of the closing Rondo al Espagnol. Spohr's second clarinet concerto, the only one of the four written in a major key (E-flat Major) is the other main work on the disc; while not as consistently exhilarating as its E Minor companion, it manages to sustain an acceptable level of interest throughout. The

Georg Solti:
Born György Stern on October 12, 1912, in Budapest, Hungary, Georg Solti studied piano with Béla Bartók and Ernst von Dohnányi and composition with Zoltán Kodály before starting his career in 1930 as a vocal coach with the State Opera in Budapest. After serving as an assistant to Bruno Walter and Arturo Toscanini, Solti made his conducting debut on March 11, 1938 with a production of Wolfgang Amadeus Mozart's *Le Nozze di Figaro.* Adolph Hitler's troops invaded Austria that same day and it was apparent that Hungary, and thus Solti, was in danger. His Jewish heritage made him a potential target for the death camps and he quickly made arrangements for travel to Lucerne, Switzerland. There he found work with Walter, Toscanini, and Adolf Busch at a festival they were organizing there. Swiss work-permit laws were structured so that Solti couldn't make a living as a conductor but he was able to generate income by giving piano lessons and hiring himself out as an accompanist.

After the end of World War II, Solti moved into a series of European positions before winning his first American appointment in 1953, becoming conductor of the San Francisco Opera. Three years later he was in Chicago, working with the Opera Theatre Association there. His next important position was back in Europe, as musical director at Covent Garden from 1961 to 1971. After the completion of his stint there, the conductor was knighted and became a British citizen. 1971 was also the year that Solti began working with the Chicago Symphony Orchestra as their conductor. His other important associations during the 1970s included a two-year engagement as music director of l'Orchestre de Paris and his relationship with the London Philharmonic Orchestra, with whom he worked as principal guest conductor, principal conductor, and artistic director.

While Solti continued to work with other organizations, including the Vienna Philharmonic, with whom he made the very first studio recording of Richard Wagner's *Ring* cycle, his twenty-two-year-long association with the Chicago Symphony Orchestra was to be his most fruitful. Before he died on September 5, 1997, Solti recorded more than one hundred albums with the CSO and won more Grammy Awards (thirty-two) than any other artist in history.

It is fitting, given his earliest experiences as a conductor, that operas play a dominant part in his recorded legacy. Grammy Award-winning performances in this category include renditions of Wagner's *Lohengrin* (Decca 421053) and *Der Meistersinger von Nürnberg* (Decca 452606), and Wolfgang Amadeus Mozart's *Le Nozze di Figaro (The Marriage of Figaro)* (Decca 410150). He was also known as a persuasive advocate for Gustav Mahler's oeuvre, especially the composer's eighth and ninth symphonies, performances of which are available as part of Solti's complete set of Mahler symphonies (Decca 430804). As a pianist, Solti can be heard in a fine performance of Bartók's Sonata for Two Pianos and Percussion (Sony Classics 42625) along with fellow pianist Murray Perahia and the percussion duo of Evelyn Glennie and David Corkhill.

William Gerard

composer's *Fantasie and Variations on a Theme of Danzi* in B-flat Major for Clarinet and Strings, op. 81, rounds out this budget package.

Concerto no. 8 in A Minor for Violin and Orchestra, op. 47—*In modo si Scena Cantante*
what to buy: [Ulf Hoelscher, violin; Christian Fröhlich, cond.; Berlin Radio Symphony Orchestra] (CPO 999187) ♪ ♪ ♪

Spohr wrote virtuoso solo sections for this work, but he structured the score along the lines of an operatic scene and aria, creating instrumental recitatives to go along with instrumental arias that took into account the supposedly bad Italian orchestra he was going to be soloing with. The resulting music has a haunting, lyrical quality that Hoelscher exploits most convincingly. While the engineering places the violin even more forward in the mix than usual, it doesn't take away from the basic attractiveness of the performance. Spohr's twelfth and thirteenth violin concertos are also included on the disc.

Chamber
Nonet in F Major for Strings and Winds, op. 31—*Grand*
what to buy: [members of the Gaudier Ensemble] (Hyperion 66699) ♪ ♪ ♪ ♪

Spohr's nonet marks the high-water mark in his chamber music; the adagio's fluid, graceful writing for violin is especially notable. The Gaudier Ensemble's Marjeke Blankestijn does admirable work in that solo role and throughout this well-recorded program. The composer's octet is also included here, and if the Gaudier Ensemble's playing doesn't quite erase memories of the Vienna Octet's wonderful performance of that pleasant score (available in remastered splendor on Decca 4665880), the results are still commendable.

what to buy next: [members of the Nash Ensemble] (CRD 3354) ♪ ♪ ♪

This rendition of the nonet is quite good, and it is purely a matter of taste whether this performance is better than the one on the Hyperion disc cited above. Both albums feature the same program, and the Nash Ensemble gives a marginally finer rendering of the octet, but either set will provide pleasure.

Vocal
Mass in C Major for Five Vocal Soloists and Double Chorus, op. 54
what to buy: [Juliane Claus, Beate Timm, sopranos; Christiane Oertel, alto; Martin Petzold, tenor; Wolfgang

Dersch, bass; Michael Gläser, cond.; Rundfunkchor Berlin, choir] (CPO 999149) ♪ ♪ ♪ ♪

Spohr's singular take on this a cappella mass demands that the choir take the composer's not inconsiderable vocal challenges in stride without making mush out of the intricately woven parts. In this instance Gläser's choir is disciplined, their diction is fairly clean, and the tempos are magisterial, making this the finest available version of what is a surprisingly magnificent score. Two of the movements in the Mass, the Sanctus and the Agnus Dei, deserve ♪ ♪ ♪ ♪ ♪ ratings by themselves. The composer's *Three Psalms* for Two Four-Part Choirs, op. 85, performed here by the same choir but with a different conductor (Dietrich Knothe) and different soloists, is an intriguing, often upbeat setting of Moses Mendelssohn's translation. The Psalms set are 8, 23, and 130.

what to buy next: [Ludmila Vernerová-Nováková, Milada Cejková, sopranos; Agáta Hauserová, alto; Viktor Bytchek, tenor; Roman Vocel, bass; Jaroslav Brych, cond.; Prague Philharmonic Choir] (Praga Digitals 250117) ♪ ♪ ♪

The singing here is not as idiomatic as it is with the Rundfunkchor (see above), but the performance is acceptable and gives the listener a sense of what the piece might sound like if only the group could navigate the score a tad better. As on the German choir's recording, Spohr's *Three Psalms* is included, but so too is Felix Mendelssohn's own *Three Psalms* for Soloists and Two Eight-Part Choirs, op. 78, which sets Psalms 2, 22, and 43.

influences: Wolfgang Amadeus Mozart, Luigi Cherubini, Felix Mendelssohn-Bartholdy, Carl Maria von Weber

Garaud MacTaggart

Carl Stamitz
Born Carl Philipp Stamitz c. May 8, 1745, in Mannheim, Germany. Died November 9, 1801 in Jena, Germany

period: Classical

Carl Stamitz was the descendant of a musical family; his brother and father were both famous composers and instrumentalists. Renowned during his lifetime as a violinist and violist, Stamitz was also a prolific writer of instrumental music, with some 150 orchestral works to his credit, although his thirty-eight contributions to the symphonie concertante genre would seem to outweigh his sixty concertos and fifty or so symphonies.

Like the Bachs before them and the Strausses after them, the Stamitz family—Johann Wenzel Stamitz and his two sons, Carl and Anton—made a name throughout Europe. The elder Stamitz led one of the most famous orchestras in Europe out of the relatively modest court of Mannheim, but this orchestra was celebrated for its virtuoso players and set the standard of instrumental proficiency for years to come. Papa Stamitz was a firm, demanding but loving taskmaster who first gave Carl music instruction. He died when Carl was eleven, and the younger Stamitz continued his studies with the leading musicians of Mannheim, including Christian Cannabich and Ignaz Holzbauer. At an early age Stamitz established himself as a gifted violin and viola player.

The two Stamitz brothers traveled to Paris, where they performed regularly in public concerts from 1770 to 1772. Trips as a virtuoso performer, either with his brother or on his own, then took Carl Stamitz all over Europe—to Vienna, Salzburg, London, and the leading courts in Germany and France. He moved to the Netherlands in 1779, staying for about five years and performing often as a viola soloist at the court of William, Prince of Orange. His travels were reduced considerably after his marriage to Maria Joseph Pilz in 1790. When his daughter was born in 1792 and his wife's health declined, the devoted husband curtailed his plans for future concerts in distant locales. The lack of touring put a strain on the family finances, and though commissions continued to come in for his compositions, especially from the orchestra at Mannheim, Stamitz was unsuccessful in achieving any type of permanent post or regular stipend. When he died at the age of fifty-six, he was completely penniless. Even though his name was famous and he had traveled throughout Europe to great critical acclaim, his possessions had to be auctioned off to pay his debts.

As a composer, Carl Stamitz took full advantage of the rising ability of orchestral players such as those of the orchestra at Mannheim by making greater technical and musical demands on the players he wrote for and played with. He learned well from his father the importance of asking for more from an ensemble than they would normally give, and his firsthand knowledge of an orchestra's inner workings gave him the ability to channel the musi-

cians' individual and collective virtuosity toward a unified goal. This was a tradition that was to continue with Wolfgang Amadeus Mozart and then Ludwig van Beethoven. The lengthy crescendo made famous by the Mannheim orchestra was in sharp contrast to the more static terraced dynamics of the typical baroque ensemble; when coupled with the clean, sharply defined phrase structure of Stamitz's music, it makes a wonderful sonic impression that still has great impact today.

Orchestral
Concerto no. 3 in B-flat Major for Clarinet and Orchestra
what to buy: [Sabine Meyer, clarinet; Iona Brown, cond.; Academy of St. Martin-in-the-Fields, orch.] (EMI Classics 54842) ♪ ♪ ♪ ♪

The luminous sound of Sabine Meyer unites the music of Carl Stamitz with that of his father, Johann Wenzel Stamitz. You can find many recordings featuring one or two pieces by Stamitz, but Meyer and friends seem to have understood the intrinsic value of putting together a disc containing nothing but music from this remarkable family. Carl contributes three of the four concertos heard here, two (nos. 3 and 10) in B-flat Major and one (no. 11) in E-flat Major, while Johann is represented by yet another clarinet concerto in B-flat Major. The playing and sound are first-rate, with both disc and repertoire deserving high recommendations.

Symphony in D Major—*La Chasse*
what to buy: [*Four Symphonies*; Matthias Bamert, cond.; London Mozart Players, orch.] (Chandos 9358) ♪ ♪ ♪ ♪

All the clarity and grace of the rococo period can be heard in this symphony, subtitled *The Hunt*. In addition to the famous slow crescendos beloved by Mannheim composers, Stamitz gave a prominent role to the valveless hunting horns—hence the work's moniker. The other three Stamitz symphonies in this set are just as delightful.

Chamber
Octet no. 1 in B-flat Major for Wind Instruments
what to buy: [Consortium Classicum, ensemble] (CPO 999081) ♪ ♪ ♪ ♪

Like the Orpheus Chamber Orchestra, the Consortium

Classicum is a conductorless ensemble, but unlike the former group, it focuses on the music of lesser-known yet deserving composers. Listening to this album reminds one that it is not just Haydn and Mozart who were masters of the chamber music genre. The program also contains two more octets by Stamitz and a pair of his partitas (multi-movement works that share thematic material), all of which maintain their delightful, fresh qualities.

influences: Johann Wenzel Stamitz, Anton Stamitz, Christian Cannabich, Franz Danzi, Ignaz Holzbauer

Dave Wagner

Charles Villiers Stanford

Born September 30, 1852, in Dublin, Ireland. Died March 29, 1924, in London, England.

period: Romantic

Although it is not of major international importance, the music of Charles Villiers Stanford embodies both English and Irish nationalism during the late Romantic period. His prolific output includes orchestral works, operas, songs, chamber music, and keyboard music, while his choral music in both large and small forms has been a staple of the Anglican sacred repertoire. Stanford was an important teacher as well, subtly influencing the shape of twentieth century English music via the host of composition students that passed through his classes.

Stanford's interest in music came from his father, who was a lawyer as well as an amateur cellist and singer. Despite showing an early aptitude for music (he gave his first piano recital when he was nine years old), Stanford's parents wanted him to follow in his father's footsteps as a lawyer. Still, they permitted him to attend Queens College, Cambridge as a choral scholar in 1870, fully intent on pursuing a career as a musician. This he did with a vengeance, switching to Trinity College in 1873 and adding to an already-growing list of professional accomplishments by being appointed organist there in 1874. Stanford then spent portions of the next two years in Germany and France, studying composition with Carl Reinecke, meeting such famous composers as Johannes Brahms, Jacques Offenbach, and Camille Saint-Saëns, and attending the opening of the Bayreuth Festival Theatre—all activities that made major impressions on the young man.

By this time, many of Stanford's first published works were garnering acclaim from the British academic community, and his reputation for composing music used in Anglican church services was blooming. In 1883, when there was an opening to join the teaching staff at the Royal College of Music, he took the position as professor of composition. This was followed in 1887 with the offer of a slot as professor of music at Cambridge, a post he was to hold concurrently with the one at the Royal College of Music. From these two perches (both of which he held until his death in 1924) Stanford could oversee the development of British music, influencing generations of young composers, including Ralph Vaughan Williams, Gustav Holst, John Ireland, Herbert Howells, and Frank Bridge. Knighted in 1902 for advancing the cause of English music, Stanford's abilities as a teacher were unquestioned and his impact on Anglican religious music was considerable. When he died, his ashes were laid to rest in Westminster Abbey next to those of Henry Purcell. In a tribute to him that appeared in the July 1924 issue of *Music and Letters,* Ralph Vaughan Williams noted that Stanford's "music is in the best sense of the word Victorian . . . ."

Orchestral
Symphony no. 7 in D Minor, op. 124
what to buy: [Vernon Handley, cond.; Ulster Orchestra] (Chandos CHAN 8861) ♪ ♪ ♪ ♪

Chandos has been a champion of Stanford's orchestral music and this recording is as good as the previous ones. Both the Ulster Orchestra and the recording site of Ulster Hall in Belfast give a nod toward Stanford's Irish roots. The performances are polished and the recording spacious, enabling the beauty of this music to shine so obviously that it makes one wonder why more people don't know it. This all-Stanford disc also includes the *Concert Piece* for Organ and Orchestra performed with Gillian Weir, and the *Irish Rhapsody* no. 3 for Cello and Orchestra, featuring Raphael Wallfisch as soloist.

Chamber
various organ sonatas
what to buy: [*Sonatas for Organ*, Joseph Payne, organ] (Marco Polo 8.223754) ♪ ♪ ♪ ♪

Although Stanford began his career as an organist, all but one of his organ works were composed after he had given up performing for teaching and composing. His five sonatas represent a significant portion of his music for organ and the three works heard here are based on tunes from either France (*La Marseillaise*), England (*St. Mary, Benedictus, Hanover*), or Ireland (*St. Patrick's Breastplate*). Payne performs these pieces in an authoritative manner and with great musicianship. The four-manual Garland organ, built in 1993, at St. Stephen Presbyterian Church, Fort Worth, Texas, does justice to the music, though the rather bright tonal design is not in the English style of the late Romantic organ.

Vocal
Morning Service in C Major, op. 115
what to buy: [*The Complete Morning and Evening Services and Offices for Holy*

Communion, vol. 1; Keith Wright, organ; James Lancelot, cond.; Durham Cathedral Choir] (Priory 437) ♪ ♪ ♪ ♪

Stanford has long been known for his liturgical music for the Anglican Church, introducing the use of thematic repetition throughout an entire setting to provide a sense of musical unity not theretofore found in English service music. All of the right elements (reverberant acoustics, stylistically appropriate organ, and a choir of men and boys) are combined here for a marvelous rendition of this music.

influences: Herbert Howells, John Ireland

D. John Apple

John Stanley
Born Charles John Stanley, January 17, 1712, in London, England. Died May 19, 1786, in London, England.

period: Baroque

John Stanley became one of the most respected English organists despite blindness resulting from an accident when he was two years old. His competence and inventiveness as a composer for the keyboard were such that, with the exception of George Frideric Handel, no one in England was comparable. Although Stanley wrote music in a variety of styles and genres, his reputation as a composer is based upon his concerti grossi and various works featuring the organ—most clearly influenced by Handel.

Stanley was extremely talented as a youth, being appointed organist at All Hallows Church in London before he was even into his teens. He then became music director at St. Andreas Church, Holborn when he was fourteen years old and two years after that graduated from Oxford, making him the youngest person ever to gain a Bachelor of Music degree from the school. In 1734 he became organist of the Honourable Society of the Inner Temple, a post he held simultaneously with the one at St. Andreas, until his death. This was also the year that the earliest composition attributed to Stanley, a verse anthem known as *Hear me when I call,* was written. However, some scholars believe that his first organ voluntaries—some of the works by which he is best known today—were written in the early 1730s, perhaps predating the anthem. In 1738, Stanley acquired a measure of fiscal stability by marrying the daughter of a member of the East India Company and securing a dowry of 7,000 pounds. An added attraction was the new sister-in-law who moved in with the young couple and later became his amanuensis—writing down his music for him, facilitating the publication of his compositions, and thus helping to establish Stanley as a composer. The majority of Stanley's scores were printed during the 1740s and 1750s including three sets of cantatas (fifteen in all), three books of keyboard voluntaries (ten per tome), a few chamber pieces for flute or violin, and the six concertos for strings that make up his op. 2.

While he was considered an excellent organist whose playing attracted the attention of many London notables (including Handel, who later became a close friend), Stanley was also reputed to be an admirable violinist and extremely popular with the public. Music historian Charles Burney called him "a neat, pleasing and accurate performer, a natural and agreeable composer, and an intelligent instructor." It is no wonder then that he was considered to be one of the best musicians of his day in terms of generating cash flow. When Handel died in 1759, Stanley reduced his teaching load so that he could direct performances of the annual Lenten Oratorio that his friend had led. He also tried his hand at writing a pair of oratorios during the next few years, but neither were very popular and he didn't attempt another one until 1774. In 1779 Stanley was appointed Master of the King's Band of Musicians, succeeding William Boyce and contributing odes on demand to the royal household for the balance of his life.

Orchestral
Concertos for Strings, op. 2
what to buy: [Roy Goodman, cond.; Parley of Instruments, orch.] (Hyperion 66338) ♪ ♪ ♪ ♪

These concertos are probably Stanley's most important instrumental works and were designed to be performed as concerti grossi or as keyboard concertos with the three solo (concertino) parts performed by strings or keyboard. The pattern of movements is similar to that of a suite, instead of the normal concerto grosso blueprint. Performances by Goodman and the Parley of Instruments are buoyant, particularly with regard to making the dance-like qualities of this music shine forth. Since these recordings use original instruments, the clarity and lightness of texture is especially evident.

what to buy next: [Simon Standage, cond.; Collegium Musicum 90, orch.] (Chandos 638) ♪ ♪ ♪ ♪

Standage's version of these works is similar to the Goodman recording in that his forces use original instruments. While Standage offers a different interpretation of these pieces and a good performance, the resulting disc does not have quite the transparency of the Goodman version.

Chamber
various organ voluntaries
what to buy: [*11 Voluntaries*; Ton Koopman, organ] (Capriccio 10256) ♪ ♪ ♪ ♪ ♪

These organ pieces consist of two to four movements with contrasting tempi and contrasting organ registration. This recording presents a uniting of two forces that are perfect for this music; Koopman, as a specialist in Baroque keyboard music, is well-acquainted with the style popular in England during Stanley's lifetime, and the John Byfield II organ of three manuals and twenty-one stops (built in 1764—5 for St. Mary Rotherhithe, London) is one of the few remaining (and best-preserved) English instruments from the eighteenth century. The eleven voluntaries heard on this wonderful disc were selected from Stanley's opp. 5, 6, and 7.

influences: George Frideric Handel, William Boyce, Charles Avison, Thomas Arne, Archangelo Corelli

D. John Apple and Garaud MacTaggart

Max Steiner
Born Maximilian Raoul Walter Steiner on May 10, 1888, in Vienna, Austria. Died December 28, 1971 in Los Angeles, CA.

period: Twentieth century

Perhaps the single most influential composer in Hollywood history, and also one of the most prolific, Steiner brought keen dramatic insight and a warmly romantic style to some of world's best-loved motion pictures. Steiner reached his high point in the 1930s and early 1940s with scores to such films as *King Kong, The Informer, Dark Victory, Gone with the Wind, Casablanca,* and *Now Voyager.*

The grandson and namesake of the famed impresario of the Theatre an der Wien (who had commissioned operettas from Franz von Suppé and Johann Strauss Jr.), Max Steiner was drawn to music and the theater early in life. He studied with Robert Fuchs at the Vienna Conservatory and as a teenager wrote an operetta called *The Beautiful Greek Girl,* which ran for more than a year. Steiner didn't stay in Vienna, however, leaving for London in 1906 to conduct a production of Franz Lehár's *The Merry Widow.* He liked England so well that he stayed until 1914, when fear of being interned as an enemy alien during World War I caused him to emigrate to America. Since his savings in London had been impounded, he arrived in New York with precisely thirty-two dollars in his pocket.

Steiner, however, was resourceful and industrious, and he built up a reputation as a first-rate arranger and conductor in the thriving New York musical theater community. During the next fifteen years he worked with such well-known composers as Victor Herbert, Vincent Youmans, Jerome Kern, and George Gershwin. One of the shows Steiner worked on was *Rio Rita,* and when it was bought by RKO for the movies, the producer took his conductor/arranger out West. It was 1929, the very beginning of the talking pictures era, and musicals were all the rage. Steiner found himself in great demand and never went back to the theater.

Gradually, as recording and editing technology improved, movie makers began experimenting with original dramatic scores for motion pictures, and Steiner wound up being one of the pioneers. He signed a contract with RKO and soon allied himself with a young producer named David Selznick, who sympathized with Steiner's ideas about using continuous musical commentary instead of just a few bars of music at the beginning and end of each film. Steiner was encouraged to write extensive scores for such early talkies as *The Garden of Allah, Symphony for Six Million,* and *Bird of Paradise.* Probably his most significant score from this period was *King Kong,* still considered a landmark as one of the earliest examples of music completely altering the public perception of a motion picture. Preview audiences had laughed at the giant ape, but with the addition of Steiner's vivid symphonic score, they were caught up in the excitement of the story and moved to tears at the end when Kong died atop the Empire State Building.

As time went on, the prolific and indefatigable Steiner became less satisfied with conditions at RKO (not enough work!), and in 1936 he signed a contract with Warner Brothers. Until the mid-1960s this remained his home, the place where he did his finest and most characteristic work, turning out full-length scores at the rate of more than eight a year and often working on several films at one time. In 1939 alone, Steiner toiled on a dozen motion pictures before being loaned out by the Warner studio to Selznick (by now an independent producer) for *Gone with the Wind,* a mammoth undertaking that required an unprecedented amount of scoring. Steiner insisted he could not possibly meet the deadline, but Selznick knew his composer well and made sure that Steiner heard rumors about plans to use other composers in case he couldn't complete the assignment. Steiner was outraged, redoubled his efforts, and finished the score on time.

A fanfare that Steiner originally wrote in 1937 for a film called *Tovarich* made such an impression on studio chief Jack Warner that for decades it accompanied the Warner Brothers emblem in nearly every film the company produced. Steiner was nominated for Academy Awards twenty-six times, winning three times for his scores to *The Informer* (1935), *Now Voyager* (1942), and *Since You Went Away* (1944). Some of his other three-hundred-odd credits include *Little Women* (1933), *Jezebel* (1938), *They Died with Their Boots On* (1941), *Casablanca* (1943), *The Big Sleep* (1946), *The Treasure of the Sierra Madre* (1948), *The Glass Menagerie* (1950), *The Searchers* (1956), and *A Summer Place* (1959). Steiner suffered from vision problems in his later years and died in 1971, a few years after his retirement.

various film scores
what to buy: [*Now Voyager: The Classic Film Scores of Max Steiner,* Charles Gerhardt, cond.; National Philharmonic Orchestra; Ambrosian Singers, choir] (RCA Victor 0136) ♪ ♪ ♪⸴

This superb overview of Steiner's art contains a spine-tingling suite from *King Kong,* the full four-hankie weep-er treatment of *Now Voyager,* and Max channeling Humphrey Bogart as Philip Marlowe in *The Big Sleep.* Also included are some gems from lesser-known scores like *The Fountainhead* and *Saratoga Trunk,* along with the *Symphonie Moderne* for Piano, Celeste, and Orchestra from *Four Wives,* featuring Earl Wild at the keyboard.

Gone with the Wind
what to buy: [Charles Gerhardt, cond.; National Philharmonic Orchestra] (RCA 0452) ♪ ♪ ♪

This is the only disc in the RCA Classic Film Score Series devoted to a single film score. The extended concert suite heard here contains about forty-four minutes of what is arguably Steiner's greatest achievement, the mammoth score for David Selznick's film version of Margaret Mitchell's best-selling novel.

influences: Franz Waxman, Erich Wolfgang Korngold

Jack Goggins

Wilhelm Stenhammar
Born Karl Wilhelm Eugen Stenhammar, February 7, 1871, in Goteborg, Sweden. Died November 20, 1927, in Stockholm, Sweden.

period: Romantic

While many European composers of his generation were looking exclusively to the harmonic daring of Wagner and Liszt, Stenhammar also admired classicists like Haydn, Mozart, and Beethoven in addition to his friends and colleagues, Jean Sibelius and Carl Nielsen. His musical language avoided the more bombastic elements loved by many of his contemporaries, and sought a relatively restrained, civilized approach that usually yielded interesting if not necessarily compelling works. This all changed during the last fifteen years of his life when his scores absorbed these influences and transcended them, making his second symphony and the later string quartets into minor masterpieces.

Young Wilhelm's father was a well-known architect and, as an amateur, had even written some religious music. His mother was heavily involved in Stockholm's social whirl and was responsible for much of the artistic discussions taking place in the Stenhammar household. Even though he was encouraged by his family to pursue his musical inclinations, Wilhelm didn't really receive his first formal piano lessons until 1887. By 1892, Stenhammar had made three debuts: as a pianist in Johannes Brahms's Piano Concerto no. 2, as a chamber musician in the Piano Quintet by Camille Saint-Saëns, and as a composer with his choral ballad *I Rosengård*. Within a few years, he had also become one of the most sought-after pianists in the country and a frequent participant in chamber music gatherings, specifically concerts with the Aulin String Quartet, an association which would last from 1894 until 1912. Stenhammar made his conductorial debut in 1897, leading the Stockholm Philharmonic Society in a performance of his concert overture, *Excelsior!*. This also marked the year when he assumed the artistic directorship of that same organization, an office he was to hold for the next three years before moving on to similar slots at the Royal Opera, the New Philharmonic Society, and the Göteborg Orchestral Society.

By 1904 Stenhammar was acknowledged as one of Sweden's finest art song composers, with part of this success directly attributable to his studies with Emil Sjögren, a major force in that genre. One of Stenhammar's most popular efforts in that direction, *Sverige*, was drawn from his cantata *Ett Folk (The People)* and has served as Sweden's unofficial national anthem in much the same way that Jean Sibelius's *Finlandia* does for Finland. Stenhammar's unique, self-taught methods of conducting and composing further evolved due to his study of Heinrich Bellermann's *Der Contrapunkt,* a text on counterpoint that was published in 1862 and basically restated much of the information contained in Johann Joseph Fux's classic tome from 1725, *Gradus ad Parnassum.*

Stenhammar's second symphony was finished and debuted in 1915, when he was still serving with the Göteborg Orchestral Society and after he had completed and digested his intensive study of counterpoint. Part of the reason he waited so long to write this score lay in his reaction to Sibelius's second symphony, a work he heard shortly before the premiere of his own first symphony in 1903. The Finn's distinctive voicings and assured handling of orchestral colors made Stenhammar realize that his own work drew too much of its substance from Bruckner, Wagner, and Brahms instead of showcasing his own unique musical personality. This observation was confirmed in 1910 when he led a program containing Carl Nielsen's first symphony and noticed, once again, another singular Northern European voice. Since Stenhammar was already considered to be

one of the finest Swedish composers of art song—primarily via his permutations of traditional melodies—it is not surprising that folk elements play a big role in the success of his second symphony, especially in the masterful fugue at the heart of the fourth movement. What is really impressive, however, is the artistic maturity shown in the work's crafting, a sense that the composer was ready to move past his influences into a uniquely personal realm.

All of these experiences came to the fore in the composing of his last string quartet in 1916. At the first few performances two years later, the critics were relatively reserved, commenting on the technical assurance of the composer but concerned about the "inaccessibility" of the work itself. It wasn't until two years after his death from a stroke that a truer picture of Stenhammar's final quartet was voiced in the press. In 1929 the young Swedish composer/poet Ture Rangström noted that "Here, more perhaps than in any of his other instrumental works, Wilhelm Stenhammar bears witness to himself, his deepest self. This quartet is a confession of the tragedy of illusions and of the resignation sternly demanded of us by fate."

Orchestral
Symphony no. 2 in G Minor, op. 34
what to buy: [Paavo Järvi, cond.; Royal Stockholm Philharmonic Orchestra] (Virgin Classics 45244) ♪♪♪♪₄

Järvi's performance gives this work a majestic leanness without lessening any of the power and tuneful grace Stenhammar fit into this score. The CD gives especially good value by including the composer's gutsy early overture, *Excelsior!*, a proposed movement for his Serenade that was set aside (*Reverenza*), and an orchestration of his *2 Songs,* op. 4, sung by Anne Sofie von Otter.

what to buy next: [Peter Sundkvist, cond.; Royal Scottish National Orchestra] (Naxos 8.553888) ♪♪♪₄

Sundkvist takes this piece at a faster clip than does Järvi and the record company is not as generous with the accompanying works, only including a performance of *Excelsior!*. Still, the price is right, the engineering is pretty good, and the playing of the orchestra, especially in the strings, is very recommendable for those wishing to dabble in Stenhammar's oeuvre.

the omnibus essential guide to classical CDs

Chamber
Quartet no. 6 in D Minor for Strings, op. 35
worth searching for: [Copenhagen String Quartet, ensemble] (Caprice 21339) ♪ ♪ ♪ ♪₄

Stenhammar's six string quartets are a convenient way of tracking his development as a composer, from some-one inspired by Haydn and Beethoven to, in the last quartets, a markedly personal viewpoint that holds sur-prising rewards for chamber music aficionados. Published after his death, the sixth of his quartets is par-ticularly notable for the brevity and conciseness of its musical arguments, the palpable sense of longing pres-ent in the first movement, and the intensity of the final Presto. This performance is paired with the Fresk Quartet's worthy rendition of Stenhammar's fifth quartet (op. 29, in C Major), a work written in 1910—just after his counterpoint studies were finished.

influences: Hugo Alfvén, Wilhelm Peterson-Berger, Tor Aulin, Hilding Rosenberg, Edvard Grieg, Carl Nielsen, Jean Sibelius, Johannes Brahms

Garaud MacTaggart

William Grant Still
Born May 11, 1895, in Woodville, MS. Died December 3,1978, in Los Angeles, CA.

period: Twentieth century

William Grant Still was the first African-American com-poser/conductor to have a symphony (the *Afro-American Symphony* from 1930) performed by an American orchestra and the first African-American to have an opera (*Troubled Island*, written in 1949) staged by a major American opera company. He also created sym-phonic poems, orchestral suites, operas, ballets, and various forms of vocal and instrumental music, including works for theater, cinema, and broadcasting.

Born on a plantation near Woodville, Mississippi, William Grant Still moved with his family (after the death of his father, the town bandmaster) to Little Rock, Arkansas where he began studying the violin. To satisfy his mother, Still entered Wilberforce College in 1911 as a pre-med student. While there, he participated in musi-cal activities, teaching himself to play clarinet, saxo-phone, string bass, viola, cello, and oboe, and perform-

ing with the Wilberforce String Quartet. In 1915 he left college without graduating, got married, and ended up working in various music ensembles, including one led by W. C. Handy. He enrolled at Oberlin Conservatory in 1917 and began his first efforts at composition, but when the US entered World War I he enlisted in the Navy.

After his release from the military in 1919, Still returned to Oberlin but soon left again, this time for New York City, where he eventually found work playing oboe in theater and radio orchestras, including a stint with the pit band for *Shuffle Along,* a revue by Noble Sissle and Eubie Blake. In 1922, while in Boston with the *Shuffle Along* road company, he studied composition with George Whitefield Chadwick, director of the New England Conservatory. The next year he entered a two-year course of study in New York with the French avant-garde composer Edgard Varèse, which led to a perform-ance of his *From the Land of Dreams* by the International Composers' Guild in 1925. From that time onward, Still divided his composing time between serious concert music and scores for radio broadcasts and the cinema. He was determined not to write in the modernist idiom espoused by Varèse, seeking instead a more traditional style.

Still took a job with Paul Whiteman in 1929, creating arrangements for his band to play each week on the *Old Gold* radio show, but in his spare time he was also com-posing a ballet (*Sahdji*), an orchestral tone poem (*Africa*), and a symphony. Premiered by Howard Hanson and the Rochester Philharmonic Orchestra in 1931, the *Afro-American Symphony* was the first by an African-American to be performed by a major orchestra. The work garnered instant critical acclaim, was later per-formed by the New York Philharmonic in Carnegie Hall, and has since been given hundreds of times by major American and European orchestras.

Although the premiere of his first symphony was a suc-cess, Still's personal life was becoming increasingly dif-ficult. In 1932 his marriage broke up, and two years later the composer moved to Los Angeles on a Guggenheim fellowship, which was renewed twice. He worked on an opera begun in New York (*Blue Steel*) and hired Verna Arvey, a budding concert pianist, to be his press secre-tary. He wrote *The Seven Traceries* for her in 1939, the year they were married, and she performed it with the Los Angeles Philharmonic Orchestra. The piece was pub-lished the following year.

In 1937, Leopold Stokowski conducted the Philadelphia Orchestra in the first performance of the composer's second symphony, the *Song of a New Race.* Other important works by Still include his opera *Troubled Island,* which was performed by the New York City Opera in 1949, the first major company to stage a work by a black composer. That was also the year when Still wrote his *Songs of Separation,* a cycle of five thematically related songs set to texts by prominent Black poets: Arna Bonemps (*Idolatry*), Philippe Thoby-Marcelin (*Poème*), Paul Laurence Dunbar (*Parted*), Countee Cullen (*If You Should Go*) and Langston Hughes (*A Black Pierrot*). Still's Symphony no. 3 was written in 1958 but, despite its assigned number, was actually the last of Still's five symphonies and the only one not performed during his lifetime. (He had discarded his original Symphony no. 3 in 1945 and revised it in 1958 as his Symphony no. 5.)

Still was awarded honorary degrees by Wilberforce College (1936), Howard University (1941), Oberlin College (1947), Bates College (1954), and, towards the end of his life, from the University of Arkansas (1971), Pepperdine University (1973), the New England Conservatory of Music (1973), the Peabody Conservatory (1974), and the University of Southern California (1975).

Orchestral
Symphony no. 1—*Afro-American Symphony*
what to buy: [Neeme Järvi, cond.; Detroit Symphony Orchestra] (Chandos 9154) ♪ ♪ ♪ ♪

The Detroit Symphony delivers a magnificently expressive performance that captures the blues-tinged, swinging grandeur and warmth of this important four-movement work. Slightly suggesting Gershwin's *Porgy and Bess,* its principal theme is initiated by a solo trumpet and runs through the entire melodically rich symphony. The disc also features the DSO performing an arrangement of Duke Ellington's seven movement suite from *The River.*

Symphony no. 2 in G minor—*Song of a New Race*
what to buy: [*American Series, vol. 5*; Neeme Järvi,, cond.; Detroit Symphony Orchestra] (Chandos 9226) ♪ ♪ ♪ ♪

Still's symphonies remain among his most beautiful compositions. Järvi directs a strong reading of this powerful work, full of densely textured strings, brass and woodwinds, and fully captures the essence of Still's musical style in the bold, sweeping grandeur of the tutti

passages. The program also contains the *Negro Folk Symphony* by William Levi Dawson and an orchestral arrangement of Duke Ellington's tone poem, *Harlem.*

Symphony no. 3——*The Sunday Symphony*
[*A Festive Sunday with William Grant Still;* Carlton R. Woods, cond.; North Arkansas Symphony Orchestra] (Cambria 1060) ♪ ♪ ♪ ♪ ♪

Still's Symphony no. 3 is the main attraction here, with Woods leading this orchestra deftly through the grand, folk-influenced, four-movement work. This disc also collects an array of appetite-whetting works composed by Still, mostly from the 1950s–60s. Performed by various groups, they include Still's warm, blues-based 1954 composition *Romance* for saxophone and piano, a rousing version of his prizewinning *Festive Overture,* the sweet, sonorous *Folk Suite no. 4* for flute, clarinet, cello, and piano (based on music from Venezuela, Mexico, and Brazil) and the euphonious choral work *Three Rhythmic Spirituals.*

Chamber
Seven Traceries
what to buy: [*Black Piano: A Treasury of Works for Solo Piano by Black Composers*; Monica Gaylord, piano] (Music & Arts 737) ♪ ♪ ♪ ♪

Gaylord delivers a lush, passionate interpretation of Still's impressionistic *Seven Traceries.* She also plays, in splendid style, the composer's piano score for *Three Visions,* a tone painting which begins with rhythmic horses hooves in *Dark Horsemen,* slows dreamily to *Summertime,* and simmers to a close with *Radiant Pinnacle.* Works by Robert Nathaniel Dett, Samuel Coleridge-Taylor, Edward "Duke" Ellington, and others are also included on the disc.

Vocal
various songs for voice and orchestra
worth searching for: [*Witness, vol. 2*; Yolanda Williams, soprano; Hilda Harris, mezzo-soprano; William Warfield, narrator; Philip Brunelle, cond.; Plymouth Music Series Orchestra and Chorus; Leigh Morris Chorale] (Collins Classics 14542) ♪ ♪ ♪ ♪

Brunelle elicits a poignant reading by Yolanda Williams of *Wailing Woman,* with lush accompaniment from chorus and orchestra. The ensemble singers perform a moving version of Still's *Swanee River (Old Folks At Home).*

Brunelle also performs the composer's light, playful, *Miss Sally's Party,* an orchestral work full of scintillating jazz-tinged themes and dance tempos that culminates with a cakewalk finale. However, the centerpiece of the album is an authoritative performance of Still's 1940 composition *And They Lynched Him on a Tree.* Brunelle leads a magnificent rendering of this six-movement work featuring narrator Warfield, soloists, chorus, and orchestra. Two short works for organ, *Reverie* and *Elegy,* round out the selection.

influences: Samuel Coleridge-Taylor, Robert Nathaniel Dett, William Levi Dawson, Edward "Duke" Ellington, Adophus Hailstork, Wendell Logan, Leslie Adams

Nancy Ann Lee and Ellen Kokko

Karlheinz Stockhausen

Born August 22, 1928, in Mödrath, Germany.

period: Twentieth century

Karlheinz Stockhausen is a leader in the electronic avant-garde movement, an uncompromising master standing on an obscure pinnacle of musical philosophy. The austere "throw out the baby with the bathwater" technique of his revolutionary youth has mellowed into a rarefied esthetic.

Stockhausen was not a prodigy, but he did study piano when he was five years old, adding violin and oboe to his arsenal soon after that. He was orphaned during World War II, and worked as a farmhand, a hospital orderly, and a dance-band pianist while furthering his education. In 1947 Stockhausen entered the Cologne Musik-Hochschule, where he studied piano in addition to attending Frank Martin's composition classes. He also took theory classes at Cologne University, before passing a civil service examination allowing him to teach piano at the high school level.

The post-war era was a heady time for young composers with serious musical pretensions. The old world of music, art, literature, and philosophy—the whole edifice of modern thinking, in fact—was undergoing a dramatic reassessment and rebuilding. Stockhausen and others were searching for two seemingly contradictory ideals—complete artistic freedom and a new set of rules by which to navigate these uncharted waters. By 1950 he had begun analyzing scores by Arnold

Isaac Stern:
Isaac Stern's family moved from Russia to San Francisco in 1921, before he had even reached his first birthday. Although he began playing the piano when he was six years old, the violin claimed Stern's full attention two years later. In 1936 he made his debut as a soloist in Johannes Brahms's violin concerto under the baton of Pierre Monteux with the San Francisco Symphony. Stern's initial New York City appearance occurred at Town Hall in 1937, but it wasn't until his 1943 Carnegie Hall recital that he was able to convincingly establish his reputation as a violin soloist.

Stern has since acquired a reputation as one of the foremost musicians of the twentieth century, both as a soloist and within the context of a chamber ensemble. In addition, he has served as a mentor to some of the finest violinists to come after him, including Itzhak Perlman, Pinchas Zukerman, Shlomo Mintz, and Midori. He didn't restrict himself to encouraging players of his own instrument, however, performing key roles in the careers of cellist Yo-Yo Ma and pianists Emanuel Ax and Yefim Bronfman.

Stern's passion for music and its place in society led him to advocate governmental support for music and arts education in the United States. During the 1960s he not only played a crucial role in the formation of the National Endowment for the Arts but was in the forefront of the battle to defend Carnegie Hall from developers, successfully seeking to preserve the venerable institution by convincing New York City to purchase the building. Stern's affiliation with that hallowed venue continued until his death on September 22, 2001, serving as president of Carnegie Hall for over forty years.

Although he had been a strong supporter of twentieth century music throughout his career, and his recordings of violin concerti by Paul Hindemith and Kryzsztof Penderecki (Sony Classics 64507) and Béla Bartók's violin sonatas (Sony Classics 64535) amount to solid works of advocacy, Stern's bread-and-butter interpretations are more likely to be found in the standard repertoire. Among his many fine recordings in the latter category are his readings of Antonio Vivaldi's *Four Seasons* (Sony Classics 42526), in which he conducts the Jerusalem Music Centre Chamber Orchestra in addition to playing the violin, and a classic rendition of Ludwig van Beethoven's ten piano trios (Sony Classics 46738), with pianist Eugene Istomin and cellist Leonard Rose, that won a Grammy Award in 1970 for Best Chamber Music Performance. Stern also won Grammys for Best Instrumental Soloist with Orchestra many times during the 1960s, most notably for his performance of Igor Stravinsky's Concerto in D Major for Violin and Orchestra (Sony Classics 64505) with the composer leading the Columbia Symphony Orchestra, and a pair of recordings with Eugene Ormandy and the Philadelphia Orchestra: Sergei Prokofiev's Concerto no. 1 for Violin and Orchestra (Sony Classics 38525) and Béla Bartók's Concerto no. 1 for Violin and Orchestra (Sony Classics 64502).

Garaud MacTaggart

Schoenberg, Anton Webern, and Béla Bartók as a way of furthering his education beyond the boundaries of what he was being taught at the University. During this time Stockhausen also attended the Darmstadt International Summer School, where he was exposed to even more modern trends in serialism. The result of all this intellectual processing was the first work heralding the "post-Webern" brand of serialism that Stockhausen would espouse later—the *Kreuzspiel (Crossplay)* for piano, oboe, bass clarinet, and percussion.

In 1952 Stockhausen moved to Paris, France—the hotbed of "new music" at that time—to study with Olivier Messiaen, whose *Quatre Études de Rythme* had made a big impression on the younger composer. While there he met Pierre Boulez and began experimenting with *musique concrète,* using natural sound sources recorded directly to tape. These studies induced him to reorganize his approach to composition and influenced the completion of his next important breakthrough work, *Kontra-Punkte* for ten instruments. Stockhausen returned to Cologne in 1953 to premiere his new piece and work at the Westdeutsche Rundfunk (West German Radio) electronic music studio.

Stockhausen began moving away from his "post-Webern" serialism and toward indeterminacy in the later half of the 1950s. This brought his theories of composition closer to the ideas espoused by John Cage, and required that Stockhausen develop a new system of notation for people playing his works. By the time he won appointment to the Cologne Musik-Hochschule staff as a composition teacher in 1971, Stockhausen had seemingly turned has back on prior methods of working and re-invented his approach once more. While he still used some of the notational devices he had developed earlier, Stockhausen was experimenting with musical ideas from other cultures and large blocks of melody broken up into phrases. This development marked the beginnings of the major operatic project that he has been working on since 1977, *Licht: Die sieben Tage der Woche (Light: The Seven Days of the Week.)* Actually a projected cycle of seven interlocking operas with socio-religious underpinnings, *Licht* reflects Stockhausen's evolving ideas about meditation and spirituality as personified by four characters—Michael (an angel), Eve (representing womankind), a wise man, and Lucifer.

In his heyday during the 1960s and early '70s, Stockhausen was considered a giant in the avant-garde music world. Since then his appeal has lessened somewhat, though he still has a solid, almost worshipful following. These acolytes are certain that Stockhausen is a master of acoustical space whose orchestral pieces are splendidly engineered, while other voices believe his spiritual mannerisms may be charlatanism personified. Quite unrelated to his music, the composer found him-

self shunned as never before in late 2001, after highly publicized remarks which seemed to trivialize the events of September 11. The ultimate impact of this episode on his reputation was unforeseeable at the time of writing. Stockhausen maintains his own CD catalog, Stockhausen-Verlag, through which almost everything he ever wrote is available. Titles may be ordered from: Stockhausen-Verlag, Kettenberg 15, 51515 Kürten, Germany.

Vocal
Gesang der Jünglinge (Song of the Youths)
what to buy: [*Elektronische Musik 1952 to 1960;* Karlheinz Stockhausen, electronics] (Stockhausen-Verlag Disc 3) ♪ ♪ ♪ ♪ ♪

Speech fragments emerge from the "sound symbols" of the musical fabric, quoting from the Old Testament story of Daniel. A powerful and unique emotional experience full of innocence, bravery, and fire, this piece is essential for any collection of twentieth century art music. The other works on the album include *Étude*—an example of the composer's *musique concrète*—and the electronic pieces *Studie I, Studie II,* and *Kontakte.*

Stimmung (Tuning) for Six Vocalists
what to buy: [Gregory Rose, cond.; Singcircle, choir] (Hyperion 66115) ♪ ♪ ♪ ♪

Written in 1968, this work is in the forefront of minimalist sprechgesang (song/speech), containing seventy minutes' worth of vocalists dwelling on six notes. Some will find it intriguing while others will find it numbing.

Donnerstag aus LICHT (Thursday from LIGHT)
[Karlheinz Stockhausen, cond.; various ensembles and soloists] (Stockhausen-Verlag Disc 30) ♪ ♪ ♪ ♪

LICHT will be an operatic cycle (incomplete at this writing) consisting of a week of music-theater with specific segments to be performed on the day for which they are named. The principal character in the cycle is the Archangel Michael, and the complete work is meant to evoke a spiritual voyage. Originally released on Deutsche Grammophon 473379, this four-CD set has been remastered by the composer, who also designed the packaging and compiled the extensive accompanying booklet.

Karlheinz Stockhausen

Unsichtbare Chöre (Invisible Choirs)

what to buy: [Karlheinz Stockhausen, cond.; West German Radio Chorus] (Stockhausen-Verlag Disc 31) ♪ ♪ ♪ ♪₈

Excerpted from the *Michaels Jugend* section of *Donnerstag aus LICHT,* this piece for electronically processed voices is very inventive and surprisingly moving. This performance was originally released on Deutsche Grammophon 419432, but the new packaging includes both cover art and ample notes by the composer.

influences: György Ligeti, Pierre Boulez, John Cage, Anton Webern, Milton Babbitt

Gerald Brennan and Garaud MacTaggart

Johann Strauss II

Born Johann Baptist Strauss, October 25, 1825, in Vienna, Austria. Died June 3, 1899, in Vienna, Austria.

period: Romantic

An Austrian composer, conductor, and violinist, he was the son of Johann Strauss and is known as the "Waltz King" by virtue of the massive popularity of his works at a time when waltzes were sweeping the European capitals. Johannes Brahms was friends with Strauss and once autographed the fan of an admirer by writing the first few bars of *An der schönen, blauen donau (The Blue Danube)* and signing it with the message: "Alas, not by Brahms." Strauss wrote over 400 opus numbers and some of his most popular works include the aforementioned *Blue Danube* and *Kaiser-Walzer (Emperor Waltz),* both of which remain concert staples today. Strauss was also famous for his operettas, with his best-known works in that genre, *Die Fledermaus (The Bat)* and *Der Zigeunerbaron (The Gypsy Baron),* still garnering performances widely every year.

Johann Strauss I preceded his eldest son with the title of "Waltz King" but his son would surpass his reputation. The father initially wanted his eldest son to pursue a banking career and was not supportive of Johann's musical ambitions, perhaps because he wished to spare his son the uncertain life of a musician. This despite his son's demonstrated gift for music as evidenced by the rudimentary waltz (*Erster Gedanke (First Idea)*) written when he was only six years old. Bowing to the will of his father, Strauss studied at the Schottengymnaisium and the Polytechnic Institute, preparing himself to become a banker. This all changed after his father abandoned the family in 1842 to live with another woman. His mother had arranged for him to study the violin with Franz Amon, her husband's concertmaster, even before his father changed households and now, with the senior Strauss off playing house with someone else, Strauss junior was free to follow in his father's footsteps as a musician.

At the age of nineteen he made his debut conducting his own orchestra, and after the death of his father in 1849 he merged the two groups, meshing the musicians into a powerful musical organization that would dominate the Vienna cultural scene. He began composing at a furious rate and, in 1853—after collapsing from exhaustion during a grueling tour—gave some of his conducting responsibilities to his brothers, Josef and Eduard. Strauss was appointed to the rank of Hofballmusikdirektor (Director of Music at the Court Balls) in 1863 and often traveled abroad promoting his music, leaving the bulk of day-to-day business operations in the hands of his brothers.

In 1867 Strauss wrote what is undoubtedly his most famous composition, *The Blue Danube.* He had been approached by Johann Herbeck, the man who conducted the very first performance of Franz Schubert's *"Unfinished"* symphony two years earlier, to write a waltz for a choral society concert. Strauss wrote the beautiful motif, bestowing on it a title inspired by a poem from Karl Isidor Beck, and gave it to Herbeck, who then prevailed upon Joseph Weyl to write lyrics which would mesh with the music. The initial performance of the choral version of *The Blue Danube* was a relative failure, but six months later Strauss was in Paris conducting the non-vocal version at a dinner and the response was overwhelming. It seemed like every orchestra on the planet wanted to have this piece in its repertoire. Soon the publisher of the work had to ship thousands of copies of the score all around the world, helping to promulgate what has since become the most famous waltz in history.

The decade from 1870 to 1880 saw him at the artistic apex of his career but there was still one more genre to explore. Strauss had no intention of writing for the musical theater initially, as he was satisfied composing waltzes and enjoying his reputation as the Waltz King, but his first wife (Jetty Trefez) and Jacques Offenbach were both responsible for persuading Strauss to write for the stage. His first attempts at opera proved to be only a modest success, but in 1874 he was given a good libretto by Richard Genee and Karl Haffner. In six weeks of total immersion in the score, Strauss composed *Die Fledermaus*. Its premiere was not a great success in Vienna since the populace, who would normally flock to the halls at the hint of a new Strauss work, were preoccupied with the effects of the Austrian/Prussian war and stock exchange problems. They had no spirit for champagne songs and merriment. Fortunately, however, *Die Fledermaus* found fame in Berlin, where it ran for one hundred consecutive performances. His next well-known operetta, *Der Zigeunerbaron,* was written in 1885. This extraordinary and successful work depicted Gypsy life, buried treasure, and romance through a judicious blend of drama and comedy with music employing Gypsy tunes, csárdás, and Viennese waltz. The premiere was an event unmatched in the history of operetta, with encores demanded several times that evening. Such was the work's popularity that it was repeated eighty-five times during the season.

When Strauss died he was working on a revision of his ballet *Aschenbrödel (Cinderella)* at the request of Gustav Mahler, who had become director of the Court Opera in 1897. Strauss had already been diagnosed with pneumonia and pleurisy by the family doctor and, on May 22, 1899, exhibited some dizziness while conducting a performance of *Die Fledermaus,* a fact which caused him, shortly after the overture, to abdicate his role to another conductor. He died less than two weeks later, but the same can never be said for his legacy.

Orchestral
various waltzes
what to buy: [Herbert von Karajan, cond.; Berlin Philharmonic Orchestra] (Deutsche Grammophon 437255) ♪ ♪ ♪ ♪₄

In this well-chosen collection of Strauss waltzes, production values go hand-in-hand with Karajan's polished (but not overly slick) rendition of Viennese masterpieces. The sonic heft of the Berlin Philharmonic provides a powerful engine for these performances but the conductor keeps the players focused on crisp, to-the-point playing that helps their rendition of the *Emperor Waltz* glide effortlessly from the CD player. Also included are impeccable versions of the composer's other big hits *Perpetuum mobile, Wiener Blut (Vienna Blood),* and *The Blue Danube.*

[*Johann Strauss: Waltzes*; Willi Boskovsky, cond.; Vienna Philharmonic Orchestra] (Decca/Eloquence 467413) ♪ ♪ ♪ ♪₄

With the exception of the *Anna Polka, In the Krapfen Woods,* and *Perpetuum mobile,* all of which were recorded during the 1970s, this fourteen-cut sampler features classic performances from the late 1950s to mid-1960s. The engineers have done an impeccable job of remastering and the budget pricing is almost too good to be true. Boskovsky leads the orchestra in interpretations that breathe a bit more than do Karajan's, and it is interesting (and affordable) to compare the two versions on the eight duplicated works, especially such warhorses as the *Emperor Waltz, The Blue Danube,* and *Perpetuum mobile.*

what to buy next: [*Vienna*; Fritz Reiner, cond.; Chicago Symphony Orchestra] (RCA Victor 68160) ♪ ♪ ♪ ♪

Fritz Reiner captures the music fittingly in this disc featuring recordings dating from 1957 to 1960. Most of the music belongs to Johann Strauss II (although Carl Maria von Weber is represented with his *Invitation to the Dance* and Richard Strauss's *Der Rosenkavalier* waltzes also appear), and Reiner's rendition of the *Emperor Waltz* is very rhythmic. The Chicago Symphony has a very rich sound from their string section without sacrificing accuracy. *The Blue Danube* also receives a faithful stylistic performance.

[*Johann Strauss II: Waltzes*; Rudolph Kempe, cond.; Vienna Philharmonic Orchestra] (EMI/ Seraphim 68535) ♪ ♪ ♪₄

This two-disc budget recording offers brilliant sound by Kempe and the Vienna Philharmonic Orchestra on the *Emperor Waltz,* a performance which displays the lilt and schmaltz characteristic of that orchestra in this material. The balance of the recording contains more Strauss by Kempe, but also some fine renditions of the composer's oeuvre by Willi Boskovsky and the great Johann Strauss Orchestra, Vienna. Johann Strauss I's *Radetzky March* closes out the proceedings.

Chamber
various waltz transcriptions
worth searching for: [*Strauss and Lanner Waltzes*; Alfred Mitterhofer, harmonium; Heinz Medjimorec, piano; Wolfgang Schulz, flute; Ernst Ottensamer, clar-

inet; Alban Berg Quartet, ensemble] (EMI Classics 54881) ♪ ♪ ♪ ♪

Proving that you may be wrong to write off "The Waltz King" as mere fluff are three transcriptions of his works by twentieth century twelve-tone masters Anton von Webern, Alban Berg, and Arnold Schoenberg. The basic float of these pieces is still present and serial methods aren't necessarily applied but there are definitely moments when the tonal centers get a tad fuzzy. Berg's version of *Wein, Weib, und Gesang (Wine, Women, and Song)* is especially interesting. The other six works on the album are arrangements by Alexander Weinmann of material originating with either Joseph Lanner or Johann Strauss I.

Vocal Music
Die Fledermaus
what to buy: [Anneliese Rothenberger, soprano; Brigitte Fassbaender, mezzo-soprano; Nicolai Gedda, tenor; Dietrich Fischer-Dieskau, baritone; Walter Berry, bass-baritone; Otto Schenk, narrator; Willi Boskovsky, cond.; Vienna Philharmonic Orchestra; Vienna State Folk Opera Chorus] (EMI Classics 69354) ♪ ♪ ♪ ♪ ♪

This set boasts one of the most well-regarded conductors of Viennese music; Boskovsky gives the perfect sparkle to Strauss along with an unmistakable Viennese style. Some of the finest singers of the twentieth century round off a perfect *Die Fledermaus*, producing an excellent interpretation of this work.

what to buy next: [Kiri Te Kanawa, soprano; Edita Gruberová, soprano; Brigitte Fassbaender, mezzo-soprano; Richard Leech, tenor; Olaf Bär, baritone; Tom Krause, baritone; Wolfgang Brendel, baritone; André Previn, cond.; Vienna Philharmonic Orchestra; Vienna State Opera Chorus] (Philips 432157) ♪ ♪ ♪ ♪

This recording has a cast of renowned singers giving a solid reading of the operetta, but the performance lacks the true Viennese style and flair that Boskovsky overwhelmingly brings to his recording. Fassbaender is an excellent Prince Orlofsky and she can be heard on the Boskovsky recording in the same role.

Der Zigeunerbaron
what to buy: [Pamela Coburn, soprano; Christiane Oelze, soprano; Júlia Hamari, mezzo-soprano; Elisabeth von Magnus-Harnoncourt, contralto; Herbert Lippert, tenor; Rudolf Schasching, tenor; Jurgen Flimm, baritone;

Wolfang Holzmair, baritone; Robert Florianschütz, bass; Nikolaus Harnoncourt, cond.; Vienna Symphony Orchestra; Arnold Schoenberg Choir] (Teldec 94555) ♪ ♪ ♪ ♪

Harnoncourt has researched and restored the work as it was initially conceived, changing the style in which it is usually performed and transforming it from an operetta into an opera. This solid, more serious interpretation deserves to be heard. The sound quality is a bit on the dry side but not enough to inhibit Harnoncourt's vision.

influences: Franz Lehár, Jacques Offenbach, Josef Strauss, Joseph Lanner

Tim Kennedy and Ellen Kokko

Josef Strauss
Born August 20, 1827, in Vienna, Austria. Died July 22, 1870, in Vienna, Austria.

period: Romantic

Josef was the younger brother of Johann Strauss Jr., and though he was an accomplished composer in his own right, he relied more on his technical skills than on the kind of inspiration that propelled his older sibling to popularity. His well-crafted scores include a number of fine waltzes and polkas that were very popular during their heyday, including "Delirien" (Delirium) and "Aquarellen" (Water Colors), but he may be best known today for collaborating with his brother on the "Pizzicato Polka."

The second child of Johann and Maria Anna Strauss exhibited signs of brain and spinal chord damage at an early age, a condition that would later lead to severe headaches and near-constant fatigue. Josef was also quieter and more subdued in temperament than his boisterous, outgoing older brother, the future Waltz King. While the Johann Jr. had already decided to follow in his father's footsteps and pursue a musical career, Josef wasn't sure he wanted to work as a musician. When both brothers were admitted to the Polytechnic Institute in 1841, Josef delved into mathematics and other classes that would lead him to a degree in mechanical engineering.

Despite his scientific bent, Josef didn't neglect the rich musical life Vienna offered, attending piano performances by Franz Liszt and Clara Schumann and hearing works by Hector Berlioz, Giaccomo Meyerbeer, and Franz von Suppé. After the death of their father, Johann Jr. took over the leadership of his orchestra and set about making it the most acclaimed musical organization in Vienna. Josef, however, attempted a variety of careers (including that of playwright) before finally joining in the family enterprise in 1852 when his older brother returned from a concert tour of Germany exhausted and sick.

Josef made his debut as conductor of the orchestra in the summer of 1853 and soon succumbed to the pressure to write his own music, despite having had no lessons in harmony or counterpoint. His sympathies were with such "advanced" composers as Berlioz and Richard Wagner, but after taking composition and violin lessons, he ended up writing in the traditional waltz fashion Viennese audiences had grown to expect and demand from the Strauss family. The orchestra was now an ongoing concern, and Josef would often lead the ensemble when his brother was away from Vienna. He began inserting more modern works next to the standard waltzes in the programs, including scenes from Wagner's *Lohengrin* and *Tristan und Isolde,* along with works by Liszt and Giuseppe Verdi. He also introduced lighthearted scores by Jacques Offenbach as a way of counterbalancing the heftier intellectual content of his other new additions.

By 1862 the Strauss organization had made room for Eduard, the younger brother of Johann and Josef. This troika shared the leadership of the orchestra until the following year, when Johann accepted a position as Hofballmusikdirektor (Director of Music at the Court Balls). Eduard was the best conductor of the three brothers but also the most likely to stir up trouble, butting heads with Josef most of all. This was of concern not only because of the sibling relationship but because all the Strauss sons had married, and the various orchestras performing under their guidance were sources of income for their families and their mother, who was still alive. Josef, never a well man, had to fight off both illness and his younger brother's increasingly worrisome demands. He also filled in for Johann on tours of Russia, Poland, and Austria, and it was during one such concert in Warsaw that Josef, after arguing with an orchestra member who disagreed with some edits made to his solo parts, collapsed on the podium. He suffered a severe concussion and was rushed home to Vienna, where he died little more than two months later. Upon his brother's death, Johann noted that "Josef was the most gifted among the three of us. I am only the more popular one."

Orchestral
"Pizzicato Polka" for Orchestra
what to buy: [*Walzer & Polkas*; Herbert von Karajan, cond.; Berlin Philharmonic Orchestra] (Deutsche Grammophon 437255) ♪ ♪ ♪ ♪₅

"Delirien," one of Josef's most popular works, is grafted onto an album featuring his older brother's waltzes and polkas, but so too is the bouncy, vivacious "Pizzicato Polka," a collaboration between the two siblings that remains the most frequently performed composition that Josef had a hand in writing. Von Karajan's performance with the BPO makes a strong case for both of the Josef Strauss pieces on this disc, even if they are included merely as afterthoughts.

what to buy next: [*Weekend in Vienna: Strauss Favorites*; Willi Boskovsky, cond.; Vienna Philharmonic Orchestra] (Preiser 90046) ♪ ♪ ♪ ♪

Boskovsky is one of the finest interpreters of the Waltz King and the rest of the Strauss family. This performance has all the lift and lilt one should expect from him, but as is usually the case with this work, it has found its way onto an album celebrating the accomplishments of Josef's older brother. However, along with a solid collection of Johann's classic tunes, Boskovsky manages to sneak in one other tune by Josef, the rarely heard "Brennende Liebe," in addition to their father's "Radetzky March." In any event, the polkas and waltzes on this set are marvelous, and the playing sparkles.

"Aquarellen," op. 258
what to buy: [*Josef Strauss Edition, vol. 18*; Karl Geyer, cond.; Slovak State Philharmonic Orchestra] (Marco Polo 8.223620) ♪ ♪ ♪₅

This is part of a twenty-volume series devoted to Josef Strauss, a set geared toward academia and people enamored with the whole Strauss mystique. That said, there is some pretty decent playing to be found throughout the cycle, not least on Geyer's take of "Aquarellen." Other gems from Josef's oeuvre to be found here include "Brennende Liebe," "Die Libelle," and "Im Fluge."

influences: Johann Strauss Jr., Joseph Lanner, Emile Waldteufel

Garaud MacTaggart

Johann Strauss, Sr.

Born Johann Baptist Strauss, March 14, 1804, in Vienna, Austria.
Died September 25, 1849, in Vienna, Austria.

period: Romantic

The patriarch of the Strauss family influenced Frédéric Chopin in addition to his trio of sons: Josef, Eduard, and—most famous of them all—Johann, Jr., the "Waltz King." Although he was a prolific composer of waltzes, galops, and quadrilles, Strauss is best known today for the *Radetzky March* (a work published the year before he died) and for siring a ballroom-music dynasty.

Waltzes emerged out of the Ländler, a slow-paced country dance of which both Ludwig van Beethoven and Franz Schubert provided numerous examples in their catalog of works. The next step in the evolutionary process was taken by Josef Lanner and his compatriot Johann Strauss. Lanner was the more talented musician of the two, playing the violin with a facility that few on the dance-hall circuit could match, and creating compositions which would be characterized as "violet-scented melodies" by the influential Viennese music critic, Eduard Hanslick. Lanner was already making a solid reputation for himself as a musician when he took his trio to the Café "Zum grünen Jäger" for a better-paying engagement in 1823. Later that year, Johann Strauss came on board as the group's violist and within a few years the quartet had expanded to a small orchestra of a dozen or so musicians, playing in the choicest of Viennese venues. Strauss was already experimenting with writing his own tunes and crafting arrangements for the orchestra to play, but his greatest attribute may have been his fierce drive to succeed. By 1825 Lanner had appointed Strauss as his second-in-command and included a number of Strauss's works in the orchestra's set-list.

With the publication and success of his *Kettenbrückenwalzer (Chain Bridge Waltz)* in 1827, Strauss began entertaining ideas of starting his own orchestra and splitting off from Lanner, which he did two years later when the first incarnation of the Strauss Orchestra was formed. The new group got off to a good start in 1830 when Strauss entered into a long-term, non-exclusive agreement to play at a dance hall (Zum Sperlbauer) that was popular with Vienna's cultural elite. This proved especially fortuitous for the young entrepreneur, as he was starting a family and already

had two children, Johann, Jr. and Josef. Strauss proved, over the next couple of years, to be a most industrious bandleader and composer, cramming his calendar with engagements (in Vienna and in other cities), and writing an amazing amount of music. He also introduced spectacle and crowd-pleasing antics into his programs, having fireworks shot off during some of his performances and conducting every concert in an animated manner that entertained the masses.

By the mid-1830s, Strauss's industrious ways and entertaining style enabled him to field over 200 musicians in six orchestras, all bearing his name. With his self-imposed workload, it is also no wonder that his marriage began breaking up around that time. While their six children were at home with his wife, Strauss began an affair in 1833 with the woman who would eventually become his second wife and the mother of seven more children. He also began taking one of his orchestras on the road to other countries—traveling to Hungary, Germany, France, Belgium, and Britain, playing before members of the ruling class, and generating interest in his compositions among other musicians and various music publishers.

In 1848, Strauss was the toast of Europe's upper crust, a fact that no doubt caused him to write his single most enduring piece, the *Radetzky March*. Composed in honor of the Austrian army, this work placed the author squarely on the side of the reactionaries and conservatives led by Prince Metternich during the Revolution of 1848. When Strauss died a year later, it was supposedly because of the scarlet fever he contracted during a performance of this march three days earlier.

Orchestral
Radetzky March for Orchestra, op. 228
what to buy: [*New Year's Concert: Live From Vienna*; Willi Boskovsky, cond.; Vienna Philharmonic Orchestra] (Preiser 90045) ♪ ♪ ♪ ♪₵

Boskovsky's flair for Viennese waltzes is undeniable, something that makes his performances of Strauss family music such a joy to listen to. In this case, the *Radetzky March* is a bit of classy filler for an album featuring his oldest son's material, including a variety of overtures, waltzes, polkas, and selections from the rarely performed operetta, *Ritter Pázmán*.

what to buy next: [*Great Marches*; Leonard Bernstein, cond.; New York Philharmonic Orchestra] (Sony Classics 63154) ♪ ♪ ♪ ♪

Once again, the *Radetzky March* is the only composition by the elder Strauss on the album but the rest of the disc is pretty exciting stuff too. Included are pulse raisers by Georges Bizet (*March of the Toreadors*), Thomas Arne (*Rule Britannia*), Edward Elgar (*Pomp and Circumstance March no. 1*), a fistful of John Philip Sousa works, and more.

various works
what to buy: [*Orchestral Works*; Mika Eichenholz, cond.; Slovak State Philharmonic Orchestra (Kosice)] (Marco Polo 8.223617) ♪ ♪ ♪⅛

While there is no *Radetzky March* here, the dozen mid-length works heard in this collection can give a better idea of why Strauss was such an effective composer for his time. The *Moldau-Klänge* Waltz and the *Orpheus-Quadrille* are fine examples of period music, displaying an unforced yet decorous gaiety that has its own charms. Ditto for the other ten selections on the set. Eichenholz and the orchestra do a solid if unspectacular job in performing these works but the rarity of the material makes it worth checking out if one wishes to explore Strauss's sound world further.

Chamber
various works
what to buy: [*Strauss Dances*; Gaudier Ensemble, orch.] (Hyperion 67169) ♪ ♪ ♪ ♪

For a historically valid survey of the elder Strauss's oeuvre, this well-produced, well-played album is the ticket. While there are four of Junior's compositions on the program, Papa gets the lion's share of space with the *Cachucha Galopp,* his debonair *Salon Polka,* and ten more selections. The Gaudier Ensemble is actually an octet and the performances have a definite chamber music feel about them but one that is wholly appropriate, given the intimate functions at which many of them were performed.

influences: Joseph Lanner, Eduard Strauss, Josef Strauss, Johann Strauss, Jr., Frédéric Chopin

Ellen Kokko

Richard Stoltzman:
Although Richard Stoltzman is now considered to be one of the foremost modern classical clarinet players, his early years often found him playing in his father's jazz groups. It is no wonder then that one of his earliest musical heroes was Benny Goodman, the jazz clarinetist who was able to cross over and play music by Wolfgang Amadeus Mozart and Béla Bartók with equal conviction. Stoltzman's own ability to swing freely between classical and jazz idioms probably stems from Goodman's example, though he has also expressed admiration for Bill Evans, Gary Burton, and Chick Corea, other jazz players who have experimented with aspects of classical music.

After graduating with a Bachelor of Music degree from Ohio State University in 1964, Stoltzman took clarinet lessons with Robert Marcellus, the principal clarinetist for the New York Philharmonic Orchestra, and then continued his studies with Keith Wilson at Yale University and Kalmen Opperman at Columbia University. In 1967, after auditioning twice and being passed over both times, Stoltzman began a ten-year stint of playing summers at the prestigious Marlboro Festival, where he studied with Harold Wright. In 1977 Stoltzman became the first woodwind player to win an Avery Fisher Career Grant, a fact that probably made it easier for him to get beyond failing a number of orchestra auditions during the years prior. While he was performing at the Marlboro Festival, Stoltzman became acquainted with Peter Serkin, Ida Kavafian, and Fred Sherry, the musicians with whom he would establish the chamber music ensemble Tashi. The group, whose name means "good fortune" in Tibetan, was originally created for a performance of Olivier Messiaen's *Quatuor pour la fin du temps (Quartet for the End of Time),* a piece which they later recorded (RCA Victor Gold Seal 7835).

Since then, Stoltzman has become one of the most prolifically-recorded classical clarinet soloists of the twentieth century, performing elements of the standard repertoire in addition to playing newly-created scores and working on different projects with a variety of non-classical musicians. He has won Grammy Awards for Best Chamber Music Performance for 1982 and 1996, working in the first case with pianist Richard Goode on a recording of the two sonatas for clarinet and piano by Johannes Brahms (RCA Victor Gold Seal 60036) and then with cellist Yo-Yo Ma and pianist Emanuel Ax for an album of trios by Brahms, Ludwig van Beethoven, and Wolfgang Amadeus Mozart (Sony Classical 57499). On the orchestral front, Stoltzman has recorded Aaron Copland's great Concerto for Clarinet and Orchestra several times, including his most recent performance with Michael Tilson Thomas conducting the London Symphony Orchestra (RCA Victor Red Seal 61790).

Stoltzman is also active with regard to recording music from lesser-known contemporary American composers, performing clarinet concertos by William Thomas McKinley, Burt Fenner, and John Carbon (*Alchemy,* MMC 2031) and playing on a collection of compositions by Frederick Speck, Frank Graham Stewart, Burton Beerman, and Mark Philips (MMC 2078). On a somewhat lighter note, *Worldbeat Bach* (RCA Records 63544) finds Stoltzman in the company of jazz vibraphonist Gary Burton, bassist Eddie Gomez, and others, playing arrangements of Bach works set to samba, flamenco, calypso, and other dance rhythms.

Ian Palmer

Richard Strauss

Born Richard Georg Strauss, June 11, 1864, in Munich, Germany. Died September 8, 1949, in Garmisch-Partenkirchen, Germany.

period: Romantic/twentieth century

Richard Strauss was a exceptionally talented young German musician who first startled the music world with his modern orchestral works and then went on to compose some of the finest operas of the 20th century.

Franz Strauss, Richard's father, was the principal horn player in the Munich court orchestra when his son was born and would rise to the position of *Kammermusiker* at the Bavarian court by 1873. Thus it was that the young Richard found himself surrounded by music and the accoutrements of the musical profession at an early age. Before reaching his teen years he had already begun taking piano lessons, writing his first pieces, and learning to play the violin. By the time he entered Munich University in 1882, Strauss had already composed a violin concerto and was soon to finish his first horn concerto. His higher education was to be brief however and he left the university in 1883, eventually landing up in Berlin where he met the famous conductor Hans von Bülow. Impressed by some of Strauss's scores, Bülow commissioned the Suite in B flat major for woodwinds from the young composer. This piece, the Horn Concerto, and his budding abilities as a conductor convinced Bülow to appoint Strauss as his assistant with the Meiningen Orchestra in 1885.

Strauss, whose early compositions owed much to the model provided by Johannes Brahms, was now coming more and more under the sway of Richard Wagner, perhaps due in part to the influence of Bülow who had conducted the premieres of *Tristan und Isolde* in 1865 and *Die Meistersinger von Nürnberg* in 1868 (although Bülow had plenty of reason to be upset with Wagner, who had stolen his wife). Another factor may have his friendship with Alexander Ritter, a violinist in the orchestra who was married to Wagner's niece and, in addition to being an ardent Wagnerite and a devoted fan of Franz Liszt, in 1882 became one of Strauss's earliest contacts with that musical faction. None of this was occurring in a vacuum however, since the young composer had been exposed to Wagner's music as far back as 1878, when he attended performances of *Die Walküre* and *Siegfried* in Munich. He had also heard his father perform in the premiere of *Parsifal* at Bayreuth in 1882.

Strauss left Meiningen in 1886 to take up a new post with the Munich Court Opera but not before touring Italy, the inspiration for his first tone poem, *Aus Italien.* When he finally went to Munich, Strauss stepped into an uncomfortable situation as third conductor, working with an administration that was opposed to much of the music that he held dear. Within a year however, his stock had risen with other orchestras, both as a composer and as a conductor. As a result, he began accepting conducting engagements throughout Germany, including Weimar where, in 1889, he became *Kapellmeister.* Works from this time include two of his most arresting tone poems: *Don Juan* and *Tod und Verklärung (Death and Transfiguration).* As his conducting career began flourishing, Strauss was even invited by Cosima Wagner (in 1891) to conduct *Tannhäuser* and *Parsifal* at the festival devoted to Richard Wagner's works at Bayreuth.

Shortly thereafter, Strauss began working on the first of his Wagner-inspired operas, *Guntram,* completing it in 1893. Like *Feuersnot,* the 1901 opera which followed it in Strauss's canon, it failed to find an audience. Meanwhile his tone poems were proving to be increasingly successful—such popular works as *Till Eulenspiegels lustige Streiche (Till Eulenspiegel's Merry Pranks* (1894-95), *Also sprach Zarathustra* (1896), and *Ein Heldenleben (A Hero's Life)* (1897-98). Then, in 1905, came the premiere of his opera, *Salome,* which shook up German and other audiences when it was first performed. Basing it on Oscar Wilde's play about King Herod's daughter, one of the Bible's most idealized temptresses, Strauss gave her and the court an unprecedented sensuous, propulsive, hard-edged, and dissonant musical setting. In one long act, he moved beyond Wagner's Romantic chromaticism into the 20th century. The composer also produced an orchestral arrangement of *Salomes Tanz (Salome's Dance)* from *Salome* that same year.

In 1909 Strauss composed *Elektra,* based the Greek myths of the House of Atreus; his score for this opera is wildly dissonant, expressing the rage, jealousy, and murderous impulses of the characters. (Many sopranos have been made famous by their portrayal of the title character.) His first-time librettist was Hugo von Hofmannsthal, a Viennese poet and dramatist who would later provide tenderer, lighter, wittier libretti for Strauss's most suc-

cessful opera, the sublime *Der Rosenkavalier* (1909-1910), and *Ariadne auf Naxos* (1911-12, revised in 1916). The composer also wrote *Eine Alpensinfonie* during this same period (1911-15) but most of the scores written from then until his death in 1949 (with the notable exception of *Metamorphosen* for strings from 1945 and the poignant *Vier letzte Lieder* (*Four Last Songs* for soprano and orchestra of 1948), though well constructed, are of lesser importance than his works of the late 19th and early 20th centuries.

Orchestral
Also sprach Zarathustra (Therefore Spake Zarathustra, op. 30
what to buy: [*Richard Strauss In Hi-Fidelity*, Fritz Reiner, cond.; Chicago Symphony Orchestra] (RCA Living Stereo 61494) ♪ ♪ ♪ ♪

The music is, of course, more famous to the world of popular culture from Stanley Kubrick's film *2001, a Space Odyssey*. Fritz Reiner's recording has its ardent supporters and is a fine choice, especially as it is combined with a fine performance of the composer's *Ein Heldenleben*, op. 40.

[Herbert von Karajan, cond.; Berlin Philharmonic Orchestra] (Deutsche Grammophon 447441) ♪ ♪ ♪ ♪

Often accused of favoring surface sheen over substance, Karajan turns in a well-recorded version of this tone poem that combines both those qualities to produce a wallop. His conducting in the other Strauss works included here (*Don Juan*, *Till Eulenspiegels lustige Streiche*, and *Salomes Tanz*) is almost as powerful, making this a very strong recommendation.

what to buy next: [*Richard Strauss: 5 Great Tone Poems*; Bernard Haitink, cond.; Royal Concertgebouw Orchestra] (Philips 442281) ♪ ♪ ♪ ♪

Two discs at a budget price featuring Haitink and the marvelous orchestra with which he has done some of his best work sounds like it should be a winner—and it is. While his rendition of *Also Sprach Zarathustra* doesn't have quite the drama of the versions by Reiner or Karajan, the package does include exemplary performances of *Ein Heldenleben*, *Tod und Verklärung*, *Don Juan*, and *Till Eulenspiegel* plus two suites of waltzes drawn from *Der Rosenkavalier*.

Tod und Verklärung (Death and Transfiguration), op. 24
what to buy: [Herbert von Karajan, cond.; Berlin Philharmonic Orchestra] (Deutsche Grammophon 447422) ♪ ♪ ♪ ♪

All the strength, drama, and glory hinted at in the title of this remarkable tone poem can be found in Karajan's interpretation. The strings are marvelous here and in the *Metamorphosen* that is also included in this set. There is also a solid version of the *Vier letzte Lieder* featuring Gundula Janowitz as the soloist.

worth searching for: [Otto Klemperer, cond.; Philharmonia Orchestra] (EMI Classics Imports 66823) ♪ ♪ ♪ ♪

Klemperer's approach to the score isn't as flashy as Karajan, but it is far from stolid, offering its own rewards for those who prefer a performance of more inward, personalized majesty. The same sort of interpretive skills are also applied to the other Strauss scores heard here: *Don Juan*, *Salomes Tanz*, and, especially, an incredibly moving version of the *Metamorphosen* for 23 solo strings.

Till Eulenspiegels lustige Streiche (Till Eulenspiegel's Merry Pranks) for Orchestra, op. 28
what to buy: [Leonard Bernstein, cond; New York Philharmonic Orchestra] (Sony Classical 47626) ♪ ♪ ♪ ♪

If you want emotional impact, Bernstein delivers. The coupling of this work with two of Strauss's other tone poems (*Don Juan*, and *Also sprach Zarathustra*) is felicitous and, given the price, quite affordable.

Vocal
Der Rosenkavalier, op. 59
what to buy: [Elisabeth Schwarzkopf, soprano; Ljuba Welitsch, soprano; Christa Ludwig, mezzo-soprano; Teresa Stich-Randall, mezzo-soprano; Kerstin Meyer, mezzo-soprano; Nicolai Gedda, tenor; Paul Kuen, tenor; Eberhard Wächter, baritone; Otto Edelmann, bass; Herbert von Karajan, cond.; Philharmonia Orchestra; Philharmonia Chorus; Bancroft School Children's Chorus; Loughton High School for Girls Choir] (EMI Classics 56113) ♪ ♪ ♪ ♪

Even now, 40 or so years later, Elisabeth Schwarzkopf is *the* Marschallin; her crystalline soprano and inimitable emotional inflection still hold sway and are the primary reasons for selecting this recording.

Elektra, op. 58
what to buy: [Inge Borkh, soprano; Lisa della Casa, soprano; Lisa Otto, soprano; Anny Felbermayer, soprano; Audrey Gerber, soprano; Marilyn Horne, mezzo-soprano; Jean Madeira, mezzo-soprano; Kerstin Meyer, mezzo-soprano; Sieglinde Wagner, mezzo-soprano; Max Lorenz, tenor; Erich Majkut, tenor; Kurt Böhme, bass; Georg Littasy, bass; Alois Pernerstorfer, bass; Dimitri Mitropoulos, cond.; Vienna Philharmonic Orchestra; Vienna State Opera Chorus] (Orfeo d'Or 456972) ♪ ♪ ♪ ♪

This live recording from 1957 documents a stunningly intense performance. Based purely on the quality of the orchestral playing heard here, Mitropoulos is the star of the production. That isn't meant to detract from what is essentially a fine cast, especially Borkh who is terrifyingly good in her characterization of Elektra, but to emphasize the committed performances to which the conductor drives his forces.

worth searching for: [Birgit Nilsson, soprano; Marie Collier, soprano; Regina Resnik, mezzo-soprano; Gerhard Stolze, tenor; Tom Krause, baritone; Georg Solti, cond.; Vienna Philharmonic Orchestra] (London 417345) ♪ ♪ ♪ ♪ ♪

Birgit Nilsson all but owns the title role; in it she capped a brilliant career. The voice is capable of the lunging, demanding tessitura and the dramatic inflection is chilling, with her solo passage *Allein! Weh, ganz allein!* demonstrating her superb control and characterization. This one has bite, heft and Solti's propulsive conducting.

Vier letzte Lieder (Four Last Songs) for Soprano and Orchestra
what to buy: [Jessye Norman, soprano; Kurt Masur, cond.; Leipzig Gewandhaus Orchestra] (Phillips 411052) ♪ ♪ ♪ ♪

The sumptuous tones of Jessye Norman are well suited to this work, composed when Strauss was 84. The disc also includes six orchestrated songs drawn from the composer's opp. 10, 14, 27, and 37. A recent, sonically updated reissue (Philips 464742) couples the Four Last Songs with Norman's recording of Wagner's

Wesendonck Lieder.

what to buy next: [Elisabeth Schwarzkopf, soprano; George Szell, cond.; Berlin Radio Symphony Orchestra] (EMI Classics 66960) ♪ ♪ ♪

This reissue of the famous Schwarzkopf/Szell version of the Four Last Songs also includes the German soprano singing 12 orchestral songs with Szell conducting the London Symphony Orchestra.

[Barbara Bonney, soprano; Malcolm Martineau, piano] (London 460812) ♪ ♪ ♪

Bonney performs these songs in the piano/voice reduction created by Max Wolff, which concentrates on vocal color and line instead of the lustrous orchestral setting Strauss originally created. It's an interesting experiment, made more valuable by the inclusion of a fine selection of other songs for soprano and piano by the composer. Of particular note is Bonney's singing in the composer's early eight Lieder, op. 10.

influences: Johannes Brahms, Franz Liszt, Richard Wagner

Michael H. Margolin and Garaud MacTaggart

Igor Stravinsky
Born Igor Fyodorovich Stravinsky, June 17, 1882, Oranienbaum, near St. Petersburg, Russia. Died April 6,1971, New York City, NY.

period: Twentieth century

Stravinsky was a towering figure in the history of music, and one of two 20th-century composers (Arnold Schoenberg is the other) whose work forever altered the musical landscape. Stravinsky is still best known for his early ballets, *L'Oiseau de feu (The Firebird)* and *Le Sacre du printemps (The Rite of Spring)*, but the neo-classical period of the 1920s and 1930s as well as his experiments with serial techniques towards the end of his life also have rewards for the adventurous listener.

Igor was the third of Fyodor Stravinsky's four sons. The eminent bass-baritone, one of the finest Russian opera singers of his day, and his wife Anna Kholodovskaya provided surroundings for their children that were decidedly theatrical and very musical. Studying piano from the age of nine (he would always be a first-rate pianist), Igor later took lessons in harmony and counterpoint. In accordance with his father's wishes however, he studied law at St. Petersburg University from 1901-05.

A pivotal move for him, one that turned him decisively towards music, was the private instruction Stravinsky began receiving from Rimsky-Korsakov after meeting him in 1902. He composed several piano pieces, songs, and studied orchestration with a man who was himself a master of instrumentation. Bringing his own genius to what he learned from Rimsky-Korsakov, Stravinsky's unique manner of scoring would remain a distinct feature of his music. Intensifying studies with Rimsky-Korsakov after 1905, Stravinsky composed the *Scherzo fantastique* and *Feu d'artifice (Fireworks), which are polished enough to avoid being labeled "student works" and are still performed.*

Stravinsky had quickly discovered his voice and was just as quickly establishing relationships that would be pivotal in music history. The triumphant premieres of the *Scherzo fantastique* and *Fireworks* in 1909 prompted Sergei Diaghilev to engage him for the upcoming season of his newly formed Ballets Russes in Paris, commissioning the fairy-tale ballet *L'Oiseau de feu (The Firebird),* and premiering the completed score in June of 1910. The music, which shows the influence of Rimsky-Korsakov in its skillful, exciting orchestration, was highly successful and helped establish the young composer as a major talent. Stravinsky followed it with another ballet based on a Russian folk tale, *Petrushka,* whose use of polytonality and asymmetrical rhythms expanded the musical language still further. It too became a popular work for Diaghilev's ballet company after its successful premiere in 1911. Another piece already in gestation *(Le Sacre du printemps)* would culminate the musical upheaval.

At its premiere (May 29, 1913) a riot broke out in the audience, a reaction to the choreography by Nijinsky as well as to Stravinsky's music, which was more dissonant and violent than anything ever heard before. Lavishly orchestrated, densely polytonal, asymmetrical in its rhythmic design, it is propelled by driving rhythms that charge the dissonances with raw energy. *The Rite* has worked its way into the standard repertoire with a vengeance, becoming standard fare for ballet companies and in the concert hall as one of the most important pieces of orchestral music of the entire twentieth century.

For the 1914 season of the Ballet Russes, Stravinsky completed his opera *The Nightingale* and began preparing for 1915 with the vocal-orchestral ballet *Les Noces (The Wedding),* but the outbreak of the First World War delayed its production. With the 1917 Bolshevik coup his ties with his homeland were severed and return was no longer possible. At this point, with Stravinsky now settled in Switzerland, a change occurs in his style of composition: his scoring becomes more spare and Russian nationalism for its own sake ceases to be a major theme. 1918 saw *Histoire du soldat,* a frugally scored theater piece, and *Ragtime* for eleven instruments, with Stravinsky still drawing upon his tonal and rhythmic innovations from the pre-war years. Other pieces from this time include the light-hearted *Piano-Rag Music* (1919) and the stark, solemn *Symphonies of Wind Instruments* (1920).

Moving to France after the war, he was commissioned by Diaghilev to write a ballet *(Pulcinella,* based on Italian Baroque music then attributed to Giovanni Battista Pergolesi) and the buffo opera *Mavra,* and was also occupied by work on a drastically reduced version of *Les Noces (The Wedding),* a score which Stravinsky had originally completed in 1917 but would tinker with until its eventual premiere in 1923. Perhaps inspired by his brush with 18th century music in *Pulcinella,* the Octet of 1923 embraced both the manner and form of this older period, creating a neoclassical style that would permeate his compositions through the early 1950s.

In 1925, Stravinsky also began appearing more regularly as a conductor and pianist in his own music and the next decade saw him create a number of important works either as commissions or as scores for him to perform: the opera/oratorio *Oedipus Rex* (1926-27), the ballet *Apollon Musagète* (1927-28), the *Symphony of Psalms* (1930), and the Concerto in D major for Violin and Orchestra (1931), the ballet *Jeu de cartes (The Card Game)* (1935-36), the *Dumbarton Oaks* chamber concerto (1937-38), and the Symphony in C (1938-40). He also published his autobiography (*Chroniques de ma vie*) in 1936.

The decade ended and the next one began with Stravinsky giving the Charles Eliot Norton Lectures at Harvard University in 1939-40 and applying for American citizenship in 1940. During the coming years he wrote a few major pieces (the *Symphony in Three Movements* and the ballet *Orpheus*) but seemed to save most of his creative juices for *The Rake's Progress.* Begun in 1948 and finished three years later, this English-language opera features a libretto by W.H. Auden and Chester Kallman and is strongly neoclassical in its use of arias, duets, recitative, and chorus. Premiered in Venice in 1951, it won immediate critical acclaim.

By this time, a young Juilliard School graduate named Robert Craft had entered the picture. Starting in 1948, he quickly became an amanuensis who would remain the composer's assistant for the rest of Stravinsky's life. Craft was greatly intrigued by the music of Arnold Schoenberg, and this interest, along with Schoenberg's death in 1951, prompted Stravinsky to study twelve-tone procedures (especially as used by Anton Webern). Many compositions after *The Rake* show a concern with these serial techniques (though, with tonal implications) and are often densely constructed, spare, and miniature in scale. They are perhaps the least understood portion of the composer's output. Stravinsky was still writing larger-scale music at this time, and some of these works—the ballet *Agon* 1953-57), the choral *Canticum sacrum* (1955) and *Threni* (1957-58), and *The Flood* (1961-62), a biblically based dramatic piece commissioned by CBS television—are marvelous gems of orchestration. His last major work was the spare, moving *Requiem Canticles* of 1966, a setting of the requiem text that was written as his health was failing.

Orchestra
various ballets
what to buy: [Claudio Abbado, cond., London Symphony Orchestra] (Deutsche Grammophon 453085) ♪♪♪♪♪

This two-disc set contains a fabulous recording of the complete *L'Oiseau de feu (The Firebird)* along with fine performances of Stravinsky's *Jeu de cartes (The Card Game)*, *Petrushka*, *Pulcinella*, and the ever popular *Le Sacre du Printemps (The Rite of Spring)*.

[Pierre Boulez, cond.; Cleveland Orchestra] (Deutsche Grammophon 435769] ♪♪♪♪♪

Boulez brings an intense concentration to Stravinsky's masterpiece *(The Rite of Spring)*, and to this disc's companion piece, *Petrushka*.

what to buy next: [*Stravinsky: The Great Ballets*; Bernard Haitink, cond.; London Philharmonic Orchestra] (Philips 438350) ♪♪♪♪

This is one of Haitink's most invigorating outings, a two-CD package including his performances of *The Firebird*, *Petrushka* and *The Rite of Spring*, while Igor Markevitch does the honors (with the London Symphony Orchestra) for *Apollon Musagète*.

worth searching for: [Pierre Boulez, cond. New York Philharmonic Orchestra] (Sony Classics 42396) ♪♪♪♪♪

Boulez's direction is superb and likewise the playing of the New York Philharmonic. This disc contains solid, probing performances of *The Firebird* and *Le Chant du rossignol (The Song of the Nightingale)*.

Firebird Suite no. 1 for orchestra (revised 1911)
what to buy: [Vladimir Ashkenazy, cond.; St. Petersburg Philharmonic Orchestra] (Decca 448812) ♪♪♪♪

The playing in this program of four early Stravinsky compositions is strong throughout, containing just enough raw energy to make one realize that this is a Russian score being performed by a Russian orchestra. Ashkenazy returns to the 1911 version of the suite, with fuller orchestration than in later revisions. There are also sparkling performances of Stravinsky's early *Feu d'artifice (Fireworks)*, *Scherzo fantastique,* and the Symphony no. 1 in E flat major, op. 1, which shows the strong influence of his teacher Rimsky-Korsakov.

Firebird Suite no. 2 for Orchestra (revised 1919)
what to buy: [*Bernstein Conducts Stravinsky*; Leonard Bernstein, cond., Israel Philharmonic] (Deutsche Grammophon 445538) ♪♪♪♪♪

Bernstein's very fine set offers the second suite which Stravinsky carved from the original ballet along with *The Rite of Spring*, *Petrushka*, the *Symphony in Three Movements,* and the witty *Scenes de ballet* from 1944.

Firebird Suite no. 3 for Orchestra (revised 1945)
[Josep Pons, cond.; Orquesta Ciudad de Granada] (Harmonia Mundi 901728) ♪♪♪♪

Here is a surprisingly effective recording of the downsized 1945 suite from a totally unexpected source. Usually one expects performances of this caliber from major orchestras but Pons and his forces give a suitably taut rendering that should please most listeners. Their version of *Jeu de cartes* makes an admirable pairing for the more familiar work.

Concerto in D Major for Violin and Orchestra

what to buy: [Itzhak Perlman, violin, Seiji Ozawa, cond., Boston Symphony Orchestra] (Deutsche Grammophon 447445) ♪ ♪ ♪ ♪⸍

A wonderful recording of this modern masterpiece, coupled with one of the finest versions of Alban Berg's Violin Concerto. The disc also has Perlman playing Maurice Ravel's *Tzigane* (with Zubin Mehta conducting the New York Philharmonic).

what to buy next: [*Stravinsky: Symphonies and Concertos*; Arthur Grumiaux, violin; Ernest Bour, cond.; Royal Concertgebouw Orchestra] (Philips 442583) ♪ ♪ ♪⸍

This orchestra is habitually great, as is the violinist, but here the conductor seems to be buoyed along by the forces he is supposed to be leading instead of the other way around. Be that as it may, this is still a sturdy performance of the Violin Concerto but the two-disc set's main attraction is the plethora of other outstanding performances it contains. This is probably the package to get if you want good (but relatively inexpensive) renditions of the Symphony in C, the *Symphony in Three Movements,* the *Symphony of Psalms,* the *Symphonies of Wind Instruments,* and the *Ebony Concerto* that Stravinsky wrote for clarinetist Benny Goodman.

various works

what to buy: [*Igor Stravinsky: The Edition*; Igor Stravinsky, cond., Robert Craft, cond.; various orchestras; various ensembles; various vocalists] (Sony Classical 46290) ♪ ♪ ♪ ♪ ♪

Sony has packaged these performances of Stravinsky's music (conducted by the composer and Robert Craft) in 12 volumes containing 22 CDs. The project was originally released on LPs in 1982 and is now expanded to bring in even more pertinent material so that most of the composer's scores are included here. The recordings in this set are also available separately.

Vocal
Oedipus Rex

what to buy: [Jessye Norman, soprano; Peter Schreier, tenor; Robert Swensen, tenor; Michio Tatara, baritone; Bryn Terfel, bass-baritone; Harry Peeters, bass; Seiji Ozawa, cond.; Saito Kinen Orchestra; Shinyukai Choir] (Philips 438865) ♪ ♪ ♪ ♪⸍

This version of Stravinsky's opera/oratorio hybrid is a classic, prize-winning recording (*International Classical Music Award, 1993* and the *Choc du Monde de la Musique, 1994*) by Ozawa. Norman is spectacular as usual and the rest of the cast is marvelous.

The Rake's Progress

what to buy: [Sylvia McNair, soprano; Jane Henschel, contralto; Anthony Rolfe Johnson, tenor; Ian Bostridge, tenor; Paul Plishka, bass; Donald Adams, bass; Seiji Ozawa, cond.; Saito Kinen Orchestra; Tokyo Opera Singers] (Philips 454431) ♪ ♪ ♪ ♪ ♪

Simply put, this is the best recorded performance of this delightful opera.

Symphony of Psalms

what to buy: [Pierre Boulez, cond.; Berlin Philharmonic Orchestra; Berlin Radio Chorus] (Deutsche Grammophon 457616) ♪ ♪ ♪ ♪⸍

Boulez has long been one of the most ardent advocates for this composer and his latest traversal of the *Symphony of Psalms* has a lean but fiery approach. The other works on this disc, the *Symphony in Three Movements* and Stravinsky's brief, acerbic *Symphonies of Wind Instruments,* receive similar treatments.

what to buy next: [James O'Donnell, cond., City of London Sinfonia, orch.; Westminster Cathedral Choir] (Hyperion 66437) ♪ ♪ ♪ ♪

There are three major sacred choral works on this disc: the *Symphony of Psalms, Canticum sacrum,* and the Mass. Each work is distinctive, and shows the composer as a man of deep faith. They are all done very well, making this an album that's both representative and a joy to listen to.

worth searching for: [Herbert von Karajan, cond.; Berlin Philharmonic Orchestra; Chor der Deutschen Oper Berlin] (Deutsche Grammophon 423252) ♪ ♪ ♪ ♪ ♪

Perfectly balanced in every way and accompanied by an astounding version of Stravinsky's masterful Symphony in C and a fine rendering of the 1946 revision of his Concerto in D Major for String Orchestra, this is a wonderful recording to have and cherish.

influences: Arnold Schoenberg, Sergei Prokofiev, Dmitri Shostakovich

Frank Retzel and Ian Palmer

Josef Suk

Born January 4, 1874, in Krecovice, Bohemia. Died May 29, 1935, in Prague, Czechoslovakia.

period: Romantic/twentieth century

Josef Suk's earliest scores were pleasant rather than inspired, but this changed with the death in 1904 of his close friend and father-in-law, Antonín Dvořák. Grief motivated Suk to start writing a five-movement symphony he named *Asrael,* after the angel of death. This work evolved into a doubly tragic memorial when his wife, Dvořák's daughter Ottilie, died in 1905.

Suk's father was a teacher and church choirmaster whose home was filled with instrumental and vocal music. Growing up in a musically congenial atmosphere and learning to play piano and violin at an early age helped prepare Suk to enter the Prague Conservatory as a novice scholar in 1885.

Suk graduated from the conservatory in 1890 but stayed for an extra year so that he could attend the composition classes taught by Antonín Dvořák, who had just joined the faculty. The young man had already started a portfolio of compositions, including a few piano pieces and some small chamber works—enough to show Dvořák his potential. Suk rapidly became one of Dvořák's favorite students, and when the teacher prodded him to stretch his writing beyond what Suk was used to, the student responded with his Serenade in E-flat Major for String Orchestra, op. 6. This work became Suk's first big success, even attracting the attention of Johannes Brahms, who convinced his publisher, Simrock, to print the score in 1892. That same year, Suk joined the Czech Quartet as second violinist, a position he would retain until 1933, playing over four thousand concerts on a multitude of international stages.

When Suk met Dvořák's daughter Ottilie, there was a definite attraction between the two, but they waited until the Dvořák family returned from the composer's famous sojourn in America before getting married. The union took place on Dvořák's silver wedding anniversary. During this period Suk composed lyrical works in a Dvořákian mode, including the Symphony in E Major, op. 14 (1897), the Suite for Piano, op. 21 (1900), and the Fantasy in G Minor for Violin and Orchestra, op. 24 (1903). A time of profound spiritual and emotional crisis for Suk began in 1904, when his father-in-law died. The two men had been very close, and Suk started work on

Antonio Stradivari:

Stradivarius (the Latinized version of Stradivari) is a name that has become almost synonymous with greatness in the craft of violin construction, a name that is more familiar to general audiences than that of Antonio Stradivari's fellow violin makers, the Amatis and the Guarneris. Born in Cremona, Italy during the middle of the seventeenth century, Stradivari may very well have served an apprenticeship with Niccoló Amati, but he established his own shop in 1665, continuing to make or supervise the construction of violins, violas, cellos, and other stringed instruments until his death in 1737.

From 1665 until 1685, most of his violins were constructed on patterns he had adapted from Amati's examples. Stradivari gradually began experimenting with modifications to the sound holes (situating them in a slightly different position), trying out different formulas for the varnishes he used, enlarging the resonance box of the violin, and lengthening the body of the instrument. The period from 1695 until 1725 is when his greatest violins seem to have been produced. By this time Stradivari had settled on the varnishes, the various woods he would use in constructing the violins, and the basic structural features most closely associated with him. From 1726 until his death in 1737, Stradivari's abilities were starting to erode and he left more and more of the details of his shop's products to the hands of his apprentices, including his sons Francesco and Omobono.

The reasons why a prized Stradivarius violin sounds as good as it does have been subjected to much debate, scientific and otherwise. There are those who ascribe its fabled tone to the varnish Stradivari used—for example, some credit Stradivari's use of tung oil as a defining factor, while some claim that he had developed a specific mixture of lye-soaked chitin (the outer shells of insect bodies and/or shrimp shells) which he then strained, rinsed, and dissolved in vinegar. Others assert that the woods utilized—taken from forests that no longer exist or smoked in ammonia fumes for several weeks or treated with potassium silicate and calcium—aided the structural composition of Stradivari's violins and their ability to produce such a glorious sound.

Another bone of contention among scholars and auction houses alike relates to counterfeiting, the creation of violins whose pedigree as a Stradivarius is in doubt. When prices for these instruments run into the hundreds of thousands of dollars—and, for some particularly well-documented specimens, well more than a million—the confirmation of a violin's origins can have distinct financial ramifications. The most current controversy revolves around the "Messiah" Strad, a violin on permanent display at the Ashmolean Museum in Oxford, England. The instrument's lineage has some uncomfortable gaps in it, including ownership by a French violin dealer named Jean-Baptiste Vuillaume who purchased it from the prior owner's estate in 1855. Vuillaume based his statement of the violin's origin upon a previously-published description of the violin which he said matched one of the instruments he bought. Two recent analyses of tree ring patterns visible on the front of the violin came up with conflicting opinions as to whether the wood used was contemporaneous with Stradivari's lifetime or if it was harvested after his death, although it would appear that most scholarly opinion lines up on the side of the "Messiah" being Stradivari's creation.

Ian Palmer

a musical memorial for Dvořák, a symphony entitled *Asrael*. While he was working on the fourth movement of the piece, Suk's wife died, and *Asrael* evolved into a poignant testimony to the two most important people in his life, Antonín Dvořák and Ottilie.

The emotional complexity of Suk's work after this double tragedy was undeniable, although he would rarely approach the intensity reached in *Asrael*. However, it can still be rewarding to listen to his later orchestral works *A Summer Tale* (1909), *Ripening* (1917), and *Epilogue* (1933) or his String Quartet, op. 31 (1909–10) and the cycle of ten short piano pieces titled *Things Lived and Dreamed* (1909). They stand as a testament to Suk's ability to move from music overtly influenced by Dvořák to his own unique style. As one of Czechoslovakia's foremost composers (not to mention his special relationship with his teacher/father-in-law) Suk also helped revise and prepare Dvořák's *Cypresses* for string quartet in 1921.

In addition to his work as a composer and a member of one of the early twentieth century's most famous string quartets, Suk was a professor of composition at the Prague Conservatory, beginning in 1922. During his tenure there he taught Bohuslav Martinu, thus perpetuating a distinguished line of twentieth-century Czech composers. Suk eventually became rector of the conservatory and remained at the school until his death in 1935.

Orchestral
Asrael, op. 27
what to buy: [Vaclav Neumann, cond.; Czech Philharmonic Orchestra] (Supraphon FL 0278) ♪ ♪ ♪ ♪⅛

While the recording may not have the sonic advantages of more recent performances, this version by Neumann is incredibly moving, wringing every last bit of soul from the piece. Perhaps only Charles Mackerras, the renowned Czech music specialist, might approach the greatness of Neumann's performance—that is, if he ever gets around to recording this work.

what to buy next: [Peter Schneider, cond.; Orchestre Philharmonique de Montpellier Lanquedoc-Roussillon] (Naïve 34105) ♪ ♪ ♪ ♪

Live recordings, if all goes right, can be more exciting than their studio counterparts. Here, Schneider and his French orchestra take the full measure of Suk's tormented score, communicating the despair at the core of this

heart-wrenching piece. It just proves that you don't have to be Czech to play this music with conviction and skill.

[Jiri Belohlavek, cond.; Czech Philharmonic Orchestra] (Chandos 9640) ♪ ♪ ♪⅛

Belohlavek's version of this work has wonderful sonics, and the performance is certainly a worthwhile alternative to the Neumann and Schneider recordings, especially since it has the added advantage of wider distribution than either of the others. To make things even more attractive, the label included Suk's youthful Serenade in E-flat Major for Strings and the mid-period *Fairy Tale,* a selection that gives the listener a timeline for the composer's development.

Serenade in E-flat Major for Strings, op. 6
what to buy: [*Summer Evening: Works by Kodály and Suk*; Orpheus Chamber Orchestra) (Deutsche Grammophon 447109) ♪ ♪ ♪ ♪

Probably Suk's most played score, this sunny student work was written in response to Dvořák's advice to give up "those minor-key monumentalities" the young composer had been handing in. The Serenade is bracketed on this album by two relatively minor pieces by Zoltán Kodály—the work that gives the album its name and the *Hungarian Rondo*.

Chamber
String Quartet no. 2, op. 31
what to buy: [Suk Quartet] (Supraphon 111531) ♪ ♪ ♪ ♪

Cast in a single movement, this piece hovers close to the half-hour mark and is one of the finest (and least performed) Czech chamber works of the early twentieth century. The album also features a marvelously played *Meditation on the Old Czech Chorale "St. Wenceslas,"* op. 35a, and three other Suk compositions for string quartet.

influences: Antonín Dvořák, Vitezslav Novák

Garaud MacTaggart

Arthur Sullivan
Born Arthur Seymour Sullivan on May 13, 1842, in Lambeth, London, England. Died November 22, 1900, in Westminster, London, England.

period: Romantic

Arthur Sullivan achieved musical immortality for his collaborations with librettist William Schwenck Gilbert. Their many enduring light English operas, such as *The Mikado, H.M.S. Pinafore,* and *Pirates of Penzance,* are full of social satire, burlesque, and witty, sophisticated, parody.

Composer, conductor, and organist Arthur Seymour Sullivan was the son of an Irish bandmaster; by the time he was ten years old he had mastered all the wind instruments. Four years later he was a soloist with the Chapel Royale choir, had written and published an anthem on his own, and won his first scholarship. He then attended several prominent academies and conservatories, including the Leipzig Conservatory in Germany, where Franz Liszt was one of the judges at Sullivan's final thesis presentation. At age twenty Sullivan returned to England, where he wrote an opera based on William Shakespeare's *The Tempest* and garnered a measure of fame. By 1870, Sullivan had written a ballet, a cantata, his Symphony in E-flat (formerly known as the *Irish Symphony*), a few pieces of chamber music, a bevy of songs, and a host of hymn tunes. His short hymn "St. Gertrude" (1871) was set to an 1865 poem by Sabine Baring-Gould and became famous as "Onward, Christian Soldiers."

Sullivan and Gilbert originally met in 1869 at an operetta rehearsal; their first work together was a relatively unsuccessful light opera, *Thespis* (1871). The English impresario Richard D'Oyly Carte commissioned and produced their successful (and only) one-act opera, *Trial by Jury* in 1875 and later leased the Opera Comique especially to present their opera productions. *Trial by Jury,* about a courtroom trial where the bride sues for breach of promise, premiered at the Royalty Theatre in 1875 and ran for three hundred performances. Sullivan was kept busy with his composing, with his duties as conductor, and (beginning in 1876) as an administrator at the newly founded National Training School of Music (now the Royal College). Still, his scores for operas with librettos by Gilbert were his most financially rewarding efforts. In 1877, *The Sorcerer* began a run of 175 nights, followed by the successful runs of *H.M.S. Pinafore, Pirates of Penzance,* and *Patience.*

One of Gilbert and Sullivan's "big three" operas, *H.M.S. Pinafore* opened at the Opera Comique on May 28, 1878, and ran for 571 performances. It was their first major success. Alternately titled *The Lass That Loved a Sailor,* the two-act comic opera is a political and social satire with a story line that swirls around the love between a sailor (Ralph Rackstraw) and the captain's daughter (Josephine), with the added complication of attempts by the villain (Dick Deadeye) to foil their relationship. Probably the most familiar tune in the score is "When I Was a Lad," sung by the Rt. Hon. Sir Joseph Porter, the First Lord of the Admiralty. This comic opera features some of Gilbert's wittiest lyrics, paired with Sullivan's well-crafted choral and instrumental music.

After a New York City premiere in 1879, the London production of the comic opera *The Pirates of Penzance* opened in 1880 and ran for 363 performances at the Opera Comique in the Strand. Another of the duo's big three, *Pirates of Penzance,* is a delightful satire about the idiocy of mindless devotion to a perceived obligation. Also titled, *The Slave of Duty,* it pokes fun at the military, the police, and the duty-bound Frederic—a young apprentice pirate who expects to be freed from his service to marry Mabel, the daughter of Major-General Stanley. In a plot twist, it is revealed that because he was born on February 29 in a leap year, he won't come of age until 160 years later! The familiar chorus of "A Rollicking Band of Pirates We" was later appropriated by Theodore F. Morse and refashioned as a march for band, with lyrics by his wife (Theodora Terris, writing as D.A. Esrom), under the new title "Hail! Hail! The Gang's All Here."

Premiered in 1885 at the Savoy Theatre, *The Mikado* was the longest-running Gilbert and Sullivan opera, with 672 performances. The two-act opera begins in the courtyard of Ko-Ko, a tailor who becomes the Lord High Executioner for the Japanese town of Titipu (Pooh-Bah is the Lord High Everything Else). Emperor Mikado's son, Nanki-Poo, wants to marry Yum-Yum, Ko-Ko's ward. The situation becomes complicated when Ko-Ko condemns Nanki-Poo to death for flirting (made a capital offense by the Mikado). This opera contains unforgettable songs such as "A Wand'ring Minstrel I," "Three Little Maids from School Are We," "The Flowers That Bloom in the Spring," and "Willow, Tit-Willow."

The nearest Gilbert and Sullivan ever came to grand opera was *The Yeomen of the Guard (or The Merryman and His Maid)* (1888). One of the best loved and most serious of the Savoy operas, it was an instant success, enjoying an initial run of over 450 performances. Within the space of two acts, Gilbert's libretto (set in the Tower of London around the sixteenth century) tells the tale of Colonel Fairfax's woes. Sentenced to die on a false charge of sorcery, Fairfax tells Sir Richard (the Tower lieutenant) that he wishes to marry before he is put to death; Sir Richard then persuades Elsie to become Fairfax's bride for one day. Much intrigue ensues before Fairfax is released and claims Elsie as his wife.

For his illustrious contributions, Sullivan was knighted in 1883, but six years later, during the run of *The Gondoliers,* the two partners quarreled and separated. Sullivan's next opera, *Haddon Hall,* was composed to a libretto by Sydney Grundy, and two years later *Ivanhoe,* with a story line by Julian Sturgis, was unveiled. This attempt at grand opera enjoyed a meager run of 160 performances at the new Royal English Opera House built by D'Oyly Carte. Sullivan eventually reconciled with Gilbert, and in an attempt to recapture the magic of their finest collaborations, they wrote *Utopia Limited* (1896) and *The Grand Duke* (1896). Toward the end of his life, Sullivan finally admitted that his real genius could be found in the Savoy Theatre operettas he wrote between 1882 and 1896 with Gilbert. His happy melodies, light orchestrations, and gifts for musical parody and pastiche gave England and the world a unique, cult-drawing form of musical entertainment.

Vocal
The Mikado (or The Town of Titipu)
what to buy: [Valerie Masterson, soprano; Peggy Ann Jones, Pauline Wales, mezzo-sopranos; Lyndsie Holland, contralto; Colin Wright, tenor; Michael Rayner, John Reed, Kenneth Sandford, baritones; John Ayldon, bass-baritone; John Broad, bass; Royston Nash, cond.; Royal Philharmonic Orchestra; D'Oyly Carte Chorus] (Decca/London, 425190) ♪ ♪ ♪ ♪ ♪

This two-disc reissue of Gilbert and Sullivan's *The Mikado,* originally recorded in 1973 and reissued on CD in 1989, ranks among the best complete versions done by the D'Oyly Carte Opera Company. Nash directs a production with singing that is full of vitality in both solo and choral segments. The soloists, supported by the fine orchestra, are convincing in their roles.

what to buy next: [Elsie Morison, Jeannette Sinclair, sopranos; Marjorie Thomas, Monica Sinclair, contraltos; Richard Lewis, tenor; Geraint Evans, Ian Wallace, John Cameron, baritones; Owen Brannigan, bass; Malcolm Sargent, cond.; Pro Arte Orchestra; Glyndebourne Festival Chorus] (EMI 64403) ♪ ♪ ♪ ♪

While it is enjoyable for the precision and splendor of the soloists, vocal ensembles, and chorus, this 1957 recording (despite its digital remastering) lacks depth of sound in some orchestral passages. Sargent's interpretation is deliberate though not plodding, and his non-intrusive focus is on the singers, something especially notable in accompanied choral passages and solos. Sargent and chorus master Peter Gellhorn aptly capture the satire of this Gilbert and Sullivan opera. Although all these talented singers are appropriately pompous, Evans as the Lord High Executioner delivers a particularly waggish, convincing performance. The absence of a full libretto costs this version half a bone.

[Marie McLaughlin, Janice Watson, sopranos; Felicity Palmer, Anne Howells, mezzo-sopranos; Anthony Rolfe Johnson, Richard Suart, Nicolas Folwell, baritones; Richard Van Allan, Donald Adams, basses; Charles Mackerras, cond.; Welsh National Opera Orchestra; Welsh National Opera Chorus] (Telarc 80284) ♪ ♪ ♪ ♪

This single-disc version of the complete opera skips the overture (which wasn't composed by Sullivan anyway) and begins with the "Chorus of Nobles" (also known as "If You Want to Know Who We Are"). Mackerras draws rich performances full of dramatic verve from all participants. Although the ensemble passages are zestfully delivered, the orchestra sometimes overpowers the singers, especially in the male chorus passages, where the singers seemingly crank up the volume to be heard. Still, the soloists convey wit and sentiment, and the wonderful melodies and rhythms keep the production lively. The enclosed libretto makes it an attractive package.

The Pirates of Penzance (or The Slave of Duty)
what to buy: [Rebecca Evans, soprano; Gillian Knight, mezzo-soprano; John Mark

Ainsley, tenor; Nicholas Folwell, Richard Suart, baritones; Richard Van Allan, Donald Adams, basses; Charles Mackerras, cond.; Welsh National Opera Orchestra; Welsh National Opera Chorus] (Telarc, 80353) ♪ ♪ ♪ ♪ ♪

A top-notch version of this opera is captured here. The fine soloists, especially the plump-toned soprano Rebecca Evans in the role of Mabel, display just the right touch of comic aplomb. The choruses are superbly blended, and "When a Felon's Not Engaged in His Employment," sung by the Sergeant and a chorus of police, is especially delightful.

H.M.S. Pinafore (or The Lass That Loved a Sailor)
what to buy: [Rebecca Evans, soprano; Felicity Palmer, mezzo-soprano; Michael Schade, tenor; Thomas Allen, Richard Suart, baritones; Donald Adams, Richard Van Allan, basses; Charles Mackerras, cond.; Welsh National Opera Orchestra; Welsh National Opera Chorus] (Telarc 80374) ♪ ♪ ♪ ♪

Tight choruses, splendid orchestral passages, and top-notch solos by singers who fall nicely into their characterizations make this complete version of *Pinafore* an appropriately stuffy and satisfying listen from start to finish.

Iolanthe (or The Peer and the Peri)
what to buy: [Mary Sansom, Dawn Bradshaw, Jennifer Toye, sopranos; Gillian Knight, Yvonne Newman, Pauline Wales, mezzo-soprano; Thomas Round, tenor; John Reed, Kenneth Sandford, Alan Styler, baritones; Donald Adams, bass; Isidore Godfrey, cond.; New Symphony Orchestra; Grenadier Guards Band; D'Oyly Carte Opera Chorus] (London 414145) ♪ ♪ ♪ ♪

Iolanthe, a fairy, is exiled by the Queen of the Fairies for twenty-five years because she married a mortal. Her son, Strephon, has grown up as a shepherd—half fairy, half mortal. Strephon loves and wants to marry Phyllis, a ward of the Court of Chancery who is unaware of his mixed origins. With interference from the House of Lords, the Lord Chancellor, and the band of fairies, the situation takes hilarious twists and turns characteristic of Victorian-era light opera. Sweet, melodious music blends with the libretto's comic lyrics and dialogue to help tell the fanciful story, with Godfrey's interpretation of the score providing a most satisfying listen. Recorded in 1960, the album has been nicely remastered for this two-disc reissue. The singing is superb, the music is rife with appropriate pomp and circumstance, and the usual complications and absurdities prevail throughout this flawless performance.

The Yeoman of the Guard (or The Merryman and his Maid)
what to buy: [Felicity Palmer, Alwyn Mellor, Clare O'Neill, Pamela Helen Stephens, sopranos; Neil Archer, Ralph Mason, Peter Lloyd Adams, tenors; Donald Maxwell, Peter Savidge, baritones; Donald Adams, Richard Suart, basses; Charles Mackerras, cond.; Welsh National Opera Orchestra; Welsh National Opera

Chorus] (Telarc 80404) ♪ ♪ ♪ ♪

This two-CD set contains this opera as well as the one-act Gilbert and Sullivan opera, *Trial by Jury,* performed by the same company. Only a couple of recorded versions of *Yeoman of the Guard* exist, and this 1995 performance, led by Mackerras, captures the seriousness of the plot in solid solos, especially by the dignified Palmer. Many highlights contribute to the enjoyment of *Yeoman,* but while the music is good, it doesn't quite match up to that of Gilbert and Sullivan's more popular operas.

various songs
what to buy: [*Here's A Howdy Do!: A Gilbert and Sullivan Festival*; Wild Ray Snurck, keyboards; Mamadi Kamara, percussion, Chris Laurence, bass violin; King's Singers, choir] (RCA Victor 61885) ♪ ♪ ♪ ♪

On eleven of the fifteen tracks here, the exceptionally well blended a cappella vocal harmonies of the King's Singers make for charming listening. The remaining four tracks feature light instrumental accompaniment, providing overall variety but almost detracting from the splendid choral singing. Included are selections drawn mostly from *H.M.S. Pinafore, The Mikado,* and *Pirates of Penzance.* The animated, witty version of "A Wand'ring Minstrel I" from *The Mikado* and the authoritative take on "The Pirate King" from *Pirates of Penzance* are each worth the price of the album by themselves.

what to buy next: [*Gilbert and Sullivan Highlights*; Rebecca Evans, Marie McLaughlin, Janice Watson, Alwyn Mellor, Pamela Helen Stephen, sopranos; Felicity Palmer, Anne Howells, mezzo-sopranos; John Mark Ainsley, Neill Archer, Barry Banks, tenors; Anthony Rolfe Johnson, Thomas Allen, Richard Suart, Nicolas Folwell, Gareth Rhys-Davies, Peter Savidge, baritones; Eric Garrett, bass-baritone; Richard Van Allan, bass; Charles Mackerras, cond.; Welsh National Opera Orchestra; Welsh National Opera Chorus] (Telarc 80431) ♪ ♪ ♪

If you wish to hear Gilbert and Sullivan hits without listening to all of the operas, you'll find this twenty-eight-track compilation attractive. With classic selections from *The Mikado, Pirates of Penzance, H.M.S Pinafore, The Yeoman of the Guard,* and *Trial by Jury,* it is a perfect introductory sampler to the music of Gilbert and Sullivan.

influences: Jacques Offenbach, Felix Mendelssohn-Bartholdy, Johann Strauss II, Giuseppe Verdi, Frederic

Clay, John Philip Sousa, Victor Herbert, Jerome Kern, George M. Cohan

Nancy Ann Lee

Franz von Suppé

Born Francesco Ezechiele Ermenegildo Cavaliere Suppé Demelli on April 18, 1819, in Spalato, Dalmatia (now Split, Croatia). Died May 21, 1895, in Vienna, Austria.

period: Romantic

The bulk of Franz von Suppé's career was spent in the theater, where he churned out incidental music and other such fare for a variety of venues. Even though he had a strong run of popularity in the middle to late nineteenth century, with frequent performances of his most celebrated operetta, *Boccaccio*, he is best known to modern audiences for potboiler overtures like *Dichter und Bauer* (Poet and Peasant), *Leichte Kavallerie* (Light Cavalry), and *Die schöne Galatea* (The Beautiful Galatea). The *Light Cavalry* overture is particularly familiar to viewers of vintage animated cartoons because of the trumpet riff that always signals a character about to ride off into who knows what mischief.

Suppé's story is the familiar one of the talented young man who wants a career in music but is actively discouraged from seeking such a frivolous livelihood by more practical members of his family. Fortunately, outside influences conspired to bring the budding musician to a fuller awareness of his potential. Even though he wrote a Mass when he was only thirteen years old, his family pressed him to study law and forget about music except as recreation. Somehow he managed to travel to Milan, where he met the major Italian opera composers of the day—Gioachino Rossini, Gaetano Donizetti (a distant relative), and Giuseppe Verdi. Since being a lawyer didn't seem to be in the cards for her son, his mother then fastened on the hope that he would become a doctor. All this familial planning went for naught in 1840 when the Suppé took an unpaid job as the third-string director at a theater in Josefstadt, Austria.

Things got better when he wrote a comedic review in 1841 that made it to the stage and received good responses from the local critics. He remained a mainly regional musical hero, churning out compositions for a variety of medium-market venues until he moved to Vienna in 1845. Although still employed by the same company of theater owners he had worked for back in

Josefstadt, Suppé was now working in a big city that rewarded composers who gave audiences what they wanted. Another of his responsibilities was to conduct operas that were booked into the theater, giving him a chance to study what other, more successful composers were writing. In 1860 his years of study paid off with *Das Pensionat*, a prototypical Viennese operetta that served to counterbalance the inroads French composers such as Giacomo Meyerbeer and Jacques Offenbach were making with the local populace. From that point on, Suppé had a solid record of success with his theater works, topped off by *Boccaccio* in 1879. Although he retired from his position as kapellmeister three years later, he kept writing music until his death from cancer in 1895.

Nowadays few revivals of his operettas are staged, but the sizable number of overtures Suppé wrote for these works provide likable, well-crafted sonic appetizers for concerts and accompaniments for cartoons and advertisements.

Orchestral
various overtures
what to buy: [Paul Paray, cond.; Detroit Symphony Orchestra] (Mercury Classics 434309) ♪ ♪ ♪ ♪

Despite its age, this disc, recorded in the late 1950s, is filled with the kind of verve and spunk one wants for this material, complete with a string sound that is surprisingly full and tempos that bounce and sway beguilingly under Paray's direction. In addition to the "big three" overtures (*Light Cavalry, Beautiful Galatea,* and *Poet and Peasant*), there are the fairly popular *Ein Morgen, ein Mittag, ein Abend in Wien* (Morning, Noon, and Night in Vienna), *Pique Dame,* and the intro to Suppé's most popular operetta, *Boccaccio.* Wonderful renditions of three overtures written by Daniel-François Auber (including the one for *Fra Diavolo*) fill out the album.

what to buy next: [Otmar Suitner, cond.; Dresden Staatskapelle, orch.] (Berlin Classics 2153) ♪ ♪ ♪♪

Suitner's takes on these works are on the fast side, but his orchestra is up to the task, and the engineering lets every little nuance come through; despite the speed involved in his performances, subtle shadings of orchestral texture are maintained. Just as on the Paray recording above, the "big three" are represented, as is *Pique Dame,* but Suitner also conducts the rarely heard *Flotte Bursche* (Gay Blades) and the slightly more popular

Banditenstreiche (Jolly Robbers).

[Alfred Walter, cond.; Slovak State Philharmonic Orchestra] (Naxos 8.553935) ♪ ♪ ♪ ♪

Where Suitner dashes, Walter and Paray prance. The tempos are more relaxed here, but the playing still manages to remain taut, a tribute to how well Walter has this ensemble under control. Once again, all the big overtures are represented, but little-known gems such as *Fatinitza, Die Kartenschlägerin* (Queen of Spades), and *Irrfahrt um's Glück* (Fortune's Labyrinth) make this collection stand out just a bit more.

influences: Franz Lehár, Jacques Offenbach

Garaud MacTaggart

Karol Szymanowski

Born Karol Maciej Szymanowski, October 6, 1882, in Tymoszówka, Ukraine. Died March 29, 1937, in Lausanne, Switzerland.

period: Twentieth century

Poland has provided its fair share of world-class composers, from Frédéric Chopin to such modern masters as Witold Lutoslawski, Krzysztof Penderecki, and Henryk Górecki. In this line of succession Karol Szymanowski was an important transitional figure. He was a fine pianist whose solo piano pieces found advocates in Artur Rubinstein and Ignace Paderewski, while his later opera, chamber music, choral and orchestral works feature lush textures awash in chromatic and harmonic subtleties.

The son of wealthy landowners in what is now the Ukraine, Karol Szymanowski was also lucky to be born into a household where music was a major part of family life. His parents played piano and Szymanowski received his first lessons at home. He prospered in this supportive environment, showing enough talent so that, at the age of 10, young Karol was turned over to the noted pedagogue Gustav Neuhaus for further instruction. This instruction, grounded in the works of Chopin, Richard Wagner, and Ludwig van Beethoven, was to influence Szymanowski's earliest compositions. In 1901 he became a student at the Warsaw Conservatory, where he formed an important, lifelong friendship with pianist Artur Rubinstein. By the time Szymanowski was 20 years old, he (along with Rubinstein) was part of a loose knit batch of young musicians known as "Young

Poland in Music." Another member of this organization was the violinist Pawel Kochánski, for whom Szymanowski was to write many of his violin works.

After his father died in 1906 Szymanowski traveled around Europe and North Africa, performing in concerts, soaking up the atmosphere and developing an interest in a lusher, more ecstatic music, as envisioned by Claude Debussy, Alexander Scriabin, and Richard Strauss. He returned to the family homestead in 1914 on the eve of World War I and remained there composing steadily for the next three years. It was during this period that Szymanowski became acquainted with the texts of the Sufi mystic poet Jalal al-Din Rumi—founder of the order of whirling dervishes—whose words seemed a perfect fit for the exotic harmonies with which the composer was beginning to work. These years saw the creation of his First Violin Concerto, the Third Symphony, the *Metopes,* op. 29, and the *Masques* op. 34 for piano, *Mythes* for violin and piano, op. 30, and his First String Quartet. He also began work on the opera *King Roger,* one of his most important works, which was not completed until 1924.

With the end of the war came the Russian Revolution and the destruction of the Szymanowski family estate. Although he was away from home at the time, the event was a source of heartsickness and financial stress for the composer. He started traveling again, even visiting the USA, but Poland, an independent state after the war, was now the country of Szymanowski's allegiance. He spent much of his time at Zakopane, a resort in the Tatra Mountains where, like Leoš Janáček in Czechoslovakia and Béla Bartók in Hungary, he became enamored of his country's folk music. It was during this period that an increasingly nationalistic flavor began creeping into his music and blending with the mystic overtones of his earlier works. These elements helped shape his *Stabat Mater* in 1926 and, in 1932, his Second Violin Concerto and the ballet *Harnasie.*

Szymanowski had accepted the directorship of the Warsaw Conservatory in 1926 but left the position two years later with his health deteriorating. Despite ever worsening tuberculosis, he continued touring (and performing) through 1936. He died the next year in a sanatorium in Lausanne, Switzerland.

Orchestral
Violin Concerto no. 1, op. 35
what to buy: [Lydia Mordkovitch, violin; Vassili

Sinaisky, cond.; BBC Philharmonic Orchestra] (Chandos 9496) ♪ ♪ ♪ ♪

Szymanowski's two violin concertos deserve a wider audience, and this well-engineered set has in Mordkovitch the most convincing soloist in the mystical First Concerto since Wanda Wilkomirska's version (see below). Sinaisky's accompaniment is adequate, although the work would have benefited from more vigorous conducting. Also included in this recital is a fine reading of Szymanowski's Second Violin Concerto and the somewhat slighter *Concert Overture* in E major, op. 12.

worth searching for: [Wanda Wilkomirska, violin; Witold Rowicki, cond.; Warsaw National Philharmonic Symphony Orchestra] (Muza-Polskie Nagrania 64) ♪ ♪ ♪ ♪₄

This is a difficult set to find but Wilkomirska's performances of both concertos are fluid, daring, and, at times, almost wild, lending them a visceral quality not found in some more commonly available recordings. Also included are her versions of Szymanowski's early Sonata in D minor for Violin and Piano, op. 9 and an arrangement of *Roxana's Song* from the opera *King Roger*.

Symphony no. 3, op. 27—*Song of the Night*
what to buy: [Wieslaw Ochman, tenor; Karol Stryja, cond.; Polish State Philharmonic Orchestra; Polish State Philharmonic Chorus] (Naxos 8.553684) ♪ ♪ ♪ ♪₄

Inspired by the composer's reading of texts by the Sufi poet Jalal al-Din Rumi, this symphony is imbued with ecstasy on various levels. The text is given to a tenor soloist with a choir and Szymanowski's impressionist writing for strings. There are echoes of Scriabin, Debussy, and Stravinsky in the work, but also hints of Arab mysticism. Stryja, almost by default, is the premier Polish conductor of Szymanowski and this is one of his best recordings.

Chamber
Mythes for violin and piano, op. 30
what to buy: [Lydia Mordkovitch, violin; Marina Gusak-Grin, piano] (Chandos 8747) ♪ ♪ ♪ ♪

Szymanowski wrote some of the twentieth century's most ecstatic tunes and these three pieces for violin and piano are among his most intense. Mordkovitch is a good player and her version of the composer's Sonata in D minor for Violin and Piano, op. 9 (also on the album) is

the best one currently available.

worth searching for: Kaja Danczowska, violin; Krystian Zimerman, piano] (Deutsche Grammophon 431469) ♪ ♪ ♪ ♪ ♪

Danczowka's playing is a wonderful blend of clarity and passion and Zimerman is a superb accompanist. The coupling of Franck's Sonata for Violin and Piano in A major is just as stunningly performed.

Vocal
King Roger
what to buy: [Barbara Zagórzanka, soprano; Anna Malewicz-Madey, contralto; Wieslaw Ochman, tenor; Andrzej Hiolski, baritone; Henryk Grychnik, tenor; Leonard Andrzej Mróz, bass; Karol Stryja, cond.; Polish State Philharmonic Orchestra; Polish State Philharmonic Orchestra Chorus; Cracow Philharmonic Orchestra Boys Chorus] (Naxos 8.660062/63) ♪ ♪ ♪ ♪

Szymanowski's gorgeous music, sense of Dionysian drama, and brilliant orchestration make this work a must-have for opera lovers. Stryja is a more than competent conductor, the soloists are uniformly fine (especially Hiolski in the title role), and the choral singing is solid throughout.

Stabat Mater for soprano, contralto, baritone, orchestra and chorus, op. 53
what to buy: [Christine Goerke, soprano; Marietta Simpson, mezzo-soprano; Victor Ledbetter, baritone; Robert Shaw, cond.; Atlanta Symphony Orchestra; Atlanta Symphony Chorus] (Telarc 80362) ♪ ♪ ♪ ♪

The only area where Shaw's performance has a definite edge over the Stryja recording (cited below) is in the engineering. Telarc's audio magicians allow the listener to bathe in the gorgeous choral singing—despite occasional lapses in diction, this is a marvelous experience. Francis Poulenc's Stabat Mater makes a more than worthy disc-mate.

what to buy next: [Jadwiga Gadulanka, soprano; Krystyna Szostek-Radkowa, contralto; Andrzej Hiolski, baritone; Karol Stryja, cond.; Polish State Philharmonic Orchestra and Chorus] (Naxos 8.553687) ♪ ♪ ♪ ♪₄

This is Szymanowski's supreme choral work and Stryja's forces have the full measure of it. The rest of the album contains four other choral pieces by the composer including a beautiful performance of the *Veni Creator,* op. 57. Excellent value in a budget recording.

influences: Alexander Scriabin, Richard Strauss, Claude Debussy

Ellen Kokko

Toru Takemitsu

Born October 8, 1930, in Tokyo, Japan. Died February 20, 1996, in Tokyo, Japan.

period: Twentieth century

Toru Takemitsu, arguably Japan's greatest composer, had a prolific career, though only a small segment of it was widely heard in the West until recently. It's no surprise that his titles often refer to dreams and the sea, as Takemitsu could easily be dubbed the last Impressionist. However, he actually had a number of distinct but related styles, not all of which are as limpid and hazy as the works that have recently been given prominence.

Takemitsu's musical education and development were unusual. Although he did study for a while with Yasuji Kiyose (a student of Alexander Tcherepnin, who spent a significant amount of time living in Asia), Takemitsu was largely self-taught. Furthermore, he first became familiar with Western classical music through twentieth century composers, initially Claude Debussy and Olivier Messiaen and then the Viennese serialists Arnold Schoenberg, Anton Webern, and Alban Berg. His exposure to the Western music of previous centuries came much later. His musical thought was also permeated by the striking spareness of traditional Japanese music, classical itself rather than a folk form. His combination of those influences into his own distinctive styles was such a unique amalgam of influences that he cannot be called the product of any single school of thought, either Western or post-war Japanese.

In 1950 Takemitsu co-founded, with composer Jogi Yuasa and conductor Kazuyoshi Akiyama, the *Jikken Kobo (Experimental Workshop),* a group that promoted mixed-media collaborations unifying traditional Japanese techniques with modern approaches. At times (in the 1960s) his music was constructed in ways that went beyond traditional notation, with sonic effects sim-

ilar to those being explored halfway around the world by Polish composers, most notably Krzysztof Penderecki, though with somewhat less radical results. He also wrote some quite effective electronic music, though that has barely circulated outside of Japan. Before, during, and after this period Takemitsu also produced music that is both accessible and communicative. His highly individual organization of thematic materials, treatment of sounds as ends in themselves, and kaleidoscopic orchestrations could make even relatively mainstream harmonic material sound fresh and daring.

A turning point in Takemitsu's career came when his 1957 composition *Requiem for Strings*—one of his more mainstream creations, though not without its original points—was heard by Igor Stravinsky, whose praise of the work brought Takemitsu to international attention. This was amplified greatly in 1967 when the New York Philharmonic Orchestra commissioned a work for its 125th anniversary. The result, *November Steps,* immediately raised Takemitsu's international profile considerably thanks to its then-unique juxtaposition of traditional Japanese instruments (biwa and shakuhachi) with the Western orchestra. From that point on, Takemitsu was a respected, if never really mainstream, figure in modern music, beloved both for his compositions and for his gentle personality. He became just as prolific in his writing as his composing, with twenty books to his credit; he also lectured around the world and was showered with honors (membership in France's Académie des Beaux-Arts, the UNESCO/IMC Music Prize in 1991, the Grawemeyer Award in 1994, and much more), composer-in-residence posts (Tanglewood, Berliner Festwochen, and other international festivals), and the like.

In later years his music became increasingly quiet, dream-like, and attractive to an audience (and record labels) looking for high-class mood music. The promulgation of these works over the sometimes-tougher earlier ones has left newcomers to his music with a somewhat skewed conception of his style. Nonetheless, this most Impressionistic element was a genuinely important part of his repertoire—but it does have to be understood within the context of his whole career.

Orchestral
November Steps
what to buy: [Hiroshi Wakasugi, cond.; Tokyo Metropolitan Symphony Orchestra] (Denon 79441) ♪ ♪ ♪ ♪ ♪

Denon's invaluable four-CD series of Takemitsu's orchestral works (put together in the 1990s) is the best and easiest source for Takemitsu's most famous piece. Proving that East can meet West, Takemitsu balances the delicate sounds of biwa (Japanese four-string lute), shakuhachi (vertical bamboo flute), and a Western orchestra—not in the manner of a concerto, but by having these very different forces alternate. Furthermore, the biwa and shakuhachi have a considerable improvisatory element, whereas the orchestra's parts are entirely written out. The effect is startling at times and quite evocative. The biwa and shakuhachi players on the premiere recording (see below) returned over two decades later for the Denon recording, in crystalline digital sound. Also included is the *Requiem* for strings, *Far Calls, Coming, Far!* for violin and orchestra, and the contemplative *Visions,* inspired by two late paintings of Odilon Redon.

worth searching for: [Seiji Ozawa, cond.; Toronto Symphony Orchestra] (RCA Victor Red Seal 7051) ♪ ♪ ♪ ♪♪

It's not impossible (even now) to track down this premiere recording of *November Steps,* the fourth side on a two-LP set issued in 1968. Biwa player Kinshi Tsuruta and shakuhachi player Katsuya Yokoyama had worked with Takemitsu before and there is a certain *frisson* to this first performance, a focused concentration, that makes it worthy of reissue on CD.

Autumn
what to buy: [Ryusuke Numajiri, cond.; Tokyo Metropolitan Symphony Orchestra] (Denon 18032) ♪ ♪ ♪ ♪

Autumn, dating from 1973, could easily be seen as a continuation of the interests displayed in *November Steps,* since they are both for biwa, shakuhachi, and orchestra and both include improvisational sections for the Japanese instruments. However, the emphasis (heard here) on the intervals of the minor second and the tritone are identified with Schoenberg's move from tonality, and there is more emphasis on the orchestra, with oboe and trombone solos. Denon's sub-indexing is most useful for pointing out to listeners the key points in this sixteen-minute work. Also included are the string orchestra arrangement of *A Way a Lone, I Hear the Water Dreaming* for flute and orchestra, and *Twill by Twilight.*

various orchestral works
what to buy: [*Quotation of Dream*; Paul Crossley, piano; Peter Serkin, piano; Oliver Knussen, cond.; London Sinfonietta, orch.] (Deutsche Grammophon 453495) ♪ ♪ ♪ ♪♪

Quotation of Dream (1991), for two pianos and orchestra, is subtitled *Say sea, take me!* Quoting Debussy's *La Mer,* though not ostentatiously, it takes in not only Takemitsu's frequent Impressionist influence but also a certain degree of Hollywood soundtrack melodrama as bold gestures emerge from an orchestral haze. This is the premiere recording, and, at sixteen minutes, the longest on this program. The other significant work here is *Dream/Window* (1985), the orchestral pinnacle of Takemitsu's late period, and one of the very finest works of the last two decades. Takemitsu's fragmentary structures cohere gradually in an intuitively logical manner suggesting great profundity. This disc also includes *How Slow the Wind* (1991) for chamber orchestra (built on a seven-note motif that slowly evolves through varieties of texture and thickness); the stately yet sensuous *Twill by Twilight* (1988), which was dedicated to the memory of Morton Feldman; *Archipelago S.* for twenty-one players (1993), which uses as an organizing principle the image of small islands being separate yet contributing to an overall shape; and antiphonal fanfares for two brass groups: *Day Signal* and *Night Signal* from 1987, collectively known as *Signals from Heaven I & II. Night Signal* is dedicated to Oliver Knussen, the sympathetic conductor of this program.

what to buy next: [Hiroshi Wakasugi, cond.; Tokyo Metropolitan Symphony Orchestra] (Denon 78944) ♪ ♪ ♪ ♪

These world premiere recordings display the thornier and more austere side of Takemitsu, with the influence of Messiaen partly giving way to more Stockhausen-esque concerns, though serialism directly and obliquely shapes these pieces. The explorations of sonic color and musical gestures seem to take place on a microscopic level, rewarding only concentrated listening, with the tiniest details granted great weight. Alas, even with great speaker separation, some of the effect of the double orchestras and soloists in the four-movement *Gémeaux (Twins)*—for oboe (Masashi Honma), trombone (Christian Lindberg), two orchestras, and two conductors (adding Ryusuke Numajiri)—seems lost on CD. The twelve-tone *Spirit Garden,* wistfully nostalgic, doesn't have this problem. This disc also includes *Dream/Window.*

[*Toru Takemitsu: Orchestral Works, vol. 4*; Yuzo Toyama, cond.; Tokyo Metropolitan Symphony Orchestra] (Denon 18073) ♪ ♪ ♪ ♪

This set includes some of Takemitsu's most radical, challenging music and most imaginatively colorful orchestrations, often achieving spatial effects through the division of the orchestra into subgroups spread around the stage (inevitably diluted in a recording, though Denon preserves sufficient sense of those separations). The pointillistically built *The Dorian Horizon* (1966) emphasizes stark timbral, textural, and dynamic contrasts. *Coral Island* (1962), for soprano (in only two of its five sections) and orchestra, uses sparse textures and soprano melodies with wide intervallic leaps. Based on the roughly triangular image of a flock of birds, *A flock descends into the pentagonal garden* (1977) is denser and more dissonant, though not without lyrical melodies. Also included is *Archipelago S.* Throughout, the playing is distinguished by great precision of rhythm and articulation, so needed in music that becomes quite ineffective without these characteristics.

Woman in the Dunes (film score)
worth searching for: [*Film Music by Toru Takemitsu, vol. 4*] (Japanese Victor 5127) ♪ ♪ ♪ ♪ ♪

Takemitsu scored ninety-three soundtracks, a high proportion of his work yet largely unheard by Western audiences (and certainly the most soundtracks written by a composer of his repute). Perhaps the best-known of these is the one he wrote for Hiroshi Teshigawara's classic 1964 film *Woman in the Dunes*. The movie's hallucinatory, shadowed style works in synergy with Takemitsu's eerie, modernistic effects and unsettling dissonances, utterly Japanese in character, sounds for the sake of themselves. This import CD also includes music from other Teshigawara films: *The Face of Another, Summer Soldiers, The Pitfall, White Morning,* the jazzy *José Torres,* and *The Man without a Map.* Takemitsu aficionados will want to track down the six volumes in this film-score series from 1990–91, catalog numbers 5124 through 5129, with separate volumes dedicated to Takemitsu's widely varying scores for movies of Masahiro Shinoda and Masaki Kobayashi as well as mixed volumes including scores for films directed by Akira Kurosawa, Noboru Nakamura, and others.

Chamber
various piano works
what to buy: [*Toru Takemitsu: Complete Notated Piano*

Works; Peter Serkin, piano] (RCA Victor Red Seal 68595) ♪ ♪ ♪ ♪₄

Takemitsu's solo piano music, though occupying just one CD, is an extremely important segment of his productivity, since some of the composers who most influenced him—most significantly Debussy, Messiaen, Alexander Scriabin, and John Cage—were major writers for the piano. Takemitsu's influences are also most clear in his piano music, since his highly individual orchestrations can divert attention from similarities. Serkin's delicate touch and affinity for Impressionist music makes him well-suited to Takemitsu's style; in the 1960s, the pianist began an association with the composer that lasted until Takemitsu's death, with seven compositions written specifically for Serkin. The tracks on this disc were done over a considerable period of time ranging from 1978 to 1996, with *Uninterrupted Rest, Piano Distance, For Away,* and *Les Yeux clos* recorded under the composer's supervision. However, Serkin omits (as the album title indicates) the two graphic works (which Woodward, below, includes). Nonetheless, were one to recommend just one album ideally suited to introduce neophytes to the special sound-world of Takemitsu, this could be it.

[Roger Woodward, piano] (Etcetera 1103) ♪ ♪ ♪ ♪₆

This collection by the excellent Australian pianist Roger Woodward, recognized as a talented proponent of contemporary music (though he has also established himself as an interpreter of mainstream repertoire such as Chopin), is especially noteworthy for including the 1962 graphic compositions *Corona* and *Crossing*. These improvisational works are left off of other Takemitsu piano collections, for they allow the performer such vast leeway as to entirely blur the meaning of composition. However, note that because this 1990 set was recorded before Takemitsu's career concluded, it's missing the 1992 work *Rain Tree Sketch II* (found on the Peter Serkin disc, above). Woodward's touch is a tad more percussive than Serkin's, which is a valid approach and one the composer presumably found amenable, since he dedicated two solo piano works to Woodward.

various chamber works
what to buy: [*Toru Takemitsu: Chamber Music*; Ensemble Kaï] (BIS 920) ♪ ♪ ♪ ♪

This collection of Takemitsu's mostly little-known chamber music offers a distinctly different face than his "serious" orchestral works, his film scores, or his solo piano music. Less colorful in its interplay of timbres, it seems more abstract. The elegiac and tuneful *Between Tides* (1993), for violin, cello, and piano, recalls Messiaen, especially the chiming piano. *Landscape I* (1961), for string quartet, must be performed without vibrato, which emphasizes its spare character à la early Feldman and early Cage. *Distance de fée* (1951), for violin and piano, has a surprisingly Romantic violin part. The four-movement *Rocking Mirror Daybreak* (1983), for violin duo, is more varied, angular, and modern. *Hika* (1966), for violin and piano, isn't serial, but its atonality, gestures, and cellular development recall Webern. *A Way a Lone* (1980), for string quartet, is built from a small motivic cell (E-flat, E natural, A) and also recalls Webern, but with long slides. The various ensemble members excel in transparent scores that hide no flaws.

influences: Claude Debussy, Olivier Messiaen, Alexander Scriabin, Arnold Schoenberg, Anton Webern,

Morton Feldman, John Cage

Steve Holtje

Thomas Tallis
Born c. 1505, in England. Died c. November 23,1585, in Greenwich, England.

period: Renaissance

While he did write some works for the keyboard, Tallis's a cappella choral works are more plentiful and rewarding. One of them, a setting of the hymn tune *God, grant we grace,* was at the core of Ralph Vaughan Williams's famous composition *Fantasia on a Theme by Thomas Tallis* for Orchestra.

Not much is known of Thomas Tallis's early life, but he did manage to acquire a reputation as a fine singer and organist during stints at the Benedictine Priory at Dover, St. Mary-at-Hill, Billingsgate, and Waltham Abbey. When Henry VIII ordered the monasteries shuttered in 1540, Tallis became organist at Canterbury Cathedral, finally joining the Chapel Royal itself around 1543. He served there for over forty years, bridging the religious fluctuations of England's monarchy during the tumultuous period between King Henry VIII and Queen Elizabeth I.

Most of Tallis's compositions that have come down through history seem to stem from the period after his installation in the Chapel Royal. These comprise a whole range of liturgical settings for both Anglican and Catholic services including anthems, motets, psalms, masses, and responses. Pride of place should go to the *Lamentations of Jeremiah*—a setting of two separate texts from the Biblical book of *Jeremiah* that was written for pre-Easter holy week services—and the astonishing musical architecture of the beautiful, complex forty-part motet *Spem in alium*. In 1560, at the front end of Queen Elizabeth's reign, some of Tallis's pieces were included in the first printed collection of part-music for the Anglican service. He, along with his pupil William Byrd, received a monopoly from the queen in 1575 which gave them the sole right to print music books and music paper for the next twenty-one years. They got this favor from the crown despite the duo's papist sympathies at a time when English Catholics were being persecuted by the monarchy for their religious beliefs. The two composers then compiled a collection of thirty-four motets (seventeen apiece) called *Cantiones Sacrae* which was dedicated to the queen. Evidently the monopoly wasn't exactly a license to print money, contributing little to the income of either man, although Tallis (according to his will) ended up owning his own house and accumulating a fair number of possessions by the time he died in 1585.

Vocal
various choral works
what to buy: [Andrew Davis, organ; John Langdon, organ; Peter White, organ; Stephen Cleobury, cond.; George Guest, cond.; David Willcocks, cond.; Cambridge University Musical Society, choir.; Cambridge King's College Choir; Cambridge St. John's College Choir] (Decca 455029) ♪ ♪ ♪ ♪ ♪⅜

When the Willcocks-conducted versions of the *Lamentations of Jeremiah* and *Spem in alium* were first released, they garnered much critical acclaim. Years later those performances are still among the first rank of choices available to the consumer, via this handsome two-disc reissue. The bonuses are many, including solo keyboard works played by Davis and White and a stunning *Te Deum* conducted by Guest. For those potential listeners wishing to explore the full range of Tallis's art in one convenient package, this is the place to start.

The Lamentations of Jeremiah
what to buy: [Paul Hillier, cond.; the Theatre of Voices, choir] (Harmonia Mundi 907154) ♪ ♪ ♪ ♪

This well-performed, well-recorded alternative to the Kings College performance (cited above) also features nine other motets and a sampling of the composer's instrumental music played by The King's Noyse under the direction of violinist David Douglass.

worth searching for: [Peter Phillips, cond.; the Tallis Scholars, choir] (Gimell 454925) ♪ ♪ ♪ ♪⅜

There are many fine recordings of this work available, but the Tallis Scholars version was probably the best all-around choice when it was still in print. The antiphon *Salve intemerata* and a well-sung sampling of motets were nice, well-performed bonuses on this CD.

Spem in alium
what to buy: [Peter Phillips, cond.; the Tallis Scholars, choir] (Gimell 006) ♪ ♪ ♪ ♪⅜

This piece deserves a taut, suspenseful performance

and that is exactly what Phillips and his forces give. The other motets on the album are beautiful but overpowered by this work and its magnificence.

what to buy next: [David Hill, cond.; Winchester Cathedral Choir; Vocal Arts Choir] (Harmonia Mundi 20400) ♪ ♪ ♪ ♪

Demanding eight separate choirs of five parts each, this fluent blend of chordal and polyphonic writing stands as one of the Elizabethan era's aural glories. Hill and his choirs complement their performance of the mighty motet with yet another well-sung rendition of Tallis's *Lamentations of Jeremiah* in addition to a fine selection of the composer's choral works.

[*Black Angels*; Kronos Quartet, ensemble] (Elektra/Nonesuch 79242) ♪ ♪ ♪⅜

Set amidst twentieth century compositions by Dmitri Shostakovich, George Crumb, and Charles Ives is a multi-tracked string quartet attempting to tackle Tallis's complexities. Surprisingly effective, the Kronos Quartet's rendering of this masterpiece is an interesting experiment even if it doesn't supplant the choral version.

influences: William Byrd, Christopher Tye, John Sheppard, Robert White

Garaud MacTaggart

Tan Dun
Born August 18, 1957, in Simao, Hunan province, China.

period: Twentieth century

A composer globally known not only for his stage works (*Nine Songs*, *Marco Polo*, and *Peony Pavilion*) but also for his inherently dramatic chamber and orchestral works (such as the *Orchestral Theatre* series), Tan Dun has created unique sound worlds through his explorations of East and West. The premiere of his *Symphony 1997*, commissioned for the ceremony for the transfer of Hong Kong to China, was televised globally.

Tan Dun grew up in the 1960s; during the period of the Cultural Revolution in China, when schools were closed and youths were sent to rural areas, he spent several years in a commune planting rice. However, this experience had a positive influence: the rich cultural heritage of the countryside, especially the rituals and ceremonies in which he participated, became one of the major sources for the composer's philosophy. He learned to play the *erhu,* or Chinese violin, and joined a local Peking opera troupe as fiddler and arranger. Tan was not exposed to any Western classical music until he was nineteen, when he was accepted to study at the Central Conservatory of Music in Beijing. He wrote his first symphony (*Li Sao*) while a student there. Another student composition, his String Quartet *Feng Ya Song,* was awarded the Weber Prize in Dresden in 1983, making Tan the first Chinese composer to receive an international accolade since 1949. However, 1983 was also the year that the Chinese government attacked "spiritual pollution," as the country suddenly recoiled from opening its doors to the world. Tan's music was withdrawn from performance and broadcasts of his music were temporarily suspended.

A fellowship to study at Columbia University in New York City brought Tan to the United States in 1986. He quickly immersed himself in the "downtown" avant-garde music scene, collaborating in performance art as well as experimental music. Tan's output during the latter half of the 1980s was wide-ranging, including some works written for the "uptown" academic world and others for the downtown audience. *Eight Colors for String Quartet* (1986–1988) was inspired by Peking opera: many of the instrumental gestures were percussive (imitating Chinese instruments), and pitch materials were dominated by harmonics and sliding tones. Cast as eight vignettes (with descriptive titles such as "Black Dance," "Drum and Gong," and "Red Sona"), this work is the result of Tan's synthesis of East and West. *Ghost Opera* (1994), a later piece that also employs a string quartet, is a five-movement work in which a Bach quotation (the opening of the Prelude and Fugue in C-sharp Minor from Book 1 of the *Well-Tempered Clavier*) was juxtaposed with a famous Chinese folk tune (*Xiao Baicai*). A *pipa* soloist joins the string quartet, and the musicians not only play their own instruments but also vocalize and extract sounds from a water bowl, Chinese one-stringed lutes, cymbals, gongs, stones, and paper.

Tan's first stage work for New York audiences, *Nine Songs (Ritual Opera)* (1989), employs ceramic instruments that are struck, blown and bowed. This "opera" is not constructed as a narrative but as a musical distillation of the essence of poet Qu Yuan (340-277 B.C.). The singers are required to whisper, shout, murmur, and

vocalize in unusual ways, extending the auditory experience for performer and audience alike. Tan's next large-scale stage work, *Marco Polo* (1995), with a libretto by Paul Griffiths, is subtitled "an opera within an opera." It is a spiritual journey that explores the musical cultures of Europe and Asia, with inhabitants that represent memory, beings, nature, and shadows. *Peony Pavilion,* a collaboration with director Peter Sellars, reinterprets the classic Chinese *kun* opera, mixing worldwide compositional styles of the past millennium. Gregorian chants, organum, and melismatic vocal lines (occasionally resembling Chinese folksong) are juxtaposed with MIDI horns, elaborate percussion, and electronic samples and ornamented by traditional Chinese instruments (*pipa, zun,* and *dizi*). The sound of water is written into the score, as are the special effects of the water gong.

Tan's acute sense of drama is not restricted to works involving singers and stagecraft. His Violin Concerto (1987, revised 1994), entitled *Out of Peking Opera,* is a search for balance between East and West. Using fragments of Peking opera melodies and percussive gestures, Tan creates a work that is vibrant and truly multicultural. His command of orchestration is superb, particularly in string and percussive writing; a good example is his work in *Death and Fire: Dialogue with Paul Klee* (1992). A smaller-scale work, *Circle with Four Trios, Conductor, and Audience* (1992), is based on a haunting fragment of ancient Greek music. Tan's output has attracted the attention of twentieth-century masters such as John Cage and Toru Takemitsu.

Among Tan's major orchestral works since 1990 is the *Orchestral Theatre* series, in which the composer combined ancient ritual and multimedia effects, requiring orchestral musicians and audience members to sing and chant; of special note is the second in the series, *Re* (1993). *Red Forecast: Orchestral Theatre III* (1996) explored the extremes of the human spirit in the 1960s through video and audio arts. Tan also wrote and conducted *Symphony 1997: Heaven, Earth, Mankind,* the premiere of which (featuring cellist Yo-Yo Ma) was globally telecast from the ceremony of Hong Kong's reunification with China on July 1, 1997. The *Symphony 1997* employs solo cello, children's choir, symphony orchestra, and ancient Chinese bells (*bianzhong*) and directly quotes the children's song that Giacomo Puccini used in *Turandot.* Tan's commissions for major international orchestras and opera companies (including the Metropolitan Opera) continue into the new millennium. He made his debut as a Hollywood film composer in

Fallen (1998), a movie starring Denzel Washington, and won an Academy Award in 2001 for scoring the Ang Lee production *Crouching Tiger, Hidden Dragon.*

Orchestral
Symphony 1997: Heaven, Earth, Mankind
what to buy: [Yo-Yo Ma, cello; Tan Dun, cond.; Imperial Bells Ensemble of China; Hong Kong Philharmonic Orchestra; Yip's Children's Choir] (Sony 63368) ♪♪♪♪

A ceremonial piece for a unique political occasion, this symphony is an amalgam of Tan's many approaches to composition. A grand-scale work, it includes field recordings the composer made on Hong Kong's Temple Street, where Cantonese opera singers performed in the open air. In addition to fragments of the children's chorus emblematic of Puccini's exotic *Turandot,* Tan's paraphrases of Beethoven and contemporary popular music are also thought-provoking.

Out of Peking Opera for Violin and Orchestra
what to buy: [Cho-Liang Lin, violin; Muhai Tang, cond.; Helsinki Philharmonic Orchestra] (Ondine 864) ♪♪♪♪

This premiere recording of Tan's revised violin concerto is excellent. Dramatic gestures, written as musical figures, are very suggestive of opera in this piece. The two other orchestral works heard on this all-Tan album are *Death and Fire: Dialogue with Paul Klee* and *Orchestral Theatre II: Re.*

Chamber
Ghost Opera for Pipa and String Quartet with Water, Stones, Paper and Metal
what to buy: [Wu Man, pipa, Kronos Quartet, ensemble] (Nonesuch 79445) ♪♪♪♪♪

As recorded by the group for whom the piece was written, *Ghost Opera* is mesmerizing masterpiece. The interplay of Bach's Prelude and Fugue in C-sharp Minor and the Chinese folk tune *Xiao Baicai* in the center of the five-movement work is astoundingly beautiful. Shakespeare is also quoted here, when members of the quintet whisper, shout, and sing texts such as, "We are such stuff as dreams are made on and our little life is rounded with a sleep."

various chamber works
what to buy: [*Snow in June*; Nieuw Ensemble; Arditti

String Quartet, ensemble; Anssi Karttunen, cello; Talujon Percussion Quartet, ensemble; Susan Botti, soprano; Keri-Lynn Wilson, piccolo; Gillian Benet, harp; Tan Dun, bass drum] (CRI 655) ♪♪♪♪

This is a worthy introduction to Tan's chamber music, including *Circle with Four Trios, Conductor, and Audience* performed by the Nieuw Ensemble (conducted by Ed Spanjaard) and *Eight Colors for String Quartet* performed by the Arditti String Quartet. *Silk Road,* sung superbly by soprano Susan Botti, shows Tan in a more reflective mode. Tan's personal reaction to the events of

Tiananmen Square in 1989 resulted in *Elegy: Snow in June* for Cello and Percussion, played here by Anssi Karttunen and the Talujon Percussion Quartet.

Vocal
Peony Pavilion: Bitter Love
what to buy: [Ying Huang, soprano; Tan Dun, cond.; NChiCa Orchestra; New York Virtuoso Singers, choir] (Sony 61658) ♪ ♪ ♪ ♪

Tan's latest stage works embrace more contemporary popular styles. The Gregorian chant fragments are well sung, although the MIDI/rhythm-machine seems too persistent throughout most of this album. Ying Huang's voice is mellifluous (the text is in English). A departure from Tan's earlier work, this piece shows an even wider musical vista that is hauntingly mesmerizing, perfectly befitting the ghost story in *Peony Pavilion.*

Marco Polo
what to buy: [Shi-Zheng Chen, Susan Botti, Nina Warren, sopranos; Alexandra Montano, mezzo-soprano; Thomas Young, tenor; Stephen Bryant, baritone; Dong-Jian Gong, bass; Tan Dun, cond.; Netherlands Radio Chamber Orchestra; Cappella Amsterdam, choir] (Sony Classical 62912) ♪ ♪ ♪ ♪

Paul Griffiths wrote the libretto for *Marco Polo,* a work that was named Opera of the Year in 1996 by Germany's *Opera* magazine and awarded the Grawemeyer Award for Music Composition in 1998. This live two-CD premiere recording is an adventurous journey into many musical styles of the world throughout the ages.

Nine Songs
worth searching for: [Tan Dun, cond.] (CRI 603) ♪ ♪ ♪ ♪

Tan's first full-length stage work, the "ritual opera" *Nine Songs,* involves musical sounds created by ceramic instruments—symbolic of the earth. Released in 1990 but no longer available through CRI, this disc is a valuable musical document.

influences: Toru Takemitsu, Chen Yi, Zhou Long

Joanna Lee

Tan Dun

Sergei Taneyev
Born Sergei Ivanovich Taneyev on November 25, 1856, in Vladimir-na-Klyaz'me, Russia. Died June 19, 1915, in Dyud'kovo, Russia.

period: Romantic

While Sergei Taneyev was a technically proficient composer of well-crafted scores, his impact on Russian music came mostly through his theoretical research and pedagogy. A conservative internationalist in an age of radical nationalism, he sought inspiration in the baroque structures of George Frederic Handel and the works of Renaissance contrapuntalists such as Orlando de Lassus rather than the folk music of his homeland. As a teacher, Taneyev had a decisive effect on the early careers of such disparate musical personalities as Alexander Scriabin, Sergei Rachmaninoff, and Nicolai Medtner—composers whose works are more familiar to modern audiences than are Taneyev's.

Taneyev's displayed early musical aptitude, so much so that he was admitted to the Moscow Conservatory just shy of his tenth birthday. There he studied piano with Nicholas Rubinstein and composition with Piotr Illyich Tchaikovsky, the single most important creative figure in the young man's life. In fact, relations between the two would become so close that Taneyev debuted all of Tchaikovsky's works for piano and orchestra after the first concerto. He also seemed to be the only member of Tchaikovsky's immediate circle who could criticize his teacher's scores with relative impunity. He likened Tchaikovsky's fourth symphony to "a symphonic poem to which three movements have been appended to make up a symphony" and stated that the first movement seemed "disproportionately long when compared with the others."

After graduating with honors in 1875, Taneyev performed in various Russian cities and began traveling around Europe, exposing himself to a variety of cosmopolitan experiences. Three years later he was called back to Moscow, where he reluctantly assumed Tchaikovsky's old position at the conservatory. Taneyev's initial misgivings about teaching were based on his perception that he had not really learned enough about the art of composing to impart that kind of knowledge to others. With that in mind he began an intensive study of counterpoint that delved deeply into the music of Orlando de Lassus, Josquin Des Prez, and other Flemish masters of the Renaissance. In 1885 he was made director of the conservatory despite his self-perceived lack of potential. The results were quietly triumphant, since he totally revamped the teaching system, exercising the kind of fiscal responsibility that had been missing for years and creating more performance opportunities for the students. Although he was an effective administrator, Taneyev resigned his directorship in 1889 (while maintaining his spot on the faculty as an instructor in counterpoint) so that he could devote more time to composing. He finally left the school for good in 1905 and resumed his career as a concert pianist. Ten years later, Taneyev suffered a heart attack and died, shortly after attending the funeral of his former pupil Alexander Scriabin.

The majority of Taneyev's orchestral compositions were written at the tail end of the nineteenth century, while the bulk of his finest chamber pieces (including his two piano trios) appeared in the 1900s. The most impressive portion of his oeuvre, however, remains in the vocal realm, where he created an impressive number of a cappella scores and set a surprising number of texts in Esperanto—an artificial language intended for international use by its creator, Russian linguist Ludwik Lazar Zamenhof.

Orchestral
Symphony no. 4 in C Minor, op. 12
what to buy: [Neeme Järvi, cond.; Philharmonia Orchestra] (Chandos 8953) ♪ ♪ ♪ ♪

Taneyev's fourth symphony is a powerful piece filled with the kind of heart-on-sleeve emotions so prevalent in Russian symphonic fare from this era (1896-1898). That said, this is not a work that wallows in sentiment to the extent that form and content take a backseat to rampant romanticism. By including a fiery performance of the overture from Taneyev's most popular opera, *The Oresteia*, along with Järvi's excellent rendition of the symphony, Chandos has created a wonderful sampler of the composer's best orchestral works.

what to buy next: [Stephen Gunzenhauser, cond.; Polish State Philharmonic Orchestra, Katowice] (Marco Polo 8.223196) ♪ ♪ ♪ ♪

While not as well recorded as the Järvi version of this work, Gunzenhauser's forces certainly make an exciting and convincing case for Taneyev as a composer worth exploring. Their take on Taneyev's Symphony no. 2 in B-flat Minor from 1888 may even whet a listener's appetite for more of the composer's symphonic repertoire.

Chamber
Trio in D Major for Piano, Violin, and Cello, op. 22
what to buy: [Borodin Trio, ensemble] (Chandos 8592) ♪ ♪ ♪ ♪

A master of melody and counterpoint, Taneyev created a gem of a work with this effort. Timing out at just under forty-six minutes with a host of felicitous tunes and beautiful playing from the Borodin Trio, the piece just seems to zip along. The recording itself is remarkably clean without being antiseptic, a sonic virtue that seems to be traditional at Chandos.

Vocal
various choral works
what to buy: [*Choruses for Men's Voices*; Valery Rybin, cond.; Valery Rybin Male Choir] (Le Chant du Monde 288074) ♪ ♪ ♪ ♪

The prevalence of male choirs in Russian music is a historical fact and, truth be told, there is a great sense of power to be gained from the traditional Slavic blend of bass vocals and robust melodies. Rybin's forces are quite polished and the massed vocals are quite impressive although Yurlov's choir (see below) gave more definitive performances.

worth searching for: [*Taneyev: Music for Chorus*; Aleksander Yurlov, cond.; U.S.S.R. Russian Chorus] (Angel/Melodiya 40151) ♪ ♪ ♪ ♪

Drawn from the pre-Glasnost days of vinyl, this album contains only three of the songs heard on the Rybin disc and contributes seven other gems. The singing is impeccable throughout, revealing Taneyev as a master of scoring for the human voice and Yurlov as a fine choral conductor.

influences: Nicolai Rimsky-Korsakov, Piotr Tchaikovsky, Alexander Scriabin, Nicolai Medtner

Garaud MacTaggart

Francisco Tárrega
Born Francisco Tárrega y Eixea, November 21, 1852, in Villareal, Castellón, Spain. Died December 15, 1909, in Barcelona, Spain.

period: Romantic

Through his playing, composition, and transcriptions,

Francisco Tárrega made possible the resurrection of the guitar as an instrument of substance in modern composition and performance. In this fashion he was paving the way for Andrés Segovia, Sabicas, and countless other guitarists. Although his name may not be well-known by the general public, his most famous guitar work, the *Recuerdos de la Alhambra,* is beloved by classical guitarists and audiences everywhere for the subtle, flamenco-inspired tune at its core.

When Tárrega displayed musical talent as a child, he wanted to learn guitar, but his father insisted he study piano as well. That was a reasonable choice at the time because the guitar had fallen out of use as a serious instrument. Although Tárrega became an accomplished performer on both instruments, his future became apparent when he acquired a guitar which was constructed in such a manner that it was able to project sound much better than any other guitar available at the time. After studies in theory and harmony at the Madrid Conservatory, Tárrega began earning his living as a teacher and concert performer. He also became friends with Isaac Albéniz and Enrique Granados, two other composers interested in using the indigenous music of Spain in classical contexts, and transcribed many of their pieces for guitar.

Tárrega's most enduring legacies are as a teacher (his students included Emilo Pujol and Miguel Llobet) and an advocate for the guitar's place within classical music. His plethora of compositions and transcriptions, most of which are imbued with Spanish folk influences, have taught later generations of musicians to approach the guitar with the respect Tárrega sought for his beloved instrument.

Chamber
Recuerdos de la Alhambra
what to buy: [*Christopher Parkening Celebrates Segovia*; Christopher Parkening, guitar] (Angel/EMI 56730) ♪ ♪ ♪ ♪

The Moorish influences of southern Spain which Tárrega portrayed in the three pieces heard here are evocatively presented by Christopher Parkening. They are part of the program found on this interactive CD that also includes a twelve-minute video about Parkening and Segovia. Besides the *Recuerdos de la Alhambra,* the guitarist also performs Tárrega's *Capricho árabe* and *Estudio brillante.* Albeniz, Granados, Ponce, and Sor are among the other composers whose works fill out this disc.

what to buy next: [*19th Century Guitar Favorites*; Norbert Kraft, guitar] (Naxos 8.553007) ♪ ♪ ♪ ♪

Kraft is a very good guitarist, one worth noting. His excellent, budget-priced recital features works by Fernando Sor and Dionysio Aguado but listeners are also exposed to far more of Tárrega's music here than on any other disc on the market. In addition to the *Recuerdos de la Alhambra,* Kraft plays a baker's dozen of the composer's works including the Mazurkas, a nice selection of Preludes, and the *Grand Valse.*

influences: Issac Albeniz, Enrique Granados, Fernando Sor, Emilo Pujol, Miguel Llobet

Kerry Dexter and Garaud MacTaggart

Giuseppe Tartini
Born April 8, 1692, in Pirano, Italy. Died February 26, 1770, in Padua, Italy.

period: Baroque/Classical

Tartini flourished as a concert violinist, performing throughout Italy for nearly four decades. A master musician, prolific composer, and pioneering theorist, Tartini is best known for his violin sonata, the *Devil's Trill.* His expressive "galant" style bridged the baroque and classical periods.

A composer of more than one hundred violin sonatas, over 150 concertos, and copious amounts of chamber music and sacred vocal pieces, Giuseppe Tartini is best remembered for his contributions to the art of violin playing during the transition between the baroque and classical periods. After a childhood spent living in a monastery and preparing for the priesthood, Tartini began studying law at the University of Padua in 1709. A scandalous, secret marriage in 1710 forced him into exile in Assisi, where he studied music and eventually found employment with an opera orchestra. Soon he was made violin soloist and conductor at Saint Anthony's in Padua and reunited with his wife. Five years later, after a visit to Venice where he heard a violin recital by the renowned virtuoso Francesco Maria Veracini, he felt compelled to work even harder at the art of playing the violin. By 1720, he was an acknowledged expert and his reputation was strong enough that he was a highly sought-after musician. Tartini formed a music school in Padua in 1728 and counted future composer/virtuosos Pietro Nardini, Gaetano Pugnani, and

Johann Gottlieb Graun among his students. A mild stroke in 1768 ended his playing career and he suffered from an ulcerated foot in 1770 which lead to his death from gangrene.

Glimpses of the early classical style were emerging in the 1740s, with a new approach being taken to overall form, phrase structure, and the nature of the accompaniment. Also, the differentiation between chamber and orchestral music became more pronounced. An ardent and passionate theorist, Tartini wrote a number of treatises on harmony, performance practice, and music theory, absorbing these new advances in addition to making important contributions to the advancement of violin technique. His fingering innovations enabled the violinist to shift more efficiently among different positions on the fingerboard, and his advancements in bowing technique are still used today. Extreme virtuosity became a vehicle for greater emotional expression. In fact, Tartini frequently included poetic quotes in the score, evidence of the mid-eighteenth century preoccupation with the "expressive style" (*empfindsamer Stil*). His technical insights are clearly apparent in his compositions for violin; the legendary Sonata for Violin in G Minor, known as the *Devil's Trill,* exhibits complete mastery of the instrument. The nickname of this piece refers to a dream the composer had in which Satan played the "devilishly" challenging passage of trills found in the last movement of the work.

Orchestral
Concertos for Violin, Strings, and Continuo, op. 2
what to buy: [*Violin Concertos, vol. 2*; Giovanni Guglielmo, violin; L'Arte dell Arco, orch.] (Dynamic 190) ♪♪♪♪

According to the liner notes provided, this is the first recording of Tartini's second opus number. Utterly delightful, with moments of gravity (as in the dramatic unison opening of the second movement), this concerto looks fondly back at Antonio Vivaldi and bravely ahead to the Bach brothers. Performing on period instruments, Guglielmo and L'Arte dell Arco exhibit wonderful technique and imagination.

Chamber
Sonata in G Minor for Violin and Piano (*Devil's Trill*)
what to buy: [Andrew Manze, violin] (Harmonia Mundi 907213) ♪♪♪♪♪

Andrew Manze, one of today's finest early violin repertoire specialists, presents Tartini's signature work. Most commonly heard with piano or orchestral accompaniment, Manze presents the sonata in its original solo version. Thanks to his mastery of embellishment and improvisation, Manze's performance possesses a feeling of spontaneous invention. Refreshing and often revelatory, this recording makes an excellent case that great virtuosity and expression can walk hand-in-hand. As always, the Harmonia Mundi recorded sound is splendid.

worth searching for: [*The Romantic Baroque Violin;* Aaron Rosand, violin. Hugh Sung, piano] (Biddulph 006) ♪♪♪♪

Serving as perfect contrast to Manze's recording, Rosand and pianist Sung present the 1905 Fritz Kreisler edition of the *Devil's Trill.* Rosand's Tartini receives a full, lush approach in the late nineteenth/early twentieth century style of virtuoso violin playing associated with Leopold Auer, Efrem Zimbalist, Eugène Ysaÿe, and Jascha Heifetz. Works by Arcangelo Corelli, Niccolo Pasquali, Giovanni Pergolesi, Antonio Vivaldi, and others round out this recital.

influences: Arcangelo Corelli, Antonio Vivaldi, Carl Philipp Emanuel Bach

Christine L. Cody and Mona C. DeQuis

John Tavener
Born John Kenneth Tavener, January 28, 1944, in London, England.

period: Twentieth century

John Tavener stands as one of Great Britain's most influential composers of the last third of the twentieth century. His innovative, mystical style remains most apparent in the realm of sacred music, where he has proven himself a worthy successor to Benjamin Britten, Ralph Vaughan Williams, and Herbert Howells.

Tavener's music aptitude surfaced early and, by the time he entered London's Highgate School on a scholarship, he displayed considerable ability as a pianist and organist. His father, the organist at St. Andrew's Presbyterian Church, Hampstead, provided further encouragement by inviting his son to submit compositions for the church's worship services. Later training included study at the

Royal Academy of Music with special studies in composition under David Lumsdaine and Lennox Berkeley. While at the Academy, Tavener's reputation as a promising composer was both established and further encouraged through a number of composition projects and ensuing prizes. Originally intent on a career as concert pianist, Tavener now turned his attentions fully to composition. Ensuing meetings with luminaries such as Olivier Messaien, Pierre Boulez, and Gyorgy Ligeti further influenced his decision.

Tavener's early employment helped provide a proving ground for his first serious efforts at composition. While organist and choirmaster at St. John's Presbyterian Church, Kensington, in the 1960s, he composed several smaller choral works, performed his own piano concerto, and saw the premiere of his one-act opera, *The Cappemakers*. Also, his *Three Holy Sonnets of John Donne* received performances as did his cantata *Cain and Abel*, this by the London Bach Society. The 1968 premiere of *The Whale* marks Tavener's point of entry into the ranks of established British composers. Part of the inaugural performance of the London Sinfonietta under David Atherton, *The Whale* led a long string of subsequent works that employed both acoustic and electronic media. Scored for orchestra, tape, and electronically enhanced percussion and chorus, it takes the form of a dramatic, semi-staged hybrid of oratorio and opera, all with compelling if somewhat dated effects.

Other successes quickly followed, such as *In Alium* (1968) and *Celtic Requiem* (1969). Both works' general mood and style paralleled the prevailing transcendental movement made so popular in the British consciousness by the Beatles. It was just such a subliminal connection that brought Tavener and his works to the attention of the Beatles themselves, resulting in a recording relationship with Apple Records. Added to *The Whale* and *Celtic Requiem*, then, were recordings of *Coplas* (1970) and *Nomine Jesus* (1970), all on the Apple label.

In 1969 Tavener accepted the position of professor of composition at Trinity College. From the start of his tenure, he received many commissions for a wide variety of works suited to particular performance needs and venues. Resulting were his *Ultimos Ritos* (1972), a sophisticated multi-media work for the Cathedral of St. Bavo, Haarlem; *Therese* (1973–1976), an opera with libretto by Gerard McLarnon; and the chamber opera *A Gentle Spirit* (1977), after a short story of Dostoyevsky. In 1977 Tavener, in a bold personal statement, aligned

himself with the Russian Orthodox Church and was received into its membership. His conversion can be traced to an earlier friendship with Father Malachy Lynch, a member of the Carmelite Order with close ties to the head of the western Orthodox Church. Influences of the Orthodox faith, its liturgical traditions, and its theology readily appear throughout works such as *Orthodox Vigil Service* (1984); *Akathist of Thanksgiving* (1986), premiered in Westminster Abbey; *The Protecting Veil* (1987); *Resurrection* (1989), first given at Glasgow Cathedral; and the opera *Mary of Egypt* (1991), for the Aldeburgh Festival. Other smaller choral anthems reflecting moods of the Eastern rite include *The Lamb* and *The Tiger,* both based on poems of William Blake, and *A Hymn to the Mother of God* (1985) for a cappella double choir.

Vocal
Eternity's Sunrise
what to buy: [Patricia Rozario, soprano; Paul Goodwin, cond.; The Academy of Ancient Music, orch.; The Academy of Ancient Music, choir] (Harmonia Mundi 907231) ♪ ♪ ♪ ♪

Four of the composer's larger choral settings and one short alleluia (*Song of Angel*) are offered here in performances of tonal purity and restraint. Among the finest of the big works is Patricia Rozario's homage to the morning of man's afterlife in *Eternity's Sunrise*, a simple yet mysteriously structured work for instruments and solo voice dedicated to the memory of Princess Diana. One can easily envision the film version of this highly descriptive work as the soloist flies above the ensemble's block harmonies in sweet, fragile descant. Temple Church's temperamental acoustics present no threat to the superb clarity and control of the orchestral and vocal forces.

Innocence
what to buy: [Patricia Rozario, soprano; Alice Neary, cello; Martin Baker, organ; Charles Fullbrook, bells; Martin Neary, cond.; Westminster Abbey Choir] (Sony Classics 66613) ♪ ♪ ♪♪

The great cavernous frame of the Abbey takes some of the fine edge off of the vocalists' diction in some of these otherwise lovely and well-crafted performances. On the other hand, such sonic cover also gives to other works a ghost-like patina most appropriate to their style. *Innocence* is the work from this collection that benefits most clearly from this. From its opening peal of the great organ and restless groans of the choir to the plaintive whispers of the soprano soloist, *Innocence* easily matches the most dramatic overture or film score in its theatrical explosiveness. Primordial chaos swirls around the souls of those in agony as solo voices cry out from the far reaches of the Abbey's nave to proclaim both the good and evil that struggle for victory. Among the seven other scores heard here are *The Lamb, The Tiger,* and (with the English Chamber Orchestra) the *Little Requiem for Father Malachy Lynch.*

various choral works

what to buy: [*English Choral Music: John Tavener,* Christopher Robinson, cond.; Choir of St. John's College, Cambridge] (Naxos 8.555256) ♪ ♪ ♪ ♪ ♪

Here is a splendid performance of several of Tavener's smaller choral works, many of them staples of today's worship services in the Roman and Anglican churches. Christopher Robinson is able to alter the sound of the excellent St. John's Choir to meet the composer's changing demands of color and voicing. *The Lamb* and *The Tiger* glisten with superb diction and phrasing, allowing the spare vocal lines of each work to flow freely from sorrowful dissonance to sublime unison proclamations. A fitting vessel in which to contain the poet's message. *A Hymn to the Mother of God* sends hypnotic waves of double choir harmonies over the listener, creating the acoustic sense of vast open spaces just large enough to allow the work's great forte ending to bloom in full. Tim Hugh's cello contributes the loveliest voice to *Svyati* as the choral accompaniment blankets his plaintive melody with a hushed lamentation.

what to buy next: [*Sacred Music by John Tavener,* Christopher Robinson, cond.; Choir of St. George's Chapel, Windsor Castle] (Hyperion 66464) ♪ ♪ ♪ ♪♪

Again Mr. Robinson creates magic, this time with a different choir. Many of the same works found in the Naxos collection (see above) are repeated here, allowing a fascinating "control factor" against which to compare and contrast differences in choral timbre and chapel acoustics. The anthem *Love bade me welcome* joins this mystic composer to his poetic counterpart, George Herbert, with neither artist suffering from the union. Each line of text is set to an amalgam of plainsong and homophonic sweetness, creating an ethereal frame for this loveliest of verses. The *Ode to St. Andrew of Crete* begins with a bold baritone sentence in unison that sets

the text against rich melismatic lines and later fractures into two and three-part episodes of dissonant organum. The upper voices then add lightness and an antiphonal backing to Matthew Brook's rich solo chanting.

influences: Gustav Holst, Arvo Pärt, Peteris Vasks, Veljo Tormis

Frank Scinta

John Taverner

Born c. 1490 in Lincolnshire, England. Died October 18, 1545, in Lincolnshire, England.

period: Renaissance

Taverner was one of the leading composers of English sacred music during the first part of the sixteenth century. He is best known for his *Western Wynde* Mass, a work based on a secular tune often attributed to Henry VIII. There is reason to believe that Taverner had close ties to the Chapel Royal and may have known Henry VIII personally.

There is much conflicting information about John Taverner, and only by comparing a number of sources can a partial picture of his life be constructed. Due to the most recent research, it is now believed that the first mention of Taverner was around the year 1525, when his name appears as a singer at the Collegiate Church in Tattershall. He must have made quite a reputation there as both a musician and teacher, since he was invited by Bishop Longland to take over the choir director's duties at the newly formed Cardinal College (now Christ Church) at Oxford. Cardinal Woolsey had started the school and spared no expense on the sumptuous music performed there. As a result, Taverner was in charge of some fine musical forces, and much of his surviving music was written during his tenure there (1526–30). In 1528 certain members of the Cardinal College choir were influenced by Lutheran thought, and Taverner was accused of heresy, but there is no proof that he was briefly imprisoned, as some have stated. He appeared to have a pleasant, easygoing personality, and Cardinal Woolsey protected him from any legal repercussions from this supposed challenge to Catholic orthodoxy.

However, Woolsey fell from Henry VIII's favor by 1530 and was replaced by Sir Thomas Moore, the Lord

Chancellor who would later lose his head for not supporting Henry's claim to the spiritual leadership of the Church of England. With this change in administration, Taverner's association with the college was ended, and he was obliged to seek employment elsewhere. His next position was as instructor of choristers at the Church of St. Botolph in Boston, Lincolnshire, where he served from 1530 to 1537. It appears that his professional music career ended at this point. Due to the considerable wealth he was able to accumulate as a church musician, Taverner moved in aristocratic circles and became a well-respected local citizen; as a result of his good relationship with Henry VIII's minister Thomas Cromwell, he enjoyed close ties to the Crown. Reports that Taverner had a change of heart later in life, denouncing all things connected with the Catholic Church and disavowing his earlier sacred music, seem to stem from errors propagated by earlier historians.

England, before Henry's break with Rome, was a devoutly Catholic country, and the celebration of liturgies was very elaborate and done with the greatest attention to the use of music. One technique was the writing of Masses using popular or secular tunes as the basis for structural unity. Of the eight Masses set by Taverner, six of them use this method. Taverner was also fluent in the use of motivic development of small musical ideas, long series of notes set to single syllables (melismas), and the grouping of high and low voices common among medieval English composers.

Vocal
Western Wynde for Four Voices
what to buy: [Harry Christophers, cond; The Sixteen, choir] (Helios 55056) ♪♪♪♪⁴

This group was founded by Christophers in 1997, and its recordings have already won some impressive prizes. A warm, full sound characterizes the group's performance of the *Western Wynde* setting, with careful attention to detail when highlighting the nuances of imitative counterpoint. You'll also find solid performances of the antiphon *O splendor gloriae* and Taverner's conception of the Te Deum.

worth searching for: [*The John Taverner Anniversary Album*; Peter Philips, cond.; Tallis Scholars, choir] (Gimell 454995) ♪♪♪♪⁴

This is a superb recording in all respects; in addition to Taverner's setting of *Western Wynde*, it contains the

---

Tapes and Computers in Classical Music: A Brief Snapshot

Ferruccio Busoni was the first major composer of the twentieth century to propose using "nonmusical" sounds within the context of music, and in 1907 he published his thoughts on the matter in a pamphlet called *Entwurf einer neuen Äesthetik der Tonkunst (Sketch of a New Esthetic of Music)*. The *Manifesto dei musicisti futuristi (Futurist Manifesto)* of 1909 by Filippo Tommaso Marinetti and Francesco Balilla Pratella, and *L'arte dei rumori (The Art of Noise)* by Luigi Russolo from 1913, were other important texts espousing the adoption of new definitions for what was and was not music.

Although George Antheil's *Ballet Mécanique* of 1926 may have been the score that first exposed a measure of the "noise as music" aesthetic to a fairly wide audience, it was John Cage and his 1939 work *Imaginary Landscape no. 1* for muted piano, cymbal, and two variable-speed phonographs playing test recordings, which really foreshadowed the approach later taken by other adventurous musical artists. Edgard Varèse's compositions from 1954 (*Déserts* for winds, brass, percussion and electronic tape) and 1956 (the *Poème électronique,* a piece meant for tape machines feeding information over telephone relays through fifteen channels to more than 400 speakers in the Philips Pavilion at the 1958 World's Fair in Brussels) were also important milestones.

Pierre Schaeffer, the French theoretician and composer, developed the world's first electronic music studio in 1948. The earliest of his works created there used only variable-speed tape recorders and phonographs, microphones, and sound-effects records for their realization. The product of using this equipment and manipulating the resulting sounds has since been termed *musique concrète*. American composers who've also done important work within this category include Otto Luening and Vladimir Ussachevsky.

The development of the RCA Mark II Synthesizer at the Columbia-Princeton Electronic Music Center (and Milton Babbitt's use of it) paved the way for portable electronic instruments like the Moog and ARP synthesizers as well as the digital samplers which since have been used in ad jingles, hip-hop music, and other artistic avenues. During the middle of the twentieth century, work with computers and tape was also being done at various American academic centers by Morton Subotnick, Lejaren Hiller, Robert Ashley, Charles Wuorinen, and others. In France, the Centre d'Études de Mathematique et Automatique Musicales (directed by Iannis Xenakis) and the Institut de Recherche et Coordination Acoustique/Musique (founded by Pierre Boulez) were the major centers of work on computer-assisted music, while Karlheinz Stockhausen was the most influential figure at the radio studios of Germany's Nordwest Deutsche Rundfunk; Luciano Berio headed up the Milan Studio de Fonologia RAI in Italy; Krzysztof Penderecki led the way at Polish Radio, Warsaw; and Toshio Mayuzumi established similar operations at the NHK Studio in Tokyo, Japan.

A good overview of the genre's history is *OHM: The Early Gurus of Electronic Music, 1848–1980* (Ellipsis Arts 3670), a three-CD set which features seminal works by Schaefer, Cage, Varèse, Stockhausen, Xenakis, Terry Riley, Steve Reich, Pauline Oliveros, and others.

Mathilde August

Mass for Six Voices entitled *Gloria tibi trinitas* and the Kyrie *Leroy* for Four Voices. While this could be the starting point anyone seeking to appreciate the music of Taverner, the same sterling performance was also released on an album (Gimell 454927) featuring versions of the *Western Wynde* Mass by Taverner, Christopher Tye, and John Sheppard.

Mater Christi sanctissima

what to buy: [*English Choral Music: 1514–1682*; Stephen Darlington, cond.; Christ Church Cathedral Choir, Oxford] (Nimbus 1762) ♪ ♪ ♪ ♪⅞

It is only fitting that Stephen Darlington, a successor of Taverner, should lead the musical forces in the very place where the composer lived and composed nearly five hundred years ago. In addition to Taverner's *Mater Christi sanctissima*, the choir sings his Mass *Mater Christi* (a parody of the antiphon, scored for five voices), plus a reconstruction of the antiphon *O Wilheme, pastor bone.* When all is said and done, Darlington has put together an impressive budget-priced eight-disc survey of English choral music that magically captures this highly symbolic sacred music and transports the listener to another place and time. Other composers heard on this compilation include Thomas Weelkes, William Byrd, John Blow, Henry Purcell, Matthew Locke, John Sheppard, and Pelham Humfrey.

influences: John Sheppard, Christopher Tye

Dave Wagner

Piotr Ilyich Tchaikovsky

Born c. May, 7, 1840, in Kamsko-Votkinsk, Russia. Died c. November 6, 1893, in St. Petersburg, Russia.

period: Romantic

Though his life was a strange mixture of success and failure and his musical style has been described as eclectic, Tchaikovsky was a distinguished exponent of the Russian national school during the late Romantic period, often drawing inspiration from native Russian sources. The strong melodies found in his first piano concerto, the Concerto in D Major for Violin and Orchestra, the *Nutcracker* and *Swan Lake* ballets, and his fifth and sixth symphonies, hold enduring appeal.

Piotr Ilyich Tchaikovsky grew up in an unmusical upper-

class family that moved to St. Petersburg when he was eight years old. As a youngster he developed his love of music by improvising at the piano but, at the tender age of ten, he was enrolled in the preparatory class of St. Petersburg School of Jurisprudence where, for ten years, he bowed to his parent's wishes for a law career. At the age of nineteen Tchaikovsky obtained a position as law clerk in the Ministry of Justice in St. Petersburg, working at this job from June 1859 until September 1863 and continuing musical studies in his spare time; in 1862 he became one of the first students at the newly opened St. Petersburg Conservatory, remaining there for two and a half years. During this time Tchaikovsky went frequently to the Italian operas which were popular on the Russian stage but, still in his early twenties, the budding composer actually knew little about other composers of his day. Despite this fact, he accepted a post in 1865 as teacher of harmony at the Russian Musical Society's Moscow branch, an organization which would become the Moscow Conservatory one year later.

It was while living in Moscow that Tchaikovsky first met some great contemporaries (including Hector Berlioz, Franz Liszt, Camille Saint-Saëns, and Richard Wagner), suffered through an abortive love affair with opera singer Desiree Artot, and produced distinctive works with a flair for resplendent orchestral coloring. At the end of 1867 Tchaikovsky met Mily Balakirev, one of a group of composers including Nicolai Rimsky-Korsakov, Modest Mussorgsky, Alexander Borodin, and César Cui who were collectively known as "The Five" or "The Mighty Handful." These men were fanatical nationalists who believed that music began and ended with folk song. All but Rimsky-Korsakov were rather amateurish in technique and most of them tended to regard the formally-trained Tchaikovsky with suspicion. Balakirev, however, encouraged the young composer and out of their friendship came Tchaikovsky's first masterpiece, the fantasy overture *Romeo and Juliet.*

From August 1875 until April 1876, he worked on the score for his first ballet, *Swan Lake,* a commission by the director of the Moscow Imperial Theatres that premiered at the Bolshoi Theatre in March, 1877. Tchaikovsky once told Rimsky-Korsakov that he undertook the project because he needed the money and because he'd long wanted to try his hand at writing a ballet. At a time when music for the ballet theater was usually supplied by staff composers who shaped it to the needs of the ballet-master choreographing the dances, Tchaikovsky worked on this particular ballet independently. This piece is structured like a four-part tone poem but divided into the short Pas de deux, ensembles, character-dances, and mime scenes necessary to dancing; symphonically, its rich musical content is unified by carefully conceived key structure and melodic shapes. Shortly after that score's debut, Tchaikovsky began work with librettist Konstantine Shilovsky on a three-act opera based on an Alexander Pushkin poem, *Eugene Onegin*. The opera was completed in nine months and the world premiere (March 17, 1879) featured students of the Moscow conservatory singing the roles at Moscow's Chamber Theater (the site selected by the composer).

Tchaikovsky had interrupted work on *Onegin* to compose his fourth symphony, completing it in January 1878 and dedicating it to his patroness, Nadezhda von Meck. His credentials as a master of lyrical themes and melodic invention had already been established, but never before in such overtly Romantic material as his fourth symphony and his violin concerto, compositions that were completed the same year as *Eugene Onegin*. The widow of a wealthy railway engineer, Meck had become enraptured with Tchaikovsky's music the year before, had given him loans, and began a lengthy correspondence with the composer in 1878. It is said they never spoke to each other, though they regularly corresponded. Secure with this situation and the 6,000-ruble annuity Meck provided him, Tchaikovsky resigned from his Moscow professorship in 1878.

His next big work, the *1812 Overture*, quotes the Tsarist national anthem and the French *Marseillaise*, with trumpets rising every few seconds. One of his most popular scores and a surprisingly regular feature of American July Fourth celebrations, it was written in 1880 to commemorate Napoleon's defeat in Russia and published two years later. Tchaikovsky had traveled in Europe almost every year since 1870, but toured as a conductor for the first time in 1888. In the spring of that year, he returned from a visit to England and France where he'd met Johannes Brahms, Antonin Dvořák, Edvard Grieg, and others. He then settled into his country home between Moscow and Kiln and began working on his fifth symphony, conducting the first performance of that piece in St. Petersburg on November 17, 1888. Though well-received by the audience, critics panned it, and it languished in oblivion until after his death when it was revived by Arthur Nikisch in 1895. The work subsequently gained broader acceptance in overseas performances with other conductors. Today it is considered one

of Tchaikovsky's finest symphonies for its warmth, an abundance of melodies, and rich colorful harmonies. During the same period he also completed his great ballet score, *The Sleeping Beauty*.

At the end of 1890, three years before his death, came the inevitable break with Madame von Meck. By that time he was financially independent, yet the separation affected his spirits more than his music. In 1893 he wrote his most famous work, the *Pathétique* symphony, and conducted it at St. Petersburg on Oct. 28. It stands as a fitting end to the career of a tragic man who displayed his deepest feelings in music, often with tremendous emotional power. It was coolly received, and he did not live to witness its success. He died of cholera on November 6, 1893.

Orchestral
Concerto no. 1 in B-flat Minor for Piano and Orchestra, op. 23
what to buy: [Emil Gilels, piano; Zubin Mehta, cond.; New York Philharmonic Orchestra] (Sony Classics 46339) ♪♪♪♪

Probably one of the most familiar works in the history of classical music, this dramatic concerto was recorded live at Avery Fisher Hall and features Gilels, one of the greatest Russian pianists, in tandem with conductor Mehta and the New York Philharmonic. The disc also contains an awesome performance of Tchaikovsky's Concerto in D Major for Violin and Orchestra (op. 35) with David Oistrakh as soloist and Eugene Ormandy conducting the Philadelphia Orchestra. While lacking the light-handed touch and infinite orchestral detail of the Heifetz recording of this score (see below), it is still a remarkable listen. This double-bill offers a splendid opportunity to hear these two major Tchaikovsky works on one disc.

what to buy next: [André Watts, piano; Yoel Levi, cond.; Atlanta Symphony Orchestra] (Telarc 80386) ♪♪♪⸲

Watts offers a robust performance of this piece under Levi's direction, with sound quality that is best in softer passages. A bit brighter sound would have been preferable, hence the half-bone deduction. The disc also contains a solid performance of the Concerto no. 2 in G Minor for Piano and Orchestra by Camille Saint-Saëns.

Concerto in D Major for Violin and Orchestra, op. 35
what to buy: [Jascha Heifetz, violin; Fritz Reiner, cond.; Chicago Symphony Orchestra] (RCA Red Seal 5933)
♪ ♪ ♪ ♪ ♪

Reiner brings forth a performance that is resounding in potency and warmth and full of detail. Recorded in 1957, this breathtaking rendering remains a vital item in Heifetz's discography as well as a reflection of Tchaikovsky's compositional gifts. The violinist delivers an awesome technical performance and the tonal qualities of his instrument are exceptionally pleasing, especially in those honeyed upper-register notes. The disc also contains Tchaikovsky's *Sérénade Mélancolique* in B Minor (op. 25) and the Waltz from his Serenade In C Major (op. 48) in addition to Felix Mendelssohn's Concerto in E Minor for Violin and Orchestra (op. 64).

what to buy next: [Gidon Kremer, violin; Lorin Maazel, cond.; Berlin Philharmonic Orchestra] (Deutsche Grammophon 431609) ♪ ♪ ♪ ♪

Kremer is a virtuoso violinist with talent, technique, and fervent feeling comparable to Heifetz; he's definitely the star here. Maazel takes an overly sensitive approach in some parts and creates power without passion in others. Kremer's reading belongs in your collection in spite of the orchestra's relatively lackluster performance.

worth searching for: [Itzhak Perlman, violin; Zubin Mehta, cond.; Israel Philharmonic Orchestra] (EMI Classics 54108) ♪ ♪ ♪ ♪⅛

For their debut performances in the Soviet Union (May 2,1990), Mehta and Perlman bring forth a passionate rendering of this gorgeous Tchaikovsky work. Recorded in concert at Leningrad's Bolshoi Philharmonic Hall, their sterling performance with this orchestra marked the 150th anniversary of Tchaikovsky's birth. From the beginning of the first movement *Allegro moderato* with its gentle string motif, Perlman's proficiency and passion hold your attention.

The Nutcracker for Orchestra, op. 71
what to buy: [Seiji Ozawa, cond.; Boston Symphony Orchestra; American Boys Choir] (Deutsche Grammophon 435619) ♪ ♪ ♪ ♪

Piotr Ilyich Tchaikovsky

Ozawa conducts a glorious version of the complete ballet, with notable renderings of the second act's divertimento containing the familiar sweeping themes of *Waltz of the Flowers* and the delicate passages of *Dance of the Sugar Plum Fairy.* This disc also contains the suite (op. 66a) from Tchaikovsky's ballet *The Sleeping Beauty.*

what to buy next: [Antal Dorati, cond.; Royal Concertgebouw Orchestra; St. Bavo Cathedral Boys' Choir] (Philips 442562) ♪ ♪ ♪ ♪

This is a fulfilling complete version of Tchaikovsky's familiar ballet, rendered with energy, heartfulness, and splendid sound quality that captures the tiniest detail, including the brightly tapping triangle in the Overture. There's not too much that could really improve on Dorati's splendid interpretation, since he captures all of the jaunty section and tutti passages with utmost finesse. The two-CD set also includes selected highlights from a 1962 recording of Tchaikovsky's *The Sleeping Beauty* featuring Anatole Fistoulari leading the London Symphony Orchestra.

Nutcracker Suite for Orchestra, op. 71a
what to buy: [Neville Marriner, cond.; Academy of St. Martin-in-the-Fields, orch.] (Philips 411471) ♪ ♪ ♪ ♪⅛

Marriner brings particular life to *Dance of the Sugar-Plum Fairy,* the *Chinese Dance (Tea),* the bright and lively *Dance of the Reed Pipes,* and a splendid version of *Waltz of the Flowers.* The disc also contains Marriner's sensitive, lovely interpretation of the composer's expansive, harmonious Serenade in C Major for String Orchestra, op. 48.

1812 Overture in E-flat Major for Orchestra, op. 49
what to buy: [Charles Dutoit, cond.; Montreal Symphony Orchestra] (London 417300) ♪ ♪ ♪ ♪⅛

With sensitivity and full authority, Dutoit achieves a masterful reading of Tchaikovsky's popular work which slowly and melodiously builds through brass fanfares to an exciting finish with swirling strings, lots of brassy verve, and, in this case, booming canons of the Canadian Forces Base (Valcartier, Quebec), the *Gros Bourdon* bell of the Basilique Notre-Dame, Montreal, and the peal of the Basilique Sainte Anne de Beaupre, Quebec. A worthy purchase, this disc also contains an insightful reading of the composer's *Capriccio Italien* (op. 45), popular selections from the *Nutcracker Suite* (op. 71a), and a stimulating rendering of the robust *Marche slave* (op. 31).

[Leonard Slatkin, cond.; St. Louis Symphony Orchestra] (RCA Red Seal 68045) ♪ ♪ ♪ ♪⁸

Slatkin's reading is serious, powerful, and appealing, enhanced by a real cannon and the chiming carillon of Culver Military Academy. The CD cover featuring a discretely veiled, boudoir photo of a half-naked male with a female peeking over his shoulder belongs on a romance novel but plugs the central feature here: the 1993 recording of Tchaikovsky's fantasy overture *Romeo and Juliet*. The disc also contains a highly satisfying reading of the composer's second symphony (the *Little Russian*), not one of his most popular, but mastered here with utmost finesse.

what to buy next: [Eric Kunzel, cond.; Cincinnati Symphony Orchestra] (Telarc 80041) ♪ ♪ ♪ ♪

Kunzel brings forth an enthusiastic reading, though it seems somewhat rushed during the softer passages when compared with the above-mentioned versions. This disc also contains an authoritative reading of Tchaikovsky's *Capriccio Italien* and the less-often-heard *Cossack Dance* from *Mazeppa*.

Swan Lake, op. 20
what to buy: [Charles Dutoit, cond.; Montreal Symphony Orchestra] (London 436212) ♪ ♪ ♪ ♪⁸

This complete two-disc version of the ballet is a sensitively rendered performance. Although Tchaikovsky's music for this ballet is not quite as powerfully engaging as that which he wrote for his *Nutcracker*, Dutoit skillfully brings out many beautiful highlights. *Dance of the Swans* features pleasing violin and cello solos backed lightly by strings and woodwinds.

Symphony no. 4 in F Major, op. 36
what to buy: [David Zinman, cond.; Baltimore Symphony Orchestra] (Telarc 80228) ♪ ♪ ♪ ♪

Zinman achieves a performance resplendently demonstrating the full power and delicate detail of Tchaikovsky's work. This masterful reading is a memorable listen, especially in the energetic tutti passages and the shifting dynamics of the first movement. Zinman also conducts a glorious performance of Tchaikovsky's fantasy overture *Romeo and Juliet*, making this CD a

splendid buy.

Symphony no. 5 in E Minor, op. 64
what to buy: [Claudio Abbado, cond.; Chicago Symphony Orchestra] (Sony Classics 42094) ♪ ♪ ♪ ♪⁸

It's always Tchaikovsky's sixth symphony (the *Pathétique*) that's recommended in books on building your classical collection. However, his fifth symphony is equally engaging and perhaps more melodically upbeat. Under Abbado's baton, all the sweeping romanticism and brawny muscle of this magnificent work is evident.

what to buy next: [Lorin Maazel, cond.; Cleveland Orchestra] (Sony Classics 44785) ♪ ♪ ♪ ♪

This version of Symphony no. 5 is a satisfying listen but lacks some of the spirit of the Abbado version until you get to the Finale. There, Maazel elicits from the orchestra a robust, grandiose finish full of brassy fury and swirling strings, making this CD an attractive choice. The disc also features Maazel conducting the National Orchestra of France in Sergei Prokofiev's first symphony.

Symphony no. 6 in B Minor, op. 74 (*Pathétique*)
what to buy: [Christoph von Dohnanyi, cond.; Cleveland Orchestra] (Telarc 80130) ♪ ♪ ♪ ♪

Recorded in 1986 using the fine acoustics of Cleveland's Masonic Auditorium, the Cleveland Orchestra under Dohnanyi delivers a performance that captures all of the softest passages as well as the majestic power of this highly popular symphony. The disc includes the brief *Polonaise* from *Eugene Onegin* as filler.

what to buy next: [*The Solti Collection, vol. 6*; Georg Solti, cond.; Chicago Symphony Orchestra] (London 430442) ♪ ♪ ♪⁸

Under Solti's direction, the rendering by the Chicago Symphony Orchestra (recorded in 1976 at Medinah Temple in Chicago, Illinois) sparkles throughout, though the inconsistent sound reproduction on this version could have been improved. This disc also includes a better-sounding performance of Tchaikovsky's complete *Romeo and Juliet* recorded nearly a decade later in Chicago's Orchestra Hall.

Chamber
Trio in A Minor for Piano, Violin, and Cello, op. 50
what to buy: [*Smetana and Tchaikovsky Piano Trios*;

David Golub, piano; Mark Kaplan, violin; Colin Carr, cello] (Arabesque 6661) ♪ ♪ ♪ ♪

This acclaimed trio has toured the United States and Europe together, appeared with top symphony orchestras, and pursued solo careers. Their 1994 performance of this piece, recorded in the SUNY Purchase Recital Hall, is technically proficient and elegant, especially when Kaplan and Carr join in some deep-toned, melodic duets in the first movement. Smetana's only piano trio is also included on this disc.

what to buy next: [Arensky Piano Trio, ensemble] (Naxos 8.550467) ♪ ♪ ♪♪

The Arensky Piano trio, formed from veteran soloists early in 1990, presents a satisfying performance of this challenging piece that shimmers with melodious innovation, potency, and luxuriance. The CD also contains one of the piano trios by Anton Arensky, a younger colleague of Tchaikovsky. Both pieces yield most of the central themes to the cello.

Vocal
Eugene Onegin, op. 24
what to buy: [Anna Tomowa-Sintow, soprano; Rossitza Troeva-Mircheva, contralto; Nicolai Gedda, tenor; Yuri Mazurok, baritone; Nicola Ghiuselev, bass; Emil Tchakarov, cond.; Sofia Festival Orchestra; Sofia National Opera Chorus] (Sony 45539) ♪ ♪ ♪ ♪♪

Throughout, Tchakarov ignites a masterful rendering of this score from the orchestra, chorus, and soloists, drawing dramatically beautiful work from the participants. Yet while the rich, heavy voices of Tomowa-Sintow and Troeva-Mircheva (first heard in their opening duet) seem fitting for Russian opera, they're not so appropriate for the young women they portray. Still, Tomowa-Sintow's emotional *Let me die* aria in Act One is full of anguish and matched by impassioned orchestral passages.

various songs
what to buy next: [*Complete Songs, volume 1*; Ljuba Kazarnovskaya, soprano; Ljuba Orfenova, piano] (Naxos 8.554357) ♪ ♪ ♪ ♪♪

Kazarnovskaya is a spunky soprano with a sterling range and full-throated delivery. You'll want to crank up the sound to hear this magnificent dramatist who puts emphasis in all the right places. Texts and English translations are included in the liner booklet of this highly recommended CD.

what to buy next: [Julia Varady, soprano; Aribert Reimann, piano] (Orfeo 53851) ♪ ♪ ♪ ♪

Varady's richly expressive soprano voice (with just the right amount of vibrato) engages throughout this collection of eighteen songs, including the six from Tchaikovsky's op. 65, presented here in their original French version. While Tchaikovsky's songs don't approach the melodiousness of his other works and were criticized as being nothing more than parlor pieces, Varady is a versatile songbird who adds much to them in these attractive performances.

influences: Nikolai Rimsky-Korsakov, Alexander Borodin, Modest Mussorgsky, César Cui

Nancy Ann Lee

Georg Philipp Telemann
Born March 14, 1681 in Magdeburg, Germany. Died June 25, 1767, in Hamburg, Germany.

period: Baroque

Widely regarded by his contemporaries as one of Germany's leading musicians, Telemann was an extremely prolific composer whose voluminous output bridges the late Baroque style and early Classicism. Among his most important works are the three books of concertos, trios, and sonatas known as *Musique de Table (Tafelmusik).*

Georg Philipp Telemann came from an upper middle-class family. His father, brother, and maternal grandfather were all clergymen —a path that Telemann might also have followed had it not been for his exceptional musical ability. As a child, he mastered the violin, flute, zither, and keyboard and even began composing an opera (*Sigismundus*) when he was only twelve years old. Though his mother's side of the family disapproved of music as an occupation, such resistance only reinforced Telemann's determination to persevere in his studies. In 1694 his mother sent him to Zellerfeld where he was entrusted to the educational guidance of Caspar Calvoer, an old friend of Telemann's father. Unbeknownst to Georg's mother, it would be through this new teacher that the young man would discover the relationship

between mathematics and music, and revel in the concepts of music theory.

After four years, Telemann entered the Hildesheim Gymnasium where he continued his science education and learned to play even more instruments, including the oboe, viola da gamba, and trombone. Then, in 1701, he went to Leipzig University where, at the insistence of his mother, he began studying law. Telemann was already so capable a musician that within a year of his arrival he founded and gave public concerts with the student Collegium Musicum, wrote works for and became musical director of the Leipzig Opera, and was appointed organist at the Neukirche. Telemann did not stay long in Leipzig however. In 1705 he accepted an appointment as Kapellmeister to the cosmopolitan court of Count Erdmann II of Promnitz at Sorau (now Zary, Poland), where the count's taste for the French and Italian styles provided him with new challenges.

By 1708 Telemann had been appointed Konzertmeister to Duke Johann Wilhelm at Eisenach and plunged into composing church cantatas and much instrumental music for the court orchestra. A year later, he married Louise Eberlin, a lady-in-waiting to the Countess of Promnitz and daughter of the musician Daniel Eberlin. However, her tragic death in January 1711 following the birth of their first daughter led to an emotionally necessary change of scenery. He headed to Frankfurt-am-Main to take up appointments as municipal director of music and Kapellmeister of the Barfüsserkirche. Telemann's new posts suited his talents; he composed music for civic ceremonies, church cantatas, oratorios, orchestral music, and abundant chamber music, much of which was published. The freedom he enjoyed in his civic appointment also allowed him time to help shape the city's musical life and he quickly assumed the directorship of the Collegium Musicum of the Frauenstein Society, which presented weekly concerts in Frankfurt. During this period he was also appointed Kapellmeister to the Prince of Bayreuth and, while on a visit to Eisenach in 1716, was honored with an appointment as visiting Kapellmeister. His increasing stature was further enhanced the following year when Duke Ernst of Gotha invited him to become Kapellmeister of all his various courts, but he remained in Frankfurt, using this offer to force improvements in his situation.

In 1721, Telemann was invited to succeed Joachim Gerstenbüttel in the coveted post of Kantor of the Johanneum, a leading Hamburg school, which tradition-

ally carried with it teaching responsibilities, as well as the directorship of the city's five principal churches. This was a prestigious appointment which would provide him with seemingly unlimited opportunities to compose and perform. As Kantor, he was required to write two cantatas a week, produce a new Passion annually, and generate occasional works for church and civil ceremonies. Initially there was strong opposition among the city officials to Telemann's active involvement in the Hamburg Opera, especially since his own opera *Der geduldige Socrates* had been performed there earlier that year. Telemann threatened to resign and, applying for the post of Kantor of the Leipzig Thomaskirche, he was selected over five other candidates in 1722. But the Hamburg City Council refused to grant his release, ultimately increasing his stipend and withdrawing their objections to his association with the Hamburg Opera. He would continue to live in that city for the rest of his life.

Telemann's eventual output (more than 3,000 works) surpassed Johann Sebastian Bach's in part because he chose to not be confined by his official duties. His swift rise to power and wealth as the most famous composer in Germany was partly accomplished through the publication of his works, many of which were also known and loved throughout Europe. His output was so vast that musicologists have only recently undertaken the huge task of identifying and cataloging all of Telemann's works.

Orchestral
Concerto in D Major for Trumpet and Strings
what to buy: [*Virtuoso Trumpet*, Rolf Smedvig, trumpet; Jahja Ling, cond.; Scottish Chamber Orchestra] (Telarc 80227) ♪ ♪ ♪ ♪

Jahja Ling extracts a lush, richly sonorous version of this splendid piece from American trumpeter Rolf Smedvig and the British orchestra. Smedvig's crisp, precise technique and passion (immediately apparent in the gorgeous Adagio) make this one of the most attractive works on an album that also contains pieces by J. S. Bach and Leopold Mozart.

various concertos for stringed instruments
what to buy: [*Violin and Viola Concertos*; Paul Peabody, violin, viola; Richard Kapp, cond.; Philharmonia Virtuosi] (ESS.A.Y 1016) ♪ ♪ ♪ ♪

All Telemann albums recorded by this group under

Kapp's leadership sparkle with passion and charm. This CD featuring soloist Paul Peabody performing six concerti for violin or viola, with strings and continuo is no exception. Peabody is a pleasing soloist, but the emphasis falls equally on the orchestra in these superbly played performances of four violin concertos, a concerto for two violins, and a viola concerto.

various works for flute or recorder and orchestra
what to buy: [*Complete Double Concertos with Recorder*, Claas Pehrsson, recorder; Olof Larsson, viola da gamba; Nils-Erik Sparf, cond.; Drottningholm Baroque Ensemble, orch.] (BIS 617) ♪ ♪ ♪ ♪₄

Sparf evokes sympathetic playing from the orchestra and the world-class soloists on this period-instrument performance of the Double Concerto in A minor for recorder, viola da gamba, and string orchestra. For its rich, deep sonorities, catchy melody and rhythms in the first movement, this piece is widely admired. An appealing Telemann collection (recorded in 1983, 1984 and 1993), this disc contains four other sprightly concerti, including a pair for two tenor recorders and string orchestra.

[*Les Plaisirs: Chamber Concertos*; Marion Verbruggen, recorder; Sarah Cunningham, viola da gamba; Monica Huggett, cond.; Orchestra of the Age of Enlightenment] (Harmonia Mundi 7907093) ♪ ♪ ♪ ♪₄

The dance movements in two suites included here are performed with gay enthusiasm and crisp precision by these world-class players, and the rest of this all-Telemann program is also engaging.

what to buy next: [Susan Milan, flute; Leonard Friedman, cond.; St. Andrew Camerata, orch.] (Omega Classics 1006) ♪ ♪ ♪ ♪

Telemann's Suite for Flute and Strings in A minor was also scored by him for solo recorder or flute, strings and continuo. Resembling a work by J. S. Bach, it reflects the popularity in German-speaking lands of the French-style suite, basically an overture plus several shorter, lighter movements, including stylized dances and characteristic pieces in the same key. In this 1987 recording Milan and the Camerata deliver a lovely interpretation of this seven-movement work and two others by Telemann (the suite from *Don Quichotte* and a concerto for flute, violin, cello, and strings).

various orchestral suites
what to buy: [Akademie für Alte Musik, Berlin, orch.] (Harmonia Mundi 901654) ♪ ♪ ♪ ♪ ♪

Three of Telemann's royal suites in the French style (plus two overtures) receive glorious readings by this original-instrument orchestra. Their attractive performance of Suite in F major—*Alster*, engages the listener from the galloping horn quartet in the overture to the final notes. There is also a majestic reading of the Suite in G minor—*La Musette*, intriguing with its various dances and the deep, droning fifths of simulated bagpipes in the sixth movement that gives the piece its name. The Suite in F major—*La Chasse*, was written entirely for wind instruments and is deftly performed, capturing the delightful upbeat mood that reaches a peak in *Les Plaisirs*, a movement detailing the prince's pleasure in the chase. These are first-rate performances.

what to buy next: [*Suites for Orchestra*; Richard Kapp, cond.; Philharmonia Virtuosi, orch.] (ESS.A.Y. 1017) ♪ ♪ ♪ ♪₄

This recording is pure pleasure. From his magnificent orchestra, Kapp elicits profoundly expressive performances of Telemann's Suite in C major—*La Bouffonne*, the Suite in G minor—*La Changeante;* and the Suite in G major—*La Bizarre*.

Chamber
***Musique de Table—"Tafelmusik"* (complete)**
what to buy: [Robert Glenton, cond.; members of the Orchestra of the Golden Age] (Naxos 8.504022) ♪ ♪ ♪ ♪ ♪

Telemann's three books of *Musique de table* for a variety of instrumental combinations rank among his most important and well-known works. Although he chose a French title for the three volumes, the music also contains elements of the Italian, German, and Polish styles. Superior, detailed sound quality on this period-instrument package combines with a budget price to give this four-disc set an edge over the other recordings recommended here. For anyone wishing to sample the works, these performances are also available as single discs. (Naxos 8.553724, 8.553725, 8.553731, and 8.553732)

what to buy next: [Frans Brüggen, cond.; members of the Concerto Amsterdam] (Teldec Das Alte Werk 95519) ♪ ♪ ♪ ♪

This is an older recording than the Glenton-led set and the sound is a bit "drier" than Naxos provides. Still, these are quite beguiling performances from the era when recordings of authentic-instrument ensembles were still a novelty. Especially notable are the Quartet in D minor from Book 2 and the Trio in E flat major from Book 1.

Paris Quartets (selections)

what to buy: [*Nouveaux Quatuors en six suites*; Quadro Amsterdam, ensemble] (Teldec Das Alte Werk 92177) ♪ ♪ ♪ ♪ ♪

The six quartets Telemann composed in 1730 and his *New Quartets* of 1738 have together become known as the *Paris Quartets*, because their successful performances there earned Telemann wider acclaim. He used characteristics of the French style, but he also injected them with liveliness, a witty conversational quality, supple German counterpoint, and a personal sensitivity to instrumental sonority. This stunning two-disc set has been around for decades in one form or other and still sounds good. Part of that has to do with the performers, longtime stalwarts of the original-instrument movement (Frans Brüggen, Jaap Schröder, Anner Bylsma, and Gustav Leonhardt), who present this music with all the skill and verve it deserves.

what to buy next: [*Paris Quartets*; members of Florilegium, ensemble] (Channel Classics 13598) ♪ ♪ ♪ ♪

Members of Florilegium, an award-winning British group, do a fine job of navigating through four of the 1730 quartets in addition to the Fantasies for solo flute (Ashley Solomon), violin (Rachel Podger), and harpsichord (Neal Peres DaCosta).

[Christopher Krueger, baroque flute; Boston Museum Trio, ensemble] (Centaur 2260) ♪ ♪ ♪ ♪

Launching the album with the colorful *Concerto Primo in G major*, these four gifted musicians render engaging readings of six of Telemann's 1738 quartets. While their performances are technically well executed and sonorously pleasing, there's an element of warm congeniality missing when compared to the Florilegium performances. Still, because there are so few recordings of the *quadri* exist, these elegant, harmonious renderings warrant serious listening.

influences: Antonio Vivaldi, Johann Sebastian Bach, Franz Joseph Haydn, Wolfgang Amadeus Mozart

Nancy Ann Lee

Virgil Thomson

Born November 25, 1896, in Kansas City, MO, USA. Died September 30, 1989, in New York City, NY, USA.

period: Twentieth century

Composer and music critic Thomson's collaborations with the expatriate writer Gertrude Stein resulted in his best-known works, specifically *Four Saints in Three Acts* and *The Mother of Us All*. These operas, along with the film scores to *Louisiana Story* and *The Plow That Broke the Plains*, secured Thomson his place in the twentieth century American classical canon.

Thomson grew up in the heartland of America, in a home steeped in Southern Baptist traditions. He began to play the piano at the tender age of five and took formal lessons with local teachers at the age of twelve. Thomson next studied the organ, progressing well enough that he eventually took a position as the organist in his family's church. This was the beginning of his lifelong connection with sacred music. In 1917 the United States declared war on Germany and Thomson enlisted; he never took part in combat, however, as the armistice was signed before he received his final orders. Abandoning his military career, he moved back to Kansas City prior to studying music full-time at Harvard University. At Harvard, he trained with Edward Burlingame Hill, the influential composer who also instructed Walter Piston, Elliott Carter, and Leonard Bernstein. Thomson's other mentor was S. Foster Damon, an English instructor and founder of the *Harvard Musical Review*. It was Damon who introduced Thomson to the writings of Gertrude Stein and to the music of Erik Satie. In 1921 the Harvard Glee Club toured Europe, with Thomson taking up the role of assistant conductor. When the tour ended, he remained in Paris under a fellowship, studying counterpoint and organ with Nadia Boulanger. During this period Thomson also began his parallel career as a music critic. He frequently wrote reviews of the concerts he attended in Paris and mailed these pieces to the *Boston Evening Transcript*, an experience foreshadowing his later appointment as chief music critic of the *New York Herald Tribune*.

max. Tippett served three months' imprisonment in 1943 as a result of his pacifist principals, refusing on principle to do the alternative farm work assigned him. Enduring prison for his beliefs turned out to be a positive experience for Tippett and his music, encouraging him to continue evolving his own technique, one using complex rhythms and long phrases. Using this methodology he established his own brand of dynamism and lyricism, efforts that resulted in his Symphony no. 1 from 1945 and, a year later, in his third string quartet.

After the war ended, Tippett worked for six years on his first mature opera (again to his own libretto), the exorbitantly lyrical *The Midsummer Marriage*. The richly symbolic text—heavily influenced by the psychology of Carl Jung, the drama of Bernard Shaw, and the poetry of T.S. Eliot—largely baffled the critics at its 1955 Covent Garden debut though the superb quality of the music was generally recognized. The opera was not fully appreciated for being the jewel that it is until its 1968 Covent Garden revival directed by Colin Davis. Tippett hit his stride after this, composing several masterpieces including *Fantasia Concertante on a Theme of Corelli* for String Orchestra and culminating with the superb Symphony no. 2—perhaps his most completely satisfying excursion in that format.

Tippett's next opera (*King Priam*) is a taut, stark tragedy written in an abrasive style contrary to the expansive music heard in *Midsummer Marriage* and representing a change of direction. Tippett's music, including the Sonata no. 2 for Piano and the Concerto for Orchestra, now generally followed this more austere course even though he continued to write less complex pieces for public occasions. Often utilizing choruses, such works as the *Magnificat and Nunc Dimittis* and the *Praeludium* for Brass, Bells, and Percussion followed the earlier *Suite for the Birthday of Prince Charles* as examples of his continuing political commitment to occasionally compose music accessible to the general public. Tippett's second oratorio, *The Vision of Saint Augustine*, comes from 1965 and reaches out toward a state of ecstasy, attempting to present Augustine's vision of eternity. *The Knot Garden*, Tippett's third opera, uses an almost cinematic technique as large orchestral forces comment on the complex, fragmented interrelationships of the seven characters. The Symphony no. 3 for Soprano and Orchestra is Tippett's ambitious reply to Beethoven's Ninth; the brotherhood of the *Ode to Joy*, no longer possible in the late twentieth century, is replaced by the compassion of the *St. Louis Blues*. *The Ice Break*,

Bryn Terfel:
Born Bryn Terfel Jones, this bass/baritone vocalist has had what could safely be called a meteoric rise to the top of his profession. Before he was eighteen years old he rarely left the Welsh village where he grew up, but after years of entering and winning local singing festivals called *eisteddfodau*, Terfel was finally convinced by his high school music teacher to audition for London's Guildhall School of Music and Drama. There the young man who would later make his mark in opera studied fencing, acting, and languages while working with his voice teachers, Arthur Reckless and Rudolf Piernay. In 1989, when Terfel was only twenty-three years old and after winning a number of prizes at the Guildhall School, he entered the Cardiff Singer of the World Competition. Although he came in second overall to the young Russian baritone Dmitri Hvorostovsky, Terfel did take home the Lieder Prize and impress many of the professional musicians in attendance.

With an abundance of natural talent, a willingness to keep perfecting his craft, and a hardy, pleasant personality, Terfel proceeded to carefully make his way through the operatic repertoire, eventually appearing in most of the major European venues before making his Carnegie Hall recital debut in 1996. By this time his performances in operas by Wolfgang Amadeus Mozart (*Die Zauberflöte [The Magic Flute]*, *Don Giovanni*, and *Le Nozze di Figaro [The Marriage of Figaro]*); Richard Strauss (*Salome* and *Die Frau ohne Schatten [The Woman without a Shadow]*); and Jacques Offenbach (*Les Contes d'Hoffmann [Tales of Hoffman]*) were welcomed by fans and critics alike. It comes as no surprise, then, that his impressive album of opera arias by Mozart, Richard Wagner, Giuseppe Verdi, and others (Deutsche Grammophon 445866) won a Grammy Award in 1997 for Best Vocal Soloist Performance.

Terfel has also developed quite a reputation as a recitalist, usually accompanied by Malcolm Martineau, the pianist with whom he has worked since the two of them met at the Guildhall School. On disc, this pairing is well-represented by an outstanding recording of Robert Schumann's *Liederkreis* and excerpts from other song cycles by the composer (Deutsche Grammophon 447042), and *The Vagabond* (Deutsche Grammophon 445946), a fine selection of songs by English composers Ralph Vaughan Williams, Gerald Finzi, George Butterworth, and John Ireland. Terfel has also, as many current classical singers are wont to do, released a few albums for the crossover market, including a salute to the tunes of Rodgers and Hammerstein (*Something Wonderful*, Deutsche Grammophon 440163) and a program of songs inspired by Terfel's Welsh heritage and the spirit of the eisteddfodau, *We'll Keep a Welcome: The Welsh Album* (Deutsche Grammophon 463593).

William Gerard

Tippett's most topical opera, is even more condensed and sped up than *The Knot Garden*. Influenced by the composer's increasing involvement with American idioms, the work is a not completely successful political and social commentary on stereotypes and the need for individual rebirth. Tippett's fourth symphony returned to a purely instrumental (albeit programmatic) conception, being a single-movement work that traces one's life experience from birth to death, using a wind machine to simulate breathing. His fourth and fifth string quartets demonstrated his continuing passion for the music of Beethoven, while the dramatic setting for soprano and orchestra of Yeats's five-stanza poem *Byzantium* (1991) showcased his still-vital ability to set words to music.

Orchestral

Fantasia Concertante on a Theme of Corelli for String Orchestra

what to buy: [*The English Collection*; Neville Marriner, cond.; Academy of St. Martin-in-the-Fields, orch.] (ASV 518) ♪ ♪ ♪ ♪

Marriner gets an absolutely first-rate performance from the strings of the Academy in the *Fantasia,* as well as in Edward Elgar's *Serenade for Strings* and two works by Ralph Vaughan Williams (the *Fantasia on a Theme By Thomas Tallis* and *The Lark Ascending*).

what to buy next: [William Boughton, cond.; English String Orchestra] (Nimbus 7026) ♪ ♪ ♪⅝

The collection from which this selection comes is a well-played, admirably programmed sampler of Tippett's orchestral and vocal pieces. In addition to the composer's most delightful, audience-friendly work (the *Fantasia Concertante*), there are splendid renditions of his Concerto for Double String Orchestra, the *Little Music* for String Orchestra, and two choral works: the *Evening Canticles* and the five *Negro Spirituals* drawn from his oratorio, *A Child of Our Time.*

Symphony no. 2

what to buy: [Colin Davis, cond.; London Symphony Orchestra] (London 425646) ♪ ♪ ♪ ♪

Davis gives this symphony, Tippett's best, the reading that it deserves, demonstrating why he is the ideal conductor of Tippett's music. This set also contains the first and third symphonies conducted by Davis, with the fourth under Solti.

Vocal

The Midsummer Marriage

worth searching for: [Joan Carlyle, soprano; Elizabeth Harwood, soprano; Elizabeth Bainbridge, mezzo-soprano; Helen Watts, contralto; Stuart Burrows, tenor; Alberto Remedios, tenor; Stafford Dean, bass; Raymund Hericnx, bass; Colin Davis, cond.; Royal Opera House Orchestra, Covent Garden; Royal Opera House Chorus,

Covent Garden] (Lyrita 2217) ♪ ♪ ♪ ♪

Davis leads his well-balanced cast of soloists through an exciting performance of Tippett's finest opera, with Helen Watts a standout as Sosostris. This reissue on CD of the Philips recording from the early 1970s still conveys sonic excitement.

Byzantium

what to buy: [Faye Robinson, soprano; Georg Solti, cond.; Chicago Symphony Orchestra] (London 433668) ♪ ♪ ♪⅜

These same artists premiered this work, the score of which was commissioned by the Chicago Symphony to celebrate its centenary. Robinson, well-supported by Solti, does full justice to a vocal line which is often more declamatory than lyrical. Additionally, Solti leads an effective performance of Tippett's Symphony no. 4, another work which was commissioned and premiered by the Chicago Symphony.

influences: Henry Purcell, Igor Stravinsky

Jan Jezioro

Joan Tower

Born September 6, 1938, in New Rochelle, NY

period: Twentieth century

Joan Tower's experiences as a performer have, to a large extent, influenced the course she has pursued as a composer. Her early compositions, scored primarily for solo instruments or chamber ensembles, reflect the pointillistic and rhythmically complex music she played with various groups during the 1960s. These works also hinted at her future path, a time when she would concentrate more on tonal color, compositional balance, the exploration of musical space, and the shape and energy of a musical line. Among her best works are the orchestral piece *Silver Ladders,* and *Night Fields* for string quartet.

Though born in New Rochelle, New York, Tower grew up in South America where her father was a mining engineer. After absorbing the native culture and playing piano and percussion in family music sessions, she returned to the United States at age eighteen. She attended Bennington College and later received a doctorate in composition from Columbia University. In 1969, Tower founded the Da Capo Chamber Players, serving as pianist for its first fifteen years. This prestigious ensemble won the Naumburg Award for Chamber Music in 1973 in addition to commissioning and premiering many of her most popular works including *Platinum Spirals, Hexachords, Wings, Petroushskates,* and *Amazon I.*

Music for Cello and Orchestra, Tower's one-movement concerto from 1984, is typical of her large-style works. Written for her long-time collaborator André Emelianoff and the conductor Gerard Schwarz, this dramatic piece is surprisingly reminiscent of Vivaldi in its use of moving rhythms. In September 1985, Tower was appointed by Leonard Slatkin to a three-year period as composer-in-residence with the Saint Louis Symphony. Her piano concerto from that year (subtitled *Homage to Beethoven*) was inspired by three Beethoven sonatas (the *Tempest,* the *Waldstein,* and op. 111) and is stylistically similar to the cello piece, even sharing some musical materials. In the late 1980s Tower exhibited a new musical assertiveness and penchant for taking risks in many of her compositions, including the concertos for clarinet (1988) and flute (1989). Tower has said that she tries to see how high she can push a work's energy level without making it chaotic or incoherent, a methodology evident in both of those works. Another piece written during her St. Louis residency, *Silver Ladders,* received the prestigious Grawemeyer Award for Music Composition in 1990 and has been hailed by critics as "a well-built, well-crafted...exciting piece.... a dynamic contribution to the modern orchestral literature." Tower's work during this period also includes *Island Rhythms,* a celebratory overture for orchestra; *Clocks* (for solo guitar), which draws inspiration from both Franz Joseph Haydn and flamenco music; and *Fanfare for the Uncommon Woman,* a chamber work honoring both Aaron Copland and adventurous, risk-taking women.

This last-mentioned piece continues to stimulate Tower's imagination and she has thus far composed a series of five *Uncommon Woman* works, each for different instrumental combinations. The *Third Fanfare for the Uncommon Woman,* commissioned by Carnegie Hall for its centennial celebration, premiered during the televised concert on May 5, 1991. *For the Uncommon Woman* (for orchestra) was originally titled *Fanfare No. 4,* but changed by Tower when she felt she'd stretched the fanfare definition too far. Nonetheless, *Fanfare for the Uncommon Woman No. 5* was commissioned by the

Michael Tilson Thomas:
Born in Los Angeles, California on December 21, 1944, Michael Tilson Thomas learned to play piano while attending the University of Southern California's prep school. He continued his musical education at the University of Southern California, where he studied with Ingolf Dahl and John Crown. While still a student there, Thomas also managed to take part in premieres of works by Aaron Copland, Igor Stravinsky, Pierre Boulez, Karlheinz Stockhausen, and Dahl, his composition teacher. In 1968 Thomas moved to the East Coast, where he had a conducting fellowship at the Boston Symphony Orchestra's summer home, the Berkshire Music Center at Tanglewood. During the next year, Thomas won the Koussevitzky Prize and was then appointed assistant conductor of the BSO. He later became associate conductor for that orchestra and took part in one of the finest recordings of his career with them, an album containing music by three American composers: Charles Ives (*Three Places in New England*), Carl Ruggles (*Sun Treader*), and Walter Piston (Symphony no. 2).

Thomas was named music director of the Buffalo Philharmonic Orchestra in 1971. For some time after leaving that position in 1979, despite holding other posts with the Los Angeles Philharmonic Orchestra and the Great Woods Music Festival, most of his career was spent as a guest conductor at numerous venues in North America and Europe. In 1988 he helped establish the New World Symphony, an ongoing organization based in Miami, Florida which helps prepare selected music students for life as orchestra musicians, offering intensive three-year fellowship programs that include tours to other cities in the United States and around the world. Thomas has also taken these students into the recording studio, where he has led them in highly acclaimed performances of music by Heitor Villa-Lobos (*Alma Brasileira*, RCA Victor Red Seal 68538) and Morton Feldman (*Coptic Light,* Argo 448513), and a program featuring jazz-oriented scores by George Gershwin, Leonard Bernstein, Darius Milhaud, and others (*New World Jazz,* RCA Victor Red Seal 68798). When all is said and done, there is a distinct possibility that this ever-evolving ensemble (which he still serves as artistic director) will be Thomas's most enduring legacy.

In 1995 he joined the San Francisco Symphony Orchestra as their music director, and it is with them that he appears to have found his greatest degree of commercial acceptance, winning Grammy Awards first in 1996 with a recording of Sergei Prokofiev's ballet *Romeo and Juliet,* and again in 1999 for performances of Igor Stravinsky's three ballets, *L'Oiseau de feu (The Firebird), Le sacre du printemps (The Rite of Spring),* and *Perséphone* (RCA Victor Red Seal 68898).

William Gerard

Aspen Music Festival for the inaugural concert of the Joan and Irving Harris Concert Hall in 1993.

Throughout the 1990s Tower continued to create vibrant works. Her first ballet score, *Stepping Stones,* was created with choreographer Kathryn Posin and premiered by the Milwaukee Ballet in April 1993. She also composed her first piece for string quartet: *Night Fields,* a one-movement work that was commissioned by Hancher

Auditorium, the University of Iowa, and the Snowbird Institute for the Arts and Humanities. The same year Tower composed *Très Lent* for Cello and Piano (subtitled *Hommage à Messiaen*) in honor of the French composer Olivier Messiaen, whose radical and mystical music revealed an alternate path to the strict serialism in which Tower had been trained. Modeled after Messiaen's *Quartet for the End of Time,* which Tower had performed with the Da Capo Chamber Players, her piece mirrors Messiaen's long, broad melodic lines. Other scores written during the 1990s include her one-movement chamber work *Turning Points,* which once again draws inspiration from Beethoven, and her first piece for organ, *Ascent.*

Orchestral
Silver Ladders for Orchestra
worth searching for: [Leonard Slatkin, cond.; Saint Louis Symphony Orch.] (Nonesuch 79245) ♪ ♪ ♪ ♪ ♪

A work of sheer power and subtle delicacy, the twists and turns of this piece are eloquently presented by the Saint Louis Symphony under Slatkin's capable direction. The orchestra is also featured in excellent performances of Tower's *Sequoia* for Orchestra (a re-release of the 1984 recording); *Island Prelude* for Oboe and String Orchestra (with soloist Peter Bowman); and *Music for Cello and Orchestra* (with the cellist Lynn Harrell). There's rarely gaiety or playfulness in Tower's complex and intriguing music but her earnestness and formidable talent allow the composer to create brawny compositions full of excitement, color, and texture.

Chamber
Night Fields for String Quartet
what to buy: [*Black Topaz,* Muir Quartet, ensemble] (New World Records 80470) ♪ ♪ ♪ ♪ ♪

This is a string quartet piece of churning, dark intensity, a quality which the Muir Quartet realizes with the fullest passion and stunning virtuosity. The album contains a treasure chest of modern Tower works, including *Snow Dreams* for Flute and Guitar performed by flautist Carol Wincenc and guitarist Sharon Isbin; *Black Topaz* for Piano and Six Instruments played by the Group for Contemporary Music with pianist Robert Miller; *Très Lent* for Cello and Piano performed by Tower and cellist André Emelianoff; and the two-piano version of *Stepping Stones* featuring Edmund Niemann and Nurit Tilles. Varied pieces and performers showcasing Tower's

extraordinary compositional skills in a variety of formats make this a must-own album.

influences: Arnold Schoenberg, Olivier Messiaen, Elliott Carter

Nancy Ann Lee

Joaquín Turina
Born Joaquín Turina y Perez, December 9, 1882, in Seville, Spain. Died January 14, 1949, in Madrid, Spain.

period: Twentieth century

Even though much of Turina's music utilizes Spanish folk elements as a core, the composer consciously brought in Impressionist influences that he picked up during his studies in Paris. This made his compositions closer to the pan-European model subtly espoused by Manuel de Falla than the specifically Spanish style adopted by their near-contemporaries Isaac Albéniz and Enrique Granados. However, like his three compatriots, Turina's oeuvre contains a healthy dose of music written for the piano, either solo or in small groups, and it is for these works that he is best known.

Turina first began taking piano lessons upon demonstrating a passion for music (something which manifested itself soon after he received an accordion when he was four years old), and in 1894 he began studying counterpoint at the Colegio de San Miguel with Evaristo García Torres. Turina's first orchestral work, *Las Coplas al Señor de Pasión,* was premiered and conducted by the composer in 1900, but it was part of his juvenilia, and Turina later refused to acknowledge any of the works he wrote prior to 1907 as part of his official canon. He had begun studying music in Madrid with José Tragó in 1904 prior to leaving for Paris in 1905; he enrolled at the Schola Cantorum there in January of the following year. It was at this institution that the young composer studied with Vincent d'Indy, became enamored of Claude Debussy's works, and was introduced to Paul Dukas, Manuel de Falla, and Isaac Albéniz. The young Spaniard's Quintet for Piano and Strings was given its first performance in 1907 and Albéniz was so impressed with the piece (and its composer's musical potential) that he subsidized the initial press run for the work. He also suggested that Turina explore the music of his homeland for ideas upon which to base future scores, a concept that the young composer would adapt in his own fashion without abandoning the Impressionist fla-vorings he had picked up during his Parisian studies. After graduating in 1913, Turina returned to Spain, final-ly establishing Madrid as his home in 1914.

By this time Turina had married and established a fami-ly, which meant that he needed to find some way of bringing cash into the household. Thus, the young com-poser set about generating income by developing his reputation as an artist and establishing himself as a con-ductor, pianist, music critic, and teacher. To this end, he worked as a conductor with Sergei Diaghilev's Ballets Russes, served as pianist for both the Cuarteto Francés and the Quinteto de Madrid, and signed an agreement with the Unión Musical Española to compose piano works for them. This last turn of events resulted in a lot of weak material churned out to satisfy the terms of his contract, but one of his best-known works, a piano reduction of his earlier *Danzas fantásticas,* also came out of this period. Turina's career in academia started in 1920 when he taught some music history classes at the Circulo de Belles Artes.

In 1921, Turina developed the first in a series of unspec-ified illnesses which would interfere with his ability to work free from pain during the remaining course of his life. This was not to be his only tribulation, however. In 1932, just one year after he had won an appointment to the Madrid Conservatory faculty as chair of the compo-sition department, the second of his five children (María) died when she was only nineteen years old. With the eruption of the Spanish Civil War, Turina—who was not a particular favorite of the Republicans—stopped com-posing and teaching altogether. During this time he joined the staff of the British consulate as an archivist, which saved him from overt persecution, and his illness became increasingly distressful.

Finally, after the end of the war, Turina emerged into public life again, resuming his teaching duties at the Conservatory and adding to them some teaching respon-sibilities at the Real Academia de Bellas Artes de San Fernando. By 1940, Turina, who was a generally pleas-ant person and well-liked by the bulk of his contempo-raries, became one of the three members of the Comisaría General de la Música, a division of the Ministry of Education that oversaw music instruction throughout the country. Most of his finest works—the *Danzas fantásticas,* his piano quartet (op. 67), and the second piano trio (op. 76)—had already been written, and though Turina would continue composing music up

until 1946, the bulk of his energies were absorbed by his academic work and the writing of his two-volume *Tratado de composición (Treatise on Composition).* While he meant to produce a third volume of this text, he was only able to complete about eight pages before entering a clinic to undergo an experimental treatment for his increasingly devastating illness. Despite the best hopes of his family and friends, this effort was not suc-cessful and Turina died just over a month after beginning the therapy.

Chamber
Quartet for Piano and Strings, op. 67
what to buy: [Ensemble Variable] (CPO 999609) ♪ ♪ ♪ ♪

Turina packed the first movement of this piece with a winning combination of drama and hummable, memo-rable melodies. The wonder of this work is that the com-poser could keep up that level of inspiration from begin-ning to end. It is difficult to imagine a more right-sound-ing performance of this piece than the one given by the Ensemble Variable and, by tossing in excellent rendi-tions of Turina's Sonata no. 2 for Violin and Piano as well as an excerpt from his *Musas de Andalucia,* op. 93, they have made this one of the best discs to introduce the composer to the listener. Two pieces by Granados, his *Romanza* for Violin and Piano and the Quintet for Piano and Strings, fill out this fine set.

Danzas fantásticas for Piano, op. 22
what to buy: [*Obras para piano*; Albert Guinovart, piano] (Harmonia Mundi France 987009) ♪ ♪ ♪ ♪

Guinovart's articulation is clear yet supple all through this recital, and there might not be a finer version of Turina's *Danzas fantásticas* than his. Another plus is the basic programming of the disc, which makes sure to include most of the composer's finest works for solo piano, especially the two sets (opp. 55 and 84) of *Danzas gitanas* and the intriguing, seldom-played *Concierto sin orquesta,* op. 88.

worth searching for: [*Obras para piano*; Alicia de Larrocha, piano] (EMI Classics 64528) ♪ ♪ ♪ ♪

De Larrocha's dedication to exposing Spanish piano music has long been documented, and while her efforts on behalf of Turina fail to reach the heights of her work on scores by Albéniz, de Falla, or Federico Mompou, this is still an admirable collection. While she includes only excerpts from the *Danzas andaluzas* and *Danzas gitanas* (the full versions of which are on Guinovart's disc), she does present *Sanlúcar de Barrameda,* an interesting score written shortly after the *Danzas fantásticas.*

influences: Federico Mompou, Conrado del Campo, Manuel de Falla, Isaac Albéniz, Enrique Granados

Garaud MacTaggart

Edgard Varèse

Born Edgard Victor Achille Charles Varèse, December 22, 1883, in Paris. Died November 6, 1965, in New York City, NY

period: Twentieth century

One of the twentieth century's true musical visionaries, Varèse sought a music entirely free of reliance upon past masters and the constraint and limitations of conventional instruments. Varèse was the first to use electronics in compositions, and his influence has been acknowledged by a number of successors, most notably Pierre Boulez and Frank Zappa.

The wildly-coiffured Varèse was a radical from the get-go. After leaving his studies in science at the École Polytechnique, he began his formal musical training in Paris at the Schola Cantorum and later the Paris Conservatoire. Around 1912 he fell under the spell of Arnold Schoenberg's music while living in Berlin and he then introduced Schoenberg's works to his compatriot, Claude Debussy. Varèse was also close with Ferruccio Busoni, whom he had met in Berlin and whose theories on modern music the impressionable composer took with him to New York City in the winter of 1915. His earliest surviving works show a fascination with percussion and novel sounds inspired by the harsh urban landscape of what was soon to be his adoptive home. *Amériques,* a bold and propulsive work for a 142-player orchestra, was as uncompromising as anything yet written, and it was certain from that point onward that the composer would never enjoy any commercial success. As the United States was largely unaware of developments in modern music, Varèse helped found the International Composers Guild and later the Pan-American Association of Composers, securing an audience for

both his music and the scores of his contemporaries in musical experimentation.

In *Intégrales,* first heard in 1925, Varèse makes use of the giant "blocks of sound" that can be found in his subsequent works. There is no trace here of melody or of dissectible harmony—rather a simultaneity of sonority—and he uses an instinctual, polarizing process of layering sounds to create a violent effect, capped by a loud and visceral barrage of percussion. The pioneering *Ionisation* came in 1931, scored for percussion alone, and is considered to be the first Western work for such an instrumentation. In addition to a whirring siren and a wild assortment of pitched and non-pitched percussion, Varèse uses the resonant piano in this work for its percussive properties. The performer is asked to hurl his fists and level his forearms to create the violent tone clusters used largely by later composers (though none with Varese's gallant assurance).

The primal *Ecuatorial,* a Mayan incantation scored for bass voice, brass, percussion, organ, and the ondes martenot—a French electronic invention—was followed by a piece for solo platinum flute with the curious title *Density 21.5* (the molecular density of the element platinum). Along with Debussy's *Syrinx,* this work with its harmonic implications became a prototype for later pieces that used an unaccompanied melody instrument.

Nearly a decade of compositional silence halted in 1954 with the premiere of *Déserts* for winds, brass, percussion, and electronic tape. This riot-provoking premiere was surpassed only by Igor Stravinsky's *Rite of Spring,* which had coincidentally had its first staging forty-one years earlier in the same venue, Paris' fabled Théâtre des Champs-Elysées. It was clear now, if there had ever been any doubt, that Varèse was charting heretofore unexplored areas. Indeed, he scorned most of his contemporaries, including Schoenberg and Stravinsky, the musical giants of the twentieth century's tumultuous first half. Varèse was calling for a new energy of "organized sound" and his apocalyptic vision sought new ways to give voice to the palpable landscape of his imagination. Electronics were a means to this end and the pre-recorded tape for *Déserts* includes sounds from factories, sawmills, and foundries—all mechanical noises that the composer found disturbingly beautiful.

Now in his 70s, Varèse repeated his electronic experiments with the influential *Poème électronique,* a work that was meant to be played over 400 spatially-distributed speakers at the Philips Pavilion, a structure designed by Le Corbusier and Iannis Xenakis for the 1958 World's Fair in Brussels. Varèse was hailed as a modernist genius by (among others) Pierre Boulez, who brought Varèse's music to the American public and regularly conducted it (particularly with the New York Philharmonic).

Even the best music of Varèse is difficult to listen to. Horns, whistles, clanging percussion, taped noises—these are the elements that make up the unique sound-world of this intrepid explorer. But Varèse sought to reinvent the public's definition of music and his pieces sound as fresh and as novel today as they did when they were premiered. His ideas influenced whole generations of composers and musicians, from the members of the French and German avant-garde to Frank Zappa, who claimed that Varèse did more to shape his own musical visions than any other musician. The aging enfant terrible was continually searching for a wider, more diverse means of musical expression—something littered with the kinetic noises of industry and aided by the newest developments in technology—envisioning and constructing a futuristic sound-world seemingly beyond possibility.

Orchestral
various compositions
what to buy: [*Varèse: The Complete Works*; Ricardo Chailly, cond; ASKO Ensemble, Royal Concertgebouw Orchestra] (London 460208) ♪ ♪ ♪ ♪

The two-CD complete edition of Varèse's work features some incredible playing under the baton of one of the world's great conductors and was nominated for a Grammy Award. The first disc uses the forces of the Royal Concertgebouw Orchestra for the larger pieces, while the second disc belongs to the smaller ASKO Ensemble and is a near duplicate of the Attacca set mentioned below.

Intégrales for Eleven Winds and Four Percussionists
what to buy: [ASKO Ensemble] (Attacca Babel 9263) ♪ ♪ ♪♪

Though it is tough to find, this CD features some incredible playing on four of Varèse's compositions including *Déserts, Ionisation,* and a *Poème électronique* that utilizes the original stereo versions of the four-track electronic tape the composer made for this piece.

Ecuatorial for Orchestra
what to buy: [Maurice Abravanel, cond.; Utah Symphony Orchestra] (Vanguard Classics 4031) ♪ ♪ ♪♪

This early recording (1968) by an underrated American orchestra finds this key work coupled with two other pieces by Varèse (*Amériques* and *Nocturnal* for Soprano and Orchestra), with Arthur Honegger's *Pacific 231* completing this program featuring masterworks of the machine age.

Ionisation for Thirteen Percussionists
what to buy: [*The Works of Edgar Varèse, vol. 2*; Kent Nagano, cond.; Orchestre National de France] (Erato 14332) ♪ ♪ ♪♪

Still one of the greats, Nagano's penetrating reading of this piece and five other Varèse works (including *Déserts*) is brazen and exciting. The percussion barrage is wonderfully fierce.

influences: Pierre Boulez, Karlheinz Stockhausen, André Jolivet, George Antheil, Iannis Xenakis, Frank Zappa

Sean Hickey

Ralph Vaughan Williams
Born October 12, 1872, in Down Ampney, England. Died August 26, 1958, in London, England.

period: Twentieth century

Ralph Vaughan Williams was a remarkable musical personality—not only the most important English composer of his generation, but also a key figure in the modern revival of English music. He was one of the finest symphonists of the 20th century, a towering figure whose accomplishments grow only greater with the passage of time. He is perhaps best known to American audiences for the lush string writing heard in *The Lark Ascending, Fantasia on "Greensleeves,"* and the strikingly beautiful *Fantasia on a Theme of Thomas Tallis.*

VW (as he is often called) studied at the Royal College of Music and at Cambridge University, where he eventually earned a doctorate—a most unusual accomplishment for a composer at the time. He studied briefly with the great French Impressionist composer Maurice Ravel in 1908 and this influence can be heard in a number of

his later compositions, particularly the hauntingly beautiful *Flos Campi* for solo viola, wordless chorus, and orchestra. He enlisted in the British Army at the outbreak of World War I, and some of his personal impressions and experiences in France while serving with the medical corps found expression in his lovely Third Symphony, subtitled the *Pastoral*. Following the war he returned to the Royal College of Music, where he taught from 1919 to 1938. Vaughan Williams visited the United States in 1922, 1932, and 1954, conducting his own works and lecturing at such institutions as Bryn Mawr College and Cornell University. Just as Benjamin Britten was to do years later, he refused a knighthood, but was given the Order of Merit in 1935 (the year he produced the Fourth Symphony).

His nine symphonies, written between 1906 and 1958, cover an enormous range of musical and emotional expression, and in this regard are comparable to the 15 symphonies of the great 20th-century Russian master, Dmitri Shostakovich. Vaughan Williams conducted the first-ever recording of one of his symphonies in 1937, the Fourth with the BBC Symphony Orchestra. Although he was not a first-rate conductor in the usual sense—the power, thrust, and almost demonic fury which he elicited from the orchestra on this occasion have never been surpassed. During Word War II he helped organize the celebrated lunchtime concerts at the National Gallery in London and contributed much to the organization which is now the Arts Council of Great Britain. Following its premiere in 1948, his Sixth Symphony was performed 100 times during the next two years—a record for an English symphony surpassed only by Edward Elgar's First in 1908 and a remarkable accomplishment for any symphony in the 20th century.

Vaughan Williams developed slowly, both musically and technically, and it was not until the 1920s that his unique and unmistakable personality began to emerge. As a measure of his wide-ranging genius, it is interesting to note that at every stage of his development he wrote works ranging from the simple to the complex and even visionary. He helped to re-create an English musical language, and was a founder of what is now referred to as the English Nationalist Movement. Vaughan Williams wrote in every form, and virtually all of his mature works were permeated by English folksong, as well as influences from early English music. While he

Ralph Vaughan Williams

Tokyo String Quartet:
Although this group started off in 1969 as four Japanese musicians playing the music of European composers, it has evolved into a more internationally diverse ensemble, albeit one with the same high reputation for technical expertise. The current membership includes violinists Mikhail Kopelman and Kikuei Ikeda, violist Kazuhide Isomura, and cellist Clive Greensmith.

The original quartet studied with members of the Juilliard String Quartet when they first came to the United States, and this was reflected in much of their repertoire from that time, including works by Béla Bartók and members of the Second Viennese School. Most of the quartet's programs since then, however (with the notable exception of Toru Takemitsu's *A Way a Lone*, which was written specifically for them), seem to lean heavily toward classics by Franz Joseph Haydn, Ludwig van Beethoven, and Wolfgang Amadeus Mozart, with a smattering of Romantic and early twentieth century works thrown in.

Since 1976, the members of the group have been on the faculty at the Yale School of Music, but they have also worked with students at the University of Cincinnati's College-Conservatory of Music, taken a residency at Stanford University, and taught various master classes throughout the United States. In 1995 they began playing on instruments made by Stradivarius which were loaned to them by the current owner (the Nippon Music Foundation) and were once the property of the fabled violinist/composer Niccolò Paganini.

Their recording of Bartók's six string quartets won the *Gramophone* magazine award for Chamber Music in 1981 but, like most of the Grammy Award-nominated recordings the group has done (including their treatment of Takemitsu's *A Way a Lone*, RCA Victor Red Seal 61387), it is out of print domestically—though still available as an import (Deutsche Grammophon 445241). Of the group's discs which still are in print, the recording of Johannes Brahms's three string quartets and Franz Schubert's *Death and the Maiden* quartet and *Quartettsatz* (Vox 5179) is excellent, and dates from the early 1980s when Peter Oundjian was first violinist and Sadao Harada was their cellist. The clarinet quintets by Brahms and Carl Maria von Weber (RCA Victor Red Seal 68033) find the quartet meshing their talents with Richard Stoltzman's fluid clarinet artistry in exquisite performances.

Ian Palmer

seldom used actual folksongs in his orchestral and instrumental works, he had absorbed the idiom so thoroughly that it affected practically everything he wrote. He never adopted any particular method of composition but sampled from a great variety of procedures, welding them into his own distinctive style.

He also had a life-long love for the poetry of the great American writer Walt Whitman, and this inspired some of his finest choral compositions, including the vocal section of his First Symphony and the cantata *Dona nobis pacem*. In addition, Vaughan Williams wrote eleven movie scores, with the best-known being the one he created for the 1948 film *Scott of the Antarctic*. He eventually worked some of the material from this score into his Seventh Symphony, the *Sinfonia antartica*. His creative powers kept expanding in his old age, and towards the end of his life he began experimenting with unusual instruments and sonorities. Three of the most interesting works from this period are the Romance in D flat major for Harmonica and Orchestra, the Concerto in F minor for Bass Tuba and Orchestra, and the Eighth Symphony, which features a huge percussion section. As a teacher, VW had a great gift for encouraging and showing pupils how to be themselves, and was always greatly supportive of and helpful to younger composers.

The man took part in a wide range of musical activities throughout all of his life as composer, conductor, teacher, writer, and lecturer. His outlook was human and social: he felt strongly that music was for people and was interested in every situation in which music played a part. This "extraordinary ordinary man" (as biographer Michael Kennedy so beautifully put it) became an English institution, and when he died his loss was felt all over the country, both musically and personally.

Orchestral
Fantasia on a Theme by Thomas Tallis for double string orchestra
what to buy: [*The English Connection*; Neville Marriner, cond.; Academy of St. Martin-in-the-Fields, orch.] (ASV 518) ♪ ♪ ♪ ♪

Based on a melody by the 16th-century English composer Tallis, this justly famous piece set the standard for the English "Pastoral" school of composers. Marriner is afforded a clean, spacious recording for this well chosen recital, and the members of the Academy provide a marvelous string section for the headline work and another short gem from the composer's pen, *The Lark Ascending*. Edward Elgar's Serenade for Strings in E minor, op. 20 and Michael Tippett's *Fantasia concertante on a Theme of Corelli* fill up the balance of the program.

The Lark Ascending for violin and orchestra
what to buy: [Hugh Bean, violin; Adrian Boult, cond.; New Philharmonia Orchestra] (EMI Classics 64022) ♪ ♪ ♪ ♪

In addition to a wonderful rendition of the composer's

romance, *The Lark Ascending*, there are five other fine examples of VW's short orchestral works included here: the *Serenade to Music, English Folksong Suite, Norfolk Rhapsody no. 1, Fantasia on Greensleeves*, and *In the Fen Country*. Boult, who knew the composer intimately, conducted many first performances, and was a tireless champion of his music, has the measure of all of these pieces. This is an outstanding introduction to the works of one of the greatest of all 20th-century composers.

Symphony no. 1 for soprano, baritone, orchestra, and chorus—*A Sea Symphony*
what to buy: [Sheila Armstrong, soprano; John Carol Case, baritone; Adrian Boult, cond.; London Philharmonic Orchestra; London Philharmonic Chorus] (EMI Classics 64016) ♪ ♪ ♪ ♪

Boult has a long history with this work, having first recorded it during the early '50s under the composer's supervision. Vaughan Williams's respect for Walt Whitman's poetry shows in the sensitive manner with which he set the texts that provide the heart of this intriguing work. The performances are solid, as could be expected from such a well-known advocate for the composer, and so is the engineering.

worth searching for: [Isobel Baillie, soprano; John Cameron, baritone; Adrian Boult, cond.; London Philharmonic Orchestra; London Philharmonic Chorus] (Belart 450144) ♪ ♪ ♪ ♪

This performance of the early *A Sea Symphony* is extraordinarily fine, and in many respects has never been surpassed. The recording was re-issued by Belart, a mid-price reissue subsidiary of Decca/London, but a label which has never been made regularly available in the United States. These magnificent readings, conducted by one of the composer's greatest interpreters, are of prime importance to anyone interested in Vaughan Williams and his symphonic output.

Symphony no. 4 in F Minor
what to buy: [André Previn, cond.; London Symphony Orchestra] (RCA Gold Seal 60583) ♪ ♪ ♪ ♪

Previn couples the savage and violent Fourth Symphony with Vaughan Williams's lovely, lyrical, and almost mystical Third Symphony (the *Pastoral*), presenting two contrasting sides of the composer's multi-faceted personality. When Symphony no.4 was premiered under Adrian Boult's direction in 1935, it startled an entire nation.

Previn, who has proven to be a great champion of 20th-century British music, elicits fine performances from the LSO and the recording is clear but atmospheric.

Symphony no. 5 in D Major
what to buy: [Vernon Handley, cond.; Royal Liverpool Philharmonic Orchestra] (Classics for Pleasure 9512) ♪ ♪ ♪ ♪₈

For many, the beautiful and radiant Fifth is the greatest of all of Vaughan Williams's symphonies, and this superb performance under Handley's direction ranks along with the finest recordings ever made of this inspired work. The composer's lovely suite for solo viola, orchestra, and chorus, *Flos Campi,* is a wonderful addition to the program.

Symphony no. 7 for Soprano, Orchestra, and Chorus—*Sinfonia antartica*
what to buy: [Sheila Armstrong, soprano; Bernard Haitink, cond.; London Philharmonic Orchestra] (EMI Classics 47516) ♪ ♪ ♪ ♪₈

Although some are wont to dismiss this unusual work as merely dressed-up film music, it is anything but that, as this powerful and magisterial performance demonstrates. It is a world of unique atmosphere and haunting impressions, and the wide-ranging sound only serves to underscore the greatness of the music and the performance.

Job (masque for dancing) for Orchestra
what to buy: [Vernon Handley, cond.; London Philharmonic Orchestra] (EMI Classics For Pleasure 4603) ♪ ♪ ♪ ♪₈

Job is one of Vaughan William's greatest works—some would even say his masterpiece. This is perhaps its finest-ever recording, revealing the true power and inspiration of the score. Handley and company have delivered an outstanding achievement in every way and, at mid-price, one well worth seeking out.

influences: Frederick Delius, Gerald Finzi, Peter Warlock, Gustav Holst, Maurice Ravel

Charles Greenwell and Dave Wagner

Giuseppe Verdi
Born Giuseppe Fortunino Francesco Verdi, c. October 10, 1813, in Roncole, Italy. Died January 27, 1901, in Milan, Italy.

period: Romantic

Giuseppe Verdi essentially took the bel canto (beautiful singing) style pioneered by Gaetano Donizetti and Vincenzo Bellini and injected it with heroics, family drama, and great clashes of melodrama, thereby becoming one of the most popular Italian opera composers in history. His innovations in handling text would later result in the creation of the verismo (truth) sub-genre which found its fullest expression in the works of Giacomo Puccini, Ruggero Leoncavallo, and Pietro Mascagni.

A gifted youngster, Verdi was born in the village of Roncole, took music lessons from the local organist, and, upon the death of his teacher, acquired some of the responsibilities for that position; he was only nine years old at the time. Antonio Barezzi, a merchant who had become a driving force in the local Philharmonic Society, saw the young man's talent and more or less subsidized him for the next few years, taking Verdi into his household where the young man lived with Barezzi's own children and began creating his first rudimentary compositions.

At the age of nineteen, he was rejected for admission to the Milan Conservatory, in part due to lack of room on the rolls for someone over the age-limit for entry, a circumstance which Verdi would subsequently "remember" as a comment on his lack of musical talent rather than accepting the decision at face value. In his later years, this single-minded sense of self would also allow Verdi to use his rejection as an opportunity to rail against conservatory training and promote the myth of his having been mostly self-taught. (Verdi's attitude toward reality and legend-building would be elucidated more directly in 1883 when he wrote a letter to his publisher about the libretto to *Don Carlos* in which he noted, "To copy truth can be good, but to invent truth is better, far better.") With the Milan Conservatory now beyond his reach, he began studying composition and counterpoint privately with Vincenzo Lavigna, a former member of the orchestra at La Scala.

In 1839, at the age of twenty-six, Verdi's first opera, *Oberto, Conte di San Bonifacio* premiered at La Scala, followed a year later by his second, *Un giorno di regno.* Neither of these scores were big hits though *Oberto* showed box office promise, but *Un giorno di regno* became his first massive flop, and the source of a deep depression for the young composer. The manager of La

Scala had evidently realized Verdi's potential, however, and managed to persuade him to take the libretto for what would become his first great success, *Nabucco,* in 1842. For the next eight years, Verdi churned out a number of solidly received operas including the first of his works based on Shakespearean sources, 1847's *Macbeth.*

Verdi was a composer who worked closely with librettists, driving them to create texts which would best serve the music he had in mind for the projects. Francesco Maria Piave was the person with whom Verdi worked the most during the years of his greatest fame, 1851–1869, supplying the words for such popular favorites as *Rigoletto, La traviata,* and *La forza del destino.* The only great opera from this period which Piave did not supply the text for was *Il trovatore* (1853), which had a script by Salvatore Cammarano, who had worked with Verdi on three of his earlier projects—*Alzira* (1845), *La battaglia de Legnano* (1849), and *Luisa Miller* (1849)—but whose greatest artistic achievement up to that point had been his libretto for Donizetti's *Lucia di Lammermoor.*

Verdi's next major opera, *Don Carlos,* was the third of his works (after 1855's *Les vêpres siciliennes* and the revised version of *Macbeth* from 1865) to be premiered in Paris—unless one counts *Jérusalem* which reset the libretto for the composer's earlier work, *I lombardi,* in 1847. Along with *Aida, Otello,* and *Falstaff, Don Carlos* marks the high water mark of Verdi's oeuvre, if not from a popularity standpoint, certainly from an artistic one. In fact, the five acts of *Don Carlos* proved to be a formidable drawback to performance, with the Parisian run that began in 1867 proving briefer than usual (given the status of the composer) as costs mounted and receipts dwindled; cuts in the first act and the exclusion of the ballet proved to be the only way that some opera houses would even consider mounting productions of this work.

Aida was a commission by the Khedive of Egypt that was originally set to premiere in Cairo in celebration of the opening of the Suez Canal. Perhaps his most monumental work, the famous triumphal scene in *Aida* has been a source of great excess in productions the world over. The opera's arias and beautiful chorus writing are its heart and soul; a love triangle and a father-daughter relationship its raison d'etre. The success that *Aida* has had since its debut in 1871 could not have been foreseen given the logistic difficulties of mounting the composer's

elaborate staging; in fact, the Khedive was subsequently recalled for administrative incompetence.

After the initial staging of *Aida,* Verdi more or less "retired" from life as an operatic composer but this didn't mean that he stopped creating music. The following years saw him concentrating to a large degree on sacred works such as his setting of the *Requiem* (1874–1875) and the *Quattro pezzi sacri,* four separate works which were written between 1889 and 1898 and published as one in the latter year. First, however, he completed his Quartet in E Minor for Strings in 1873. This was a score which Verdi probably didn't wish to see published, though a few people were aware of the music, especially the friends who attended a private performance of the revised edition in 1884.

Otello and *Falstaff* are the final hurrahs of a great opera composer, with librettos by Arrigo Boito fashioned from Shakespeare's plays. *Otello* was actually begun in the late 1870s when Verdi was in the midst of his "retirement," but the chance to set another work by his favorite playwright proved to be more attractive than he could resist. Eventually the project premiered at La Scala in 1887. *Falstaff,* a blend of Shakespeare's *The Merry Wives of Windsor* and *King Henry IV,* was the first comedic opera in Verdi's oeuvre since his first big box office failure *Un giorno di regno,* and debuted, also at La Scala, in 1893.

Orchestral
various overtures
what to buy: [*Verdi: Overtures and Preludes*; Herbert von Karajan, cond.; Berlin Philharmonic Orchestra] (Deutsche Grammophon 453058) ♪ ♪ ♪ ♪ ♪

This two-disc set is an affordable, well-recorded collection of Verdi's most accessible orchestral music. Scores from some of his most popular operas (*Rigoletto, Aida, La Traviata,* etc.) are represented, but so too are selections from his earlier, less well-known works including *Giovanna d'Arco, Alzira,* and *I masnadieri.*

Quartet in E Minor for Strings (arranged for orchestra by Arturo Toscanini)
what to buy: [André Previn, cond.; Vienna Philharmonic Orchestra] (Deutsche Grammophon 463579) ♪ ♪ ♪ ♪

Toscanini's reworking of Verdi's lone major chamber work is finely crafted and worth more than a few listens, especially when performed and recorded as well as it is in this set. It is also something that Verdi himself once toyed with, saying "there are certain passages which require a fuller sonority than a mere quartet can furnish." The accompanying orchestration of Beethoven's Quartet in C-sharp Minor for Strings (op. 131) by Dimitri Mitropoulos is a bit more of a stretch, despite the committed performances by all concerned. The orchestration of Beethoven gilds the lily and doesn't work as well.

Chamber
Quartet in E Minor for Strings
what to buy: [Juilliard String Quartet, ensemble] (Sony Classics 48193) ♪ ♪ ♪ ♪

This recording pairs two distinct composers whose reputations were made in totally different fields: Jean Sibelius and Giuseppe Verdi. Neither of their scores for string quartet are performed all that often, though Sibelius has the edge in that regard. Still, it is good to hear Verdi's own, well-crafted essay in the form, a work that is more than a souvenir and one that fleshes out the composer's oeuvre quite well. The Juilliard String Quartet offers taut performances of both pieces with the nod actually going to Verdi, partially because there are better renditions of the Sibelius work available.

what to buy next: [Melos Quartett, ensemble] (Harmonia Mundi 901671) ♪ ♪ ♪♪

The Melos Quartett duplicates the program of the Juilliard Quartet on this set. While not quite as lean and acerbic in the Sibelius as is the other group, the Melos Quartett offers a rather full-sounding recording that compares quite favorably in Verdi's sole quartet.

Vocal
Requiem Mass for Soprano, Alto, Tenor, Bass, Orchestra, and Chorus (*In Memory of Mazoni*)
what to buy: [*Arturo Toscanini, vol. 11: Verdi and Cherubini Choral Works*; Herva Nelli, soprano; Fedora Barbieri, mezzo-soprano; Giuseppe di Stefano, tenor; Cesare Siepi, bass; Arturo Toscanini, cond.; NBC Symphony Orchestra; Robert Shaw Chorale] (RCA Victor 72373) ♪ ♪ ♪ ♪♪

The remastering process for this *Requiem* has returned one of the finest Toscanini performances to the catalog. Partnering it with his conducting in Verdi's *Quattro pezzi sacri (Four Sacred Pieces)* makes sense, but the real bonus in this two-disc set is Toscanini's amazing version of Luigi Cherubini's *Requiem* in C Minor.

Arturo Toscanini:

By the end of his career it had been apparent for decades that Arturo Toscanini was an elemental force to be reckoned within the concert hall or the recording studio. His shows of temper when the orchestra (or soloists) didn't give him the response he was looking for were ofttimes monumental, and have become an accepted element of the Toscanini legend. British violinist Bernard Shore, in his book *The Orchestra Speaks* (Longmans, Green, and Co., 1938), recalled an instance of Toscanini's rage during a rehearsal, noting that the conductor "seized the open score as if it were going to be torn to bits, loose pages flying out, and stamped round the rostrum, a torrent of Italian streaming from his lips, appealing to all the saints and to the Deity himself…. His face, of rare beauty in repose, becomes almost terrifying in fury."

Before he became one of the twentieth century's most famous conductors, it looked as if Toscanini would carve out a career as an orchestra cellist. That all changed in 1886 when, during a South American tour with an Italian opera company, the nineteen-year-old filled in as a last-minute substitute conductor during a production of Giuseppe Verdi's *Aïda*. The conducting classes Toscanini had taken during his student days at the Parma Conservatory served him well in this instance, as did the phenomenal memory which he used then—and would continue to use throughout his career—to conduct the score without resorting to a printed copy.

His next important position, as principal conductor at one of the world's foremost opera houses (La Scala in Milan, Italy), lasted from 1898 until 1909, the year after Toscanini also accepted an appointment to direct at the Metropolitan Opera House in New York City, where he stayed until 1915. From 1920 through 1929, he found himself employed once more at La Scala, though he continued to direct on the other side of the ocean as well, conducting for the Philharmonic Society of New York from 1926 until 1936. Toscanini was also the first foreign conductor to perform at the Bayreuth Festival in Germany, leading performances of *Tannhäuser* and *Tristan und Isolde* there in 1930.

By 1933, however, the National Socialists were in power in Germany, and though he conducted all-Mozart programs at the Salzburg Festival from 1934 until 1938, Toscanini was increasingly disturbed by the Nazi social agenda. When Benito Mussolini came to power in Italy, Toscanini, due to his worldwide notoriety, had been one of the few Italian musicians who could stand up to the Fascist leader and make it stick. Toscanini finally moved to New York City in 1937 to conduct both the New York Philharmonic Orchestra and an ensemble of studio musicians known as the NBC Symphony Orchestra.

It was with the NBC Symphony Orchestra that Toscanini made some of his most revered performances, despite the almost continual use of a recording studio with notoriously bad acoustics. Certainly among the finest of Toscanini's accomplishments with this orchestra were his versions of Ludwig van Beethoven's nine symphonies from the late 1940s and early 1950s (RCA Victor Gold Seal 60324) and his conducting of Giuseppe Verdi's *Requiem* (RCA Victor Red Seal 72373).

Ian Palmer

what to buy next: [Elisabeth Schwarzkopf, soprano; Christa Ludwig, mezzo-soprano; Nicolai Gedda, tenor; Nicolai Ghiaurov, bass; Carlo Maria Giulini, cond.; Philharmonia Orchestra; Philharmonia Chorus] (EMI Classics 67563) ♪♪♪♪

Some swear by this work; some swear off of it. It does seem a bit dry, lacking the great flashes of drama which Verdi epitomizes. But unlike other requiems, it is down-to-earth rather than rarefied, and Giulini is the perfect conductor. The disc also includes a fine recording of Verdi's *Four Sacred Pieces* featuring Janet Baker as soloist with Wilhelm Pitz leading the Philharmonia Choir.

[Leontyne Price, soprano; Rosalind Elias, mezzo-soprano; Jussi Björling, tenor; Giorgio Tozzi, bass; Fritz Reiner, cond.; Vienna Philharmonic Orchestra; Singverein der Gesellschaft der Musikfreunde, Vienna] (Decca 467119) ♪♪♪♪

Reiner's thoughtful 1960 recording of the *Requiem* has been released at a budget price and his soloists are quite good. As in the other recommendations for this music, Verdi's *Four Sacred Pieces* is the accompanying work; however, Zubin Mehta is the conductor (of the Los Angeles Philharmonic Orchestra) for that score, and he just doesn't do it justice. His direction, despite a fine soloist (Yvonne Minton) and a superb chorus master (Robert Shaw), leans heavily on surface beauty to the detriment of substance.

Rigoletto
what to buy: [Maria Callas, soprano; Giuse Gerbino, soprano; Elvira Galassi, mezzo-soprano; Luisa Mandelli, mezzo-soprano; Adriana Lazzarini, contralto; Giuseppe di Stefano, tenor; Renato Ercolani, tenor; Tito Gobbi, baritone; William Dickie, baritone; Plinio Clabassi, bass; Carol Forti, bass; Vittorio Tatozzi, bass; Nicola Zaccaria, bass; Tullio Serafin, cond.; Orchestra of La Scala, Milan; Chorus of La Scala, Milan] (EMI Classics 56327) ♪♪♪♪♪

Here we have the esteemed Tito Gobbi in a great acting/singing role; by the time the last-act tenor aria *La donna e mobile* and the quartet arrive, you will have been transported. This monaural performance from 1955 marks the third time that Callas recorded *Rigoletto*.

what to buy next: [Joan Sutherland, soprano; Kiri Te Kanawa, soprano; Gillian Knight, soprano; Huguette Tourangeau, mezzo-soprano; Josephte Clément, mezzo-soprano; Luciano Pavarotti, tenor; Ricardo Cassinelli, tenor; Sherrill Milnes, baritone; Christian DuPlessis, baritone; John Gibbs, baritone; John Noble, baritone; Martti Talvela, bass; Clifford Grant, bass; Richard Bonynge, cond.; London Symphony Orchestra; Ambrosian Opera Choir] (Decca 414269) ♪♪♪♪♩

This recording dates from the period when Sutherland and Pavarotti were *the* operatic duo of choice. Never much of one for diction, Sutherland still sang beautifully here while Pavarotti was a wonderful, full-throated Verdian tenor when he needed to be. The supporting cast is marvelous and Bonynge actually gives one of his better performances as a conductor.

Il trovatore
what to buy: [Aprile Millo, soprano; Dolora Zajick, mezzo-soprano; Sondra Kelly, contralto; Placido Domingo, tenor; Anthony Laciura, tenor; Tim Willson, tenor; Vladimir Chernov, baritone; James Morris, bass; Glenn Bater, bass; James Levine, cond.; Metropolitan Opera Orchestra; Metropolitan Opera Chorus] (Sony Classics 48070) ♪♪♪♪

There is no winning—one wants Leontyne Price as Leonora, Leonard Warren as the Count di Luna, Franco Corelli as the troubadour. Unfortunately they can't be found together in any one recording, so go for the more recent one with the good, often fine sounds of a top-notch Metropolitan Opera cast.

worth searching for: [Leontyne Price, soprano; Roseland Elias, mezzo-soprano; Richard Tucker, tenor; Leonard Warren, baritone; Giorgio Tozzi, bass; Arturo Basile, cond.; Rome Opera Orchestra; Rome Opera Chorus] (RCA Gold Seal 60560) ♪♪♪♪♩

Basile's production with Price, Tucker, and Warren runs a close second to the Levine set cited above, partially due to overall sound quality which isn't as kind.

La traviata
what to buy: [Joan Sutherland, soprano; Marjon Lambriks, soprano; Della Jones, mezzo-soprano; Luciano Pavarotti, tenor; Alexander Oliver, tenor; Matteo Manuguerra, baritone; William Elvin, baritone; Ubaldo Gardini, baritone; Jonathan Summers, baritone; Giorgio Tadeo, bass; John Tomlinson, bass; David Wilson-

Johnson, bass; Richard Bonynge, cond.; National Philharmonic Orchestra; London Opera Chorus] (Decca 411877) ♪ ♪ ♪ ♪ ♪

Sutherland is the technical wizard as Violetta, and her pairing with Pavarotti provides all the vocal fireworks that one could ask for in this work. Bonynge's direction is solid throughout, securing a steady platform for the singing to take flight.

what to buy next: [Maria Callas, soprano; Silvana Zanoli, soprano; Luisa Mandelli, soprano; Giuseppe Zampieri, tenor; Giuseppe di Steffano, tenor; Franco Ricciardi, tenor; Ettore Bastianni, baritone; Arturo La Porta, bass-baritone; Silvio Maionica, bass; Antonio Zerbini, bass; Carlo Maria Giulini, cond.; La Scala Orchestra; La Scala Chorus] (EMI Classics 66450) ♪ ♪ ♪ ♪

The sound is not up to today's standards (or even those of twenty years ago) but this 1955 recording has a performance by Callas as Violetta which is a high-water mark.

Don Carlos
what to buy: [Galina Gorchakova, soprano; Elizabeth Norberg-Schulz, soprano; Sylvia McNair, soprano; Olga Borodina, mezzo-soprano; Richard Margison, tenor; Robin Leggate, tenor; Dmitri Hvorostovsky, baritone; Roderick Williams, baritone; Robert Lloyd, bass-baritone; Roberto Scanduzzi, bass; Ildebrando d'Arcangelo, bass; Bernard Haitink, conductor; Orchestra of the Royal Opera House, Covent Garden; Chorus of the Royal Opera House, Covent Garden] (Philips 454463) ♪ ♪ ♪ ♪₂

This is the five-act, 1886 Modena version, featuring singers from Russia who have, since the fall of the USSR, come Westward to sing. They all seem to have an uncanny knack in the Verdian repertory. Also on tap is Richard Margison, the Canadian tenor who is often mentioned as slipping into the Luciano Pavarotti vacuum.

what to buy next: [Mirella Freni, soprano; Edita Gruberova, soprano; Barbara Hendricks, soprano; Agnes Baltsa, mezzo-soprano; José Carreras, tenor; Horst Nitsche, tenor; Piero Cappuccilli, baritone; Carlo Meletti, baritone; Nicolai Ghiaurov, bass; Ruggero Raimondi, bass; José Van Dam, bass; Roberto Banuelas, bass; Josef Becker, bass; Walton Grönroos, bass; Klaus Lang, bass; Manfred Röhrl, bass; Ivan Sardi, bass; Herbert von Karajan, cond.; Berlin Philharmonic Orchestra; Berlin

Deutsche Opera Chorus] (EMI Classics 69304) ♪ ♪ ♪ ♪

This is the later four-act version of the opera with an exquisite cast and fairly decent sound. Karajan keeps everybody focused on the task at hand, thus making this one of the best opera recordings in his canon. Freni and Carreras are great and the confrontation scene between the Grand Inquisitor (Raimondi) and Philip II (Ghiaurov) is wonderfully intense to say the least.

Aida
what to buy: [Leontyne Price, soprano; Grace Bumbry, mezzo-soprano; Placido Domingo, tenor; Bruce Brewer, tenor; Sherill Milnes, baritone; Ruggero Raimondi, bass; Hans Sotin, bass; Erich Leinsdorf, cond.; London Symphony Orchestra; John Alldis Choir] (RCA Victor Red Seal 39498) ♪ ♪ ♪ ♪ ♪

This 1970 production features Price, arguably the finest Verdian soprano, combined with a young, splendid Domingo and Bumbry (before she ruined her voice singing soprano roles). Milnes had not yet developed the convincing acting skills he would display a decade or so later, and his diction was suspect at times, but in general his singing doesn't detract from the overall greatness of the production.

Otello
[Leonie Rysanek, soprano; Jon Vickers, tenor; Florindo Andreolli, tenor; Mario Carlin, tenor; Tito Gobbi, baritone; Ferruccio Mazzoli, bass; Franco Calabrese, bass; Tullio Serafin, cond.; Rome Opera House Orchestra; Rome Opera House Chorus] (RCA Victor Living Stereo 63180) ♪ ♪ ♪ ♪ ♪

The work is a splendid reduction of William Shakespeare's play; the measure of a tenor can be taken in this role. Vickers is still available and is the best choice. You may find his sound a trifle harsh (it requires some adjusting to) but the first-rate vocal drama tells all. Both Rysanek and Gobbi are splendid here, too.

what to buy next: [Renatta Scotto, soprano; Jean Kraft, mezzo-soprano; Placido Domingo, tenor; Peter Crook, tenor; Frank Little, tenor; Sherill Milnes, baritone; Paul Plishka, bass; Malcolm King, bass; James Levine, cond.; National Philharmonic Orchestra, London; National Philharmonic Chorus, London] (RCA Red Seal 39501) ♪ ♪ ♪ ♪₂

This is the next best choice for this work since Milnes

floats in and out of pitch occasionally. Domingo is quite good, however, and Scotto's performance is well-characterized.

Falstaff
what to buy: [Elisabeth Schwarzkopf, soprano; Anna Moffo, soprano; Fedora Barbieri, mezzo-soprano; Nan Merriman, mezzo-soprano; Renato Ercolani, tenor; Tomaso Spataro, tenor; Luigi Alva, tenor; Tito Gobbi, baritone; Rolando Panerai, baritone; Nicola Zaccaria, bass; Herbert von Karajan, cond.; Philharmonia Orchestra; Philharmonia Chorus] (EMI Classics 67162) ♪ ♪ ♪ ♪ ♪

It is the towering Falstaff of Gobbi that fueled this 1956 recording under Herbert von Karajan's baton. The final work of Verdi's career, *Falstaff* has wit, charm, and real comedy. The overall vocal blend is important as there are many ensembles, and this is where the Karajan/Gobbi version pulls ahead of its competitors.

what to buy next: [Hillevi Martinpelto, soprano; Rebecca Evans, soprano; Eirian James, mezzo-soprano; Sara Mingardo, contralto; Antonello Palombi, tenor; Peter Bronder, tenor; Francis Egerton, tenor; Jean-Philippe Lafont, baritone; Anthony Michaels-Moore, baritone; Gabriele Monici, bass; John Eliot Gardiner, cond.; Orchestre Révolutionnaire et Romantique; Monteverdi Choir] (Philips 462603) ♪ ♪ ♪ ♪

With the exception of Lafont's Falstaff and the Ford of Michaels-Moore, characterization gives way to the glories of the human voice in this production. This is not a bad thing on the whole, since all of the principals are very good and the recorded sound is clear and forthright. Gardiner's period-instrument orchestra gives the work an interesting tonal picture that brings it closer to the composer's time, and although the tempos can be a bit brisk, nothing is really out of place.

worth searching for: [Anna Moffo, soprano; Renata Tebaldi, soprano; Anna Maria Canali, mezzo-soprano; Giulietta Simionato, mezzo-soprano; Mariano Caruso, tenor; Alvino Misciano, tenor; Tito Gobbi, baritone; Cornell MacNeil, baritone; Tullio Serafin, cond.; unknown orchestra] (Legato Classics 206) ♪ ♪ ♪ ♪

This 1958 concert recording benefits from some fine performances, though the sound quality is mediocre.

influences: Giacomo Puccini, Vincenzo Bellini, Gaetano Donizetti, Gioachino Rossini

Michael H. Margolin and Ellen Kokko

Tomás Luis de Victoria
Born c. 1548, in Avila, Spain. Died August 20, 1611, in Madrid, Spain.

period: Renaissance

Tomás Luis de Victoria stands as the major representative of sixteenth century polyphonic choral style in Spain. Like his contemporaries William Byrd, Thomas Tallis, and Orlando Gibbons in England and Orlando di Lasso and Giovanni Palestrina in Italy, Victoria claims membership in that exclusive circle of Renaissance masters who shaped the identity of sacred choral music during its most exalted period.

Little documentation remains about Victoria's youth and education, except for his presence as a chorister at the Cathedral in Avila. He later lived for a significant period in Rome, studying for the priesthood under the Jesuits and, more significantly, composition under Palestrina himself. Victoria's years in Rome culminated in an appointment to the directorship of the Collegium Romanum, most likely as Palestrina's successor. While in that post, Victoria composed the bulk of his most significant motets and Mass settings. More importantly, these works quickly and easily found their way to publication, an advantage that had eluded even his most illustrious predecessors. In 1586, at the conclusion of his Roman period, Victoria returned to Spain and served as both chaplain and choirmaster to the Nuns of St. Clare in Madrid. The Dowager Empress Maria, widow of Maximilian II and sister of Philip II, was a resident and benefactor of the convent. She held the composer in high esteem, encouraging his last great compositions, and ensuring his tenure there until his death in 1611.

Victoria's compositions are limited exclusively to sacred choral music for the church. His intense concentration on this genre is what perhaps accounts for the focused brilliance of his polyphonic style and the dramatic intensity of his text settings. In nearly all of his twenty masses and forty motets, Victoria perfects the art of contrapuntal writing and uses its inherent rhythmic energy to paint vivid depictions of highly emotional prayers and scriptural passages. His most famous motet, *O Magnum Mysterium,* for example, recounts the birth of Christ, not simply by setting the usual historical narrative, but rather by focusing upon the mystical nature of the virgin birth and incarnation of God. Each voice successively combines the uncharacteristic *descending* fourth opening with a sudden upturn of a semitone on the word "mysterium" to evoke an expression of wonderment and disbelief. Such dramatic treatment extends to similar motets including *Ave Maria* (two settings: one for four voices and another for double choir and organ), *Ecce sacerdos magnus,* and *Quan pulchri sunt.* Even the more repetitive and formulaic texts of the Mass benefit from such treatment, in particular his *Officium defunctorum,* a setting of the Matins of the Dead and Requiem Mass composed in 1605 for the memorial of the Empress Maria.

The Requiem, by its very nature, evokes man's most feared yet most exalted experience. Death and its aftermath link physical with spiritual, temporal with eternal. Thus any responsible setting of these rites for the dead relies upon a necessary melding of music, drama, ritual, gesture, and prayer. Victoria's Requiem captures all of that and more. The "more" stems from the fact that Victoria sets not merely the Ordinary of the Mass, but many significant parts of the Office of the Dead, which would have accompanied the prayers and practices of the Requiem Mass in committing the soul to its creator.

Vocal
Requiem
what to buy: [David Hill, cond.; Choir of Westminster Cathedral] (Hyperion 66250) ♪ ♪ ♪ ♪₄

The Choir of Westminster Cathedral, London, artfully weaves these two great liturgical forms into what would have been the correct sequential pattern heard at the funeral of an exalted figure—in this case, the Dowager Empress Maria. Cavernous acoustics lend the requisite "disembodied" feel while never dulling the choir's exquisite diction and sense of line. Rapturous episodes of each occur in the *Ego sum resurrection* of Lauds and the *Agnus Dei.*

Missa O magnum mysterium
what to buy: [Jeremy Summerly, cond.; Oxford Camerata, choir] (Naxos 8.550575) ♪ ♪ ♪ ♪

Summerly and his choir bring a sense of structural awareness and architectural intelligence to this most moving treatment of the Ordinary of the Mass. One of Victoria's many "parody Masses," this setting evolves,

as do all such parodies, out of the melodic material from the composer's best-known motets. The singers carefully etch and outline the themes of the motet that support and sustain each movement, and they do so not with a forced vocal emphasis upon the hidden melodies, but by reserving a specific tonal color for motivic episodes. Thus it seems that two separate choirs spring from one vocal source, giving a rare depth and dimension to each movement. This set is a testament to the ensemble's gift for "building" a work as they perform it. It also includes a performance of Victoria's *Missa O quam gloriosum* and Alonso Lobo's motet, *Versa est in luctum.*

influences: Giovanni Palestrina, Orlando di Lasso, Alonso Lobo, William Byrd, Thomas Tallis, Orlando Gibbons

Frank Scinta

Louis Vierne

Born Louis-Victor-Jules Vierne, October 8, 1870, in Poitiers, France. Died June 2, 1937, in Paris, France.

period: Romantic/Twentieth century

Vierne is most remembered today for six symphonies and several collections that make up the majority of his organ works. His compositional style, built upon those of his teachers César Franck and Charles Marie Widor, gradually evolved toward the use of a wider chromatic harmonic vocabulary without losing a basically conservative viewpoint.

Vierne demonstrated an extraordinary talent in music despite being born with cataracts which almost completely blinded him. When he was three, his family moved to Paris as a result of his father being appointed Editor in Chief of the *Paris Journal.* There he met his uncle, Charles Colin, who was an organist working at the Paris Conservatoire as professor of oboe. It was Colin who confirmed Vierne's musical gifts and encouraged his music study. Later, Vierne studied at the Institution Nationale des Jeunes Aveugles (National Institute for Blind Youths), receiving first prizes in violin, organ, and piano. His prodigious talents had already attracted the attention of Franck by then and, in 1888, the older musician began teaching Vierne the disciplines of counterpoint, fugue, and composition in addition to encouraging the youngster to audit his organ class at the

Paris Conservatoire. Vierne actually enrolled at the school in October 1890, roughly a month before Franck died. When Charles-Marie Widor was appointed professor of organ and improvisation at the Conservatoire shortly after Franck's death, Vierne became infatuated with his new instructor's techniques, eventually assisting Widor by teaching plainsong accompaniment and technique to some of the newer students.

In 1894, Vierne received a first prize in organ from the Conservatoire and became a full-fledged teaching assistant there. By this time he was also taking lessons in composition from Widor, serving as assistant organist to his teacher at Saint Sulpice, and performing similar duties for Albert Périlhou at Saint Séverin. Two years later, when Widor gave up the organ class to become a professor of composition, he did so with the provision that Vierne stay on as assistant to the new teacher, Félix-Alexandre Guilmant. Vierne also premiered Widor's Symphony no. 3 for Organ and Orchestra earlier that same year. In 1900, with Widor's encouragement, Vierne entered and won the competition—over ninety-seven applicants—to become chief organist at Notre-Dame. This was a good thing for the young musician since not only was this one of the most prestigious (albeit poorly-paid) positions in France, but he had just married in the preceding year and his first child (Jacques) had been born mere months before the new posting.

In 1911, Vincent d'Indy offered Vierne a professorship at the Schola Cantorum, a school devoted to church music. By this time Vierne had written his impressive *Messe solennelle,* his second organ symphony, and a batch of well received chamber music pieces. Since he had been passed over for a similar position at the Conservatoire after Guilmant died, he was urged by Widor to accept the offer. He did so and retained that post for nearly twenty years, taking four years off (1916–1920) to shuttle between Switzerland, where he went to receive treatment for glaucoma, and the homes of various friends throughout France. While he was undergoing this series of procedures to stabilize his vision, Vierne also had to leave his post at Notre-Dame in the hands of a substitute, the formidable organist Marcel Dupré. After returning to Notre-Dame, Vierne began raising money to restore the organ, which had been deteriorating from neglect during World War I.

During the 1920s his concert tours throughout Europe and North America were the subject of great acclaim. In 1927, while Vierne was on tour in New York City, he cut

five player organ rolls for the Aeolian Organ Company, including the *Légende* and *Berceuse* from his *24 Pièces en style libre,* op. 31. A year later Vierne, playing the organ at Notre-Dame, recorded six short pieces by Johann Sebastian Bach plus two improvisations and one of his own compositions (the *Andantino* from *24 Pièces de Fantaisie*) for Odéon. He was named a Chevalier of the Légion d'Honneur at the beginning of 1931 and had his sixth organ symphony published later that year. By now he was suffering increased ill health and becoming noticeably frailer. He still managed to play at the re-inauguration of the newly renovated organ at Notre-Dame, but by 1935 the number of concerts he played was declining and he began making plans ensuring that the person succeeding him in his position at Notre-Dame went through the same sort of competition that he had undergone in 1900. The composer had already decided that his 1,750th recital was to be his last, since he was suffering from a variety of heart problems and, at times, even had to be carried up into the loft so that he could play the organ. When the evening came, his students, Maurice Duruflé and Jean Fellot, were beside him in the loft at Notre-Dame, pulling stops for their former teacher. He had just finished playing the *Triptyque,* his last published piece, and was about to perform one of his famous improvisations when Vierne collapsed onto the keyboard and died.

Chamber
Complete Organ Symphonies, opp. 14, 20, 28, 32, 47, 59
what to buy: [Ben van Oosten, organ] (MD and G 3160732) ♪♪♪♪⸴

This four-CD collection contains some of the greatest of twentieth century organ music. The pieces are recorded on three of the nineteenth century Cavaillé-Coll organs (St. Francois des Sales in Lyon [symphonies 1 and 4], St. Sernin in Toulouse [3 and 5], and St. Ouen in Rouen [2 and 6]) that were such an influence on Vierne's compositional style. The booklet is unusually informative and contains photos and specifications of the organs. The performance is exciting but is stylistically in keeping with the period. The recording was made a bit distantly and therefore lacks some clarity, but it captures the sound of these organs in their resonant spaces.

Symphony no. 3 in F-sharp Minor for Organ, op. 28
what to buy: [Michael Murray, organ] (Telarc 80329) ♪♪♪♪♪

If somebody were to buy a single CD sampling of the symphonies, this would be the one! Murray is an American organist who studied with Marcel Dupré, a student of Vierne, and the organ is the Cavaillé-Coll instrument at St. Ouen, Rouen, built in 1890. The artist plays this music with rhythmic drive and sensitivity to the style, tossing in a fine performance of Vierne's initial organ symphony (no. 1 in D Minor, op. 14) as a bonus.

24 Pièces de Fantaisie, opp. 51–54
what to buy: [Olivier Latry, organ] (BNL 112742) ♪♪♪♪₄

Latry's playing will make any listener a lover of this music. As the titular organist at Notre-Dame de Paris, he has access to one of the most wonderful-sounding organs in France to go along with his undeniable technique and flair for performance. His rendition of the *Carillon de Westminster,* the finale of which is a true speaker-buster, is slightly faster than van Oosten's (see below). The *Marche nuptiale* is suitably dignified, the *Aubade* is appropriately delicate, and the recital as a whole is one of the finest Latry has recorded.

what to buy next: [Ben van Oosten, organ] (MD and G 3160847) ♪♪♪₄

The most popular of the pieces in this cycle, the *Carillon de Westminster,* maintains a deliberate, bell-like clarity even as the organist weaves his way through the majestic textures and intriguing harmonies to the crashing display of pedal power at its end. Van Oosten performs this recital on the same Cavaillé-Coll organ he used for his recording of Vierne's second and sixth organ symphonies.

Choral
Messe solennelle for Vocal Soloists, Organ, Orchestra, and Chorus, op. 16
what to buy: [Michel Bouvard, organ; Yasuko Uyama-Bouvard, organ; Joël Suhubiette, cond.; Les Éléments, ensemble] (Tempéraments 316008) ♪♪♪♪♪

This piece, composed in 1899 at age twenty-nine, is Vierne's largest choral work both in length and in forces. The large organ is heard in dialogue with the small organ and choir. This performance was recorded partially on an 1889 Cavaillé-Coll organ, and benefits from the reverberant acoustics of its home at St. Sernin, Toulouse. The French choral sound from Les Éléments exhibits a wonderful purity not associated with typical French choirs, while the organ performance is all one could want in style and sound. In addition, there are four shorter organ works by Vierne plus Widor's Symphony no. 10 for Organ (the *Symphonie Romane*).

influences: Charles-Marie Widor, Marcel Dupré, Maurice Duruflé, Charles Tournemire

D. John Apple and Ian Palmer

Henri Vieuxtemps
Born February 17, 1820, in Veviers, Belgium. Died June 6, 1881, in Mustapha, Algiers.

period: Romantic

Nicknamed *le roi du violon,* Henri Vieuxtemps exemplified the French school of violin playing during the romantic period. A master teacher as well as a world-renowned performer and composer, Vieuxtemps endowed his compositions with an elegant, flowing style that perfectly showcased the French romantic approach to performance.

One often hears of the "child prodigy syndrome," in which a talented performer begins his career so early, studies so assiduously, and finally is so overworked (by an overbearing parent, as often as not) that he either burns out or breaks down before the age of thirty. Vieuxtemps was one child prodigy who seems to have escaped this malady, although he certainly had a right to suffer from it. From the earliest age until nearly the end of his life, Vieuxtemps enjoyed a successful performing career. He began his studies with his father and had his debut recital at the age of six. He went on the road soon afterward, performing in Liège at seven and giving several concerts in Brussels the following year. The great violinist and teacher Hector de Bériot accepted him as a pupil, and he remained with Bériot until 1831.

A second concert tour took him to Germany with his father; at the tour's end in 1833, the young violinist began his education anew in Vienna. While this experience further aided Vieuxtemps's career as a violinist (his 1834 Viennese debut as soloist in the Beethoven Violin Concerto was a huge success), his studies in counterpoint with the renowned theorist Simon Sechter awakened a new interest in composition. It soon became evident that Vieuxtemps would be equally talented as both a performer and a composer. Later in 1834 he made his

British debut with the Philharmonic Society in London and soon began a two-year course of study in composition with Anton Reicha in Paris.

The ensuing years brought concert tours that eventually took him throughout Europe and America (each twice), with a five-season rest as a professor at the St. Petersburg Conservatory. During all these trips, Vieuxtemps performed his many new compositions, in addition to the standard repertoire, to great acclaim. Eventually these works themselves became part of the canon. A return to Belgium as professor of violin at the Brussels Conservatory further confirmed Vieuxtemps's "third career" as a teacher, and he continued to teach even after paralysis of the left side forced him to end his concert career. He finally left the Conservatory in 1873 and retired in Algiers, where he died in 1880 with his gifted pupil Jeno Hubay at his side.

Orchestral
Concerto no. 5 in A Minor for Violin and Orchestra, op. 37—*Grétry*
what to buy: [Jascha Heifetz, violin; Sir Malcolm Sargent, conductor; New Symphony Orchestra of London] (RCA Red Seal 6214) ♪ ♪ ♪ ♪ ♪

The technical impeccability of a Heifetz performance is simply not to be missed, and Sargent's interpretation of this piece is equally clean while still exploring every romantic avenue the work has to offer. This historic re-release (originally recorded in London in 1961) also includes Bruch's *Scottish Fantasy* and Violin Concerto no. 1. Forty years later, Heifetz is still the standard to which violinists are held.

influences: Henryk Wieniawski, Camille Saint-Saëns

Melissa M. Stewart

Heitor Villa-Lobos
Born March 5, 1887, in Rio de Janeiro, Brazil. Died November 17, 1959, in Rio de Janeiro, Brazil.

period: Twentieth century

Heitor Villa-Lobos, Brazil's most important twentieth century composer, wrote prolifically, balancing European stylistic training with the native rhythms and melodies of his country. At the time of his death, Villa-Lobos had

over 2,000 pieces in his catalog, and a substantial number of them were quite compelling.

Villa-Lobos didn't receive much in the way of formal musical training during his early youth. He started playing the cello at the instigation of his father, an amateur cellist, but when the senior Villa-Lobos died in 1899, things changed. Heitor's mother apparently didn't think that the life of a musician was suitable for her son and tried steering him toward a career in medicine. This didn't sit too well with the impetuous youth and he spent much of his time wandering the streets of Rio de Janeiro in the company of like-minded souls, playing cello, piano, or guitar in theaters, restaurants, and other venues in need of live music.

Eventually, Villa-Lobos did study cello at the National Music Institute of Rio de Janeiro, but not until after he had begun venturing into the Brazilian hinterlands, supposedly conducting his own semi-formal research on the musical elements and traditions of native cultures. He had also taken some classes in composition, attempting to gain a better technical grasp on the process instead of just relying on his raw talents. This blend of factors resulted in a series of songs and small chamber pieces that were unveiled publicly during a concert in 1915. His suite for piano, *A Prole do Bebê (The Child's Dolls)*, no. 1, dates from 1918 and is the earliest of his works to garner standing among international musicians, due in part to the advocacy of pianist Artur Rubinstein. That piece also contained bitonal elements commonly found in Brazilian folk music, a concept which the French composer Darius Milhaud would later adopt for his own scores. Villa-Lobos's mélange of influences continued inflecting his works, helping him garner acclaim from some Brazilian critics and disapproval from others. The end result, however, was that he received a grant from the state (and a few wealthy backers) that let him travel to Europe in 1923.

Using Paris as a base of operations, Villa-Lobos roamed the world, meeting people and exposing himself to the music of other cultures. By the time he returned to Brazil in 1930, Villa-Lobos had already assembled a series of important works that would solidify his reputation at home and abroad. Among them were *Rudepoêma*, a piano piece he created for Rubinstein, and the cycle of fourteen *Chôros* he wrote for a variety of forces. (Every one of the *Chôros* was built around a Brazilian musical genre calling for group improvisations around a specific set of rhythms.) Villa-Lobos had also published a text in

1929 (*Alma do Brasil*) examining Brazilian folk music and this scholarly effort, combined with his increasing reputation as a nationalist composer, may have played a role in getting him his jobs supervising musical education in São Paulo and Rio de Janeiro. During the next few decades, Villa-Lobos practically re-shaped the entire music education system in Brazil, establishing conservatories and reforming the bureaucracy. Despite the weight of his administrative duties, however, Villa-Lobos was still as hyperactive as ever from a compositional standpoint.

While in Europe Villa-Lobos had been exposed to the music of Johann Sebastian Bach more than at any other time of his life. This led to a heightened appreciation for Bach's genius and a remarkable assortment of works (the various *Bachianas brasileiras*) attempting to meld Brazilian-style chôros with the spirit of the earlier composer. Villa-Lobos's unique *Bachianas brasileira* no. 5 for Soprano and Cellos once caused the eminent musicologist Wilfred Mellers to comment that "... the remarkable work for eight cellos does achieve, at least in the slow movement, a sustained line and an extraordinary depth and richness of harmony." Villa-Lobos was so enamored of Bach that he conducted the first Brazilian performance of Bach's Mass in B Minor and even transcribed Bach's *Das wohltemperirte Klavier (The Well-tempered Clavier)* for cello ensemble.

Toward the end of his life, many of Villa-Lobos's compositions were being developed with instruction and practice in mind. Still, he did manage to deliver on commissions like the batch he received from Andres Segovia, who wanted Villa-Lobos to write various pieces for an instrument of his youth, the guitar. The results included a concerto, some études, and a few preludes, all among his most frequently-performed compositions.

Orchestral
Concerto for Guitar and Orchestra
what to buy: [Julian Bream, guitar; André Previn, cond.; London Symphony Orchestra] (RCA Victor Gold Seal 6525) ♪ ♪ ♪ ♪

A classic performance from Bream and Previn is paired with five of the composer's Preludes for solo guitar and Joaquin Rodrigo's ever-popular *Concierto de Aranjuez*, with Bream as soloist and John Eliot Gardiner guiding the Monteverdi Orchestra through their paces. The budget price of this package makes it an even better deal.

what to buy next: [John Williams, guitar; Daniel Barenboim, cond.; English Chamber Orchestra] (Sony Classical 33208) ♪ ♪ ♪

Williams is a bit more analytical-sounding than Bream, and the engineering is a bit steely, but the playing is never less than expert. Once again, Rodrigo's *Concierto de Aranjuez*, the world's most-programmed work for guitar and orchestra, receives top billing on the CD cover.

Bachiana brasileira no. 2 for Orchestra
what to buy: [Jésus López-Cobos, cond.; Cincinnati Symphony Orchestra] (Telarc 80393) ♪ ♪ ♪ ♪

López-Cobos draws a fine performance from one of America's great (if overlooked) orchestras. Their rendering of the piece's popular last movement (the *Little Train of Caipira*) is brilliant. They also play two other works from the *Bachiana brasileiras*: no. 4 for Piano and Orchestra and the infrequently-heard no. 8 for Orchestra.

Chamber
Rudepoêma
what to buy: [*Villa-Lobos Piano Music*; Marc-André Hamelin, piano] (Hyperion 67176) ♪ ♪ ♪ ♪

Rudepoêma is about polytonality and power; even in its reflective moments this piece harbors an underlying, somewhat savage pulse. There is plenty of technical filagree here but Hamelin is more than up to the task, making everything sound, not easy, but right. Aficionados of the old Nelson Freire and Roberto Szidon recordings of the vinyl era should note that Hamelin and Szidon are about equal in the timing department but Freire is a tad faster—coming in closer to eighteen minutes than nineteen. The other Villa-Lobos works on this disc (both books of *A Prole do Bebê* and the short but graceful trilogy *As Três Marias*) are more immediately appealing, leading the listener up to the thornier masterpiece.

Vocal
Bachiana brasileira no. 5 for Soprano and Cellos
what to buy: [Victoria de los Angeles, soprano; Heitor Villa-Lobos, cond.; Orchestre National de la Radiodiffusion Française, orch.] (EMI Classics 66964) ♪ ♪ ♪ ♪

The sonics of this recording may be a bit outdated in some respects (read: monaural) but the remastering is fine and the performances are, without question, definitive. De los Angeles is superb. The rest of the disc includes more of Villa-Lobos's conducting, working his way through three more of his *Bachiana brasileiras:* nos. 1 (for eight cellos), 2 (for orchestra), and 9 (for string orchestra).

what to buy next: [Anna Moffo, soprano; Leopold Stokowski, cond.; American Symphony Orchestra] (RCA Gold Seal 7831) ♪ ♪ ♪ ♪

Nearly three generations of listeners have been introduced to Villa-Lobos with this performance. Even though the focus of the disc is more on Moffo than on Villa-Lobos, her singing is certainly beautiful enough. Sergei Rachmaninoff's *Vocalise* and selections from Joseph Canteloube's lovely *Songs of the Auvergne* fill out the rest of the program.

influences: Darius Milhaud, Ernesto Nazareth, Egberto Gismonti, Leo Brouwer

Gary Barton and Ellen Kokko

Antonio Vivaldi

Born Antonio Lucio Vivaldi, March 4, 1678, in Venice, Italy. Died c. July 28, 1741, in Vienna, Austria.

period: Baroque

Antonio Vivaldi is probably best known for his works for strings, especially his eighth opus, *Il cimento dell'armonia e dell'inventione (The Contest Between Harmony and Invention),* a compilation which includes the four violin concertos subtitled *Le quattro stagioni (The Four Seasons).* In many ways, Vivaldi's importance as a composer has more to do with his mastery of compositional form and his application of this mastery to the development of the concerto than it does with any of the other idioms in which he worked. The most direct evidence of this is the attention paid to his scoring by such contemporaries as Frantisek Benda, Johann Joachim Quantz, and, most famously of all, Johann Sebastian Bach, who studied some of those works carefully, even arranging a few of Vivaldi's concertos for keyboard.

Many of the facts surrounding Vivaldi's early life are fairly, albeit not completely, obscure. It is known that he was a sickly child who entered training to become a priest around 1693 but never ended up taking his final vows even though he was ordained ten years later. The most likely explanation for this failure was Vivaldi's inability to say mass with any degree of consistency due to what many modern scholars believe was acute asthma. It has also been posited by some historians that he studied music with his father (a musician in the orchestra of San Marco) and Giovanni Legrenzi, the maestro di cappella of San Marco, prior to being handed over to the church by his parents.

Vivaldi became violin teacher at an orphanage for girls (the Seminario dell'Ospedale della Pietà) in 1703 and within a few years had published his first opus, a set of twelve trio sonatas. Although the Board of Governors of Pietà gave him a raise in 1704, for some unknown reason (perhaps a power struggle of some sort) Vivaldi was voted out of office in 1709, only to be reinstated in 1711. Both before his unemployed interlude and after regaining his position, he substituted frequently for the maestro di coro, Francesco Gasparini, who was often ill or busy working on the operas for which he was so famous at that time. Vivaldi's talents were such that in 1713 he ended up assuming the functions associated with not only the maestro di coro but those of the maestro de concerti as well, directing all vocal and instrumental forces at the institution. By this time, Vivaldi was already a respected musician and composer, having published two highly-regarded and influential books of twelve concerti each (*L'Estro Armonico,* op. 3, and *La Stravaganza,* op. 4) and developed the orchestra at the orphanage to the point where it was considered one of the finest in Italy.

1713 was also the year when Vivaldi's first opera, *Ottone in villa,* was produced. This was the composer's initial foray into a field to which he would contribute well over forty examples, many to popular acclaim in their heyday but most of which have disappeared from the current repertoire. He also published another well-received batch of works (the six sonatas of op. 5, the six concertos of op. 6, and the dozen concertos of op. 7) and composed a couple of oratorios, with *Juditha triumphans* being his one true standout in that genre. Three years later, however, Vivaldi was once again voted off the staff, this time to be reinstated within two months. This on-again, off-again relationship with the orphanage must have gotten tiresome for the composer, since he left the Pietà in 1717 and, a year later, turned up in Mantua as the maestro di cappella da camera for Prince Philip of Hesse-Darmstadt.

By 1723 the board of the orphanage reappeared in Vivaldi's life, asking him to compose and direct the performance of two new concertos every month, apparently coming to the realization that the composer's reputation would reflect favorably on the institution and that without him their standing as a musical organization was lessened. The resulting agreement stipulated that Vivaldi rehearse the orchestra "three or four times in person for each concert in such a way that they perform well whenever he is in Venice," essentially freeing the composer to travel and promote his artistry in non-Venetian venues. Vivaldi also spent many of his years in operatic endeavors: writing, conducting, and acting as agent for a number of singers, particularly Anna Girò (sometimes written as Giraud). She, along with her sister, who later acted as Vivaldi's nurse, lived and traveled with him from 1726 until 1741, causing a great deal of moral consternation amongst rumor mongers and those who professed to care about the potential conflict of interest for a priest. He didn't neglect instrumental forms during this time, publishing the concerto collections *Il cimento dell'armonia e dell'inventione* (op. 8) in 1725 and *La centra* (op. 9) in 1728, and the six flute concertos of op. 10 in 1730, plus numerous concertos and sonatas for diverse instruments ranging from bassoons and oboes to mandolins and lutes.

As a priest, musician, and composer, Vivaldi's responsibilities at the Pietà also necessitated his writing a number of pieces for worship services and various ecclesiastical ceremonies. Composed mainly between the mid-1720s and the early 1730s, most of Vivaldi's sacred vocal music was operatic in nature. This includes the aforementioned oratorio *Juditha triumphans,* which is, essentially, a liturgical drama sans costuming and staging. This sense of operatic drama isn't missing from his popular choral work, the *Gloria* in D Major, either, since the score places the arias of the soloists against a concerto-derived background in four of its dozen movements even as the chorus takes the lead in the other eight.

Throughout Vivaldi's life he traveled around Italy in addition to taking side trips to Germany, Austria, and the Netherlands. He was a shrewd businessman in some ways, always seeking to acquire wealthy students and cajoling them into dispensing a portion of their funds directly to him since the music piracy of his day assured fairly wide distribution of his scores without necessarily

Antonio Vivaldi

increasing his income. One of his favorite tactics involved getting prospective violinists from the upper classes to take lessons from him, and giving them a copy of an unpublished score which he then claimed was specifically created for their use. Despite his ability to generate cash flow through his talents as a violinist, teacher, conductor, and, to some extent, composer, Vivaldi apparently spent money to an amazing degree of profligacy, which probably explains why he died in poverty while in Austria on a promotional junket.

Orchestral
Concertos for Violin(s), Strings, and Continuo, op. 3, nos. 1–12 (*L'estro armonico*)
what to buy: [Neville Marriner, cond.; Academy of St. Martin-in-the-Fields, orch.] (London 443476) ♪ ♪ ♪ ♪ ♪

This felicitously priced two-disc set is a lovely-sounding project that, while it doesn't follow period-instrument practices, offers plenty of delights on its own. The recording dates from the period when Iona Brown and Alan Loveday provided most of the violin solos for this ensemble and Christopher Hogwood had not yet left his harpsichord bench to take up the baton. As filler, the label also tosses in four of Vivaldi's concertos for wind instruments.

[Christopher Hogwood, cond.; Academy of Ancient Music, orch.] (London 458078) ♪ ♪ ♪ ♪ ♪

On the other hand, if you want these works done with a semblance of period authenticity then this rendering by Hogwood as conductor should fit the bill quite nicely. It also makes a nice contrast to the modern-instrument version by Marriner, and also includes fine performances of the six flute concertos from op. 10 with Stephen Preston as soloist.

Concertos for Violin, Strings, and Continuo, op. 8, nos. 1–4 (*Le Quattro Stagioni [The Four Seasons]*)
what to buy: [Gidon Kremer, violin; Claudio Abbado, cond.; London Symphony Orchestra] (Deutsche Grammophon 431172) ♪ ♪ ♪ ♪ ♪

Kremer is such a virtuoso that his solos make this 1980-recorded version with Abbado and the elegant London Symphony Orchestra sizzle with fresh invigoration and beauty. Though sound quality leans to the brighter side, it serves to deliciously set off the softest parts of Kremer's solos, the wonderfully delicate harpsichord solo in the *Adagio molto* of *L'autunno (Autumn)*, and infinitesimal orchestral detail. Abbado's conducting of the delightful Allegro movement in *L'estate (Summer)*, ferociously shifting tempos back and forth to feature the LSO in full force and Kremer's playing at its fiercest, is a gem.

what to buy next: [Paul Peabody, violin; Richard Kapp, cond.; Philharmonia Virtuosi, orch.] (ESS.A.Y. 1001) ♪ ♪ ♪ ♪₈

Peabody is a splendid soloist who has performed, toured, and recorded as concertmaster and resident soloist for this group. Founder-conductor Kapp shows infinite sensitivity with this stellar ensemble, whose individual and collective expertise is evident on this well-produced album and outshines many other recorded performances of this piece.

[Michel Schwalbé, violin; Herbert von Karajan, cond.; Berlin Philharmonic Orchestra] (Deutsche Grammophon 415301) ♪ ♪ ♪ ♪₈

It's easy to understand the popularity of the first four concertos from Vivaldi's opus 8 when you hear this beautiful version featuring Schwalbé playing a "King Maximilian" Stradivarius which dates from 1709. Schwalbé, Karajan, and the BPO seem cohesively made for each other as they majestically convey elements of the changing seasons: the birdsongs, approaching thunder, wind and storm, icy winter chills, lazy autumn days, and more. The addition of Tomaso Albinoni's popular Adagio in G Minor makes this an especially felicitous purchase.

[Joseph Silverstein, violin; Seiji Ozawa, cond.; Boston Symphony Orchestra] (Telarc 80070) ♪ ♪ ♪ ♪

Ozawa achieves a responsive reading from the orchestra on this 1981-recorded performance. But it is violinist Silverstein, a regular with the BSO since 1955 (and assistant conductor), who truly captures your heart and ears with his impeccable technique and powerful, resplendent playing on his 1742 Guarnerius del Jesu violin.

[Amsterdam Guitar Trio, ensemble] (RCA Gold Seal 61652) ♪ ♪ ♪₈

For fans seeking variety, this is a novel version of the four famous Vivaldi works, adapted for three guitars.

While the reading by these conservatory-trained musicians fails to capture the excitement and lacks the colorful textures of the violin/orchestra performances above, it is a lovely recording in itself and you have to commend these talented musicians for taking the risk.

Concertos for Flute and Orchestra, op. 10, nos. 1–6
what to buy: [Jean-Pierre Rampal, flute; Claudio Scimone, cond.; I Solisti Veneti, orch.] (Sony Classics 39062) ♪ ♪ ♪ ♪

Flautist Rampal is a graceful, sensitive veteran who has recorded many Vivaldi works. On these half-dozen sumptuously light and airy concertos he offers enchanting performances, judiciously using vibrato. Rampal's lightsome approach is supported by an excellent orchestra which aptly showcases, in a most unified manner, Vivaldi's genius for arranging strings.

Concerto in C Minor for Cello and Orchestra (RV 401)
what to buy: [*Vivaldi: Concertos pour violoncelle*; Roel Dieltiens, cello; Ensemble Explorations] (Harmonia Mundi 901655) ♪ ♪ ♪ ♪

Dieltiens displays crisp, muscular virtuosity in RV 401, one of the prettiest pieces on this CD. Richly textured solos by Dieltiens, especially in the colorfully orchestrated *Allegro non molto*, are sensitively rendered and the work seemingly glides on air. The musicians bring passion and understanding to their performances of the six other cello concertos by the composer in this set.

worth searching for: [*Vivaldi: Cello Concertos, vol. 2*; Ofra Harnoy, cello; Paul Robinson, cond.; Toronto Chamber Orchestra] (RCA Victor Red Seal 60155) ♪ ♪ ♪ ♪₈

Displaying great feeling and warmth, Harnoy's mastery of her rich-toned instrument makes this CD a glorious listen as she wends her way with great grandeur and sprightliness through RV 401, three world-premiere recordings (RV 402, RV 403, and RV 412), and three other Vivaldi cello concertos.

Concerto in G Major for Two Mandolins, Strings, and Continuo (RV 532)
what to buy: [*The Miraculous Mandolin: Concertos and Sonatas for Mandolin and Guitar*, Peter Press, mandolin; Scott Kuney, mandolin; Richard Kapp, cond.; Philharmonia Virtuosi, orch.] (ESS.A.Y 1004) ♪ ♪ ♪ ♪₈

Kapp always extracts the best from the musicians of this New York-based ensemble formed in the 1970s, and this performance is no exception. Press and Kuney are highly skilled instrumentalists who render technically-precise and passionate readings of this sprightly, ear-satisfying piece. Their double mandolin solo in the *Andante* sparkles with meaning and musicianship.

what to buy next: [James Tyler, mandolin; Douglas Wootton, mandolin; Neville Marriner, cond.; Academy of St. Martin-in-the-Fields, orch.] (Philips 412892) ♪♪♪♪

In their double mandolin solo, Tyler and Wootton give the *Andante* movement at Bela Fleck flavor. The fifty-minute CD is a charming listen that includes five other Vivaldi concertos featuring stately solos on horns, trumpets, flutes, and oboes.

[*Vivaldi: Guitar Concertos*; Angel Romero, guitar; Pepe Romero, guitar; Iona Brown, cond.; Academy of St. Martin-in-the-Fields, orch.] (Philips 412624) ♪♪♪♪

The composer never actually wrote anything for guitar, but guitarists have been playing arrangements of his various concertos for decades, and this performance is one of the best available programs of its kind. In addition to some suave playing in RV 532, the two brothers team up with their father (Celedonio) and other brother (Celín) in an arrangement of the tenth concerto from *L'estro armonico*, which was originally meant for four violins. Celín, who is rarely heard on his own, is the soloist in RV 93 while Pepe, probably the finest musician in the quartet, covers RV 425 and joins Angel in RV 532. Brown and the orchestra provide sensitive accompaniment throughout.

Concerto in C Major for Recorder and Strings (RV 444)

[Michala Petri, sopranino recorder; Claudio Scimone, cond.; I Solisti Veneti, orch.] (RCA Victor 7885) ♪♪♪♪

Right from her launch of the initial *Allegro non molto*, Copenhagen-born Petri plays the high-pitched sopranino recorder with ear-catching, astonishing agility and precision, supported splendidly by this world-class chamber orchestra. Petri evenly splits her sure-handed performances on the six concertos (RV 108 and RV 441–445) of this set between sopranino and treble recorder. Scimone is sensitive to his soloist and evokes the best from orchestra members on this 1988 recording.

Concerto in C Major for Two Trumpets, Strings, and Continuo (RV 537)

what to buy: [*Vivaldi Concertos*; John Wilbraham, trumpet; Philip Jones, trumpet; Neville Marriner, cond.; Academy of St. Martin-in-the-Fields, orch.] (Decca 425721) ♪♪♪♪

This is a sprightly, well-played performance of Vivaldi's popular concerto. Wilbraham and Jones had a long association with each other in the Philip Jones Brass Ensemble, and their sparkling interplay has a lot to do with the success of this venture. The five other works on this mid-priced set display fine soloists in a program which covers a number of scores featuring violins, horns, oboes, and cellos.

what to buy next: [*Baroque Music for Trumpets*; Wynton Marsalis, trumpets; Raymond Leppard, cond.; English Chamber Orchestra] (Sony Classics 42478) ♪♪♪♪

Marsalis proves that talented jazz musicians can play classical music with no real drop-off in quality on either side of the artistic divide. This disc cheats a bit, however, since the wonder of overdubbing lets Marsalis play both trumpets in the Vivaldi piece, three trumpets in two concertos by Georg Philipp Telemann and an arrangement of the infamous "Canon" by Johann Pachelbel, and eight trumpets in the Heinrich von Biber sonata heard here. About the only "normal" work is Michael Haydn's popular concerto, which features only one trumpet. Despite the gimmickry, the playing works surprisingly well and Leppard's conducting keeps the textures of the music relatively uncluttered.

[*Favorite Trumpet Concertos*; Maurice André, trumpet; Bernard Soustrot, trumpet; Neville Marriner, cond.; Academy of St. Martin-in-the-Fields, orch.] (EMI Seraphim 69731) ♪♪♪♪

Budget recordings aren't often thought of when quality performances by major-league artists are bandied about by connoisseurs, but the lineup and playing on this incredibly inexpensive disc are too good to pass up for anyone interested in baroque trumpet playing. While André may be the biggest "name" associated with this collection (he also solos in Tomaso Albinoni's F Major Trumpet Concerto), John Wilbraham (featured in works by Franz Joseph Haydn and Georg Philipp Telemann) and Edward H. Tarr (the soloist for pieces by Leopold Mozart and Johann Nepomuk Hummel) are also in the pantheon of trumpeters and deserve to be heard by more people.

Various concertos for diverse instruments
what to buy: [*Vivaldi Favorites, vol. 1*; Richard Kapp, cond.; Philharmonia Virtuosi, orch.] (ESS.A.Y 1022) ♪ ♪ ♪ ♪ ♪

The six concertos on this album do not overlap with those on the recording below, but display Vivaldi's genius through diverse interpretations using various pairs and configurations of instruments. A superb conductor who achieves performances full of feeling, Kapp is in charge of this wonderful ensemble and uncovers an especially remarkable readings throughout. He calls the colorful Concerto in C Major (RV 558) a "Noah's Ark concerto for pairs of just about everything...."

what to buy next: [*Concerti for Diverse Instruments*; Robert King, cond.; King's Consort, orch.] (Hyperion 67073) ♪ ♪ ♪ ♪

While they please diehard Vivaldi fans with well-executed, attractive versions of the seven versatile pieces heard on this set, leader King fails to inspire his musicians to a performance exuding all-around, bright spirit. Still, the works assume proper earnestness and dignity, both for fans who prefer robust, blended sounds and those who like their Vivaldi slightly on the lighter side. Vivaldi's Concerto in B-flat Major for Violin, Oboe, Salmo, Three Violas, Strings, and Continuo (RV 579)—subtitled *Funebre*—ranks high as the most lithesome and synergistic rendering on this disc, especially in the first two movements and in the attention-grabbing, fiery violin solo from Elizabeth Wallfisch that highlights the third movement.

Vocal
Juditha triumphans
what to buy: [*Vivaldi: Sacred Music, vol. 4* Maria Cristina Kiehr, soprano; Ann Murray, mezzo-soprano; Susan Bickley, mezzo-soprano; Sarah Connolly, mezzo-soprano; Jean Rigby, mezzo-soprano; Robert King, cond.; King's Consort, orch.; Choir of King's Consort] (Hyperion 67281/82) ♪ ♪ ♪ ♪ ♪

The (Apocryphal) Biblical theme of Vivaldi's sole surviving oratorio relates to Judith, a young widow of

strong faith who beheaded Holofernes (one of Nebuchadnezzar's generals) in the aftermath of a banquet where he drank to excess after receiving false information from her about how to destroy the Jews in the town he was intent on capturing. Murray provides a wonderful characterization of the heroine while Bickley's Holofernes is an admirably despicable partner for Murray in the duets. King's forces are well-recorded and their playing is beyond reproach. Since Vivaldi's overture for *Juditha* has been lost, the conductor has substituted excerpts from the composer's C Major concerto, RV 555.

Gloria in D Major for Chamber Orchestra and Chorus (RV 589)
what to buy: [Nancy Argenta, soprano; Ingrid Attrot, soprano; Catherine Denley, contralto; Ashley Stafford, alto; Stephen Varcoe, bass; Trevor Pinnock, cond.; English Concert, orch.; English Concert Choir] (Deutsche Grammophon Archiv 423386) ♪ ♪ ♪ ♪

The well-blended chorus, the splendid singers, skillful instrumental soloists, and authentic instrumentation make this version of Vivaldi's *Gloria* a keeper. Denley's deep-toned, luxuriant *Domine Deus, Agnus Dei* is pure exaltation, worth the album price alone. There are many highlights that will lead you to replay this work as well as the performance of Alessandro Scarlatti's *Dixit Dominus,* also included in this set.

[Dawn Upshaw, soprano; Penelope Jensen, soprano; Marietta Simpson, mezzo-soprano, David Gordon, tenor; William Stone, baritone; Robert Shaw, cond.; Atlanta Symphony Orchestra; Atlanta Symphony Chamber Chorus] (Telarc 80194) ♪ ♪ ♪ ♪

A master of vocal performance, conductor Shaw extracts a ravishing performance of this Vivaldi work and J.S. Bach's *Magnificat.* For the wonderful soloists, the grandeur of the vocal chorus, and the graceful beauty of the orchestrations, this performance ranks among the best.

influences: Johann Sebastian Bach, George Frideric Handel, Alessandro Scarlatti, Domenico Scarlatti, Wolfgang Amadeus Mozart, Guiseppe Tartini, Pietro Locatelli, Arcangelo Corelli

Ellen Kokko and Nancy Ann Lee

Richard Wagner

Born Wilhelm Richard Wagner, May 22, 1813, in Leipzig, Germany. Died February 13, 1883, in Venice, Italy.

period: Romantic

Known for his "music dramas" (in particular the tetralogy, *Der Ring des Nibelungen*) and for his use in them of leitmotifs to musically (and subliminally) convey the various levels of meaning, Wagner was the ultimate magician of 19th-century theater. In addition to music, he was involved with poetry, drama, and painting. His works are a "dramatic synthesis" of these various art forms, for which he also crafted the texts, involved himself in the production, and designed the ideal theater for presenting them at Bayreuth.

Richard Wagner was the ninth child of Carl Friedrich Wagner and Johanna Wagner, née Paetz. When his father died six months after Wagner's birth, his mother married the actor and painter Ludwig Geyer and shortly afterwards the family moved to Dresden where Geyer was a member of the Court Theater. Not surprisingly Geyer was influential in his stepson's developing love of the theater. Wagner's early musical activities consisted of teaching himself to play the violin and copying out the scores to Beethoven's Fifth and Ninth Symphonies. He took harmony lessons from Christian Gottlieb Müller, a local musician, before entering Leipzig University in 1831 to study music.

After years of holding minor posts at various theaters, debt forced Wagner to flee his creditors (in 1839) by secretly slipping away to Russia and then England. On the journey to London, the ship on which he had booked passage was forced to seek refuge from a storm in a Norwegian fjord. This incident supposedly inspired Wagner's 1841 opera, *Der fliegende Holländer (The Flying Dutchman)* even though it was based on a tale by the famous poet Heinrich Heine. Following an extended period in Paris, Wagner went to Dresden in 1842 when the Court Theater accepted his opera *Rienzi* for production. Its success there led to his appointment there as Saxon court conductor in 1843 and to a Berlin staging of *Der fliegende Holländer* in 1844. Further opera scores (*Tannhäuser* and *Lohengrin*) soon followed. Wagner then worked on the poem *Siegfrieds Tod (The Death of*

Siegfried), which was to form the basis of his masterpiece, *Der Ring des Nibelungen (The Ring of the Nibelung)*. This project was temporarily halted when he was forced to flee to Switzerland following his participation in the Dresden uprising of 1848-49. Settling in Zurich, Wagner remained active by preparing an edition (lost) of Mozart's *Don Giovanni,* and conducting. While there, he also completed an anti-Semitic treatise entitled *Das Judenthum in der Musik (Judaism in Music)*, following that up in 1851 with a theoretical text entitled *Oper und Drama (Opera and Drama)*. Incorporating a rabid antipathy to Judaism in his theoretical writings, Wagner distinguished "German music" from the contributions of Germanic composers and musicians of Jewish descent.

While he had been surviving mainly on the generosity of friends, in 1855 poverty forced Wagner to accept a four-month conducting engagement in London, but the revenue that he anticipated from the productions was greater than the actual receipts and he returned to Zurich and work on the *Ring*. Two years later he moved into a cottage outside the city owned by Otto Wesendonck. Inspired by his love for Wesendonck's wife Mathilde, Wagner interrupted composition of *Siegfried* to begin work on the opera *Tristan und Isolde,* which was revolutionary in its orchestral sweep and use of dissonance. He also set five poems of Mathilde Wesendonck to music, some of which served as studies for *Tristan und Isolde*. In 1864, Ludwig II, the young king of Bavaria, became Wagner's patron, granting him a stipend to complete the *Ring,* a yearly allowance, and payment of his debts. In return, Ludwig was given original scores and drafts of various of Wagner's operas and other works. *Tristan und Isolde* was premiered in Munich in 1865 under Hans von Bülow, but a conspiracy against Wagner, fomented by Ludwig's cabinet, resulted in his temporary banishment from Bavaria and a return to Switzerland later that year. In Lucerne, Wagner resumed work on his opera *Die Meistersinger von Nürnberg (The Mastersingers of Nuremberg)* which was completed in 1867 and premiered under Bülow the following year. In 1868, Wagner began an open relationship with Cosima von Bülow, daughter of Franz Liszt and wife of the conductor who had done so much to promote his music dramas. She moved in with Wagner at Tribschen and gave birth to a son (Siegfried), their third child, in 1869. Following the Bülows' divorce, Wagner married Cosima in 1870 and premiered his *Siegfried Idyll* with a chamber orchestra playing on the stairway of the family home as a combined Christmas and birthday present for Cosima.

The first installments of the *Ring* cycle, *Das Rheingold* and *Die Walküre,* were premiered in Munich in 1869 and 1870 respectively. But dissatisfaction with the staging and differences with King Ludwig led Wagner to the building of a new theater in Bayreuth to showcase his music dramas. Funds for the construction were raised through the selling of certificates of patronage, a loan from Ludwig, and a concert tour. In 1872 Wagner moved into his new home (*Wahnfried*) at Bayreuth and construction of the theater was begun. Three performances of the complete *Der Ring des Nibelungen* were given at Bayreuth in 1876 with Hans Richter conducting, initiating the Wagner festival that would come to be known universally as the Bayreuth Festival. Debt incurred from the project nearly resulted in the sale of the theater and *Wahnfried,* but Wagner was bailed out by King Ludwig, with a loan to be repaid through the festival proceeds. *Parsifal,* his music drama, was premiered at Bayreuth (perhaps surprisingly, considering the composer's anti-Semitism, by the Jewish conductor Hermann Levi, who greatly admired Wagner) in 1882. Levi conducted sixteen performances, but Wagner personally took the baton and conducted the final scene of its last performance of the season.

In September 1882, Wagner took up residence in the villa *Palazzo Vendramin* on the Grand Canal in Venice. He suffered a fatal heart attack there on February 13, 1883, and his body was brought back to Bayreuth to be buried in the garden of his home at *Wahnfried.* Following Wagner's death, Cosima continued operating the annual summer Wagner Festival at Bayreuth. Under her strict tutelage, Bayreuth became a German nationalistic center. Upon the death of both Cosima and Siegfried in 1930, Siegfried's English-born wife Winifred took over the directorship of Bayreuth. With his ascension to power in 1933, Adolph Hitler was welcomed to Bayreuth by Winifred and the festival was used by the Nazis as a national socialist shrine until the end of the Second World War. With its reopening in 1951 under the composer's grandsons (Wolfgang and Wieland Wagner), the Festival was stripped of much of its chauvinistic baggage.

Influenced by the classical drama of ancient Greece, the German symphonic tradition, Lisztian romanticism, and the philosophy of Arthur Schopenhauer (via the text of *Die Welt als Wille und Vorstellung [The World as Will and Representation]*), Wagner aimed to create a new aesthetic and national art form for the German-speaking nations. This he envisioned as something lofty and seri-

ous, as distinguished from what he considered the frivolous character of Italian and French opera at that time. Wagner believed that the German peoples, if not the world, would be redeemed through listening to his "music dramas." In the "music dramas," as distinct from his earlier operas, and opera generally, Wagner put emphasis on his text (the drama) rather than on the musical aspect of the composition, introducing a declamatory singing style into his own works. He also had the orchestra playing continuously, as opposed to the discrete musical numbers of traditional opera such as aria, recitative, ensembles, and finales. He conceived these works on a symphonic scale, drastically increasing the size of his orchestra, most notably the brass section. Of particular importance was Wagner's development and use of "leitmotifs," repeated musical archetypes that characterize or symbolize various aspects of the drama being enacted on stage.

Orchestral
various overtures
what to buy: [*The Klemperer Legacy—Wagner: Orchestral Works, vol. 1*; Otto Klemperer, cond.; Philharmonia Orchestra] (EMI Classics 66805) ♪♪♪♪♪

[*The Klemperer Legacy—Wagner: Orchestral Works, vol. 2*; Otto Klemperer, cond.; Philharmonia Orchestra] (EMI Studio 66806) ♪♪♪♪♪

A lifetime of conducting Wagner in the theater is summed up in these orchestral excerpts from the operas. While Klemperer was to record only one of the Wagner operas to disc (*Die fliegende Holländer*), his experience and commitment to this music is preserved in these memorable excerpts. The original three LPs have been transferred to two CDs, and at mid-price, these collections are a bargain.

Prelude and *Good Friday Spell* from *Parsifal*
what to buy: [Bruno Walter, cond.; Columbia Symphony Orchestra] (Sony Classics 42038) ♪♪♪♪♪

A stunning performance in outstanding recorded sound, together with Antonín Dvořák's Eighth Symphony, this mid-price release is a treasurable recording.

Vocal
Die Meistersinger von Nürnberg (The Mastersingers of Nuremberg)

what to buy: [Helen Donath, soprano; Ruth Hesse, mezzo-soprano; René Kollo, tenor; Peter Schreier, tenor; Geraint Evans, baritone; Theo Adam, bass; Karl Ridderbusch, bass; Herbert von Karajan, cond; Dresden State Opera Chorus; Leipzig Radio Chorus; Dresden Staatskapelle, orch.] (EMI Classics 67148) ♪ ♪ ♪ ♪

Karajan's second recording, with fine cast and orchestra, is a more studied account than his freer Bayreuth performance. (see below) While in stereo, the atmosphere of the recording is less natural than on the earlier monaural accounts, and EMI balances the singers less favorably and at times places them on separate tracks, detracting from the warmth of the performance. Nevertheless, with a new generation of singers, striving after a more modern performance style, this is one of the finer available *Meistersinger* recordings, recently reissued at mid-price.

worth searching for: [Elisabeth Schwarzkopf, soprano; Ira Malaniuk, mezzo-soprano; Hans Hopf, tenor; Gerhard Unger, tenor; Otto Edelmann, baritone; Erich Kunz, baritone; Friedrich Dalberg, bass; Herbert von Karajan, cond.; Bayreuth Festival Orchestra; Bayreuth Festival Chorus] (EMI Classics 63500) ♪ ♪ ♪ ♪

Die Meistersinger, his only major "comedy," is the composer's most glorious and human opera, and Karajan's "live" performance is as much a tribute to Wagner's genius as a document of the 1951 reopening of the Bayreuth Festival. Its characterizations, singing and orchestral playing are wonderfully free, and its cast features many of the finest post-war era Wagnerian voices. With the performance's joyous singing and orchestral playing, as well as EMI's superb refurbishing and transfer to disc, one easily transcends the extraneous audience and stage noise and sound limitations of this recording. Schwarzkopf is radiant in this classic of the gramophone.

[Elisabeth Grümmer, soprano; Marga Höffgen, mezzo-soprano; Rudolf Schock, tenor; Gerhard Unger, tenor; Ferdinand Frantz, bass; Gottlob Frick, bass; Benno Kusche, baritone; Rudolf Kempe, cond; Berlin Philharmonic Orchestra] (EMI Classics 64154) ♪ ♪ ♪ ♪

This wonderful recording from the 1950s features some outstanding Wagnerian singers of the post-war era. The vocalists are balanced up-front in a natural sound environment for emphasis on the vocal line, creating a concert atmosphere. Though Grümmer, as Eva, does not

sound as young as Schwarzkopf in the earlier Karajan account, the dramatic delivery and beauty of tone of the cast are treasurable. This account, one of the last to capture an older Wagnerian style, makes us painfully aware of the absence of great Wagnerian voices on the stage today.

Der fliegende Holländer (The Flying Dutchman)
what to buy: [Marianne Schech, soprano; Sieglinde Wagner, contralto; Rudolf Schock, tenor; Fritz Wunderlich, tenor; Dietrich Fischer-Dieskau, baritone; Gottlob Frick, bass; Franz Konwitschny, cond.; Berlin Staatskapelle, orch.; Berlin State Opera Chorus] (Berlin Classics 2097) ♪ ♪ ♪ ♪

This 1960 recording (licensed from EMI), though it suffers some steely sound distortion, is as fine a performance of Wagner's tale of redemption through love as any on disc. It features a powerful cast of vocalists. Frick is a superb, melodious Daland, and Fischer-Dieskau, contrary to expectation, is a wonderfully dark, brooding *Holländer.* Schech gives a powerful account of Senta, equalled by few others on disc, while Wunderlich elevates the minor role of Daland's Steersman.

what to buy next: [Anja Silja, soprano; Annelies Burmeister, mezzo-soprano; Ernst Kozub, tenor; Gerhard Unger, tenor; Theo Adam, bass; Martti Talvela, bass; Otto Klemperer, cond.; New Philharmonia Orchestra; BBC Chorus] (EMI Classics 67405) ♪ ♪ ♪ ♪

Klemperer's famous recording offers an outstanding cast, but it is most notable for the wonderfully emotive Senta of Anja Silja. Though Silja's tone is not as beautiful as that of Schech for Konwitschny, her Senta has a tragic intensity. Klemperer's tempos are slower than most, but the performance never drags.

Lohengrin
what to buy: [Elisabeth Grümmer, soprano; Christa Ludwig, mezzo-soprano; Jess Thomas, tenor; Dietrich Fischer-Dieskau, baritone; Gottlob Frick, bass; Otto Wiener, bass; Rudolf Kempe, cond.; Vienna Philharmonic Orchestra; Vienna State Opera Chorus] (EMI Classics 67411) ♪ ♪ ♪ ♪

Kempe's famous stereo recording boasts a strong cast and dramatic performances in Wagner's morality play on the theme of good and evil. Jess Thomas makes a powerful Lohengrin, while Fischer-Dieskau and Christa Ludwig convincingly embody the evil of Friedrich and

Ortrud. Grümmer sings well, though she does not make for an appropriately young-sounding Elsa. Unfortunately, EMI attempted to duplicate sound effects pioneered on the Decca *Ring* cycle, and Lohengrin's distant entrance sounds as if he was recorded in an electronic box (which was most likely the case). This strong account, recently reissued at mid-price, is very good value.

worth searching for: [Maud Cunitz, soprano; Margarete Klose, mezzo-soprano; Rudolf Schock, tenor; Josef Metternich, baritone; Gottlob Frick, bass; Horst Günter, bass; Wilhelm Schüchter, cond.; Northwest German Radio Orchestra, Hamburg; Northwest German Radio Chorus, Hamburg; Cologne Radio Chorus] (EMI Classics 65517) ♪ ♪ ♪ ♪

Sadly, this outstanding performance appears to have been recently deleted from EMI's international catalog. While recorded in monaural sound and marred by a cut of 157 bars in the third act, Schüchter's account offers some of the best singing of this opera on record. In this, his earlier recording of the part, Frick's very precise performance of Heinrich is arguably unsurpassed, while Metternich is an outstanding Friedrich. Schock's account of Lohengrin is distinguished, while Cunitz is an appropriately young-sounding Elsa. The mono sound is very good and the atmosphere is more natural than that of the later Kempe stereo account. (see above)

Tristan und Isolde
what to buy: [Kirsten Flagstad, soprano; Blanche Thebom, mezzo-soprano; Ludwig Suthaus, tenor; Edgar Evans, tenor; Rudolf Schock, tenor; Josef Greindl, baritone; Dietrich Fischer-Dieskau, baritone; Wilhelm Furtwängler, cond.; Philharmonia Orch.; Chorus of the Royal Opera House, Covent Garden] (EMI Classics 56254) ♪ ♪ ♪ ♪ ♪

This classic recording of Wagner's most romantic and pioneering opera, conducted by its most authoritative modern interpreter, is distinguished for Flagstad's powerful Isolde. Suthaus is a vigorous Tristan, though not as effortless as was Melchior for Beecham. The lovers are marvelously supported by a fine cast and orchestra, and Furtwängler opts for a long, sustained dramatic line and slower tempos that usual. The 1953 monaural sound is superb.

what to buy next: [Brigit Nilsson, soprano; Christa Ludwig, mezzo-soprano; Wolfgang Windgassen, tenor; Peter Schreier, tenor; Erwin Wohlfahrt, tenor; Eberhard

Wächter, baritone; Claude Heater, baritone; Martti Talvela, bass; Gerd Nienstedt, bass; Karl Böhm, cond.; Bayreuth Festival Orchestra; Bayreuth Festival Chorus] (Deutsche Grammophon 449772) ♪ ♪ ♪ ♪ ♪

If Flagstad was the mid-20th century's great Isolde, then Nilsson was her worthy successor. Finely pairing Nilsson's powerful Isolde with the heroic Tristan of Wolfgang Windgassen, this "live" performance from the 1966 Bayreuth Festival delivers one of the most visceral recorded accounts of Wagner's retelling of this classical tale. The supporting cast is outstanding, Wächter delivering a wonderfully mellifluous Kurwenal. Under Böhm's vigorous direction, tempos are faster than commonly taken, allowing DG to accommodate each act on a single disc.

Der Ring des Nibelungen (The Ring of the Nibelung)
what to buy: [Kirsten Flagstad, soprano; Birgit Nilsson, soprano; Berit Lindholm, soprano; Vera Schlosser, soprano; Régine Crespin, soprano; Joan Sutherland, soprano; Lucia Popp, soprano; Gwyneth Jones, soprano; Anita Valkki, soprano; Oda Balsborg, soprano; Claire Watson, soprano; Ira Malaniuk, mezzo-soprano; Christa Ludwig, mezzo-soprano; Brigitte Fassbaender, mezzo-soprano; Helga Dernesch, mezzo-soprano; Maureen Guy, mezzo-soprano; Grace Hoffman, mezzo-soprano; Jean Madeira, mezzo-soprano; Marga Höffgen, contralto; Vera Little, contralto; Claudia Hellmann, contralto; Marilyn Tyler, contralto; Helen Watts, contralto; Hetty Plumacher, contralto; James King, tenor; Wolfgang Windgassen, tenor; Gerhard Stolze, tenor; Set Svanholm, tenor; Waldemar Kmentt, tenor; Paul Kuen, tenor; Eberhard Wächter, baritone; Dietrich Fischer-Dieskau, baritone; Gustav Neidlinger, baritone; Kurt Böhme, baritone; Hans Hotter, bass-baritone; George London, bass-baritone; Gottlob Frick, bass; Georg Solti, cond.; Vienna Philharmonic Orchestra; Vienna State Opera Chorus] (Decca 455555) ♪ ♪ ♪ ♪

Wagner's *Ring* tetralogy, a Schopenhauerian parable of the struggle for and fall from power, derived from Norse mythology, was Wagner's magnum opus. Solti's *Ring* for Decca was the first studio-recorded integral *Ring* cycle, and in its day it was a marvel, as it remains in ours. But as with any other *Ring* cycle, it has its pluses and minuses. Its strengths were its generally strong cast, out-

Richard Wagner

standing orchestral accompaniment and stunning recorded sound. Decca scored a coup when it secured Hans Hotter and Kirsten Flagstad, who unfortunately lived long enough only to record *Das Rheingold*. The downside of this *Ring* was its electronic gimmickry, pioneered by producer John Culshaw, which selectively distorted the singing voice in an attempt to simulate stage effects. In spite of its variability, this set remains a testament to Wagner's greatest achievement.

what to buy next: [Gundula Janowitz, soprano; Régine Crespin, soprano; Helen Donath, soprano; Edda Moser, soprano; Liselotte Rebmann, soprano; Catherine Gayer, soprano; Catarina Ligendza, soprano; Helga Dernesch, soprano; Christa Ludwig, mezzo-soprano; Josephine Veasey, mezzo-soprano; Anna Reynolds, mezzo-soprano; Oralia Dominguez, contralto; Jon Vickers, tenor; Donald Grobe, tenor; Jess Thomas, tenor; Gerhard Stolze, tenor; Erwin Wohlfahrt, tenor; Helge Brilioth, tenor; Robert Kerns, baritone; Zoltan Kélémen, baritone; Thomas Stewart, baritone; Dietrich Fischer-Dieskau, bass-baritone; Martti Talvela, bass; Karl Ridderbusch, bass; Herbert von Karajan, cond.; Berlin Philharmonic Orchestra; Chorus of the Deutsche Oper, Berlin] (Deutsche Grammophon 457780) ♪ ♪ ♪ ♪

While Karajan characteristically slimmed down the voices and interpretatively reigned in the strengths of his singers, this *Ring* cycle nevertheless offers some outstanding singing and orchestral accompaniment, notably in its very fine *Die Walküre* and *Götterdämerung*. While overall not as strong an effort as offered by Solti's *Ring* for Decca, this more natural-sounding integral cycle is not overpowered by electronic effects. Recently released at mid-price, it is nicely packaged and a wonderful buy.

Die Walküre (The Valkyrie)

what to buy: [Martha Mödl, soprano; Leonie Rysanek, soprano; Gerda Scheyrer, soprano; Erika Köth, soprano; Hertha Töpper, mezzo-soprano; Margarete Klose, mezzo-soprano; Ruth Siewert, contralto; Dagmar Hermann, contralto; Ludwig Suthaus, tenor; Ferdinand Frantz, baritone; Gottlob Frick, bass; Wilhelm Furtwängler, cond.; Vienna Philharmonic Orchestra] (EMI Classics 63045) ♪ ♪ ♪ ♪ ♪

Furtwängler recorded this classic 1954 monaural account of the great drama of forbidden love and sacrifice, the second part of the *Ring* tetralogy, as the first installment of his planned studio *Ring* cycle, but sadly

didn't live to complete the project. While missing Hans Hotter, then the reigning Wotan, this performance nevertheless boasts spot-on singing from a wonderful cast and marvelous playing from the glorious Vienna Philharmonic. The pairing of the young Leonie Rysanek with a heroic Ludwig Suthaus makes for a strong pair of Wälsung lovers, contrasting sharply with Gottlob Frick's appropriately dark Hunding. Furtwängler nicely paces the performance, and EMI manages to fit it on three discs, rather than the usual four. At mid-price, that makes for an unrivaled bargain.

Parsifal

what to buy: [Lucia Popp, soprano; Kiri Te Kanawa, soprano; Alison Hargan, soprano; Rotraud Hansmann, soprano; Christa Ludwig, mezzo-soprano; Birgit Finnilä, mezzo-soprano; Anne Howells, mezzo-soprano; Margarita Lilowa, mezzo-soprano; Gillian Knight, mezzo-soprano; Marga Schiml, contralto; René Kollo, tenor; Robert Tear, tenor; Heinz Zednik, tenor; Ewald Aichberger, tenor; Dietrich Fischer-Dieskau, baritone; Hans Hotter, baritone; Zoltan Kélémen, baritone; Gottlob Frick, bass; Herbert Lackner, bass; Georg Solti, cond.; Vienna Philharmonic Orchestra; Vienna State Opera Chorus; Vienna Boys Choir] (Decca 417143) ♪ ♪ ♪ ♪

Parsifal is Wagner's mystery play, descendant of the great medieval dramas, and Solti's effort is a strong one. Despite undeserved disparagement of his leadership in favor of Karajan's glitzier production, this remains the stronger performance. Its overall strength lies in its superb casting and orchestral playing, and though the quality of Kélémen's singing style may be an acquired taste, his characterization of the magician Klingsor is one of pure evil. The major flaw in this recording, and it is a serious one, is Decca's shameful electronic distortion of Hans Hotter's Titurel, in a misguided effort to create the effect of his being at stage rear. In spite of this glaring fault, this is a winning performance.

Tristan und Isolde: Prelude and Liebestod

what to buy: [*Wagner: Karajan*; Jessye Norman, soprano; Herbert von Karajan, cond; Vienna Philharmonic Orchestra] (Deutsche Grammophon 423613) ♪ ♪ ♪ ♪

In this love-death final scene from *Tristan und Isolde*, Jessye Norman is a powerhouse of sound and the VPO soars under Karajan in this and the *Siegfried Idyll*, a serenade first performed on the stairway of the Wagner home as a surprise birthday/Christmas present for his wife Cosima. The other work in this "live" concert recording is the overture to *Tannhäuser*.

Wesendonck Lieder
what to buy: [*The Klemperer Legacy*, Christa Ludwig, mezzo-soprano; Otto Klemperer, cond.; Philharmonia Orchestra] (EMI 67037) ♪ ♪ ♪ ♪

Inspired by his forbidden love for Mathilde Wesendonck while residing on her husband's estate, these love songs served as fertile ground for the music of Wagner's later *Tristan und Isolde*. Ludwig's superb attention to the text and her passionate commitment make this a strong recommendation. The *Wesendonck Lieder* are heard here with Klemperer's impressive rendition of Anton Bruckner's Sixth Symphony but it can also be found on a four-disc set dedicated to Ludwig's early and lesser-known recordings, *Les Introuvables de Christa Ludwig* (EMI Classics 64074).

excerpts from various operas
what to buy: [*Hans Hotter: The Early EMI Recordings*; Hans Hotter, baritone; Meinhard von Zallinger, cond.; Vienna Philharmonic Orchestra] (Testament 1199) ♪ ♪ ♪ ♪ ♪

Hotter's 1948 excerpts (two from *Die Meistersinger von Nürnberg* and *Wotan's Farewell* from *Die Walküre*) are not complete, but these fragments are wonderful samples of the art of one of the great Wagner interpreters of the 20th century. Coupled with arias from Handel and songs of Schubert, Schumann, Brahms, and others, this is a marvelous issue.

what to buy: [*Lauritz Melchior, Helen Traubel Sing Wagner: Excerpts from "Tristan und Isolde," "Lohengrin," and "Rienzi"*; Helen Traubel, soprano; Astrid Varnay, soprano; Herta Glaz, mezzo-soprano; Lauritz Melchior, tenor; Kurt Baum, tenor; Torsten Ralf, tenor; Herbert Janssen, baritone; Lorenzo Alvary, bass; Erich Leinsdorf, cond.; Artur Rodzinski, cond.; Fritz Busch, cond.; Roberto Kinsky, cond.; New York Philharmonic Orchestra; Columbia Symphony Orchestra; Metropolitan Opera Orchestra; Orchestra of the Teatro Colón] (Sony Classical 60896) ♪ ♪ ♪ ♪

Who's afraid of Wagner? This collection by two of the great Wagnerian voices of the Metropolitan Opera in the 1940s, together with superb supporting singers, is mellifluously and sensitively sung, dispelling the image of Wagner's music as overbearing and inaccessible. Though suffering some distortion, Traubel's delivery of

Isolde's *Liebestod* is powerful. This mid-priced limited edition is beautifully packaged with wonderful period photos and is sure to satisfy both neophyte and connoisseur. Sony's transfer to disc is outstanding.

influences: Franz Liszt, Hector Berlioz, Hugo Wolf

Gerald B. Goldberg

William Walton
Born William Turner Walton on March 29, 1902, in Oldham, England. Died March 8, 1983, in Ischia, Italy.

period: Twentieth century

William Walton, a distinctive and compelling musical voice in twentieth-century music, is often considered the most significant English composer between Ralph Vaughan Williams and Benjamin Britten. In addition to writing major concertos for violin and viola, Walton also wrote a string of impressive film scores and a series of provocative choral works, including the oratorio *Belshazzar's Feast* and the quirky *Façade*, constructed around the idiosyncratic lyrics of Edith Sitwell.

Walton became a boy chorister at the Christ Church Cathedral Choir School at Oxford when he was ten, having sung in his father's choir prior to that. His early training in the lofts probably influenced his decision to start writing works for unaccompanied chorus, a genre that he returned to frequently, with increasing skill, through the years.

By 1920 Walton had formed an attachment to the remarkable Sitwell siblings, Edith, Osbert, and Sacheverell, and had gone to live with them in London. This close and productive friendship broadened his cultural and artistic horizons, particularly in literature and the visual arts. His relationship with the Sitwells fostered his first significant work, an extraordinary "entertainment" for speaker and chamber ensemble called *Façade*, set to poems by Edith and musically influenced by many of the popular songs and forms of the day. The first performances of this work, both private and public, created a minor-grade scandal but also served notice that the nineteen-year-old Walton possessed a remarkable and highly original talent. *Façade* earned the young man a reputation as one the "bad boys" of contemporary music. By the time he was twenty, Walton had branched out into different formats, including a pungent avant-garde string quartet that was premiered at the first meeting of the International Society for Contemporary Music in Salzburg. This composition made the European musical community sit up and take notice, but he later withdrew the work, although he did not destroy the parts. Comfortable though his situation with the Sitwells was, Walton did not actually begin earning money from his composing until the mid-1920s, when he started writing music for films, a medium in which he was to achieve great distinction.

His next major work was the lyrical and bittersweet Viola Concerto of 1929, first performed by the composer/viola player Paul Hindemith. In 1931 came his powerful and exciting oratorio *Belshazzar's Feast,* which was first performed at the Leeds Festival. The piece only lasts about thirty-five minutes, but it was considered the greatest work in English choral music since Edward Elgar's *The Dream of Gerontius* and has since been recognized as one of the great oratorios of all time. Walton's uniqueness became even more evident when his monumental First Symphony was finally completed in 1935 and his lyrical, moving Violin Concerto (commissioned by the great Jascha Heifetz) was unveiled in 1939. With these accomplishments, Walton was firmly established as a major international composer.

The only writing that brought the composer any real income during the 1930s was the work he did for films. Starting in 1934 and continuing through 1970, Walton displayed a particular flair for the genre, honing his skills to their finest in 1944 with his brilliant score to the first of Laurence Olivier's three Shakespeare films, *Henry V.* This music, considered one of the greatest cinema scores ever composed, brought Walton new acclaim. He wrote some interesting chamber music works in the late 1940s, including a powerful yet understated string quartet, and was finally knighted for his contributions to British cultural life in 1951. Walton's next major work was his first opera, *Troilus and Cressida,* initially produced at the Royal Opera House in 1954. That first production was deemed unsatisfactory in several ways, not least of which was the apparently backward compositional step Walton was taking, veering away from the essentially romantic viewpoint many critics thought the story line deserved. Even though there have been good productions since, and the score is highly regarded by opera buffs and musicians, the work has never caught on with the general public. After that, Walton wrote almost exclusively to commissions, his final major

pieces being the Cello Concerto of 1957 (written for the great Gregor Piatigorsky), the Partita for Orchestra (written for the fortieth anniversary season of the Cleveland Orchestra in 1958), and the *Variations on a Theme by Hindemith* from 1963.

Walton's comparatively small output is of the highest quality, and a good deal of it is of major importance. He remained mostly untouched by mid-twentieth-century styles and techniques: he broke no new ground, did no musical exploration, and remained highly consistent (too consistent, some might say) throughout his life. He certainly accepted new musical techniques but never abandoned basic tonality and clarity of form. The hallmarks of his musical style include technical virtuosity (particularly in the orchestral works), great rhythmic drive, pungent harmonies, wide-ranging melodies, a humorous element bordering on the sardonic, and a strong melancholy cast, which is just one of his links with the music of Edward Elgar.

Orchestral
Concerto for Viola and Orchestra
what to buy: [Nigel Kennedy, viola; André Previn, cond.; Royal Philharmonic Orchestra] (EMI Classics 49628) ♪♪♪♪

This album contains remarkable performances of Walton's two greatest concertos—showcases for viola and violin—superlatively played by the young Kennedy and given great support by Previn and the orchestra. Rich, finely detailed sound makes this disc a winner.

what to buy next: [William Primrose, viola; William Walton, cond.; Philharmonia Orchestra] (Avid Master Series 604) ♪♪♪♪

Walton was a decent conductor and Primrose a masterly violist. The combination of the two makes this one of the finest early recordings of the composer's superb concerto. Also heard on this disc is his Violin Concerto, with Eugene Goossens conducting the Cincinnati Symphony Orchestra and Jascha Heifetz as soloist, as well as his Sinfonia Concertante, with Walton leading the City of Birmingham Symphony Orchestra.

Symphony no. 2
worth searching for: [George Szell, cond.; Cleveland Orchestra] (CBS 46732) ♪♪♪♪♪

Szell and the Clevelanders became great advocates of

Walton's music in the late 1950s and early 1960s, and these performances document a very special relationship between composer, conductor, and orchestra. In addition to the second symphony, this all-Walton project includes his *Variations on a Theme by Hindemith* and the *Partita for Orchestra*. There are not many recordings which can truly be called definitive, but this is one of them, and the interpretations will stand for all time as paragons of the pieces involved.

Vocal

Belshazzar's Feast for Baritone, Orchestra, and Chorus

what to buy: [Stephen Roberts, baritone; Gwynne Howell, bass; David Willcocks, cond.; Philharmonia Orchestra; Bach Choir] (Chandos 8760) ♪ ♪ ♪ ♪

There are number of good recordings of this extraordinary work, but Willcocks's account, featuring fine singing by the choir and riveting playing by the orchestra, is probably the best available. The inclusion of Walton's *Gloria* and the *Coronation Te Deum* help make this a solid overall program, and the engineering is spectacular.

Façade for Two Speakers and Chamber Ensemble

worth searching for: [Dame Edith Sitwell, narrator; Peter Pears, narrator; Anthony Collins, cond.; English Opera Group Ensemble, orch.] (London 425661) ♪ ♪ ♪ ♪

This, the first modern recording of the complete post-1922 final version, is remarkable for Dame Edith's reading of her own verses. Pears is an admirable partner, and Collins's direction has never been bettered.

Henry V: A Shakespeare Scenario

what to buy: [*Scenes from Shakespeare*; Christopher Plummer, narrator; Sir Neville Marriner, cond.; Academy of St. Martin-in-the-Fields, orch.; Choristers of Westminster Cathedral; Academy of St. Martin-in-the-Fields Chorus] (Chandos Enchant 7041) ♪ ♪ ♪ ♪

Most of the music Walton wrote for *Henry V* shows up in this arrangement by Christopher Palmer; while not totally authentic, the setting hews fairly closely to the original score. Plummer is grand, Marriner guides his forces convincingly, and the sonics are clear. Excerpts from other Shakespearean scores by Walton—*As You Like It*, *Hamlet*, and *Richard III*—also appear on this set.

influences: Edward Elgar, Benjamin Britten

Charles Greenwell and Dave Wagner

Peter Warlock

Born Philip Arnold Heseltine, October 30, 1894, in London, England. Died December 17, 1930, in London, England.

period: Twentieth century

Philip Heseltine was not only a musician, he was a prolific writer and critic who published more than nine books and nearly one hundred articles on music. He also worked as an editor and transcriber of early music, taking a keen interest in the music of Elizabethan and Jacobean times. His artistic alter ego, Peter Warlock, wrote music that is a unique mix of Impressionistic harmony and folk-like melodies. His best-known song cycle, *The Curlew*, is based on texts by the Irish poet William Butler Yeats, while the jaunty *Capriol Suite* for String Orchestra and the supple Serenade for String Orchestra have more than a touch of Frederick Delius (an early mentor) about them.

Philip Heseltine was born at the ultra-exclusive Savoy Hotel in the heart of London, to a wealthy family of English bankers and stockbrokers. It was assumed that he would follow in the family tradition as a financier, but he had taken piano lessons when he was six years old and, by the time he was nine, displayed an interest in music that would soon supplant any thoughts of a financial career. While attending Eton, Heseltine was introduced to the music of Delius and became obsessed with it. He managed to finagle an introduction to the composer in 1910 and this meeting led to a friendship between the young lad and the older man which would last until Heseltine's death. Although he attempted a formal education—first in Germany, where he studied piano and the German language, then in a brief period at Oxford University and an even shorter one at the University of London—Heseltine's training was self-generated, through the study of older musical scores and the influence of certain twentieth century composers, specifically Delius and (after 1916) the Dutch composer Bernard van Dieren.

Heseltine's decision to use a pseudonym when writing music has raised some questions with his biographers, and there are almost as many opinions about his reasoning in this matter as there are songs in his oeuvre. No clear answer was ever given by the composer as to why he chose this particular alias and the issue has never been definitively resolved, though he often expressed a great interest in the occult and it is possible that the name "Warlock" had a special meaning for him.

The young Heseltine's lifestyle leaned toward the profligate and, as a result, despite the wealth of his family financial worries followed him for the rest of his life. In the best Romantic tradition, he insisted on living the bohemian life of a young musician. He married an artist's model in 1917 (after having had a child with her) and, outside of a six-month period as music critic for the *London Daily Mail* in 1915 and a short stint as editor at a journal called *The Sackbut* the following year, never held a regular job. He also briefly became good friends with the writer D.H. Lawrence, but their friendship ended when Lawrence used a rather unflattering characterization of Heseltine and his wife in his novel *Women in Love.* Only the threat of legal action caused Lawrence to rewrite the sections of the book dealing with his portrayal of the Heseltines. From 1925 Heseltine ran something of an open-door artists' colony out of his home in Eynsford, where he continued to write songs, edit early music, and write a book on the life and music of Carlos Gesualdo, one of the most musically audacious composers of Italian madrigals in the late Renaissance period. The last year of Heseltine's life was filled with financial problems and fits of depression. He was found dead in his Chelsea flat, the victim of carbon monoxide poisoning. There is still some question as to whether his death was accidental or self-inflicted.

Orchestral
Capriol Suite
what to buy: [Vernon Handley, cond.; Ulster Orchestra] (Chandos 8808) ♪ ♪ ♪ ♪♪

This is a delightful disc, presenting a wonderful combination of music from Warlock with that of his contemporary E.J. Moeran. The complete *Capriol Suite* is played with real verve by the Ulster ensemble, as is Warlock's Serenade for String Orchestra. A pair of works by Moeran—the Nocturne for Baritone and Orchestra (with soloist Hugh Mackey) and the Serenade in G Major for Orchestra—round out the disc.

Vocal
The Curlew for Tenor and Instruments

what to buy: [John Mark Ainsley, tenor; Martyn Brabbins cond.; Nash Ensemble] (Hyperion 66938) ♪ ♪ ♪ ♪♪

The mark of Delius is everywhere in this music and Ainsley's wonderfully clear and sweet tenor fits perfectly with these hauntingly beautiful songs. The disc also includes another handful of songs by the composer plus a rendition of the Serenade for String Orchestra and selections from the *Capriol Suite.*

various songs
what to buy: [James Griffett, tenor; Haffner String Quartet, ensemble] (ASV Quicksilva 6143) ♪ ♪ ♪ ♪♪

Here is another superb disc, with the surprisingly dark, rich quality of Griffett's voice adding extra depth to *The withering of the boughs* and three other songs taken from *The Curlew* plus ten more songs selected from Warlock's oeuvre. Alan Barstow and the Royal Philharmonic Orchestra add their rendition of the *Capriol Suite* to the program.

influences: George Butterworth, Frederick Delius, E.J. Moeran

Dave Wagner

Franz Waxman
Born December 24, 1906, in Königshütte, Germany (now part of Poland). Died February 24, 1967, in Los Angeles, CA

period: Twentieth century

Noted for the consistent high quality of his work, Waxman was a gifted and painstaking master of the art of film scoring. He wrote the music for almost 200 movies, won two Oscars, and (in 1947) founded the Los Angeles International Music Festival.

The child of a steel manufacturing executive, Waxman became interested in music at an early age but, despite his obvious talents, his father insisted that he take a job as a bank teller after finishing the German equivalent of high school. Determined to make music his career, Franz enrolled in the Dresden Music Academy prior to transferring to the Berlin Conservatory. In order to make ends meet while studying in Berlin, Franz began working in a popular jazz band called the Weintraub Syncopators, eventually becoming their chief arranger. Friedrich Hollaender (who, like Waxman, would eventually make his way to America) was one of the composers whose tunes the band played. In 1930 when Hollaender got an assignment to write music for a movie called *The Blue Angel* (starring a little-known actress named Marlene Dietrich), he thought of Waxman and the Syncopators. He introduced Waxman to producer Erich Pommer, who soon hired the young man to arrange and conduct the soundtrack. The movie became a great success and Waxman soon began considering other film projects. One assignment he took on was Fritz Lang's screen adaptation of Ferenc Molnar's play *Liliom*. (Molnar's work was also the basis for the celebrated Rodgers and Hammerstein musical *Carousel*.)

Things were looking up for Waxman professionally, but the situation was bad politically and showed no signs of improvement. In 1934 Waxman was assaulted by a thug on a Berlin street and beaten because he was a Jew; he resolved to leave Germany before things got worse. When Pommer got an offer to leave for America and make movies there, he took Waxman and the young screenwriter Billy Wilder with him. Their first project in Hollywood, an adaptation of a Jerome Kern/Oscar Hammerstein musical called *Music in the Air,* got a good response and enabled Waxman to obtain a job with Universal Pictures. Said job turned out to be *The Bride of Frankenstein* for director James Whale, who had seen *Liliom* and admired Waxman's music. His work on *The Bride of Frankenstein* was so good (arguably the greatest score ever written for a horror film) that Waxman was immediately offered the job of running the entire music operation at the studio. He eventually decided that the non-musical aspects of running a studio department were not to his liking and, after a short time, left the company to concentrate on composing. For the rest of his career in Hollywood, Waxman worked under contract to MGM or Warner Brothers before becoming a freelancer upon the dismantling of the great studio "assembly lines."

As one of the top composers in the motion picture industry, Waxman was expected to write music for every conceivable kind of film but, unlike many of his colleagues, he apparently did not draw distinctions between quality projects that were worthy of his finest efforts and routine pictures that could be dashed off without a great deal of work. Such was the composer's sense of integrity that every project got his very best. The result of his efforts meant that many of Waxman's most subtle and effective scores were written for movies that really aren't very good.

Nevertheless, among all the potboilers and programmers, a number of truly remarkable scores for good films stand out: *Captains Courageous* (1937), Alfred Hitchcock's *Rebecca* (1940), *Humoresque* (1946), the Oscar-winning *Sunset Boulevard*—directed by his old friend Wilder—(1950), *A Place in the Sun* (1951), *Peyton Place* and *The Spirit of St. Louis* (both from 1957), and *The Nun's Story* (1958). In the 1960s Waxman's work with the Los Angeles Music Festival (which he founded) occupied him more and more, and film assignments became fewer. He died in 1967, a couple of years after writing *The Song of Terezin,* a work based on poems found in a World War II concentration camp near Prague.

Orchestral
various film scores
what to buy: [*Sunset Boulevard: The Classic Film Scores of Franz Waxman*; Charles Gerhardt, cond.; National Philharmonic Orchestra] (RCA Victor 0708) ♪ ♪ ♪ ♪ ♪

Another spectacular disc by Gerhardt and the guys from the *RCA Classic Film Scores* series. This album includes a fine suite from the titular motion picture, as well as outstanding selections from *The Bride of Frankenstein, Prince Valiant, Rebecca, The Philadelphia Story,* and the exciting *Ride to Dubno* from *Taras Bulba*. This is, quite simply, one of the finest film score recordings ever made.

Sinfonietta for String Orchestra and Timpani
what to buy: [*Goyana*; Roxan Jurkevich, timpani; Lawrence Foster, cond.; Orquestra Sinfònica de Barcelona i Nacional de Catalunya] (Koch International Classics 7444) ♪ ♪ ♪ ♪

The film scores are Waxman's greatest legacy but he also wrote some worthwhile concert works, including the Sinfonietta for String Orchestra and Timpani. It would be a shame to disregard the non-cinematic aspect of his career, and the eight relatively short works on this disc turn the album into a nice broad sampler of Waxman's more "serious" side. The arrangements of the *Carmen Fantasy* (for trumpet and orchestra) and the *Tristan und Isolde Love Music* (for violin and piano) heard here have their roots in the movies.

Carmen Fantasy for Violin and Orchestra
what to buy: [*Humoresque*; Nadia Salerno-Sonnenberg, violin; Andrew Litton, cond.; London Symphony

Orchestra] (Nonesuch 79464) ♪ ♪ ♪₄

The album is a modern-day remake utilizing elements of Waxman's great film score from the 1940s. In addition to his own scoring (including an arrangement for violin, piano, and orchestra of the *Libestod* from Richard Wagner's *Tristan und Isolde*) there are renditions of works by Antonín Dvořák, Édouard Lalo, George Gershwin, and Cole Porter. While there is not a lot of original Waxman to be found here, it is a fine example of what a great film composer and arranger can do with a musical hodgepodge.

influences: Bernard Herrmann, Erich Wolfgang Korngold, Elmer Bernstein

Jack Goggins and Garaud MacTaggart

Carl Maria von Weber

Born Carl Maria Friedrich Ernst von Weber, c. November 18, 1786, in Eutin, Germany. Died June 5, 1826, in London, England.

period: Classical

Carl Maria von Weber's operatic masterpiece, *Der Freischütz,* is seen by many admirers as the predecessor to the German Romantic era typified by such disparate types as Robert Schumann and Richard Wagner. However, it is the works Weber wrote for the clarinet virtuoso Heinrich Joseph Bärmann—the two concertos and the Quintet in B-flat Major for Clarinet and Strings—plus the orchestral arrangement that Hector Berlioz made of his piano work *Invitation to the Dance* which receive the most performances today.

Carl was the son of Franz Anton Weber from his second marriage. The father was a violinist, an impresario, and the founder of his own theater company. Carl's mother, Genofeva, was a singer in the troupe and his two step-brothers (Fridolin and Edmund, both of whom had studied with Franz Joseph Haydn) were musicians in the band. This was the ensemble with whom Weber spent his formative years, touring the German-speaking countries and presenting various plays and operas. This musical and theatrical background only hints at the kind of childhood Carl must have had since there aren't many documents available to detail the reality of his life at that time. What is known is that his health was never very strong, he had a problem with his hips that caused

him to limp when he walked, and his father desired to turn him into a piano prodigy. Young Weber studied counterpoint with Michael Haydn and piano, singing, and composition with a number of Salzburg and Munich-based teachers. After his mother's death (in 1798) and until late in 1803, much of his life revolved around concert tours, though he did manage to compose a trio of operatic juvenilia and some short piano works.

In 1803 he moved to Vienna and began studying composition with Abbé Georg Joseph Vogler. The well-connected Vogler introduced Weber to the wonders of German folksong (elements of which would show up in later compositions) and some of the more important musicians around town at that time, including Antonio Salieri and Johann Nepomuk Hummel. In addition, Vogler was instrumental in helping Weber secure a position as theater conductor in Breslau a year later. There the youngster took it upon himself to revamp and upgrade the orchestra and chorus, taking special care to program a number of works by German composers or in German translations. His official duties left little time for composition but he did manage to "digest the many different ideas and artistic principles that I had, as it were, swallowed perhaps too hastily, and so gradually to develop my own musical personality." He also ticked off the musicians, who weren't used to the kinds of musical demands Weber made on them, and upset theater management with the costs of the changes he sought to make.

He resigned two years later and moved on to Carlsruhe, where he composed his two symphonies but little else until 1807, when he was employed by Duke Ludwig of Württemberg as his secretary. It was while in this position that he wrote much of his next opera, *Silvana.* 1810 found Weber working as a concert pianist, touring the circuit of theaters around Mannheim and Heidelberg, and continuing his studies with Vogler at Darmstadt. He also managed to sell several of his compositions, including *Silvana,* which premiered later that year. In 1811, Weber returned to the road and, later that year, premiered his next opera (*Abu Hassan*), wrote his two clarinet concertos (inspired by the virtuosity of Heinrich Joseph Bärmann), and composed the second of his piano concertos.

Weber's reputation as an orchestra builder and shaper had reached the management of the Estates Theatre in Prague and, in 1813, they offered him the position of Music Director in hopes that he would effect the necessary changes to make their operation a better, more profitable one. While he was able to upgrade the orchestra's performances and schedule a number of important works for their season programs, Weber was basically unhappy in Prague, plagued by ill health and an inability to find the time necessary to compose. About the only good things to come out of his years there (1813–1816) were his introduction to Caroline Brandt—with whom he engaged in a tumultuous courtship before eventually marrying her in 1818—and the completion of his second piano sonata and the Quintet in B-flat Major for Clarinet and Strings. After leaving Prague, Weber moved to Dresden, where he took up an appointment as Kapellmeister with a directive to build a company specifically for the performance of German operas. This too proved a problematic way station for Weber since his administrative duties and the connivance of the resident Italianate opera company helped thwart his mandate.

Things didn't appear to be getting much better for him on a personal level, either; Caroline's difficult pregnancy, the ensuing death of their baby daughter, and his own lengthy illness in 1819 were disheartening experiences. Despite these setbacks, Weber persevered and later that year wrote a piano piece for his wife—*Aufforderung zum Tanze (Invitation to the Dance)*—which, according to music historian Konrad Huschke, was "not the typical superficial and sentimental waltz of the early nineteenth century but a programmatic dance-poem with an unusually long and rich slow introduction." Weber also began writing his fourth piano sonata and what would become the high point of his career, *Der Freischütz*. In between the completion of that opera and its premiere he began working on *Die drie Pintos*. When *Der Freischütz*—a mystical tale involving the devil, magic bullets, and a misguided hunter—finally debuted in Berlin (June 18, 1821) the reaction from the audience was tremendous, a response that would be echoed by others through the ensuing years.

Weber's next opera (*Euryanthe*) suffered in comparison to *Der Freischütz*, both from the a weak libretto and the expectations of his audiences, who wanted more of the same and got a work more difficult to assimilate instead. The premiere in 1823 received mixed notices while *Der Freischütz* went on to play all the major opera houses in Europe, garnering its most fevered support in London. *Oberon,* his last completed opera, was premiered on April 12, 1826, almost two months before he finally fell to tuberculosis after conducting some concerts in London and just prior to his intended date for

heading home. *Die drie Pintos* was finally completed by another of Weber's admirers, Gustav Mahler, in 1888.

Orchestral
Concerto no. 1 in F Minor for Clarinet and Orchestra, op. 73
what to buy: [Emma Johnson, clarinet; Yan Pascal Tortelier, cond.; English Chamber Orchestra] (ASV 747) ♪ ♪ ♪ ♪

Johnson's playing is as close to perfect as one has any right to expect in the F Minor concerto, with nary a let-down for the follow-up E-flat Major concerto found in the same program. Tortelier gets the ECO to play with plenty of sensitive flair, and that is hardly an oxymoronic statement. Gerard Schwarz's conducting in the op. 74 Clarinet Concerto is just about as good. Ditto for Johnson's takes on the Concertino for Clarinet and Orchestra (with Charles Groves conducting) and, in the smaller format, the *Grand Duo Concertant* (with pianist Gordon Back), which is tossed in as an agreeable makeweight.

what to buy next: [Janet Hilton, clarinet; Neeme Järvi, cond.; City of Birmingham Symphony Orchestra] (Chandos 8305) ♪ ♪ ♪♪

The sonics of this recording are another tribute to Chandos's engineering staff, putting the soloist in a most favorable position vis-a-vis the orchestra. Hilton's playing is steady and conservative throughout, which means no great interpretive chances are taken even though her technique could probably handle greater challenges. The same material covered on the Johnson album gets a solid run-through in this set with the exception of the *Grand Duo Concertant*, which isn't heard here.

[Ernst Ottensamer, clarinet; Johannes Wildner, cond.; Czecho-Slovak State Philharmonic Orchestra] (Naxos 8.550378) ♪ ♪ ♪♪

Ottensamer is not exactly a household name in retail circles but his performances deserve a hearing. Both of Weber's clarinet concertos are included here and benefit from some wonderful playing, and with the Concertino for Clarinet and Orchestra also on the program this package duplicates the works heard on the Hilton disc.

various overtures
what to buy: [Roy Goodman, cond.; Hanover Band, orch.] (Nimbus 7062/63) ♪ ♪ ♪ ♪ ♪

In addition to a fine selection of Weber's operatic overtures (including the one to *Der Freischütz*) this set features the added pleasure of Hector Berlioz's orchestration of Weber's *Invitation to the Dance*. Period instruments are used but the sound is still amazingly full and the performances are very noteworthy. The two-disc set also includes fine renditions of Weber's symphonies in addition to a respectable version of the composer's Concertino in E Minor for Horn and Orchestra (op. 45) with soloist Anthony Halstead.

what to buy next: [Neeme Järvi, cond.; Philharmonia Orchestra] (Chandos 9066) ♪ ♪ ♪ ♪

Järvi has generally been a good, solid conductor who occasionally will create a great performance. Things haven't changed with this set, although one would be hard pressed to assign greatness to it. Still, there are virtues, not least of which are the sonics with which the Chandos engineers blessed this project. The overture to *Der Freischütz* is included, but the clincher may be the punchy overture and march from Weber's incidental music to Schiller's play *Turandot*.

Chamber
Sonatas for Piano (complete)
what to buy: [Garrick Ohlsson, piano] (Arabesque 6584) ♪ ♪ ♪ ♪

Ohlsson's two-disc survey of Weber's four piano sonatas displays the virtues of completeness and consistently excellent technique, falling short only when compared to Emil Gilels's emotional artistry in the second (A-flat Major) sonata and Leon Fleisher's superbly-crafted fourth (E Minor). Ohlsson also includes three lovely bonbons by the composer: the original piano version of *Invitation to the Dance* (op. 65), the *Rondo Brillante* (op. 52), and the *Momento Capriccioso* (op. 12).

Quintet in B-flat Major for Clarinet and Strings, op. 34
what to buy: [Walter Boeykens, clarinet; Walter Boeykens Ensemble] (Harmonia Mundi Musique d'Abord 1951481) ♪ ♪ ♪ ♪

Boeykens is a marvelous clarinet player and this is one of his finest recorded moments. Rarely has the dark,

woody feel of the second movement *Fantasia* been conveyed so well, and his performance in the *Grand Duo Concertante* is wonderful too. Weber's seven *Variations on a Theme from "Silvana"* for Clarinet and Piano also benefit from Boeykens's skill.

what to buy next: [Kálmán Berkes, clarinet; Auer Quartet, ensemble] (Naxos 8.553122) ♪ ♪ ♪ ♪

The price is a bargain, with performances worth far more than some costlier versions. In addition to a wonderfully played Quintet, there is a fine *Introduction, Theme, and Variations*, a really good *Variations on a Theme from "Silvana,"* and a good, but not great, version of the *Grand Duo Concertante*.

Vocal
Der Freischütz
what to buy: [Gundula Janowitz, soprano; Edith Mathis, soprano; Pete Schreier, tenor; Bernd Weikl, baritone; Theo Adam, bass-baritone; Franz Crass, bass; Günter Leib, bass; Siegfried Vogel, bass; Carlos Kleiber, cond.; Dresden Staatskapelle, orch.; Leipzig Radio Choir] (Deutsche Grammophon 457736) ♪ ♪ ♪ ♪ ♪

There are newer versions of Weber's most popular opera but Kleiber's conception of how the work should sound, his marvelous cast, and the engineers at Deutsche Grammophon have made this vintage 1970s production the one to beat. The Wolf's Glen scene, where the magic bullets are created, is awesome in its diabolical power.

what to buy next: [Anne Constantin, soprano; Cécile Perrin, soprano; Françoise Soulet, tenor; Jacques Perroni, baritone; Didier Henry, baritone; Francis Dudziak, baritone; Fernand Bernadi, bass; Jean-Marie Lenaerts, bass; Jean-Paul Penin, cond.; Hungarian Philharmonic Chamber Orchestra; Chœurs de Saint-Eustache, choir] (l'Empreinte digitale 13100/01) ♪ ♪ ♪ ♪

Berlioz, despite his initial reluctance to touch the perfection of Weber's score, did so to assure that the debut production of this work at the Paris Opéra would have musical recitatives in accordance with the dictates of the venue (where no spoken dialog was permitted) and in keeping with the spirit of the music. Penin and company treat the work just as it would have been handled at that performance, singing in French instead of German and following Berlioz's musical directives in the recitatives. The cast is good but not great and the set is geared toward those Weber aficionados looking more for historical context than a definitive version.

influences: Wolfgang Amadeus Mozart, Franz Liszt, Hector Berlioz, Richard Wagner

William Gerard

Anton Webern

Born Anton Friedrich Wilhelm von Webern, December 3, 1883, in Vienna, Austria. Died September 15, 1945, in Mittersill, Austria.

period: Twentieth century

". . . to convey a novel through a single gesture, or felicity by a single catch of the breath: such concentration exists only when emotional self-indulgence is correspondingly absent." Arnold Schoenberg wrote these words in 1924 as part of the foreword to Anton Webern's six *Bagatelles* for String Quartet, op. 9. No words could better express Webern's music than these, for although his style was brevity itself and his whole output takes just a few hours to perform, this is not simple music.

Anton Webern spent much of his later youth in Klangenfurt. The years 1884–1902 were the years of formation, with Anton studying piano, cello, and some theory with a local teacher. In 1902 he enrolled at the University of Vienna to study with the great musicologist Guido Adler, but Webern was also focusing on harmony and counterpoint and composing songs, chamber music, and an orchestral work, *Im Sommerwind*. After receiving his Ph.D. in 1906—his dissertation was an edition of part 2 of Heinrich Isaac's *Choralis Constantinus*—he went to Arnold Schoenberg, seeking further instruction in composition. Alban Berg found the master that same year and the three composers would become lifelong friends and colleagues.

Webern would compose a number of pieces in these early years, including *Langsamer Satz* (1905), the Piano Quintet (1907), and *Passacaglia* for Orchestra, op. 1 (1908). The style of these works is post-Romantic and quite chromatic in its use of harmony, though there are hints of the stylistic transformation to come. Schoenberg's *Verklärte Nacht* is an influence in Webern's next score, also from 1908—the nearly atonal choral work, *Entfliecht auf leichen Kähnen*, op. 2—but his studies of Isaac's oeuvre could also be counted in that regard. Webern's next compositions were the two sets of songs *Five Songs from "Der siebente Ring"* by

Stefan George, op. 3, and *Five Songs on poems of Stefan George,* op. 4; the five *Movements* for string quartet, op. 5; and the six *Pieces for Orchestra*, op. 6. The orchestral work makes great use of something that Schoenberg would term *Klangfarbenmelodie* ("melody of color"), and this focus on the coloristic possibilities of the orchestra would become a stylistic trait of the Second Viennese School, especially Anton Webern.

Brevity in Webern's music becomes more pronounced during the period of 1910–1914. In compositions such as the four *Pieces* for Violin and Piano (op. 7), the six *Bagatelles* for string quartet (op. 9), and the five *Pieces for Orchestra* (op. 10), the music is so concise that six measures can convey a complete movement (as it does in the fourth piece of op. 10). Between 1913 and 1926, Webern's predominant genre was song—voice and piano, or voice with a small instrumental group, featuring texts ranging from those of Georg Trakl (op. 14) to the *Five Sacred Songs* (op. 15). Texts from the liturgy also play a part in *Three Songs* (op. 18). Use of canonic and contrapuntal devices, simplicity and directness of expression—all are hallmarks of the composer's style at this point. A number of the later works from this period exhibit traces of something that Schoenberg was working out—a "method of composition with twelve notes related only to one another." Schoenberg "officially" announced this to his students in February of 1923, though we can see it clearly marked in Webern's sketches for op. 15 in 1922.

After World War I Webern became more active in Schoenberg's Society for Private Musical Performances and found work conducting several choral groups. Universal Edition began publishing his music in 1920 and by the end of that decade he had an international reputation. As Webern adopted the twelve-tone method, he felt free to work again with instrumental groups and with larger forms. His compositions would not achieve the expanse of someone like Gustav Mahler, but Webern was satisfied that his music was moving toward a truly symphonic nature. He even used traditional forms such as rondo and sonata-allegro in his String Trio (op. 20) while employing an ever-increasing degree of serial technique. Webern's friend Hildegard Jone supplied the texts for his vocal compositions in the 1930s. These include the sets of songs (opp. 23 and 25), *Das Augenlicht* (op. 26), Cantata no. 1 (op. 29), and Cantata no. 2 (op. 31). Instrumental compositions include his *Variations* for Piano (op. 27) and the orchestral *Variations* (op. 30).

"Entartete Musik!" ("degenerate music"), a branding of music (and art) that would forever alter the course of Europe and the twentieth century, made its impact in March of 1938 when Austria was incorporated into the Third Reich. Music so branded was banned from publication and performance. This blacklisting would include many composers, and Webern was one of them. He lost his position as conductor, his music could not be performed, and he was forced to earn a living by teaching and doing occasional arrangements for Universal Edition. In March of 1945, with the Russian army approaching Vienna, Webern fled with his wife to Mittersill in the American Zone. On September 15, 1945, he was mistaken for a black marketeer and killed by an American soldier.

The end of the war saw a shift in musical composition, one that looked to the Second Viennese School for guidance. Though only Schoenberg was still alive, their musical legacy was already quite valuable. Webern in particular became an important influence on several prominent postwar composers; Pierre Boulez, Karlheinz Stockhausen, Luigi Nono, Luciano Berio, and Milton Babbitt would be only a small number of those who saw the future in Anton Webern. Even after the twelve-tone "rage" ended Webern's music remained, esteemed as a great expression of the twentieth century.

Orchestral
various works
what to buy: [Complete Works, opp. 1–31; Pierre Boulez, cond.; London Symphony Orchestra; John Alldis Choir] (Sony Classical 45845) ♪ ♪ ♪ ♪ ♪

These performances are from 1967 to 1972. The soloists for various chamber (Juilliard String Quartet, Isaac Stern, Gregor Piatigorsky, Charles Rosen) and vocal works (Heather Harper, Halina Lukomska) included in this set are first-rate, but the repertoire covered in this collection consists basically of works with opus numbers. The early pieces are not there, but that's a small price to pay for this fine three-disc collection.

[Complete Webern; Pierre Boulez, cond.; Berlin Philharmonic Orchestra; Ensemble Intercontemporain; BBC Singers, choir] (Deutsche Grammophon 457637) ♪ ♪ ♪ ♪ ♪

For those seeking a fuller sampling of Webern, Deutsche Grammophon offers this more recent cache of recordings made from 1992 to 1996. Most of the composer's

early material can be found on this six-CD set, including Im Sommerwind and arrangements he made of works by Johann Sebastian Bach and Franz Schubert. The Johann Strauss, Jr. settings are not here, however. The non-orchestral scores in this set are handled by the Emerson String Quartet, pianist Krystian Zimerman, violinist Gidon Kremer, soprano Christiane Oelze, and a host of other worthies.

Passacaglia for Orchestra, op. 1
worth searching for: [Claudio Abbado, Vienna Philharmonic Orchestra] (Deutsche Grammophon 431774) ♪ ♪ ♪ ♪ ♪

This is a fine collection, wonderfully played. Several other works by Webern are presented here: the five Pieces of op. 10, the six Pieces of op. 6, and his Variations for Orchestra (op. 30), along with Schoenberg's stunning A Survivor from Warsaw.

Vocal
various vocal works
what to buy: [Complete Vocal Chamber Music; Dorothy Dorow, soprano; Reinbert DeLeeuw, cond.; Schönberg Ensemble, orch.; Netherlands Chamber Choir] (Koch Schwann 314005) ♪ ♪ ♪ ♪ ♪

Dorow is heard as the soloist for most of the album, most notably in a stunning rendition of the two Rilke Lieder, op. 8. The Netherlands Chamber Choir can be best heard on the two Entfliecht auf leichen Kähnen, op. 2, which bracket the balance of the album. DeLeeuw is an outstanding conductor of twentieth century materials and nearly outdoes himself here.

influences: Arnold Schoenberg, Alban Berg, Igor Stravinsky

Frank Retzel

Kurt Weill
Born Kurt Julian Weill, March 2, 1900, in Dessau, Germany. Died April 3, 1950, in New York City, NY

period: Twentieth century

Kurt Weill composed chamber music, symphonic scores, and a number of vocal works, but is best-known for his labors in the field of musical theater, supplying the music for a number of popular songs. His days in Germany saw the production of "Moritat" (better known among English speakers as "Mack the Knife") and "Alabama Song" while the American years supplied such well-crafted pop gems as "Speak Low" and "September Song."

Depending on the orientation of the musical historian speaking, it is just as easy to halve Weill's creative life into European and American periods as it is to split it into three parts: pre-Bertold Brecht, works with Brecht, and later works without Brecht. Perhaps the key piece in this set of options is *Die Dreigroschenoper (The Threepenny Opera)*, the most popular production of the partnership and one that has gifted the world with "Mack the Knife."

Prior to the advent of their affiliation, Weill was already establishing himself as both a promising conductor and a composer of music with non-tonal tendencies. His early string quartet (op. 8) had received the blessings of his teacher Ferruccio Busoni (who recommended it to the publishing firm Universal Edition in 1923) and the influences of Paul Hindemith, Igor Stravinsky, Gustav Mahler, and Arnold Schoenberg could be heard in the impressive Concerto for Violin and Wind Orchestra (op. 12). Weill was also beginning to make a mark in the world of German opera with the successful production of *Der Protagonist (The Protagonist)* in 1926, the same year he married the woman who was to be his most formidable adherent, the singer/actress Lotte Lenya.

The following year Brecht and Weill met and began discussing future collaborations, in particular the *Mahagonny Songspiel* which included "Alabama Song" and set previously-existing poetry by Brecht to newly created music from Weill. This process also held true for *Vom Tod im Wald (The Death in the Forest)*, a score for bass vocalist and ten wind instruments, which was likewise a product of 1927. The texts that Brecht was providing to the partnership generally espoused humanist and socialist viewpoints that frequently needled capitalist power structures; his lyrics also supplied the vocal sting to the duo's next important works, the opera *Aufstieg und Fall der Stadt Mahagonny (The Rise and Fall of Mahagonny City)*—a piece which was partially based on the earlier *Mahagonny Songspiel*—and *Die Dreigroschenoper (The Threepenny Opera)*, an updated adaptation of John Gay's eighteenth century English stage work *The Beggar's Opera*.

The Threepenny Opera opened to rave reviews in 1928 and has continued to amaze and please audiences with its verbal audacity, its skillful characterizations, and most of all its music. Over time the score went through a number of permutations, including having some songs and dialog that were originally assigned to one character showing up in the mouth of another during a subsequent production. The most blatant change involves "Seeräuberjenny (Pirate Jenny)," which went from Polly Peachum in 1928 to Jenny (played by Lenya) in the 1930 revision; lines for Mrs. Peachum also went to Jenny, and Lucy Brown briefly gained Polly's "Barbara Song" during the initial Berlin run of the work. (After Weill's death, Brecht, who in addition to being a talented poet and playwright had garnered a modicum of fame as a cabaret singer/guitarist, claimed to have written the music for "Pirate Jenny" and "Barbara Song," but there are significant differences between Weill's published score and the materials found in the Brecht Archive that would seem to minimize his musical contribution though not necessarily his inspiration.)

The Rise and Fall of Mahagonny City didn't fare as well at its premiere in 1930, or in any of the subsequent revisions that took place later that year. In fact, the political climate in Germany was becoming increasingly difficult for artists like Brecht and Weill, particularly for the composer, a Jew. Despite the unpleasant reaction of the populace to that opera, the pair had better luck with the debut of another stage work, *Der Jasager (The Yes-Sayer)*, a few months later. By 1933, however, Adolph Hitler became chancellor and Weill again suffered public anti-Semitic abuse, this time during a performance of an opera with text by Georg Kaiser, *Der Silbersee (The Silver Lake)*. By the end of February 1933 the Nazis had seized power and a month later Weill left for France. Not only would the composer become a virtual exile from the country of his birth, but his marriage to Lenya was over, his publishing contract with Universal Edition was suspended, and the premiere of another Brecht/Weill collaboration, *Die sieben Todsünden (The Seven Deadly Sins)*, made little apparent impression on Parisian audiences.

By 1935 Weill and Lenya had reconciled and the pair left Europe for the United States, arriving in September. Within a year, Weill was engaged in creating a score for the Paul Green play *Johnny Johnson*. This was a work which, in a way, stepped on Brecht's artistic toes because it was an Americanized version of the Jaroslav Hasek novel *The Good Soldier Schweik*, a dramatized

production of which Brecht had contributed to in 1928. Weill and Lenya remarried in 1937, the same year that the composer started working for films in Hollywood and took steps to acquire American citizenship. The Broadway show he wrote with Maxwell Anderson, *Knickerbocker Holiday,* became a hit in 1938 and contributed the hit tune "September Song" to generations of pop singers. With the exception of *The Firebrand of Florence* from 1944, all of his subsequent Broadway shows—including *Lady in the Dark* (1941), *One Touch of Venus* (from which the classic song "Speak Low" comes, 1943), and *Lost in the Stars* (1949)—opened to good if not excellent reviews and box office sales.

Orchestral
Suite for Wind Orchestra from *The Threepenny Opera*
what to buy: [David Atherton, cond.; London Sinfonietta, orch.] (Deutsche Grammophon 459442) ♪ ♪ ♪ ♪ ♪

The most fun-filled example of Weill's work in the wind-band medium is the suite he created from material found in *The Threepenny Opera,* and Atherton's performance is the finest rendition of this setting currently in catalog. It is only part of a wonderful two-disc set containing definitive modern versions of Weill's two key works for wind orchestra (the suite and the Concerto for Violin and Wind Orchestra—the latter featuring Nona Liddell as soloist) and superbly-crafted renditions of his major non-operatic vocal pieces: *Happy End* (minus *Bilbao Song*), the *Berliner Requiem,* the *Mahagonny Songspiel,* and *Vom Tod im Wald (The Death in the Forest),* plus the first *Pantomime* from *The Protagonist.*

Concerto for Violin and Wind Orchestra, op. 12
what to buy: [Elisabeth Glab, violin; Philippe Herreweghe, cond.; Ensemble Musique Oblique, orch.] (Harmonia Mundi France 901422) ♪ ♪ ♪ ♪

Weill worked wonders with this unlikely combination of instruments and his solutions to the problems posed by a string instrument soloing over a mass of woodwinds are ingenious and worth repeated hearings. While it isn't the headlining work on this disc (that honor goes to the composer's *Berliner Requiem*), Glab is a marvelous violinist ably abetted by Herreweghe's pacing and his clear delineation of textures.

Kurt Weill

Gillian Weir:
Born in New Zealand and educated at the Royal College of Music in London, Gillian Weir has inspired a number of today's organists through her solid musical technique and instincts informed by scholarly research. She is in constant demand, not only as a player but as a judge at a number of leading international competitions. Weir has also tried her hand at broadcasting, teaching, and writing. In 1996 she was the first organist to be made a Dame Commander of the British Empire.

Dame Gillian has a repertoire that is exceptional for both its wide range and its individual focus on musical periods from the Renaissance through the contemporary era. She has also been known as an advocate for a more continental style of organ-building than is generally accepted in Great Britain, and has continually championed encased mechanical action instruments as the ideal organ for expressive and musical players.

Weir has recorded the complete organ works of Olivier Messiaen (Collins Classics 7031, out of print), and has written articles on the unique approach to music that Messiaen embraced (including incorporation of birdsongs). Along with solo recordings, look for one of the Camille Saint-Säens Symphony no. 3 with the Ulster Orchestra conducted by Yan Pascal Tortelier (Chandos 8822). Weir also joins the Ulster Orchestra with Vernon Handley directing in the seldom-heard *Concert Piece* for Organ and Orchestra, op. 181, by the English composer Charles Villier Stanford (Chandos 8861). Weir's most recent disc at this writing is a recital on the Aeolian-Skinner organ of the First Church of Christ, Scientist in Boston, including Joseph Jongen's *Sonata Eroica,* Paul Hindemith's *Sonata 1,* and Healy Willan's *Introduction, Passacaglia, and Fugue* (Priory 751). One of the best surveys of Weir's talents, and definitely worth searching for, is the five-CD box set *King of Instruments: The Art of Gillian Wier* (Argo 460185, out of print).

Organ recordings can be difficult to find, so consult the Organ Historical Society at P.O. Box 26811, Richmond, VA 23261, or on the web at www.ohscatalog.org. Here you will find almost the complete Weir discography, including the Argo set.

Dave Wagner

---

what to buy next: [Daniel Hope, violin; William Boughton, cond.; English Symphony Orchestra] (Nimbus 5582) ♪ ♪ ♪⸴

With violin works from Weill, Toru Takemitsu, and Alfred Schnittke, it is apparent that the focus of the album is the brilliant young violinist Daniel Hope. There is more technical muscle here than in Glab's performance but there is also less magic.

Vocal
Die Dreigroschenoper (Threepenny Opera)
what to buy: [Ute Lemper, soprano; Helga Dernesch, mezzo-soprano; Susanne Tremper, singer; Milva, narrator; René Kollo, tenor; Mario Adorf, singer; Wolfgang Reichmann, singer; Rolf Boysen, singer; John Mauceri,

cond.; RIAS Sinfonietta, orch.; RIAS Berlin Sinfonietta Chamber Choir] (Decca 430075) ♪ ♪ ♪ ♪₈

This isn't a perfectly performed *Threepenny Opera*, but it will do until Teresa Stratas goes in the studio to make one. Tempos are good throughout, the recording itself is top-notch, and Lemper is much better than Lenya from a technical standpoint although her characterizations aren't quite as worldly-wise or world-weary. Kollo's trained tenor seems a bit out of place when compared to the cast of German theater veterans.

what to buy next: [Lotte Lenya, soprano; Jo Sullivan, soprano; Beatrice Arthur, singer; Charlotte Rae, singer; Jo Sullivan, singer; Scott Merrill, singer; George Tyne, singer; Martin Wolfson, singer; Paul Dooley, singer; John Astin, singer; Gerald Price, narrator; Mark Blitzstein, piano; Samuel Matlowsky, cond.; The Threepenny Opera Orchestra] (Decca Broadway 159463) ♪ ♪ ♪ ♪

Composer Marc Blitzstein adapted Bertold Brecht's text for American audiences, translating the core of the work but deleting the profanity and sugar coating much of Brecht's political ideology. Still, many Americans were introduced to "Mack the Knife" and "Pirate Jenny" through this production, and that was a good thing.

[Gabriele Ramm, soprano; Ulrike Steinsky, soprano; Jolanta Kuznik, soprano; Jane Henschel, contralto; Peter Nikolaus Kante, tenor; Walter Raffeiner, tenor; Rolf Wollrad, baritone; Reinhard Firchow, baritone; Jan Latham-König, cond.; König Ensemble, orch.; Händel Collegium Köln, choir] (Capriccio 60058) ♪ ♪ ♪ ♪

The tempos in the opening overture are slower than in other versions but Latham-König and his colleagues take that pacing and make it convincing. Not a great first choice, but certainly a worthy second option.

[Lotte Lenya, soprano; Erika Helmke, soprano; Kurt Gerron, narrator; Theo Mackeben, cond.; Lewis-Ruth Band, orch.] (Teldec 72025) ♪ ♪ ♪

Lenya recorded other versions of this work but the performances here feature the original German cast from 1930 in an abridged version of the score that was arranged by Mackeben. Get past the dated sonics (the source of the relatively low bone rating) and you will be rewarded with Weill's intensely new vision on the eve of Nazi Germany. German and French cabaret songs from

Marlene Dietrich and Curt Bois help fill out the balance of the program.

Die sieben Todsünden (The Seven Deadly Sins)
what to buy: [Teresa Stratas, soprano; Nora Kimball, soprano; Howard Haskin, tenor; Frank Kelley, tenor; Herbert Perry, baritone; Peter Rose, bass; Kent Nagano, cond.; Lyon Opera Orchestra] (Nonesuch 17068) ♪ ♪ ♪ ♪ ♪

Stratas is one of the premier Weill interpreters of modern times, and her performance in this wonderfully decadent cycle makes this disc a core holding for anyone interested in the composer. Nagano consistently proves himself to be one of the finest American conductors, and the male quartet is quite good. Weill's second symphony, a work that attempts more than it succeeds, fills up the balance of the program.

what to buy next: [Marianne Faithful, soprano; Hugo Munday, tenor; Mark Bleeke, tenor; Peter Becker, baritone; Wilbur Pauley, bass; Dennis Russell Davies, cond.; Vienna Radio Symphony Orchestra] (RCA Victor 60119) ♪ ♪ ♪ ♪

Lenya and Faithful have pretty much the same vocal qualities, which means that the term "soprano" assigned to either is about a step or so above reality. Still, this is a marvelous, gritty performance of the English-language version which serves as a useful adjunct to the original German setting. Faithful also sings four of Weill's classic songs ("Alabama Song," "The Ballad of Sexual Dependency," "Bilbao Song," and "Pirate Jenny") most convincingly.

various songs
what to buy: [*The Unknown Kurt Weill*; Teresa Stratas, soprano; Richard Woitach, piano] (Nonesuch 79019) ♪ ♪ ♪ ♪ ♪

Lotte Lenya, Weill's widow, felt that Teresa Stratas was the only modern singer able to perform Weill's material in the way it was supposed to be done. This disc makes a pretty good case for Lenya's argument; Stratas is marvelous throughout, doing a splendid job on songs that were rarely performed at the time of this recording including "Die Muschel von Margate (The Mussel of Margate)" and "Schickelgruber," tunes now afforded classic status.

[*Ute Lemper Sings Kurt Weill*; Ute Lemper, soprano;

John Mauceri, cond.; RIAS Berlin Sinfonietta, orch.] (London 425204) ♪ ♪ ♪ ♪ ♪

Lemper manages to cross the great divide between the cabaret/theater and the opera house, something that Stratas, as great as she is, has not been able to do. As a result, Lemper makes downtown ("Speak Low") sit next to uptown ("Nannas Lied" from the composer's *Berliner Requiem*) better than just about any other singer.

what to buy next: [*Lotte Lenya Sings Kurt Weill— American Theatre Songs*; Lotte Lenya, soprano; Maurice Levine, cond.; anonymous orchestra; anonymous chorus] (Sony Classics 60647) ♪ ♪ ♪ ♪⸰

[*Lotte Lenya Sings Kurt Weill's "The Seven Deadly Sins" and Berlin Theater Songs*; Lotte Lenya, soprano; Roger Bean, cond.; anonymous orchestra] (Sony Classics 63222) ♪ ♪ ♪ ♪⸰

It is no secret that Weill wrote most of his material for a higher voice and his songs had to be arranged downward to fit within Lenya's constricted range. That said, this pair of discs contains palpable proof that her cigarette-scarred voice was the most effective vehicle for conveying the blend of decadence and longing filling these songs. The tunes themselves are among the best-known in Weill's canon, including "Moritat (Mack the Knife)" and "Surabaya Johnny" from the Berlin theater days and, from his time spent on Broadway, "Speak Low" and "September Song."

[*Berlin im Licht (Berlin Lit Up)*; Rosemary Hardy, soprano; Heinz Karl Gruber, tenor; Heinz Karl Gruber, cond.; Ensemble Modern, orch.] (Largo 5114) ♪ ♪ ♪ ♪

The arrangements featured on this album are for a "jazz band" similar in sound to the military-style bands Weill often wrote for during the 1920s in Berlin. The music is redolent of decadent dance halls, but the performances have the tautness of a well-honed pit orchestra playing twelve "tone bonbons." In addition to a finely chosen selection of relatively rare songs and instrumental pieces, this set includes an excellently-written 199-page book printed in three languages.

influences: Stephen Sondheim, Leonard Bernstein, Alban Berg, Hans Werner Henze, Nikos Skalkottas

William Gerard

Charles-Marie Widor

Born Charles-Marie-Jean-Albert Widor, February 21, 1844, in Lyons, France. Died March 12, 1937, in Paris, France.

period: Romantic

More than any other single composer, Charles-Marie Widor is responsible for the development of the organ "symphony," utilizing the multitude of sounds made available to him by the advances in organ construction developed by Aristide Cavaillé-Coll—an organ builder whose largest instrument (built in 1862 with five manuals and one hundred stops) was built for the church of St. Sulpice, Paris, where Widor was organist. Widor used Cavaillé-Coll's new instruments to create a wide range of timbres which, in effect, treated the organ like a miniaturized orchestra. Although he wrote scores in a variety of formats, almost none of Widor's works featuring instruments other than the organ are performed today.

Widor was born into a family of organists and organ-builders. His early training from his father revealed such talent and ability that the young musician received his first position as organist when he was only eleven years old. Later, upon the recommendation of Cavaillé-Coll, Widor went to Brussels to study organ with Jacques-Nicolas Lemmens, one of Europe's most prominent teachers and performers, and composition with François Fétis, the director of the Brussels Conservatoire. In 1869, Widor became assistant to Camille Saint-Saëns at the Madeleine in Paris, and a year later the church of St. Sulpice awarded Widor (based on recommendations by Cavaillé-Coll and Charles Gounod) a provisional one-year appointment as titular organist that turned into a stay of sixty-four years.

His first four organ symphonies were bound together as his opus 14 in 1872, but it is quite possible that they were not created as unified works and were cobbled together out of disparate instrumental movements created over a long period of time for various church services and recitals. Gabriel Fauré was also employed by the church during this time, playing the smaller organ in the choir loft, and the two men often engaged in informal contests against each other (while services were going on) for a little over two years before Fauré left to become Saint-Saëns's assistant in January 1874. Widor's superbly fashioned Mass (op. 36) was created for two organs and double choir four years later, while the next set of his organ symphonies (op. 42) was published in 1887 and seems to have been developed in a more orderly, coherent fashion than his earlier set. This is the group of compositions containing what is probably Widor's most popular work, the final movement from his Symphony no. 5 in F Minor: the mighty, powerful *Toccata*.

He began his teaching career at the Paris Conservatoire first as professor of organ (1890) and then as professor of composition (1896). Numbered among his many organ students were Louis Vierne, Charles Tournemire, Albert Schweitzer, and Marcel Dupré, while his composition students included such future luminaries as Edgard Varèse, Darius Milhaud, and Arthur Honegger. Widor's Symphony no. 9 in C Minor, op. 70 (a.k.a. the *Gothique*) was the product of 1895 while his last in this important series of works, his tenth symphony (*Romane*, op. 73), was published five years later. Other than these two scores and the Symphony no. 3 for Organ and Orchestra (op. 69) which, like the *Gothique*, dates from 1895, there is little of real, lasting substance that flowed from Widor's pen despite his position as a composition teacher. Part of the reason for this might have been his increased activity as a writer on and cataloger of music. In 1904 he published his *Technique de l'orchestre moderne*—an important supplement to Hector Berlioz's treatise on orchestration, the *Grand traité d'instrumentation et d'orchestration modernes*—and since Johann Sebastian Bach's works provided the underpinning for much of Widor's teaching, he collaborated with Schweitzer (between 1912 and 1914) on an edition of Bach's organ compositions. Widor also wrote a standard text on the art of organ-playing called *L'orgue moderne* in 1929, nearly two years after he finally retired from his professorship. He kept his position at St. Sulpice until he turned ninety years old, leaving the bench for one of his pupils, Marcel Dupré.

Orchestral
Symphony no. 3 for Organ and Orchestra, op. 69
what to buy: [*The Complete Symphonies, vol. 8: Symphonies for organ and orchestra*; Paul Wisskirchen, organ; Volker Hempling, cond.; Philharmonia Hungarica, orch.; Cologne Gürzenich Chorus] (Motette 40071) ♪ ♪ ♪ ♪

Here is a recording of these important works (the *Sinfonia Sacra*, op. 81, is also included) demonstrating that Widor knew not only how to compose for the organ, but for the orchestra as well. The organ, built in 1981 by Klais for the Altenberg Cathedral, works well in spite of

its non-French tonal character. The performances are exemplary; the recording of this live concert gives much detail within the reverberant acoustic.

Chamber
Symphony no. 5 in F Minor for Organ, op. 42, no. 1
what to buy: [David Hill, organ] (Hyperion 66181) ♪ ♪ ♪ ♪ ♪

There are several recordings of Widor's most popular symphony, the one containing the famous *Toccata*. This performance was recorded on the 1932 Willis organ at Westminster Cathedral, London, and while it is not a French organ, it has many of the tonal colors called for in this music. The sound of the organ is greatly enhanced by the reverberant acoustics of the hall, and Hill's performance is quite buoyant and very musical. The recording captures all of these elements well, making for a wonderful listening experience. Two other works by Widor flesh out the recital: the *Marche Pontificale* from Symphony no. 1 in C Minor for Organ, op. 13, no. 1, and *Mystique*, the second of his three *Nouvelles Pièces*, op. 87.

worth searching for: [Olivier Latry, organ] (BNL Productions 112617) ♪ ♪ ♪ ♪ ♪

Recorded at the Cathedral Notre-Dame de Paris on an organ remarkably similar to the one Widor used to play at Saint-Sulpice, the *Toccata* is heard in a full-bodied performance that excites the senses. Latry is one of the finest organists playing this repertoire, and it shows in exemplary renditions of Widor's fifth and sixth organ symphonies.

Symphony no. 9 in C Minor for Organ, op. 70 (*Gothique*)
what to buy: [*Charles Widor: The Organ Works, vol. 4*; Ben van Oosten, organ] (MD&G 3160404) ♪ ♪ ♪ ♪ ♪

This is one of seven volumes by van Oosten covering all of Widor's organ works. The series has the organist performing on instruments built by Cavaillé-Coll, with this volume recording the organ at St. Ouen de Rouen which was built in 1890. The *Gothic Symphony*, composed specifically for this organ, was meant to evoke the Gothic architecture of this medieval abbey church and is based on Gregorian themes. Widor's austere and rarely heard Symphony no. 7 for Organ (op. 42, no. 3) is also included on this disc. These performances, the organ, and the enclosed booklet with handsome pictures and a thematic analysis make for an excellent combination.

Vocal
Mass for Two Organs and Double Chorus, op. 36
what to buy: [Joseph Cullen, organ; Andrew Reid, organ; James O'Donnell, cond.; Westminster Cathedral Choir; Hyperion Baritone Chorus] (Hyperion 66898) ♪ ♪ ♪ ♪ ♪

Widor was a master at composing for choral forces that would complement the organ, especially in a large reverberant space. This piece (and its accompanying works, the *Messe solennelle,* op. 16 by Vierne and Marcel Dupré's *Four Motets,* op. 9) is among the best French Catholic church music of this period. The choir and the Willis organ deliver this little-performed music with fluency and style. The recording captures the inspiring sound in the wonderful acoustics of this cathedral.

influences: César Franck, Louis Vierne, Marcel Dupré, Charles Tournemire, Maurice Duruflé, Johann Sebastian Bach, Jacques Nicolas Lemmens

D. John Apple and Ian Palmer

Henryk Wieniawski
Born July 10, 1835, in Lublin, Poland. Died March 31, 1880, in Moscow, Russia.

period: Romantic

A child prodigy on the violin, Wieniawski was acknowledged in his own time as one of the foremost virtuosos of the nineteenth century. His skill as a violinist certainly influenced Wieniawski's compositions, which include many short pieces and studies for the violin (as well as two concertos) that are still performed today.

Henryk Wieniawski, one of the most important founding fathers of the Franco-Belgian school of violin technique, was as influential a composer and performer as he was a teacher. He entered the Paris Conservatory as an eight-year-old and graduated by the age of eleven with the first prize in violin, the youngest person in Conservatory history to do so. He made his Paris debut in January 1848, following that with other concerts in Russia, Finland, the Baltic States, and Poland. Almost from the first, his extraordinary technique was noted by performing composer/musicians, including Henri Vieuxtemps and Stanislaw Moniuszko, whom he befriended in Warsaw. In 1849 he returned to the Paris Conservatory, this time to study composition with Hippollyte Collet; he finished his formal training the following year, graduating with an *accessit* prize (honorable mention) in composition. He was not quite fifteen years old.

With school over, the young violinist embarked upon a two-year tour of Russia, with his brother Joszef as accompanist. The hectic concert schedule might have exhausted a lesser (or perhaps older) performer, but the two Wienawskis seemed to enjoy the life of traveling virtuosos. Henryk used what spare time he had to compose works for the violin, and by the time he reached his eighteenth birthday, he had composed fourteen opus numbers, though some of these were probably written while he was still in school. His Concerto no. 1 in F-sharp Minor for Violin and Orchestra, arguably the most important of these early works, was composed and published in 1850, and he gave its debut performance at the Leipzig Gewandhaus three years later. Although this piece reflects the impact of Henryk's tour, perhaps to the point of being overly virtuosic in spots, it was a huge success with the Leipzig audience and can be said to be the turning point in Wienawski's career as a composer.

As Wienawski's fame as an artist and composer grew, his tour schedule became more and more extensive, and he might have enjoyed a life on the road until the end but for two important events. First, in 1858, he returned to Paris and appeared with the noted pianist Anton Rubinstein, a prophetic performance that foreshadowed a long and close collaboration to come. Then, in 1859, he appeared with the London Quartet Society and met the woman who was to become his wife, Isabella Hampton. It was his infatuation with Isabella that led Wienawski to write what is probably his best-known piece, the *Légende* for Violin and Orchestra. While both his concertos are familiar as larger works, the *Légende* enjoys an even wider audience because of its frequent use as an encore or short recital piece. In any case, when Wieniawski asked for Isabella's hand, her father refused to let her marry him. In despair, Wieniawski went back to his rooms and composed the *Légende,* premiering the piece at his next concert. When Isabella's father heard the work and the story behind it, he relented and from then on treated Wieniawski as his son. After the marriage, the idea of settling down must have appealed to Wieniawski, for he accepted a post in St. Petersburg as solo violinist to the czar in 1860, remaining for the next eight years and becoming professor of violin at the new

St. Petersburg Conservatory in 1862. It was there that he wrote and premiered his second violin concerto, with Rubinstein conducting. In 1872 he embarked upon another successful tour with Rubinstein, this time to the United States. Two years later the pair returned to Paris for another concert series, and Wieniawski succeeded Henri Vieuxtemps as professor of violin at the Brussels Conservatory. He had to resign the post in 1877 due to a serious heart condition, although he continued to perform in Russia. In April of 1879 he gave his farewell concert in Odessa, and less than a year later he died at the home of Madame von Meck, Piotr Tchaikovsky's patroness.

Besides the *Legende,* Wieniawski is best known today for his two violin concertos, for his *Scherzo Tarantelle* (another short character piece for violin and orchestra), and for a particularly difficult set of etudes whose popularity (or infamy) is surpassed only by Niccolò Paganini's twenty-four *Caprices* for Solo Violin. In addition to their pedagogical use, these etudes, like the *Caprices,* are often performed as solo recital pieces.

Orchestral
Concerto no. 2 in D Minor for Violin and Orchestra, op. 22
what to buy: [Gil Shaham, violin; Lawrence Foster, cond. London Symphony Orchestra] (Deutsche Grammophon 431815) ♪ ♪ ♪ ♪

This collection contains both violin concertos, as well as the *Légende* and Pablo de Sarasate's *Zigeunerweisen,* making it an excellent introduction to Wieniawski's best-known works as well as two shorter classics of the violin repertoire. Shaham's performance here is excellent, not dripping with romanticism but not dry either. The London Symphony is always technically accurate, but this performance is particularly clean, especially when compared with the Paris rendition below.

what to buy next: [Itzhak Perlman, violin; Daniel Barenboim, cond.; Orchestre de Paris] (Deutsche Grammophon 410526) ♪ ♪ ♪ ♪

While there can be no argument against Perlman's performance here, it is just a little predictable. Barenboim gets a distinctively French sound from the orchestra, but the playing is a bit sloppy. Still, you'll probably want to be familiar with Perlman's interpretation, which has become the standard for violinists.

influences: Camille Saint-Saëns, Niccolò Paganini, Henri Vieuxtemps

Melissa M. Stewart

John Williams
Born John Towner Williams, February 8, 1932, in Queens, New York.

period: Twentieth century

There are "A-List" film composers and then there is John Williams. He has written music for many of the biggest blockbusters of the second half of the 20th century, creating memorable music for such films as *Jaws, Star Wars, Indiana Jones,* and *Schindler's List.* Also famous as conductor of the Boston Pops Orchestra (1980-95), this master musician is familiar to millions and probably the most recognizable film composer today.

Williams is the son of a professional drummer who used to play with the Raymond Scott Quintet before moving his family to Los Angeles in 1948 and becoming a Hollywood studio musician. After finishing high school, John attended the University of California at Los Angeles (UCLA) with the intention of studying music. Instead, he ended up joining the Air Force for three years, getting first-hand experience conducting and arranging for a variety of military bands. After being discharged in 1954, he moved back to New York City where he studied piano with Rosina Lhévinne at the Juilliard School of Music and played jazz piano at various clubs and on recording dates. A year later, he returned to Los Angeles where he re-enrolled at UCLA and began studying composition with Mario Castelnuovo-Tedesco. Williams also continued to pick up gigs as a session pianist, eventually working in various film studios with Bernard Herrmann, Alfred Newman, Franz Waxman, and other key cinema composers of the 1950s.

The first film that he contributed music to was *My Gun Is Quick* in 1957 but the first all-Williams soundtrack was *Daddy-O* from 1958. Most of his early work was for television, however, and from 1958-65, Williams scored hundreds of hours of dramatic music, mostly for Revue Studios, a branch of Universal. He contributed theme songs or background music to numerous shows, including *Playhouse 90, Wagon Train, Bachelor Father, Checkmate, Gilligan's Island,* and *Lost In Space.* More recent work for the small screen includes his music for Steven Spielberg's *Amazing Stories* and the famous theme for NBC News, *The Mission.*

It didn't take Williams long to get up to speed in motion-picture composition, and from 1960 onwards (with a couple of exceptions), he managed at least one score a year, sometimes working on as many as four. To date, Williams has written the music and served as music director for more than seventy-five films. These include *The Reivers* (1969), *The Paper Chase* (1973), *Earthquake* (1974), *Jaws* (1975), the *Star Wars* trilogy (1977/1980/1983), *Close Encounters of the Third Kind* (1977), the three *Indiana Jones* sagas (1981/1984/1989), *E.T.: the Extra-Terrestrial* (1982), *The Witches of Eastwick* (1987), *JFK* (1991), *Schindler's List* (1993), *Nixon* (1995), *Seven Years in Tibet* (1997), *Amistad* (1997), *Saving Private Ryan* (1998), *Angela's Ashes* (1999), *Star Wars, the Phantom Menace* (1999), *The Patriot* (2000), and *Harry Potter and the Sorcerer's Stone* (2001).

As of 2001 John Williams has won five Oscars (with thirty-six nominations), sixteen Grammys, three Golden Globe Awards, and two Emmys. He also holds honorary doctorates from fourteen American universities.

A return to the grand tradition of film scoring is what best describes Williams's more commercial work. Besides the impact of composers with whom he worked directly (Herrmann, Newman, and Waxman), he also displays the distinct influences of Richard Wagner, Dmitri Shostakovich and Sergei Prokofiev. He uses leitmotif with a master's touch, identifying characters, moods, and underlying tensions. His melodies are beautiful, harmonies rich, development creative, forms inventive, and then there's that gorgeous orchestration!

David Shire, a film composer in his own right, was quoted by David Morgan in the book *Knowing the Score,* as saying of Williams, "…he's much more versatile than Hollywood lets him be most of the time. He can write anything, and he's written some very avant-garde things…stuff that wasn't necessarily a symphony orchestra pumping away." With that in mind, it should also be mentioned that Williams has written at least two symphonies, eight concertos, and numerous works for chamber music ensembles of varying sizes, in addition to arranging many of his film scores into orchestral suites.

Orchestral
various film scores
what to buy: [*Star Wars Trilogy,* John Williams, cond.; London Symphony Orchestra] (Arista 11012) ♪ ♪ ♪ ♪ ♪

One of the greatest film scores of all time, and this is the anthology to get. It is as epic as the series, and contains soundtracks from each movie in the trilogy. Four discs provide the music for *Star Wars, The Empire Strikes Back,* and *Return of the Jedi,* with a disc devoted to previously unreleased material from all three films. The package includes a booklet with an essay on the music, track-by-track synopsis and a biographical note about Williams.

[*Jaws: The Anniversary Collector's Edition* John Williams, cond.; unknown orchestra] (Decca 467045) ♪ ♪ ♪ ♪ ♪

This is a reissue of the original recording but with five previously unreleased tracks, some of which were not in the original film. The score is a classic, with some of the most dramatic and thrilling music ever written.

[*Raiders of the Lost Ark,* John Williams, cond.; London Symphony Orchestra] (DCC Compact Classics 090) ♪ ♪ ♪ ♪ ♪

This is a wonderful score with drama, action, humor, and this expanded recording shows it to good advantage.

[*Schindler's List,* Itzhak Perlman, violin; Giora Feidman, clarinet; John Williams, cond.; Boston Symphony Orchestra; Li-Ron Herzeliya Children's Choir; Ramat Gan Chamber Choir] (MCA 10969) ♪ ♪ ♪ ♪ ♪

Williams has developed a darker, more passionate tone in more recent scores. This is a stunningly beautiful, heartbreaking work, and features solo performances played to perfection by Perlman. It won the Oscar for 1993 and in 1995 was awarded the Grammy for Best Instrumental Composition Written for a Motion Picture or for Television.

[*Seven Years in Tibet,* Yo-Yo Ma, cello; John Williams, cond.; unknown orchestra; Gyuto Monks, choir] (Sony Classical 60271) ♪ ♪ ♪ ♪ ♪

This is a movie that holds you in the theater until the last sounds have died away. The soundtrack is gorgeous, one

of Williams's best efforts, with a sterling solo performance by Yo-Yo Ma. Add to this, the distinctive flavor of
Eastern sound and chanting by the Gyuto Monks. What
a mix!

worth searching for: [*The Reivers*; John Williams,
cond.; Boston Pops Orchestra] (Sony Legacy 66130)
♪ ♪ ♪ ♪ ♪

This is Williams's first major film score (1969). It is
robust and full of wonderful music with a charming feel
of "Americana." It was reissued on CD in 1995 but has
since been deleted from the catalog.

influences: Jerry Goldsmith, John Corigliano, Bernard
Herrmann, Erich Wolfgang Korngold, Sergei Prokofiev,
Dmitri Shostakovich, Richard Wagner, Franz Waxman

Frank Retzel

Dag Wirén
Born Dag Ivar Wirén on October, 15, 1905, in Stridsberg, Sweden.
Died April 19, 1986, in Danderyd, Sweden.

period: Twentieth century

When many of Dag Wirén's Scandinavian contemporaries were dabbling in serialism and other twentieth-
century compositional trends, he flirted with neoclassicism before carving out a style that emphasized melodic content and more traditional harmonic virtues. The
resulting scores have a pungent grace, similar in many
respects to like-minded pieces by Benjamin Britten or
Sergei Prokofiev but with a touch of Igor Stravinsky's
aesthetic. These are qualities that could make Wirén's
music accessible to a wider audience if that larger pop-
ulation of listeners ever gets to hear it. Today, with the
exception of his 1937 Serenade in G Major for Strings,
little of Wirén's music is heard outside northern Europe.

Wirén, after taking classes at the State Academy of
Music in Stockholm (1926–1931), moved to Paris, where
he studied composition and orchestration with Leonid
Sabaneev. Although a streak of Scandinavian romanticism would always tinge his work, the young Swede had
already come into contact with French neoclassicism in
the form of Arthur Honegger's oratorio *Le Roi David*. In
Paris he also absorbed the music of Igor Stravinsky and
Sergei Prokofiev, whose scores were revolutionizing
musical concepts for a whole generation of composers.

His Parisian years yielded a characteristically small
batch of well-crafted orchestral works, including his first
symphony (op. 3) and a sinfonietta (op. 7a), plus some
rudimentary chamber music pieces. When Wirén
returned to Sweden in 1935, he took a job as librarian of
the Swedish Composer's Association for three years, followed by a stint as music critic for the newspaper
Svenska Morgonbladet until 1946. During this period,
Wirén continued writing music, penning his most popular piece, the vibrant, energetic Serenade in G Major for
Strings of 1937, along with two more symphonies, a violin concerto, and a third string quartet.

This last work was a forerunner of the kind of material
Wirén would write during the balance of his career.
Although the scores he had written prior to 1941 reveal
the composer's "acerbic scoring of basically warm
melodies" (as Antony Hodgson noted in an overview of
Scandinavian music), he was slowly moving toward an
even more economical and individualistic style. By the
late 1940s Wirén was experimenting with a technique in
which the basic theme of the work underwent a gradual
metamorphosis through the studied application of non-
repetitive variations. However, despite the dry methodology this process would seem to entail, Wirén's music
develops an endearing bloom, rewarding the ears as it
intrigues the intellect. Arguably the finest example of
this new way of composing was his fifth string quartet
(op. 41), where his musical argument is tightly edited,
with no extraneous clutter. He only gave opus numbers
to three more works after that—his Quintet for Winds,
op. 42, the *Little Suite* for Piano, op. 43, and his
Concertino for Flute and Small Orchestra, op. 44. In 1972
his meager flow of melodic, intriguing, well-constructed
scores stopped.

Orchestral
Serenade in G Major for Strings, op. 11
what to buy: [Johannes Somary, cond.; English
Chamber Orchestra] (Vanguard Classics 45) ♪ ♪ ♪ ♪

The sonics on this 1973 recording may not be as fresh as
those on Studt's budget version (below), but Somary's
conducting is quite reliable. His program casts a wide
international net, reeling in Benjamin Britten's *Simple
Symphony* and two pieces by Edvard Grieg—the *Elegiac
Melodies* and the *Holberg Suite*—giving listeners a
chance to compare Wirén's skills to those of more familiar composers.

what to buy next: [*Scandinavian String Music*; Richard

Studt, cond.; Bournemouth Sinfonietta, orch.] (Naxos 8.553106) ♪ ♪ ♪₄

In addition to Wirén's delightful work, Studt's orchestra presents a fine selection of ear-friendly works by Edvard Grieg (the *Holberg Suite*), Carl Nielsen (his *Little Suite*), and the lesser-known Johan Severin Svendsen. The orchestral playing is respectable, the engineering is decent, and the budget price makes this an easy choice if you want to check out Wirén's single most popular piece within the context of his Scandinavian predecessors.

Symphony no. 4, op. 27
what to buy: [Thomas Dausgaard, cond.; Norrköping Symphony Orchestra] (CPO 999563) ♪ ♪ ♪ ♪

Written in 1951 and standing at the juncture between earlier works such his popular Serenade and the more intellectually rigorous pieces of Wirén's later years, this short, tautly orchestrated work is one of the finest Scandinavian symphonies of the twentieth century. It would be a shame if listeners wishing to explore Wirén's oeuvre were not afforded the opportunity to acquaint themselves with this delightful symphony, which remains relatively unknown outside of Sweden, Dausgaard is a solid conductor, his orchestra is filled with some of Sweden's best musicians, and the music is concise and melodic without pandering to sentimentality. The earlier ballet suite, *Oscarsbalen*, and the composer's somewhat harder-edged fifth symphony (from 1964) close out the program.

Chamber
Quartet no. 5 for Strings, op. 41
what to buy: [*CCS #21*; Ferro Quartet, ensemble] (Caprice 21413) ♪ ♪ ♪ ♪

In many ways, this work mirrors the bulk of Wirén's post-Serenade music. It is succinct in its musical argument and far more intellectually rigorous than his earlier material, a result of the composer's growth from the late 1930s, when he wrote the Serenade, until the 1960s and 1970s, when he composed his more mature works. The balance of the collection is a superb primer on Wirén's chamber music that traces his development as a composer and serves as a wonderful introduction to his work in general. Other pieces here include his second string quartet (a sibling, chronologically speaking, of the Serenade), the *Little Serenade* for Guitar from 1964, and the wondrously fluid Quartet for Flute, Oboe, Clarinet,

---

Where Have I Heard That? Classical Music in Movies
While many twentieth century composers have made a living writing film scores, there are times when movie directors have dipped into the classical repertoire for snippets of themes to help set a mood and/or provide an appropriate audio backdrop. Here is a short list of works by well-known composers and some of the films they appeared in.

Composer: Johann Sebastian Bach
Work: *Toccata and Fugue* in D Minor (BWV 565)
Movies: *Fantasia, Rollerball, Sunset Boulevard*

Composer: Samuel Barber
Work: *Adagio for Strings*
Movies: *The Elephant Man, Platoon, The Scarlet Letter*

Composer: Ludwig van Beethoven
Work: *Für Elise*
Movies: *Bill and Ted's Excellent Adventure, Death in Venice*

Composer: Felix Mendelssohn
Work: *Wedding March from (A Midsummer Night's Dream)*
Movies: *The Father of the Bride, Four Weddings and a Funeral, Wayne's World 2*

Composer: Wolfgang Amadeus Mozart
Work: *Eine kleine nachtmusik*
Movie: *Alien, Amadeus, Fame*

Composer: Jacques Offenbach
Work: *Can Can from the opera Orphée aux enfers*
Movies: *Day of the Jackal, Robin Hood: Men In Tights, Titanic*

Composer: Carl Orff
Work: *O fortuna! from Carmina Burana*
Movies: *Detroit Rock City, The Doors, The General's Daughter*

Composer: Johann Strauss II
Work: *An der schönen, blauen donau (The Blue Danube)*
Movies: *Heaven's Gate, Titanic, 2001: A Space Odyssey*

Composer: Richard Strauss
Work: *Also sprach Zarathustra (Also Spake Zarathustra),* op. 30
Movies: *Clueless, Toy Story 2, 2001: A Space Odyssey*

Composer: Giuseppe Verdi
Work: *Anvil Chorus from the opera Il trovatore*
Movies: *D2: The Mighty Ducks, How to Make an American Quilt, A Night at the Opera*

Composer: Richard Wagner
Work: *Ride of the Valkyries*
Movies: *Apocalypse Now, The Blues Brothers*

Composer: Kurt Weill
Work: *Moritat (a.k.a. Mack the Knife)*
Movies: *The Butcher Boy, Quiz Show, What Women* Want

Mathilde August

and Cello from 1956.

influences: Arthur Honegger, Igor Stravinsky, Carl Nielsen, Jean Sibelius

Garaud MacTaggart

Hugo Wolf

Born Hugo Filipp Jakob Wolf, March 13, 1860, in Windischgraz, Styria (now Slovenjgradec, Slovenia). Died February 22, 1903, in Vienna, Austria.

period: Romantic/twentieth century

A master songsmith, Hugo Wolf introduced new psychological sensitivity to the lied with a superbly crafted balance of voice and accompaniment that remains unmatched to this day. Wolf was emotionally unstable, eventually resulting in confinement in asylums towards the end of his life, but the enormity of his passions lent a characteristic expressiveness and empathy to his songs.

As a student, Wolf was fiery and impatient—all of his energies were devoted to music, to the detriment of other subjects. In 1875, after much pleading with his father, who loved music but considered it an avocation, he was finally allowed to enter the Vienna Conservatory where he studied piano under Wilhelm Schenner and harmony and composition under Robert Fuchs, and made friends with fellow-student Gustav Mahler. He developed a life-long penchant for the works of Richard Wagner and had the good fortune to meet Wagner in December 1875. The meeting was inspiring to Wolf, as his idol praised the boy's work and encouraged him to continue his studies with patience and discipline. These were not, however, Wolf's strongest attributes and, within two years, the youngster had outworn whatever welcome he once might have had at the Conservatory. Expelled for various disciplinary offenses, he returned to Windischgraz in disgrace.

Eight months later, however, in November 1877, he returned to Vienna and attempted to eke out a living as a teacher. Since Wolf had neither the predilection nor the temperament for teaching, he lived by the patronage of friends, family, and wealthy benefactors—composer Adalbert von Goldschmidt in particular. Goldschmidt took the young Wolf to concerts and operas, and also to a brothel, where he undoubtedly contracted the syphilis that caused the dementia afflicting his last years.

By 1880 the symptoms of syphilis that had been plaguing him for the past two years had ebbed and with a summer of rest at a benefactor's home, Wolf's dramatic mood swings subsided into a semblance of tranquillity. However, these periods of serenity would be infrequent and brief. Seeking to ease and distract his friend, Goldschmidt secured him a post as second conductor at Salzburg; but even this job ended less than a year later following Wolf's bitter quarrels with the director and he returned to a bohemian life of relying his friends' generosity.

In 1883 Wolf attended the premiere of *Parsifal* in Bayreuth, which made a deep impression on Wolf. He was also inspired by a meeting with Franz Liszt to tackle larger forms and began work on *Penthesilea,* a symphonic poem based on the German poet Heinrich von Kleist's story about violence unleashed by female sexuality. Neither work was completed as Wolf entered another phase of barren depression. After finally finishing the string quartet he had been working on intermittently since 1878, Wolf tried his hand at music criticism from 1884 until the beginning of 1887—an occupation that would earn him many enemies in the more conservative, pro-Brahms camp.

Wolf actually returned to composition in the fall of 1886 with the *Intermezzo* in E flat major and vigorous work on several other projects, including the original string quartet version of his *Italian Serenade.* This phase of creativity was interrupted with the death of his father in May 1887. With the help of a friend, Wolf published six lieder dedicated to his father in 1888, heralding the most productive period of the composer's life. This tribute to his father sparked a creative wildfire in Wolf. He was now producing as many as two or three songs a day, including *Der Tambour,* one of his first masterpieces. Soon he was performing his works for the Wagner Society, where he attracted the attention of several influential members, including the famous tenor Ferdinand Jäger, who would become a devoted supporter. During the next year his complete collection of *Mörike-Lieder* was published, and this, combined with successful concert performances of his songs, had an energizing effect on the composer who began work on his *Spanisches Liederbuch.* By mid-1890 Wolf had composed more than 174 songs, begun the *Italienisches Liederbuch,* and seen the publication of his masterful *Goethe Lieder.*

The fever pitch at which Wolf had been working for the

past two and a half years left him thoroughly exhausted by 1892. While his fame was spreading across Europe, he nursed depression and complications of syphilis and completed only the orchestral arrangement of his *Italian Serenade* before he stopped composing completely. Two years later his determination to complete a larger-scale work erupted and Wolf labored tirelessly on his first and only opera, *Der Corregidor.* Wolf then battled his own disintegrating mental state to complete the *Italienisches Liederbuch* and settings of Reinick, Byron, and Michelangelo.

In 1897 Wolf was planning a second opera but, by this time, his mind had deteriorated past the point of reason, much less coherent composition. Refusing to submit to his affliction, Wolf secluded himself and began composing with an obsessive intensity that yielded over 60 pages of score in three weeks before he suffered a complete mental breakdown. He was committed to an asylum after claiming to be the new director of the Vienna Opera and then discharged during a brief period of lucidity in early 1898. He re-committed himself later that year and died after four and a half more years in the institution. Wolf was buried beside Schubert and Beethoven in the Central Cemetery in Vienna.

Orchestral
Italian Serenade in G Major for String Quartet (orchestral arrangement)
what to buy: [*Rossini: The Complete String Sonatas*; I Musici, orch.] (Philips 456330) ♪ ♪ ♪ ♪

The orchestral version of this piece (arranged by the composer in 1892) is a most charming makeweight for a program of works for string ensemble. In addition to the Rossini compositions ballyhooed in the album title, the recital also includes Felix Mendelssohn's Octet (op. 20) and Giovanni Bottesini's short, sweet, *Grand Duo Concertante* for violin, double bass, and orchestra. The Wolf and Mendelssohn scores are the most substantial works in this two-disc set.

Chamber
Italian Serenade in G Major for string quartet
what to buy: [Takács Quartet, ensemble] (Decca 460034) ♪ ♪ ♪ ♪

Although this work may be the least substantial of the three on this disc (Schubert's *Trout* Quintet and Mozart's *Eine Kleine Nachtmusik* are the others), it receives the

John Williams:
Born in 1941 in Melbourne, Australia, Williams initially began learning to play the guitar from his father, a jazz musician, but after the family moved to Great Britain in 1952, John began studying more formally, eventually displaying enough talent to attract the attention of Andrés Segovia and become one of the master guitarist's students. Williams also attended the Royal College of Music, where he took classes in piano and music theory from 1956 to 1959.

Although he was trained in part by Segovia and later acclaimed by his instructor as a stylistic successor, Williams eventually rejected Segovia's approach to performing in favor of a more rhythmically secure style, avoiding the Romantic-era tendency toward big, emotional gestures favored by his teacher. Williams also branched out in terms of the material that he would play, working within a variety of contexts that had little to do with the tradition established, in part, by Segovia. As a result, Williams has recorded not only many of the staples of classical guitar literature (in addition to compositions written specifically for him by contemporary composers), but has sought out other frameworks within which to play.

His recordings of Johann Sebastian Bach's lute suites (Sony Classics 42204) and his arrangements of Isaac Albéniz's piano pieces (*Echoes of Spain*, Sony Classics 36679) are among the more "traditional" pieces that Williams has recorded, but he has also been active as a persuasive advocate for the guitar works of Augustin Barrios-Mangore (*From the Jungles of Paraguay*, Sony Classics 64396) and Toru Takemitsu (Sony Classics 46720). In addition, a number of important modern works for guitar have been written specifically for Williams and he has recorded many of them, including Leo Brouwer's Concerto no. 4 for Guitar and Orchestra (the *Concerto de Toronto*, available on *The Black Decameron*, Sony Classics 63173); Peter Sculthorpe's second guitar concerto (*Nourlangie*, available on *From Australia*, Sony Classics 53361); and Richard Harvey's *Concerto antico* (Sony Classics 68337).

On a less conventional note, Williams has also performed as a member of Sky, the hybrid classical/rock group with whom he played on six albums from 1979 until leaving them in 1983. An aural document of Williams's work with them (*Squared*, Recall Records 218) is available as a British import in some outlets. Other non-classical projects that he has been involved with include performances with flamenco guitarist Paco Peña and the world-renowned Chilean folk group Inti-Illimani that have been documented in the group's albums *Fragments of a Dream* (CBS Masterworks 44574) and *Leyenda* (CBS Masterworks 45948).

William Gerard

best performance. So, if you don't mind merely adequate playing in the Schubert and Mozart pieces when looking for the delightful Wolf piece from 1887, this could be a good choice.

[Auryn Quartet, ensemble] (CPO 999529) ♪ ♪ ♪♪

The Auryn Quartet's ensemble playing isn't quite as impressive as that of the more seasoned Takács. That said, their rough and ready conception of Wolf's instrumental bon-bon is totally plausible, especially when considered in light of the other items in their program. They put the serenade right after the relatively slight *Intermezzo* in E flat major and the much more powerful (and youthful) string quartet. This lineup takes the listener through all of Wolf's completed works for string quartet.

Vocal
Spanisches Liederbuch (Spanish Songbook) (complete)
what to buy: [Elisabeth Schwarzkopf, soprano; Dietrich Fischer-Dieskau, baritone; Gerald Moore, piano] (Deutsche Grammophon 457726) ♪ ♪ ♪ ♪ ♪

Fischer-Dieskau is particularly effective in the ten *Geistliche Lieder (Sacred Songs),* but Schwarzkopf can more than hold her own there and in the thirty-four *Weltliche Lieder (Secular Songs)* that follow. Moore was one of the greatest accompanists of all time, and his work in this classic set is a model of restraint in the service of the music.

Mörike-Lieder (selections)
worth searching for: [*Fischer-Dieskau Edition;* Dietrich Fischer-Dieskau, baritone; Sviatoslav Richter, piano] (Deutsche Grammophon 463510) ♪ ♪ ♪ ♪ ♪

You can buy this disc domestically as part of the twenty-one-disc Fischer-Dieskau retrospective from Deutsche Grammophon (463500) or check various import sources for this single-disc offering of two virtuoso performers meeting in recital (Innsbruck, 1973) to perform a well-chosen selection of Wolf's intense *Mörike-Lieder.*

various songs
what to buy: [*Wolf Lieder Recital;* Hans Hotter, baritone; Gerald Moore, piano] (Testament 1197) ♪ ♪ ♪ ♪ ♪

Hotter, one of the greatest baritones in modern history and the finest Wotan in Wagner's *Ring* cycle, recorded these gems during the 1950s. His voice is magnificently shaded throughout the youthful *Der Tambour* and suitably heartsick in *Verborgenheit (Seclusion)* (nos. 5 and 12 from the *Mörike-Lieder*), but Hotter's best readings are reserved for the *Goethe-Lieder* heard in this collection, especially the 1954 recording of *Prometheus,* which tellingly captures the bitterness of the formerly naive.

what to buy next: [Elisabeth Schwarzkopf, soprano; Gerald Moore, piano] (EMI Classics Imports 65749) ♪ ♪ ♪ ♪ ♪

Schwarzkopf and Moore were a marvelous team and this disc captures their artistry in performances covering the breadth of Wolf's oeuvre—from a well-chosen sampling of the various Mörike and Goethe settings to excerpts from the *Italian* and *Spanish* songbooks. The drama that the partnership imparts to *Elfenlied* (inspired by Shakespeare's *A Midsummer Night's Dream*) and *Wer rief dich denn? (Who Called You Here Then?)* should serve as a model for the next generation of lied singers.

[*Wolf: Mörike und Goethe-Lieder;* Barbara Hendricks, soprano; Roland Pöntinen, piano] (EMI Classics 56988) ♪ ♪ ♪ ♪

Hendricks is not in the same class as Schwarzkopf, at least as far as this repertoire is concerned, but her voice is a beautiful instrument, showcased best in lighter-weight Goethe songs such as *Frühling übers Jahr (Spring all year round)* and *Die Spröde (The Coy Shepherdess)* rather than the darker, more reflective Mörike pieces such as *In der Frühe (At Daybreak)* or *Begegnung (Encounter).* Pöntinen is that rare breed, a sensitive virtuoso who uses his strength to support rather than propel a singer.

influences: Richard Wagner, Franz Schubert, Robert Schumann

Sharon L. Hoyer and Mathilde August

Iannis Xenakis
Born May 29, 1922, in Braïla, Romania.

period: Twentieth century

Mathematics and architecture are disciplines that inform the music of Iannis Xenakis. There is also a manifestly human element involved, however, which invests his computer-generated scores with vibrant passion, setting them distinctly apart from the compositions of Milton Babbit or Pierre Henry. Olivier Messiaen, in an interview conducted by Nouritza Matossian, discussed his former student, noting that Xenakis "has used mathematics, he has used architecture, in order to compose and that has given something which is totally inspired, but is completely 'outside.' Which belongs only to him. Which no one else could have done! That has an impact, a force. That is a power."

Xenakis's mother died in childbirth when he was five years old, and his father, a prosperous shipping merchant, hired a series of governesses to take care of Iannis and his two younger brothers. In 1932 Xenakis was sent to a boarding school on the Greek island of Spetsai, where he discovered a natural bent for mathematics, science, classical literature, and philosophy. Upon his graduation in 1938, his father offered to send him to England to study naval engineering, but Xenakis preferred to live in Athens and attend Athens Polytechnic School. There he pursued the same curriculum that had interested him on Spetsai and also started taking piano lessons as well as instruction in harmony and counterpoint. At the beginning of World War II, Italian forces invaded Greece, and Xenakis joined the Resistance, fighting the Italians, the Germans, and finally the British. He was imprisoned repeatedly, severely wounded in a street action (losing an eye), and even sentenced to death before managing to escape.

In 1947, with the aid of a false passport, Xenakis arrrived in Paris, where he befriended the famed architect and iconoclast Le Corbusier. He worked with Le Corbusier on a variety of architecturally important projects, including an innovative housing project, Les Habitations de Marseilles, and the convent of Sainte Marie de la Tourette. He also started attending Messiaen's composition class at the Paris Conservatory and studying with Darius Milhaud, Arthur Honegger, and Hermann Scherchen. Xenakis was still working with Le Corbusier in 1955 when his *Metastaseis,* for an orchestra of sixty-one players, premiered at Donaueschingen to a nearly equal mix of acclaim and derision. The work itself was based upon the architectural technique (graphically revealed in the Philips pavilion at the 1958 Brussels Exposition) that enabled large-scale hyperbolic parabolas to function as stable structures. Transferring his ideas into the realm of music, Xenakis constructed a score where strings arched in overlapping blocks in a manner totally unrelated to serialism or any other previously formulated style. The second work to make an impact among the avant-garde was *Achorripsis,* for twenty-one instruments, which debuted at Pleyel in 1959. According to Xenakis, the piece "constitutes a

sample of aleatoric disturbances organized with the help of the calculus of probabilities." It wasn't until the 1960 premiere of his *Pithoprakta,* for orchestra of fifty instruments, that French critics and audiences realized the worth of his efforts. Coincidently, that was the last year that Xenakis worked with Le Corbusier. By then, he was already experimenting with compositions for tape and programming computers with formulas to help generate his stochastic music, creating new soundscapes that meshed mathematical concepts with pitch and time. He was also working extensively with the applications of set theory and game theory to music. A pair of works from this period, *Duel* and *Strategie,* pitted two small orchestras and their respective conductors against each other by making the leaders choose from a specific number of possibilities assigned to them—provided that the choices of each conductor countered the selections made by the other. These works, premiered in 1959, provided the roots of John Zorn's various game pieces (e.g., *Cobra*).

By 1965 Xenakis had become a French citizen and was delving into early Greco-Roman history, attempting to mesh legends and myths, ancient music and theatrical practices, and the compositional styles he had forged. These were the ideas behind such later works as *Oresteia, Medea,* and *Nuits,* where Xenakis treated human voices with the same kinds of mathematical rules he applied to instrumental scores. Since then Xenakis has become a much-honored composer, valued for creating a radically new way of looking at what constitutes music—an approach that stands apart from every other twentieth-century style. He has served on university staffs throughout Europe and North America and won awards for various scores. Through it all, Xenakis has kept to his own seemingly unpolished but innovative art, continuing to create passionate music with the beautiful predictability of fractal geometry.

Chamber
Pleiades for Percussion Sextet
what to buy: [Strasbourg Percussion Ensemble] (Denon 73678) ♪ ♪ ♪ ♪

Potential listeners hoping for an easy way to understand Xenakis's music won't find it readily, although his numerous works for tuned percussion provide the most accessible approach to his unique rhythmic sense. The four movement *Pleiades* was premiered by the same ensemble heard on this disc. All the different instruments in the group's arsenal are heard in the first movement, while the other three sections are devoted to either drums, members of the xylophone family, or the "sixxen," a metallic percussion instrument created especially for this piece. The tonal palette involved is quite sophisticated, but as in all Xenakis works for percussion, it's the rhythm that counts, and it is the rhythms that make this such a beguiling listening experience. Maki Ishii's *Concertante,* op. 79, for marimba and six percussionists, fits right in with the Xenakis work it is paired with.

Échange for Bass Clarinet and Ensemble
what to buy: [*Xenakis: Ensemble Music 2;* Michael Lowenstern, bass clarinet; Charles Zachary Bornstein, cond.; ST-X Ensemble] (Mode 56) ♪ ♪ ♪ ♪

From a barely audible whisper to a convoluted instrumental scream, this work is a highly effective example of Xenakis's writing for winds and brass. So, too, is the rest of this impeccably performed album. There's *Xas,* for saxophone quartet; *Akrata,* for eight winds and eight brasses; and *A la Mémoire de Witold Lutoslawski,* for two horns and two trumpets, plus an immediately accessible sample of Xenakis's percussion oeuvre, *Okho,* for three West African *djembe* drums. The ensemble is obviously committed to the composer, and it is difficult to imagine more insightful renderings of these scores.

Vocal
Medea for Men's Chorus and Instrumental Ensemble
what to buy: [James Wood, cond.; Critical Band, ensemble; New London Chamber Choir] (Hyperion 66980) ♪ ♪ ♪ ♪

Dating from 1967, this work actually provided the incidental music for a French production of Seneca's *Medea.* Sung in Latin and set against a five-piece instrumental group, this twenty-three minute piece contains a variety of vocal effects, ranging from whispers and hisses to full-blown rants and raves. Not surprisingly, Xenakis has in some ways mellowed as he has grown older, and the newer vocal works on this disc, especially *Serment,* from 1981, and *Knephas,* from 1990, seem only a century ahead of their time instead of a millennium.

influences: Olivier Messiaen, Edgard Varèse, John Cage, Yuji Takahashi, John Zorn

Garaud MacTaggart

Eugène Ysaÿe
Born Eugène-Auguste Ysaÿe, July 16, 1858, in Liège, Belgium. Died May 12, 1931, in Brussels, Belgium.

period: Romantic

A master violinist and teacher, Eugène Ysaÿe was an impressive, vibrant figure. The recordings he made at the dawn of the 78 rpm era, according to former students, give no more than a glimpse of his remarkable playing. Of the many works he wrote, only the six sonatas for solo violin (op. 27) are heard with any frequency in recitals. Composers who wrote works specifically for him include Claude Debussy, Ernest Chausson, Gabriel Fauré, and César Franck.

Ysaÿe's first music lessons came from his father, reputedly a harsh, impatient man, given to occasional displays of violence. To develop his child's tone he had young Eugène draw the bow endlessly across the strings of his violin, rapping him with a cane when vibrato raised its shaky head or whenever the tonal quality was deemed to be suffering. Eugène entered the Liège Conservatory in 1865 but, basically an indifferent student, more prone to fun than studying, he left in 1869. To be fair, part of the reason he did poorly may have been his playing three nights a week (or more) in the family orchestra at the Pavillon de Flore or any number of other venues around Liège. Life on the road with his father and brothers continued until he returned to the Conservatory in 1872. By then his skills were honed via countless concerts with the orchestra and had improved to the point where, two years later, he won a prize enabling him to study with Henryk Wieniawski and Henry Vieuxtemps, two of the greatest violinists of the day.

After four years of study in Paris, Ysaÿe joined Benjamin Bilse's orchestra as concertmaster at a large Berlin beerhall called the *Konzerthaus.* He became friends with the celebrated violinist Joseph Joachim and the worldly pianist-composer Anton Rubinstein, who was able to provide Ysaÿe with contacts for a new career as a traveling soloist. Embarking on his first concert tour after leaving the Bilse Orchestra in 1882, he journeyed with Rubinstein to Norway and Russia. When he returned to Paris in 1883, it was with favorable reviews and a fatter bank account. By 1891, the violinist was famous throughout Europe (having broadened his touring to include Italy, Switzerland, Austria and England), and he was teaching at the Brussels Conservatory. Ysaÿe's reputation as a virtuoso was now such that famous composers were writing pieces for him or the string quartet he had founded. Many of these works, including César Franck's masterful violin sonata, Ernest Chausson's *Poème* for violin and orchestra (inspired by Ysaÿe's own *Poème élégiaque*), and Claude Debussy's sole string quartet, are still mainstays of the repertoire. Franck's score was particularly meaningful, since it was given to Ysaÿe as a wedding present in 1886.

After the start of World War I, giving concerts became difficult in light of the hardships faced by many in Europe. Ysaÿe was frustrated and disappointed, noting that "True creative work is almost impossible when the edifice of social life is crumbling." He was also troubled by a series of health problems which interfered with his, up until then, extraordinary technical proficiency, causing him to turn to conducting. Ysaÿe probably considered his acceptance of a four-year contract (in 1918) to conduct the Cincinnati Symphony Orchestra as a signal that his career as the world's greatest violin virtuoso was over. When he finally returned to Belgium, he resumed concertizing and teaching, but he also wrote what many violinists consider to be his magnum opus, the six solo violin sonatas (op. 27) that he finished in 1924. These virtuosic, harmonically intriguing, works were not to be his last compositions, but they have become the ones for which is best known.

Chamber
Sonatas for Violin, op. 27
what to buy: [Philippe Graffin, violin] (Hyperion 66940)
♪ ♪ ♪ ♪₄

Ysaÿe's six sonatas are music to dip into unless you happen to be a violinist or enamored of works showcasing violin virtuosity. Graffin makes the most of the melodic charms of the third sonata (*Ballade*), a popular recital piece, and the E Minor sonata, which was dedicated to Fritz Kreisler. Unlike other recordings of these scores, Graffin also includes two duos for violin and piano by Ysaÿe: the violin and piano arrangement of his *Poème élégiaque* in D minor (op. 12) and the beautiful *Rêve d'enfant*—both with Pascal Devoyon as accompanist.

what to buy next: [Oscar Shumsky, violin] (Nimbus 7715) ♪ ♪ ♪ ♪₄

Yo-Yo Ma:
Yo-Yo Ma is, by a wide margin, the most popular American cellist. His artistic integrity is such that even his "crossover" projects—so crucial to keeping major labels happy nowadays—are in good taste and maintain high artistic standards. Classical purists may not be interested in hearing him play bluegrass or tango, though they will find the soundtrack to the acclaimed Ang Lee film *Crouching Tiger, Hidden Dragon* (Sony Classics 89347)—composed by Tan Dun and featuring Ma throughout—much more to their liking. The fringe benefit is that Ma has also used his popularity to put on record the music of modern composers such as John Corigliano, Leon Kirchner, etc., and to spearhead the label/performing project Silk Road, which explores Asian and Middle Eastern music.

Though born (on October 7, 1955) in Paris, Ma was largely raised in the United States. His first cello lessons were with his father; starting at age nine, he studied with Leonard Rose at Juilliard (later, he went to Harvard). His technical skills are on the highest level, and he is utterly secure in standard repertoire, whether concertos, chamber music, or solo works. He has also recorded the Bach Cello Suites twice, the second time including components from other artistic fields, as shown in videos that correspond to each suite. He's such a high-profile performer that in December 2000 he even performed the Suite in G Major on an episode of the TV series *The West Wing*.

He's garnered thirteen Grammy Awards among his nearly fifty albums. The finest have included *Premieres: Concertos for Violincello and Orchestra* (Sony Classics 66299), containing works by Richard Danielpour, Leon Kirchner, and Christopher Rouse, performed with the Philadelphia Orchestra conducted by David Zinman, which won Grammys for Best Classical Album and Best Instrumental Soloist(s) Performance (with Orchestra); and *Solo* (Sony Classics 64114), a quite varied program of solo cello pieces by Mark O'Connor, Bright Sheng, David Wilde, Alexander Tcherepnin, and Zoltán Kodály.

Steve Holtje

Shumsky is a virtuoso who puts technique in the service of the music, much as Ysaÿe did. The recording is close, but not overly so, and the performances are masterful. The price is attractive too.

Rêve d'enfant, op. 14a
worth searching for: [*Eugène Ysaÿe, violinist and conductor: The Complete Violin Recordings*; Eugène Ysaÿe, violin; Camille De Creus, piano] (Columbia Masterworks 62337) ♪ ♪ ♪

Ysaÿe recorded during the acoustic era, but the extraneous noise doesn't totally mask the lovely tone he was able to generate despite playing into a horn instead of a microphone. Only two of his works are on this disc (the *Mazurka*, op. 11, no. 3 is the other one). The balance of the album showcases him as virtuoso in pieces by Brahms, Kreisler, Mendelssohn, Schubert, and others. It is also interesting, from a historical point of view, to hear Ysaÿe as a conductor; he leads the Cincinnati Symphony Orchestra through snippets from Massenet (*Navarraise* from his opera, *Le Cid*), Delibes (the Intermezzo from *Naïla*), and Maillart (the overture to *Les Dragons de Villars*).

influences: Nicolò Paganini, Henryk Wieniawski, Henri Vieuxtemps, Pablo de Sarasate

Ian Palmer

Z

Jan Dismas Zelenka

Born Jan Lukás Ignatius Dismas Zelenka c. October 16, 1679, in Lounovice, Bohemia. Died c. December 22, 1745, in Dresden, Germany.

period: Baroque

Although he was woefully underappreciated during his lifetime, there is a good case for considering Zelenka, alongside Johann Sebastian Bach, George Frederic Handel, and Antonio Vivaldi, as one of the greatest baroque composers. An intensely religious man, Zelenka created the bulk of his surviving compositions for various aspects of the Roman Catholic service, although he did write a small number of well-crafted works for instrumental ensembles of different sizes.

Much of Zelenka's early life can only be guessed at. It is known that his father was an organist, and there are records that mention his taking music theory courses from Bohuslav Cernohorsky, a monk of the Minorite order stationed in Prague who also taught Zelenka's Bohemian contemporary Frantisek Tuma and would later (during a few years spent in Italy) teach Giuseppe Tartini and Christoph Willibald Gluck. By 1709, Zelenka had found employment with Count Hartig, joining the royal orchestra in Dresden a year later as a double bassist. In the interest of maintaining a high-quality musical organization, he was sent to Italy in 1715, along with some other orchestra members, for further studies in theory, composition, and performance. Two years later Zelenka took up residence in Vienna, where he continued his education. He moved back to Dresden in 1719, becoming an assistant to the Kapellmeister, Johann David Heinichen.

When Heinichen fell ill, Zelenka took over many of his duties. Upon Heinichen's death in 1733, many composers actively sought the Kapellmeister position, including Johann Sebastian Bach and Zelenka. The Dresden court opted instead for Johann Adoph Hasse, a German composer who had studied with Alessandro Scarlatti and specialized in *opera seria,* an extremely popular art form that that the royal household wished to be associated with. Thus, Bach had to remain content with his position in Leipzig, and Zelenka, despite having written a battery of secular arias, was relegated to composing church music. After Zelenka was passed over for the position of court conductor, he worked on a cycle of six Masses as an exercise that, because of the time needed to perform them, may never have been meant for use in a service. He didn't complete the cycle, but the *Missa Dei Patris,* along with the *Gloria* and *Kyrie* sections of his projected *Missa Dei Fillii,* were completed and did survive.

Zelenka's music was not very fashionable in its time, dealing in lengthy themes of marked complexity instead of relying on the simple formulas employed by many of his contemporaries. His rhythms were often eccentric and his harmonies were advanced, but he never applied these characteristics in a careless manner, preferring instead to frame them within the basic context of the day and for the use they were intended.

Orchestral
Hipocondrie à 7 concertanti in A Major
what to buy: [*Complete Orchestral Works, vol. 1;* Jürgen Sonnentheil, cond.; Das Neu-Eröffnete Orchestre] (CPO 999 458) ♪ ♪ ♪

Superficially speaking, Zelenka may have been writing baroque music, but he was constantly composing material that tweaked the status quo in subtle ways. That is the case for his short but sweet *Hipocondrie à 7 concertanti,* heard here in a brisk performance by Sonnentheil's band of period-instrument musicians. Balancing out the program are three other attractive orchestral works by the composer.

Chamber
Trio Sonatas for Two Oboes and Continuo
what to buy: [*Sonatas Pour Deux Hautbois et Basson, vol. II;* Ensemble Zefiro] (Astrée 8563) ♪ ♪ ♪ ♪

For fans of instrumental music, this set of pieces is the

way to get acquainted with Zelenka. These beautiful and utterly delightful performances rank among the finest baroque recordings of the past decade. The Ensemble Zefiro benefits from warm sonics and magical group interplay.

[Heinz Holliger, oboe; Maurice Bourgue, oboe; Thomas Zehetmair, violin; Klaus Thunemann, bassoon; Klaus Stoll, bass violin; Jonathan Rubin, lute; Christiane Jaccottet, harpsichord] (ECM 1671/72) ♪ ♪ ♪ ♪₈

Holliger recorded these same charming yet challenging works more than two decades ago with some of the same personnel as on this newer set. Here he presents an even leaner vision than on the earlier recordings (see below), with Rubin's lute utilized as a companion and alternative to Jaccottet's harpsichord in the continuo. ECM's engineers have done marvelous work on the sound of these performances, giving them a clear yet comfortable presence that makes the music more intimate.

what to buy next: [*Six Trio Sonatas*; Heinz Holliger, oboe; Maurice Bourgue, oboe; Saschko Gawriloff, violin; Klaus Thunemann, bassoon; Lucio Buccarella, bass violin; Christiane Jaccottet, harpsichord] (Deutsche Grammophon 423937) ♪ ♪ ♪ ♪

This pioneering package from 1973 by the great oboist Heinz Holliger and friends is back in print. The recording is a bit harsher than on the Ensemble Zefiro's recording or Holliger's later set (see above), but the performances are quite good and definitely worth a listen.

Vocal
Missa Dei Fillii in C Minor (incomplete)
what to buy: [Heike Hallaschka, soprano; Kai Wessel, alto; Marcus Ullmann, tenor; Frank Schiller, bass; Hans-Christoph Rademann, cond.; Dresdner Barockorchester, orch.; Dresdner Kammerchor, choir] (Raumklang 9702) ♪ ♪ ♪ ♪ ♪

The disc starts out with a bit of mediocrity (Johann Adolf Hasse's *Miserere* in C Minor) before unfolding the glory of Zelenka's supreme masterpiece. Although not a completed work, the forty-plus minutes of *Gloria* and *Kyrie* make one wonder how the Dresden court could have picked Hasse over Zelenka. Rademann and company make a convincing case for Zelenka being considered in the same breath as Bach.

Missa Circumcisionis Domini Nostri Jesu Christi
what to buy: [Andrea Ihle, soprano; Brigitte Pfretzschner, alto; Ekkehard Wagner, tenor; Matthias Henneberg, bass; Konrad Wagner, cond.; Dresdner Kapellknaben, choir; Dresdner Kathedralchor, choir; Staatskapelle Dresden, orch.] (Christophorus 87) ♪ ♪ ♪ ♪

Zelenka was interim court composer at Dresden when he wrote this Mass celebrating the circumcision of Jesus. The music is glorious from start to finish. Wagner's ensembles are well recorded, and it is difficult to imagine anyone bettering this performance anytime soon.

influences: Johann Sebastian Bach, Wilhelm Friedemann Bach, Frantisek Tuma, Johann Joachim Quantz

Garaud MacTaggart

Alexander Zemlinsky

Born Alexander von Zemlinsky, October 14, 1871 in Vienna, Austria. Died March 15, 1942, in Larchmont, New York.

period: Twentieth century

Alexander Zemlinsky represents a fascinating chapter in the progression of music history from the 19th century to the 20th. He was acquainted with Johannes Brahms (the last great classicist among the Romantic composers), friends with Gustav Mahler (the titan who straddled the two eras), and taught Arnold Schoenberg (the prophet of atonality). While Zemlinsky was admired by several members of the Second Viennese School, he charted a more conservative path, one that displayed a deliberate movement forward without ever abandoning traditional tonality or formal dimensions.

Zemlinsky studied piano and composition at the Vienna Conservatory (1887-92) and enjoyed early success with his chamber music, some of which attracted the attention of Brahms. While the master's influence was evident in the younger composer's music, Mahler was also one of his early champions, introducing his opera *Es war einmal* at the Court Opera in 1900 and sponsoring the younger man's entry into Viennese musical life. Schoenberg first became acquainted with him through an amateur orchestra in 1895 and later became one of his students. The bond was further enhanced in 1901 when Schoenberg married Zemlinsky's sister, Mathilde.

By this time Zemlinsky was also beginning his career as a conductor in Vienna, first at the Carltheater (1899) and then at the Volksoper (1904). He proved to be an adventurous, first-rate conductor, leading the Vienna premiere of Richard Strauss's *Salome* in 1910 and—after moving to Prague in 1911 to become principal conductor of the German Theater—the Czech premieres of Mahler's Eighth Symphony and Schoenberg's *Erwartung.* Zemlinsky also taught composition at the German Music Academy while living in Prague. During this time he maintained close contact with Schoenberg and other members of the Second Viennese School, even engaging Anton Webern to conduct at the German Theater.

In 1927, Zemlinsky moved to Berlin to take a conducting position at the Kroll Opera and to teach at the Musikhochschule. The rise to power of Hitler and his National Socialists six years later prompted him to move to Vienna, and after the Anschluss in 1938 he fled to the United States. When he died in poverty in Larchmont,

New York a few years later, he had been forgotten as a composer. Not until the early 1970s were his works rediscovered for the gems they are.

"He was too modern for the conservatives, and he did not manage to catch up with the 'New Music,' despite his close personal relationship to Schoenberg." Thus musicologist Horst Weber described the peculiarity of Zemlinsky's music, even during his own lifetime. In the early years of the 20th century, his compositional style was chromatic and intensely lyrical, with harmony and form deriving from thematic content. However, as Schoenberg began publicizing his twelve-tone method, Zemlinsky reverted to the use of established tonal centers and traditional forms, though the music does not sound reactionary. There is always a sense of fresh discovery about his scores. Within Zemlinsky's catalog, there are three acknowledged masterworks: his Second String Quartet (1914), the *Lyrische Symphonie (Lyric Symphony)* (1922-23), and the opera *Der Zwerg (The Dwarf)* (1920-21). (Alban Berg, another member of the Second Viennese School, quoted the *Lyric Symphony* a few years later in his own *Lyric Suite* for string quartet). Zemlinsky also composed four operas (and most of a fifth), two symphonies (1892 and 1897), a symphonic poem *Die Seejungfrau (The Mermaid)* (1902-03), the *Sinfonietta* (1934), three other string quartets (1895, 1923, and 1936), the *Maeterlinck Songs* for mezzo soprano or baritone and piano (1910, orchestrated in 1913), and his *Symphonische Gesänge* for voice and orchestra (1929). Zemlinsky's scores are being performed and recorded with greater frequency these days, and more of them will undoubtedly join the pantheon of acknowledged masterworks.

Orchestral
Lyrische Symphonie, op. 18
[Vlatka Orsanic, soprano; James Johnson, baritone; Michael Gielen, cond.; Southwest German Radio Symphony Orchestra] (Arte Nova 27768) ♪ ♪ ♪ ♪

Gielen is a master at getting the most out of Zemlinsky's works, and the singing is superb. A special treat in this album is its pairing of the Zemlinsky with two scores by Alban Berg: the *Altenberg Lieder,* and three pieces from his *Lyric Suite.*

worth searching for: [Elisabeth Söderström, soprano; Thomas Allen, baritone; Michael Gielen, cond.; BBC Symphony Orchestra] (IMP 5691852) ♪ ♪ ♪ ♪ ♪

Zemlinsky's *Lyrische Symphonie* is charmingly sung and superbly played by these artists. That also applies to the 1916 orchestration of the composer's six *Maeterlinck Songs*. The conductor really knows his way around these pieces and the result is fabulous.

Die Seejungfrau (The Mermaid)
what to buy: [Thomas Dausgaard, cond.; Danish National Radio Symphony Orchestra] (Chandos 9601) ♪ ♪ ♪ ♪ ♪

To have such wonderful performances of *The Mermaid*, Zemlinsky's Sinfonietta and the overture to his first opera (*Sarema*) on one album is a joy.

Chamber
Quartet no. 2 for Strings, op. 15
what to buy: [Schoenberg String Quartet] (Koch Schwann 310118) ♪ ♪ ♪ ♪♪

This 1992 release of Zemlinsky's second and third string quartets is a perfect place to begin exploring his chamber music. While, from a compositional standpoint, the second quartet is exceptional, both works are given stirring performances here.

Vocal
various choral works
what to buy: [*Sämtliche Chorwerke (Complete Choral Works)*; Deborah Voigt, soprano; Donnie Ray Albert, baritone; James Conlon, cond.; Gürzenich-Orchester, orch.; Kölner Philharmoniker, orch.; Chor des Städt. Musikvereins zu Düsseldorf, choir; Mülheimer Kantorei, choir] (EMI Classics 56783) ♪ ♪ ♪ ♪ ♪

Included on this album is a live, world premiere recording of the revised version of Zemlinsky's *Frühlingbegräbnis* featuring Voigt and Albert as soloists. Throughout this disc you will find superb singing, orchestral playing and fine conducting. The whole project was long overdue, and shows Zemlinsky as a composer of vast talents. Enjoyable for study or for pleasure—either way, you can't go wrong.

Der Zwerg, op. 17
worth seaching for: [Soile Isokoski, soprano; Juanita Lascarro, soprano; Iride Martinez, soprano; Machiko Obata, soprano; Anne Schwanewilms, soprano; David Kuebler, tenor; Andrew Collis, bass; James Conlon, cond.; Gürzenich-Orchester Kölner Philharmoniker] (EMI

Classics 56208) ♪ ♪ ♪ ♪ ♪

Based on Oscar Wilde's *The Birthday of the Infanta*, this is a masterwork. It is also a wonderful introduction to Zemlinsky's operas (if you find a copy), since Conlon and company bring it to life with exciting performances.

influences: Gustav Mahler, Arnold Schoenberg, Erich Wolfgang Korngold, Alban Berg

Frank Retzel

John Zorn
Born September 2, 1953, in New York City, NY

period: Twentieth century

The multiplicity of musical styles with which John Zorn is involved ranges from avant-garde cut-ups to Japanese bar bands, from chamber music to hardcore punk rock, from film music to klezmer to jazz, with the boundaries between his many endeavors often rather blurred. A visionary entrepreneur, he has founded several labels dedicated to cutting-edge music, most notably Tzadik, which has released vast quantities of his music as both performer and composer and also features the important Radical Jewish Culture sub-series.

Boundary-crossing composer/performer John Zorn was already playing a variety of instruments by the time he studied saxophone and composition at Webster College in St. Louis in the early 1970s. He has apparently never particularly worried about what the "academy" thinks of his music, and certainly doesn't work within its strictures. Still, there are some recognizable precedents in his work. Classical compositional influences he has cited include Charles Ives, John Cage, and Harry Partch, along with cartoon composer Carl Stalling for his genre-hopping style and Duke Ellington for his propensity to compose for specific musicians in his band. Zorn has frequently lived in Japan for extended periods, and Japanese culture informs some of his work. However, in recent years Zorn has placed special emphasis on his Jewish heritage.

Zorn's best-known group is his jazz quartet Masada, named for the fortress in Israel where besieged Jews chose to commit communal suicide rather than submit to captivity. He has also used the moniker for chamber

John Zorn

groups of varying membership (Masada Chamber Ensemble, Masada String Trio), along with the related Bar Kokhba Sextet (the leader of the Jews at Masada was named Bar Kokhba). Before Masada, Zorn's quintet Naked City (Zorn, alto sax; Bill Frisell, lead guitar; Wayne Horvitz, keyboards; Fred Frith, electric bass guitar; Joey Baron, drums; occasionally augmented by Yamatska Eye, screaming vocals), which lasted from 1989 to 1993, was most prominent. Extremely eclectic and open-minded, it drew on jazz, hardcore thrash, surf, movie themes, funk, and contemporary classical—sometimes several within the same short piece. Zorn was the main composer, but the band's repertoire included covers of movie themes, jazz, and early and modern classical music (Claude Debussy, Alexander Scriabin, Orlando di Lasso, Charles Ives, Olivier Messiaen). There was also the shock value of the occasional screaming vocals by Eye, and cover art depicting violence, domination, torture, death, and sex. In fact, Zorn left the major label Nonesuch when it refused to release *Torture Garden* due to its violent cover art, with the rock indie label Shimmy-Disc issuing it instead. But however much the brutality of the punk/thrash influence may have provoked some listen-

ers, the predominant effect was of superb musicians playing with extreme discipline and without regard to boundaries and categories. Zorn was also active in creating cued improvisations, the most-performed of which is probably *Cobra*.

An attempt has been made in the recommendations below to focus on works which lean more toward "classical music," however loosely. However, whatever vague boundary exists between classical improvisation and jazz improvisation is frequently crossed or just plain ignored by Zorn.

Chamber
Redbird
what to buy: [Carol Emanuel, harp; Jill Jaffee, viola; Erik Friedlander, cello; Jim Pugliese, percussion] (Tzadik 7008) ♪ ♪ ♪ ♪ ♪

This is a forty-one-minute piece for harp, viola, cello, and percussion that recalls the spare textures and slow-moving development of Morton Feldman's proto-minimalist music. The other track on this CD, *Dark River,* is for percussionist (the late, lamented Jim Pugliese) playing four bass drums in an exploration of subtle timbres.

The Book of Heads
what to buy: [Marc Ribot, electric guitar] (Tzadik 7009)
♪ ♪ ♪ ♪ ♪

These thirty-five guitar études, written in 1978 for Eugene Chadbourne, use a multiplicity of extended techniques drawn from improvised music, the contemporary avant-garde, and Zorn's "own sick imagination" (his words). Nowhere is the concern for texture more prominent in Zorn's music; these short pieces are like Zen exercises in hearing, free of preconceptions. In their complex yet completely notated variety and virtuosity they are on a par with John Cage's technique-stretching *Freeman Études* for violin.

Duras
what to buy: [*Duras: Duchamp*; Mark Feldman, violin; Cenovia Cummins, violin; Erik Friedlander, cello; Anthony Coleman, piano; John Medeski, organ; Christian Bard, percussion; Jim Pugliese, percussion] (Tzadik 7023)
♪ ♪ ♪ ♪ ♪

Duras (inspired by the writer Marguerite Duras) starts out sounding like Harold Budd's California Minimalism, but—as one would expect of Zorn—doesn't stay in that sound throughout. The long, calmly ecstatic third section shows Zorn's debt to Messiaen most explicitly, with the drawn-out harmonies strongly recalling parts of the French composer's famous *Quartet for the End of Time*. The *Duchamp* half of this 1997 album's title comes from *Étant Donnés: 69 paroxyms for Marcel Duchamp* for violin, cello, and percussion. All sixty-nine "paroxyms" (sic) in total require just twelve minutes and seventeen seconds, and to a certain extent blend into each other; the emphasis—masterfully so—is on instrumental color and texture.

Trembling Before G*d (soundtrack)
what to buy: [*Filmworks IX*; Jamie Saft, piano; Jamie Saft, organ; Chris Speed, clarinet; Cyro Baptista, percussion] (Tzadik 7331) ♪ ♪ ♪ ♪

On this Zorn-penned soundtrack for a movie about gay Hasidic Jews, the performances are largely by clarinetist Chris Speed and keyboardist Jamie Saft (mostly on organ), with percussionist Cyro Baptista making a few appearances and Zorn delivering a demented vocal on the giddy/silly *Simen Tov/ Mazel Tov*, which definite-

ly isn't typical of the overall mood of otherworldly spirituality and quiet joy. Speed's keening clarinet wails, strongly modal and occasionally microtonal, are the sonic key to the album. A few Masada tunes show up, quite transformed by the different sonic garb.

Angelus Novus
what to buy: [Stephen Drury, cond.; Callithumpian Consort of New England Conservatory, ensemble] (Tzadik 7028) ♪ ♪ ♪ ♪

The five-movement *Angelus Novus,* for wind octet (pairs of oboes, clarinets, bassoons, and French horns), is the main attraction on this set. It is a strongly etched, mature work recommended to fans of Toru Takemitsu's middle period but distinctively Zorn-ish in many ways. Other works on this disc include *For Your Eyes Only, Carny,* and Zorn's student composition *Christabel*—a work for five flutes and viola that brings early Morton Feldman to mind in its juxtaposition of minimal textures with hyperkinetic passages.

Issachar
what to buy: [*The Circle Maker*; Masada String Trio] (Tzadik 7122) ♪ ♪ ♪ ♪

Zorn's scoring here is strongly flavored by the rhythms and modal scales of Eastern European Jewish music, though also with a bit of Brazilian or jazz feeling in some of the bass lines. The most striking movement is the brief, dissonant, energetic *Karet*, with the violin/cello counterpoint of *Mispar* also attractive and the mournful *Yatzah* quite successful on a slightly larger scale. Erik Friedlander gets the spotlight on *Elilah,* which cellists looking for new solo repertoire would be well advised to investigate. The same could hold true for violinists in *Aravot,* which Mark Feldman gives a bravura reading. The other piece in this two-disc set, *Zevulun,* is even more heavily influenced by Brazilian music and performed by the Bar Kokhba Sextet.

various works
what to buy: [*Bar Kokhbah*; John Zorn, cond.; members of the Masada Chamber Ensemble] (Tzadik 7108) ♪ ♪ ♪ ♪

The music on this two-CD set is performed not by the Masada jazz quartet, but by a chamber ensemble, sometimes without drums, and with Zorn acting as composer and leader but not playing. *Tannaim,* for instance, is a contemplative string trio while the following tune, *Nefesh,* is swinging piano-trio bop. This music is more low-key than that performed by the quartet, with a corresponding increase in restful beauty during the strings-only numbers and in plaintive soulfulness when the clarinetists wail.

what to buy next: [*Music for Children*; various performers] (Tzadik 7321) ♪ ♪ ♪ ♪

Don't be deceived by this album's title; this is not watered-down Zorn in the slightest. Three typically-brief, previously-unrecorded Naked City compositions are played by the group Prelapse; *Fils des Etoiles* for celeste, percussion, and vocals expands on early Steve Reich; the title track (for violin, piano, and percussion) sports many stark textural juxtapositions; *Dreamer of Dreams,* for guitar, cello, and bass, spins out lounge-y music halfway between cool jazz and hip '60s soundtrack themes. The most significant piece heard herein may be *Cycles du Nord*, for three wind machines and two acoustic feedback systems, dedicated to Edgard Varèse and a fascinating tangent from Zorn's usual procedures and styles.

Vocal
Aporias: Requia for Piano, Boy Sopranos, and Orchestra
what to buy: [Stephen Drury, piano; Dennis Russell Davies, cond.; American Composers Orchestra; Hungarian Children's Choir] (Tzadik 7037) ♪ ♪ ♪ ♪⅛

Although thirty-three minutes is extremely short for a full-price CD, this eclectic ten-movement composition is quite striking at times, mixing spirited hijinks and an affecting use of silence and near-silence.

influences: John Cage, Olivier Messiaen, Edgard Varèse, Henry Mancini, John Barry, Carl Stalling

Steve Holtje

Ellen Taaffe Zwilich
Born April 30, 1939, in Miami, FL.

period: Twentieth century

In 1975, Zwilich became the first woman to receive a doctorate in composition from the Juilliard School of Music; in 1983, she became the first female composer to win the Pulitzer Prize in music. She is one of the most popular of today's postmodernist composers, and her

work has enjoyed frequent performances by major performing organizations in America and abroad.

Miami-born Ellen Taaffe Zwilich learned to play piano, trumpet, and violin at an early age and wrote her first musical composition by the time she was ten. At Florida State University she studied composition with John Boda and violin with Richard Burgin. Composer and pianist Ernst von Dohnanyi, grandfather of conductor Christoph von Dohnanyi, was also a mentor of hers.

After receiving her degrees, Zwilich moved to New York City to study violin with Ivan Galamian. From 1965 to 1972 she played in the American Symphony Orchestra under the leadership of Leopold Stokowski. She was admitted to the Juilliard School in 1970, where her primary teachers were Elliot Carter and Roger Sessions. Recognition of her composing talents soon followed. Pierre Boulez conducted the Juilliard Orchestra in a performance of *Symposium* (1973), followed by the premiere of her Quartet for Strings (1974) at the prestigious ISCM (International Society for Contemporary Music) World Music Days in Boston. Her husband, violinist Joseph Zwilich, championed the Sonata in Three Movements for Violin and Piano (1974), and in 1975, Zwilich became the first woman in Juilliard's history to graduate with a Doctor of Musical Arts degree in composition.

Her early works were more atonal and complex, but after the untimely death of her husband in 1979, Zwilich moved toward a simpler style in order to communicate more directly. In 1982, Gunther Schuller conducted the American Composers Orchestra at Lincoln Center in the premiere of Zwilich's Symphony No. 1. The piece was awarded the Pulitzer Prize for music in 1983, making Zwilich the first woman to win in this category.

Stylistically, Zwilich is a descendant of postmodernist composer George Rochberg. In the mid-1960s, Rochberg rejected academic serialism, re-embraced tonality, and liberated the next generation of composers, who then divided into two camps. One faction, including John Corigliano, David Del Tredici, Jacob Druckman, and William Bolcom, followed Rochberg's lead in using musical quotation, collage, and references to older musical styles. The other group, including Stephen Albert, Bernard Rands, Joseph Schwantner, and Zwilich, explored new ways to utilize the tools of the past without direct quotation (an exception is her *Concerto Grosso 1985* for Orchestra, based on Handel's Sonata in D major for Violin and Continuo). Consequently, most of these composers have enjoyed much greater public success than their predecessors. In fact, Zwilich's work is in such demand that she is able to make a full-time living from composition.

Besides the Pulitzer Prize, Zwilich has been honored with the Elizabeth Sprague Coolidge Chamber Music Prize, the Arturo Toscanini Music Critics Award, the Ernst von Dohnanyi Citation (from Florida State University), a Guggenheim Fellowship, and three Grammy Award nominations.

Orchestral
Symphony No. 1
what to buy: [John Nelson, cond; Indianapolis Symphony Orchestra] (New World Records 80336) ♪ ♪ ♪ ♪ ⅛

The historical significance of this piece cannot be overstated but must not obscure the pure artistry at work. Skilled at orchestration, Zwilich taps the potential of each instrument. After a tentative opening, the strings soar with a thrilling lushness of melody. The middle movement is atmospheric and introspective, with occasional colorful outbursts, while the rhythmic energy in the last movement creates a palpable intensity. Nelson and his Hoosiers perform this and two other short works by Zwilich (*Celebration* and *Prologue and Variations*) with great vitality and virtuosity.

Symbolon for Orchestra
what to buy: [Zubin Mehta, cond.; New York Philharmonic Orchestra] (New World Records 80372) ♪ ♪ ♪ ♪

Composed for the New York Philharmonic's 1988 concert tour of the former Soviet Union, *Symbolon* may have been the first American work to be premiered in that country. The name is derived from an ancient Greek custom where two parties break a piece of pottery, a stone, or a coin, and each keeps a half (*symbolon*) as a token of friendship. The work is dramatic and angular, perhaps symbolizing the tension between the two superpowers at the time, and it receives a gripping performance by the New York Philharmonic, for whom it was written. Also on this all-Zwilich program are versions of her *Concerto Grosso 1985,* the Double Quartet for Strings, and the *Concerto for Trumpet and Five Players.*

Concerto Grosso 1985 for Orchestra
what to buy: [James Sedares, cond.; Louisville Orchestra] (Koch 7278) ♪ ♪ ♪ ♪ ⅛

For this work, commissioned by the Washington Friends of Handel to commemorate the three-hundredth anniversary of George Frideric Handel's birth, Zwilich borrowed from the consummate borrower himself. Using material from his Sonata in D Major for Violin and Continuo (which Handel cribbed from earlier pieces), she fashioned a work that is neoclassical in form yet neoromantic in temperament. The opening triadic melody serves as a unifying device, as it is transformed throughout the other four movements. There is a recurring Coplandesque unison string passage, as well as glimpses of Sergei Prokofiev and Dmitri Shostakovich, particularly in the "Largo" movement. Sedares leads a wonderful performance of this work, which is both sparkling and vivacious yet somehow ominous.

influences: Roy Harris, Samuel Barber, Joan Tower

Christine L. Cody and Mona C. DeQuis

The following albums by individual artists or groups achieved the highest rating possible—5 notes—from our discriminating writers. You can't miss with any of these recordings.

Valentin Alkan
Grande sonate for piano, op. 33—Les quatre âges
Marc-André Hamelin, piano (Hyperion 20794)

Johann Sebastian Bach
Brandenburg Concertos (BWV 1046–1051)
Herbert von Karajan, cond.; Berlin Philharmonic Orchestra (Deutsche Grammophon 453001)

Trevor Pinnock, cond.; English Concert, orch. (Deutsche Grammophon Archiv 423492)

Die Kunst der Fuge (The Art of the Fugue) (BWV 1080)
Christopher Hogwood, harpsichord; Neville Marriner, cond., Academy of St. Martin-in-the-Fields, orch. (Philips 442556)

Sonatas and Partitas for Solo Violin (BWV 1001–1006)
Itzhak Perlman, violin (EMI Classics 49483)

Henryk Szeryng, violin (Deutsche Grammophon 453004)

Suites for Solo Cello (BWV 1007–1012)
Yo-Yo Ma, cello (Sony Classics 37867)

Pablo Casals, cello (EMI Classics 66215)

Pierre Fournier, cello (Deutsche Grammophon 449711)

Sonatas for Flute and Continuo (BWV 1030–1035)
Jean-Pierre Rampal, flute; Trevor Pinnock, harpsichord; Roland Pidoux, cello (Sony Classics 39746)

Chromatic Fantasy and Fugue in D Minor for Harpsichord (BWV 903)
Wanda Landowska, harpsichord (EMI Classics 67200)

Rosalyn Tureck Collection, Vol. IV; Rosalyn Tureck, harpsichord (VAI Audio 1139)

Partitas for Harpsichord
Glenn Gould Edition; Glenn Gould, piano (Sony Classical 52597)

Das wohltemperirte Clavier (The Well-Tempered Clavier), (BWV 846–893)
Book 1; Andras Schiff, piano (London 414388) and *Book 2*; Andras Schiff, piano (London 417236)

Book 1; Wanda Landowska, harpsichord (RCA Red Seal 6217) and *Book 2*; Wanda Landowska, harpsichord (RCA Red Seal 7825)

various organ works
The Biggs Bach Book; E. Power Biggs, organ (Sony Classics 30539)

Bach: Great Organ Works; Helmut Walcha, organ (Deutsche Grammophon 453064)

Mass in B Minor for Orchestra and Chorus (BWV 232)

John Eliot Gardiner, cond., English Baroque Soloists, orch; Monteverdi Choir (Deutsche Grammophon 415514)

St. Matthew Passion (Matthäus Passion) (BWV 244)

Elisabeth Schwarzkopf, soprano; Christa Ludwig, mezzo-soprano; Peter Pears, tenor; Nicolai Gedda, tenor; Dietrich Fischer-Dieskau, baritone; Walter Berry, bass-baritone; Otto Klemperer, cond.; Philharmonia Orchestra; Philharmonia Choir; Hampstead Parish Church Boy's Choir (EMI Classics 63058)

Sibylla Rubens, soprano; Andreas Scholl, countertenor; Ian Bostridge, tenor; Werner Güra, tenor; Franz-Josef Selig, bass; Dietrich Henschel, bass; Philippe Herreweghe, cond.; Orchestre du Collegium Vocale, Choir du Collegium Vocale (Harmonia Mundi 901676.78)

Schweigt stille, plaudert nicht (BWV 211) (Coffee Cantata)

Emma Kirkby, soprano; David Thomas, bass; Christopher Hogwood, cond.; Academy of Ancient Music, orch. (L'Oiseau-Lyre 417621)

Weichet nur, betrübte Schatten (BWV 202) (Wedding Cantata)

Emma Kirkby, soprano; David Thomas, bass; Andrew Parrott, cond.; Taverner Players, orch. (Hyperion 66036)

various cantatas
The Bach Cantatas, vol. 16; Helmut Rilling, cond.; Stuttgart Bach Collegium, orch.; Gächinger Kantorei, choir (Hanssler Classics 98867)

Samuel Barber
Adagio for Strings
Neville Marriner, cond.; Academy of St. Martin-in-the-Fields (Argo 417818)

Concerto for Piano and Orchestra, op. 38
John Browning, piano; Leonard Slatkin, cond.; St. Louis Symphony Orchestra (RCA Red Seal 60732)

John Browning, piano; George Szell, cond., Cleveland Orchestra (Sony Classics 61621)

various piano works
The Complete Solo Piano Music; John Browning, piano (Music Masters 67122)

Knoxville: Summer of 1915
Leontyne Price Sings Barber; Leontyne Price, soprano; Thomas Schippers, cond.; New Philharmonia Orchestra (RCA Gold Seal 61983)

Dawn Upshaw, soprano; David Zinman, cond.; Orchestra of St. Luke's (Nonesuch 79187)

various songs
Secrets of the Old: Complete Songs of Samuel Barber; Cheryl Studer, soprano; Thomas Hampson, baritone; John Browning, piano; Emerson String Quartet, ensemble (Deutsche Grammophon 435867)

Vanessa, op. 32
Eleanor Steber, soprano; Regina Resnik, mezzo-soprano; Rosalind Elias, mezzo-soprano; Nicolai Gedda, tenor; Robert Nagy, tenor; George Cehanovsky, baritone; Giorgio Tozzi, bass; Dimitri Mitropoulos, cond.; Metropolitan Opera Orchestra; Metropolitan Opera Chorus (RCA Gold Seal 7899)

Béla Bartók
Concerto for Orchestra
Fritz Reiner, cond.; Chicago Symphony Orchestra (RCA Victor Living Stereo 61504)

James Levine, cond.; Chicago Symphony Orchestra (Deutsche Grammophon 429747)

Music for Strings, Percussion, and Celesta
Pierre Boulez, cond.; Chicago Symphony Orchestra (Deutsche Grammophon 447747)

The Wooden Prince
Pierre Boulez, cond.; Chicago Symphony Orchestra (Deutsche Grammophon 435863)

Quartets for Strings (nos. 1–6, complete)
Emerson String Quartet, ensemble (Deutsche Grammophon 423657)

Tokyo String Quartet, ensemble (RCA Red Seal 68286)

Bluebeard's Castle, op. 11
Jessye Norman, soprano; Laszlo Polgár, baritone; Pierre Boulez, cond.; Chicago Symphony Orchestra (Deutsche Grammophon 447040)

Contrasts for Clarinet, Violin, and Piano
Benny Goodman: Collector's Edition; Benny Goodman, clarinet, Joseph Szigeti , violin, Béla Bartók, piano (Sony Classics 42227)

Ludwig van Beethoven
Symphony no. 5 in C Minor, op. 67
Carlos Kleiber, cond.; Vienna Philharmonic Orchestra (Deutsche Grammophon 447400)

Symphony no. 6 in F Major, op. 68 Pastoral
Karl Böhm, cond.; Vienna Philharmonic Orchestra (Deutsche Grammophon 447433)

Symphony no. 9 in D Minor, op. 125 Choral
Carol Vaness, soprano; Janice Taylor, mezzo-soprano; Siegfried Jerusalem, tenor; Robert Lloyd, bass; Christoph von Dohnányi, cond.; Cleveland Orchestra; Cleveland Orchestra Chorus (Telarc 80120)

Concertos for Piano and Orchestra (complete)
Wilhelm Kempff, piano; Paul van Kempen, cond.; Berlin Philharmonic Orchestra (Deutsche Grammophon 435744)

Vladimir Ashkenazy, piano; Georg Solti, cond.; Chicago Symphony Orchestra (London 443723)

Concertos for Piano and Orchestra (nos. 1–4)
Emil Gilels, piano; George Szell, cond.; Cleveland Orchestra (EMI Classics 69506)

Concerto no. 5 in E-flat Major for Piano and Orchestra, op. 73 Emperor
Walter Gieseking, piano; Artur Rother, cond.; Greater Berlin Radio Orchestra (Music & Arts 815)

Great Pianists of the 20th Century—Edwin Fischer II; Edwin Fischer; Wilhelm Furtwängler, cond.; Philharmonia Orchestra (Philips 456769)

Concerto in D Major for Violin and Orchestra, op. 61
Jascha Heifetz, violin; Charles Munch, cond.; Boston Symphony Orchestra (RCA Living Stereo 68980)

Jascha Heifetz, violin; Arturo Toscanini, cond.; NBC Symphony Orchestra (Naxos 8.110936)

Concerto in C major for Violin, Cello, Piano, and Orchestra, op. 56 Triple Concerto
David Oistrakh, violin; Mstislav Rostropovich, cello; Sviatoslav Richter, piano; Herbert von Karajan, cond.; Berlin Philharmonic Orchestra (EMI Classics 66954)

Quartets for Strings (complete)
Alban Berg Quartet, ensemble (EMI Classics 54587, 54592)

Sonatas for Piano (complete)
Richard Goode, piano (Nonesuch 79328)

Vladimir Ashkenazy, piano (London 443706)

Sonata no. 29 in B-flat Major for Piano, op. 106 Hammerklavier
Sviatoslav Richter, piano (BBC Legends 4052)

Sonatas for Piano, nos. 28-32 (selections)—The Late Piano Sonatas
Richter in Leipzig—The 28 November 1963 Recital at the Leipzig Gewandhaus; Sviatoslav Richter, piano (Music & Arts 1025)

various "name" sonata collections
Beethoven: Favourite Piano Sonatas; Vladimir Ashkenazy, piano (Decca 452952)

various piano sonatas
Sviatoslav Richter, piano (Praga 354022/25)

Sonatas for Violin and Piano (complete)
Beethoven: Complete Violin Sonatas; Aaron Rosand, violin; Eileen Flissler, piano (Vox 3503)

various sonatas for violin and piano
Artur Rubinstein Collection, vol. 40: Beethoven Violin Sonatas; Henryk Szeryng, piano; Artur Rubinstein, piano (RCA Red Seal 63040)

Fidelio

Christa Ludwig, mezzo-soprano; Ingeborg Hallstein, soprano; Jon Vickers, tenor; Gerhard Unger, tenor; Gottlob Frick, bass; Walter Berry, bass; Franz Crass, bass; Kurt Wehofschitz, tenor; Raymond Wolansky, baritone; Otto Klemperer, cond; Philharmonia Orchestra and Chorus (EMI Classics 67361)

Vincenzo Bellini

Norma

Maria Callas, soprano; Christa Ludwig, mezzo-soprano; Franco Corelli, tenor; Nicola Zaccharia, bass; Tullio Serafin, cond.; La Scala Orchestra; La Scala Chorus (EMI Classics 66428)

I Puritani

Joan Sutherland, soprano; Luciano Pavarotti, tenor; Piero Cappuccilli, baritone; Nicolai Ghiaurov, bass; Richard Bonynge, cond.; London Symphony Orchestra; London Symphony Orchestra Chorus (London 417588)

Alban Berg

Concerto for Violin and Orchestra—To the Memory of an Angel

Itzhak Perlman, violin, Seiji Ozawa, cond., Boston Symphony Orchestra (Deutsche Grammophon 447445)

Sonata for Piano, op. 1

Glenn Gould, piano (CBC 2008)

Altenberg Lieder, op. 4

Jessye Norman Sings Alban Berg; Jessye Norman, soprano; Pierre Boulez, cond.; London Symphony Orchestra (Sony Classical 66826)

Wozzeck, op. 7

Hildegard Behrens, soprano; Philip Langridge, tenor; Walter Raffeiner, tenor: Heinz Zednik, tenor; Franz Grundheber, baritone; Aage Haugland, bass; Alfred Zramek, bass; Claudio Abbado, cond.; Vienna Philharmonic Orchestra, Vienna State Opera Chorus; Vienna Boys Choir (Deutsche Grammophon 423587)

Evelyn Lear, soprano; Gerhard Stolze, tenor; Helmut Melchert, tenor; Dietrich Fischer-Dieskau, baritone; Karl Böhm, cond.; German Opera Orchestra, Berlin; German Opera Chorus (Deutsche Grammophon 138991/92)

Lulu

Teresa Stratas, soprano; Hanna Schwarz, mezzo-soprano; Yvonne Minton, mezzo-soprano; Robert Tear, tenor; Kenneth Riegel, tenor; Franz Mazura, baritone; Gerd Nienstedt, bass; Pierre Boulez, cond., Paris Opera Orchestra (Deutsche Grammophon 415489)

Evelyn Lear, soprano; Patricia Johnson, mezzo-soprano; Donald Grobe, tenor; Dietrich Fischer-Dieskau, baritone; Karl Böhm, cond.; German Opera Orchestra, Berlin; German Opera Chorus (Deutsche Grammophon 435705)

Hector Berlioz

Harold in Italy, op. 16

William Primrose, viola; Serge Koussevitzky, cond.; Boston Symphony Orchestra (Dutton Laboratories 5013)

Leonard Bernstein

West Side Story: Symphonic Dances

Leonard Bernstein, cond.; New York Philharmonic (Sony Classics 63085)

West Side Story

Carol Lawrence (Maria); Larry Kert (Tony); Chita Rivera (Anita); Mickey Calin (Riff); Ken LeRoy (Bernardo); Max Goberman, cond.; Original Broadway Cast recording (Columbia Broadway 60724)

Candide

Jerry Hadley, tenor; June Anderson, soprano; Della Jones, mezzo-soprano; Christa Ludwig, mezzo-soprano; Nicolai Gedda, tenor; Kurt Ollmann, baritone; Adolph Green; Leonard Bernstein, cond.; London Symphony Orchestra and Chorus (Deutsche Grammophon 449656)

Ernest Bloch

Schelomo for Cello and Orchestra

Leonard Rose, cello, Eugene Ormandy, cond., Philadelphia Orchestra (Sony Classical 48278)

Luigi Boccherini

Concerto in B-flat Major for Cello and Orchestra

Erling Blondal Bengtsson, cello; Ilya Stupel, cond.; Artur Rubinstein State Philharmonic Orchestra (Danacord 416)

William Bolcom
Symphony no. 4 for Mezzo-Soprano and Orchestra
Joan Morris, mezzo-soprano, Leonard Slatkin, cond., St. Louis Symphony Orchestra (New World 80356)

Twelve New Études for Piano
Marc-André Hamelin, piano (New World 80345)

Rags for Piano (complete)
Knight Hubert, John Murphy, piano (Albany TROY 325/26)

various songs by other composers
After the Ball: A Treasury of Turn-of-the-Century Popular Songs; Joan Morris, mezzo-soprano; William Bolcom, piano (Nonesuch 79148)

Johannes Brahms
Symphonies (complete)
Furtwängler Conducts Brahms; Wilhelm Furtwängler, cond.; North German Radio Orchestra; Berlin Philharmonic Orchestra; Vienna Philharmonic Orchestra (Music & Arts 4941)

Symphony no. 4 in E major, op. 98
Carlos Kleiber, cond.; Vienna Philharmonic Orchestra (Deutsche Grammophon 457706)

Concerto no. 2 in B flat major for Piano and Orchestra, op. 83
Sviatoslav Richter, piano; Erich Leinsdorf, cond.; Chicago Symphony Orchestra (RCA Victor Gold Seal 56518)

Artur Rubinstein Collection, vol. 1 Artur Rubinstein, piano; Albert Coates, cond.; London Symphony Orchestra (RCA Red Seal 63001)

Artur Rubinstein Collection, vol. 71; Artur Rubinstein, piano; Eugene Ormandy, orch.; Philadelphia Orchestra (RCA Red Seal 63071)

Concerto in D major for Violin and Orchestra Concerto, op. 77
Jascha Heifetz, violin; Fritz Reiner, cond.; Chicago Symphony Orchestra (RCA Living Stereo 61495)

Nathan Milstein, violin; Anatole Fistoulari, cond.; Philharmonia Orchestra (EMI Classics 67021)

Serenades for Orchestra, opp. 11 (D major) and 16 (A major)
Jirí Belohlávek, cond.; Czech Philharmonic Orchestra (Supraphon 1992)

Sextets (complete)
Isaac Stern, violin; Cho-Liang Lin, violin; Jaime Laredo, viola; Michael Tree, viola; Yo-Yo Ma, cello; Sharon Robinson, cello (Sony Classics 45820)

Sonatas for Violin and Piano (complete)
Artur Rubinstein Collection, vol. 41: Brahms Violin Sonatas; Henryk Szeryng, violin; Artur Rubinstein, piano (RCA Red Seal 63041)

various works for solo piano
The Glenn Gould Edition: Brahms; Glenn Gould, piano (Sony Classics 52651)

Yaara Tal, piano; Andreas Groethuysen, piano (Sony Classics 53285)

Ein Deutsches Requiem (A German Requiem), op. 45
Elisabeth Schwarzkopf, soprano; Dietrich Fischer-Dieskau, baritone; Otto Klemperer, cond.; Philharmonia Orchestra and Chorus (EMI Classics 66955)

various sacred choral works
Brahms: Motets; Philippe Herreweghe, cond.; La Chapelle Royale de Paris, choir; Collegium Vocale, choir (Harmonia Mundi 901122)

Benjamin Britten
Instruments of the Orchestra
Malcolm Sargent, narrator and cond.; London Symphony Orchestra (Beulah Video RT 152)

Suites for Solo Cello, opp. 72, 80, and 87
Britten: Cello Suites 1 & 2; Mstislav Rostropovich, cello (London 421859)

Peter Grimes, op. 33
Peter Pears, tenor; Claire Watson, soprano; James Pease, baritone; Geraint Evans, baritone; Benjamin Britten, cond.; Orchestra and Chorus of the Royal Opera House, Covent Garden (London 414577)

Billy Budd, op. 50
Peter Glossop, baritone; Peter Pears, tenor; Michael Langdon, bass; John Shirley-Quirk, baritone; Owen Brannigan, bass; Benjamin Britten, cond., London Symphony Orchestra; Ambrosian Opera Chorus (London 417428)

A Ceremony of Carols for Treble voices, Harp, and Chorus, op. 28
Britten: The Choral Works, vol. III; Harry Christophers, cond.; The Sixteen, choir (Collins Classics 1370)

Leo Brouwer

Concerto no. 3 for Guitar and Orchestra—*Elegíaco*
The Guitar Concertos of Leo Brouwer, Ricardo Cobo, guitar; Richard Kapp, cond.; Pro Musica Kiev, orch. (ESS.A.Y. 1040)

El Decamerón negro
Tales for Guitar, Ricardo Cobo, guitar (ESS.A.Y 1034)

Anton Bruckner

Symphony no. 4 in E-flat Major (*Romantic*)
Eugen Jochum, cond.; Berlin Philharmonic Orchestra (Deutsche Grammophon 449718)

Symphony no. 7 in E Major
Herbert van Karajan, cond.; Vienna Philharmonic Orchestra (Deutsche Grammophon 439037)

Ferruccio Busoni

various piano transcriptions
Ferruccio Busoni, piano; Egon Petri, piano (Pearl 9347)

John Cage

various works for piano and ensemble
The Piano Concertos; Stephen Drury, piano; Charles Peltz, cond.; Callithumpian Consort, orch.; David Tudor, piano; Ingo Metzmacher, cond.; Ensemble Modern, orch. (mode 57)

Concert for Piano and Orchestra
The 25-Year Retrospective Concert of the Music of John Cage; David Tudor, piano; Merce Cunningham, cond.; anonymous orchestra (Wergo 6247)

Music of Changes
Herbert Henck, piano (Wergo 60099-50)

Sonatas and Interludes for Prepared Piano
Philipp Vandré, prepared piano (mode 50)

Aleck Karis, prepared piano (Bridge 9081A/B)

Nigel Butterley, prepared piano (Tall Poppies 025)

The Perilous Night
Margaret Leng Tan, prepared piano (New Albion 037)

Etudes Australes
Grete Sultan, prepared piano (Wergo 6152)

various works for prepared piano
Daughters of the Lonesome Isle; Margaret Leng Tan, piano, prepared piano, and toy piano (New Albion 070)

various dance pieces
Music for Merce Cunningham; David Tudor, electronics; Takehisa Kosugi, pizzicato amplified violin, bamboo flute, percussion; Michael Pugliese, percussion (mode 24)

Elliott Carter

Sonata for Cello and Piano
Rhonda Rider, cello; Lois Shapiro, piano (Centaur 2267)

Quartet no. 1 for Strings
Composers String Quartet, ensemble (Nonesuch 71249)

Ernest Chausson

Chanson perpétuelle for Soprano and Orchestra, op. 37
La Bonne Chanson: French Chamber Songs; Anne Sophie von Otter, mezzo-soprano; Bengt Forsberg, piano; Nils-Erik Sparf, violin; Ulf Forsberg, violin; Matti Hirvikangas, viola; Mats Lindström, cello (Deutsche Grammophon 447752)

Frédéric Chopin

Nocturnes for piano (complete)
Ivan Moravec, piano (Nonesuch 79233)

various piano works
Great Pianists of the 20th Century, vol. 85: Artur Rubinstein I; Artur Rubinstein, piano (Philips 456955)

Aaron Copland

various ballets and concert suites
Copland the Populist; Michael Tilson Thomas, cond.; San Francisco Symphony Orchestra (RCA Victor Red Seal 63511)

John Corigliano

Symphony no. 1
Leonard Slatkin, cond.; National Symphony Orchestra, Washington D.C. (RCA Victor Red Seal 68450)

Daniel Barenboim, cond.; Chicago Symphony Orchestra (Erato 45601)

various film scores
The Red Violin: Music from the Motion Picture; Joshua Bell, violin; Esa-Pekka Salonen, cond.; Philharmonia Orchestra; Shanghai Film Studio Children's Chorus (Sony Classical 63010)

Henry Cowell

various piano works
Henry Cowell, piano (Smithsonian/Folkways 40801)

Claude Debussy

Images for Orchestra
Pierre Boulez, cond.; Cleveland Orchestra (Deutsche Grammophon 435766)

La Mer for Orchestra
Pierre Boulez, cond.; Cleveland Orchestra (Deutsche Grammophon 439896)

various orchestral and vocal works
Oeuvres Orchestrales; Daniel Barenboim, cond.; Orchestre de Paris (Deutsche Grammophon 437934)

Quartet in G minor for Strings, op. 10
Emerson String Quartet, ensemble (Deutsche Grammophon 445509)

Preludes for Piano, Books 1 and 2
Walter Gieseking, piano (EMI Classics 67262)

Etudes for Piano
Paul Jacobs, piano (Elektra/Nonesuch 79161)

Images for Piano
Paul Jacobs, piano (Nonesuch 71365)

Children's Corner for Piano
Arturo Benedetti Michelangeli, piano (Deutsche Grammophon 415372)

Pelléas et Mélisande
Frederica von Stade, mezzo-soprano; Richard Stilwell, baritone; José van Dam, baritone; Ruggero Raimondi, bass; Herbert von Karajan, cond.; Berlin Philharmonic Orchestra; Chorus of the Deutsche Oper, Berlin (EMI Classics 67168)

Maria Ewing, soprano; François Le Roux, baritone; José van Dam, baritone; Jean-Philippe Courtis, bass; Claudio Abbado, cond.; Vienna Philharmonic Orchestra; Vienna State Opera Chorus (Deutsche Grammophon 435344)

various songs
Complete Mélodies; Elly Ameling, soprano; Frederica von Stade, mezzo-soprano; Michele Command, soprano; Mady Mesplé, soprano; Gerard Souzay, baritone; Dalton Baldwin, piano (EMI Classics 64095)

Frederick Delius

various orchestral works
Beecham Conducts Delius; Thomas Beecham, cond.; Royal Philharmonic Orchestra (EMI Angel 47509)

Gaetano Donizetti

Lucia di Lammermoor
Joan Sutherland, soprano; Luciano Pavarotti, tenor; Ryland Davies, tenor; Sherill Milnes, baritone; Nicolai Ghiairov, bass; Richard Bonynge, cond.; Royal Opera House Orchestra, Covent Garden; Royal Opera House Chorus, Covent Garden (London 410193)

Maria Callas, soprano; Luisa Villa, mezzo-soprano; Giuseppe di Stefano, tenor; Giuseppe Zampieri, tenor; Mario Carlin, tenor; Rolando Panerai, baritone; Nicola

Zaccaria, bass; Herbert von Karajan, cond.; Berlin RIAS Symphony Orchestra; La Scala Chorus (EMI Classics 66441)

L'elisir d'amore

Joan Sutherland, soprano; Maria Casula, soprano; Luciano Pavarotti, tenor; Dominic Cossa, baritone; Spiro Maias, bass; Richard Bonynge, cond.; English Chamber Orchestra; Ambrosian Opera Chorus (London 414461)

Marcel Dupré

various works

The Organ Encyclopedia—Dupré: Works for Organ, Vol. 3: Complete Music for Organ and Orchestra; Daniel Jay McKinley, organ; David Bowden, cond.; Columbus Indiana Philharmonic, orch. (Naxos 8.553922)

various works

Organ Music by Marcel Dupré; John Scott, organ (Hyperion 67047)

Dupré joue Dupré; Marcel Dupré, organ (Philips 446648)

Antonín Dvořák

Quintet in A Major for Piano and Strings, op. 81

Tucson Winter Chamber Music Festival: March 1996, vol. 2; Ralph Votapek, piano; Joseph Suk, violin; Ani Kavafian, violin; Cynthia Phelps, viola; Peter Rejto, cello (Arizona Friends of Chamber Music 96.102)

Edward Elgar

Concerto in E Minor for Cello and Orchestra, op. 85

Jacqueline du Pré, cello; John Barbirolli, cond; London Symphony Orchestra (EMI Classics 56219)

Edward Kennedy "Duke" Ellington

Black, Brown, and Beige

Mahalia Jackson, singer; Duke Ellington, cond.; the Duke Ellington Orchestra (Columbia 65566)

Gabriel Fauré

Arthur Grumiaux, violin; Paul Crossley, piano (Philips 426384)

Quartets for Piano and Strings, opp. 15 and 45

Domus, ensemble (Hyperion 66166)

various songs

La Chanson d'Eve; Janet Baker, mezzo-soprano; Geoffrey Parsons, piano (Hyperion 66320)

Stephen Foster

various songs

Stephen Foster Songbook; Robert Shaw, cond.; Robert Shaw Chorale (RCA Living Stereo 61253)

César Franck

Complete Works for Organ; Jeanne Demessieux, organ (Festivo 155-156)

Kaja Danczowska, violin; Krystian Zimerman, piano (Deutsche Grammophon 2531330)

George Gershwin

Rhapsody in Blue for Piano and Orchestra

Gershwin and Grofé; George Gershwin, piano; Paul Whiteman, cond.; Paul Whiteman Orchestra (Pearl 22)

James Levine, piano; James Levine, cond.; Chicago Symphony Orchestra (Deutsche Grammophon 431625)

various piano works

Gershwin: 'S Wonderful; Ralph Grierson, Artie Kane, pianos (EMI Classics 69119)

Porgy and Bess

Clamma Dale, Betty Lane, Wilma Shakesnider, sopranos; Shirley Baines, Phyllis Bash, Carol Brice, Myra Merritt, mezzo-sopranos; Steven Alex-Cole, Larry Marshall Glover Parham, Alexander B. Smalls, Bernard Thacker, Mervin Wallace, tenors; Donnie Ray Albert, Hartwell Mace, Cornel Richie, Andrew Smith, baritones; Raymond Bazemore, bass; John DeMain, cond.; Houston Grand Opera Orchestra; Houston Grand Opera Chorus (RCA Red Seal 2109)

Crazy for You

Beth Leavel, Stacey Logan, Judine Hawkins Richard, Paula Leggett, Ida Henry, Jean Marie, Penny Ayn Maas, Louise Ruck, Pamela Everett, Michele Pawk, Jalle Connell, Harry Groener, Bruce Adler, Geryy Burkhardt,

Briarl M. Nalepka, Tripp Hanson, Hal Shane, Casey Nicholaw, Fred Anderson, Michael Kubala, singers; Paul Gemignani, cond.; unknown orchestra (Angel Broadway 54618)

various songs
Crazy for Gershwin; George Gershwin, Fred Astaire, Adele Astaire, Judy Garland, Helen Forrest, singers; Duke Ellington, cond.; Duke Ellington Concert Choir (Memoir Classics 502)

Carlo Gesualdo
various madrigals
Madrigaux a cinq voix; William Christie, cond.; Les Arts Florissants Ensemble, choir (Harmonia Mundi France 901268)

Orlando Gibbons
various choral anthems
Anthems by Orlando Gibbons; Robin Blaze, countertenor; Stephen Varcoe, baritone; Stephen Farr, organ; Sarah Baldock, organ; David Hill, cond.; Winchester Cathedral Choir (Hyperion 67116)

Alberto Ginastera
Concerto for Piano and Orchestra
Hilde Somer, piano; Ernst Marzendorfer, cond.; Vienna Philharmonic Orchestra (Phoenix USA 110)

Philip Glass
Symphony no. 5 for Soloists, Chorus, and Orchestra—*Requiem, Bardo, Nirmanakaya*
Ana Maria Martinez, soprano; Denyce Graves, mezzo-soprano; Michael Schade, tenor; Eric Owens, baritone; Albert Dohmen, bass-baritone; Dennis Russell Davies, cond.; Vienna Radio Symphony Orchestra; Morgan State University Choir; Hungarian Radio/TV Children's Chorus (Nonesuch 79618)

Einstein on the Beach
Patricia Schuman, soprano; Lucinda Childs, speaker; Gregory Dolbashian, speaker; Jasper McGruder, speaker; Sheryl Sutton, speaker; Michael Riesman, cond.; Philip Glass Ensemble, orch (Nonesuch 79323)

La Belle et la Bête (Beauty and the Beast)
Ana Maria Martinez, soprano; Hallie Neill, soprano; Janice Felty, mezzo-soprano; John Kuether, baritone; Gregory Purnhagen, baritone; Zheng Zhou, baritone; Michael Riesman, cond.; Philip Glass Ensemble, orch. (Nonesuch 79347)

Kundun (soundtrack)
Michael Riesman, cond.; anon. orch.; Gyuto Monks, choir; Monks of the Drukpa Order, choir (Nonesuch 79460)

Henryk Górecki
Symphony no. 3 for Soprano and Orchestra— *Symphony of Sorrowful Songs*
Dawn Upshaw, soprano; David Zinman, cond.; London Sinfonietta, orch. (Nonesuch 79282)

Quartet no. 1 for Strings, op. 62—*Already It Is Dusk*
Kronos Quartet, ensemble (Nonesuch 79319)

Sofia Gubaidulina
Stimmen. . .verstummen. . .
Gennady Rozhdeshvensky, cond.; Royal Stockholm Philharmonic Orchestra (Chandos 9183)

Offertorium for Violin and Orchestra
Gidon Kremer, violin; Charles Dutoit, cond.; Boston Symphony Orchestra (Deutsche Grammophon 427336)

Howard Hanson
Symphony no. 3, op. 33
Gerard Schwarz, cond.; Seattle Symphony Orchestra (Delos 3092)

Roy Harris
Symphony no. 3
Bernstein Century: American Masters; Leonard Bernstein, cond.; New York Philharmonic Orchestra (Sony Classical 60594)

Karl Amadeus Hartmann
Symphonies, nos. 7 and 8
Ingo Metzmacher, cond.; Bamberg Symphony Orchestra (EMI Classics 56427)

Quartets for Strings
Pellegrini Quartet, ensemble (CPO 999219)

Franz Joseph Haydn
Symphonies nos. 93-102 (The London Symphonies)
The 12 "London" Symphonies; Eugen Jochum, cond.; London Philharmonic Orchestra (Deutsche Grammophon 437201)

Quartets for Strings, op. 76, nos. 1–6 (*Erdödy Quartets*)
Tátrai String Quartet, ensemble (Hungaroton 12812/13)

Quartet for Strings in G Major, op. 76, no. 1
Kodály Quartet, ensemble (Naxos 8.550129)

Quartets for Strings, op. 77 (*Lobkowitz Quartets*)
Tátrai String Quartet, ensemble (Hungaroton 11776)

Hans Werner Henze
Symphony no. 7
Simon Rattle, cond.; City of Birmingham Symphony Orchestra (EMI Classics Imports 54762)

Hildegard von Bingen
various works
900 Years—Hildegard von Bingen; Sequentia, ensemble (Deutsche Harmonia Mundi 77505)

Paul Hindemith
Mathis der Maler for Orchestra
Herbert von Karajan, cond.; Berlin Philharmonic Orchestra (EMI Classics 69242)

Charles Ives
Contemplations no. 1: The Unanswered Question for Orchestra
Gerhard Samuel, cond.; Cincinnati Philharmonia Orchestra (Centaur 2205)

Leoš Janáček
Quartet no. 1 for Strings—*The Kreutzer Sonata*
Janáček String Quartet, ensemble (Supraphon 3460)

Jerome Kern
various songs
Silver Linings: Songs by Jerome Kern; Joan Morris, mezzo-soprano; William Bolcom, piano (Arabesque 6515)

Aram Khachaturian
Gayane
Yuri Temirkanov, cond.; Royal Philharmonic Orchestra (EMI Classics 47348)

Symphony no. 2 in E minor—*The Bell*
Neeme Järvi, cond.; Royal Scottish National Orchestra (Chandos 8945)

Concerto in D Minor for Violin and Orchestra
Lydia Mordkovitch, violin; Neeme Järvi, cond., Royal Scottish National Orchestra (Chandos 8918)

Zoltán Kodály
Sonata for Solo Cello, op. 8
Starker Plays Kodály; Janos Starker, cello (Delos 1015)

Charles Koechlin
Les Heures Persanes (Persian Hours)
Herbert Henck, piano (Wergo 60 137-50)

Franz Lehár
various songs
Fritz Wunderlich: The Great German Tenor, Melitta Muszely, soprano; Liselotte Schmidt, soprano; Lisa Otto, soprano; Pilar Lorengar, soprano; Anneliese Rothenberger, soprano; Edith Mathis, soprano; Elisabeth Grummer, soprano; Sieglinde Wagner, contralto; Friz Wunderlich, tenor; Rudolf Schock, tenor; Hermann Prey, baritone; Marcel Cordes, baritone; Frick Gottlob, bass; various conductors; various orchestras (EMI Classics 62993)

Elisabeth Schwarzkopf Sings Operetta; Elisabeth Schwarzkopf, soprano; Otto Ackermann, cond.; Philharmonia Orchestra; Philharmonia Chorus (EMI Classics 47284)

Edward MacDowell

Van Cliburn, piano; Walter Hendl, cond.; Chicago Symphony Orchestra (RCA Gold Seal 60420)

Gustav Mahler

Symphony no. 1 in D major—*Titan*

Bruno Walter, cond.; New York Philharmonic Orchestra (Sony Classical Masterworks 63328)

Symphony no. 2 for soprano, mezzo-soprano, orchestra, and chorus—*Resurrection*

Barbara Hendricks, soprano; Christa Ludwig, mezzo-soprano; Leonard Bernstein, cond.; New York Philharmonic Orchestra; Westminster Choir (Deutsche Grammophon 423395)

Symphony no. 3 for mezzo-soprano, orchestra, and chorus

Christa Ludwig, mezzo-soprano; Leonard Bernstein, cond.; New York Philharmonic Orchestra (Deutsche Grammophon 427328)

Symphony no. 4 for soprano and orchestra

Judith Raskin, soprano; George Szell, cond.; Cleveland Orchestra (Sony Essential Classical Classics 46535)

Symphony no. 5

Leonard Bernstein, cond.; Vienna Philharmonic Orchestra (Deutsche Grammophon Panorama 469154)

Symphony no. 6 in A minor—*Tragic*

Leonard Bernstein, cond.; Vienna Philharmonic Orchestra (Deutsche Grammophon 427697)

Symphony no. 7—*Song of the Night*

Leonard Bernstein, cond.; New York Philharmonic Orchestra (Sony Classics 60564)

Symphony no. 8—*Symphony of a Thousand*

Arleen Augér, soprano; Heather Harper, soprano; Yvonne Minton, mezzo-soprano; Lucia Popp, mezzo-soprano; Helen Watts, mezzo-soprano; Rene Kollo, tenor; John Shirley-Quirk, bass-baritone; Martti Talvela, bass; Georg Solti, cond.; Chicago Symphony Orchestra; Vienna Singverein; Vienna State Opera Chorus; Vienna Boys Choir (Decca Legends 460972)

Lieder und Gesänge aus der Jungendzeit (Songs of Youth) for Voice and Piano

Bernstein Century: Mahler Lieder; Dietrich Fischer-Dieskau, baritone; Leonard Bernstein, piano (Sony Classical 61847)

Anne Sofie von Otter, mezzo-soprano; Ralf Gothoni, piano (Deutsche Grammophon 423666)

Des Knaben Wunderhorn (The Youth's Magic Horn) for Voice and Orchestra

Elisabeth Schwarzkopf, soprano; Dietrich Fischer-Dieskau, baritone; George Szell, cond.; London Symphony Orchestra (EMI Classics 67256)

Das Lied von der Erde (The Song of the Earth) for Solo Voices and Orchestra

Christa Ludwig, mezzo-soprano; Fritz Wunderlich, tenor; Otto Klemperer, cond.; Philharmonia Orchestra; New Philharmonia Orchestra (EMI 66944)

Kathleen Ferrier, contralto; Julius Patzak, tenor; Bruno Walter, cond.; Vienna Philharmonic Orchestra (Decca 466576)

various orchestral songs

Dietrich Fischer-Dieskau, baritone; Rafael Kubelik, cond.; Bavarian Radio Symphony Orchestra; (in the *Lieder eines Fahrenden Gesellen*) Karl Böhm, cond.; Berlin Philharmonic Orchestra (in the *Kindertotenlieder* and the *Rückert Lieder*) (Deutsche Grammophon 415191)

Marin Marais

Pièces de viole

Pièces de viole du second Livre, 1701; Jordi Savall, viola da gamba; Anne Gallet, harpsichord; Hopkinson Smith, theorbo (Auvidis Fontalis 7770)

Frank Martin

Petite Symphonie Concertante for Harp, Harpsichord, Piano, and Two String Orchestras

Armin Jordan, cond.; Orchestre de la Suisse Romande (Erato 45694)

Jules Massenet

Manon

Victoria de los Angeles, soprano; Liliane Berton, soprano; Raymonde Notti, soprano; Marthe Serres, soprano; Henri Legay, tenor; René Hérent, tenor; Michel Dens, baritone; Jean Vieuille, baritone; Jean Borthayre, bass; Pierre Monteux, cond.; Orchestre du Théâtre National de l'Opéra Comique; Chœurs du Théâtre National de l'Opéra Comique (Testament 3203)

Nicolai Medtner

Concerto no. 2 in C Minor for Piano and Orchestra, op. 50

The Romantic Piano Concerto, Vol. 2; Nikolai Demidenko, piano; Jerzy Maksymiuk, cond.; BBC Scottish Symphony Orchestra (Hyperion 66580)

Olivier Messiaen

various organ works
Organ Works; Olivier Messiaen, organ (EMI Classics 67400)

Messiaen: Complete Organ Music; Gillian Weir, organ (Collins Classics 7031)

Messe de la Pentecôte
Things Visible and Invisible; Catherine Crozier, organ (Delos 3147)

Federico Mompou

Música Callada
Mompou Plays Mompou, vol. 1; Federico Mompou, piano (Ensayo 9716)

Spanish Songs and Dances; Alícia de Larrocha, piano (RCA Victor 62554)

various works for piano
Mompou Plays Mompou, vol. 3; Federico Mompou, piano (Ensayo 9726)

Wolfgang Amadeus Mozart

Serenade no. 13 in G Major for Strings and Continuo (K. 525) (Eine kleine Nachtmusik)
Christoph von Dohnányi, cond.; Cleveland Orchestra (London 443175)

Mozart: Great Serenades; Neville Marriner, cond.;

Academy of St. Martin-in-the-Fields, orch. (Philips 464022)

Concerto no. 20 in D Minor for Piano and Orchestra (K. 466)
Murray Perahia, piano; Murray Perahia, cond.; English Chamber Orchestra (Sony Classics 42241)

Concertos for Horn and Orchestra (K. 412/386b, 417, 447, 495)
Dennis Brain, horn; Herbert von Karajan, cond.; Philharmonia Orchestra (EMI Classics 66950)

Quartets for Strings, nos. 14–19 (the Haydn Quartets K. 387, K. 421, K. 428, K. 458, K. 464, K. 465)
Complete Mozart Edition, vol. 12: String Quartets; Quartetto Italiano, ensemble (Philips 422 512)

Missa in C Minor (K. 427) (The Great Mass)
Sylvia McNair, soprano; Diana Montague, mezzo-soprano, Anthony Rolfe Johnson, tenor; Cornelius Hauptmann, bass; John Eliot Gardiner, cond.; English Baroque Soloists, orch.; Monteverdi Choir, London (Philips 420210)

Sylvia McNair, soprano; Delores Ziegler, mezzo-soprano; Hans Peter Blochwitz, tenor; Andreas Schmidt, baritone; James Levine, cond.; Berlin Symphony Orchestra; Berlin RIAS Chamber Choir (Deutsche Grammophon 435853)

Don Giovanni (K. 527)
Elisabeth Schwarzkopf, soprano; Joan Sutherland, soprano; Graziella Sciutti, soprano; Luigi Alva, tenor; Eberhard Wächter, baritone; Piero Cappuccilli, baritone; Gottlob Frick, bass; Giuseppe Taddei, bass; Carlo Maria Giulini, cond.; Philharmonia Orchestra; Philharmonia Chorus (EMI Classics 56232)

Così fan tutte (K. 588)
Véronique Gens, soprano; Bernarda Fink, soprano; Graciela Oddone, soprano; Werner Gura, tenor; Marcel Boone, baritone; Pietro Spagnoli, baritone; René Jacobs, cond.; Concerto Köln, orch.; Köln Chamber Choir (Harmonia Mundi 951663)

Die Zauberflöte (The Magic Flute) (K. 620)
Irmgard Seefried, soprano; Wilma Lipp, soprano; Sena Jurinac, soprano; Emmy Loose, soprano; Anton Dermotta, tenor; Erich Majkut, tenor; Peter Klein, tenor; Erich Kunz, baritone; George London, bass-baritone;

Ludwig Weber, bass; Harald Pröglhöf, bass; Ljubomir Pantscheff, bass; Herbert von Karajan, cond.; Vienna Philharmonic Orchestra; Vienna Singverein, choir (EMI Classics 67165)

Conlon Nancarrow
Studies for Player Piano, Vols. 1–5
Conlon Nancarrow, player piano (Wergo 6907)

Carl Nielsen
Symphony no. 5, op. 50
Leonard Bernstein, cond.; New York Philharmonic Orchestra (Sony Classics 47598)

Quintet for Winds, op. 43
Favorite Music for Wind Quintet; Frösunda Wind Quintet, ensemble (BIS 136)

Niccolò Paganini
Concerto no. 1 in D Major for Violin and Orchestra, op. 6
Itzhak Perlman, violin; Lawrence Foster, cond.; Royal Philharmonic Orchestra (EMI Classics 47101)

Giovanni Palestrina
Missa "Papae Marcelli"
Peter Phillips, cond.; Tallis Scholars, choir (Gimell 454939)

Hubert Parry
Symphony no. 3 in C Major (*The English*)
Matthias Bamert, cond.; London Philharmonic Orchestra (Chandos 8896)

Arvo Pärt
Tabula Rasa for Violin, Prepared Piano, and String Orchestra
Gidon Kremer, violin; Tatiana Grindenko, violin; Alfred Schnittke, prepared piano; Saulus Sondeckis, cond.; Lithuanian Chamber Orchestra (ECM 1275)

Kanon Pokajanen for Chorus
Tõnu Kaljuste, cond.; Estonian Philharmonic Chamber Choir (ECM 1654/55)

Litany for Solo Voices, Orchestra, and Chorus
David James, alto; John Potter, tenor; Rogers Covey-Crump, tenor; Gordon Jones, bass; Tõnu Kaljuste, cond.; Tallinn Chamber Orchestra; Estonian Philharmonic Chamber Choir (ECM 1592)

Berliner Messe (Berlin Mass) for Organ and Chorus
Te Deum; Tõnu Kaljuste, cond.; Tallinn Chamber Orchestra; Estonian Philharmonic Chamber Choir (ECM 1505)

Magnificat for Chorus
De Profundis; Christopher Bower-Broadbent, organ; Paul Hillier, cond.; Theatre of Voices, choir (Harmonia Mundi 907182)

Stabat Mater for Vocal Ensemble
Arbos; Gidon Kremer, violin; Vladimir Mendelssohn, viola; Thomas Demenga, cello; Dennis Russell Davies, cond.; Hilliard Ensemble, choir (ECM 1325)

Harry Partch
Delusion of the Fury: A Ritual of Dream and Delusion
Victoria Bond, soprano; John Stannard, tenor; Paul Bergen, bass; Danlee Mitchell, cond.; various musicians (Innova 406)

Allan Pettersson
Symphony no. 7
Antal Doráti, cond.; Stockholm Philharmonic Orchestra (Swedish Society Discofil 1002)

Sergei Prokofiev
Concertos for Piano and Orchestra
Prokofiev: The Five Piano Concertos; Vladimir Ashkenazy, piano; André Previn, cond.; London Symphony Orchestra) (London 452588)

Sonata no. 7 in B-flat Major for Piano, op. 83
Maurizio Pollini, piano (Deutsche Grammophon 447431)

Giacomo Puccini
Tosca
Maria Callas, soprano; Alvaro Cordova, treble; Giuseppe

di Stefano, tenor; Angelo Mercuriali, tenor; Tito Gobbi, baritone; Melchiorre Luise, bass-baritone; Franco Calabrese, bass; Dario Caselli, bass; Victor de Sabata, cond.; La Scala Theatre Orchestra; La Scala Theatre Chorus (EMI Classics 56304)

Turandot

Birgit Nilsson, soprano; Renata Scotto, soprano; Franco Corelli, tenor; Angelo Mercuriali, tenor; Piero de Palma, tenor; Franco Ricciardi, tenor; Giuseppe Morresi, bass-baritone; Bonaldo Giaiotti, bass; Guido Mazzini, bass; Francesco Molinari-Pradelli, cond.; Rome Opera Orchestra; Rome Opera Chorus (EMI Classics 69327)

Sergei Rachmaninoff

Preludes, opp. 23 and 32

Vladimir Ashkenazy, piano (London 443841)

various solo piano works

A Window in Time; Sergei Rachmaninoff, piano (Telarc 80489)

Horowitz in Moscow; Vladimir Horowitz, piano (Deutsche Grammophon 419499)

Maurice Ravel

Rhapsodie Espagnole for Orchestra

Fritz Reiner, cond.; Chicago Symphony Orchestra (RCA Gold Seal 60179)

Daphnis et Chloe

Pierre Boulez, cond.; Berlin Philharmonic Orchestra; Berlin Radio Choir (Deutsche Grammophon 447057)

Concerto in G Major for Piano and Orchestra

Martha Argerich, piano; Claudio Abbado, cond.; Berlin Philharmonic Orchestra (Deutsche Grammophon 447438)

Tzigane

Gil Shaham, violin; Gerhard Oppitz, piano (Deutsche Grammophon 429729)

Poèmes de Stéphane Mallarmé for Voice and Ensemble (or Piano)

La Bonne Chanson: French Chamber Songs; Anne Sofie von Otter, mezzo-soprano; Peter Rydström, flute/piccolo; Andreas Alin, flute; Lars Paulsson, clarinet; Per Billman, clarinet/bass clarinet; Nils-Erik Sparf, violin; Ulf

Forsberg, violin; Matti Hirvikangas, viola; Mats Lindström, cello; Bengt Forsberg, piano (Deutsche Grammophon 447752)

Max Reger

String Quartets, opp. 54 (nos. 1 and 2), 74, 109, 121, and the D Minor (1889)

Complete String Quartets; Berner String Quartet (CPO 999069)

various organ works

Die Grosse Sauer-Orgel Im Berliner Dom; Michael Pohl, organ (Motette 11781)

Hannes Kastner, organ (Ars Vivendi 2100187)

Steve Reich

Different Trains for String Quartet and Pre-Recorded Tape

Kronos Quartet, ensemble (Nonesuch 79176)

Music for 18 Musicians for Voices and Ensemble

Steve Reich Ensemble, orch. (Nonesuch 79448)

The Cave

Cheryl Rowe Bensman, soprano; Marion Beckenstein, soprano; James Bassi, tenor; Hugo Munday, baritone; Paul Hillier, cond.; Steve Reich Ensemble, orch. (Nonesuch 79327)

Terry Riley

Cadenza on the Night Plain for String Quartet

Kronos Quartet, ensemble (Gramavision 79444)

Nikolai Rimsky-Korsakov

Scheherazade for Orchestra, op. 35

Charles Mackerras, cond.; London Symphony Orchestra (Telarc 80208)

Ned Rorem

Nantucket Songs for Voice and Piano

American Masters: Ned Rorem; Phyllis Bryn-Julson, soprano; Ned Rorem, piano (CRI 657)

Gioachino Rossini

various overtures

Rossini Overtures; Roger Norrington, cond.; London Classical Players, orch. (EMI Classics 54091)

Il Barbiere di Siviglia (The Barber of Seville)

Maria Callas, soprano; Luigi Alva, tenor; Tito Gobbi, baritone; Carl Maria Giulini, cond.; La Scala Orchestra; La Scala Chorus (Melodram 20038)

Tancredi

Sumi Jo, soprano; Anna Maria di Micco, soprano; Lucretia Lendi, mezzo-soprano; Ewa Podles, contralto; Stanford Olsen, tenor; Pietro Spagnoli, baritone; Alberto Zedda, cond.; Collegium Instrumentale Brugense, orch.; Capella Brugensis, chorus (Naxos Opera Classics 8.660037)

Camille Saint-Saëns

Concerto no. 1 in A Minor for Cello and Orchestra, op. 33

Yo-Yo Ma, cello; Lorin Maazel, cond.; French National Orchestra (Sony Classical 35848)

Concertos for Piano and Orchestra, opp. 17, 22, 29, 44, and 103

Aldo Ciccolini, piano; Serge Baudo, cond.; Orchestre de Paris (EMI Classics 69443)

Erik Satie

Trois Gymnopédies

Satie: The Early Piano Works; Reinbert de Leeuw, piano (Philips 462161)

Alfred Schnittke

Concerto no. 2 for Cello and Orchestra

Alexander Ivashkin, cello; Valéri Polyansky, cond.; Russian State Symphony Orchestra (Chandos 9722)

Quintet for Piano and Strings

Gary Graffman, piano; Lark Quartet, ensemble (Arabesque 26707)

Franz Schubert

Symphony no. 8 in B Minor (*Unfinished, D. 759*)

Bruno Walter, cond.; New York Philharmonic Orchestra (Sony Classical 64487)

Symphony no. 9 in C Major (*The Great,* D. 944)

Wilhelm Furtwängler, cond.; Berlin Philharmonic Orchestra (Deutsche Grammophon 447439)

Piano Quintet in A Major for Piano and Strings, op 114 (*The Trout,* D. 667)

Marlboro Festival 40th Anniversary; Rudolf Serkin, piano; Jaime Laredo, violin; Philipp Naegele, viola; Leslie Parnas, cello; Julius Levine, double bass (Sony Classical 46252)

Trios for Piano, Violin, and Cello, opp. 99 (D. 898) and 100 (D. 929)

Isaac Stern: A Life In Music; Eugene Istomin, piano; Isaac Stern, violin; Leonard Rose, cello (Sony Classics 64516)

Sonata in A Minor for Piano, op. 143 (D. 784)

Stephen Hough, piano (Hyperion 67027)

Piano Sonatas in A major, D.959; in B-flat major, D.960

Alfred Brendel, piano (Philips 456573)

Fantasie in C Major, op. 15 (*"Wanderer" Fantasy,* D. 760)

Sviatoslav Richter, piano (EMI Classics 64429)

The Rubinstein Collection: vol. 54; Artur Rubinstein, piano (RCA Red Seal 63054)

Winterreise (Winter Journey), op. 89 (D. 911)

Hans Hotter, baritone; Gerald Moore, piano (EMI Classics 67000)

Schwanengesang (D. 957)

Hans Hotter, baritone; Gerald Moore, piano (EMI Classics 65196)

Dietrich Fischer-Dieskau, baritone; Gerald Moore, piano (Deutsche Grammophon 463503)

various lieder

Franz Schubert: 21 Lieder; Dietrich Fischer-Dieskau, baritone; Gerald Moore, piano (EMI Classics 69503)

Alexander Scriabin

Symphony no. 5, op. 60—*Prometheus, Poem of Fire*

Pierre Boulez, cond.; Anatol Ugorski, piano; Chicago Symphony Orchestra; Chicago Symphony Chorus (Deutsche Grammophon 459647)

Sonata no. 5 in F sharp major for Piano, op. 53— *Poem of Ecstasy*

Svjatoslav Richter In Prague: Frédéric Chopin; Sviatoslav Richter, piano (Praga 254056)

Dmitri Shostakovich

Symphony no. 5 in D Minor, op. 47 (Revolution)

Bernard Haitink, cond.; Concertgebouw Orchestra (Decca 425066)

Symphony no. 10 in E Minor, op. 93

Herbert von Karajan, cond.; Berlin Philharmonic Orchestra (Deutsche Grammophon 439036)

Concerto no. 1 in A Minor for Violin and Orchestra, op. 77

David Oistrakh, violin; Evgeny Mravinsky, cond.; Czech Philharmonic Orchestra (Le Chant du Monde 7250052)

Preludes and Fugues, op. 87

Tatiana Nikolayeva, piano (Hyperion 66441/3)

String Quartets (complete)

Fitzwilliam String Quartet, ensemble (London 455776)

Emerson String Quartet, ensemble (Deutsche Grammophon 463284)

Jean Sibelius

Symphony no. 4 in A Minor, op. 63

Osmo Vänskä, cond.; Lahti Symphony Orchestra (BIS 861)

Bedrich Smetana

Má Vlast (My Fatherland)

Charles Mackerras, cond.; Czech Philharmonic Orchestra (Supraphon 3465)

Smetana Quartet, ensemble (Denon 7339)

John Philip Sousa

The Dwellers in the Western World

Sousa for Orchestra; Richard Kapp, cond.; Philharmonia Virtuosi of New York, orch. (ESS.A.Y. Recordings 1003)

John Philip Sousa: At the Symphony; Keith Brion, cond.; Razumovsky Symphony Orchestra (Naxos 8.559013)

Charles Villiers Stanford

***Morning Service* in C Major, op. 115**

The Complete Morning and Evening Services and Offices for Holy Communion, vol. 1; Keith Wright, organ; James Lancelot, cond.; Durham Cathedral Choir (Priory 437)

John Stanley

various organ voluntaries

11 Voluntaries; Ton Koopman, organ (Capriccio 10256)

William Grant Still

Symphony no. 3—*The Sunday Symphony*

A Festive Sunday with William Grant Still; Carlton R. Woods, cond.; North Arkansas Symphony Orchestra (Cambria 1060)

various songs for voice and orchestra

Witness, vol. 2; Yolanda Williams, soprano; Hilda Harris, mezzo-soprano; William Warfield, narrator; Philip Brunelle, cond.; Plymouth Music Series Orchestra and Chorus; Leigh Morris Chorale (Collins Classics 14542)

Karlheinz Stockhausen

Gesang der Jünglinge (Song of the Youths)

Elektronische Musik 1952 to 1960; Karlheinz Stockhausen, electronics (Stockhausen-Verlag Disc 3)

Johann Strauss II

Die Fledermaus

Anneliese Rothenberger, soprano; Brigitte Fassbaender, mezzo-soprano; Nicolai Gedda, tenor; Dietrich Fischer-Dieskau, baritone; Walter Berry, bass-baritone; Otto Schenk, narrator; Willi Boskovsky, cond.; Vienna Philharmonic Orchestra; Vienna State Folk Opera Chorus (EMI Classics 69354)

Richard Strauss
Der Rosenkavalier, op. 59

Elisabeth Schwarzkopf, soprano; Ljuba Welitsch, soprano; Christa Ludwig, mezzo-soprano; Teresa Stich-Randall, mezzo-soprano; Kerstin Meyer, mezzo-soprano; Nicolai Gedda, tenor; Paul Kuen, tenor; Eberhard Wächter, baritone; Otto Edelmann, bass; Herbert von Karajan, cond.; Philharmonia Orchestra; Philharmonia Chorus; Bancroft School Children's Chorus; Loughton High School for Girls Choir (EMI Classics 56113)

Birgit Nilsson, soprano; Marie Collier, soprano; Regina Resnik, mezzo-soprano; Gerhard Stolze, tenor; Tom Krause, baritone; Georg Solti, cond.; Vienna Philharmonic Orchestra (London 417345)

Igor Stravinsky

various ballets
Claudio Abbado, cond., London Symphony Orchestra (Deutsche Grammophon 453085)

Pierre Boulez, cond.; Cleveland Orchestra (Deutsche Grammophon 435769

Pierre Boulez, cond. New York Philharmonic Orchestra (Sony Classics 42396)

Firebird Suite no. 2 for Orchestra (revised 1919)
Bernstein Conducts Stravinsky; Leonard Bernstein, cond., Israel Philharmonic (Deutsche Grammophon 445538)

various works
Igor Stravinsky: The Edition; Igor Stravinsky, cond.; Robert Craft, cond.; various orchestras; various ensembles; various vocalists (Sony Classical 46290)

The Rake's Progress
Sylvia McNair, soprano; Jane Henschel, contralto; Anthony Rolfe Johnson, tenor; Ian Bostridge, tenor; Paul Plishka, bass; Donald Adams, bass; Seiji Ozawa, cond.; Saito Kinen Orchestra; Tokyo Opera Singers (Philips 454431)

Herbert von Karajan, cond.; Berlin Philharmonic Orchestra; Chor der Deutschen Oper Berlin (Deutsche Grammophon 423252)

Arthur Sullivan
The Pirates of Penzance (or The Slave of Duty)

Rebecca Evans, soprano; Gillian Knight, mezzo-soprano; John Mark Ainsley, tenor; Nicholas Folwell, Richard Suart, baritones; Richard Van Allan, Donald Adams, basses; Charles Mackerras, cond.; Welsh National Opera Orchestra; Welsh National Opera Chorus (Telarc, 80353)

Karol Szymanowski
Mythes for violin and piano, op. 30

Kaja Danczowska, violin; Krystian Zimerman, piano (Deutsche Grammophon 431469)

Toru Takemitsu
November Steps

Hiroshi Wakasugi, cond.; Tokyo Metropolitan Symphony Orchestra (Denon 79441)

Woman in the Dunes (film score)
Film Music by Toru Takemitsu, vol. 4 (Japanese Victor 5127)

Tan Dun
Ghost Opera for Pipa and String Quartet with Water, Stones, Paper and Metal

Wu Man, pipa, Kronos Quartet, ensemble (Nonesuch 79445)

Giuseppe Tartini
Sonata in G Minor for Violin and Piano (Devil's Trill)

Andrew Manze, violin (Harmonia Mundi 907213)

John Tavener

various choral works
English Choral Music: John Tavener; Christopher Robinson, cond.; Choir of St. John's College, Cambridge (Naxos 8.555256)

Piotr Ilyich Tchaikovsky
Concerto in D Major for Violin and Orchestra, op. 35

Jascha Heifetz, violin; Fritz Reiner, cond.; Chicago Symphony Orchestra (RCA Red Seal 5933)

Georg Philipp Telemann

various orchestral suites
Akademie für Alte Musik, Berlin, orch. (Harmonia Mundi 901654)

***Musique de Table—"Tafelmusik"* (complete)**
Robert Glenton, cond.; members of the Orchestra of the Golden Age (Naxos 8.504022)

***Paris Quartets* (selections)**
Nouveaux Quatuors en six suites; Quadro Amsterdam, ensemble (Teldec Das Alte Werk 92177)

Joan Tower

***Silver Ladders* for Orchestra**
Leonard Slatkin, cond.; Saint Louis Symphony Orch. (Nonesuch 79245)

***Night Fields* for String Quartet**
Black Topaz, Muir Quartet, ensemble (New World Records 80470)

Giuseppe Verdi

Rigoletto
Maria Callas, soprano; Giuse Gerbino, soprano; Elvira Galassi, mezzo-soprano; Luisa Mandelli, mezzo-soprano; Adriana Lazzarini, contralto; Giuseppe di Stefano, tenor; Renato Ercolani, tenor; Tito Gobbi, baritone; William Dickie, baritone; Plinio Clabassi, bass; Carol Forti, bass; Vittorio Tatozzi, bass; Nicola Zaccaria, bass; Tullio Serafin, cond.; Orchestra of La Scala, Milan; Chorus of La Scala, Milan (EMI Classics 56327)

La traviata
Joan Sutherland, soprano; Marjon Lambriks, soprano; Della Jones, mezzo-soprano; Luciano Pavarotti, tenor; Alexander Oliver, tenor; Matteo Manuguerra, baritone; William Elvin, baritone; Ubaldo Gardini, baritone; Jonathan Summers, baritone; Giorgio Tadeo, bass; John Tomlinson, bass; David Wilson-Johnson, bass; Richard Bonynge, cond.; National Philharmonic Orchestra; London Opera Chorus (Decca 411877)

Aida
Leontyne Price, soprano; Grace Bumbry, mezzo-soprano; Placido Domingo, tenor; Bruce Brewer, tenor; Sherill Milnes, baritone; Ruggero Raimondi, bass; Hans Sotin, bass; Erich Leinsdorf, cond.; London Symphony Orchestra; John Alldis Choir (RCA Victor Red Seal 39498)

Otello
Leonie Rysanek, soprano; Jon Vickers, tenor; Florindo Andreolli, tenor; Mario Carlin, tenor; Tito Gobbi, baritone; Ferruccio Mazzoli, bass; Franco Calabrese, bass; Tullio Serafin, cond.; Rome Opera House Orchestra; Rome Opera House Chorus (RCA Victor Living Stereo 63180)

Falstaff
Elisabeth Schwarzkopf, soprano; Anna Moffo, soprano; Fedora Barbieri, mezzo-soprano; Nan Merriman, mezzo-soprano; Renato Ercolani, tenor; Tomaso Spataro, tenor; Luigi Alva, tenor; Tito Gobbi, baritone; Rolando Panerai, baritone; Nicola Zaccaria, bass; Herbert von Karajan, cond.; Philharmonia Orchestra; Philharmonia Chorus (EMI Classics 67162)

Louis Vierne

Symphony no. 3 in F-sharp Minor for Organ, op. 28
Michael Murray, organ (Telarc 80329)

***Messe solennelle* for Vocal Soloists, Organ, Orchestra, and Chorus, op. 16**
Michel Bouvard, organ; Yasuko Uyama-Bouvard, organ; Joël Suhubiette, cond.; Les Éléments, ensemble (Tempéraments 316008)

Henri Vieuxtemps

Concerto no. 5 in A Minor for Violin and Orchestra, op. 37—*Grétry*
Jascha Heifetz, violin; Sir Malcolm Sargent, conductor; New Symphony Orchestra of London (RCA Red Seal 6214)

Heitor Villa-Lobos

***Bachiana brasileira no. 5* for Soprano and Cellos**
Victoria de los Angeles, soprano; Heitor Villa-Lobos, cond.; Orchestre National de la Radiodiffusion Française, orch. (EMI Classics 66964)

Antonio Vivaldi

Concertos for Violin, Strings, and Continuo, op. 8, nos. 1–4 (*Le Quattro Stagioni The Four Seasons*)
Gidon Kremer, violin; Claudio Abbado, cond.; London

Symphony Orchestra (Deutsche Grammophon 431172)

Various concertos for diverse instruments
Vivaldi Favorites, vol. 1; Richard Kapp, cond.; Philharmonia Virtuosi, orch. (ESS.A.Y 1022)

Richard Wagner

various overtures
The Klemperer Legacy—Wagner: Orchestral Works, vol. 1; Otto Klemperer, cond.; Philharmonia Orchestra (EMI Classics 66805)

The Klemperer Legacy—Wagner: Orchestral Works, vol. 2; Otto Klemperer, cond.; Philharmonia Orchestra (EMI Studio 66806)

Prelude and Good Friday Spell from Parsifal
Bruno Walter, cond.; Columbia Symphony Orchestra (Sony Classics 42038)

Tristan und Isolde
Kirsten Flagstad, soprano; Blanche Thebom, mezzo-soprano; Ludwig Suthaus, tenor; Edgar Evans, tenor; Rudolf Schock, tenor; Josef Greindl, baritone; Dietrich Fischer-Dieskau, baritone; Wilhelm Furtwängler, cond.; Philharmonia Orch.; Chorus of the Royal Opera House, Covent Garden (EMI Classics 56254)

Brigit Nilsson, soprano; Christa Ludwig, mezzo-soprano; Wolfgang Windgassen, tenor; Peter Schreier, tenor; Erwin Wohlfahrt, tenor; Eberhard Wächter, baritone; Claude Heater, baritone; Martti Talvela, bass; Gerd Nienstedt, bass; Karl Böhm, cond.; Bayreuth Festival Orchestra; Bayreuth Festival Chorus (Deutsche Grammophon 449772)

Die Walküre (The Valkyrie)
Martha Mödl, soprano; Leonie Rysanek, soprano; Gerda Scheyrer, soprano; Erika Köth, soprano; Hertha Töpper, mezzo-soprano; Margarete Klose, mezzo-soprano; Ruth Siewert, contralto; Dagmar Hermann, contralto; Ludwig Suthaus, tenor; Ferdinand Frantz, baritone; Gottlob Frick, bass; Wilhelm Furtwängler, cond.; Vienna Philharmonic Orchestra (EMI Classics 63045)

excerpts from various operas
Hans Hotter: The Early EMI Recordings; Hans Hotter, baritone; Meinhard von Zallinger, cond.; Vienna

Philharmonic Orchestra (Testament 1199)

William Walton

Symphony no. 2
George Szell, cond.; Cleveland Orchestra (CBS 46732)

Franz Waxman

various film scores
Sunset Boulevard: The Classic Film Scores of Franz Waxman; Charles Gerhardt, cond.; National Philharmonic Orchestra (RCA Victor 0708)

Carl Maria von Weber
Der Freischütz

Gundula Janowitz, soprano; Edith Mathis, soprano; Pete Schreier, tenor; Bernd Weikl, baritone; Theo Adam, bass-baritone; Franz Crass, bass; Günter Leib, bass; Siegfried Vogel, bass; Carlos Kleiber, cond.; Dresden Staatskapelle, orch.; Leipzig Radio Choir (Deutsche Grammophon 457736)

Anton Webern

various works
Complete Works, Opp. 1–31; Pierre Boulez, cond.; London Symphony Orchestra; John Alldis Choir (Sony Classical 45845)

Complete Webern; Pierre Boulez, cond.; Berlin Philharmonic Orchestra; Ensemble Intercontemporain; BBC Singers, choir (Deutsche Grammophon 457637)

Passacaglia for Orchestra, op. 1
Claudio Abbado, Vienna Philharmonic Orchestra (Deutsche Grammophon 431774)

Kurt Weill
Suite for Wind Orchestra from The Threepenny Opera

David Atherton, cond.; London Sinfonietta, orch. (Deutsche Grammophon 459442)

Die sieben Todsünden (The Seven Deadly Sins)
Teresa Stratas, soprano; Nora Kimball, soprano; Howard Haskin, tenor; Frank Kelley, tenor; Herbert Perry, bari-

tone; Peter Rose, bass; Kent Nagano, cond.; Lyon Opera Orchestra (Nonesuch 17068)

various songs
The Unknown Kurt Weill; Teresa Stratas, soprano; Richard Woitach, piano (Nonesuch 79019)

Ute Lemper Sings Kurt Weill; Ute Lemper, soprano; John Mauceri, cond.; RIAS Berlin Sinfonietta, orch. (London 425204)

Charles-Marie Widor
Symphony no. 5 in F Minor for Organ, op. 42, no. 1
David Hill, organ (Hyperion 66181)

Olivier Latry, organ (BNL Productions 112617)

Symphony no. 9 in C Minor for Organ, op. 70 (*Gothique*)
Charles Widor: The Organ Works, vol. 4; Ben van Oosten, organ (MD&G 3160404)

Mass for Two Organs and Double Chorus, op. 36
Joseph Cullen, organ; Andrew Reid, organ; James O'Donnell, cond.; Westminster Cathedral Choir; Hyperion Baritone Chorus (Hyperion 66898)

John Williams
various film scores
Star Wars Trilogy; John Williams, cond.; London Symphony Orchestra (Arista 11012)

Jaws: The Anniversary Collector's Edition John Williams, cond.; unknown orchestra (Decca 467045)

Raiders of the Lost Ark; John Williams, cond.; London Symphony Orchestra (DCC Compact Classics 090)

Schindler's List; Itzhak Perlman, violin; Giora Feidman, clarinet; John Williams, cond.; Boston Symphony Orchestra; Li-Ron Herzeliya Children's Choir; Ramat Gan Chamber Choir (MCA 10969)

Seven Years in Tibet; Yo-Yo Ma, cello; John Williams, cond.; unknown orchestra; Gyuto Monks, choir (Sony Classical 60271)

The Reivers; John Williams, cond.; Boston Pops Orchestra (Sony Legacy 66130)

Hugo Wolf
Spanisches Liederbuch (Spanish Songbook) (complete)
Elisabeth Schwarzkopf, soprano; Dietrich Fischer-Dieskau, baritone; Gerald Moore, piano (Deutsche Grammophon 457726)

various songs
Wolf Lieder Recital; Hans Hotter, baritone; Gerald Moore, piano (Testament 1197)

Jan Dismas Zelenka
Missa Dei Fillii in C Minor (incomplete)
Heike Hallaschka, soprano; Kai Wessel, alto; Marcus Ullmann, tenor; Frank Schiller, bass; Hans-Christoph Rademann, cond.; Dresdner Barockorchester, orch.; Dresdner Kammerchor, choir (Raumklang 9702)

Alexander Zemlinsky
Lyrische Symphonie, op. 18
Elisabeth Söderström, soprano; Thomas Allen, baritone; Michael Gielen, cond.; BBC Symphony Orchestra (IMP 5691852)

Die Seejungfrau (The Mermaid)
Thomas Dausgaard, cond.; Danish National Radio Symphony Orchestra (Chandos 9601)

various choral works
Sämtliche Chorwerke (Complete Choral Works); Deborah Voigt, soprano; Donnie Ray Albert, baritone; James Conlon, cond.; Gürzenich-Orchester, orch.; Kölner Philharmoniker, orch.; Chor des Städt. Musikvereins zu Düsseldorf, choir; Mülheimer Kantorei, choir (EMI Classics 56783)

Der Zwerg, op. 17
Soile Isokoski, soprano; Juanita Lascarro, soprano; Iride Martinez, soprano; Machiko Obata, soprano; Anne Schwanewilms, soprano; David Kuebler, tenor; Andrew Collis, bass; James Conlon, cond.; Gürzenich-Orchester Kölner Philharmoniker (EMI Classics 56208)

John Zorn

Redbird

Carol Emanuel, harp; Jill Jaffee, viola; Erik Friedlander, cello; Jim Pugliese, percussion (Tzadik 7008)

The Book of Heads

Marc Ribot, electric guitar (Tzadik 7009)

Editor
Garaud MacTaggart

Assistant Editor
David Wagner

Contributors
D. John Apple
Gary Barton
Suzanne Bona
Gerald Brennan
Christine Cody
Mona DeQuis
Kerry Dexter
Chris Felcyn
Jack Goggin
Gerald B. Goldberg
Charles Greenwell
Sean Hickey
Steve Holtje
Sharon L. Hoyer
Jan Jezioro
Kevin Kazmierczak

Tim Kennedy
Joanna Lee
Nancy Ann Lee
Michael H. Margolin
Linette Popoff-Parks
Polly Rapp
Frank Retzel
Frank Scinta
Melissa Stewart
Craig Scott Symons
Marijim Thoene
Herman Trotter
Paul Wintemute

Photo Credits
Pages 40, 65, 73, 121, 149, 203, 208, 220, 288, 303, 306, 310, 318, 334, 387, 461, 494, 518, 531, 572, 587, 595, 642, 680, and 700: **Corbis**

Page 473: **RCA**

Pages 2, 12, 16, 19, 37, 78, 106, 127, 153, 158, 190, 228, 242, 258, 278, 378, 421, 450, 541, and 616: **Courtesy: G. Schirmer/AMP Archives.**